EXEGETICAL DICTIONARY OF THE NEW TESTAMENT

EXEGETICAL DICTIONARY OF THE NEW TESTAMENT

VOLUME 3

παγιδεύω – ὠφέλιμος

edited by
Horst Balz and
Gerhard Schneider

WILLIAM B. EERDMANS PUBLISHING COMPANY
GRAND RAPIDS, MICHIGAN

Originally published as
Exegetisches Wörterbuch zum Neuen Testament
Band III, Lieferungen 1-10
Copyright © 1982-83 by
Verlag W. Kohlhammer GmbH, Stuttgart, Germany

English translation copyright © 1993 by
William B. Eerdmans Publishing Company
255 Jefferson Ave. SE, Grand Rapids, Michigan 49503
All rights reserved

Library of Congress Cataloging-in-Publication Data

Exegetical dictionary of the New Testament.

    Translation of: Exegetisches Wörterbuch zum Neuen Testament.
    Includes bibliographical references and index.
    Contents: v. 1. — Aarōn-Henōch — v. 2. Ex-opsōnion — v. 3. Pagideuō-ōphelimos.
    1. Bible. N.T. — Dictionaries — Greek. 2. Bible. N.T. — Criticism, Interpretation, etc.
3. Greek language, Biblical — Dictionaries — English.   I. Balz, Horst Robert.
II. Schneider, Gerhard, 1926-
BS2312.E913   1990   225.4′8′03   90-35682
ISBN 0-8028-2409-9 (v. 1)
ISBN 0-8028-2410-2 (v. 2)
ISBN 0-8028-2411-0 (v. 3)

CONTENTS

EDITORS' FOREWORD

It was in December 1979 that we wrote the foreword for the first volume of the *Exegetisches Wörterbuch zum Neuen Testament*. Now the final volume of the English translation is ready to appear. Thanks to the reliability of the coauthors, translators, and publisher the *Exegetical Dictionary of the New Testament (EDNT)* represents the status of exegetical knowledge of a relatively short span of time.

Although *EDNT* is not a "theological dictionary," but proceeds rather from an "exegesis" of the words in their contexts, it is certainly no less theologically oriented. But unlike the *Theological Dictionary of the New Testament*, it covers all the words of the Greek New Testament (including the most important textual variants) and all proper names. And comparison with other dictionaries treating the entire New Testament vocabulary throws the theological orientation of *EDNT* into sharp relief: Wherever it has been appropriate, key words are treated in the context of individual writings or groups of writings. In this way the contours of the different New Testament "theologies" can be seen clearly.

The index at the end of this final volume lists the English translations of every Greek word treated in all three volumes, thus making possible use of the dictionary by those who have not studied Greek or have not yet mastered it sufficiently to allow them direct access to the articles of the dictionary.

May *EDNT* find many grateful users! Without doubt, it will both help and encourage them to hear the Word itself in the words.

Bochum, August 1983/November 1992   *Horst Balz*
                                                             Gerhard Schneider

Our special thanks go to the translators of this final volume of the *Exegetical Dictionary of the New Testament*. John W. Medendorp's work is seen from the beginning of the volume through παρουσία 1.b. Douglas W. Stott translated the rest of the volume, beginning with παρουσία 1.c. Our thanks also go to Professors Balz and Schneider for updating the bibliographies in this volume to include works published through 1990.

                                                             The Publishers

INTRODUCTION

The *Exegetical Dictionary of the New Testament (EDNT)* is a guide to the forms, meaning, and usage of every word in the text of the third edition of *The Greek New Testament (UBSGNT),* which is equivalent to the text of the twenty-sixth edition of the Nestle-Aland *Novum Testamentum Graece (NTG)* and the text followed in the *Vollständige Konkordanz zum griechischen Neuen Testament (VKGNT;* see abbreviations list for full publication data on these works). Words in the most important textual variants in *UBSGNT* and *NTG* are also included, and the authors of *EDNT* articles have been granted the freedom to depart from the basic text of these two editions where they have deemed it appropriate.

The *heading* of each *EDNT* article, along with identifying the word to be discussed, supplies the following information:

- The gender of common nouns is identified by inclusion of the nominative singular article.
- The declension of nouns is identified by inclusion of the genitive singular ending.
- Whether an adjective has one, two, or three sets of endings (corresponding to the three genders) is specified by a boldface number.[1]
- The word is transliterated.
- The meaning of the word is indicated by one or more English translations (sometimes divided according to verb voice or adjectival or substantival use of an adjective).[2]
- An asterisk (*) appears at the end of the heading line if all New Testament occurrences of a word are at least mentioned in the body of the article.

A group of words related by form and meaning is sometimes treated in one article with multiple heading lines. In that case, a cross reference (→) is placed at each word's normal alphabetical location.

πλούσιος, **3** *plousios* rich*
πλουσίως *plousiōs* abundantly, richly*
πλουτέω *plouteō* be (or become) rich*
πλουτίζω *ploutizō* make rich*
πλοῦτος, ου, ὁ/τό *ploutos* wealth, abundance*

πλουσίως *plousiōs* abundantly, richly
→ πλούσιος.

πλουτέω *plouteō* be (or become) rich
→ πλούσιος.

πλουτίζω *ploutizō* make rich
→ πλούσιος.

πλοῦτος, ου, ὁ/τό *ploutos* wealth, abundance
→ πλούσιος.

1. **1:** third declension adjectives in which the three genders have the same forms; **2:** adjectives in which masculine and feminine forms are identical, including second declension adjectives in -ος, -ον and third declension adjectives in -ης, -ες and -ων, -ον; **3:** adjectives in which the three genders have different forms, including first and second declension adjectives in -ος, -η/-α, -ον and -οῦς, -ῆ/-ᾶ, -οῦν, first and third declension adjectives in -υς, -εια, -υ and those formed like πᾶς, πᾶσα, πᾶν, and a few adjectives which combine declensional patterns in ways not listed here.

2. The headings of articles are usually not a complete guide to meaning, since in some cases only a selection of documented meanings is included and since the bodies of articles discuss the meanings of words as they appear in context in different usages.

INTRODUCTION

The *body* of a shorter article normally mentions all New Testament occurrences of a word, grouped, if appropriate, according to different usages and different kinds of contexts in which the word is found, and discusses the more interesting, difficult, or controversial occurrences. Shorter articles also often include some bibliography listing discussions in reference works, journal articles, monographs, and commentaries of New Testament usage of the word and of passages in which the word plays a decisive role.

More is provided for more significant words — actually many of the words in the New Testament, including both words of great frequency and words that express significant New Testament concepts. *Longer articles* are usually divided into numbered sections, sometimes with lettered subsections, and often include an outline listing the sections and subsections. An extended bibliography, which emphasizes recent works, usually precedes the body of a longer article.

παρθένος, ου, ἡ (ὁ) *parthenos* virgin; young woman of marriageable age; chaste man*

1. Occurrences in the NT — 2. "Young woman" — 3. Mary as virgin — 4. 1 Corinthians 7 — 5. 2 Cor. 11:2 — 6. Acts 14:4

Lit.: R. A. BATEY, *NT Nuptial Imagery* (1971). — O. BECKER and C. BROWN, *DNTT* III, 1071-73. — G. DELLING, *TDNT* V, 826-37. — J. M. FORD, "The Meaning of 'Virgin,'" *NTS* 12 (1965/66) 293-99. — W. G. KÜMMEL, "Verlobung und Heirat bei Paulus (I. Kor 7,36-38)," FS Bultmann (1954) 275-95. — L. LEGRAND, "Saint Paul et le célibat," *Sacerdoce et célibat* (BETL 28, ed. J. Coppens; 1971) 315-31. — K. NIEDERWIMMER, "Zur Analyse der asketischen Motivation in 1 Kor 7," *TLZ* 99 (1974) 241-48. — H. M. ORLINSKY, *IDBSup* 939f. — A. SCHULZ, "'Almā,'" *BZ* 23 (1935) 229-41. — R. H. A. SEBOLDT, "Spiritual Marriage in the Early Church," *CTM* 30 (1959) 103-19, 176-86. — F. A. STROBEL, "Zum Verständnis von Mt XXV 1-13," *NovT* 2 (1957) 199-227. — G. J. WENHAM, "*Bᵉtûlâh* 'A Girl of Marriageable Age,'" *VT* 22 (1972) 326-48. — For further bibliography see *TWNT* X, 1217-20.

The body of a longer article generally proceeds from a statistical summary of the word's New Testament occurrences, through discussion of the word's range of meanings and of the variety of usages in which it is found in the New Testament, to treatment of the exegetical and theological significance of the word in the different blocks of New Testament literature. Included where relevant is treatment of the background of New Testament usage of the word in classical Greek, the Septuagint, post-Old Testament Judaism, and Hellenistic literature. For names of persons and places, consideration is given to the historical background of the person's or place's significance in the New Testament. Where one of these longer *EDNT* articles touches on matters of significant disagreement among scholars, the author of the article summarizes and enters into the discussion.

Both shorter and longer articles include cross-references (→) to other articles where further treatment of words or exegetical problems under discussion are touched on. The index to all three volumes of *EDNT* appears on page 513.

CONTRIBUTORS

Horst Balz, Bochum, Germany
Gerhard Barth, Wuppertal, Germany
Johannes B. Bauer, Graz, Austria
Günther Baumbach, Berlin, Germany
Wolfgang Beilner, Salzburg, Austria
Klaus Berger, Heidelberg, Germany
Roland Bergmeier, Weingarten, Germany
Otto Betz, Tübingen, Germany
Johannes Beutler, Frankfurt, Germany
Otto Böcher, Mainz, Germany
Udo Borse, Bonn, Germany
Gijs Bouwman, Tilburg, Netherlands
Jan-Adolf Bühner, Tübingen, Germany
Willi Egger, Brixen, Italy
Winfried Elliger, Tübingen, Germany
Wolfgang Feneberg, Munich, Germany
Peter Fiedler, Freiburg, Germany
Gottfried Fitzer, Vienna, Austria
Joseph A. Fitzmyer, Washington, D.C., USA
Hubert Frankemölle, Paderborn, Germany
Johannes H. Friedrich, Jerusalem, Israel
Heinz Giesen, Hennef, Germany
Horst Goldstein, Lilienthal, Germany
Klaus Haacker, Wuppertal, Germany
Wolfgang Hackenberg, Witten, Germany
Ferdinand Hahn, Munich, Germany
Victor Hasler, Bern, Switzerland
Günter Haufe, Greifswald, Germany
Harald Hegermann, Munich, Germany
Otfried Hofius, Tübingen, Germany
Harm W. Hollander, Haarlem, Netherlands
Traugott Holtz, Halle, Germany
Axel Horstmann, Hamburg, Germany
Hans Hübner, Göttingen, Germany
Ulrich Hutter, Bonn, Germany
Ulrich Kellermann, Mülheim, Germany
Wilhelm Köhler, Wuppertal, Germany
Heinrich Kraft, Kiel, Germany
Reinhard Kratz, Bensheim, Germany
Jacob Kremer, Vienna, Austria
Armin Kretzer, Würzburg, Germany

Horst Kuhli, Königstein, Germany
Heinz-Wolfgang Kuhn, Munich, Germany
Hugolinus Langkammer, Lublin, Poland
Edvin Larsson, Oslo, Norway
Hermann Lichtenberger, Münster, Germany
Gerd Lüdemann, Göttingen, Germany
Helmut Merkel, Osnabrück, Germany
Helmut Merklein, Bonn, Germany
Otto Michel, Tübingen, Germany
Paul-Gerd Müller, Trier, Germany
Gottfried Nebe, Bochum, Germany
Johannes M. Nützel, Münster, Germany
Wolf-Henning Ollrog, Darmstadt, Germany
Angela Palzkill, Bochum, Germany
Elisabeth Palzkill, Bochum, Germany
Hermann Patsch, Munich, Germany
Henning Paulsen, Hamburg, Germany
Rudolf Pesch, Munich, Germany
Eckhard Plümacher, Berlin, Germany
Wolfgang Pöhlmann, Lüneberg, Germany
Wiard Popkes, Hamburg, Germany
Felix Porsch, St. Augustin, Germany
Karl-Heinz Pridik, Wuppertal, Germany
Hermann Probst, Erlangen, Germany
Walter Radl, Augsburg, Germany
Walter Rebell, Siegen, Germany
Mathias Rissi, Stonington, ME, USA
Hubert Ritt, Regensburg, Germany
Joachim Rohde, Berlin, Germany
Monika Rutenfranz, Bochum, Germany
Alexander Sand, Bochum, Germany
Dieter Sänger, Flensburg, Germany
†Karl Hermann Schelkle, Tübingen, Germany
Wolfgang Schenk, Eppstein, Germany
Gottfried Schille, Borsdorf bei Leipzig, Germany
Gerhard Schneider, Bochum, Germany
Franz Schnider, Regensburg, Germany
Tim Schramm, Hamburg, Germany
Gerd Schunack, Marburg, Germany
Benedikt Schwank, Beuron, Germany, and
    Jerusalem, Israel

CONTRIBUTORS

Günther Schwarz, Wagenfeld, Germany
Eduard Schweizer, Zurich, Switzerland
Johannes Thomas, Bremerhaven, Germany
Peter Trummer, Graz, Austria
Martin Völkel, Dortmund, Germany
Nikolaus Walter, Jena, Germany

Alfons Weiser, Vallendar, Germany
Martin Winter, Wetter-Oberrosphe, Germany
Michael Wolter, Bayreuth, Germany
Dieter Zeller, Mainz, Germany
Josef Zmijewski, Fulda, Germany

ABBREVIATIONS

1. The Bible and Other Ancient Literature

a. Old Testament

Gen	Genesis	Cant	Canticles
Exod	Exodus	Isa	Isaiah
Lev	Leviticus	Jer	Jeremiah
Num	Numbers	Lam	Lamentations
Deut	Deuteronomy	Ezek	Ezekiel
Josh	Joshua	Dan	Daniel
Judg	Judges	Hos	Hosea
Ruth	Ruth	Joel	Joel
1–2 Sam	1–2 Samuel	Amos	Amos
1–2 Kgs	1–2 Kings	Obad	Obadiah
1–2 Chr	1–2 Chronicles	Jonah	Jonah
Ezra	Ezra	Mic	Micah
Neh	Nehemiah	Nah	Nahum
Esth	Esther	Hab	Habakkuk
Job	Job	Zeph	Zephaniah
Ps(s)	Psalm(s)	Hag	Haggai
Prov	Proverbs	Zech	Zechariah
Eccl	Ecclesiastes	Mal	Malachi

b. Apocrypha and Septuagint

1–4 Kgdms	1–4 Kingdoms	1–4 Macc	1–4 Maccabees
Add Esth	Additions to Esther	Pr Azar	Prayer of Azariah
Bar	Baruch	Pr Man	Prayer of Manasseh
Bel	Bel and the Dragon	Sir	Sirach (Ecclesiasticus)
1–2 Esdr	1–2 Esdras	Sus	Susanna
4 Ezra	4 Ezra	Tob	Tobit
Jdt	Judith	Wis	Wisdom of Solomon
Ep Jer	Epistle of Jeremiah		

c. New Testament

Matt	Matthew	1–2 Thess	1–2 Thessalonians
Mark	Mark	1–2 Tim	1–2 Timothy
Luke	Luke	Titus	Titus
John	John	Phlm	Philemon
Acts	Acts	Heb	Hebrews
Rom	Romans	Jas	James
1–2 Cor	1–2 Corinthians	1–2 Pet	1–2 Peter
Gal	Galatians	1–3 John	1–3 John
Eph	Ephesians	Jude	Jude
Phil	Philippians	Rev	Revelation
Col	Colossians		

ABBREVIATIONS

d. Pseudepigrapha and Early Church Writings

Acts John	Acts of John	Smyrn.	Smyrnaeans
Acts Pet.	Acts of Peter	Trall.	Trallians
Acts Phil.	Acts of Philip	Irenaeus	
Acts Pil.	Acts of Pilate	Haer.	Adversus Haereses
Acts Thom.	Acts of Thomas	Jos. As.	Joseph and Aseneth
Apoc. Abr.	Apocalypse of Abraham	Jub.	Jubilees
Apoc. Elijah	Apocalypse of Elijah	Justin	
Apoc. Mos.	Apocalypse of Moses	Apol.	Apologia
Apoc. Paul	Apocalypse of Paul	Dial.	Dialogue with Trypho
Apoc. Pet.	Apocalypse of Peter	Mart. Andr.	Martyrdom of Andrew
Apoc. Zeph.	Apocalypse of Zephaniah	Mart. Isa.	Martyrdom of Isaiah
Asc. Isa.	Ascension of Isaiah	Mart. Pol.	Martyrdom of Polycarp
Athenagoras		Odes Sol.	Odes of Solomon
Suppl.	Supplicatio	Origen	
2–3 Bar.	Syriac, Greek Apocalypse of Baruch	Cels.	Contra Celsum
Barn.	Barnabas	De Prin.	De Principia
Bib. Ant.	Pseudo-Philo Biblical Antiquities	Frag. in Prov.	Fragmenta in Proverbia
1–2 Clem.	1–2 Clement	Orat.	De Oratione
Clement of Alexandria		Pol.	Polycarp
Quis Div. Salv.	Quis Dives Salvetur	Phil.	Epistle to the Philippians
Strom.	Stromata	Prot. Jas.	Protevangelium of James
Did.	Didache	Ps.-Clem. Hom.	Pseudo-Clementine Homilies
Diog.	Epistle to Diognetus	Ps.-Clem. Rec.	Pseudo-Clementine Recognitions
1–3 Enoch	Ethiopic, Slavonic, Hebrew Enoch	Pss. Sol.	Psalms of Solomon
Ep. Arist.	Epistle of Aristeas	Sib. Or.	Sibylline Oracles
Epiphanius		T. Abr.	Testament of Abraham
Haer.	Haereses	T. Isaac	Testament of Isaac
Eusebius		T. Job	Testament of Job
HE	Historia Ecclesiastica	T. Mos.	Testament ("Assumption") of Moses
Onom.	Onomasticon	T. Sol.	Testament of Solomon
PE	Praeparatio Evangelica	T. 12 Patr.	Testaments of the Twelve Patriarchs
Gos. Eb.	Gospel of the Ebionites	T. Ash.	Testament of Asher
Gos. Eg.	Gospel of the Egyptians	T. Benj.	Testament of Benjamin
Gos. Pet.	Gospel of Peter	T. Dan	Testament of Dan
Gos. Phil.	Gospel of Philip	T. Gad	Testament of Gad
Gos. Thom.	Gospel of Thomas	T. Iss.	Testament of Issachar
Gos. Truth	Gospel of Truth	T. Jos.	Testament of Joseph
Herm.	Shepherd of Hermas	T. Jud.	Testament of Judah
Man.	Mandates	T. Levi	Testament of Levi
Sim.	Similitudes	T. Naph.	Testament of Naphtali
Vis.	Visions	T. Reu.	Testament of Reuben
Hippolytus		T. Sim.	Testament of Simeon
Haer.	Refutatio Omnium Haeresium	T. Zeb.	Testament of Zebulun
Ign.	Ignatius	Tatian	
Eph.	Ephesians	Or. Graec.	Oratio ad Graecos
Magn.	Magnesians	Thund.	The Thunder: Perfect Mind (NHC VI, 2)
Phld.	Philadelphians	Vit. Proph.	Lives of the Prophets (Vitae
Pol.	Polycarp		Prophetarum)
Rom.	Romans		

e. Qumran and Related Texts

The standard abbreviations are used (see J. A. Fitzmyer, *The Dead Sea Scrolls: Major Publications and Tools for Study* [Sources for Biblical Study 8, ²1977]).

f. Rabbinic Literature

m.	Mishnah		b.	Babylonian Talmud
t.	Tosefta		y.	Jerusalem Talmud

'Abot	'Abot	Nazir	Nazir
'Arak.	'Arakin	Ned.	Nedarim
'Abod. Zar.	'Aboda Zara	Neg.	Nega'im
B. Bat.	Baba Batra	Nez.	Neziqin
Bek.	Bekorot	Nid.	Niddah
Ber.	Berakot	Ohol.	Oholot
Beṣa	Beṣa (= Yom Ṭob)	'Or.	'Orla
Bik.	Bikkurim	Para	Para
B. Meṣ.	Baba Meṣi'a	Pe'a	Pe'a
B. Qam.	Baba Qamma	Pesaḥ.	Pesaḥim
Dem.	Demai	Qinnim	Qinnim
'Erub.	'Erubin	Qidd.	Qiddušin
'Ed.	'Eduyyot	Qod.	Qodašin
Giṭ.	Giṭṭin	Roš Haš.	Roš Haššana
Ḥag.	Ḥagiga	Sanh.	Sanhedrin
Ḥal.	Ḥalla	Šabb.	Šabbat
Hor.	Horayot	Šeb.	Šebi'it
Ḥul.	Ḥullin	Šebu.	Šebu'ot
Kelim	Kelim	Šeqal.	Šeqalim
Ker.	Keritot	Soṭa	Soṭa
Ketub.	Ketubot	Sukk.	Sukka
Kil.	Kil'ayim	Ta'an.	Ta'anit
Ma'aś.	Ma'aśerot	Tamid	Tamid
Mak.	Makkot	Tem.	Temura
Makš.	Makširin (= Mašqin)	Ter.	Terumot
Meg.	Megilla	Ṭohar.	Ṭoharot
Me'il.	Me'ila	Ṭ. Yom	Ṭebul Yom
Menaḥ.	Menaḥot	'Uq.	'Uqṣin
Mid.	Middot	Yad.	Yadayim
Miqw.	Miqwa'ot	Yebam.	Yebamot
Mo'ed	Mo'ed	Yoma	Yoma (= Kippurim)
Mo'ed Qaṭ.	Mo'ed Qatan	Zabim	Zabim
Ma'aś. Š.	Ma'aśer Šeni	Zebaḥ.	Zebaḥim
Našim	Našim	Zer.	Zera'im
'Abot R. Nat.	'Abot de Rabbi Nathan	Midr.	Midrash
Bar.	Baraita	Midr. Qoh.	Midrash Qoheleth
Meg. Ta'an.	Megillath Ta'anith	Pesiq.	Pesiqta
Mek.	Mekilta	Rab.	Rabbah

g. Targums

Tg.	Targum	Tg. Yer. I	Targum Yerušalmi I (Pseudo-Jonathan)

h. Other Ancient Authors and Writings

Aeschylus
    A. — *Agamemnon*
    Ch. — *Choephori*
    Eu. — *Eumeniaes*
    Th. — *Septem contra Thebas*
Appian
    BC — *Bella Civilia*
Apuleius
    Met. — *Metamorphoses*
Aristides
    Or. — *Orationes*
Aristophanes
    Ec. — *Ecclesiasuzae*
    V. — *Vespae*

Aristotle
    De An. — *De Anima*
    EN — *Ethica Nicomachea*
    Metaph. — *Metaphysica*
    MM — *Magna Moralia*
    PA — *De Partibus Animalium*
    Ph. — *Physica*
    Po. — *Poetica*
    Pol. — *Politica*
    Rh. — *Rhetorica*
Cornutus
    Theol. Graec. — *Theologia Graeca*
    Corp. Herm. — *Corpus Hermeticum*

ABBREVIATIONS

Demosthenes
  - *Cor.* — *De Corona*
  - *Or.* — *Orationes*

Dio Chrysostom
  - *Or.* — *Orationes*

Epictetus
  - *Diss.* — *Dissertationes*

Euripides
  - *Alc.* — *Alcestis*
  - *Andr.* — *Andromache*
  - *IA* — *Iphigenia Aulidensis*
  - *IT* — *Iphigenia Taurica*
  - *Med.* — *Medea*
  - *Tr.* — *Trodes*

Hesiod
  - *Op.* — *Opera et Dies*
  - *Th.* — *Theogonia*

Hippocrates
  - *Art.* — Περί ἄρθρων ἐμβολῆς
  - *Prog.* — Προγνωστικόν

Homer
  - *Il.* — *Iliad*
  - *Od.* — *Odyssey*

Iamblichus
  - *VP* — *De Vita Pythagorica*

Josephus
  - *Ant.* — *Antiquitates Judaicae*
  - *Ap.* — *Contra Apionem*
  - *B.J.* — *De Bello Judaico*
  - *Vita* — *Vita Josephi*

Libanius
  - *Decl.* — *Declamationes*

Lucian
  - *Alex.* — *Alexander sive Pseudomantis*
  - *Im.* — *Imagines*
  - *JTr.* — *Juppiter Tragoedus*
  - *Macr.* — *Macrobii*
  - *Peregr.* — *De Morte Peregrini*
  - *Philops.* — *Philopseudes*
  - *Sacr.* — *De Sacrificiis*
  - *Sat.* — *Saturnalia*
  - *Symp.* — *Symposium*
  - *Tim.* — *Timon*
  - *VH* — *Verae Historiae*

Ovid
  - *Am.* — *Amores*

Philo
  - *Abr.* — *De Abrahamo*
  - *All.* — *Legum Allegoriae*
  - *Cher.* — *De Cherubim*
  - *Conf.* — *De Confusione Linguarum*
  - *Decal.* — *De Decalogo*
  - *Det.* — *Quod Deterius Potiori insidiari soleat*
  - *Ebr.* — *De Ebrietate*
  - *Exsec.* — *Exsecrationibus*
  - *Flacc.* — *In Flaccum*
  - *Gig.* — *De Gigantibus*
  - *Her.* — *Quis Rerum Divinarum Heres Sit*
  - *Imm.* — *Quod Deus Sit Immutabilis*
  - *Jos.* — *De Josepho*
  - *Leg. Gai.* — *Legatio ad Gaium*
  - *Migr.* — *De Migratione Abrahami*

  - *Mut.* — *De Mutatione Nominum*
  - *Omn. Prob. Lib.* — *Quod Omnis Probus Liber Sit*
  - *Op.* — *De Opificione Mundi*
  - *Plant.* — *De Plantatione*
  - *Praem.* — *De Praemiis et Poenis*
  - *Post.* — *De Posteritate Caini*
  - *Prov.* — *De Providentia*
  - *Quaest. Ex.* — *Quaestiones et Solutiones in Exodum*
  - *Quaest. Gen.* — *Quaestiones et Solutiones in Genesim*
  - *Sacr.* — *De Sacrificiis Abelis et Caini*
  - *Som.* — *De Somniis*
  - *Spec. Leg.* — *De Specialibus Legibus*
  - *Virt.* — *De Virtutibus*
  - *Vit. Cont.* — *De Vita Contemplativa*
  - *Vit. Mos.* — *De Vita Mosis*

Philostratus
  - *VA* — *Vita Apollonii*

Plato
  - *Ap.* — *Apologia*
  - *Chrm.* — *Charmides*
  - *Cra.* — *Cratylus*
  - *Euthphr.* — *Euthyphro*
  - *Grg.* — *Gorgias*
  - *La.* — *Laches*
  - *Lg.* — *Leges*
  - *Lys.* — *Lysis*
  - *Mx.* — *Menexenus*
  - *Phd.* — *Phaedo*
  - *Phdr.* — *Phaedrus*
  - *Plt.* — *Politicus*
  - *R.* — *Republic*
  - *Smp.* — *Symposium*
  - *Sph.* — *Sophista*
  - *Tht.* — *Theaetetus*
  - *Ti.* — *Timaeus*

Pliny
  - *HN* — *Historia Naturalis*

Plutarch
  - *Ant.* — *Antonius*
  - *Apophth. Lac.* — *Apophthegmata Laconica*
  - *Brut.* — *Brutus*
  - *Cam.* — *Camillus*
  - *Cat. Mi.* — *Cato Minor*
  - *Cons. ad Apoll.* — *Consolatio ad Apollonium*
  - *Cor.* — *Coriolanus*
  - *De Def. Orac.* — *De Defectu Oraculorum*
  - *Demetr.* — *Demetrius*
  - *Lib. Educ.* — *De Liberis Educandis*
  - *Luc.* — *Lucullus*
  - *Lyc.* — *Lycurgus*
  - *Mar.* — *Marius*
  - *Pel.* — *Pelopidas*
  - *Per.* — *Pericles*
  - *Pomp.* — *Pompeius*
  - *Pyth.* — *De Pythiae Oraculis*
  - *Quaest. Conv.* — *Quaestiones Convivales*
  - *Rect. Rat.* — *De Recta Ratione Audiendi*
  - *Sept. Sap.* — *Septem Sapientum Convivum*
  - *Superst.* — *De Superstitione*

Ptolemy
  - *Apotel.* — *De Apotelesmatibus (Tetrabiblos)*

Seneca			*Hist.*	*Historiae*
Ben.	*De Beneficiis*		Theophrastus	
Ira	*De Ira*		*CP*	*De Causis Plantarum*
Marc.	*De Consolatione ad Marciam*		*Sens.*	*De Sensu*
Sophocles			Virgil	
Aj.	*Ajax*		*Aen.*	*Aeneid*
Ant.	*Antigone*		Xenophon	
El.	*Electra*		*An.*	*Anabasis*
OT	*Oedipus Tyrannus*		*Cyr.*	*Institutio Cyri (Cyropaedia)*
Suetonius			*HG*	*Historia Graeca (Hellenica)*
Caes.	*De Vita Caesarum*		*Mem.*	*Memorabilia*
Tacitus				
Ann.	*Annales*			

i. Inscriptions, Fragments, Papyri, and Anthologies

ÄgU	Ägyptische Urkunden aus den Staatlichen Museen zu Berlin, Griechische Urkunden I-XI (1895-1970)
CIG	*Corpus Inscriptionum Graecarum* I-IV (ed. A. Boeckh, et al.; 1828-77)
CIJ	*Corpus Inscriptionum Judaicarum* I-II (1936, 1952)
CIL	*Corpus Inscriptionum Latinarum* I-XVI (1862-1943, [2]1893-)
CPJ	*Corpus Papyrorum Judaicarum* (1957ff.)
Diehl, *Anthologia*	E. Diehl, *Anthologia Lyrica Graeca* I-III ([2]1949-52 = 1954-64)
Diels, *Fragmente*	H. Diels and W. Kranz, *Die Fragmente der Vorsokratiker* ([11]1964)
FAC	*Fragments of Attic Comedy* I-IIIB (ed. J. M. Edmonds; 1957-61)
FGH	*Fragmente der griechischen Historiker* (1923ff.)
IG	*Inscriptiones Graecae* (1873-1939)
NHC	*Nag Hammadi Codices*
OGIS	*Orientis Graeci Inscriptiones Selectae* I-II (ed. W. Dittenberger; 1903, 1905, reprint 1960)
Pap.	Papyrus, Papyri
Pap. Fayûm	*Fayûm Towns and the Papyri,* ed. B. P. Grenfell, A. S. Hunt, and D. Hogarth (1900)
Pap. Flor.	*Papiri Florentini, Papiri Greco-Egizii* I-III (1906-15)
Pap. Leipzig	*Griechische Urkunden der Papytussamlung zu Leipzig* (ed. L. Miteis; 1906)
Pap. London	*Greek Papyri in the British Museum* I-II (ed. F. G. Kenyon; 1893, 1898), III (ed. F. G. Kenyon and H. I. Bell; 1907), IV-V (ed. H. I. Bell; 1910, 1917)
Pap. Oxy.	*The Oxyrhynchus Papyri* I-XLI (ed. B. P. Grenfell, A. S. Hunt, et al.; 1898-1972)
Pap. Petrie	*The Flinders Petrie Papyri* I-II (ed. J. P. Mahaffy; 1891), III (ed. J. P. Mahaffy and J. G. Smyly; 1905)
Pap. Tebt.	*The Tebtunis Papyri* I-III (ed. B. P. Grenfell, A. S. Hunt, et al.; 1902-38)
Pap. Zenon	*Zenon Papyri: Business Papers of the 3rd Century B.C.* I (ed. W. L. Westermann and E. S. Hasenoehrl; 1934), II (ed. W. L. Westermann, C. W. Keys, and H. Liebesny; 1940)
PGM	*Papyri Graecae Magicae. Die griechischen Zauberpapyri* (ed. K. Preisendanz, et al.; [2]1973, 1974)
Preisigke, *Sammelbuch*	F. Preisigke, F. Bilabel, and E. Kiessling, *Sammelbuch griechischer Urkunden aus Ägypten* I-XI (1915-73)
SIG	*Sylloge Inscriptionum Graecarum* I-IV (ed. W. Dittenberger; [3]1915-24, reprinted 1960)
von Arnim, *Fragmenta*	J. von Arnim, *Stoicorum Veterum Fragmenta* I-IV (1903-24 = 1964)

2. Modern Writings

Commentaries on biblical books are identified by the abbreviations for the names of the biblical books (p. xi above) in italics.

AAWLM.G	Abhandlungen der Akademie der Wissenschaften und der Literatur in Mainz. Geistes- und sozialwissenschaftliche Klasse
AB	Anchor Bible
Abel, *Géographie*	F.-M. Abel, *Géographie de la Palestine* I-II (1933-38)
ABR	*Australian Biblical Review*
ACJD	Abhandlungen zum christlich-jüdischen Dialog
AGJU	Arbeiten zur Geschichte des antiken Judentums und des Urchristentums
AGSU	Arbeiten zur Geschichte des Spätjudentums und Urchristentums
AJA	*American Journal of Archaeology*
AJT	*American Journal of Theology*
ALGHL	Arbeiten zur Literatur und Geschichte des hellenistischen Judentums

ABBREVIATIONS

AnBib	Analecta Biblica
ANET	*Ancient Near Eastern Texts Relating to the OT* (ed. J. B. Pritchard; ³1969)
Ang	*Angelicum*
AnGr	Analecta Gregoriana
ANRW	*Aufstieg und Niedergang der römischen Welt*
ANTJ	Arbeiten zum NT und Judentum
ASGW(PH)	Abhandlungen der sächsischen Gesellschaft der Wissenschaft (Philologisch-historische Klasse)
AsSeign	*Assemblées du Seigneur*
ASNU	Acta seminarii Neotestamentici Upsaliensis
ASTI	*Annual of the Swedish Theological Institute*
ATANT	Abhandlungen zur Theologie des Alten und Neuen Testaments
ATR	*Anglican Theological Review*
AuA	*Antike und Abendland*
AuC	*Antike und Christentum. Kultur- und religionsgeschichtliche Studien*
AUSS	*Andrews University Seminary Studies*
AzT	Arbeiten zur Theologie
BA	*Biblical Archaeologist*
BAGD	W. Bauer, W. F. Arndt, F. W. Gingrich, and F. Danker, *A Greek-English Lexicon of the NT and Other Early Christian Literature* (²1979)
BBB	Bonner biblische Beiträge
BBET	Beiträge zur biblischen Exegese und Theologie
BDF	F. Blass, A. Debrunner, and R. W. Funk, *A Greek Grammar of the NT and Other Early Christian Literature* (1961)
BeO	*Bibbia e oriente*
Beginnings	*The Beginnings of Christianity,* Part I: *The Acts of the Apostles* (ed. F. J. Foakes-Jackson and K. Lake; 1920-33)
BETL	Bibliotheca ephemeridum theologicarum Lovaniensium
BEURU	Bibliotheca Ekmaniana Universitatis Regiae Upsaliensis
BEvT	Beiträge zur evangelischen Theologie
Beyer, *Syntax*	K. Beyer, *Semitische Syntax im NT* I/1 (1962)
BFCT	Beiträge zur Förderung christlicher Theologie
BGBE	Beiträge zur Geschichte der biblischen Exegese
BHH	*Biblisch-historisches Handwörterbuch* I-III (single pagination; ed. B. Reicke and L. Rost; 1962-66)
BHT	Beiträge zur Historischen Theologie
Bib	*Biblica*
BibLeb	*Bibel und Leben*
BibS(F)	Biblische Studien (Freiburg)
BibS(N)	Biblische Studien (Neukirchen)
Bijdr.	*Bijdragen. Tijdschrift voor philosophie en theologie*
BiLi	*Bibel und Liturgie*
Billerbeck	(H. Strack and) P. Billerbeck, *Kommentar zum NT aus Talmud und Midrasch* I-IV (1922-28)
BJRL	*Bulletin of the John Rylands University Library of Manchester*
BK	*Bibel und Kirche*
BL	*Bibel-Lexikon,* ed. H. Haag (²1968)
Black, *Approach*	M. Black, *An Aramaic Approach to the Gospels and Acts* (³1967)
BNTC	Black's NT Commentaries
Bornkamm, *Aufsätze*	G. Bornkamm, *Gesammelte Aufsätze.* I: *Das Ende des Gesetzes. Paulusstudien;* II: *Studien zu Antike und Urchristentum;* III-IV: *Geschichte und Glaube* (1952-1971)
Bousset/Gressmann	W. Bousset, *Die Religion des Judentums im späthellenistischen Zeitalter* (ed. H. Gressmann; ⁴1966 = ³1926)
BR	*Biblical Research*
Braun, *Qumran*	H. Braun, *Qumran und das NT* I-II (1966)
BRL	*Biblisches Reallexikon* (ed. K. Galling; ²1977)
BSac	*Bibliotheca Sacra*
BT	*The Bible Translator*
BTB	*Biblical Theology Bulletin*
BTN	Bibliotheca Theologica Norvegica
BU	Biblische Untersuchungen
Bultmann, *Glauben*	R. Bultmann, *Glauben und Verstehen. Gesammelte Aufsätze* I-IV (1933-65)
Bultmann, *History*	R. Bultmann, *History of the Synoptic Tradition* (1963)
Bultmann, *Theology*	R. Bultmann, *Theology of the NT* I-II (1951, 1955)
BVC	*Bible et vie chrétienne*

BWANT	Beiträge zur Wissenschaft vom Alten und Neuen Testament
BZ	*Biblische Zeitschrift*
BZAW	Beihefte zur *Zeitschrift für die alttestamentliche Wissenschaft*
BZNW	Beihefte zur *Zeitschrift für die neutestamentliche Wissenschaft*
CB.NT	Coniectanea biblica, NT Series
CBQ	*Catholic Biblical Quarterly*
CGTC	Cambridge Greek Testament Commentary
CiW	Christ in der Welt
CNT	Commentaire du NT
Colloquium	*Colloquium: Australia and New Zealand Theological Review*
Compendia	Compendia Rerum Judaicarum ad Novum Testamentum
Conzelmann, *Theology*	H. Conzelmann, *An Outline of the Theology of the NT* (1969)
Cremer/Kögel	H. Cremer and J. Kögel, *Biblisch-theologisches Wörterbuch des neutestamentlichen Griechisch* (^{11}1923)
CTM	Calwer Theologische Monographien
CTM	*Concordia Theological Monthly*
CV	*Communio Viatorum*
Dalman, *Arbeit*	G. Dalman, *Arbeit und Sitte in Palästina* I-VII (1928-42, reprinted 1964)
Dalman, *Words*	G. Dalman, *The Words of Jesus* (1902)
DBSup	*Dictionnaire de la Bible, Supplément* (1928-)
DBT	*Dictionary of Biblical Theology* (ed. X. Léon-Dufour; 1967, ^{2}1972)
Deissmann, *Light*	A. Deissmann, *Light from the Ancient East* (^{2}1927)
Dibelius, *Botschaft*	M. Dibelius, *Botschaft und Geschichte. Gesammelte Studien* I-II (1953, 1956)
Dibelius, *Tradition*	M. Dibelius, *From Tradition to Gospel* (n.d.)
DNTT	*New International Dictionary of NT Theology* I-III (ed. C. Brown; 1975-78)
Dupont, *Béatitudes*	J. Dupont, *Les Béatitudes* I-III (1969, 1973)
EAEHL	*Encyclopedia of Archaeological Excavations in the Holy Land* I-IV (ed. M. Avi-Yonah and E. Stern; 1975-78)
ÉBib	Études Bibliques
EdF	Erträge der Forschung
EHS	Europäische Hochschulschriften
EKKNT	Evangelisch-katholischer Kommentar zum NT
EKKNT (V)	EKKNT Vorarbeiten
EncJud	*Encyclopaedia Judaica* I-XVI (1971-72)
EncPh	*Encyclopedia of Philosophy* I-VIII (ed. P. Edwards, et al., 1967)
EPRO	Études préliminaires aux religions orientales dans l'empire romain
ErJb	*Eranos-Jahrbuch*
EstBib	*Estudios biblicos*
ETL	*Ephemerides theologicae Lovanienses*
EvQ	*Evangelical Quarterly*
EvT	*Evangelische Theologie*
EWG	J. B. Hofmann, *Etymologisches Wörterbuch des Griechischen* (reprinted 1950)
ExpTim	*Expository Times*
Frisk, *Wörterbuch*	H. Frisk, *Griechisches etymologisches Wörterbuch* I-III (1960-72)
FRLANT	Forschungen zur Religion und Literatur des Alten und Neuen Testaments
FrRu	*Freiburger Rundbrief*
FS	Festschrift
FS Bardtke	*Bibel und Qumran* (FS H. Bardtke; 1968)
FS Black (1969)	*Neotestamentica et Semitica* (FS M. Black; 1969)
FS Black (1979)	*Text and Interpretation* (FS M. Black; 1979)
FS Bornkamm	*Kirche* (FS G. Bornkamm; 1980)
FS Braun	*Neues Testament und christliche Existenz* (FS H. Braun; 1973)
FS Bultmann (1954)	*Neutestamentliche Studien* (FS R. Bultmann; 1954)
FS Bultmann (1964)	*Zeit und Geschichte* (FS R. Bultmann; 1964)
FS Conzelmann	*Jesus Christus in Historie und Theologie* (FS H. Conzelmann; 1975)
FS Cullmann (1962)	*Neotestamentica et Patristica* (FS O. Cullmann; 1962)
FS Cullmann (1972)	*Neues Testament und Geschichte* (FS O. Cullmann; 1972)
FS Dahl	*God's Christ and His People* (FS N. A. Dahl; 1977)
FS Daube	*Donum Gentilicium* (FS D. Daube; 1978)
FS de Zwaan	*Studia Paulinum in honorem Johannis de Zwaan* (1953)
FS Dinkler	*Theologia Crucis — Signum Crucis* (FS E. Dinkler; 1979)
FS Dupont	*À cause de l'évangile* (FS J. Dupont; 1985)

ABBREVIATIONS

FS Ellis	*Tradition and Interpretation in the NT* (FS E. E. Ellis; 1987)
FS Fuchs	*Festschrift für Ernst Fuchs* (1973)
FS Gingrich	*Festschrift to Honor F. W. Gingrich* (1972)
FS Greeven	*Studien zum Text und zur Ethik des NT* (FS H. Greeven; 1986)
FS Haenchen	*Apophoreta* (FS E. Haenchen; 1964)
FS Jeremias (1960)	*Judentum, Urchristentum, Kirche* (FS J. Jeremias; 1960)
FS Jeremias (1970)	*Der Ruf Jesu und die Antwort der Gemeinde* (FS J. Jeremias; 1970)
FS Käsemann	*Rechtfertigung* (FS E. Käsemann; 1976)
FS Kilpatrick	*Studies in NT Language and Text* (FS G. D. Kilpatrick; 1976)
FS Kuhn	*Tradition und Glaube. Das frühe Christentum in seiner Umwelt* (FS K. G. Kuhn; 1971)
FS Kümmel (1975)	*Jesus und Paulus* (FS W. G. Kümmel; 1975)
FS Kümmel (1985)	*Glaube und Eschatologie* (FS W. G. Kümmel; 1985)
FS Michel	*Abraham unser Vater. Juden und Christen im Gespräch über die Bibel* (FS O. Michel; 1963)
FS Moule	*Christ and Spirit in the NT* (FS C. F. D. Moule; 1973)
FS Mussner	*Kontinuität und Einheit* (FS F. Mussner; 1981)
FS Ratzinger	*Weisheit Gottes—Weisheit der Welt* (FS J. Cardinal Ratzinger; 1987)
FS Rengstorf (1973)	*Theokratia II* (FS K. H. Rengstorf; 1973)
FS Rengstorf (1980)	*Wort in der Zeit. Neutestamentliche Studien* (FS K. H. Rengstorf; 1980)
FS Rigaux	*Mélanges Bibliques en hommage au B. Rigaux* (1970)
FS Schelkle	*Wort Gottes in der Zeit* (FS K. H. Schelkle; 1973)
FS Schmid (1963)	*Neutestamentliche Aufsätze* (FS J. Schmid; 1963)
FS Schmid (1973)	*Orientierung an Jesus* (FS J. Schmid; 1973)
FS Schnackenburg	*Neues Testament und Kirche* (FS R. Schnackenburg; 1974)
FS Schürmann	*Die Kirche des Anfangs* (FS H. Schürmann; 1977)
FS Stählin	*Verborum Veritas* (FS G. Stählin; 1970)
FS Vögtle	*Jesus und der Menschensohn* (FS A. Vögtle; 1975)
FS Zimmermann	*Begegnung mit dem Wort* (FS H. Zimmermann; 1980)
FTS	Frankfurter theologische Studien
Fuchs, *Aufsätze*	E. Fuchs, *Gesammelte Aufsätze* I-III (1959-65)
FzB	Forschungen zur Bibel
GCS	Die griechischen christlichen Schriftsteller
Glotta	*Glotta. Zeitschrift für die griechische und lateinische Sprache*
Goppelt, *Theology*	L. Goppelt, *Theology of the NT* I, II (1981, 1982)
GTA	Göttinger Theologische Arbeiten
GTB	Van Gorcum's theologische bibliotheek
GuL	*Geist und Leben*
Hahn, *Titles*	F. Hahn, *The Titles of Jesus in Christology* (1969)
Haenchen I-II	E. Haenchen, *Gesammelte Aufsätze*. I: *Gott und Mensch* (1965); II: *Die Bibel und wir* (1968)
Harnack, *Mission*	A. Harnack, *The Mission and Expansion of Christianity in the First Three Centuries* I-II (1904-05)
Hatch/Redpath	E. Hatch and H. A. Redpath, *A Concordance to the Septuagint* I-III (1897-1906)
Hengel, *Judaism*	M. Hengel, *Judaism and Hellenism* I-II (1974)
Hennecke/ Schneemelcher	E. Hennecke, *New Testament Apocrypha* I-II (ed. W. Schneemelcher and [English translation] R. McL. Wilson; 1963, 1965)
Hermeneia	Hermeneia—A Critical and Historical Commentary on the Bible
HKNT	Handkommentar zum NT
HNT	Handbuch zum NT
HNTC	Harper's NT Commentaries
HTG	*Handbuch theologischer Grundbegriffe* I-II (ed. H. Fries; 1962, 1963)
HTKNT	Herders theologischer Kommentar zum NT
HTR	*Harvard Theological Review*
HUCA	*Hebrew Union College Annual*
ICC	International Critical Commentary
IDB	*Interpreter's Dictionary of the Bible* I-IV (ed. G. A. Buttrick, et al.; 1962)
IDBSup	*Interpreter's Dictionary of the Bible, Supplementary Volume* (ed. K. Crim; 1976)
IEJ	*Israel Exploration Journal*
IKZ	*Internationale kirchliche Zeitschrift*
Int	*Interpretation*
ISBE	*The International Standard Bible Encyclopedia* I-IV (ed. G. W. Bromiley, et al.; 1979-88)
JAAR	*Journal of the American Academy of Religion*
JAC	Jahrbuch für Antike und Christentum
JBL	*Journal of Biblical Literature*
Jeremias, *Parables*	J. Jeremias, *The Parables of Jesus* (^{2}1972)

Jeremias, *Theology*	J. Jeremias, *NT Theology* (1971)
JES	*Journal of Ecumenical Studies*
JJS	*Journal of Jewish Studies*
Johannessohn, *Präpositionen*	M. Johannessohn, *Der Gebrauch der Präpositionen in der Septuaginta* (1926)
JQR	*Jewish Quarterly Review*
JR	*Journal of Religion*
JSHRZ	*Jüdische Schriften aus hellenistisch-römischer Zeit* I-V (ed. W. G. Kümmel; 1973-)
JSJ	*Journal for the Study of Judaism*
JSNT	*Journal for the Study of the NT*
JSS	*Journal of Semitic Studies*
JTC	*Journal for Theology and the Church*
JTS	*Journal of Theological Studies*
JTSA	*Journal of Theology for South Africa*
Judaica	*Judaica. Beiträge zum Verständnis des jüdischen Schicksals in Vergangenheit und Gegenwart*
Jülicher I-II	A. Jülicher, *Die Gleichnissreden Jesu* I-II (1910)
Kairos	*Kairos. Zeitschrift für Religionswissenschaft und Theologie*
Käsemann, *Versuche*	E. Käsemann, *Exegetische Versuche und Besinnungen* I-II (⁴1965, ³1968)
KD	*Kerygma und Dogma*
KEK	Kritisch-exegetischer Kommentar über das NT
KlT	Kleine Texte
KNT	Kommentar zum NT
Kopp, *Places*	C. Kopp, *The Holy Places of the Gospels* (1963)
KP	*Der Kleine Pauly. Lexikon der Antike* I-V (ed. Ziegler and Sontheimer; 1964-75)
Kühner, *Grammatik*	R. Kühner, *Ausführliche Grammatik der griechischen Sprache* I by F. Blass, II by B. Gerth (1890-1904)
Kümmel I, II	W. G. Kümmel, *Heilsgeschehen und Geschichte* I-II (1965, 1978)
Kümmel, *Introduction*	W. G. Kümmel, *Introduction to the NT* (²1975)
Kuss I-III	O. Kuss, *Auslegung und Verkündigung* I-III (1963-71)
LAW	*Lexikon der Alten Welt* (ed. C. Andresen, H. Erbse, et al.; 1965)
Leipoldt/Grundmann	*Umwelt des Urchristentums* I-III (ed. J. Leipoldt and W. Grundmann; I: ²1967, II: ³1972, III: 1966)
Levy I-IV	J. Levy, *Wörterbuch über die Talmudim und Midraschim* (²1924 = 1963)
Lietzmann I-III	H. Lietzmann, *Kleine Schriften* I-III (1958-62)
LQ	*Lutheran Quarterly*
LSJ	H. G. Liddell, R. Scott, H. S. Jones, and R. McKenzie, *A Greek-English Lexicon* (⁹1940)
LTK	*Lexikon für Theologie und Kirche* I-XI (ed. J. Höfer and K. Rahner; ²1957-67)
LuM	*Liturgie und Mönchtum*
Maier/Schreiner	*Literatur und Religion des Frühjudentums. Eine Einführung* (ed. J. Maier and J. Schreiner; 1973)
Mayser, *Grammatik*	E. Mayser, *Grammatik der griechischen Papyri aus der Ptolemäerzeit* I-II (1906, 1934)
MGWJ	*Monatsschrift für Geschichte und Wissenschaft des Judentums*
MH	*Museum Helveticum*
Moore, *Judaism*	G. F. Moore, *Judaism in the First Centuries of the Christian Era* I-III (1927, 1930)
Morgenthaler, *Statistik*	R. Morgenthaler, *Statistik des neutestamentlichen Wortschatzes* (1958)
Moule, *Idiom-Book*	C. F. D. Moule, *An Idiom-Book of NT Greek* (²1959)
Moulton, *Grammar*	*A Grammar of NT Greek:* I by J. H. Moulton (²1908), II by W. F. Howard (1963), III, IV by N. Turner (1963, 1976)
Moulton/Milligan	J. H. Moulton and G. Milligan, *The Vocabulary of the Greek Testament, Illustrated from the Papyri and Other Non-literary Sources* (1930)
MTS	Münchener theologische Studien
MTSt	Marburger theologische Studien
MTZ	*Münchener theologische Zeitschrift*
MySal	*Mysterium Salutis*
NAWG.PH	Nachrichten der Akademie der Wissenschaften in Göttingen. Philogisch-historische Klasse
NCE	*New Catholic Encyclopedia* I-XV (ed. M. R. P. McGuire, et al.; 1967)
NEB	New English Bible
Neot	*Neotestamentica*
N.F.	Neue Folge
NGWG.PH	Nachrichten der Gesellschaft der Wissenschaften in Göttingen. Philologisch-historische Klasse
NIGTC	New International Greek Testament Commentary
NKZ	*Neue Kirchliche Zeitschrift*
NovT	*Novum Testamentum*
NovTSup	*Novum Testamentum* Supplements

ABBREVIATIONS

NRT	*La nouvelle revue théologique*
NTAbh	Neutestamentliche Abhandlungen
NTD	Das Neue Testament Deutsch
NTF	Neutestamentliche Forschungen
NTG	*Novum Testamentum Graece* (ed. E. Nestle and K. Aland; [25]1963; ed. K. Aland, M. Black, C. M. Martini, B. M. Metzger, and A. Wikgren; [26]1979)
NTL	New Testament Library
NTS	*New Testament Studies*
NTSR	NT for Spiritual Reading
OBL	*Orientalia et Biblica Lovaniensia*
OBO	Orbis Biblicus et Orientalis
OCD	*The Oxford Classical Dictionary* (ed. H. G. L. Hammond and H. H. Scullard; [2]1970)
OLZ	*Orientalische Literaturzeitung*
OrSyr	*L'orient Syrien*
ÖTK	Ökumenischer Taschenbuch-Kommentar
OTS	*Oudtestamentische Studiën*
Passow I-II	F. Passow, *Handwörterbuch der griechischen Sprache* I-II ([5]1841, 1857)
PEQ	*Palestine Exploration Quarterly*
PG	J.-P. Migne, *Patrologiae cursus completus. Series Graeca* (1857-1936)
PGL	G. W. H. Lampe, *A Patristic Greek Lexicon* ([4]1976)
PL	J.-P. Migne, *Patrologiae cursus completus. Series Latina* (1841-64)
PoTh	*Point Théologique*
Preisigke, *Wörterbuch*	F. Preisigke, *Wörterbuch der griechischen Papyrusurkunden* I-III (1925-31), Supplement I (1971)
Preisker, *Zeitgeschichte*	H. Preisker, *Neutestamentliche Zeitgeschichte* (1937)
Prümm, *Handbuch*	K. Prümm, *Religionsgeschichtliches Handbuch für den Raum der altchristlichen Umwelt* (1943 = 1954)
PW	(A.) *Paulys Real-Encyclopädie der classischen Altertumswissenschaft* (ed. G. Wissowa and W. Kroll; 1893-)
QD	Quaestiones Disputatae
QLP	*Questions liturgiques et paroissiales*
RAC	*Reallexikon für Antike und Christentum* (ed. T. Klauser; 1941-)
Radermacher, *Grammatik*	L. Radermacher, *Neutestamentliche Grammatik* ([2]1925)
RAr	*Revue Archéologique*
RB	*Revue Biblique*
RCB	*Revista de cultura bíblica*
RE	*Realencyclopädie für protestantische Theologie und Kirche* I-XXIV ([3]1896-1913)
Reicke, *NT Era*	B. Reicke, *The NT Era* (1968)
RevistBib	*Revista bíblica*
RevQ	*Revue de Qumran*
RevScRel	*Revue des sciences religieuses*
RevThom	*Revue Thomiste*
RGG	*Die Religion in Geschichte und Gegenwart* I-VI (ed. K. Galling, et al.; [3]1957-62)
RHPR	*Revue d'histoire et de philosophie religieuses*
RIL.L	*Rendiconti Instituto Lombardo. Classe di lettere e scienze morali e politiche*
Ristow/Matthiae	*Der historische Jesus und der kerygmatische Christus* (ed. H. Ristow and K. Matthiae; [3]1964)
RivB	*Rivista Biblica*
RMP	*Rheinisches Museum für Philologie*
RNT	Regensburger Neues Testament
Robertson, *Grammar*	A. T. Robertson, *A Grammar of the Greek NT in the Light of Historical Research* ([4]1934)
RSPT	*Revue des sciences philosophiques et théologiques*
RSR	*Recherches de science religieuse*
RSV	Revised Standard Version
RTL	*Revue théologique de Louvain*
RTP	*Revue de théologie et de philosophie*
SacVb	*Sacramentum Verbi* (= Encyclopedia of Biblical Theology; ed. J. B. Bauer; [3]1967)
SANT	Studien zum Alten und Neuen Testament
SBB	Stuttgarter biblische Beiträge
SBFA	Studii biblici Franciscani analecta
SBLDS	Society of Biblical Literature Dissertation Series
SBLMS	Society of Biblical Literature Monograph Series
SBLSBS	Society of Biblical Literature Sources for Biblical Study

SBS	Stuttgarter Bibelstudien
SBT	Studies in Biblical Theology
ScEc	Sciences Ecclésiastiques
ScEs	Science et esprit
Schelkle, Theology	K. H. Schelkle, Theology of the NT I-IV (1971-78)
Schlier I-IV	H. Schlier, Exegetische Aufsätze und Vorträge I-IV (1956-72)
Schmidt, Synonymik	J. H. H. Schmidt, Synonymik der griechischen Sprache I-IV (1876-86, reprinted 1967-69)
Schnackenburg I-II	R. Schnackenburg, Christian Existence in the NT (1968, 1969)
Schnackenburg, Botschaft	R. Schnackenburg, Die sittliche Botschaft des NT (²1962)
Schreiner/Dautzenberg	Gestalt und Anspruch des NT (ed. J. Schreiner and G. Dautzenberg; 1969)
Schulz, Q	S. Schulz, Q. Die Spruchquelle der Evangelisten (1972)
Schürer, History	E. Schürer, The History of the Jewish People in the Age of Jesus Christ I-III/1-2 (revised and ed. G. Vermes, F. Millar, and M. Black; 1973-87)
Schürmann I-III	H. Schürmann, Traditionsgeschichtliche Untersuchungen zu den synoptischen Evangelien (1968-76)
Schwyzer, Grammatik	E. Schwyzer, Griechische Grammatik I-IV (1939-71)
SE	Studia Evangelica (= TU 73, 87, 88, etc.)
SEÅ	Svensk exegetisk årsbok
SGU	Studia Graeca Upsaliensia
SHAW	Sitzungsberichte der Heidelberger Akademie der Wissenschaften. Philosophisch-historische Klasse
SJ	Studia Judaica
SJLA	Studies in Judaism in Late Antiquity
SJT	Scottish Journal of Theology
SNT	Studien zum NT
SNTSMS	Society for NT Studies Monograph Series
SNTU	Studien zum NT und seiner Umwelt
SO	Symbolae Osloenses
Sophocles, Lexicon	E. A. Sophocles, Greek Lexicon of the Roman and Byzantine Periods I-II (³1888)
SPAW	Sitzungsberichte der Preußischen Akademie der Wissenschaft zu Berlin. Philosophisch-historische Klasse
SPB	Studia postbiblica
SPCIC	Studiorum Paulinorum Congressus Internationalis Catholicus
Spicq, Notes	C. Spicq, Notes de lexicographie néo-testamentaire I-II, Suppl. (1978-82)
SSA	Schriften der Sektion für Altertumswissenschaft (Deutsche Akademie der Wissenschaft zu Berlin)
ST	Studia theologica
StOr	Studia Orientalia (Societas orientalis Fennica)
SUNT	Studien zur Umwelt des NT
SWJT	Southwestern Journal of Theology
TBer	Theologische Berichte
TBl	Theologische Blätter
TBü	Theologische Bücherei
TCGNT	B. Metzger, A Textual Commentary on the Greek NT (1971)
TDNT	Theological Dictionary of the NT I-X (ed. G. Kittel and G. Friedrich; 1964-76)
TDOT	Theological Dictionary of the OT (ed. J. Botterweck and H. Ringgren; ²1974-)
TEH	Theologische Existenz heute
TF	Theologische Forschung
TGl	Theologie und Glaube
THAT	Theologisches Handwörterbuch zum AT I-II (ed. E. Jenni and C. Westermann; 1971, 1976)
Theokratia	Theokratia. Jahrbuch des Institutum Judaicum Delitzschianum
ThGL	Thesaurus Graecae Linguae ab H. Stephano constructus I-IX (ed. Hase and Dindorf; 1831-65)
THKNT	Theologischer Handkommentar zum NT
TLZ	Theologische Literaturzeitung
TP	Theologie und Philosophie
TQ	Theologische Quartalschrift
TRE	Theologische Realenzyklopädie (ed. G. Krause and G. Müller; 1976-)
Trench, Synonyms	R. C. Trench, Synonyms of the NT (⁹1880)
TRu	Theologische Rundschau
TS	Theological Studies
TTK	Tidsskrift for teologi og kirke
TTS	Trierer Theologische Studien
TTZ	Trierer Theologische Zeitschrift
TU	Texte und Untersuchungen zur Geschichte der altchristlichen Literatur

ABBREVIATIONS

TViat	*Theologia Viatorum*
TWAT	*Theologisches Wörterbuch zum AT* I- (ed. G. J. Botterweck and H. Ringgren; 1970-)
TWNT	*Theologisches Wörterbuch zum NT* I-X (ed. G. Kittel and G. Friedrich; 1933-79)
TZ	*Theologische Zeitschrift*
UBSGNT	*The Greek NT* (ed. K. Aland, M. Black, C. M. Martini, B. M. Metzger, and A. Wikgren; [3]1975)
UTB	Uni-Taschenbücher
VC	*Vigiliae Christianae*
VD	*Verbum Domini*
VKGNT	*Vollständige Konkordanz zum griechischen NT* I-II (ed. K. Aland; 1978, 1983)
Volz, *Eschatologie*	P. Volz, *Die Eschatologie der jüdischen Gemeinde im neutestamentlichen Zeitalter* (1934)
von Rad, *Theology*	G. von Rad, *OT Theology* I, II (1962, 1965)
VT	*Vetus Testamentum*
WdF	Wege der Forschung
Westcott/Hort	B. F. Westcott and F. J. A. Hort, *The NT in the Original Greek* (1881)
Wettstein, *NT*	J. J. Wettstein, *Novum Testamentum Graecum* I-II (1751-52, reprinted 1962)
Wikenhauser, *Geschichtswert*	A. Wikenhauser, *Die Apostelgeschichte und ihr Geschichtswert* (1921)
WMANT	Wissenschaftliche Monographien zum Alten und Neuen Testament
WuD	*Wort und Dienst. Jahrbuch der Kirchlichen Hochschule Bethel*
WUNT	Wissenschaftliche Untersuchungen zum NT
Zahn, *Kanon*	T. Zahn, *Forschungen zur Geschichte des neutestamentlichen Kanons und der altkirchlichen Literatur* I-IX (1881-1916)
ZAW	*Zeitschrift für die Alttestamentliche Wissenschaft*
ZBK	Zürcher Bibelkommentare
ZDPV	*Zeitschrift des deutschen Palästina-Vereins*
ZdZ	*Zeichen der Zeit*
Zerwick, *Biblical Greek*	M. Zerwick, *Biblical Greek* (1963)
ZKG	*Zeitschrift für Kirchengeschichte*
ZKT	*Zeitschrift für katholische Theologie*
ZNW	*Zeitschrift für die neutestamentliche Wissenschaft*
Zorell, *Lexikon*	F. Zorell, *Novi Testamenti Lexicon Graecum* ([2]1931)
ZPE	*Zeitschrift für Papyrologie und Epigrafik*
ZST	*Zeitschrift für systematische Theologie*
ZTK	*Zeitschrift für Theologie und Kirche*
ZVSF	*Zeitschrift für vergleichende Sprachforschung*

3. General

Sigla in textual notes are from the twenty-fifth and twenty-sixth editions of *NTG*.

acc.	accusative	g.	gram(s)
act.	active (voice)	gen.	genitive
adj(s).	adjective(s), adjectival(ly)	Germ.	German
adv(s).	adverb(s), adverbial(ly)	Gk.	Greek
Akk.	Akkadian	Heb.	Hebrew
aor.	aorist	impf.	imperfect
Aram.	Aramaic	imv(s).	imperative(s)
art.	(definite) article	ind.	indicative
AT	Altes Testament, Ancien Testament	inf(s).	infinitive(s)
ch(s).	chapter(s)	intrans.	intransitive(ly)
conj.	conjunction	kg.	kilogram(s)
dat.	dative	km.	kilometer(s)
def. art.	definite article	κτλ.	etc. (Greek)
dir. obj.	direct object	L	Material in Luke not found in Matthew or Mark
diss.	dissertation		
ed.	edition, edited, editor(s)	l(l).	line number(s)
Eng.	English	Lat.	Latin
esp.	especially	LXX	Septuagint
fem.	feminine	M	Material in Matthew not found in Mark or Luke
fig.	figurative(ly)		
frag.	fragment	m.	meter(s)
fut.	future	masc.	masculine

mg.	marginal reading	prep(s).	preposition(s), prepositional
mid.	middle	pres.	present
mm.	millimeter(s)	pron(s).	pronoun(s)
ms(s).	manuscript(s)	Q	Hypothetical source of material
MT	Masoretic Text		common to Matthew and Luke but
neut.	neuter		not found in Mark
nom.	nominative	rel.	relative
NT	New Testament, Neues Testament,	sg.	singular
	Nouveau Testament	subj.	subject, subjective
obj(s).	object(s), objective	subjunc.	subjunctive
opt.	optative	subst.	substantive, substantivally
OT	Old Testament	tr.	translated, translation
p(p).	page(s)	TR	Textus Receptus
par.	parallel	trans.	transitive(ly)
partc.	participle	t.t.	technical term
pass.	passive	v(v).	verse(s)
pf.	perfect	vb(s).	verb(s)
pl.	plural	Vg.	Vulgate
plupf.	pluperfect	v.l.	variant reading
pred.	predicate	voc.	vocative

TRANSLITERATION SCHEME

Greek

α	*a*	η	*ē*		ϱ	*r*	
ᾳ	*ą*	ῃ	*ę̄*		ῥ	*rh*	
β	*b*	θ	*th*		σ, ς	*s*	
γ	*g*	ι	*i*		τ	*t*	
γγ	*ng*	κ	*k*		υ	*y (u in diphthongs)*	
γκ	*nk*	λ	*l*		φ	*ph*	
γξ	*nx*	μ	*m*		χ	*ch*	
γχ	*nch*	ν	*n*		ψ	*ps*	
δ	*d*	ξ	*x*		ω	*ō*	
ε	*e*	ο	*o*		ῳ	*ǭ*	
ζ	*z*	π	*p*		ʽ	*h*	

Hebrew and Aramaic

Consonants

א	*ʾ*	ח	*ḥ*		פ	*p̲*	
ב	*b̲*	ט	*ṭ*		פּ	*p*	
בּ	*b*	י	*y*		צ	*ṣ*	
ג	*g̲*	כ	*k̲*		ק	*q*	
גּ	*g*	כּ	*k*		ר	*r*	
ד	*d̲*	ל	*l*		שׂ	*ś*	
דּ	*d*	ם, מ	*m*		שׁ	*š*	
ה	*h*	ן, נ	*n*		ת	*t̲*	
ו	*w*	ס	*s*		תּ	*t*	
ז	*z*	ע	*ʿ*				

Vowels

ֲ	*a*	ֻ	*u*	(vocal)	*e*
ָ	*ā, o*	וּ	*â*		*a*
ֶ	*e*	ֵי	*ê*		*ĕ*
ֵ	*ē*	ִי	*î*		*o*
ִ	*i*	וֹ	*ô*		
	ō	וּ	*û*		

Π π

παγιδεύω *pagideuō* lay a snare, catch (in a snare)*

In Matt 22:15 fig. of the plan of the Pharisees to "*catch him [Jesus] in his words*" (ὅπως αὐτὸν παγιδεύσωσιν ἐν λόγῳ), where λόγος is both the words provoked and the "snare" or "trap"; cf. 1 Kgs 28:9; Prov 6:2 Symmachus (LXX παγίς). J. Schneider, *TDNT* V, 595f.

παγίς, ίδος, ἡ *pagis* snare, trap*

5 occurrences in the NT, always fig. or as a metaphor for a sudden and unexpected danger or evil: Luke 21:35 of the day of the Son of man, which comes suddenly on the unprepared "like a snare" (for catching a bird; cf. Isa 24:17f.); according to Rom 11:9 (quoting Ps 68:23 LXX) the altar will become a snare for those of Israel who remain unrepentant. In 1 Tim 3:7 παγὶς τοῦ διαβόλου (with ὀνειδισμός) is a metaphor for the dangerous consequences for a bishop of a bad reputation among outsiders; cf. also CD 4:17f.; likewise 2 Tim 2:26: → ἀνανήφω ἐκ τῆς τοῦ διαβόλου παγίδος, "be sobered by/ wriggle out of the snare of the devil"; 1 Tim 6:9 with πειρασμός and ἐπιθυμίαι. J. Schneider, *TDNT* V, 593-95; H. Wildberger, *BHH* 1702f.

πάγος, ου, ὁ *pagos* mountain, hill
→ Ἄρειος πάγος.

πάθημα, ατος, τό *pathēma* suffering, misfortune; passion*

1. Occurrences and meaning — 2. "Passions" — 3. The suffering of Christians and of Christ

Lit.: W. MICHAELIS, *TDNT* V, 930-35. — H. MILLAUER, *Leiden als Gnade. Eine traditionsgeschichtliche Untersuchung zur Leidenstheologie des 1 Petrus* (EHS 23/56, 1976). — P. VON DER OSTEN-SACKEN, *Römerbrief 8 als Beispiel paulinischer Soteriologie* (FRLANT 112, 1973) 260-309. — C. H. PROUDFOOT, "Ihitation or Realistic Participation," *Int* 17 (1963) 140-60. — P. SIBER, *Mit Christus leben. Eine Studie zur paulinischen Auferstehungshoffnung* (ATANT 61, 1971). — R. C. TANNEHILL, *Dying and Rising with Christ. A Study in Pauline Theology*

(BZNW 32, 1967). — For further bibliography → θλίβω, → πάσχω, see *TWNT* X, 1224f.; *DNTT* III, 725f.

1. πάθημα has the basic meaning *what a person experiences* (→ πάσχω), does not occur in the LXX, and occurs 16 times in the NT. Twice it designates passion experienced as a force (→ 2), elsewhere the *suffering/torment* of Christians and of Jesus Christ (→ 3). It should be kept in mind that under the influence of later atonement theology and Passion piety the translation "suffering of Christ" was often understood in the narrow sense of bitter physical or spiritual torments.

2. According to Rom 7:5 the "*passions* of sin" (that which leads to sin or is experienced as a result of sin) characterize life "in the flesh"; they become so powerful "through the law . . . in our members" that they cause death (cf. 6:12). Those who belong to Christ have in faith and baptism "crucified the flesh with its *passions* and desires" (Gal 5:24; cf. Rom 6:6; 8:13; Col 3:5). Πάθημα is found here with → ἐπιθυμία and is distinct from it in that it characterizes more the power exercised by the σάρξ, while ἐπιθυμία characterizes more the active strivings of the person (cf. H. Schlier, *Gal* [KEK] ad loc.).

3. In several instances τὰ παθήματα (like → θλῖψις) clearly indicates the *sufferings* to which Christians and esp. the apostles are subject in this world and which result primarily from persecution (thus 2 Cor 1:6, 7; Col 1:24a; 2 Tim 3:11; 1 Pet 5:9; Heb 10:32; cf. the more precise definition in 10:33f.). In Rom 8:18 Paul uses the pl. of the suffering of Christians in general and sees these sufferings in line with Jewish-apocalyptic conceptions in close connection with the eschatological condition of the world (cf. vv. 19ff.); Christians experience this suffering in fellowship with Christ; it is the precondition for participation in his glory (v. 17).

Τὰ παθήματα τοῦ Χριστοῦ in 2 Cor 1:5 could be the difficulties experienced by Paul for Christ's sake (Michaelis 930f.; L. Goppelt, *1 Pet* [KEK] 298). But it is more probably Jesus' own *suffering* (rejection and crucifiction; see the sentence structure and cf. Phil 3:10; 2 Cor

4:10). Paul was able to see his own torments as closely related to these sufferings because of his communion (mediated by the → πνεῦμα) with Christ. As such they were profitable for the "comfort" (παράκλησις) and "salvation" (σωτηρία) of the readers (v. 6; cf. 4:10-12).

"Knowing" (experiencing) "the fellowship of his sufferings," according to Phil 3:10, in conjunction with the daily experience of the "power of his resurrection" (cf. 2 Cor 4:10; 13:4) is the way to become one with Christ and to attain the resurrection. The παθήματα are Christ's own sufferings (cf. "his resurrection"), in which the apostle, through his daily afflictions (cf. 1 Cor 15:31; 2 Cor 4:10f.), shares (→ κοινωνία) and in this way is "conformed to his death" (συμμορφίζω).

In 1 Peter, τὰ παθήματα designate *"the* [painful] *suffering"* that Christ encountered (1:11) and that Christians share (in imitation of the crucified Christ, 4:13; cf. 2:21: → πάσχω 3; differently Phil 3:10) in contrast to the future glory. The "witness" (→ μάρτυς) of these sufferings is Peter, according to 5:1 (whether as "eyewitness"—using the status of "eyewitness" as an element of pseudepigraphal construction?—or as a witness who attests to the Christ's suffering by bearing his own afflictions; cf. N. Brox, *1 Pet* [EKK] ad loc.).

In Heb 2:9 πάθημα τοῦ θανάτου clearly refers to the death of Jesus (τοῦ θανάτου is epexegetical gen.), which points to the extraordinary aspect of his suffering (πάθημα is therefore not simply a synonym for "death" [contra Michaelis 933f.]). Christ had to be led in this way "through suffering to perfection" (2:10; cf. 5:8f., → πάσχω 4). The formula τὰ παθήματα, which points to the painful, humiliating death, is not used here, as in Paul and in 1 Peter, with a view toward the lot of Christians (cf. the v.l. of D* in 2:14; cf. esp., however, 11:26; 13:13: "disgrace of Christ").   J. Kremer

παθητός, 3 *pathētos* exposed to suffering, capable of suffering*

In Acts 26:23 in Paul's defense speech before Festus and Agrippa: εἰ παθητὸς ὁ Χριστός, "that the Christ would have *to suffer*" (see BDF §65.3; cf. also Luke 24:26, 46; Acts 3:18; 17:3; with the antonym ἀπαθής, likewise of Christ in Ign. *Eph.* 7:2; *Pol.* 3:2; not in the LXX). W. Michaelis, *TDNT* V, 923; → πάσχω.

πάθος, ους, τό *pathos* passion; suffering*

There are 3 occurrences in the NT, all with the meaning *(sexual) passions:* In Rom 1:26 πάθη ἀτιμίας (→ ἄτιμος 3) is used of Gentiles who because of their godless "shameful *passions"* (homosexuality, cf. vv. 26b, 27) are abandoned; in Col 3:5 πάθος with πορνεία, ἀκαθαρσία, ἐπιθυμία κακή, πλεονεξία as an urge still belonging to this

earth (cf. *T. Jos.* 7:8); 1 Thess 4:5: πάθος ἐπιθυμίας, of covetous *passion* that characterizes the former sexual conduct of the Gentiles. W. Michaelis, *TDNT* V, 926-30.

παιδαγωγός, οῦ, ὁ *paidagōgos* child's attendant, disciplinarian, supervisor*

1. Occurrences and meaning — 2. Gal 3:24f. — 3. 1 Cor 4:15.

Lit.: BAGD s.v. (older bibliography). — G. BERTRAM, *TDNT* V, 620f. — D. GORDON, "A Note on παιδαγωγός in Gal. 3,24-25," *NTS* 35 (1989) 150-54. — W. H. GROSS, *KP* IV, 408. — D. J. LULL, "'The Law Was Our Pedagogue': A Study in Gal. 3, 19-25," *JBL* 105 (1986) 481-98. — A. OEPKE, *Gal* (THKNT) 86-88. — G. RINALDI, "La legge 'pedagogo' (Gal 3,23-26a)," *Chiesa per il mondo* I (Miscellanea M. Pellegrino, 1974) 157-66. — E. SCHUPPE, PW XVIII, 2375-85. — SPICQ, *Notes* II, 639-41. — N. H. YOUNG, "*Paidagogos:* The Social Setting of a Pauline Metaphor," *NovT* 29 (1987) 150-76.

1. The subst. παιδαγωγός is attested from Euripides and Herodotus on and was a common loanword in rabbinic usage. It is found in the NT only in Gal 3:24, 25; 1 Cor 4:15. In accordance with its etymology παιδαγωγός means "child-leader" and designates in the world of the NT that man—usually of the slave class (Plato *Lys.* 208c; Plutarch *Moralia* 4a, b)—who was in charge of the external education (conduct, courtesy, table manners, and general deportment) of boys of about six to sixteen years of age. The παιδαγωγός was distinguished from the "teacher," the διδάσκαλος (Plato *Lys.* 208c; Diogenes Laertius iii.92; Philo *Leg. Gai.* 53). Thus the παιδαγωγός should be understood as a *supervisor/disciplinarian.* The negative evaluation of the παιδαγωγός—despite his usefulness (see references in Oepke 87)—is also assumed in the two NT occurrences (→ 2, 3): There is a longing for an end to supervision by the παιδαγωγός (Gal 3:23-26), and παιδαγωγοί are compared negatively to the "father" (namely, Paul, 1 Cor 4:14-16).

2. In Gal 3:24 the → νόμος (4.b) is compared to a παιδαγωγός: "So the law has become a *disciplinarian* until Christ, so that we might be justified by faith." This does not mean that the Mosaic law should have "pedagogically" trained us with a view toward Christ, but that we were in a way kept in custody (protective custody?) by the law "until faith (→ πίστις 6) came" (v. 23: ἐφρουρούμεθα συγκλειόμενοι). Therefore, v. 25 can state: "But since faith came, we are no longer subject to a disciplinarian (ὑπὸ παιδαγωγόν ἐσμεν)." Through this comparison (Plutarch also occasionally brought together law and the παιδαγωγός: *Quaest. Conv.* iii, proem; *Moralia* 645b, c) Paul not only characterizes the negative aspect of the law, its enslaving function; he is also able to make clear the temporary nature of its task. Through

faith, and with the coming of Christ, we are now no longer slaves (4:1-7) but "sons" of God (v. 26).

3. In 1 Cor 4:15 παιδαγωγοί are mentioned as persons who along with πατέρες are deserving of respect (cf. Plutarch *Lyc.* 17.1). After Paul has emphasized that he is admonishing the Corinthians as his "beloved children" (v. 14), he underscores his unique relationship with the Corinthian congregation. He is the "father" of the Corinthians, since he "begat" them: "Although you may have ten thousand *disciplinarians* in Christ, you will not have many fathers; for I (ἐγώ) begat you in Jesus Christ through the gospel" (v. 15). The difference between fatherly admonition (v. 14b: νουθετέω) and the berating of a παιδαγωγός (v. 14a: ἐντρέπω) is found in the fact that the father summons the children to imitation of himself (v. 16)

G. Schneider

παιδάριον, ου, τό *paidarion* boy, youth*

Diminutive of παῖς, which can designate a (male) *child* or a *youth* (cf. Gen 37:30; Tob 6:2) as well as a "young slave" (cf. 1 Kgs 25:5; *Mart. Pol.* 6:1). John 6:9: ἔστιν παιδάριον ὧδε, "there is a boy here"; see A. Oepke, *TDNT* V, 638.

παιδεία, ας, ἡ *paideia* training, reprimand, discipline*

1. Occurrences and meaning — 2. Heb 12:4-11 — 3. Ephesians and 2 Timothy

Lit.: G. BERTRAM, *TDNT* V, 596-624. — P. BLOMENKAMP, *RAC* VI, 502-59. — G. BORNKAMM, "Sohnschaft und Leiden. Hebr 12,5-11," FS Jeremias (1960) 188-98 (= Bornkamm, *Aufsätze* IV, 214-24). — H. VON CAMPENHAUSEN, "Faith and Culture in the NT," *idem, Tradition and Life in the Church* (1968) 19-41. — H. DÖRRIE, *KP* IV, 408f. — W.-D. HAUSCHILD, "Erziehung und Bildung als theologisches Problem der frühen Christenheit," FS Ratzinger I, 615-35. — M. HENGEL, *Judaism and Hellenism* (1974), index s.v. — W. JAEGER, *Paideia* (1959). — W. JENTSCH, "Erziehung und Bildung im NT," *Pastoralblätter* 108 (1968) 206-22. — O. MICHEL, *Heb* (KEK, [6]1966), esp. 439f. — O. MICHEL and N. OSWALD, *TRE* VI, 582-95. — I. SCHINDLER, *Paideia nach dem Zeugnis des NT* (Diss. Munich, 1958). — TRENCH, *Synonyms* 111-14.

1. The term παιδεία, which possessed a unique character and great breadth in the Greek world (Jaeger; Bertram 597-603), a character that also found its way into the conceptual world of (Hellenistic) Judaism (Betram 607-17; Hengel), has a much narrower sense and but minor significance in the NT. This is due simply to its infrequent use: In addition to the 4 occurrences in Hebrews (12:5, 7, 8, 11) the abstract noun is found only in Eph 6:4 and 2 Tim 3:16 (esp. frequent though in *1 Clement*). In all 6 instances παιδεία is used actively of *training* (2 Tim 3:16) or of *reprimand/discipline,* not in the (pass.)

sense of "education" (thus, however, Sir 1:27; Josephus *Vita* 196, 359; Apollonius Rhodius i.73; *Herm. Vis.* iii.9.10).

2. Heb 12:4-11 forms a parenetic address built on Prov 3:11f. within the whole "exhortation" of Hebrews. As in wisdom literature, sonship and discipline are "viewed as a divinely ordained training process" (Michel 426). The author of Hebrews begins 12:5f. with a quotation from Prov 3:11f. LXX consisting of the exhortation (with the address "my son") not to despise the παιδεία κυρίου, i.e., *discipline* from God, since God disciplines (παιδεύει) those whom he loves. Therefore, if God exercises παιδεία on the readers of Hebrews, i.e., disciplines them, it is because he regards them "as sons" (v. 7). If the discipline of God were absent, this would be evidence that the readers were "illegitimate children and not sons" (v. 8). All παιδεία ultimately produces the "peaceful fruit of righteousness" (v. 11).

3. Eph 6:4 contains the only exhortation in the "domestic code" addressed to "fathers": " . . . do not provoke your children to anger, but bring them up (ἐκτρέφετε) in the *discipline* and admonition of the Lord (ἐν παιδείᾳ καὶ νουθεσίᾳ κυρίου)." Gen. κυρίου characterizes "discipline and admonition" as "Christian" acts (BAGD s.v. παιδεία). The writer associates παιδεία more with fatherly "guidance, instruction, and teaching," and less with "discipline" (J. Gnilka, *Eph* [HTKNT] ad loc.).

2 Tim 3:16 states that all γραφή (→ θεόπνευστος) is useful "for teaching, convicting, correcting, and *training* in righteousness." The words διδασκαλία, ἐλεγμός, ἐπανόρθωσις, and παιδεία stand in a series; for παιδεία the tr. *training* suggests itself.

G. Schneider

παιδευτής, οῦ, ὁ instructor, teacher, disciplinarian*

In Rom 2:20 of the Jew who on the basis of his knowledge of the law considers himself "an instructor of the foolish" (παιδευτὴς ἀφρόνων, with διδάσκαλος νηπίων); in Heb 12:9 of the "earthly fathers" who have been our *instructors,* disciplining as they thought best (cf. v. 10a; → ὀλίγος 2); D. Fürst, *DNTT* III, 778 (bibliography 780f.); G. Bertram, *TDNT* V, 621ff.; Spicq, *Notes* III, 639-41.

παιδεύω *paideuō* train; reprimand; discipline*

1. Occurrences and meaning — 2. "Train" — 3. "Reprimand" — 4. "Discipline"

Lit.: G. BERTRAM, *TDNT* V, 596-625. — D. FÜRST, *DNTT* III, 775-81. — For further bibliography → παιδεία; see *TWNT* X, 1208f.

1. The vb. παιδεύω is found 13 times in the NT, esp. in Lukan writings (Luke twice, Acts twice) and in the Pauline

corpus (5 times), also in Hebrews (3 times) and Revelation (3:19). The meaning *train, instruct, educate* is only evident in Acts. The remaining occurrences should be interpreted as *discipline*. Of these, only Luke 23:16, 22 (possibly?) refers to physical *discipline* (flogging; → 4).

2. Moses was, according to Acts 7:22, "*trained/instructed* in all the wisdom of Egypt" (on the education and knowledge of Moses see Philo *Vit. Mos.* i.20-24). In Acts 22:3 "Paul" describes his upbringing: "I am a Jew, born in Tarsus of Cilicia, but raised in this city [*sc.* Jerusalem], *trained* (πεπαιδευμένος) at the feet of Gamaliel in the rigor of the law of the fathers. . . . " See on this W. C. van Unnik, *Sparsa Collecta* I (1973) 259-320 (= *Tarsus or Jerusalem: The City of Paul's Youth* [1962]), 321-27. Only in Luke does the vb. παιδεύω express the aspect of "education."

3. Between παιδεύω = *train* and παιδεύω = *discipline* lies a broad spectrum of meaning. Παιδεύω in the sense of (spiritual) correction and guidance is found in the Pastorals (2 Tim 2:25; Titus 2:12; likewise *1 Clem.* 21:6; 59:3; *Herm. Vis.* ii.3.1; iii.9.10). Discipline in the form of punishment from God is mentioned in Heb 12:6 (→ παιδεία 2) and Rev 3:19 (also *1 Clem.* 56:3, 4, 5); it is expressed in the pass. in 1 Cor 11:32; 2 Cor 6:9 (also *1 Clem.* 56:16). 1 Tim 1:20 has in mind saving discipline (by Satan?). Heb 12:7, 10a speak of the discipline of a son by a father (cf. Prov 19:18; 28:17a; 29:17; → παιδεία 2).

4. BAGD (s.v. 2.b.γ) proposes the meaning *discipline* = "flogging" for Luke 23:16, 22 (with reference to 3 Kgdms 12:11, 14; 2 Chr 10:11, 14 LXX). In light of the fact that Luke 23:16, 22 is a substitution for Mark 15:15 (par. Matt 27:26 φραγελλώσας), it is doubtful that Luke intended with the phrase παιδεύσας οὖν αὐτὸν ἀπολύσω (Luke 23:16, 22) to express an actual and intentional "flogging" of Jesus (cf. παιδεύω in Acts → 2). Luke does, in any case, avoid any report of "discipline" administered to Jesus (cf. J. Blinzler, *The Trial of Jesus* [1959] 225f.)

G. Schneider

παιδιόθεν *paidiothen* from childhood on*

In Mark 9:21 in the phrase ἐκ παιδιόθεν, "*from childhood on/since his childhood*" (cf. Gen 47:3 A).

παιδίον, ου, τό *paidion* (small) child

1. Occurrences in the NT — 2. Concern for children — 3. Comparisons involving children — 4. Lists

Lit.: DUPONT, *Béatitudes* II, 145-218. — G. HAUFE, "Das Kind im NT," *TLZ* 104 (1979) 625-38. — G. KRAUSE, ed., *Das Kind im Evangelium* (1973). — S. LÉGASSE, *Jésus et l'enfant. "Enfants," "Petits" et "Simples" dans la tradition synoptique* (1969). — A. LINDEMANN, "Die Kinder und die Gottesherrschaft.

Mk 10,13-16 und die Stellung der Kinder in der späthellenistischen Gesellschaft und im Urchristentum," *WuD* 17 (1983) 77-104. — H. MERKLEIN, *Die Gottesherrschaft als Handlungsprinzip* (1978) 115-34. — A. OEPKE, *TDNT* V, 636-54. — C. PERROT, "La lecture d'un texte exégétique. Essai méthodologique à partir de Mc 10,13-16," *PoTh* 2 (1972) 51-130. — G. RINGSHAUSEN, "Die Kinder der Weisheit. Zur Auslegung von Mk 10,13-16 par.," *ZNW* 77 (1983) 60-72. — D. ZELLER, "Die Bildlogik des Gleichnisses Mt 11,16f; Lk 7,31," *ZNW* 68 (1977) 252-57. — For further bibliography → βρέφος, → τέκνον.

1. The noun παιδίον appears 52 times in the NT, esp. in the Synoptic Gospels: 18 times in Matthew, 12 in Mark, and 13 in Luke. The remaining occurrences are divided between John (3 occurrences), Hebrews (3), 1 John (2), and 1 Cor 14:20. The NT speaks of the child (παιδίον) under the following headings (→ 2-4).

2. Jesus grants to children the right of blessing: Children are among those to whom the beatitudes of Jesus apply (cf. Luke 6:20-23) and in whom Jesus is present (Matt 25:40, 45). Therefore Jesus grants them a blessing (Mark 10:14); the disciples should serve them (Mark 9:37).

3. The comparison with children is intended to lead to new conduct: The hearers of Jesus should not be like children, who in their listlessness refuse the invitation to play both wedding and funeral; the hearer should recognize the grace of the hour (Mark 11:16f.; par. Luke 7:32).

According to Mark 10:15 entrance into the Kingdom of God depends on becoming "like a child." The point of comparison, which is debated, arises from the form and contemporary background of the saying: Mark 10:15 is a paradoxical provocation. Jesus makes use of the "requirements for entrance" common to the Judaism of his day, in which certain rewards were granted for certain acts (cf. H. Windisch, "Die Sprüche vom Eingehen in das Reich Gottes," *ZNW* 27 [1928] 163-92), but where the mention of a law-fulfilling act was expected, Jesus names instead a "child"—i.e., a person who was not able to fulfill the law. In this way, in spite of the implications of the form, the connection between act and reward is ruptured. The statement gives no explicit indication of what should be done, but rather provokes the hearer to reflect anew on the connection of act and reward by contending that the act is not decisive.

The parallel passage in Matt 18:4 turns the provocation into a teaching by interpreting "being a child" as humility and by placing the whole discourse on the household of God under the banner of the child (18:1f.). In the further development of this tradition, the entrance into the Kingdom of God was only possible through renewal (John 3:3, 5) or by overcoming the differentiation of the sexes (*Gos. Thom.* 22).

In Mark 7:28 the metaphor of the Syrophoenician

woman, in which she recognizes the primary position of Israel (the "children") and yet stresses the handout for the "dogs," gains her the healing of her daughter.

The origin of these traditions (→ 2, 3) is to be found in the historical Jesus. In favor of this is: a) the diversity among the witnesses in the sources and in the various forms in which the traditions are found (narratives and sayings), b) the diverse development of the related saying, c) the consternation of Jesus over the treatment of children revealed in the saying, and d) its proximity to the core of Jesus proclamation. There is too little evidence for the assumption that baptism of children was the setting of this saying; cf. J. Sauer, *ZNW* 72 (1981) 27-50.

4. In spite of the extant Synoptic parallels, children are mentioned in the miracle stories only in Matt 14:21; 15:38; Mark 5:39-41; 7:30; 9:24; John 4:49. In the infancy narratives, παιδίον is used of Jesus—in Matthew 9 times and in Luke 3 times—and of John the Baptist in Luke 1:59, 66, 76, 80.   W. Egger

παιδίσκη, ης, ἡ *paidiskē* servant girl, maid, slave girl*

The 13 occurrences in the NT are limited to the Gospels (6 occurrences), Acts (2), and Gal 4:22-31 (5). In each case παιδίσκη refers to a young woman in a position of servitude, whether a slave or a servant: Matt 26:69; Mark 14:66, 69; Luke 22:56; John 18:17, of a maid of the high priest in response to whose questions Peter denied Jesus; Luke 12:45: παιδίσκαι with παῖδες, "male and female servants" (cf. Lev 25:44); Acts 12:13: "a *servant girl* named Rhoda" (παιδίσκη . . . ὀνόματι Ῥόδη) in the house of Mary the mother of John Mark; 16:16, more probably of a *slave girl* with a divining spirit (cf. v. 19: οἱ κύριοι αὐτῆς [D: τῆς παιδίσκης]); Gal 4:22, 23, 30 (bis), 31: the two sons of Abraham born of the παιδίσκη (Hagar) and of the ἐλευθέρα (Sarah; cf. Gen 16:1ff., 15f.; 21:1ff., 10; Philo *All.* iii.244): Paul assumes in accordance with the slave laws of his day that the offspring of slaves were also slaves; παιδίσκη therefore means here *female slave.* G. Kittel, *TDNT* I, 55f.; K. Cramer, *BHH* 623; F. Mussner, *Gal* (HTKNT) 319ff.

παίζω *paizō* play, dance*

The inf. is found in 1 Cor 10:7 in the description of the idolatry of Israel: καὶ ἀνέστησαν παίζειν, "and they rose up to dance" (quoting Exod 32:6 LXX); see H. Conzelmann, *1 Cor* [Hermeneia] 167.n.33; G. Bertram, *TDNT* V, 625-29; B. Reicke and E. Esking, *BHH* 1832-35.

παῖς, παιδός, ὁ (ἡ) *pais* servant; child, son

1. Occurrences, meaning, and semantic field — 2. παῖς θεοῦ as a christological designation

Lit.: G. BRAUMANN and C. BROWN, *DNTT* I, 283-85. — O. CULLMANN, *The Christology of the NT* (1963) 51-82. — J. D. M. DERRETT, "Law in the NT: The Syro-Phoenician Woman and the Centurion of Capernaum," *NovT* 15 (1973) 161-86. — J. P. FLOSS, *Jahwe Dienen—Göttern Dienen* (BBB 45, 1975). — R. T. FRANCE, "Herod and the Children of Bethlehem," *NovT* 21 (1979) 98-120. — N. FÜGLISTER, "Alttestamentliche Grundlagen der neutestamentlichen Christologie," *MySal* III/1 (ed. J. Feiner and M. Löhrer; 1970) 105-224, esp. 147-77, 206-8. — W. GRIMM, *Weil ich dich liebe. Die Verkündigung Jesu und Deuterojesaja* (²1981). —W. C. HOFHEINZ, *An Analysis of the Usage and Influence of Isaiah Chapters 40-66 in the NT* (Diss. Columbia University, 1964) 586-633. — M. D. HOOKER, *Jesus and the Servant* (1959). — J. JEREMIAS, "Παῖς (θεοῦ) im NT," *idem, Abba* (1966) 191-216. — E. KRÄNKL, *Jesus der Knecht Gottes. Die heilsgeschichtliche Stellung Jesu in den Reden der Apostelgeschichte* (BU 8, 1972) 125-29. — E. LOHMEYER, *Gottesknecht und Davidsohn* (1953). — R. N. LONGENECKER, *The Christology of Early Jewish Christianity* (1970) 104-9. — J. E. MÉNARD, "Pais Theou as Messianic Title in the Book of Acts," *CBQ* 19 (1957) 83-92. — O. MICHEL and I. H. MARSHALL, *DNTT* III, 607-13. — J. MORGENSTERN, *Some Significant Antecedents of Christianity* (SPB 10, 1966) 41-60. — L. S. MUDGE, *The Servant Christology in the NT* (Diss. Princeton University, 1961). — A. OEPKE, *TDNT* V, 636-54. — M. RESE, *Alttestamentliche Motive in der Christologie des Lukas* (SNT 1, 1969) 128-31. — *idem*, "Überprüfung einiger Thesen von Joachim Jeremias zum Thema des Gottesknechtes im Judentum," *ZTK* 60 (1963) 21-41. — I. RIESENER, *Der Stamm ʿābad im AT* (BZAW 149, 1979). — U. WILCKENS, *Die Missionsreden der Apostelgeschichte* (WMANT 5, 1974) 163-70. — W. ZIMMERLI and J. JEREMIAS, *TDNT* V, 654-713. — For further bibliography see *TWNT* X, 1209-12.

1. The word παῖς is found 24 times in the NT, but only in the writings of Luke (Gospel and Acts) and Matthew. It is a collective term for all members of a household subordinate to the master of the house and can have the corresponding meanings: In Matt 2:16; 17:18 par. Luke 2:43; Acts 20:12 παῖς designates a *young boy,* one younger than an adolescent; in Luke 8:51, 54 a young girl is intended; Matt 21:15 groups *children* under pl. παῖδες. In typical fashion Matt 8:6-13 par. Luke 7:2-10/ John 4:46-53 interchanges παῖς with δοῦλος, υἱος and παιδίον. While Matthew consistently uses παῖς, *boy/child* (of the centurion, cf. on the background Derrett 174f.), Luke interprets the παῖς as a δοῦλος in order to express the nonfamilial relation between the one who commands and the one who obeys; John emphasizes υἱός as a generic term: It should be kept in mind that in Palestine the servant belonged to the family and the "son of the household" did not have to be a natural-born son (cf. Lohmeyer 3). In Luke 12:45 παῖς and παιδίσκαι refer to male and female household servants; Luke 15:26 appears not to

distinguish between παῖς and δοῦλος, although here, too, belonging to the οἶκος is fundamental to the distinction between παῖς and μίσθιος. In Matt 14:2 Herod expresses his opinion of Jesus to his παῖδες ("members of the court /counselors," i.e., his "cabinet"; cf. the *'abdey hammelek* /παῖδες τοῦ βασιλέως in 2 Sam 11:24; 15:15; cf. Riesener 150-59).

2. The expression παῖς θεοῦ, "*servant* of God," derives from the cultic language of the ancient Orient and corresponds to the ideological usage of the royal court (cf. Michel; Riesener 268-71; differently Floss, who assumes a special salvation-historical and religious usage in the OT). In Luke 1:54 παῖς, as a "liturgical expression" (Lohmeyer 6) and honorific title, refers according to Isa 41:8f. to the eschatological Israel, which experiences the saving work of God, the exaltation of the lowly, in the sending of Jesus and so takes on the redemptive form of the servant of God. In Luke 1:69 David bears this honorific title, which expresses both proximity and subordination to God. From the time of deutero-Isaiah, individual and collective features were combined in the expression παῖς θεοῦ (cf. Riesener 246f.); Jesus as the παῖς θεοῦ is therefore the messianic successor of the house of David and the fulfillment of Israel's messianic expectations.

Matthew summarizes in 12:18-21, by means of an independent tr. of Isa 42:1-4, the leading features of his view of Christ: He is the one who shapes the sabbath Halakah to the contours of his merciful authority and who is secretly at work as Savior. He is the παῖς θεοῦ who brings the eschatological kingdom of God as one who does not seek conflict, nor who clamorously proclaims the great message, nor delights in the final destruction of humans, but who in his hiddenness points to the mercy of God and therefore to hope for those who stand on the outside. The messianic uniqueness of Jesus' prophetic mission, conformed as he is to the image of the suffering servant of God of deutero-Isaiah, places him in a close proximity to God that corresponds to the security and hiddenness of the Son in unity with the Father (cf. Matt 11:25-27).

In the missionary discourse in Acts 3, the title παῖς θεοῦ is related in vv. 13 and 26 to the risen and glorified Jesus. The context in this instance is not as clearly influenced by deutero-Isaiah, since resurrection does not here mean exaltation after a time of humiliation. Indeed, christological authority and humiliation are not consistent with one another. Rather, rejection by the Jews and confirmation of the παῖς by God are placed in direct opposition. Jesus is the servant of God, the eschatological, messianic prophet, the one who was sent and appointed to work miracles, to bring about conversion, and to bless; this prophetic task, not in any special way linked with the suffering servant of God, determines not only his earthly

mission, but also that of the earthly community that bears his name; their mutual mission is salvation-historically anchored in the resurrection.

In the prayer in Acts 4:24-30 Jesus' fate in Jerusalem is interpreted in terms of Ps 2:1f.: He is the Christ of God, who fell victim to the attack of the opponent; as such he is the holy παῖς, who stands on God's side, whose fate was guided by God's providence. The context throws a christological glance toward the baptism of Jesus. There may be present in this reference traces of a view of baptism as anointing by the Spirit to be the servant of God, based on Isa 42:1.

Present in παῖς θεοῦ christology is an old Palestinian tradition that was once well developed but had by this time been eclipsed by the christological title found in the Hellenistic congregations, υἱὸς τοῦ θεοῦ (thus Bousset and, more recently, among others, Cullmann, Jeremias, Lohmeyer, Füglister, and Grimm). Or it could also represent a secondary, supposedly ancient, amplification of an older christology, which originally arose from the Son of man teaching (thus Harnack, more recently E. Haenchen, *Acts* [Eng. tr., 1971] at 3:13, Hofheinz, Hooker, Ménard, Mudge, Rese). Whatever the case, it is certain that the tradition previously possessed no fixed connection between the suffering Messiah of Isaiah 53 and other Suffering Servant songs and that the deutero-Isaianic motif of righteous, suffering Israel and the eschatological establishment of the holy congregation that has passed through humiliation was very active in the self-understanding of the pious of Israel (cf. Mudge 99-147). Any attempt to demonstrate the presence of παῖς θεοῦ christology as a teaching of the suffering Messiah already with Jesus and in the initial stages of the formation of the kerygma must, therefore, rest on a broader group of motifs (thus most recently esp. Grimm) and philological echoes of the servant songs (thus, e.g., Jeremias 194f.: Aram. *talyā'* = 1. "servant," 2. "son," 3. "lamb"; cf. reference to δοῦλος in Mark 10:44 and the ὑπέρ-formulas in Mark 14:24 and John 6:51; with further references Michel 1152f.).

One can theologically assert that the παῖς teaching makes visible the characteristic features of the humiliation and hiddenness of Jesus, his messianic work of mercy, and his authority through his unity with the hidden Father.

J.-A. Bühner

παίω *paiō* strike, hit*

This vb. occurs 5 times in the NT: *hit* (in the face, with the fist or the open hand; see Billerbeck I, 1024) of the abuse of Jesus at the trial before the Sanhedrin in Matt 26:68 (cf. v. 67) par. Luke 22:64 (cf. v. 63); *strike/wound* (with the sword) in Mark 14:47; John 18:10 (at the arrest of Jesus); *sting* (of a scorpion) in Rev 9:5. It is also used figuratively of the "blows of God" in Job 4:19; 5:18; *1 Clem.* 39:5.

Παχατιανός, 3 *Pakatianos* Pacatacian

In the NT only in the subscription of 1 Timothy in the mss. of the Koine text tradition as a late designation for a portion of Phrygia whose capital was Laodicea, from which the letter was supposedly sent.

πάλαι *palai* formerly, long ago, previously; for a long time, already (for a long time)*

This adv. occurs 7 times in the NT: Of a specific point in the past (Matt 11:21 par. Luke 10:13, in the cry of woe over the Galilean cities): *long ago/already a long time ago;* with the meaning *once* (Heb 1:1); αἱ πάλαι ἁμαρτίαι, *"the former sins"* (2 Pet 1:9); οἱ πάλαι προγεγραμμένοι εἰς τοῦτο τὸ κρίμα, of the false teachers "who *already long ago* were marked for this judgment [described in the following statements]" (Jude 4); *already* (Mark 15:44: εἰ πάλαι ἀπέθανεν). 2 Cor 12:19 refers to a time in the more distant past: πάλαι δοκεῖτε, "you have thought *already for a long time.*" H. Seesemann, *TDNT* V, 717; H. Haarbeck, *DNTT* II, 713f.

παλαιός, 3 *palaios* old; obsolete*

1. Occurrences in the NT — 2. "Old" in contrast to νέος and καινός — 3. The "old person"

Lit.: O. Betz, "Neues und Altes im Geschichtshandeln Gottes. Bemerkungen zu Mt 13,51f.," FS Schelkle 69-84. — H. Haarbeck, *DNTT* I, 713-16. — J. Kremer, " 'Altes und Neues.' Zu dem Logion über den christlichen 'Schriftgelehrten' (Mt 13,52)," *Die Zukunft der Glaubensunterweisung* (FS A. Heuser; 1971) 84-101. — E. Larsson, *Christus als Vorbild* (1962) 61-69, 197-210. — O. Linton, " 'Gammalt' och 'nytt,' " *SEÅ* 5 (1940) 43-55. — B. Rey, "L'homme nouveau d'après s. Paul," *RSPT* 48 (1964) 603-29; 49 (1965) 161-95. — H. Seesemann, *TDNT* V, 717-20. — D. Zeller, "Zu einer jüdischen Vorlage von Mt 13,52," *BZ* 20 (1976) 223-26. — For further bibliography → καινός, → νέος.

1. The adj. παλαιός is found 19 times in the NT, each time in opposition to → νέος or → καινός (→ 2). It indicates that which is *old,* in the sense of *having been in existence for a long time* (in contrast to νέος) or in a somewhat derived sense *obsolete* (in contrast to καινός; cf. BAGD s.v.). The occurrences are concentrated in the Synoptic Gospels (11), the Pauline letters (4), and the tradition influenced by Paul (once each in Colossians and Ephesians). Elsewhere παλαιός is found only in 1 John 2:7a, b (the *"old"* commandment"). Mark 2:21a (b) par. Matt 9:16/Luke 5:36a, b speak of an *"old* garment" and Mark 2:22 par. Matt 9:17/Luke 5:37 of *"old* wineskins." For the double metaphorical saying about the new patch and the new wine and for Luke 5:39a, b ("*old* wine") → νέος 3.a. Matt 13:52 characterizes the righteous scribe as one who "brings out of his treasure things new and *old."* The Pauline occurrences speak of the *"old* person" (Rom 6:6; thus also Col 3:9; Eph 4:22), of *"old* yeast," i.e., leaven (1 Cor 5:7, 8, → νέος 3.b), and of the *"old*

covenant" (2 Cor 3:14); cf. also παλαιότης γράμματος (Rom 7:6).

2. As an antonym of νέος, "fresh, young," παλαιός primarily means *old* (= in existence for a long time): Mark 2:21a par. Matt 9:16: "the *old* garment" in contrast to the "unshrunk (new)" patch; Mark 2:22 par. Matt 9:17 /Luke 5:37: "new wine in *old* wineskins" (contrast Mark 2:22 par.: ἀσκοὶ καινοί); Luke 5:39a, b "*old*—new wine"; 1 Cor 5:7, 8 "*old* yeast" (leaven) in contrast to νέον φύραμα. Col 3:9, unlike Rom 6:6 (see below), contrasts the "*old* person" to the νέος (v. 10).

The following passages have καινός, "new, never having existed," as an antonym and παλαιός is understood primarily as *obsolete, superseded:* Luke 5:36a, b: "new —*old* garment"; cf. Mark 2:21b: "the new from the *old.*" The righteous scribe, according to Matt 13:52, brings out καινὰ καὶ παλαιά (→ θησαυρός 3.d). Rom 6:6: "our *old* person was crucified with Christ" (cf. v. 4: καινότης ζωῆς); this is picked up in Eph 4:22: "the *old* person" (v. 24: ὁ καινὸς ἄνθρωπος; see also Col 3:10; → 3). In 2 Cor 3:14 "the *old* διαθήκη" is contrasted to the new (v. 6, → διαθήκη 4.b) and represents that for which there were books or documents to be "read." In Rom 7:6 καινότης πνεύματος stands over against παλαιότης γράμματος. In 1 John 2:7a, b "the *old* commandment" is distinguished from the new (→ ἐντολή 6).

The distinction between νέος and καινός is, of course, not always strictly preserved, and the significance of παλαιός is similarly often fluid; cf., e.g., Col 3:9f. (παλαιός—νέος with ἀνακαινόομαι); Eph 4:22-24 (παλαιός—καινός with ἀνανεόομαι); Matt 13:52 (παλαιά without negative connotations).

3. The statement regarding the crucifixion of "our *old* person" with Christ is found in Rom 6:6 in connection with other indicative statements about baptism: "We have died to sin" (v. 2), "have been baptized into his [Jesus Christ's] death" (v. 3), and "have been buried with him . . . in his death" (v. 4). "Our *old* person" is to be interpreted within this context. Paul is apparently drawing on traditional baptismal teaching (v. 6: τοῦτο γινώσκοντες; see E. Käsemann, *Rom* [Eng. tr., 1980] ad loc., who assumes that παλαιὸς ἄνθρωπος originated in the Adam-Christ typology).

With the phrase "with his deeds" Col 3:9 characterizes the "*old* person" as a doer of evil, who (in baptism) is "put off"; at the same time the "new" is "put on" (like a garment, v. 10). Therefore one must now "put off" all blasphemy (v. 8) and "put on" the virtues listed in v. 12. Following the indicatives come corresponding imperatives.

Eph 4:22 also stands in a parenetic context: the "*old* person" is the one φθειρόμενος κατὰ τὰς ἐπιθυμίας τῆς ἀπάτης. It must be "put off" and the καινὸς ἄνθρωπος "put on" (v. 24). Here the opposing term "new person" is mentioned explicitly. This new person is "created by God [cf. Gen 1:26f.] in true righteousness and holiness."

G. Schneider

παλαιότης, ητος, ἡ *palaiotēs* old age; old state of affairs*

Rom 7:6: δουλεύειν . . . οὐ (ἐν) παλαιότητι γράμματος, "not to serve in *the old state of affairs* under the letter [of the law]" (opposed to ἐν καινότητι πνεύματος; → παλαιός 2). H. Seesemann, *TDNT* V, 720; H. Haarbeck, *DNTT* II, 715.

παλαιόω *palaioō* make old; declare old (obsolete); pass.: age, grow old*

This vb. occurs 4 times in the NT (outside LXX and NT only pass.): Luke 12:33, pass.: *become old* (i.e., *lose its usefulness,* as frequently in the LXX; cf. H. Seesemann, *TDNT* V, 720): "purses that do not *wear out*" (βαλλάντια μὴ παλαιούμενα, parallel to θησαυρὸς ἀνέκλειπτος ἐν τοῖς οὐρανοῖς); Heb 1:11, pass.: "*wear out* like a garment" (πάντες ὡς ἱμάτιον παλαιωθήσονται, quoting Ps 101:27 LXX; cf. Deut 8:4; Sir 14:17; Isa 51:6; etc.); Heb 8:13 (bis) of God, who with the proclamation of the new covenant "*has declared* the first *obsolete*" (act.: πεπαλαίωκεν τὴν πρώτην, v. 13a), whereupon "the *obsolete* and outmoded . . . [is] near its end" (τὸ παλαιούμενον καὶ γηράσκον ἐγγὺς ἀφανισμοῦ). H. Seesemann, *TDNT* V, 220; H. Haarbeck, *DNTT* II, 716.

πάλη, ης, ἡ *palē* battle*

Fig. in Eph 6:12 of the eschatological *battle* of believers against the "attacks of the devil" (v. 11), which is not a "*battle* against flesh and blood" (πάλη πρὸς αἷμα καὶ σάρκα) and therefore is to be conducted with the "armor of God" (vv. 11, 13; cf. also Rom 13:12; 1 Thess 5:8; used often in Greek of the spiritual battle of the ascetics, etc.: cf. Philo *Abr.* 243). H. Greeven, *TDNT* V, 721 (bibliography).

παλιγγενεσία, ας, ἡ *palingenesia* rebirth*

1. Greek usage — 2. NT terms — 3. Matt 19:28 — 4. Titus 3:5 — 5. Relation to usage in mystery religions

Lit.: BAGD s.v. — F. BÜCHSEL, *TDNT* I, 686-89. — F. W. BURNETT, "Παλιγγενεσία in Matt. 19:28: A Window on Matthean Community?" *JSNT* 17 (1983) 60-72. — idem, "Philo on Immortality: A Thematic Study of Philo's Concept of παλιγγενεσία," *CBQ* 46 (1984) 447-70. — A. CHARBEL, "O Conceito de 'Palingenesia' ou Regeneração em Mt 19,28," *RCB* 7 (1963) 13-17. — P. CHRISTOU, *The Idea of Regeneration in the NT* (Diss. Boston, 1950). — J. DEY, ΠΑΛΙΓΓΕΝΕΣΙΑ (NTAbh 17/5, 1937). — M. DIBELIUS and H. CONZELMANN, *The Pastoral*

Epistles (Hermeneia, 1972) 148-50. — FRISK, *Wörterbuch* II, 468. — W. C. GRESE, *Corpus Hermeticum XIII and Early Christian Literature* (1979). — J. GUHRT, *DNTT* I, 184-86. — PRÜMM, *Handbuch* 332f. — R. REITZENSTEIN, *Poimandres* (1904). — T. RIISE-HANSSEN, "Gjenfødelsesbegrepet i det NT," *TTK* 5 (1958) 186-98. — R. SCHNACKENBURG, *Das Heilsgeschehen bei der Taufe nach dem Apostel Paulus* (MTS 1/1, 1950) 8-14. — K.-W. TRÖGER, "Die hermetische Gnosis," *Gnosis und NT* (ed. K.-W. Tröger; 1973) 97-119. — P. TRUMMER, *Die Paulustradition der Pastoralbriefen* (BBET 8, 1978) 185-89.

1. This noun, composed of πάλιν, "again, back," and γένεσις, "become, come about," designates various forms of *rebirth* or renewal, e.g., restoration of health, the beginnning of the new life of an individual or a people, the anticipated restoration of the world, or the reincarnation of souls, among many others (LSJ 1291).

2. In contrast to the usage of παλιγγενεσία in the world of the NT, the NT itself, with only 2 occurrences (Matt 19:28; Titus 3:5), shows more reserve, even though the metaphor itself is more frequently alluded to in the NT (cf. → ἀναγεννάω, 1 Pet 1:3, 23; γεννηθῆναι → ἄνωθεν, "be born from above" or "be born again," John 3:3, 7; ἐκ θεοῦ γεννηθῆναι, "be born of God" in contrast to natural birth, John 1:13; 1 John 5:1, etc.; cf. also ἀποκυέω, Jas 1:18). Belonging to the same conceptual field are such expressions as "new person," "new creation," "restoration" (ἀποκατάστασις, Acts 3:21; cf. also 1:6), etc., hopes that were already expressed in the OT salvation oracles involving both the individual (esp. Job 14:14 LXX!) and the entire world (Isa 65:17).

3. As a reward for the sacrifice made by the disciples in following Jesus, Matt 19:28 promises them participation in the judgment by the Son of man ἐν τῇ παλιγγενεσίᾳ, "at the rebirth," which is understood by Mark 10:30 and Luke 18:30 as "the age to come." The context in Matthew connects παλιγγενεσία primarily with the Son of man and his final revelation and judgment, and implies hopes for the future that point beyond individual, personal, or purely spiritual dimensions.

4. Titus 3:5, taking up and transforming the Pauline tradition, speaks of our salvation "not by works . . . but because of his mercy . . . through the washing of *rebirth* and renewal by the Holy Spirit." In this way the Pastorals reject even works "that we do in righteousness" (v. 5) as the foundation of redemption, and identifies the true foundation as an act of God alone mediated in symbolic fashion "through (διά) the bath of rebirth," which is in essence, however, a renewal (ἀνακαίνωσις), brought about by the Spirit of God. The parenetic intention of the section refuses any ecstatic mystical speculation or any purely personal interpretation of παλιγγενεσία (cf. "we" and "us," vv. 3-7); it summons to sober and active demonstration of the redeemed existence granted in connec-

tion with the appearing of "the kindness and love of God our Savior" (v. 4).

5. The question under discussion since Reitzenstein whether the NT concept of rebirth is dependent on the mystery religions (esp. *Corp. Herm.* xiii.1: "No one can be saved before rebirth") demands methodological discretion: On the one hand, the chronology of Gnostic and NT documents—and consequently the lines of dependence—can be determined only approximately. On the other hand, in instances of possible conceptual correspondence or derivation, the respective contexts of the statements remain decisive for the actual meaning of the statements. What the NT actually means with παλιγγενεσία eludes all possible historical and natural experience. It designates faith in a new creative act of God and the "hope of eternal life" (Titus 3:9), which transcends all that has gone before while at the same time not excluding it.　　　　　　　　　　　P. Trummer

πάλιν *palin* back; again; furthermore; on the other hand

This adv. appears 141 times in the NT with special frequency in John (45 occurrences, including 8:2, 8), Mark (28 occurrences), Matthew (17), Hebrews (10), and Galatians (9).

With vbs. of motion or cause often with the meaning *back:* ἀποστέλλω πάλιν, "send *back*" (Mark 11:3); ἔρχομαι πάλιν, "come *back*" (Matt 26:43; John 4:46); ἄγω πάλιν, "turn *back*" (John 11:7); πάλιν λαμβάνω, "get *back*" (10:17); pleonastic in Acts 18:21; Gal 1:17; with obvious stress on the return in ἐπιστρέφω πάλιν (Gal 4:9; cf. BDF §484).

Usually the translation *again* is used when reference is made to a previous state of affairs or the like (Mark 11:27; Rom 8:15; 11:23; 1 Cor 7:5; Gal 2:18; Phil 2:28). *Once again, once more* is employed with recurring circumstances or actions (Matt 4:8; 19:24; 21:36; Mark 2:13; 8:1; Luke 23:20; John 1:35): πάλιν ἐκ δευτέρου (Matt 26:42; Acts 10:15; cf. John 4:54); εἰς τὸ πάλιν (2 Cor 13:2) is an Atticism for simple πάλιν.

πάλιν is also frequently used in series with the meaning *furthermore, moreover* (Matt 5:33; 13:45, 47; John 9:27; 12:39; Rom 15:10, 11, 12; Rev 10:11); the intent of Mark 15:13 and John 18:40 is also probably to place in series (in response), without the explicit mention of a previous cry by the people.

The contrasting use *on the other hand, by way of contrast, in turn* is seen in Matt 4:7; Luke 6:43; 1 Cor 12:21; 2 Cor 10:7; 1 John 2:8.

παλιγγενεσία, ας, ἡ *palingennesia* rebirth
Variant form of → παλιγγενεσία.

παμπληθεί *pamplēthei* all together*

According to Luke 23:18, the high priests, the elders, and the people (cf. v. 13) shouted *all together* (ἀνέκραγον δὲ πάλιν λέγοντες) for Pilate to free Barabbas; see BDF §122.

πάμπολυς, 3 *pampolys* very large

Πάμπολυς ὄχλος in Mark 8:1 A K Koine, etc., instead of πάλιν πολὺς ὄχλος.

Παμφυλία, ας *Pamphylía* Pamphylia*

A coastal region on the southern coast of Asia Minor west of Lycia, south of Pisidia, and east of Cilicia, connected at different times with Lycia, Cilicia, and Galatia, an independent province from 25 B.C. to A.D. 43 (cf. Dio Cassius liii.26). According to 1 Macc 15:23 Jewish communities inhabited Pamphylia; cf. Acts 2:10. Paul went through Pamphylia more than once on his "first missionary journey," visiting the major port city of Perga (Acts 13:13; cf. 15:38) and later Perga again and Attalia, another port city (14:24[f.]; cf 27:5). W. Ruge, PW XVIII, 354-407; D. Magie, *Roman Rule in Asia Minor* (1950) 260ff., 1132ff.; A. H. M. Jones, *OCD* 773; T. Lohmann, *BHH* 1381; *BL* 1289; *KP* IV, 441-44.

πανδοχεῖον, ου, τό *pandocheion* inn, lodging*

In Attic and Hellenistic texts one usually finds the older form πανδοκεῖον (see BAGD s.v.; BDF §33); also as a loanword in Jewish texts (see Billerbeck II, 183). Luke 10:34, in the parable of the good Samaritan, who brought the man who had been assaulted to an *inn* (ἤγαγεν αὐτὸν εἰς πανδοχεῖον; cf. G. Stählin, *TDNT* V, 19n.135; B. Reicke, *BHH* 693f.; J. R. Royse, *NovT* 23 (1981) 193f.

πανδοχεύς, έως, ὁ *pandocheus* innkeeper

According to Luke 10:35 the good Samaritan turned the man who had been attacked over to the innkeeper for further care and at his departure paid two denarii in advance.

πανήγυρις, εως, ἡ *panēgyris* assembly*

Heb 12:22(f.), in the description of the new covenant: πανήγυρις καὶ ἐκκλησία πρωτοτόκων, "the *assembly* and congregation of the firstborn," in which πανήγυρις emphasizes more the cultic (cf. Josephus *B.J.* v.230; Philo *Vit. Mos.* ii.159; Amos 5:21; also Isocrates *Panegyricus* 43, 46) and ἐκκλησία more the constitutional character of the gathering; in the service of God the Church considered itself one with the heavenly Jerusalem and the hosts of angels. O. Michel, *Heb* (KEK) ad loc.; R. Williamson, *Philo and the Epistle to the Hebrews* (ALGHL 4, 1970) 64-70; A. Strobel, *Heb* (NTD) ad loc.; Spicq, *Notes* II, 642-46.

πανοικεί *panoikei* with the entire household, with the whole family*

Acts 16:34, of the jailer in Philippi: ἠγαλλιάσατο πανοικεί, "he rejoiced *with his entire household*" (because he had become a believer; cf. v. 33: αὐτὸς καὶ οἱ αὐτοῦ); cf. *Mart. Pol.* 20:2. BDF §§23; 122.

πανοπλία, ας, ἡ *panoplia* full armor, armaments*

The noun occurs 3 times in the NT and designates the full armor of a heavily armed foot soldier (shield, sword, spear, helmet, armor, shin guards, etc.; see A. Oepke, *TDNT* V, 295). Fig. use of the motif of war and armor is typical in biblical texts and texts influenced by the Bible (with reference to God in Isa 42:13; 59:17; Ps 35:1ff.; Wis 5:17ff.

In the NT literal use of πανοπλία is found only in the image of the defeat of the strong man in combat by one stronger (Luke 11:22, redactional): τὴν πανοπλίαν αὐτοῦ αἴρει (contrast Matt 12:29/Mark 3:27; cf. also 2 Kgs 2:21).

Πανοπλία is used metaphorically of putting on or taking up the πανοπλία τοῦ θεοῦ in Eph 6:11, 13 (cf. also 1 Thess 5:8; Rom 13:12; 16:20; 1 Cor 16:13; 2 Cor 6:7; 10:4f.; Phil 1:27, 30; 1 Pet 4:1), where Eph 6:14-17 bears out the weapon allegory in detail. The model is the armor of the Roman soldiers. In this case, however, God himself (gen. τοῦ θεοῦ) is viewed as the one who actually supplies the spiritual weapons in the eschatological battle against the onslaughts of the devil (6:11) and against the evil powers of this world and in the heavenly realms (under God, 6:12). Eph 6:10-20 shows in connection with 1:20-23 that the lordship of Christ over the world has in principle already been secured. In the present age, however, in which the evil one is still active, the cosmos must be recovered for the lordship of the Creator through the deployment of all the gifts of the Spirit (H. Conzelmann, *Eph* [NTD] ad loc.; see also 1 QM 1:1, 10; 3:1ff.; 4:1; 5:1; 6:1ff.; 14:1ff., etc.). Behind this, therefore, is not the Greek concept of the "battle" of the ascetic against self, but the apocalyptic hope of the powerful triumph of the kingdom of God, manifest already now, according to Ephesians 6, in the baptized believer's earthly struggle of faith.

BAGD s.v. (bibliography); A. Oepke and K. G. Kuhn, *TDNT* V, 295-302; G. Fohrer, *BHH* 2124-27; F. Mussner, "Beiträge aus Qumran zum Verständnis des Epheserbriefes," FS Schmid (1963) 185-98; A. E. Travis, *SWJT* 6 (1963) 71-80; P. F. Beatrice, *Studia Patrologia* 19 (1972) 359-422; K. M. Fischer, *Tendenz und Absicht des Epheserbriefs* (FRLANT 111, 1973) 165-72; A. Lindemann, *Die Aufhebung der Zeit* (SNT 12, 1975) 63-66. For further bibliography see *TWNT* X, 1203f.   H. Balz

πανουργία, ας, ἡ *panourgia* craftiness, cunning, treachery*

This noun is found 5 times in the NT, always (in contrast to the LXX) with negative connotations: Luke 20:23: *cunning* (κατανοήσας δὲ αὐτῶν τὴν πανουργίαν); 1 Cor 3:19 (quoting Job 5:13, cf. 5:12f. LXX), of God, who "catches the wise in their own *craftiness*" (ὁ δρασσόμμενος τοὺς σοφοὺς ἐν τῇ πανουργίᾳ αὐτῶν); 2 Cor 4:2, of Paul, who "does not walk in *craftiness*" (μὴ περιπατοῦντες ἐν πανουργίᾳ . . .); 2 Cor 11:3, of the *cunning* of the snake that tempted Eve (ἐν τῇ πανουργίᾳ αὐτοῦ; cf. Gen 3:1 A S Theodotion: πανοῦργος[-ότερος], in contrast to LXX: φρονιμώτατος); Eph 4:14: ἐν πανουργίᾳ πρὸς τὴν μεθοδείαν τῆς πλάννης, "by *craftiness* in deceitful scheming." O. Bauernfeind, *TDNT* V, 722-27; H. D. Betz, *Der Apostel Paulus und die sokratische Tradition* (BHT 45, 1972) 104-6.

πανοῦργος, 2 *panourgos* cunning, sly*

In 2 Cor 12:16, Paul speaks of himself (ironically— or assuming the accusations of the opponents; see R. Bultmann, *2 Cor* [Eng. tr., 1985] ad loc.) as *cunning*: ὑπάρχων πανοῦργος, "*cunning*, as I am, I have caught you with craftiness"; v. 17 points toward an accusation that Paul enriched himself on the collection; cf. further *Herm. Vis.* iii.3.1. O. Bauernfeind, *TDNT* V, 722-27.

πανταχῇ *pantachē* everywhere*

Acts 21:28: πάντας πανταχῇ διδάσκων, of Paul, "who brings a teaching to all people *everywhere*" that is directed against the people of God, the law, and the temple; BDF §§26; 103.

πανταχοῦ *pantachou* everywhere, in all places*

This adv. occurs 7 times in the NT, in the sense of *everywhere* in Mark 16:20 (ἐκήρυξαν πανταχοῦ); Luke 9:6 (εὐαγγελιζόμενοι καὶ θεραπεύοντες πανταχοῦ); Acts 28:22; frequently with πᾶς: 17:30 (πάντας πανταχοῦ μετανοεῖν); 24:3 (πάντη τε καὶ πανταχοῦ . . . μετὰ πάσης εὐχαριστίας, rhetorical paronomasia; see BDF §488.1a: "at all times/ in all ways and *in all places* . . . "); 1 Cor 4:17 (πανταχοῦ ἐν πάσῃ ἐκκλησίᾳ). With the meaning *in all directions* in Mark 1:28 (πανταχοῦ εἰς ὅλην τὴν περίχωρον).

παντελής, 2 *pantelēs* absolute, complete, perfect, total*

This adj. occurs only twice in the NT, both times in the expression εἰς τὸ παντελές, *completely/totally,* which is a substitute for the adv. παντελῶς. Heb 7:25: σῴζειν εἰς τὸ παντελὲς δύναται, "he is able to save *completely*"—in light of v. 24 and v. 25b, there could also be an emphasis on the temporal aspect ("forever"), but for the theology of Hebrews, the two belong together (cf. O. Michel, *Heb* [KEK] ad loc.). In Luke 12:11 (μὴ δυναμένη ἀνακύψαι εἰς τὸ παντελές) the phrase can modify either the inf. ("to straighten herself *completely*") or the partc. ("she was not *completely* able to straighten herself"; thus the Vg.). BAGD s.v.

πάντη *pantē* in every way, at all times*

Acts 24:3: πάντη τε καὶ πανταχοῦ, "*at all times* and in all places"; → πανταχοῦ.

πάντοθεν *pantothen* from all sides, all around, everywhere*

This adv. occurs 3 times in the NT: Mark 1:45: *from everywhere;* Luke 19:43: *from all sides;* Heb 9:4: *all around/on all sides.*

παντοκράτωρ, ορος, ὁ *pantokratōr* almighty, ruler over all*

1. Occurrences in the NT and religious-historical background — 2. Usage — 3. παντοκράτωρ in Revelation

Lit.: P. BIARD, *La puissance de Dieu* (1960). — T. BLATTER, *Macht und Herrschaft Gottes* (1962). — A. DE HALLEUX, " 'Dieu le Père tout-puissant,' " *RTL* 8 (1977) 401-22. — D. L. HOLLAND, "Παντοκράτωρ in NT and Creed," *SE* 6 (1973) 256-66. — H. HOMMEL, "Pantokrator," *TViat* 5 (1953/54) 322-78. — *idem, Schöpfer und Erhalter* (1956), esp. 81-137. — W. MICHAELIS, *TDNT* III, 914f. — A. S. VAN DER WOUDE, *THAT* II, 498-507.

1. The noun παντοκράτωρ appears 10 times in the NT: in 2 Cor 6:18 at the close of a series of OT quotations and 9 times in Revelation. 6 of the occurrences in Revelation appear to be inspired by the OT (Amos 4:13?); the first 3 (1:8; 4:8; 11:17; cf. also 16:5, 7) are similar in form and content. Rev 4:8 and Amos 4:13 appear to translate the divine predicate *s^e bā'ôt* as παντοκράτωρ. One could therefore assume that this was determinative for the παντοκράτωρ passages as well. In the research *s^e bā'ôt* is usually viewed as an intensive abstract pl. (like, e.g., *'ēṣôt*, "true wisdom"; *dē'ôt*, "fundamental knowledge," etc.)

This interpretation of the epithet as "Yahweh the powerful" or "Yahweh the almighty" corresponds to the primary translation found in the LXX, κύριος παντοκράτωρ. Moreover, *yhwh s^e bā'ôt* is a designation for the divine king sitting on the throne of the cherubim (e.g., 1 Sam 4:4; 2 Sam 6:2), he who is endowed with the power of dominion. The LXX also translates (*'ēl) šadday* with παντοκράτωρ The idea of dominion also seems to play a role here in some way. In any case, the LXX introduces a Greek term that appeared around the third century B.C. and could actually be derived from an older (Stoic) model, παγκρατής, with the primary sense of "almighty" (πᾶν κράτος ἔχων/παντὸς κρατῶν, from κρατέω plus gen.).

2. In Rev 1:8; 4:8; 11:17, the (variously) repeated expression "the one who was, who is, and who is to come" sounds formulaic. Since in 11:17 we are dealing with a heavenly song of praise upon the realization of the reign of God, the third element is lacking. God's "coming" is viewed as already having taken place (cf. 16:5). Lying behind this three-part formula is Exod 3:14 and Isa 41:4. The divine appellatives from these passages appear to have been combined and placed in chronological order in Rev 4:8. Thus, God is the beginning, middle, and end, a sentiment also expressed in the abbreviated symbol A-Ω in 1:8 (→ Ἄλφα). This is then expressly interpreted in 21:6 with πρῶτος καὶ ἔσχατος and in 22:13 with ἡ ἀρχὴ καὶ τὸ τέλος. The beginning-middle-end formula is also known among the Stoics. In Rom 11:36; 1 Cor 8:6; Col 1:16; and Heb 2:10 it appears in the form of a threefold πᾶν-formula (ἐξ αὐτοῦ—δι' αὐτοῦ [ἐν αὐτῷ]—εἰς αὐτόν), which also has a Stoic ring to it (cf. Marcus Antonius iv.23). Nevertheless, one should not assume direct Stoic influence on Revelation, since the OT background is rather evident. Consequently, one probably should not assign to the παντοκράτωρ of Revelation the "sustainer" motif contained esp. in the middle element (with ἐν) of the Stoic formula; cf. → 3.

3. Rev 1:8 is a divine saying. It is asyndetically joined to the preceding clause, which is intended to demonstrate that the end of the world is in God's hands (v. 7). Rev 4:8 presents the confession of the "four living creatures" (modeled after Ezek 1:6), who are endowed with knowledge of earthly things (see the description of the many "eyes"). They intone the trisagion (cf. Isa 6:3), in which the holiness, omnipotence, and eternity of God are praised. The heavenly prayer of the twenty-four elders (representatives of the OT righteous) begins in 11:17: God's almighty power has been fully brought to bear, and the eschatological kingdom has been created (cf. the throne concept of *s^e bā'ôt*).

According to 15:3, the "victors" whom the Antichrist was not able to defeat sing the song of Moses (cf. Exod 15:1-8) and the lamb. In this way it is pointed out that the hymn is sung already now in communion with Christ. As in the song of Moses, the majesty, omnipotence, and righteousness of God, and the fulfillment of promises and the eternal kingdom are praised (cf. the ruler motif of *s^e bā'ôt*). In Rev 16:7 the altar speaks the παντοκράτωρ-predicate (a metaphor for the martyrs?). The motif of "being" and of "the one who was there" appears already in v. 5 (acclamation of the "Angel of the waters"). The ὁ ἐρχόμενος element is lacking, since God has already appeared as judge. No acclamation is contained in 16:14. The text deals with the eschatological slaughter, in which the παντοκράτωρ will reveal his omnipotence.

In Rev 19:6 a voice from heaven commands the "servants" of God to sing a song of praise to God. This hymn, the last in Revelation, is sung by a mass choir of all believers. After an introductory Hallelujah (cf. 11:17), God the *Almighty* is given thanks for finally establishing his reign. In 19:15 the absolute power of God to rule is emphasized, although 19:6 and 19:15 are imbedded in a christological realm of thought that is already manifest in 1:8.

In 21:22 the temple vision of Ezekiel 48 is viewed as realized in God, the ruler over all, and in the lamb. By way of summary one can say that the παντοκράτωρ passages of Revelation intend to make visible the omnipotence and absolute reign of God.   H. Langkammer

πάντοτε *pantote* always, at all times

This adv. occurs 41 times in the NT, usually as a substitute for the infrequent (in the NT) → ἀεί (see BDF §105), 6 times in the Synoptics, 7 times in John, 19 times in Paul, 8 times in the deutero-Pauline writings, and in Heb 7:27; it is lacking, however, in Acts, the Catholic Epistles, and Revelation: in Mark 14:7 (bis) par. Matt 26:11 (bis)/John 12:8 (bis); in Rom 1:10 with ὡς ἀδιαλείπτως (v. 9); cf. 1 Thess 5:16; in 2 Cor 2:14 with ἐν παντὶ τόπῳ; and in paronomasia (πᾶσαν . . . ἐν παντὶ πάντοτε πᾶσαν . . . εἰς πᾶν) in 2 Cor 9:8; cf. also Eph 5:20; Phil 1:4, 20; 1 Thess 1:2; in Heb 7:25 with εἰς τὸ παντελές; esp. frequent with εὐχαριστέω (esp. at the beginning of letters): 1 Cor 1:4; Eph 5:20; Col 1:3; 1 Thess 1:2; 2 Thess 1:3; 2:13; Phlm 4.

πάντως *pantōs* completely, totally, certainly, absolutely, definitely*

This adv. is found 8 times in the NT, of which 4 are in 1 Corinthians: *certainly/surely* in Luke 4:23; Acts 21:22; 28:4; *completely/totally* in 1 Cor 9:10; *absolutely /in every case* in 9:22; negated οὐ πάντως, "*absolutely not/not at all*," in Rom 3:9; πάντως οὐκ in 1 Cor 16:12; οὐ πάντως, "*not completely/not absolutely*," in 5:10 (see BDF §433.2). G. M. Lee, *ZNW* 64 (1973) 152; *idem*, *NovT* 19 (1977) 240.

παρά *para* with gen.: of, from; with dat.: at, by, in the opinion of; with acc.: at, along, alongside of, in comparison to, against

1. Occurrences in the NT — 2. With gen. — a) Local sense — b) Fig. sense — 3. With dat. — a) Local sense — b) Fig. sense — 4. With acc.— a) Local sense — b) Fig. sense — c) In fixed expressions

Lit.: On preps. in general → ἀνά. BAGD s.v. — BDF §§236f. — M. J. HARRIS, *DNTT* III, 1201-3. — JOHANNESSOHN, *Präpositionen* 226-35. — KÜHNER, *Grammatik* II/1, 509-15. — MAYSER, *Grammatik* II/2, 482-92. — MOULE, *Idiom-Book* 50-52. —

MOULTON, *Grammar* III, 272f. — RADERMACHER, *Grammatik* 137-46. — P. F. REGARD, *Contribution à l'Étude des Prépositions dans la langue du NT* (1919) 513-26. — E. H. RIESENFELD, *TDNT* V, 727-36. — SCHWYZER, *Grammatik* II, 491-98.

1. Παρά appears in the NT 194 times, placing it only in twelfth place in frequency among NT prepositions. As a verbal prefix παρά occupies only ninth position in frequency. The use of παρά is rather evenly distributed between the three cases; in contrast to ἐπί and κατά it is frequently used with gen. and dat. by John. In the NT, as everywhere in koine, there is a mixing in the use of παρά with the gen. and dat. (Radermacher 141f.). Παρά is used without distinction in response to the questions "where?" and "to where?" (BDF §236.1). Consistent with its generally less frequent usage, παρά does not appear in all NT writings (Morgenthaler, *Statistik* 17). It originally designated proximity, esp. in the spatial sense, but also in derived senses (Kühner 509). It designates, according to case, movement away from proximity (gen.), position in proximity (dat.), and movement into proximity (acc.).

2. With gen.: a) Local: *of, from, from the side of* (with verbs of coming, going, sending, pushing, departing, being, etc.; also used attributively to designate starting point or origin): Mark 14:43: coming *from;* John 15:26a: send *from;* Mark 16:9: drive *out of;* John 15:26b (ἐκπορεύεται); 16:27 (ἐξῆλθον); Luke 6:19 (ἐξήρχετο): go out *from;* John 6:46: ὁ ὢν παρὰ τοῦ θεοῦ, "the one who is *from* God"; 7:29: παρὰ αὐτοῦ εἰμι, "I am *from* him"; Luke 8:49: τις παρὰ τοῦ ἀρχισυναγώγου, "someone *from* [the house]/*of* [the family] of the ruler of the synagogue."

b) The fig. sense, derived from the local sense, cannot always be clearly distinguished from the local sense. Many times the local point of departure and author cannot be separated. Frequently, as in classical Greek, παρά replaces ὑπό as a designation of the actor with the pass.

1) Author: *from, by:* Mark 12:11 par.: παρὰ κυρίου ἐγένετο, "this occurred *from* the Lord/it was brought about *by* the Lord"; Luke 1:45: "what was said to her *by* the Lord" (BDF §237.1); John 1:6: "sent *from* God" (BAGD s.v. I.2); John 1:14: "the only begotten *of* the Father" or "the only Son of the Father" (παρά as paraphrase of gen.; cf. Mayser 487) or, when παρὰ πατρός is combined with δόξαν: "a glory that [comes] *from* the Father"; Luke 10:7: τὰ παρὰ αὐτῶν, "that which [is offered] *by* them."

2) Origin and point of departure: *from:* α) After verbs of asking and demanding: Mark 8:11: "by asking *from* him"; John 4:9: "How can you ask [a drink] *of* me"; Jas 1:5: "he should ask *from* God"; Matt 20:20 v.l. (ἀπό in text; on use of ἀπό for παρά see BDF §210): "asked something *of* him." β) After verbs of taking, receiving, and buying: Mark 12:2: "to collect [a portion] *of* the grapes"; Matt 18:19: "it will be given to you *by* my Father

in heaven"; Acts 7:16: "which he had bought *from* the sons"; Phil 4:18: "after I received your gifts *from* Epaphroditus." γ) After verbs of hearing, perceiving, and questioning: John 1:40: "who had heard the word *from* John"; 8:38b: "what you have heard *from* the Father"; 2 Tim 3:14: "since you know *from* whom [pl. in Greek] you have learned it"; Matt 2:4: ἐπυνθάνετο παρὰ αὐτῶν, "he inquired *of* them."

3) Paraphrase of gen. or possessive pron.: Mark 5:26: τὰ παρὰ αὐτῆς πάντα, "all her possessions"; Phil 4:18: τὰ παρὰ ὑμῶν, "your gifts"; Rom 11:27: αὕτη αὐτοῖς ἡ παρ' ἐμοῦ διαθήκη, "this is my covenant with them"; Mark 3:21: οἱ παρ' αὐτοῦ, "his followers."

3. With dat.: a) Local: *by, at, next to* (in reponse to "where?" or "where to?"): John 19:25: "they stood *by* the cross"; Luke 9:47: "he placed [the child] *next to* himself"; 1 Cor 16:2: παρὰ ἑαυτῷ, "*with* him [at home]"; Luke 11:37: "that he eat *with* him [at his house]"; 19:7: "he has gone to visit *with* [at the house of] a sinner"; John 14:23: "we will dwell *with* him"; Rev 2:13: "who was killed *among* you [i.e., in the place where you live]"; Matt 28:15: "*among* the Jews"; John 8:38: "what I have seen *with* my Father [sphere, close affiliation]"; 1 Cor 7:24: παρὰ θεῷ, "*to/before* God" (in communion with God/in God's presence: the local sense gives way to the fig. sense; BAGD s.v. II.2.e).

b) Fig.: 1) judgment, opinion: 2 Pet 2:11 v.l.: παρὰ κυρίῳ, "*before* God [as judge]" (text = παρὰ κυρίου, "*from* God"; see *TCGNT* ad loc.); Rom 2:13: δίκαιοι παρὰ θεῷ, "righteous *before* God [in God's judgment]"; 1 Cor 3:19: "foolishness *with* God"; Gal 3:11: "no one is justified *before* God."

2) Sphere: Luke 1:30: "you have found favor *with* God"; 1 Pet 2:20: τοῦτο χάρις παρὰ θεῷ, "this is grace *with* God"; Luke 2:52: "in favor *with* God and humans"; 1 Pet 2:4: παρὰ θεῷ ἐκλεκτόν, "elect *with* God" (overlap in meaning of παρά with gen. and dat.); Matt 19:26 par.: "*with* people this is impossible, but *with* God all things are possible" (παρά with dat. here not only indicates sphere, but also has the sense of a simple dat.; cf. Riesenfeld 733); Rom 2:11: "for there is no regard for persons *with* God"; Jas 1:17: "*with* whom there is no changing"; Matt 8:10: "*with* no one have I found such faith."

4. With acc.: a) Local: *by, at, next to, on the edge of, toward, by, along* (in response to "where?" or "where to?"): Matt 15:30; Luke 7:38; 8:35, 41; Acts 4:35, etc.: παρὰ τοὺς πόδας τινός, "*at* someone's feet" (lay, sit, stand, fall, etc.); Matt 4:18: "*alongside* the sea" (go); 13:1: "*by* the sea" (sit down); Mark 4:1: "*by* the sea[shore]" (teach); Acts 10:6: "a house *by* the sea"; Matt 15:29: "*along* the Sea of Galilee" (come); Acts 16:13: "*to* the river" (go); Matt 20:30 par.: "*by* [the side of] the road" (sit); Matt 13:4 par.: "*on* the path" or "*alongside* the path/*by* the

path" (fall); Mark 4:15: "*on* the path" (be); Heb 11:12 "*on* the seashore."

b) Fig.: 1) Comparative: *in comparison to, (more) than, (different) from, in the place of, instead of*: Luke 13:2: ἁμαρτωλοὶ παρὰ πάντας τοὺς Γαλιλαίους, "more sinful *than/in comparison to* all other Galileans"; Rom 14:5: κρίνει ἡμέραν παρ' ἡμέραν, "he values one day *more than* other days"; 12:3: μὴ ὑπερφρονεῖν παρ' ὃ δεῖ φρονεῖν, "not to think *beyond* that which one ought to think" (wordplay); Luke 3:13: πλέον παρὰ τὸ διατεταγμένον, "more *than* what is required"; Heb 3:3: παρὰ Μωϋσῆν, "*compared to* Moses"; 1 Cor 3:11: θεμέλιον ἄλλον παρὰ τὸν κείμενον, "another foundation *than* that which has already been laid"; Gal 1:8: παρ' ὃ εὐηγγελισάμεθα ὑμῖν, "*different from* the gospel that we proclaimed to you"; v. 9: παρ' ὃ παρελάβετε, "*different from* what you have received."

One of the two elements of comparison can be omitted (Riesenfeld 734): Rom 1:25: ἐλάτρευσαν τῇ κτίσει παρὰ τὸν κτίσαντα, "they worshiped the creature *instead of* the Creator"; Luke 18:14: κατέβη οὗτος δεδικαιωμένος εἰς τὸν οἶκον αὐτοῦ παρ' ἐκεῖνον, "he *rather than* the other went home justified" (Riesenfeld 735; n. 35 refers to Jeremias [*Parables* 112f.] and the exclusive Aram. *min); Heb 1:9 (Ps 44:8 LXX): παρὰ τοὺς μετόχους σου, "but not your companions/like none of your companions" or "*more than* your peers."

2) Adversative: The meaning *beside* also forms the background for the adversative sense *against, contrary to* (opposite to κατά with acc. = "according to"): Rom 1:26: παρὰ φύσιν, "*contrary to* nature/*un*natural"; 16:17: παρὰ τὴν διδαχήν, "*contradicting/against* the teaching"; 2 Cor 8:3: παρὰ δύναμιν, "*beyond* their ability" (overlap with the comparative meaning); Acts 18:13: παρὰ τὸν νόμον, "*against* the law."

3) Causal: *because of*: 1 Cor 12:15f.: οὐ παρὰ τοῦτο οὐκ (litotes), "not *because of* this not/nevertheless *because of* this."

4) Subtracting: *minus*: 2 Cor 11:24: τεσσεράκοντα παρὰ μίαν, "forty *less* one [i.e., thirty-nine]."

c) Fixed expressions: Luke 5:7 v.l. (insertion in D) and *Herm. Sim.* ix.19.3: παρά τι "*up to* something/almost /nearly"; cf. *Herm. Sim.* viii.1.14: παρὰ μικρόν, "almost."

W. Köhler

παραβαίνω *parabainō* transgress, deviate → παράβασις.

παραβάλλω *paraballō* throw down; compare; intrans.: approach; cross over*

Only intrans. in the NT, as a nautical t.t.: Acts 20:15: παρεβάλομεν εἰς Σάμον, "We *crossed over* to Samos"; *compare* in Mark 4:30 A C² D Θ Koine, etc.

παράβασις, εως, ἡ *parabasis* transgression, violation of the law*
παραβαίνω *parabainō* transgress, deviate*
παραβάτης, ου, ὁ *parabatēs* transgressor, lawbreaker*

1. Occurrences and meaning — 2. Paul — 3. Acts 1:25

Lit.: E. BRANDENBURGER, *Adam und Christus* (WMANT 7, 1962) 180-205. — R. BULTMANN, "Zur Auslegung von Gal 2:15-18," *idem, Exegetica* (1967) 394-99. — W. GÜNTHER, *DNTT* III, 583-85. — U. LUZ, *Das Geschichtsverständnis des Paulus* (BEvT 49, 1968) 186ff. — W. MUNDLE, "Zur Auslegung von Gal 2,17.18," *ZNW* 23 (1924) 152f. — J. SCHNEIDER, *TDNT* V, 736-44.

1. In the NT παραβαίνω is found only 3 times (Matt 15:2f.; Acts 1:25); παράβασις, with 7 occurrences, and παραβάτης, with 5, are found only in the Epistles (excluding the v.l. in Luke 6:4 D), 7 times in Paul (→ 2).

The word group is used in the NT, except in Acts 1:25 (→ 3), in accordance with (esp. Jewish) Hellenistic usage (cf. Schneider) of violation of the law given or sanctioned by God: παράβασις/παραβάτης (τοῦ) νόμου (i.e., the Torah): Luke 6:4 D; Rom 2:23, 25, 27; Jas 2:11. In Matt 15:2f., in response to the accusations of the Pharisees that the disciples of Jesus "transgress the tradition of the elders," Jesus objects that this tradition itself (esp. the practice of korban [vv. 5f.; → κορβᾶν]) "transgresses the command of God [the fourth commandment, v. 4]." The stylistically-rhetorically motivated Matthean replacement of two different verbs in the Markan source (Mark 7:5, 8f.) with παραβαίνω, which is then anaphorically repeated in Jesus' counter-question, lends it a pregnant sense and added emphasis. This sense is also evident in Rom 5:14; 1 Tim 2:14 (of the sin of Adam or Eve understood as transgression of the divine command [cf. 4 Ezra 3:7; *2 Bar.* 4:16; 9:7; Josephus, *Ant.* i.46; *Apoc. Mos.* 8:14, etc.]); Heb 2:2 (parallel to παρακοή in reference to the βέβαιος λόγος of God announced by angels); 9:5; Jas 2:9 (cf. v. 8: quotation of Lev 19:18 as νόμος βασιλικός).

2. In Paul, παράβασις and παραβάτης are found only in Galatians and Romans, always in discussion of the law (→ νόμος 4.b).

a) Rom 2:23, 25, and 27 are polemical. Paul makes the thematic (from 1:18) universality of sin against the law (παράβασις τοῦ νόμου) specific from v. 12 on. In so doing, Paul destroys the unique claim of the Jew over against the Gentile, a claim based on possession of the law and circumcision: In v. 23, as a summary of vv. 21f., Paul accuses the Jew of a contradiction between his καυχᾶσθαι ἐν νόμῳ and his παράβασις τοῦ νόμου: The one who boasts of God (2:17) and the law "dishonors God through a *violation* of the law" (cf. *T. Naph.* 8:4, 6; *Mek. Exod.* 15:2; *b. Yoma* 86a [see Billerbeck I, 414f.]; gener-

ally, Billerbeck I, 412ff.). In Rom 2:25-27 the accusation that the Jew is a παραβάτης τοῦ νόμου is related to the dualism of περιτομή and ἀκροβυστία and is transferred to the opposition of Jew and Gentile: As a *"transgressor* of the law"* the Jew loses the privilege gained in circumcision, which is dependent on fulfillment of the law. On the other hand, the Gentile who keeps the law gains the status of one circumcised and will pass judgment on the Jew in the final judgment (v. 27). In this way, Rom 2:1 is eschatologically inverted, as is the Jewish idea (see Matt 12:41 par.) that Israel, the righteous, will judge the godless in the final judgment (cf., e.g., Dan 7:27 LXX; *1 Enoch* 95:3; *Wis* 4:16; *Apoc. Abr.* 29, etc.; see also Billerbeck I, 650; III, 124). Here as there the keeping and transgressing of the law determine how the roles are distributed in the final judgment.

b) The word group is found elsewhere in excursive parenthetical reflections, the intention of which is directed toward abrogation of the law as the way of salvation: According to Rom 4:13-15, the law could not have been the bearer of the promise to Abraham, since it in fact only brings divine wrath in that it is violated. This would not have happened without the presence of the law (v. 15b; for the missing element in v. 15, one could point, e.g., to *Apoc. Mos.* 14). By means of this concept, Paul draws the law into the frequently attested, general context of sin and wrath (cf., e.g., 2 Macc 5:17; Rom 1:18).

In Rom 5:13f. Paul is concerned with demonstrating that even without the law or its proclamation sin existed. Here, with the help of the concept of law, he makes a salvation-historical distinction between παράβασις and ἁμαρτία: According to this distinction sin existed independently of law already in the time between the παράβασις of Adam (see → 1) and the proclamation of the law, with the result that "death also reigned over those who had not sinned after the manner of the *trespass* of Adam" (v. 14), although it did not have at the time the empirical form of παράβασις, which it received only through the law and as such also rendered people liable (→ ἐλλογέω). This observation forms the presupposition for the idea then expressed in v. 20 (see Brandenburger 251; contra Luz 202n.254): Inasmuch as through the law human sin takes on the same form as Adam's sin, Adam's sin and the ruin that follows from it are multiplied, as it were (v. 16), so that Paul is able to say that the law multiplied *transgressions* and caused sin to spread for the first time.

According to Gal 3:19(-22) the law was added "in order to provoke *transgressions"* (in stark contrast to the Jewish view, in which the Torah, as a "fence against sin," is thought to prevent sin; cf., e.g., *Lev. Rab.* 1 [106a]; Billerbeck III, 588), and is therefore also "a prisoner under sin" (v. 22).

According to Gal 2:18 (see G. Klein, *Rekonstruktion*

und Interpretation [1969] 195ff.) the reestablishment (οἰκοδομέω) of the already nullified law (cf. v. 19) as a way of salvation proves (συνιστάνω) everyone who strives after such a righteousness ἐξ ἔργων νόμου (this is the sense of the first person sg.) to be a *transgressor* (of the law), since ἐξ ἔργων νόμου οὐ δικαιωθήσεται πᾶσα σάρξ (v. 16). Therefore, it could pointedly be stated, not Christ (v. 17), but the law is a "servant of sin."

With the aid of a correlation between παράβασις and νόμος, Paul links the law, the reason for the presence of παραβάσεις, with sin, which gained its concrete form as παράβασις through the law.

3. In Acts 1:25, παραβαίνω is not related to the law; based on the construction with → ἀπό (2.a.1) and the immediate reference to τόπος, it contains rather a local component. According to this text, Judas had *removed himself* from the office of apostle assigned him by God (cf. H. Köster, *TDNT* VIII, 205-7) so that his place would now have to be filled again.

The LXX uses παραβαίνω with ἀπό or ἐξ to translate Heb. *sûr min* in Exod 32:8; Deut 9:12, 16 (cf. *1 Clem.* 53:2; CD 1:13, 15, etc.) to indicate a "deviation" from the way pointed out by God, and then also directly ἀπὸ τῶν ἐντολῶν (τοῦ θεοῦ) (Deut 17:20; 28:14).   M. Wolter

παραβάτης, ου, ὁ *parabatēs* transgressor, lawbreaker
→ παράβασις.

παραβιάζομαι *parabiazomai* apply force, coerce, urge*

Luke 24:29: "they *urged* him and said"; Acts 16:15: "they *forced* us"; cf. further *Mart. Pol.* 4.

παραβολεύομαι *paraboleuomai* venture, risk*

Phil 2:30 (as always with the dat.), of Epaphroditus, who according to vv. 26f. was close to death as a result of an illness and according to v. 30a for the sake of the work of Christ did not shrink from death: παραβολευσάμενος τῇ ψυχῇ, "*risking* his life"; cf. further Polybius ii.26.3 (τοῖς ὅλοις); Diodorus Siculus iii.36.4 (ταῖς ψυχαῖς).

παραβολή, ῆς, ἡ *parabolē* type, parable

1. Occurrences in the NT and meaning — 2. Form-critical differentiation — 3. Subject matter and structure — 4. Message and purpose of parables — 5. Interpretation

Lit.: A. M. AMBROZIC, "Mark's Concept of the Parable," *CBQ* 29 (1967) 220-27. — J. D. CROSSAN, "Parable as Religious and Poetic Experience," *JR* 53 (1973) 330-58 (revised and expanded as chapter 1 of *In Parables: The Challenge of the Historical Jesus* [1973]). — P. DSCHULNIGG, *Rabbinische*

Gleichnisse und das NT. Die Gleichnisse der PesK im Vergleich mit den Gleichnissen Jesu und dem NT (1988). — D. FLUSSER, *Die rabbinischen Gleichnisse und der Gleichniserzähler Jesus.* I: *Das Wesen der Gleichnisse* (Judaica et Christiana 4, 1981). — B. GERHARDSSON, "The Narrative Meshalim in the Synoptic Gospels: A Comparison with the Narrative Meshalim in the OT," *NTS* 34 (1988) 339-63. — W. HARNISCH, *Die Gleichniserzählungen Jesu* (UTB 1343, 1985). — F. HAUCK, *TDNT* V, 744-61. — M. S. KJÄRGAARD, *Metaphor and Parable: A Systematic Analysis of the Specific Structure and Cognitive Function of the Synoptic Similes and Parables qua Metaphors* (1986). — JÜLICHER I-II. — E. JÜNGEL, *Paulus und Jesus* (1964) 87-139. — W. S. KISSINGER, *The Parables of Jesus* (1979). — E. LINNEMANN, *Gleichnisse Jesu* (1978). — J. C. LITTLE, "Parable Research in the Twentieth Century," *ExpTim* 87 (1975/76) 356-60; 88 (1976/77) 40-43, 71-75. — C. H. PEISKER and C. BROWN, *DNTT* II, 743-60. — N. PERRIN, *Jesus and the Language of the Kingdom* (1976). — *idem,* "The Parables of Jesus as Parables, as Metaphors, and as Aesthetic Objects," *JR* 47 (1967) 340-46. — H. RÄISÄNEN, *Die Parabeltheorie im Markusevangelium* (1973). — J. W. SIDER, "The Meaning of *Parabole* in the Usage of the Synoptic Evangelists," *Bib* 62 (1981) 453-70. — E. TROCMÉ, "Why Parables? A Study of Mark IV," *BJRL* 59 (1977) 458-71. — D. O. VIA, *The Parables: Their Literary and Existential Dimension* (1967). — For further bibliography see *TWNT* X, 1212-15.

1. The NT contains 50 occurrences of this noun, of which 2 are in Hebrews, 13 in Mark, 17 in Matthew, and 18 in Luke. In Hebrews, παραβολή is a t.t. of typological exegesis: The former tabernacle is a *type* of the present time (9:9), and the return of Isaac to Abraham is a *type* of the resurrection of the dead (11:19). In the Synoptics παραβολή designates a characteristic speech form used by Jesus that in a metaphorical way expresses the fundamental principles of his proclamation. The usual translation, "parable," should not obscure the fact that form-critical distinctions must be made among the pericopes so designated (→ 2). The sg. (31 occurrences) refers to individual discourses and the pl. (17 occurrences) to the general portrayal of Jesus as the teller of parables. Not all of the discourses that might be are explicitly classified as παραβολαί.

2. In the Synoptics, παραβολή is used to identify *proverbs* (Luke 4:23; 6:39), *maxims* (Mark 7:17; Matt 15:15), *metaphorical sayings* (Mark 3:23; Luke 5:36), *enigmatic sayings* (Mark 4:11; Matt 13:10; Luke 8:10), *general rules* (Luke 14:7), *parables* (depicting a common occurrence: Mark 4:13, 30; 13:28; Matt 13:18, 31, 33, 36; 24:32; Luke 8:4, 9, 11; 12:41; 13:6; 15:3; 21:29), *parabolic stories* (depicting remarkable singular occurrences: Mark 12:12; Matt 13:24; 21:33; Luke 18:1; 19:11; 20:9, 19), and *paradigmatic illustrative stories* (Luke 12:16; 18:9). These distinctions are rather fluid. The range of usage of παραβολή corresponds to that of Heb. *māšāl* in the OT and Judaism (excluding Qumran).

3. The subject matter of the Synoptic παραβολαί is taken from the daily world of Jesus' audience, some from nature (Mark 4:26-32; 13:28f.; Luke 12:54-56, etc.), some from the multitude of social relationships. The subject matter and its formal presentation are determined by Jesus' rhetorical objective. Like the rabbis, Jesus uses contemporary metaphors (king, servant, vineyard, etc.), through which parables gain slightly allegorical features. The structures of the parables are simple and pregnant: Limited action with a maximum of three persons or groups of persons, clearly delimited scenes, individual features clearly related to the main point, obvious broader significance, and assumed truths (metaphors, parables) or unusual events (parabolic stories, illustrative stories) all arouse the interest of the hearer.

4. The original message of Jesus' parables is thematically complex and conceptually difficult to grasp with precision. It concerns the coming of the kingdom of God (Mark 4:26-32; 13:28f.; Matt 13:33), the great invitation (Luke 14:16-24), the eschatological separation (Luke 13:6-9; 17:26-29; Matt 13:24-30, 47-50), proper conduct (Mark 13:33-37; Matt 7:24-27; 18:23-35; 21:28-32; 24:45-51; Luke 14:23-32; 16:1-8), and God's reaction to the conversion of sinners (Matt 18:12-24; 20:1-16; Luke 15:11-32; 18:9-14). In certain instances the original meaning is no longer discernible (e.g., Mark 4:3-8).

Jesus' parables are thematically distinct from those of the rabbis, which primarily serve to expound the law. The objective of Jesus' parables is discernible from their indicative and imperative elements (address and demand): Their intent is to transform the hearer. Therefore, they are more than pedagogic aids, since Jesus' message functionally required the parables and Jesus' life gave the parables practical commentary.

5. The post-Easter Church knew that Jesus' παραβολαί were only accessible to those who listened attentively (Mark 4:9, 33). The setting in the Church created new audiences and new methods of interpretation. Many parables were retold in this new setting as allegories (Mark 12:1-12; Matt 22:1-14; 25:1-13); others were allegorically interpreted (Mark 4:13-20; Matt 13:36-43). The apostolic Church claimed that it alone was entrusted with the key to understanding the parables or the μυστήριον of the kingdom of God, while "those outside" encounter them as mere obscure, enigmatic sayings that cause continued hardening (Mark 4:34, 10-12; weakened in Luke 8:20 par. Matt 13:11). Matthew speaks of the "things hidden from the beginning," which are revealed in the parables of Jesus in accordance with the prophetic promises (13:35).

Critical research on the parables since Jülicher has distinguished between image and reality and has sought the *tertium comparationis*, the third point at which the two intersect. While in this view the parable and the parabolic story are understood as figurative stories, more recent linguistic theory (Ricoeur, etc.) maintains that true metaphorical language is real, in that it is functionally necessary language. Accordingly, parables should not be interpreted, only paraphrased: The truth is only present "in the parable as a parable" (Jüngel 135).   G. Haufe

παραβουλεύομαι *parabouleuomai* venture, risk

Phil 2:30 C Ψ Koine sy bo^pt for → παραβολεύομαι.

παραγγελία, ας, ἡ *parangelia* instruction, command, proclamation
→ παραγγέλλω.

παραγγέλλω *parangellō* instruct, command*
παραγγελία, ας, ἡ *parangelia* instruction, command, proclamation*

1. Occurrences — 2. Constructions — 3. Meaning — 4. Usage

Lit.: W. MUNDLE, *DNTT* I, 340f. (bibliography 342f.). — O. SCHMITZ, *TDNT* V, 759-62. — SPICQ, *Notes* II, 647-49.

1. The vb. παραγγέλλω has over 20 occurrences in the LXX and 31 in the NT. Of the latter 11 are in Acts (cf. Luke: all 4 occurrences in contrast to Mark), 4 in 2 Thessalonians, and 5 in 1 Timothy. The noun is not found in the LXX or the NT except in 1 Thess 4:2 and in the writings listed above: Acts 5:28; 16:24; 1 Tim 1:5, 18.

2. As a designation for a "command whose execution is taken for granted" (BDF §328) the vb. as preterit is always in the aor. except for the iterative impf. in 2 Thess 3:10. Except in 1 Cor 11:17 it is followed by a pres. or aor. inf. (see BAGD 613), a ἵνα-clause (in Mark 6:8; 2 Thess 3:13), or direct discourse (3:10, proverbial after ὅτι; Matt 10:5, after λέγων), also as continuation of indirect discourse in Mark 6:8f.; Luke 5:14; Acts 1:4; 23:22.

3. Both vb. and noun refer to the action of directing a person or group of persons with authority, in the sense of *instructing, commanding* (with μή: *forbid*) and instruction, order, command respectively. In 1 Thess 4:2 the noun with δίδωμι, a Hellenistic paraphrase, means the same as the vb. (cf. 1 Tim 1:18). Both words are used together to intensify the statement made in Acts 5:28: "we have *strictly forbidden*."

4. In the Gospels, only Jesus gives commands or instructions: to an unclean Spirit in Luke 8:29, to the Twelve in Mark 8:6 (R. Pesch, *Mark* [HTKNT] ad loc.: "Jesus' establishment of the rules for mission") and Matt

10:5; to the crowd in Matt 15:35 par. Mark 8:6; and the command of silence in Luke 5:14; 8:56; 9:21.

In Acts, the resurrected Jesus commands in 1:4 and 10:42. God himself commands in 17:30. Paul can now command the divining spirit "in the name of Jesus Christ" in 16:18. He and the twelve apostles are the recipients of commands and prohibitions of the Jewish and Roman authorities in 4:18; 5:28, 40; 16:23, 24; 23:22, 30.

Both Acts 15:5 and the Pauline Epistles mention commands for the Church. In the latter the authentic Paul appeals to the "Lord (Jesus)" (1 Cor 7:10; 11:17 with v. 23; 1 Thess 4:2, διά and ἐν, v. 1; 4:11). 2 Thess 3:4, 6, 10, 12, on the other hand, commands with the authority of Paul. Finally, "Paul" charges "Timothy" in 1 Tim 1:18; 6:13 to see to the correct teaching (1:3, 5) and proper conduct, esp. of widows (5:7) and the rich (6:17). These passages present instructions with universal validity (cf. N. Brox, *Die Pastoralbriefe* [RNT] on 1:5; differently Schmitz 761f.n.33), while passages referring to Jesus present commands addressed to certain situations or persons.   W. Radl

παραγίνομαι *paraginomai* arrive, come to; appear, be present*

This vb. occurs 37 times in the NT, 8 times in Luke and 20 in Acts, in Paul only in 1 Cor 16:3 (absolute: ὅταν δὲ παραγένωμαι, "when I *am with you*/after my *arrival*"), in the Pastorals only in 2 Tim 4:16 (οὐδείς μοι παρεγένετο, "no one *is present* with me/*is by my side*"); Heb 9:11 (Χριστὸς δὲ παραγενόμενος ἀρχιερεύς, "but when Christ *appeared* as high priest"); cf. the meaning *appear* in Matt 3:1; Luke 12:51; the vb. is lacking in the Catholic Epistles and Revelation. In all the remaining occurrences παραγίνομαι means *come/arrive* with place indicated by εἰς (Matt 2:1; John 8:2; Acts 9:26; 13:14; 15:4), ἐπί (Luke 22:52), πρός (Luke 7:4, 20; 8:19; 11:6; Acts 20:18), or ἐπὶ ... πρός (Matt 3:13) or not indicated (Mark 14:43; Luke 14:21; 19:16; John 3:23; Acts 5:21, 22, 25; 9:39; 10:33; 11:23; 14:27; 17:10; 18:27; 21:18; 23:16, 35; 24:17, 24; 25:7; 28:21).

παράγω *paragō* pass by, pass away, go away; pass.: pass away*

This vb. occurs 10 times in the NT, usually intrans. *pass by* (Matt 20:30; Mark 2:14; 15:21; John 9:1; with παρά in Mark 1:16 ("as he was *going* along the shore of the Sea of Galilee"), also fig. (1 Cor 7:31: παράγει γὰρ τὸ σχῆμα, "for the form of this world *is passing away*"; cf. *pertransire* in 4 Ezra 4:26). With the meaning *go away* (ἐκεῖθεν) in Matt 9:9, 27; pass. ἡ σκοτία παράγεται, "the darkness *is waning*" (1 John 2:8); ὁ κόσμος παράγεται, "the world *must pass away*" (2:17). K. L. Schmidt, *TDNT* I, 129f.

παραδειγματίζω *paradeigmatizō* expose to ridicule or scorn, disgrace*

Heb 6:6: ἀνασταυροῦντας . . . καὶ παραδειγματίζοντας, of those who have fallen away and cannot be brought again to repentance, since they "crucify [again] the Son of God and *expose* him *to scorn*"; cf. also Matt 1:19 v.l. The significance of public punishment, which plays a frequent role in the LXX (cf. Num 25:4; Jer 13:22), is lacking in Heb 6:6; on the idea of public shaming, see Ezek 28:17; 3 Macc 3:11; 7:14. H. Schlier, *TDNT* II, 32; Spicq, *Notes* II, 650.

παράδεισος, ου, ὁ *paradeisos* paradise*

Although the OT paradise narratives of Genesis 2–3 are frequently reflected in the NT (esp. in Romans: 3:23; 5:12; 8:20; also 2 Cor 11:3), παράδεισος occurs only 3 times in the NT. It is an expression for the now-hidden extraterrestrial resting place for the dead in the intermediate state between death and resurrection (Luke 23:42; 2 Cor 12:4; Rev 2:7).

Παράδεισος is a loanword from old Iranian annd generally designates a "garden" or "park." Accordingly, in the LXX it refers esp. to the "garden of God" (Gen 2:8ff.; 13:10; Ezek 31:8). From there, παράδεισος came to refer to the original *paradise*, now hidden but to be revealed again in the future (Isa 51:3; T. Lev. 18:10f.; *1 Enoch* 25:4f.; 4 Ezra 7:36; 8:52; on the present hiddenness cf. esp. *1 Enoch* 60:7f.; 61:12; 70:4; *Apoc. Abr.* 21:6f.; as the resting place of Enoch and Elijah, who were taken from this life: *1 Enoch* 60:8; 89:52; *T. Abr.* 11:3; cf. also Luke 16:9). Paradise is usually thought of as located in heaven (4 Ezra 4:7f.; *Life of Adam and Eve* 25:3; *3 Bar.* 4:8; *Apoc. Mos.* 37:5; on the NT conception cf. further Luke 16:22ff.; John 14:2ff.; 2 Cor 5:1ff.; Phil 1:23; 1 Thess 4:17; Revelation 20–22).

According to Luke 23:43 Jesus grants to the thief on the cross, in response to his request for acceptance in the final judgment (v. 42: ὅταν ἔλθῃς εἰς τὴν βασιλείαν σου [p⁷⁵ ℵ B C*, etc.]), a share already "today" in *paradise* (σήμερον μετ’ ἐμοῦ ἔσῃ ἐν τῷ παραδείσῳ). In this way the thief's guilt is definitively forgiven and salvation is opened to him in a hidden sphere beyond death (cf. also Acts 7:59; Rom 8:38f.; 2 Cor 5:1ff.; Phil 1:23).

Rev 2:7 speaks of παράδεισος τοῦ θεοῦ: The original *paradise* with the tree of life (Gen 2:9; 3:3ff.) will return in the eschaton (paradise is probably thought of here in connection with the new Jerusalem, cf. 21:2; 22:1ff.).

Paul speaks in 2 Cor 12:4 of being taken up into *paradise* (ἡρπάγη εἰς τὸν παράδεισον; cf. ἕως τρίτου οὐρανοῦ, v. 2), which he classifies in 12:1 among ὀπτασίαι καὶ ἀποκαλύψεις κυρίου. He probably speaks here of an ecstatic state, one obviously unconnected with the expected state of salvation after the parousia, which happened to Paul as though to a stranger (cf. R. Bultmann, *2 Cor* [Eng. tr., 1985] ad loc.).

See also generally BAGD s.v. (bibliography); J. Jeremias, *TDNT* V, 765-73; *TWNT* X, 1215 (bibliography); H. Ringgren, *BHH* 1386f.; *BL* 1297-1300; P. Hoffmann, *Die Toten in Christus* (NTAbh N.F. 2, 1969) index s.v.; H. Bietenhard and C. Brown, *DNTT* II, 760-64 (bibliography); G. Schneider, *Luke* II (ÖTK) on 23:43 (bibliography).

H. Balz

παραδέχομαι *paradechomai* receive, accept, adopt*

This vb. occurs 6 times in the NT: Mark 4:20: τὸν λόγον παραδέχομαι (with ἀκούω); Acts 16:21: ἔθη παραδέχομαι, "customs that we as Romans cannot *adopt*"; 22:18: μαρτυρίαν παραδέχομαι; 1 Tim 5:19: κατηγορίαν παραδέχομαι, "*entertain* a charge"; Heb 12:6, with a person as obj.: act. *accept/love* (quoting Prov 3:12, corresponding to Heb. *rāṣâ*); pass. in Acts 15:4: *be accepted*.

παραδίδωμι *paradidōmi* hand over; pass on*

1. Occurrences in the NT — 2. Meaning — 3. Tradition history in connection with the Passion — 4. Usage — a) Mark — b) Matthew — c) Luke-Acts — d) John — e) The Pauline corpus — f) The Catholic Epistles

Lit.: M. BLACK, "The 'Son of Man' Passion Sayings in the Gospel Tradition," *ZNW* 60 (1969) 1-8. — F. BÜCHSEL, *TDNT* II, 169-71. — GOPPELT, *Theology* I, 224-28. — M.-L. GUBLER, *Die frühesten Deutungen des Todes Jesu* (1977). — HAHN, *Titles* 37-67. — P. HOFFMANN, "Mk 8,31," FS Schmid (1973) 170-204. — J. JEREMIAS, *Abba* (1966) 191-216, 216-29. — *idem*, *Theology* 295-97. — K. KERTELGE, ed., *Der Tod Jesu. Deutungen im NT* (1976). — H. KESSLER, *Die theologischen Bedeutungen des Todes Jesu* (1970). — W. KRAMER, *Christ, Lord, Son of God* (1966). — B. LINDARS, *NT Apologetic* (1961). — E. LOHSE, *Märtyrer und Gottesknecht* (1963). — K. LÜTHI, "Das Problem des Judas Iskariot—neu untersucht," *EvT* 16 (1956) 98-114. — H.-J. VAN DER MINDE, *Schrift und Tradition bei Paulus* (1976). — H. PATSCH, *Abendmahl und historischer Jesus* (1972). — N. PERRIN, "The Use of (παρα)διδόναι in Connection with the Passion of Jesus in the NT," FS Jeremias (1970) 204-12. — *idem*, "Towards an Interpretation of the Gospel of Mark," *Christology and a Modern Pilgrimage* (ed. H. D. Betz, 1971) 23f., 71-73. — W. POPKES, *Christus Traditus* (1967). — J. ROLOFF, "Anfänge der soteriologischen Deutung des Todes Jesu," *NTS* 19 (1972/73) 38-64. — K. ROMANIUK, *L'amour du Père et du Fils dans la sotériologie de Saint Paul* (1961). — L. SCHENKE, *Studien zur Passionsgeschichte des Markus* (1971). — E. SCHWEIZER, "Der Menschensohn in der synoptischen Überlieferung," *idem*, *Neotestamentica* (1963) 56-84. — G. STRECKER, "Die Leidens- und Auferstehungsvoraussagen im Markusevangelium," *ZTK* 64 (1967) 16-39. — P. STUHLMACHER, "Vicariously Giving His Life for Many, Mark 10:45 (Matt. 20:28)," *idem*, *Reconciliation, Law, and Righteousness* (1986) 16-29. — H. E. TÖDT, *Der Menschensohn in der synoptischen Überlieferung* (1963). — K. WENGST, *Christologische Formeln und Lieder des Urchristentums* (1972). — For further bibliography see *TWNT* X, 1047f.

1. Παραδίδωμι appears in the NT 119 times, with greatest frequency in the Gospels and Acts (Matthew has 31 occurrences, Mark 20, Luke 17, John 15, Acts 13, total 96). There are 19 occurrences in the Pauline corpus (6 in Romans and 7 in 1 Corinthians) and 4 in the Catholic Epistles.

2. As an intensified form of "give," παραδίδωμι designates the act whereby something or someone is transferred into the possession of another. While OT Hebrew is familiar only with a simple *ntn*, the later *msr* (Hebrew and Aramaic) is a synonym of παραδίδωμι; Lat. *tradere* also corresponds completely with παραδίδωμι (W. Bacher, *ZAW* 29 [1909] 219). In Greek, (παρα)τίθημι often has a similar sense. The simple and compound forms are frequently interchanged.

The great breadth of meaning displayed by παραδίδωμι is best divided according to the implied degree of possession and esp. the degree of threat to the existence of the one who or that which is given over: a) entrust/commend/give for safekeeping; as a t.t. *hand down*, almost *command;* b) *hand over an area of authority/authorize/permit;* c) *hand over for judgment/punishment,* etc. (the act is a threat to the one concerned, but follows a prescribed course), again a t.t.; d) *deliver/hand over;* e) *risk one's existence* or even *sacrifice* (esp. as a self-sacrifice; similarly τίθημι τὴν ψυχήν, John 10:15); f) *hand over to death/destruction.*

Under d) we can include the always concise and stereotyped statements on the act of Judas (all in the Gospels), for which the basic meaning is *deliver over,* though redacted modifications do appear. Παραδίδωμι does not mean "betray something (esp. secrets)." At the most it means, in a derived sense, "deliver, surrender" and thereby "betray (a person)" (Popkes 217ff.).

A considerable portion of the NT passages, esp. in connection with Jesus' Passion, defy simple classification, since their precise formulation is uncertain: the tradition of John the Baptist (Mark 1:14 par.) and of the Son of man (Mark 9:31, etc.: divine pass.? Judas? someone else?); likewise 1 Cor 11:23b; Rom 4:25; cf. John 3:16. Different expressions are also combined, which also leads to ambiguity. Moreover, interpretation appears to vary in traditional materials.

3. The most significant portion of NT uses of παραδίδωμι are connected with the Passion accounts. The following attempts to reconstruct a tradition history have been made (excluding the overly speculative proposal of K. Barth, *Church Dogmatics* II/2 [1957] 480-506):

a) The essential impulses come from Isaiah 53. The earliest formulation is perhaps found in Mark 9:31a (a mashal using divine pass.; cf. Rom 4:25), possibly coming from Jesus. The reflexive expressions in Mark 10:45, etc. are also very old. Isaiah 53 also had its impact in Hellenistic circles (various text forms; among others Rom

8:32). The setting was scriptural proof (thus esp. Jeremias, *Abba* 204ff.).

b) The Synoptic Passion accounts and the pre-Pauline traditions arose independently of each other. In the pre-Pauline (and pre-Johannine) form of the tradition παραδίδωμι was found in one of three types of sonship formulas ("delivered up," along with "adopted" and "sent") and was not limited to the death of the Son of God, but also included his coming. The oldest form of the tradition is found in Rom 8:32 and John 3:16, while the form in Rom 4:25 is late (thus Kramer, van der Minde).

c) The nontheological (trial, Judas) and theological (action of God/Jesus) statements have an independent origin; their overlap came about only later. It is not easy to demonstrate a common origin for the various theological statements; most probably a saying like that of Mark 9:31a was the point of departure. In its wake followed soteriological explanation (Rom 4:25) and transformation into a self-surrender formula (Mark 10:45, etc.) with a degree of dependence on Isaiah 53 (thus Popkes; to a certain extent already Hahn).

d) Originally, παραδίδωμι was used in a purely descriptive fashion in the account of Jesus' trial (Mark 15:1, etc.; also for the act of Judas). Then in the early Passion apologetic it came to be used as a divine pass. (Mark 9:31; 14:21, 41, etc.). From this apologetic developed the soteriological use of the vb., esp in Hellenistic circles and under the influence of Isaiah 53 (Rom 4:25; Mark 10:45, etc.; thus Perrin).

e) The Pauline and Synoptic sayings arose independently. The Passion-theological use of παραδίδωμι first appears in Mark (not in proto-Mark). Redaction criticism of Mark shows that 8:31, not 9:31, contains early material. Use of παραδίδωμι derives from the trial account (esp. the actions of Judas). Mark was the first consciously to formulate ambiguous statements (in the same vein as the messianic secret), such as 9:31; he sees God's hand behind the actions of unbelievers. The theologizing may be influenced by Pauline language (thus Hoffmann, Schenke; cf. already Strecker).

f) Already in the pre-Markan Passion account there was a concatenation of the various παραδίδωμι acts—that of Judas, the Sanhedrin, Pilate, and the executioners. Prior to all the human acts of "delivering up," however, stands the act of God (Mark 9:31; perhaps this saying even occasioned the account of the betrayal; thus Goppelt).

In light of the ongoing discussion of the nature of the problem it is not possible at the present time to reconstruct definitively the tradition history. Thus it is unclear to what extent one can assume pre-Pauline, pre-Markan, or perhaps pre-Lukan and pre-Johannine material (esp. at Mark 9:31; Rom 4:25). The tradition-historical classification of the "Son of Man" sayings and Isaiah 53 (text

forms, influence) is still a matter of debate. Also questions concerning the form (mashal, "delivered up" formula) and the setting (Lord's Supper, scriptural proof) of fixed phrases have not yet produced any clear answers. The same is true of the relationship between the different interpretations of the death of Jesus (Roloff, etc.).

The fixed points of the tradition history, which are at best only relatively certain, are probably the broad, stereotypical statements concerning the actions of Judas, such as the note in 1 Cor 11:23b. The earliest παραδίδωμι passages are therefore historically as well as tradition-historically linked with the Last Supper. Judas's act would then be the original fact underlying the use of παραδίδωμι. Another very early line is found in the words of institution of the Lord's Supper, which are Jesus' self-surrender, at least according to the sense of the passage (also Mark 10:45; cf. John 13 and 15, Galatians, Ephesians, the Pastorals) and also a reference to that "holy night" (cf. the Passover).

The stages of development are uncertain. Presumably there was further soteriological development (under the influence of Isaiah 53) and possibly also development in the direction of the vicariously borne judgment of God (in the OT παραδίδωμι is found strikingly often in connection with God's judgment). Other, originally independent, παραδίδωμι statements (esp. trial terminology) were added to the tradition, resulting in reciprocal influence on various levels. The contribution of the final redactor (special Mark) should not be underestimated. The course of the tradition needs further clarification; skepticism is appropriate toward derivations that posit a single source.

4. a) In Mark only two occurrences (4:29: *permit*; 7:13: *pass on*) have nothing to do with suffering; three deal with the suffering of the community (13:9, 11, 12: *take before the court:* unnatural enmity), another with a prefiguring of the destiny of Jesus (1:14: John the Baptist).

The remaining Markan occurrences deal with Jesus' Passion. Mark intertwines in these passages three different trajectories: the enigmatically intimated "delivering up" of the Son of man (9:31; 10:33; 14:21, 41; cf. 8:31), the "handing over" by Judas (3:19; 14:10f., 18, 21, 42), and the "delivery" of Jesus by the Jewish authorities to the Gentiles (10:33; 15:1, 10) and by the Gentiles to death (15:15). We are dealing here with the essential elements of the Markan Passion theology, in which the messianic secret is gradually revealed. If a tradition also stands behind 9:31, etc., which speaks apocalyptically of the eschatological surrender of the Son of man to humans, Mark himself saw in it, on the historical level, the rejection by Judas and the Jewish authorities, at the same time preserving the theological dimension (the will of God, in accordance with the Scriptures).

b) Matthew follows by and large the Markan formulations regarding Jesus' Passion (also with regard to John the Baptist in 4:12): the handing over of the Son of man (17:22; 20:18f.; 26:2, 24, 45), the handing over by Judas (10:4; 26:15f., 21ff., 46ff.; 27:3f.), and transfer to and by Pilate (27:2, 18, 26). In the process Matthew closely connects the first two and places the blame entirely on Judas (frequency of mention, content and position of 27:3-10). Judas is the archetype of those who reject Jesus and understand their act only too late.

This tone of warning is well suited to another group of Matthean passages where the community is admonished with respect to the gifts that have been bestowed (25:14, 20, 22) and with respect to the persecutions under which they must not yield (10:17-21; 24:9f.). The unrepentant are threatened with being delivered to judgment (5:25; 18:34). Matthew also uses παραδίδωμι to emphasize the authority of Jesus (11:27, cf. 28:18).

c) In Luke-Acts παραδίδωμι possesses a wide range of meanings. In addition to the Passion-theological statements, we find: the tradition of the eyewitnesses (Luke 1:2), *grant authority* (10:22; weakened in 4:6: "I possess"), *deliver* to the officer (12:58), *command* (Acts 6:14; 16:4), abandonment by God (7:42), *commit* to grace (14:26; 15:40), and *commit oneself* (15:26). The breadth of meaning corresponds to the linguistic variation in the Markan source (Luke 6:16: Judas) and to the ample use of synonyms (e.g., Acts 2:23). Παραδίδωμι is not as important to Luke as it is to Mark and Matthew. He frequently replaces it with logical clarifications (thus Luke 3:20: "incarcerate") and glosses (see 18:31f.; 21:16). Nevertheless, παραδίδωμι also appears frequently in the Lukan Passion accounts: the delivering up of the Son of man (9:44; 18:32; 22:22; 24:7) and the handing over by Judas (22:4, 6, 21f., 48), Pilate (23:25), and the Jewish authorities (20:20; Acts 3:13). God's plan is fulfilled (Luke 24:7; cf. 17:25). But Luke places responsibility on the Jews (Acts 3:13; cf. 2:36; 7:51f.), though the power of the devil is never underestimated (Luke 4:6; cf. 22:3; Acts 26:18). Acts ultimately depicts the suffering Church as an imitation of its Lord: prison and delivery into the hands of the Gentiles and to death (8:3; 12:4; 21:11; 22:4; 27:1; 28:17; see also Luke 21:12, 16).

d) John uses παραδίδωμι for the act of Judas (9 or 10 occurrences) and for the handing over of Jesus to Pilate by the Jews (18:30, 35, possibly 19:11) or the reverse (18:36; 19:16). Παραδίδωμι signals delivery to a different sphere of power. Those who should be "his" end up rejecting Jesus; their deed is Satanic (6:71, etc.; 19:11). Ultimately, of course, the handing over of Jesus is not successful; Pilate gives Jesus back (19:16); what remains is the rejection. The evil game cannot, however, contest the sovereignty of Jesus (he predicted it: 6:64, etc.; his

kingdom is of a different world: 18:36; nothing happens without the will of God: 19:11).

Beyond these passages lies only 19:30 (Jesus *transfers* the Spirit). The unusual formulation (R. Schnackenburg, *John* III [Eng. tr., 1982], 284) emphasizes active submission to the Father. The statement in 3:16 belongs to the Johannine theology of giving (→ δίδωμι 8); it is doubtful that John has reworked an older "delivered-up" formula.

e) The usage of the Pauline corpus is not consistent: God *abandons* the sinner to his fate (Rom 1:24, 26, 28, more resignation than punishment); *be entrusted* to a form of teaching (Rom 6:17, cf. the Jewish practice of entrusting a student to the teaching of a rabbi: see E. Käsemann, *Rom* [Eng. tr., 1980] 181); *deliver* a sinner to Satan for punishment (1 Cor 5:5; 1 Tim 1:20; no exact parallels: see Popkes 138-40); *pass on* teaching and modes of conduct (for faithful observance, 1 Cor 11:2, 23a; 15:3); *surrender* one's body to be burned (13:3: martyrdom by fire? as a mark of slavery?); experience imitation of the death of the cross (2 Cor 4:11); and *abandon* oneself to sensuality (Eph 4:19).

Παραδίδωμι also appears in 1 Cor 15:24 in a christological sense (*return* or *transfer* power), in the first place as an interpretation of the surrender of Jesus' life ("out of love of": Gal 2:20; Eph 5:2, 25, probably traditional; cf. Gal 1:4; 1 Tim 2:6; Titus 2:14, which are connected with Mark 10:45).

Christ is the object of παραδίδωμι in 1 Cor 11:23b, which is pre-Pauline. Paul might understand it here as delivering up by God, as is explicitly formulated in Rom 8:32. Rom 4:25 is then certainly divine pass. (pre-Pauline? cf. U. Wilckens, *Rom* I [EKK], 279f.). Παραδίδωμι refers to the death on the cross, not generally to the work of Christ (contra Kramer). The saving significance is emphasized; the death took place because of our sins or for our good and is the pledge of divine love (Rom 8:32-39; Galatians 2; Ephesians 5).

f) In the Catholic letters παραδίδωμι is found in the first place in connection with divine judgment. The abused Christ leaves "it" (the object is lacking) to the "righteous judge" (1 Pet 2:23; cf. Rom 12:19). 2 Pet 2:4 emphasizes by way of warning that the judgment of God is sure; the fallen angels are an example (Genesis 6; cf. *1 Enoch* 10-11, 18-19, 21-22).

Jude 3 and 2 Pet 2:21 stress in opposition to the false teachers "the faith that was once for all *handed down*" and "the command that *was given*" to Christians. The one who gives the command is probably the apostle (2 Pet 3:2; cf. Pol. *Phil.* 7:2). Doctrine and conduct belong together (cf. "way of righteousness," 2 Pet 2:21; "straight way," 2:15). One should not leave the foundation (Jude 20; cf. 1 Tim 1:19, etc.; also already Rom 16:17).   W. Popkes

παράδοξος, 2 *paradoxos* unbelievable, incredible*

Luke 5:26: εἴδομεν παράδοξα σήμερον, "we have seen *incredible things* today" (literally, "that which contradicts one's views and expectations"; cf. Mark 2:12: οὕτως οὐδέποτε εἴδαμεν); cf. also Wis 5:2; 16:17; 19:5; 3 Macc 6:33. G. Kittel, *TDNT* II, 255.

παράδοσις, εως, ἡ *paradosis* tradition; regulation*

1. Occurrences in the NT — 2. Meaning — 3. Mark and Matthew — 4. The Pauline corpus

Lit.: H. R. Balz, *Methodische Probleme der neutestament-lichen Christologie* (1967) 176-203. — K. Berger, *Die Gesetzesauslegung Jesu* I (1972), index s.v. — F. Büchsel, *TDNT* II, 172f. — L. Cerfaux, "Die Tradition bei Paulus," *Catholica* 9 (1953) 94-104. — O. Cullmann, *Die Tradition als exegetisches, historisches und theologisches Problem* (1954). — E. Dinkler, *RGG* VI, 970-74. — L. Goppelt, "Tradition nach Paulus," *KD* 4 (1958) 213-33. — W. G. Kümmel, "Jesus und der jüdische Traditionsgedanke," Kümmel I, 15-35. — F. Mussner, *LTK* X, 291-93. — J. Roloff, *Apostolat-Verkündigung-Kirche* (1965) 84-90. — K. Wegenast, *Das Verständnis der Tradition bei Paulus und in den Deuteropaulinen* (1962; for critical reviews see W. G. Kümmel, *TLZ* 89 [1964] 753-55; W. Gerber, *TZ* 25 [1969] 81-90). — For further bibliography see *TWNT* X, 1047f.

1. This noun is found 13 times in the NT—8 times in Mark 7:3-13 par. and elsewhere only in the Pauline corpus.

2. a) The noun consistently means *traditional regulation* (Cerfaux: "rule-tradition"), that which is handed down from generation to generation with an authoritative demand for compliance and is received accordingly. It thus approaches the sense of rule, command, law (cf. Gal 1:14 with Phil 3:6; analogous to ἐντολή and λόγος in Mark 7:8f. par.; v.l. νόμος in Matt 15:1). The regulation is "learned, passed on, received, obeyed, grasped"; one either "walks" in accord with it or "transgresses" it. The semantic structure remains unaffected by the sphere of application (Jewish παράδοσις in Mark 7 par. and Galatians 1, Christian in 1 Corinthians and 2 Thessalonians, heretical in Colossians 2) and any negative or positive evaluation. Παράδοσις is rejected when it is human in form and stands against the will of God.

b) In Greek usage, παράδοσις means "tradition" in the broader sense. The focus on *regulation* in the NT corresponds with Jewish practice, where tradition and law are closely associated (tradition as Halakah; references in Kümmel; Billerbeck I, 691-94; Wegenast 30-33; F. Mussner, *Gal* [HTKNT] 80).

c) The secondary literature usually operates with "tradition" as a generic term, a term that only partially coincides with the NT term (see on this Balz and Dinkler).

3. Why did the disciples of Jesus not follow the παράδοσις of the elders, i.e., the ways of Scripture (Mark 7 par. Matthew 15)? The polemical response is: The pharisaic tradition obstructs the command and word of God. Mark 7 disqualifies the παράδοσις on the basis of its origin (from humans, v. 8) and three times stresses its irreconcilability with God's true will (vv. 8, 9, 13). The prophets and the Torah contradict the παράδοσις, which is thereby exposed as a later, illegitimate distortion; this fulfills the prophecy concerning the eschatological falling away of Israel (Berger 15f., 498f.). Matthew 15 clarifies the counterquestion (v. 3): The important thing is to obey the command of God; the pharisaic regulations only provide means of avoiding that command.

4. The absolute formulation and contextual problems hamper the interpretation of *regulation* in 1 Cor 11:2. In connection with 11:3-16 (the question of head coverings) παράδοσις refers to Christian regulations pertaining to life and conduct. Since 11:3-16 is undoubtedly an interpolation (L. Cope, *JBL* 97 [1978] 435f.), v. 2 actually refers to the instructions regarding the Lord's Supper (see v. 23).

2 Thess 2:15; 3:6 summon to the keeping of the *regulations,* as taught by Paul (example in 3:7ff., also 1 Cor 11:1). Doctrinal as well as ethical traditions are intended (2:17: work and word). The statements are not necessarily signs of a later construction of tradition; see already 1 Thess 4:2 (cf. W. Schrage, *Die konkrete Einzelgebote* . . . [1961] 19, 59, 79, 135f.).

According to Gal 1:14 Paul's earlier life was lived in strict accordance with Jewish practices ('Ιουδαϊσμός) and with zeal for the "*regulations* of the fathers." This formulation accentuates the broadest possible compliance with the law, not differences between Pharisees and Sadducees regarding the oral tradition.

According to Col 2:8 the false teaching is not κατὰ Χριστόν, but κατὰ τὴν παράδοσιν τῶν ἀνθρώπων and κατὰ τὰ στοιχεῖα τοῦ κόσμου. In its *prohibitions* (cf. 2:14, 20-22) the Jewish background and the connection with Mark 7 are obvious: purity, "from humans" (v. 22; quoting Isa 29:13; cf. Titus 1:14; see also Berger 471; E. Schweizer, *Col* [Eng. tr., 1985] 137).

W. Popkes

παραζηλόω *parazēloō* rouse, make jealous/zealous*

This vb. occurs 4 times in the NT, all in Paul: Rom 10:19, of God who *wants to make* his people *jealous* (ἐγὼ παραζηλώσω ὑμᾶς, quoting Deut 32:21); likewise 11:11 (εἰς τὸ παραζηλῶσαι αὐτούς); 11:14, with reference to Paul's διακονία: εἰ πῶς παραζηλώσω μου τὴν σάρκα, ". . . my fellow people"; 1 Cor 10:22: ἢ παραζηλοῦμεν τὸν κύριον, "or *do* we *want to rouse/provoke* the Lord *to jealousy?"*

(by taking part in sacrificial meals to idols, which bind believers to demons; cf. Isa 65:11f.); → ζῆλος 6.

παραθαλάσσιος, 2 *parathalassios* by the sea/lake*

This adj. is found only in Matt 4:13, where it refers to Capernaum, which was *located by the sea* (i.e., in the valley, unlike Nazareth, which was just mentioned): εἰς Καφαρναοὺμ τὴν παραθαλασσίαν (on the fem. gender see BDF §59.1; also §123.1; cf. Luke 4:31 D: τὴν παραθαλάσσιον).

παραθεωρέω *paratheōreō* overlook, neglect*

Acts 6:1, in reference to the widows of the Hellenists (→ Ἑλληνιστής), who were neglected in the daily care (παρεθεωροῦντο . . . αἱ χῆραι αὐτῶν).

παραθήκη, ης, ἡ *parathēkē* property entrusted to another*

παρατίθημι *paratithēmi* set before, present; place next to; hand over, entrust; expound*

1. Meanings — 2. The vb. in the NT — 3. The noun in the Pastorals

Lit.: BAGD 616, 622f. — N. BROX, *Die Pastoralbriefe* (RNT) 235f. — M DIBELIUS and H. CONZELMANN, *The Pastoral Epistles* (Hermeneia) 32, 92. — FRISK, *Wörterbuch* II, 897f. — G. LOHFINK, "Die Normativität der Amtsvorstellungen in der Pastoralbriefen," *TQ* 157 (1977) 93-106, esp. 95ff. — P. TRUMMER, *Die Paulustradition der Pastoralbriefe* (BBET 8, 1978) 219-22. — K. WEGENAST, *Das Verständnis der Tradition bei Paulus und in den Deuteropaulinen* (WMANT 8, 1962) 132-58.

1. Vb. and noun are constructed from παρά + τίθημι, where the basic meaning of the vb., "set (down), lay (down), (re)establish," etc. (Frisk 897), is nuanced by the prep. παρά, "from the side of, from," in the sense of a motion's (local) point of departure.

2. The vb., which occurs 19 times in the NT, designates the serving of food as a sign of hospitality (Luke 10:8; 11:6; Acts 16:34; 1 Cor 10:27), which Jesus himself affirmed by providing food in abundance (Mark 6:41; 8:6 bis, 7; Luke 9:16). It also stands in connection with the "presenting" of parables (Matt 13:24, 31), the presentation and explanation of the proclamation (Acts 17:3), and the personal propagation of the apostolic proclamation (1 Tim 1:18; 2 Tim 2:2) and refers (in the act.) to committing apostolic representatives to the Lord (Acts 14:23; 20:32) or to the final surrender of the spirit (Luke 23:46) or of one's life (1 Pet 4:19) to God. Luke 12:48 uses the vb. in the sense of a position of responsibility or legal liability: "from him to whom much *has been entrusted,* more will be demanded."

3. The Pastorals use the noun, which originally arose in connection with the law governing deposits and possessions (Attic → παρακαταθήκη), 3 times of the gospel, which the addressee, the post-Pauline officebearer (Timothy), is to "guard" (1 Tim 6:20; 2 Tim 1:14). This *deposit* is further delineated in 1 Tim 6:20 as consisting of avoidance of "unholy idle talk and the antitheses of what is falsely called knowledge." According to 2 Tim 1:14 it is produced by "the Holy Spirit who lives in us" and comes about ultimately only through trust in God, "who is able to guard my *tradition* until that day" (v. 12). The frequent assertion that the concept of tradition in the Pastorals is static coheres neither with the context nor with its overall intention (Trummer 220ff.).

P. Trummer

παραινέω *paraineō* command, admonish, advise*

Lit.: M. DIBELIUS and H. GREEVEN, *Jas* (Hermeneia) 3-5. — E. HAENCHEN, "Acta 27," FS Bultmann (1964) 235-54. — G. STÄHLIN, *TDNT* V, 817. — For further bibliography see → παρακαλέω.

1. Παραινέω occurs in the NT only in Acts 27:9, 22. More general than the ancient rhetorical term παραίνεσις, "practical hortatory speech" (in contrast to προτρεπτικός or παράκλησις, "speech intended fundamentally to influence"), and the modern exegetical t.t. "admonitions of general ethical content" addressed to a specific audience (Dibelius and Greeven 3), παραινέω in the NT means *give urgent advice,* without per se the weight of authority, but entirely practical (with acc. ὑμᾶς instead of classical dat. ["persuade"] and without the friendly tone of the παρα- [see Stählin]). Παραινέω is located in meaning somewhere between the commanding → παραγγέλλω (11 occurrences in Acts) and the warm παρακαλέω (22 occurrences in Acts).

2. Since the description of impf. παρήνει in Acts 27:9 as "literary language" (BDF §328) is insufficient, we must interpret the author's unusual word choice (two occurrences in ch. 27) in conjunction with the deliberate doubling of παρεκάλει/παρακαλῶ . . . μεταλαβεῖν τροφῆς (vv. 33f.): In v. 34 Paul admonishes in a reassuring way, and is immediately successful (v. 22: παραινέω ὑμᾶς εὐθυμεῖν; v. 36: εὔθυμοι δὲ γενόμενοι). According to v. 9, Paul previously intervened without success: When advising those in charge he simply *warned* them. What then follows λέγων (v. 10) is not the content of the warning (cf. vv. 33f.), but the reason for it (cf. Luke 7:4).

When Paul then speaks to the entire group (27:22), the precondition for the use of παρακαλέω is lacking, i.e., the combination of extreme need and imminent change in circumstances. Καὶ τὰ νῦν indicates the divine consequence rather than the result of guilt: "But now I am urging you to be of good courage." Paul is here the prophetic man of God who through a word of rebuke and promise establishes his authority in the matter, an authority that those in charge lack.   J. Thomas

παραιτέομαι *paraiteomai* request for oneself, excuse oneself; reject, avoid, refuse*

This vb. occurs 12 times in the NT: 4 times each in the Gospels and the Pastorals and in Acts 25:11; Heb 12:19, 25 (bis); it does not appear in the Pauline corpus. Mark 15:6: *request* (a prisoner on the occasion of the Passover); this basic meaning is altered in Luke 14:18a: *excuse oneself* (from an invitation), i.e., *decline* (cf. 1 Kgs 20:6, 28); vv. 18b, 19, pass.: ἔχε με παρῃτημένον, "consider me *excused*." In the broader meaning *reject/refuse* "the prefix παρ- gives a nuance of aversion or repudiation" (G. Stählin, *TDNT* I, 195) occasionally in the sense of a refusal. Heb 12:19: at Sinai Israel *sought* (by request) *to avoid/rejected* God speaking to them any more in the thunder (cf. Exod 19:16ff.; μή functions pleonastically, see BDF §429); Acts 25:11: Paul *does* not *want to avoid* a deserved death (by begging for pardon; οὐ παραιτοῦμαι τὸ ἀποθανεῖν; cf. Josephus *Vita* 141). The meaning *reject* also appears, esp. in the Pastorals (always in imv. παραιτοῦ): 1 Tim 4:7; 5:11; 2 Tim 2:23; Titus 3:10; and in in Heb 12:25a, b in a warning against falling away: The God who ultimately has revealed himself from heaven (ὁ λαλῶν) must not (as the people of the old covenant sought to do with the one who revealed himself at Sinai) be *rejected*. G. Stählin, *TDNT* I, 195; H. Schönweiss, *DNTT* II, 855, 858f.

παρακαθέζομαι *parakathezomai* sit down beside*

Luke 10:39, aor. pass. partc. παρακαθεσθεῖσα reflexively of Mary, "*who had sat down* at the feet of the Lord" (v.l. παρακαθίσασα).

παρακαθίζω *parakathizō* sit down beside Luke 10:39 v.l. in place of → παρακαθέζομαι.

παρακαλέω *parakaleō* request, urge; comfort
παράκλησις, εως, ἡ *paraklēsis* admonition, encouragement, comfort, request*

1. Occurrences — 2. Meanings — a) Development — b) Delimitation — 3. The Synoptics — 4. Form-critical concerns — 5. Paul — a) General remarks — b) 1 Thessalonians — c) 2 Corinthians — d) The theological place of paraclesis in Paul — 6. The other Epistles — 7. Acts

Lit.: C. ANDRESEN, "Zum Formular frühchristlicher Gemeindebriefe," *ZNW* 56 (1965) 233-59. — R. ASTING, *Die Verkündigung des Wortes im Urchristentum* (1958) 171ff., 716-29. — K. BERGER, "Apostelbrief und apostolische Rede. Zum Formular frühchristlicher Briefe," *ZNW* 65 (1974) 190-231. — C. J.

BJERKELUND, *Parakalō* (BTN 1, 1967) (bibliography). — N. BROX, *Paulus und seine Verkündigung* (1966) 55. — R. BULTMANN, "Das Problem der Ethik bei Paulus," *ZNW* 23 (1924) 123-40. — idem, *Der Stil der paulinischen Predigt und die kynisch-stoische Diatribe* (FRLANT 13, 1910) 96-107. — A. CAVALLIN, "(τὸ) λοιπόν," *Eranos. Acta Philologica Suecana* 38 (1941) 121-44. — C. H. DODD, *Gospel and Law* (1951) 3-24. — G. FRIEDRICH, *RGG* V, 1137-44, esp. 1142. — A. GRABNER-HAIDER, *Paraklese und Eschatologie bei Paulus* (NTAbh N.F. 4, 1968). — GOPPELT, *Theology*, II, 136f., 167-74, 224-31. — K. GRAYSTON, "A Problem of Translation. The Meaning of *parakaleō, paraklēsis* in the NT," *Scripture Bulletin* 11 (1980) 27-31. — F. HAHN, "Die christologische Begründung urchristlicher Paränese," *ZNW* 72 (1981) 88-99. — W. JOEST, *Gesetz und Freiheit* (1961). — E. KAMLAH, *Die Form der katalogischen Paränese im NT* (WUNT 7, 1964). — E. KÄSEMANN, "Worship and Everyday Life: A Note on Romans 12," *idem, NT Questions of Today* (1969) 188-95. — E. LOHSE, "Paränese und Kerygma im 1. Petrusbrief," *ZNW* 45 (1954) 68-89. — U. B. MÜLLER, *Prophetie und Predigt im NT* (SNT 10, 1975) 118-30, 162-233. — E. REINMUTH, *Geist und Gesetz. Studien zu Voraussetzungen und Inhalt der paulinischen Paränese* (1985). — J. T. SANDERS, "The Transition from Opening Epistolary Thanksgiving to Body in the Pauline Corpus," *JBL* 81 (1962) 348-62. — H. SCHLIER, "Die Eigenart der christlichen Mahnung nach dem Apostel Paulus," *idem* II, 340-59. — E. SCHLINK, "Gesetz und Paraklese," *Antwort* (FS K. Barth, ed. E. Wolf, C. von Kirschbaum, and R. Frey; 1956) 323-35. — O. SCHMITZ and G. STÄHLIN, *TDNT* V, 773-99. — W. SCHRAGE, *Die konkreten Einzelgebote in der paulinischen Paränese* (1961) 71-115. — E. G. SELWYN, *1 Pet* (1955) 365-466. — F. SELTER and G. BRAUMANN, *DNTT* I, 567-71. — H. D. WENDLAND, *Ethik des NT* (NTD Ergänzungsband 4, 1970) 84ff. — P. WENDLAND, *Die urchristlichen Literaturformen* (HNT, 1912) 276-81, 286f., 290-92. — For further bibliography see *TWNT* X, 1215.

1. On the basis of statistics alone, παρακαλέω/ παράκλησις are among the most important terms for speaking and influencing in the NT. The vb. (109 occurrences) is used in the Synoptics 25 times, predominantly as *request* in the sense of petition, in Paul about 44 times, and in the other Epistles about 18 times, overwhelmingly as *request* in the sense of a summoning address and as *exhort* and *comfort*. It is lacking in John, 1–3 John, Revelation, James, 2 Peter, and Galatians (!). The noun (29 occurrences) is found only in Luke (2 occurrences), Acts (4), Paul (19), 1 Timothy (1), and Hebrews (4). Only once does it have the sense of *request* (*"appeal,"* 2 Cor 8:17). The concentration of vb. and noun in Acts, 2 Corinthians, 1 Thessalonians, Philemon, and Hebrews leads us to emphasize the root meaning "comfort," and to interpret its further occurrences in prominent passages (Rom 12:1; 1 Cor 1:10; Eph 4:1; Jude 3; Phil 2:1) on that basis.

Παρακαλέω is found only 10 times in the pass., otherwise always in the act. The *nomen actionis,* too, has a pass. sense only 7 times. Paul's preference for noun constructions is evident in the large number of occurrences of παράκλησις in his writings.

2. a) In spite of the purely secular meaning, παρακαλέω /παράκλησις "are very freely set in the service of testimony to the NT event of salvation" (Schmitz 799), although its subsequent theological significance remains slight and bears a variety of nuances. Nowhere is it possible to establish a special significance for the terms (unlike διδαχή, εὐαγγέλιον, and κήρυγμα). Consequently, the syntax is equally varied (cf. BAGD s.v. παρακαλέω 1-4). The word overwhelmingly expresses a personal and often emphatic concern.

1) The simple *summon/request* is "always in some way related to the proclamation of salvation" (Schmitz 791; e.g., Heb 13:19). It is used of response to the revealed saving power of Jesus (Acts 8:31; contrast Mark 5:10, 12, 17)—and can take on the sense of *recommend* for a third party (Mark 7:32; 8:22; Luke 7:4 par.; cf. Phlm 10) or *invite* (acc. of the person; → 7). When the speaker does not desire anything for himself (or for a third party), but desires something for the person addressed, the meaning *encourage* arises (Acts 27:33f.; → παραινέω; negatively *warn/advise against*, Acts 19:31; 21:12); it then easily develops into *friendly, exhorting comfort* (2) or *comfort/console* (3).

2) In most cases a statement of or reference to the content of the exhorting comfort is expressed through a parallel vb. (→ 2.b) and/or an inf. construction (less frequently through a final clause, which is more frequent with requests). When the exhortation follows without grammatical connection (or is introduced only by direct discourse), it has the tone of a specific *command* (e.g., regarding the task of exhorting in 1 Thess 5:14; 1 Pet 5:1f.; or the support of the apostle in Rom 15:30; with the tone of an instruction using the aor. in 1 Tim 1:3; 2 Tim 4:2; contrast Titus 2:15; → 4.g). When used absolutely, παρακαλέω can also point to the development of the t.t. "application of the message of salvation (the doctrinal tradition) to the addressed individuals (the actual situation)" in the sense of *applicatio*.

3) The older Jewish usage "eschatological consolation" (→ 3) is preserved, but retreats completely behind the help brought by present salvation—in word (2 Cor 7:7) or in deed (Acts 20:12). Since the biblical sense of *consoling* always connotes an element of the fulfillment of blessing (not a mere pacification: Matt 2:18), the combination of consolation and exhortation suggests the sense *give a departing blessing* (Acts 16:40; 20:1; contrast 15:32; 2 Thess 2:16: παράκλησις; cf. Rom 15:5).

4) The meanings easily flow into one another: request and exhortation (Acts 16:15; 2 Thess 3:12); exhortation and encouragement (Col 2:2); consolation and exhortation (2 Cor 2:7- 8). In the NT this is due esp. to the unique nature of the gospel: As παράκλησις it creates a crisis, in which it also displays its power—both as a claim to

victory in the crisis it creates and as encouragement in that crisis.

5) In the pass. παρακαλέω shows a slight preference for the meanings *console* (5 times in 2 Corinthians 1 and 7 and also in Luke 16:25; Acts 20:12; and with an OT source Matt 2:18; 5:4) and *encourage* (1 Thess 3:7), rather than *invite* (Acts 28:14) and *exhort* (1 Cor 14:31; *be exhorted,* 2 Cor 13:11). Παράκλησις also less frequently has a pass. meaning (obj. gen., 2 Cor 1:5-7; 7:13; further Luke 6:24 [fig.]; Phlm 7).

6) Παράκλησις in the act. sense takes various subjects: the coming Messiah (Luke 2:25), God (Rom 15:5; 2 Cor 1:3), the Spirit of God (Acts 9:31), the Scriptures (Rom 15:4; Heb 6:18; 12:5), the missionary (1 Thess 2:3), the charismatic (Rom 12:8; 1 Cor 14:3; 1 Tim 4:13; Acts 4:36), the Church (Phil 2:1), or a letter (Acts 13:15).

7) The dual act.-pass. function of παράκλησις in 2 Cor 1:4; 7:7 (connected to παρεκλήθη and ἀναγγέλλων) makes evident Paul's ability to construct terms in this area as well.

8) The tenses are used carefully (→ 3). The impf. (and pres. partc.) indicates uncertain results (Acts 21:12) or an ongoing address (Acts 2:40; *persuade,* directed toward Paul, 19:31; after the closing of a letter, ἔγραψα παρακαλῶν in 1 Pet 5:12: "I have written and *even now am exhorting* and testifying . . ."). The aor. indicates assured results (Acts 16:15; contrast 1 Cor 16:12: *decisive* and yet negatively granted *request),* something new (Acts 16:39 with impf.), something eventful (2 Cor 7:6f. with pres. partc. and with pf. in v. 13), or the close of a discourse (Acts 16:40; cf. 2:40 διεμαρτύρατο with παρεκάλει, → 2.b).

9) Also unique to the NT are the attributes of παρακαλέω introduced by Paul in the form of appositions to the subject (Phlm 9; Eph 4:1; 1 Pet 5:1) or to those addressed (with ὡς 1 Pet 2:11) or prepositional phrases (→ 5.d.2).

10) The history of the word is strongly influenced by Greek rhetoric (P. Wendland) as well as the form of the Greek letter (Bjerkelund). The current t.t. *paraclesis* only remotely corresponds to the old rhetorical generic term ("a speech seeking to win assent to a specific fundamental point of view"). The development of the Greek term converges with that of the LXX in Judaism and the NT. The LXX displays an interest in developing a religious vocabulary in which certain Greek terms consistently represent certain concepts in Scripture. The translators link παρακαλέω with Heb. *nhm* ("console") and its equivalents (Isa 40:1-11 LXX). From the consoling address and the consoling event come the consoling words of God.

In the NT "consoling in light of the end times" becomes specifically the proclamation of Christ in light of the end times, which has two forms: the persuasive missionary proclamation and Church paraclesis.

b) The specific content of παρακαλέω/παράκλησις can be determined by comparison with parallel terms (which frequently are found in groupings: 1 Cor 14:3; 2 Cor 13:11; Phil 2:1; 1 Thess 4:13; 2 Tim 4:2; cf. 1 Thess 5:14): *paraclesis* makes use of information (Col 4:8 par. with γινώσκοντες) or the proclamation of a firm conviction (1 Pet 5:12 with ἐπιμαρτυρῶν). In the Church it is done in accordance with the doctrinal tradition (Rom 16:17; 1 Cor 4:13ff.; Titus 1:9). In the proclamation of salvation παρακαλέω marks the transition from kerygma (διεμαρτύρατο [aor.!] in Acts 2:40) to application (παρεκάλει [impf.!]), the fulfillment of which Luke sums up with "save yourselves!" (see also emphatic μαρτυρεῖν with παρακαλέω in 1 Thess 2:12). Thus, παρακαλέω documents the dual character of the word as indicative and imperative (Schmitz 779f.).

Παρακαλέω/παράκλησις with παραγγέλλω (and the like) makes a command more personal and urgent (2 Thess 3:12; 2 Cor 10:1, 6; by way of contrast, *request* replaces *command* in Phlm 8f.; Ign. *Rom.* 4:1, 3), with νουθετέω it makes the harshness of the pastoral care more fatherly (1 Cor 4:14, 16), and with δέομαι it makes the request more reserved (2 Cor 8:4).

Παρακαλέω/παράκλησις with ἐλέγχω becomes more serious (Titus 1:9; 2:15; cf. 2 Tim 4:2), with ἐρωτάω more cooperative, relying more on voluntary compliance (1 Thess 4:1; 5:12; Phil 4:2f.), with παραμυθέομαι/παραμυθία(ιον) even more friendly (1 Thess 2:12; Phil 2:1f.). The intended effect is emphasized by στηρίξαι (with παρακαλέω τὰς καρδίας, 2 Thess 2:17; cf. Acts 14:22; 1 Thess 3:2), οἰκοδομεῖτε/οἰκοδομή (1 Thess 5:11/1 Cor 14:3: edification through exhortation and consolation) and χαρά (2 Cor 7:4; Phlm 7). In 1 Cor 14:31 παρακαλῶνται after προφητεύειν and ἵνα μανθάνωσιν is nearly identical with οἰκοδομεῖσαι.

3. Mark (this is weaker in Matthew and Luke) uses παρακαλέω, *(humbly) request with manifest urgency,* as a formulaic opening of healing accounts. In addition the meanings *urge* (5:17) and *desire* (v. 18; on vv. 10 and 12 → 2.a.1) are found. *Request with assurance of response* (Matt 26:53) is slightly distinguished by its use of the aor. from *request without assurance of response* (impf.: Luke 8:41; → 2.a.8). Matthew and Luke also pick up on the ring of eschatological consolation (→ 2.a.3), which is found in the proclamation of the actions of God: "Blessed are those who mourn, for *they shall be comforted* [by God's intervention on their behalf]" (Matt 5:4), or by overcoming the distress of this world (Luke 16:25). Luke already stands in the *paraclesis* tradition of Paul (→ 5): "John *exhorted* many other things (παρακαλέω used of the preaching of repentance) and in this way continued the proclamation of the gospel for the people (παρακαλῶν εὐηγγελίζετο)" (3:18). The invitation of the father in 15:28 could be an echo of the pleading proclamation (the addressees are found in v. 2).

4. a) The NT Epistles are a "word of *comfort,*" λόγος παρακλήσεως (Heb 13:22). With this brief formula one can summarize the purpose (actual aid), the structure (interplay of teaching and exhortation), and the content (encouragement and warning) of NT Epistles. Cf. Acts 15:31; 1 Pet 5:12; Jude 3 (Schmitz 795f.).

b) The epistles define the *paraclesis* practiced in the community (1 Cor 1:6; 1 Thess 5:11b; Col 2:1f.). It revolves around mutual comfort: συμπαρακληθῆναι (Rom 1:11). For that reason, authors unfamiliar with their readers appeal for mutual recognition (Heb 13:22; Jude 3; Rom 15:30). There is no other condition set down for the form of Christian παράκλησις than compliance with this mutuality. Παρακαλέω opens the way for all possible forms—ranging from the spontaneous, incidental word to institutionalized address for the sake of agape.

c) Paraclesis comes more clearly to expression within the community than it does in the one-sided missionary proclamation (nevertheless → 5.d.1). Παρακαλέω (almost) always assumes a believing or assenting response.

d) Paraclesis speaks personally, persuasively, and directly (in contrast to popular philosophy and aphoristic wisdom). It possesses an imperative character as a result of 1) the OT words of God (with following ind. "establishment clause"; on the imv. of the household code cf. Goppelt II, 170), 2) the compassionate character of the mission of Jesus, and 3) the χάρις that was intended to lead to personal χάρισμα.

e) Paraclesis is not established on legal norms (cf. Acts 15:28 with v. 32; however → j) and softens the demand for obedience to a *request* (differently James; Galatians 5–6). Its language by and large blurs the distinction between tradition and contemporary comment (unlike the rabbis) and between norm and advice (cf., however, 1 Corinthians 7—without παρακαλέω). Authority is wielded in a fatherly way (1 Cor 4:13-17; Schlier 342).

f) The practical character of paraclesis does not leave much room in most Epistles for a separate, "dogmatic" section (cf., e.g., 1 Cor 1:10; 1 Pet 2:11). The didactic is more frequently imbedded in the thanksgiving (e.g., Ephesians 1–3; Col 1:3ff.) or in the paraclesis (e.g., Eph 4:7-16; Phil 2:5ff.). The exceptions are Romans and Hebrews.

g) Spiritual comfort has as its goal continuing effects (Eph 6:22/Col 4:8; 1 Cor 16:15; 1 Pet 5:1; Heb 3:13; 10:25; cf. Rom 15:30, etc.). The paracletic chain of concern extends from God (in Christ; 2 Cor 5:20), through the proclaimer, to the people (→ b) and causes ever anew the acceptance and propagation of the exhortation (Phil 2:1).

h) The chain of concern also works retroactively as a comfort that reinforces experience (παρεκλήθημεν, 1 Thess 3:7; 2 Cor 7:4-7, 13) and as praise to God (2 Cor

1:11, cf. v. 3: εὐλογητός). Paraclesis is also in this regard anchored in religion (cf. παρακαλέω as generic term in blessings, 2 Thess 2:16f.; Rom 15:5; 2 Cor 13:11).

i) In the official Greek letter the "*p[arakalō]*-clauses" ("I urge that . . .") give "dignified and urbane expression to a petition that is well removed from both commanding (sc., imperial letters) and subservience (sc., by the one making the proposal)" and introduce a specific request (Bjerkelund 110). "Request" can accordingly be an expression of apostolic authority. The division of the occurrences between this (originally) secular use and a religious use, however, denies 1) the close connection between oral and epistolary paraclesis, 2) the generic function of παρακαλέω (→ 5.b), 3) the difficult definition of the "typical" παρακαλέω-clause (cf. the synonymity of λέγω, μαρτύρομαι, ἐρωτάω, etc.), and 4) the "emphasis" of the prepositional phrases directly connected with the παρακαλέω-clauses in Rom 12:1 (E. Käsemann [Eng. tr., 1981] ad loc.); 15:30 (→5.d.2).

j) Paraclesis and the teaching tradition stand in close reciprocal relation. Παρακαλέω is often followed by portions of the letter made up in large part of parenetic tradition. The sermon and the epistle often take the form of application of the tradition to the contemporary audience—as suggested by the youth (1 Thess 4:1ff.) or the persecution of the community (persecution paraclesis in Heb 10:32ff.; 12:1ff. with dependence on the tradition of Jas 1:2-12 par.; on the relation between doctrinal norms and the work of the Spirit cf. H. D. Wendland). The Pastorals and Jude develop further the Pauline line: to preserve and make relevant his instruction, and to apply the message—as the ethical will of God—to themselves and the readers (1 Cor 4:13-17; Rom 16:17f.)

5. a) The high degree of modulation and theological relevance for παρακαλέω/παράκλησις in the NT is attested esp. in Paul (and Acts). Only once does Paul express the summons of the kyrios with παρακαλέω (2 Cor 12:8), although he often allows exhortation to become *request* (cf. Phlm 8 with v. 10). On the specific emphases of asking see → 2.a.2. In most instances the persuasive tone of παρακαλέω contains undeniable echoes of the message of salvation.

b). 1 Thessalonians shows the proclamation to be a contemporary, practical renewal of the appeal. In the thanksgiving and Paul's "rendering-of-account" in chs. 1-3, Paul describes the initial proclamation and its effects. "Our preaching" (ἡ παράκλησις ἡμῶν, 2:3) means not only the words but also the disposition of the one who proclaimed them—his freedom won through persecution and his complete devotion to the readers and to the ministry (vv. 1-12), whose fruit is a purer faith, made stronger by suffering (vv. 13f.) and—retroactively— the comfort of the one who made the proclamation (3:7). The sum-

mons to faith is not directed toward a religious-dogmatic thought world, but rather toward "everyday life" (Käsemann 190f.). Here the old and new aeons meet. "*We* further ask and *urge* you" introduces—with formulaic λοιπόν (4:1; see Cavallin)—not an ethical appendix to the letter, but the contemporary renewal of the appeal with increase as its goal. Paul calls this 1) brotherly (v. 1), 2) the devotion of Christ himself ἐν κυρίῳ, 3) a reminder of the tradition received, and 4) assurance of preservation in judgment (v. 6; 5:9). The ensuing holiness (v. 7) is the fruit, not the condition of comfort and assurance. The paraclesis embeds the contemporary—which is mentioned frequently and without veiled allusion (esp. in 4:10b-12, 13-18)—in the traditional on five separate occasions (5 occurrences of παρακαλέω with varying nuance in 4:1ff.) and consequently always aims at mutual comfort in the congregation over and above clarity of doctrine (4:15-18) and its moral application (5:1-11) as well as the order of the Church, within which framework in particular the paraclesis becomes the theme (5:12-25). The series of brief instructions to the suffering (vv. 14-15a) goes without transition directly over into instructions for the life of the community, standing as they usually do at the end of the paraclesis (Phil 4:2-9; Col 4:2-6; Heb 13:1-21; Eph 6:18-20; cf. Rom 15:30-33; 16:17-20). The paraclesis flows into the blessing (vv. 23f.), which attests to its concern as God's own affair.

c) 2 Corinthians points to παρακαλέω/παράκλησις as God's fruitful presence and support in situations of human crisis (1:3-4). The means of divine paraclesis are: 1) words—as the message of salvation (5:20), as brotherly (1:4), forgiving (2:7), warning (6:2), mutually (13:11) comforting, as the example of Jesus (10:1), as good news (7:4-7, 13), and as ecclesiastical task (8:6, 17; cf. 9:5)—and 2) experiences, i.e., the comfort of God (1:3), esp. for the downcast (7:6a), the consoling effect of faith (1:4) and the blessing of suffering (1:6f.). Παρακαλέω is the bridge that spans the gap between the saving call and the future glory, combining and holding in tension doubt and faith (4:13-17).

d) 1) Missionary message and Church paraclesis retain this similarity, that the hearer (continually) experiences the crisis of the times as a personal experience. Therefore Paul can call to those who have already been reconciled to God: "We implore you [by this means now] as Christ's helpers: be reconciled (imv.) with God" (2 Cor 5:20). The imperative address is grounded not only in sin's threat to mankind, but primarily in the human person, human election to be God's coworker, and human dependence on God's call.

2) Christ himself blesses by establishing the παράδοσις in the heart; in this way God gives courage for the future: παράκλησιν αἰωνίαν (2 Thess 2:15f.). This is why short theological phrases, esp. prep. phrases with διά

(κυρίου), ἐν (κυρίῳ) among others (cf. ὑπέρ in 2 Thess 2:1), characterize the παράκλησις (→ 4.i). Paul brings the full weight of the knowledge of salvation to bear when giving content to this term (→ 5.b on 1 Thess 4:1; for an overview of the expressions with διά see Bjerkelund 163-73).

3) Law and paraclesis stand in tension, not because the deed has become secondary (to faith-doubt), but because in God's economy of salvation, his saving mercy itself has become the norm of action. Thus the exhortation to serving love is the concrete application of the gospel (Rom 15:1-6; Friedrich).

4) Prophecy is a reliable, but not the decisive means of παράκλησις (1 Cor 14:3, [24f.], 31). The charisma of παράκλησις is itself conclusive. "Whoever *comforts* should dedicate himself to it [i.e., to the word and the person] totally" (Rom 12:8).

6. In the tradition that developed from Paul παρακαλέω /παράκλησις appears with less variety and without the close relation to θλῖψις.

Ephesians 4-6 contains the most consistently full and complete parenesis in the NT. After the thanksgiving section in chs. 1–3, the parenetic section is programmatically introduced by the παρακαλέω clause (→ 4.i) with the contemporizing of the event of falling (4:1; cf. 1 Cor 7:20-24). The letter closes with the commendation of the paraclesis of Tychicus, as in Col 4:8. By way of contrast, in 1 Timothy the instruction (1:3, aor.) to Timothy to admonish precedes "Paul's" own hortatory concerns (2:1: παρακαλέω οὖν). According to the Pastorals παρακαλέω 1) is done in a kindly way ἐν μακροθυμίᾳ (2 Tim 4:2), directed toward old (1 Tim 5:1) and young (Titus 2:6), 2) is a word that brings about repentance (ἔλεγξον) and a new attitude (ἐπιτίμησον; 2 Tim 4:2), 3) is always in accordance with doctrine (1 Tim 4:13; 6:2), and 4) is in harmony with the conduct of the officebearer who has been called to comfort (4:13-16).

1 Peter fits fully into the Pauline line: 1) in its introduction of primary pastoral concerns by means of παρακαλέω (2:11, continuing through 4:19), 2) in its exhortation to exhort (5:1ff.), and 3) in its identification of epistolary paraclesis with community paraclesis (5:12).

Hebrews is the oldest known sermon, which connects in rigid succession the sections of imv. address (with παρακαλέω and equivalents) with those of ind.-doctrinal application. The author calls his letter λόγος παρακλήσεως (13:22), because in spite of all present concerns he is focused on his trust in the power of the word spoken by God's command and in the willingness of the community to hear (!—cf. 6:9). Παρακαλέω is indeed a daily task (3:13) and conceptually summarizes all pastoral ministry

(10:23-25). The "strong impetus" of those who "have fled in order to gain the hope that stands ready" is imbedded in the *comfort* of the unchangeable saving acts and in the ensuing *demand* (6:18). And it speaks in order to help, "as with sons" (12:5). The author contends for the unity of the biblical word and contemporary witness as παράκλησις.

"Jude" indicates his intentions with παρακαλεῖν (Jude 3), introduces it with a spiritually based *captatio benevolentiae* (ἀνάγκην ἔσχον, → 4.b), and mentions—after the "reminder" (the primary doctrinal section in vv. 5-19) —traditionally, albeit in condensed form, the imperative of his exhortation (vv. 20-30).

7. Acts offers the entire spectrum of meanings from *request* (25:2; ingratiatingly proposed *request* in 24:4; *summon* in 28:20 after v. 17), to *urgently dissuade* (19:31; 21:12), to missionary *call to salvation* (2:40), as well as *consolation* (20:12) and *encouragement* in light of the threat of the eschaton (14:22, see below). Under *invite* we may include the tone and direction of the requests in 8:31; 9:38; 13:42; and 28:14; moreover, with an obligatory accent, 16:9f., 15. Παρακαλέω never designates the missionary kerygma per se, but rather its exhorting-inviting application (2:40, → 2.b). The acceptance of the word (v. 41) includes both the ind. of διεμαρτύρατο (*fides quae creditur*) and the imv. of παρεκάλει (*fides qua creditur*).

In the remaining occurrences Luke follows the specific usage of παρακαλέω as spiritual comfort *within* the community (13:15) derived from the synagogue tradition. The prophets Judas and Silas reinforce *the command and encouragement* of the Jerusalem letter (15:31f.). Moreover, the Church was "increased by the comfort of the Holy Spirit" (9:31). Three times παρακαλέω designates a blessing and consoling *farewell speech* (14:22, with a line that links faith and suffering [cf. 2 Corinthians]; 16:40; 20:1); twice it is used of the *open* (15:32) or *intensive act of preaching* (20:2, G. Stählin, *Acts* [NTD] ad loc.): "He spoke the word to them extensively (παρακαλέσας αὐτοὺς λόγῳ πολλῷ)."

                                                    J. Thomas

παρακαλύπτω *parakalyptō* hide*

Luke 9:45, of the (second) proclamation of the suffering of Jesus (v. 44), which remained *hidden/veiled* to his disciples (ἦν παρακεκαλυμμένον ἀπ' αὐτῶν).

παρακαταθήκη, ης, ἡ *parakatathēkē* entrusted possessions

1 Tim 6:20; in 2 Tim 1:14 TR has the Attic form παρακαταθήκη in place of → παραθήκη (3).

παράκειμαι *parakeimai* be ready, be at one's disposal, be available*

Rom 7:18, 21, in the description of a person before faith, for whom the desire to do good *was available/was already there* (τὸ γὰρ θέλειν παράκειταί μοι, v. 18), but when it came to doing good only evil *was at his disposal* (ὅτι ἐμοὶ τὸ κακὸν παράκειται, v. 21). F. Büchsel, *TDNT* III, 656.

παράκλησις, εως, ἡ *paraklēsis* admonition, encouragement, comfort, request
→ παρακαλέω.

παράκλητος, ου, ὁ *paraklētos* legal adviser, advocate, counselor, helper*

1. Meaning — 2. 1 John — 3. John — 4. Origin of the title "Paraclete"

Lit.: J. BEHM, *TDNT* V, 800-14. — O. BETZ, *Der Paraklet* (AGSU 2, 1963). — J. BLANK, *Krisis* (1964) 316-39. — G. BORNKAMM, "Der Paraklet im Johannesevangelium" (1949), *idem, Aufsätze* III, 68-89. — R. E. BROWN, "The Paraclete in the Fourth Gospel," *NTS* 13 (1966/67) 113-32. — *idem*, "The 'Paraclete' in Light of Modern Research," *SE* IV, 158-65. — R. BULTMANN, *John* (Eng. tr., 1971) 566-72. — D. A. CARSON, "The Function of the Paraclete in John 16:7-11," *JBL* 98 (1979) 547-66. — A. CASURELLA, *The Johannine Paraclete in the Church Fathers. A Study in the History of Exegesis* (1983). — C. DIETZFELBINGER, "Paraklet und theologischer Anspruch im Johannesevangelium," *ZTK* 82 (1985) 389-408. — J. T. FORESTELL, "Jesus and the Paraclete in the Gospel of John," *Word and Spirit* (FS D. M. Stanley, ed. J. Plevnik; 1975) 151-97. — G. JOHNSTON, *The Sprit-Paraclete in the Gospel of John* (SNTSMS 12, 1970). — A. M. KOTHGASSER, "Die Lehr-, Erinnerungs-, Bezeugungs-, und Einführungsfunktion des johanneischen Geist-Parakleten gegenüber der Christusoffenbarung," *Salesianum* 33 (1971) 557-98; 34 (1972) 3-51. — M. MIGUÉNS, *El Paráclito (Juan 14-16)* (SBFA 2, 1963). — U. B. MÜLLER, "Die Parakletenvorstellung im Johannesevangelium," *ZTK* 71 (1974) 31-77. — F. MUSSNER, "Die johanneischen Parakletsprüche und die apostolische Tradition," *BZ* 5 (1961) 56-70. — F. PORSCH, *Pneuma und Wort* (FTS 16, 1974). — I. DE LA POTTERIE, *La vérité dans Saint Jean* I (AnBib 73, 1977) 330-466. — R. SCHNACKENBURG, *John* III (Eng. tr., 1982) 138-54. — *idem*, "Die johanneische Gemeinde und ihre Geisterfahrung," FS Schürmann 277-306. — J. VEENHOF, *De Parakleet* (1977). — U. WILCKENS, "Der Paraklet und die Kirche," FS Bornkamm 185-203. — For further bibliography → παρακαλέω, πνεῦμα, see Porsch; *DNTT* I, 91f.; *TWNT* X, 1215-17.

1. According to its grammatical form, παράκλητος is a pass. verbal adj. from παρακαλέω. It means primarily "called (by someone for something)" (BAGD 618). When used as a noun, it means "one called upon for support, one called in for assistance" (BAGD s.v.), thus an *advocate*. The Latin Fathers therefore often translate παράκλητος as *advocatus* (Augustine, Tertullian, Cyp-

rian). Outside the NT one finds "the clear picture of a legal adviser or helper or advocate in the relevant court" (Behm 803; further references in Behm 800-806; Porsch 227f.; de la Potterie 330ff.). Παράκλητος is not found in the LXX (in Job 16:2 *mᵉ nahamim* is translated παρακλή-τορες, in Aquila and Theodotion as παράκλητος).

2. Παράκλητος appears in the NT only in the Johannine writings (John and 1 John). In 1 John 2:1 Jesus Christ is called παράκλητος, since after his exaltation to the Father he intercedes on behalf of sinners. Here the term is not a title; it corresponds to the Jewish conception of an advocate before God (cf. Betz 36-116).

3. Johannine usage is distinct from this concept in that the Paraclete does not intercede on behalf of (the sins of) believers before God (in heaven) and in that the term is clearly used as a title for the "Spirit of Truth" or for the "Holy Spirit" (14:26). As such it is found exclusively (4 occurrences) in the Paraclete sayings of the farewell discourse (14:16f.; 14:26; 15:26; 16:7-11; implicitly in 16:13-15).

In John 14:16, the "Spirit of Truth" is immediately introduced as "another Paraclete" (ἄλλος παράκλητος) with the promise that he will be "with," "by," and "in" the disciples, generally describing his function as helper. The context shows that he is "given" to replace the physical absence of Jesus with a new presence "in the Spirit" and thereby to avoid leaving the disciples as orphans. He is at the same time a representative of Jesus to his own (cf. 14:18ff.). By way of contrast, there is no connection between the Paraclete and the "world" (14:17). The reference to "another Paraclete" assumes that Jesus himself was already a Paraclete for the disciples, although this title is never applied to the earthly Jesus. Nevertheless, the Gospel writer consciously places in parallel the work of Jesus and that of the παράκλητος (cf. Porsch 239f., 242f.).

In 14:26 (and 16:13ff.) the revelatory functions of teaching and reminding (διδάσκειν, ὑπομμνήσκειν), which advance the revelatory work of Jesus are attributed to the παράκλητος. The two concepts form a unit: The παράκλητος teaches by reminding. What is meant is a later recollection of the message of Jesus ("that which I have said"; cf. 2:22; 12:16; 16:4).

16:13-15 in particular demonstrates that the Paraclete brings no new teaching, but rather continues the revelatory work of Jesus. According to v. 12 there was "much" that Jesus could not yet say to his disciples since they would not yet (before the sending of the Spirit) be able to "bear" it. It would be the gift of the Spirit-Paraclete that would "lead" (ὁδηγεῖν) them "into the whole truth," into the yet unknown depths and nuances of the truth. This truth is Jesus' revelation, ultimately Jesus himself (cf. 1:18; 14:6; 17:18). This leading into the "whole truth" includes also the proclamation of "that which is to come" (τὰ ἐρχόμενα). This does not point to future revelations in the apocalyptic sense, but to interpretation of the "signs of the times" as that which the Church will always have in store for it. Since the παράκλητος proclaims Jesus as the exalted one and points to him as the source of salvation, he glorifies him (16:14f.).

The characteristic function of the παράκλητος as advocate is most clearly expressed in 15:26 and 16:7-11. Both sayings stand in a context governed by the enmity and hostility of the world (15:18–16:4a). In this situation the παράκλητος will bear witness to Jesus (in believers), thereby also making the disciples capable of witness (15:27). The saying could be tradition-historically connected with Mark 13:9-13 par. According to John 16:8, the παράκλητος (v. 7) will take on the function of one who convicts and exposes (→ ἐλέγχω) in the clash between believers and the world, in that he furnishes proof that Jesus has been glorified, while the world and its "prince" have been judged for their unbelief in sin (vv. 8-12). In this way the Spirit proves to be an advocate for Jesus and believers.

4. The origin of the title ὁ παράκλητος, which is introduced without further explanation in John's Gospel, is still a matter of debate. Attempts to derive the term from the Gnostic "helper" figure (Bultmann), from the Jewish concept of an advocate (Behm, Betz) or from Son of man expectation (Bornkamm) are not very satisfying. Nor does recourse to the conceptual field of paraclesis (→ παρακαλέω) provide an explanation. The title should probably be explained in terms of the "trial context" of John. In the clash with the "world" believers experience the work of the Spirit as that of a παράκλητος, i.e., as an *advocate* and *legal adviser* (see Porsch 306-24; Schnackenburg 144-50 for details).   F. Porsch

παρακοή, ῆς, ἡ *parakoē* disobedience, failure to listen*

This noun occurs 3 times in the NT: Rom 5:19, of Adam, through whose παρακοή "the many" became sinners (antonym of ὑπακοή); 2 Cor 10:6: Paul is prepared to punish every *disobedience* (antonym of ὑπακοή); Heb 2:2: *disobedience* (with παράβασις) of the law enacted at Sinai by angels (cf. Gal 3:19f.). G. Kittel, *TDNT* I, 223; H. Opitz, *BHH* 2048; Spicq, *Notes* II, 656f.

παρακολουθέω *parakoloutheō* accompany; investigate (a matter)
→ ἀκολουθέω 5.

παρακούω *parakouō* (over)hear; pay no attention to, not listen to*

Mark 5:36 (ὁ δὲ Ἰησοῦς παρακούσας τὸν λόγον λαλούμενον) can mean either that Jesus *ignored/did not*

wish to listen to, or that he *overheard/happened to hear* the report (of the death of the daughter of the ruler of the synagogue); the link to vv. 35 and 36b makes the second more likely. The vb. appears twice in Matt 18:17 with the meaning *be disobedient/not listen to* (ἐὰν δὲ [. . .] παρακούσῃ); cf. also *2 Clem.* 3:4; 15:5; T. Hirunuma, "*Parakouō:* 'To Overhear, to Refuse to Hear,'" *Shinyaku Kenkyū* (Osaka) 147 (1978) 1223f.; G. Kittel, *TDNT* I, 223.

παρακύπτω *parakyptō* bend over (in order to look into), look into*

This vb. occurs 5 times in the NT. The original meaning *bend over (in order to look into)* is present in the combination καὶ παρακύψας βλέπει in Luke 24:12 (of Peter) and in John 20:5 (of the "other disciple"); cf. παρέκυψεν εἰς τὸ μνημεῖον in 20:11 (of Mary Magdalene). Fig. *look into* ("the perfect law of freedom") in Jas 1:25 (cf. the image in vv. 23f.); *steal a glance* (into the saving events of the proclamation of the gospel) in 1 Pet 1:12. W. Michaelis, *TDNT* V, 814-16; R. Neirynck, *ETL* 53 (1977) 113-52.

παραλαμβάνω *paralambanō* receive, take; draw to oneself; take over*

1. NT occurrences and syntax — 2. Use in the world of the NT, esp. in conjunction with tradition — 3. Exegetical emphases and perspectives —a) As a term for community-building — b) In christological contexts — c) As a t.t. for apostolic handing on of tradition

Lit.: BAGD s.v. — BDF, index s.v. (294). — H. CONZELMANN, *1 Cor* (Hermeneia) on 11:23; 15:1-3. — G. DELLING, *TDNT* IV, 5-15. — B. GERHARDSSON, *Memory and Manuscript* (ASNU 22, 1961), esp. 262-323 (on 3.c). —E. LOHSE, *Col/Phlm* (Hermeneia) on Col 2:6; 4:17. — F. MUSSNER, *Gal* (HTKNT) on 1:9, 12. — K. WEGENAST, *Das Traditionsverständnis bei Paulus und in den Deuteropaulinen* (WMANT 8, 1962). — For further bibliography see *TWNT* X, 1154.

1. Παραλαμβάνω is attested 50 times in the NT. The narrative writings of Matthew (16 ocurrences) and Luke-Acts (13), and the Epistles of Paul (8) show a numerical preponderance, while the later witnesses are represented only sparingly (e.g., Hebrews, with 1 occurrence), albeit significantly, from a theological perspective (e.g., John, with 3 occurrences). The aor. partc. παραλαβών can be used pleonastically (Acts 15:39; 21:32) or intensively (Luke 9:10). While in the papyri and inscriptions παραλαμβάνω is frequently found with παρά, in 1 Cor 11:23 it is found with ἀπό as a reference to origin. Mark 7:4 is also noteworthy, where παραλαμβάνω is followed by an inf. of purpose (BDF §391).

2. For the NT understanding of παραλαμβάνω, esp. in con-

junction with tradition, a look at the LXX and nonbiblical writings is informative. In the LXX παραλαμβάνω (ca. 50 occurrences) is frequently used as an intensification of the simple form of the vb. (e.g., Gen 22:3) and can take both personal (Gen 31:23) or nonpersonal (Num 23:20) objects. It can have the meanings "take along with" (in a friendly sense: Gen 47:2; in a situation of war: 1 Macc 4:1); "take away" (Wis 16:4); "obtain, achieve" (e.g., a kingdom: Dan 6:1, 29; the eschatological kingdom: 7:18).

In Greek literature as well παραλαμβάνω is found both in the personal sense ("accept, receive someone," Herodotus, Plato) and the objective sense ("take over the government, a business," Aristophanes, Plutarch). It could especially be used as a t.t. for the process of tradition along with παραδιδόναι. Over against the general tradition-related understanding (Herodotus, Isocrates) is the verb's special use in the description of the school tradition, e.g., in conjunction with the definition of the teacher-student relationship (Plato *Tht.* 198b) or the designation of intellectual property and influence (Plato *La.* 197d), which is usually traceable to the paramount position of the person of the philosopher (Plato *R.* vii.520). "For this reason the παραλαμβάνων finds in him absolute authority" (Delling 11). This authority assumes a relationship of trust and requires a certain way of life (cf. Paul). The understanding of παραλαμβάνω in the mystery cults and Gnosticism can be shown to be no less personally formative and religiously profound, often with an esoteric character (Conzelmann 195f. with nn. 29 and 30).

In Jewish writings the accent of παραλαμβάνω is on the content of the teaching, on the Torah and its interpretation. The absolute authority of the tradition is guaranteed primarily by its unbroken derivation from Moses and even from God himself ('*Abot* 1.1). The piel *qibbel* ("take, receive") and the niphal *māsar* ("be handed down") are found almost formulaically in this connection for the handing down of the content of the tradition (Delling 12f.).

3. a) Παραλαμβάνω as a term for community-building can refer in the first place to the family: Joseph *takes* Mary to be his wife (Matt 1:20, 24), *accepts* the child and its mother (2:13f.), and provides them protection and security (2:20f.). Matthew here uses a fixed schema: command— revelation—compliance, in which παραλαμβάνω is always combined with ἐγερθείς as a sign of completion.

As a community-building term in the broader sense, παραλαμβάνω is applied to the disciple-Jesus relationship (Mark 4:36) and includes both the sphere of glorification (Mark 5:40; 9:2 par.: Jesus takes three disciples along with him) and the experience of the crucifixion (Mark 10:32 par. Matt 17:1/Luke 9:28: Jesus takes the disciples aside and speaks to them of his suffering; cf. Mark 14:33 par. Matt 26:37: the scene on the Mount of Olives).

The communal sense of παραλαμβάνω can even include the demonic realm, thus Matt 4:5, 8 (the devil *takes* Jesus with himself) and 12:45 par. Luke 11:26 (the unclean spirit and his entourage). It can also take on a forensic orientation—Matt 18:16 (*take* witnesses along); 27:27 (the soldiers present Jesus; cf. John 19:16)—and have eschatological significance—Matt 24:40, 41 par. Luke 17:34, 35, 36 (obviously with divisive consequence: *take* vs. leave behind); cf. also Heb 12:28 (*receive* the kingdom, in accordance with Dan 7:18). In this range of meanings are included almost without distinction the occurrences in Acts, e.g., 15:39 (Barnabas *takes* Mark along); 16:33 *(take in);* 21:24 (*take along* to fulfill a vow); see also 21:26, 32; 23:18 (and see C. Burchard, *ZNW* 69 [1978] 156f.).

b) Παραλαμβάνω as a term for community-building takes on a special nuance in christological contexts, esp. in John 1:11 (his own did not *receive* the word) and 14:3 ("I *will take* you to myself"). This is given existential depth in Col 2:6: You *have accepted* Christ Jesus as Lord. Therefore also live in him. "Thus Christology and ethics are intimately conjoined" (Lohse 93n.7). This disposition is also to characterize the ministry of Archippus, received by commission of the Lord (4:17).

c) Παραλαμβάνω is also used by Paul as a t.t. for the apostolic paradosis. The context reveals that both the community-building event and the christological aspect are included here. In one group of occurrences the content of the tradition remains unspecified (1 Thess 2:13: *receive* the proclaimed word of God; Gal 1:9: the gospel) and the accent lies more on the value of that which has been learned (1 Thess 4:1; cf. Phil 4:9; 2 Thess 3:6).

But the essential elements of the paradosis are explicitly mentioned in 1 Cor 11:23; 15:1-3. These passages deal with the weighty matter of the celebration of the eucharist and the confessional formulation of the Christ experience in death and resurrection, i.e., with the "primitive gospel" (cf. 15:1f.). These materials of the faith (oral and/or written) are both firmly anchored in the tradition of the community (e.g., in the celebration of the Lord's Supper: Mark 14:22-25; esp. Luke 22:19f.) and considered universally binding because they were established by the Lord himself (1 Cor 11:23).

Both the polemical-apologetic aspect, which plays a role, e.g., in Gal 1:12 (cf. 1:10f.), and the apparent tension between revelation and tradition can perhaps be explained as follows: "As a result of Paul's experience of the 'revelation of Jesus Christ,' he recognized that the Christian kerygma rightly exists so that he could now himself 'receive it' and 'pass it on' as paradosis. And so the irreducibility of the 'revelation of Jesus Christ' is retained while room continues to exist for a communication of this revelation and paradosis" (Mussner 66n.116; see also further his bibliography).

The idea of tradition in the purely Jewish sense is present in Mark 7:4, where the regulations for purification are explicitly mentioned. Παραλαμβάνω here proves to be a term that in its various expressions and nuances is essentially christologically based (community, unity with Jesus) and thus guarantees the binding and vibrant character of the primitive Christian tradition, not least due to the realization in faith of the Christian community.   A. Kretzer

παραλέγομαι *paralegomai* sail along(side)*

A maritime t.t. in Acts 27:8: μόλις τε παραλεγόμενοι αὐτήν (= τὴν Κρήτην; cf. v. 7), "since we *sailed along* its coast with difficulty"; 27:13: τὴν Κρήτην.

παράλιος, 2 *paralios* situated by the sea, subst.: coastal area*

Luke 6:17: among the crowd of people listening to Jesus were those "from the *coastal region* of Tyre and Sidon," as well as people from all Judea and Jerusalem (cf. Mark 3:8: περὶ Τύρον καὶ Σιδῶνα).

παραλλαγή, ῆς, ἡ *parallagē* change (noun)*

An astronomical t.t. used fig. in Jas 1:17: God, "the Father of 'lights' [cf. Ps 135:7 LXX], with whom there is no change or darkness caused by turning" (παρ' ᾧ οὐκ ἔνι παραλλαγὴ ἢ τροπῆς ἀποσκίασμα). In contrast to the change in the stars, therefore, which is subject to a particular order, God is unchangeable (in his goodness: v. 17a).

παραλογίζομαι *paralogizomai* deceive, cheat*

Col 2:4: παραλογίζομαι ἐν πιθανολογίᾳ, "*deceive/mislead* with false pretenses"; Jas 1:22: παραλογίζομαι ἑαυτόν, "*deceive* oneself" (by only hearing and not doing the word); cf. also *2 Clem.* 17:6.

παραλύομαι *paralyomai* be an invalid; subst. pf. partc.: cripple (noun)*

This vb. occurs 5 times in the NT, 4 times in the Lukan writings and in Heb 12:12, always as the pf. pass. partc. παραλελυμένος, used as a noun in Luke 5:24; Acts 8:7. In the Lukan writings it always refers to a *cripple* who is healed by Jesus (Luke 5:18, 24) or by an apostle (Philip in Acts 8:7; Peter in 9:33). In Heb 12:12 it appears in the exhortation to strengthen again the *weak/disabled* knees (τὰ παραλελυμένα γόνατα); cf. Isa 35:3; → γόνυ 2.a. Also → παραλυτικός.

παραλυτικός, 3 *paralytikos* lame*

1. Occurrences and meaning in the NT — 2. The healing of the lame man in Mark 2 par. — 3. The healing of the officer's servant in Matthew 8 par.

Lit.: P. J. ACHTEMEIER, "Toward the Isolation of Pre-Markan Miracle Catenae," *JBL* 89 (1970) 265-91. — R. W. FUNK, ed., *Early Christian Miracle Stories* (= *Semeia* 11 [1978]). — H. J. HELD, "Matthew as Interpreter of the Miracle Stories," G. Bornkamm, G. Barth, and H. J. Held, *Tradition and Interpretation in Matthew* (NTL, 1963) 165-299, esp. 175ff., 193ff. — K. KERTELGE, *Die Wunder Jesu im Markusevangelium* (1970), esp. 75-82, 85-89, 185ff. — J. D. KINGSBURY, "Observations on the

Miracle Chapters of Matthew 8-9," *CBQ* 40 (1978) 559-73. — X. LÉON-DUFOUR, ed., *Les Miracles de Jésus* (1977), esp. 227-47. — H. VAN DER LOOS, *The Miracles of Jesus* (1965), esp. 435-63, 530-50. — I. MAISCH, *Die Heilung des Gelähmten* (1971). — R. PESCH, *Jesu ureigene Taten?* (1970) 135ff. — B. REICKE, "The Synoptic Reports on the Healing of the Paralytic, Matthew 9,1-8 and Parallels," FS Kilpatrick 319-29. — E. SCHWEIZER, "Die Heilung des Königlichen: Joh 4,46-54," *EvT* 11 (1951/52) 64-71. — E. F. SIEGMANN, "St. John's Use of the Synoptic Material," *CBQ* 30 (1968) 182-98. — G. THEISSEN, *Urchristliche Wundergeschichten* (1974) 114ff., 165f.

1. Παραλυτικός occurs 10 times in the NT. It is used as both adj. and noun and is found in the Matthean summary report in 4:23-25 (describing the work of Jesus as proclamation and healing) among other disorders (v. 24), in Mark 2:1ff. (5 occurrences) par. Matt 9:2ff. (3 occurrences; healing of the "man with palsy"), and in Matt 8:6 (healing of the lame servant of the Gentile officer). The Lukan writings (and Heb 12:12) use instead παραλελυμένος, the pf. pass. partc. of παραλύω (the Gospels and Hebrews also use χωλός, but except in Luke 14:13; Acts 3:2; 14:8; John 5:3, only in Synoptic summaries and in a fig. sense). A precise diagnosis of the disabilities described in the healing accounts in the NT is impossible. In Matt 8:6 reference is made to a lame man who is crippled with severe pains. The Lukan parallel in 7:2 simply refers to the patient as κακῶς ἔχων, but intensifies the gravity of the illness to the point of death (also John 4:47). The form of the NT miracle story is borrowed from the typical schema of the Hellenistic world. There is, therefore, nothing decisive about the historicity of such accounts.

2. The striking difference in vocabulary and details of the narrative in Mark 2:1-12 par. Matt 9:1-8/Luke 5:17-26 makes difficult the traditional assumption that Matthew and Luke used Mark (see Reicke).

Mark has taken over the pericope for the most part unchanged from Church tradition. The dialogue in vv. 5b-10a was already combined with the miracle story at the pre-Markan level. V. 11 (all praise God, the opponents of Jesus are no longer mentioned) shows that the narrative originally was independent. The dialogue (inserted later, as v. 12 and the stylized transition at v. 10b demonstrate), however, never circulated independently of the miracle story, since v. 10 is inextricably connected with the healing. The miracle story stresses the all-conquering faith of the four men. The dialogue assumes a link between sickness and sin (already in the OT and Judaism; cf. *b. Ned.* 41a: "The sick person does not rise from his sickness until all his sins are forgiven [by God]"; see Billerbeck I, 495f.), but contains no doctrine of correspondence (severity of illness = degree of sin). Jesus first frees the παραλυτικός from what separates him from God and then from his physical disability, which—like all illness—is an expression of the distorted human relationship with God. The question in v. 9 is, therefore, not simply a "teasing question" (contra Dibelius, *Tradition* 66), but points to the inexpressible difficulty of forgiveness, the reality of which is reflected by the less difficult healing in v. 11.

Matthew reduces the account (as he frequently does) to a few essential details. As a result, the saying of Jesus in 9:6 has a dominant position. By means of the "choral" closing in 9:8, Matthew connects the account with a concern that goes beyond Mark: The Church, too, has authority to forgive sins (cf. 16:19; 18:18).

Luke alters the exposition by introducing the opponents immediately in 5:17. At the same time Luke inserts an element that is of importance to him, namely, the charismatic interpretation of Jesus' power of healing (cf. 4:14; 6:19; 8:46). As in Matthew, the saying tradition in Luke stays fairly close to Mark.

3. In Matt 8:5-13 par. Luke 7:1-10 (John 4:46-53) the wording and flow of the accounts (unlike the sayings tradition: Matt 8:8b-10, 13 par. Luke 7:6b-9) are so different that it is difficult to imagine a single source (Q) for the two Synoptic compositions.

Matthew introduces the report of the request concerning the lame servant (παῖς = δοῦλος). 8:6 should be read as a question: "Should I come [to the impure house of a Gentile]?" But the Gentile does not allow himself to be put off (v. 9; cf. Matt 15:26f.). Jesus does not refuse such faith among the Gentiles, and accordingly the time of salvation begins for the "many" (vv. 11f. [Q: see Luke 13:28-30]; cf. Isa 2:2f.; Mic 4:1).

Luke focuses more on the humility of the Gentiles, and therefore has the officer represented by Jewish elders and later by friends so that there is no direct encounter with Jesus. The reason for this is not the impurity of the Gentile, but the overwhelming majesty of Jesus.

M. Rissi

παράλυτος, 2 *paralytos* lame; subst.: cripple

Mark 2:9 D subst. ὁ παράλυτος in place of → παραλυτικός.

παραμένω *paramenō* remain, continue*

This vb. occurs 4 times in the NT: 1 Cor 16:6, of Paul, who wants *to stay* (for a time) with the Corinthians (v.l. καταμένω); Phil 1:25: μενῶ καὶ παραμενῶ πᾶσιν ὑμῖν, "I will remain and *will continue to remain* with you all"; absolute in Heb 7:23, of the levitical priests, who (in contrast to Jesus) are prevented from *remaining* (in office) by death; absolute in Jas 1:25: *continuing* in the perfect law of freedom. Cf. Ign. *Eph.* 2:1; *Herm. Vis.*

ii.3.2; *Man.* v.2.3. F. Hauck, *TDNT* IV, 577f.; K. Munzer and C. Brown, *DNTT* III, 223, 228.

παραμυθέομαι *paramytheomai* comfort, encourage, console*

This vb. occurs 4 times in the NT. It gains its meaning from παρά ("to, toward") and μυθέομαι ("speak"): *speak (in a friendly way) to someone*. Its meaning is similar to that of → παρακαλέω; "both are characterized by the twofoldness of admonition and comfort" (G. Stählin, *TDNT* V, 821).

John 11:19, 31, of the Jews who *comfort* Mary and Martha (αὐτάς/αὐτήν) on the death of their brother (for comfort/condolence in situations of mourning, cf. Thucydides ii.44.1; Plutarch *Cons. ad Apoll.* 104c; behind John 11:19ff. lies the imperative to comfort the mourning, which in the Jewish tradition is viewed as one of the greatest acts of love; see Stählin 821f.; O. Schmitz and G. Stählin, *TDNT* V, 790-93; Billerbeck IV, 582ff.; Spicq, *Notes* II, 659nn.2, 3); 1 Thess 2:12, in Paul's account of his work in the Church, which he has "exhorted, *consoled,* and implored" (παρακαλοῦντες ὑμᾶς καὶ παραμυθούμενοι καὶ μαρτυρόμενοι); 5:14 used parenetically: "*encourage/comfort* the timid" (παραμυθεῖσθε τοὺς ὀλιγοψύχους, with νουθετεῖτε τοὺς ἀτάκτους). BAGD s.v. (bibliography); G. Stählin, *TDNT* V, 816-23; H. Schlier, *GuL* 36 (1963) 327-40; G. Braumann, *DNTT* I, 328f.; Spicq, *Notes* II, 658-63.

παραμυθία, ας, ἡ *paramythia* comfort, encouragement*

1 Cor 14:3, of prophetic speech in the congregational assembly, which "speaks to people to give them upbuilding, comfort/courage, and admonition" (λαλεῖ οἰκοδομὴν καὶ παράκλησις καὶ παραμυθίαν). H. Greeven, *ZNW* 44 (1952/53) 1-43, esp. 11, 37; G Stählin, *TDNT* V, 816-23; G. Braumann, *DNTT* I, 328f.; Spicq, *Notes* III, 658-63.

παραμύθιον, ου, τό *paramythion* comfort, consolation*

Phil 2:1, in a call to unity and mutual love: "loving comfort/comfort nurtured by love" (παραμύθιον ἀγάπης, with παράκλησις ἐν Χριστῷ, κοινωνία πνεύματος, σπλάγχνα καὶ οἰκτιρμοί).

παράνοια, ας, ἡ *paranoia* foolishness, nonsense 2 Pet 2:16 v.l. in place of → παραφρονία.

παρανομέω *paranomeō* act contrary to the law*

According to Acts 23:3, the high priest, *acting contrary to the law,* has Paul slapped (παρανομῶν κελεύεις με τύπτεσθαι); the opposite expression is κρίνων με κατὰ τὸν νόμον, v. 23a. W. Gutbrod, *TDNT* IV, 1091.

παρανομία, ας, ἡ *paranomia* evil deed, lawless deed, wrongdoing*

2 Pet 2:16, of Balaam, who (according to the context) "received a rebuke for his *wrongdoing*" from his donkey (ἔλεγξις . . . παρανομίας); cf. Num 22:22ff., where, however, the angel of the Lord meets Balaam, a meeting of which the seer was only initially unaware; cf. Jude 11. W. Gutbrod, *TDNT* IV, 1090.

παραπικραίνω *parapikrainō* rebel, revolt*

This vb. is attested only from the time of the LXX. Absolute in Heb 3:16 of the disobedient (vv. 18f.), who *rebelled/revolted* (against God) in the desert (τίνες . . . παρεπίκραναν;); cf. v. 15; Exod 17:1ff.; Deut 31:27; Ps 105:7, and *passim* in the LXX. W. Michaelis, *TDNT* VI, 125-27; P. Walters, *The Text of the Septuagint* (1973) 150-54.

παραπικρασμός, οῦ, ὁ *parapikrasmos* rage, rebellion, revolt*

The noun, like the vb., is attested only from the time of the LXX. Heb 3:8, 15, of the *rebellion* of the people of the Exodus against God: μὴ σκληρύνητε τὰς καρδίας ὑμῶν ὡς ἐν τῷ παραπικρασμῷ (quoting Ps 94:8 LXX; cf. further Exod 15:23ff.; 17:1ff.; Num 20:2ff.). W. Michaelis, *TDNT* VI, 125-27.

παραπίπτω *parapiptō* miss, fall away, fall*

Absolute and fig. in Heb 6:6 of former believers who *have fallen* again (καὶ παραπεσόντας); cf. 3:12; 10:26; Wis 6:9; 12:2; *1 Clem.* 51:1. Hebrews has in mind here a fundamental and conscious rejection of the Church (cf. 6:6b-8). W. Michaelis, *TDNT* VI, 170-73; W. Bauder, *DNTT* I, 608-11; Spicq, *Notes* II, 692-94; → παράπτωμα 3.

παραπλέω *parapleō* sail past*

A maritime t.t. in Acts 20:16: παραπλεῦσαι τὴν Ἔφεσον, "*to sail past* Ephesus."

παραπλήσιος, 3 *paraplēsios* approaching, almost the same, similar*

In the NT only the neut. occurs and is used as an adv. Phil 2:27: Epaphroditus had an illness "that *approached* death," i.e., he was "deathly ill" (παραπλήσιον θανάτῳ). Spicq, *Notes* II, 664f.

παραπλησίως *paraplēsiōs* approaching, similarly, in the same way, likewise*

Heb 2:14: Jesus took on flesh and blood *in the same way* as others (καὶ αὐτὸς παραπλησίως μετέσχεν τῶν αὐτῶν); cf. 4:15. In spite of the ambiguity of the expression, the thought is not simply of a "similarity"; O. Michel, Heb (KEK) ad loc.; Spicq, *Notes* II, 665: "without any difference."

παραπορεύομαι *paraporeuomai* pass by; pass through*

This vb. occurs 5 times in the NT: absolute *pass by* in Mark 11:20; οἱ παραπορευόμενοι, "those *who passed by*" in 15:29 par. Matt 27:39; with διά, *pass through*: διὰ τῶν σπορίμων, "through the wheat fields" in Mark 2:23; παραπορεύομαι διὰ τῆς Γαλιλαίας, "*pass through* Galilee" in 9:30.

παράπτωμα, ατος, τό *paraptōma* offense, failure, sin, fall (noun)*

1. Occurrences and meaning — 2. Παράπτωμα and ἁμαρτία — 3. "Fall" from grace

Lit.: E. BRANDENBURGER, *Adam und Christus* (WMANT 7, 1962). — E. JÜNGEL, "Das Gesetz zwischen Adam und Christus," idem, *Unterwegs zur Sache* (BEvT 61, 1972) 145-72. — U. LUZ, *Das Geschichtsverständnis des Paulus* (BEvT 49, 1968) 202f. — W. MICHAELIS, *TDNT* VI, 170-73.

1. Παράπτωμα occurs 19 times in the NT (excluding the v.l. in Mark 11:26). Of the 11 Pauline occurrences 6 are in Rom 5:15-20.

The verbal noun παράπτωμα is first attested in secular Greek in Hellenistic literature (Polybius ix.10.6; Pap. Tebt. I, 5, 9). As a *nomen rei actae,* as can be seen by the ending -μα, it refers to *sin* as individual (acts of) transgression (usually pl. and usually against God). In this connection it falls in part within the semantic range of ἁμάρτημα. The LXX uses the ἁμάρτημα word group to render the same Hebrew terms as are represented by παράπτωμα (and παραπίπτω). But Heb. ḥāṭā'/ḥaṭṭā'ṭ, by far and away most frequently rendered by ἁμαρτάνω/ἁμαρτία, etc., are not translated with παράπτωμα, etc.

2. In Pauline usage, παράπτωμα, as a specific sinful act, is clearly distinguished from ἁμαρτία, which is understood as a controlling power. The pl. appears in Paul almost exclusively in quotations and traditional expressions, as also in non-Pauline texts in similar contexts (Rom 4:25: Christ παρεδόθη διὰ τὰ παραπτώματα [Isa 53:12 LXX: τὰς ἁμαρτίας] ἡμῶν; 2 Cor 5:19: μὴ λογιζόμενος τὰ παραπτώματα [Ps 31:2 LXX: ἁμαρτίαν; see also Aristophanes *Vespae* 745]). The same is true, analogically, of deutero-Pauline usage (cf. ἄφεσις τῶν

παραπτωμάτων in Eph 1:7 with the frequent Synoptic expression ἄφεσις τῶν ἁμαρτιῶν [see also Matt 6:14f. par. Mark 11:25]; Col 2:13c: χαρισάμενος ἡμῖν πάντα τὰ παραπτώματα [Josephus *Ant.* vi.114: ἁμαρτήματα]). In Eph 2:1, 5 and Col 2:13a, identical formulations occur (conversion statements; see P. Hoffmann, *TRE* IV, 484), in which death, from which those who have been baptized with Christ have been awakened through the act of baptism, is seen as caused by παραπτώματα, among other things.

In Gal 6:1 παράπτωμα appears to be used with a meaning that is distinctly weaker than that of ἁμαρτία, in the sense of a lapse that does not exclude one from the community. Comparable are *Pss. Sol.* 3:7; 13:5, 10, where παράπτωμα is used of transgressions specifically of the righteous, god-fearing, and pious and is clearly contrasted with ἁμαρτωλός, which causes damnation (cf. also Ps 18:13 LXX: παράπτωμα as tr. of *š^egî'â* ["unintentionally err"; see R. Knierim, *THAT* II, 869ff.]).

3. Here, too, belongs the reference to the *transgression* of Adam (Rom 5:15 bis, 17, 18, 20; cf. vv. 12f.). In spite of the parallelism with παράβασις in v. 14, παράπτωμα clearly differs from it here and elsewhere in that there is no connection with the law (*contra* U. Wilckens, *Rom* [EKKNT] I, 322n.1070; II, 242n.1079; Jüngel 167 and elsewhere). By referring to the sin of Adam as παράπτωμα, more focus is placed on effects and results of the παράπτωμα, esp. (as in Wis 10:1; see on this Brandenburger 111ff.) as Adam's *"fall,"* i.e., the loss of the glory of Paradise, which also resulted in the fate of death (5:15, 17) and damnation (5:16, 18; see 4 Ezra 7:118). After the proclamation of the law (v. 20) mankind sinned in the same way as Adam (→ παράβασις [2.b]), with the result that Adam's transgression was likewise "multiplied" (see v. 16; → πλεονάζω). Placed in contrast to this are terms corresponding to παράπτωμα that describe the salvation event and its effects, which far exceed the consequences of the fall into sin, such as χάρισμα (v. 15a), δικαίωμα (v. 18), and (διὰ) τοῦ Χριστοῦ (vv. 15b, 17).

This connotation clearly comes to expression in Rom 11:11f. and Heb 6:6, where παράπτωμα and → παραπίπτω (like → ἐκπίπτω in Gal 5:4; 2 Pet 3:17; Rev 2:5; *T. Jud.* 21:4; cf. also Philo, *Fragmenta* ii.648 [ed. T. Mangey, 1742]) are used of the fall from the realm of salvation— in Rom 11:11f., Israel's *fall* from election because of its rejection of the gospel (cf. v. 9) and in Heb 6:6 the *falling away* of the Christian community (contra Michaelis 171). In the LXX (Ezekiel) this meaning is proper to both expressions, when they describe Israel's sin as a turning away from God (with ἀποστρέφω or as tr. of Heb. *mā'al* ["be unfaithful"; noun "faithlessness/fall"]; see Ezek 3:20; 14:11, 13; 15:8; 18:24, 26; 20:27).

M. Wolter

παρραρρέω *pararreō* flow by, drift away*

Fig. in Heb 2:1: μήποτε παραρυῶμεν (2nd aor. pass.), "so that we *do* not *drift away/are* not *driven off course.*"

παράσημος, 2 *parasēmos* conspicuous, distinguished*

According to Acts 28:11 Paul and his companion traveled on an Alexandrian ship that was "*distinguished* by the divine twins [as figureheads]" (ἐν πλοίῳ . . . παρασήμῳ Διοσκούροις, probably instrumental dat., perhaps also associative: "with the twins as the *insignia of the ship*"; see BAGD s.v.; BDF §198.7). E. Haenchen, *Acts* [Eng. tr., 1971] 714n.2; → Διόσκουροι.

παρασκευάζω *paraskeuazō* prepare, make ready; mid.: prepare oneself, get ready*

This vb. occurs 4 times in the NT. Absolute in Acts 10:10: παρασκευαζόντων δὲ αὐτῶν (sc. δεῖπνον), "while [the meal, cf. v. 10a] *was being prepared*"; mid. in 1 Cor 14:8: παρασκευάζομαι εἰς πόλεμον, "*prepare oneself* for battle"; pf. mid. in 2 Cor 9:2, of the preparation of the "collection": Ἀχαΐα παρεσκεύασται ἀπὸ πέρυσι, "Achaia *has been prepared* [already] since last year"; 9:3: ἵνα . . . παρεσκευασμένοι ἦτε, "so that you may be *ready.*" F. Thiele, *DNTT* III, 118-20.

παρασκευή, ῆς, ἡ *paraskeuē* preparation; Day of Preparation*

This noun occurs 6 times in the NT: According to Mark 15:42 (ἦν παρασκευὴ ὅ ἐστιν προσάββατον) par. Luke 23:54 (ἡμέρα ἦν παρασκευῆς καὶ σάββατον ἐπέφωσκεν); cf. John 19:42 (διὰ τὴν παρασκευὴν τῶν Ἰουδαίων), Jesus' crucifixion and burial took place on the *Day of Preparation* before the sabbath (Heb. *'ereb haššabbāt*); Matt 27:62 assumes the same time frame (τῇ δὲ ἐπαύριον . . . μετὰ τὴν παρασκευήν), since the guard at the grave (vv. 63ff.) was placed on the day after the burial (vv. 59f.), which therefore took place on the *Day of Preparation.* Likewise in John 19:31 Jesus' death is dated on the *Day of Preparation* for the sabbath (ἐπεὶ παρασκευὴ ἦν, ἵνα μὴ μείνῃ ἐπὶ τοῦ σταυροῦ τὰ σώματα ἐν τῷ σαββάτῳ); the legs of those who were crucified would be broken so that their bodies could be taken away before the sabbath (cf. Deut 21:22f.; Ps 33:21 LXX). In John this *Day of Preparation* (= Friday) is for the sabbath and also (in contrast to the Synoptics) for the Passover (Nisan 14): 19:14: ἦν δὲ παρασκευὴ τοῦ πάσχα (Heb. *'ereb pesaḥ;* cf. also 18:28). Therefore, Jesus' death took place, according to the Fourth Gospel, at the same time as the sacrifice of the Passover lamb. In early Christian writings παρασκευή is likewise used of Friday (*Mart. Pol.* 7:1;

Did. 8:1: the day of Jesus' death as a day of fasting). Billerbeck II, 829ff.; BAGD s.v.; A. B. du Toit, *BHH* 1625f.; R. Bultmann, *John* (Eng. tr., 1971) 651n.6, 664n.5, 676n.6; E. Lohse, *TDNT* VII, 1-35; P.-E. Bonnard, *DBT* 409; F. Thiele, *DNTT* III, 118-20.   H. Balz

παραστάτις, ιδος, ἡ *parastatis* (female) helper Rom 16:2 v.l. in place of προστάτις (of Phoebe).

παρατείνω *parateinō* extend, expand*

Acts 20:7: Paul "*continued* his speech" in Troas (v. 6) through the evening "until midnight" (παρέτεινέν τε τὸν λόγον).

παρατηρέω *paratēreō* carefully observe, guard*

This vb. occurs 6 times in the NT: act. in Mark 3:2 of the opponents of Jesus, who *carefully/furtively observed* him (παρετήρουν αὐτόν); mid. in the same sense in Luke 6:7 (παρετηροῦντο δὲ αὐτόν); 14:1 (ἦσαν παρατηρούμενοι αὐτόν); absolute παρατηρήσαντες ἀπέστειλαν ἐγκαθέτους, "they sent observers *to wait for an opportunity/to spy* [on Jesus]" in Luke 20:20 (v.l. ἀποχωρήσαντες; see also H. Riesenfeld, *TDNT* VIII, 147n.10); *guard* in Acts 9:24 (παρετηροῦντο δὲ καὶ τὰς πύλας); *observe/keep* in Gal 4:10 (ἡμέρας παρατηρεῖσθε καὶ μῆνας καὶ καιροὺς καὶ ἐνιαυτούς), concerning the regression of the Galatians into the observance of a (Jewish?) festal calendar and consequently also into renewed slavery to the orders and powers of this world (cf. similarly on cultic observance Josephus *Ap.* ii.282; *Ant.* iii.91; xiv.264; τοὺς καιρούς in Philodemus Περὶ οἰκονομίας xvii.10f.; see also Riesenfeld 147f., where an anxious observance of favorable or unfavorable times is assumed [bibliography]; cf. further Rom 14:5; Col 2:16). A. Strobel, *ZNW* 49 (1958) 157-96, esp. 163ff.; H. Riesenfeld, *TDNT* VIII, 146-48; BDF §316; H.-G. Schütz, *DNTT* II, 132f.

παρατήρησις, εως, ἡ *paratērēsis* observation*

According to Luke 17:20 Jesus rejects the question of the Pharisees concerning the time of the coming of the kingdom of God as inappropriate: οὐκ ἔρχεται ἡ βασιλεία τοῦ θεοῦ μετὰ παρατηρήσεως, "the kingdom of God does not come *in a way that can be observed [by external signs]*." The noun, which does not occur in the LXX, was also used of scientific "observation" (Sextus Empiricus *Adversus Mathematicos* i.153), esp. astronomical (Diodorus Siculus i.9.6; Clement of Alexandria, *Strom.* i.135.2 and *passim*), and generally for any critical observation (Origen *Orat.* iii.1), and also the keeping of the law and precepts (Josephus *Ant.* viii.96). In Luke 17:20 the issue may be less that of calculating a specific time

than the view (of the Pharisees) that the coming and the presence of the kingdom of God must be recognizable by clearly discernible phenomena. Jesus' reply is that the kingdom can only be experienced as present reality and cannot be ascertained as some objectively accessible or inevitably coming entity (→ ἐντός 2). BAGD s.v.; A. Strobel, *ZNW* 49 (1958) 157-96; 51 (1960) 133f.; H. Riesenfeld, *TDNT* VIII, 148-51 (bibliography); G. Schneider, *Luke* II (ÖTK) on 17:20f. (bibliography); H.-G. Schütz, *DNTT* II, 132f.   H. Balz

παρατίθημι *paratithēmi* set before, present; place next to; hand over, entrust; expound
→ παραθήκη 2.

παρατυγχάνω *paratynchanō* happen to be present*

According to Acts 17:17 Paul spoke daily in the market in Athens to those *who happened to be there* (πρὸς τοὺς παρατυγχάνοντας); cf. Josephus *Ant.* ii.226.

παραυτίκα *parautika* presently, momentarily, currently*

This adv. appears in 2 Cor 4:17 with the art. and is used adjectivally: τὸ παραυτίκα ἐλαφρὸν τῆς θλίψεως, "the present light burden of our affliction" (in the sense of "only in the present"; cf. πρόσκαιρα, v. 18); see R. Bultmann, *2 Cor* (Eng. tr., 1985) ad loc.

παραφέρω *parapherō* carry away; lead away; take away*

This vb. occurs 4 times in the NT: act. only fig. *take away, cause to pass* in Mark 14:36 par. Luke 22:42 (παρένεγκε τοῦτο τὸ ποτήριον ἀπ᾽ ἐμοῦ); pass. *be driven by/driven away* in Jude 12: "waterless clouds *driven away* by storms"; fig. in Heb 13:9: "*do* not *let yourselves be carried away/thrown off course* (μὴ παραφέρεσθε)"; cf. 2 Pet 2:17. Spicq, *Notes* II, 666f.

παραφρονέω *paraphroneō* be foolish, behave foolishly*

2 Cor 11:23: παραφρονῶν λαλῶ; Paul asserts with *senseless/foolish* presumption his superiority over his opponents (cf. ἐν ἀφροσύνῃ λέγω, v. 21).

παραφρονία, ας, ἡ foolishness, madness*

2 Pet 2:16: the *madness* of Balaam (ἡ τοῦ προφήτου

παραφρονία), who wanted to curse the people of God (cf. Num 22:22ff.).

παραφροσύνη, ης, ἡ *paraphrosynē* craziness, nonsense

2 Pet 2:16: v.l. in place of → παραφρονία.

παραχειμάζω *paracheimazō* spend the winter*

This vb. occurs 4 times in the NT: Acts 27:12; 28:11, of ships that *spend the winter* in a harbor. According to 1 Cor 16:6, it was Paul's desire on his trip to "stay or even *spend the winter"* with the Corinthians; according to Titus 3:12 "Paul" decided to *spend the winter* in Nicopolis.

παραχειμασία, ας, ἡ *paracheimasia* wintering (noun)*

Acts 27:12, of the harbor → Καλοὶ λιμένες (v. 8), which "was not suitable for *wintering"* (ἀνεύθετος . . . πρὸς παραχειμασίαν).

παραχράομαι *parachraomai* misuse

Absolute παραχρώμενοι in 1 Cor 7:31 L in place of → καταχρώμενοι.

παραχρῆμα *parachrēma* immediately, right away, at once, instantly*

This adv. occurs 18 times in the NT, with 10 occurrences in Luke and 6 in Acts and in Matt 21:19, 20. In 15 instances παραχρῆμα (literally παρὰ τὸ χρῆμα, "in the course of the event/act") is used in miracle stories (healings: Luke 1:64; 4:39; 5:25; 8:44, 47, 55; 13:13; 18:43; Acts 3:7; miracles of punishment: Matt 21:19f.; Acts 5:10; 12:23; 13:11; a miracle of opening doors: Acts 16:26) of the immediate or instantaneous occurrence of the miracle. Elsewhere, Luke 19:11: *at once/immediately;* 22:60: *at that very moment;* Acts 16:33: *on the spot.* L. Rydbeck, *Fachprosa, vermeintliche Volkssprache und NT* (SGU 5, 1967) 167-76; BDF §102.2; → εὐθύς (3).

πάρδαλις, εως, ἡ *pardalis* panther, leopard*

In Rev 13:2 in the description of the apocalyptic animal that was "like a *leopard"* (ὅμοιον παρδάλει); cf. Dan 7:6. K. Hanhart, *NTS* 27 (1980/81) 576-83.

παρεδρεύω *paredreuō* sit beside; be (continually) occupied with

1 Cor 9:13, of those "who *perform the duties* at the altar" (οἱ τῷ θυσιαστηρίῳ παρεδρεύοντες along with οἱ τὰ ἱερὰ ἐργαζόμενοι), i.e., the priests who serve in the temple at the altar of burnt sacrifice and are entitled to a share of the offering (cf. Num 18:8ff.; Deut 18:1ff.; → θυσιαστήριον 3). Cultic usage is also evident in Diodorus Siculus iv.3.3; *SIG* 695.27; but not in the LXX.

παρεῖδον *pareidon* overlook(ed)
2nd aor. of → παροράω.

πάρειμι *pareimi* be present/in attendance; have come*

1. Occurrences in the NT — 2. Of persons — a) "be present/in attendance" — b) "have come" — 3. Of things

Lit.: BAGD s.v. — A. OEPKE, *TDNT* V, 858-71.

1. The vb. πάρειμι, from which → παρουσία is derived, appears in the NT 24 times and is distributed in several NT writings with no particular discernible pattern. It is absent from Mark, Romans, Ephesians, the Pastorals, James, and 1–3 John. Concentrations of usage are discernible in Acts (5 occurrences) and 2 Corinthians 10–13 (5 occurrences; a total of 9 in Paul's letters).

2. Of persons:
a) In 18 of the NT occurrences, including all those in Paul and Luke-Acts, the reference is to the presence of persons: John 11:28 (ὁ διδάσκαλος); Acts 10:33 (ἡμεῖς); 24:19 (ἐπὶ σοῦ παρεῖναι). In Paul usually the partc. παρών is used: 2 Cor 10:2; 11:9; with the antonym ἀπών in 1 Cor 5:3a, b; 2 Cor 10:11 (pl.); 13:2, 10. In Gal 4:18, 20 Paul refers to his own presence with the inf.: ἐν τῷ παρεῖναί με πρὸς ὑμᾶς/ἤθελον δὲ παρεῖναι πρὸς ὑμᾶς ἄρτι. In Rev 17:8 the revealing angel says: "The beast (→ θηρίον) that you have seen was, and is not, and will come [again] from the abyss . . . and the inhabitants of the earth will be astonished . . . when they see that the beast was, and is not, and *will have come into existence* [again; fut. παρέσται]."

b) The pres. of πάρειμι sometimes has a pf. sense, *have come:* Matt 26:50 (contrast par. Mark; not as question, but elliptically): "Friend, [do now] that for which *you have come"* (see F. Rehkopf, *ZNW* 52 [1961] 109-15; W. Eltester, FS Cullmann [1962] 70-91); Acts 10:21; 17:6; Luke 11:6 D. Impf. παρῆσαν can be translated "they *had come"* in Luke 13:1; Acts 12:20.

3. Πάρειμι has a nonpersonal subj. in a few passages: John 7:6: καιρός, "my time *has* not yet *come";* Col 1:6: the gospel τοῦ παρόντος εἰς ὑμᾶς, "that *has come* to you"; also participles in Heb 12:11: πρὸς τὸ παρόν, "for the *present moment";* 13:5: τὰ παρόντα, *"that which is available/possessions";* 2 Pet 1:9: ᾧ μὴ πάρεστιν ταῦτα, "to whom these things [*sc.* the virtues of vv. 5-7] *are* not *available";* 1:12: ἡ παροῦσα ἀλήθεια, "the truth *available* [to you]."

G. Schneider

παρεισάγω *pareisagō* bring in, smuggle in*

2 Pet 2:1, in the warning against false teachers, who *"(secretly) introduce* corrupting heresies (παρεισάξουσιν αἱρέσεις ἀπολείας)"; cf. Jude 4; Eusebius *HE* iv.22.5. W. Michaelis, *TDNT* V, 824-26.

παρείσακτος, 2 *pareisaktos* brought in secretly, smuggled in*

The verbal adj. of → παρεισάγω is found very infrequently outside the Bible and in the NT only in Gal 2:4 of the "false brothers *who have sneaked in*" (παρείσακτοι ψευδάδελφοι), i.e., those who were requiring circumcision of Gentile Christians in opposition to the Pauline gospel (cf. παρεισῆλθον, v. 4b; Acts 15:1ff.; 2 Pet 2:1). Hesychius, Photius *(Lexicon),* and Suidas interpret παρείσακτος as ἀλλότριος. BAGD s.v. (bibliography); F. Mussner, *Gal* (HTKNT) ad loc. (bibliography); W. Michaelis, *TDNT* V, 824-26.

παρεισδύω *pareisdyō* secretly penetrate, sneak in*

In Jude 4 in a warning against intruders in the churches who long ago have received the final condemnation: παρεισέδυσαν γάρ τινες ἄνθρωποι (according to the context probably libertines). The aor. act. form could be derived either from a first person 1st aor. (pres. -δύω) or from 2nd aor. -ἔδυν (pres. -δύνω). The v.l. -ἐδύησαν (B C) is 2nd aor. pass. with the same intrans. meaning; cf. BDF §§76.2; 101. Outside the NT the vb. usually appears in the mid.

παρεισέρχομαι *pareiserchomai* enter on the side, slip in between; sneak in*

This vb. is used in Gal 2:4 with → παρείσακτος of the "false brothers who *have sneaked in/have infiltrated* (παρεισῆλθον)," probably radical Jewish Christians who appeared in Antioch (cf. Acts 15:1ff.), and perhaps also in the assembly in Jerusalem and in the Galatian churches, in opposition to the Pauline message of freedom (cf. J. Becker, *Gal* [NTD] ad loc.).

According to Rom 5:20 the law has no independent saving function in the Adam-Christ antithesis (vv. 12-18), but, as an entity that entered the world "after" Adam and "before" Christ, still belonged to the side of Adam, sin, and death: νόμος δὲ παρεισῆλθεν, "but the law *slipped in between/came in addition.*" This means not that the law was an "unauthorized addition," but that it was a temporarily and circumstantially necessary "interim entity" that had the function of ultimately preparing the way from Adam and sin to grace in Christ. Cf. E. Käsemann, *Rom* (Eng. tr., 1980) ad loc. (bibliography); E. Jüngel, *ZTK* 60 (1963) 145-72, esp. 159f., 169ff.: "Thus the law proves to be a provisional regulation between Adam and Christ that is theologically necessary for the Adam-Christ correspondence" (171f.); U. Wilckens, *Rom* I (EKKNT) ad loc. (bibliography); J. Schneider, *TDNT* II, 682.

H. Balz

παρεισφέρω *pareispherō* bring to, apply*

2 Pet 1:5, in a parenetic context: σπουδὴν πᾶσαν παρεισενέγκαντες, *"by applying* all diligence/*bringing* every effort *to bear";* widespread usage in Koine: cf. *OGIS* II, 438, 5ff.; *SIG* II, 656, 14; 667, 10; 694, 16; Josephus *Ant.* xx.204. Spicq, *Notes* II, 668.

παρεκτός *parektos* except, other than*

1. As a substantivized adv. (BDF §226) in 2 Cor 11:28, τὰ παρεκτός designates "that which *remains outside* (i.e., *unmentioned*)." The litotes χωρὶς τῶν παρεκτός cuts off the series of peristases from v. 27 and accentuates paraleptically the two following anacolutha as a concluding climax ("not to mention . . ."). See J. Zmijewski, *Der Stil der paulinischen "Narrenrede"* (BBB 52, 1978) 264-70.

2. As an improper prep. with gen. (BDF §216.2), *except/excluding,* in Matt 5:32; Acts 26:29. The "adultery clause," παρεκτὸς λόγου πορνείας, in Matt 5:32 (in 19:9 v.l. for μὴ ἐπὶ πορνείᾳ), *"except* in the case of adultery," is of Jewish Christian origin, shaped by rabbinic casuistry (see B. Schaller, FS Jeremias [1970] 226-38, esp. 237; on the somewhat controverial discussion cf. H. Baltensweiler, *Die Ehe im NT* [ATANT 52, 1967] 59-72, 87-102; A. Sand, *MTZ* 20 [1969] 118-29; G. Schneider, *TTZ* 80 [1971] 78-83; E. Schweizer, *Matt* [Eng. tr., 1975] ad loc.; G. Strecker, *ZNW* 69 [1978] 52-56; → πορνεία 3). The exclusive understanding of παρεκτός (and μή in 19:9; on the inclusive interpretation see, among others, A. Ott, *Die Ehescheidung im Matthäusevangelium* [1933]; K. Berger, *Die Gesetzesauslegung Jesu* [WMANT 40, 1972] 562n.1 [bibliography]) no longer demands discussion, even among Catholic exegetes (see P. Hoffmann, "Jesus' Saying about Divorce and Its Interpretation in the NT Tradition," *The Future of Marriage as Institution* (Concilium 55, ed. F. Böckle; 1970) 51-66.

R. Bergmeier

παρεμβάλλω *paremballō* set up, erect*

In Luke 19:43 as a military t.t.: "Your enemies *will erect* a wall against you (παρεμβαλοῦσιν . . . σοί)" (v.l. περιβαλοῦσιν A B Koine, etc.; ἐπιβαλοῦσιν G, etc.; βαλοῦσιν D); found frequently in the LXX as a t.t.: "encamp" (e.g., Gen 33:18; Judg 6:33); "besiege" (2 Kgdms 12:28; Jer 27:29; cf. further also Isa 29:3; Ezek 4:2; 26:8).

παρεμβολή, ῆς, ἡ *parembolē* camp; barracks; battle line, army*

10 occurrences in the NT, always as a military t.t.: In Acts always in the expression εἰς τὴν παρεμβολήν, referring to the Roman barracks in the fortress of Antonia in Jerusalem (21:34, 37; 22:24; 23:10, 16, 32). Elsewhere usually referring to a (fortified) camp, e.g., in the expression ἔξω τῆς παρεμβολῆς of the camp of the Israelites (Exod 29:14; 33:7; Lev 4:12, 21, etc.) and in Heb 13:11 (quoting Lev 16:27) of the flesh of the animal sacrificed on the Day of Atonement, which was burned "outside the *camp,*" with reference to Jesus' death outside the city (v. 12); therefore the servants of the old covenant have no right to participate in the salvation (v. 10) mediated through the death on the cross (sacramentally in the communal meal?), while believers "go outside the camp" to the crucified outcast (13:13: ἐξερχώμεθα πρὸς αὐτὸν ἔξω τῆς παρεμβολῆς; Lev 24:14; Num 15:35ff.), since they have here no "enduring city," but rather seek the city that is to come (v. 14; cf. *1 Clem.* 4:11; Philo *Gig.* 54). Also influenced by the OT is the expression παρεμβολὴ τῶν ἁγίων (Rev 20:9) in connection with the eschatological stream of nations to "the *camp* of the saints and the beloved city" (cf. Jer 12:7; Ps 78:68; Ezek 39:6). Heb 11:34: *battle line/army:* παρεμβολαὶ . . . ἀλλοτρίων, "*armies* of foreign peoples" (cf. on the meaning Judg 4:16; 8:11; on the subject 7:7f.; 2 Kgs 19:6ff., etc.). R. Hentschke and B. Reicke, *BHH* 1041f.; D. Lührmann, *ZNW* 69 (1978) 178-86.   H. Balz

παρενοχλέω *parenochleō* (further) burden (vb.), make things (more) difficult*

According to Acts 15:19 James did not want *to (further) burden* (with circumcision and the law) those who had turned to God from among the Gentiles (cf. vv. 10f.). Παρα- intensifies ἐνοχλέω and emphasizes the aspect of addition (cf. Passow II/1 s.v.; differently E. Haenchen, *Acts* [Eng. tr., 1971] ad loc.).

παρεπίδημος, 2 *parepidēmos* dwelling among people as a stranger; subst.: stranger*

This adj. occurs 3 times in the NT, always subst. of believers, who have in this world only a passing dwelling place, but not their actual home. In Heb 11:13 ξένοι καὶ παρεπίδημοι . . . ἐπὶ τῆς γῆς, "aliens and *strangers* on earth" (cf. Gen 23:4; 1 Chr 29:15), originally designated Abraham and those with him as strangers in the land and in principle refers to their traveling in search of the true heavenly home (Heb 11:14-16; cf. also Ps 38:13 LXX). In 1 Pet 1:1 the churches are addressed as ἐκλεκτοὶ παρεπίδημοι διασπορᾶς, i.e., as those who have been set apart in the world by God's election and who are *strangers* in the present "diaspora." In both passages παρεπίδημος is fig. and refers to the isolation of the congregations and their critical distance from the world (cf. Phil 3:20; Jas 1:1; 4 Ezra 8:39; 14:13f.). According to 1 Pet 2:11 believers, as πάροικοι καὶ παρεπίδημοι, "aliens and *strangers*" (quoting Gen 23:4; cf. Ps 38:13 LXX), can no longer have anything to do with the ἐπιθυμίαι of this world; the word is also fig. here, though the distinction between παρεπίδημος (a *foreigner* without the rights of a citizen or resident alien) and a → πάροικος (a foreigner who has lived for a long time in the land, i.e., a resident alien) is without significance. W. Grundmann, *TDNT* II, 64f.; R. Gyllenberg and B. Reicke, *BHH* I, 498f.; J. H. Elliott, *A Home for the Homeless: A Sociological Exegesis of 1 Peter* (1981); L. F. Mercado, *The Language of Sojourning in the Abraham Midrash in Hebrews 11:8-19* (Diss. Harvard, 1967); H. Bietenhard, *DNTT* I, 690; L. Goppelt, *1 Pet* (KEK) 79f.; Spicq, *Notes* II, 669-72.   H. Balz

παρέρχομαι *parerchomai* come up to; pass by, pass away*

Lit.: I. BROER, *Freiheit vom Gesetz und Radikalisierung des Gesetzes* (SBS 98, 1980) (bibliography on Matt 5:18). — W. MUNDLE, *DNTT* I, 319-22. — J. SCHNEIDER, *TDNT* II, 681f. — D. P. SENIOR, *The Passion Narrative According to Matthew* (BETL 39, 1975) 100-119. — For further bibliography see *TWNT* X, 1086.

1. a) παρέρχομαι occurs 30 times in the NT, 23 times in the Synoptics, 2 (or 3) times in Acts (24:7 is an interpolated "invective against Lysias": H. Conzelmann, *Acts* [Hermeneia] 199), and 4 times in the Epistles (2 Cor 5:17; Jas 1:10; 1 Pet 4:3; 2 Pet 3:10). The primary meaning is local: *pass by:* Jesus *passed by* the disciples (Mark 6:48) and the blind man of Jericho (Luke 18:37); Paul and Timothy *sailed past* Mysia (partc. in Acts 16:8); no one dared *pass by* on the road when they met the two demoniacs (Matt 8:28). The meaning *come up to* is present in Luke 12:37: The partc. modifies "serve" and does not mean "pass by" (*contra* R. Pesch, ed., *Synoptisches Arbeitsbuch zum NT* III [1980] 51). The imv. in Luke 17:7 commands the servant to *come*.

b) A temporal aspect is present in Matt 14:15: The hour *passes by/away,* i.e., it is getting late in the day. According to Acts 27:9, the fast (the time of fasting) was *past.* In Mark 14:35 Jesus prays that "the hour" (as the time of threat) *might pass by;* the vb. gains already here a theological significance, as it also does in 2 Cor 5:17: Paul states that the old (τὰ ἀρχαῖα—not temporally, but qualitatively) has *passed away;* "The ἀρχαῖα comprises everything under the old aeon" (R. Bultmann, *2 Cor* [Eng. tr., 1986] 158). Likewise 1 Pet 4:3 speaks of time *past,* of the time before the conversion of the Christian, which was characterized by profligacy. Concerning the rich man it is said that he *passes away* like a flower of the field (Jas 1:10; cf. Isa 40:6b, etc.).

A temporal designation is also present in apocalyptic occurrences of the vb.: This generation (Mark 13:30 par. Matt 24:34/Luke 21:32) as well as heaven and earth (Mark 13:31 par. Matt 24:35/Luke 21:33, in each instance twice) *will pass away;* in contrast, the words of Jesus will definitely not (οὐ μή) *pass away* (Mark 13:31 par. Matt 24:35 / Luke 21:33, in each instance twice). The apocalyptic reference to the future in 2 Pet 3:10 has a primarily temporal meaning, though because of the reference to the "day of the Lord" only the temporal aspect is registered.

2. Luke 11:42, where the Pharisees are reproached because they carelessly *pass by* justice and God's love by taking their scrupulous tithing as a pretext for defying God, also has theological relevance. In Luke 15:29 the older son contends that he *has* never *passed by* a single command.

In Matt 26:36-42 Jesus prays three times that his "suffering" *might pass by:* The prayer is twice quoted word for word, while the third time reference is made to the wording already cited (v. 44); in the first Jesus asks that the cup *might pass away* (aor. imv.) and in the second, "if this cannot *pass away.* . . ." Matthew makes the cup that is to be taken away from Jesus by God (Mark 14:36) into a cup that is to *pass away;* through the repetition in direct discourse, the negative formulation, the specification of the content of the statement concerning the cup, and not least through the inclusion of the suffering as a whole (τοῦτο), the second request undergoes an intensification that also comes to expression through verbal similarities with the third petition of the Lord's Prayer.

In Matt 5:18 (bis; cf. Luke 16:17) it is stressed that the validity of the law continues "until heaven and earth *pass away.*" Here "heaven and earth" refer to the present aeon, in which the law has indissoluble validity. Therefore, in the foreground is "the positive and unwavering validity of the law and not its essential dissolubility and imminent dissolution" (Broer 44).   A. Sand

πάρεσις, εως, ἡ *paresis* letting go; letting go unpunished, forgiveness*

This noun, which does not appear in the LXX and is usually used in extrabiblical literature of "release" from debts or requirments (Phalaris *Epistulae* 81.1; Dionysius of Halicarnassus *Antiquitates Romanae* vii.37.2), is found in Rom 3:25 in the expression πάρεσις τῶν . . . ἁμαρτημάτων, which should be translated "*remission/forgiveness* of sins" (Vg. *remissio*), hardly in the sense of "letting go unpunished/overlooking" (cf. Plutarch *Com-*

paratio Dionysii Bruti 2). In contrast to the more common ἄφεσις (→ ἀφίημι 1) πάρεσις stresses the universal salvation-historical aspect of remission (cf. → ἔνδειξις, used twice in Rom 3:25f.; see also U. Wilckens, *Rom* I [EKKNT] ad loc. [bibliography]; similarly with emphasis of the juridical aspect E. Käsemann, *Rom* [Eng. tr., 1980] ad loc. [bibliography]); it concerns the forgiveness of all sins that occurred before Christ. R. Bultmann, *TDNT* I, 509-12, esp. 511; J. M. Creed, *JTS* 41 (1940) 28-30; S. Lyonnet, *VD* 28 (1950) 282-87; Kümmel I, 260-70.

παρέχω *parechō* grant, present; cause; mid.: show oneself to be; grant*

This vb. occurs 16 times in the NT, 4 times in Luke and 5 times in Acts, in Paul only in Gal 6:17 (Col 4:1), and not in the Catholic Epistles or Revelation.

The act. is used most frequently with these meanings: *grant/furnish/render:* Acts 17:31: πίστιν παρέχω, "*grant /furnish* an affirmation"; 22:2: παρέχω ἡσυχίαν, "*keep silent/become quiet*"; 28:2: παρέχω οὐ τὴν τυχοῦσαν φιλανθρωπίαν, "*show* exceptional hospitality"; 1 Tim 6:17: παρέχω πάντα πλουσίως, God "richly *grants* us all things"; *present, hold out:* Luke 6:29: παρέχω τὴν ἄλλην (σιαγόνα); *cause, bring about:* κόπους παρέχω, "*make* trouble, *cause* problems/difficulties, *bother*" (Matt 26:10; Mark 14:6; Luke 11:7; Gal 6:17); Luke 18:5: παρέχω κόπον; Acts 16:16: ἐργασίαν πολλὴν παρέχω, "*bring in* much profit"; 1 Tim 1:4: ἐκζητήσεις παρέχω, "*cause* speculation."

The mid. has the meaning *provide/grant:* Acts 19:24: παρέχω οὐκ ὀλίγην ἐργασίαν; on the relation of "masters" to slaves: Col 4:1: τὸ δίκαιον καὶ τὴν ἰσότητα παρέχω, "*provide* what is right and fair"; Luke 7:4: ἄξιός ἐστιν ᾧ παρέξῃ τοῦτο, "he is worthy that you should *grant* this to him"; Titus 2:7: σεαυτὸν παρεχόμενος τύπον, "by *showing yourself to be* an example." BAGD s.v.; BDF §316.3.

παρηγορία, ας, ἡ *parēgoria* comfort, consolation*

Col 4:11, of the fellow workers of "Paul": ἐγενήθησάν μοι παρηγορία, "they have become a *comfort* to me here."

παρθενία, ας, ἡ *parthenia* virginity*

Luke 2:36, of the prophetess Anna, "who lived with a man [i.e., was married] seven years after/from the time of her *virginity* (ἀπὸ τῆς παρθενίας αὐτῆς)."

παρθένος, ου, ἡ (ὁ) *parthenos* virgin; young woman of marriageable age; chaste man*

1. Occurrences in the NT — 2. "Young woman" — 3. Mary as virgin — 4. 1 Corinthians 7 — 5. 2 Cor. 11:2 — 6. Acts 14:4

Lit.: R. A. Batey, *NT Nuptial Imagery* (1971). — O. Becker and C. Brown, *DNTT* III, 1071-73. — G. Delling, *TDNT* V, 826-37. — J. M. Ford, "The Meaning of 'Virgin,'" *NTS* 12 (1965/66) 293-99. — W. G. Kümmel, "Verlobung und Heirat bei Paulus (I. Kor 7,36-38)," FS Bultmann (1954) 275-95. — L. Legrand, "Saint Paul et le célibat," *Sacerdoce et célibat* (BETL 28, ed. J. Coppens; 1971) 315-31. — K. Niederwimmer, "Zur Analyse der asketischen Motivation in 1 Kor 7," *TLZ* 99 (1974) 241-48. — H. M. Orlinsky, *IDBSup* 939f. — A. Schulz, "'Almā,'" *BZ* 23 (1935) 229-41. — R. H. A. Seboldt, "Spiritual Marriage in the Early Church," *CTM* 30 (1959) 103-19, 176-86. — F. A. Strobel, "Zum Verständnis von Mt XXV 1-13," *NovT* 2 (1957) 199-227. — G. J. Wenham, "*B^etûlâh* 'A Girl of Marriageable Age,'" *VT* 22 (1972) 326-48. — For further bibliography see *TWNT* X, 1217-20.

1. Παρθένος occurs 15 times in the NT: 6 times in 1 Corinthians, 4 times in Matthew, twice in Luke, and once each in Acts, 2 Corinthians, and Revelation. The abstract noun παρθενία, "virginity," is found only in Luke 2:36.

2. Occasionally παρθένος refers just to a *young woman of marriageable age*. This is the case, e.g., in the parable of the ten παρθένοι (Matt 25:1, 7, 11), the *young women* who are waiting for the bridegroom and are as yet unmarried. The point of the parable does not depend on their "virginity" in the strict sense. Likewise, according to Acts 21:9, the four daughters of Philip are παρθένοι προφητεύουσαι, i.e., *young* (sexually mature) *women* (perhaps virgins); they are mentioned because of their prophetic gift.

3. "Virgin" in the strict sense (ἄπειρος ἀνδρός, Menander) is intended by παρθένος in Luke 1:27a, b: Mary is described as "a *virgin* pledged to be married to a man named Joseph" (cf. 2:5). This is also the sense of παρθένος in Matt 1:23, where Isa 7:14 LXX (ἡ παρθένος ἐν γαστρὶ ἕξει) is applied to Mary. The LXX narrowed the broader sense of Heb. *'almâ* (a young woman of marriageable age) and translated it as παρθένος. In this narrower sense παρθένος is applied to Mary, although the corresponding NT statements are related only to Mary's virginity *ante partum*.

4. In 1 Corinthians 7 a distinction must be made between use of παρθένος in vv. 25-34 and use of it in vv. 36-38. Vv. 25, 28, and 34 speak generally of παρθένοι: Paul gives his own advice in lieu of a command from the Lord (v. 25), apparently without knowledge of Matt 19:10-12. With παρθένος he refers to the virgin state of unmarried men and women. His ascetic advice for them, as for those who are married, is: Remain as you are, taking into consideration the present crisis. In 7:34 the various textual variants make the interpretation more difficult, but the generally preferred reading refers to the "unmarried woman" (παρθένος) as one who is not dis-tracted from the service of the Lord. The παρθένος in these verses has nothing to do with the persons spoken of in 7:2-5.

In 7:36-38, however, Paul uses παρθένος in a specific sense, which unfortunately remains ambiguous. He obviously refers to a *virgin*, but her relation to the man referred to (τίς ὅς, αὐτοῦ) depends on how one interprets → ὑπέρακμος (masc. or fem.) and on the more specific meaning of γαμείτω(σαν) and γαμίζων (→ γαμέω 2). There have been various attempts to interpret παρθένος here as "virgin daughter," a "virgin minor or ward," a "virgin wife or fiancée" in spiritual marriage, or even as the *virgo subintroducta* of the later monastic communities (obviously an anachronism!). The interpretation of παρθένος that best fits is either the *virgin* that the man is engaged to or his *virgin* wife.

5. In 2 Cor 11:2 Paul applies παρθένος in a fig. collective sense to the Corinthians to whom he proclaimed the gospel for Christ: "I have betrothed you as pure *virgins* to one husband (ἑνὶ ἀνδρὶ παρθένον ἁγνήν)," i.e., to Christ, who will come at the parousia; in the meantime, however, Paul is jealously afraid that the Corinthians will be led astray, i.e., that they might give up their believing dependence on him.

6. In an even stronger fig. sense the 144,000 redeemed followers of the lamb in Rev 14:4 are called παρθένοι ("virgins"), those who have not "defiled themselves with women," i.e., have not lapsed into idol worship (the emperor cult). This usage reflects the OT identification of idol worship as fornication (2 Kgs 9:22; Ezek 23:11). In this context, παρθένος is an antonym of → πόρνη (5) (Rev 17:1, 5, 15f.).

J. A. Fitzmyer

Πάρθος, ου, ὁ *Parthos* Parthian*

In Acts 2:9, in the list of Jews from the Diaspora who were residing in Jerusalem at the time of the feast of Pentecost (v. 5). The Πάρθοι are the first of the fourteen (originally twelve) names (probably as the people living farthest to the east; immediately followed by Μῆδοι καὶ Ἐλαμῖται). The Parthians ruled Mesopotamia and Iran from the 2nd cent. B.C. and were feared enemies on the eastern border of the Roman Empire. Their rule was ended in A.D. 227 by the Sassanids. W. Hinz, *BHH* 1394; *BL* 1304; on the list of nations see H. Conzelmann, *Acts* (Hermeneia) ad loc.; G. Schneider, *Acts* I (HTKNT) ad loc.

παρίημι *pariēmi* omit, neglect; pass.: become weak, tired*

Luke 11:42: ποιῆσαι . . . μὴ παρεῖναι, "*do . . . not neglect*"; pass. in Heb 12:12: τὰς παρειμένας χεῖρας . . .

ἀνορθώσατε, "strengthen *weakened* hands" (cf. Sir 2:12; 25:23; Isa 35:3). The meaning "remit" (cf. → πάρεσις) is lacking in the NT (see, however, Sir 23:2; Josephus, *Ant.* xv.48). R. Bultmann, *TDNT* I, 509f., 511f.

παρίστημι, παριστάνω *paristēmi, paristanō* set down; come beside; present, subject*

Lit.: N. Baumert, *Täglich sterben und auferstehen* (SANT 34, 1973) 284-99. — H. Frankemölle, *Das Taufverständnis des Paulus* (SBS 47, 1970). — O. Kuss, *Röm* I (1957) 307-19 (excursus on baptism). — K. Munzer, *DNTT* I, 474f. — B. Reicke and G. Bertram, *TDNT* V, 837-41.

1. This compound form of → ἵστημι is found 41 times in the NT, esp. in Acts (13 occurrences) and Romans (8 occurrences). In the later writings the vb. is found only 5 times (twice each in Colossians and 2 Timothy, once in Ephesians). In the act. it means *make available, place at one's disposal* (trans.) and *come beside, approach (someone)* (intrans.). The mid. has the meanings *present, subject, conquer*. The broad diversification of meaning in secular Greek is carried over into the NT, so that it is necessary to consider the context in each case. The pres. form παριστάνω that is dominant is found in the LXX and in nonbiblical Greek from about the 2nd cent. B.C. (cf. BAGD s.v.).

2. The NT authors use the vb. primarily in the same senses as it is used in secular Greek. The Father can *place at the* Son's *disposal* more than twelve legions of angels (Matt 26:53); likewise in Acts 23:24 the soldiers had to *make available* mounts. According to Acts 24:13 the Jews could *provide* no evidence against Paul. The meaning *present oneself as* is found in Acts 1:3; 9:41: Those who had been dead before now showed that they were alive. Intrans. *approach (someone)* is found in 4:26 (in a hostile sense; cf. Ps 2:2 LXX); 9:39 (the mourning widows); and 27:23 (an angel of God). The vb. means *stand by, be present* (frequently substantivized) in Mark 15:35, 39; 14:47, 69, 70; Luke 19:24; Acts 1:10; 4:10; 23:2, 4; John 18:22; 19:26. The harvest is said to *be present*, i.e., its time has arrived, in Mark 4:29. The meaning *present, give* is found in Acts 23:33; 27:24. In Rom 16:2; 2 Tim 4:17 παρίστημι has the sense of *assist, help*.

3. a) All Christians *are placed* before the judgment of God according to Rom 14:10 (v.l.: before the judgment of Christ), since God is the ruler and king before whom every knee must bow (v. 11). The angel Gabriel identifies himself as the one who *stands* before God (Luke 1:19; not "who waits on God," *contra* Reicke 840). Here we see the Jewish idea that no one sits in God's presence: "All that has been created must stand before him" (Munzer 474).

Trans. use is present in Luke 2:22: The parents bring their child to Jerusalem to *present* him to the Lord in accordance with the requirements of the Mosaic law. Although there was no legal basis for presenting the firstborn in the temple, "the actual emphasis" lies on παρίστημι (G. Schneider, *Luke* I [ÖTK] 71).

b) Of theological import are texts in which παρίστημι has the sense of *make, create, present*. Humanity separated from God is made into a holy people through Christ's death (Col 1:22); everyone who has become perfect in Jesus Christ *is presented* to him (1:28). Just as Jesus presented himself to the apostles as the living one (Acts 1:3; → 2), so also God will resurrect believers with Jesus and will *present* them (in his presence; 2 Cor 4:14). According to 2 Cor 11:2, Paul wants to *present* the Church to Christ as a pure virgin (as one who *presents* a royal bride: Psalm 44 LXX). Christ *presents* the Church in glory in Eph 5:27. Timothy must takes pains to present himself approved by God (2 Tim 2:15). In contrast, food is not able *to place* the believer before God (1 Cor 8:8): "No work, not even freedom practiced as a work, makes us acceptable before God" (H. Conzelmann, *1 Cor* [Hermeneia] 148).

c) Παρίστημι occurs 5 times in Romans 6 (vv. 13 bis, 16, 19 bis). The consequence for conduct arising from baptism is that members (τὰ μέλα) that *were* previously *at the disposal of* impurity must now (vv. 19, 21) *be placed* in the service of righteousness. The pres. in v. 13a, "which indicates a continuation in the old existence," corresponds to the aor. imv. in v. 13b (cf. BDF §337), which postulates a decision (Kuss 383f.). Paul calls "the readers to the realization of the received salvation, to the 'service of righteousness' " (Frankemölle 95). It is up to each person *to place* himself *at the disposal of* the good or evil power (v. 16); nevertheless, baptism is such an important break in a person's life that he must now place his members, i.e., himself, in subjection to the service of righteousness (v. 19). Παρίστημι entails the freedom of will and decision, so that the imv. demands *presenting* bodily existence in the comprehensive sense as a well-pleasing sacrifice to God (12:1). The vb. thus signals a change in human existence through a change in the relationship of service.

A. Sand

Παρμενᾶς, ᾶ *Parmenas* Parmenas*

The name (a shortened form of Παρμενίδης, Παρμένων, and the like) of one of the members of "the seven" in Acts 6:5. Parmenas, like the other members of the group (with the exception of Nicolaus) was a Jewish Christian. BDF §125.1.

πάροδος, ου, ἡ *parodos* passing; passageway*

According to 1 Cor 16:7 Paul wanted to see the

Corinthians "not only on *the way through* (ἐν παρόδῳ)," but also perhaps spend the winter with them (v. 6).

παροικέω *paroikeō* live next to; live as a foreigner, take up residence as a foreigner*

This vb. is a t.t. in the LXX for the habitation of resident aliens, i.e., foreigners without the rights of citizens, in Israel (2 Kgdms 4:3) and for the habitation of Israelites in foreign lands (Gen 12:10; 19:9; Exod 6:4; tr. of Heb. *gûr*). In contrast to the → παρεπίδημος, who stays in a foreign land for only a limited time, the → πάροικος lives continually among the natives and enjoys a certain degree of legal protection (R. Meyer, *TDNT* V, 842ff.).

Heb 11:9 should be understood in this light: Abraham "*settled as a foreigner* in the land of promise (παρῴκησεν εἰς γῆν . . . ὡς ἀλλοτρίαν)," albeit only in tents, since he was still waiting for the firmly established city (the heavenly Jerusalem, vv. 9b-10; cf. Gen 23:4; 26:3; Heb 11:13 [→ παρεπίδημος]). In Luke 24:18 Cleopas asks σὺ μόνος παροικεῖς Ἰερουσαλήμ . . . ; This could mean either "*live* in Jeusalem" (cf. Thucydides I.71.2) with no further nuance or *be present* in Jerusalem *as a foreigner* ("are you the only foreigner [i.e., pilgrim at the feast] in Jerusalem?"). R. Meyer, K. L. Schmidt, and M. A. Schmidt, *TDNT* V, 841-53; H. Bietenhard, *DNTT* I, 690f.; for further bibliography see *TWNT* X, 1220.   H. Balz

παροικία, ας, ἡ *paroikia* foreign lands; life abroad, life as a foreigner*

Acts 13:17, of Israel's growth "during the *stay in the foreign land* of Egypt" (ἐν τῇ παροικίᾳ ἐν γῇ Αἰγύπτου; cf. Exod 6:1, 6; Deut 5:15); fig. in 1 Pet 1:17: "while you *live as foreigners* (ὁ τῆς παροικίας χρόνος)," i.e., while still bound to this world (cf. *2 Clem.* 5:1; Philo *Conf.* 80). R. Meyer, K. L. Schmidt, and M. A. Schmidt, *TDNT* V, 841-53; H. Bietenhard, *DNTT* I, 690f.; for further bibliography see *TWNT* X, 1220; → παρεπίδημος, → παροικέω.

πάροικος, 2 *paroikos* foreign; subst.: foreigner, resident alien*

This adj. appears 4 times in the NT. It occurs twice in the literal sense (LXX for Heb. *gēr*) in Stephen's speech in Acts 7 (v. 6, adj. for the σπέρμα of Abraham as πάροικον ἐν γῇ ἀλλοτρίᾳ [cf. Gen 15:13]; v. 29, subst. of Moses who after his flight from Egypt was a πάροικος in Midian [cf. Exod 2:15, 22]).

In Eph 2:19 it is used fig. of baptized Gentiles, who are no longer ξένοι καὶ πάροικοι, but συμπολῖται τῶν ἁγίων καὶ οἰκεῖοι τοῦ θεοῦ ("fellow citizens with the saints and fellow members of God's household"). Here the image of the foreigner or resident alien (→ παροικέω)

is applied in a striking way to the already existing state of the Gentile Christians, who formerly did not belong to God's people, and then depicts the Church, under the image of a national or household community, as reconciled with God and unified. The statement in 1 Pet 2:11, on the other hand (Christians are πάροικοι καὶ παρεπίδημοι in the world) links up with the widespread NT tradition concerning the eschatological foreign existence of believers (→ παρεπίδημος, → παροικέω). BAGD s.v. (bibliography); R. Meyer, K. L. Schmidt, and M. A. Schmidt, *TDNT* V, 841-53; H. Bietenhard, *DNTT* I, 690f.; R. Gyllenburg and B. Reicke, *BHH* 498f.; for further bibliography see *TWNT* X, 1220.   H. Balz

παροιμία, ας, ἡ *paroimia* proverb, metaphorical saying, puzzling saying*

This noun occurs 4 times in the NT. It has the sense *proverb* (that can be quoted) only in 2 Pet 2:22: τὸ τῆς ἀληθοῦς παροιμίας, "what the true *proverb* says," followed by a quotation of Prov 26:11 and a further expanded proverb. Similar quotations, though without παροιμία, are found in Luke 4:23 (→ παραβολή 2); John 4:37; 1 Cor 15:33; Titus 1:12, etc.

Παροιμία is used in John 10:6 (παροιμίαν λέγω, of the "good shepherd" discourse); 16:25 (bis, ἐν παροιμίαις λαλέω), 29 (παροιμίαν λέγω) of Jesus' sayings, which for the time being are still veiled and obscured (in images, Heb. *māšāl;* cf. Sir 47:17), though someday they will be spoken openly and will be intelligible to those who hear (παρρησίᾳ . . . ἀπαγγελῶ ὑμῖν, 16:25b; νῦν ἐν παρρησίᾳ λαλεῖς, v. 29). The Synoptic expression ἐν παραβολαῖς in Mark 4:11 par., etc., is comparable (παραβολή does not appear in John), but in John it is not a question of hardening the hearers by means of veiled parabolic sayings but of uncovering the inability to hear and understand among those who have not yet participated in the change brought about by the eschatological "hour" (cf. John 10:24f.; 11:11-14). For the disciples this hour of openness has begun with faith (16:29-33)—but still in the uncertainty and risk of pre-Easter existence. It is only after the coming of the Paraclete that it will be in the certainty of the presence of the exalted one (16:13ff.). BAGD s.v. (bibliography); F. Hauck, *TDNT* V, 852-56; R. Bultmann, *John* (Eng. tr., 1971), and R. Schnackenburg, *John* III (Eng. tr., 1982), both on 16:25; → παρρησία.   H. Balz

πάροινος, 2 *paroinos* drunk, drunkenly dissolute; subst.: drunkard*

1 Tim 3:3; Titus 1:7, in lists of requirements for leaders of the Church (ἐπίσκοπος): μὴ πάροινον, "not a *drunkard*" (in both cases with μὴ πλήκτην).

παροίχομαι *paroichomai* pass by, pass away*

Acts 14:16: ἐν ταῖς παρῳχημέναις γενεαῖς, "in *past* generations/times" (cf. 15:21).

παρομοιάζω *paromoiazō* be (almost) alike, be similar*

In Matt 23:27 in the woes spoken by Jesus against the Pharisees: "You *are like* white-washed graves" (παρομοιάζετε; cf. Luke 11:44: ἐστὲ ὡς . . .).

παρόμοιος, 2 (3) *paromoios* (almost/quite) alike, similar*

Mark 7:13: καὶ παρόμοια τοιαῦτα πολλὰ ποιεῖτε, "and you do many [more] *similar* things"; cf. 7:8 v.l.

παροξύνω *paroxynō* irritate; pass.: let oneself be carried away (in anger), get excited*

In the NT only pass.: Acts 17:16, of Paul: παρωξύνετο τὸ πνεῦμα αὐτοῦ ἐν αὐτῷ, "his spirit *became agitated/angry* within him"; 1 Cor 13:5, of ἀγάπη: οὐ παροξύνεται, "it *does* not *get carried away,*" i.e., "in anger" (cf. LXX Num 14:11; Deut 1:34; Hos 8:5; Zech 10:3). H. Seesemann, *TDNT* V, 857.

παροξυσμός, οῦ, ὁ *paroxysmos* provocation, rage, heated conflict*

Acts 15:39, in a negative sense: ἐγένετο δὲ παροξυσμός, "and there arose a *heated dispute*" between Paul and Barnabas (cf. on the meaning Deut 29:27); positively in Heb 10:24: παροξυσμὸς ἀγάπης καὶ καλῶν ἔργων, "*motivation* for love and good works" (cf. Vg. "in provocationem caritatis"; a positive sense is attested for the vb. → παροξύνω: LXX only in Prov 6:3; elsewhere, e.g., Xenophon *Mem.* iii.3.13). H. Seesemann, *TDNT* V, 857.

παροράω *paroraō* overlook, not consider

Acts 17:30 D Vg., παριδών, in place of → ὑπεροράω (cf. Wis 11:23).

παροργίζω *parorgizō* make angry, provoke to anger*

Rom 10:19, with God as subj.: ἐπ᾽ ἔθνει ἀσυνέτῳ παροργιῶ ὑμᾶς, "I *will make* you *angry* toward a people who do not understand" (quoting Deut 32:21), as a scriptural justification (among others) for the acceptance of the ἔθνη (brought about by God) taking place in the Gentile mission and announced already by Moses (v. 19).

Eph 6:4: "*Do* not *provoke* your children *to anger*" (μὴ παροργίζετε); cf. Col 3:21 v.l.

παροργισμός, οῦ, ὁ *parorgismos* anger; provocation to anger*

Eph 4:26: "Do not let the sun set on your *anger* (ἐπὶ [τῷ] παροργισμῷ ὑμῶν)"; this pass. sense also in Jer 21:5 LXX (παροργισμὸς μέγας with θυμός and ὀργή).

παροτρύνω *parotrynō* stir up, incite*

Acts 13:50: the Jews *stir up* the God-fearing women and other respected persons in Antioch (in Pisidia) against Paul and Barnabas (παρώτρυναν).

παρουσία, ας, ἡ *parousia* presence; arrival*

1. a) Occurrences — b) Meaning — c) Origin of the t.t. — 2. The parousia of Christ — a) The idea — b) The expectation — c) The content

Lit.: J. BAUMGARTEN, *Paulus und die Apokalyptik* (1975)— BOUSSET/GRESSMANN 202-301. — G. BRAUMANN and C. BROWN, *DNTT* 898-935. — DEISSMANN, *Light* 368-73. — A. FEUILLET, *DBSup* VI, 1331-1419. — T. F. GLASSON, "Theophany and Parousia," *NTS* 34 (1988) 259-70. — E. GRÄSSER, *Das Problem der Parusieverzögerung in den synoptischen Evangelien und in der Apostelgeschichte* (1977). — H. GREEVEN, "Kirche und Parusie Christi," *KD* 10 (1964) 113-35. — W. HARNISCH, *Eschatologische Existenz* (1973). — E. KÄSEMANN, "An Apology for Primitive Christian Eschatology," idem, *Essays on NT Themes* (1964) 169-95. — F. LAUB, *Eschatologische Verkündigung und Lebensgestaltung nach Paulus* (1973). — D. M. MAXWELL, *The Significance of the Parousia in the Theology of Paul* (1968). — A. L. MOORE, *The Parousia in the NT* (1966). — A. OEPKE, *TDNT* V, 858-71. — A. C. PERRIMAN, "Paul and the Parousia: 1 Cor. 15,50-57 and 2 Cor. 5,1-5," *NTS* 35 (1989) 512-21. — R. PESCH, *Naherwartungen* (1968). — W. RADL, *Ankunft des Herrn. Zur Bedeutung und Funktion der Parusieaussagen bei Paulus* (1981). — J. A. T. ROBINSON, *Jesus and His Coming* (1962). — G. SCHNEIDER, *Parusiegleichnisse im Lukasevangelium* (1975). — P. SIBER, *Mit Christus Leben* (1971). SPICQ, *Notes* II, 673-75. — A. STROBEL, *Untersuchungen zum eschatologischen Verzögerungsproblem* (1961). — P. VOLZ, *Die Eschatologie der jüdischen Gemeinde im neutestamentlichen Zeitalter* (1934) 135-229. — For further bibliography see *TWNT* X, 1220-22.

1. a) παρουσία occurs in the NT 24 times, 4 times in Matthew 24 and the balance in the Epistles: 11 times in the authentic Pauline letters, 3 times in 2 Thessalonians 2, and 6 times in the Catholic Epistles. In the genuine Pauline letters, except in 2 Cor 10:10, it is always part of a prep. phrase. In Matt 24:27, 37, 39 (cf. v. 3) it is part of a fixed formula.

b) The basic meaning of the word is to be derived from the vb. → πάρειμι, "be present." Thus παρουσία originally meant *presence*. Since, however, πάρειμι can take on the sense of "come, approach" (e.g., Judg 19:3 LXX), παρουσία frequently means *arrival as the onset of presence*" (BAGD s.v. 2). This is the sense that παρουσία usually has in the NT; only in 1 Cor 16:17; 2 Cor 10:10; Phil 2:12 (1:26?) is the presence of the apostle or his fellow worker intended.

In regard to the meaning *arrival* one can further distinguish between the general concept and the specific use of the word. Only 2 Cor 7:6, 7 (Phil 1:26) speaks of a common arrival. In 2 Thess 2:9 and 2 Pet 3:12, where the Antichrist and the Day of the Lord respectively are the subjects of the coming, the use of παρουσία approaches the more specific usage. In the remaining 16 occurrences παρουσία is a t.t. for Christ's coming at the end of time.

c) The use of παρουσία as a t.t. cannot be derived from the LXX, where it occurs as such only in 3 Macc 3:17 (the word occurs otherwise only in Neh 2:6; Jdt 10:18; 2 Macc 8:12; 15:21). But Hellenistic literature uses παρουσία as a t.t. in both sacral and official contexts: It refers to both the epiphany of God or a god (Diodorus Siculus iv.3.3; Aristides *Or.* ii.30, 31; *SIG* III, 1169, 34; Josephus *Ant.* iii.5.2; iii.8.5; ix.4.3; xviii.8.6) and to the official visit of an emperor or some other high-ranking official to a provincial city (Pap. Petri II, 39e; Pap. Tebt. 48, 14; 116, 57; 121, 95; 182; 253; *SIG* 495, 85f.; 741, 21, 30; 1169, 34; *CIG* 4896, 8f.; Polybius xviii.31.4). Whether Christian technical usage arose from sacral or administrative usage cannot be answered with certainty. Christ is anticipated as savior and as Lord. Since, however, the emperor, too, could be received not just as a ruler, but also as a savior, official παρουσία terminology with its sacral elements probably stands closest to Christian usage.

2. The NT does not attest any unified conception or attitude concerning Christ's parousia.

a) The Parousia itself (apart from accompanying events such as resurrection of the dead or world judgment) is described more specifically only in Mark 13:24-27 par. Matt 24:29-31/Luke 21:25-27; 1 Thess 4:16f.; 2 Thess 1:7-10; 2:8; Rev 14:14-16; 19:11-16. The motifs treated in these texts are derived from OT and Jewish salvation expectations, which anticipate an earthly personality such as the messianic king (cf. Num 24:7, 17 LXX with *T. Jud.* 24:1; CD 7:19-21; 1QM 11:6; 4QTestim 9-13; further 2 Sam 7:12f., 16; Jer 23:5; Mic 5:1; *T. Levi* 18:2; *Pss. Sol.* 17:21; 18:5), or Yahweh himself (cf. Mic 1:3; Isa 59:20; 63:19; 64:1; 66:15), or a transcendent redeemer figure with human features (cf. *Sib. Or.* iii.49f., 286f., 652-54; 2 Esdr 7:28; 12:31f.; *2 Bar.* 29:3; 53:8-11), whose arrival, esp. in apocalyptic writing, is portrayed in vivid colors. The figure of the coming Son of man is of decisive influence (cf. Dan 7:13 LXX; *1 Enoch* 46:1; 53:6; 2 Esdr. 13:3f., 32). His advent from heaven (cf. Acts 3:20f.; Phil 3:20; 1 Thess 1:10; 2 Thess 1:7) is the heart of the NT concept of parousia.

b) Jesus himself anticipated the imminent establishment of the kingdom of God (Mark 1:15; 13:28f.; Luke 6:20-23; 11:20), but the early Church specifically anticipated his impending parousia on the basis of the Easter experience and the possession of the Spirit. This near expectation, already focusing on the exalted Jesus, is reflected by traditional formulas (1 Cor 16:22; Phil 4:5) and texts (1 Thess 4:16-17a).

Paul shares the horizon of apocalyptic hope and appropriates the corresponding formulas of Church language (1 Cor 15:23; 1 Thess 2:19; 3:13; 4:15; 5:23: παρουσία; cf. 1 Cor 1:7: "revelation"; 1:8; 3:13; 5:5; 2 Cor 1:14; Phil 1:6, 10; 2:16; 1 Thess 5:2, 4: "day" of the Lord or of Christ; 1 Cor 4:5; 11:26; 16:22; Phil 4:5: his "coming" or "nearing"; 1 Cor 1:7; 1 Thess 1:3, 10: his "expectation"). Paul does, however, emphasize the present aspects of eschatology (2 Cor 5:14–6:2) and sees as the decisive element the new life that is a reality in the present "in" Christ (5:16) and that in the future will be a reality "with" Christ (1 Thess 4:14, 17; 5:10; Phil 1:23; cf. 2 Cor 5:8).

The Synoptics testify to the problem of the delay of the parousia (Mark 13 par.; Matt 25:1-13; Luke 12:35-46; Acts 1:6-8). What according to Paul is a future condition "with Christ" is according to Eph 2:5f.; Col 1:5; 2:12f.; 3:1-4 already a present reality, though not here below, but rather in heaven above. John thinks in a radical fashion of present reality (3:19; 5:19-30). In contrast, the anticipation of the parousia is preserved (at least verbally) in the Pastorals (ἐπιφάνεια instead of παρουσία: 1 Tim 6:14; 2 Tim 4:1, 8; Titus 2:13), in the Catholic Epistles (παρουσία: Jas 5:7, 8; 2 Pet 1:16; 3:4, 12; 1 John 2:28), and in Hebrews (10:37f. with reference to Hab 2:3f. LXX; 9:28); 2 Thessalonians must practically calm down such expectation (παρουσία: 2:1, 8), whereas 1 Peter (1:5-7, 13, 20; 4:7, 17; 5:10) and Revelation (1:1, 3; 3:10f.; 10:6; 22:20) seek to revivify it and 2 Pet 3:1-13 finally must expressly defend it.

c) It is difficult to identify the absolutely essential features concerning the diverse and apocalyptically influenced views of the Parousia. In any event, the Christian anticipates an encounter with the Christ revealing himself as Lord (cf. Paul → b).

W. Radl

παροψίς, ίδος, ἡ *paropsis* (small) dish*

Actually a "small plate for a side dish" or the food thus served: Matt 23:25: τὸ ἔξωθεν . . . τῆς παροψίδος, "the outside of the cup and of the *plate*," in a portrayal of the hypocrisy fostered by the regulations for purity, hypocrisy that seeks to draw attention away from total inner impurity by means of external cleansing (23:26 v.l.). Billerbeck I, 934-36.

παρρησία, ας, ἡ *parrēsia* openness, publicness, candor; (joyous) confidence*

παρρησιάζομαι *parrēsiazomai* speak openly/ freely; gain courage*

1. Occurrences in the NT — 2. Greek and Jewish texts — 3. NT usage — a) General usage — b) The public sphere (John; Col 2:15) — c) Openness (John; Mark 8:32) — d) Bold proclamation (Acts) — e) Apostolic authority and frankness (Paul and deutero-Pauline texts) — f) Certainty, confidence (deutero-Pauline texts, Hebrews, 1 John)

Lit.: G. J. M. BARTELINK, "Quelques observations sur παρρησία dans la littérature paléo-chrétienne," *Graecitas et Latinitas Christianorum* Suppl. 3 (1970) 7-57. — BAGD s.v. — W. BEILNER, *ΠΑΡΡΗΣΙΑ. Ein neutestamentliches Wortfeld mit aktuellen Implikationen* (1979), esp. 5-49. — A.-M. DENIS, "L'apôtre Paul, prophète 'messianique' des gentils," *ETL* 33 (1957) 245-318, esp. 251-59. — L. J. ENGELS, *RAC* VII, 839-77. — H. C. HAHN, *DNTT* II, 734-37. — H. HOLSTEIN, "La Parrêsia dans le NT," *BVC* 53 (1963) 45-54. — H. JAEGER, "Παρρησία et fiducia," *Studia Patristica* (ed. K. Aland and F. L. Cross; TU 63, 1957) I, 211-39. — P. JOÜON, "Divers sens de παρρησία dans le NT," *RSR* 30 (1940) 239-42. — A. J. MALHERBE, " 'Gentle as a Nurse': The Cynic Background to 1 Thess II," *NovT* 12 (1970) 203-17. — S. B. MARROW, "*Parrhēsia* and the NT," *CBQ* 44 (1982) 431-46. — O. MICHEL, *Heb* (KEK, ⁷1975) on 3:6. — E. PETERSON, "Zur Bedeutungsgeschichte von παρρησία," *Zur Theorie des Christentums* (FS R. Seeberg, 1929) I, 283-97. — G. SCARPAT, *Parrhesia. Storia del termine e delle sue traduzioni in latino* (1964). — H. SCHLIER, *TDNT* V, 871-86. — R. SCHNACKENBURG, *LTK* VII, 110f. — SPICQ, *Notes* Suppl. 526-33. — W. STÄHLIN, "Parousia und Parrhesia," *Wahrheit und Verkündigung* (FS M. Schmaus, 1967) 229-35. — G. STRECKER, *1–3 John* (KEK, 1989) 144-46, 197f. — W. C. VAN UNNIK, "The Christian's Freedom of Speech in the NT," *BJRL* 44 (1961/62) 466-88. — *idem*, "The Semitic Background of παρρησία in the NT" (1962), *idem, Sparsa Collecta* (1980) II, 290-306. — W. S. VORSTER, "The Meaning of παρρησία in the Epistle to the Hebrews," *Neot* 5 (1971) 51-59. — For further bibliography see *TWNT* X, 1222; Beilner.

1. Παρρησία occurs 31 times in the NT, though in the Synoptics only in Mark 8:32; it occurs more frequently in John (9 times) and 1 John (4), Acts (5), Hebrews (4); Paul uses it only in 2 Cor 3:12; 7:4; Phil 1:20; Phlm 8; it occurs otherwise in Eph 3:12; 6:19; Col 2:15; 1 Tim 3:13. The vb. (9 occurrences) is found most frequently in Acts (7 times) and in 1 Thess 2:2; Eph 6:20.

2. Παρρησία refers properly to one's freedom to say anything (cf. πᾶς, ῥῆσις) and thence to straightforwardness and openness in speech. In the Greek realm this word group occurs above all among political authors. Παρρησία is virtually the equivalent of the "freedom (of speech)" of free citizens in the Attic democracy (Demosthenes *Or.* 111.3f.), which admittedly existed only among equals, and, when usurped by slaves (cf. Acts 4:29) and aliens, was quickly perceived as dangerous "audacity" (cf. Isocrates 7.20; Plato *R.* viii.557b). Among the Cynics the orig-inally aristocratic ideal of παρρησία, probably in rejection of political misuse, became a moral concept: Together with ἐλευθερία, it was viewed as the highest good of the reflective, morally secure person who lives in full "openness" toward his fellow citizens, friends, and enemies, and who both praises and severely reproves them (cf. Aristotle *EN* 1124b, 1165a; Diogenes Laertius vi.69; also Philo *Spec. Leg.* i.321, 323; *Her.* 14; see further Peterson 280-89; Malherbe 204ff.; Denis 251ff.).

In Jewish texts παρρησία (with 12 occurrences in the LXX, παρρησιάζομαι with 5) acquires new and unique significance (see esp. van Unnik): Just as God leads those delivered from bondage "in freedom/with raised heads" (ἤγαγον ὑμᾶς μετὰ παρρησίας: Lev 26:13; cf. further Jaeger 223f.), so also does the righteous person and the person accepted by God have "freedom, confidence, and joyous trust" (cf. Job 22:26: παρρησιασθήσῃ ἔναντι κυρίου ἀναβλέψας εἰς τὸν οὐρανὸν ἱλαρῶς; eschatological in Wis 5:1), while the godless person does not (Job 27:10; Prov 13:5; *T. Reu.* 4:2f.). God also manifests himself openly in both word and judgment (Pss 93:1 LXX; 11:6 LXX; concerning wisdom cf. Prov 1:20; see Schlier 876f.), brings about justice for the despised so that they can call upon him confidently, and at the same time reins in the blasphemer. Hence the παρρησία of the righteous person has its origin in God's own παρρησία (Philo *Her.* 27; →3.d-f) and shows itself to be the true boldness of the wise and of God's friends (such as Moses and Abraham, *Her.* 14, 21, and elsewhere). It is thus eschatological trust and assurance of future joy with God (cf. *1 Enoch* 61:1ff.; 62:15f.; 69:26; 2 Esdr 7:98ff.).

3. a) In about half (about 22) of the NT occurrences of both vb. and noun, they refer to publicness or openness of speech and action (→ b, c). In the other occurrences the element of candor and confidence in God predominates (→ d-f). 16 times the noun appears with λαλέω, and 6 times with λέγω. Other important associations include λόγος, ἐλπίς, εὐαγγέλιον, πίστις, and ὁμολογία (Hebrews). Those who exhibit παρρησία include Jesus (7 times), Paul in Acts (8 times), other preachers and apostles (5 times), and Christians in general (10 times; cf. further Beilner 36-41). Παρρησία is thus part of the semantic field involving proclamation and relationship to God.

Genuinely unequivocal English renderings can be formulated in only a few instances (cf. Vg. and Old Latin: *fiducia, confidentia, audere, palam, constantia,* and other expressions; see Engels 853, 856f., 859; Jaeger 222; fundamental observations in Scarpat; παρρησία is transliterated in the Peshitta and also occurs in Aramaic and Syriac as a loanword). The language of proclamation within early Christianity never consolidated the term formulaically, though the particularity of biblical παρρησία terminology does resonate unmistakably in ancient ecclesiastical literature (esp. after the end of the 2nd cent.: Bartelink 11ff.; see also Engels 860ff.; Jaeger 228ff.; Peterson 293ff.; Schlier 884f.; cf. esp. *Diog.* 11:2; *1 Clem.* 34:1ff.; *Mart. Pol.* 10:1; *Acts Thom.* 46, 81, 103; *Acts John* 22, 30; Eusebius *HE* v.1.18; 2.4).

b) According to John 7:4 Jesus' brothers try to lure him (with a general adage) into a public demonstration of his miraculous power before the world: ἐν παρρησίᾳ εἶναι, "find *public recognition*" (opposite: ἐν κρυπτῷ). They thereby fail to recognize his real significance as a witness against the world (v. 7), know nothing of the eschatological hour (v. 8), and betray their own unbelief (v. 5). Here παρρησία refers concretely to the public sphere of the Jews in Jerusalem, as also in 7:13, 26 (παρρησίᾳ λαλέω, "speak *openly*," i.e., without fear of the Jews); 11:54 (παρρησίᾳ περιπατέω, "[no longer] go about *openly*"). In 18:20 ἐγὼ παρρησίᾳ λελάληκα τῷ κόσμῳ also refers in context to Jesus' speaking *openly* (v. 20b: in the synagogue, the temple, and before all Jews), though its real opposite is found in the expression ἐν κρυπτῷ (v. 20c; cf. 7:4). All this has in mind Jesus' self-revelation before the world, not in demonstrative acts (7:4), but in open and therefore public speech, which nonetheless remains (and will remain) concealed before the world because the world has not genuinely opened itself to the word in the time of the revelation. Jesus' public openness thus judges the world.

A similar idea occurs in Col 2:15 (and only there) in view of God's acts of deliverance (vv. 13ff.): By raising Jesus from the cross (v. 14) God has announced his ultimate victory over the powers (disarming, making a public example, triumphal procession) *in public* (ἐδειγμάτισεν ἐν παρρησίᾳ). The public sphere referred to here is thus provided by the event of the cross, though also by the eschatological salvation reality of the Church baptized into Christ's death and exaltation (cf. 2:20; 3:1ff.).

c) Speaking openly and without concealment plays a role esp. in connection with central christological statements. According to John, Jesus' open self-confession is not an earthly but an eschatological possibility; only believers are able (in the time of the Spirit) genuinely to hear it: οὐκέτι ἐν παροιμίαις λαλήσω ὑμῖν, ἀλλὰ παρρησίᾳ [plainly/openly] περὶ τοῦ πατρὸς ἀπαγγελῶ ὑμῖν (16:25; cf. v. 29). This is so not because the message is incomprehensible or puzzling, but because of the listeners (cf. 11:14 with 11:11-13, 15). Although unbelief has perceived Jesus' confession, it still thinks it cannot get along without legitimation and assurances (cf. 10:24: εἰπὲ ἡμῖν παρρησίᾳ, "tell us *plainly*," with 10:25ff.). Jesus in his public ministry (→ b), the one who confesses openly his mission, is precisely in this openness not revealed, except perhaps as → κρίσις for the world and its unbelief (cf. R. Schnackenburg, *John* II [Eng. tr., 1978] 139f. on 7:4f.).

Similar misunderstanding accompanies Jesus' predictions of suffering in Mark 8:32. Whereas according to 4:33 the people were able to hear the λόγος only ἐν παραβολαῖς, the disciples now hear it *plainly/without concealment* (παρρησίᾳ τὸν λόγον ἐλάλει, 8:32), though it (still) remains incomprehensible to them (8:32b-33), since Christ's suffering becomes the heart of the salvation

proclamation only in the post-Easter situation (cf. ἤρξατο διδάσκειν in v. 31), constituting the distinction between the time of seeing and that of believing.

d) In Acts the *openness* of the mission proclamation plays a role in the sense of *fearlessness, candor,* and *joyous confidence* over against (esp. Jewish) critics and adversaries. According to 2:29 Peter takes the liberty of referring the life hope of the "patriarch" David (Ps 16:8ff.) to the resurrection of Christ as his descendant (v. 30; cf. Ps 132:11): ἐξὸν εἰπεῖν μετὰ παρρησίας, "in *[all] openness/candor*"; cf. in 4:13 the reference to the *frankness* of Peter's proclamation of Christ (vv. 8-12), almost in the sense of "rhetorical skill" (Schlier 882; cf. v. 7), and in any case not in dependence on learnedness and formal authority (v. 13b). The Spirit of the exalted Christ himself authorizes his δοῦλοι (see also Philo *Her.* 5ff.) to preach in boldness and fearlessness (4:29): μετὰ παρρησίας πάσης λαλεῖν τὸν λόγον σου (cf. 4:31, and in 28:31 the reference to Paul: κηρύσσων . . . καὶ διδάσκων . . . μετὰ πάσης παρρησίας ἀκωλύτως, "in all *candor* and unhindered"). Here, too, it is less a matter of "public openness" than of the power and fearlessness with which the exalted Christ endows his messengers.

The vb. is used similarly, most often by Paul, as a t.t. for frank or bold proclamation: According to Acts 9:27 Paul's own bold proclamation in Damascus is grounded in the Lord himself: ἐπαρρησιάσατο ἐν τῷ ὀνόματι τοῦ Ἰησοῦ; similarly v. 28; cf. in 13:46 the reference to Paul and Barnabas (παρρησιασάμενοι); 14:3 (παρρησιαζόμενοι ἐπὶ τῷ κυρίῳ, "they *proclaimed* the Lord *full of trust* in him"); 19:8 (Paul in the synagogue); 26:26 (Paul before Agrippa); 18:26 (Apollos in the synagogue).

e) The Pauline and deutero-Pauline occurrences exhibit a unique understanding. Paul always uses παρρησία with πᾶς or πολύς: According to Phil 1:20 he hopes never to become ashamed in any respect; he hopes rather that as always before, so also now Christ might be glorified in his body (that of a prisoner) ἐν πάσῃ παρρησίᾳ. After ἀποκαραδοκία and ἐλπίς (v. 20a) a subjective interpretation of παρρησία (in the sense of "confidence") is not possible here. It refers rather to the glorification of Christ in oneself. Paul's hope is that through his own body, either in missionary activity or by suffering death itself for Christ, the glorification of Christ might be furthered, glorification open in every respect, inhibited by nothing, and thus carried out for all to see (see esp. E. Lohmeyer, *Phil* [KEK] ad loc.; cf. also in 4 Macc 10:5: the παρρησία of a martyr).

In 2 Cor 3:12 as well apostolic *boldness* or *openness* is based on πεποίθησις (v. 4), trust in the service to the new covenant of glory (πολλῇ παρρησίᾳ χρώμεθα). In contrast to Moses' veiled face (vv. 13ff.), Paul presents Christ "unveiled" (3:18; 4:3; in this context cf. esp. van Unnik 292ff.) and has the freedom to dispense with all means of self-confirmation and assurance (cf. the accusations in 4:1ff.). Here, too, it is not a matter of the openness or confidence of Paul himself, but rather of the uninhibited reflection of Christ's glory in the existence of his proclaimer (4:5). Paul enters into the eschatological παρρησία of this new ministry (Denis 254).

2 Cor 7:4 is more personal: πολλή μοι παρρησία πρὸς ὑμᾶς, πολλή μοι καύχησις ὑπὲρ ὑμῶν. Paul has παρρησία in the sense of open and trusting appropriation of apostolic authority (cf. 6:11) over against a church of which he can be proud and to which he can thus also give consolation and joy (παράκλησις, χαρά, v. 4b). Phlm 8f. is also to be understood from this perspective: πολλὴ παρρησία . . . ἐπιτάσσειν is countered by διὰ τὴν ἀγάπην μᾶλλον παρακαλῶ (v. 9).

In 1 Thess 2:2 the expression ἐπαρρησιασάμεθα ἐν τῷ θεῷ ἡμῶν λαλῆσαι is to be translated: "We *gained the courage* through our God to preach the gospel to you." This refers to the eschatological παρρησία of God's emissaries (cf. 2:1-8 with 2 Cor 3:12ff.; 4:1ff.; also Wis 5:11; see Denis 256ff.; Malherbe discusses the background in Cynic philosophy, 204ff.). Cf. further Eph 6:19: *candor, boldness;* 6:20: *gain courage;* here, too, the gospel is accompanied by its own παρρησία, so that its emissary can only ask God for the ability to do justice to this power of the gospel in openness and in the public sphere.

f) Whereas in the passages discussed under → d-e it is often difficult to distinguish between παρρησία toward human beings and toward God or Christ, another series of statements does emphasize the direct reference of παρρησία to God. In Eph 3:12 παρρησία is used with προσαγωγὴ ἐν πεποίθησει ("trusting access to God" through faith in Christ), and thus likely means *ingenuousness, joyous confidence* (toward God). 1 Tim 3:13 encourages the "good" deacons to acquire πολλὴ παρρησία ἐν πίστει . . . in addition to βάθμος καλός (cf. vv. 8-12)—probably "abundant *confidence*/full *redemptive trust* in faith in Jesus Christ"; after βάθμος ("high standing" before God), παρρησία probably refers both to one's confident relationship to God (in prayer) and to candor in relation to other persons.

In Hebrews παρρησία is one of God's salvation gifts, "the real identifying feature of Christian existence" (Stählin 233; see further Vorster). As the *assurance of faith* given through Christ, together with καύχημα τῆς ἐλπίδος ("advantage [possibly: joy] of hope") it characterizes the Church (3:6). One should determinedly hold fast (κατασχῶμεν) to this παρρησία, as to the ὁμολογία (3:1; also 4:14; 10:23) and to one's initial ὑπόστασις (3:14). Heb 4:16 is concerned with the *confidence/certainty* of one's free access to God through the true high priest Christ (παρρησία in a cultic image applied to the Church's life before God: προσερχώμεθα οὖν μετὰ παρρησίας τῷ θρόνῳ τῆς χάριτος). 10:19 (also a cultic image:

παρρησία εἰς τὴν εἴσοδον τῶν ἁγίων ἐν τῷ αἵματι Ἰησοῦ) can be understood either in the sense of *authority* (cf. also Sir 25:25 B: ἐξουσία) to enter the sanctuary through Jesus' blood, or in the sense of the corresponding *confidence/certainty.* Here as in 10:35, where the warning μὴ ἀποβάλητε corresponds to the exhortation κατασχῶμεν in 3:6, the certainty of faith on the one hand, and the exhortation to preserve such confidence, are inseparably interwoven. Παρρησία thus refers to this freedom and to the immediacy of one's access to God as a sign of eschatological salvation; losing this would be irrevocable loss for oneself.

In 1 John παρρησία occurs twice in eschatological contexts. In connection with the parousia it refers in 2:28 to *confidence* in deliverance: ἵνα . . . σχῶμεν παρρησίαν καὶ μὴ αἰσχυνθῶμεν (cf. Wis 5:1; 2 Esdr 7:98ff.; → 2); similarly 4:17: ἵνα παρρησίαν ἔχωμεν ἐν τῇ ἡμέρᾳ τῆς κρίσεως; this *confidence* or *forthrightness* has its basis in God's ἀγάπη, since love excludes the presence of fear in believers as well (vv. 16-18). 3:21 (παρρησία . . . πρὸς τὸν θεόν) and 5:14 (παρρησία . . . πρὸς αὐτόν) speak of the *confidence* and *trust* a person has regarding prayers being answered (→ 2), which 3:21 grounds in "the good conscience of the righteous person" (cf. Prov 13:5; 20:9; Philo *Spec. Leg.* i.203f.; *T. Reu.* 4:2f.; see also Peterson 293), and which 5:14f. limits to requests "according to the will of God." The eschatological certainty of deliverance and of having one's prayers heard is grounded in the loving concern of God toward believers, concern experienced as the gift of the Spirit (3:21-24; 4:17-19).

H. Balz

παρρησιάζομαι   *parrēsiazomai*   speak candidly/ openly; gain courage
→ παρρησία.

πᾶς, πᾶσα, πᾶν   *pas, pasa, pan*   every; the whole; pl.: all
ἅπας, ασα, αν   *hapas*   the whole; pl.: all

1. Occurrences in the NT — 2. General meaning — 3. Cosmological-soteriological associations — 4. The cosmological-ecclesiological sense — 5. Jesus' claim to full authority

Lit.: P. BENOIT, "Body, Head, and *Pleroma* in the Epistles of Captivity," *idem, Jesus and the Gospel* (1974) 51-92. — J. G. GIBBS, *Creation and Redemption* (1971). — W. GRUNDMANN, "Matth XI.27 und die johanneischen 'Der Vater—der Sohn'-Stellen," *NTS* 12 (1965/66) 42-49. — H. HEGERMANN, *Die Vorstellung vom Schöpfungsmittler im hellenistischen Judentum und Urchristentum* (TU 82, 1961). — H. S. HWANG, *Die Verwendung des Wortes πᾶς* in den paulinischen Briefen (Diss. Erlangen, 1985). — H. LANGKAMMER, "Die Einwohnung der 'absoluten Seinsfülle' in Christus. Bemerkungen zu Kol 1,19," *BZ* 12 (1968) 258-63. — *idem,* "Literarische und theologische Einzelstücke in

1 Kor VIII.6," *NTS* 17 (1970/71) 193-97. — F. MUSSNER, *Christus, das All und die Kirche. Studien zur Theologie des Epheserbriefs* (²1968), esp. 29-39. — E. SCHWEIZER, "Kolosser 1,15-20," EKKNT (V) 1 (1969) 7-31. — W. THÜSING, *Per Christum in Deum. Studien zum Verhältnis von Christozentrik und Theozentrik in den paulinischen Hauptbriefen* (1965). — K. WENGST, *Christologische Formeln und Lieder des Urchristentums* (²1973). — For further bibliography see *TWNT* X, 1222f.

1. Πᾶς occurs 1244 times in the NT, to which can be added 34 occurrences of ἅπας.

Used adjectivally, πᾶς occurs either in the predicate position or in the attributive position. In the predicate position the art. is placed after πᾶς and frequently in the demonstrative sense yields an implicit meaning, e.g., in Mark 5:33: πᾶσα ἡ ἀλήθεια. In Matt 18:31 πᾶς is used with a subst. partc.: πάντα τὰ γενόμενα, and in Matt 5:15 with a subst. prep. phrase: πάντες οἱ ἐν τῇ οἰκίᾳ. A generic art. gives πᾶς a distributive sense, e.g., in 1 Cor 10:25: πᾶν τὸ πωλούμενον; the elative sense should also be noted, e.g., in 2 Cor 1:4: ἐπὶ πάσῃ τῇ θλίψει ἡμῶν. This meaning can often be discerned where πᾶς is used without the art., though only in connection with abstract concepts, e.g., in Matt 28:18: πᾶσα ἐξουσία. The distributive sense is usually generic (e.g., Luke 3:6) or indefinite (e.g., Titus 1:16).

Πᾶς is used subst. both with and without the art. When the art. is used demonstratively, πᾶς has an implicit meaning (e.g., Mark 14:64: οἱ πάντες, "they all"; Rom 11:32; 1 Cor 9:22); when it is used generically, πᾶς then often has a formulaic meaning: for "all things/the All (in the broadest sense)" (e.g., Rom 11:36; 1 Cor 8:6; Col 1:16f.; Heb 1:3). Οἱ πάντες κτλ. functions in a summarizing sense as an explicative appositive to a noun (e.g., Acts 19:7: ἦσαν δὲ οἱ πάντες ἄνδρες ὡσεὶ δώδεκα, "there were about twelve of them *in all*"). Without the art. subst. πᾶς has a distributive sense, indefinitely or generically in the sg. in the sense of *every person, each one, all* (e.g., Luke 14:33: πᾶς ἐξ ὑμῶν, "each one"), in the pl. in the sense of *all* (e.g., Matt 10:22: πάντες, "all people").

Adv. expressions are constructed with considerable variety: partitive gen. πάντων with superlatives (e.g., Matt 22:27: ὕστερον πάντων, "last of all"), acc. of respect (e.g., Acts 20:35: πάντα [ὑπέδειξα], "in all respects"), with several preps. (e.g., 2 Cor 2:9: εἰς πάντα, "in every respect"). The adv. πάντως must be interpreted on the basis of context (e.g., 1 Cor 5:10: πάντως οἱ πόρνοι, "immoral people *in general*").

Ἅπας is a secondary form amplified by ἅ- (indicating totality). It is used in the NT primarily when something special is to be emphasized. As a rule it occurs after a consonant. Luke shows a particular preference for it (e.g., Luke 3:21; 4:6; 8:37; Acts 2:44; 4:32).

2. The occurrence of πᾶς in the NT exhibits first a completely normal sense, or can signal a narrative style that reports a certain event with exaggeration. This includes primarily motifs of assembly such as "*all* Jerusalem" (Matt 2:3), "*all* Judea" (3:5), "*all* who were suffering" (4:24). In certain instances, however, one can discern an author's redactional intentions, e.g., Mark 1:5 ("*all* Judea went out to him and *all* the people of Jerusalem") probably implies the fulfillment of Isaiah's corresponding prediction.

3. Πᾶς often has a quite specific cosmological-soteriological sense. 1 Cor 8:6 can serve as an example: The text's parallelism attests formulaic treatment; this treatment either existed already before Paul, was composed by him for his own mission proclamation, or was constructed by him ad hoc, the apostle appropriating an older cosmological statement and giving it a soteriological orientation. This last possibility is supported esp. by the frequent appearance of purely cosmological formulations in the NT:

Paul uses a πᾶς formula (modeled on Isa 40:13) in Rom 11:36: ἐξ αὐτοῦ—δι' αὐτοῦ—εἰς αὐτὸν πάντα. This formula is related to the Stoic formula in Marcus Antoninus iv.23, but the OT conviction of faith in God's transcendence and personal nature displaces the pantheistic element. The prep. ἐν is replaced by διά. God is the cause, mediator, and ultimate goal of all things.

This conception of a cosmologically oriented pre-Pauline formula in 1 Cor 8:6 is further confirmed by the purely cosmic coloring of the first strophe of the Christ hymn in Col 1:15-18a, where both τὰ πάντα δι' αὐτοῦ and εἰς αὐτόν are applied to Christ, God's εἰκών. Heb 1:2 is also cosmologically conceived; there the OT creation-oriented manner of expression is preserved. God created the all through the Son. Instead of τὰ πάντα, αἰῶνες appears with the vb. ποιέω. Finally, one should probably interpret John 1:3, 10 cosmologically as well. In sum, whenever the NT uses διά with πάντα, Christ is praised *only* as the mediator of creation, which is probably also the case in 1 Cor 8:6. He is presented as εἷς κύριος.

In 1 Cor 8:6 Paul has conceived a formal connection between creation and salvation. The immediate occasion for this was the situation of the Church itself, which is formulaically reminded here that it separates itself from its pagan surroundings and proclaims the one God, the Father, the only cause of the all, and the ultimate goal of Christians, as well as the one Lord, the mediator of the first creation and of the Church's salvation existence. This weakens the strict distinction between creation and salvation. It is not the all itself that stands at the center of these statements. This is not a attempt at cosmogony, but a concern rather with the fact that all creatures are dependent on God (Rom 9:5) and were created through the "Lord," and that this Jesus Christ has already completed his redemptive work, and the redeemed have already been turned toward their Creator, which 2 Cor 5:17 also illustrates by referring τὰ πάντα to the καινά, the new creation that emerges from God's work of reconciliation.

One can observe a similar attempt to link creation and salvation in Col 1:15-20. Interpreters generally assume that we are dealing here with a preexisting Christ hymn. Yet only the first strophe (vv. 15-18a) appears to be pre-Pauline, assuming Pauline authorship of Colossians. This first strophe has some form of πᾶς five times. "In him," "through him," "for him," "before all things," and "all things" are cosmological predicates of the "firstborn of all creation." They govern this first strophe and characterize it as a creation hymn. In the second strophe (vv. 18b-20) πᾶς appears in v. 18b: "so that in *everything* he might be preeminent," v. 19: "for it pleased the *whole* fullness" (literally), and v. 20: "through him to reconcile *all things* to him." In v. 18 the expression ἐν πᾶσιν has the same universal salvation-historical sense as in v. 20.

V. 19 is variously interpreted. The meaning of πᾶς depends on what is identified as the subj. of the sentence. Πᾶν τὸ πλήρωμα as the subj. presents considerable difficulties, which is why many exegetes identify θεός as the subj., though here, too, one encounters difficulties. The last previous occurrence of "God" is in v. 12. If one considers, however, that the second strophe is soteriologically cast and substantively related to 1:13f., one might perhaps translate: "Because it pleased (God) to have the whole pleroma indwell." The accent would then fall on "in him" (cf. 1:16a). The pron. αὐτός, which is the subj. in v. 18b, is taken up, altered to αὐτῷ, placed before εὐδόκησεν, and carried further in v. 20 twice in the variation δι᾽ αὐτοῦ. One further element accompanies πᾶν, going back to the preceding ἐν πᾶσιν in v. 18c and continuing on in the expression τὰ πάντα in v. 20a. This shows that Paul (or the letter's author) wants to maintain Christ's cosmic *prae* from the first strophe to the second and establishes connections to this second strophe.

Just as Christ as the image of God fashioned the first creation, so also was he able (filled with this absolute creative power) through his own death and resurrection to bring about the new creation of the all as a universal reconciliation through his blood. V. 18a offers post-Pauline ecclesiology a model for the Church's cosmic dimension.

4. This idea is picked up esp. in Eph 1:22f. God is the subj. of the sentence: "And he has put *all things* under his feet and has made him the head over *all things* for the Church, which is his body, the fullness of him who fills *all in all*." The first πάντα is referred in the OT context (Ps 8:7 LXX) to the preeminence of human beings in creation. Here Christ's universal exaltation is described. According to 1 Cor 15:27 Christ's ultimate universal dominion is yet to come, whereas according to Eph 1:22f. it has already begun. The cosmic perspective is consolidated through this fundamental conception into an ecclesiological conception. Because Christ is the head over all things (v. 22a, b), he is also given as such to the Church. As the body of Christ the Church is his pleroma (v. 23). Thus cosmological statements are merged into ecclesiological statements. Into this Church flows the love of Christ that surpasses human understanding (3:18f.).

5. Πᾶς appears in statements concerning Christ's claims to full authority also in Q and in John. Q includes esp. the messianic "cry of exultation" in Matt 11:27 par. Luke 10:22: "*All things* have been delivered to me by my Father. . . ." The fourth Gospel appears not to have deviated completely in its πᾶν-formulations from the prologue (John 1:3, 10). The cosmological accent continues to play a role. John 3:31 speaks of Christ, who comes from above and "is above *all*," in contrast to human beings on earth. "Above" and "earth" are cosmological and dualistic concepts in John, though here the concern is to deny the right of any human being of this world to step forth as revealer. Only Christ has this authority.

Matt 11:27 is related to John 6:37: "*All* that the Father has given me. . . ." Both texts first speak cosmologically and then narrow the focus to the human condition. This is understandable in John's thought: Human beings belong to the world and are in need of redemption. This world, which did not recognize the Logos—and thus the human world—was created through the Logos (1:3, 10). In 13:3 the Evangelist says about Christ: "Although he knew that the Father had given *all things* into his hands . . ."—one more testimony to the fact that Jesus was conscious of his position as Son and Messiah in God's universal redemptive plan. This witness is followed in 16:30 by a statement of faith on the part of the disciples: "Now we know that you know *all things*. . . ." John's statements concerning Christ's full authoritative power culminate in 17:2: "You have given him power over *all* flesh, to give eternal life to *all* whom you have given him." The one who has become flesh exercises power over all flesh. The ultimate glory is revealed that Christ already had as the preexistent Logos, through whom all things were created. Though John proclaims Christ's position of power in various ways, he always does so in such a way that Christ maintains his cosmic *prae*. This does, of course, exhibit a strong soteriological orientation.

After the resurrection the Gospel of John attests no other emphatic πᾶν-formulations, though Thomas does confess: "My Lord and my God." This confession of Christ is singular in the NT. It expresses what John's Gospel has anticipated in its entirety. Here again one can recall the formulation in 1 Cor 8:6: "one God and one Lord." Jesus' claim to authority in Matt 28:18 is similar to the Johannine claim, and serves in Matthew to inaugurate the worldwide mission activity.   *H. Langkammer*

πάσχα, τό *pascha* Passover celebration, Passover meal; paschal lamb*

1. Occurrences and meaning — 2. The Gospels — 3. Hebrews and Paul

Lit.: BILLERBECK, IV, 41-76. — A. DAUER, *Die Passionsgeschichte im Johannesevangelium* (SANT 30, 1972). — R. LE DÉAUT, *La Nuit Pascale* (AnBib 22, 1963). — R. FENEBERG, *Christliche Passafeier und Abendmahl* (SANT 27, 1971). — N. FÜGLISTER, *Die Heilsbedeutung des Pascha* (SANT 8, 1963). — H. HAAG, *Vom alten zum neuen Pascha* (SBS 49, 1971). — J. HALBE, "Passa-Massot im deuteronomistischen Festkalender," *ZAW* 87 (1975) 147-68. — W. HUBER, *Passa und Ostern* (BZNW 35, 1969). — J. JEREMIAS, *The Eucharistic Words of Jesus* ([2]1966). — *idem, TDNT* V, 896-904. — H. PATSCH, *Abendmahl und historischer Jesus* (1972). — B. SCHALLER, *DNTT* I, 632-34. — R. SCHNACKENBURG, *John* III (Eng. tr., 1982). — B. N. WAMBACQ, "Pesaḥ—Maṣṣôt," *Bib* 62 (1981) 499-518. — M. WEISE, "Passionswoche und Epiphaniewoche im Johannesevangelium," *KD* 12 (1966) 48-62. — For further bibliography see *DNTT* I, 634f.; *TWNT* X, 1223f.

1. This indeclinable noun derived from Aram. *pasḥā'* (for Heb. *pesaḥ*) occurs 29 times in the NT, with few exceptions (Acts 12:4; 1 Cor 5:7; Heb 11:28) only in the Gospels. It refers to the first of the great pilgrimage festivals (Exod 23:15) for which Israel assembled each year in Jerusalem (Luke 2:41). From the time of the reforms of Josiah (2 Kgs 23:21-23) a year-old male animal without defect, usually a lamb or kid (Exod 12:5), was ritually slain in the temple on the afternoon of the fourteenth of Nisan (March/April) and then after sundown, i.e., as the fifteenth of Nisan began, eaten in gatherings in private houses. Because of its connection with the Feast of Unleavened Bread (→ ἄζυμος, Nisan 15-21), a connection familiar since OT times (Exodus 12; Numbers 9; Deuteronomy 16; cf. *Jub.* 49:22), the Passover was considered the beginning of the festival week (see Mark 14:12; Luke 22:7); τὸ πάσχα can refer to the entire seven-day festival (Luke 22:1; Acts 12:4). Mark 14:1 mentions the two festivals separately. Ἡ ἑορτὴ τοῦ πάσχα, "the feast of the *Passover*" (Luke 2:41; John 13:1; cf. 2:23; 6:4), is a fixed expression, occasionally abbreviated to → ἑορτή (2) (John 4:45 and elsewhere), though always referring to the festival week. Absolute πάσχα refers to the nocturnal *Passover celebration* (Matt 26:18; Heb 11:28), the *meal* of which must be prepared (Mark 14:16; Matt 26:19; Luke 22:8, 13). The use of πάσχα for the *paschal lamb* is specifically biblical, where it occurs in connection with the vbs. *slaughter* (Mark 14:12a; Luke 22:7; 1 Cor 5:7—from *šāḥaṭ hapesaḥ,* Exod 12:21 and elsewhere) and "eat" (Mark 14:12b, 14; Matt 26:17; Luke 22:11, 15; John 18:28—from *'ākal hapesaḥ,* 2 Chr 30:18 and elsewhere).

The ritual of the Passover Seder is described in the Mishnah (tractate *Pesaḥim*); in its basic features this can be presupposed for the NT era. Theologically the meal had a dual orientation: Though it directed its attention to an event in the past, it was nonetheless colored by eschatological anticipation. It was based on the successful deliverance from bondage in Egypt; the household's father was obligated to tell the story of the exodus in connection with Deut 26:5-11 and to interpret the various parts of the meal (lamb, unleavened bread, bitter herbs) from the perspective of this occurrence (cf. *m. Pesaḥ.* 10:4f.). This past historical action on God's part had significance for the present (10:5), though it also represented a model for future redemption (*Mek. Exod.* 12:42). The expectation that the Messiah would come during the night of Passover (*Tg. Exod.* 12:42) is probably pre-Christian.

2. Mark's redactional dating of Jesus' death sentence two days before Passover and the Feast of Unleavened Bread is characterized by historicizing intentions (14:1). Mark has no theological interest in the Passover; the legend of seeking the room (vv. 12-16), with its fourfold mention of the Passover, is pre-Markan, and has thus merely been appropriated by Mark. (The mention of the Passover Hallel in v. 26 is also a pre-Markan relic.) If, as is probable, Jesus' final meal was indeed a Passover meal, then the Passover motif can be explained on the basis of the tradition itself.

Matthew avoids (unlike Mark) any mention of the sacrifice of the Passover lamb (26:17), and otherwise refers only to the Passover motif itself: In 26:2 it is immediately followed by the reference to the crucifixion of the Son of man, and in 26:18 it is expanded by the reference to the proximity of the καιρός. Matthew's theological interest is not in the Passover itself, but rather in the obedient group of disciples, all of whom Jesus sends (vv. 18f.).

Luke basically follows Mark's framework, though he does delete the dating (22:1, 7) and has Jesus immediately issue the order, and then identifies Peter and John as the two emissaries (v. 8) who carry out the instructions (vv. 11, 13). Luke, too, has no particular interest in the Passover motif as such. His account of the institution of the eucharist in 22:15-20 is in material unique to him, which is intended not etiologically (as a cult legend of an early Christian Passover celebration), but rather in the final analysis in a historicizing-catechetical sense. Among the NT accounts of the institution of the eucharist, only this one speaks explicitly of the Passover lamb (v. 15). One can no longer determine philologically whether Luke or his source thought of Jesus' wish as an unfulfillable or fulfilled wish.

In John we can differentiate various layers of tradition. In addition to general chronological data (2:13, 23; 6:4; cf. 4:45) and elements corresponding to the Synoptic tradition (11:55a: death decree; 13:1: tradition of the meal), there is also a very specific Passover chronology: The anointing in Bethany occurs six days before the feast of Passover (12:1), i.e., on the tenth of Nisan, the day on which the Passover lambs were selected (Exod 12:3). The interrogation and handing over of Jesus are set on the day of preparation for

Passover, i.e., on the fourteenth of Nisan (19:14). This explains the Jews' ritual reservations before Pilate (18:28) and the Passover amnesty (v. 39). The dating of Jesus' death (*contra* the Synoptics) on the fourteenth of Nisan (19:31, 42) derives from a pre-Johannine chronology. This chronology is first interpreted as an actual typology (Jesus as the Passover lamb) probably only in the latest layer of tradition, in 19:36, when allusion is made to Exod 12:46 or Num 9:12 (*contra* MT and LXX!), i.e., to the Passover lamb whose bones may not be broken (though a reference to the suffering righteous person [Ps 34:21] is also possible). That is, the Passover chronology is older than the Passover typology.

3. The author of Hebrews reflects on the history of the Passover sacrifice when he traces it back to Moses' faith (11:28). Paul employs the traditional image of Christ as the sacrificial lamb in his parenesis (1 Cor 5:7), using the indicative-imperative scheme: The Passover lamb typology (only here is it unequivocal) grounds Paul's exhortation to the Corinthian church to commit itself to its status as "new dough," "unleavened" (v. 7a), whereupon the cleansing of immorality (vv. 1f.) must follow (v. 8). Here Paul presupposes an acquaintance with Jewish Passover customs and with the Passover typology, but not necessarily a Christian Passover feast.

H. Patsch

πάσχω *paschō* experience, undergo; suffer (death), endure*

1. Occurrences, basic meaning — 2. General meanings — 3. The suffering of Christians — 4. Christ's suffering

Lit.: → θλίβω; πάθημα; also: W. J. BENNETT, JR., " 'The Son of Man Must . . . ,' " *NovT* 17 (1975) 113-29. — L. BOREHAM, "The Semantic Development of πάσχω," *Glotta* 49 (1971) 231-44. — D. DORMEYER, *Der Sinn des Leidens Jesu. Historisch-kritische und textpragmatische Analysen zur Markuspassion* (SBS 96, 1979). — B. GÄRTNER, *DNTT* III, 719-25. — P. HOFFMANN, "Mk 8,31. Zur Herkunft und markinischen Rezeption einer alten Überlieferung," FS Schmid (1973) 170-204. — K. T. KLEINKNECHT, *Der leidende Gerechtfertigte. Die alttestamentlich-jüdische Tradition vom "leidenden Gerechten" und ihre Rezeption bei Paulus* (WUNT II/13, ²1988). — E. LARSSON, *Christus als Vorbild. Eine Untersuchung zu den paulinischen Tauf- und Eikontexten* (ASNU 23, 1962). — D. MEYER, "Πολλὰ παθεῖν," *ZNW* 55 (1964) 132. — J. R. MICHAELIS, "Eschatology in I Peter III.17," *NTS* 13 (1966/67) 394-401. — W. MICHAELIS, *TDNT* V, 904-26. — W. REBELL, "Das Leidensverständnis bei Paulus und Ignatius von Antiochien," *NTS* 32 (1986) 458-65. — L. RUPPERT, *Jesus als der leidende Gerechte? Der Weg Jesu im Lichte eines alt- und zwischentestamentlichen Motivs* (SBS 59, 1972) 44-71. — G. STRECKER, "Die Leidens- und Auferstehungsvoraussagen im Markusevangelium," *ZTK* 64 (1967) 16-39. — A. STROBEL, "Macht Leiden von der Sünde frei? Zur Problematik von 1Petr 4,1f," *TZ* 19 (1963) 412-25. — For further bibliography see *DNTT* III, 725f.; *TWNT* X, 1224f.

1. The act. vb. πάσχω with the pass. basic meaning *undergo, experience, suffer* occurs 42 times in the NT (esp. in the Synoptics, 1 Peter, and Hebrews), about 7 of those in the general sense (→ 2) and 35 times (like → πάθημα) referring to the suffering of Christians (→ 3) or of Christ (→ 4). Πάσχω occurs 21 times in the LXX, but 150 times in Philo. Hebrew does not attest the juxtaposition expressed by πάσχω and δράω and similar terms in the sense of "suffer/undergo" on the one hand, and "do" on the other, but rather uses more concrete expressions for "suffer."

2. The general meaning occurs in Gal 3:4: "Did you *experience* such things [signs of reception of the Spirit] in vain?" It lies behind Luke 13:2 even though this is a concrete reference to a negative experience of the kind Acts 28:5 presents explicitly: "He *experienced* [suffered] no harm." In Matt 17:15 the adv. κακῶς characterizes πάσχω, which is actually conceived in a neutral sense (v.l. ἔχει), so that the translation is: *be badly off*." In 1 Cor 12:26, with no more specific characterization, πάσχω means *suffer* (in contrast to "be honored"). In Mark 5:26 and Matt 27:19 the expression πολλὰ πάσχω means "*go through/endure* much."

3. In the earliest NT occurrence, 1 Thess 2:14, πάσχω refers to the suffering of Christians in persecution. According to Phil 1:29 it is a grace "*to suffer* . . . for him [Christ]," i.e., to be subjected to persecution for the sake of Christ (v. 28), since this points toward the coming glory (cf. Rom 8:17) and to the special bond with the crucified Christ (cf. Phil 3:10, → πάθημα). Only in 2 Cor 1:6 does Paul refer to his own afflictions with πάσχω (cf. συμπάσχομεν in Rom 8:17).

According to Acts 9:16 Christ will show Paul, who until now has persecuted "all who call upon his name" (v. 14), "how much he must *suffer* for the sake of my name." These sufferings are unavoidably (δεῖ; cf. 14:22) bound to his new task and will come from persecutions (cf. 5:41; 15:26; 21:13). This hardly asserts (as does 2 Corinthians 4) that Paul must proclaim the gospel precisely through suffering (Michaelis 919; objections from E. Haenchen, *Acts* [Eng. tr., 1971] ad loc.). Πάσχω also refers to the sufferings of persecution in 2 Tim 1:12; 2 Thess 1:5; Rev 2:10.

In 1 Pet 2:19, 20 πάσχω means *endure* with reference to unjust treatment of slaves, though beyond this also to the analogous lot of all Christians, as shown by the following general reference to Christ's own exemplary suffering (vv. 21f.). The blessing in 3:14 (cf. v. 13 [κακόω] and Matt 5:11) and the note in 3:17 seek to strengthen Christians, who because of their faith must apparently endure disadvantages and reproach. This encouragement is again underscored by reference to Christ's own example, who "*suffered* as a righteous person for the unrighteous," thereby opening their way to God (v. 18, → 4).

In 1 Pet 4:1, along with the reference to the attitude with which Christ took suffering upon himself (→ 4), an enigmatic, gnomic-sounding statement is made: "For whoever *suffers* in the flesh has ceased from sin" (or: "is free from sin"). The subj. of this sentence can hardly be Christ (Strobel 420; objections from N. Brox, *1 Pet* [EKKNT] ad loc. [bibliography]). Nor is πάσχω used here fig. in reference to baptism in accord with Rom 6:3, 7 (so Michaelis 922f.). Most likely the meaning is: Whoever suffers in following Jesus announces thereby his break from sin. Beyond this, the close association between "flesh" and "sin" during this period may have influenced the formulation of this statement (cf. Rom 7:18, 24; 6:7; 8:13; L. Goppelt, *1 Pet* [KEK] ad loc.).

Jewish thought also contributes to the presentation in 1 Pet 4:12-19, where the suffering of Christians— which resembles punishment (vv. 15-19)—is viewed in connection with the beginning of God's judgment, which unbelievers will certainly not be able to escape (cf. Goppelt 312ff., and 299-304 concerning the motif of joy at suffering). According to 5:10, what the readers *must suffer* (aor. παθόντας referring to the present) is only "a little" (for only a little while; cf. 1:6) compared to "eternal glory."

4. In Jesus' first prediction of the Passion (Mark 8:31 par. Matt 16:21/Luke 9:22; cf. Luke 17:25), πολλὰ πάσχω means "*endure* many things." The content of this suffering—which stands in Mark and Luke as a collective term —is characterized more specifically by "rejection" and "be killed" (cf. Mark 5:26; Matt 27:19). The expression is probably influenced by the motif of the afflictions of the righteous person from Ps 34:20 (see the context), though also by the way in which the afflictions of Christians were spoken of (cf. 1 Thess 2:14-16). It is questionable whether this Passion prediction originally referred (cf. Luke 17:25) in a general fashion to Jesus' rejection and persecution during his ministry (Hoffmann 181f.). In the present context (esp. in Matthew) it predicts the sufferings associated with the trial itself (arrest, trial, crucifixion; cf. Josephus *Ant.* xiii.268: πολλὰ πάθων . . . ἀπέθανεν, "after he had endured many things . . . he died"). Mark 9:12 explicitly refers the announcement ἵνα πολλὰ πάθη to Scripture; as the addition "and be treated with contempt" (→ ἐξουδενέω) suggests, this might be thinking beyond Pss 34:20; 188:22 to Ps 88:39 LXX (ἐξουδένωσας . . . τὸν χριστόν σου) and of other statements concerning the suffering righteous person (also Isaiah 53? cf. R. Pesch, *Mark* [HTKNT] II ad loc.). The parallel Matt 17:12 views the necessary suffering of the Son of man in connection with statements about Elijah. Considering the other uses of πάσχω one cannot deduce

from the vb. alone any particular theological connotation or "uniqueness of the passion of Jesus" (Michaelis 915f.).

Without further specification, πάσχω refers in Luke 22:15; 24:16, 46; Acts 1:3; 3:18; 17:3 to the events preceding Christ's resurrection or glorification. Even if this refers essentially to Jesus' death, πάσχω here is not simply the equivalent of "die" (*contra* Michaelis 913), but rather characterizes the end of Jesus' life as the disgraceful fate of rejection. It is disputed whether this manner of speaking (esp. Luke 22:15) derives from a tradition independent of Mark 8:31 (and perhaps even older?). The active form παθεῖν emphasizes the active element in Jesus' dying or resurrection as little as do → εἰσελθεῖν or ἀναστῆναι (→ ἀνάστασις 5).

In 1 Peter statements using πάσχω for Christ's suffering are closely associated with statements concerning the disgraceful suffering of Christians. In 2:21, 23 πάσχω characterizes Jesus' Passion as exemplary suffering: "He *suffered* for you, leaving an example for you"; "*when he suffered,* he did not threaten" (the v.l. ἀπέθανεν, as also in 3:18, is probably inserted here from the Pauline letters; cf. Brox ad loc.). The words "for you" (2:21), apparently already present in the text, are not given any particular attention (→ ὑπέρ). In 3:18 the probably genuine reading ἔπαθεν refers at least in the present context to the exemplary acceptance of suffering (cf. v. 17) in connection with the death of atonement (cf. 2:24). That the author here is not just thinking of death can also be seen from 4:1a ("*suffered* in his flesh"; cf. 3:18: "put to death in the flesh"), since there the reference is to the attitude characterizing Jesus' exemplary behavior (2:22f.; cf. Phil 2:6ff.; on 4:1b → 3).

In Hebrews πάσχω is the only vb. used of Jesus' death. In 2:18 πάσχω characterizes his death from the perspective of a test. 5:8 interprets this test (patient perseverance in the face of apparent abandonment by God) in the wordplay ἔμαθεν—ἔπαθεν, which appropriates a general adage from experience: πάθει—μάθος: "He learned obedience from what he *suffered*" (cf. Phil 2:8). Heb 9:26 portrays Jesus' dying as a sacrificial act (cf. προσφέρω, vv. 9, 14, 25, 28). Πάσχω is also closely associated with the idea of sacrifice in 13:12 (cf. v. 11): "He also *suffered* [a sacrificial death] outside the gate in order to sanctify the people through his own blood." What follows ("bearing his reproach") shows that πάσχω here refers to his voluntary death, accepted in obedience and successfully endured, which, in addition to its sacrificial character serving sanctification (the extirpation of sins), also possessed the character of disgrace, and is thus presented to the readers as an encouraging example.   J. Kremer

Πάταρα, ων *Patara* Patara*

A port city on the southwest coast of Lycia that Paul

visited on his last journey from Corinth to Jerusalem (via Kos and Rhodes; Acts 21:1). W. Bieder, *BHH* 1400; A. van den Born, *BL* 1324; E. A. Judge, *ISBE* III, 687.

πατάσσω *patassō* strike, hit, slay*

This vb. occurs 10 times in the NT, 3 of those in OT citations (Acts 7:24 [Exod 2:12]; Mark 14:27 par. Matt 26:31 [Zech 13:7]). It occurs over 400 times in the LXX, usually translating the hiphil of Heb. *nākâ*. Acts 12:7: "*strike* on the side"; Matt 26:51 par. Luke 22:50: *strike out at* someone/*vehemently strike* someone (with a sword); used absolutely in Luke 22:49: *begin striking (at random)* (ἐν μαχαίρῃ πατάσσω); Acts 7:24: *strike down/slay* (of Moses: πατάξας τὸν Αἰγύπτιον); Mark 14:27 par. Matt 26:31, of God: πατάξω τὸν ποιμένα (cf. Zech 13:7; *Barn.* 5:12). Fig. of divine chastising or punitive *striking, smiting* (cf., e.g., Gen 8:21; Exod 7:20): Acts 12:23: an angel *smites* Herod (Agrippa I) to death; Rev 11:6: the two witnesses (Moses and Elijah) "*smite* the earth with every plague" (πατάσσω τὴν γῆν ἐν πάσῃ πληγῇ; cf. 2 Macc 9:5; Exod 7:19f.); Rev 19:15: Christ the victorious king and judge (v. 13: ὁ λόγος τοῦ θεοῦ) *smites* the nations with the sharp sword issuing from his mouth (cf. 1:16; Isa 11:4; 49:2; Ps 2:9; Wis 18:15ff.; *Pss. Sol.* 17:24, 35; 2 Esdr 13:9; *1 Enoch* 62:2): ἵνα ἐν αὐτῇ πατάξῃ τὰ ἔθνη. H. Seesemann, *TDNT* V, 939f.

πατέω *pateō* tread on, trample*

This vb. occurs 5 times in the NT, 4 of those (as frequently in the LXX: cf. Joel 4:13; Isa 63:2f., 18; Zech 12:3) speaking of God's activity of punishing and judging: *Trample:* pass. in Luke 21:24: Ἰερουσαλὴμ ἔσται πατουμένη ὑπὸ ἐθνῶν (cf. Zech 12:3; Dan 8:10, 13); similarly Rev 11:2: τὴν πόλιν τὴν ἁγίαν πατήσουσιν (*sc.* τὰ ἔθνη; cf. esp. Dan 8:10ff.; Isa 63:18), possibly with the particular sense of "desecrate"; pass. in Rev 14:20; 19:15: "*tread* the wine press" (πατέω τὴν ληνόν), a metaphor for God's wrathful judgment (cf. Joel 4:13; Isa 63:1ff.; → ληνός).

Only Luke 10:19 uses the vb. in the neutral or positive sense of the authority Jesus gives the disciples "to *tread* on serpents and scorpions" (πατέω ἐπάνω), i.e., to be protected from satanic assault (as a sign of the time of salvation; cf. v. 19b; Ps 90:13 LXX; *T. Levi* 18:12). BAGD s.v.; G. Bertram, *TDNT* V, 940-43.

πατήρ, τρός, ὁ *patēr* father

1. Occurrences in the NT — 2. Background — 3. Jesus' relationship to the Father — 4. OT and Judaism — 5. Diaspora Judaism, esp. Philo and Josephus — 6. Liturgical and doxological tradition in Judaism and early Christianity — 7. Jesus' use of "Father" as an address

and his statements concerning the "Father" — 8. Human fathers in the NT

Lit.: BILLERBECK I, 392-96. — P. A. H. DE BOER, *Fatherhood and Motherhood in Israelite and Judean Piety* (1974). — G. BORNKAMM, H. G. GADAMER, W. LEMKE, and L. PERLITT, *Das Vaterbild in Mythos und Geschichte* (1976). — DALMAN, *The Words of Jesus* (1909) 184-94. — *idem, Die Worte Jesu* (²1930) 296-304. — W. GRUNDMANN, "Matth XI.27 und die johanneischen 'Der Vater—Der Sohn'-Stellen," *NTS* 12 (1965/66) 42-49. — R. GYLLENBERG, *Gott der Vater im AT und in der Predigt Jesu* (StOr 1, 1926) 3-140. — E. HAENCHEN, " 'Der Vater, der mich gesandt hat,' " Haenchen I, 68-77. — O. HOFIUS, *DNTT* I, 615-21. — E. HÜBNER, "Credo in Deum patrem?" *EvT* 23 (1963) 646-72. — J. JEREMIAS, *The Prayers of Jesus* (SBT 6, 1967), esp. 108-15. — J. JEREMIAS and W. JANNASCH, *RGG* VI, 1235-38. — G. KITTEL, *Die Religionsgeschichte und das Urchristentum* (1932) 92-95. — T. W. MANSON, *The Teaching of Jesus* (²1935) 89-115. — W. MARCHEL, *Abba, Père! La prière du Christ et des Chrétiens* (AnBib 19, 1963). — G. MENSCHING, H. J. KRAUS, and J. JEREMIAS, *RGG* VI, 1232-35. — MOORE, *Judaism* II, 201-11. — K. H. RENGSTORF, *Mann und Frau im Urchristentum* (1954) 32-46. — *idem,* "Vaterschaft im NT," *Familienrechtsreform* (ed. H. A. Dombois and F. K. Schumann; Glaube und Forschung 8, 1955) 34-41. — F. ROSENZWEIG, *The Star of Redemption* (1972) 199f., 317ff., 349ff. — A. SCHLATTER, "Wie sprach Josephus von Gott?" *idem, Kleinere Schriften zu Flavius Josephus* (1970) 65-142, esp. 74-76. — G. SCHRENK and G. QUELL, *TDNT* V, 945-1022. — M. SMITH, *Jesus the Magician* (1978) 132. — W. STAERK, *Altjüdische liturgische Gebete* (KIT 58, ²1930). — G. VERMES, *Jesus the Jew* (1973) 78ff. — H. W. WOLFF, *Was sagt die Bibel von Vater und Mutter?* (Gespräche 23, ³1966). — D. ZELLER, "God as Father in the Proclamation and in the Prayer of Jesus," *Standing before God* (FS J. M. Oesterreicher, 1981) 117-29. — For further bibliography → ἀββά; see also *DNTT* I, 621; *TWNT* X, 1225.

1. Πατήρ occurs 414 times in the NT, referring more than 250 times to God and 150 times to men. The greatest number of occurrences are in John (136), then Matthew (63), Mark (19), Luke (56), Acts (35), Paul (40), 1 John (14), and Hebrews (9). Jesus himself speaks of God as Father 3 times in Mark, 4 in Q, 4 in L, 31 in Matthew (not counting material from Q and Mark), and 100 in John (see Hofius 619f.).

2. Both the concept and standing of the father are part of the patriarchal structure of antiquity and are oriented toward the idea of household, family, and dominion. The father is the protector, nourisher, and helper. From the time of Homer the biological father, forefather, and ancestor of a race are called πατήρ (*Il.* vi.209), though both the teacher in one's philosophical education (Epictetus *Diss.* iii.22.81ff.) and the mystagogue within a cult (Apuleius *Met.* xi.25.7) can be called "father." As a metaphor πατήρ is used of the king and of God. A king in northern Syria (825 B.C.) boasts that he has cared for his tenants like a father, a mother, and a brother (M. Lidzbarski, *Ephemeris für Semitische Epigraphik* III [1915] 237f.; cf. *ANET* 653f.). The address in prayer, e.g., in a Sumerian wisdom text, acquires significance in this context: "My God, you who are my father who begot me" (*ANET* 590). Sirach calls upon the Lord, "Father and Ruler" of

his life (Sir 23:1-4; 51:10 [Hebrew text]), though this God himself can also be addressed as ἀπάτωρ (*Apoc. Abr.* 17:9). The Qumran community praises God: "Yet you are a father to all who know your truth; you will rejoice over them like a mother over her infant and will feed all your works as a nurse feeds her charge at the bosom" (1QH 9:35f.). Aram. *'abbā'* as a form of address for one's father replaced the older Hebrew and Aramaic address *'āḇî*, "my father" (*b. Ber.* 40a par.; *b. Sanh.* 70b; cf. *b. Ta'an.* 23b; → ἀββά).

3. The mystery of Jesus points to a fixed father-son relationship based on seeing and hearing, receiving and giving (= offering). This relationship resonates in rhythmic sayings such as Matt 11:27; 24:36. The Father who sees into what is secret or is himself hidden (6:4, 6) demands the same behavior from humans. He is "the Lord of heaven and earth" and controls both the concealing and revealing of his will (11:25; see further → 7).

4. The connection between "God" and "father" is biblically bound by election, covenant, and the promise of salvation to Israel (cf. Deut 32:6; see also E. Jenni, *THAT* I, 15). Through a historical process God has become Father through his love, care, and instruction (Jer 31:9). Promises to the line of David point toward the law of adoption (2 Sam 7:14: "I will be his father, and he will be my son"; Ps 2:7: "You are my son, today I have begotten you"). The OT does, however, employ such God-Father statements only with some reservation. Israel did not really appropriate such mythic talk of a conceiving and procreating God: Even in the messianic adoption formula the statement "today I have begotten you" reflects protocol in the sense of divine right and expresses a privilege, a relationship of protection, and a commission. The metaphor of God as "father" shows its meaning in Ps 103:13 ("as a father pities his sons") and Prov 3:12 ("for Yahweh reproves him whom he loves"): God's mercy and instruction are directed to the person standing in misery and temptation: Such an experience is part of the legitimizing process of sonship. The biblical Father-son relationship (Deut 14:1: "You are the children of Yahweh, your God") is always qualified by accompanying prerequisites and is to be kept in obedience and faithfulness.

Carrying Ps 22:11 further, the supplicant in 1QH 9:35f. confesses: "My father has renounced me, and my mother has abandoned me to you. Yet you are a father to all who know your truth. You will rejoice over them like a mother over her infant." Although such knowledge of God as "father" is by no means rare in Judaism thereafter, its origin is probably liturgical (Tob 13:4; Sir 51:10 [Hebrew text]; *Jub.* 1:24f., 28; 19:29). The future revelation will bring about a holy spirit, purity and obedience, and a new relationship with God as Father (*Jub.* 1:25). *T. Jud.* 24 heralds a new period of salvation with a new pouring out of the Spirit and a new kingship (messianic fragments). A new priesthood will come (*T. Levi* 18:6). It should be noted, however, that the text of the *T. 12 Patr.* was reworked later.

In Hellenistic Judaism the relationship with God as Father of the individual righteous person emerges more strongly (e.g., Sir 23:4 [Greek text]: "Lord, my father"). In the struggle between the worldly person and the righteous person the latter calls himself God's servant or child and boasts that God is his Father (Wis 2:13-20). One can consider this the continuation of biblical

motifs in Diaspora Judaism. Tob 13:4 boasts quite self-evidently: "For he is our Lord and God, he is our Father forever."

In accord with this, rabbinic material reaching back perhaps to the time of Jesus attests the address in prayer: "Our Father, our King" (*'ahaḇâ rabbâ;* New Year's liturgy: *'aḇînû malkēnû;* cf. Staerk 6, 27ff.): The address of God as Father now occupies the first position!

In a further sense the beginning of the Hekhalot literature and the continued influence of OT theophanies in apocalyptic writings (God's throne and temple, God's appearance, the tradition of angels, and the heavenly cult) are of significance: the ascent and descent of angels and human beings, the transformation of the body, and the superiority of the ascending person over the angels (*1 Enoch* 14:5; 71:1-17; *T. Levi* 3). The Hekhalot literature is a continuation of the bond with the Torah and Israel and thus belongs within the framework of the piety of Judaism. Its beginnings extend back into the period before the destruction of the temple (A.D. 70).

It must be asked whether Jesus is best understood from the perspective of wisdom teaching (or prophecy) or from the fundamental motifs of the Hekhalot literature. In the latter case Jesus' Father-son relationship with God is unique (cf. John 20:17); "Father" is not just a metaphor, but, like kingship and will or decree, is part of revelation itself. The Son brought it down from heaven. This constitutes its difference from OT and rabbinic thought (→ 3, 7).

5. The Hellenistic synagogue carries on the LXX view of God with strong accentuation from the Palestinian tradition. 1 Chr 29:16 LXX can be compared with Josephus *Ant.* vii.380: David praises God as the "Father and source of the universe, as creator of things human and divine, with which he had adorned himself, and as the protector and guardian of the Hebrew race and of its prosperity and of the kingdom which he had given him." A priestly doxological tradition follows closely the model of the LXX, though it employs its own language, which includes new Greek terms. Philo, too, speaks of the "Father of all and creator of the all" (*Op.* 89; *Decal.* 64; *Spec. Leg.* i.96; ii.6; *Ebr.* 81). The common element here is a Jewish Diaspora theology with Palestinian accentuation; Josephus as a politician inquires concerning the origin of power, whereas Philo as a philosopher inquires concerning the origin of the world. In this context the Father can be understood as the creator and caretaker (Josephus: God is addressed as πατήρ, δημιουργός, προστάτης, and κηδεμών; Philo: God is πατήρ and ποιητής).

In Philo this Father motif can also take on particularity: Certain persons such as Moses are "sons of God" (*Vit. Mos.* ii.288); Josephus, on the other hand, says only that the patriarchs were "creatures of God himself" (*Ant.* i.106). According to Josephus those who are "beloved of God" have a special course of life. Philo, however, adds his own philosophical interpretation: Creation has its own source (πηγή and αἰτία) in God through the formative power (δύναμις ποιητική) and through agreement with him through the Logos (ὁ θεῖος λόγος). The doctrine of the creation of the invisible world becomes decisive here (*Op.* 19f.). Platonic and Stoic elements constitute the background in Philo. Above all, God pervades the world as "Creator, Father, and Preserver" of mankind (cf. Epictetus *Diss.* i.9.7; Cleanthes' hymn to Zeus).

The question arises whether such elements found their way into the Diaspora Jewish tradition at other points as well. Significant here is the frequent doxological occurrence of the address "God (δέσποτα) of the fathers" (1 Esdr 4:60: δέσποτα τῶν πατέρων), either abbreviated as in Philo or emphasized as in Josephus. Statements concerning the Lord or Creator exercise a certain primacy over those concerning the Father. The development of Jewish liturgy stands in the foreground, and only secondarily the philosophical influence in Philonic Halakah. Nonetheless, the address in prayer, "Father," asserted itself in Judaism alongside statements concerning the Father (3 Macc 6:3, 8; Wis 14:3; *Apocryphon of Ezekiel* frag. 3), which probably reflect an abbreviated liturgical tradition. In Hellenistic Judaism statements concerning the Father penetrated into cosmic relationships, and even into the realm of heaven and earth, though in the OT and the Palestinian tradition this concept already contains the seeds of such development. The care and help Israel experiences as a people stands next to the guidance of the fathers and the concerns of the individual pious person.

6. The fathers and the God of the fathers, the promises to the fathers, and the blessing of the fathers all constitute the background of the NT message and give it legitimacy. Eph 3:14f. occupies a central position: "I bow my knees before the *Father,* from whom every family has its name. . . ." This statement is liturgical and presupposes a Palestinian, not a Greek cosmos: the angelic world as the upper family, and the human world as the lower family are both encompassed by God as Father and Lord, as the creator of an order encompassing heaven and earth. The Father is the master of the house (Billerbeck III, 594; see also → πατριά 2). As the creator he is also the redeemer.

A related concept here is abbreviated from the Palestinian tradition (Num 16:22; 27:16): "*Father* of all spirits," encompassing both heaven and earth (Heb 12:9). Here, too, it is a matter of obedience to the Father, who alone creates life. The attribute "*Father* of lights" recalls the thought forms of the Hellenistic synagogue (Jas 1:17): With him there is neither variation nor darkening. The older message of 1 John 1:5 is rendered here in a younger form (cf. the expressions: "light of the all" and "Father of light" in *Apoc. Mos.* 36:3). The heritage of synagogal liturgy manifests itself here as well.

With the founding of the Church we encounter a new liturgical and didactic form (prayer, blessing, confession). Paul speaks of "God the Father," "God our Father," "God the Father of our Lord Jesus Christ" (cf. Rom 1:7; 1 Cor 1:3; 2 Cor 1:2; Gal 1:3, and elsewhere). This doctrinal form is bipartite where confession of God as Father is expanded to include Jesus' lordship. In the fashion of the Jewish Diaspora (1 Chr 29:16 LXX), formulas of omnipotence can be added doxologically to this bipartite confession of God and Lord (as in 1 Cor 8:6). In the style of the Shema (Deut 6:4 LXX) the unity of God the Father is emphasized, and the confession of Christ's lordship then appears as an expansion and explication, not as a limitation of the confession of God as Father. This recalls Exod 4:16, where Moses is to speak for Aaron in God's stead, or the ascending Moses, who lingers in conversation with God (Exod 24:15-18). This also calls to mind the Johannine connection between the Father-Son relationship and the authorization of the messenger by the person sending him (John 17:1-3).

By no means, however, does designation of God as Father occur in every confessional statement (cf. 1 Tim 2:5). Emphasis on God's unity and on the one mediator between God and mankind, the man Christ Jesus, exhibits Jewish Christian features following OT tradition. Confession of the one Kyrios and the one God and Father, with its accompanying formula of omnipotence, appears even richer (Eph 4:5-6). Here, too, the rule applies: expansion and supplement, but not limitation. The reservation of Revelation over against such Father statements is interesting (2:28; 3:5, 21; 14:1): Although the address in prayer "Father" does not occur, the addresses prompting reverence ὁ δεσπότης (6:10) and κύριε ὁ θεὸς ὁ παντοκράτωρ (15:3), shortened to κύριε (15:4), all point to the analogy with Judaism.

The formulaic material in Matthew's Gospel deserves special attention. The Lord's Prayer begins with the address: "Our *Father* in heaven" (Matt 6:9). This might, like the synagogal prayers of the period, have been formulated originally in Hebrew or Aramaic. The address reaches back into Jesus' own prayers and prayer instruction (cf. Mark 11:25; Luke 11:13). According to the baptism command (Matt 28:19; *Did.* 7:2) the name of the *Father,* the Son, and the Holy Spirit is pronounced over the person baptized: The name invokes surrender to the dominion of the Father, who reveals himself in creation, as the full authority of Jesus, and in the gift of the Holy Spirit. The formula in Matthew is triadic, intended as an expansion and supplement, not as a limitation (cf. 2 Cor 13:13 as a wish for blessing). The same Gospel speaks in a summary fashion of the Father as the creator and elector of Israel, of Jesus as the crucified, resurrected, and exalted one, and of the Spirit of the *Father* speaking in the disciples (Matt 10:20). The address in prayer "*Father* in heaven" and the corresponding statement about God ("your Father in heaven," 6:14) carry the entire message of the Gospel of Matthew.

In prayer and instruction "Father" becomes an important fundamental designation that does, however, encompass the entire gospel. One calls upon God as Father, remembering that he is also the judge exhorting one to embrace holy conduct in life (1 Pet 1:17). The address in prayer carries the entire message, including the apostle's discourse of admonition. The development in prayer and in the Spirit of early Christianity prompts a resurgence also in the "Father" address and "Father" statements, though one should also note the analogy to Jewish prayer custom; it should not be developed into an antithesis, as it usually has been.

7. Aram. *'abbā'* (Mark 14:36; Rom 8:15; Gal 4:6) is a prayer invocation and renders the familiar address for God used by Jesus and Aramaic-speaking Christians (cf. in addition to the examples in → 1 also *Tg. Isa* 8:14; see Hofius 614; → ἀββά). It means something like "dear father." The Hebrew address is by no means entirely displaced (Mark 15:34, e.g., takes up Ps 22:2 in the Aramaic vernacular, and Matt 27:46 takes it up in the original Hebrew version).

The term of address *'abbā'* does not stand in tension with the address "ruler of the world" (*b. Ta'an.* 23b), but rather finds its parallel in Jesus' own cry of rejoicing (Matt 11:25; Luke 10:21), where "Father" is supplemented and expanded by "Lord" (*'adōnāy*). This is an exceptional, indeed exclusive Father-Son relationship. The closest parallel is in Galilean hasidic Judaism (Vermes). The derivation of Jesus' mystery is traced back to a vision and a heavenly voice (Mark 1:11; 9:7) and finds its parallel in tradition in *b. Ber.* 7a (the address "Hananiah, my son" during a vision).

Jesus' identification by the vision and voice (Matt 3:17 par.) is of fundamental importance for him. His prayer, his obedience, his miraculous gifts, and his separation from persons and parties are all based on this primal event. It makes him the elect and beloved, the servant of God, and the Son of God. The combination of Spirit and voice is of legal provenance (two witnesses); the words directed to him recall Ps 2:7 and Isa 42:1. John's Gospel makes this primal event into a witness of John the Baptist, analogous to the understanding of the messianic witness: He is himself taken into the process of seeing and hearing that is actually meant for Jesus of Nazareth (1:32f.)

Jesus himself knows of both heavenly and earthly things because he alone has ascended into heaven and descended again (John 3:12f.). He thus has both direct and indirect legitimacy. The fundamental earthly events become a heavenly process. Jesus acquires his legitimacy from heaven and stands in an immediate relationship to heaven itself (1:51). With this we are standing in the realm of Hekhalot apocalyptic thought (→ 4).

This does not remove Jesus from his full existence as a human being; he remains rather in an exemplary fashion the teacher of his disciples and the preacher before the people. There is a difference between his address of God as Father and his instruction concerning God's fatherhood, but no antithesis: Jesus receives and then passes on to his disciples (Matt 6:9: "our *Father*" as a term of

alliance, in John 20:17 as differentiation). Later, Heb 2:11ff. describes him as a liturgical prayer leader before his "brethren." Yet precisely this context amplifies the difference between the prayer leader, who stands like a father over against his children, and the congregation. This differentiation is carried through in the father-teacher relationship.

Again, according to John's Gospel, Jesus calls on the "Father" (cf. Matt 11:25; Luke 10:21; John 11:41; 12:27f.; 17:1ff.; 17:25: "righteous *Father*"). In the prayer of thanksgiving in 11:41 Jesus is among those supplicants whose prayers the Father regularly answers and who thus have authority from the Father; this is based on an Aramaic source. In Jesus' statements about the Father the contexts of 4:34 and 5:19 probably also point back to an older source: The Son is only able to act in full obedience with the Father; thus does the Father love him and give him authority. Today an apocalyptic Halakah describing the heavenly and earthly world in the interaction between the Son and the Father permeates the entire Gospel of John. The Father confirms the Son's total obedience and legitimizes him: The authority he claims is none other than the very manner in which the Father himself operates. Whereas Philo thinks metaphysically (→ 5), John wants to be understood metaethically (3:35; 5:20). The fourth Gospel is strongly polemical and counters the Jewish claim to be Abraham's seed, or indeed sons of God, with the antithesis: "You are of your *father* the devil, and your will is to do your *father's* desires" (8:44: Jews hostile to Jesus are excluded from the Father's world, as their actions prove). The statements about God as Father in the Johannine writings stand within a framework of metaethical dualism, though in the sense of the OT they far transcend that dualism (1 John 1:5; John 8:12).

8. The title "father" can be applied to the priest (Judg 17:10; 18:19), the prophet (2 Kgs 6:21; 13:14), and the teacher (Matt 23:8f. forbids the address "rabbi" and the title "father"). In Acts 7:2 the members of the Sanhedrin and in 22:1 the people are called "brethren and *fathers*." Israel's ancestors are specifically mentioned (such as Abraham, Isaac, Jacob— even David as king) when Jews and Christians are permitted to invoke them (Matt 3:9; John 8:39; Rom 4:1ff.; 9:5). Both Jewish and early Christian traditions, of course, want to invoke the fathers, and each knows of common affiliation under the auspices of common origin. Reverence before one's teacher is considered as important as reverence before heaven itself (*m. 'Abot* 4:12).

Paul reminds the Corinthians: "For though you have countless guides in Christ, you do not have many *fathers*. For I became your father in Christ Jesus through the gospel" (1 Cor 4:15). The rabbi becomes a "father" of believers as a teacher, the mystagogue through initiation into the mysteries, and Paul by proclaiming the gospel. In his mission he seeks people that they might be begotten and born (Gal 4:19; Phlm 10). The missionary himself becomes a "father": When "Paul" calls Timothy and Titus "legitimate child" (1 Tim 1:2; Titus 1:4), this also refers to the transmission of Pauline doctrine and engagement in mission activity. 1 Pet 5:13 shows just how much "Peter" also thinks of faithful transmission of doctrine and engagement in the churches (Mark is "my son"). The son walks in the father's footsteps and represents him before the congregation. In the face of human ambition, contentiousness, and trust in authority, Matt 23:8-10 remains an urgent warning. The honor given a father should be reserved for God alone. As a metaphor this also applies to the apostle.

The castigation for misuse of corban and the attempt to expose one's parents leads into a different context (Mark 7:9ff. par. Matt 15:3ff.). Here in Jesus' words the misuse of Pharisaic tradition becomes a reason to hold up God's commandment and reject the tradition of the elders altogether. Exod 20:12 is fundamental here, a commandment strengthened by the threat of judgment in 21:17. The background of this story can only be the institution of a new kind of obedience. Love for God must be so strong that it fulfills to the very end the commandment to honor one's parents (Mark 12:28-34 par. Matt 22:35-40). In a reverse fashion, this love can require that in discipleship the bonds to father and mother, sons and daughters recede (Matt 10:37; Luke 14:26). The crisis into which Jesus places a person can break the bonds to one's parents. Thus does Jesus heighten the seriousness of the decision before us.

In Colossians and Ephesians the household codes are structured in three parts: Wife and husband, children and fathers, slave and master are all exhorted as classes to take seriously their various tasks and duties toward the others. What is appropriate and required is illuminated and deepened by baptism and by the new human existence (Col 3:18–4:1; Eph 5:22–6:9). The foundation established in creation (husbands and wives) includes parental relationships (Eph 6:1). The commandment to honor one's parents (Exod 20:12/Eph 6:2) is supplemented and deepened by the corresponding obligations of fathers not to provoke their children, but to bring them up with discipline and exhortation. A new standard emerges: that which is "pleasing" in the Lord, "just and fair" (Col 3:20; 4:1).

The three-part appeal to children, fathers, and young men in 1 John 2:12ff. is to be understood differently. The "children" are the entire readership (cf. 2:1, 18); the term is a didactic stylistic device. But *fathers* and "young men" are different age groups. The message of forgiveness and of the special knowledge of the Father applies to all members of the congregation. The "old ones"—the

fathers—have recognized him who is from the beginning, which is stated twice. The "young men," as bearers of the word and of the Spirit, have overcome the evil one. This appeal is not part of a household code, since it does not address women.

If we review the whole, our attention repeatedly returns to the parable of the prodigal son (Luke 15:11-32). The merciful father who divides his property and attends to his sons, but who receives his lost son with rejoicing, leads into the whole wealth of earthly and heavenly fathership.

O. Michel

Πάτμος, ου *Patmos* Patmos*

According to Rev 1:9 the seer John received his calling and commission on the "Lord's day" (v. 10) on the small, sparsely populated, and rocky island of Patmos, situated among the southern Sporades in the Aegean Sea off the Ionian coast, about 70 km. west of Miletus: ἐγενόμην ἐν τῇ νήσῳ τῇ καλουμένῃ Πάτμῳ. According to his own statement, John came to Patmos when Christians in Asia Minor were being persecuted (probably in Ephesus *ca.* A.D. 95 under Domitian; cf. v. 9a), "on account of God's word and Jesus' testimony" (v. 9b). There, separated from his churches, he composed the seven open letters (vv. 10f.) and his entire revelation (v. 19). Later tradition says that John was an exile or prisoner on Patmos (Clement of Alexandria *Quis Div. Salv.* 42; Eusebius *HE* iii.18.1ff.; 23.6; Tertullian *De Praescriptione Haereticorum* 36; according to Pliny *HN* 12.13 Patmos was a place of exile). Exile, however, is historically as improbable as, e.g., the choice of Patmos as a mission region. H. Kraft (*Rev* [HNT] on 1:9) suggests a private time for reception of revelation far from other people (42). BAGD s.v.; B. Reicke, *BHH* 1400f. (bibliography); A. van den Born, *BL* 1325; E. Meyer, *KP* IV, 549; A. A. Bell, "The Date of John's Apocalypse: The Evidence of Some Roman Historians Reconsidered," *NTS* 25 (1978/79) 93-102 (Revelation composed after Nero's death in A.D. 68-69?).

πατϱιά, ᾶς, ἡ *patria* people, nation; division of a nation*

Lit.: BAGD s.v. — H. Schlier, *Eph* ([6]1968) 167f. — G. Schrenk, *TDNT* V, 1015-19.

1. Πατϱιά occurs 3 times in the NT (Luke 2:4; Acts 3:25; Eph 3:15). The noun is derived from πατήϱ as a designation of origin from the same father or ancestor.

2. According to the report in Luke 2:1-5 concerning the census of Augustus, all Jewish inhabitants of Palestine reported for the counting not in their actual place of residence, but rather in the place of origin of their family line. According to v. 4 Joseph, because of his Davidic

lineage, went "to the city from which his progenitor came" (G. Schneider, *Luke* [ÖTK] I ad loc.).

In Peter's discourse in Acts 3:25, composed by Luke, the expression πᾶσαι αἱ πατριαὶ τῆς γῆς, "all the *races* of the earth," occurs as a scriptural quotation which does not, however, appear in the LXX. Luke probably took Gen 22:18; 26:4 and changed ἔθνη (LXX) into πατριαί, since he could not let his t.t. for Gentiles (ἔθνη) remain in a speech to Jews.

In the "wordplay conceived in Greek" (Schlier 168) in Eph 3:14f. (πρὸς τὸν πατέρα ἐξ οὗ πᾶσα πατριά, "to the Father from whom every *people . . .*") the meaning of πατριά must probably be inferred from the LXX. There, however, πατριά exhibits several meanings (race, kinship group; nation, cf. Schrenk 1016), and the statement does not find any key in rabbinic literature. A narrowed rendering such as that in the Vg. (πατριά = *paternitas*) misses the real meaning. Schrenk (1017f.) is correct when in this context he explicates πατριά with "people," since Eph 3:15 is referring to Israel and the "Gentiles," who are now united in one Church.   U. Hutter

πατριάρχης, ου, ὁ *patriarchēs* father of a nation, ancestor, patriarch*

This noun occurs 4 times in the NT. Acts 7:8: Jacob's twelve sons as the δώδεκα πατριάρχαι (cf. Gen 29:31ff.; 35:16ff.); 7:9: οἱ πατριάρχαι (cf. Gen 37:11); Heb 7:4, of Abraham: Ἀβραάμ . . . ὁ πατριάρχης (cf. Gen 14:20); Acts 2:29: a special honorific title for David: περὶ τοῦ πατριάρχου Δαυίδ, whose tomb "is with us to this day" (cf. Josephus *Ant.* vii.392ff.).

πατρικός, 3 *patrikos* handed down from one's father(s), paternal*

Gal 1:14: αἱ πατρικαί μου παραδόσεις, "my *paternal* traditions" (thinking of Paul's parents) or (more likely) "the traditions *of my ancestors*" (cf. Mark 7:5; Acts 22:3; 23:6; Phil 3:5), among whom Paul's own father (μου) is included as a mediator. G. Schrenk, *TDNT* V, 1021f.

πατρίς, ίδος, ἡ *patris* fatherland; hometown*

Lit.: BAGD s.v. — H. BRAUN, "Das himmlische Vaterland bei Philo und im Hebräerbrief," FS Stählin 319-27. — E. GRÄSSER, "Jesus in Nazareth (Mk 6,1-6a)," *idem, Text und Situation* (1973) 13-49. — F. LAUB, *Bekenntnis und Auslegung* (1980) 257ff. — R. PESCH, *Mark* (HTKNT, ³1980) I, 316. — R. L. STURCH, "The 'ΠΑΤΡΙΣ' of Jesus," *JTS* 28 (1977) 94-96. — For further bibliography see Grässer 27, 37.

1. Πατρίς occurs 8 times in the NT, 6 of those in the pericope Mark 6:1ff. par. Luke 4:16ff./Matt 13:54ff.; cf. John 4:44; further Heb 11:14.

2. Mark 6:1 par. Matt 13:54 mentions Jesus' home-

town without naming the place (unlike Luke 4:16: εἰς Ναζαρά), presumably in anticipation of Jesus' "regulative statement" (cf. Pesch 320) concerning the prophet's fate in Mark 6:4 par. Matt 13:57. This biographical apophthegm is an expression of general experience also attested in Jewish, Greek, and Hellenistic writings (documentation in Pesch 320). R. Bultmann (*History* 31 n.2) refers to an Arabic proverb: "The piper has no friends (of his art) in his own town." Matt 13:54-58 makes lesser, Luke 4:16-30 greater changes in the Markan original. *Gos. Thom.* 31 and Pap. Oxy. no. 1, ll. 31-36 (logion 6) offer extracanonical parallels to the proverb (texts in Hennecke /Schneemelcher I, 109). These are secondary expansions on the model of Luke 4:23f. (G. Schneider, *Luke* [ÖTK] I ad loc.).

John 4:44 takes the Synoptic statement from oral tradition, probably not from the Synoptic tradition itself since his statement is formulated too independently. Πατρίς refers to Jesus' *native country* here, again doubtlessly Galilee (cf. 1:45f.; 6:42; 7:3, 41, 52). Jesus goes there in order to avoid clashes with the Pharisees (cf. 4:1-4).

Heb 11:14 stands within the summary of vv. 3-12 (the first seven witnesses). Πατρίς is used in the sense of *fatherland/homeland*. The author of Hebrews wants to show that the attainment of the "heavenly πατρίς" anticipated by the fathers (cf. v. 16) is first made accessible only in Christ's own redemptive activity (cf. Laub 261).   U. Hutter

Πατροβᾶς, ᾶ *Patrobas* Patrobas*

A Christian in Rome (a shortened form of Πατρόβιος; cf. BDF §125.1) who in Rom 16:14 receives a greeting from Paul. Patrobas occurs elsewhere as the name of freedmen; see R. Knippenberg, *BHH* 1402.

πατρολῴας, ου, ὁ *patrolǭas* one who murders his father*

1 Tim 1:9, in a catalog of vices with → μητρολῴας.

πατροπαράδοτος, 2 *patroparadotos* received from the father/forefathers*

1 Pet 1:18: ἡ ματαία ὑμῶν ἀναστροφὴ πατροπαράδοτος, "your futile ways *inherited from your fathers/after the manner of your [pagan] fathers*" (cf. the antithesis in vv. 14, 17: God as Father; 4:3; Eph 4:17).

πατρῷος, 3 *patrǭos* paternal, inherited from one's father/forefathers*

3 occurrences in the NT, all in Acts: 22:3: ὁ πατρῷος νόμος, "the law *of our fathers/given to our fathers*" (cf.

3 Macc 1:23; 4 Macc 16:16; further → πατρικός in Gal 1:14); 24:14: ὁ πατρῷος θεός, "the God *of our fathers*" (cf. 4 Macc 12:17; Josephus *Ant.* ix.256); 28:17: τὰ ἔθη τὰ πατρῷα, "the laws/customs *of our fathers*." The LXX uses πατρῷος in the same sense as πάτριος, which Josephus esp. favors. Perhaps Luke uses πατρῷος (always in the context of Paul's self-defense) in order to emphasize the close relationship between the Pauline proclamation and the "fathers," whereas πάτριος would have emphasized more strongly the connection with Israel as a people; cf. G. Schrenk, *TDNT* V, 1014.

Παῦλος, ου *Paulos* Paul

1. Occurrences in the NT — 2. The Pauline material — a) Biographical material — b) Theological material — 3. Paul in Acts — 4. Paul in the deutero-Pauline writings (Colossians, Ephesians, 2 Thessalonians) — 5. Paul in the Pastorals and in 2 Peter — 6. Sergius Paulus

Lit.: S. Ben-Chorin, *Paulus. Der Völkerapostel in jüdischer Sicht* (1970). — C. K. Barrett, "Paulus als Missionar und Theologe," *ZTK* 86 (1989) 18-32. — J. Becker, *Paulus. Der Apostel der Völker* (1989). — J. C. Beker, *Paul the Apostle: The Triumph of God in Life and Thought* (1980). — O. Betz, "Paulus als Pharisäer nach dem Gesetz," *Treue zur Thora* (FS G. Harder, 1977) 54-64. — G. Bornkamm, *RGG* V, 166-90. — *idem, Paul,* (1971). — F. F. Bruce, *Paul: Apostle of the Heart Set Free (= Paul: Apostle of the Free Spirit)* (1977). — Bultmann, *Theology* I, 185-352. — C. Burchard, *Der dreizehnte Zeuge* (1970). — H. J. Cadbury, *The Book of Acts in History* (1955) 69ff. — L. Cerfaux, *The Spiritual Journey of St. Paul* (1968). — C. Dietzfelbinger, *Die Berufung des Paulus als Ursprung seiner Theologie* (WMANT 58, 1985). — J. D. G. Dunn, "The New Perspective on Paul," *idem, Jesus, Paul, and the Law* (1990) 183-214. — G. Eichholz, *Die Theologie des Paulus im Umriß* (²1977). — W. Elliger, *Paulus in Griechenland. Philippi, Thessaloniki, Athen, Korinth* (SBS 92/93, 1978). — J. A. Fitzmyer, *Paul and His Theology* (1989). — V. P. Furnish, "Pauline Studies," *The NT and Its Modern Interpreters* (ed. E. J. Epp and G. W. MacRae; 1989) 321-50. — G. A. Harrer, "Saul Who Also Is Called Paul," *HTR* 33 (1940) 19-34. — M. Hengel, *The Pre-Christian Paul* (1991). — H. Hübner, "Paulusforschung seit 1945," *ANRW* II, 25/4 (1987) 2649-2840. — N. Hyldahl, *Die paulinische Chronologie* (Acta theologica Danica 19, 1986). — J. Jervell, *Luke and the People of God* (1972). — *idem,* "Paulus in der Apostelgeschichte und in der Geschichte des Urchristentums," *NTS* 32 (1986) 378-92. — R. Jewett, *A Chronology of Paul's Life* (1979). — K. Kertelge, ed., *Paulus in den neutestamentlichen Spätschriften* (1981). — O. Kuss, *Paulus* (1971) = Kuss III. — A. Lindemann, *Paulus im ältesten Christentum* (BHT 58, 1979). — K. Löning, *Die Saulustradition in der Apostelgeschichte* (NTAbh 9, 1973). — G. Lohfink, *The Conversion of St. Paul: Narrative and History in Acts* (1976). — G. Luedemann, *Opposition to Paul in Jewish Christianity* (1989). — *idem, Paul, Apostle to the Gentiles: Studies in Chronology* (1984). — D. P. Moessner, "Paul in Acts: Preacher of Eschatological Repentance to Israel," *NTS* 34 (1988) 96-104. — J. Munck, *Paul and the Salvation of Mankind* (1959).

— F. Mussner, *Petrus und Paulus—Pole der Einheit* (1976). — W.-H. Ollrog, *Paulus und seine Mitarbeiter* (WMANT 50, 1979). — W. Radl, *Paulus und Jesus im lukanischen Doppelwerk* (1975). — W. Rebell, *Gehorsam und Unabhängigkeit. Eine sozialpsychologische Studie zu Paulus* (1986). — K. H. Rengstorf and U. Luck, ed., *Das Paulusbild in der neueren deutschen Forschung* (WdF 24, ²1969). — B. Rigaux, *The Letters of St. Paul: Modern Studies* (1968). — J. Roloff, "Die Paulusdarstellung des Lukas," *EvT* 39 (1979) 510-31. — E. P. Sanders, *Paul and Palestinian Judaism: A Comparison of Patterns of Religion* (1977). — *idem, Paul, the Law, and the Jewish People* (1983). — K. H. Schelkle, *Paulus. Leben—Briefe—Theologie* (1981). — H.-M. Schenke, "Das Weiterwirken des Paulus und die Pflege seines Erbes durch die Paulus-Schule," *NTS* 21 (1974/75) 505-18. — G. Schille, *Das älteste Paulus-Bild* (1980). — H. Schlier, *Grundzüge einer paulinischen Theologie* (1978). — J. Schmid, *LTK* VIII, 216-20. — W. Schmithals, *Die Briefe des Paulus in ihrer ursprünglichen Form* (1984). — G. Schneider, *Acts* (HTKNT, 1982) II, 41-45. — H. J. Schoeps, *Paul: The Theology of the Apostle in the Light of Jewish Religious History* (1961). — J. N. Sevenster, *BHH* 1402-9. — W. Stegemann, "War der Apostel Paulus ein römischer Bürger?" *ZNW* 78 (1987) 200-229. — V. Stolle, *Der Zeuge als Angeklagter. Untersuchungen zum Paulusbild des Lukas* (BWANT 102, 1973). — A. Suhl, *Paulus und seine Briefe* (SNT 11, 1975). — W. C. van Unnik, *Tarsus or Jerusalem: The City of Paul's Youth* (1962) = *idem, Sparsa Collecta* I (1973) 259-320; cf. also 321-27. — U. Wilckens, "Lukas und Paulus unter dem Aspekt dialektisch-theologisch beeinflußter Exegese," *idem, Rechtfertigung als Freiheit* (1974) 171-202.

1. The name of the apostle Paul (Παῦλος is probably his Roman *cognomen:* so Harrer) occurs 157 times in the NT. 127 of these are in Acts 13–28, and 11 in the post-Pauline letters (2 in Ephesians, 8 in Colossians, 2 in 2 Thessalonians, 3 in the Pastorals, and 1 in 2 Peter). Paul mentions his own name 19 times in his letters (once in Romans, 8 times in 1 Corinthians, twice each in 2 Corinthians and Galatians, once in Philippians, twice in 1 Thessalonians, and 3 times in Philemon), with 7 of these at the beginning of the letters (Παῦλος . . . ἀπόστολος: Rom 1:1; 1 Cor 1:1; 2 Cor 1:1; Gal 1:1 [in post-Pauline letters: Eph 1:1; Col 1:1; 1 Tim 1:1; 2 Tim 1:1; Titus 1:1]; without ἀπόστολος in Phil 1:1; 1 Thess 1:1; Phlm 1 [in a post-Pauline letter: 2 Thess 1:1]). Emphatic ἐγὼ Παῦλος draws attention either to the apostle's authority in paraclesis (2 Cor 10:1; Phlm 9), or to the uniqueness of his proclamation (Gal 5:2; cf. Eph 3:1; Col 1:23), and appears further in organizational notices (1 Thess 2:18) and in conclusions to letters (1 Cor 16:21; Phlm 19; cf. Col 4:18; 2 Thess 3:17). Paul also mentions his own name 6 times (with other names) in the dispute with the Corinthian groups (1 Cor 1:12, 13 bis; 3:4, 5, 22). In contrast, his Jewish name → Σαῦλος is used only in Acts (15 times), as is also the case (only in the voc.) with its Hebrew form Σαούλ (9 times). Acts 13:7 mentions the Roman proconsul Sergius Paulus (→ 6).

2. a) Our sources for Paul's life are first and foremost those letters recognized as genuine (Romans, 1–2 Corinthians, Galatians, Philippians, 1 Thessalonians, Philemon), even though they offer but little biographical information. Concerning the period before his calling, we learn that Paul was a (Diaspora) Jew, a Pharisee from the tribe of Benjamin (Phil 3:5; cf. Rom 11:1; 2 Cor 11:22; Gal 2:15) who was esp. zealous regarding his ancestral traditions (Gal 1:14) and who therefore vehemently persecuted (esp. in Damascus? cf. Gal 1:17) the (Hellenistic) Christian churches (Gal 1:13, 23; Phil 3:6; 1 Cor 15:9), during which he was able to employ the synagogal punishment of expulsion and scourging. Gal 1:14 reveals something of the religious significance of Paul's parental home (→ πατρικός). Paul probably acquired the Roman *cognomen* Παῦλος (on his Jewish name *Šā'ûl* → Σαῦλος), by which he always refers to himself, already at his circumcision.

Paul experienced his call through an appearance (probably in Damascus, cf. Gal 1:17) of the resurrected Christ (Gal 1:12, 15; 1 Cor 9:1; 15:8; Phil 3:7ff.). This call immediately made him the apostle to the Gentiles (Gal 1:11-17). With this Paul completely discarded his previous self-understanding (Phil 3:7-9; Gal 1:15-17). After his initial activity in Nabatean Arabia (Gal 1:17) he returned to Damascus (1:17), from which, however, he had to flee (2 Cor 11:32), whereupon he came—after an intervening two-week stay with Peter in Jerusalem (Gal 1:18f.: "after three years")—into the region of Syria and Cilicia (Gal 1:21) with its center at Antioch (cf. 2:11; Acts 11:26; and the list of fellow workers in 13:1), probably for about fourteen years (Gal 2:1). Through his missionary success and through the energetic defense of his "gospel to the uncircumcised" at the Jerusalem "apostolic council" (Gal 2:7; cf. Acts 15) and on the occasion of what is known as the "incident at Antioch" with Peter (Gal 2:11ff.), Paul soon became the decisive representative of the early Christian (Antiochian) mission to the Gentiles. A portrayal of the Pauline mission activity solely on the basis of the Pauline corpus is still a desideratum of scholarship (Luedemann).

Paul emerged first as an itinerant apostle (→ ἀπόστολος 2, 5). In cities in Asia Minor and Greece he founded (initially probably quite small: cf. 1 Cor 1:14, 16) churches that met in the homes of individual Christians (cf. 1 Cor 16:15, 19; Rom 16:5). He communicated actively with his churches, received inquiries and news (1 Cor 1:11; 7:1; 16:17) and support (Phil 2:25, 30; 4:10ff.). The number of his fellow workers increased rapidly (cf. the prescripts and greetings of the letters). Paul did, however, also experience serious opposition, particularly from Jewish congregations and the civil authorities (1 Cor 4:9ff.; 15:32; 16:9; 2 Cor 6:4ff.; 11:23ff.). Moreover, he was subjected to numerous other dangers and privations (1 Cor 4:11ff.; 2 Cor 1:8f.; 4:7ff.). He wrote the letter to the Philippians from prison (1:7, 13, 20ff.), probably in Ephesus (cf. 1 Cor 4:9; 15:32). At the same time he carried on what were in part quite vehement struggles in many churches against competing itinerant missionaries (2 Corinthians 10–13; Phil 3:2ff.) and against the distortion of "his" gospel (Gal 1:6ff.). He usually oversaw the churches he founded only for a short period, then left them as independent entities under the care of his fellow workers. He did, however, remain in constant contact with them through his letters and occasional visits, though he avoided mission activity in churches founded by others (Rom 15:20).

During his main period of activity in Greece he vigorously solicited a collection of money for Jerusalem (Gal 2:10; 1 Cor 16:1; 2 Cor 8:1ff.; Rom 15:25ff.), which was probably intended as a sign of ecumenical unity between the Jewish and Gentile Christian churches. At the end of his own activity he was planning to expand his missionary work as far as Spain (Rom 15:23) and thus wrote (from Corinth) the letter to the Romans in order to gain the support of the Roman church (which he did not found) for this mission. But before that mission he wanted to deliver the "collection" to Jerusalem. This concludes the Pauline reports of his own activity. Paul was possibly executed in Rome (*1 Clem.* 5:5-7; *Acts of Paul* 10). Soon, however, the veneration of Paul and legends surrounding him developed, as shown by the deutero-Pauline writings and the traditions used in Acts. The customary Pauline chronology is taken largely from the portrayal in Acts and relies esp. on the mention of Gallio in Acts 18:12f.

b) Through his restless mission work Paul decisively furthered the early Christian mission to the Gentiles—which was under way before him—and brought about the rapid expansion of early Christianity beyond the boundaries of Palestine and Asia Minor. For him the transition of the world toward eschatological salvation took place in the Christ-event (cf. 2 Cor 5:16ff.). This salvation he regarded as no longer bound to the law and righteousness according to the law (Rom 10:4), applying, rather, to all who in faith in Christ (Rom 10:9ff.) allow themselves to be taken into God's grace, i.e., into liberation from the power of sin and death (Rom 5:12ff.), and into the new life before God in the Spirit (Gal 5:1ff.; Rom 8:1ff.) as a guarantee of the eschaton (Rom 8:23). The community of believers is the true eschatological people of God (Gal 6:16; Rom 4:16), which came into being with Christ out of Israel, though it will eventually include Israel as well (Rom 11:11ff., 25ff.).

Despite all this, Paul did not put forth any self-enclosed theological structure in his letters, but rather responded to concrete inquiries, uncertainties, and attacks. His concluding letter to the Romans, though, must be considered Paul's missionary and theological "testament" (Bornkamm, *Paul* 88ff.; *idem,* "The Letter to the Romans as Paul's Last Will and Testament," *The Romans Debate* [ed. K. P. Donfried; [2]1991] 16-28). For further discussion of Paul's theology see Bultmann, Eichholz, Kuss, Schlier; see also → ἁμαρτία 4.a; δικαιοσύνη 4; δικαιόω 3, 4; ἐλπίς 3; νόμος 4.b; πίστις 6; πνεῦμα 3.b; σάρξ 3; χάρις.

3. Along with many valuable individual bits of tradition, the portrayal of Paul in Acts also exhibits amplification and redistribution of emphasis in the direction of a legend of Paul. What we see is the image of the post-Pauline period, clearly influenced also by Luke's theological interests (see esp. Burchard, Kertelge, Radl, Roloff, Wilckens). Only Acts reports that Paul came from Tarsus in Cilicia (9:11; 21:39; 22:3; cf. 9:30; 11:25), that he was a Roman citizen by birth (22:28), that (after a very brief period in Tarsus: so van Unnik) he lived in Jerusalem, where he had relatives (23:16ff.), that he was a pupil of Rabbi Gamaliel (I) (22:3), and that he learned the trade of tentmaking (18:3). As a young man he witnessed the stoning of Stephen (7:58). In the middle of his journey to Damascus to persecute the Christians there (9:1f.) he experienced conversion through a vision of Christ (9:3ff.; 22:6ff.; 26:12ff.) and subsequently received the Spirit duːing baptism there (9:17f.). After his flight from Damascus (9:25; cf. 2 Cor 11:32) Barnabas allegedly introduced him to the apostles (9:26f.); he then journeyed back to Tarsus by way of Caesarea (9:30).

The portrayal of the Pauline mission in Acts displays elements of Luke's amplification. From the very beginning Paul emerges from the group of fellow workers (Acts 13:1) and occupies the more important role over against Barnabas already during the "first missionary journey" (cf. 13:13: οἱ περὶ Παῦλον; see also 15:36). Before the "second missionary journey" he leaves Barnabas (v. 39) and continues his mission independently in the cities of Asia Minor and finally (16:9ff.) of Macedonia and Greece, with new fellow workers of his own choosing (15:40; 16:1ff.), guided by the Holy Spirit (16:6-8) and in faithful observance of the Jerusalem decisions (v. 4). The portrayal of Paul as a mighty miracle worker (13:9ff.; 14:8ff.; 16:18; 19:11ff.; 20:7ff.; 28:3ff., 8ff.) can be reconciled with Paul's own behavior only with difficulty; though he, too, could perform the "signs of an apostle" (2 Cor 12:12), he did not regard such miraculous deeds as the decisive element of his mission. In contrast to the Paul of the letters (cf. 1 Cor 2:1ff.; 2 Cor 10:10), the Paul of Acts is an excellent speaker who can preach to the educated men of Athens (17:22ff.) with the same facility that he silences a furious mob in Jerusalem (21:40; 22:1f.) and commands respect and recognition from his adversaries in court (24:10ff.). In Acts Paul always finally experiences success before his enemies

and those in power (13:7ff.; 18:12ff.; 19:35ff.; 24:23; 26:24ff.) and at the end in Rome is still able to preach the gospel to both Jews and Gentiles for an extended period of time (28:23ff.).

This portrayal also exhibits certain abbreviations. Whereas Paul himself mentions three shipwrecks and several beatings (five times at the hands of the Jews, three otherwise: 2 Cor 11:24f.), Acts knows of only one shipwreck (27:27ff.) and one beating (16:22ff.).

With this portrayal, then, Paul, who for Luke is not an "apostle" in the same way as the Twelve (1:21f.), is nonetheless characterized by the idea of an "apostle" held by the post-Pauline generation. His untiring and successful proclamation alone brought about the expansion from Jerusalem to Rome of the path of salvation grounded in God's will and in the Jew's rejection of salvation (cf. 13:45ff.; 14:2ff.; 17:5ff.; 18:5ff.; 22:22ff.; 28:17ff.).

4. In the deutero-Pauline letters Colossians and Ephesians the gospel (for the Gentiles) and the apostle himself are so inextricably bound together that this gospel can only be brought to expression as the "Pauline" gospel. This intention is served by emphatic ἐγὼ Παῦλος (Col 1:23; Eph 3:1) and by the fundamental determination of the function of the apostolic office in Eph 4:11f. (cf. 2:20).

A similar process is seen in the use of Colossians by the author of Ephesians (cf. 1:1, 7, 10f., 15f., 19f.; 3:2ff., 17; 4:16, 22ff.; 6:21f.) as in the use of the Pauline letter 1 Thessalonians by the author of the pseudepigraphal 2 Thessalonians: The apostolic word is available to the post-Pauline generation as a received (written) tradition (2 Thess 2:15), and in contrast to 1 Cor 16:21 (though also to Col 4:18) the author's own signature in greeting in 2 Thess 3:17 now confirms the letter's "apostolic" authenticity.

The reception and critical continuation of Pauline theology in Colossians and Ephesians can best be understood in some connection with the idea of a Pauline school (in Ephesus? [so Schenke]; see the contributions of H. Merklein and W. Trilling in Kertelge).

5. In the Pastorals Paul is *the* apostle. His name appears only in the prescripts, and his apostolate is primarily oriented toward office, doctrine, and conduct (1 Tim 1:15f.; 4:12; 2 Tim 1:13; 3:10). Thus the gospel shows its power not only in Paul's historical uniqueness, but also in his personal life (2 Tim 1:8). In a later and different theological climate one can now teach with the authority of the apostolic gospel in the name of Paul, i.e., apostolically.

The author of 2 Pet 3:15f. similarly already looks back at the Pauline writings from an appropriate distance with respect and veneration. He places them on the same level as the γραφαί (3:16), even though they are no longer immediately comprehensible to all readers and have occasioned their share of false teaching. An initial collection of Pauline letters can probably be presupposed as standing behind both the Pastorals and 2 Peter. "Peter" and ὁ ἀγαπητὸς ἡμῶν ἀδελφὸς Παῦλος represent the totality of the older apostolic tradition (cf. the contributions of G. Lohfink and P. Trummer in Kertelge).

6. → Σέργιος (nomen gentilicium) Παῦλος (cognomen) is the name of the Roman proconsul of Cyprus who according to Acts 13:7 hears Barnabas and Saul and according to v. 12 becomes a believer.
                                                                        H. Balz

παύω pauō trans.: stop, quiet; mid.: cease*

1. Occurrences — 2. Act. — 3. Mid.

Lit.: BAGD s.v. — BDF §§180.6; 414.2.

1. Of the 15 occurrences of παύω in the NT, 9 are in Luke-Acts (3 in the Gospel, 6 in Acts), the rest in the Epistles (1 Cor 13:8; Col 1:9 par. Eph 1:16; Heb 10:2; 1 Pet 3:10; 4:1).

2. Only 1 Pet 3:10 attests act. usage of this term in the NT (as in 1 Clem. 22:3 an approximate quotation from Ps 33:14 LXX): "let him keep his tongue from evil (παυσάτω). . . ."

3. Mid. usage occurs esp. in Luke-Acts: With a following pres. partc. in Luke 5:4 (λαλῶν); Acts 21:32 (τύπτων). Negated (οὐ παύομαι) with pres. partc. ("[do something] without ceasing") in Acts 5:42 (διδάσκων); 6:13 (λαλῶν); 13:10 (διαστρέφων); 20:1 (νουθετῶν), so also Eph 1:16 (εὐχαριστῶν); Col 1:9 (προσευχόμενοι καὶ αἰτούμενοι); Heb 10:2 (προσφερόμεναι). In 1 Pet 4:1 followed by gen. of separation (BDF §180.6): πέπαυται ἁμαρτίας, "he has ceased from sin."

Absolute in Luke 8:24, of wind and waves, which "subsided" (cf. Homer Od. xii.168; Herodotus vii.193); 11:1, of Jesus at the conclusion of prayer: "and when he ceased" (absolute usage also in Ep. Arist. 293; Sib. Or. v.458); further Acts 20:1, of a riot: (θόρυβος); 1 Cor 13:8, of glossolalia (γλῶσσαι).
                                                                        G. Schneider

Πάφος, ου Paphos Paphos*

A port city on the southwest coast of Cyprus (New Paphos), from the time of Augustus the metropolis of Cyprus bearing the honorific title Augusta. During the time of Paul (from ca. A.D. 46-48) the seat of a Roman proconsul. Paul visited Paphos during his "first missionary journey" together with Barnabas (Acts 13:6: ἀχρὶ Πάφου), defeated a Jewish magician, and converted the proconsul → Σέργιος Παῦλος there (vv. 6ff.). He then journeyed on to Perga in Pamphylia (v. 13: ἀπὸ τῆς Πάφου). BAGD s.v.; H.-E. Wilhelm, BHH 1382f.; A. van

den Born, BL 1290; E. Meyer, KP IV, 484-87 (bibliography); T. B. Mitford, OCD 777.

παχύνω pachynō make firm/dull/impervious*

Lit. "make fat" (from παχύς, "fat"), in the NT always pass. and fig. become dull/impervious in citations of Isa 6:10 LXX (Heb. šāmān hiphil): ἐπαχύνθη γὰρ ἡ καρδία τοῦ λαοῦ τούτου (Matt 13:15; Acts 28:27; here as in the LXX this dulling is God's work, in the MT it is the goal of the prophet's message; cf. further John 12:40; Rom 11:8). K. L. and M. A. Schmidt, TDNT V, 1022-25, esp. 1025; TWNT X, 1226 (bibliography).

πέδη, ης, ἡ pedē fetter*

Mark 5:4 (bis) par. Luke 8:29: πέδαι καὶ ἁλύσεις, "fetters and chains."

πεδινός, 3 pedinos flat, in the plain*

Luke 6:17: ἐπὶ τόπου πεδίνου, "in a place/an area in the plain" (in contrast to the hills, vv. 12, 17a).

πεζεύω pezeuō travel by land/on foot*

Acts 20:13: Paul wanted to travel from Troas to Assos along the shorter route by land or on foot (μέλλων αὐτὸς πεζεύειν), while the others (vv. 5f.) went by ship. E. Haenchen, Acts (Eng. tr., 1971) 587.

πεζῇ pezē by land, on foot*

Mark 6:33 par. Matt 14:13: the crowd followed Jesus and the disciples on foot to the far shore of the Sea of Galilee (in contrast to ἐν [τῷ] πλοίῳ).

πεζός, 3 pezos going by land/on foot
Matt 14:13 א L Z, etc., in place of → πεζῇ.

πειθαρχέω peitharcheō obey, be obedient, listen to*

4 occurrences in the NT. Literally "obey an authority /power (ἀρχή)," used absolutely of the obedient behavior of believers (in personal relationships and before God; cf. 2 Tim 3:2; Titus 1:10; 3:3): Titus 3:1, with ὑποτάσσεσθαι; Acts 5:29: θεῷ μᾶλλον ἢ ἀνθρώποις, "obey God rather than people" (cf. 4:19; Plato Ap. 29d: πείσομαι δὲ μᾶλλον τῷ θεῷ ἢ ὑμῖν); 5:32: οἱ πειθαρχοῦντες αὐτῷ (θεῷ) as a designation for believers; 27:21: πειθαρχήσαντάς μοι, "listen to me." R. Bultmann, TDNT VI, 9f.; TWNT X, 1226 (bibliography); Spicq, Notes II, 676-78.

πειθός, 3 *peithos* convincing, persuasive*

This adj., which does not occur elsewhere, appears in 1 Cor 2:4 ([א*] B D 33, etc.) in the expression ἐν πειθοῖς σοφίας λόγοις, "in *persuasive* words of wisdom" (cf. BDF §§47; 112). Πειθοῖς also occurs in otherwise different formulations in, among others, 𝔓⁴⁶ א² A C Ψ Koine. The minuscules 1, 42, 440, and others have dat. πειθοῖ (from → πειθώ); see also *TCGNT* ad loc.; BAGD s.v.; R. Bultmann, *TDNT* VI, 8f.; H. Conzelmann, *1 Cor* (Hermeneia) 54f.

πείθω *peithō* persuade, convince; trust, believe

1. Occurrences and meanings — 2. "Convince, persuade" — 3. Πείθομαι — 4. Πέποιθα

Lit.: O. BECKER, *DNTT* I, 588-93. — R. BULTMANN, *TDNT* VI, 1-7. — For further bibliography see *TWNT* X, 1226.

1. This vb. occurs 52 times in the NT. It is a favorite word in the Lukan double work (4 occurrences in the Gospel, 17 in Acts) and in Paul (19 occurrences, none of those in 1 Corinthians). It does not occur in, among others, Mark, John's Gospel (once in 1 John [3:19]), or Revelation.

In act. usage the vb. means *convince, persuade* (or negatively: *induce, cajole;* cf. BAGD s.v. 1.b), *conciliate, pacify.* In the pass. it means *trust,* then also *obey.* Second pf. πέποιθα preserves its act. form the original intrans. meaning *fully trust in, depend on,* i.e., persevere in a condition of trust. The mid. pass. first pf. maintains the pres. sense of *be convinced* (see Becker 588f.). The spectrum of meaning is wide, and the nuances many; a consideration of the various tenses and esp. of the context best discloses the meaning in a given instance.

2. Matt 27:20; Acts 12:20; 14:19; 19:26 use πείθω in the aor. in the (positive) sense of *persuade;* in Matt 27:20 and Acts 14:19 the negative sense of *mislead* is associated with it, probably also in Acts 19:26. This usage is closely related to the statements in Acts 13:43; 18:4; 19:8: Paul attempts to *persuade* the Jews in a positive sense. This is esp. so in 28:23: Having arrived in Rome, the apostle endeavors to *convince* the leaders of the Jews (v. 17), i.e., to *win* them over to the gospel of Jesus. Acts 26:28, a passage with an uncertain textual tradition (see *NTG* ad loc.) can be variously interpreted; the sense is probably that Paul makes Agrippa into a Christian through *persuasion* (cf. Bultmann 2 n.4; → ὀλίγος 4). An exact meaning is difficult to determine for 2 Cor 5:11 and Gal 1:10 (pres. ind.). In 2 Cor 5:11 the vb. probably means seek to *win* people in the execution of one's apostolic office; this may also be the meaning in Gal 1:10. Finally, the act. fut. means *persuade* in the sense of *conciliate* (Matt 28:14; 1 John 3:19; on the text-critical difficulties

and the two most significant interpretive possibilities cf. R. Schnackenburg, *1-3 John* [HTKNT] 179f.; Schnackenburg translates: "we *will reassure* our hearts before him").

3. Pass. πείθομαι occurs 3 times in the aor. (Acts 5:39; 17:4; 23:21 [μή with subjunc. = negative imv.]) referring to the result (the success) of *persuading.* One allows oneself to be *convinced* by someone: one follows and *obeys* him. The impf. has the same meaning in Acts 27:11 and 28:24; ἀπιστεῖν in 28:24 suggests that πείθομαι has the sense of *believe* here. Luke 16:31 uses the vb. in the fut. and asserts that a person refusing his assent will also not be *convinced* if someone should rise from the dead. The pres. expresses the sense of *being convinced* (Acts 21:14; 26:26; Heb 13:18); in Gal 5:7; Heb 13:17; Jas 3:3 it takes on the meaning *obey.* In Rom 2:8 the vb. already exhibits a stronger theological sense: The appropriate behavior before God is *obedience* (cf. the antithetical formulation and → ἀπειθέω) in the *certainty of faith* (Rom 8:38 and elsewhere).

4. Πέποιθα with ἐπί means *depend on* after one has already been securely convinced (Luke 18:9; 2 Cor 1:9; 2:3; 2 Thess 3:4). In the later addition to Mark 10:24 (Koine, several minuscules) the rich *depend* on their wealth. The use of πέποιθα in Phil 1:25 and 2:24 makes it clear that "at the same time this expresses a hope in the future" (Becker 592). The second pf. occurs with ἐν only in Phil 3:3, 4; this *dependence* on the flesh is the Jews' false confidence, which stands in contrast to faith in Christ (v. 9). Finally, πέποιθα with the dat. (Phil 1:14) means *trust in* (ἐν κυρίῳ refers to the vb.; J. Gnilka, *Phil* [HTKNT] 54, 58f.): The brethren draw their own confidence from the fact that Paul is imprisoned. Paul speaks of *trust* in God only in 2 Cor 1:19 and Phil 1:6, just as the NT as a whole rarely speaks of trust in God (in Matt 27:43 it is Jesus who trusts in God; cf. Ps 21:9 LXX: ἤλπισεν ἐπὶ κύριον; cf. H. Windisch, *2 Cor* [KEK] 47). The NT speaks so rarely of trust in God because it is concerned "with the common distress of mankind and with eschatological salvation. With this reference, however, confidence takes the form of faith" (Bultmann 7).

A. Sand

πειθώ, οῦς, ἡ *peithō* persuasion, the art of persuasion

1 Cor 2:4 v.l. (d: ἐν πειθοῖ σοφίας λόγου; g: ἐν πειθοῖ σοφίας, also in Origen and Ambrose); if πειθώ is preferred over → πειθός one can assume dittography of the σ or an auditory error. On the use of πειθώ with λόγος cf. Plato *R.* 411d; Philo *Virt.* 217; see further BAGD s.v.; H. Conzelmann, *1 Cor* (Hermeneia) 54f. with nn. 21 and 24.

Πειλᾶτος, ου *Peilatos* Pilate*

A secondary form of → Πιλᾶτος.

πεινάω *peinaō* hunger (vb.), hunger for*

This vb. occurs 23 times in the NT, 9 of those in Matthew and 5 each in Luke and Paul; in John (6:35) it is fig.

21 occurrences are literal: Jesus *was hungry* (ἐπείνασεν) after his forty-day fast in the wilderness (Matt 4:2 par. Luke 4:2); David and his companions *were hungry* (Mark 2:25 par. Matt 12:3/Luke 6:3; cf. 1 Sam 21:1ff.); cf. further ἐπείνασεν of Jesus (Mark 11:12 par. Matt 21:18), the disciples on the sabbath (Matt 12:1), *remaining hungry* at the Lord's Supper in Corinth: ὃς μὲν πεινᾷ ὃς δὲ μεθύει (1 Cor 11:21; cf. v. 34). As a general term for lack and need: πεινῶντας ἐνέπλησεν ἀγαθῶν (in contrast to πλουτοῦντες, Luke 1:53; cf. 1 Sam 2:5; Ps 106:9, 36 LXX); with διψάω (cf. Jer 38:25 LXX; Ps 106:5 LXX) in Jesus' judgment discourse (Matt 25:35, 37, 42, 44; the opposite is satiation or assistance: ἐδώκατέ μοι φαγεῖν, vv. 35, 42; ἐθρέψαμεν, v. 37; οὐ διηκονήσαμέν σοι, v. 44); cf. Rev 7:16: οὐ πεινάσουσιν ἔτι οὔτε διψήσουσιν ἔτι (citing Isa 49:10 LXX); Rom 12:20: ἐὰν πεινᾷ ὁ ἐχθρός σου . . . ἐὰν διψᾷ (citing Prov 25:21); 1 Cor 4:11: πεινῶμεν καὶ διψῶμεν καὶ γυμνιτεύομεν; Phil 4:12: χορτάζεσθαι καὶ πεινᾶν; in the blessings and woes of the Sermon on the Plain: οἱ πεινῶντες νῦν (Luke 6:21; antithesis: χορτασθήσεσθε); πεινάσετε (v. 25; antithesis: οἱ ἐμπεπλησμένοι νῦν); in contrast, Matt 5:6 exhibits fig. usage: οἱ πεινῶντες καὶ διψῶντες τὴν δικαιοσύνην . . . χορτασθήσονται (see Amos 8:11; Isa 55:1f.; Ps 42:3; Bar 2:18); cf. John 6:35: ὁ ἐρχόμενος . . . οὐ μὴ πεινάσῃ, καὶ ὁ πιστεύων εἰς ἐμὲ οὐ μὴ διψήσει (see Sir 24:21).

Hunger in the NT is thus a sign of distress and poverty and is used as a metaphor for dependence on God; just as believers have learned to endure hunger and distress for the sake of the Lord and in their works of love to turn their attention to those who are hungry (and in them to the Lord himself), so also will God still their "hunger," while those who are "satiated" will go away empty. L. Goppelt, *TDNT* VI, 12-22; *TWNT* X, 1226 (bibliography); W. Bauder, *DNTT* II, 265-68.   H. Balz

πεῖρα, ας, ἡ *peira* attempt, test, experience (noun)*

In the NT only in πεῖραν λαμβάνω, "make *an attempt*" (Heb 11:29); "acquire *experience with/make the acquaintance of* mocking and scourging (v. 36). H. Seesemann, *TDNT* VI, 23-28.

πειράζω *peirazō* try; tempt*
ἐκπειράζω *ekpeirazō* challenge (vb.)*
πειρασμός, οῦ, ὁ *peirasmos* test, temptation*

1. Occurrences in the NT — 2. Meaning — 3. Usage —
4. OT and Jewish tradition — 5. Tempting God — 6. Testing Jesus — 7. Temptation of the pious

Lit.: G. BAUMBACH, *Das Verständnis des Bösen in den synoptischen Evangelien* (1963). — E. BEST, *The Temptation and the Passion* (1965). — N. BROX, *HTG* II, 778-82. — BULTMANN, *History* 253-57. — H. CONZELMANN, *The Theology of St. Luke* (1960) 27-29, 233f. — P. H. DAVIDS, "The Meaning of ἀπείραστος in James 1:13," *NTS* 24 (1977/78) 386-99. — J. DUPONT, *Les Tentations de Jésus au désert* (1968; Germ. tr.: *Die Versuchungen Jesu in der Wüste* [1969]). — E. FASCHER, *Jesus und der Satan* (1949). — *idem,* "Jesus und die Tiere," *TLZ* 90 (1965) 561-70. — A. FEUILLET, "Die Versuchungen Jesu," *Internationale katholische Zeitschrift* 8 (1979) 226-37. — W. FOERSTER, *TDNT* II, 72f., 75-81; VII, 151-63. — G. FRIEDRICH, "Beobachtungen zur messianischen Hohepriestererwartung in den Synoptikern," *idem, Auf das Wort kommt es an* (1978) 56-102. — B. GERHARDSSON, *The Testing of God's Son* (1966). — P. HOFFMANN, "Die Versuchungsgeschichte in der Logienquelle," *BZ* 13 (1969) 207-23. — C. B. HOUK, "ΠΕΙΡΑΣΜΟΣ, The Lord's Prayer, and the Massah Tradition," *SJT* 19 (1966) 216-25. — B. M. F. VAN IERSEL, *"Der Sohn" in den synoptischen Jesusworten* (1961) 165-71. — JEREMIAS, *Theology* 68-75. — K.-P. KÖPPEN, *Die Auslegung der Versuchungsgeschichte unter besonderer Berücksichtigung der Alten Kirche* (1961). — J. H. KORN, *ΠΕΙΡΑΣΜΟΣ. Die Versuchung des Gläubigen in der griechischen Bibel* (1937). — K. G. KUHN, "Πειρασμός—ἁμαρτία—σάρξ im NT und die damit zusammenhängenden Vorstellungen," *ZTK* 49 (1952) 200-222. — *idem,* "Jesus in Gethsemane," *EvT* 12 (1952/53) 260-85. — H.-G. LEDER, "Sündenfallerzählung und Versuchungsgeschichte," *ZNW* 54 (1963) 188-216; see the concluding remarks by J. Jeremias, 278f. — E. LOHMEYER, "Die Versuchung Jesu," *idem, Urchristliche Mystik* (²1956) 81-122. — U. LUCK, "Weisheit und Leiden," *TLZ* 92 (1967) 253-58. — H. MAHNKE, *Die Versuchungsgeschichte im Rahmen der synoptischen Evangelien* (1978). — U. MAUSER, *Christ in the Wilderness* (1963). — W. NAUCK, "Freude im Leiden," *ZNW* 46 (1955) 68-80. — F. NEUGEBAUER, *Jesu Versuchung. Wegentscheidung am Anfang* (1986). — P. POKORNÝ, "The Temptation Stories and their Intention," *NTS* 20 (1973/74) 115-27. — J. A. T. ROBINSON, "The Temptations," *idem, Twelve NT Studies* (1962) 53-60. — R. SCHNACKENBURG, "Der Sinn der Versuchung Jesu bei den Synoptikern," *idem, Schriften zum NT* (1971) 101-28. — C. SCHÜTZ, *Mysterium Salutis: Grundriß heilsgeschichtlicher Dogmatik* III/2 (ed. J. Feiner and M. Löhrer; 1969) 75-90. — SCHULZ, *Q* 177-90. — H. SEESEMANN, *TDNT* VI, 23-36. — H. THIELICKE, *Between God and Satan* (1969). — J. THOMAS, "Anfechtung und Vorfreude," *KD* 14 (1968) 183-206. — W. WILKENS, "Die Versuchungsgeschichte Lk 4,1-13 und die Komposition des Evangeliums," *TZ* 30 (1974) 262-72. — For older bibliography see BAGD s.v.; Seesemann; for more recent bibliography see *TWNT* X, 1226-28; Mahnke.

1. Πειράζω and ἐκπειράζω occur 38 and 4 times respectively in the NT, πειρασμός 21 times. The distribution varies: The terms do not occur in Romans, Ephesians, Philippians, Colossians, 2 Thessalonians, 2 Timothy, Titus, Philemon, 1–3 John, or Jude, and hardly at all in John; they occur most frequently in the Synoptics, Acts, 1 Corinthians 10, Hebrews 2–4, James 1, Revelation 2–3.

2. The fundamental meaning of the stem πειρα- corresponds to a large extent to that of English *test* and *try* and Heb. *nsh* (G. Gerleman, *THAT* II, 69-71): *put to some sort of test.* This testing is accompanied by burdening, risk, uncertainty, and even danger and mistrust. Depending on the intention at hand, the test can be, positively, a test in which one proves oneself or, negatively, an enticement to failure. Since persons are virtually the only object of such testing in the NT, trust, faithfulness, and obedience usually play a role as well. Ἐκπειράζω, on the other hand, means *challenge,* and is always in the NT directed toward God or Christ. The spectrum of meaning of πειράζω is wider: 1) examine with sincere intentions; 2) test critically with less than serious intentions; 3) threaten, burden, tempt; 4) mislead, seduce; 5) challenge, doubt, mistrust; 6) arrange for or plan something. The nuances can, of course, overlap.

Πειρασμός, rare in secular Greek, exhibits less extensive variations in meaning. It largely refers to some burden or threat by humans or other powers (affliction, persecution, snares, etc.), i.e., an expressly human experience (only in Heb 3:8 possibly God). Objectively the πειρασμός (only 4 occurrences are pl.) is some danger threatening to cause a person to depart from the correct path. Subjectively this threat is perceived in part as the occasion for worry (God's help is necessary, petition for protection), and in part as a stimulus (opportunity for proving oneself).

3. In Mark, Q, and Matthew we find three areas of usage: the temptation of Jesus, interrogation by Jesus' adversaries (also in John 8:6), and the disciples' petition in prayer. A unique expression is ὁ πειράζων in Matt 4:34, which occurs otherwise only in 1 Thess 3:5.

Luke is more independent. 2 further occurrences speak of Jesus' *temptation(s)* (4:13; 22:28); Luke also emphasizes the temptation of Christians (8:13; Acts 20:19). In contrast, πειράζω is twice not used in interrogations of Jesus, while in one instance (Luke 10:25) probably blasphemy is emphasized; similarly also in Acts 5:9 and 15:10. Πειράζω can also, however, simply mean *prepare to/want to* (Acts 9:26; 16:7; 24:6).

John 6:6: pedagogically *put to the test.*

The Pauline occurrences usually associate a negative sense with πειρα-: sin, transgression, opposition (1 Cor 7:5; 10:6ff.; Gal 6:1; 1 Thess 3:5; 1 Tim 6:9), burdening (1 Cor 10:13), taking offense (Gal 4:14). Only 2 Cor 13:5 uses it more positively (*"examine* oneself").

Hebrews mentions Israel's rebellion (3:8f.) and emphasizes the test of obedience in suffering (2:18; 4:15; 11:17).

Jas 1:2, 12; 1 Pet 1:6; 4:12 also fit into this context: heavily burden; cf. in contrast Jas 1:13f.: mislead into sin.

The temptation set before faith by suffering is also the concern in 2 Pet 2:9; Rev 2:10; 3:10; critical examination in Rev 2:2.

4. Israel's understanding of this word group exhibits a "distinctly religious" interest (Seesemann 24, with details). The most important elements for the NT are: a) God's often painful testing of the pious (Abraham, Job, etc.); this topos is associated with that of the suffering righteous person and that of wisdom pedagogy (e.g., Wis 3:5; Sir 2:1; *Jub.* 19:8f.); b) Adam's fall (even though πειράζω/*nsh* does not occur in Genesis 3); c) Satan's increasing significance and the heightened situation of struggle (Kuhn, "Πειρασμός," esp. in Qumran, though more as a topos than an emphasis on this specific terminology); d) expectation of great eschatological tribulation, though here, too, πειράζω only rarely appears (Seesemann 26; the most frequently mentioned occurrence is Rev 3:10 [cf. *1 Enoch* 94:5]; Dan 12:10 speaks of testing and sanctification; πλανάω κτλ. are used more frequently: H. Braun, *TDNT* VI, 238ff.); e) the idea of the "evil impulse" (see Billerbeck IV, 466-83); and f) Israel's provocation of God (Exodus 17, Numbers 20, Psalms 78, 95, and 106).

5. The testing of God is characterized by Israel's rebellion in the wilderness (1 Cor 10:9; Heb 3:8f.; also Matt 4:7 par.). One provokes God by "subjecting to doubt his goodness and his perfect power through challenging greedy wishes" (H.-J. Kraus, *Pss* II [Eng. tr., 1989] on 78:18). Such provocation of the Spirit or of God is also mentioned in Acts 5:9 and 15:10: Through deception or misunderstanding human beings strain God's kind forbearance.

6. a) It is uncertain whether Heb 2:18 and 4:15 stand in context with the Synoptic material. Jesus' temptation appears here in the same context as the afflictions affecting all human beings, specifically suffering (see 5:7; 11:1ff.). Πειρασμός is the threat of being misled into disobedience and resignation. As one who has suffered thus, Jesus is qualified to offer assistance; as a sinless person he shows that πειρασμός "does not necessarily lead to sin" (H. Zimmermann, *Das Bekenntnis der Hoffnung* [1977] 173).

b) The temptations by earthly adversaries constituted an originally independent tradition (Mark 8:11 par.; 10:2 par.; 12:15 par.; Matt 22:35 par.; John 8:6). They include critical interrogation, intrigue, and deceit.

c) The tradition-critical and literary-critical problems of Mark 1:12f. and Matt 4:1-11 par. can no longer be unequivocally resolved (cf. also John 6:15ff.: the miracle of the bread). The common point of departure seems to have been a situation of physical need (wilderness). The development then followed two different lines in regard to form, connection with the OT, and understanding. Any attempts at reconstruction regarding the original form and development remain without real support, as do attempts to trace the event back to the historical Jesus and the accompanying attempt to locate it historically. The association with baptism was not necessarily a constituent part from the very beginning (reservations, e.g., from Lohmeyer; J. Gnilka, *Mark* [EKKNT] I ad loc.; Mahnke; different views, e.g., from Gerhardsson; R. Pesch, *Mark* [HTKNT] I ad loc.). Quite apart from the question of any historical core, we are dealing primarily with a Christ-narrative in two forms whose understanding was determined by changing tradition-historical interests. All the traditions note that Jesus was tempted, though usually in a general sense at the beginning (Matthew and Luke one more time each); according to Matt 4:7 par. temptation of God is also involved.

d) Mark 1:12f. is not the core of a longer narrative. Πειραζόμενος . . . is not a Markan addition, and the whole can be characterized only with qualification as a temptation story (Mahnke). The motif-historical background points (despite Leder's concerns) to the context surrounding paradise and Adam (not to the Elijah tradition; details in Mahnke; Jeremias; Pesch, *loc. cit.;* Gnilka, *loc. cit.*). The temptation seeks to bring about an act of disobedience and disloyalty on the part of Jesus that would disqualify him from his eschatological office. By resisting, Jesus wins back paradise. Mark 1:12f. is not an incomplete piece the ending of which was added later (3:27: Best, Pokorný, Schütz; 1:14f.; resurrection). Admittedly, the motif of the victorious struggle against Satan becomes essential for Mark.

e) The parallel tradition in Matt 4:1-11 and Luke 4:1-13 contains numerous problems. Despite various questions, it is probably a product of Q; the divergences are in part already pre-redactional. The Matthean sequence is almost certainly the older. Other disputed elements include: uniformity, form (suggestions include midrash, haggadah, dispute, apology, catechism, etc.), references to the OT (Israel, Adam, Abraham, Job, etc.?), religious-historical background (the Jewish righteous person, Hellenistic θεῖος ἀνήρ, etc.?), christological scope (specifically messianic or universally human temptation?), opposing fronts (Zealotism, magic, show-miracles?), motif-historical aspects (prophet-priest-king; prophetic, priestly, apocalyptic expectation?), relationship to baptism (original? parenetic scheme?), and the kind and sense of the temptation: *probatio, deceptio, seductio?* (Augustine). Dupont and Mahnke offer overviews of scholarship.

The network of citations in Jesus' answers offers the most secure point of departure: Deut 8:3b and 6:16; 6:13 from the context of the Shema. All refer to Israel's critical phase in the wilderness in chronologically correct order: manna (Exodus 16), turmoil at Massah (Exodus 17), and land acquisition (Exodus 23, 34). The combination of citations also supports the unity of the temptation account: Scenes two and three in any case probably never existed separately. That the LXX is quoted points to a Hellenistic Jewish formulation, but not to a late date.

The obedient Jesus is an antitype to Israel in the wilderness, is simultaneously an exemplary righteous person, and in both respects is the proven Son of God and a true human being. He withstands the devil's seduction to disobedience and his indirect testing of God.

The Israel (and Moses) typology suspends the alternatives "messianic temptation or not" and "messianic work or personal conduct." Salvation-historical perspective and individual focus are inseparable here. There is more here than just the rejection of a magical understanding of miracles. The fundamental feature is that Jesus as an exemplary Israelite can complete the eschatological work (cf. Mahnke).

The three scenes probably also allude to Jesus' threefold role as prophet, priest, and king. Though in form and content originally a christological didactic discourse, at various levels of tradition the piece also acquired relevance for delimitation esp. over against Zealotism (political Messiah) and a θεῖος ἀνήρ christology (a magical understanding of miracles). Despite Jesus' uniqueness, his own act of proving himself also became the model for Christians (see the association with baptism, Israel typology, 1 Corinthians 10).

f) Matthew "tells us about Jesus, Luke about the devil" (Dupont 61). Here, too, Jesus is for Matthew the one who "fulfills all righteousness" (3:15), remains in submission to God and does not seize the opportunity to help himself (see 27:40!), and simultaneously legitimizes himself as a correct interpreter of Scripture. God rewards obedience (4:11).

Luke directs everything toward Jerusalem; 4:13 additionally accentuates the Passion. Jesus offers resistance to the devil's position of power (4:6; cf. 4:14), and the result is an "initial skirmish" (Dupont 67). As one filled with the Spirit who vanquishes his adversary when challenged, Jesus also becomes a prototype for the missionary (Baumbach). 4:13 is probably not pointing to a "period free of Satan" lasting up to the Passion, since 22:28 is more retrospective than forward-looking. It remains correct that the Passion is the time determined by God when Satan again vehemently attacks Jesus.

7. a) "If you come forward to serve the Lord, prepare your soul εἰς πειρασμόν" (Sir 2:1). This line of admonition continues in the NT; the Christian must preprare himself for temptation (πειρασμός as a burden, esp. suffering: 1 Pet 1:6; 4:12; Jas 1:2, 12; Heb 2:18; 4:15; 11:17; more frequent terminology: affliction, persecution, etc.). Though it is not a pleasant experience, one can see it as a means of divine instruction and find a positive sense in it; cf. the topos "joy in suffering" (Nauck; cf. also N. Brox, *1 Pet* [EKKNT] 64 n.213), instruction of neophytes (relationship to baptism), and the perseverance sayings (Matt 10:22 etc.).

b) The accent can also fall on the pernicious character of temptations; the devil is often suspected as being behind them (Matt 6:13; Luke 8:13; 1 Cor 7:5; 1 Thess 3:5). For this reason deliverance is often promised from or in the πειρασμός (1 Cor 10:13; 2 Pet 2:9; Rev 2:10; 3:10).

c) The interpretation of Matt 6:13a par. and Mark 14:38 par. is difficult. The petition in the Lord's Prayer is interpreted both apocalyptically (preservation in—not from—the great tribulations; e.g., J. Jeremias, *Abba* [1966] 169f.) and from the perspective of wisdom (may God not put us to the test; e.g., E. Schweizer, *Matt* [Eng. tr., 1975] 156). Matthew (threatened by evil: 6:13b) and Luke (daily endangerment of the converted: J. Ernst, *Luke* [RNT] 365) apparently already differed. In view of the general findings (see above) and the missing article, the apocalyptic interpretation is problematic.

Again with regard to the Gethsemane prayer one must ask whether Jesus faces apocalyptic-satanic temptation (e.g., W. Schenk, *Der Passionsbericht nach Markus* [1974] 202f.) or a testing (in the sense of wisdom: e.g., Gnilka, *op. cit.* II, 262)? The context suggests a situation of apocalyptic struggle (see Kuhn, "Πειρασμός"); one should persevere in the face of coercion and betrayal. According to Mark and Matthew the πειρασμός begins with the weakness of the flesh; the ἵνα clause indicates the purpose of watchfulness and prayer; this is not the case in Luke 22:40, 46 (content of the prayer; Kuhn, "Jesus" 285).

d) The source of temptation is also located in the person himself, specifically in his or her ἐπιθυμία (Jas 1:14; similarly 1 Cor 10:6ff.; 1 Tim 6:9; cf. Mark 14:38b). This view is apparently related to the Jewish doctrine of the "evil impulse," with additional Hellenistic motifs (further discussion in F. Mussner, *Jas* [HTKNT] on 1:14).

e) These various aspects of temptation were perceived together as a cluster of problems, specifically for theodicy. The more strongly one understood πειρασμός as a burden or as satanic affliction, the more questionable did its character as testing in the sense of wisdom and God's role in it become. This is most clear in James 1: The traditional motif of joy in πειρασμός (vv. 2, 12) is countered by exoneration of God (v. 13) and the individual's own responsibility (v. 14). These same factors appear in 1 Corinthians 10: Paul incriminates evil human inclinations, which themselves lead to a testing of God (v. 9; cf. Heb 3:8f.). But according to 1 Cor 10:13 the πειρασμός comes to us from outside, whereby God keeps watch over the limits of our capacity for burdens; thus here it exhibits more the character of testing. The question of the originator of the πειρασμός—as is frequently the case in the NT—remains unclear, presumably because of the sense that it touches on the problem of the *opus Dei alienum*.　　　　　　　　　　　　　W. Popkes

πειράομαι *peiraomai* try, endeavor*

Only mid. in the NT: Acts 26:21: ἐπειρῶντο διαχειρίσασθαι, "they *tried* to kill [me]" (cf. 9:26 TR); on Heb 4:15 TR (πεπειραμένος) see BAGD s.v.; → πειράζω 6.a.

πειρασμός, οῦ, ὁ *peirasmos* test, temptation → πειράζω.

πεισμονή, ῆς, ἡ *peismonē* persuasion*

Gal 5:8: ἡ πεισμονὴ οὐκ ἐκ τοῦ καλοῦντος ὑμᾶς, "this persuasion," i.e., not to turn from truth (v. 7), "is not from him who called you" (cf. Ign. *Rom.* 3:3). This tr. assumes derivation from → πείθω. The v.l. in Gal 5:7 (ἀληθείᾳ μὴ πείθεσθαι μηδενὶ πείθεσθε, "obey no one in such a way as to disobey the truth," F G a b, etc.) is weakly attested; therefore, the tr. of πεισμονή as "obedience/observance" (derivation from πείθομαι) is excluded (see further BAGD s.v.; BDF §488.1). R. Bultmann, *TDNT* VI, 9.

πέλαγος, ους, τό *pelagos* open sea, deep sea; sea*

Matt 18:6: ἐν τῷ πελάγει τῆς θαλάσσης, "on the *high seas*/in the *depth* of the sea"; Acts 27:5: τὸ πέλαγος τὸ κατὰ τὴν Κιλικίαν . . . , "the *sea* along the coast of Cilicia."

πελεκίζω *pelekizō* behead*

Rev 20:4: αἱ ψυχαὶ τῶν πεπελεκισμένων, "the souls of those who had been beheaded" (referring to Roman execution with axe or sword; cf. Acts 12:2; *m. Sanh.* 7:1, 3; according to 9:1 also a Jewish punishment; see further Billerbeck I, 270).

πεμπταῖος, 3 *pemptaios* lasting five days

Acts 20:6 D: ἤλθομεν . . . πεμπταῖοι, "*in five days* we came [to Troas]," in place of ἄχρι ἡμερῶν πέντε.

πέμπτος, 3 *pemptos* fifth*

4 occurrences in the NT, all in Revelation: 6:9: ἡ πέμπτη σφραγίς; 9:1: ὁ πέμπτος ἄγγελος (cf. 8:2, 6); 16:10: ὁ πέμπτος (ἄγγελος) (cf. 15:1, 6-8; 16:1); 21:20: ὁ πέμπτος σαρδόνυξ (referring to the foundation stones in the wall of the heavenly Jerusalem; cf. v. 19; Ezek 28:13; Exod 28:17-20). Πέμπτη (σαββάτων), the "fifth day of the week /Thursday," is according to *Did.* 8:1 a Jewish day of fasting (along with Monday; for Christians Tuesday and Friday).

πέμπω *pempō* send

1. Occurrences in the NT — 2. Human communication — 3. The soteriology of Rom 8:3 — 4. Theocentricity in John

Lit.: H. BÜRKLE, *Missionstheologie* (1979). — HAENCHEN I, 68-77. — J. KUHL, *Die Sendung Jesu und der Kirche nach dem Johannesevangelium* (1967). — H. RITT, *Das Gebet zum Vater* (1979) 319-23. — E. SCHWEIZER, "Zum religionsgeschichtlichen Hintergrund der 'Sendungsformel' Gal 4,4f; Röm 8,3f; Joh 3,16; 1 Joh 4,9," *ZNW* 57 (1966) 199-210. — J. SEYNAEVE, "Les verbes ἀποστέλλω et πέμπω dans le vocabulaire théologique de saint Jean," *L'Évangile de Jean* (ed. M. de Jonge; BETL 44, 1977) 385-89. — M. WALDSTEIN, "The Mission of Jesus and the Disciples in John," *Communio/International Catholic Review* 17 (1990) 311-33. — S. G. WILSON, *The Gentiles and the Gentile Mission in Luke-Acts* (1973). — For further bibliography → ἀπόστολος (Miranda, Rengstorf, Schneider).

1. Of the 79 occurrences of this vb. in the NT, the 32 in John (24 of those referring to the sending of Jesus) are noteworthy, as are the 21 in Luke-Acts. While ἀποστέλλω occurs 42 times in Mark and Matthew together, πέμπω occurs in Mark and Matthew only 5 times.

2. Use of πέμπω for human communication:
a) Sending of persons to communicate (usually) important messages: Matthew always uses the partc. πέμψας with a finite vb. (2:8; 11:2; 14:10; 22:7). But in the Synoptic parallels we encounter redactional formulations (Luke 7:19: ἔπεμψεν πρός) or synonymous use of ἀποστέλλω (Mark 6:27). The transferral to legal proceedings (Acts 23:20; 25:25, 27: Paul's trial before the governor's court in Caesarea) or the order to send men to Joppa, given to Cornelius in an angelophany in Caesarea before his baptism (Acts 10:5, 32, 33), both contain special commissions for sending.

For Paul the sending of fellow workers constitutes a mandate to carry out certain functions in the churches with authority. Thus Timothy is to strengthen the Thessalonians in their lives of faith (1 Thess 3:2, 5), remind the Corinthians of the Pauline teachings (1 Cor 4:17), and inform Paul concerning the church at Philippi (Phil 2:19, 23; on Epaphroditus cf. Phil 2:25, 28). The primary tasks of those sent out (e.g., Tychicus: Col 4:8; Eph 6:22; Titus 3:12) are to take care of the collection (1 Cor 16:3; 2 Cor 9:3) and to gather news. The parallelism of "choose" (ἐκλέγομαι) and *send* (πέμπω) emphasizes the responsibility of the "leading men among the brethren" at the Apostolic Council (Acts 15:22, 25). Luke in particular always traces πέμπω back to the initiative of someone bearing authority (the centurion in Luke 7:6, 10; a citizen in 15:15; Abraham in 16:24, 27; the owner of the vineyard in 20:11, 12, 13).

b) Sending of objects of value: "Collections" (Phil 4:16; Acts 11:29) connect the churches to one another (cf. Rev 11:10), and God's word communicated in the "book" (Rev 1:11; cf. Germ. *Sendschreiben*) encourages the churches.

In addition, exorcism of demons (Mark 5:12: πέμψον) and sending of divine messengers (Rev 22:16; Luke 4:26) carry the image of "empowered" commissioning— analogous to earthly bearers of power (1 Pet 2:14) or to "powers" coming from God (2 Thess 2:11).

3. Rom 8:3 interprets soteriologically the sending of God's Son into the world of creaturely human existence and mortality under the prerequisite of preexistence (cf. Gal 4:4-6; Phil 2:6-11) and with anticipation of the sacrifice in death (Rom 8:32): To stand under Christ's dominion means to be liberated from the power of sin and death.

4. In John the actual historical sending of the Son by the Father is expressed in Jesus' own words in the formula ὁ πέμψας με (4:34; 5:24, 30, 37; 6:38, 39, 44; 7:16, 28, 33; 8:16, 18, 26, 29; 9:4; 12:44, 45, 49; 13:20; 14:24; 15:21; 16:5). These 22 occurrences, along with statements in the third person referring to the Father or God *"who sent* him" (5:23; 7:18), reveal the christological theocentricity of the Father-Son relationship. The initiative for this sending comes *from* the Father and remains present *in* the Son's work. The continuation of this sending by Jesus involves the believing disciples (cf. the "Synoptic" logion in 13:20); the Jewish legal principle that the messenger bears the same authority as the one who sent him comes into play. Juxtaposed with passages expressing the same idea with ἀποστέλλω (4:38; 17:18), the logion 20:21 is to be considered primary and has (in the pres.!) the resurrected Lord transmit the authoritative power of divine redemptive activity to the community of disciples. Thus also can follow the sending of the Paraclete by the Father (14:26; cf. the sending of the Spirit as a continuation of the sending of the Son in Gal 4:6: ἐξαπέστειλεν) or by the Son himself (John 15:26; 16:7). The words and deeds of the earthly Jesus become fully efficacious only in the witnessing Spirit of the present Christ in the life of the Church.

H. Ritt

πένης, ητος, ὁ *penēs* poor/needy person*

Subst. in the NT: 2 Cor 9:9, of the conduct of the "God-fearing person": ἔδωκεν τοῖς πένησιν, "he has given to the *poor*," quoting Ps 111:9 LXX. The LXX uses πένης in this Psalm and elsewhere frequently to render Heb. *'ebyôn;* with → πτωχός it appears as a designation for the pious in Pss 39:18 LXX; 85:1 LXX, and elsewhere; it is usually a general designation for actual poverty. BAGD s.v. (bibliography); F. Hauck, *TDNT* VI, 37-40; L. Coenen, *DNTT* II, 820f.

πενθερά, ᾶς, ἡ *penthera* mother-in-law*

6 occurrences in the NT. Of Simon Peter's *mother-in-law* in Mark 1:30 par. Matt 8:14/Luke 4:38; in a Q logion (Matt 10:35), referring to estrangement among family members: διχάσαι . . . νύμφην κατὰ τῆς πενθερᾶς αὐτῆς (similarly Luke 12:53 bis; cf. Mic 7:6).

πενθερός, οῦ, ὁ *pentheros* father-in-law*

John 18:13: Annas, the *father-in-law* of Caiaphas; → Ἅννας 2; R. Schnackenburg, *John* III (Eng. tr., 1982) ad loc.

πενθέω *pentheō* grieve, lament, mourn*

This vb. occurs 10 times in the NT, of which 3 are in Revelation 18 (which also has 3 of the 5 occurrences of the noun → πένθος) and 6 are with → κλαίω (Mark 16:10; Luke 6:25; Jas 4:9; Rev 18:11, 15, 19; cf. also in the LXX 2 Kgdms 19:2; 2 Esdr. 18:9 [= MT Neh 8:9]). The LXX frequently uses the vb. to refer to grief (in the face of death or God's punishment) that expresses itself in tears, lament, and mourning ritual (lament for the dead: Gen 23:2; the people's grief after the death of the spies: Num 14:39; the grief of the afflicted and rejected: Ps 34:14 LXX; the grief of the earth: Isa 24:4, 7; 33:9).

In the NT πενθέω can refer to the disciples' lament for the dead Jesus (Mark 16:10: πενθοῦντες καὶ κλαίοντες). But the time of rejoicing (at the presence of the bridegroom) excludes grief (Matt 9:15: μὴ δύνανται . . . πενθεῖν, contra Mark 2:19 par. Luke 5:34: νηστεύειν/ νηστεῦσαι). In 1 Cor 5:2 it refers to *mourning/lamenting* over a serious transgression (incest) in the church as a sign of self-reflection and resulting purification: καὶ οὐχὶ μᾶλλον ἐπενθήσατε, in contrast to καὶ ὑμεῖς πεφυσιωμένοι ἐστέ; cf. also 2 Cor 12:21 (trans.: *mourn*), of Paul's (publicly expressed) grief over sinners in the church who have not yet repented (cf. also *2 Clem.* 2:6). Jas 4:9 uses it similarly in the context of a call to penitence (vv. 1-8, 10): ταλαιπωρήσατε καὶ πενθήσατε καὶ κλαύσατε (cf. Isa 32:11ff.; Jer 4:8; Mic 1:8; also Luke 6:25; → κλαίω 3; → πένθος). Revelation 18 speaks of the mourning (for the dead) on the part of the merchants (vv. 11, 15) and sailors (v. 19) over the fall of "Babylon" (cf. Ezekiel 26–27) as a sign of the terror among men of this world at God's judgment.

In the blessing in Matt 5:4 (μακάριοι οἱ πενθοῦντες, ὅτι αὐτοὶ παρακληθήσονται) πενθέω is an expression for the grief of those who suffer under this world and place their hope in God alone (→ κλαίω 3; cf. Isa 49:13; 61:2f.; 66:10; Ps 125:5 LXX); this is countered by the apocalyptic cry of woe in Luke 6:25 to "those who laugh now" (→ γελάω): ὅτι πενθήσετε καὶ κλαύσετε (cf. v. 21; Matt 8:12; Jas 5:1; *1 Enoch* 94:8ff.; Rev 18:9ff. [see

above]). BAGD s.v.; R. Bultmann, *TDNT* VI, 40-43; *TWNT* X, 1228 (bibliography); → κλαίω (bibliography).

H. Balz

πένθος, ους, τό *penthos* mourning, grief*

This noun occurs 5 times in the NT, 4 of which are in Revelation. It also occurs in Jas 4:9 (ὁ γέλως ὑμῶν εἰς πένθος μετατραπήτω) in a call to penitence addressed to the arrogant (cf. vv. 6-8), who are to seek humility before God (v. 10; → γέλως; → πενθέω). Revelation speaks of the eschatological punishment of "Babylon" (18:7a: βασανισμὸς καὶ πένθος; v. 8: θάνατος καὶ πένθος καὶ λιμός), which arrogantly claims that it "does not know *grief/mourning*": πένθος οὐ μὴ ἴδω (v. 7b; cf. Isa 47:7-10). In contrast to this stands God's eschatological elimination of the suffering of this world: ὁ θάνατος οὐκ ἔσται ἔτι οὔτε πένθος οὔτε κραυγὴ οὔτε πόνος, ". . . neither *mourning* nor crying nor pain" (Rev 21:4; cf. Isa 35:10; 51:11; 65:19). → πενθέω.

πενιχρός, 3 *penichros* poor*

Luke 21:2: χήρα πενιχρά (par. Mark 12:42: πτωχή), referring to a "*poor/wretched* widow," with particular emphasis on her neediness (cf. Philo *Som.* i.98; ii.213). F. Hauck, *TDNT* VI, 40. → χήρα.

πεντάκις *pentakis* five times*

According to 2 Cor 11:24, *five times* Paul had to endure at the hands of the Jews the (synagogal) punishment (not mentioned in Acts) of the forty less one lashes (or blows with a rod: A. van den Born, *BL* 533f.; cf. the three beatings by the Romans [v. 25]; see also Acts 16:22); for further discussion see Billerbeck III, 527-30.

πεντακισχίλιοι, 3 *pentakischilioi* five thousand*

6 occurrences in the NT, always in reference to the miraculous feeding of the *five thousand*. Matt 14:21: ἄνδρες ὡσεὶ πεντακισχίλιοι χωρὶς γυναικῶν καὶ παιδίων; 16:9; Mark 6:44: πεντακισχίλιοι ἄνδρες; 8:19; Luke 9:14: ὡσεὶ ἄνδρες πεντακισχίλιοι; John 6:10: οἱ ἄνδρες τὸν ἀριθμὸν ὡς πεντακισχίλιοι; cf. also Acts 4:4: χιλιάδες πέντε.

πεντακόσιοι, 3 *pentakosioi* five hundred*

Luke 7:41: δηνάρια πεντακόσια (with πεντήκοντα); 1 Cor 15:6: ὤφθη ἐπάνω πεντακοσίοις ἀδελφοῖς, ". . . more than *five hundred* brethren" (see H. Grass, *Ostergeschehen und Osterberichte* [⁴1970] 99-101; H. Conzelmann, *1 Cor* [Hermeneia] ad loc.).

πέντε *pente* five*

There are 38 occurrences in the NT, 12 of those in Matthew, 3 in Mark, 9 in Luke, 5 each in John and Acts, and 3 in Revelation; Paul uses the word only in 1 Cor 14:19.

The number *five* is a favorite round number for a smaller quantity (cf. the five fingers of a hand), e.g., in the OT in Exod 22:1; Lev 26:8; Judg 18:2; 1 Sam 17:40; 21:4 (*five* loaves), and elsewhere. In the NT, too, it is usually a round number: *five* loaves (Matt 14:17, 19; 16:9; Mark 6:38, 41; 8:19; Luke 9:13, 16; John 6:9, 13), maidens (Matt 25:2 bis), talents (Matt 25:15, 16 bis, 20 [4 occurrences]), minas (Luke 19:18), months (Luke 1:24; as a time of torment in Rev 9:5, 10), days (Acts 20:6; 24:1), sparrows (Luke 12:6), persons in one house (3 + 2, Luke 12:52), oxen (14:19), brothers (16:28), cities (19:19), husbands of one woman (John 4:18), and words (with one's understanding, in contrast to ten thousand in tongues: 1 Cor 14:19). It is also used with larger round numbers (Acts 4:4: χιλιάδες πέντε; 19:19: μυριάδες πέντε), in a specification of location (John 5:2: πέντε στοὰς ἔχουσα), and in historical allusions (Rev 17:10: οἱ πέντε [βασιλεῖς]). In number combinations: εἴκοσι πέντε, *twenty-five* (John 6:19); ἑβδομήκοντα πέντε, *seventy-five* (Acts 7:14). G. Kittel, *Rabbinica* (1919) 31-47, esp. 39ff.; E. Hommel, *ZNW* 23 (1924) 305-10.

πεντεκαιδέκατος, 3 *pentekaidekatos* fifteenth*

Luke 3:1: ἐν ἔτει πεντεκαιδεκάτῳ, referring to the *fifteenth* year of the reign of Emperor Tiberius (A.D. 27/28); see G. Schneider, *Luke* (ÖTK) I ad loc.

πεντήκοντα *pentēkonta* fifty*

5 occurrences in the NT. Mark 6:40: κατὰ ἑκατὸν καὶ κατὰ πεντήκοντα; cf. Luke 9:14: ἀνὰ πεντήκοντα; 7:41: πεντήκοντα (δηνάρια), in contrast to five hundred; 16:6: πεντήκοντα (βάτοι ἐλαίου), in contrast to one hundred. According to John 8:57, πεντήκοντα ἔτη οὔπω ἔχεις means that Jesus has not yet reached full maturity (cf. also Num 4:3; 8:24f.).

πεντηκοστή, ῆς, ἡ *pentēkostē* fiftieth (day), Pentecost*

Lit.: N. ADLER, *Das erste christliche Pfingstfest* (1938). — idem, *LTK* VIII, 422f. — A. ARENS, *LTK* VIII, 421f. — BAGD s.v. — J. D. COLLINS, "Discovering the Meaning of Pentecost," *Scripture* 20 (1968) 73-79. — M. DELCOR, *DBSup* VII (1966) 858-79. — J. D. G. DUNN, *DNTT*, II, 783-87. — W. GRUNDMANN, "Der Pfingstbericht der Apostelgeschichte in seinem theologischen Sinn," *SE* II (1964) 584-94. — K. HRUBY, "La fête de la Pentecôte dans la tradition juive," *BVC* 63 (1965) 46-64. — P. VAN IMSCHOOT and H. HAAG, *BL* 1370f. — J. KREMER, *Pfingst-*

bericht und Pfingstgeschehen (1973). — G. KRETSCHMAR, "Himmelfahrt und Pfingsten," *ZKG* 66 (1954/55) 209-53. — E. KUTSCH and H. D. WENDLAND, *RGG* II, 910-19. — E. LOHSE, *TDNT* VI, 44-53. — I. H. MARSHALL, "The Significance of Pentecost," *SJT* 30 (1977) 347-69. — P. MATTA-EL-MESKIN, "La Pentecôte," *Irénikon* 50 (1977) 5-45. — P. H. MENOUD, "La Pentecôte lucanienne et l'histoire," *RHPR* 42 (1962) 141-47. — B. NOACK, "The Day of Pentecost in Jubilees, Qumran, and Acts," *ASTI* 1 (1962) 73-95. — J. POTIN, *La fête juive de la Pentecôte* (1971). — G. SCHNEIDER, *BL* 1371f. — For further bibliography see *DNTT* II, 787f.; *TWNT* X, 1228f.

1. The designation for the OT Feast of Weeks, *ḥag šābu'ōt* (= ἑορτὴ ἑβδομάδων, "Feast of Weeks") is rendered in Tob 2:1; 2 Macc 12:32; and in Hellenistic Jewish writings (e.g., Philo *Decal.* 160; Josephus *Ant.* iii.252) by πεντηκοστή. It was originally a harvest festival celebrated seven weeks after the beginning of the harvest (Deut 16:9f.) or "after the sabbath" (Lev 23:15f.). In early Judaism the seven weeks or the fiftieth day began with Passover. After the destruction of the temple in A.D. 70 one could no longer bring offerings there, so a different focus for the festival came to the fore, already attested in *Jubilees* 6 and probably also in 1QS 1:18–2:23: the giving of the law on Sinai (for rabbinic sources see Billerbeck II, 601). This content emerged from the reference to Passover and from the time reference in Exod 19:1.

2. In all 3 NT occurrences πεντηκοστή refers to the Jewish Feast of Weeks. In 1 Cor 16:8 Paul writes that he wishes to remain in Ephesus until the Jewish festival designated as πεντηκοστή; in Acts 20:16 he says that he wants to have returned to Jerusalem from his third missionary journey before πεντηκοστή. According to Acts 2:1 the descent of the Holy Spirit accompanied by cosmic phenomena and the miracle of foreign languages occurred "when the day of Pentecost had come," indicating that what occurred was salvation-historical fulfillment. It is disputed whether the dating of this scene to the feast day, which is heavy with motifs of theophany, originally comes from Luke himself (so among others E. Haenchen, *Acts* [Eng. tr., 1971] 172f.; M. Dömer, *Das Heil Gottes* [1978] 151f.), or from pre-Lukan tradition (so among others Menoud 144f.; Kremer 94), from which one could assume a connection with a historical event in Jerusalem during the Jewish Feast of Weeks after Jesus' resurrection (so among others Kretschmar 248; Kremer 260f.; G. Lohfink, *TQ* 160 [1980] 172-74; G. Schneider [justifiably more reserved], *Acts* [HTKNT] I, 242-48).

A. Weiser

πεποίθησις, εως, ἡ *pepoithēsis* trust, confidence*

This noun is a later construction occurring variously in Hellenistic Jewish writings. In the NT it occurs only in the Pauline corpus and refers to trust in others (2 Cor 1:15; 8:22; cf. Phil 3:4: ἐν σαρκί), in God (Eph 3:12), and in oneself (2 Cor 3:4; 10:2). R. Bultmann, *TDNT* VI, 7f.; O. Becker, *DNTT* I, 588-93.

περαιτέρω *peraiterō* beyond this*

This adv., from the adj. περαίτερος, occurs in the NT only in Acts 19:39: "if you seek (ἐπιζητεῖτε) anything *beyond this/further.*"

πέραν *peran* on the other side*

This adv. of place is used subst. with the art.: τὸ πέραν, *the shore on the other side* (Matt 8:18, 28; 14:22; 16:5; Mark 4:35; 5:21; 6:45; 8:13). It also occurs as an improper prep. with gen. responding to the questions "whither" (John 6:1, 17; cf. 10:40; 18:1) and "where" (Matt 19:1; John 1:28; 3:26; 6:22, 25; cf. BDF §184) and with both art. and gen. (Mark 5:1; Luke 8:22). Πέραν τοῦ Ἰορδάνου functions as an indeclinable proper name (Matt 4:25; Mark 3:8; cf. Matt 4:15; Mark 10:1).

πέρας, ατος, τό *peras* boundary, end*

Pl. in Matt 12:42 par. Luke 11:31: ἐκ τῶν περάτων τῆς γῆς; Rom 10:18, quoting Ps 18:5 LXX: εἰς τὰ πέρατα τῆς οἰκουμένης. In addition to the spatial meaning attested here, πέρας also designates the *conclusion* or *end,* in Heb 6:16 referring to the oath that is the *end* of all objection.

Πέργαμος, ου *Pergamos* Pergamum*

The NT mentions the city of Pergamum only in Rev 1:11 and 2:12, in the first instance in an enumeration of the seven Christian churches in Asia Minor (in third position), in the second instance in the formulaic commission: "And to the angel of the church in *Pergamum* write. . . ." Both occurrences possibly attest the form τὸ Πέργαμον, also attested elsewhere. The city was in Mysia and was the center of numerous cults (including Zeus Soter; cf. E. Meyer, *KP* IV, 626-31; D. Boyd, *IDBSup* 653f.; G. T. Griffith, *OCD* 799f.). Persecution of Christians in Pergamum probably began early (cf. Rev 2:13). Rev 2:14-16 admonishes the Christians of Pergamum to turn away from the false teachings of the Nicolaitans. H. Kraft, *Rev* (HNT) 63-67.

Πέργη, ης *Pergē* Perga*

Paul visited the city of Perga in Pamphylia during his "first missionary journey" (Acts 13:13, 14; 14:25). W. Ruge, *PW* XIX/1, 694-704; E. Olshausen, *KP* IV, 631f.; G. E. Bean, *OCD* 800.

περί *peri* with gen.: about, concerning, because of, with regard to, for; with acc.: about, around, with regard to

1. Occurrences in the NT — 2. With gen. — a) Direction — b) Reason — c) Reference — d) Interest — 3. With acc. — a) Local — b) Temporal — c) Fig.

Lit.: On preps. in general → ἀνά. — BAGD s.v. — E. BAASLAND, "Die περί-Formel und die Argumentation(ssituation) des Paulus," *ST* 42 (1988) 69-87. — BDF §§228f. — JOHANNESSOHN, *Präpositionen* 219-26. — KÜHNER, *Grammatik* II/1, 491-95. — MAYSER, *Grammatik* II/2, 445-56. — MOULE, *Idiom-Book* 62f. — MOULTON, *Grammar* III, 269f. — RADERMACHER, *Grammatik* 137-46. — P. F. REGARD, *Contribution à l'Étude des Prépositions dans la langue du NT* (1919) 527-44. — E. H. RIESENFELD, *TDNT* VI, 53-56. — SCHWYZER, *Grammatik* II, 499-505.

1. Περί occurs 333 times in the NT and occupies tenth place in frequency among NT preps. As a prefix with compound vbs. περί *(around, beyond, very)* occupies twelfth place in frequency in the NT. Περί no longer occurs with the dat. in the NT or the papyri (περί with dat. 4 times in the LXX). This ends a development that began in classical Greek. Περί occurs in almost all NT writings (except Galatians, James, and 2 John) and is used most often, by far, with the gen. (Morgenthaler, *Statistik* 160). Περί with gen. is a typical feature of the Lukan and Johannine writings (though not of Revelation). As with other preps., NT use of περί represents the emergence of prep. phrases in the place of the simple cases (Radermacher 125, 135). Περί and ὑπέρ with gen. often overlap, with περί replacing ὑπέρ more often than vice versa (BDF §§229.1; 231).

Περί means something like *through* and *beyond,* but its original meaning is not quite clear (Frisk, *Wörterbuch* II, 512f.; Schwyzer 499). This meaning is also seen in the intensive enclitic particle περ, which in the NT only occurs in compound words. From this fundamental meaning comes the spatial meaning *about/around,* designating the act of lingering in the vicinity of something or movement around something. At an early stage this spatial meaning was increasingly displaced by fig. meanings.

2. With gen. a) Designating the object or person toward which an activity is directed: *about, concerning, with,* after vbs. of speaking, teaching, writing, hearing, knowing, meaning, thinking, witnessing, asking, inquiring, overhearing, caring, etc. This field of meaning cannot always be clearly distinguished from others (reason, reference, interest). Matt 11:7: "Jesus began to speak *concerning* John"; Acts 8:34: "*about* whom does the prophet say this, *about* himself or *about* someone else?"; John 1:22: "what do you say *about* yourself?"; 1 John 2:27: "as his anointing teaches you *about* everything"; Acts 25:26: "but I have nothing definite to write to my lord *about* him"; 1 John 2:26: "I write this to you *about* those who would deceive you"; Acts 24:24: ἤκουσεν αὐτοῦ περὶ τῆς εἰς Χριστὸν Ἰησοῦν πίστεως, "He heard from him *concerning* faith in Christ Jesus"; Mark 13:32 (Matt 24:36): "but *of* that day or hour no one knows";

1 Thess 4:13: οὐ θέλομεν ὑμᾶς ἀγνοεῖν περὶ τῶν κοιμωμένων, "we do not want you to know nothing *of* those who are asleep/to be ignorant *concerning* those who are asleep"; Acts 26:26: ἐπίσταται περὶ τούτων ὁ βασιλεύς, "the king knows *about* these things/understands *concerning* these things"; Matt 22:42: τί ὑμῖν δοκεῖ περὶ τοῦ Χριστοῦ, "what do you think *concerning* the Christ?"; John 1:7f.: ἵνα μαρτυρήσῃ περὶ τοῦ φωτός, "to bear witness *concerning* [or *for:* → 2.d] the light"; Acts 23:20: "as though they were going to inquire somewhat [learn something] more closely *about* him (πυνθάνεσθαι)"; John 19:24: λάχωμεν περὶ αὐτοῦ τίνος ἔσται, "let us cast lots *concerning* whose it shall be"; Matt 22:16: οὐ μέλει σοι περὶ οὐδενός, "you care *for* no man/ask *about* no one"; Matt 6:28: περὶ ἐνδύματος τί μεριμνᾶτε, "why are you anxious *about* clothing."

b) Indicating the reason for an action: *because of, for,* after vbs. of charging, convicting, condemning, punishing, and praising and vbs. of emotion, etc. Acts 24:13: περὶ ὧν κατηγοροῦσίν μου, "the things *because of* which they charge me"; John 8:46: τίς ἐλέγχει με περὶ ἁμαρτίας, "Which of you convicts me *of* sin?"; Acts 25:20: κρίνεσθαι περὶ τούτων, "be judged *because of* them"; 23:6: "*because of* the hope and the resurrection of the dead I am on trial (κρίνομαι)"; in contrast John 8:26: πολλὰ ἔχω περὶ ὑμῶν λαλεῖν καὶ κρίνειν, "I have much to say *about* you and to judge" (i.e., "I could say much *about* you and condemn you"); 10:33: "not *because of* a good work do we stone you, but *for* blasphemy"; Luke 19:37: αἰνεῖν τὸν θεὸν περὶ πασῶν δυνάμεων, "praise God *for* all the mighty works"; Matt 20:24: "They were indignant *at* the two brothers"; Luke 2:18: "They wondered *at* the words."

c) Of reference: *in reference to, with respect to, concerning* (similar in meaning to περί with acc. [→ 3.c.2]). 1 Cor 7:1: περὶ ὧν ἐγράψατε, "*with regard to* the matters about which you wrote"; Luke 24:19: τὰ περὶ Ἰησοῦ, "that which *concerns* Jesus/what happened to Jesus"; Luke 24:27: τὰ περὶ ἑαυτοῦ, "the things *concerning* himself/dealing with himself"; Phil 1:27; 2:19: τὰ περὶ ὑμῶν, "your situation/circumstances"; Eph 6:22: τὰ περὶ ἡμῶν, "our circumstances"; Acts 24:10: τὰ περὶ ἐμαυτοῦ, "my matter"; Luke 22:37: τὸ περὶ ἐμοῦ, "what *concerns* me," possibly "what is written about me/what is determined for me/my life" (so Riesenfeld 54); 3 John 2: περὶ πάντων, "*in* every respect" (BDF §229 considers "*above* all" possible); John 15:22: "they have no excuse *with respect to/for* their sin."

d) Designating the object or person in whose interest or on whose behalf something happens (like ὑπέρ with gen.), esp. with vbs. of asking and praying: *for, on account of.* Luke 4:38: "They besought him *for* her"; 6:28: "pray *for* those who abuse you"; Col 1:3: περὶ (v.l. ὑπέρ) ὑμῶν προσευχόμενοι, "when we pray *for* you"; 2:1 v.l.: ἀγῶνα ἔχω περὶ (in the text: ὑπέρ) ὑμῶν, "I have a struggle

to endure for you" (περὶ ὑμῶν as v.l. also in 1 Cor 1:13); Matt 26:28: τὸ περὶ πολλῶν ἐκχυννόμενον (Mark 14:24/Luke 22:20: ὑπέρ), "that which is poured out *for* the many"; Acts 26:1: "you have permission to speak *for* yourself (περὶ σεαυτοῦ; v.l. ὑπέρ)."

In the phrase περὶ ἁμαρτίας (Rom 8:3), "*because of* sin," περί takes on the sense "for the elimination/atonement of (sin)." 1 Pet 3:18: Χριστὸς ἅπαξ περὶ ἁμαρτιῶν ἔπαθεν (v.l. ἀπέθανεν), "Christ suffered *for* [the atonement of] sins once for all"; Heb 10:18: προσφορὰ περὶ ἁμαρτίας, "sin offering"; so also 10:6, 8; 13:11: περὶ ἁμαρτίας (προσφορά to be supplied); 5:3: περὶ ἁμαρτιῶν, "sin offering"; 10:26: οὐκέτι περὶ ἁμαρτιῶν ἀπολείπεται θυσία, "there no longer remains a sacrifice *for* sins."

3. With acc. a) Local: *about, around, in the vicinity of:* Luke 13:8: ἕως ὅτου σκάψω περὶ αὐτήν (i.e., συκῆν), "till I have dug [the ground] *around* it"; Acts 22:6: περιαστράψαι φῶς περὶ ἐμέ, "a light shone *about* me" (the verbal prefix strengthens the prep.); Matt 3:4 and Mark 1:6: "*around* his waist"; Mark 9:42 par.: "*around* his neck"; Mark 3:8: "[the region] *around* Tyre and Sidon"; Acts 28:7: ἐν τοῖς περὶ τὸν τόπον ἐκεῖνον, "in the area *around* that place/*in the vicinity of* that place"; Mark 3:32, 34: "[sitting] *about* him."

Local περί with a personal acc. can refer to people around a person (companions, followers). As in classical Greek, the person involved can also be included in the action (whether this is the case can only be determined from context). Occasionally, as in Hellenistic Greek, this manner of expression refers only to the intended person (so perhaps John 11:19 v.l.: πρὸς τὰς περὶ Μάρθαν καὶ Μαριάμ, "to Martha and Mary," or "to Martha and Mary and their people" [cf. Riesenfeld 56 n.25]): Mark 4:10 and Luke 22:49: οἱ περὶ αὐτόν, "his companions/disciples"; Acts 13:13: οἱ περὶ Παῦλον, "Paul and his companions."

b) Temporal (approximate designation of time): *around, toward.* Matt 20:3: "*about* the third hour"; Mark 6:48: "*about* the fourth watch"; Acts 22:6: "*about* noon." In classical and Hellenistic Greek περί with acc. also designates various other approximate indications of time.

c) Fig.: 1) *Being occupied with, taking trouble for:* Acts 19:25: οἱ περὶ τὰ τοιαῦτα ἐργάται, "the workers *who were occupied with* such things"; Luke 10:40: περιεσπᾶτο περὶ πολλὴν διακονίαν, "she was occupied *with* much service [preparing the meal]"; v. 41: θορυβάζῃ περὶ πολλά, "you are troubled *about* many things" (literally: "you trouble yourself *about* many things"); Mark 4:19: αἱ περὶ τὰ λοιπὰ ἐπιθυμίαι, "desires *for* other things."

2) *In reference to, with respect to, concerning* (similar in meaning to περί with gen. [→ 2.c]): Phil 2:23: τὰ περὶ ἐμέ, "that which *concerns* me/my circumstances"; 1 Tim 1:19; 6:21; 2 Tim 3:8: περὶ τὴν πίστιν, "*with respect to*

faith" (become shipwrecked, err from the path, not prove oneself); 2 Tim 2:18: *"regarding* truth" (err from the path); 1 Tim 6:4: νοσῶν περὶ ζητήσεις καὶ λογομαχίας, "ill *with* [or *from*] [nothing but] controversy and disputes about words"; Titus 2:7: περὶ πάντα, *"in* all respects."

W. Köhler

περιάγω *periagō* lead around; intrans.: go about*

Trans. *lead around with oneself/have with oneself* in the NT only in 1 Cor 9:5: *"have* a sister [Christian] as a wife *with oneself."* Otherwise intrans.: of Jesus in Mark 6:6b par. Matt 9:35; Matt 4:23; of journeys of the scribes and Pharisees in Matt 23:15; of the blind man who *went about* in Acts 13:11.

περιαιρέω *periaireō* take away; destroy*

2 Cor 3:16: the veil *is removed;* Acts 27:40: the anchors (on both sides of the ship) *are taken away/cut away;* 28:13: *weigh* the anchors (→ περιέρχομαι); Heb 10:11: sacrifices cannot *destroy/take away* sins (cf. Exod 8:4, 27); pass. in Acts 27:20: "All hope of our being saved *grew weaker and weaker* [impf. περιῃρεῖτο]." Spicq, *Notes* II, 679f.

περιάπτω *periaptō* kindle*

Luke 22:55 (cf. par. Mark 14:54): "when they *had kindled* a fire in the middle of the courtyard" (the denial narrative).

περιαστράπτω *periastraptō* shine around; intrans.: become illuminated all around*

Trans. περιαστράπτω τινά in Acts 9:3; 22:6 D: Light from heaven *shone around* the persecutor Saul; intrans. in 22:6, of the same event: "From heaven a light *shone* all around me (περὶ ἐμέ)."

περιβάλλω *periballō* throw around, put on; mid.: get dressed*

Always literal in the NT, usually of putting on clothing. Luke 19:43 v.l., of the bank with which the enemies *will surround* (περιβαλοῦσιν) Jerusalem. In regard to putting on clothing the following constructions occur: 1) with τί τινι, *"put* something *on* someone" or mid. *"put* something *on* oneself" (Mark 14:51; 16:5; Matt 6:31; Acts 12:8; Rev 7:9, 13; 10:1; 11:3; 12:1; 17:4; 18:16; 19:8, 13); 2) with τινά τινι, *"clothe* somebody with something" (Rev 17:4 v.l.); 3) mid. with ἔν τινι, *"clothe oneself* with something" (Rev 3:5; 4:4); 4) with double acc., *"put* something *on* someone" (John 19:2; cf. Luke 23:11); 5) with τινά without mentioning the garment, *"clothe*

someone" (Matt 25:36, 38, 43) or mid., *get dressed* (Matt 6:29 par. Luke 12:27; Rev 3:18).

περιβλέπομαι *periblepomai* look around (in a circle)*

In the NT only in Mark 3:5 par. Luke 6:10; Mark 3:34; 5:32; 10:23; 11:11, variously referring to Jesus; in 9:8, of the disciples at Jesus' transfiguration.

περιβόλαιον, ου, τό *peribolaion* cloak, mantle, covering*

Heb 1:12 (cf. Ps 101:27 LXX): ὡσεὶ περιβόλαιον ἑλίσσω, "roll up like a *mantle*"; 1 Cor 11:15: "Her [a woman's] hair is given to her for a *covering* (ἀντὶ περιβολαίου)."

περιδέω *perideō* wrap around*

John 11:44: "His face *was wrapped* (περιεδέδετο) with a cloth."

περιεργάζομαι *periergazomai* do useless things, appear busy*

In the NT only in 2 Thess 3:11 (see also → περίεργος): "For we hear that some of you are leading idle lives, not doing any work, but rather *doing useless things.*" Here ἐργαζόμενοι and περιεργαζόμενοι are antonyms. W. Trilling, *2 Thess* (EKKNT) 150-53 (on the motif of disinclination toward work).

περίεργος, 2 *periergos* curious; magic (adj.)*

1 Tim 5:13, of the "younger widows" who are "not only idlers, but also gossips and *given to prying.* . ." (cf. *Herm. Vis.* iv.3.1); Acts 19:19: τὰ περίεργα πράσσω, "practice *magic arts.*"

περιέρχομαι *perierchomai* go about*

Acts 19:13, of itinerant exorcists; Heb 11:37, of persecuted persons who *wander about;* with acc. of place in 1 Tim 5:13 (cf. Acts 13:6 D); Acts 28:13 v.l., of the passengers on a ship: περιελθόντες, "they made a circuit" (B ℵ*: περιελόντες, "they weighed [the anchors]"; see E. Haenchen, *Acts* [Eng. tr., 1971] 564ff.). J. Schneider, *TDNT* II, 682f.

περιέχω *periechō* encompass, contain*

Luke 5:9 (cf. Dan 7:28 LXX): θάμβος περιέσχεν αὐτόν, "fear *befell* him"; Acts 15:23 D: the letter *"containing* the following"; intrans. in 1 Pet 2:6: περιέχει ἐν γραφῇ, "it *stands/we read* in Scripture."

περιζώννυμαι *perizōnnymai* gird (someone); mid.: gird oneself*

Act. in Rev 1:13 (perhaps also in 15:6); absolute περιεζωσμέναι in Luke 12:35: "let your loins *be girded*"; absolute with mid. meaning in 12:37; 17:8, possibly also Rev 1:13 and 15:6. Eph 6:14 names the girded body part in the acc.: τὴν ὀσφὺν ὑμῶν. A. Oepke, *TDNT* V, 302-6; F. Selter, *DNTT* III, 120f.

περίθεσις, εως, ἡ *perithesis* putting on (noun)*

1 Pet 3:3: περίθεσις χρυσίων, "*adornment* with gold."

περιΐστημι *periïstēmi* place around; mid.: turn around, avoid*

Acts 25:7: The Jews "*placed themselves [stood] around* him"; John 11:42: ὁ ὄχλος ὁ περιεστώς, "the people *standing around*"; mid. in parenesis in 2 Tim 2:16; Titus 3:9.

περικάθαρμα, ατος, τό *perikatharma* refuse, filth*

1 Cor 4:13: "We have become as the *dregs* of the world (περικαθάρματα τοῦ κόσμου)." F. Hauck, *TDNT* III, 430f.; H.-G. Link, *DNTT* III, 102f.; Spicq, *Notes* II, 681f.

περικαθίζω *perikathizō* sit around
Luke 22:55 D in place of → συγκαθίζω.

περικαλύπτω *perikalyptō* cover, conceal*

Mark 14:65, of covering Jesus' face; par. Luke 22:64, of covering Jesus himself (αὐτόν); Heb 9:4 (cf. Exod 28:20): the ark of the covenant was *covered/adorned* completely with gold.

περίκειμαι *perikeimai* lie around; pass.: be surrounded*

Mark 9:42, of a millstone *hung round* one's neck (cf. Luke 17:2); Heb 12:1, of a crowd of people (νέφος μαρτύρων) *surrounding* someone; Acts 28:20, of chains that someone *bears;* fig. in Heb 5:2: "*beset* with weakness." F. Büchsel, *TDNT* III, 656.

περικεφαλαία, ας, ἡ *perikephalaia* helmet*

Fig. in virtue parenesis: 1 Thess 5:8: the hope of σωτηρία as a *helmet;* Eph 6:17: "the *helmet* of salvation (τοῦ σωτηρίου)." Cf. Ign. *Pol.* 6:2: πίστις as a helmet. A. Oepke, *TDNT* V, 314f.

περικρατής, 2 *perikratēs* powerful, in control*

Acts 27:16: περικρατὴς τῆς σκάφης, "*in control* of the boat," i.e., having power over it.

περικρύβω *perikrybō* hide*

Luke 1:24, of Elizabeth: "She *hid* herself (περιέκρυβεν ἑαυτήν) for five months."

περικυκλόω *perikykloō* surround*

With acc., of a besieged city (Josh 6:13; 4 Kgdms 6:14) in Luke 19:43 (Jesus' prediction regarding Jerusalem).

περιλάμπω *perilampō* shine around (someone)*

Luke 2:9: "the glory of the Lord *shone around* them"; Acts 26;13: "a light *shone around* me [sc. Paul]." A. Oepke, *TDNT* IV, 16, 24; H. C. Hahn, *DNTT* II, 484-86.

περιλείπομαι *perileipomai* (pass.) remain behind*

1 Thess 4:15, 17: "we, the living, *who are left behind* [until the Lord's parousia]." Spicq, *Notes* II, 683.

περιλείχω *perileichō* lick all around, lick
Luke 16:21 v.l. in place of ἐπιλείχω (of dogs that lick wounds).

περίλυπος, 2 *perilypos* very sad*

Mark 6:26: περίλυπος γενόμενος; Luke 18:23 περίλυπος ἐγενήθη (cf. v. 24); Mark 14:34 par. Matt 26:38: "My soul is *deeply grieved,* even unto death" (cf. Ps 41:6, 12 LXX). R. Bultmann, *TDNT* IV, 323; J. Beutler, *NTS* 25 (1978/79) 33-57.

περιμένω *perimenō* await*

Acts 1:4: await the fulfillment of the promise in Jerusalem. F. Hauck, *TDNT* IV, 578f.

πέριξ *perix* all around*

Acts 5:16: αἱ πέριξ πόλεις, "the towns *all around*," i.e., in the vicinity (of Jerusalem).

περιοικέω *perioikeō* dwell in the neighborhood*

Luke 1:65: οἱ περιοικοῦντες αὐτούς, "their *neighbors*."

περίοικος, 2 *perioikos* living in the neighborhood (adj.)*

Only subst. in the NT: οἱ περίοικοι, the *neighbors;* Luke 1:58, with οἱ συγγενεῖς ("the relatives").

περιούσιος, 2 *periousios* chosen, elect*

Titus 2:14: Jesus Christ "gave himself for us to redeem us from all guilt and to create for himself a pure people *that belongs to him as his special possession.*" Λαὸς περιούσιος is to be interpreted here against the background of Exod 19:5; 23:22; Deut 7:6; 14:2; 26:18. H. Preisker, *TDNT* VI, 57f.; E. Beyreuther, *DNTT* II, 838-40.

περιοχή, ῆς, ἡ *perioche* content (noun); section*

In Acts 8:32 περιοχή can refer either to the *content/wording* of the scriptural passage in question or to the relevant *section (passage)* of the biblical book, either "the *passage* of Scripture" or "what it said in the Scripture" (ἡ περιοχὴ τῆς γραφῆς) "that he was reading was this. . . ."

περιπατέω *peripateo* go about, walk; conduct oneself, live (in a certain way)*

1. Occurrences in the NT — 2. *Walk (about)* — 3. *Conduct oneself/live*

Lit.: BAGD s.v. — G. BERTRAM and H. SEESEMANN, *TDNT* V, 940-45. — O. BÖCHER, *Der johanneische Dualismus im Zusammenhang des nach-biblischen Judentums* (1965) 76-106, 149ff. — G. EBEL, *DNTT* III, 943-45. — R. G. WARD, *Paul's Use of the Root* περιπατέω (Diss. Dallas, 1953).

1. This vb. occurs 95 times in the NT, though in its fig. meaning *conduct oneself, live*—apart from Mark 7:5; Acts 21:21; Heb 13:9 referring to Jewish regulations— only in the Johannine writings and esp. in the Pauline and deutero-Pauline letters.

2. *Walk (about):* Healing of the lame (Mark 2:9 par.; John 5:8, 11f.; Acts 3:6, 12; 14:8), so also in the characterization of the time of salvation (Matt 11:5 par., motifs from Isa 35:6; cf. H.-W. Kuhn, *Enderwartung und gegenwärtiges Heil* [1966] 196), in Matthew and Luke in enumeration of Jesus' deeds (cf. also 15:31); esp. in demonstration of the success of a miracle (Mark 5:42; 8:24; John 5:9; Acts 3:8f.; 14:10; cf. G. Theissen, *Miracle Stories of the Early Christian Tradition* [1983] 66f.).

Rev 9:20: idols that "cannot *walk*" (cf. Ps 113:15 LXX); 1 Pet 5:8: the devil *"prowls around* [cf. Job 1:7; 2:2] like a roaring lion." In descriptions of setting: *walk by* (John 1:36); *on one's way* (Mark 16:12; Luke 24:17); *"walk* over" (11:44); περιπατέω παρὰ τὴν θάλασσαν etc., *"walk* along" (Matt 4:18); περιπατέω ἐν, stay around,

linger (Mark 11:27; John 7:1a, b; 10:23; 11:54); περιπατέω ἐν μέσῳ, etc. (Rev 2:1 [cf. 1:13]). "They no longer *went about* with him" (John 6:66).

In the manner of theophanies (cf. Job 9:8b): περιπατέω ἐπὶ τῆς θαλάσσης (Mark 6:48f.; Matt 14:26; John 6:19); περιπατέω ἐπὶ τὴν θάλασσαν/τὰ ὕδατα (Matt 14:25, 29). With an indication of one's clothing (cf. ἐν στολίῳ περιπατέω, Marcus Antoninus i.7.4; ἐν κοκκίνοις περιπατέω, Epictetus *Diss.* iii.22.10): ἐν στολαῖς (Mark 12:38 par.; → στολή); ἐν λευκοῖς (Rev 3:4; cf. *1 Enoch* 62:16; *Herm. Sim.* viii.2.3; → λευκός); in contrast to "*going* naked" (16:15). In a unique variation of Isa 60:3, according to Rev 21:24 the nations *will stroll* in the light of the divine city (literally "through its light").

The transition from literal to metaphorical usage (in Paul cf. 2 Cor 12:18: περιπατέω τοῖς αὐτοῖς ἴχνεσιν) can be seen in John: *be on one's way* during the day or night (John 11:9f.); "you *walked* wherever you wanted" (21:18); in contrast to dualistic terminology (cf. 1QS 3:21; 4:11; *Barn.* 19:1), περιπατέω ἐν τῇ σκοτίᾳ (8:12; 12:35c). "*Walk* while you have the light" (12:35b) is interpreted by πιστεύετε εἰς τὸ φῶς (v. 36; on these passages cf. R. Bergmeier, *Glaube als Gabe nach Johannes* [1980] 231, 235, 272 n.598).

3. *Conduct oneself, live,* as a rule more closely specified by the manner of such conduct (1 Thess 4:1a, b; Eph 5:15; on the relationship to wisdom and folly cf. 1QS 4:24; see K. G. Kuhn, *NTS* 7 [1960/61] 341) specifically:

a) with ἐν designating the condition or sphere of the "walking": ἐν καινότητι ζωῆς (Rom 6:4; cf. 7:6); ἐν πανουργίᾳ (2 Cor 4:2); in sins (Eph 2:2; Col 3:7; → ποτέ); in good works (Eph 2:10); ἐν ἀγάπῃ (5:2; cf. 2 John 6b, possibly also with reference to ἐντολή); in the Lord (the Christ Jesus of the apostolic proclamation, Col 2:6; see E. Schweizer, *Col* [Eng. tr., 1982] 123f.); ἐν σοφίᾳ (4:5); in dietary regulations (Heb 13:9); in darkness (John 8:12; 12:35c [→ 2]; 1 John 1:6; 2:11); in the light (1:7); ἐν (τῇ) ἀληθείᾳ (2 John 4; 3 John 3f., i.e., "believing and acting as a Christian"; see R. Bergmeier, *ZNW* 57 [1966] 96-100; *idem, Glaube als Gabe nach Johannes* [1980] 200ff.);

b) by the associative dat. (see BDF §198): τοῖς ἔθεσιν (Acts 21:21); μὴ κώμοις, etc. (Rom 13:13b); τῷ αὐτῷ πνεύματι, etc. (2 Cor 12:18); πνεύματι (Gal 5:16; cf. F. Mussner, *Gal* [HTKNT] 374f.);

c) by κατά with acc. to designate a norm: κατὰ τὴν παράδοσιν (Mark 7:5, referring to the Pharisaic halakah; 2 Thess 3:6c, referring to the apostolic tradition); κατὰ σάρκα (Rom 8:4; 2 Cor 10:2); κατὰ ἄνθρωπον (1 Cor 3:3); κατὰ πνεῦμα (Rom 8:4); κατὰ ἀγάπην (14:15); "according to his commandments" (2 John 6a);

d) by an adv.: εὐσχημόνως (Rom 13:13a; 1 Thess

4:12); ἀξίως with gen. (1 Thess 2:12; Eph 4:1; Col 1:10); ἀτάκτως (2 Thess 3:6, 11); or

e) by comparison: Phil 3:17 (18); Eph 4:17; 5:8 (J. Gnilka, *Eph* [HTKNT] 251ff.: "walk as children of the light"); 1 John 2:6.

Like ζῆν ἐν σαρκί (Gal 2:20; Phil 1:22), ἐν σαρκὶ περιπατέω (2 Cor 10:3) refers to earthly existence (cf. *1 Enoch* 108:11; *Barn.* 10:11). A similar correspondence obtains between ζῆν ἐν πίστει (Gal 2:20) and διὰ πίστεως περιπατοῦμεν οὐ διὰ εἴδους (2 Cor 5:7). 1 Cor 7:17: "*let each person [continue to] live*" as God's call has assigned him or her (cf. vv. 20, 24). R. Bergmeier

περιπείρω *peripeirō* pierce through*

Fig. in 1 Tim 6:10: ἑαυτὸν περιπείρειν ὀδύναις, "cause themselves piercing pain."

περιπίπτω *peripiptō* fall into/get involved with*

Luke 10:30: περιπίπτω λῃσταῖς, "*fall into the hands of* robbers"; Acts 27:41: περιπίπτω εἰς τόπον διθάλασσον, "*strike/hit* upon a shoal/sandbank"; fig. in Jas 1:2: περιπίπτω πειρασμοῖς ποικίλοις, "*encounter* various trials." W. Michaelis, *TDNT* VI, 173; Spicq, *Notes* II, 684-86.

περιποιέομαι *peripoieomai* acquire/gain for oneself*

Luke 17:33: τὴν ψυχήν, "*gain* one's life"; Acts 20:28, of "church of God" which God "*obtained* with his own Son's blood"; 1 Tim 3:13: "*gain* good standing for oneself." E. Beyreuther, *DNTT* II, 838ff.; Spicq, *Notes* II, 687-89.

περιποίησις, εως, ἡ *peripoiēsis* preservation; acquisition; possession*

With obj. gen. in 1 Thess 5:9 (σωτηρίας); 2 Thess 2:14 (δόξης τοῦ κυρίου ἡμῶν). In Heb 10:39 εἰς περιποίησιν ψυχῆς (antithesis: εἰς ἀπώλειαν) refers to the preservation of life (cf. Luke 17:33, → περιποιέομαι). 1 Pet 2:9: "a people for his *possession*"; Eph 1:14: ἀπολύτρωσις τῆς περιποιήσεως, "redemption through which we become [God's] *possession*." E. Beyreuther, *DNTT* II, 838ff.; Spicq, *Notes* II, 687-89.

περιραίνω *perirainō* sprinkle around
Rev 19:13 ℵ(c): περιρεραμμένον after ἱμάτιον (in place of βεβαμμένον, from βάπτω). *TCGNT* ad loc.

περιρήγνυμι *perirēgnymi* tear off all around*

Acts 16:22: In Philippi they "*tore* the clothes *off* the bodies (περιρήξαντες αὐτῶν τὰ ἱμάτια)" of Paul and Silas before the missionaries were beaten with rods.

περισπάομαι *perispaomai* be distracted/busy*

Luke 10:40, of Martha: περιεσπᾶτο περὶ πολλὴν διακονίαν, "she *was extremely busy* with much service," i.e., she was completely occupied with caring for Jesus. → περί 3.c.1.

περισσεία, ας, ἡ *perisseia* surplus, abundance*

Absolute only in 2 Cor 10:15: "increase to a *vast extent*." Otherwise an object is specified in the gen.: Rom 5:17: τῆς χάριτος; 2 Cor 8:2: τῆς χαρᾶς; Jas 1:21: κακίας. F. Hauck, *TDNT* VI, 63.

περίσσευμα, ατος, τό *perisseuma* surplus, what remains behind, leavings*

2 Cor 8:14a, b, contrasted to → ὑστέρημα, "deficiency," referring to the Corinthians' collection for Jerusalem. Matt 12:34 par. Luke 6:45: ἐκ (τῆς) περισσεύματος (τῆς) καρδίας, "out of the *abundance* of the heart. . . ." *Scraps, leftovers*, Mark 8:8: περισσεύματα κλασμάτων (Matt 15:37 has τὸ περισσεῦον τῶν κλασμάτων). F. Hauck, *TDNT* VI, 63.

περισσεύω *perisseuō* exceed, be present in superabundance, prove to be extremely rich, have a superabundance; trans.: make extremely rich*

1. Occurrences of the root περισσ- in the NT — 2. Usage and meaning of περισσεύω — 3. The Gospels — 4. Paul — 5. The other NT writings

Lit.: BAGD s.v. — N. BAUMERT, *Täglich sterben und auferstehen. Der Literalsinn von 2Kor 4,12–5,10* (SANT 34, 1973) 300-310. — T. BRANDT, *DNTT* I, 728-31. — F. HAUCK, *TDNT* VI, 58-63. — B. NOACK, "A Note on II Cor. IV.15," *ST* 17 (1963) 129-32. — M. THEOBALD, *Die überströmende Gnade. Studien zu einem paulinischen Motivfeld* (Diss. Bonn, 1980).

1. In the NT, words of the stem περισσ- occur, in addition to περισσεύω itself, esp. in the authentic Pauline letters (NT as a whole/Paul/other NT writings): περισσεύω (39/24/15), περισσεία (4/3/1), περίσσευμα (5/2/3), περισσός (6/2/4), περισσότερος (17/6/11), περισσοτέρως (12/10/2), περισσῶς (4/0/4), ὑπερεκπερισσοῦ (3/2/1), ὑπερπερισσεύω (2/2/0), ὑπερπερισσῶς (1/0/1). Of the 93 total occurrences, 51 are in Paul, 42 in other NT writings. In the LXX the stem περισσ- almost always renders the Hebrew root *ytr* (niphal: "be left over," hiphil: "leave over or behind").

2. Περισσεύω is largely used intrans., and in the case of things means *exceed, be left over, be present in superabundance*, though also *be exceedingly rich*. In reference to persons περισσεύω means *have more than enough, be rich* (in something). The less frequent trans. meaning

make exceedingly rich occurs with reference to things only in Matt 13:12; 25:29; 2 Cor 4:15; 9:8a; Eph 1:8, and with reference to persons in 1 Thess 3:12 and perhaps Luke 15:17, if περισσεύονται is pass. rather than mid. (→ 3). The (intrans.) meaning noted by BAGD (s.v. 1.a.δ, for Acts 16:5 and Phil 1:9), *grow,* renders only inexactly the sense of περισσεύω with dat. or with ἐν.

3. In the Gospels, περισσεύω with the meaning *be left over* (in the feedings of the four and five thousand) refers to the κλάσματα left over (Matt 14:20; 15:37; Luke 9:17; John 6:12, 13; Mark 8:8 has περισσεύματα). In both instances Matthew has τὸ περισσεῦον, *what was left over,* Luke τὸ περισσεῦσαν αὐτοῖς, *"what they had left over."* In Mark 12:44 par. Luke 21:4 τὸ περισσεῦον (with dat.) refers to the *surplus* a person has in the way of material goods (antonyms: Mark ὑστέρησις, Luke: ὑστέρημα).

Matthew, with 5 occurrences, exhibits a definite preference for περισσεύω. In 5:20 (M) the δικαιοσύνη of Jesus' disciples is the subj.: "Unless your righteousness *exceeds* (περισσεύσῃ . . . πλεῖον) that of the scribes and Pharisees." The logion in 13:12 is repeated in 25:29 (both passages use περισσεύω trans.): "For to him who has will more be given, and *will be granted in superabundance*" (καὶ περισσευθήσεται does not occur in par. Mark 4:25).

Luke has 2 occurrences in L. The warning against covetousness in 12:15 concludes with: "For a man's life does not consist in the *superabundance* of his possessions (ἐν τῷ περισσεύειν τινί)." Περισσεύονται in 15:17 is probably to be understood as the pass. of trans. περισσεύω: They *are brought to overflow/receive more than enough* (with gen.); BAGD s.v. 1.b considers this a mid. use of intrans. περισσεύω, which cannot be excluded. In 15:17 א Koine and others read (probably simplifying) περισσεύουσιν.

4. Expressly mentioned subjects of περισσεύω in Paul include: "God's truth" (Rom 3:7), "God's grace" (5:15), "Christ's παθήματα" (2 Cor 1:5a), "our παράκλησις" (1:5b), "the διακονία of righteousness" (3:9), "the περισσεία of their joy and their extreme πτωχεία" (8:2), "the διακονία of this service" (9:12), "your love" (Phil 1:9), and "your glory" (1:26). Subjects of trans. περισσεύω include "the Lord" (1 Thess 3:12), "grace" (2 Cor 4:15), and "God" (9:8a).

Use of περισσεύω with εἰς is characteristic of Paul (Baumert 300f.; Rom 3:7; 5:15; 2 Cor 1:5a; 4:15; 8:2; 9:8a, b; 1 Thess 3:12 [in the NT otherwise only Eph 1:8]). Περισσεύω with μᾶλλον is also noteworthy (2 Cor 3:9; Phil 1:9; 1 Thess 4:1, 10).

One area of concentration emerges in the use of περισσεύω meaning *have a superabundance of* for Christians' wealth of present salvation possessions (besides the instances already mentioned see also Rom 15:13: "of hope"; 2 Cor 8:7a: "of everything"; 9:8a, 12) and the

resulting challenge to *excel* (1 Cor 14:12; 15:58; 2 Cor 8:7b; 9:8b; 1 Thess 4:1, 10). The vb. exhibits more neutral meaning in 1 Cor 8:8 *(be at an advantage)* and Phil 4:12a, b, 18 *(have enough and to spare;* antonym: ὑστερέομαι, v. 12b).

Περισσεύω can be used of "not only the specifics of a particular condition, but also the dynamics of a particular process" (Baumert 300). Paul uses περισσεύω to characterize the dynamics of Christian existence, the superabundance of incipient salvation over against pre-Christian existence (Rom 5:15, 17, 20f.), the wealth of the Church in gifts, powers, and service, and Christians' spiritual growth (Rom 15:13; 1 Cor 14:12; 15:58).

5. The other NT writings attest περισσεύω only in three instances. Acts 16:5 reports concerning the growth of the Christian churches (ἐκκλησίαι): ἐπερίσσευον τῷ ἀριθμῷ καθ' ἡμέραν. In Col 2:7 περισσεύοντες ἐν εὐχαριστίᾳ means that the addressees should *excel* in thanksgiving (cf. 1 Thess 4:1, 10). Eph 1:8 stands in the Pauline tradition (cf. Rom 5:15; 2 Cor 4:15) and asserts of χάρις that God *"has richly lavished* [it] upon us [ἐπερίσσευσεν trans.] in all wisdom and insight."

G. Schneider

περισσός, 3 *perissos* exceeding (the usual number or the usual measure), superfluous*

Matt 5:47: "What are you doing *that is special?*"; v. 37: τὸ περισσόν, *"anything more than this* [sc. than simple yes or no]"; John 10:10: περισσὸν ἔχω, "have *in superabundance*"; 2 Cor 9:1: περισσόν μοί ἐστιν with inf., *"it is superfluous* for me [to write]"; Rom 3:1: τὸ περισσόν, referring to the *advantage* the Jew enjoys over the Gentile; Mark 6:51: adv. ἐκ περισσοῦ, "exceedingly." F. Hauck, *TDNT* VI, 61f.

περισσότερος, 3 *perissoteros* greater, more*

The comparative of περισσός is used with nouns in 1 Cor 12:23a, 24 (τιμή); 12:23b (εὐσχημοσύνη); 2 Cor 2:7 (λύπη); Mark 12:40 par. Matt 23:14 v.l./Luke 20:47 (κρίμα). Neut. περισσότερον occurs in Luke 12:48; 1 Cor 15:10; περισσότερόν τι, "something *more,*" in Luke 12:4; 2 Cor 10:8; with gen. of comparison in Mark 12:33; cf. also Matt 11:9 par. Luke 7:26 *(greater / more* than a prophet). Adv. περισσότερον in Mark 7:36; Heb 6:17; 7:15.

περισσοτέρως *perissoterōs* more (adv.), especially*

Used in the NT comparatively *(to a far greater measure:* 2 Cor 11:23 bis; 12:15; Gal 1:14; Phil 1:14; Heb

2:1; 13:19) and elatively (*especially:* 2 Cor 1:12; 2:4; 7:13, 15; 1 Thess 2:17).

περισσῶς *perissōs* beyond measure, exceedingly; more*

Περισσῶς is used comparatively (*even more*) in Mark 10:26 (with ἐκπλήσσομαι); Mark 15:14 par. Matt 27:23 (with κράζω). Only Acts 26:11 shows the meaning *exceedingly:* Paul "raged *exceedingly/beyond all measure*" against the Christians.

περιστερά, ᾶς, ἡ *peristera* dove, pigeon*

1. Occurrences in the NT and general usage — 2. The dove at Jesus' baptism

Lit.: H. BRAUN, "Entscheidende Motive in den Berichten über die Taufe Jesu von Markus bis Justin," *ZTK* 50 (1953) 39-43. — J. DE COCK, "Het Symbolisme van de Duif bij het Doopsel van Christus," *Bijdr.* 21 (1960) 363-74. — A. FEUILLET, "Le symbolisme de la colombe dans les récits évangéliques du baptême," *RSR* 46 (1958) 524-44. — S. GERO, "The Spirit as Dove at the Baptism of Jesus," *NovT* 18 (1976) 17-35. — E. R. GOODENOUGH, *Jewish Symbols in the Greco-Roman Period* VIII (1958) 27-46. — H. GREEVEN, *TDNT* VI, 63-72. — L. E. KECK, "The Spirit and the Dove," *NTS* 17 (1970/71) 41-67. — O. KEEL, *Vögel als Boten* (OBO 14, 1977). — F. LENTZEN-DEIS, *Die Taufe Jesu nach den Synoptikern* (1970) esp. 12-14, 20, 46, 133f., 170-83, 265-70. — G. RICHTER, "Zu den Tauferzählungen Mk 1,9-11 und Joh 1,32-34," *ZNW* 65 (1974) 42-56, esp. 42-46. — H. SCHÜRMANN, *Luke* (HTKNT, 1969) I. — M. SMITH, *Jesus the Magician* (1978) 96-104. — For further bibliography see *TWNT* X, 1229.

1. The 10 NT occurrences of this noun are in four Gospel pericopes (Mark 1:10 par. Matt 3:16/Luke 3:22/ John 1:32; Mark 11:15 par. Matt 21:12/John 12:14, 16; Matt 10:16; Luke 2:24).

In the narrative of the cleansing of the temple, Mark 11:15 par. mentions the doves offered for sale as sacrificial animals in the concessionary trade. Their sale in the temple forecourt made it possible for temple visitors to acquire cultically pure animals. Luke 2:24 refers to the sacrifice of two doves prescribed for the purification of a new mother, quoting the clause regarding the poor from Lev 12:8; the context here is imprecise as far as the Halakah is concerned and has been christologically heightened in a priestly direction (cf. Schürmann 121f.). In Matt 10:16, taking up traditional imagery (cf. Billerbeck I, 574f.; Goodenough 39), Jesus compares the sending of the disciples to the behavior of wise serpents and guileless doves: The disciples are like defenseless sheep among marauding wolves and yet in their dealings with people exhibit the guilelessness of doves as a sign of their wisdom; they know of the radical eschatological transition.

2. According to the the Gospels' reports of Jesus'

baptism (on the early Christian material cf. Braun), the Spirit descended upon him "as a *dove.*" The adv. interpretation (the Spirit descended from heaven in the way that doves descend during flight) is recently supported again by Keck. But it is not in accord with the genre of vision, in which heavenly elements as unified phenomena become "actual" as form and in specific forms. The dove must be understood as a formed symbol that "actualizes" the significance of the bestowing of the Spirit within the framework of baptism and the voice from heaven.

Antiquity customarily associated three elements of symbolism with the dove (cf. Goodenough): It was a manifestation and sympathetic bird of the (usually feminine) deity (on the etymology of περιστερά cf. the Semitic form *perach-ishtar,* "bird of Ishtar"), a manifestation of the human soul, and in Judaism a symbol for Israel. There is probably no basis for exegesis in the fact that in Judaism the dove was traditionally a symbol of the spirit (cf. Billerbeck I, 123ff.). The dove as a symbol for Israel, emphasized by Lentzen-Deis and Feuillet, also finds no support in the Gospel texts and can at most merely resonate there.

The second aspect of this symbolism, the dove as the bird of the soul, implies that Jesus was united with his heavenly soul, an interpretation that seems to stand in some proximity to the Son-of-Man traditions (esp. in the Gospel of John). The first-mentioned symbolic level (the dove as one of God's manifestations) can imply that the πνεῦμα/*rûah* itself is a manifestation (in Semitic usage usually feminine) of God: The figure of the dove then expresses the visionary, apocalyptic "realization" of God's manifestation as πνεῦμα (associated in the history of religion with elements of magic and with shamanistic initiation; cf. Smith); through this dove the "beloved Son" is dealing with the Spirit's actual presence, and in a referential sense with God's own μορφή.

This interpretation can refer to 2 Esdr 5:23ff.: The objects of creation mentioned there are chosen because they are symbols of Israel's historical election. At the same time, according to priestly historical understanding (cf. *Jubilees* 2: creation prefigures the election) they stand in a creation-oriented sympathetic relationship to God himself, a relationship that is continued in the realm of the history of nations in Israel's election: The dove appears thus as a sympathetic bird of Israel's God.

The Spirit in the form of a dove, as a charismatic-visionary reality, bears the bond between Father and Son described by the heavenly voice.

J.-A. Bühner

περιτέμνω *peritemnō* cut off around, circumcise → περιτομή.

περιτίθημι *peritithēmi* construct around; bestow, invest*

Mark 12:1 par. Matt 21:33: φραγμόν "*surround* [the vineyard] with a hedge" (Isa 5:2 LXX); Mark 15:36 par.

Matt 27:48: σπόγγον καλάμῳ, *"place* a sponge *on* a reed"; John 19:29: σπόγγον ὑσσώπῳ περιθέντες; Matt 27:28: the soldiers *hung* a scarlet robe *around* Jesus (χλαμύδα κοκκίνην περιέθηκαν αὐτῷ); Mark 15:17: putting on the crown of thorns; fig. only in 1 Cor 12:23: τιμὴν περι-τίθημι, *"show* honor."

περιτομή, ῆς, ἡ *peritomē* circumcision; the circum-cised (i.e., Jews)*
περιτέμνω *peritemnō* circumcise*

1. Occurrences in the NT and meanings — 2. Luke-Acts and John — 3. The Pauline corpus

Lit.: BILLERBECK, IV, 23-40. — O. CULLMANN, *Baptism in the NT* (1950) 56-80. — H.-C. HAHN, *DNTT* I, 307-11. — W. KORNFELD, *SacVb* I, 116-18. — O. KUSS, *Rom* (1. Lieferung, 1957) 92-98. — F. R. LEHMANN and K. GALLING, *RGG* I, 1090f. — N. J. McELENEY, "Conversion, Circumcision, and the Law," *NTS* 20 (1973/74) 319-41. — R. MEYER, *TDNT* VI, 72-84. — J. SCHMID, *LTK* II, 289-91. — T. R. SCHREINER, *Circumcision: An Entrée into "Newness" in Pauline Thought* (Diss. Fuller Theological Seminary, Pasadena, 1983). — F. STUMMER, *RAC* II, 159-69. — R. DE VAUX, *Ancient Israel* (1961) I, 46-48. — H. WISSMANN, O. BETZ, and F. DEXINGER, *TRE* V, 714-24. — For further bibliography see *TWNT* X, 1229f.; Schreiner; Wissmann, et al.

1. In the NT the vb. occurs 17 times, the noun 36 times, esp. in Romans and Galatians, where Paul deals with Judaism or with Judaizing Christians. In the NT the noun, like the rabbinic term *mîlâ,* refers to a) the rite of *circumcision* (John 7:22, 23; Acts 7:8; Rom 2:25a, 27; 4:11; Phil 3:5; Col 2:11 bis; Eph 2:11), and b) the *state of having been circumcised* as it characterizes the Jews (Rom 2:25b, 26, 28; 4:10 bis; 1 Cor 7:19; Gal 5:6, 11; 6:15; fig. in Rom 2:28 and Col 2:11). What is new in the NT is: c) the concrete meaning *"(circumcised) Jews"* (Rom 3:1, 30; 4:9, 12; 15:8; Gal 2:7, 8, 9; Col 3:11) and "Jewish Christians" (οἱ ἐκ [τῆς] περιτομῆς: Acts 10:45; 11:2; Rom 4:12; Gal 2:12; Col 4:11; Titus 1:10). In Phil 3:2 Paul mocks the Judaizers as κατατομή, "cutting, muti-lation"; v. 3 says of the Christians: "We are the περιτομή."

The vb. occurs 26 times in the LXX rendering Heb. *mûl;* the noun occurs 4 times, in Exod 4:26 for *mûlâ.* Passages of signif-icance include Exod 4:24f. (J), Genesis 17 (P), and Exod 12:44-50 (P). Fig. references to circumcision (of the heart) occur in Deut 10:16; 30:6; Jer 4:4 (cf. 1QS 5:5f.; 1QH 18:20). On the basis of prohibition of circumcision under Antiochus IV and Hadrian, circumcision acquired confessional significance: The rabbinic literature emphasizes the atoning power of the blood of circumcision (*Tg. Exod.* 4:25), the performance of which even overrides the sabbath (*b. Šabb.* 132a).

2. Luke presupposes circumcision on the eighth day in the case of Jewish and Jewish Christian infants, so with John the Baptist (Luke 1:59), Jesus (2:21), and Isaac (Acts 7:8; cf. Gen 21:4). More important to him, though,

is the giving of the name associated with this rite (Luke 1:59f.; 2:21). Out of consideration for Jews Paul circum-cised the half-Jew Timothy (Acts 16:1-3); the objection raised against him in Jerusalem, namely, that he elim-inated circumcision for Diaspora Jews (21:21; cf. *Sifre Num.* 15:31 §112), was thus unjustified. The demand brought by former Pharisees that Gentile Christians be circumcised (15:1, 5) was rejected at the "Apostolic Council," as its decree shows (15:20, 29; 21:25). Stephen uses the expression "covenant of *circumcision*" (7:8; = *bᵉrît mîlâ, b. Menaḥ.* 53b, following Gen 17:13), of which Paul also probably thinks when he mentions "the covenants" in Rom 9:4 and in his rendering of the words of institution, "the new covenant in my blood" (1 Cor 11:25; cf. Sir 44:20; Rom 2:28). The metaphor of uncir-cumcised heart and ears (Acts 7:51) refers to obduracy (cf. Deut 10:16; Jer 6:10; 1QH 18:20; 1QS 5:5f.).

According to John 7:22-24 Jesus justified healing on the sabbath from the obligation to circumcise a child also on the sabbath (v. 22): If a single bodily part may on the day of rest be put into the condition willed by God, how much more must this hold true for the whole body (cf. *b. Šabb.* 132a). Though circumcision does goes back to the patriarchs, it was legally regulated by Moses (John 7:22; cf. Acts 15:1).

3. Paul includes his circumcision on the eighth day among his God-given distinctions (Phil 3:5). In a salva-tion-historical sense it is the sign that God's words, i.e., law and promise, were entrusted to Israel (Rom 3:1f.; cf. Eph 2:11-13). Thus also did Christ serve circumcision (Rom 15:8) and invested Peter with the "apostolate *of the circumcision*" (Gal 2:7-9). As with the rabbis and Pharisaic Christians, so also with Paul, circumcision and law are the characteristic features of Judaism (cf. Rom 4:12 with v. 16); the former obligates a man to observe the entire Torah (Gal 5:3; 6:13; Rom 2:25; 1 Cor 7:19; cf. Acts 15:5; Sir 44:20). Observance of the Torah is the standard in the final judgment and determines the value of one's circumcision, which counts as uncircumcision for Jews who violate the Torah and vice versa (Rom 2:25f.). With God, who sees into a person's heart, it is not the visible sign in the flesh "made by hands" (Eph 2:11) that counts, but rather *"circumcision* of the heart in the Spirit" (Rom 2:28f.; cf. 1QpHab 11:13); here Paul is thinking esp. of Ezek 36:26f. and Jer 31:31-34.

The eschatological events of cross, resurrection, and new creation in the Spirit eliminate the salvation-histori-cal advantage of circumcision (Gal 5:6; 6:15). Against the Judaizers Paul emphasizes that even for Abraham circumcision was not the prerequisite but the "seal" of righteousness in faith (Rom 4:9-11). Thus Abraham be-came the heir of the promise in Gen 17:5f., 16 and a father of both Jews and Gentiles who follow his example of faith (Rom 4:12; cf. 3:30; Gal 3:6-9). Baptism is the visible confirmation of justification by faith and is therefore called "the *circumcision* of Christ made without hands" (Col 2:11), and Gentile Christians are the (spiritual) circumcision (Phil 3:3). Paul did not need to circumcise Titus (Gal 2:3), no longer preached circumcision (5:11), and considered the demand that Gentile Christians be circumcised (6:12) a vote of no confidence against the redemptive significance of the cross (5:2; 3:1-3), an anachronism, as also was reversing circumcision (→ ἐπισπάομαι) among Jewish Christians (1 Cor 7:18). In Christ the distinction between circumcision and uncircumcision is eliminated (Gal 5:6; 6:15; Col 3:11).

O. Betz

περιτρέπω *peritrepō* turn, place (into a condition)*

Acts 26:24: Festus says to Paul: "Your great learning *is turning* you mad (εἰς μανίαν περιτρέπει)."

περιτρέχω *peritrechō* run about*

Mark 6:55: περιέδραμον ὅλην τὴν χώραν ἐκείνην, the people "*ran about* the whole neighborhood."

περιφέρω *peripherō* carry around*

Literal in Mark 6:55, of sick persons carried around in order to bring them to Jesus; 2 Cor 4:10: Paul *carries* Jesus' → νέκρωσις *around* on his own body, i.e., probably: he lives in continual mortal danger; fig. and pass. in Eph 4:14: "*carried to and fro* by every wind of doctrine."

περιφρονέω *periphroneō* disregard, despise*

Titus 2:15: μηδείς σου περιφρονείτω, "*let no one disregard* you." The words of the officeholder are binding for the Church, not optional (cf. 1 Tim 4:12 [with καταφρονέω]). N. Brox, *Die Pastoralbriefe* (RNT) ad loc.; C. Schneider, *TDNT* III, 633; Spicq, *Notes* II, 690f.

περίχωρος, 2 *perichōros* neighboring*

This adj. is largely used subst.: ἡ περίχωρος (γῆ), *the surrounding area* (Matt 14:35; Mark 6:55 TR; Luke 4:14, 37; 7:17; Acts 14:6). Matt 3:5 and Luke 3:3 use it with gen. τοῦ Ἰορδάνου, similarly also Luke 8:37: "of the Gerasenes"; Mark 1:28: "of Galilee" (epexegetical gen.: "the region, i.e., Galilee"). Matt 3:5 uses περίχωρος of those dwelling in a particular region.

περίψημα, ατος, τό *peripsēma* rubbish, scum*

1 Cor 4:13: "We are the refuse of the world, the *scum* of all things until now." G. Stählin, *TDNT* VI, 84-93; BAGD s.v.; Spicq, *Notes* II, 681f.

περπερεύομαι *perpereuomai* boast*

1 Cor 13:4, of ἀγάπη: οὐ περπερεύεται, "it *does not boast*." H. Braun, *TDNT* VI, 93-95.

Περσίς, ίδος *Persis* Persis*

A Christian woman greeted in Rom 16:12: "Greet beloved *Persis,* who has worked hard in the Lord."

πέρυσι(ν) *perysi(n)* last year (adv.)*

2 Cor 8:10; 9:2: ἀπὸ πέρυσι, "since *last year.*"

πετάομαι *petaomai* fly (vb.)
A secondary form of → πέτομαι as v.l. in TR (Rev 4:7; 8:13; 14:6; 19:17).

πετεινόν, οῦ, τό *peteinon* bird*

This noun usually occurs in the pl. (always in the NT), frequently in the expression "the *birds* of the air" (Matt 6:26; 8:20; 13:32; Mark 4:32; Luke 8:5; 9:58; 13:19; Acts 10:12; 11:6). 10 of the 14 NT occurrences are in sayings of Jesus: Mark 4:4 par. Matt 13:4/Luke 8:5 (the parable of the sower); Mark 4:32 par. Matt 13:32/Luke 13:19 (the parable of the mustard seed); Matt 6:26 (cf. par. Luke): "Look at the *birds* of the air" (cf. Luke 12:24); Matt 8:20 par. Luke 9:58: "Foxes have holes, and *birds* of the air have nests. . . ." From the Jewish and biblical tradition come lists such as those in Acts 10:12; Rom 1:23 (τετράποδα, ἑρπετά, πετεινά); Acts 11:6 (the same three terms with θηρία); Jas 3:7 (θηρία, πετεινά, ἑρπετά, ἐνάλια).

πέτομαι *petomai* fly (vb.)*

In Revelation (usually partc.) referring to the flying eagle (4:7; 8:13), the apocalyptic "woman" (12:14: ἵνα πέτηται εἰς τὴν ἔρημον), an angel (14:6), and birds (19:17: ὄρνεα).

πέτρα, ας, ἡ *petra* rock*

1. Occurrences in the NT — 2. Usage and meanings — 3. Matt 16:18

Lit.: H. CONZELMANN, *1 Cor* (Hermeneia, 1975) on 10:4. — O. CULLMANN, *TDNT* VI, 95-99. — L. GOPPELT, *1 Pet* (KEK, 1978) on 2:8. — H. HALTER, *1Kor 10,1-13: Sakramentale Rettung unter ethischem Vorbehalt* (1977). — E. KÄSEMANN, *Rom* (Eng. tr., 1980) on 9:33. — R. PESCH, *Mark* (HTKNT, 1980). — idem, *Simon Petrus. Geschichte und geschichtliche Bedeutung des ersten Jüngers Jesu Christi* (1980). — R. PESCH and R. KRATZ, *So liest man synoptisch* (1980) chs. 4f. — M. RIEHL, *Auferstehung Jesu in der Stunde seines Todes? Zur Botschaft von Mt 27,51b-53* (1978). — For further bibliography see *TWNT* X, 1230; Pesch, *Simon.*

1. Of the 15 NT occurrences, 9 are in the Synoptic Gospels (5 in Matthew, 1 in Mark, 3 in Luke), 3 in Paul, 1 in 1 Peter, and 2 in Revelation. The sg. occurs 12 times, the pl. 3 times (Matt 27:51; Rev 6:15, 16). Of the Synoptic occurrences 3 are from the Q tradition (Matt 7:24f. par. Luke 6:48), 2 from the pre-Markan Passion narrative (Mark 15:46 par. Matt 27:60), 2 from M (Matt 16:18; 27:51), and 2 from the Lukan redaction of Mark (Luke 8:6, 13 contra Mark 4:5, 16 [τὸ πετρῶδες or τὰ πετρώδη]). Among the Pauline occurrences 1 is in an OT citation (Rom 9:33 = Isa 28:16; 8:14; similarly 1 Pet 2:8). Rev 6:15f. alludes to OT passages (Isa 2:10, 19, 21; 4:29).

2. Πέτρα refers to matured rock, a *sturdy stone foundation*, a *rock gorge,* and *boulders.* The concluding parable in the Sermon on the Mount/Plain makes emphatic mention of *rock* as a firm foundation (Matt 7:24f. par. Luke 6:48) and compares the person who does Jesus' words with one who builds his house on a stone foundation that guarantees the sturdiness of the construction; similarly also in the promise to Peter in Matt 16:18 (→ 3). Luke 8:6, 13 redactionally mentions *rocky ground* as unfruitful land lacking the moisture necessary for plant growth. Luke alters his Markan source probably because he is presupposing sowing on a steep, hilly field (instead of on a field partially covered with fieldstone), where the seed falls on lower fieldstones; although it can indeed sprout in such thin soil, it cannot grow properly because of lack of moisture. The interpretation of the parable does not address itself to the "hardness" of the listeners, but rather (so also Luke 8:13 par. Mark 4:17 despite Luke 8:6 contra Mark 4:5f.) to their "rootlessness."

Jesus' tomb "hewn from *rock*" (sealed by a stone rolled across its entrance) is an example of (archaeologically well-attested) tombs for the wealthy (Mark 15:46 par. Matt 27:60). The splitting of the *rocks* mentioned in Matt 27:51 in the context of an earthquake and the opening of tombs is an eschatological signal (cf. *T. Levi* 4:1) at Jesus' death (a theophany motif) serving the eschatological-universal interpretation of this death as the opening of salvation by the "Immanuel."

The "*rock* of offense" causing one to fall (Isa 8:14, cited in Rom 9:33 and 1 Pet 2:8) is an obstacle over which a person stumbles. Both Paul and the author of 1 Peter employ an early Christian interpretive tradition in which Jesus, as the rock laid by God as the foundation of the eschatological Zion, the edifice of the Church, is also the stumbling stone for unbelieving Israel obstructing or confusing faith: Obdurate unbelief does not recognize that stone as the "cornerstone" (Isa 28:16). Paul's heightening of the combined quotation to refer to Israel's lack of faith is in 1 Peter expanded by inclusion of the world of nations, which also stumbles in disobedience to the word of God given in proclamation. Whereas 1 Peter is prob-

ably following a "stone-rock" testimonial collection, Rom 9:33 inserts Isa 8:14 into Isa 28:16 and changes the salvation promise into a prophecy of disaster.

In 1 Cor 10:4 Paul interprets the water-giving *rock* (Exod 17:6; Num 20:7-13) by recalling the Jewish tradition that spoke of the rock wandering with Israel in the desert (*Bib. Ant.* 10:7; *t. Sukk.* 3:11ff.) and that identified the rock with preexistent wisdom (Philo *All.* ii.86). Paul identifies the rock with the preexistent Christ as πέτρα πνευματική dispensing the pneumatic drink (a typological interpretation of the eucharist).

In its apocalyptic portrayal of judgment, Rev 6:15f. speaks of caves as a refuge and *rocks* as a (paradoxically mortally dangerous) covering before the annihilating countenance of the judgment of God and his Messiah.

3. In Matt 16:18 (→ Κηφᾶς, Πέτρος) Jesus refers to Peter as the stone foundation of the edifice of the eschatological people of salvation (composed of Jews and Gentiles), as the decisive mediator of the revelation tradition. This pronouncement from the Easter epiphany tradition in Jesus' words of promise concerning the construction of his Church "on this *rock*" (= the noble rock "Peter") has been set by Matthew into the portrayal of Peter's messianic confession. What we probably have here is an expansion of the authoritative claim of the leader of the three "pillars" (Gal 2:9) in the eschatological temple edifice through reference to Abraham traditions attesting that ancestor as a "pillar of Israel" and "rock." This expansion comes from the conflict in Antioch (Gal 2:11ff.) and is interpreted through a play on words— probably in Greek (not Aramaic): Πέτρος = πέτρα. Peter's name is interpreted in the sense of Peter's being. This occurs within the genre "investiture of the mediator of the revelation tradition." Matthew's reception of the investiture confirms the significance of Peter as the mediator and guarantor of that tradition.

                                   R. Pesch

Πέτρος, ου *Petros* Peter*
Σίμων, ος *Simōn* Simon

1. Origin of the names — 2. Usage — a) Mark — b) Matthew — c) Luke-Acts — d) John — e) The rest of the NT — 3. Peter in the individual NT writings — a) Mark — b) Matthew — c) Luke-Acts — d) John — e) The rest of the NT — 4. Significant passages — 5. The life of Peter

Lit.: K. Berger, "Unfehlbare Offenbarung. Petrus in der gnostischen und apokalyptischen Offenbarungsliteratur," FS Mussner 261-326. — J. Blank, "Neutestamentliche Petrus-Typologie und Petrusamt," Concilium 9 (1973) 173-79. — *idem,* "Petrus und Petrus-Amt im NT," *Papsttum als ökumenische Frage* (1979) 59-103. — R. E. Brown, et al., *Peter in the NT* (1973). — C. C. Caragounis, *Peter and the Rock* (BZNW 58, 1989). — O. Cullmann, *Peter: Disciple, Apostle, Martyr* (1953).

— *idem, TDNT* VI, 100-112. — W. DIETRICH, *Das Petrusbild der lukanischen Schriften* (1972). — E. DINKLER, *RGG* V, 247-49. — J. ERNST, "Die Petrustradition im Markusevangelium—ein altes Problem neu angegangen," FS Zimmermann 35-65. — J. H. ELLIOTT, "Peter, Silvanus, and Mark in I Peter and Acts: Sociological-Exegetical Perspectives on a Petrine Group in Rome," FS Rengstorf (1980) 250-67. — R. FELDMEIER, "The Portrayal of Peter in the Synoptic Gospels," *The Gospel and the Gospels* (ed. P. Stuhlmacher; 1991) 252-56 (= M. Hengel, *Studies in the Gospel of Mark* [1985] 59-63, 161f.). — P. GAECHTER, *Petrus und seine Zeit* I (1958). — E. GRÄSSER, "Neutestamentliche Grundlagen des Papsttums," *Papsttum als ökumenische Frage* (1979) 33-58. — E. HAENCHEN, "Petrus-Probleme," *NTS* 7 (1960/61) 187-97. — C. KÄHLER, "Zur Form- und Traditionsgeschichte von Matthäus XVI.17-19," *NTS* 23 (1976/77) 36-58. — O. KARRER, *Peter and the Church* (1963). — *idem,* "Petrus im paulinischen Gemeindekreis," *ZNW* 80 (1989) 210-31. — J. D. KINGSBURY, "The Figure of Peter in Matthew's Gospel as a Theological Problem," *JBL* 98 (1979) 67-83. — O. KNOCH, "Petrus und Paulus in den Schriften der Apostolischen Väter," FS Mussner 240-60. — F. MUSSNER, *Petrus und Paulus—Pole der Einheit* (1976). — R. PESCH, *Der reiche Fischfang* (1969). — *idem,* "The Position and Significance of Peter in the Church of the NT," *Papal Ministry in the Church* (Concilium 64, ed. H. Küng; 1971) 21-35. — *idem,* "Das Messiasbekenntnis des Petrus (Mk 8,27-30). Neuverhandlung einer alten Frage," *BZ* 17 (1973) 178-95; 18 (1974) 20-31. — *idem,* "Die Verleugnung des Petrus. Eine Studie zu Mk 14,54.66-72 (und Mk 14,26-31)," FS Schnackenburg 43-62. — *idem,* "Peter in the Mirror of Paul's Letters," *Paul de Tarse* (FS Pope Paul VI, 1979) 291-309. — *idem, Mark* (HTKNT, 1980). — *idem, Simon-Petrus. Geschichte und geschichtliche Bedeutung des ersten Jüngers Jesu Christi* (1980). — B. RIGAUX, "St. Peter in Contemporary Exegesis," *Progress and Decline in the History of Church Renewal* (Concilium 27, ed. R. Aubert; 1967) 147-79. — R. SCHNACKENBURG, "Petrus im Matthäusevangelium," FS Dupont 107-25. — G. SCHNEIDER, " 'Stärke deine Brüder!' (Lk 22,32). Die Aufgabe des Petrus nach Lukas," *Petrus und Papst* (ed. A. Brandenburg and H. J. Urban; 1977) 36-42. — T. V. SMITH, *Petrine Controversies in Early Christianity* (WUNT II/15, 1985). — C. P. THIEDE, ed., *Das Petrusbild in der neueren Forschung* (1987). — W. TRILLING, "Ist die katholische Primatslehre schriftgemäß?" *Zum Thema Petrusamt und Papsttum* (1970) 36-50. — *idem,* "Zum Petrusamt im NT," *TQ* 151 (1971) 110-33. — A. VÖGTLE, "Der Petrus der Verheißung und der Erfüllung. Zum Petrusbuch von O. Cullmann," *MTZ* 5 (1954) 1-47. — *idem, LTK* VIII, 334-40. — *idem,* "Messiasbekenntnis und Petrusverheißung," *idem, Das Evangelium und die Evangelien* (1971) 137-70. — *idem,* "Zum Problem der Herkunft von Mt 16,17-19," FS Schmid (1973) 137-70. — H. ZIMMERMANN, "Die innere Struktur der Kirche und das Petrusamt nach Mt 18," *Petrus und Papst* (ed. A. Brandenburg and H. J. Urban; 1977) 4-19. — For further bibliography → Κηφᾶς; see further *TWNT* X, 1230-32; Pesch, *Simon-Petrus.*

1. Σίμων is the Greek name that in the Hellenistic period had become the equivalent of the Hebrew patriarchal name *Šim'ôn,* which is transliterated into Greek in Acts 15:14 and 2 Pet 1:1 (Συμεών). Like his brother Andrew, Peter probably received a Greek name from his father John (cf. Matt 16:17; John 1:41; 21:15-17) in Hellenistically influenced Bethsaida (John 1:44).

Πέτρος is not attested as a Greek proper name before the Christian era. It occurs as a term for an object from Homer until the NT period: "stone." It came to be regarded as a name, as the tr. of the epithet given to Simon by Jesus, *kyp'* (= "precious stone"), which is preserved in Greek transliteration (with the Greek proper name ending ς) as → Κηφᾶς. This epithet or surname in its transliterated or translated form early became the proper name itself, increasingly displacing the original name Simon, presumably because the epithet became esp. important as an "official name" (cf. the analogy in the development of the Messiah title into the proper name "Christ"). The original name Simon was combined with Peter into the double name "Simon Peter" (cf. the double name "Jesus Christ").

2. Peter's original name Σίμων (on Συμεών → 1) occurs in all the Gospels as well as in later noncanonical sources.

a) Up to the account of the bestowal of the name Peter (3:16), Mark uses "Simon" (1:16, 29, 30, 36; 3:15). Thereafter Πέτρος is used (except once, when Jesus addresses Peter as "Simon," 14:37); Peter has, therefore, become the proper name (5:37; 8:29, 32, 33; 9:2, 5; 10:28; 11:21; 13:3; 14:29, 33, 37, 54, 66, 67, 70, 72; 16:7).

b) Matthew identifies Simon already at his first appearance as the one "who is called Peter" (4:18; cf. 10:2). Jesus addresses him as "Simon" only twice (16:17 [with Bar-Jona]; 17:25). Matthew otherwise always introduces him as Peter (8:14; 14:28, 29; 15:15; 16:18, 22, 23; 17:1, 4, 24; 18:21; 19:27; 26:33, 35, 37, 40, 58, 69, 73, 75).

c) The Gospel of Luke follows its Markan source with the name "Simon" (4:38; 5:3, 4, 5, 10) up to Simon's designation as Peter (6:14), except in his use of the double name "Simon Peter" in 5:8 (following the tradition of the miraculous catch of fish; cf. John 21:1ff.). Thereafter, except for the address "Simon, Simon" (22:31) and the Easter confession "appeared to Simon" (24:34), Luke uses Πέτρος (8:45, 51; 9:20, 28, 32, 33; 12:41; 18:28; 22:8, 34, 54, 55, 58, 60, 61; 24:12), so also throughout Acts (1:13, 15; 2:14, 37, 38; 3:1, 3, 4, 6, 11, 12; 4:8, 13, 19; 5:3, 8, 9, 15, 29; 8:14, 20; 9:32, 34, 38, 39, 40 bis, 43; 10:5, 9, 13, 14, 17, 18, 19, 21, 25, 26, 32, 34, 44, 45, 46; 11:2, 4, 7; 12:3, 5, 6, 7, 11, 14 bis, 16, 18; 15:7). "Peter" also occurs in address (10:13; 11:7). Four times in the story of Cornelius, Peter is referred to as "Simon who is called Peter" (10:5, 18, 32; 11:13). James uses the form "Symeon" (Hebraizing? 15:14).

d) In the Gospel of John "Simon" is immediately given the name "Cephas" ("which means Peter/rock") when he meets Jesus (1:42). "Simon" without "Peter" appears only in the words of Jesus (21:15, 16, 17, each time with "son of John"). The disciple is introduced in narrative as "Peter" or as "Simon Peter": The double name (1:41; 6:8, 68; 13:6,

9, 24, 36; 18:10, 15, 25; 20:2; 21:2, 3, 7, 11, 15) always precedes the single name (1:44; 13:8, 37; 18:11, 16, 17, 18, 26, 27; 20:3, 4, 6; 21:7, 17, 20, 21).

e) The double name "Simon Peter" occurs otherwise only in Luke 5:8; Matt 16:16 (in a tradition related to John 21:15-17); and 2 Pet 1:1 ("Symeon Peter"), later also in noncanonical writings. In addition to the usual form Κηφᾶς, Paul uses Πέτρος only twice (Gal 2:7, 8). Finally, 1 Pet 1:1 uses the name "Peter" as a pseudonym.

3. a) Of the 16 occurrences in Mark of the names Simon or Peter, 9 belong to the pre-Markan Passion narrative, which reflects the history of the leading disciple and his leadership role in the early Church. As the spokesperson of the disciples (8:27-33) and of the Twelve (11:21), the first among Jesus' three confidants (9:2; 14:33) as well as their spokesperson (9:5) and protagonist (14:37), Peter occupied a secure leadership role. Therefore, Mark could unsparingly tell of Peter's failures (14:29, 33, 54, 66-72) and summarize in Peter's protest the initial lack of understanding among the community of disciples regarding the Son of man's suffering (8:31-33; 9:5). Peter is responsible for the messianic confession (8:29) and is the most significant Easter witness (9:2; 16:7). Through his failings he learns to concentrate on "God's matters" (8:33). Mark introduces Peter redactionally as the spokesperson of the willing disciples (10:28) and gives him as one of Jesus' three confidants a place next to Andrew, whom the tradition probably mentioned alone, as a recipient of Jesus' eschatological discourse (13:3). Along with the sons of Zebedee Mark probably also redactionally makes Peter one of the witnesses of Jesus' greatest miracle (5:37). The Markan portrayal of Simon as the first-called disciple (1:16-18), the first among the Twelve, and the one who received the epithet Peter (3:16) on the whole follows the main features of the tradition. Along with the Twelve, Peter is for the Gospel of Mark (as appropriately preserved in Papias of Hierapolis, at least in view of the Markan portrayal of Peter) the guarantor of the Jesus tradition as a witness of Jesus' own ministry from the very beginning.

b) Matthew alters the portrayal of Peter by means of omissions, use of other traditions, and redactional introduction of Peter. Matthew does not tell how "Simon and his companions" followed Jesus outside Capernaum (Mark 1:35-39); along with the three confidants Peter disappears from the Jairus narrative (Mark 5:37); replaced by "disciples," Peter is no longer specifically mentioned in Matt 21:19 contra Mark 11:21 or (along with the other three mentioned by name) in 24:3 contra Mark 13:3; he is no longer specifically mentioned in 28:7 contra Mark 16:7. Matthew redactionally introduces Peter as a spokesperson in 15:15 contra Mark 7:17 and Matt 18:21 contra Luke 17:4 (Q), as well as in 26:35 contra

Mark 14:31. The context-oriented omissions thus are not intended to diminish Peter's role. Matthew identifies Simon from the very beginning as "Peter" (4:18 contra Mark 1:16) and as the "first" among the Twelve (10:2 contra Mark 3:16); Matthew no longers relates that Jesus bestowed the epithet Peter upon Simon (Mark 3:16), since he predates the Easter tradition concerning Jesus' interpretation of the name Peter (16:18; → πέτρα). On the whole Matthew spares Peter (except in 26:72 contra Mark 14:70: the oath occurs already at the second denial) in his alteration of Peter's role in Jesus' Passion (cf. 26:33 contra 14:29; 26:40 contra Mark 14:37; 26:58 contra Mark 14:54; 26:75 contra Mark 14:72; cf. also 17:4 contra Mark 9:5f.). What Matthew underscores is Peter's orientation toward Jesus, his dependence on the "Lord."

Peter's role is amplified by three traditions unique to Matthew: Peter's walk on the water (16:16-19), the promise to Peter (16:16-19), and the story of the shekel in the fish's mouth (17:24-27). The understanding of Matt 16:16-19 (cf. → 4) involves the question of how Matthew interprets Peter's special role. As the mediator of the revelation tradition Peter is the guarantor of the Jesus tradition in its correct interpretation (cf. his role as the questioner in Jesus' doctrinal halakah decisions: 15:15; 18:21). But as such he is completely attached to Jesus himself as the mediator of revelation. Wherever the Church is grounded in Jesus' doctrine, it is according to Matthew constructed on the foundation of Peter as the mediator of that revelatory tradition, to whom the authoritative keys of binding and loosing were given (in the present exercised by the unified community as a whole; 18:19). Because Matthew wants to emphasize the Church's dependence on Jesus' doctrine, he heightens Jesus' reproach of Peter (16:21-23 contra Mark 8:31-33), further typifying thereby his person, into which he engraves, as it were, the Church's apostolic norm.

c) Luke alters more extensively the traditional Markan portrayal of Peter. Instead of Simon and his companions (Mark 1:36), it is "the people" (Luke 4:42) who seek Jesus. Peter is no longer the spokesperson, and the episode of the fig tree is dropped (Mark 11:20); cf. Luke 21:7 contra Mark 13:3. In the Gethsemane narrative (22:39-46), Jesus' confidants, including Peter, do not play any special role. The angelic commissioning (Mark 16:7) is replaced by a recollection of the prophecies of suffering and resurrection (24:6f.). Luke unburdens Peter and shows him in a positive function (8:45 contra Mark 5:31) and has him use the title of sovereignty "Master" (5:5; 9:33 contra Mark 9:5). Luke 12:39-43 alludes to Peter as the "faithful and wise steward," since he (contra Mark) appears as the questioner. Luke 22:8 contra Mark 14:13 has "Peter and John," the two leaders of the early Church (Acts 1-8; cf. John's second position in the lists of disciples), prepare the Passover meal. Peter (9:20 contra

Mark 8:29) confesses Jesus as "the Christ *of God*," but does not reproach Jesus and in his own turn is not reproached as "Satan" (Mark 8:23f. is dropped).

In the Lukan arrangement of the Last Supper farewell discourse Peter does not react (*contra* Mark 14:27) to a prediction of the disciples' falling away, but reacts rather to Jesus' pledge with a heightened declaration of commitment (22:33 *contra* Mark 14:29). He does not dispute that he will deny Jesus (Mark 14:31 is dropped). In the palace of the high priest he stays near Jesus (22:54f. *contra* Mark 14:53f.; 22:61 *contra* 14:72) and at the third denial does not curse and swear (22:60 *contra* Mark 14:71; cf. also 22:62). At the beginning of Luke Jesus enters Simon's house (4:38) even before the disciple is called in connection with the miraculous catch of fish (5:1-11); the saying concerning fishers of people, *contra* Mark 1:17, is addressed to Peter alone (5:10: a prefiguration of the early Church's missionary role).

In the Lukan portrayal (including Acts) "Simon," whom Jesus "also named Peter" (6:14 *contra* Mark 3:16), is the leader of "the Twelve, whom he also named apostles" (6:13). Peter's denial is in the final analysis not a cessation of his faith (22:32); on the contrary, he will strengthen his brethren. He runs to the tomb (24:12), and "the Lord appeared" to him (24:34); the Easter faith is bound to his testimony. The Lukan portrayal of Peter acquires a significant amplification through the traditions taken up in 5:1-11 and 22:31f.

In Acts Peter stands at the head of the Eleven (1:13) and reestablishes the circle of the Twelve (1:15ff.). He is the leader of the early Church and the initiator of the missions to the Jews and Gentiles (Acts 2ff., 10–11, 15). As a miracle worker (3:1-10; 5:15; 9:32-34, 36-43) he follows Jesus' missionary commissioning (9:1f.), and as a persecuted disciple (4:1-22; 12:1-17) he represents with all frankness the fate of disciples foretold by the Lord (Luke 12:4ff.; 21:12ff.). He dispenses discipline within the Church with full charismatic authority (Acts 5:1-11), and as an apostolic legate in Samaria he exposes the greedy sorcerer Simon Magus (8:9-25).

The essential feature of the portrayal of Peter appears to be that in him is presented the normative "eyewitness and minister of the word" (Luke 1:2) who guarantees the faithfulness of the Christian tradition (v. 4) for the following era, which commences with the Pauline mission. Peter, the disciple and eyewitness "from the beginning" (v. 2), commissioned with leading the Church (22:31f.), allows himself to be led ever anew by the Spirit poured out by the resurrected Lord and in the opening of the missions to the Jews and Gentiles lays the foundation for the path of God's Word, the history of the Church.

d) The Gospel of John mentions Peter more frequently than do the Synoptics (34 times), but in fewer passages (9 in John 1–20, 3 in the supplementary ch. 21). He is not the first disciple called, but is rather brought to Jesus (1:41) by his brother Andrew (cf. 1:44; 6:8), then is distinguished by Jesus through the promise of the name Cephas (1:42). During the crisis following the discourse on the bread he is the spokeperson of the twelve who remain with Jesus (6:68f.). At the footwashing (13:6-9), the prediction of the denial (vv. 36-38), and in the Garden of Gethsemane, where he is identified as the one wielding the sword (18:9f.), Peter is portrayed as an uncomprehending disciple (cf. also 18:11 with Mark 8:31-33 par.). Even though Peter expresses his willingness to lay down his life for Jesus (13:37), he denies being Jesus' disciple three times in the palace of the high priest (in two scenes in the Johannine version: 18:15-18, 25-27).

The "beloved disciple" appears to stand closer than Peter to Jesus (13:34): He is the disciple who stands beneath the cross (19:25-27), the only one who does not abandon Jesus, who comes to faith in the empty tomb, and who after hurrying ahead of Peter allows him to enter the tomb first (20:3-10). In the supplementary ch. 21 the beloved disciple identifies Jesus as "the Lord" (21:7), and Peter is again dependent on him. Since 21:15-17 relates the installation of Peter into the shepherd's office (→ 4) and presupposes his death (alluding to crucifixion: vv. 18f.), the question of his successor suggests itself, but remains unanswered. Without diminishing Peter's ecumenical authority, the Johannine circle appears to be interested in strengthening the reputation of the beloved disciple as its normative authority (through his tense relationship with Peter).

e) Paul speaks more frequently and extensively of Cephas/Peter (→ Κηφᾶς) than of all other persons of the apostolic era. In 1 Pet 1:1 apostolic authority is claimed for the pseudonymous writing through a reference to the Roman (5:13) Peter. 2 Peter offers supplementary support for Peter's authority with a reference to the Synoptic tradition's assertion that he was an eyewitness (1:16-19). The "servant and apostle of Jesus Christ" (1:1) is a consecrated witness (1:16) to whom Christ granted a special revelation concerning his impending death (1:14f.: the letter is a testament). Peter appears as a guardian of the true faith who in view of the assault by false teachers in the post-apostolic era possesses full interpretive authority concering both Scripture (letters of "brother Paul," 3:15f.; also 1:20) and tradition.

4. Concerning the bestowal of the epithet or surname (Mark 3:16) and the promise of the name (John 1:42) → Κηφᾶς.

Despite various objections, Peter's messianic confession in Caesarea Philippi (Mark 8:27-30) might be historically credible in view of the text as a narrative report with temporal and religio-historical details that can be correlated. Nonetheless, Peter should not be associated with any Jewish national-political messianism (not least because of Jesus' own criticism, 12:35-37). His confession more likely picked up on prophetic traditions of the eschatological teacher, prophet, and revealer anointed by the Spirit.

Tradition-critical examination shows that the tradition of the denial (Mark 14:54, 66-72) is also told from a basis of historical information concerning the life of Peter.

The story, found only in Matthew, of walking on water (Matt 14:28-31) is a legend of faith standardizing the figure of Peter.

Matthew works an Easter tradition into Mark 8:27ff. The result (Matt 16:16-19, → πέτρα), with its promise to Peter concerning the building of the Church, is an epiphany narrative establishing Peter's authority (prompted probably by the Antiochian conflict) for the Church composed of Jews and Gentiles by portraying his "investiture as the mediator of the revelation tradition": He commits himself to the confession of Christ and God revealed to him (16:16f.), is the rock foundation of the edifice of the eschatological Church, and is equipped with the authoritative keys of binding and loosing, i.e., with full interpretive authority concerning "conditions for entry" into the βασιλεία ("in heaven"), which are already in effect for the ἐκκλησία ("on earth") in which the salvation community is gathered.

The story unique to Luke of the miraculous catch of fish (Luke 5:1-11), redactionally merged with the call narrative (Mark 1:16-20; perceivable in a different version behind John 21:1-14, with a connection to an Easter appearance narrative), exhibits elements of legend.

Jesus' final words to Simon (Luke 22:31f.), on the other hand, could go back to authentic words focusing on Peter's role in view of Jesus' impending Passion: Peter's own faith and repentance are to strengthen the community of disciples, which will be shaken as in a sieve by public opposition (Satan!) to God's work as represented by Jesus.

The dependability of the Peter tradition in Acts remains esp. difficult to evaluate (and correspondingly controversial).

Within the specifically Johannine material the Easter scene portraying the transmission of the shepherd's office to Peter (John 21:15-17) is esp. important, portraying Peter's early Church function as the "Church leader" (possibly in competition with claims to authority made by the Lord's brother James, alluded to perhaps in the "ritual" employed).

5. A brief biography of Peter can include the following adequately attested information: He was from Bethsaida (John 1:44), married in Capernaum (1 Cor 9:5; Mark 1:29), was a fisherman by occupation (Mark 1:16-18; John 21:3), was probably brought into contact with John

the Baptist's penitential movement by his brother Andrew (John 1:35-37, 40), with Andrew was probably Jesus' first disciple (Mark 1:16-18; John 1:41f.), and was at the formation of the circle of the Twelve distinguished by Jesus as a leading disciple with the epithet "(precious) stone" (Mark 3:13-16). After his messianic confession (Mark 8:27-30) and failure during the Passion (14:54, 66-72) he became the normative Easter witness (Mark 16:7; Luke 24:34; 1 Cor 15:5) and the leader of the early Church. As such he was also the one responsible for the mission to the Jews (Acts 1–12; Gal 2:8), who after being forced to leave Jerusalem also opened himself to the mission to the Gentiles. He was a decisive mediator in the Jerusalem agreements and the Antiochian conflict (Galatians 2; Acts 15), and later undertook missionary journeys (1 Cor 9:5). Finally, he died a martyr's death in Rome. His actual pan-ecclesiastical authority, established against James and Paul, is broadly reflected in the overall NT witness.

R. Pesch

πετρώδης, 2 *petrōdēs* stony, rocky*

Subst. τὸ πετρῶδες (Mark 4:5) or τὰ πετρώδη (Matt 13:5, 20; Mark 4:16). In all instances the reference is to *rocky ground* over which at most a thin layer of soil lies (→ πέτρα 2).

πήγανον, ου, τό *pēganon* rue*

Luke 11:42 mentions πήγανον among herbs that are "tithed" (cf. par. Matt 23:23).

πηγή, ῆς, ἡ *pēgē* spring (noun)*

Literal in Jas 3:11; Rev 8:10; 14:7; 16:4; in 2 Pet 2:17 as a metaphor for sinners: "waterless *springs*"; John 4:6a(b), of Jacob's well; Mark 5:29: "the *source* of his blood" (Lev 12:7); Rev 21:6: "the *fountain* of the water of life" (cf. ζωῆς πηγαὶ ὑδάτων in 7:17); John 4:14: "a *spring* of water welling up to eternal life." W. Michaelis, *TDNT* VI, 112-17; O. Böcher, *DNTT* III, 985-88; for further bibliography see *TWNT* X, 1232f.

πήγνυμι *pēgnymi* make firm, fix; set up*

Heb 8:2, of the erection of the tabernacle (cf. Exod 33:7; 38:26).

πηδάλιον, ου, τό *pēdalion* steering rudder*

Sg. in Jas 3:4; pl. in Acts 27:40.

πηλίκος, 3 *pēlikos* how large*

This correlative pron. occurs in the NT in exclamations: Gal 6:11: πηλίκοις γράμμασιν ἔγραψα, "*with what large* letters I am writing"; fig. in Heb 7:4: πηλίκος οὗτος, "*how great* he [*sc.* Melchizedek] is."

πηλός, οῦ, ὁ *pēlos* loam, clay*

Clay as the potter's material is mentioned in Rom 9:21 (cf. Wis 15:7). In John 9:6 πηλός is used of soft earthen material: Jesus "spat on the ground and made a *paste* of the spittle and anointed the [blind] man's eyes with the *paste*" (cf. vv. 11, 14, 15). K. H. Rengstorf, *TDNT* VI, 118f.

πήρα, ας, ἡ *pēra* traveler's bag/pouch*

Mark 6:8 par. Luke 9:3; Matt 10:10 par. Luke 10:4; Luke 22:35: Jesus directs his disciples not to take along a traveler's bag (beggar's pouch? cf. in contrast Luke 22:36; also H. Schürmann, *Jesu Abschiedsrede* [1957] 138). W. Michaelis, *TDNT* VI, 119-21.

πηρόω *pēroō* cripple; blind (vb.)
An occasional v.l. in place of πωρόω (so Mark 8:17; John 12:41; Rom 11:7). K. L. and M. A. Schmidt, *TDNT* V, 1025-28.

πήρωσις, εως, ἡ *pērōsis* crippling; blindness
Fig. in Mark 3:5 v.l.: πήρωσις (instead of πώρωσις) τῆς καρδίας. K. L. and M. A. Schmidt, *TDNT* V, 1025-28.

πῆχυς, εως, ὁ *pēchys* cubit; small span of time(?)*

Lit.: G. DALMAN, *Aramäisch-neuhebräisches Handwörterbuch zu Targum, Talmud und Midrasch* (1938 = 1967) 87. — JEREMIAS, *Parables* 171. — J. SCHNEIDER, *TDNT* II, 942. — G. SCHWARZ, "προσθεῖναι ἐπὶ τὴν ἡλικίαν αὐτοῦ πῆχυν ἕνα," *ZNW* 71 (1980) 244-47.

1. Πῆχυς occurs 4 times in the NT, twice apparently as a unit of time (Matt 6:27 par. Luke 12:25 in one of Jesus' fig. sayings: "lengthen by a small span of time") and twice as a unit of length (John 21:8, indicating the distance from the boat to the shore: "about two hundred *cubits*"; Rev 21:17 indicating the height of the wall of the new Jerusalem: "144 cubits").

2. The πῆχυς was a linear measure based on the distance from the tip of the elbow to the tip of the middle finger; according to the "Philetarian system of measurement" used in Palestine at the time of Jesus it measured 525 mm. (J. Jeremias, *Jerusalem in the Time of Jesus* [1969] 11 n.20). In John 21:8 and Rev 21:17 its meaning is clear from the context.
In Jesus' saying in Matt 6:27 par. Luke 12:25 it is "debated" (Schneider): As a linear measure it is "much too large" and is thus understood as "a minimal measure of time"; "then the logion may have an eschatological reference," referring to the impossibility of "prolonging

the span of life" in view of the impending catastrophe (Jeremias 171).
It is also possible, however, to trace πῆχυς in the saying back to a mistranslation from Aramaic based on either mishearing or misreading *garmît'ā*, "little bone," as *garmîd'ā*, "cubit." If this mistake (and a second one involving ἡλικία) is corrected, the following (presumably original) wording emerges for Jesus' saying: "Who among you can add a single bone to himself [literally: to his skeleton]?" If this is correct, Jesus might have addressed this saying to listeners whose arrogance, which he found unbearable, he wanted to throw into relief with sharp irony.

G. Schwarz

πιάζω *piazō* hold, take hold of, arrest*

Πιάζω corresponds in Doric and colloquially to Attic → πιέζω. It is neutral in Acts 3:7: "he *took* him by the hand," and otherwise hostile: *seize, arrest* (of Jesus in John 7:30, 32, 44; 8:20; 10:39; 11:57; of Peter or Paul in Acts 12:4; 2 Cor 11:32). The vb. is also used of capturing animals (John 21:3, 10: fish; Rev 19:20: τὸ θηρίον).

πιέζω *piezō* press*

Luke 6:38: pf. pass. partc. πεπιεσμένον, "*(firmly) pressed* measure (μέτρον)."

πιθανολογία, ας, ἡ *pithanologia* art of persuasion*

In Col 2:4 πιθανολογία occurs in the negative sense: "I say this in order that no one may delude you with *beguiling speech*." Moulton/Milligan s.v.; O. Becker, *DNTT* I, 588, 592.

πιθός, 3 *pithos* persuasive
A secondary form of → πειθός (in Westcott/Hort).

πικραίνω *pikrainō* make bitter*

Literal in Rev 10:9, 10, of ἡ κοιλία: The little scroll that the seer eats "*makes* his stomach *bitter*," i.e., spoils his stomach or his digestive organs; 8:11, of water made into wormwood or *made bitter;* fig. and pass. in Col 3:19 (*let oneself become embittered*): Husbands should not *become bitter* toward their wives (cf. *Herm. Man.* x.2.3). W. Michaelis, *TDNT* VI, 122-25.

πικρία, ας, ἡ *pikria* bitterness*

Acts 8:23 says of the magician that he was in χολὴ πικρίας (i.e., χολὴ πικρά, "bitter gall"; see G. Schneider, *Acts* [HTKNT] ad loc.). In Heb 12:15 ῥίζα πικρίας is a "*bitter root*," i.e., a root from which bitter fruits grow. Πικρία is fig. in the catalog of vices in Eph 4:31 and in the citation (Ps 9:28 LXX?) in Rom 3:13. W. Michaelis, *TDNT* VI, 122-25.

πικρός, 3 *pikros* bitter*

Jas 3:11, of undrinkable water (cf. Exod 15:23); fig. in 3:14: ζῆλον πικρὸν ἔχω, "have *bitter* jealousy [in one's heart]." W. Michaelis, *TDNT* VI, 122-25.

πικρῶς *pikrōs* bitterly*

With κλαίω (as in Isa 22:4; 33:7 LXX), "weep *bitterly*" at the end of the story of Peter's denial (Matt 26:75 par. Luke 22:62 (*contra* Mark!).

Πιλᾶτος, ου *Pilatos* Pilate
Πόντιος, ου *Pontios* Pontius*

1. Pilate's life — 2. The NT — a) Luke 3:1; 13:1 — b) The Passion

Lit.: A. BAJSIC, "Pilatus, Jesus und Barabbas," *Bib* 48 (1967) 7-28. — E. BAMMEL, *RGG* V, 383f. — *idem*, "The Trial before Pilate," *Jesus and the Politics of His Day* (ed. E. Bammel and C. F. D. Moule; 1984) 415-51. — J. BLINZLER, *Der Prozeß Jesu* (⁴1969) 260-83. — *idem*, "Die Niedermetzelung von Galiläern durch Pilatus," *NovT* 2 (1957) 24-49. — J. BLINZLER, J. MICHL, and E. LUCCHESI PALLI, *LTK* VIII, 504-6. — A. VAN DEN BORN, *BL* 1388f. — A. DAUER, *Die Passionsgeschichte im Johannesevangelium* (1972) 100-164. — M. DIBELIUS, "Herodes und Pilatus," *idem, Botschaft* I, 278-92. — A. EHRHARDT, "Pontius Pilatus in der frühchristlichen Mythologie," *EvT* 9 (1949/50) 433-47. — E. FASCHER, PW XX / 2 (1950) 1322f. — A. FROVA, "L'iscrizione di Ponzio Pilato à Cesarea," *RIL.L* 95 (1961) 419-34. — B. KANAEL, "Ancient Jewish Coins and Their Historical Importance," *BA* 26 (1963) 38-62. — J.-P. LÉMONON, *Pilate et le gouvernement de la Judée. Textes et monuments* (1981). — REICKE, *NT Era* 140f., 175f., 190f. — L. ROTH, *EncJud* XIII, 848. — G. SCHNEIDER, *Verleugnung, Verspottung und Verhör Jesu nach Lukas 22,54-71* (1969) 211-20. — SCHÜRER, *History* I, 383-87. — A. N. SHERWIN-WHITE, "The Trial of Jesus," *Historicity and Chronology in the NT* (ed. D. Nineham; 1965) 97-116. — *idem, Roman Society and Roman Law in the NT* (1963) 24-47. — *idem, ISBE* III, 867-69. — E. M. SMALLWOOD, "The Date of the Dismissal of Pontius Pilate from Judaea," *JJS* 5 (1954) 12-21. — R. STAATS, "Pontius Pilatus im Bekenntnis der frühen Kirche," *ZTK* 84 (1987) 493-513. — M. STERN, "The Province of Judaea," *The Jewish People in the First Century* I (Compendia 1/1, 1974) 308-76. — A. STROBEL, *Die Stunde der Wahrheit. Untersuchungen zum Strafverfahren gegen Jesus* (1980) 95-142. — H. WANSBROUGH, "Suffered Under Pontius Pilate," *Scripture* 18 (1966) 84-93. — P. WINTER, *On the Trial of Jesus* (1961). — G. WIRSCHING, *KP* IV, 1049f.

1. Pilate, a Roman equestrian soldier from the line of Pontius, was the governor of Judea A.D. 26-36. The inscription found in Caesarea in 1961 calls him *praefectus*. Philo (*Leg. Gai.* 38) characterizes him as "inflexible and relentlessly severe." Several conflicts accord with this description: Contrary to the usual practice of Roman troops, he had the army march into Jerusalem with imperial standards (Josephus *Ant.* xviii.55-59), he used funds from the temple treasury to finance the building of a water supply (Josephus *Ant.* xviii.60-62; *B.J.* ii.175-77), he erected shields of dedication with the name of the emperor in the former Herodian palace (Philo *Leg. Gai.* 38), and he attacked an assembly of Samaritans on Mt. Gerizim (Josephus *Ant.* xviii.85-89). Pilate was removed from office because of this last transgression and was sent to Rome to answer for it. The date and manner of his death are uncertain. Several Christian apocryphal writings focus on him (cf. Hennecke/Schneemelcher I, 444-70, 481-84). Tacitus *Ann.* xv.44 mentions Jesus' crucifixion by Pilate.

2. a) Luke 3:1 (redactional) mentions Pontius Pilate's governorship of Judea and by this reference to secular history alludes to the universal nature of Jesus' offer of salvation. 13:1 reports that Pilate killed Galilean festival pilgrims while they were involved in a rite of sacrifice. Although this event is not attested by extrabiblical sources, it does fit Pilate's behavior.

b) All other NT passages in which Pilate is mentioned refer to Jesus' Passion. Mark 15 reports the interrogation by Pilate (vv. 1-5), the release of Barabbas and handing over of Jesus for scourging and crucifixion (vv. 6-15), and the release of Jesus' corpse for burial to Joseph of Arimathea (vv. 42-46).

Matthew 27 takes up the Markan accounts while emphasizing more strongly the Jews' guilt in Jesus' death: In v. 19 Matthew adds the warning by Pilate's wife, in v. 24 Pilate's own disavowal of any responsibility, and in v. 25 the Jewish people's acceptance of responsibility. One further insertion reflects apologetic interests: the report that Pilate secured the tomb (vv. 62-66).

Luke 23 also takes up from Mark the sections mentioning Pilate. Luke adds that Pilate had Jesus brought before Herod Antipas, who sent him back to Pilate, whereupon Pilate and Herod became friends (vv. 6-12). Luke probably composed this scene on the basis of a historical reminiscence. In the communal prayer in Acts 4:27 ("Herod and Pontius Pilate") Luke redactionally refers again to this scene (*contra* Dibelius). Luke emphasizes his own agenda by having Pilate three times attest Jesus' innocence and in that way defend both Jesus and Christians before the Roman state (Luke 23:4, 14f., 22).

In John the trial before Pilate is "the heart of the entire account" (R. Schnackenburg, *John* III [Eng. tr., 1982] 241). Jesus is shown to be the true king while Pilate appears as the helpless plaything of the powers hostile to God (18:28–19:16a). In John 19:19-22 Pilate testifies to Jesus' kingship by composing the inscription for the cross and defending its content against Jewish objections. In 19:31-38 the Evangelist takes up two competing traditions: According to the first, the Jews ask Pilate that the crucified men's legs be broken and that they be brought down from the crosses; according to the second, Joseph of Arimathea asks Pilate for the body of Jesus.

Pilate is mentioned in early Christian preaching and confessional statements concerning Jesus' death in Acts 3:13; 13:28; 1 Tim 6:13 ("Pontius Pilate").   A. Weiser

πίμπλημι *pimplēmi* fill up, make full*

Literal in Matt 22:10; 27:48; Luke 5:7; Acts 19:29; of being filled with the Holy Spirit in Luke 1:15, 41, 67; Acts 2:4; 4:8, 31; 9:17; 13:9 (thus characteristic of Luke-Acts); of a person being filled with some emotion (again characteristic of Luke-Acts) in Luke 4:28 (θυμοῦ); 5:26 (φόβου); 6:11 (ἀνοίας); Acts 3:10 (θάμβους καὶ ἐκστάσεως); 5:17 and 13:45 (ζήλου); fig. of fulfilled prophecies in Luke 21:22 (cf. 1:20 v.l.) and of a span of time coming to its end in Luke 1:23, 57; 2:6, 21, 22. G. Delling, *TDNT* VI, 128-31; R. Schippers, *DNTT* I, 733-41.

πίμπραμαι *pimpramai* swell up*

The pass. of πίμπρημι in Acts 28:6 probably means *become distended, swell up:* "They waited, expecting him [*sc.* Paul, after being bitten by the snake] to *swell up* or suddenly fall dead."

πινακίδιον, ου, τό *pinakidion* small tablet*

Derived from πίναξ; Luke 1:63, of a writing *tablet*. Billerbeck II, 108-10.

πινακίς, ίδος, ἡ *pinakis* small writing tablet Luke 1:63 v.l. in place of → πινακίδιον.

πίναξ, ακος, ἡ *pinax* platter, dish*

With ποτήριον in Luke 11:39: "You cleanse the outside of the cup and the *dish*"; Mark 6:25, 28 par. Matt 14:8, 11: the head of John the Baptist ἐπὶ πίνακι. On the presentation of a head during a banquet cf. Diogenes Laertius ix.58.

πίνω *pinō* drink*

1. Occurrences in the NT — 2. Eating and drinking — 3. Table fellowship — 4. The Lord's Supper — 5. Drinking the living water (John) — 6. Further occurrences

Lit.: H. Bardtke and B. Reicke, *BHH* 208f. — J. Betz, "Der Abendmahlskelch im Judenchristentum," *Abhandlungen über Theologie und Kirche* (FS K. Adam, 1952) 109-37. — G. Braumann, *DNTT,* II, 274-77. — F. M. Braun, "Avoir soif et boire (Jn 4,10-14; 7,37-39)," FS Rigaux 247-58. — L. Goppelt, *TDNT* VI, 135-60. — E. J. Kilmartin, "The Eucharistic Cup in the Primitive Liturgy," *CBQ* 24 (1962) 32-43. — H. Schürmann, "Das apostolische Interesse am eucharistischen Kelch," Schürmann II, 188-96. — For further bibliography see *TWNT* X, 1233.

1. The vb. πίνω occurs 73 times in the NT: 15 times in Matthew, 8 in Mark, 17 in Luke, 3 in Acts, 11 in John, 15 in the authentic Pauline letters (once in Rom 14:21, 14 in 1 Corinthians), 3 in Revelation, and once in Heb 6:7. In 39 of these occurrences it is with → ἐσθίω, 24 of those in the expression ἐσθίω (τρώγω) καὶ πίνω. The compound καταπίνω ("drink down") occurs 7 times.

2. "Eating and drinking" serve to satisfy physical hunger and thirst. The NT warns against a life focused primarily on earthly enjoyment (eating and drinking). Matt 6:25-32 par. Luke 12:22-32 emphasize that it is not necessary to worry about food and clothing, eating and *drinking* (Matt 6:25, 31 par. Luke 12:29); it is only important to seek "the kingdom of the Father." Otherwise what happened in the days of Noah and Lot (Matt 24:37-39 par. Luke 17:26-30) will happen again: "They were eating and *drinking*" and did not reckon with the sudden end. Thus they overlooked the signs of the time.

The parable of the rich fool (Luke 12:13-21) warns against limiting one's interests to earthly goods without considering that such wealth ends with death. "This very night" God will call to account the rich man who wants to "take his ease, eat, *drink*, and be merry" (v. 19). The parable of the watchful and neglectful servants (Matt 24:45-51 par. Luke 12:42-46) points out the wrongful behavior of the servant who does not reckon with the delay of the parousia: He beats his fellow servants and eats and *drinks* with drunks.

Even though the Christian has a "right to food and *drink*" (1 Cor 9:4; cf. also 11:22), he is nonetheless obligated to show consideration for his fellow Christians and "not eat meat or *drink* wine" or anything that might cause a brother to take offense (Rom 14:21). By quoting the exhortation "let us eat and *drink*" 1 Cor 15:32 characterizes the behavior of those who seek fulfillment in this life.

With warnings against a lifestyle focused on eating and drinking occur also statements about abstinence. John the Baptist came "neither eating nor *drinking*" (Matt 11:18; cf. par. Luke 7:33: "eating no bread and drinking no wine"). Already at the promise of his birth the assertion is made: "He shall *drink* no wine or strong drink" (Luke 1:15). These statements characterize the Baptist's (prophetic?) lifestyle. Jesus himself hears the objection that his own disciples eat and *drink* while those of John and the Pharisees fast (Luke 5:33; cf. Mark 2:18 par. Matt 9:14).

After his Damascus experience Paul neither ate nor *drank* for three days (penitence and preparation for baptism; Acts 9:9; cf. v. 19a). Acts portrays the actions of those planning to attack Paul: They bound themselves by an oath and declared they would neither eat nor *drink* until they had killed him (Acts 23:12, 21).

3. The expression "eating and drinking" is frequently used as an expression for table fellowship. In contrast to John the Baptist (→ 2) Jesus came "eating and *drinking*"

(Matt 11:19 par. Luke 7:34). With Jesus the time of rejoicing commences; Jesus strikes up the music, as it were, for the wedding itself. During this time the guests cannot fast (Luke 5:33f.). Jesus' own eating and drinking with his table fellows is a sign of the inbreaking of the time of salvation. Because of John's ascetic behavior people assert that he is possessed, and then they disqualify Jesus as a glutton and drunkard (Matt 11:19 par. Luke 7:34). Jesus "eats and *drinks*" with tax collectors and sinners (Luke 5:30; cf. Mark 2:16 par. Matt 9:11), i.e., he enjoys table fellowship with them, stands on their side, and establishes solidarity with them.

Jesus instructs his messengers to remain in a hospitable house and there to eat and *drink* what is set before them (Luke 10:7).

The parable of the narrow and closed door (Luke 13:22-30) presupposes the motif of the eschatological meal (cf. vv. 25, 28f.). Those knocking on the door will be turned back and will seek recourse in the fact that as Jesus' contemporaries they ate and *drank* with him (v. 26). For Luke's readers this means that participation in the meal of the worship service does not yet entitle a person to enter the kingdom of God.

To those disciples who have continued with Jesus in his trials he makes the promise: "You will eat and *drink* at my table in my kingdom and sit on thrones judging the twelve tribes of Israel" (Luke 22:30; cf. Matt 19:28). In Jesus' kingdom the disciples will enjoy table fellowship and rule together with him.

4. The accounts of the institution of the eucharist use πίνω a total of 9 times (Mark 14:23, 25 bis; Matt 26:27, 29 bis; Luke 22:18; 1 Cor 11:25, 26). The vb. must be interpreted here in the context of the accounts of the Last Supper, so that the eucharistic rites of bread and cup belong together. After the bread ritual Jesus takes the cup and speaks a thanksgiving prayer. It is emphasized that Jesus tells those present to "take the cup and divide it among yourselves" (Luke 22:17b), since the communal cup was *not* the usual practice at celebration meals, at which each participant normally drank from his own cup. Mark accordingly emphasizes: "and they all *drank* from it" (14:23). Jesus does not drink from the cup. The cup ritual with the exhortation to drink is grounded—like the bread ritual—in the announcement of death (Luke 22:18; cf. Mark 14:25 par. Matt 26:29). In the coming kingdom of God Jesus will "*drink* anew" of the fruit of the vine (Mark 14:25 par. Matt 26:29). In this drink Jesus offers his own redemptive death, and the physical act of drinking is made part of the reception of redemption. Thus "this drinking, as the accounts of the institution portray it, is sacramental" (Goppelt 141).

Along with the account of the institution in 1 Cor 11:23-26 Paul describes eating and drinking at the Lord's Supper in 10:3-5, 18-21. This eating and drinking he compares to the receiving of the manna in the wilderness and of the water from the rock during the time of Moses (πίνω, v. 4 bis). Eating and drinking at the Lord's Supper is consciously distinguished from normal eating and drinking (10:18, 21; 11:27-32). Paul warns against eating and drinking as the people did in the wilderness (10:7). Eating and drinking, like all other activity, should be done to the glory of God (v. 31).

John 6 speaks of an eating and drinking that brings eternal life. Whoever eats Jesus' flesh and *drinks* his blood (vv. 53, 54) has eternal life. His flesh is true food and his blood true drink (v. 55). Whoever eats this flesh and *drinks* this blood abides in Jesus and Jesus in him (v. 56). Πίνω here is to be viewed in the context of the bread discourse (vv. 48-58), which is open to a eucharistic interpretation. The gift that Jesus gives thus consists— as in the accounts of the Last Supper—of himself.

5. In addition to the eating and drinking of the eucharistic gifts (→ 4), John also speaks of *drinking the living water* (4:7-14; 7:37). To the woman at Jacob's well Jesus promises water that will satisfy thirst forever. Whoever drinks this water, which brings eternal life, will never thirst again (4:10-14). All who thirst should come to Jesus (7:37), and whoever believes in him, from that person rivers of living water will flow (v. 38). Drinking of living water should be viewed as parallel to eating the bread of life (6:35, 50f.; cf. 4:32). Jesus is himself the gift that one can receive through faith.

6. Πίνω is used metaphorically in statements about the cup of suffering and the cup of wrath. One who willingly takes on himself the fate ordained by God is prepared to "*drink* the cup" (Matt 26:42; John 18:11; cf. Mark 10:38f. par. Matt 20:22f.: → ποτήριον). Revelation speaks of *drinking* the wine of God's wrath (Rev 14:10; 18:3) poured into the "cup of wrath" (cf. also 16:6).

According to Matt 27:34 the soldiers gave the crucified Jesus "wine to *drink* mingled with gall"; he tasted it, but did not want to *drink*. Mark 16:18 promises to Jesus' disciples the capacity to "*drink* any deadly thing" without it harming them.

To the question regarding fasting Luke adds a wine precept making clear why many people reject the new that Jesus brings (Luke 5:39). The old is much more suitable in the view of many, and hence one can understand the Jews' negative response to Jesus' claims. The parable of the unworthy servant (17:7-10) makes it clear that the servant first serves his master. Only when the master has "eaten and *drunk*" can the servant "eat and *drink*" (v. 8). This parable directs itself against false expectation of reward.

Heb 6:7 asserts that land that "has drunk the rain" participates in God's blessing.   A. Palzkill

πιότης, ητος, ἡ   piotēs   fatness*

Rom 11:17: ἡ ῥίζα τῆς πιότητος, literally "the root of fatness," i.e., the fat-giving root of the cultivated olive tree (cf. *T. Levi* 8:8; Judg 9:9 LXX).

πιπράσκω   pipraskō   sell*

With the acc. of thing in Matt 13:46; Acts 2:45, of selling all one's possessions; pass. in Acts 4:34; 5:4 in the same context; with gen. of price: Mark 14:5: "for more than three hundred denarii"; Matt 26:9: πολλοῦ; John 12:5: "for three hundred denarii"; of selling of slaves: in a parable in Matt 18:25; also, metaphorically, in Rom 7:14: "*sold* under sin [as the slaveholder]." H. Preisker, *TDNT* VI, 160f.

πίπτω   piptō   fall down; fall to pieces, collapse; falter (morally); become invalid*

1. Occurrences in the NT and basic meaning — 2. Fall down, fall into, fall off, fall upon — 3. Collapse, fall to pieces — 4. Fall down, throw oneself down (and worship) — 5. Lose one's life, be killed, die, fall over dead — 6. Falter (morally); become invalid

Lit.: W. BAUDER, *DNTT* I, 608-11. — W. MICHAELIS, *TDNT* VI, 161-66. — Spicq, *Notes* II, 692-94.

1. Πίπτω occurs 90 times in the NT, most frequently in Revelation (23 times), and 47 times in the Gospels (19 times in Matthew, 8 in Mark, 17 in Luke, 3 in John), 9 in Acts, 3 in Romans, 4 in 1 Corinthians, 3 in Hebrews, and once in Jas 5:12. The NT also has the compounds ἐκπίπτω, καταπίπτω, παραπίπτω, and περιπίπτω. In the LXX πίπτω (over 400 occurrences) is almost always the tr. of *npl,* "fall." Its basic meaning is *fall, fall down, plunge.*

2. In most instances the vb. speaks of unintentional falling. The stars *fall down* from heaven (Mark 13:25 par. Matt 24:29; Rev 6:13; 8:10 bis; 9:1). Satan *fell down* "like lightning from heaven" (Luke 10:18). Crumbs *fall* from the table of the rich (Matt 15:27; Luke 16:21).
Seeds *fall* into the soil (Mark 4:4-8 par. Matt 13:4-8/ Luke 8:5, 7, 8, 14; John 12:24). Animals *and persons fall* (Matt 10:29: sparrows; Luke 14:5: ox and human). Matt 15:14: "If a blind man leads a blind man, both *will fall* into a pit." An epileptic "often *falls* into the fire and into the water" (17:15). An evil spirit "*fell* on the ground" (Mark 9:20). People call to the mountains and rocks: "*Fall* on us" (Luke 23:30; Rev 6:16).
Twice πίπτω is used in the sense *fall on, come to:*

"*and the lot fell* on Matthias" (Acts 1:26); "the sun will no longer *fall* on them" (Rev 7:16). In Acts 13:11 πίπτω takes on the meaning *surround:* "Immediately dimness and darkness *fell* on him."

3. Πίπτω is used of structures with the meaning *collapse, fall to pieces* in Matt 7:25, 27; Luke 11:17 (houses); 13:4 (tower); Heb 11:30 (walls); Acts 15:16; Rev 11:13; 14:8 (bis); 16:19; 18:2 (bis: parts of cities and cities themselves, e.g., Babylon). People *collapse* from astonishment (John 18:6: the people who arrested Jesus; Acts 9:4; 22:7: Paul before Damascus; Rev 1:17: the seer at the vision).

4. The meaning *fall down, throw oneself down* (intentional falling) occurs 12 times in the context of "worship" (→ προσκυνέω). In 6 of these instances God is worshiped (1 Cor 14:25; Rev 4:10; 5:14; 7:11; 11:16; 19:4) and twice angels (Rev 19:10 and 22:8). The wise men *fall down* before the child and worship him (Matt 2:11). The devil says to Jesus: "if you *fall down* and worship me" (4:9). The parable of the unmerciful servant refers to the proskynesis of a slave before his master (18:26). According to Acts 10:25 Cornelius fell down before Peter.
Falling without worship is spoken of in Rev 5:8; Matt 18:29 (the parable of the unmerciful servant); and Mark 5:22 par. Luke 8:41 (raising of the daughter of Jairus). In Luke 5:12 (healing a leper) a petition follows this falling, and in Luke 17:16 (the grateful Samaritan) gratitude. Mary of Bethany *falls* at Jesus' feet in greeting (John 11:32). The disciples *fell* on their faces at Jesus' transfiguration and were filled with fear (Matt 17:6). Before his arrest Jesus *fell* to the ground in order to pray (Mark 14:35 par. Matt 26:39).

5. 11 times πίπτω occurs in connection with death: Luke 20:18 par. Matt 21:44 (fig.: death by *falling* on the stone or through the *falling* of the stone itself); Luke 21:24 (*fall* by the edge of the sword); Acts 5:5, 10 (*fall over dead);* 20:9 (death by *plunging* from the third story); 1 Cor 10:8 ("and twenty-three thousand *fell* in a single day"); Heb 3:17 (*die* in the wilderness); Rev 17:10 ("five have *fallen*"). Except in Acts 20:9 death thus spoken of comes as the result of guilt.

6. Guilt is also expressed by πίπτω in Heb 4:11 ("so that no one *fall* by the same sort of disobedience"). The people of Israel are again referred to in Rom 11:11 ("have they stumbled so as to *fall*?"), 22 ("severity toward those who have *fallen*"); 1 Cor 10:12 ("let any one who thinks that he stands take heed lest he *fall*"). Rom 14:4 is also concerned with the antithesis between standing and falling: "It is before his own master that he stands or *falls.*"
James appeals for honesty: "so that you may not *fall* under condemnation" (5:12). In the letter to Ephesus

Revelation reminds the congregation of its fall and admonishes them to repent: "Remember then from what height you have *fallen*, repent and do the works you did at first" (2:5).

Luke 16:17 asserts that not a single "serif [→ κεραία] *will become invalid.*" The Torah will thus remain in effect in its entire form. According to 1 Cor 13:8 love will not *become invalid*, i.e., will never cease.   E. Palzkill

Πισιδία, ας *Pisidia* Pisidia*

The mountainous region west of the Taurus mountains, visited by Paul and Barnabas (Acts 14:24). Acts 13:14 TR reads Ἀντιόχεια τῆς Πισιδίας, "Antioch of *Pisidia*." A. van den Born, *BL* 1390f.; G. Neumann, *KP* IV, 868-70; G. E. Bean, *OCD* 835f.; W. H. C. Frend, *ISBE* III, 873f.

Πισίδιος, 3 *Pisidios* Pisidian*

The older text of Acts 13:14 (𝔓^{45, 74} ℵ A B al) does not attest the name → Πισιδία, but rather the adj. Πισίδιος: Ἀντιόχεια ἡ Πισιδία, "Pisidian Antioch." The adj. Πισίδιος is not, however, otherwise attested, though there is an adj. form Πισιδικός. Therefore the v.l. with the name → Πισιδία is perhaps to be preferred. *TCGNT* ad loc.

πιστεύω *pisteuō* believe, have faith
→ πίστις.

πιστικός, 3 *pistikos* faithful; genuine(?)*

According to Mark 14:3 and John 12:3 the vessel for anointing Jesus contained (costly) nard ointment (μύρου νάρδου). The adj. πιστικός, modifying νάρδος, probably means here *genuine, unadulterated* (Spicq, *Notes* II, 696: "a perfume of *genuine* nard" or "*extremely pure* nard"). Possibly, however, πιστικός derives from a name (Theophylact, *PG* CXXIII, 645B; cf. John 12:3 Vg.: *pisticus*). BAGD s.v. 3; Spicq, *Notes* II, 695f.

πίστις, εως, ἡ *pistis* faith, trust; faithfulness*
πιστεύω *pisteuō* believe, have faith*

1. Occurrences in the NT and linguistic background — 2. General usage — 3. Christian usage — 4. In the words of Jesus — 5. Faith and miracles — 6. Paul — 7. The Gospel of John and 1 John — 8. Hebrews — 9. James — 10. The Pastorals

Lit.: → ἀπιστέω; ὀλιγοπιστία; also: G. BARTH, "Pistis in hellenistischer Religiosität," *ZNW* 73 (1982) 110-26. — M. BARTH, "The Faith of the Messiah," *Heythrop Journal* 10 (1969) 363-70. — H. BINDER, *Der Glaube bei Paulus* (1968).

— G. BORNKAMM, *Jesus of Nazareth* (1960) 129-37. — *idem, Paul* (Eng. tr., 1971) 141-46. — J. E. BOTHA, "The Meanings of *pisteuō* in the Greek NT," *Neot* 21 (1987) 225-40. — E. BRANDENBURGER, "Pistis und Soteria. Zum Verstehenshorizont von 'Glaube' im Urchristentum," *ZTK* 85 (1988) 165-98. — H. BRAUN, *RGG* II, 1590-97. — R. BULTMANN, *Jesus and the Word* (1934 = 1958) 172-91. — *idem, Theology* I, 314-30; II, 70-92. — H. CONZELMANN, "Was glaubte die frühe Christenheit," *idem, Theologie als Schriftauslegung* (1974) 106-16. — C. E. B. CRANFIELD, "Μέτρον πίστεως in Romans 12:3," *NTS* 8 (1961/62) 345-51 (= *idem, The Bible and Christian Life* [1985] 203-14). — A. DELACHARLERIE, *Foi et miracles dans les évangiles synoptiques* (Diss. Louvain, 1960). — A. VON DOBBELER, *Glaube als Teilhabe. Historische und semantische Grundlagen der paulinischen Theologie und Ekklesiologie* (WUNT II/22, 1987). — H. DÖRRIE, "Zu Hebr. 11,1," *ZNW* 46 (1955) 196-202. — G. EICHHOLZ, *Jakobus und Paulus* (TEH 39, 1953). — *idem, Glaube und Werk bei Paulus und Jakobus* (TEH 88, 1961). — G. FRIEDRICH, "Muß ὑπακοὴ πίστεως Röm 1,5 mit 'Glaubensgehorsam' übersetzt werden?" *ZNW* 72 (1981) 118-23. — GOPPELT, *Theology* II, 124-34. — W. GRUNDMANN, "Verständnis und Bewegung des Glaubens im Johannesevangelium," *KD* 6 (1960) 131-54. — F. HAHN, "Das Glaubensverständnis im Johannesevangelium," FS Kümmel (1985) 51-69. — *idem,* "Jesu Worte vom bergeversetzenden Glauben," *ZNW* 76 (1985) 149-69. — *idem,* "Sehen und Glauben im Johannesevangelium," FS Cullmann (1972) 125-42. — D. M. HAY, "*Pistis* as 'Ground for Faith' in Hellenized Judaism and Paul," *JBL* 108 (1989) 461-76. — R. B. HAYS, *The Faith of Jesus Christ* (SBLDS 56, 1983), esp. 139ff. — H.-J. HERMISSON and E. LOHSE, *Faith* (1981). — M. D. HOOKER, "Πίστις Χριστοῦ," *NTS* 35 (1989) 321-42. — G. HOWARD, "On the 'Faith of Christ,'" *HTR* 60 (1967) 459-65. — A. J. HULTGREN, "The *Pistis Christou* Formulation in Paul," *NovT* 22 (1980) 248-63. — A. JEPSEN, *TDOT* I, 292-323. — E. KÄSEMANN, "The Faith of Abraham in Romans 4," *idem, Perspectives on Paul* (1971) 79-101. — *idem, Rom* (Eng. tr., 1980) 106ff. — J. KÖRNER, "Das Wesen des Glaubens nach dem AT," *TLZ* 104 (1979) 713-20. — W. KRAMER, *Christ, Lord, Son of God* (1966) 45-64. — O. KUSS, "Der Glaube nach den paulinischen Hauptbriefen," Kuss I, 187-212. — M. LAUTENSCHLAGER, "Der Gegenstand des Glaubens im Jakobusbrief," *ZTK* 87 (1990) 163-84. — H. LJUNGMAN, *Pistis: A Study of Its Presuppositions and Its Meanings in Pauline Use* (1964). — E. LOHSE, "Glaube und Werke," *ZNW* 48 (1957) 1-22. — *idem,* "Emuna und Pistis," *ZNW* 68 (1977) 147-63. — D. LÜHRMANN, *Glaube im frühen Christentum* (1976). — O. MERK, "Glaube und Tat in den Pastoralbriefen," *ZNW* 66 (1975) 91-102. — O. MICHEL, *DNTT* I, 593-605. — M. PEISKER, *Der Glaubensbegriff bei Philon* (Diss. Breslau, 1936). — W. REBELL, *Alles ist möglich dem, der glaubt. Glaubensvollmacht im frühen Christentum* (1989). — J. ROLOFF, *Das Kerygma und der irdische Jesus* (²1973) 152-207. — W. SCHENK, "Die Gerechtigkeit Gottes und der Glaube Christi," *TLZ* 97 (1972) 161-74. — E. SEIDEL, *Πίστις in der griechischen Literatur bis zur Zeit des Peripatos* (Diss. Innsbruck, 1952). — T. SÖDING, *Glaube bei Markus. Glaube an das Evangelium, Gebetsglaube und Wunderglaube im Kontext der markinischen Basileiatheologie und Christologie* (SBB 12, 1987). — R. SMEND, "Zur Geschichte von *h'mjn,*" *Hebräische Wortforschung* (FS W. Baumgartner, 1967) 284-90. — SPICQ, *Notes* II, 697-703. —

J. Swetnam, "The Meaning of πεπιστευκότας in John 8:31," *Bib* 61 (1980) 106-9. — G. M. Taylor, "The Function of πίστις Χριστοῦ in Galatians," *JBL* 85 (1966) 58-76. — C. Thomassen, *Der Glaube nach Paulus, dargestellt an den Hauptbriefen des Apostels* (1970). — L. Walter, *Foi et Incrédulité selon Saint Jean* (Diss. Paris, 1975). — N. Walter, "Christusglaube und heidnische Religiosität in paulinischen Gemeinden," *NTS* 25 (1978/79) 422-42. — W. Wiefel, "Glaubensgehorsam? Erwägungen zu Röm 1,5," *Wort und Gemeinde* (FS E. Schott, 1967) 137-44. — H. Wildberger, " 'Glauben' im AT," *ZTK* 65 (1968) 129-59. — *idem, THAT* I, 177-209. — S. K. Williams, "Again *Pistis Christou*," *CBQ* 49 (1987) 431-47. — *idem,* "The Hearing of Faith: ΑΚΟΗ ΠΙΣΤΕΩΣ in Gal. 3," *NTS* 35 (1989) 82-93. — E. Wissmann, *Das Verhältnis von πίστις und Christusfrömmigkeit bei Paulus* (1926). — J. Zmijewski, "Der Glaube und seine Macht," FS Zimmermann 81-103. — For further bibliography see *DNTT* I, 605f.; *TWNT* X, 1233-36.

1. Noun and vb. occur 243 times each in the NT. Neither occurs in 2–3 John. Since John uses only the vb. and Colossians, Philemon, 2 Peter, and Revelation use only the noun, and since the same statement can often be expressed either by the vb. or the noun, the two words must be treated together. Their frequency and esp. their particular usage show that we are dealing here with a central theological concept, one that represents the correct relationship to God and ultimately the essence of the Christian religion itself.

Πιστεύειν and πίστις exhibit this kind of significance in neither the Hellenistic nor the Jewish world of the NT, nor in the OT. They were not Hellenistic catchwords of religions engaging in propaganda, but contemporary Greek was familiar with the use of πιστ- in religious contexts (besides the documentation in BAGD s.v. cf. Plato *Ti.* 40d, e; Plutarch *Superst.* 2, 4; *De Pythiae Oraculis* 17.25; *De Genio Socratis* 24; *Consolatio ad Uxorem* 11; *De sera numinis vindicta* 3; Lucian *Alex.* 30, 38; *JTr.* 40; *Philops.* 10, 38; *Sat.* 5; *Sacr.* 15).

As a rule, the LXX uses words from the stem πιστ- (except in Jer 25:8) only to translate the Hebrew stem *'mn,* esp. hiphil and niphal. Yet *'mn* does not occupy the central position that πιστεύειν and πίστις do in the NT, but rather characterizes the relationship between humans and God along with other words such as *bṭḥ, ḥsh, qwh, yḥl,* and *ḥkh.* It is questionable (Jepsen 309) whether *'mn* (hiphil) acquired a more central significance from its setting in the sacred oracle of holy war (so Wildberger). In any case, *'mn,* with its meanings "acquire firmness/stability," "depend on someone without qualification," and "give credence to a message," strongly influenced the understanding of πιστ-both in Judaism and the NT.

Only in a few Jewish writings does πιστ- emerge more strongly as a designation for relationship to God (so esp. Sir 2:6, 8, 10; 4:16; 11:21; Wis 16:26; 4 Macc 7:19, 21; 15:24; 16:22; Philo *Abr.* 262ff., 268ff.; *Her.* 90ff.; *Vit. Mos.* i.83, 90; *All.* ii.89), now associated with conversion to Judaism (Wis 12:2; Jdt 14:10; Philo *Abr.* 69f.) and with the νόμος (Sir 32:24; 33:3; 2 Esdr 7:24; *2 Bar.* 54:5).

How πιστεύειν and πίστις became *the* central theological terms for the appropriate relationship to God and for the Christian religion itself cannot be clarified from the perspective of this Jewish background alone. Here one must take account of a further, independent Christian development prompted by events themselves.

2. a) **Πιστεύω.** 1) "Give credence to a message and/ or its bearer." Purely secular usage (cf. Gen 45:26; 3 Kgdms 10:7; Job 4:19; Prov 14:15; Jer 12:6, and elsewhere) is rare (John 9:18; Acts 9:26; 1 Cor 11:18: καὶ μέρος τι πιστεύω, "and I partly *believe* it"). The main focus is religious. Depending on the context, πιστεύω can mean *consider true, obey,* or *trust.*

With the dat. of the person (cf. Exod 4:1, 8f.; 19:9) in Mark 16:13: "neither *did* they *believe* them"; 16:14; 11:31 par. Matt 21:25/Luke 20:5: "Why then *did* you not *believe/obey* him [*sc.* John the Baptist]?"; similarly Matt 21:32; further John 5:46; 8:45f.; 10:38a; Acts 8:12; 26:27; 1 John 4:1. With dat. of the thing (cf. Pss 105:24 LXX; 118:66 LXX; Tob 14:4): "give credence to someone's words or message": Luke 1:20; John 2:22; 4:50; 5:47b; 12:38; Rom 10:16 (citing Isa 53:1); "*believe* Scripture": John 2:22; 5:47a; Acts 24:14; John 10:38b (τοῖς ἔργοις, their witness); 2 Thess 2:11, 12 (*believe* lies or the truth). With a ὅτι clause: "*believe* that . . ." (cf. Exod 4:5; Isa 43:10; 4 Macc 7:19): Luke 1:45; John 4:21; Acts 27:25; Heb 11:6; Jas 2:19. With acc. of thing: John 11:26: πιστεύεις τοῦτο; "*do* you *believe* this?" Acts 13:41 (citing Hab 1:5); 1 Cor 13:7; 1 John 4:16; with inf. in Acts 15:11: πιστεύομεν σωθῆναι; pass. in 2 Thess 1:10b: ἐπιστεύθη τὸ μαρτύριον ἡμῶν, "our testimony to you *was believed.*" With prep. phrases: Luke 24:25: πιστεύειν ἐπὶ πᾶσιν οἷς ἐλάλησαν . . . , "*to believe* everything they have spoken"; Mark 1:15: ἐν τῷ εὐαγγελίῳ (cf. Ps 105:12 LXX), ". . . in the gospel." Used absolutely with the context supplying the specifics: Mark 13:21 par. Matt 24:23; Matt 24:26: "*do* not *believe* it"; Luke 22:67; John 3:12; 10:25f.; 12:39; 19:35; 20:8, 25, 29; Jas 2:19b; Jude 5; the context also explains Rom 14:2: πιστεύει φαγεῖν πάντα, ". . . *believes* that he may eat anything."

2) God is the obj. of faith in Rom 4:3; Gal 3:6; Jas 2:23: τῷ θεῷ, "Abraham *believed* God" (citing Gen 15:6); Rom 4:17: κατέναντι οὗ ἐπίστευσεν θεοῦ (= κατέναντι θεοῦ ᾧ ἐπίστευσεν; BDF §294.5); John 5:24; Acts 27:25; 1 John 5:10b; cf. in contrast Acts 16:34; Titus 3:8: "*come to faith* in God."

3) "*Entrust* something to someone," τινί τι (cf. Xenophon *Mem.* iv.4.17; 1 Macc 8:16; 4 Macc 4:7; Josephus *B.J.* iv.492): Luke 16:11: "Who will *entrust* to you the true riches?"; John 2:24: *entrust* oneself to someone. Pass. πιστεύομαί τι, "*receive* something *in trust/be entrusted with* something (cf. Josephus *B.J.* v.567; *Vita* 137): Rom 3:2: "the oracles of God *were entrusted* to them"; Gal 2:7: the gospel; 1 Thess 2:4; 1 Tim 1:11; Titus 1:3; 1 Cor 9:17: οἰκονομίαν πεπίστευμαι.

b) **Πίστις.** 1) "That which elicits trust, faith": α. *Faithfulness, dependability* (cf. Xenophon *An.* i.6.3;

1 Kgdms 26:23; Jer 5:1, 3; Sir 1:27; 1 Macc 10:27): with κρίσις and ἔλεος in Matt 23:23: *faithfulness* (to God's will as revealed in Scripture); Rom 3:3: τὴν πίστιν τοῦ θεοῦ καταργέω, "nullify God's [covenantal] *faithfulness*" (cf. Ps 32:4 LXX; Hos 2:22); Titus 2:10: πᾶσαν πίστιν ἐνδείκνυσθαι ἀγαθήν, "show entire and true *fidelity*." With other virtues in Gal 5:22; 2 Tim 4:7: "I have kept *faithfulness*" (τηρέω πίστιν, Josephus *B.J.* ii.121). β. *Solemn promise, oath* (cf. Xenophon *Cyr.* vii.1.44; Plato *Lg.* iii.701c; 3 Macc 3:10; Josephus *Ant.* xii.382): 1 Tim 5:12: τὴν πρώτην πίστιν ἠθέτησαν, "they violated their first [= earlier] *pledge*." γ. *Proof* (cf. Plato *Phd.* 70b; Epictetus *Diss.* i.28.3; Josephus *Ant.* xv.69): Acts 17:31: πίστιν παρασχὼν πᾶσιν ἀναστήσας αὐτὸν ἐκ νεκρῶν (God appointed Jesus to judge the world), "he has given *proof* [of his choice of Jesus] to all by raising him from the dead."

2) *"Trust which one puts into practice, faith."* α. With God named as the obj. of faith: Mark 11:22: πίστις θεοῦ (obj. gen.; cf. Plutarch *Superst.* 2: ἀπιστία τοῦ θείου), *"faith/trust in God"*; Heb 6:1: πίστις ἐπὶ θεόν; 1 Thess 1:8: πρὸς τὸν θεόν; 1 Pet 1:21: εἰς θεόν. β. Even without God named, the context often shows God to be the obj. of πίστις: Matt 17:20 par. Luke 17:5f.; Matt 21:21; Col 2:12: *faith* in God's power; Heb 11:3-33, 39; Jas 1:6; 5:15.

3. Though one cannot proceed on the assumption of a uniform concept of faith standing at the beginning of the NT development, one that was then developed in various ways, one can nonetheless ascertain in the majority of NT traditions and writings a usage clearly distinguishing itself from that of the OT and Jewish environment but attesting also a certain continuity and agreement. Only in the NT did "faith" first become the central and comprehensive designation for one's relationship to God, and esp. that faith now entered into an indissoluble relationship to Jesus as the crucified and exalted Lord of the Church.

a) This orientation of faith toward Jesus is usually spoken of as "faith in" him: πιστεύω εἰς Ἰησοῦν (John 12:11); εἰς Χριστὸν Ἰησοῦν (Gal 2:16); εἰς τὸν υἱὸν (τοῦ θεοῦ) (John 3:36; 1 John 5:10); εἰς τὸν υἱὸν τοῦ ἀνθρώπου (John 9:35); εἰς αὐτόν/όν (John 2:11; 3:16, 18; 4:39; 6:29, 40; 7:5, 31, 39, 48; 8:30; 9:36; 10:42; 11:45, 48; 12:37, 42; Acts 10:43; 14:23; Rom 10:14; Phil 1:29; 1 Pet 1:8); εἰς ἐμέ (Matt 18:6; Mark 9:42 v.l.; John 6:35; 7:38; 11:25f.; 12:44, 46; 14:1, 12; 16:9; 17:20); εἰς τὸ ὄνομα . . . (John 1:12; 2:23; 3:18; 1 John 5:13); εἰς τὸν ἐρχόμενον (Acts 19:4); πιστεύω ἐν αὐτῷ (John 3:15 [v.l. εἰς αὐτόν]); Eph 1:15. It is questionable, however, whether in Gal 3:26 ἐν Χριστῷ Ἰησοῦ belongs with διὰ τῆς πίστεως. Πιστεύω ἐπί . . . (Matt 27:42; Acts 9:42; 11:17; 16:31; 22:19; 1 Tim 1:16; in Rom 9:33; 10:11; and 1 Pet

2:6 citing Isa 28:16). Πιστεύω τῷ κυρίῳ (Acts 5:14; 18:8); τῷ ὀνόματι . . . (1 John 3:23). In absolute usage, too, the context can disclose Christ as the obj. of πιστεύειν: Mark 15:32; John 1:7; 4:41f., 53; 5:44; 6:36, 47, 64; 9:38; 11:15, 40; 14:29; 16:31; 20:31b; Acts 13:39; 18:8b; 21:25; Rom 3:22; 10:4, 10; 1 Cor 1:21; Gal 3:22; Eph 1:19; 1 Tim 3:16 (pass.). Πίστις εἰς . . . (Acts 20:21; 24:24; 26:18; Col 2:5). Πίστις πρός . . . (Phlm 5). Gal 2:16 shows unequivocally that the gen. construction πίστις Χριστοῦ (Rom 3:22, 26; Gal 2:20; Phil 3:9) is to be understood as obj. gen. (*"faith* in Christ"; cf. further Acts 3:16; Eph 3:12; Jas 2:1; Rev 2:13; 14:12; cf. the analogous obj. gen. in Mark 11:22: *"faith* in God"; Phil 1:27: *"faith* in the gospel," as well as Col 2:12 and 2 Thess 2:13.

b) Ὅτι clauses express the content of faith in Christ, often in fixed traditional formulations: that God raised him from the dead (Rom 10:9), that he died and was resurrected (1 Thess 4:14; cf. Rom 6:8), that God sent him (John 11:42; 16:27, 30; 17:8, 21), that he is the Holy One of God (John 6:69), the Christ, and the Son of God (John 11:27; 20:31; 1 John 5:1, 5; cf. also the inf. construction in Acts 8:37 v.l.). Faith in Jesus is thus not belief in another deity, but rather belief that only in Jesus has God brought about salvation through his actions and self-revelation. Hence faith in Jesus (John 12:44; 14:1, 10f.; 1 Thess 1:8) is simultaneously faith in God or a turning to God (Acts 20:21), since it is faith in the God who raised Jesus from the dead (Rom 4:24; Col 2:12) and thus faith in God's own redemptive revelation in Christ, faith in the light (John 12:36). Faith is thus acceptance of the salvation proclamation of God's action in Christ; in Mark 1:15 and Phil 1:27 this faith is associated with the gospel (cf. also Mark 16:15f.; Rom 1:16; 1 Cor 15:1f.; Eph 1:13) and is certainly also part of the mission proclamation to Jews and Gentiles (Acts 10:43; 13:39; 16:31; 20:21; 24:24; cf. Rom 1:5; John 17:20f.; Luke 8:12f.; Acts 14:27). It is by no means, however, mere acceptance of certain facts; rather, πιστεύειν ὅτι . . . (Rom 10:9) is inseparably bound to the confession κύριος Ἰησοῦς with which the believing person subordinates himself to Jesus as his Lord. It encompasses a self-understanding and attitude governing one's entire existence, just as faith is associated (Mark 1:15; Acts 11:21; 20:21) with repentance and is understood as an act of obedience (Rom 10:16; ὑπακοὴ πίστεως: Rom 1:5; 16:26 [explicative gen.]), as is shown esp. by comparison of Rom 1:8 and 1 Thess 1:8 with Rom 15:18 and 16:19 and of 2 Cor 10:5 with v. 15, and by the antithesis to → ἀπειθέω (1) in John 3:36; Acts 14:2; Rom 11:30f.; 1 Pet 2:8; 3:1; 4:17.

c) In the aor. πιστεύω becomes a t.t. for *coming to faith* = becoming a Christian (Luke 8:12; Acts 4:4; 8:13; 11:21; 13:12, 48; 14:1; 15:7; 17:12, 34; 18:8; 19:2; Rom 13:11; 1 Cor 3:5; 15:2, 11; Gal 2:16; Eph 1:13); similarly the pf. (Acts 14:23; 15:5). Christians are πιστεύοντες (Mark 9:42 v.l.; Acts 2:44; 1 Cor 14:22; 1 Thess 1:7; 2:10, 13; 1 Pet 2:7), πιστεύσαντες (Mark 16:17; Acts 4:32; 2 Thess 1:10), πεπιστευκότες (Acts 18:27; 19:18; cf. 21:20), or οἰκεῖοι τῆς πίστεως (Gal 6:10).

d) Beyond this, πίστις can also refer to the *condition of (having) faith*. Luke 22:32: ". . . that your *faith* may not fail"; 1 Cor 2:5: "that your *faith* might not rest in human wisdom"; so esp. when the reference is to standing or abiding in faith (Acts 14:22; 1 Cor 16:13; 2 Cor 1:24b; 13:5; Col 1:23), though also Acts 14:27: θύρα πίστεως, "a door to *[the condition of] faith*" (cf. further Acts 15:9; 1 Cor 15:14, 17; 2 Cor 4:13; Eph 2:8; Col 2:7; 1 Thess 3:2, 5ff.; 2 Thess 1:4; 3:2; 1 Tim 3:13; Jas 2:5; 1 Pet 1:5, 7, 9; 5:9; Rev 13:10) or to the breastplate of *faith* (1 Thess 5:8) or shield of *faith* (Eph 6:16). The inf. ἐν τῷ πιστεύειν (Rom 15:13) can have the same sense.

Often the reference is less to the existence than to the vitality or intensity of one's faith, so when one speaks of the growth of faith (2 Cor 10:15; 2 Thess 1:3), of strengthening in faith (Acts 16:5), excelling (→ περισσεύω) in faith (2 Cor 8:7), or of works of faith (1 Thess 1:3; 2 Thess 1:11; cf. also 2 Pet 1:5 and Rev 2:19), and when persons are described as πλήρης πίστεως καὶ πνεύματος (Acts 6:5; 11:24). This group should probably also include Rom 1:12; 14:22; Eph 4:13; Rom 12:3 (→ μέτρον πίστεως); it is debatable whether Phlm 6 (→ κοινωνία τῆς πίστεως) belongs here. This group certainly includes, however, instances in which *faith* and love are associated (Eph 3:17; 6:23; Col 1:4; 2 Thess 1:3; 1 Tim 1:14; 2:15; 4:12) and the trio of *faith,* love, and hope (1 Cor 13:13; 1 Thess 1:3; 5:8; on this trio cf. H. Conzelmann, *1Cor* [Hermeneia] on 13:13). Luke 18:8 should probably also be understood in this sense: "When the Son of man comes, will he find [living] *faith* on earth?"

e) In some cases πίστις already refers to the *fides quae creditur,* the content of faith itself, the Christian religion (in Plutarch *Pyth.* 18; *Amatorius* 13 πίστις already designates the religion handed down by the fathers: ἡ πάτριος καὶ παλαιὰ πίστις). We find the beginnings of this already in Paul (Gal 1:23): "He is now preaching the *faith* [= the religion] he once persecuted." Πίστις should probably also be understood as *fides quae creditur* in the expression κατὰ τὴν ἀναλογίαν τῆς πίστεως (Rom 12:6). Further Acts 6:7: become obedient to the *message of faith,* or obediently accept the *faith;* Eph 4:5: "one *faith,* one baptism . . ."; further 1 Tim 1:19; 2:7; 3:9; 4:1, 6; 6:21; Titus 1:1; 2 Pet 1:1; Jude 3:20.

4. The central significance of πιστεύειν and πίστις in the post-Easter Church prompts the question to what extent one can discern evidence of a "basis" in Jesus' own proclamation. To be sure, Jesus did not demand that one believe in his person (πιστεύειν εἰς ἐμέ in Matt 18:6

and Mark 9:42 v.l. is redactional). He apparently did, however, call for and encourage a faith that in its radical nature went far beyond what contemporary theology was able to say concerning faith. The assertion that all things are possible to one who believes (Mark 9:23) and the variously transmitted saying about "faith as a grain of mustard seed" or "able to move mountains" allow the believer to participate in God's omnipotence (Matt 17:20 par. Luke 17:6; Matt 21:21 par. Mark 11:23; cf. 1 Cor 13:2; on the history of tradition cf. G. Barth, *ZTK* 72 [1975] 271-82; Zmijewski 81-101; the central elements of Matt 17:20 possibly contain the oldest version). The contrast between faith as small as a mustard seed and results possible only as a result of God's own creative power makes it clear that such faith is not a human accomplishment, but is rather trust in God's limitless goodness. This faith is, therefore, explicitly defined in Mark 11:24 par. Matt 21:22 as the faith of prayer, and the answer Mark attributes to the petitioning father ("I *believe,* help my unbelief," 9:24) shows that he has correctly understood this: A person does not "possess" such faith; it is a constant movement from unbelief to belief and thus the only appropriate attitude toward the offer of God's goodness.

5. Jesus speaks of faith in a series of miracle stories (Mark 2:5 par. Matt 9:2/Luke 5:20; Mark 5:36 par. Luke 8:50; Matt 8:10 par. Luke 7:9; Matt 9:29; 15:28); the expression ἡ πίστις σου σέσωκέν σε occurs in Mark 5:34 par. Matt 9:22/Luke 8:48; Mark 10:52 par. Luke 18:42; Luke 17:19 (cf. also 7:50); cf. further Mark 4:40 par. Luke 8:25. Since the form and language of the miracle stories are shaped by the narrating community, one cannot straightforwardly verify such statements as words of the earthly Jesus.

But they exhibit such an exceptional understanding of the relationship between faith and miracle that they are hardly comprehensible apart from some influence from Jesus' proclamation: Whereas a miracle usually precedes faith— with faith understood as the result of that miracle —both in the surrounding culture (Lucian *Philops.* ix.13; cf. Exod 4:8f.; 14:31; Ps 78:22; further documentation in O. Weinreich, *Antike Heilungswunder* [1909] 87, 119) and in a broad stream of the Christian miracle tradition itself (John 2:11, 23; 4:53; 11:15, 42, 45; 20:31; Acts 5:12ff.; 9:42; 13:12; 19:17f.; *Acts Pet.* 2:4, 12f., 23, 28, 32; *Acts John* 22:30, 42, 56f.; *Acts Thom.* 6ff., 53), the Synoptic tradition exhibits exactly the opposite relationship: Supplicating faith precedes miraculous healing and receives the miracle itself. For this reason the demand for signs (Matt 12:38ff. par.; Mark 8:11f. par.) and demonstration miracles (Matt 4:5ff. par.; Mark 15:32 par.) is strictly rejected, and Jesus performs no miracles where he comes up against unbelief (Matt 13:58 par.). This understanding of faith and miracles, which is thus at odds with the thinking of its own environment and with the broad stream of later Christian miracle tradition, can best be explained by assuming a basis in Jesus' own activity.

A relatively narrow stream of early Christian tradition carried this understanding of faith further; Matthew esp. emphasized it with the expressions ὡς ἐπίστευσας γενηθήτω σοι (8:13) and κατὰ τὴν πίστιν ὑμῶν γενηθήτω ὑμῖν (9:29; cf. also 15:28; Acts 3:16; 14:9). In contrast, the wider stream of early Christian miracle tradition viewed the miracle as a propaganda device that should elicit or strengthen faith. Itinerant charismatics and miracle workers (cf. Mark 6:7; 1 Cor 12:9) were probably the main bearers of this understanding.

6. Πιστεύειν and πίστις are right in the center of Paul's theological thinking, where he takes over the general Christian meaning of the acceptance of the proclamation of God's salvation activity in Christ (Rom 10:9, 14; 13:11; 1 Cor 1:21; 2:5; 15:2, 11; Gal 2:16, and elsewhere). Thus faith always comes from the word itself (Rom 10:14) and is πίστις ἐξ ἀκοῆς (v. 17), so that Paul can speak of the ῥῆμα τῆς πίστεως (v. 8) or the ἀκοὴ πίστεως (Gal 3:2, 5).

Though faith does, indeed, find its basis in proclamation of God's salvation activity, Paul thinks through the consequences of this event in a much more radical fashion: If God has acted for salvation once and for all in Christ's cross, then the human response can only consist in obedient acceptance, in trust in God's χάρις, and in receiving this gift with and in a life lived from within the gift itself. Thus πίστις belongs together with χάρις (Rom 4:4f., 16) and for the same reason is antithetical to ἔργα νόμου (Rom 3:28; 9:32; Gal 2:16) and to the νόμος understood as the principle of performance (Rom 3:21f.; Gal 3:12; Phil 3:9).

The salvation gift of δικαιοσύνη can only be received ἐκ πίστεως (Rom 1:17; 5:1; 9:30; 10:6; 14:23; Gal 3:7ff., 22, 24; 5:5) or διὰ πίστεως (Rom 3:25, 31; Gal 2:16; 3:14, 26; Phil 3:9; ἐκ πίστεως and διὰ πίστεως are equivalents in Rom 3:30; Rom 5:2 uses dat. τῇ πίστει). Therefore Paul can speak of the δικαιοσύνη πίστεως (Rom 4:13), which as δικαιοσύνη θεοῦ (10:3) or ἐκ θεοῦ δικαιοσύνη (Phil 3:9) is the complete antithesis of δικαιοσύνη ἐκ νόμου (3:9) or ἰδία δικαιοσύνη (Rom 10:3).

Just as righteousness can only be received ἐκ πίστεως, so also its revelation in the gospel aims εἰς πίστιν (Rom 1:17); i.e., this redemptive path of faith disclosed by Christ is the actual and original will of God (Gal 3:15ff.). Paul sees it proclaimed in the OT (in the context of Rom 1:17 and Gal 3:11, Hab 2:4 should probably be translated: "He who through faith is righteous shall live") and prefigured in Abraham's faith (Gen 15:6): The promise and sonship of Abraham are made available to believers (Ro-

mans 4; Gal 3:6ff.). Paul does not understand Abraham's faith, as in Judaism, as a virtue (Philo Her. 90ff.; cf. 1 Macc 2:52), and certainly not as a meritorious work (Mek. Exod. 14:15), but rather as an act of holding fast to God's promise without consideration for oneself, one's possibilities, or one's accomplishments. Just as Abraham held fast, even when no hope was left, to the promise of the God "who gives life to the dead and calls into existence what does not exist" (Rom 4:17ff.), so also is Christian faith the act of holding to the word of him who raised Christ from the dead and who justifies the ungodly in Christ (vv. 5, 24).

Since faith lives from the word, it stands in opposition to seeing (2 Cor 5:7), to dependence on what is visible (4:18), and to the immediacy of things that can be proven. Therefore it never reaches the goal of salvation perfection, but is rather always in a process of becoming (Phil 3:9ff.).

It has been thought that Gal 3:23, 25 regards πίστις as "the actuality of a divine event, a transsubjective quantity" (Binder 53) or "a comprehensive supra-individual phenomenon" (P. Stuhlmacher, Gerechtigkeit Gottes bei Paulus [1965] 81). But this is contradicted by the frequent occurrence of πίστις ὑμῶν (Rom 1:8; 1 Cor 2:5; 2 Cor 1:24; Phil 2:17; 1 Thess 1:8; 3:2, 5ff., 10; cf. Phlm 5), by the interchangeable use of the noun and vb. (→ 1), and above all by the fundamental binding of faith to the hearing of the word. Rather, Gal 3:23, 25 personifies faith in much the same way that Rom 10:6ff. personifies righteousness. The coming of πίστις in Gal 3:23, 25 refers in substance to the redemptive path of faith that has come with Christ.

As the appropriate human reponse to the salvation proclamation, faith shapes the Christian's existence (Rom 14:22f.; 1 Cor 13:13; 2 Cor 4:13; Gal 2:10; 5:5f.) and is the basis of the Christian's new life. Faith thus manifests itself in love (Gal 5:6) and results in a certain demeanor (Rom 14:23; 2 Cor 4:13). As life lived from the gift of grace, the attitude of the believer stands in opposition to any trust or boasting in one's own accomplishments (Rom 3:27; 4:2). Thus Paul can speak of a νόμος πίστεως in contrast to the νόμος τῶν ἔργων (3:27). Since, however, faith as the seizing of χάρις is never a fixed, accessible possession, one can also speak of being weak in faith (14:1) and of growing in faith (Phil 1:25; 2 Cor 10:15; cf. 1 Thess 3:10). Because it holds fast to the word against all appearances, it is, like Abraham's faith (Rom 4:19f.), repeatedly under attack, which is why Paul can exhort his readers to stand fast in faith (11:20; 1 Cor 16:13; 2 Cor 1:24; cf. Gal 5:1), though also to examine oneself to determine whether one is, indeed, in faith (2 Cor 13:5).

7. In Johannine theology πιστεύω (98 occurrences in the Gospel, 9 in 1 John; πίστις only in 1 John 5:4) oc-

cupies a position of central importance. Nonetheless, John's statements are characterized by a certain tension. He has apparently taken up a tradition for which πιστεύειν is bound to Jesus' miracles: Jesus' σημεῖα lead to faith or at least should lead to faith (John 2:11, 23; 4:53; 7:31; 11:15, 42, 45; 12:37; 20:31; according to 10:25, 37f.; 14:11 Jesus' ἔργα should do this). John both subjects this understanding of faith to severe criticism and tries to interpret it positively:

On the one hand, the demand for miracles to ground faith is exposed as the attitude of the unbelieving world (John 2:18; 4:48; 6:26f., 30); Jesus says to the doubting Thomas: "*Have* you *believed* because you have seen me? Blessed are those who have not seen and yet *believe*" (20:29). John repeatedly emphasizes that faith is bound to Jesus' word or to witness concerning Jesus (1:7; 4:39, 41f., 50; 5:24, 47; 8:30f.; 17:20; cf. 10:3, 16, 27; 18:37).

On the other hand, there is a faithful seeing, or a seeing in faith, for which Jesus' miracles become signs for the gift Jesus is actually bringing. Thus John 6:40 brings seeing and believing together, 12:44f. uses them as complete parallels, and 1:14, 50f.; 14:19; 16:16 speak simply of seeing, clearly referring to a process of faith. This indicates that the structure of faith includes an element of recognition and knowledge, which is why πιστεύω and γινώσκω (6:69; 8:31f.; 10:38; 17:8; 1 John 4:16; cf. οἴδαμεν in John 16:30) are also associated; and when the sequence is reversed, it becomes clear that knowledge is not a more advanced stage than faith, but is rather itself a structural element of faith.

Such faith is oriented toward the assertions that Jesus is sent by the Father (5:24, 38; 6:29; 12:44; 17:8, 21), went out from the Father (16:27, 30; 17:8), is in the Father and the Father in him (14:10f.; 17:21), is the Christ, the Son of God (3:18; 11:27; 1 John 3:24; 5:1, 5), and is he who came into the world (John 11:27; 12:46). It is thus oriented less toward the soteriological significance of Jesus' death and resurrection than to the fact that God has revealed himself in Jesus, which means that he has revealed himself as the power of love (3:16; 1 John 4:8, 10, 16). This is why the content of faith can be given simply as ὅτι ἐγώ εἰμι (John 8:24; 13:19) and that believing in Jesus can be equated with believing in God (12:44; 14:1). The statement that God has revealed himself ἐν σαρκί (1 John 4:2), in a man whose origin one knows, is the offense that Jesus' claim constitutes for the world (John 6:42, 60; 7:27, 41f.), an offense that faith overcomes.

A series of partly metaphorical circumlocutions shows how the believer is bound to Jesus: Πιστεύω can be replaced by: coming to Jesus (John 5:40; 6:35, 37, 44f., 65; 7:37), receiving him (1:12; 5:43), drinking of the water he offers (4:13f.; cf. 6:35; 7:37), following him (8:12), and loving him (14:15, 21, 23f.; 16:27). What John 11:25

says of the πιστεύων εἰς ἐμέ also applies in 8:51f. to the person who "keeps" his word (cf. 14:23; 17:6; 1 John 2:5). Since God's eschatological revelation has come in Jesus, the believer already participates in eschatological salvation (John 3:18, 36; 5:24; 6:40, 47; 11:25f.; 17:3). Yet it is necessary to "abide" in Jesus (15:4, 7; 1 John 2:6, 28; 3:6), which means nothing other than to abide in his word (John 8:31) and thus in his love (15:9) and to keep his commandments (15:10; 14:15, 21; 1 John 2:3f.; 3:24). Since the knowledge bequeathed to faith is knowledge of God's love, faith must necessarily lead to love (John 17:26; 1 John 3:23; 4:16), a love directed above all toward one's brother.

8. Of the 34 occurrences of πιστεύω and πίστις in Hebrews, two-thirds are in ch. 11. Various tensions within the text itself suggest that the author has probably picked up and reworked a (Jewish?) source. The other occurrences should, therefore, provide the point of departure.

It is striking that πίστις always occurs in parenetic contexts, and never in the christological sections. This accords with the fact that though πίστις ἐπὶ θεόν, *faith* in God, is mentioned once among basic Christian doctrines (6:1), Christ never appears as the object of faith. Christ is rather the author and perfecter of faith (12:2), and one might best call faith a persevering in the way opened by Christ. Thus 6:12 associates πίστις with μακροθυμία and contrasts it with becoming fatigued. While 10:38f. contrasts it with "shrinking back" (ὑποστολή) and 4:2f. with "falling behind" (ὑστερέω, 4:1), 12:1f. parallels it with δι' ὑπομονῆς τρέχειν and 10:22f. with holding fast to one's confession. Thus also 13:7 exhorts believers to imitate the faith of the Church's leaders in view of their fate.

Although 11:1 appears to offer a definition of faith, the tr. here is disputed: ἔστιν δὲ πίστις ἐλπιζομένων ὑπόστασις, πραγμάτων ἔλεγχος οὐ βλεπομένων. Luther's tr. of → ὑπόστασις, "gewisse Zuversicht," i.e., "certain confidence," is not possible. The etymologically derived interpretation of ὑπόστασις preferred by many, "standing under" = standing firm, founders on the second clause, where faith is characterized as ἔλεγχος (proof, conviction —not pass. being convicted!). Therefore in the parallel first clause ὑπόστασις should be translated, in accord with use of the word as it developed in the philosophical tradition, as "realization" (cf. Dörrie; Lührmann 72ff.; H. Köster, *TDNT* VIII, 572-89), yielding the paradoxical assertion: "*Faith* is the realization of one's hopes and the proof of things that one cannot see."

Therefore, Heb 11:1 does not define faith, but makes an assertion about the object of faith: The invisible gifts of promise constitute a secure reality for faith. This establishes the basis of that faithful perseverance solicited in the admonition, which the following list of witnesses of faith illustrates. For those witnesses the blessings of the promise were a dependable reality to which they held fast. That the author has reworked a source handed down to him can be seen among other ways in the fact that in this list πίστις does not always exhibit this meaning, but rather often means simply *trust* in God's promise (vv. 7, 11, 20, 21, 22, 23, 24, 27, 29), obedient *acceptance* of God's word (vv. 8; 17:28), *belief* in God's existence (vv. 3, 6)—or simply remains indeterminate.

9. The letter of James does not exhibit a unified concept of faith. 2:1 mentions Jesus Christ, the Lord of glory, as the object of faith (obj. gen.). Πίστις in 1:6 and 5:15 refers to the prayer of faith, to trust without doubt. When 1:3 mentions trials as the means of testing faith, this presupposes that πίστις involves consequences for one's life and prompts a certain attitude; similarly 2:5, which characterizes the poor as being rich ἐν πίστει.

The understanding of faith in 2:14-26 is different. There the author polemicizes against the thesis that a person is justified ἐκ πίστεως μόνον (v. 24). He counters this by emphasizing that works must be added to faith (vv. 17, 20, 26) and that faith is completed only by works (v. 22). Since the juxtapostion of faith and works (πίστις χωρὶς ἔργων, vv. 18, 20, 26) is found only in Paul and his school (Eph 2:9; 2 Tim 1:9; Titus 3:5), this polemic in James must have been directed against misunderstood Pauline doctrine. It does not really involve Paul himself, since for Paul faith is life from God's grace in Christ, not from one's own accomplishments, and does, indeed, involve consequences for the way one conducts one's life. In contrast, the πίστις James addresses is, according to 2:19, faith in the existence of the one God, faith that one finds even among demons. It is thus simply considering something to be true, with no consequences for one's life. In view of this kind of dead (vv. 17, 26) and useless (v. 20) faith, vv. 14-26 emphasizes the necessity of works.

10. Although the Pastorals clearly want to remain in the Pauline tradition, they do exhibit over against Paul a noteworthy shift and late further development. Here, too, Christ is the primary object of faith (1 Tim 3:16 pass.), though instead of πιστεύω εἰς Χριστόν the Pastorals use πιστεύω ἐπί . . . (1:16), πίστις ἐν Χριστῷ (3:13; 2 Tim 3:15; cf. 1 Tim 1:14). This faith issues from the proclamation of the gospel, of sound doctrine (1 Tim 1:5, 10; 2 Tim 2:2, 15ff.; 4:3); it is not merely acceptance of the salvation proclamation, but also trust directing itself toward God (2 Tim 1:12; Titus 3:8). It leads to σωτηρία (2 Tim 3:15) and to eternal life (1 Tim 1:16).

In the anti-Gnostic agenda πίστις becomes not only *fides quae creditur,* but also correct faith as opposed to false doctrine (1 Tim 1:19; 4:1, 6; 6:21; 2 Tim 2:18; 3:8; Titus 1:13f.; cf. vv. 1, 4). Characteristic expressions in-

clude ὑγιαίνειν τῇ πίστει (Titus 1:13; 2:2), πίστις καὶ ἀλήθεια (1 Tim 2:7), λόγοι τῆς πίστεως καὶ τῆς καλῆς διδασκαλίας (4:6), and μυστήριον τῆς πίστεως (3:9). One can be shipwrecked in faith (1:19), fall away or wander from faith (1:4; 6:10, 21), and destroy it (2 Tim 2:18).

Despite this orientation toward correct doctrine, faith is in the Pastorals an attitude characterizing one's entire existence, the genuinely Christian demeanor that one should preserve amid struggle (1 Tim 6:12). Πίστις is therefore often mentioned in a series including other virtues (1:5, 14, 19; 2:15; 4:12; 6:11; 2 Tim 1:13; 2:22; 3:10f.; Titus 2:2), and one reads of "sincere *faith*" (1 Tim 1:5; 2 Tim 1:5) and of faith with a "clear conscience" (1 Tim 3:9). Inadequate care for relatives constitutes a "denial" of faith (5:8). The increasingly established ecclesiastical nature of this view also manifests itself in the assertions that such faith already dwelled in the addressee's mother and grandmother (2 Tim 1:5) and that it is nourished by the sacred writings (3:15) and in the fact that ἐν πίστει is occasionally used formulaically (1 Tim 1:2, 4; Titus 3:15).

G. Barth

πιστός, 3 *pistos*   faithful; believing*

1. Occurrences in the NT — 2. Faithful, dependable, credible — 3. Believing, full of faith*

Lit.: → ἀπιστέω; πίστις; also: J. M. Bover, "Fidelis sermo," *Bib* 19 (1938) 74-79. — G. W. Knight, *The Faithful Sayings in the Pastoral Letters* (1968).

1. Πίστις occurs 67 times in the NT, though in only 16 of these instances with the meaning *faithful* in the sense of *believing*. The majority of occurrences thus follow the meaning predominant in non-Christian usage: *faithful* in the sense of *dependable*. It is striking that John uses it only with the meaning *believing*.

2. *Faithful, dependable, credible* (= prompting faith or trust):

a) Of persons (cf. Homer *Il.* 15.331; Xenophon *An.* i.5.15; 1 Kgdms 22:14; Sir 44:20; Josephus *Ant.* vi.256, and elsewhere): Matt 24:45 par.: ὁ πιστὸς δοῦλος; Luke 12:42: πιστὸς οἰκονόμος, "*faithful/dependable* servant or steward"; Matt 25:21, 23: δοῦλε ἀγαθὲ καὶ πιστέ. That toward which one is thus said to be dependable or faithful is introduced with ἐπί (Matt 25:21, 23) or ἐν (Luke): Luke 19:17; 16:10: ἐν ἐλαχίστῳ πιστός, "*dependable* in small matters"; 16:11: ἐν τῷ ἀδίκῳ μαμωνᾷ, "in matters of unrighteous mammon"; v. 12: ἐν τῷ ἀλλοτρίῳ, "with someone else's matters/in dealing with someone else's concerns." 1 Cor 4:2, in a general sense: "It is required of stewards that they be found *trustworthy*." Paul is referring here to the office of preacher. In the same way, reference is also made to faithfulness and dependability in the apostle or preacher (1 Tim 1:12; 2 Tim 2:2), in wives of preachers (1 Tim 3:11), in Moses (Heb 3:5, citing Num 12:7; cf. Philo *All.* ii.67).

Πιστός is used of various fellow workers as an honorific title (Timothy in 1 Cor 4:17; Onesimus in Col 4:9; Silvanus in 1 Pet 5:12; Epaphras and Tychicus, πιστὸς διάκονος in Col 1:7; 4:7; Eph 6:21). When "Paul explains in 1 Cor 7:25 that the Lord graciously granted him the privilege of being πιστός, and uses this as a basis for his claim to be heard with respect" (BAGD 664), πιστός here not only means *trustworthy/dependable,* but is also being used almost as a title: "trusted man/commissioner" *(ibid.).* Πιστός often occurs in this sense in inscriptions (documentation *ibid.;* also E. Peterson, *ΕΙΣ ΘΕΟΣ* [1926] 32f.), just as πίστις also occurs with the meaning "position of trust" or "office of trust" (cf. E. Seidl, *Πίστις in der griechischen Literatur* [Diss. Innsbruck; 1952] 200).

In Revelation πιστός occurs in connection with martyrdom: 2:10 admonishes: "Be *faithful* unto death," and 2:13 characterizes Antipas as ὁ → μάρτυς μου ὁ πιστός, just as Christ is called ὁ μάρτυς ὁ πιστός (1:5) and πιστὸς καὶ ἀληθινός (3:14; cf. 19:11; Prov 14:5: μάρτυς πιστός, *"faithful* witness"; cf. Jer 49:5; Philo *Sacr.* 17). Hence πιστοί in Rev 17:14 probably means the *faithful.* In addition to Rev 1:5 and 3:14, Christ's faithfulness is also mentioned in 2 Thess 3:3; 2 Tim 2:13 (→ ἀπιστέω 2.a); Heb 2:17: *"faithful* high priest"; 3:2: πιστὸν ὄντα τῷ ποιήσαντι αὐτόν, "he is *faithful* to him who made [or appointed] him."

In accord with OT and Jewish understanding (Deut 7:9; 32:4; Isa 49:7; Ps 144:13a LXX; cf. Philo *Her.* 93; *Sacr.* 93; *All.* iii.204), emphatic mention is made of God's faithfulness. So Heb 10:23: "He who promised is *faithful"* (similarly 11:11). 1 Pet 4:19 admonishes the readers to entrust themselves to the πιστῷ κτίστῃ, "to the *faithful* Creator," and according to 1 John 1:9 God is *"faithful* and just" when in view of our confession of sin he forgives those sins. Formulaic features are already discernible in the expression πιστὸς ὁ θεός (1 Cor 1:9: "God is *faithful,* by whom . . ."; 10:13: "God is *faithful,* who . . ."); 1 Thess 5:24: "he who calls you is *faithful* and will do it" (cf. the similar expression in 2 Thess 3:3, applied to Christ). In contrast, πιστὸς δὲ ὁ θεός (2 Cor 1:18), because of the following ὅτι clause, is probably to be understood as an oath formula: "As surely as God is *faithful,* our word to you has not been yes and no at the same time."

b) Of things, esp. words (Josephus *Ant.* xix.132; Plato *Ti.* 49b; Plutarch *Sept. Sap.* 17; Dio Chrysostom 45.3): *trustworthy/credible.* So Rev 21:5, 6: "These words are *trustworthy* and true"; Titus 1:9: the *trustworthy* word corresponding to doctrine. Esp. important here is the formula πιστὸς ὁ λόγος (1 Tim 3:1; 2 Tim 2:11; Titus 3:8), sometimes expanded by καὶ πάσης ἀποδοχῆς ἄξιος:

"The saying is *credible* and worthy of all acceptance" (1 Tim 1:15; 4:9). Since only in 1 Tim 1:15 does this expression refer to what follows, otherwise referring to preceding material, one should probably view it less as a citation formula than as a formula of asseveration (on this matter cf. Bover; Knight; G. Kittel, *TDNT* IV, 118 n.199; M. Dibelius and H. Conzelmann, *The Pastoral Epistles* [Hermeneia] 28f. [excursus on 1 Tim 1:15]). 3 John 5: πιστὸν ποιεῖς ὃ ἐὰν ἐργάσῃ, "what you do, do *dependably"* (= "as something that is dependable"; predicate position). On Acts 13:34 (δώσω ὑμῖν τὰ ὅσια Δαυὶδ τὰ πιστά, citing Isa 55:3 LXX), cf. → ὅσιος 2.

3. *Faithful* in the sense of *believing* (cf. Wis 3:9; Sir 1:14): Thus does Gal 3:9 speak of Abraham, *who had faith* (cf. 2 Macc 1:2; Philo *Post.* 173); in John 20:27 the resurrected Jesus admonishes: "Do not be unfaithful, but *believing";* Acts 16:15: πιστὴν τῷ κυρίῳ εἶναι, "to believe in the Lord"; 1 Tim 4:3: τοῖς πιστοῖς καὶ ἐπεγνωκόσι . . . , "for those *who believe* and have recognized the truth"; similarly 1 Pet 1:21: τοὺς . . . πιστοὺς εἰς θεόν, "who . . . *believe* in God."

Certain persons are described as *believing* in reference to their conversion to Christianity: Thus Acts 16:1 describes Timothy as the son of a Jewish woman *who had become a believer* (γυναικὸς Ἰουδαίας πιστῆς); Col 1:2 speaks of *faithful* brethren, 1 Tim 6:2 of *believing* masters, and Titus 1:6 of *believing* children. Finally, used absolutely πιστοί simply means *believers* = Christians (so 2 Cor 6:15; Eph 1:1; 1 Tim 4:10, 12; 5:16). In Acts 10:45 οἱ ἐκ περιτομῆς πιστοί are "the *Christians* from among the circumcised" (= Jewish Christians).

G. Barth

πιστόω *pistoō* come to trust, be persuaded*

2 Tim 3:14: "But as for you, continue in what you have learned and *acquired in faith* (ἐπιστώθης)." A. Weiser, *TDNT* VI, 178f.; R. Bultmann, *TDNT* VI, 204.

πλανάω *planaō* mislead, deceive*
ἀποπλανάω *apoplanaō* mislead, deceive*

1. Occurrences in the NT — 2. The OT and Jewish background — 3. Πλανάω in the Pauline corpus and in Hebrews — 4. Πλανάω in the Synoptics — 5. Πλανάω in the Johannine writings (including Revelation) — 6. Πλανάω in the Catholic Epistles (except 1/3 John) — 7. Ἀποπλανάω — 8. Πλάνη — 9. Πλάνος — 10. Summary

Lit.: W. Bauer, *Orthodoxy and Heresy in Earliest Christianity* (1971). — O. Böcher, *Der johanneische Dualismus im Zusammenhang des nach-biblischen Judentums* (1965) 77-96, and *passim.* — H. Braun, *TDNT* VI, 228-53. — W. Günther, *DNTT* II, 457-61. — K. Koch, *TDOT* IV, 309-19. — O. Michel, *BHH* 2080f. — M. Sæbø, *THAT* II, 495-98. — For further bibliography see *TWNT* X, 1236.

1. Πλανάω occurs 39 times in the NT, the synonymous compound ἀποπλανάω twice. The occurrences of πλανάω are distributed relatively equally among the various groups of NT writings: 8 occurrences in Matthew, 4 in Mark, 1 in Luke, 2 in John, 2 in 1 Corinthians, 1 in Galatians, 2 in 2 Timothy, 1 in Titus, 3 in Hebrews, 2 in James, 1 in 1 Peter, 1 in 2 Peter, 3 in 1 John, 8 in Revelation; Mark and 1 Timothy use ἀποπλανάω once each. 2 of the occurrences of πλανάω are in quotations from the LXX (Heb 3:10 [Ps 94:10]; 1 Pet 2:25 [Isa 53:6]). The frequent occurrence of πλανάω in Matthew and Revelation (8 occurrences each) is noteworthy.

2. The LXX translates various Hebrew vbs. with πλανάω or πλανάομαι *(hātā', pātâ, tā'â)*. In addition to the literal, geographical meaning "mislead" (e.g., Deut 27:18), "cause to stagger" (e.g., Isa 19:13f.; 28:7, and elsewhere), mid. and pass. "wander about" (e.g., Deut 22:1; Isa 13:14; 53:6, and elsewhere, of sheep), "stagger" (e.g., Job 12:25; Isa 19:4; 28:7, and elsewhere, of the inebriated), the LXX also uses πλανάω fig. of religious "misleading" and "deceiving": Yahweh himself misleads the people (Isa 63:17), Gentiles (Job 12:23), rulers (v. 24), or lying prophets (Ezek 14:9). Above all, however, pagan gods (Hos 8:6; Amos 2:4) and their idols (Wis 14:12, 27; 15:4-6), false prophets (Deut 13:6; Jer 23:13, 32; cf. Isa 31:20f.; 41:29), and unfaithful kings (2 Kgs 21:9 par. 2 Chr 33:9) seduce Israel into worship of idols. Mid. and pass. πλανάομαι is used of Israel's "going astray" or "having gone astray," its giving in seduction to disobedience, sacrilege, and idolatry (Deut 4:19; 11:28; 30:17; Prov 21:16; Ezek 14:11; 44:10-15; Wis 5:6, and elsewhere); this is frequently set against the background metaphor of sheep gone astray (Ps 118:176 LXX; Isa 53:6; Ezek 34:4, 16).

The writings of postbiblical Judaism attribute such seduction into sin and esp. into idolatry to demonic powers. Older monistic conceptions that could see God and his emissaries as the deceivers (cf. 2 Sam 24:1 with 1 Chr 21:1; further 1 Kgs 22:22f.; → δαιμόνιον) are overcome by the dualism found generally in antiquity. Demons, i.e., the fallen celestial angels of Gen 6:1-4 or their descendants (cf. *1 Enoch* 6–11; 15:3-12; *Jub.* 5:1-10; 10:5-11; *T. Reu.* 5:1-7, and elsewhere), are viewed as those who seduce into sin (*1 Enoch* 10:7-16; 64:2, 6-11), esp. into idolatry (19:1; cf. 8:1-3). For the pious in Qumran sin is based on the rule of Belial (1QS 1:22-24); through the angel of darkness "error" (Heb. *tā'ût*) comes also over the sons of righteousness, leading to sin (3:21-23).

In the *T. 12 Patr.* the πνεῦμα τῆς πλάνης (*T. Sim.* 3:1; *T. Jud.* 14:8; 20:1, and elsewhere) and the πνεῦμα τῆς ἀληθείας (*T. Jud.* 20:5) stand opposite one another (20:1). The spirit or spirits of deception (πνεύματα τῆς πλάνης, *T. Reu.* 2:1f.; 3:2, 7; *T. Sim.* 6:6, and elsewhere) are the instruments of Beliar (→ Βελιάρ) and of Satan, by whom Satan, as the prince of deception (*T. Sim.* 2:7; *T. Jud.* 19:4), tries to bring people away from the right path. The object of this seduction (πλανᾶν) is always the Israelites, i.e., the patriarchs (who are addressed) and their descendants (*T. Reu.* 4:6; 5:3; *T. Lev.* 10:2; *T. Jud.* 14:5; *T. Iss.* 1:13, and elsewhere); only *T. Naph.* 3:3 speaks of the Gentiles having been seduced into idolatry. Usually readers are warned against idolatry (*T. Reu.* 4:6; *T. Levi* 16:1; *T. Zeb.* 9:7, and elsewhere) and profligate behavior (*T. Reu.* 4:6; 5:3; *T. Jud.* 14:1, 8; 17:1, and elsewhere). Mid. and pass. πλανάομαι is used of living in this

deception (*T. Levi* 16:1; *T. Zeb.* 9:7 v.l.; *T. Naph.* 3:3). According to *T. Levi* 10:2; 16:1 πλανᾶν and πλανᾶσθαι will characterize the end time.

3. The three occurrences in the genuine Pauline letters (1 Cor 6:9; 15:33; Gal 6:7) all admonish: μὴ πλανᾶσθε, "Do not err" (cf. Luke 21:8; Jas 1:16). In 1 Cor 6:9 this introduces a catalog of vices, in 15:33 a citation from Menander, and in Gal 6:7 what is perhaps a proverbial warning: The formal connection with OT-Jewish tradition (despite Isa 41:10; 44:8 v.l.; *T. Gad* 3:1) is of less significance than that with Stoic diatribe (Braun 243f.). This forbidden self-deception consists in failure to recognize God's "penal severity" (Braun 244; Gal 6:7), which manifests itself in bad company (1 Cor 15:33) and immoral behavior (6:9f.).

A life in the service of vice, typical of the existence of Gentiles, can be compared to the disoriented lives of those who have gone astray (πλανώμενοι, Titus 3:3). The evil men and imposters whom 2 Tim 3:13 characterizes as *deceived deceivers* (πλανῶντες καὶ πλανώμενοι), are according to 1 Tim 4:1 the false teachers of the end time; in what was originally a pagan proverb πλανάω has acquired eschatological implications (cf. *T. Levi* 10:2; 16:1).

Of the 3 occurrences of πλανάω in Hebrews, 11:38 uses πλανάω in the original geographical sense of *wander about* (cf. LXX). 3:10 cites Ps 94:10 LXX in view of Israel's disobedience; 5:2 extols the high priest's ability to bring understanding to the ignorant and *wayward* (πλανώμενοι), i.e., to atone for sins of weakness and ignorance. Since according to 4:14f. Jesus Christ is the Christians' high priest, the πλανώμενοι of 5:2 also include those Christians whose sins can be atoned.

4. For the Synoptics πλανάω has above all the sense of eschatological deception. In Mark 13:5 par. Matt 24:4 /Luke 21:8 Jesus warns his listeners against the deception which according to Mark 13:6 par. Matt 24:5 will come from messianic false teachers; according to Matt 24:11 many ψευδοπροφῆται will *lead* many *astray*. According to Matt 24:24 it is the ψευδόχριστοι καὶ ψευδοπροφῆται whose deception will even threaten the elect (par. Mark 13:22: ἀποπλανάω, → 7).

Jesus answers the Sadducees' question by accusing his adversaries of error (πλανᾶσθε, Mark 12:24 par. Matt 22:29; Mark 12:27) on the basis of their inadequate knowledge of Scripture and God's power. In the parable of the lost sheep (Matthew: sheep gone astray) Matthew has introduced πλανάω 3 times (Matt 18:12 bis, 13), where the Lukan parallel speaks of losing or getting lost (→ ἀπόλλυμι 2, Luke 15:4-6); the metaphor of the sheep gone astray, which comes from the LXX (→ 2), characterizes Israel's guilt of disobedience—here that of unfaithful Church members—and perhaps also belongs in the context of eschatological deception (cf. Matt 24:11, 24).

5. The Fourth Gospel exposes the blindness of the "Jews" (→ Ἰουδαῖος 5) who are hostile to Jesus, which consists in the fact that they describe Jesus as a deceiver of the people (John 7:12) and of the court officials (v. 47); this reflects both intramural Jewish polemic against heretics and the process of Christian separation from Judaism (cf. 8:37-59).

The dualism of "spirit of truth" and "spirit of error" seen in the *T. 12 Patr.* (*T. Jud.* 20:1; → 2) is also seen in 1 John (4:6; → 8); thus the occurrences of πλανάω in 1:8, 2:26, and 3:7 are also to be interpreted dualistically. The διάβολος (3:8) is at work in the christological false teachers (2:26; 3:7); they are identical with the πλάνοι, indeed with the πλάνος (→ 9) and the ἀντίχριστος himself (2 John 7). Whoever follows the false path of the heretics deceives himself and separates himself from the ἀλήθεια (1 John 1:8).

Revelation refers to the dragon/devil/Satan as a deceiver (12:9; 20:3, 8, 10). Again, the devil employs false teachers: Jezebel *seduces* the Christians in Thyatira to "idolatry" (2:20). The devil (12:9, 18) has invested the two anti-Christian beasts (ch. 13) with power. He stands behind the deceiving signs of the "second beast" and false prophet (13:14; 19:20), i.e., behind the successful propaganda for the imperial Roman cult. "Babylon" (= Rome) has seduced all the nations into idolatry (18:23). False teaching and apostasy brought about by the devil and his deceivers are, like the war incited by Satan (20:8; cf. 16:14 and *1 Enoch* 56:5f.), signs of the end time. They conclude with the destruction of the devil and of the diabolical powers (19:20; 20:10).

6. Jas 1:16, like Paul (→ 3), admonishes: *"Do not err."* The readers are warned against believing that something bad (such as temptation, v. 13) might come from God (v. 17). The occurrence in 5:19 belongs with 1 John 1:8; the path of πλάνη (Jas 5:20; → 8) is opposed to that of ἀλήθεια. Retrieving one who has gone astray brings about eschatological salvation both for the sinner and for his rescuer (5:20).

1 Peter, picking up on Isa 53:6, speaks of sheep *gone astray* (2:25; cf. Matt 18:12f.), using the metaphor of the time before the conversion of the Gentiles to Christ as their shepherd and guardian. 2 Pet 2:15 asserts that the false teachers have forsaken the right way, have gone astray, and have chosen Balaam as their model (on Balaam as a false teacher, cf. Jude 11; Rev 2:14; → Βαλαάμ).

7. Ἀποπλανάω occurs in the act. only in Mark 13:22 as a synonymous parallel to πλανάω in Matt 24:24 (→ 4). 1 Tim 6:10 uses pass. ἀπεπλανήθησαν: The greedy are threatened by deception leading them away from πίστις, the new norm (Braun 249f.).

8. **Πλάνη**, *error, deception**, occurs 10 times in the NT, 4 of those in the Pauline corpus and 5 in the Catholic Epistles. The dualistic background (→ 2) is clear at almost every point. The idolatry God punishes by giving a person up to vice (Rom 1:21-27) is πλάνη (v. 27). Just as truth and love belong together (Eph 4:15), so also do error and craftiness (v. 14). Behind Paul's proclamation (1 Thess 2:3) there stands no πλάνη, which as a power hostile to truth leads to false doctrine (2 Thess 2:10f.) and shows that the Church now lives in the end time.

The only Synoptic occurrence, Matt 27:64, belongs with John 7:12, 47 (→ 5): The Jews accuse Jesus and his disciples of deception (on πλάνος, e.g., in Matt 27:63, → 9). In a context of strict dualism 1 John 4:6 contrast the spirit of truth with the spirit of error, the correct confession with christological false doctrine. James describes sin as a wandering from the truth (Jas 5:19; → 6) and the way of error (v. 20); again, ἀλήθεια and πλάνη stand opposed. In the remaining 3 occurrences in the Catholic Epistles (2 Pet 2:18; 3:17; Jude 11), πλάνη refers to false doctrine; Jude 11 mentions Balaam as the author of πλάνη (cf. 2 Pet 2:15; Rev 2:14) and avarice as its basis (cf. 1 Tim 6:10; → 7).

9. **Πλάνος**, *leading astray,* subst. *deceiver**, appears in the NT 5 times. Paul, who according to human and esp. Jewish reckoning is a deceiver, is on the contrary truthful (2 Cor 6:8); the antithesis between πλάνη and ἀλήθεια (→ 8) corresponds to that between πλάνος and ἀληθής. Jewish polemic calls Jesus' messianic claim a πλάνη (Matt 27:64; → 8), and Jesus himself a πλάνος (v. 63). 1 Tim 4:1 and 2 John 7 (bis) speak of the demonic character of false doctrine.

10. NT use of this word group is related to OT and Jewish usage. Like Israel (LXX), Christians can also be compared to sheep gone astray (Matthew, 1 Peter). A person is deceived into sin, and esp. into idolatry and false doctrine. This is the work of the devil and his demons. Dualism inherited from Judaism (cf. *1 Enoch, Qumran, T. 12 Patr.*) sets πλάνη over against ἀλήθεια (Paul, James), the spirit of πλάνη over against the spirit of ἀλήθεια (1 John). The spirit of error brings self-deception, against which μὴ πλανᾶσθε warns Christians (Paul, James). Diabolical blinding can even expose Jesus (Matthew, John) and his apostles (2 Corinthians) to the charge of being deceivers. Idolatry and false teaching characterize the end time; they cease only when along with the devil himself his demonic accomplices are also destroyed (Revelation).

O. Böcher

πλάνη, ης, ἡ *planē* erring, error, deception → πλανάω 8.

πλάνης, ητος, ὁ *planēs* wanderer
Jude 13 v.l. in place of πλανήτης.

πλανήτης, ου, ὁ *planētēs* wanderer, roamer*

Πλανήτης is also used adj., as in the only NT occurrence, Jude 13: ἀστέρες πλανῆται, *"wandering stars"* (cf. v. 11: πλάνη). H. Braun, *TDNT* VI, 228f., 234f., 250.

πλάνος, 2 *planos* leading astray; subst.: deceiver → πλανάω 9.

πλάξ, πλακός, ἡ *plax* tablet*

Heb 9:4: πλάκες τῆς διαθήκης, of the *tablets* of the law; so also 2 Cor 3:3: ". . . written not on *tablets* of stone, but on *tablets* in hearts of flesh (ἐν πλαξὶν καρδίαις σαρκίναις)."

πλάσμα, ατος, τό *plasma* something formed, creation*

Rom 9:20: "Does perhaps *what is created* say to its creator. . . ?" (cf. Isa 29:16 LXX). H. Braun, *TDNT* VI, 254-62.

πλάσσω *plassō* form, construct, create*

Rom 9:20: "Will perhaps what is molded say to the *molder* (τῷ πλάσαντι): Why have you made (ἐποίησας) me thus?"; 1 Tim 2:13: "Adam was *formed/created* (ἐπλάσθη) first (πρῶτος), then Eve" (cf. Gen 2:7, 8, 15 LXX; on the priority of man see also 1 Cor 11:8). H. Braun, *TDNT* VI, 254-62, esp. 260f.

πλαστός, 3 *plastos* made up, false*

2 Pet 2:3: "In their greed they will exploit you with *fabricated* words (πλαστοῖς λόγοις)," referring to false teachers. H. Braun, *TDNT* VI, 262.

πλατεῖα, ας, ἡ *plateia* wide road, street*

Matt 6:5: ἐν ταῖς γωνίαις τῶν πλατειῶν, "at the *street* corners"; 12:19: "hear his voice in the *streets*." Luke 10:10 and 14:21 speak of the streets of a town, 13:26 of streets as the location of Jesus' teaching. Acts 5:15: The people carried the sick out into the streets so that Peter's shadow might fall upon them; Rev 11:8 and 21:21: "the *street(s)* of the city" (cf. 22:2: αὐτῆς). The street of the heavenly Jerusalem is made of pure gold (21:21); 22:2 also speaks of the one (main) street of the new Jerusalem.

πλάτος, ους, τό *platos* breadth*

Rev 21:16a, b: τὸ πλάτος with τὸ μῆκος (length) and τὸ ὕψος (height), in reference to the new Jerusalem; Eph 3:18 adds βάθος (depth) to these three dimensions; Rev 20:9, of Satan's final assault: "They marched up over the *broad surface* of the earth and surrounded the camp of the saints."

πλατύνω *platynō* make broad, expand*

Matt 23:5, of the scribes and Pharisees, who *make* their φυλακτήρια (phylacteries) *broad;* 2 Cor 6:11: "Our mouth has opened to you . . . our heart *has opened itself wide* (πεπλάτυνται)"; v. 13 petitions: "*Open* yourselves wide also (πλατύνθητε)."

πλατύς, 3 *platys* broad, wide*

Matt 7:13: "The gate (ἡ πύλη) is *wide* and the road is broad (εὐρύχωρος) that leads to destruction."

πλέγμα, ατος, τό *plegma* something woven or braided*

1 Tim 2:9, in an exhortation to women: "that they adorn themselves with honorable apparel . . . not with *braided hair* or gold or pearls. . . ."

πλεῖστος, 3 *pleistos* most, very much*

The NT uses the superlative of → πολύς both adj. and subst. Adj. in Matt 11:20: *"most* of his mighty works"; 21:8 (elative): "the *very great* crowd"; Mark 4:1: ὄχλος πλεῖστος. Subst. in οἱ πλεῖστοι, *"most of them"* (Acts 19:32 D); 1 Cor 14:27: neut. τὸ πλεῖστον, *at most.*

πλείων (πλέων), 2 *pleiōn (pleōn)* more

1. Occurrences in the NT — 2. Forms and meaning — 3. Specifically theological usage

Lit.: → πολύς.

1. Πλείων is the comparative of the positive → πολύς (cf. superlative → πλεῖστος) and occurs 55 times in the NT, including 7 times in Matthew, 1 in Mark, 9 in Luke, 5 in John, 19 in Acts, 3 in 1 Corinthians, 3 in 2 Corinthians, 1 in Philippians, 2 in 2 Timothy, 4 in Hebrews, and 1 in Revelation; it is thus not as widely distributed as the positive degree.

2. Πλείων is built on the abbreviated stem πλε(ι)- and the consonantal declension with two endings (gen. πλείονος). Πλείους (derived from ἴοσες and analogously ἴοσας, instead of πλείονες, πλείονας) and πλείω (derived from ἴοσα, instead of πλείονα), forms built on the s-stem, are both attested. Πλεῖον (18 NT occurrences) occurs more frequently than πλέον (3 occurrences), which it replaces. The nom. sg. masc./fem. and the dat. sg. do not appear in the NT; except for πλέον, all extant case forms are constructed from πλει-.

The point of departure for the various meanings in the NT is *more,* from which in a fashion partly analogous to that in the positive degree a development in meaning takes place that cannot always be easily and smoothly rendered in English (e.g., Acts 2:40) depending on whether and how πλείων is used adj., subst., or adv., and with or without the art. Thus in the sense of numerical heightening (cf. local, temporal, metaphorical) it means *more, more numerous* (Matt 21:36; John 4:1; 7:31; 15:2; Acts 4:22); developed more in the sense of gradation or intensification it means *several* (Acts 13:31; 24:17; 27:20); or in the sense of direct gradation-intensification and qualified heightening it means *more* in the sense of *greater, more abundant, longer,* etc., and in some cases also *quite great, abundant,* or very great, etc. (Luke 11:53; John 15:2; 21:15; Acts 15:28; 18:20; 24:4; 2 Tim 2:16; 3:9; Heb 3:3; 11:4; cf. the meanings suggested in BAGD 689). This suggests that in the NT the comparative can be used for the superlative (cf. superlative as elative "very large," e.g., in Mark 4:1; comparative for the real superlative) and like the positive (cf. slightly elative *quite /rather;* cf. also BDF §§60-62; 244-46). From this perspective its meaning often appears ambiguous, though it is unequivocal in combination with the comparative gen. (Matt 21:36), ἤ (Luke 9:13), παρά (Luke 3:13), and πλήν (Acts 15:28).

Subst. (οἱ) πλείονες (or πλείους; neither occurs in the Gospels) as a collective term presents problems similar to those accompanying the positive (οἱ) πολλοί. Whereas Acts 19:32; 27:12; and 1 Cor 15:6 refer to the *majority, most,* as an expressed part of the total number, this is not so clearly the case in 2 Cor 2:6 (something like "full assembly"; cf. BAGD s.v. πολύς II.2.a.γ: "the others, the rest," i.e., it is not a matter of a majority decision, but of a unanimous vote [excluding the person censured]); 4:15. Noteworthy occurrences in this context also include 1 Cor 9:19 and 10:5 (partitive with πάντες?); 2 Cor 9:2; Phil 1:14 (partitive with οἱ λοιποὶ πάντες?); Heb 7:23 (with Jesus, the one priest). In any case, pl. πλείονες can delimit upward (the majority of a total number) and downward (without the art. but with ἤ and similar constructions: Matt 21:36; Acts 28:23); or, in accord with other gradal-intensive and qualifying uses of the comparative, it can refer collectively to a plurality (cf. BDF §244.3: "the majority," or "others, even more"), as opposed to an individual or a few, though it can also stand next to πάντες (on the distinction between Semitic and Greek usage cf. also Josephus *B.J.* ii.146; O. Michel and O. Bauernfeind, ed., *De Bello Judaico* [²1962] I, 437 n.71).

Special idioms and figures of speech: paronomasia (2 Cor 4:15), litotes (1 Cor 10:5), constructions with ἄλλος, ἕτερος (Matt 21:36; Acts 2:40), special congruent relationships (Matt 6:25 par.; Luke 9:13), (strengthening)

combinations with the positive (John 4:41), prep. phrases (Luke 11:53; Acts 4:17).

3. Within specifically theological usage numerous features emerge analogous to the positive degree (cf., e.g., the historical report). Conceptions noteworthy regarding the comparative include: a) special heightening: the demand for better righteousness in Matthew (Matt 5:20; though cf. also Mark 12:43 par.; John 15:2; Acts 15:28); the argument in Q concerning being anxious about the "soul" and the body (Matt 6:25 par.; cf. also 6:33 par.); christological elevation of the Son of man over Jonah and Solomon, also from Q (Matt 12:41f. par.; cf. also Heb 3:3); the problem of "equal" and *more* in statements such as Matt 20:10; Luke 7:42f.; John 21:15; Heb 11:4; progress in both good and bad (2 Cor 4:15; 2 Tim 2:16; 3:9); b) collective usage (→ 2 on πλείων as a collective term).

G. Nebe

πλέκω *plekō* plait, twist*

Mark 15:17 par. Matt 27:29/John 19:2: *plaiting* Jesus' crown of thorns: Mark: ἀκάνθινον στέφανον; Matthew/John: στέφανον ἐξ ἀκανθῶν.

πλεονάζω *pleonazō* be/become more, multiply; trans.: cause to become rich*

Πλεονάζω occurs intrans. *(be present in abundance, multiply)* esp. in Paul (Rom 5:20a, b: παράπτωμα, ἁμαρτία; 6:1; 2 Cor 4:15: χάρις; Phil 4:17: καρπός; further also 2 Thess 1:3: ἀγάπη; 2 Pet 1:18). It also occurs in the sense of *having more* (than is necessary) in 2 Cor 8:15: "He who gathered much *had* no *surplus* (ἐπλεόνασεν)." Trans. in 1 Thess 3:12: "*May* the Lord *make* you *rich* in love." G. Delling, *TDNT* VI, 263-66; W. Bauder and D. Müller, *DNTT* II, 130f.

πλεονεκτέω *pleonekteō* take advantage of, outwit*

2 Cor 7:2; 12:17, 18; 1 Thess 4:6, of those who take advantage of others; pass. in 2 Cor 2:11, of Satan: "lest we may *be outwitted* by Satan." G. Delling, *TDNT* VI, 266-74; G. Finkenrath, *DNTT* I, 137-39.

πλεονέκτης, ου, ὁ *pleonektēs* greedy person, avaricious person*

In lists of wicked persons: 1 Cor 5:10, 11; 6:10; Eph 5:5. G. Delling, *TDNT* VI, 266-74; G. Finkenrath, *DNTT* I, 137-39.

πλεονεξία, ας, ἡ *pleonexia* greediness, avarice*

In catalogs of vices in Mark 7:22 (pl.); Rom 1:29; Eph 4:19; 5:3; Col 3:5 (see A. Vögtle, *Die Tugend- und*

Lasterkataloge im NT [1936], esp. 223-25). Luke 12:15 warns against "all *covetousness*." The context in 2 Cor 9:5 suggests that πλεονεξία is there a "gift wrested away [laboriously] from avarice." 1 Thess 2:5: "a pretext for *greed*." 2 Pet 2:3, 14 attributes greed to the false teachers. G. Delling, *TDNT* VI, 266-74; G. Finkenrath, *DNTT* I, 137-39; Spicq, *Notes* II, 704-6.

πλευρά, ᾶς, ἡ *pleura* side*

In the NT this term is always used of a side of a human body. John 19:34: the side of the crucified Jesus, into which (after death) a soldier stabbed his spear (par. Matt 27:49 v.l.); John 20:20, 25, 27: the wounded *side* that the resurrected Jesus shows to his disciples; Acts 12:7: The angel strikes the sleeping Peter on the *side* (πατάξας τὴν πλευράν) to wake him.

πλέω *pleō* travel by sea, sail*

Apart from Rev 18:17 all NT occurrences are in Luke-Acts (Luke 8:23 *contra* Mark, 4 times in Acts): Luke 8:23 and Acts 27:24, with no indication of the journey's goal; the goal expressed by εἰς in Acts 21:3 and 27:2, 6; Rev 18:17: ὁ ἐπὶ τόπον πλέων, perhaps *"one who sails* along the coast" (see BAGD s.v.; H. Kraft, *Rev* [HNT] 236, considers the text corrupted and reads κώπην, "galley," or πρῷραν, "forecastle," in place of τόπον; cf. Ezek 27:29 LXX).

πληγή, ῆς, ἡ *plēgē* blow; wound; plague (noun)*

Lit.: A. VAN DEN BORN, *BL* 533f. — J. JANSSEN, *BL* 1391f. — J. LEVY, *Chaldäisches Wörterbuch über die Targumim und einen großen Theil des rabbinischen Schriftthums* [³1866 = 1959] II, 114. — C. MAURER, *TDNT* VIII, 159. — H. P. MÜLLER, "Die Plagen der Apokalypse," *ZNW* 51 (1960) 268-78.

1. Of the 22 occurrences of πληγή in the NT, 16 are in Revelation and 2 each in Luke, Paul, and Acts.

The partc. expression πληγὰς ἐπιθέντες (Luke 10:30; Acts 16:23), "inflicting *blows*," is attested both in Greek (Maurer) and Aramaic (Levy: 'assēḇ kûprê, literally "allow to receive lashes"). The expression occurs in the parable of the Good Samaritan (Luke 10:30) in connection with a robbery and in Acts 16:23, in a report of Paul's activity in Philippi, in connection with "lynch justice" involving Paul and Silas (on Rev 22:18 → 2).

2. Luke 12:48: the beating a slave receives for doing something "deserving *blows*"; Acts 16:23; 2 Cor 6:5; 11:23: the beating that Paul (in one instance with Silas) received in the service of the Lord; Acts 16:33: the results, i.e., *wounds*. This last usage corresponds to the "mortal sword *wound*" (Rev 13:3, 12, 14) that the anti-Christian

"beast" (cf. Dan 7:11ff.) received and from which it was healed.

Πληγή in all other NT occurrences deviates from this usage and is to be rendered *plague* (Rev 9:18, 20; 11:6; 15:1, 6, 8; 16:9, 21 bis; 18:4, 8; 21:9; 22:18). This usage can be interpreted correctly only against the background of the "plagues of Egypt" in Exodus (MT: *nega'*; LXX: πληγή) and in the context of the exodus event. This understanding is supported by the occurrence in both Revelation and Exodus of "ten *plagues*" (cf. Exod 7:14–12:36 with Rev 9:18 [three plagues]; 15:1, 6, 8 [seven plagues]), followed in both instances by the exodus (cf. Exod 12:31 with Rev 18:4).

G. Schwarz

πλῆθος, ους, τό *plēthos* crowd, host, great number, populace, assembly; community (assembly), church*

1. Occurrences — 2. NT usage — a) Basic meaning — b) With and without the art. — c) Indications of what is referred to — d) Specific meanings — 3. As a Lukan designation for the Christian community — a) Salvation-historical continuity — b) Growth — c) Unity

Lit.: W. BAUDER, *DNTT* I, 731-33. — G. DELLING, *TDNT* VI, 274-79. — E. HAENCHEN, *Acts* (Eng. tr., 1971) 263, esp. n.7. — G. SCHNEIDER, *Acts* (HTKNT, 1980) I, esp. 251 n.71, 381 n.23, 424 n.31. — H. SCHÜRMANN, *Luke* (HTKNT, 1969) I, 320 (on Luke 6:17). — P. ZINGG, *Das Wachsen der Kirche* (OBO 3, 1974) esp. 65ff. — For further bibliography see *TWNT* X, 1236.

1. Of the 31 unmistakable occurrences in the NT, 24 are in Luke-Acts (8 in the Gospel, 16 in Acts). This is thus one of Luke's "preferred words" (Schneider 381 n.23). Indeed, only in Luke 6:17 can the word be traced back to Mark (Mark 3:7f., used there, however, absolutely). 3 times it is redactional: In 8:37 ἅπαν τὸ πλῆθος (with gen.) is an elucidating addition to Mark 5:17; in 19:37 and 23:1 the same expression replaces complex enumerations of groups of persons in Mark (11:9; 15:1); the other occurrences in Luke's Gospel (1:10; 2:13; 5:6; 23:27) are in material unique to Luke and have no Synoptic parallel (cf. Luke 5:6 with John 21:6). Except in Acts 5:14 all NT occurrences are sg.

2. a) Etymologically (from the root *plē-*) the noun means *fullness* (cf. πίμπλημι, πλήρης, Lat. *plēnus*). Used in the NT as a (collective) indication of quantity, its basic meaning corresponds approximately to English *large number* (general synonyms: *multitude, crowd, mass*) and exhibits (as already in the LXX; cf. Delling 276ff.) a larger scope of meaning and a wide field of usage.

b) Without the art. πλῆθος designates a numerically larger but indeterminate quantity (plurality) and is occasionally equivalent to the adj. πολλοί (Delling 279). The exceptional size of an (indeterminate) πλῆθος is as a rule expressed by the adj. πολύ (Mark 3:7f.; Luke 5:6;

6:17; 23:27; Acts 14:1; 17:4); pl. πλήθη ἀνδρῶν τε καὶ γυναικῶν in Acts 5:14 has an almost "hyperbolic" effect (Zingg 65). A limiting indication of quantity (with τι) occurs in Acts 28:3: "a *handful* of sticks" (Delling 279). Πλῆθος with the art. refers to the whole body of a (self-enclosed) gathering or assembly (under certain circumstances = οἱ πολλοί; cf. Delling 278). With regard to certain gatherings of persons, Luke occasionally gives special emphasis to their "uniformity" (Zingg 67) or "unanimity" of disposition (Delling 279) by πᾶν (Luke 1:10; Acts 6:5; 15:12) or ἅπαν (Luke 8:37; 19:37; 23:1; Acts 25:24; cf. ὅλον in Acts 14:7 v.l.).

c) Usually a gen. indicates that to which (τὸ) πλῆθος refers. But even when there is no gen. (so Mark 3:7f.; Acts 2:6; 6:5; 14:7 v.l.; 19:9; 23:7; cf. Heb 11:12, where τῷ πλήθει is used adj. in the sense of "numerous"), the specific reference can be established unequivocally from the context. Usually the noun is used of persons (often with the *constructio ad sensum* characteristic of collectives; cf. BDF §§134.1; 296), and only a few times in reference to nonpersonal quantities (fish: Luke 5:6; John 21:6; sticks: Acts 28:3; stars: Heb 11:12; sins: Jas 5:20; 1 Pet 4:8).

d) When not referring to persons, the noun always exhibits the usual meaning *large quantity, abundance*. In reference to persons, on the other hand, several variations in meanings can occur:

In the general sense, as a designation for a *crowd, throng* of persons: e.g., Luke 2:13: "a *multitude* of the heavenly host"; John 5:3: "a *multitude* of invalids"; Acts 5:14: "*crowds* of men and women"; 14:1: "a great *company* [so RSV] of Jews and Greeks"; 17:4: "a great *many* of the god-fearing Greeks" (with "and not a few of the leading women" [οὐκ ὀλίγαι synonymous with πλῆθος πολύ!]). This group includes those occurrences in which (τὸ) πλῆθος refers to (the) *people* or (the) *crowd;* the noun occurs absolutely with this meaning only in Mark 3:7f. ("a great *multitude*" = "many people"; cf. par. Matt 4:25: ὄχλοι πολλοί), otherwise it always appears with τοῦ λαοῦ: Luke 1:10 (cf. simple ὁ λαός in v. 21); 6:17: ("a great *multitude* of people," here set off from ὄχλος πολὺς μαθητῶν); 23:27 (note here the division: "a great *multitude* of people and of women"); Acts 21:36 (here negatively: "the mass/mob crying out"; cf. simple ὁ ὄχλος in vv. 27, 34, ὁ λαός in vv. 30, 39f.).

Only in Luke does τὸ πλῆθος sometimes exhibit a more comprehensive sense (usually emphasizing the aspect of totality) and designate the entire *populace* of a city or region (Luke 8:37: of the region of the Gerasenes; Acts 5:16: of the cities around Jerusalem; 14:4: of Iconium; cf. [with exaggeration] 25:24: "the whole Jewish people"; further 2:6, where along with "the multitude" [τὸ πλῆθος absolutely!] the context [vv. 5, 14] suggests the reference is to the entire populace of Jeru-

salem along with the Diaspora Jews living there); twice (Luke 23:1; Acts 23:7) the reference is to (the whole body of) the *assembly* of the Sanhedrin.

Also only in Luke does the noun, in accord with the usage of religious communities (BAGD s.v.; Schneider 424 n.31), occur as a t.t. for the religious *community (assembly)* as a whole. This usage is consistent with two exceptions: In Luke 1:10 πᾶν τὸ πλῆθος is used of the community assembled for worship in the temple forecourt (as opposed to the priests offering incense in the temple itself), and Acts 19:9 uses τὸ πλῆθος absolutely of the assembly of the Ephesian synagogue community (from which "the disciples" are distinguished). Otherwise, the reference is either to the pre-Easter company of disciples (so Luke 19:37: ἅπαν τὸ πλῆθος τῶν μαθητῶν; cf. 6:17, where the synonymous expression ὄχλος πολὺς μαθητῶν αὐτοῦ is used of Jesus' closer circle of disciples, which is distinguished both from the "Twelve" and from the πλῆθος πολύ of the people), or, (always in Acts) to the Christian community (assembly), i.e., the early Jerusalem congregation in Acts 4:32 (τὸ πλῆθος τῶν πιστευσάντων); 6:2 (τὸ πλῆθος τῶν μαθητῶν), 5; 15:12 (πᾶν τὸ πλῆθος) and the congregation in Antioch in 15:30 (συναγαγόντες τὸ πλῆθος).

3. Several theologically relevant ideas are associated with the Lukan use of the noun for the *Christian community* (with → ἐκκλησία: cf., e.g., Acts 4:32 with 5:11; 15:12 with 15:22).

a) Salvation-historical continuity: Luke 19:37 (the entry into Jerusalem) gives the disciples accompanying Jesus the same designation (πλῆθος τῶν μαθητῶν) as Acts 6:2 gives the early Jerusalem church. It thus clearly characterizes the disciples as "the model and prototype of the early Christian Church" (Schürmann 320). In Luke 6:17, too, "the great company of his disciples" mentioned among Jesus' followers (with the "Twelve") appears at least "symbolically as a prophetic sign . . . for the post-Easter community of disciples," just as in a corresponding fashion "the great multitude of people"—anticipating the post-Easter mission situation—already presents "the masses of people of the oikoumene to be targeted by the mission, and thus potentially also . . . already prefigures the NT people of God" (Schürmann 321). A similar understanding suggests itself for Luke 2:10 and 23:27 and esp. for 5:6 (the rich catch of fish as an anticipatory portrayal of the post-Easter mission success; cf. v. 10).

b) Growth: This is already alluded to in Luke's Gospel. While in 6:17 the ὄχλος πολύς of the disciples is distinguished from the πλῆθος πολύ of the people (which is apparently thought of as larger: Zingg 65), the expression ἅπαν τὸ πλῆθος in 19:37 might already refer to the company of disciples expanded by "the adherents of Jesus from the masses" (Schürmann 321 n.7). Acts (esp.

in the three summaries describing the life of the first Christians: 2:41-47; 4:32-35; 5:11-16) also portrays how the early community continually grew after the first Pentecost, at which from the assembled *multitude* (2:6) the first company of Christians was formed (cf. v. 41, at the beginning of the first summary). The report of growth in 5:14 (in the third summary) is formulated almost hyperbolically: "More than ever believers were added by the Lord (προσετίθεντο), *multitudes* both of men and women" (cf. Zingg 38f.). The summoning of the "*company* of disciples" mentioned in 6:2, leading to the election of the seven by "the entire *company*" (v. 5), results from difficulties caused by the increased growth of the community (v. 1: "when the number of disciples increased" [→ πληθύνω]). The Church then grows even more through the missionary activity of Paul and his companions. According to 14:1 they preached so successfully in the synagogue at Iconium that "a great *company* believed, both of Jews and of Greeks"; according to 17:4, in Thessalonica they succeed in winning over to the faith "a great *many* of the god-fearing Greeks and not a few of the leading women."

c) The Church's (self-enclosed, but also structured) unity: Luke 19:37 already characterizes (with ἅπαν) the company of Jesus' disciples as a closed fellowship, and this is esp. the case concerning the post-Easter community of Christians. Their unity manifests itself esp. in the fact that they live together (Acts 4:32: "*The company* of those who had come to believe was of one heart and soul. . . . They had everything in common") and in their unanimous disposition in important decisions (the election of the seven: 6:5; at the Apostolic Council: 15:12, 22, 25). In this context the community, in accord with its pre-Easter model (cf. the separate emphasis of the "Twelve" over against the larger circle of "disciples" in Luke 6:17), appears as a structured unity: Acts 6:2 distinguishes the "*company* of disciples" from the "Twelve" (which summons and presides over the full assembly). The report of the Apostolic Council mentions Church (ἐκκλησία!), apostles, and elders (15:4; cf. v. 22). The apostles and elders are thus esp. emphasized as the leadership within the full Church assembly (15:12: πᾶν τὸ πλῆθος).

J. Zmijewski

πληθύνω *plēthynō* make full, multiply, grow, increase*

1. Occurrences and usage in the NT — 2. Formulaic expressions — 3. Acts

Lit.: W. BAUDER, *DNTT* I, 731-33. — G. DELLING, *TDNT* VI, .279-83. — G. SCHNEIDER, *Acts* (HTKNT, 1980) I, esp. 422 n.14, 457 n.108. — P. ZINGG, *Das Wachsen der Kirche* (OBO 3, 1974). — For further bibliography see *TWNT* X, 1236.

1. This vb. occurs 12 times in the NT (*ca.* 200 occurrences in the LXX), 5 times in Acts alone (Schneider 457 n.108: "a preferred word in Acts") and (as already in the LXX; cf. Delling 280f.) is used both trans. and intrans.

The trans. act., meaning *make full, multiply,* occurs in only two passages, in both referring to God: 2 Cor 9:10: God will supply the Corinthians with "seed" and *multiply* the seed (i.e., material goods, enabling them to undertake the work of love for Jerusalem [or which grows out of this work?]); Heb 6:14 (bis), citing God's promise to Abraham from Gen 22:17: "Truly I will bless you in blessing and *multiply* (πληθυνῶ) you [LXX: your seed] in multiplying (πληθύνων) [= abundantly]."

The intrans. act., with the meaning *grow (in number), increase,* occurs only in Acts 6:1 (in reference to the community of disciples; cf. also 19:20 D).

The remaining 8 occurrences (Matt 24:12; Acts 6:7; 7:17; 9:31; 12:24; 1 Pet 1:2; 2 Pet 1:2; Jude 2) are pass. with the meaning *be multiplied, be allotted in abundance* (so esp. with God as the logical subj.) or mid. (following the intrans. act. sense): *multiply, increase, grow* (e.g., Matt 24:12, which mentions among the signs of the end time the *proliferation* of → ἀνομία precipitated by deception [v. 11], which will cause the → ἀγάπη of many to "grow cold").

2. The combination "[let] increase and *multiply*" (αὐξάνω καὶ πληθύνω: Acts 6:7; 7:17; 12:24; 2 Cor 9:10) is already a fixed expression in the LXX (13 occurrences, e.g., Gen 1:22, 28; 47:27; Exod 1:7). The two vbs. have different fundamental connotations (despite their synonymity; cf. Zingg 26) and might be used together to express a heightening (i.e., superabundance and consistency of growth) or to indicate growth from two perspectives (αὐξάνω emphasizing more the inner power bringing about growth [cf. Delling 281f.] and πληθύνω external effects).

In three epistolary prescripts opt. πληθυνθείη ("may it grow" or "may it be allotted in abundance") is added to the formula of greeting, probably under LXX influence (cf. Dan 4:37c LXX; 4:1; 6:26 Theodotion): 1 Pet 1:2: χάρις ὑμῖν καὶ εἰρήνη πληθυνθείη; similarly 2 Pet 1:2, though with the redactional addendum ἐν ἐπιγνώσει τοῦ θεοῦ κτλ.; Jude 2: ἔλεος ὑμῖν καὶ εἰρήνη καὶ ἀγάπη πληθυνθείη. "The wish is at all events that the fulness of the divine gifts of salvation may be at work in the churches" (Delling 283).

3. Πληθύνω is one of the characteristics vbs. (along with αὐξάνω, ἰσχύω, προστίθημι, and others) used in reports of growth in Acts. Two of these notices frame the report of the election of the seven (6:2-6): The first (v. 1) is gen. absolute (πληθυνόντων τῶν μαθητῶν: "when [or since] the disciples *increased in number*") and refers to the (temporal and objective) background of the difficulties

that (according to v. 2) prompted the summoning of the full community assembly (→ πλῆθος 3; the noun with the vb. as in Exod 1:9f.; Deut 1:10; 1 Chr 4:38 LXX). The second (v. 7) portrays in three clauses with parallel structures the success brought by the appointment of the seven (and the consequent liberation of the apostles for "service to the word"; cf. v. 4): "And the word of God increased (ηὔξανεν), and the number of disciples *multiplied* greatly (σφόδρα) in Jerusalem, and a great many (πολὺς ὄχλος) of the priests came to be obedient to the faith." This summary unmistakably represents a heightening after v. 1 (cf. σφόδρα [as in Exod 1:7, and elsewhere], the impf. tense [underscoring the continuity of the growth], the expansion of the circle to include the "great company of priests," and esp. the clear reference to the connection between the growth of the logos and the increase in the number of disciples that growth brings about).

A further heightening occurs in 9:31 ("the Church throughout all Judea and Galilee and Samaria . . . *was multiplied* by the παράκλησις of the Holy Spirit"). Here reference is already made to an → ἐκκλησία (a "regional Church," extending beyond the original community), whose continued steady growth (again impf.!) is also traced back to the special intervention of the Holy Spirit.

The final notice (12:24: "but the word of the Lord grew and *multiplied*") marks a final heightening, not only because of its formulation (the logos is now the only subj.), but also because of its positioning: Luke has consciously placed it between the report of Herod's persecution of the Church and his death (vv. 1-23) and the report of Paul's first missionary journey (from 13:1 on) in order to make it clear that the growth of the logos and thus of the Church—despite persecution—goes on unabated (again impf.!), in accord with the Lord's commission (1:8).

Acts 7:17, with its allusion to Gen 47:27 or Exod 1:7 (in Stephen's words), stands exactly between the four notices of growth just discussed. If according to Luke the "growth and multiplication" of the old people of God in Egypt mentioned there refers to the beginning of the fulfillment of the promise to Abraham (cf. 7:5), then the growth of the logos and of the Church constitutes its new and ultimate realization (cf. Zingg 174).   J. Zmijewski

πλήκτης, ου, ὁ *plēktēs* bully, quarrelsome man*

The enumeration of bishops' qualities in the Pastorals contains among other things that the ἐπίσκοπος not be a *quarrelsome man* (μὴ πλήκτην; 1 Tim 3:3; Titus 1:7).

πλήμμυρα, ης, ἡ *plēmmyra* high water, flood*

Luke 6:48 (cf. par. Matt 7:25), in the concluding parable of the "Sermon on the Plain" (the house built on a rock foundation): πλημμύρης γενομένης, "when a *flood* arose."

πλήν *plēn* adv.: but, however; improper prep. with gen.: except*

1. Adv. usage (as a conjunction) at the beginning of a sentence or clause: *however, nonetheless:* Introducing Jesus' sayings: πλὴν λέγω ὑμῖν (Matt 11:22, 24; 26:64) and πλὴν οὐαί (Matt 18:7; Luke 6:24; 17:1; 22:22); also in Matt 26:39 par. Luke 22:42 (cf. par. Mark); Luke 6:35; 10:11, 14, 20; 11:41; 12:31; 13:33; 18:8; 19:27; 23:28. Also concluding a discussion and emphasizing what is important, e.g., in Paul (1 Cor 11:11; Phil 3:16; 4:14; cf. Eph 5:33; Rev 2:25). Πλὴν ὅτι, "*except* that," in Acts 20:23; Phil 1:18. In Luke 22:21 πλήν breaks off the train of thought and provides the transition to something new.

2. As improper prep. with gen.: *except*, usually after negative statements (Mark 12:32; John 8:10 TR; Acts 15:28; 27:22). After a positive statement in Acts 8:1: πάντες διεσπάρησαν πλὴν τῶν ἀποστόλων.

πλήρης, 2 *plērēs* full*

1. Occurrences in the NT — 2. Meanings — 3. Luke-Acts

Lit.: G. DELLING, *TDNT* VI, 283-86. — G. M. LEE, "Indeclinable ΠΛΗΡΗΣ," *NovT* 17 (1975) 304. — For further bibliography → πληρόω.

1. Πλήρης occurs 16 times in the NT, most of those in Luke-Acts (2 occurrences in the Gospel, 8 in Acts), otherwise twice each in Matthew and Mark, once each in John and 2 John.

2. Πλήρης (in the NT partly indeclinable, as generally in vernacular Hellenistic Greek; see BDF §137.1) means *full, filled,* first of all in a purely spatial sense: "twelve baskets *full*" (Matt 14:20; similarly Matt 15:37; Mark 8:19), "the *full* grain in the ear" (Mark 4:28). It is also used fig.: "that you may win a *full* reward" (2 John 8). Luke's usage is theologically relevant (→ 3), as is John 1:14: πλήρης χάριτος καὶ ἀληθείας, "*full* of grace and truth" (→ ἀλήθεια 4.b; πλήρωμα 3.c).

3. Πλήρης exhibits special theological significance in Luke. The pre-Easter Jesus is *the* bearer of the Spirit; he is πλήρης πνεύματος ἁγίου, "*full* of the Holy Spirit" (Luke 4:1; cf. H. Conzelmann, *The Theology of St. Luke* [1961] 180; see also vv. 16ff.). Use of πλήρης in Acts shows that after Pentecost the Holy Spirit is the real power for the time of the Church. Acts 6:3 describes "the seven" (→ ἑπτά 2.e) as "*full* of the Spirit and of wisdom," though hardly in the sense of "worldly prudence" (*contra* E. Haenchen, *Acts* [Eng. tr., 1971] 262; justified criticism from G. Schneider, *Acts* [HTKNT] I, 426 n.45 with

reference to Acts 6:10). The assertion that Stephen is "a man *full* of faith and of the Holy Spirit" (6:5) is developed in two directions: He is 1) "*full* of grace and power (→ δύναμις 6)" (6:8), and thus a miracle worker, and 2) he speaks "with wisdom and the Spirit" in the dispute with the adversaries of the Christian faith (6:10; see Schneider 434f.). In 7:55, "*full* of the Holy Spirit," Stephen sees the glory (→ δόξα 3.b) of God in heaven and Jesus at God's right hand (Haenchen 295: "The Holy Spirit opens the eyes of Stephen . . . to the heavenly Reality so infinitely raised above all earthly polemics"). 11:24 describes Barnabas as "*full* of the Holy Spirit and of faith": "A stock terminology of pious language is in process of crystallization" (Haenchen 366). The florid characterization of Tabitha as "*full* of good works and acts of charity" (9:36) should perhaps also be understood in this sense (see Haenchen 338f.).

Luke uses πλήρης in a disqualifying sense in Acts 13:10: "*full* of all deceit and villainy" (of the magician Elymas), and in 19:28: "*full* of rage" (of the Ephesians during the riot of Demetrius); see also Luke 5:12: "a man *full* of leprosy."

H. Hübner

πληροφορέω *plērophoreō* fill completely, fulfill; pass. also: be convinced*
πληροφορία, ας, ἡ *plērophoria* fullness; conviction*

1. Occurrences and meaning of πληροφορέω — 2. Occurrences and meaning of πληροφορία — 3. Luke 1:1 — 4. Rom 14:5

Lit.: J. BECKER, "Quid πληροφορεῖσθαι in Rom 14,5 significet," *VD* 45 (1967) 11-18. — *idem,* "Zu πληροφορεῖσθαι in Röm 14,5," *Bib* 65 (1984) 364. — DEISSMANN, *Light* 86f. — G. DELLING, *TDNT* VI, 309-311. — H. SCHÜRMANN, *Luke* (HTKNT, 1969) I, 1-19. — Spicq, *Notes* II, 707-9. — For further bibliography → πληρόω.

1. Because of its double meaning *fill completely* (a strengthening of → πληρόω) and *be firmly convinced* (pass.) and because of its shifting character, the late Greek vb. πληροφορέω sometimes resists an unequivocal translation. It occurs 6 times in the NT: Luke 1:1: τὰ πεπληροφορημένα ἐν ἡμῖν πράγματα, "the events *brought to fulfillment* among us [by God]" (from the German translation by Schürmann 4); Rom 4:21; 14:5: πληροφορηθείς /πληροφορείσθω, *fully convinced*/*let every one be fully convinced;* Col 4:12: πεπληροφορημένοι, *fulfilled,* or, as in Paul: *fully convinced;* 2 Tim 4:5: "*fulfill* your ministry"; v. 17: ἵνα δι' ἐμοῦ τὸ κήρυγμα πληροφορηθῇ, "so that through me the task of preaching [enjoined to me] *might be carried through to its goal*" (somewhat weakened in M. Dibelius and H. Conzelmann, *The Pastoral Epistles* [Hermeneia] 124: "that through me the preaching might be proclaimed far and wide").

2. The difficulties in translation are even greater with the equally late Greek noun πληροφορία with its double meaning *fullness* and *firm conviction, absolute certainty.* It occurs in the NT only in 3 of the letters.

1 Thess 1:5: "The gospel went out . . . not only in word, but also in power and in the Holy Spirit and [ἐν] πληροφορίᾳ πολλῇ." The contrast here between πληροφορία and "the word" and the coordination of πληροφορία with power and Spirit might suggest the tr. "in great *fullness of divine working*" (so Delling 311; differently E. von Dobschütz, *1-2 Thess* [KEK] ad loc.: "inner confidence brought about by the Spirit"; BAGD 670: probably "wealth of assurance").

Col 2:2 is unequivocal: εἰς πᾶν πλοῦτος τῆς πληροφορίας τῆς συνέσεως, "to all the riches of the *fullness* of understanding" (M. Dibelius, *Col* [HNT] 24: "to have full, rich understanding"; Delling 311: "tautologously with πλοῦτος the term denotes . . . *superabundance*").

A certain tr. is probably not possible for σπουδὴν πρὸς τὴν πληροφορίαν τῆς ἐλπίδος (Heb 6:11): neither "zeal for the *full development* of hope" (cf. O. Michel, *Heb* [KEK] ad loc.) nor "zeal which leads to *full preservation* of the final hope" (Delling 311). The meaning of ἐν πληροφορίᾳ πίστεως (10:22) is undisputed: "in full faith" (Michel 342, 346: "the unbrokenness of faith"). Delling (311) correctly sees that πληροφορία here is similar theologically to παρρησία ("confidence").

3. Τὰ πεπληροφορημένα ἐν ἡμῖν πράγματα in Luke 1:1 contains a bit of the theological and historical agenda that comes to expression in Luke's prologue. Schürmann probably correctly recognizes that πληροφορέω here is "used ambiguously": Like πληρόω it refers first to completion: For Luke "the christological events of salvation have 'come to completion' in the resurrection and exaltation of Jesus . . ."; but Luke also wants to bring the "fulfillment character" of those events to expression (Schürmann 5). Therefore, he makes theological use of the terminological ambiguity inherent in πληροφορέω. The fulfillment of what is written about the works of salvation corresponds to the fulfillment of those acts themselves (Luke 24:44, → πληρόω 3.a).

4. In the basic premise that "every one should *be fully convinced* according to his own judgment" (Rom 14:5) Paul seeks to make it possible to arrive at different views on the ticklish question of cultic purity, a question involving the validity of the Mosaic law (→ νόμος 4.b). This statement suggests that Paul is probably exercising greater "tolerance" in Romans than earlier in Galatians in questions concerning the cultic side of the law. The idea of theological development in Paul thus suggests itself (J. W. Drane, *Paul: Libertine or Legalist?* [1975] 132-36; H. Hübner, *Law in Paul's Thought* [1984], esp. 51ff., 101ff.). E. Käsemann (*Rom* [Eng. tr., 1980] 371)

justifiably criticizes Becker, who interprets πληρο-
φορείσθω here as mid.: "take pleasure in."   H. Hübner

πληροφορία, ας, ἡ *plērophoria* fullness; conviction, certainty
→ πληροφορέω 2.

πληρόω *plēroō* fill completely, fulfill, bring to completion, realize
ἀναπληρόω *anaplēroō*   fulfill, make complete, fill
up
ἀνταναπληρόω *antanaplēroō*   (vicariously) complete, fulfill

1. Occurrences in the NT — 2. Meanings — 3. Theologically relevant usage — a) The Gospels and Acts — b)
Paul — c) The deutero-Pauline writings

Lit.: R. BANKS, *Jesus and the Law in the Synoptic Tradition*
(SNTSMS 28, 1975) 204-13. — G. BARTH, "Matthew's Understanding of the Law," in G. Bornkamm, G. Barth, and H. J.
Held, *Tradition and Interpretation in Matthew* (1963) 64-69. —
M. DELCOR, *THAT* I, 897-900. — G. DELLING, *TDNT* VI, 286-98;
305f. — O. EISSFELD, "Πληρῶσαι πᾶσαν δικαιοσύνην in Mt
3,15," *ZNW* 61 (1970) 209-15. — J. A. FITZMYER, "The Use of
Explicit OT Quotations in Qumran Literature and in the NT,"
NTS 7 (1960/61) 297-333 (= *idem, Essays on the Semitic Back-
ground of the NT* [SBLSBS 5, 1974] 3-58). — F. HAHN, "Mt
5,17—Anmerkungen zum Erfüllungsgedanken bei Matthäus,"
Die Mitte des NT (FS E. Schweizer, 1983) 42-54. — H. HÜBNER,
Das Gesetz in der synoptischen Tradition (1973) 32-35, 196-211,
233-35. — *idem, Law in Paul's Thought* (1984) 36-42, 83-87.
— R. HUMMEL, *Die Auseinandersetzung zwischen Kirche und
Judentum im Mattäusevangelium* (BEvT 53, ²1966) 66-75. —
J. KREMER, *Was an den Leiden Christi noch mangelt* (BBB 12,
1956) 156-63. — H. LJUNGMAN, *Das Gesetz erfüllen. Mt 5,17ff
und 3,15 untersucht* (1954). — R. S. McCONNELL, *Law and
Prophecy in Matthew's Gospel* (1969) 6-58, 101-41, 128-32.' —
J. P. MEIER, *Law and History in Matthew's Gospel* (AnBib 71,
1976) 65-89, 120-24. — G. MIEGGE, *Il Sermone sul monte* (1970)
83-90. — W. ROTHFUCHS, *Die Erfüllungszitate des Matthäusevangeliums* (BWANT 88, 1969) 27-56, 151-283. —
R. SCHIPPERS, *DNTT* I, 733-38. — E. SCHWEIZER, "Matthäus
5,17-20, *idem, Neotestamentica* (1963) 399-406. — G. M.
SOARES PRABHU, *The Formula Quotations in the Infancy Narrative of Matthew* (AnBib 63, 1976). — SPICQ, *Notes* II, 707-9.—
G. STRECKER, *Der Weg der Gerechtigkeit* (FRLANT 82, ³1971)
49f., 143-47, 178-81. — H. T. WREGE, *Die Überlieferungsgeschichte der Bergpredigt* (WUNT 9, 1968) 35-47. — For
further bibliography → γραφή; νόμος; see also *TWNT* X, 1236f.

1. Πληρόω occurs 87 times in the NT and is esp.
prominent in Luke (9 occurrences in the Gospel, 16 in
Acts). It occurs 16 times in Matthew, 15 in John, 13 in
Paul, 3 times in Mark, 6 in deutero-Paul and the Pastorals,
once each in 1 Peter and 1/2 John, and twice in Revelation. Ἀναπληρόω occurs once in Matthew and 5 times
in Paul. Ἀνταναπληρόω occurs only in Col 1:24.

2. Πληρόω is a causative vb. from the stem of →
πλήρης and means basically *fill* or *make full* in a purely
spatial sense, e.g., jugs (Euripides *Ion* 1192), and then
metaphorically, e.g., *fill* with joy (Philo *Abr.* 108), e.g.,
Wis 1:7: πνεῦμα κυρίου πεπλήρωκε τὴν οἰκουμένην, "the
Spirit of the Lord has filled the world" (cf. also Aristides
Or. 45.21, of Zeus Serapis: τὸ πᾶν πεπλήρωκε).

The spatial meaning is relatively infrequent in the NT
(e.g., Matt 13:48, of a net; Acts 2:2, of a house). Πληρόω
first acquires its real theological importance in metaphorical usage (→ 3): One *fulfills* the law and its demands,
realizes it, or *fulfills* Scripture or its word. Πληρόω is
usually pass. in these cases and always pass. when it is
used of the end of an era (e.g., Acts 7:30: πληρωθέντων
ἐτῶν τεσσεράκοντα, "when forty years *had passed*").
Mark 1:15 uses it in a qualitative sense: πεπλήρωται ὁ
καιρός, "the time *is fulfilled*" (see also John 7:8). The
christological statement in Eph 4:10 lies somewhere between purely spatial usage and metaphorical usage: ἵνα
πληρώσῃ τὰ πάντα, "that he [Christ] might fill all things."
5:18 can be understood similarly: πληροῦσθε ἐν πνεύματι,
"be filled with the Spirit." In Acts 13:52, on the other
hand ("the disciples were filled with joy and with the
Holy Spirit"), we encounter metaphorical usage only.
"That your joy may be full" and similar phrases are
characteristic of the Johannine writings (e.g., John 15:11;
16:24; 1 John 1:4; 2 John 12).

Ἀναπληρόω is merely πληρόω intensified. Therefore,
as far as the vb. is concerned there is no real difference
between πληρόω τὸν νόμον, "*fulfill* the law," and ἀναπληρώσετε τὸν νόμον τοῦ Χριστοῦ, "*fulfill* the law of
Christ" (Gal 6:2). In 1 Thess 2:16 εἰς τὸ ἀναπληρῶσαι
αὐτῶν τὰς ἁμαρτίας πάντοτε is best translated "so as always *to fill up the measure* of their sins." Ἀντανα-
πληρόω in Col 1:24 similarly means *complete* or *fulfill*.

3.a) In Matthew one needs to distinguish between contextual quotations and formula or fulfillment quotations.
The latter are introduced by "fulfilment formulas built
round the vb. πληροῦν, which present an OT text as having
been 'fulfilled' in an event or episode narrated" (Soares
Prabhu 46). These formulas usually take the form ἵνα/
ὅπως πληρωθῇ τὸ ῥηθὲν (ὑπὸ κυρίου) διὰ . . . τοῦ προφήτου
λέγοντος, "to *fulfill* what was spoken [by the Lord] through
the prophet" (1:22; 2:15, 23; 4:14; 8:17; 12:17; 13:35;
21:4; τότε ἐπληρώθη τὸ ῥηθὲν διὰ Ἰερεμίου τοῦ προφήτου
λέγοντος, "then *was fulfilled* what was spoken by the
prophet Jeremiah," in 2:17; 27:9). Fulfillment quotations
introduced by fulfillment formulas are essential to the
redactional purposes of the author. Neither Q nor Mark
contains genuine fulfillment quotations (Mark 15:28 is a
historically secondary text). Mark 14:49 makes only a
general reference to the fulfillment of the Scriptures in
Jesus' life (likewise the par. Matt 26:56 with redactional

"but all this has taken place"; cf. also 1:22). Significantly, πληρόω does not stand in Mark 1:2, though the idea of fulfillment is probably implied by ἐγένετο in v. 4.

Whereas Matthew typically associates τὸ ῥηθέν (→ λέγω 3) with the aor. pass. of πληρόω, the subj. changes in the Johannine fulfillment formula: ἡ → γραφή (4) (John 13:18; 17:12; 19:24, 36), ὁ λόγος Ἡσαΐου τοῦ προφήτου (12:38), and ὁ λόγος ὁ ἐν τῷ νόμῳ αὐτῶν γεγραμμένος (15:25). Twice it concerns the fulfillment of something Jesus himself said (18:9, 32). Hence the Johannine fulfillment formula is not as consistent as the Matthean. The author always uses λόγος when the quotation is made more specifically or exactly (Rothfuchs 153). Only the phrase ἵνα πληρωθῇ is used consistently. Above all, however, whereas Matthew employs only prophetic texts in his fulfillment quotations (except in Matt 13:35, where a Psalm is introduced as a prophetic text), John cites passages from both the Prophets and the Psalms (in John 15:25 νόμος refers not to the Law in the stricter sense but to the Scriptures in general).

The fulfillment quotations introduced by fulfillment formulas can be distinguished from other OT quotations in Matthew —quotations with parallels in the other Synoptics—in that they are based not on the LXX but for the most part on the Hebrew text of the OT, even though the influence of the LXX is also unmistakable (e.g., Isa 7:14 with παρθένος in Matt 1:23). The discussion of the fulfillment quotations has not yet been resolved. The question is still open whether the Evangelist is using a testimonial collection (Strecker 83, among others). K. Stendahl, *The School of St. Matthew* (²1968), assumes that these quotations originated within the tradition of a certain school. Soares Prabhu, using Stendahl, R. H. Gundry, and Rothfuchs as his point of departure, speaks of "free targumic translations made from the original Hebrew by Matthew, in view of the context into which he has inserted them" (104), and may well have thus pointed the way to a solution to the problem. Nonetheless, this addresses only the formal features. The theological question remains whether it is the case that "the formula quotations . . . are a kind of proof of the legitimacy of Jesus' messiahship," and thus "it is not so much the fulfillment that determines the promise, but rather . . . the promise that determines the fulfillment" (H.-M. Schenke and K. M. Fischer, *Einleitung in die Schriften des NT* [1979] II, 100) or that the formula quotations show "how in Matthew the reference to Scripture and thus Scripture itself acquires its real legitimacy from the perspective of the Christ-event," particularly since the unity of the scriptural quotations gathered by Matthew is constituted only through the Christ-event, which has already occurred (H. Hübner, *KD* 27 [1981] 13).

Πληρόω is also a redactional code word in Matt 3:15 and 5:17, though the meaning of these occurrences should not be equated with the meaning of the vb. in the fulfillment formulas. In 5:17 τὸν νόμον καὶ τοὺς προφήτας . . . πληρῶσαι means first "*to establish* the Law [and the prophets who expound the Law] *through teaching*," but then also refers to modification of the law through teaching (Strecker 143-47; Hübner, *Gesetz in der synoptischen*

Tradition 34 and *passim*). Πληρῶσαι πᾶσαν δικαιοσύνην in 3:15 includes both πληρόω and the key theological concept δικαιοσύνη (→ δικαιοσύνη 5), which Strecker correctly interprets as "appropriate behavior": Jesus *realizes* righteousness not only by teaching but also through action (179). Consideration of 3:15 and 5:17 together thus discloses the Matthean conjunction of christology and ethics.

Luke 4:21 changes the programmatic πεπλήρωται ὁ καιρός of Mark 1:15 (cf. W. Marxsen, *Mark the Evangelist* [1969] 133f.) into the equally programmatic πεπλήρωται ἡ γραφὴ αὕτη: The time of Jesus' earthly activity as the middle of time is the fulfillment of Isa 61:1f., for Jesus' earthly activity is activity by the power of the Spirit. According to Luke 24:44 everything written in the Law, the Prophets, and the Psalms, namely, Jesus' suffering and resurrection, had to (→ δεῖ 5) *be fulfilled* (cf. also Acts 1:16; 3:18). An understanding of this fulfillment is possible only after the resurrection (Luke 24:44). The interpretation of Luke 22:16 is disputed (cf. Delling 295, 29ff.).

b) Paul never uses the idiom "to fulfill the Scriptures." He does, however, speak of the law being *fulfilled*. According to Gal 5:14 the law as a whole (ὁ πᾶς νόμος) is *fulfilled* in a single word, namely, the commandment of love (Lev 19:18). Thus "the law as a whole" stands in contrast to "the whole law" (ὅλον τὸν νόμον, v. 3), i.e., the Torah, which precisely as a whole, i.e., as the sum of all the individual commandments, should not be observed because this would lead to a fall from grace (cf. 5:3f. within the context of 3:10). Therefore, fulfillment of the "whole" law (5:14) as a function of the commandment of love is clearly not identical with following the entire Mosaic law, and thus the "whole" law (5:14) is not identical with the entire Mosaic law (Hübner, *Law in Paul's Thought* 36ff.). The clause ὁ πᾶς νόμος πεπλήρωται (5:14) is in substance related to ἀναπληρώσετε τὸν νόμον τοῦ Χριστοῦ, "*fulfill* the law of Christ" (6:2).

Rom 13:8-10 is a different story. Here to *fulfill* the law is clearly to keep the Mosaic law. Hence a theological development must have taken place between the two letters if this difference between Gal 5:14 and Rom 13:8-10 genuinely obtains (Hübner, *op. cit.* 60ff., 83ff.). Rom 8:4 ("in order that the just requirement [→ δικαίωμα] of the law *might be fulfilled*") as a theological assertion is difficult to reconcile with Galatians. In Rom 15:19 Paul uses the clause πεπληρωκέναι τὸ εὐαγγέλιον τοῦ Χριστοῦ to indicate that he has *concluded* his task of proclamation in the East.

1 Thess 2:16 also suggests that a theological development has taken place in Paul. In Rom 11:26 Paul will revise his judgment that the Jews (pl.!) "fill up the measure" of their sins and fall victim to God's wrath (→ ὀργή) (U. Wilckens, *Rom* [EKKNT] II, 184f.). Matt 23:32 is closely related to 1 Thess 2:16.

James, polemicizing against a misunderstood Paul (or Pauline theology?), no longer uses the typically Pauline πληρόω τὸν νόμον, but employs rather the Synoptic motif of the *fulfillment* of Scripture (2:23).

c) The occurrences of πληρόω in the deutero-Pauline letters are in a certain sense consistent with those in the authentic Pauline letters. Col 1:25 echoes Rom 15:19: To "Paul" as a minister of the Church the divine office is given πληρῶσαι τόν λόγον τοῦ θεοῦ, "to make the word of God *fully known*" (cf. also Col 4:17: Archippus is to *fulfill* his ministry [→ διακονία; cf. 1:25: "Paul" as διάκονος]). Pauline theology also echoes in the insistence that those addressed should be *filled* with the knowledge of God's will (Col 1:9) or with the Spirit (Eph 5:18). But Eph 3:19 ("that you may be *filled* with all the fullness [→ πλήρωμα 3.b]) goes far beyond Paul christologically. This may be a noteworthy further development of the idea in Col. 2:9f., which also goes beyond Paul: Since the entire fullness of the deity dwells within Christ (v. 9), the Colossians *are* already *fulfilled* in him (πεπληρωμένοι, v. 10). That is, they are already that which human beings should be according to God's will. Thus Paul's eschatological reservation has been overcome (cf. also Col 3:1; Eph 2:5f.). The ecclesiological agenda of Colossians and Ephesians comes to a head in Eph 1:23: The Church (→ ἐκκλησία 4.c) as the body of Christ is the fullness of him who *fills* all in all (πεπληρωμένου, mid. partc.); see also ἵνα πληρώσῃ τὰ πάντα, "that he (Christ) might fill all things" (4:10), where again the same juxtaposition of cosmic and ecclesiological perspective as in 1:23 comes to expression (J. Gnilka, *Eph* [HTKNT] 96).

The prayer of "Paul" in 2 Thess 1:11 "that God may fulfill every good resolve (→ εὐδοκία 2) and work of faith by his power," lacks any particular theological profundity (cf. Acts 3:2).

The interpretation of Col 1:24 is still disputed: "Paul" rejoices in his sufferings for the sake of the Colossians and thus *completes* (so RSV) in his own flesh what is lacking in Christ's affliction (ἀνταναπληρῶ τὰ ὑστερήματα τῶν θλίψεων τοῦ Χριστοῦ). The *crux interpretum* is the meaning of θλίψεις Χριστοῦ. Does this refer to the afflictions of the earthly Jesus, including his Passion (J. Gnilka, *Col* [HTKNT] 97f.), or in apocalyptic imagery to the eschatological tribulations as the distress of the Messiah, and thus concretely the afflictions of "Paul" (E. Lohse, *Col* [Hermeneia] 68-70; see also E. Schweizer, *Col* [Eng. tr., 1982] 105-6: "difficulties undertaken for the sake of Christ; and these difficulties alone allow the proclamation to become effective in such a way as to let faith attain its fulness among the Colossians")? If "the afflictions of Christ" refers (also) to the Passion of Jesus, then the *completion* of those afflictions through "Paul" would be a theologically untenable glorification of the apostle by one of his followers, even if 2 Cor 4:10f. also

stands behind the statement. The argument of Schweizer (*op. cit.* 84) that the Passion of Jesus cannot be meant here because θλῖψις is never used in this sense in the rest of the NT fails to see that the possible unique usage in Colossians must not necessarily be identical with the rest of the NT occurrences of the word.   H. Hübner

πλήρωμα, ατος, τό *plērōma* fullness; fulfillment*

1. Occurrences in the NT — 2. Meaning — 3. Πλήρωμα as a theological term — a) Paul — b) The deutero-Pauline material — c) John

Lit.: P. BENOIT, "Leib, Haupt und Pleroma in den Gefangenschaftsbriefen," *idem, Exegese und Theologie* (1965) 246-79. — R. BULTMANN, *John* (Eng. tr., 1971) 77, n.1. — G. DELLING, *TDNT* VI, 298-305. — J. ERNST, *Pleroma und Pleroma Christi* (BU 5, 1970). — C. A. EVANS, "The Meaning of πλήρομα in Nag Hammadi," *Bib* 65 (1984) 259-65. — A. FEUILLET, *DBSup* VIII, 18-40. — J. GNILKA, *Eph* (HTKNT, [2]1977) 97-99, 105-9. — H. HEGERMANN, *Die Vorstellung vom Schöpfungsmittler im hellenistischen Judentum und Christentum* (TU 82, 1961) 105-9. — H. JONAS, *Gnosis und spätantiker Geist* I ([3]1964) 362-75. — H. LANGKAMMER, "Die Einwohnung der 'absoluten Seinsfülle' in Christus. Bemerkungen zu Kol 1,19," *BZ* 12 (1968) 258-63. — A. LINDEMANN, *Die Aufhebung der Zeit* (SNT 12, 1975) 59-63, 201-4. — E. LOHSE, *Col / Phlm* (Hermeneia, 1971) 99-101. — J. J. MEUZELAAR, *Der Leib des Messias* (GTB 35, 1961) 130-42. — G. MÜNDERLEIN, "Die Erwählung durch das Pleroma," *NTS* 8 (1961/62) 264-76. — F. MUSSNER, *Christus, das All und die Kirche* (TTS 5, [2]1969) 46-64. — P. D. OVERFIELD, "Pleroma: A Study in Content and Context," *NTS* 25 (1978 /79) 384-96. — I. DE LA POTTERIE, "Le Christ, Plérôme de l'Église (Eph 1:22-23)," *Bib* 58 (1977) 500-524. — For further bibliography → πληρόω; see *TWNT* X, 1236f.

1. Πλήρωμα occurs 17 times in the NT: once in Matthew, 3 times in Mark, once in John, and 6 times each in Paul and the deutero-Pauline letters (Colossians and Ephesians).

2. Πλήρωμα, like πληρόω, is derived from πλήρης and in accordance with its basic meaning signifies *fullness, fulfillment.* In the NT this fundamental meaning usually has theological significance (→ 3). The subst. πλήρωμα can stand for the adj. πλήρης: δώδεκα κοφίνων πληρώματα, "twelve baskets *full*" (Mark 6:43 [Matt 14:20 changes this to δώδεκα κοφίνους πλήρεις]; similarly Mark 8:20). In Mark 2:21 par. Matt 9:16 πλήρωμα is that which "fills" the tear in a garment, thus a *patch* (in a derogatory sense). NT use of πλήρωμα has almost no background in the LXX, where it is used almost exclusively in ἡ γῆ/θάλασσα καὶ τὸ πλήρωμα αὐτῆς, "the earth/sea and its *fullness* [i.e., all that exists and dwells in it]" or in similar expressions (e.g., Ps 23:1 LXX, quoted in 1 Cor 10:26).

3.a) In Paul πλήρωμα τῶν ἐθνῶν, "the *full number* of the Gentiles" (so RSV), in Rom 11:25 is a theological concept related to Paul's mission within the framework of the discussion of Israel in Romans 9–11: Within God's salvation plan the *full number* of the Gentiles is the "prerequisite" for the saving of all Israel (vv. 11, 26). Tὸ πλήρωμα τοῦ χρόνου, "the *full* time" (Gal 4:4), is the eschatologically qualified time of salvation of the Christ-event, whereby χρόνος almost acquires the sense of → καιρός (3). Paul calls love πλήρωμα νόμου, the *"fulfilling of the law"* (Rom 13:10), and thus recalls the Pauline phrase → πληρόω (3.b) τὸν νόμον. According to Rom 15:29 Paul wants to come to the Romans ἐν πληρώματι εὐλογίας Χριστοῦ, "in the fullness of the blessing of Christ," i.e., "with all the power he has been given and therefore with the fulness of the gospel" (E. Käsemann, *Rom* [Eng. tr., 1980] 402). In 1 Cor 10:26 he strengthens his theologoumenon concerning the fundamental purity of meat sacrificed to idols (→ εἴδωλον 4.b) by referring to Ps 23:1 LXX (→ 2).

b) Πλήρωμα is a central christological term in the deutero-Pauline Epistles. In Col 1:19 πᾶν τὸ πλήρωμα is the subj. of εὐδόκησεν (*contra* Lindemann 62, n.69): It pleased the divine "fullness in its entirety" (Lohse 99: "the entire fulness of deity"; E. Schweizer, *Col* [Eng. tr., 1982] 78f., weakens it to "the whole *fulness* of the powers of grace") to dwell in Christ and thus to effect reconciliation through him (*contra* Benoit 273ff.; Langkammer 262: "the absolute fullness of being"; see also Ernst 72-105). Πᾶν τὸ πλήρωμα τῆς θεότητος, "the whole *fullness* of deity" that dwells in Christ σωματικῶς (either "actually, essentially" or in the sense of the incarnation) according to Col 2:9 interprets 1:19 by recourse to Genesis.

The ecclesiological significance of πλήρωμα already noticeable in Colossians is developed further in Ephesians. The Church as the body of Christ is τὸ πλήρωμα τοῦ τὰ πάντα ἐν πᾶσιν πληρουμένου, "the *fullness* of him who fills all in all" (1:23; → πληρόω 3.c). The addressees should be filled εἰς πᾶν τὸ πλήρωμα τοῦ θεοῦ, "with all the fullness of God" (3:19), and should advance εἰς μέτρον ἡλικίας τοῦ πληρώματος τοῦ Χριστοῦ, "to the measure of the stature [set by God] of the *fulness* of Christ" (4:13). In this way in Ephesians the *fullness* of God and the *fullness* of Christ complement one another. Eph 1:10 speaks of the πλήρωμα τῶν καιρῶν, the "fullness of time," and thus echoes Gal 4:4. In Ephesians, therefore, πλήρωμα possesses both spatial and temporal dimensions.

In dealing with the question of the origin of deutero-Pauline use of πλήρωμα, we must differentiate between its theological roots on the one hand, which doubtlessly lay with Paul himself (for passages not employing the πλήρωμα-motif cf., e.g., 1 Cor 8:6 with Col 1:15-20), and its religio-historical derivation on the other. In Valentinian Gnosticism, above all, πλήρωμα is a dominant concept. Even if, however, the Valentinian understanding of πλήρωμα could be traced back to hypothetically reconstructed pagan and pre-Gnostic movements of the 1st cent. A.D., this would still not contribute significantly to our understanding of

πλήρωμα in the deutero-Pauline letters, since in Valentinian Gnosticism God does not himself belong to the pleroma. The pleroma constitutes rather the fullness of emanations from God (Hippolytus *Haer.* vi.29.1ff.).

One could probably more easily reconstruct a common root for the deutero-Pauline πλήρωμα and that of the Hermetic writings, since in *Corp. Herm.* vi.4 God is called πλήρωμα τοῦ ἀγαθοῦ, "the fullness of the good," as opposed to the πλήρωμα τῆς κακίας, the fullness of the cosmos or world. According to xvi.3 God is identical with the πλήρωμα, though admittedly in an almost pantheistic sense. We can probably agree with Lohse (58): "The Christian community took up the word 'pleroma' from the Hellenistic milieu in order to speak of the fullness of God which decided to dwell in this One. This, however, transferred the term from the context of cosmology into that of soteriology."

c) The author of the Gospel of John operates as an essentially non-Gnostic author with (pre[?]-)Gnostic categories. But πλήρωμα in John 1:16 ("from his *fullness* have we all received, grace upon grace") should probably not be considered a Gnostic concept (correctly R. Schnackenburg, *John* [Eng. tr., 1968] I, 275).

H. Hübner

πλησίον *plēsion* near, close by; subst.: neighbor*

1. Use in the NT — 2. As a prep. — 3. As a subst. — 4. Matt 5:43; Luke 10:29

Lit.: J. BECKER, *Untersuchungen zur Entstehungsgeschichte der Test XII* (1970) 377-401.—K. BERGER, *Die Gesetzesauslegung Jesu* I: *Markus und Parallelen* (WMANT 40, 1972) 100-115 and index s.v. — E. BISER, "Wer ist mein Nächster?" *GuL* 48 (1975) 406-14. — BDF §§184; 266. — R. BULTMANN, "Das christliche Gebot der Nächstenliebe," *idem, Glauben* I, 229-44. — H. COHEN, "Der Nächste. Bibelexegese und Literaturgeschichte," *idem, Jüdische Schriften* I (1924) 182-95. — J. D. M. DERRETT, "The Parable of the Good Samaritan," *idem, Law in the NT* (1970) 208-27. — G. DOWNEY, "Who is my Neighbor? The Greek and Roman Answer," *ATR* 47 (1965) 3-15. — G. EICHHOLZ, *Jesus Christus und der Nächste* (1955). — R. EULENSTEIN, "'Und wer ist mein Nächster?' Lk 10,25-37 in der Sicht eines klassischen Philologen," *TGl* 67 (1977) 127-45. — U. FALKENROTH, *DNTT* I, 258-59. — J. FICHTNER, "Der Begriff des 'Nächsten' im AT mit einem Ausblick auf Spätjudentum und NT," *WuD* 4 (1955) 23-52. — E. FUCHS, "Was heißt: 'Du sollst deinen Nächsten lieben wie dich selbst'?" *idem, Aufsätze* II, 1-20. — H. GREEVEN and J. FICHTNER, *TDNT* VI, 311-18. — M. GÜDEMANN, "Jüdische und christliche Nächstenliebe," *MGWJ* 37 (1893) 153-64. — W. GÜNTHER, *DNTT* I, 254-58. — K. HAACKER, *DNTT* III, 449-66. — K. HRUBY, "L'amour du prochain dans la pensée juive," *NRT* 91 (1969) 493-516. — H. HÜBNER, "Das ganze und das eine Gesetz," *KD* 21 (1975) 239-56. — *idem, Law in Paul's Thought* (1984) esp. 36f., 83-87, 134-36. — M. KATTEN, "Um das Gebot der Nächstenliebe," *MGWJ* 79 (1935) 209-23. — J. KÜHLEWEIN, *THAT* II, 786-91. — O. MICHEL, "Das Gebot der Nächstenliebe in der Verkündigung Jesu," *Zur sozialen Entscheidung* (ed. N. Koch; 1947) 53-101. — G. MOLIN, "Mt 5,43 und das Schrifttum von Qumran," *FS Bardtke* 150-52. — W. MONSELEWSKI, *Der barmherzige Sa-*

mariter. Eine auslegungsgeschichtliche Untersuchung zu Lk 10,25-37 (1967). — F. MUSSNER, "Der Begriff des 'Nächsten' in der Verkündigung Jesu," *TTZ* 64 (1955) 91-99. — A. NISSEN, *Gott und der Nächste im antiken Judentum* (WUNT 15, 1974) 161-342. — G. VON RAD, "Brothers and Neighbor in the Old Testament," *idem, God at Work in Israel* (1980) 183-93. — C. H. RATSCHOW, "Agape, Nächstenliebe und Bruderliebe," *ZST* 21 (1950/52) 160-82. — B. REICKE, "Der barmherzige Samariter," FS Stählin 103-9. — H. RINGGREN, *TDOT* I, 188-93. — H. M. SCHENKE, "Jakobsbrunnen—Josephsgrab—Sychar," *ZDPV* 84 (1968) 159-84. — G. SELLIN, "Lukas als Gleichniserzähler: die Erzählung vom barmherzigen Samariter (Lk 10,25-37)," *ZNW* 65 (1974) 166-89; 66 (1975) 19-66. — J. SOUČEK, "Der Bruder und der Nächste," *Hören und Handeln* (FS E. Wolf, 1962) 362-71. — L. P. TRUDINGER, "Once Again Now, 'Who is my Neighbour?' " *EvQ* 48 (1976) 160-63. — N. H. YOUNG, "Once Again Now, 'Who is my Neighbour?' A Comment," *EvQ* 49 (1977) 178f. — For further bibliography see *TWNT* X, 1237f.

1. The adv. πλησίον is used in the NT as a prep. with gen. and as a subst. (always sg.). The NT thus offers only a limited look at the possible uses of this word during the 1st cent. A.D.

2. The only definite NT example of prep. use is in John 4:5, where John locates the place Sychar by describing it as *"near* the field that Jacob gave to his son Joseph." Today Sychar is usually identified with the contemporary town of Askar and the intended location with the area around the contemporary "well of Jacob." This is philologically possible since the distance between the two places (*ca.* 1 km.) is comparable to other verifiable distances expressed by πλησίον (cf. Josephus *B.J.* iv.158: *ca.* 5 km.; *Vita* 234: *ca.* 5 Roman miles = 7-8 km.). It is important here that the location of the well is thought of as the better-known point of orientation (John 4:6); this allusion to local tradition thus becomes literarily accessible for the first time here (cf. Gen 33:19; 48:22 LXX; Josh 24:32 LXX). Concerning the portrayal of this sort of situation cf. also Josephus *Ant.* 257 (Moses in Midian). On Luke 10:36 → 4.

3. Of the 16 occurrences of subst. use, 12 are in the context of the love commandment and the other 4 also in ethical-legal contexts.

a) Sentences with the subj. ἕκαστος and a form of ὁ πλησίον as the obj. occur in Rom 15:2; Eph 4:25; Heb 8:11 v.l. (quoting Jer 31:34 or 38:34 LXX v.l.). These derive from use of Heb. 'îš with *rēaʻ* to indicate reciprocal behavior (Kühlewein 789); cf. Josephus *B.J.* v.295; Philo *Conf.* 1; *Abr.* 40; *Vit. Mos.* i.137.

b) Without generalization and merely for the sake of reference to the rules of community life ὁ πλησίον (like → ἕτερος [2]) can designate one's *actual counterpart* in a specific interaction (so Acts 7:27; Jas 4:12).

c) The commandment to love one's *neighbor* is cited from Lev 19:18 in Matt 5:43; 19:19; 22:39; Mark 12:31;

Luke 10:27; Rom 13:9; Gal 5:14; Jas 2:8. Mark 12:33 and Rom 13:10 alter and interpret the preceding quotation. In Luke 10:29 the commandment is rendered problematical and then strengthened and interpreted in the following narrative.

In Matt 22:40 (with the commandment to love God from Deut 6:5); Rom 13:8-10; and Gal 5:14 the commandment to love one's *neighbor* represents the whole Torah. This was exegetically expedient since in many OT legal and parenetic texts ὁ πλησίον designates one's counterpart to whom ethically determined behavior is due. (This is the case four times just in the second table of the Decalogue.) The generalized commandment to love one's neighbor does not thereby replace the individual commandments concerning social matters, but rather complements them with a comprehensive positive goal, since they have largely the negative form of prohibition (cf. Matt 19:19). The historical beginnings and theoretical presuppositions of this change in understanding of the Torah are disputed (cf. Berger, Hübner, Nissen, and others). Matt 5:43 and Luke 10:29, 36 are the focal points of this discussion to the extent that it concerns the understanding of the term ὁ πλησίον (→ 4).

4.a) In Matt 5:43 ὁ πλησίον is qualified by being contrasted with ἐχθρός and by being replaced by οἱ ἀγαπῶντες ὑμᾶς in v. 46. It therefore has the meaning *friend.* Where *rēaʻ* in the OT clearly has this meaning (cf. Kühlewein 788), however, the LXX prefers other renderings (φίλος in Mic 7:5; Prov 14:20; 1 Chr 27:33; οἱ φιλοῦντες in Lam 1:2; ἑταῖρος in 2 Kgdms 15:37; 16:16; 3 Kgdms 4:5). These OT texts are not legal or parenetif; rather, "as a rule, *rēaʻ* is to be understood in the wider sense as 'fellow person, neighbor.' . . . Even if practically speaking this usually refers only to members of one's own people, *rēaʻ* thus by no means has become a technical term for members of the people of God" (Kühlewein 788f.).

A widely accepted interpretation nonetheless sees Matt 5:43-47 (in the framework of a comprehensive understanding of the "antitheses" in the Sermon on the Mount going back to F. C. Baur) as evidencing a confrontation between Jesus' ethics and the OT and Jewish tradition. Arguments to the contrary are: a) that in 5:46f. Jesus describes the behavior in question as typical of tax collectors and Gentiles, b) that there are no examples of a doctrinal tradition such as that in 5:43b in the OT or Judaism (including Qumran; cf. Molin; cf. on the other hand Exod 23:4f.; Prov 25:21; Job 31:29f.), and c) that in statements of ethical postulates by Jewish authors of the 1st cent. A.D. ὁ πλησίον clearly refers to one's fellow human beings in general (cf. among others Josephus *B.J.* vii.260; Philo *Plant.* 106; *Praem.* 100; *Som.* ii.79; *Virt.* 116; *Vit. Mos.* i.247). What is quoted in Matt 5:43 and criticized in vv. 44ff. might be a popular phrase derived from a limitation of the meaning of *rēaʻ* in the vernacular (cf. Levy IV, 447f., 458f. on *rēaʻ* and *rᵉʻût;* see also *m. 'Abot* 6:1).

b) This suggests the probable background for the question in Luke 10:29, a question that in any case should not be overrated, since Luke introduces it as an artificial complication of the commandment and not as a genuine request for instruction (cf. Eulenstein and others).

The incongruency between Luke 10:29b and 10:36 is obvious and much discussed. The surprising use of πλησίον for the active role within a specific interaction departs from the framework of the linguistic tradition associated with Lev 19:18. The usual tr. of γίνομαι πλησίον τινός in 10:36 as "be/become someone's neighbor," while certainly possible, is nonetheless extremely questionable since this turn of phrase in Josephus and Philo nowhere has any other meaning than "approach a thing or person" or "come closer to something or someone" (cf. Josephus *B.J.* vi.258, 346; *Ant.* i.254; ii.279; v.225, 245; xiv.445; without gen. in *B.J.* ii.325; *Ant.* iv.458; *Vita* 167; Philo *Virt.* 40; *Vit. Mos.* i.228). Luke 10:36 thus appears to combine the spatial-concrete fundamental meaning of πλησίον with the ethical concerns of the traditional understanding of "neighbor": One should "go toward" one's fellow human being whose need one has seen (instead of "seeing and continuing on one's way," one should "see, empathize, approach, and help"). Whereas the commandments and maxims for behavior toward one's neighbor generally end with a rule against aggression (cf. among others Rom 13:10), Luke 10:36 gives to the norm a more intensive turn toward one's fellow human being—doubtlessly in an intentional response to the question concerning eternal life (v. 25). The apparent wordplay between v. 29 and v. 36 appears at first to be possible only in Greek (J. Jeremias [*Die Sprache des Lukas-Evangeliums* (1980) 192f.] considers v. 36 redactional); it is, however, also possible on the basis of the relationship between *rēaʿ*, "neighbor," and *rāʿâ*, "associate oneself with."

The whole debate over what was alleged to be an originally particularistic concept of one's neighbor, a concept then expanded universally by Jesus, took place unfortunately under the influence of the Germ. tr. of ὁ πλησίον with a superlative form *(der Nächste)*, which implied a distinction between greater and lesser distance (cf. Cohen 193). In opposition to this is, e.g., Josephus *Ant.* xv.348, where οἱ πλησίοι are not fellow citizens (members of the predatory tribes living in Trachonitis), but the inhabitants of adjoining lands (cf. xv.345). The "kinsmen" in Ps 37:12 LXX are called οἱ ἔγγιστα (Heb. *qᵉrôbay*), and the "nearest city" in Josephus *Ant.* iv.221 is ἡ πλησιαιτάτη πόλις. In view of these passages and considering the effect this choice of words has had historically, once must ask whether the tr. of ὁ πλησίον with "neighbor" (or Germ. *der Nächste*) should be maintained.

K. Haacker

πλησμονή, ῆς, ἡ *plēsmonē*   gratification, indulgence*

Col 2:23: πρὸς πλησμονὴν τῆς σαρκός, "to indulgence of the flesh." "Indulgence is here the opposite of moderation and thus to be interpreted as over-indulgence" (J. Gnilka, *Col* [HTKNT] 161).

πλήσσω *plēssō*   strike*

Fig. and pass. in Rev 8:12, of celestial bodies that, having been struck (ἐπλήγη), lose a third of their light. → πληγή (blow; plague).

πλοιάριον, ου, τό *ploiarion*   small ship, boat*

Diminutive of → πλοῖον, though probably no longer perceived as such, since πλοιάριον is used in Mark 3:9 and πλοῖον in 4:1. John 6:22, 24; 21:8. In John 6:23 it is unclear whether one should read πλοῖα (so, e.g., 𝔭⁷⁵ ℵ B) or πλοιάρια (so, e.g., A D Koine). Luke 5:2 v.l. has πλοιάρια in place of πλοῖα. All these passages refer to boats on the Sea of Galilee. → πλοῖον 1, 3.

πλοῖον, ου, τό *ploion*   ship, boat

1. General — 2. The call narrative in Mark 1:16-20 par. — 3. The miraculous catch of fish, Luke 5:1-11; John 21:1-14 — 4. Miraculous rescues at sea, Mark 4:35-41 par.; 6:45-52 par. — 5. The pre-Markan miracles collection — 6. Acts — 7. Figurative and symbolic usage

Lit.: DALMAN, *Arbeit* VI, 351-56, 363-70. — E. HILGERT, *BHH* III, 1694-96. — *idem, The Ship and Other Related Symbols in the NT* (1962). — K. GOLDAMMER, "Navis Ecclesiae," *ZNW* 40 (1941) 76-86. — R. KRATZ, *Rettungswunder. Motiv-, traditions- und formkritische Aufarbeitung einer biblischen Gattung* (1979). — R. PESCH, *Der reiche Fischfang Lk 5,1-11/Jo 21,1-14. Wundergeschichte — Berufungserzählung — Erscheinungsbericht* (1969). — *idem, Mark* I (HTKNT, 1976). — H. RAHNER, "Antenna Crucis," *Symbole der Kirche. Die Ekklesiologie der Väter* (1964) 237-564.

1. As in classical Greek, the NT usually does not differentiate between small vessels used for fishing or inland transport and larger oceangoing vessels used for "overseas" passenger transport, distribution and trade, or military needs. Whereas Acts presupposes larger Mediterranean ships, the Gospels generally refer to smaller boats propelled by oars, perhaps augmented by sails (for details cf. Dalman). No special attention is given to dimensions or descriptions, and technical nautical details are noted only in Acts 27. Πλοῖον and its diminutive form πλοιάριον occur almost exclusively in narratives of events in sea or lake settings, usually in typical genres. Symbolic usage of πλοῖον is rare in the NT.

2. Boats naturally play a role in the setting of the call narrative in Mark 1:16-20 par. Matt 4:18-22 (Luke 5:1-11), since this narrative presupposes—in a way hardly to be doubted historically—that Simon and probably also his brother Andrew and the sons of Zebedee (?) were fishermen. Call narratives portray the person being called as he engages in his vocation. The phrase "fishers of people" in Mark 1:17 is certainly an authentic saying of Jesus, while the parallel nature of the call scenes is literary embellishment. Matthew radicalizes the concept

of discipleship further by having *only* the father remain in the boat (4:22).

3. Boats are also understandably part of the narrative of the miraculous catch of fish that occurs in two variations of an older basic form in Luke 5:1-11 and John 21:1-14. Apparently Luke combines the miracle narrative (vv. 1, 4b, 5-7, 11, 8-9) with material from Mark 2:13; 3:9; 4:1-3, 35 and the call narrative in Mark 1:16-20. The redactor of the Johannine addendum interweaves the variation he had before him (vv. 2-4a, 6, 11) and an epiphany (cf. vv. 5, 10) and subordinates these to his redactional intentions (cf. vv. 1, 2, 14) (for a reconstruction cf. Pesch, *Fischfang*). The alternation between πλοῖον and πλοιάριον does not call for literary-critical distinctions (cf. already Mark 3:9).

4. Instructions from the miracle worker to put out to sea are an aspect of narratives of miraculous sea rescues. In Mark 4:37f. (even more strongly in Matt 8:24) the boat threatened by wind and waves and Jesus asleep on a cushion in the stern (where the helmsman would be) parallel the story of Jonah: Jesus acts as the one who calms the storm, thus transcending the story of Jonah and playing the role taken by Yahweh in Jonah 1. Matthew alters the rescue miracle into a narrative concerning discipleship: He shows the Church paradigmatically that it can count on its Lord's "guidance" in all worldly storms. This constitutes a symbolic understanding of the boat as the "ship of the Church," an interpretive device extensively developed in patristic exegesis (cf. Rahner; Goldammer).

In the narrative of Jesus walking on the water (Mark 6:45-52 par. Matt 14:22-33) motifs of rescue miracles are overlaid with those of epiphany. The christological culmination occurs in Matt 14:33: "Those in the boat" confess that Jesus is the Son of God.

5. Boats serve Jesus and his disciples as a means for crossing the Sea of Galilee and appear in Mark primarily in redactional transitions (Mark 4:1 par. Matt 13:2; Mark 4:36 par. Matt 8:23/Luke 8:22; Mark 5:2, presupposed in Matt 8:28/Luke 8:26f.; Mark 5:18 par. Luke 8:37; Mark 5:21; 6:32 par. Matt 14:13; Mark 6:45 par. Matt 14:22; Mark 6:54, in the same sense Matt 14:34), which apparently served already in a pre-Markan collection of miracle stories to join individual narratives (the summaries in 3:7-12 and 6:53-56 and the narratives in 4:35-39, 41; 5:1-20, 21-43; 6:32-44; 6:45-51). Some of these narratives were already bound to a setting by or on the Sea of Galilee (→ 4). Aspects of form, content, and theology that justify the hypothesis of this collection are geographical framework, the presence of the most important miracle types, concentric structure, OT background, unified christological stylistic framework (increasingly

miraculous miracles; Jesus in the role of Yahweh), and Jewish or Jewish-Christian perspectives. The setting of the collection itself might have been a Gentile mission centered in Galilee and characterized by Jewish Christian circles (cf. esp. 5:1-20; Pesch, *Mark* I, 277-81).

6. Acts relates Paul's journeys on commercial ships: on a ship traveling to Phoenicia that unloads its cargo in Tyre (21:2), as a prisoner on a ship from Adramyttium (27:2), and on an Alexandrian grain ship under the sign of the Twin Brothers (the Dioscuri), who were known as helpers in time of distress at sea and as navigation stars (27:6; 28:11). In chapter 27, which portrays Paul's shipwreck and rescue and is enriched with both specialized nautical vocabulary and rescue miracle motifs, Luke apparently has used more extensive sources (hardly a self-contained travelogue). The idea of portraying Paul's shipwreck and rescue was precipitated perhaps by biographical material and may well be a product of Luke himself, who at the end of Acts and in a symbolic fashion wanted to create a counterpart to the death and resurrection of Jesus at the end of his Gospel. Ναῦς is used in 27:41 synonymously with πλοῖον. Σκάφη is used of the lifeboat (concerning Acts 27 cf. Kratz 320-50).

7. In Jas 3:4 tongue and speech are compared to rudder and ship. Rev 8:9 announces the eschatological destruction of a third of the sea, of living creatures, and of ships on the sea, whereby the sea and everything belonging to it (cf. Ps 104:25f.) is viewed in apocalyptic-dualistic fashion as anti-divine. In 18:19 the fall of Babylon-Rome is portrayed metaphorically with allusions to Ezekiel 27.

                                             R. Kratz

πλόος, ου, ὁ *ploos* navigation, voyage
Non-contracted form (second declension!) of → πλοῦς.

πλοῦς, οός, ὁ *plous* navigation, voyage*

For declension see BDF §52. Acts uses gen. πλοός (27:9) and acc. πλοῦν (21:7; 27:10); all three occurrences are in "we"- narratives.

πλούσιος, 3 *plousios* rich*
πλουσίως *plousiōs* abundantly, richly*
πλουτέω *plouteō* be (or become) rich*
πλουτίζω *ploutizō* make rich*
πλοῦτος, ου, ὁ/τό *ploutos* wealth, abundance*

1. Occurrences in the NT — 2. Mark — 3. Matthew — 4. Luke — 5. The Pauline corpus — a) The genuine letters — b) Colossians and Ephesians — c) The Pastoral Epistles — d) Hebrews — 6. The Catholic Epistles — 7. Revelation — a) Literal usage — b) Fig. usage

Lit.: K. BERGER, *Die Gesetzesauslegung Jesu* (1972) 396-460. — K. BORNHÄUSER, *Der Christ und seine Habe nach dem NT* (1936). — H. VON CAMPENHAUSEN, *Die Askese im Urchristentum* (1949). — R. CASSIDY, *The Social and Political Stance in Luke's Gospel* (Diss. Berkeley, 1976). — G. DAUTZENBERG, "Biblische Perspektiven zu Arbeit und Eigentum," *Handbuch der christlichen Ethik* 2 (1978) 343-62. — P. DAVIDS, "The Poor Man's Gospel," *Themelios* 1 (1976) 37-41. — H. J. DEGENHARDT, *Lukas, Evangelist der Armen* (1965). — M. DIBELIUS, "Das soziale Motiv im NT," *idem, Botschaft* I, 178-203. — M. DIBELIUS and H. GREEVEN, *Jas* (Hermeneia, 1976) 39-45. — H.-M. DION, "La notion paulinienne de 'Richesse de Dieu' et ses sources," *ScEc* 18 (1966) 139-48. — J. DUPONT, "Pour vous le Christ s'est fait pauvre (2 Co 8,7.9.13-15)," *AsSeign* 44 (1969) 32-37. — W. EGGER, *Nachfolge als Weg zum Leben* (1979). — F. HAUCK, *Die Stellung des Urchristentums zu Arbeit und Geld* (1921). — F. HAUCK and W. KASCH, *TDNT* VI, 318-32. — M. HENGEL, *Property and Riches in the Early Church* (1987). — L. T. JOHNSON, *The Literary Function of Possessions in Luke-Acts* (1977). — R. KOCH, "Die Wertung des Besitzes im Lukasevangelium," *Bib* 38 (1957) 151-69. — *idem, SacVb* 775-80. — W. G. KÜMMEL, "Der Begriff des Eigentums im NT," *idem*, I, 271-77. — S. LÉGASSE, *DBSup* X, 645-87. — *idem, L'appel du riche (Marc 10,17-31 et par.)* (1966). — E. LOHSE, "Jesu Bußruf an die Reichen," FS Kümmel (1985) 159-63. — A. DI MARCO, "La 'ricchezza' in S. Paolo," *Laurentianum* 18 (1977) 70-115. — E. NEUHÄUSLER, *Anspruch und Antwort Gottes* (1962), esp. 170-85. — B. NOACK, "Jakobus wider die Reichen," *ST* 18 (1964) 10-25. — E. PERCY, *Die Botschaft Jesu* (1953), esp. 19-115. — SCHELKLE, *Theology* III, esp. 297-312. — W. SCHMITHALS, "Lukas — Evangelist der Armen," *TViat* 12 (1973/74) 153-67. — SCHNACKENBURG, *Botschaft*, esp. 91-100, 290-95. — G. SCHNEIDER, *Luke* (ÖTK, 1977) 342-45. — *idem, Acts* I (HTKNT, 1980) 290-95. — F. SELTER, *DNTT* II, 840-45. — F. VATTIONI, *Beatitudini, Povertà, Ricchezza* (1966). — N. WALTER, "Zur Analyse von Mc 10,17-31," *ZNW* 53 (1962) 206-18. — For further bibliography → πτωχός; see *TWNT* X, 1238.

1. This word group is absent from John (including 1–3 John) and Acts. It occurs most frequently in the Synoptics (16 occurrences; 3 in the Pauline corpus, 5 in James, and 4 in Revelation). The adv. πλουσίως occurs only in Colossians, the Pastorals, and 2 Peter (4 occurrences altogether), πλουτίζω only in Paul (3 occurrences), and πλουτέω in Luke (2), in the Pauline corpus (5), and in Revelation (5).

2. The provocative statement in Mark 10:25 (cf. v. 23) should be understood in its present context as a generalization commenting on vv. 17-22 (Egger 116f.). That it does not constitute a rejection in principle of the rich can be seen from vv. 24b, 26f., according to which it is impossible in the larger sense for any human being to attain salvation. Vv. 24b-27 may have been an independently transmitted unit to which the transitional vv. 23, 24a were prefaced when it was combined with vv. 29f. or vv. 17-22. Thus in v. 25 the original "man" might have been replaced by "rich man" (Walter 209f.; cf.

Berger 403f.). The context, however, points out the particular danger for the rich person, who finds it difficult to renounce possessions (vv. 17-22), a demand that can be made on him in the concrete instance of his discipleship to Jesus (after the resurrection *imitatio* becomes the paradigm of faith; cf. also vv. 29f.). In addition, wealth in its own turn can create deceptive allegiances that can render unfruitful one's acceptance of the word (4:19). The brief mention of "many rich people" in 12:41 (par. Luke 21:1) serves to throw the contrasting example of the poor widow into relief.

3. Matthew 27:57 (unlike Mark) quite unaffectedly introduces Joseph of Arimathea, who has become a disciple, as a rich man. 13:22, however, warns against the cares of the world that make one succumb to the deception of wealth. Christian existence must be free of (secular) pagan cares and must be eschatologically directed (cf. 6:25-34), which for Matthew points to behavior in the sense of the greater righteousness of the Sermon on the Mount (cf. 5:20). It is in this sense that Matthew understands the call to discipleship to the young man (Mark 10) as a call to perfection (cf. Matt 19:21 [in contrast to Mark] with Matt 5:48), whose refusal paradigmatically illustrates the difficulty the rich have in entering into the kingdom (19:23f.).

4. Luke assumes an expressly critical posture toward the rich. Wealth, placed parallel with the cares (cf. 12:22-34) and joys of life (8:14), threatens to strangle the word of God. The rich farmer in 12:16 fails to see that the only important thing is to be rich toward God (πλουτέω, 12:21). Just how difficult it is for the rich to gain access to the kingdom of God (18:24f.) is shown by the ruler who fails to follow Jesus because he is very rich (v. 23). It is thus no accident that Jesus' opponents think and act primarily like rich people (16:14; 11:39; 20:47; cf. Hauck and Kasch 328). Luke juxtaposes the blessing of the poor (→ πτωχός) and the (probably traditional) lamentation about the rich, which is based less on the inherent danger of wealth than on the coming eschatological reversal of fortune (6:24). God sends the rich (πλουτοῦντες) away empty (1:53). Luke 16:19-31, however, shows that the Evangelist does not postulate an inescapable principle: The rich person (vv. 19, 21, 22) does not exist in isolation, but rather in the closest relationship with (in viewing distance of) the poor (vv. 20f., 23), so that the eschatological reversal (v. 25) can be understood as a heavenly establishment of the distance from the poor practiced during one's lifetime (vv. 20f., 26), i.e., it presupposes the responsibility of the rich.

In spite of all criticism, then, Luke does not reject wealth on principle. He demands rather appropriate behavior with "unrighteous mammon," behavior concerned with the heavenly future (cf. 12:21; 18:22), as he says in his comments (16:9-13) on the parable of the steward and the rich man (16:1). Above all, Luke thinks here of selfless charity (cf. 8:1-3). Hence one should invite not rich neighbors, but rather precisely the poor (14:12, 13). Just how generously those possessions (wealth) are to benefit them is illustrated by the rich tax collector Zacchaeus (19:2, 8). In other passages he even demands that one give all one's possessions to the poor (18:22; 12:33; cf. 14:33). Ascetic motives are hardly the driving force here (nor are particular instructions for officeholders, *contra* Degenhardt), but rather experiences of the Lukan community in its own distress (cf. Schmithals 159ff.): Confession of faith in Jesus could result in the loss of possessions; hence confession required at least willingness to do without possessions, just as conversely such willingness facilitated the confession itself. On Luke 21:1 par. Mark 12:41 → 2.

5. a) Characteristic of Paul's usage is the theological significance of this word group (concerning the original meaning "fullness of . . ." see Hauck and Kasch 319), in which it often functions to throw God's mercy into relief (as in Jewish tradition: cf. *2 Bar.* 59:6f.; 4 Ezra 7:132-39; and esp. 1QS 4:3; 1QH 4:32, 36f.; 6:9; 7:27, 30, 35; 9:8, 34; 10:21; 13:17; 15:16; 18:14). Rom 2:4 speaks of "the *riches* of his [God's] kindness and forbearance and patience." God makes known "the *riches* of his glory" in "the vessels of mercy" (9:23). A variation of this usage appears christologically motivated in Phil 4:19. The idea is straightforwardly christological in Rom 10:12: The Kyrios *is rich* for all (πλουτῶν εἰς πάντας) who call upon him (Jews and Greeks). In 11:12 the soteriological dimension comes into play as Paul understands the trespass of Israel, through which salvation has come to the Gentiles, as "*riches* for the world" or for the Gentiles, and on the other hand praises in 11:33 (cf. v. 32) the mystery of the salvation of all Israel (11:26) as "the depth of the *riches* and wisdom and knowledge of God."

Usage with χάρις is also understandable from the soteriological perspective. The gift of grace is seen in 1 Cor 1:5 as "enrichment" (πλουτισθῆναι) in Christ. A variation of this is then applied to the collection (which Paul understands as a result of God's grace; cf. 2 Cor 8:1; 9:8) in 2 Cor 8:2; 9:11 (*richness* of selfless giving or *enrichment* [πλουτιζόμενοι] for selfless giving).

The richness of being a Christian does, however, stand under an eschatological proviso (cf. the ironic "already you *have become rich* [ἐπλουτήσατε]!" in 1 Cor 4:8); it is embedded in the dialectic of the message of the cross (cf. 1 Cor 1:18-25; Phil 2:6-11): The grace of Christ is "that though he was *rich,* yet for your sake he became poor, so that by his poverty you might *become rich* (πλουτήσητε)" (2 Cor 8:9). Apostolic existence stands under this same dialectic (6:10, πλουτίζω).

b) Theological or christological-soteriological usage is also found in Colossians and Ephesians. Formally it is striking that almost always the neut. subst. τὸ πλοῦτος (masc. only in Eph 1:18) is used, frequently with gen. δόξης (Col 1:27; Eph 1:18; 3:16) and χάριτος (Eph 1:7; 2:7). On "the fullness of grace" cf. 1QS 4:4f.; 1QH 11:28-30; 12:14 (cf. K. G. Kuhn, *NTS* 7 [1960/61] 334-46, esp. 336f.).

As regards content, the proximity to the eschatological Christ mystery is noteworthy: Col 1:27 describes the revelation as "the *riches* of the glory of this mystery among the Gentiles." According to Eph 3:8 Paul has the task "to preach to the Gentiles the unsearchable *riches* of Christ." The cosmic extent of this event (cf. Eph 3:9f.) is a variation of the previously addressed idea that the union of all things in Christ (1:9f.) yields the dimension of the "riches of his [God's] grace" (1:7). Similarly, according to 2:7 the salvation activity of God, "who is *rich* in mercy" (2:4), has as its goal the demonstration to coming ages of "the immeasurable *riches* of his grace." The task of the Christian is a (more and more profound) knowledge of the mystery, "the *riches* of assured understanding" (Col 2:2). According to Eph 1:18 this knowledge refers to the "*riches* of his glorious inheritance in the saints." These passages also offer the context within which to understand the admonitions in Col 3:16 (adv.) and Eph 3:16 (subst.).

c) In the Pastoral Epistles, those who desire to *become rich* (1 Tim 6:9: οἱ βουλόμενοι πλουτεῖν) are strongly warned against the dangers that attend wealth. According to 1 Tim 6:17f. it is decisive for the rich that they not put their hope in the insecurity of wealth, but rather in God, who "*richly* [πλουσίως; cf. also Titus 3:6] furnishes us with everything to enjoy," and that they *be rich* (πλουτεῖν) in good deeds.

d) According to Heb 11:26 Moses became a witness of faith by sharing the ill-treatment of his people, since he considered the abuse suffered by Christ (see O. Michel, *Heb* [KEK] ad loc.) greater *wealth* than the treasures of Egypt.

6. In the Catholic Epistles this word group occurs in 2 Pet 1:11 (adv.) and James. Jas 1:10 admonishes the rich man ("brother"; cf. v. 9) to boast paradoxically in his humiliation (in death; cf. Luke 12:16-21; Psalms 49 and 73; Sir 11:18f.; *m. 'Abot* 4:4). For the *rich person* (now generic in 1:11) passes away like the grass (cf. Isa 40:6f.). Whereas 2:5 describes the poor as *rich* in faith (→ πτωχός), 2:6 characterizes the *rich* negatively by referring to prophetic motifs (cf. Amos 4:1; 8:4 and *passim*), though this is also prompted by the Church's concrete experience: The rich oppress Christians and drag them into court. 5:1 admonishes the *rich* to "weep and howl" for the miseries coming upon them (cf. Luke 6:24;

1 Enoch 96:5f.). *Riches* accumulated fraudulently (Jas 5:4-6) and senselessly rot, therefore (v. 2; cf. Matt 6:19), and will be evidence in court against the wealthy (v. 3).

7. Revelation speaks of both a) material and b) spiritual wealth.

a) In 6:15 the *rich* and the powerful and in 13:16 the *rich* and the poor are mentioned as social classes. Those from Babylon who have *grown rich* (πλουτέω, 18:3, 15, 19) cry out (v. 17) over the desolation of the wealth of the great city.

b) The church in Smyrna is *rich* in spite of its tribulation and poverty (2:9), whereas the church of Laodicea, which in 3:17 asserts "I am *rich*, I *have become rich* [πεπλούτηκα; cf. Hos 12:9; Zech 11:5]," even though in truth it is "wretched, pitiable, poor, blind, and naked," is counseled in 3:18 first to turn to God for help (H. Kraft, *Rev* [HNT] ad loc.) in order *to become rich*. In the doxology in 5:12 *wealth* (in the sense of divine abundance) is bequeathed to the Lamb.   H. Merklein

πλουσίως *plousiōs* abundantly, richly
→ πλούσιος.

πλουτέω *plouteō* be (or become) rich
→ πλούσιος.

πλουτίζω *ploutizō* make rich
→ πλούσιος.

πλοῦτος, ου, ὁ/τό *ploutos* wealth, abundance
→ πλούσιος.

πλύνω *plynō* wash*

Luke 5:2: washing of nets; Rev 7:14, of martyrs: ἔπλυναν τὰς στολὰς αὐτῶν (in the blood of the Lamb); similarly, 22:14, in a blessing: μακάριοι οἱ πλύνοντες τὰς στολὰς αὐτῶν.

πνεῦμα, ατος, τό *pneuma* breath, breeze, wind; spirit

1. Basic meaning and occurrences in the NT — 2. General usage — a) *Wind* — b) The human *spirit* — c) Evil *spirits* and other *spirits* — 3. As a t.t. for God's *Spirit* — a) Preliterary — b) Paul — c) Luke/Acts — d) John — e) Matt 28:19

Lit.: R. ALBERTZ and C. WESTERMANN, *THAT* II, 726-53. — C. K. BARRETT, *The Holy Spirit and the Gospel Tradition* (1975). — F. BAUMGÄRTEL, *TDNT* VI, 359-67. — G. R. BEASLEY-MURRAY, "Jesus and the Spirit," FS Rigaux 463-78. — H. S. BENJAMIN, "Pneuma in John and Paul," *BTB* 6 (1976) 27-48. — K. BERGER, *TRE* XII, 178-96. — W. BIEDER, "Pneumatische Aspekte im Hebräerbrief," FS Cullmann (1972) 251-59. —

P. BONNARD, "L'Esprit et l'Église selon le NT," *idem, Anamnesis* (1980) 51-60. — F. BOVON, *Luc le théologien* (1978) 211-54. — E. BRANDENBURGER, *Fleisch und Geist* (1968). — R. BULTMANN, *John* (1971) 138-40. — *idem, Theology* I, 41f., 153-64, 205-10. — H. CAZELLES, et al., *DBSup* XI, 126-398 (172-398 on the NT). — M. A. CHEVALLIER, *L'Esprit et le Messie dans le Bas-Judaisme et le NT* (1958). — *idem, Esprit de Dieu, paroles d'hommes* (1966). — *idem, Souffle de Dieu* (1978). — H. CROUZEL, *RAC* IX, 490-545. — P. DACQUINO, "Lo Spirito Santo ed il cristiano secondo Santo Paolo," *SPCIC* (AnBib 17/18, 1963) I, 119-29. — W. J. DALTON, *Christ's Proclamation to the Spirits* (1965). — G. DAUTZENBERG, *Urchristliche Prophetie* (1975) 122-48. — J. D. G. DUNN, *Baptism in the Holy Spirit* (1970). — *idem,* "2 Corinthians III.17 — 'The Lord is the Spirit,'" *JTS* 21 (1970) 309-20. — *idem,* "1 Corinthians 15:45 — Last Adam, Lifegiving Spirit," FS Moule 127-41. — *idem, Jesus and the Spirit* (1975). — *idem,* "Spirit and Fire-Baptism," *NovT* 24 (1972) 81-92. — J. DUPONT, "Ascension du Christ et don de l'Esprit, d'après Actes 2,33," FS Moule 219-28. — *idem, The Salvation of the Gentiles* (1979). — A. DUPREZ, "Note sur le rôle de l'Esprit-Saint dans la filiation du chrétien. A propos de Gal 4,6," *RSR* 52 (1964) 421-31. — A. GEORGE, "L'Esprit Saint dans l'oeuvre de Luc," *RB* 85 (1978) 500-542. — GOPPELT, *Theology* II, 118-24. — D. GREENWOOD, "The Lord is the Spirit: Some Considerations of 2 Cor 3:17," *CBQ* 34 (1972) 467-72. — F. HAHN, "Das biblische Verständnis des Heiligen Geistes," *Erfahrung und Theologie des Heiligen Geistes* (ed. C. Heitmann and H. Mühlen; 1974) 131-47. — *idem,* "Sendung des Geistes — Sendung der Jünger," *Universales Christentum angesichts einer pluralen Welt* (ed. A. Bsteh; 1976) 87-106. — G. L. HAYA-PRATS, *L'Esprit, force de l'Église. Sa nature et son activité d'après les Actes des Apôtres* (1975). — I. HERMANN, *Kyrios und Pneuma* (1961). — A. I. C. HERON, *The Holy Spirit* (1983). — M. E. ISAACS, *The Concept of Spirit. A Study of Pneuma in Hellenistic Judaism and its Bearing on the NT* (1976). — E. JACOB, *TDNT* IX, 628-31. — G. JOHNSTON, *The Spirit-Paraclete in the Gospel of John* (1970). — E. KAMLAH, *DNTT* III, 689-93. — E. KÄSEMANN, *Perspectives on Paul* (1971) 122-66. — H. KLEINKNECHT, *TDNT* VI, 334-59. — D.-A. KOCH, "Geistbesitz, Geistverleihung und Wundermacht. Erwägungen zur Tradition und zur lukanischen Redaktion in Act 8,5-25," *ZNW* 77 (1986) 64-82. — R. KOCH, "L'aspect eschatologique de l'Esprit du Seigneur d'après saint Paul," *SPCIC* (AnBib 17/18, 1963) I, 131-41. — J. KREMER, *Pfingstbericht und Pfingstgeschehen* (1973). — *idem,* "Jesu Verheißung des Geistes," FS Schürmann 247-76. — *idem,* "Denn der Buchstabe tötet, der Geist aber macht lebendig," FS Zimmermann 219-50. — G. KRETSCHMAR, "Himmelfahrt und Pfingsten," *ZKG* 66 (1954/55) 209-53. — *idem,* "Le développement de la doctrine du Saint-Esprit du NT à Nicée," *VC* 22 (1968) 5-55. — K. G. KUHN, "Jesus in Gethsemane," *EvT* 12 (1952/53) 260-85. — O. KUSS, *Der Römerbrief* II (²1963) 540-95. — E. LÖVESTAM, *Spiritus Blasphemia* (1968). — U. LUCK, "Historische Fragen zum Verhältnis von Kyrios und Pneuma bei Paulus," *TLZ* 85 (1960) 845-48. — K. MALY, "1 Kor 12,1-3, eine Regel zur Unterscheidung der Geister," *BZ* 10 (1966) 82-95. — P. W. MEYER, "The Holy Spirit in the Pauline Letters," *Int* 33 (1979) 3-18. — S. MORENZ, G. GERLEMAN, and E. KÄSEMANN, *RGG* II, 1268-79. — C. F. D. MOULE, "2Cor 3:18b. καθάπερ ἀπὸ κυρίου πνεύματος," FS Cullmann (1972) 231-37. — *idem, The Holy*

Spirit (1978). — C. D. G. MÜLLER, et al., *RAC* IX, 546-797. — K. NIEDERWIMMER, "Das Gebet des Geistes. Röm 8,26f.," *TZ* 20 (1964) 252-65. — *idem*, "Die Gegenwart des Geistes nach dem Zeugnis des NT," K. Niederwimmer, et al., *Unterscheidung der Geister* (Kirche zwischen Planen und Hoffen 7, 1972) 9-34. — R. PENNA, "Lo 'Spirito di Gesù' in Atti 16," *RivB* 20 (1972) 241-61. — F. PORSCH, *Anwalt der Glaubenden. Das Wirken des Geistes nach dem Zeugnis des Johannesevangeliums* (1978). — *idem*, *Pneuma und Wort. Ein exegetischer Beitrag zur Pneumatologie des Johannesevangeliums* (1974). — J. D. QUINN, "The Holy Spirit in the Pastoral Epistles," *Sin, Salvation, and the Spirit* (ed. D. Durken; 1979) 345-68. — H. RÄISÄNEN, "Das 'Gesetz des Glaubens' (Röm 3:27) und das 'Gesetz des Geistes' (Röm 8,2)," *NTS* 26 (1979/80) 101-17 (= *idem, The Torah and Christ* [1986] 95-118). — H. SAAKE, PW Suppl. XIV, 387-412. — *idem*, "Pneumatologia Paulina," *Catholica* 26 (1972) 212-23. — P. SCHÄFER, *Die Vorstellung vom Heiligen Geist in der rabbinischen Literatur* (1972). — F. J. SCHIERSE, "Die neutestamentliche Trinitätsoffenbarung," *MySal* II, 85-131. — H. SCHLIER, "Zum Begriff des Geistes nach dem Johannesevangelium," *idem* II, 264-71. — *idem*, "Der Heilige Geist als Interpret nach dem Johannesevangelium," *IKZ* 2 (1973) 97-108. — *idem*, "Herkunft, Ankunft und Wirkungen des Heiligen Geistes im NT," *Erfahrung und Theologie des Heiligen Geistes* (ed. C. Heitmann and H. Mühlen; 1974) 118-30. — *idem*, "Über den Heiligen Geist nach dem NT," *idem* IV, 151-64. — SCHNACKENBURG II, 99-114. — R. SCHNACKENBURG, "Christus, Geist und Gemeinde (Eph 4,1-16)," FS Moule 279-96. — *idem*, "Die johanneische Gemeinde und der Geist," FS Schürmann 277-306. — B. SCHNEIDER, "Κατὰ Πνεῦμα ῾Αγιοσύνης (Romans 1:4)," *Bib* 48 (1967) 359-88. — K. -D. SCHUNCK, "Wesen und Wirksamkeit des Geistes nach der Überlieferung des AT," *Beiträge zur Theologie in Geschichte und Gegenwart* (1976) 11-23. — E. SCHWEIZER, *TDNT* VI, 389-455. — *idem*, "Gegenwart des Geistes und eschatologische Hoffnung bei Zarathustra, spätjüdischen Gruppen, Gnostikern und Zeugen des NT," *idem, Neot* (1963) 153-79. — *idem*, "Christus und Geist im Kolosserbrief," FS Moule 297-313. — *idem, The Holy Spirit* (1980). — R. SCROGGS, "Paul: Σοφός and Πνευματικός," *NTS* 14 (1967/68) 33-35. — G. STÄHLIN, "τὸ πνεῦμα Ἰησοῦ (Apg 16,7)," FS Moule 229-52. — E. TROCMÉ, "Le Saint-Esprit et l'Église d'après le livre des Actes," *L'Esprit-Saint et l'Église* (1969) 19-44. — W. C. VAN UNNIK, "'Den Geist löscht nicht aus' (1 Thess 5:19)," *NovT* 10 (1968) 255-69. — W. WILKENS, "Wassertaufe und Geistempfang bei Lukas," *TZ* 23 (1967) 26-47. — For further bibliography see *TWNT* IX, 1238-44.

1. The verbal subst. πνεῦμα, derived from πνέω, designates the elementary power of nature and life: *wind, breeze; breath* (as such also the principle of life [like → ψυχή]), as both material and process together. In secular Greek πνεῦμα also came to be used quite early in the sense of mantic-enthusiastic inspiration and later (in Stoicism) of a cosmic-universal, divine (though existing in the world) energy or substance (Kleinknecht 334-59; Saake, "Pneuma," 387-95 [bibliography]).

In the NT πνεῦμα is essentially characterized by the Hebrew equivalent *rûaḥ* and its use in Judaism. The fundamental meaning of *rûaḥ* is also "wind" and "breath," but neither wind nor breath as materially present, but rather only

as the power inhering in breath or a gust of wind whose origin and destination remain enigmatic (Albertz and Westermann 728). In the OT *rûaḥ* often refers expressly to the "spirit" of God that acts as the life power and beyond that bestows special gifts or inspires a person (Schunck 14f.). The term "holy spirit" was adopted only in the post-exilic period. Influenced by its environment, *rûaḥ*/πνεῦμα in Judaism is often a term for *otherworldly* good or evil *beings;* in Hellenistic circles πνεῦμα is also variously thought of as substance, and often also mixed with ideas from Greek philosophy and speculation on "wisdom" (F. Baumgärtel, W. Bieder, and E. Sjöberg, *TDNT* VI, 365-89; Chevallier, *L'Esprit;* Saake, PW Suppl. XIV, 395f.).

In the NT, particularly under the influence of the early Church's experience of the Spirit, the meaning of πνεῦμα often acquired a fine nuance, even in general turns of phrase and in the rereading of OT passages.

Πνεῦμα occurs 379 times in the NT. Of those, it unequivocally yields its original meaning *(strong wind/ breeze)* only 3 times. It frequently refers to the human πνεῦμα *(ca.* 47 times) and to evil spirits *(ca.* 38 times) or the spirits of the dead or of angels *(ca.* 9 times: → 2). It is quite often clearly used of God's πνεῦμα *(ca.* 275 times), whether absolutely *(ca.* 149 times) or specified as πνεῦμα ἅγιον (92 times), πνεῦμα ἁγιοσύνης (once), πνεῦμα θεοῦ (18 times), πνεῦμα τοῦ πατρός (once), πνεῦμα τοῦ υἱοῦ αὐτοῦ (once), πνεῦμα Χριστοῦ (3 times), or πνεῦμα Ἰησοῦ (once). It is precisely as God's *Spirit* that the meaning of πνεῦμα varies among the individual NT writings (→ 3).

In determining the sense of πνεῦμα one must remember that the usual tr. *spirit* (Germ. *Geist*) often erects a barrier to understanding, since in English one often associates "spirit" with an insubstantial being (a ghost) or with understanding or reason (νοῦς). In addition, πνεῦμα is not seldom conceived under the influence of church doctrine as a "person." In order to avoid this latter misunderstanding, many exegetical writings shy away from the customary capitalization ("Holy Spirit").

2.a) Πνεῦμα has the general meaning *(powerful) wind /breeze* in John 3:8a; Heb 1:7 (cf. Ps 103:4 LXX); and 2 Thess 2:8 (cf. Isa 11:4b). This meaning does, however, betray proximity to the use of the word for God or an angel.

b) The *breath of human life* is called πνεῦμα in several passages (Matt 27:50; Jas 2:26; Rev 11:11; 13:15). Through its close, dynamic association with God (cf. Jacob 631) πνεῦμα can also be used of a manner of existence or life force that survives death (cf. 1 Pet 3:18; 4:6; 1 Tim 3:16; also Rom 1:4 [→ 3.a]; 1 Cor 5:5?). Only in individual instances is this thought of as a soul (→ ψυχή; → c).

In 1 Thess 5:23 Paul employs the language of ancient trichotomy, *"spirit,* soul, and body," not to describe three separate constituent parts of the human person, but rather the human being totally and completely. There as in Heb 4:12 ("soul and *spirit*"; cf. 2 Cor 7:1) πνεῦμα refers to the human being who is (and does not merely have) also *spirit.* The same is true in passages that use "with your *spirit*" in the sense of "with you" (Gal 6:18; Phil 4:23; Phlm 25; 2 Tim 4:22; Bultmann, *Theology* I, 153ff.).

As a term for the capacity of human beings for certain life expressions transcending what is externally ascertainable (feeling, sense, and knowledge), πνεῦμα is used several times in the NT in the sense of *the inward person* or *heart* (e.g., Mark 2:8; 8:12; Matt 5:3; Luke 1:47, 80; John 11:33; 2 Cor 2:13). Expressions such as "*spirit* of gentleness" (1 Cor 4:21; Gal 6:1; cf. 1 Pet 3:4) are also to be understood in this way. On the other hand, "the *spirit* of faith" (2 Cor 4:13) goes beyond that and implies participation in God's Spirit. The same is true of "the *spirit* is willing" (Mark 14:38 par. Matt 26:41), if the kinship between this phrase and Ps 51:14 is considered (Kuhn 274-81), and is probably also true for Rom 1:9; 8:16 ("my *spirit*"; → 3.b). Hence in Col 2:5 presence "in body" can be complemented by presence "in *spirit*," a presence that in 1 Cor 5:3f., then, appears to be one "in the Holy Spirit." Only in 1 Cor 2:11 does πνεῦμα mean *reason* (cf. 2:16, νοῦν; Eph 4:23; on the close relationship between the human πνεῦμα and νοῦς see Saake, PW Suppl. XIV, 397).

Whereas some of the passages cited clearly refer to God's spirit (e.g., also Luke 10:21), it can only be surmised in others. The inherited anthropological usage was accordingly ready to be filled with new content from the view of the OT promise of the Spirit and the NT reception of the Spirit.

c) Often, esp. in the Gospels, Acts, and Revelation, πνεῦμα is specified more closely as "unclean" (e.g., Mark 1:23, 26, 27; 3:11), "evil" (e.g., Luke 7:21), "dumb" (e.g., Mark 9:17), "dumb and deaf" (e.g., Mark 9:25), "of infirmity" (Luke 13:11), or "of demons" (Rev 16:13, 14). In Luke 8:2 "evil *spirits* and infirmities" and "seven demons" stand side by side (cf. 11:26; 4:33; Acts 16:16). In isolated instances πνεῦμα is also used absolutely in this sense (Matt 8:16; Luke 10:20; Acts 23:8f. probably also belongs here [the reference, along with "angel," is, unlike Acts 8:29, 39, cf. v. 26, hardly to God's Spirit]).

What is thought of in these passages, following the widespread understanding of the time, is beings conceived in the manner of persons (animistic) that dwell in people, rule them, and make them sick. Jesus and his disciples were able to exorcise such beings in a unique way (→ ἐκβάλλω; in principle this was also possible for others: cf. Matt 12:27); they have access to a power (God's πνεῦμα) stronger than that of the spirits. Only in Eph 2:2 does πνεῦμα, whether in apposition to ἄρχοντα or more likely to ἀέρος), refer to the power of evil or the evil one acting as "the anti-Christian pneuma" (Schlier).

Only in Luke 24:37, 39 does πνεῦμα expressly refer to a *spirit* (ghost) without flesh and blood, presumably the "soul" of a dead person (cf. Luke 8:55; 23:46; Acts 7:59; in Acts 12:15 ἄγγελος αὐτοῦ probably does not mean the same thing). In Heb 12:23 the "souls" of the righteous are called πνεύματα (cf. Rev 6:9 [→ ψυχή]; 1 Pet. 3:19 might refer to the "souls" of sinners, though also merely to evil spirits).

The divine name "Father of *spirits*" (Heb 12:9; cf. Num 16:22; 27:16) probably refers to all *spirits,* those of the angels as well as of the righteous; in Heb 1:14 the "ministering *spirits*" are angels. Rev 1:4; 3:1; 4:5; 5:6 contain related terminology; the "seven *spirits*" designate the throne angels of God (cf. the seven archangels in Tob 12:15), though they simultaneously represent God's spirit (→ 3.e).

3.a) The oldest Christian statements concerning the πνεῦμα of God transmitted in the NT writings or presupposed there assert that the OT and Jewish expectation of the inspiring and vital πνεῦμα of the eschaton (Chevallier, *L'Esprit;* Kremer, *Pfingstbericht* 63-86 [bibliography]) has now been fulfilled. The reception of the πνεῦμα is discernible from external phenomena (cf. Gal 3:2; Acts 8:18), esp. miraculous healings (1 Cor 12:9, 28, 30), ecstatic prayer (glossolalia), and prophetic speech (cf. 1 Corinthians 12 and 14; Acts 10 and 19; presumably also in the source of Acts 2:4). It is the πνεῦμα that inspired the OT authors (cf. Mark 12:36) and was active in the prophets of the early Church (their [ecstatic] utterances are later often called simply πνεῦμα, e.g., 1 John 4:1; 2 Thess 2:2; ἐν πνεύματι came to be a t.t. for prophetic ecstasy; cf. Rev 1:9). The πνεῦμα gives one courage to witness to the gospel, esp. in time of tribulation (Matt 10:20; Luke 12:12; Mark 13:11 par.; cf. Kremer, "Jesu Verheißung" 262ff.). In the distinguishing of Christian baptism from that of John the Baptist πνεῦμα is used of the power that redeems sins (Mark 1:8 par.; it is disputed whether "*spirit* and fire" in the preaching of the Baptist [Mark 3:11; Luke 3:16] originally referred only to the "storm and fire" of judgment; cf. Dunn, "Spirit and Fire-Baptism").

According to the earliest sources, Jesus' activity after his baptism (Mark 1:9-11 par.; Acts 10:37) was already characterized by the Holy Spirit (e.g., exorcism of demons, Matt 12:28; cf. Mark 3:28f. par.), and even his conception was traced back to the Spirit (Matt 1:18, 20; Luke 1:35). His postresurrection existence is pneumatic (cf. Rom 1:4; 1 Pet 3:18; 1 Tim 3:16).

It is difficult to assess the extent to which these passages about the πνεῦμα, which are oriented essentially on the OT promises, were understood in the Hellenistic environment. In any case, the various NT writings develop them further in different ways, particularly Paul, Luke-Acts, and John (→ b, c, d).

b) Paul shares the understanding of the perceivable signs of the eschatological reception of the Spirit (e.g.,

1 Thess 1:5; Gal 3:2-5; 1 Cor 12:7ff.; Rom 15:19), claims such experiences of the πνεῦμα for himself as well (1 Cor 14:18, cf. 7:40; 2 Cor 12:12; cf. Saake, "Pneumatologia" 214ff.), and warns against "quenching" (1 Thess 5:19; cf. van Unnik) the spirit that thus "manifests" itself (cf. 1 Cor 12:7). Not every effect attributed to the πνεῦμα, however, actually comes from it, and there arises the need to "distinguish between *spirits*" (1 Cor 12:10 with vv. 1-3; *contra* Dautzenberg, *Prophetie;* → διακρίνω). In response to an overestimation of the ecstatic effects of the Spirit (→ πνευματικός) Paul emphasizes the value of the less noticeable gifts of the Spirit, their origin from the one God, their variety, and their focus on the Church (1 Corinthians 12).

According to 1 Cor 12:13 all members of the Church are "baptized" and "saturated" "in/with one *Spirit*" and are thereby "one body" (→ σῶμα 6, 7). The πνεῦμα is thus an enduring gift for the baptized (cf. Rom 5:5; 1 Cor 6:19: "Your body is a temple of the Holy *Spirit* within you"; similarly 1 Cor 3:16). It is, however, not a possession for them to use, but is, rather, that which rules them. Common anthropological uses of πνεῦμα (→ 2.b) acquire thereby new content (e.g., Rom 1:9; 8:13; 9:1; 12:11; 1 Cor 7:34; 2 Cor 6:6) without the relationship between natural abilities and the πνεῦμα being more clearly delineated. Paul clearly distinguishes only the prayer of the πνεῦμα from that of the understanding (1 Cor 14:15; the entry of the Spirit "with sighs too deep for words" [Rom 8:26] is different from glossolalia and the cry "Abba! Father!" [Gal 4:6; Rom 8:15]; cf. Niederwimmer, "Gebet"). "Participation in the *Spirit*" (2 Cor 13:13) underscores the demand for unity (Phil 1:27; 2:1; 2 Cor 12:18). How little Paul conceives the gift of the πνεῦμα (despite Hellenistically flavored language) after the manner of a substance (but rather remains true to the meaning of *rûaḥ*) is suggested by his metaphors, e.g., "dwells" (1 Cor 3:16; Rom 8:11), "cries" (Gal 4:6; Rom 8:15), "intercedes" (Rom 8:26), and to be "one *spirit*" with the Lord (1 Cor 6:17).

The πνεῦμα characterizes the new covenant (2 Cor 3:6; cf. Rom 2:29; 7:6; cf. Kremer, "Buchstabe" 223-29 [bibliography]). The office of apostle is thus a διακονία τοῦ πνεύματος (2 Cor 3:8) that mediates the Spirit as a new Torah (3:3); for the πνεῦμα liberates one from rigidity of heart and fixation on the letter (3:14-17) so that one can recognize the goal or end (→ τέλος) of the Torah (3:13-18) and "that which is God's" (1 Cor 2:10-14). Hence it is possible in the πνεῦμα to confess Christ as the κύριος (1 Cor 12:3; cf. 2 Cor 4:6) and to call on God as the Father (Gal 4:6; Rom 8:14). Furthermore, the baptized person is removed from the realm of sin by the πνεῦμα and is "sanctified by the Holy Spirit" (Rom 15:16; cf. Gal 5:5; 1 Cor 6:11; Rom 14:17) and transformed by it (1 Cor 3:18). Such a person receives a portion of "God's love" (Rom 5:5; cf. 15:30) and is, therefore, no longer a "slave," but rather "son and heir" (Rom 8:15f.; cf. Gal 4:6f.; cf., however, Duprez). As "the law of the spirit of life" the πνεῦμα liberates one from enslavement to the Torah, enslavement that through the fleshly existence of human beings leads to sin and death and not, as would be in keeping with human inner destiny, to life (Rom 8:2; cf. 7:14; 2 Cor 3:6; cf. Räisänen [bibliography]). Whoever walks "according to the *Spirit*" fulfils "the law's requirment" (Rom 8:4: i.e, love, cf. Gal 5:14; Rom 13:8-10). The freedom bestowed by the πνεῦμα commands one to follow the *Spirit* (Gal 5:16, 25), to allow oneself to be guided by it as the "Torah" (cf. 2 Cor 3:3), and not to give in to the desires of the flesh (→ σάρξ; Gal 5:16f.; 6:8; Rom 8:13). "The fruit of the *Spirit*" is the sign of spiritual life (Gal 5:22).

Possession of the πνεῦμα is simultaneously "guarantee" (2 Cor 1:22; 5:5, → ἀρραβών) and "first fruits" (Rom 8:23, → ἀπαρχή) of future glory. Therefore, it is the basis of hope (cf. Rom 5:5; 8:10f.). Through the πνεῦμα the baptized person already participates in "life" (Rom 8:10) and will reap this as eternal life if he "sows to the *Spirit*" (Gal 6:8; i.e., if he lives focused on his spiritual possessions). For through the πνεῦμα God will resurrect the dead as he did Christ (Rom 8:11), and will do it through Christ, who as the new Adam can be called a "life-giving *spirit*" because of his own participation, through the resurrection, in the Creator's Spirit (1 Cor 15:45, → ζωοποιέω).

The reception of the promised Spirit is a fruit of the death of Christ (Gal 3:14). The "*Spirit* of God" or "Holy *Spirit*" is thus also called "the *Spirit* of Christ" (Rom 8:9; cf. 2 Cor 3:17), who was sent from the Father as "the *Spirit* of the Son" (Gal 4:6). Hence functioning as parallels to "Christ in you" (Rom 8:10) and "in Christ" (Rom 8:1) are statements that the Spirit "dwells" in a person or that a person is "in the Spirit" (Rom 8:9; cf. 1 Cor 3:16). Though they are by no means identical, πνεῦμα and Christ are closely related. 2 Cor 3:17 ("now the Lord is the *Spirit*") at least implies a dynamic identity of the two (cf. 1 Cor 15:45) that is simultaneously a unity with God (κύριος can refer here to both God and Christ; Dunn, "2 Corinthians"; Greenwood [bibliography]). According to Rom 5:5 God's love has been poured into the hearts of Christians through the πνεῦμα. The close relationship between God, Christ, and πνεῦμα is expressed above all in Gal 4:4-6; 1 Cor 12:4-6; and in the triadic formula in 2 Cor 13:13.

In the Epistles dependent on Paul or related to him πνεῦμα is used only rarely in the sense characteristic of Paul (so Eph 4:3f.). There, as in other NT Epistles, the inspirational meaning of πνεῦμα is striking (e.g., Col 1:18; 1 Tim 4:1; 1 Pet 1:11f. [the πνεῦμα of Christ!]; Heb 3:7; 2 Pet 1:21).

c) For Luke-Acts the πνεῦμα is indeed the Spirit already active in the Old Covenant and in the life of Jesus.

But at Pentecost (Acts 2) and later (cf., e.g., 4:31) this *Spirit* was bestowed on the disciples as the eschatological (Acts 2:17f.) "promise of the Father" (1:4; cf. 2:38f.) and as the "power from on high" (Luke 24:49; Acts 1:5, 8) promised by Jesus for the near future. The πνεῦμα is bestowed on everyone who accepts the message, normally through baptism (cf. 2:38; 8:15-17; 10:45-48; 19:2-7). Reception of the Spirit, esp. at decisive turning points for the mission, occurred amid external signs (2:1-4; 4:31; 8:17f.; 9:17f.; 10:44–11:15 [cf. 15:8]; 19:6). The most striking such sign was "speaking in tongues," a kind of inspired praise and prophetic proclamation (2:4, 11 [→ 3.a]; 4:31; 6:10; 10:45f.; 19:6; cf. Luke 1:41f., 67; 10:21; the understanding of glossolalia is different in 1 Corinthians 12 and 14; see Dupont, *Salvation* 45-52; cf. also → γλῶσσα 6). This is in keeping with the fact that in Luke-Acts the *Spirit* elicits an almost exclusively inspirational /prophetic effect. Faith, forgiveness of sins, prayer, capacity for love, and esp. miracles are not expressly attributed to the πνεῦμα (cf. Schweizer, *TDNT* VI, 407f.; *contra* Bovon 228, referring to the relationship between πνεῦμα and δύναμις), though some passages suggest that Luke was acquainted with such relationships (e.g., "full of faith and of the Holy *Spirit*," Acts 6:5; cf. 11:23; "the comfort of the Holy *Spirit*," 9:31; "filled with joy and with the Holy *Spirit*," 13:52). According to Luke 11:13 the πνεῦμα is the ultimate gift of answered prayer (cf. Schweizer, *TDNT* VI, 409).

There are no Lukan passages asserting that participation in the πνεῦμα of the resurrected Christ is already a guarantee of eternal life. Instead, the πνεῦμα is essentially the armament or strength of the Church in its task until the end (cf. G. Schneider, *Acts* [HTKNT] I, 259). It determines the life of the early Church such that it can often be described through personification, e.g., it is a witness (Acts 5:32), decides (15:28), speaks (8:29; 10:19; 13:2), sends (13:4), does not allow (16:7), makes guardians (20:28), and teaches (Luke 12:12), and one can lie to the πνεῦμα or tempt it (Acts 5:3, 9; cf. also Luke 12:10 concerning blasphemy against the Spirit [the early Church's proclamation]). It is not asserted that the baptized are molded into a community of inner life through the Spirit (as in 1 Cor 12:13; → 3.b).

In the language of Church experience Luke also portrays the activity of the πνεῦμα in the life of Jesus. Whereas John the Baptist is "filled" (Luke 1:15) with the Holy Spirit from the womb on, Jesus owes his existence to the descent of the Holy Spirit as the "power of Most High" (1:35f.); the Spirit rested on him (3:21; cf. 4:18; Acts 10:38, "anointed"); he is "led" by it (4:1; cf. 4:14; 9:39); he "rejoices in the *Spirit*" (10:21) and "chose the apostles through the Holy *Spirit*" (Acts 1:2; another possible tr. is "commissioned them through . . .").

According to Acts 2:33 the πνεῦμα is the gift of the exalted Lord that he bequeaths from the Father (Dupont, "Ascension" 226f.). Through the πνεῦμα Jesus carries forward his work, which is also the work of God (cf. Stählin 245-51). Since Luke is interested only in the function of the πνεῦμα in the Church, no conclusions can be drawn concerning the essence of the Spirit (whether merely a supernatural substance or even a person)—or concerning a closer determination of its unity with God and Christ—from the designations (e.g., "power," "gift") or from what is said about reception of the Spirit or the effects of the Spirit. This is all the more the case because Luke-Acts often employs traditional formulations (e.g., Acts 8:39 concerning Philip being "caught up") without reflecting their full meaning.

d) According to John as well the πνεῦμα is essentially a gift of the exalted Lord: "For as yet the *Spirit* had not been given, because Jesus was not yet glorified" (John 7:39c). This does not dispute the pre-resurrection existence of the πνεῦμα (cf. 1:33); rather, it points to the uniquely new reception of the Spirit by those who believe in Christ (7:39b; nor does this preclude all pre-resurrection bestowal of the Spirit; Porsch 65). The blood and water flowing from the wound in Jesus' side is fig. interpreted as this reception as a result of the glorification (19:34 [cf. 7:38f.]; the addendum in 19:35 concerning the testimony includes presumably the sending of the Spirit in the Church; cf. 1 John 5:7). According to John 20:22 the disciples receive the Spirit already on the evening of the resurrection (on the relationship to Acts 2 cf. Kremer, *Pfingstbericht* 224-28).

In keeping with the heavily symbolic portrayal in John 20:22f. ("He breathed on them, and said to them, 'Receive the Holy *Spirit*' "; cf. Gen 2:7) πνεῦμα possesses vital power. The following logion about the power to forgive sins (rescue from death; cf. 8:21, 24) presupposes this (20:23; cf. Matt 16:18; 18:18), and the exposition concerning rebirth from "water and the *Spirit*" documents it (John 3:5-8), as does the inherited formulation "it is the *Spirit* that gives life" (6:63a). Whoever is "born of the πνεῦμα" is no longer of the σάρξ (death), but is himself *spirit* (3:6) and thus capable of participating in God's life (3:5). This is reinforced by the images of "water" (7:38; cf. Ezek 36:25), "water and blood" (19:34), and probably also "living water" (4:10, 14c) as the "gift" (δωρεά) by which, as with the "wine" served in the appropriate "hour" ("now," 2:1-13), the revelation or manifestation in Christ is meant.

An inspirational effect is closely allied with this effect of giving life (though with characteristically Johannine features), since for John "life" (ζωή) and the word or truth are closely related: "The words that I have spoken to you are *Spirit* and life" (John 6:63c; cf. 1:17 and the fig. statements cited above). The mediation of truth is simultaneously the mediation of life (14:6; 17:3) granted by

Jesus, who himself is truth and life together (14:6; cf. 1 John, → ἀλήθεια). The close relationship between the revelation of truth and the giving of the πνεῦμα is also behind the passage about worshipping the Father "in Spirit and truth" (John 4:23f.; a rereading of early Christian assertions concerning Spirit-induced prayer). Influenced by the Johannine understanding of "truth," the inherited phrase "Spirit of truth" (as opposed to the "spirit of error"; 1QS 3:20, 23f.; 4:21; cf. T. Jud. 20:1, 3, 5; Wis 1:5; 1 John 4:6) within the Gospel of John also expresses the close relationship between "truth" and Spirit. As → παράκλητος the Spirit has the function (conceived as person; cf. Saake, PW Suppl. XIV, 398) that ultimately serves the enduring union with the vital truth (John 14:16f., 26; 15:26; 16:6-11, 13-15; on the interrelationships seen here between different conceptions cf. esp. Porsch 305-78). The concentration of πνεῦμα and truth in Christ is not least influenced by the dispute with adversaries (Gnostics?), who apparently claim prophetic experience of the Spirit (cf. 1 John 4:1-6).

Not without reason does John 1:33 assert that the Spirit "remains" on Jesus; there it is "without measure" (3:34; possibly also: "he [Jesus] gives the Spirit without measure"); this shows the Baptist "that this is the Son of God" (1:34). This is in keeping with the absence of any information concerning Jesus being filled with the Spirit and led by it. As the Son he is one with the πνεῦμα, though without all differentiation being suspended: The Father sends the Spirit in the name of the Son (14:26); the Son sends the Spirit from the Father (15:26), and it can be said of the πνεῦμα itself as it can of the Son that it "comes" (16:13).

e) In the early Christian baptismal formula in Matt 28:19 the πνεῦμα is named along with the Father and the Son, and it is presupposed that the Spirit, too, can be called on as the bearer of a name (on the relationship to the understanding of πνεῦμα as "angel" [cf. Rev 1:4 and passim] and "witnesses" cf. Kretschmar, "Le développement" 12f.). The early Church rightly viewed this passage as the biblical point of departure for the doctrine of the trinity; from this trinitarian perspective, in a rereading, it then reinterpreted or even changed (1 John 5:7-8 v.l.) other NT passages, esp. the triadic formulas (1 Cor 12:4-6; 2 Cor 13:13) and the Paraclete sayings (→ d; cf. Saake 398), as well as many other texts (e.g., Gal 4:6; Rom 8:15f.)

J. Kremer

πνευματικός, 3 *pneumatikos* pertaining to the spirit, spiritual*

πνευματικῶς *pneumatikōs* in a manner commensurate with the spirit, spiritually*

Lit.: → πνεῦμα. See also: U. BROCKHAUS, *Charisma und Amt* (1972). — H. CONZELMANN, *TDNT* IX, 402-6. — R. JEWETT,

Paul's Anthropological Terms (1970). — E. KÄSEMANN, "1Kor 2,6-16," *idem, Versuche* I, 267-76. — R. MORISETTE, "L'antithèse entre le 'psychique' et le 'pneumatique' en I Corinthiens XV,44 à 46," *RevScRel* 46 (1972) 97-143. — U. WILCKENS, "Zu 1 Kor 2,1-16," FS Dinkler 501-37. — M. WINTER, *Pneumatiker und Psychiker in Korinth* (1975).

1. The adj. derived from → πνεῦμα with the basic meaning *concerning the wind (the air), after the manner of the wind* (thus throughout secular Greek) occurs 28 times in the NT; the adv. occurs in 1 Cor 2:14; Rev 11:8. They are always used metaphorically (as in the Apostolic Fathers; they do not occur in the LXX). In Eph 6:12 the pl. of the adj. is used of "the *spirit hosts* of wickedness" (→ πνεῦμα 2.c). Otherwise πνευματικός always means *pertaining to the spirit, spiritual* (→ πνεῦμα 3; the tr. *spiritual* can mislead one into misunderstandings, such as "concerning reason," "religious," and that which is opposed to "corporeal").

2. In 1 Cor 12:1 (περὶ τῶν πνευματικῶν; cf. 14:1) Paul employs an already current designation for the ecstatic phenomena experienced in the Church, which were considered *effects* or *gifts of the Spirit* (→ πνεῦμα 3.a) and desirable → χάρισμα. Whoever had access to these was considered to be a person *with spiritual gifts* (πνευματικός in the sense of the ecstatics, 14:37). Using a turn of phrase derived from this, Col 3:16 and Eph 5:19 speak of "*spiritual* songs," meaning not only ecstatic, but Spirit-induced and Spirit-imparting psalms in general (cf. Col 1:9 on *spiritual* wisdom and insight).

The spirit-effected capacity for special knowledge characterizes the difference between *spiritual* (1 Cor 2:13-15) and purely secular people (→ ψυχικός); the latter are incapable of understanding *spiritual things* (2:13; cf. v. 12: "the gifts bestowed on us by God's Spirit"). The former can be judged only *spiritually* (aided by the Spirit, in a spiritual way, 2:14; a later development of this manner of expression is the use of the adv. in the sense of *commensurate with Spirit-effected* [prophetic] *interpretation* [Rev 11:8]). According to Paul, all Christians are spiritual, even if they behave "in the manner of the flesh" (→ σαρκινός) and like "babes" (1 Cor 3:1) and not like "complete, mature adults" (→ τέλειος; cf. also Gal 6:1).

The differentiation of spiritual people and secular people is characterized not least by reflection on the pneumatic existence of the resurrected Christ, an existence different from fleshly, earthly existence (cf. Rom 1:3f.; 1 Pet 3:18; 1 Tim 3:16). This is also the source of the new interpretation in 1 Cor 15:44-46 of the Jewish exegesis of Gen 2:7 that sets over against the earthly body a σῶμα πνευματικόν, a "*spirit*-body" belonging to the realm of God's Spirit and created by God (on the derivation from Gnosticism cf. Winter [bibliography]; recently, however, Wilckens).

Analogously Paul can in typological exegesis (1 Cor 10:3f.) speak of the gifts of the wilderness wanderings, because of their orientation toward participation in the Spirit of the resurrected Christ, as *"spiritual* food" and *"spiritual* drink" (perhaps already as in *Did.* 10:3 a designation for the eucharistic gifts: H. Conzelmann, *1 Cor* [Hermeneia] ad loc.) and can call Christ the *"spiritual* rock."

In that the realm of the eschatological, vital πνεῦμα stands opposed to that of the flesh (→ σάρξ), the νόμος of the Old Covenant is according to Rom 7:14 also *spiritual* (this does not refer to the νόμος τοῦ πνεύματος τῆς ζωῆς mentioned in 8:2). Paul can thus impart "a *spiritual* gift" (Rom 1:11; here probably not in the sense of charisma: so E. Käsemann, *Rom* [Eng. tr., 1980] ad loc.; *contra* Brockhaus 130ff.; cf. Rom 15:27; 1 Cor 9:11 regarding the gift of the gospel).

According to the liturgically influenced triadic formula in Eph 1:3 God blesses us "with every *spiritual* blessing . . . in Christ" (cf. Gen 49:25), i.e., through Christ God gives to us who already belong to the heavenly world (cf. Eph 2:6) his *Spirit* as the fullness of that which we hope for from the blessing of God (cf. 1:13). The Church is called as a *"spiritual* house" to offer *"spiritual* sacrifices" (a metaphor for Christian life; 1 Pet 2:5a, b).   J. Kremer

πνευματικῶς *pneumatikōs* in a manner commensurate with the spirit, spiritually
→ πνευματικός.

πνέω *pneō* blow*

Of the wind, Matt 7:25, 27; Luke 12:55; John 3:8; 6:18; Rev 7:1. In Acts 27:40 subst. ἡ πνέουσα (*sc.* αὔρα), the *blowing wind.* E. Schweizer, *TDNT* VI, 452f.

πνίγω *pnigō* strangle; pass.: be choked; intrans.: suffocate*

Literal in Matt 18:28: ἔπνιγεν (impf. of attempt), he *tried to choke* (him); 13:7, of thorns that *choke* the seeds; pass. in Mark 5:13: *drown.* H. Bietenhard, *TDNT* VI, 455-58; *idem, DNTT* I, 226.

πνικτός, 3 *pniktos* strangled, choked*

Acts 15:20, 29: ἀπέχομαι τοῦ πνικτοῦ or πνικτῶν, "abstain from *what is strangled*"; 21:25: φυλάσσομαι πνικτόν, in the same context of the Apostolic Decree. Πνικτός refers here to the flesh from animals not slaughtered according to Jewish ritual (cf. Lev 17:13f.). The "Western" text eliminates "what is strangled" in all three instances. H. Bietenhard, *TDNT* VI, 455-58; *idem, DNTT* I, 226; G. Schneider, *Acts* (HTKNT) II, excursus 12.

πνοή, ῆς, ἡ *pnoē* wind, breeze; breath*

Acts 2:2: πνοή βιαία, "a mighty *wind*"; 17:25: God gives to all (human beings) ζωὴν καὶ πνοὴν καὶ τὰ πάντα, i.e., "life and *breath* and everything"; cf. Gen 2:7 LXX: πνοὴν ζωῆς. E. Schweizer, *TDNT* VI, 453f.; E. Kamlah, J. D. G. Dunn, and C. Brown, *DNTT* III, 689f.

ποδήρης, 2 *podērēs* reaching to the feet*

Subst. in Rev. 1:13: ὁ ποδήρης (*sc.* χιτών), a garment reaching to the feet, robe; so also *Barn.* 7:9.

ποδινιπτήρ, ῆρος, ὁ *podiniptēr* basin for washing the feet
John 13:5 v.l. (p⁶⁶) in place of → νιπτήρ.

πόθεν *pothen* whence? from where? how?*

An adv. used in direct and indirect questions. With local meaning in Matt 15:33; Mark 8:4; Luke 13:25, 27; John 3:8; 4:11; 6:5; 8:14a, b; 9:29, 30; 19:9; Rev 2:5; 7:13. Asking regarding origin in Matt 13:27, 54, 56; 21:25; Mark 6:2; Luke 20:7; John 2:9; 7:27a, b, 28; Jas 4:1a, b. Asking about cause in Matt 12:37; Luke 1:43; John 1:48.

ποιέω *poieō* do, make; act

1. Occurrences — 2. Constructions — 3. Subjects of ποιέω —a) God — b) Jesus — c) Christians — d) Non-Christians acting ethically — e) Opponents of God — f) Secular actions — g) Objects

Lit.: BAGD s.v. — J. BEUTLER, "Das Theorie-Praxis-Problem in neutestamentlicher Sicht," *Theologie zwischen Theorie und Praxis* (ed. L. Bertsch; 1975) 149-78. — BDF index s.v. — H. BRAUN, *TDNT* VI, 458-84. — C. MAURER, *TDNT* VI, 632-44. — G. SCHNEIDER, "Christusbekenntnis und christliches Handeln," FS Schürmann 9-24. — F. THIELE, *DNTT* III, 1152-55. — W. WILKENS, *Zeichen und Werke* (1969). — For further bibliography see *TWNT* X, 1244.

1. Ποιέω occurs 568 times in the text of *UBSGNT* (= *NTG*), relatively frequently in Matthew (86 occurrences), John (110), James (12), and 1 John (13) and not at all in 2 John. The subj. of ποιέω in John is esp. often Jesus as the Son of God. In the Pauline letters it is Christians or Paul himself, in Hebrews it is God and Christ, and in Revelation the powers hostile to God.

2. Ποιέω is usually act., pass. only in Heb 12:27 *(what has been made),* and mid. esp. in periphrasis (e.g., Luke 13:22: πορείαν ποιούμενος instead of πορευόμενος). In Mark 2:23 ὁδὸν ποιέω can have the same force as Lat. *iter facere,* "make one's way." A definite latinism occurs in 15:15: τὸ ἱκανὸν ποιέω = *satisfacere* (similarly probably in Acts 26:28: to *make,* i.e., to *play* a Christian =

christianum agere). Ἔλεος ποιέω μετά τινος in Luke 1:72; 10:37 (cf. Gen 24:12 LXX) is a hebraism: *let* mercy *hold sway* with someone. The results of an action can be expressed by acc. with inf. (e.g., Matt 5:32), a ἵνα clause (only in John 11:37; Col 4:16; Rev 3:9; 13:12, 15, 16), or a double acc., the latter particularly striking in John 16:2 (ἀποσυναγώγους ποιέω) and Rev 12:15 (ποταμοφόρητον ποιέω).

3. Whereas πράσσω (with ποιέω in, e.g., John 3:20f.; 5:29) almost always refers to negative actions and in the NT is never used with God or Christ as subject (cf. Maurer 635-37), except in disputation concerning the action described (Luke 23:15, 41; cf. Acts 26:31), ποιέω can refer to every kind of action.

a) It is used of the creative, historical, and future eschatological action of God:

1) God appears as *Creator* in the comprehensive sense particularly in Acts. He "*made* heaven, earth, and sea and everything in them" (4:24); 14:15 (cf. 7:50; 17:24; Heb 1:2) cites Exod 20:11; Ps 145:6 LXX, similarly Rev 14:7; (κτίζω in Rev 10:6; in the LXX κτίζω is much less frequent than ποιέω for *bārā'*). More specifically, God "*made* from one every human nation" (Acts 17:26), he "*made* them male and female" (Mark 10:6; cf. Matt 19:4, where κτίζω is probably original rather than ποιέω; cf. *TCGNT* 47), he *made* "the inside and the outside" (Luke 11:40). He *made* the angels winds (Heb 1:7) and human beings "thus" (Rom 9:20), according to "his will" (v. 19).

2) Historically, according to Heb 8:9 (= Jer 31:32), God "*made* the covenant with their fathers," and according to Acts 14:27; 15:4, 12, 17; 19:11 during the time of the early Church he *did* great things through Paul's mission. Christ's death and resurrection represent the zenith of God's historical activity, according to one's perspective either the middle or the end of history. He "*made* him to be sin" (2 Cor 5:21) and "*appointed* him high priest" (Heb 3:2). Mary (Luke 1:49, 51) and Zechariah (1:68, 72; cf. 1:25) see already in Christ's advent the eschatological action of God.

3) At judgment (Matt 18:35; Luke 18:7, 8; Rom 9:28 [= Isa 10:23]; 1 Thess 5:24; Jude 15) and at the new creation: "I *make* all things new" (Rev 21:5).

b) Ποιέω is used of Jesus' activity quite frequently in John, less so in the Synoptics, and rarely in the Epistles and Revelation.

1) The Gospel of John speaks mostly of "signs" that Jesus *does* (2:11, 23; 3:2; 4:54; 6:14, 30; 7:31; 11:47; 12:18, 37; 20:30, and *passim*) and of "works" that he *does* (7:3, 21; 14:12; 15:24; cf. 17:4). It emphasizes that he *does* the Father's works (5:36; 10:25, 37, 38) and in the larger sense only the Father's will (4:34; 5:19 [4 occurrences], 27, 30; 8:28, 29; 9:33; 14:31). Some react to this activity with the objection that Jesus was "*making*

himself equal to God" and similar charges (5:18; 8:53; 10:33; 19:7). His *actions* appear exemplary (13:7, 12, 15).

2) In the Synoptics ποιέω is usually used for what Jesus should *do* or whether he should *do* it (Luke 4:23; Mark 10:35, 36; 10:51 par. Matt 20:32/Luke 18:41), what he is able to *do* (Mark 6:5 par. Matt 13:58; Matt 9:28), or what he is allowed to *do* (Mark 11:28 bis, 29, 33 par. Matt 21:23, 24, 27/Luke 20:2, 8). Mark 3:8; Luke 9:43; Acts 1:1; 10:39 contain summaries of "all that he *did*" (cf. Mark 7:37; without "all" in Mark 5:20 par. Luke 8:39); Matt 21:15 speaks of "miracles that he *did*." Pilate (Mark 15:14 par. Matt 27:23/Luke 23:22) asks what evil Jesus *has done*. Mary does not understand what Jesus *has done* to his parents (Luke 2:48). He wants to *make* his disciples into "fishers of people" (Mark 1:17); among them he *appoints* the Twelve, i.e., he *makes* the circle of Twelve (Mark 3:14, 16; without the art. in v. 14: ἐποίησεν δώδεκα).

3) In three Epistles and Revelation ποιέω refers esp. to Jesus' salvation activity: Himself without sin (1 Pet 2:22), "once for all" (Heb 7:27) he "*made* purification for sins" (1:3). He "*made* us a kingdom, priests" (Rev 1:6; 5:10). He *made* Jews and Gentiles "one" (Eph 2:14) and "*made* peace" (2:15); he "*makes* bodily growth" (4:16).

c) Commensurate with the NT genres, the activity of Christians themselves are described with ποιέω in three ways: (1) in Acts mainly in narrative, (2) in the Epistles in direct speech, and (3) in the Gospels indirectly to the extent that the addressee of the Lord's words is on the surface Jesus' listeners and at a deeper level the Church.

1) Acts, introduced by its author in 1:1 as the second book *composed* by him, portrays with ποιέω almost always the activity of individual people, e.g., *deeds* of healing by Peter and John (3:12), miraculous *deeds* by Stephen and Philip (6:8; 8:6), Tabitha's *making* of coats and garments (9:39), Christians' good acts and charity (ὧν ἐποίει, 9:36), and above all Paul's deeds (cf. 14:11). The latter do not everywhere *give* great joy as in 15:3; though Paul first considers his life "not worth a single word" (20:24; cf. BAGD s.v. λόγος 1.a.α), after he *brings* alms and offerings in Jerusalem (24:17) he must defend himself from the suspicion of having *done* something against the law (28:17) or having *incited* an insurrection (24:17).

2) In the proemium the Epistles often speak of the perpetually realized (ποιοῦμαι) thoughts or prayers of the author (Rom 1:9; Eph 1:16; 1 Thess 1:2; Phlm 4; Phil 1:4), then also of his other deeds (according to 1 Cor 9:23 grounded in the gospel [διά], esp. emphasized in the apology of 2 Corinthians: "Did I *commit* a sin . . . ? . . . And what I *do* I will continue to *do* . . . a day and a night I *have been* adrift at sea [→ βυθός; 11:7, 12, 25]). Mainly,

however, the epistolary author refers with ποιέω to the deeds of the addressees, usually in the imv., e.g., 1 Cor 10:31 (cf. Col 3:17, 23): "So, whether you eat or drink, or whatever you *do, do* all to the glory of God"; Christians should *do* the good (Rom 13:3; Eph 6:8; 1 Pet 3:11: τὸ ἀγαθόν; 2 Cor 13:7; Gal 6:9; Jas 4:17: τὸ καλόν), God's will (Eph 6:6; Heb 10:36; 13:21; 1 John 2:17), the truth (1:6), and what pleases God (3:22); they should *obey* the commandments (5:2), *do* what is right (2:29; 3:7, 10), *show* mercy (Jas 2:13), and *make* peace (3:18). Timothy should "*do* the work of an evangelist" (2 Tim 4:5) and "*do* nothing from partiality" (1 Tim 5:21). The Colossians receive the practical instructions to *see that* the letter is also read elsewhere (4:16).

3) In the Gospels Jesus, too, calls for Christians to *keep* the commandments (Matt 5:19) and to *do* the will of God (12:50; Mark 3:35; John 7:17), the word of God (Luke 8:21), the truth (John 3:21), the good (τὰ ἀγαθά, 5:29), and that which he himself says (Luke 6:46; John 15:14). Deeds are particularly emphasized wherever they stand over against mere speaking or hearing or insignificant action (Matt 7:21, 22, 24, 26 par. Luke 6:46, 47, 49; 8:21). The expressed question "What then shall we *do?*" stands in this or a similar form in Luke 3:10, 12; Matt 19:16 par. Mark 10:17/Luke 18:18; John 6:28; cf. Acts 2:37; 9:6; 22:10 (bis); Jesus discusses this with a lawyer (Luke 10:25, 28, 37 bis). According to Matt 25:40, 45 the standard of judgment will be what one has or has not *done* for others. According to John, at the Last Supper Jesus leaves behind the instruction to *do* "as I have done to you," i.e., according to the example of his love (13:15, 17), and also leaves the promise of great works for whoever believes (14:12 bis) and abides in him (15:5); according to Luke 22:19 (par. 1 Cor 11:24, 25) Jesus refers to the meal as his legacy: "*Do* this in remembrance of me."

d) Non-Christian ethical behavior is either Jewish or Gentile:

1) The most noble task of the Jews is behavior "according to the custom of the law" (Luke 2:27). Thus the Jew *brings* fruit(s) befitting repentance (Matt 3:8 par. Luke 3:8) and *makes* God's paths straight (Matt 3:3 par. Mark 1:3/Luke 3:4). Salvation would come immediately "if the Israelites would keep but two sabbaths according to the law" (*b. Šabb.* 118b; Billerbeck I, 600). Jesus' disciples create an even greater scandal when they "*do* what is not lawful to *do* on the sabbath" and must be defended with recourse to what David *did* (Matt 12:2, 3 par. Mark 2:24, 25/Luke 6:2, 3). Jesus questions the Jewish sabbath practice and other traditions (Mark 3:4; 7:12, 13) and sharply criticizes the deeds of the Pharisees themselves (Matt 23:3 ter, 5, 15 bis, 23). According to John, they do not *do* what Abraham did (8:39, 40), but rather what the devil does (8:38, 41, 44). Paul discusses

the theological problems involved with works of the law (Rom 10:5; Gal 3:10, 12; 5:3). According to him, the person dependent on the law must despair because what he does (Rom 7:15, 16, 19, 20, 21) does not correspond to what he wants.

2) Gentiles can *do* what the law requires even without the law itself (2:14); but they behave righteously as little as do the Jews (3:12) and *do* all manner of improper and objectionable things (1:28, 32; 2:3) because they *follow* the desires of body and passions (Eph 2:3).

e) Finally, hostile activity directed against the prophets, Jesus, and the Church is also theologically relevant.

1) Persecution and flattery are not new; this was already *done* to the prophets or false prophets (Luke 6:23, 26). With John they "*did* whatever they pleased" (Matt 17:12 par. Mark 9:13), i.e., Herod, "who had been reproved by him" for all the evil things that Herod had *done,* "added this to them all, that he shut up John in prison" (Luke 3:19, 20).

2) Jesus' opponents consider what they can *do* to him (6:11), but at first do not know what they should *do* (19:48; John 11:47). He himself urges Judas: "What you are going to *do, do* quickly" (13:27). The Jews *hold* a consultation (Mark 15:1; on textual criticism → ἑτοιμάζω) and decide to crucify Jesus; according to his prayer that they be forgiven, however, "they do not know what they *do*" (Luke 23:34; on textual criticism see J. Schmid, *Luke* [RNT] ad loc.).

3) The Jews also *do* evil to Jesus' disciples (12:4; John 15:21; Acts 4:16; cf. Heb 13:6), esp. to Paul (Acts 9:13; 26:10). Later a plot is *made* against him (23:12) and an ambush is *planned* (25:3). The animals and dragon representing the powers hostile to God in Revelation *wage* war against God's witnesses and his saints (11:7; 12:17; 13:7; 19:19), quite apart from their other wicked deeds against them (12:15; 13:5, 12 bis, 13 bis, 14, 15, 16; cf. 16:14).

f) Secular human deeds also have theological implications:

1) On God's *command* or *order* Joseph weds Mary (Matt 1:24). On Jesus' instruction Peter takes action (the great catch of fish, Luke 5:6; cf. his offer at the Transfiguration, 9:33 par.), as does the man with the withered hand (6:10), the disciples (before the multiplication of bread, 9:15), and the servants in Cana (John 2:5).

2) Jesus is himself *touched* or *moved* by the hemorrhaging woman (Mark 5:32), by the joy of the crowd that wants "to *make* him king" and greets him as king (John 6:15; 12:16), by the receptions with Levi and Lazarus (Luke 5:29; John 12:2), by the anointing in Bethany (Matt 26:12, 13 par. Mark 14:8, 9) and esp. during the Passion, exemplified best by the distribution of his clothes (John 19:23, 24), and in a comprehensive way in the question of Pilate, "What shall I *do* with Jesus?" (Matt 27:22 par. Mark 15:12).

3) The parables set in ordinary human life to a large extent address the situation of Jesus and finally the world of God. Such is the case in the *giving* of the marriage feast for the son (Matt 22:2), the *making* of the great feast (Luke 9:16), the paradigmatic behavior of the owner of the vineyard (Matt 20:5, 15), whom the laborers criticize (v. 12 bis), and in what the other "owner of the vineyard" "will *do* to those tenants" (21:40 par. Mark 12:9/Luke 20:15). Here the focus is on God, whereas it is on those who believe in him in the story of the steward's decisive action (Luke 16:3, 4, 8) and in the parables concerning praise and reprimand of servants (Matt 24:46 par. Luke 12:43; 25:16 v.l.; Luke 17:9; 12:47, 48). What to *do* with his wealth is the concern of the fool presented as a warning example (12:17, 18).

4) Purely secular speech can also be used of God, as the example of *making* hair white or black shows, something humanly impossible (Matt 5:36). Frequently, however, secular activity is mentioned without this reference, e.g., the normal behavior of even the tax collectors and Gentiles (5:46, 47), the obedience of the servant (8:9 par. Luke 7:8: "I say . . . '*Do* this,' and he *does* it"), the *commission* of murder (Mark 15:7), the *granting* of amnesty (15:8), the *making* of a fire (John 18:18), or the *spending* of a certain time at a place (Acts 18:23; 20:3; Jas 4:13).

g) Even objects, esp. plants mentioned in parables, "do" something. Thus the tree that *brings (forth)* and *bears* good, bad, or no fruit (Matt 3:10 par. Luke 3:9; 7:17 bis, 18 v.l. bis par. Luke 6:43 bis; 7:19; Luke 13:9; Jas 3:12; Rev 22:2), the plant that *puts forth* branches (Mark 4:32), the seed that *sets* fruit (Matt 13:26), the seed that *brings* various fruits (Luke 8:8), the spring that *brings forth* only certain water (Jas 3:12), and the pound that *makes* more pounds (Luke 19:18).   W. Radl

ποίημα, ατος, τό *poiēma* something made, constructed, creation*

Rom 1:20: what is invisible in God is perceived τοῖς ποιήμασι, in the *things that have been made* (by God); Eph 2:10: the result of the new creation in Christ is that we (Christians) are God's *workmanship/creation*. H. Braun, *TDNT* VI, 458-84.

ποίησις, εως, ἡ *poiēsis* doing, working*

Jas 1:25, in a blessing: μακάριος ἐν τῇ ποιήσει αὐτοῦ ἔσται, such a person "shall be blessed in his doing." F. Thiele, *DNTT* III, 1153-55.

ποιητής, οῦ, ὁ *poiētēs* one who does; poet*

In the sense of *poet* in Acts 17:28. Otherwise a person who does what is required (a "doer"): Rom 2:13 (νόμου);

Jas 1:22, 23 (λόγου), 25 (ἔργου); 4:11 (νόμου). The complementary term ἀκροατής occurs in Rom 2:13; Jas 1:22, 23, 25. H. Braun, *TDNT* VI, 458-84.

ποικίλος, 3 *poikilos* various, diverse*

Only in Heb 13:9 in the sense of *diverse*, i.e., *deceptive* (διδαχαὶ ποικίλαι). Otherwise in the general meaning *various*: Mark 1:34 par. Matt 4:24/Luke 4:40 (diseases); 2 Tim 3:6 (ἐπιθυμίαι); Titus 3:3 (ἐπιθυμίαι καὶ ἡδοναί); Heb 2:4 (δυνάμεις); Jas 1:2; 1 Pet 1:6 (πειρασμοί). Sg. only in 1 Pet 4:10: ποικίλη χάρις θεοῦ, the mercy of God, which manifests itself in various ways. H. Seesemann, *TDNT* VI, 484f.

ποιμαίνω *poimainō* herd (vb.), tend
→ ποιμήν.

ποιμήν, ένος, ὁ *poimēn* shepherd; pastor*
ἀρχιποίμην, ενος, ὁ *archipoimēn* chief shepherd*
ποιμαίνω *poimainō* herd (vb.), tend*

1. NT occurrences and usage — 2. Literal usage — 3. Of God — 4. Of Christ — 5. The Church — 6. Church offices

Lit.: J. B. BAUER, *SacVb* III, 844-86. — DALMAN, *Arbeit* VI, 213-87. —H. GOLDSTEIN, *Das Gemeindeverständnis des Ersten Petrusbriefs* (Diss. Münster, 1973), esp. 205-11, 240-47. — V. HAMP and J. GEWIESS, *LTK* V, 384-86. — J. JEREMIAS, *TDNT* VI, 485-90. — W. JOST, ΠΟΙΜΗΝ. *Das Bild vom Hirten in der biblischen Überlieferung und seine christologische Bedeutung* (1939). — W. NAUCK, "Probleme des frühchristlichen Amtsverständnisses (1 Ptr 5,2f.)," *ZNW* 48 (1957) 200-220. — F. PRAST, *Presbyter und Evangelium in nachapostolischer Zeit. Die Abschiedsrede des Paulus in Milet (Apg 20,17-38)* (1979) 353-433. — H. SCHÜRMANN, "Das Testament des Paulus für die Kirche. Apg 20,18-35," *idem* I, 310-40. — For further bibliography see *TWNT* X, 1244f.

1. Ποιμήν occurs 18 times, most often in the Gospels. Outside the Gospels it occurs only in Eph 4:11; Heb 13:20; 1 Pet 2:25. The vb., on the other hand, occurs only 3 times in the Gospels of a total of 11 NT occurrences (Matt 2:6; Luke 17:7; John 21:16) and 4 times in Revelation. Ἀρχιποίμην occurs only in 1 Pet 5:4 (→ 4.a).

Because of the economic situation in biblical Palestine, livestock-breeding with sheep and goat herds was an important reality along with agriculture. A small livestock herder—and this alone is what we see in the NT—thus enjoyed a respected vocation. In the entire Orient the people were referred to as "herd" and the king as "shepherd," and the OT and NT pick up this imagery. In the NT one can differentiate between the following levels of meaning, levels that at least in part are nonetheless associated closely with one another as parts of an overall picture: literal (occasionally proverbial), theo-logical, christo-logical, ecclesiological, and with reference to offices (→ 2-6).

2. The shepherds in the Lukan prehistory (2:8, 15, 18,

20), like the manger and the (assumed) stall, belong to the oldest local Bethlehem tradition of Jesus' birth. Literal, perhaps even already proverbial passages are 1 Cor 9:7; Luke 17:7; Jude 12. In John 10:2 ποιμήν is intended literally on the first level, i.e., as an element in the imagery (10:1-5), but then clearly christologically at a second level.

3. Although Jesus compares God's joy at the conversion of a sinner with the joy of one who has found a lost sheep (Luke 15:3-7), the designation of God as shepherd occurs nowhere in the NT. One can only assume that in an age when Church or community officeholders were addressed as shepherds (→ 6), so that Christ became the "great shepherd" (→ 4), the designation "shepherd" for God was perceived as ambiguous and misleading.

4. In christological usage one can differentiate three aspects:

a) In the age-old image of the renewal of the world as the gathering of a dispersed and mortally endangered flock (cf. Matt 10:6; 15:24), Jesus sees himself as the *shepherd* of a shepherdless flock (Mark 6:34; Matt 9:36). Dispersion means disaster and gathering means salvation. Later the Church also understood him in this way (Matt 2:6). Rev 7:17 uses the image of a collected flock that a shepherd leads to drink. John 10:11-18 qualifies Jesus' shepherding activity with the following characteristics: As the good shepherd he is prepared to sacrifice his own life for the sake of the flock (vv. 11, 15, 17, 18); as the owner (v. 12) he feels particularly responsible for the sheep, and—again as the good shepherd (v. 14)—he knows his sheep (vv. 15, 27) and they know him (v. 15) and follow him (v. 27; cf. vv. 4, 5). Jesus' responsibilities as shepherd, however, extend not only to the Christian community, but also to the Gentiles: As the one shepherd he is to gather them together to the one flock (v. 16). According to 1 Pet 2:25 Christ—as the shepherd and "bishop" of souls, i.e., as the shepherd who guards souls — gathers the faithful to himself, protects them in their tribulations, and leads them to the Father. Hence in Heb 13:20 he is called the "great shepherd," or "chief shepherd," which 1 Pet 5:4 designates as ἀρχιποίμην.

b) In Mark 14:27f. par. Matt 26:31f. Jesus announces his death and resurrection using the image of the shepherd (cf. Zech 13:7): The shepherd will be struck and the sheep scattered. After he is raised up Jesus will go before the disciples to Galilee.

c) The gathering of the flock is also an image for the gathering of the nations to the eschatological judgment (Matt 25:32). The shepherd then separates the (white) sheep from the (dark) goats. For the sheep as the "blessed of the Father" the kingdom of God's mercy then begins. The "cursed" (25:41) heathen, in contrast, will be "ruled

with a rod of iron," i.e., destroyed (Rev 2:27; 12:5; 19:15). → πρόβατον 3.

5. Concerning the ecclesiological meaning cf. → ποίμνη κτλ..

6. Only once in the NT are Church leaders expressly called ποιμένες, *shepherds:* "apostles, prophets, evangelists, *pastors [shepherds],* and teachers" (Eph 4:11). Since the "pastors and teachers" are introduced with a single art., one should probably assume that they constitute a single group. Ποιμήν here is thus not a title of an office, but rather refers fig. to the obligation of the teacher in his specific activity to care for the congregation.

The responsibility of congregational leaders is described elsewhere with ποιμαίνειν (John 21:16, of Simon Peter; Acts 20:28, of the "guardians"; 1 Pet 5:2, of elders). Both Acts 20:28 and 1 Pet 2:25 (→ 4.a) make clear that the association of the root forms ἐπισκοπ- and ποιμν- is traditional. Since in 1 Pet 2:25 it is Christ that is thus referred to, while in Acts 20:28 congregational leaders are addressed, one must in both passages proceed primarily on the basis of fig. imagery. But no Church leader is allowed to act as lord (1 Pet 5:3), but is always merely the steward (4:10) commissioned by the "chief shepherd" (5:4).

H. Goldstein

ποίμνη, ης, ἡ *poimnē* flock (of sheep)*
ποίμνιον, ου, τό *poimnion* flock (of sheep)*

Lit.: J. JEREMIAS, *TDNT* VI, 499-502.

1. ποίμνη occurs in the literal sense in Luke 2:8 and 1 Cor 9:7 (bis; → ποιμήν 2).

2. The image current throughout the Orient of the people as a flock, which in Israel had unequivocal religious connotations, also occurs in the NT and is behind Matt 10:6; 15:24 (cf. Mark 6:34; Matt 9:36; Luke 15:3-7). Since gen. οἴκου Ἰσραήλ (Matt 10:6; 15:24) is to be interpreted epexegetically (= the household, i.e., Israel), it likely refers to all of Israel, including the pious (cf. Luke 19:9f.). In 1 Pet 2:25, too, the "straying sheep" yield the image of a flock that in fact includes Jews and Gentiles equally. In Matt 25:32 the image refers to the totality of all nations.

3. Whereas Mark 14:27 operates only with the image of the sheep, the parallel Matt 26:31 also uses the noun ποίμνη, which designates the pre-resurrection group of disciples in the sense of the eschatological people of God. (Also in Matt 10:16 par. Luke 10:3 the disciples are described as the eschatological people of God without the word "flock," but by means of sheep imagery.) In the words of consolation in Luke 12:32 Jesus calls his disciples "little flock" (τὸ μικρὸν ποίμνιον).

4. In John, where the word ἐκκλησία does not occur, ποίμνη refers to the—post-resurrection—Church. In the context of John 10:1-30, esp. v. 16 is important: "And I have other sheep, that are not of this fold (αὐλή); I must bring them also, and they will heed my voice. So there shall be one *flock,* one shepherd." The αὐλή (v. 1) is apparently the Jewish people, whereas the ποίμνη is the *one* congregation or Church of Jews and Gentiles.

5. The Lukan farewell address of Paul in Miletus (Acts 20:17-38, ποίμνιον in vv. 28, 29) proves that ποίμνιον and ἐκκλησία in the sense of the post-resurrection Church of Jews and Gentiles are identical.

6. In 1 Pet 5:2-4 the elders are commanded, in their responsibility before Christ, who is the "chief shepherd," to tend the ποίμνιον τοῦ θεοῦ (v. 2). The reference here to the Church of Jews and Gentiles as "God's *flock*" (v. 2; cf. v. 3) asserts that the Church is both God's work and his possession (2:9).   H. Goldstein

ποίμνιον, ου, τό *poimnion* flock (of sheep)
→ ποίμνη.

ποῖος, 3 *of what kind? which?**

The interrogative pronominal adj. ποῖος occurs in direct and indirect questions.

1. The meaning *of what kind?* occurs in the NT only in combination with substantives (BDF §298.2): Luke 6:32, 33, 34; John 12:33; 18:32; 21:19; Acts 7:49; Rom 3:27; 1 Cor 15:35; Jas 4:14; 1 Pet 1:11; 2:20.

2. The meaning *which?*
a) With substantives: ἐν ποίᾳ ἐξουσίᾳ (Mark 11:28, 29, 33 par. Matt 21:23, 24, 27/Luke 20:2, 8); ποία ἐντολή (Mark 12:28 par. Matt 22:36); associated with a point in time (Matt 24:42, 43; Luke 12:39; Rev 3:3); διὰ ποῖον ἔργον (John 10:32); ἐν ποίᾳ δυνάμει ἢ ἐν ποίῳ ὀνόματι (Acts 4:7); ἐκ ποίας ἐπαρχείας (23:34).
b) With no subst. in Matt 19:18; Luke 5:19; 24:19.

πολεμέω *polemeō* wage war, fight
→ πόλεμος.

πόλεμος, ου, ὁ *polemos* war, battle; quarrel*
πολεμέω *polemeō* wage war, fight*

1. Occurrences in the NT — 2. Paul and Hebrews — 3. The Synoptics — 4. Revelation and James — 5. Πολεμέω — 6. Summary considerations

Lit.: O. BAUERNFEIND, *TDNT* VI, 502-15. — O. BETZ, "Jesu heiliger Krieg," *NovT* 2 (1957) 116-37. — H. WINDISCH, *Der messianische Krieg und das Urchristentum* (1909). — For further bibliography → εἰρήνη; see *TWNT* X, 1245f.

1. The subst. πόλεμος occurs 18 times in the NT, the vb. πολεμέω 7 times. 9 occurrences of πόλεμος and 6 occurrences of πολεμέω are in Revelation. The rest of the occurrences of πόλεμος are in the Synoptics (6, 5 of those in Mark 13:7 par.), 1 Corinthians, Hebrews, and James (1 in each); πολεμέω occurs once in James.

2. Paul uses the example of trumpeting and preparations for *battle* (1 Cor 14:8) to illustrate the uselessness of incomprehensible or uninterpreted glossolalia. Hebrews remembers how the OT witnesses of faith "became mighty in *war*" (11:34).

3. Among the examples in discipleship parenesis is also the king who undertakes to meet another king in *war* (Luke 14:31, from L). According to the Synoptic apocalypse *"wars* and rumors of *wars"* are among the signs of the eschaton that precede the τέλος (Mark 13:7 bis par. Matt 24:6 bis/Luke 21:9).

4. Revelation esp. knows of war as an element of the eschatological catastrophes. The demonic locusts are like horses arrayed for *battle* (9:7, 9). A πόλεμος in heaven between Michael and the dragon (12:7) ends with the fall of the dragon and his angels to the earth (12:9). The beast from the bottomless pit goes to *war* with the two witnesses (11:7), the dragon goes to *war* with the children of the woman of heaven, i.e., with Christians (12:17), and the antichrist "first beast" goes to *war* with the "saints," i.e., again, with Christians (13:7). Demons seduce the earthly powers into a great *war* of the end time (cf. *1 Enoch* 56:5f.): The three spirits like frogs (Rev 16:13) assemble the kings of the whole world (16:14), the beast gathers the kings of the earth (19:19; cf. 17:12), and Satan deceives Gog and Magog along with the nations at the four corners of the earth (20:8).

Unexpectedly James calls quarrels in the congregation πόλεμοι and μάχαι (4:1). Apparently the author wants to understand the conflicts among Christians as signs of the end time (cf. 1 Cor 11:18f.).

5. Use of the vb. **πολεμέω**, *wage war,* corresponds to that of the noun. Michael and his angels *fight* with the dragon and his angels (Rev 12:7 bis). Those who worship the beast believe that no one can *fight* against it (13:4); the kings (cf. 17:12; 19:19) *make war* on the messianic ἀρνίον (17:14). The victorious knight called πιστὸς καὶ ἀληθινός judges and *makes war* "in righteousness" (19:11); he is none other than the exalted one who threatens war on the heretics of Pergamum with the sword of his mouth (2:16).

Contextual considerations place the vbs. πολεμέω and μάχομαι (Jas 4:2) with the nouns πόλεμοι and μάχαι (4:1; → 4); here, too, the reference is probably to eschatological circumstances before the imminent parousia (5:7-9).

6. Πόλεμος and πολεμέω occur in the NT, therefore, most of all in eschatological contexts (the Synoptics, Revelation). Only two passages use the image of "normal" war as a parenetic example (Paul, Luke). Already Heb 11:34 possibly thinks typologically of the coming πόλεμος of the end time. Jas 4:1f. apparently considers quarrels among Christians to be eschatological wars (on heresy cf. Rev 2:16).

It is not just in the relatively small number of occurrences of πόλεμος and πολεμέω that the NT makes use of OT and Jewish imagery of the messianic war and victory (Bauernfeind 511f.; Betz 116-24). This imagery plays a role in several statements by Jesus, e.g., Matt 10:34 par. Luke 12:51 (cf. Luke 22:35-38; → μάχαιρα) and his references to "taking by storm" (Matt 11:12 par. Luke 16:16) and to the military organization of armies of angels (Matt 26:53) and demons (cf. Mark 5:9 par. Luke 8:30; → δαιμόνιον). The "spiritual armor" necessary for the battle against the demons (Eph 6:11-17; 1 Thess 5:8; → πανοπλία) also belongs to this context.   O. Böcher

πόλις, εως, ἡ *polis* city, town; capital city

1. Occurrences in the NT — 2. Greek usage and the LXX — 3. In narrative texts — 4. The heavenly city

Lit.: BAGD s.v. — W. BOUSSET, *Rev* (KEK, [2]1906, reprinted 1966) 446-55. — J. ERNST, "Die griechische Polis—das himmlische Jerusalem—die christliche Stadt," *TGl* 67 (1977) 240-58. — H. KRAFT, *Rev* (HNT, 1974) 262-75. — F. LAUB, *Bekenntnis und Auslegung* (1980) 257-61. — K. L. SCHMIDT, "Jerusalem als Urbild und Abbild," *idem, NT—Judentum—Kirche* (1981) 265-306, esp. 265-90. — *idem, Die Polis in Kirche und Welt* (1939) 11-40. — SPICQ, *Notes* II, 710-20. — H. STRATHMANN, *TDNT* VI, 516-35. — G. THEISSEN, *Untersuchungen zum Hebräerbrief* (1969), esp. 103-5. — For further bibliography see *TWNT* X, 1246; Laub.

1. Πόλις occurs 161 times in the NT: 8 times in Mark, 26 in Matthew, 39 in Luke, 8 in John, 42 in Acts. It occurs only 3 times in the genuine Pauline letters (Rom 13:26; 2 Cor 11:26, 32), only once in the deutero-Pauline letters (Titus 1:5), 4 times in Hebrews (11:10, 16; 12:22; 13:14), and in Jas 4:13; 2 Pet 2:6; and Jude 7. It occurs 27 times in Revelation.

2. Πόλις is derived from an Indo-European root that means "to fill." From Homer on πόλις had the meaning "city" or "state." This meaning as an expression of an identity of citizenship and state held until the end of the actual "city-states" during the Macedonian period.

Πόλις occurs *ca.* 1600 times in the LXX as a tr. of 'îr, "city." Nonetheless, the nature of the Israelite city was fundamentally different from that of the Greek. In the OT, e.g., every fortified height is called a "city." "City" in the sense of a fortified enclosure for the protection of the inhabitants against attack is a late concept. Jerusalem, "the city" spoken of absolutely, has special meaning in the LXX (Ezek 7:23). If the inhabitants of Jerusalem do not meet the goal of being "the city of God" or "the holy city," e.g., then the prophet calls them to repentance (22:2-4). Expectation, however, focuses on a better Jerusalem (Isa 1:26;

Jer 38:38), an anticipation arising in early Judaism. The "new Jerusalem" is expected from heaven, where it has been preserved from the very beginning (4 Ezra 7:26).

3. In the NT, too, πόλις no longer has the Greek political meaning "state." It means quite simply *city* and occurs most frequently in the Gospels and Acts, where, e.g., Bethlehem, Nazareth, Nain, Ephesus, Philippi, and Athens are called cities. The apostle Paul preached almost exclusively in the large πόλεις of the Empire, whereas Jesus and his disciples moved about in the "*cities* and villages" (κῶμαι, Matt 9:35). The hybrid term κωμόπολις in Mark 1:38 shows that the distinction between κώμη and πόλις was not strictly followed. The reference here is to a small market town that legally only occupied the position of → κώμη. Additional information is sometimes given to characterize a certain city, e.g., Acts 8:5: τὴν πόλιν τῆς Σαμαρείας; Luke 23:51: πόλεως τῶν Ἰουδαίων.

4. The NT, the LXX, and Judaism as a whole speak of Jerusalem as "the holy *city*" (Matt 4:5; 27:53; Rev 11:2). Since the fall of Jerusalem is certain (Mark 13:2ff.; Matt 24:15f.), expectation focuses entirely on the "Jerusalem above," which according to Gal 4:25f. will be juxtaposed with the present Jerusalem. Paul intends to show here that "'we are not children of the slave but of the free woman" (v. 31), i.e., that believers are free from the law" (P. Vielhauer, "Oikodome," *idem, Aufsätze* [1979] II, 210).

The occurrences in Hebrews refer even more vigorously to this "new *city*." Abraham "looked forward to the *city* that has foundations" (11:10). The witnesses of faith of the Old Covenant directed their expectation to the "heavenly homeland" (11:13-16), to the *city* prepared by God (11:16), which they have seen only from afar (11:13). In 13:14 a joyous certainty finds expression: "For here we have no lasting *city,* but we seek the *city* which is to come." The Christian knows that he has already come to this future *city* (12:22), but also knows that future salvation, the goal of the Church, is attained only with the heavenly city.

The occurrences in Revelation exhibit particular flexibility in their references to the "new Jerusalem," esp. ch. 21: The congregation of the eschaton is described as the model of the heavenly city, and the completion of that community is portrayed through rich imagery. Neither temple (as opposed to Ezek 40:2), cult, nor sacrifice will exist there. The "new Jerusalem" is the opposite of heathen Babylon, where people in their hubris once tried to climb to heaven. Now nothing more can disturb the image of the perfected heavenly city. "The upper, the new, the holy, the heavenly city of God is both the goal and the foundation of the entire salvation event from eternity to eternity" (Schmidt 289).   U. Hutter

πολιτάρχης, ου, ὁ *politarchēs* city prefect*

Acts 17:6, 8: πολιτάρχαι in Thessalonica. A plurality of "politarchs" constituted the highest authority in Macedonian cities (on Thessalonica see *CIG* II, 1967; *Bulletin de correspondances hellénistes* 18 [1894] 420; 21 [1897] 161; Moulton/Milligan s.v.) and in isolated places elsewhere. E. D. Burton, "The Politarchs," *AJT* 2 (1898) 598-632.

πολιτεία, ας, ἡ *politeia* citizenship; state*

Acts 22:28: the Roman *citizenship* bought by the χιλίαρχος; Eph 2:12: Gentile Christians were once "alienated from the *commonwealth* of Israel (ἡ πολιτεία τοῦ Ἰσραήλ)"; the synonymous parallel immediately follows: "strangers to the covenants of promise." H. Strathmann *TDNT* VI, 519f., 534f.; H. Bietenhard, *DNTT* II, 801-5; Spicq, *Notes* II, 710-15.

πολίτευμα, ατος, τό *politeuma* commonwealth, state*
πολιτεύομαι *politeuomai* be a citizen; govern the state; lead/conduct one's life*

1. Occurrences in the NT — 2. Πολιτεύομαι — 3. Πολίτευμα

Lit.: K. ALAND, "Das Verhältnis von Kirche und Staat," *idem, Neutestamentliche Entwürfe* (1979) 25-123, esp. 50-59. — BAGD s.v. — J. BECKER, "Erwägungen zu Phil. 3,20-21," *TZ* 27 (1971) 15-29. — P. C. BÖTTGER, "Die eschatologische Existenz der Christen," *ZNW* 60 (1969) 245-63. — R. R. BREWER, "The Meaning of *politeuesthe* in Philippians 1:27," *JBL* 73 (1954) 76-83. — J. GNILKA, *Phil* (HTKNT, ²1976) 96ff., 206ff. — E. HAENCHEN, *Acts* (Eng. tr., 1971) 637. — G. MENESTRINA, "πολίτευμα," *BeO* 20 (1978) 254. — H. SCHLIER, "Die Beurteilung des Staates im Neuen Testament," *idem* I, 1-16. — K. L. SCHMIDT, *Die Polis in Kirche und Welt* (1939) 15-24. — SPICQ, *Notes* II, 710-20. — H. STRATHMANN, *TDNT* VI, 516-35, esp. 534f. — N. WALTER, "Die Philipper und das Leiden," FS Schürmann 417-34, esp. 421-24. — For further bibliography see *TWNT* X, 1246.

1. The vb. occurs twice in the NT (Acts 23:1; Phil 1:27). The noun is a NT hapax legomenon (Phil 3:20).

2. In his speech before the Sanhedrin (Acts 22:30–23:10) Paul says: ἐγὼ πάσῃ συνειδήσει ἀγαθῇ πεπολίτευμαι τῷ θεῷ . . . (23:1). Almost all translators follow the Vg., which renders πολιτεύομαι with *conversatus sum*, with "lead/conduct [one's] life" (Luther: "wandeln"). Strathmann (534) believes that πολιτεύομαι would have to be translated here without any political overtones. This is not, however, entirely convincing. Considering the great scene before the Sanhedrin (22:30ff.) political implications should come to expression as well. Hence Schmidt's tr.

(15) probably comes closest: "In all good conscience up to this day I *have been a citizen* for (before) God."

Phil 1:27 is to be interpreted similarly: ἀξίως τοῦ εὐαγγελίου τοῦ Χριστοῦ, "*conduct your community life* so that it is worthy of the gospel of Christ." One should not equate πολιτεύομαι with περιπατέω, which in Judaism replaces πολιτεύομαι in the sense of "live, conduct one's life." Paul takes up a term here in common usage in the Gentile Christian community in Philippi and adapts it thus into the vocabulary of the Church.

3. In order to determine the meaning of πολίτευμα in Phil 3:20 we must first examine the context. The word stands in the large section Phil 3:2–4:1, in which Paul takes issue with the false teachings in Philippi. His adversaries were probably Christian missionaries of Jewish background, and he counters them by asserting that Christians have by no means reached their goal. The celebratory, almost liturgical language of 3:20f. is of particular importance; the contrast to τὰ ἐπίγεια φρονοῦντες in v. 19 comes in v. 20: ἡμῶν γὰρ πολίτευμα ἐν οὐρανοῖς. The tr. of the passage is not unequivocal. Luther, e.g., moved in his tr. from *Bürgerschaft* ("citizenship," 1522) to *Wandel* ("conduct," 1545). Paul probably took the term from the vocabulary of his adversaries and used it to show "that thus the earthly state is not the state in the absolute sense" (Schlier 3). Christians strive to attain not the earthly πολίτευμα, but rather the heavenly community.

U. Hutter

πολιτεύομαι *politeuomai* be a citizen; govern the state; lead/conduct one's life
→ πολίτευμα 1, 2.

πολίτης, ου, ὁ *politēs* citizen; fellow citizen*

The inhabitant of a city (Acts 21:39) or of a country (Luke 15:15). In Heb 8:11 (cf. Jer 38:34 LXX) πολίτης refers to a *fellow citizen;* similarly Luke 19:14. H. Strathmann, *TDNT* VI, 525, 533f.; H. Bietenhard, *DNTT* II, 801-5.

πολλάκις *pollakis* many times, frequently, often*

Mark 5:4; 9:22 par. Matt 17:15 (bis); John 18:2; Acts 26:11; Rom 1:13; 2 Cor 8:22; Phil 3:18. In a catalog of sufferings in 2 Cor 11:23, 26, 27 (bis). Also 2 Tim 1:16; Heb 6:7; 9:25, 26; 10:11.

πολλαπλασίων, 2 *pollaplasiōn* many times more*

Luke 18:30 (par. Matt 19:29 B L pc): πολλαπλασίονα λαμβάνω, "receive *manifold more*." E. Schwyzer, *MH* 2 (1945) 137-47.

πολυεύσπλαγχνος, 2 *polyeusplanchnos* rich in compassion

James 5:11 v.l. (in place of πολύσπλαγχνος), of God (with οἰκτίρμων). Πολυεύσπλαγχνος and πολυευσπλαγχνία occur in *Herm. Sim.* v.4.4; viii.6.1.

πολυλογία, ας, ἡ *polylogia* wordiness*

Matt 6:7, of the prayers of Gentiles, who "think that they will be heard for their *many words*" (ἐν τῇ πολυλογίᾳ αὐτῶν); cf. → βατταλογέω. C. Maurer, *TDNT* VI, 545f.

πολυμερῶς *polymerōs* in many ways*

Heb 1:1, with πολυτρόπως: "In many and various ways God spoke of old to our fathers."

πολυποίκιλος, 2 *polypoikilos* (extremely) manifold*

Eph 3:10, of God's σοφία. → ποικίλος. H. Seesemann, *TDNT* VI, 484.

πολύς, πολλή, πολύ *polys* much; many

1. Occurrences in the NT — 2. Usage and meaning — 3. Theological and other contexts — a) In a hermeneutical process (conclusions *a minore ad maius*) — b) As a cosmological and ecclesiological term? — c) In specifically soteriological statements — d) In historical narratives — e) Luke 1:1 and similar passages

Lit.: J. BAUER, "ΠΟΛΛΟΙ Lk 1,1," *NovT* 4 (1960) 263-66. — J. A. BENGEL, *Commentary on the NT (Gnomon Novi Testamenti)* (reprinted 1982), on Matt 20:28. — E. BRANDENBURGER, *Adam und Christus* (1962) 68ff. — K. BRUGMANN, *Die Ausdrücke für den Begriff der Totalität in den indogermanischen Sprachen* (1893-94). — idem, *Die distributiven und die kollektiven Numeralia der indogermanischen Sprachen* (ASGW.PH 25 /5, 1907). — J. COSTELLOE, "Pauca de 'multis,'" *Homiletic and Pastoral Review* 71 (1970/71) 417-25. — F. GRABER, *DNTT* I, 94-96. — T. HARTMANN, *THAT* II, 715-26. — J. JEREMIAS, *TDNT* VI, 536-45. — H. LAUSBERG, *Elemente der literarischen Rhetorik* (³1967). — D. MARIN, " 'Per molti' non 'per tutti' (Matth. 26, 27-28)," *Studia Florentina A. Ronconi oblata* (1970) 221-31. — B. REICKE and G. BERTRAM, *TDNT* V, 886-96. — D. J. G. ROSENMÜLLER, *Scholia in Novum Testamentum* I (1792). — G. SAUER, *THAT* I, 828-30. — J. F. SCHLEUSNER, *Novum Lexicon Graeco-Latinum in Novum Testamentum* II (1801) s.v. — O. SZEMERÉNYI, "Greek πολύς and πολλός," *ZVSF* 88 (1974) 1-31. — For further bibliography see Jeremias; *TDNT* X, 1246.

1. Πολύς occurs 359 times in the NT (418 times with comparative → πλείων and superlative → πλεῖστος) in all the writings except 2 Thessalonians and Jude (51 occurrences in Matthew, 59 in Mark, 51 in Luke, 36 in John, 48 in Acts, 21 in Romans, 18 in 1 Corinthians, 21 in 2 Corinthians, 4 in 1 Thessalonians, 5 in 1 Timothy, 7 in Hebrews, 14 in Revelation, 3 each in Galatians, Philippians, and James, 2 each in 2 Timothy, Titus, Philemon, 1 John, and 2 John, 1 each in Ephesians, Colossians, 1 Peter, 2 Peter, and 3 John).

2. In keeping with this declension nom. and acc. sg. masc. and neut. are formed from the stem πολυ- (consonant or third declension), and the rest of the forms from the stem πολλο-/α- (according to the a-/o- declension; on the etymology and word-formation see J. Pokorny, *Indogermanisches etymologisches Wörterbuch* I [1959] 798-800: root *pel-* etc., cf. there the meanings [Germ.] *füllen, Menge, viel;* cf., e.g., also Gothic *filu*). All forms of this declension are documented in the NT. Compounds and derivatives in the NT are based on both πολλο- and πολυ.

Synonymous terms or semantically related words in the NT include ὅσος, πόσος, τοσοῦτος, ἱκανός, πλῆθος, περισσεία, etc.; cf. also πᾶς (ἅπας, ὅλος). Special relationships obtain in the NT with ὀλίγος κτλ., ὑστερέω κτλ., ἐλάχιστος, εἷς, πλήρης κτλ., οὐδείς.

The point of departure for the shades of meaning in the NT is the meaning *many*. Shades of meaning develop according to whether and how πολύς is used as an adj., subst., or adv.

As an adj. it modifies a subst. (sg. or pl., with or without art.) in the numerical sense of *much, many* (Matt 7:22b; Luke 7:47), also with measurements (Matt 14:24), temporally (Luke 8:29; Acts 24:10), and fig. (Acts 26:24). Πολύς can then also mean *great* (1 Pet 1:3), intensively something like *loud* (Matt 2:18), *deep* (Acts 21:40, of a state of quiet), *late* (Mark 6:35), and similar ideas (cf. the distinctions in BAGD s.v.).

Subst. πολύς stands with and without art. in the pl. masc. and neut. (cf. Matt 7:22a; Mark 4:2; 9:26; Luke 12:48). Here the meaning *many* is esp. appropriate and actually implies *the crowd, the majority* (on the problem of inclusive usage of [οἱ] πολλοί, *all* → 3.c). Prep. usage (e.g., ἐπὶ πολύ, Acts 28:6: "long") belongs here or with adv. usage.

The advs. πολύ and πολλά are formed from subst. use in the acc. They, too, expand the meaning of *much* to *enthusiastically, loudly, passionately,* etc. (cf. BAGD s.v. I.2.b.β). Special idioms and figures include paronomasia and similar figures (Mark 12:41; John 4:41; 2 Cor 8:22; 9:12), litotes (Luke 15:13; John 2:12; Acts 1:5; 27:14; 1 Cor 1:26; 4:15), use with plerophoric καί (syndetic collocation; see Szemerényi 10) with ἄλλος, βαρύς, ἕτερος (John 20:30; Acts 25:7; Luke 3:18, without καί [asyndetic collocation] in Mark 15:41; John 21:25; Luke 8:3; Acts 15:35), and with the comparatives μᾶλλον (2 Cor 3:9; → 3.a), μᾶλλον κρεῖσσον (Phil 1:23), πλείους (John 4:41), and σπουδαιότερον (2 Cor 8:22).

3. A large part of the theological aspects and other aspects in use of πολύς derives less from the word itself than from associated terms and statements:

a) The conclusion *a minore ad maius* derives from a Jewish procedure that is documented in rabbinic writings as *qal wāḥômer* (→ μᾶλλον 3.a; cf. H. L. Strack, *Intro-*

duction to the Talmud and Midrash [1931] 94, 285). Qal waḥômer corresponds to formulaic phrases in the NT that usually use μᾶλλον (πολλῷ μᾶλλον, πόσῳ μᾶλλον, πολὺ μᾶλλον, though also implied by simple μᾶλλον, Matt 6:26) and, following the rabbinic variations of the formula (cf. Billerbeck III, 225f.), are also indicated by πόσον (Matt 6:23), πόσῳ (12:12), πολλῶν (10:31 par.), and πόσῳ χεῖρων (Heb 10:28f.). In the combination of πολύς with μᾶλλον (cf. BDF §246.1) πολύ is adv. acc., πολλῷ is dative of measure (according to Schwyzer, Grammatik II, 163 locative of degree with comparatives). Simple πολλῶν is genitive of value (cf. Kühner, Grammatik II/1, §418.7; Schwyzer, op. cit. 125ff.). Not every such phrase implies the conclusion a minore (thus not Mark 10:48; Luke 18:39; John 4:41).

In general such combinations with πολύς and ὀλίγος are found in characteristic Greek with a dative of measure. Were they, however, perceived as an expressly hermeneutical category? Ancient rhetorical theory does include a locus a minore ad maius or the reverse, above all at the level of conceptual content (cf. Lausberg §§41, 185, 192f., 198), then also in conceptual combinations (cf. ibid. §385). In such cases, however, a conscious procedure to a conclusion does not really seem intended, since a minore ad maius there does not refer to formulas of the texts themselves. In general "secular" usage here does not appear very helpful. Nonetheless, this procedure to a conclusion is clearly present in Diodorus Siculus (1st cent. B.C.) I.2 (cf. ThGL VI, 534) with εἰ . . . πόσῳ μᾶλλον. Therefore one cannot derive NT usage from the Jewish background alone, though one ought perhaps to give the latter more weight, since some NT writings did indeed originate particularly on Jewish soil (cf. the Synoptic tradition represented in Matthew and Luke along with Paul and Hebrews).

b) Unlike τὰ πάντα (cf. also ὁ κόσμος ὅλος, Matt 16:26; Luke 9:25) πολύς is not used in a universal-cosmological sense. Neither is οἱ πολλοί used as an expressly ecclesiological term (perhaps in Matt 22:14; Mark 10:45, etc.; Rom 5:12ff.; 12:5), at least not as in the Qumran community (cf. [hā-]rabbîm—not rôḇ—as the "full assembly," 1QS 6–8), particularly since in Christianity many local individual congregations (cf. the comparative in 2 Cor 2:6, πάντες in 1 Cor 14:24, specifically comprehensive, however, in 2 Cor 2:17, with the comparative in 2 Cor 4:15, etc.) and contrasting juxtaposition such as "many —few" (Matt 22:14) play a role. In characteristic Greek the pl. was then also used in the sociological sense as a designation for the "crowd, mass" and democratically for the "majority" (as opposed, e.g., to an aristocratic class).

c) In some passages we encounter a clearly soteriological usage, above all in christological statements (esp. about Jesus' suffering and death) with the intention of ὑπὲρ πολλῶν analogous to pro me/nobis. Precisely here the meaning of πολλοί becomes problematical.

Normally here as elsewhere one will want to translate simply with "many." Recently Jeremias esp. has suggested an inclusive sense that he distinguishes from an exclusive one ("many, but not all"). He considers this inclusive sense a peculiarity of Semitic languages (cf. Heb. [hā-]rabbîm, Aram. śaggî'în, "the uncountable many, the great multitude, all"; see TDNT, VI 536[ff.]; then also Graber, Hartmann). In this way a philological problem and a theological problem become one.

1) In Semitic languages there is no commonly used adj. for "all"; rather, one works with subst. (cf. Heb. kol, Aram. kōllā', and even Akk. kalû[m], kullatu[m]), so that difficulties in expressing such concepts can arise (Heb./Aram. rab to Akk. rabû[m], "much" or "great", are, on the other hand, commonly used as adjectives). On (hā)rabbîm → 3.b. In 1 Enoch 14:20 there emerges in the Aramaic, Greek, and Ethiopic versions a correspondence between rab, πᾶς, and kul. In the NT the variation from πάντες and (οἱ) πολλοί in Rom 5:12ff. is particularly striking. Nonetheless, not all the passages cited by Jeremias and others fall unequivocally under this rubric. Older lexicography (thus Schleusner) did, to be sure, assume for πολύς the sense of πᾶς, omnis, totus, universus. Today, however, this is not as a rule represented in dictionaries; one more likely only goes as far as the sense of "large crowd, mass, multitude."

In the NT the following emerges for πολύς as a term for group quantity: It can be used of a partial group (many, i.e., not all, Matt 27:52; 1 Cor 11:30) and can refer to the relationship between different partial groups (cf. "many —few," "many—one," Matt 7:13f.; 1 Cor 12:12ff.), but can also refer in summary fashion to groups with no larger group reference point (cf. "plentiful—few," "one —the many/the crowd," Matt 9:37; Luke 7:47; 1 Cor 8:4f.; 2 Cor 2:17; cf. also Mark 6:5), can be used of a larger group (Rom 8:29), can suggest the differentiation and variety within a group (Rom 12:4ff.; 1 Cor 10:17; 12:12ff.), and can alternate with the term "all" (Rom 5:12ff.; 1 Cor 10:33). Hence even in NT passages where πολύς and πᾶς stand together (cf. Rom 5:12ff.; 12:4f.; 1 Cor 10:33; 12:12ff. and correspondingly with the comparative) the question remains whether πολύς does not refer rather to a "large group" from a particular perspective (cf., e.g., a mutual relationship between two quantities or groups, a large number, differentiation) than consciously to "all." Philologically, then, unless compelling reasons exist to the contrary, perhaps one ought as a rule simply to stay with the tr. much, many, the many.

2) Paul says expressly that sin and death (through Adam) and salvation (through Christ) came to "all" (Rom 5:12ff.; v. 12: πάντες; vv. 15f., 19: πολλοί). The Pauline school (1 Tim 2:6) shows that Jesus' suffering and death ἀντί/ὑπὲρ πολλῶν (Mark 10:45 par.; 14:24 par.) are also consciously applied to "all" in the NT.

This poses the question of universal reconciliation. Perhaps the older understanding of πολλοί as "all" (cf. Rosenmüller 369 on Matt 20:28: pro universa hominum multitudine, also referring to Rom 5:12, 15, 18—contra Bengel) should be viewed in this context. Given the eschatological dualism (cf. the idea of judgment) permeating the NT both at the literary-compositional level and in the tradition-historical dimension, universal reconciliation should not carry much weight. Hence one should probably understand such passages with πολλοί and πάντες as saying that salvation has been prepared potentially for the *many* or for all, though it is realized only through acceptance of the offer.

The statements in Mark 10:45 par.; 14:24 par. doubtlessly represent old traditions. Yet even if this is a Semitism, it does not necessarily represent the *ipsissima vox* of Jesus. It can also be a manifestation of the christology of the Palestinian Church or of Hellenistic (Jewish) Christianity (cf. Isa 53:12 MT and LXX).

Rom 5:12ff. shows that πολλοί can also be understood this way in Hellenistic circles. Here the relationship of πολλοί or πάντες to εἷς (Adam or Christ) is the determining factor. Even Aristotle views τὰ πολλά not only in conjunction with τὸ ὀλίγον, but also with τὸ ἕν (*Metaph.* ix.6.1056b-57a; iv.6.1017a). Here in Paul's case, however, the tradition-historical influence is more likely the conception of a corporate personality or an Adam-primal human ancestor speculation (cf. Brandenburger): The πολλοί or πάντες are contained in this εἷς (ἄνθρωπος) or stand under his power. Perhaps in Rom 5:12ff. Paul chooses πολλοί against πάντες to express variety and differentiation within a group (cf. v. 15 following vv. 12-14). These centers of gravity are in any case part of the body-member statements in Rom 12:4f.; 1 Cor 12:12ff. to the extent that there the alternation between πολλοί and πάντες is doubtlessly intentional. The variation in perspective also plays a role in the use of πολλοί, πάντες, and similar terms; cf., e.g., the juxtaposition in Mark 10:45; 1 Tim 2:6; Rom 5:12ff.; Matt 7:13f.; 9:37; 19:30; 22:14; 1 Cor 9:19ff.; 10:33. (See also the critical considerations concerning inclusive language by Costelloe, Marin.)

d) Πολύς also occurs in historical narratives. It can be used in a more neutral fashion narratively (e.g., Matt 26:47; Acts 21:40) or as documentation (Matt 2:18; Luke 4:25, 27; Rom 4:17; 1 Cor 11:30). It can also, however, report directly and thus pose special problems. The Gospels and Acts are particularly characteristic here. Πολύς occurs in reports of the activity of John the Baptist (cf. Matt 3:7ff. par.) and in an even more pronounced fashion in reports of Jesus' activity (cf. 4:25; 8:1, 16; 9:10; 12:15; 19:2 and *passim*), on up to the resurrection (27:52f.), and of the activity of the apostles (Acts 4:4; 5:12; 6:7; 11:21; 17:4 and *passim*). In such passages we encounter above all redactional-compositional and literary activity (summaries, introductory and transitional phrases).

Whereas πολύς is not particularly striking in its reference to the disciples and apostles in the Gospels (see, however, Luke 6:17; esp. John 2:23; 6:60, 66), this is not the case concerning believers in Acts. Here the weight of pre-Easter historical circumstances or later Church circumstances may have an influence. Particularly in passages such as those which use πολύς and ὄχλος together (cf. even πᾶς in Mark 1:32) the question arises how this relates to the messianic mystery (cf. Mark 3:12) and retarding factors. Some things become clearer through the concluding events in Jerusalem: Πολύς is in part a preliminary category (cf., e.g., also Mark 6:5). Yet even after Easter this is in part still the case, since failure and suffering, relapse and desertion come to light. Here one may think of eschatological structures that under earthly conditions allow salvation to appear only in a broken and veiled fashion. This emerging dialectic manifests itself even more strikingly in Paul when he plays out

categories such as "*many*—few" in historical reports in an almost dialectical fashion (cf., e.g., 1 Cor 1:26). This dialectic weakens in the post-Pauline Epistles.

In the NT πολύς is striking in its use with the phenomenon of the future "false ones" (Mark 13:6 par.; Matt 24:10ff.; 2 Pet 2:2) or in passages reflecting current apocalyptic tradition (1 John 2:18; 2 John 7; apocalyptic vision: Rev 5:11; 8:11). If one views such quantitative aspects in historical reports, theological-eschatological influences are not the only factors to consider. Rather, combinations such as ὄχλος, used absolutely or with πολύς, πᾶς, τοσοῦτος, πλεῖστος, ἱκανός, οἱ μυριάδες (cf. Heb. *rᵉbābāh, ribbô,* Aram. *ribabtā', ribbōtā'*) or ὄχλοι, used absolutely or with πολλοί, πάντες, as well as other analogous figures of speech point toward hyperbolic and plerophoric portrayal. Such usage reflects not least also psychological-sociological (popular portrayal), doxological, or further specific, motive-bound influences (e.g., the idea of blessing, of mission with tradition-historically OT and Jewish background).

e) Πολλοί in Luke 1:1 stands out on the (form-critical) literary level. In the context of the Lukan proemium (on πολλοί as stylistic device cf. Bauer) the *many* appear between the eyewitness reports (first generation) and Luke(-Acts) himself (second or third generation) as belonging to the second generation and the second period of transmission (cf. Kümmel, *Introduction* 155-59). One can refer to Mark and Q here. Possibly, however, additional (no longer known) attempts at portrayal may be addressed. In this way it becomes clear that not only the object of portrayal itself is qualified by πολύς (→ 3.d; cf. further expressly John 20:30; 21:25; in contrast Heb 1:1f. on a different level), but also the portrayals themselves. This leads further to the hermeneutical-theological problem of the polymorphous nature of the NT witnesses and of the canon (within the canon).   G. Nebe

πολύσπλαγχνος, 2 *polysplanchnos* compassionate*

Jas 5:11, of God, with οἰκτίρμων. H. Köster, *TDNT* VII, 548-59; H. H. Esser, *DNTT* II, 599-601.

πολυτελής, 2 *polytelēs* expensive, costly*

Of ointment in Mark 14:3, clothing in 1 Tim 2:9. Fig. of the true jewel that is "πολυτελές in God's sight" (1 Pet 3:4). Spicq, *Notes* II, 721f.

πολύτιμος, 2 *polytimos* valuable, precious*

Matt 13:46, of a pearl; John 12:3, of ointment (but cf. Mark 14:3: → πολυτελής). Comparative in 1 Pet 1:7: "the genuineness of your faith, *more precious* than gold (πολυτιμότερον χρυσίου)."

πολυτρόπως *polytropōs* in many ways, variously*

In Heb 1:1 with → πολυμερῶς. E. Grässer, EKKNT (V) 3 (1971) 73-77.

πόμα, ατος, τό *poma* a drink (noun)*

Literal in Heb 9:10. Fig. in 1 Cor 12:13 v.l., probably influenced by the usage in the Last Supper: ἓν πόμα (in place of πνεῦμα) ἐποτίσθημεν; 10:4: τὸ πνευματικὸν πόμα, "the supernatural *drink*," from which the Israelites in the desert drank. L. Goppelt, *TDNT* VI, 145-48.

πονηϱία, ας ἡ *ponēria* malice, wickedness, baseness*

Lit.: BAGD s.v. — G. HARDER, *TDNT* VI, 562-66.

1. Πονηϱία occurs 7 times in the NT: 3 times in the Synoptics, twice in Paul, once each in Acts 3:26; Eph 6:12. The same writings that use πονηϱία also use the adj. → πονηϱός.

2. Πονηϱία appears exclusively in ethical-moral contexts and is used of iniquities in vice catalogs (Rom 1:29: turning away from God; Mark 7:22; Luke 11:39: the evil in human hearts; cf. 1 Cor 5:8: πονηϱία as the opposite of sincerity) and in general of utterly objectionable ethical attitudes, e.g., of the Jewish leaders opposed to Jesus (Matt 22:18: the hidden evil intent). In Acts 3:26 and Mark 7:22 the pl. is used of various sorts of iniquity. The danger of πονηϱία is underscored by its use for "the spiritual hosts of wickedness in the heavenly places" (Eph 6:12), which probably refers to "the current demonological idea of a world of ungodly spirits in the middle layer of heaven" (Harder 566) that necessitate increased attentiveness on the part of human beings (cf. 6:13).

A. Kretzer

πονηϱός, 3 *ponēros* in troubled condition, miserable; bad, worthless; evil, malicious, wicked

1. Occurrences in the NT — 2. Meaning — 3. Secular Greek and OT references — 4. NT use and meaning

Lit.: G. BAUMBACH, *Das Verständnis des Bösen in den synoptischen Evangelien* (1963). — BAGD s.v. — G. HARDER, *TDNT* VI, 546-66. — M. LIMBECK, "Satan und das Böse im NT," *Teufelsglaube* (ed. H. Haag; 1974) 271-388. — H. SCHLIER, *Principalities and Powers in the NT* (1961). — R. SCHNACKEN-BURG, "Das Geheimnis des Bösen," *idem, Maßstab des Glaubens* (1978) 205-30. — H. J. STOEBE, *THAT* II, 794-803. — For further bibliography see *TWNT* X, 1246.

1. Πονηϱός occurs 78 times in the NT. It is preferred by Matthew (26 occurrences) and occurs with relative frequency in Luke (13 occurrences in the Gospel, 8 in Acts) and in 1 John (6 occurrences), sporadically in the deutero-Pauline Epistles (e.g., Ephesians: 3 occurrences), and only sparingly in Paul (4 occurrences). Linguistic and form-critical observations yield an initial key to understanding its usage and meaning (→ 2).

2. Πονηϱός is derived from the subst. πόνος (exertion, distress, affliction, disease) and the vb. πονέω (work, exert oneself; cause pain, feel pain) or πένομαι (exert oneself, toil). Although both a trans.-act. usage ("causing evil or trouble") and an intrans.-pass. usage ("characterized by evil or trouble") emerge here, form-critical and contextual considerations disclose for πονηϱός further critical points, above all in view of the personal ethical realm (less in the neutral objective realm). Polemical and parenetic contexts (Mark 7:22f.; Matt 12:34f., 39; 16:4; 1 Thess 5:22; Rom 12:9) are as revealing in this way as eschatological-apocalyptic portayals of judgment (Matt 13:41, 49; 22:10; 25:26), not to mention symbolic phrases and ethical comparisons (Matt 6:22f.; 20:15: the eye; 13:38: sons of the kingdom/of the *evil one*), which does not exclude physical origins (7:17: the tree). These fragmentary references already reveal the strongly ethical-moral shading for πονηϱός and speak of a characteristic depravity suggesting guilt and reponsibility on the part of human beings and thus (at least indirectly) pose the question of the origin of evil (from God or from human beings?).

3. A few extrabiblical, secular Greek, and OT references can take us further here. Πονηϱός, documented in Greek literature from Hesiod on, occurs in connection with speech (Aeschylus), advice (Aristophanes), and education and character (Aeschines) in a general, straightforward fashion and clearly identifies human beings as the origin and point of departure of such objectionable behavior. In the Hellenistic period this is joined by the πονηϱὸς δαίμων or the πονηϱὸν πνεῦμα, a power exerting pernicious influence over human beings and seducing them to evil (above all in inscriptions and papyri of the 2nd cent. B.C.), perhaps already under the influence of the LXX. Most LXX occurrences (*ca.* 266) represent Heb. *r'* (bad, inferior, disadvantageous, worthless). It is clearly stated that thoughts (Gen 8:21) and the human heart (Gen 6:5; Bar 1:22) and eye (Sir 14:10) can be πονηϱός. The same is said of evil spirits (Judg 9:23; 1 Kgdms 16:14-16) and angels (Ps 77:49 LXX: sent by God himself!), though this does not exclude human responsibility: On the basis of free, if sometimes limited will, humans act "evilly, badly" both before God (Gen 2:17; 3:22) and before other humans (1 Kgdms 18:10; 19:9). What is important in this context is that in the OT ὁ πονηϱός "is not yet used for Satan" (Harder 549), but speaks rather of evil simply as "that which is contrary to God" (551). The word is used, at least as it concerns human beings, in the overwhelming majority of instances "in the moral sense" (*ibid.*).

4. Despite a certain quantitative preference for πονηϱός (esp. in Matthew, less in Luke-Acts), expressly redactional (theologically significant) accents emerge only conditionally and sporadically, and even tradition-historical (diachronic) observations contribute little that is new to our understanding. Hence we will proceed rather on the basis of a largely thematic (synchronic) disclosure of πονηϱός, examining first the neutral-objective level, then the human-ethical realm, and finally the personalized-subst. focus of πονηϱός. Sharp lines of demarcation cannot be

drawn in every instance; rather, the lines between physical and ethical, subst. and adj. use can be fluid.

a) Πονηρός has a more neutral-objective meaning in combination with the fruits of a tree (Matt 7:17: *worthless, rotten*), a person's name (Luke 6:22; cf. Matt 5:11: *slanderous, abominable*), with speech (Matt 5:37: *deceitful*), and the eye (Matt 6:23; 20:15: *malicious;* cf. Luke 11:34).

b) This last example, that of the eye, as imagery with fig. meaning, already extends into the human-ethical realm, in which πονηρός is used of both a necessary and natural fundamental disposition and human guilt. Hence polemical speech can be directed against the *evil* generation (Matt 12:39; 16:4), scribes (9:4), and Pharisees (12:34). Their wickedness can be more specifically described as stubbornness before Jesus and his works and as total rejection of Jesus, as their "deeds" also show (John 3:19; 7:7). The various manifestations and methods of evil are then revealed by individual representatives and persons (Herod, Luke 3:19; anti-Pauline agitators, Acts 17:5; the incestuous man in Corinth, 1 Cor 5:13; dangerous false doctrines, 2 John 11; 3 John 10). In contrast, Paul is accused without grounds (Acts 18:14; 25:18; 28:21: probably because of alleged trespasses against the law).

These polemical passages are joined by the parenetic passages with their urgent admonition to avoid *evil* (1 Thess 5:22; cf. Rom 10:9), and to stand fast in view of the present (Eph 5:16; cf. 6:11f.: devil, principalities and powers) and the future (6:13, probably alluding to eschatological tribulation; cf. also Rev 16:2), a realm frequently described with variations of πονηρός as the place of punishment for the irresponsible (Matt 25:26) and the wicked servant (18:32), for the sons of the *evil* one and evildoers (13:38, 49: probably trespassers against the law; cf. v. 41), as well as for unworthy guests (22:10-14). This destiny is, however, already determined in this life, in the human heart (Mark 7:22f. par. Matt 15:19; cf. Heb 3:12), in *evil* thoughts (Matt 9:4; cf. Jas 2:4: evil thoughts; 1 Tim 6:4: base suspicions); "for out of the [good or evil] abundance of the heart the mouth speaks" (Matt 12:34f. par. Luke 6:45). Thus also can we understand the concise and pessimistic assertion from the logia in Matthew 7: "You, who are *evil* . . ." (Matt 7:11 par. Luke 11:13). This series of statements that clearly address human decisions and responsibility is joined by the further series of passages speaking of a possible origin of evil outside of human beings.

c) Concerning a "personal" entity one should first mention the contemporary conception found in the logia concerning evil spirits that seduce human beings (Matt 12:45 par. Luke 11:26: perhaps as a warning to Israel; cf. Matt 12:39). The Lukan tradition in particular shows that Jesus has already declared war on these spirits (demons) and has basically already vanquished them (Luke 7:21; 8:2; also Acts 19:12f., 15f. [here accomplished by Paul]).

This element of substantivized personality is even more pronounced in Matthew in the allegorical interpretation of the parable of the sower: Satan (Mark 4:15) is in Matthew called ὁ πονηρός because he works against the power of God's word in human beings (Matt 13:19) and because through his fateful deeds (interpretation of the parable of the weeds) manages to gather "sons" named after him (13:38). The believer counters this irresistible and puzzling influence (13:25: he works when human beings sleep; cf. also 1 John 3:12; 5:18f., where lineage from the evil one and corresponding behavior are correlated, e.g., through Cain—a reference to the *mysterium iniquitatis*) with the prayer to the Father, "Deliver us from evil" (Matt 6:13b; cf. John 17:15 in a similar context; 2 Thess 3:2—clearly referring to human beings). From a purely linguistic standpoint both the masc. (personal) and the neut. meaning are possible in this petition (cf., however, 1 John 2:13f., which argues in favor of masc.). The decision for one or the other does not essentially change the Matthean intention, for at issue here is the pressing and urgent reality and activity of evil. Human beings are not defenselessly subjected to it, but neither are they permitted to stand and not fight; each person can and must endure and hold fast thanks to the faithfulness of the Lord, who preserves us from evil (2 Thess 3:3; cf. 2 Tim 4:18) and who has already liberated us by his own sacrifice (Gal 1:4), through baptism that purifies one of a bad conscience (that separates and keeps one from God: Heb 10:22). In spite of this vast reality of evil, there is no reason for pessimism and resignation; for God makes the sun rise on the *evil* and the good (Matt 5:45 par. Luke 6:35) and continues to invite both groups into the wedding hall (i.e., the Church, Matt 22:10) and reserves for himself the final decision concerning good and evil (13:30).

A. Kretzer

πόνος, ου, ὁ *ponos* work, toil; affliction*

Col 4:13: πόνον ἔχω ὑπέρ τινος; Rev 16:10, 11; 21:4, in the sense of *anguish/pain.* M. Seitz and H. G. Link, *DNTT* I, 262f.

Ποντικός, 3 *Pontikos* from Pontus*

Acts 18:2, of Aquila, who was Ποντικὸς τῷ γένει, "a native of Pontus." → Ἀκύλας (2).

Πόντιος, ου *Pontios* Pontius
→ Πιλᾶτος.

πόντος, ου, ὁ *pontos* sea, ocean
Rev 18:17 v.l.: ὁ ἐπὶ τὸν πόντον (in place of τόπον) πλέων.

Πόντος, ου   *Pontos*   Pontus*

Originally the name of the Black Sea (Πόντος Εὔξεινος), then an abbreviated designation of the empire founded by the Achaemenids and extending from the Pontus Euxinus (Black Sea) to the Caucasus. Many Greeks settled there (see R. Fellmann, *LAW* 2411). The region is mentioned with ᾿Ασία in Acts 2:9. 1 Peter is addressed to the Christians of Pontus, Galatia, Cappadocia, Asia, and Bithynia (1:1); see L. Goppelt, *1 Pet* (KEK) 27-29: Πόντος refers to the corresponding Roman province). *KP* IV, 1050f.

Πόπλιος, ου   *Poplios*   Publius*

Acts 28:7, 8 mentions a man called Publius (his Roman praenomen) as πρῶτος ("chief man") of the island of Malta. The title πρῶτος is also mentioned elsewhere in relationship to Malta (*IG* XIV, 601; *CIL* X, 7495; BAGD s.v. Πόπλιος).

πορεία, ας, ἡ   *poreia*   trip, journey*

Luke 13:22: the goal of a *journey* (Jerusalem); Jas 1:11: business *trips* of a wealthy person.

πορεύομαι   *poreuomai*   go, journey; conduct one's life
διαπορεύομαι   *diaporeuomai*   go through, pass through*

1. Occurrences — 2. Syntax — 3. Meaning

Lit.: BAGD 187, 692f. — G. EBEL, *DNTT* III, 933f. — F. HAUCK and S. SCHULZ, *TDNT* VI, 566-79. — G. SCHNEIDER, *Luke* (ÖTK, 1977) 226 (on Luke 9:51–19:27).

1. Πορεύομαι occurs in the text of the *GNT (NTG)* 154 times, 8 times in the Pauline corpus and 9 times in the Catholic Epistles, 29 times in Matthew and 16 times in John. It does not occur in Mark (see, however, Mark 16:10, 12, 15) or in Revelation. It is a preferred word, however, in Luke-Acts: The Gospel (51 occurrences) has πορεύομαι *ca.* 30 times in material not found in Matthew or Mark, 8 times (4:42; 5:24; 8:14, 48; 9:12; 22:8, 22, 39) in place of other vbs. in Mark, and 4 times (4:42; 19:36; 21:8; 22:33) in other ways different from Mark; and the vb. appears 38 times in Acts. Similarly, except for Rom 15:24, διαπορεύομαι occurs in the NT only in Luke 6:1; 13:22; 18:36; Acts 16:4.

2. Pres. and fut. of this vb. appear only in mid. forms, and aor. appears only in pass. forms. The partc. in pleonastic combination with another vb. often represents a Hebraism, though only in Matthew and Luke, and usually in material not found in Mark or found differently from Mark (except Matt 11:4 par.; cf. 12:45 par.; uncer-

tain in 18:12), e.g., Matt 9:13: "*Go* and learn. . . ." The inf. phrase ἐν (δὲ) τῷ πορεύεσθαι, "on their way," occurs in Luke 10:38; 17:11; Acts 9:3.

A dependent prep. phrase usually occurs with πορεύομαι and normally designates the goal. So used are esp. εἰς (Luke 1:39; Acts 18:6) and then (ἕως) ἐπί (Acts 17:14: "[as far as] to the sea"; on ὡς as v.l. cf. BDF §453.4) and πρός (John 14:12, 28; 16:28). A simple inf. indicates the purpose for going (only in Luke 2:3; 14:19, 31; John 14:2), as does a ἵνα clause (11:11). The path is identified with κατά (Acts 8:36; 2 Pet 3:3; Jude 16:18), ἐν (Luke 9:57; 1:6; 1 Pet 4:3; 2 Pet 2:10; "*go in peace,*" Acts 16:36 [Luke 7:50; 8:48 have εἰς instead of ἐν]), simple acc. (literal in Acts 8:39), and simple dat. (fig. in 14:16; Jude 11). Πορεύομαι is used absolutely in, e.g., Matt 2:9: they *went on their way;* 8:9 par.; Luke 13:33; 22:22.

Διαπορεύομαι occurs with διά or κατά (Luke 6:1; 13:22) and also, rendered trans. by the δια- prefix, with simple acc. (Acts 16:4). The partc. is used absolutely in Luke 18:36 to mean *going by* and in Rom 15:24, *in passing.*

3.a) The literal use of πορεύομαι can refer both to actual and fig. going:

1) Πορεύομαι expresses normal movement, e.g., in Acts 22:5; Jas 4:13. It means *go away* in Matt 11:7: "as they *went [on their way]*"; 25:41: "*Depart* from me"; Luke 4:30: he *went (away);* Acts 24:25: "*go away* for the present." The idea of *going after* (πορεύομαι ὀπίσω) is seen in Luke 21:8 (cf. 3 Kgdms 11:10). The pres. imv., used also for one-time actions (BDF §336.3), can refer to a commission to a specific task given by God (Matt 2:20; 22:9), Jesus (10:6; 21:2; John 20:17; Acts 9:15; 22:10, 21), the Spirit (10:20), or an angel (5:20; 8:26; cf. 9:11; 28:26 with aor. imv.). An immediately following πορεύομαι in the ind. in response to authoritative orders occurs only in Acts 8:27, otherwise esp. the (δια-)πορεύομαι of Paul's "missionary journeys" (16:4, 7; 17:14; 18:6; 19:21; 20:1; 21:5; Rom 15:24 bis; 1 Cor 16:4, 6; 1 Tim 1:3). Like Paul (Acts 9:16), Jesus himself, particularly in the Lukan portrayal, is driven by a divine δεῖ (Luke 13:33) that causes him to wander and preach (7:11; 9:52, 56, 57; 10:38; 13:22) and leads him into suffering. The final goal for Jesus is Jerusalem from Luke 9:51 on (cf. 9:53; 17:11; with ἀναβαίνω in 19:28; cf. Paul in Acts 19:21; 20:22; but cf. 25:20; cf. also Rom 15:25). Jesus' journey, however (cf. Paul in Acts 25:12, 20), leads further: He *goes* "as it has been determined" (Luke 22:22); as the resurrected one, however, he *went* together with the apostles from Emmaus (24:13, 28 bis), and finally from the Mount of Olives (cf. 22:39) he *went* to heaven (Acts 1:10, 11).

2) John describes Jesus' death figuratively as "*going*

to the Father" (14:12, 28; 16:28) and as *going away* (14:2, 3; 16:7; cf. 1 Pet 3:19, 22; Acts 1:25; reversed in Luke 16:30).

b) Πορεύομαι is also used in the sense of *conduct one's life:*

1) It thus refers to life as a journey toward death (e.g., Luke 22:22, 33) or as the manner in which one lives, whether positively (1:6) or negatively (Acts 14:16 and the Catholic Epistles, except in Jude 11 always with ἐπιθυμία: 1 Pet 4:3; 2 Pet 2:10; Jude 16, 18).

2) The pres. partc. in Luke 8:14 is probably patterned after Heb. *holek* (cf. Hauck and Schulz 570, 573) to express intensification (as in 1 Kgdms 2:26; 2 Kgdms 3:1 bis; cf. Judg 4:24; 2 Kgdms 5:10): "as they *go on their way,* they are [oppressed more and more and thus] choked." Similarly, Acts 9:31 refers not to conduct, but rather to the Church's incremental growth.   W. Radl

πορθέω *portheō* devastate, destroy*

Gal 1:13: "I *tried to destroy* [impf. ἐπόρθουν] the Church of God"; v. 23: Paul *tried to destroy* (impf.) the Christian faith; Acts 9:21: "Is not this the man who *devastated* (πορθήσας) in Jerusalem those who called on this name?" Spicq, *Notes* II, 723f.

πορισμός, ου, ὁ *porismos* means of gain*

1 Tim 6:5, 6, of those who think that "godliness (εὐσέβεια) is a *means of gain*" (v. 5). Understood correctly, εὐσέβεια, joined to αὐτάρκεια ("contentment"), is indeed "a great *gain*" (v. 6).

Πόρκιος, ου *Porkios* Porcius
→ Φῆστος.

πορνεία, ας, ἡ *porneia* sexual immorality
πορνεύω *porneuō* practice sexual immorality

1. Occurrences in the NT — 2. Meaning — 3. In the discussion of divorce — 4. Paul — a) Marriage — b) Basic considerations — 5. In vice catalogs

Lit.: H. BALTENSWEILER, "Die Ehebruchsklauseln bei Matthäus," *TZ* 15 (1959) 340-56. — G. FITZER, *"Das Weib schweige in der Gemeinde." Über den unpaulinischen Charakter der mulier-taceat-Verse in 1 Kor 14* (TEH 110, 1963) 30-35. — J. A. FITZMYER, "The Matthean Divorce Texts and some New Palestinian Evidence," *TS* 37 (1976) 197-226. — F. HAUCK and S. SCHULZ, *TDNT* VI, 579-95. — J. JENSEN, "Does *porneia* mean Fornication? A Critique of B. Malina," *NovT* 20 (1978) 161-84. — B. MALINA, "Does Porneia mean Fornication?" *NovT* 14 (1972) 10-17. — A. OTT, *Die Ehescheidung im Matthäus-Evangelium* (1939). — A. SAND, "Die Unzuchtsklausel in Mt 5,31.32 und 19,3-9," *MTZ* 20 (1968) 118-29. — J. SICKENBERGER, "Zwei neue Äußerungen zur Ehebruchsklausel bei Matthäus," *ZNW* 42 (1949) 202-9. — K. STAAB, "Die Unau-

flöslichkeit der Ehe und die sogenannten 'Ehebruchsklauseln' bei Mt 5,32 und 19,9," FS E. Eichmann (1940) 435-52. — A. VÖGTLE, *Die Tugend- und Lasterkataloge im NT* (1936), index s.v. — F. VOGT, *Das Ehegesetz Jesu. Eine exegetisch-kanonistische Untersuchung* (1936) 5-153. — K. WEIDINGER, *Die Haustafeln* (1928) 23-27. — S. WIBBING, *Die Tugend- und Lasterkataloge im NT und ihre Traditionsgeschichte unter besonderer Berücksichtigung der Qumrantexte* (1959) 77-117. — For further bibliography see *TDNT* X, 1246f.

1. Πορνεία occurs 26 times in the NT: 8 times with other vices, 3 times in Acts with "cultic commandments," 6 times in Paul (5 in 1 Corinthians 5–7), and 7 times in Revelation. The related vb. πορνεύω occurs 5 times in Revelation and 3 times in Paul.

2. Πορνεία means *"prostitution, unchastity, fornication,"* and is used "of every kind of unlawful sexual intercourse" (BAGD s.v.). When used of sexual infidelity on the part of a married woman it means the same as "adultery," which is normally referred to with → μοιχεύω, μοιχεία κτλ. Πορνεία and μοιχεία frequently stand next to one another in vice catalogs. Since in Rom 1:26f. Paul clearly alludes to homosexuality as sin, πορνεία can also refer to homosexuality as sexual immorality, as does ἐκπορνεύω in Jude 7 (cf. Genesis 19).

3. To the discussion of divorce in Mark 10:1-12 (par. Matt 19:1ff./Luke 16:18) Matthew adds, in reponse to the strict, absolute prohibition of divorce in Mark 10:11f. and Luke 16:18, the exception μὴ ἐπὶ πορνείᾳ (Matt 19:9; cf. 5:32). When in 19:3 Matthew completes the Pharisees' question concerning the lawfulness of divorcing one's wife with κατὰ πᾶσαν αἰτίαν ("for any cause"), he "has used his scribal learning . . . [and] again made an excellent formal correction" (Bultmann, *History* 27); he is alluding to the dispute between the schools of Hillel and Shammai concerning causes for dismissal or release of a wife. The phrase "except for unchastity" in 19:9 places a limit on "for any cause."

Much has been said concerning this Matthean adultery clause in respect to divorce (→ γαμέω 3.a, μοιχεύω 4.c, παρεκτός 2 [bibliography]). One must assume that in that age, too, a marriage was considered violated when the wife committed adultery. Only thus can we understand the assertion that whoever divorces his wife—apart from a case of adultery—and marries another commits adultery himself, namely, with respect to the earlier wife. The context reveals that πορνεία here does not refer to sexual adultery in general, but to sexual relations between a married woman and a man other than her husband, and thus to adultery. For Matthew the word probably also suggested "something shameful" or "disgraceful" (as does ῾erwâ in Deut 24:1).

According to OT law the punishment for adultery was death by stoning; at least this was the case for an engaged woman (Deut 22:23f.). Since Lev 20:10 and Deut 22:22 say nothing about the manner of execution, rabbinic tradition set this as death by strangulation. The unbinding of the hair of the woman suspected of infidelity (Num 5:18) is expanded to include the bosom as well (Billerbeck II, 519f.; III, 433). In accordance with these regulations, the woman caught in adultery (John 8:5) must have been engaged. Even if during Jesus' time the strict regulations calling for execution of both adulterers were no longer carried out, the consequences were nonetheless made more severe. Both the woman's husband and the adulterer were forbidden from having further sexual intercourse with the adulteress. Jesus' radical divorce prohibition takes no notice of these distinctions, but rather through recourse to "the more fundamental factor" declares the sexual-marital bond of man and woman to be inviolable, since "the marital bond of husband to wife is the experience of an act of God that extends into physical life as well" (E. Lohmeyer, *Matt* [KEK] 128). Just as the clause "but I say to you" in the Sermon on the Mount is used as a counter to the OT commandments, so also this radical divorce prohibition, which stands in open contradiction to Deut 24:1-3, is to be understood from the perspective of the eschatological character of Jesus' proclamation.

According to Matt 5:32 as well Jesus views divorce as adultery. In the meantime, the addition of → παρεκτὸς λόγου πορνείας ("except on the ground of unchastity") suspends the severity of the divorce prohibition. Hence Lohmeyer (*ibid.* 130) assumes that "tradition" added these words, and E. Schweizer explains: "The Matthaean addition is comprehensible on the basis of the practice of his community" (*Matt* [Eng. tr., 1975] 123). "Yet even this tradition does not consider expulsion of the wife for fornication to be possible and justified, but intends rather to avoid this severe case" (Lohmeyer, *ibid.* 130). Schweizer suggests that in this context " 'unchastity' probably means continued infidelity rather than a single instance of adultery" (124).

4.a) In 1 Corinthians 5 Paul addresses what he considers a terrible case of sexual immorality: A man had sexual relations with his father's wife, i.e., with his stepmother. Exegetes speak of "wild marriage with the escaped or divorced wife of the still-living father" (H. Lietzmann, *1 Cor* [HNT, 51969] 23) or of illegitimate concubines, whether the father has died or the wife was divorced (J. Weiss, *1 Cor* [KEK, 91977] 125). Paul himself offers no further specifics. Hence πορνεία here does not mean "adultery," but rather *(disgraceful) sexual immorality*. OT law forbade sexual relations with one's stepmother (Lev 18:8; Deut 27:20 put it under a curse; both parties are condemned to death in Lev 20:11; cf. 18:29). Marriage to one's stepmother was forbidden in Roman law in well. Paul wants the congregation to act against the man "who does such a thing" as severely as possible; he has himself "delivered him to Satan for the destruction of the flesh, that his spirit may be saved in the day of the Lord Jesus" (5:5). This harsh decision is understood as "the severe, irrevocable form of expulsion by the entire congregation" (Weiss, *op. cit.* 130; cf. the curse in Deut 27:20). If it is correct, as some exegetes maintain, that in 2 Cor 2:5-11 and 7:12 Paul addresses the same case

again, he apparently gives in and evokes the Christian motives of remorse and forgiveness.

Paul's remark concerning πορνεία in 1 Cor 7:2 is both exegetically more difficult and more important. The Corinthians have asserted in a letter that it is "good for a man not to 'touch' a woman" (v. 1). From Luther onward many exegetes (J. Weiss, H. Lietzmann, H.-D. Wendland, *1 Cor* [NTD] ad loc.) have taken this sentence as Paul's opinion, and many have concluded that Paul's own behavior was characterized by ascetic elements. NEB mg. inserts "You say" before "It is good" and thus identifies the sentence as the Corinthians' opinion—and quite justifiably so, for in 6:12 as well Paul cites the Corinthians' opinion and here the logic of the context resists the attempt to take this sentence as expressing Paul's opinion.

It would be illogical and uncharacteristic of Paul's lucid thinking for him to assert in one sentence that it is good not to "touch" a woman and in the next sentence set a rule of conduct for marriage according to which husband and wife owe one another conjugal relations (7:3) and then later advise those who cannot "exercise self-control": "It is better to marry than to burn [with passion]" (v. 9). And concerning virgins he says: "But if you marry, you do not sin, and if a girl marries, she does not sin" (v. 28). If in 7:1 Paul is quoting the Corinthians' opinion (cf. Fitzer 26-35), a clear, inherently logical position on Paul's part concerning the question of marital sexual relations emerges.

It is in this context that Paul speaks *in favor of* marriage διὰ δὲ τὰς πορνείας, "because of immorality." Pl. πορνείας, which some mss. "correct" to the sg., means "frequent fornication" and thus refers to frequent and arbitrary sexual intercourse with temple prostitutes (→ πόρνη 4).

The apostle does recommend sexual abstinence during times of prayer and fasting (1 Cor. 7:5); but here, too, he is following Jewish custom, as documented by *T. Naph.* 8: "There is a time for having intercourse with one's wife, and a time to abstain for the purpose of prayer." Similarly, in 1 Thess 4:3 he equates "sanctification" with "abstinence from immorality" and emphasizes for marital encounters the distinction between passion and honor. Sexual relations are not only a matter of passion. A related assertion occurs in 1 Cor 7:29: "Let those who have wives live as though they had none." This underscores the difference between the person living within the eschatological realm of Jesus Christ and natural social circumstances. Paul is also concerned with this distinction in his recommendation of marriage.

The distinction is intensified by the question of deity: If frequent intercourse with the πόρνη, the servant of Aphrodite, is brought into proximity with idolatry, then marriage is not merely a *remedium fornicationis,* but rather a protection against idolatry. "Shun immorality" (6:18) and "shun the worship of idols" (10:14) belong together, just as in the vice catalogs πορνεία and εἰδωλολατρία stand next to one another (similarly in the "cultic commandments" of Acts 15:20, 29). Hence for Paul πορνεία raises not only a moral question governing social behavior, but also a theological question, a question of worship, and as such belongs to a certain extent to behavior excluded by the first commandment. (In Hos 1:2 as well idolatry and prostitution are identified.)

b) Paul deals with sexuality in general terms in 1 Cor 6:12-20. There the main issue is intercourse with the → πόρνη (4).

5. Πορνεία also occurs 8 times in vice catalogs, in Matt 15:19; Mark 7:21 as part of the emanation of "evil thoughts" (with murder, adultery, theft, etc.). In Rom 1:29 one can ask whether πονηρία originally stood in place of πορνεία (thus, among others, D G Koine); the latter seems more likely, since Paul has just been speaking of sexual immorality, including homosexuality. In 2 Cor 12:21 πορνεία stands between "impurity" and "licentiousness," two sexual excesses. Paul does consider the possibility of remorse (2 Cor 2:5-11). Gal 5:19 offers a comprehensive catalog of "works of the flesh." In Eph 5:3 πορνεία stands again in the first position. Col 3:5 places the catalog under the command: "Put to death therefore what is earthly in you." In the enumeration in Rev 9:21 πορνεία appears with "murder," "sorcery," and "theft."   G. Fitzer

πορνεύω *porneuō* practice sexual immorality
→ πορνεία.

πόρνη, ης, ἡ *pornē* prostitute*

1. Occurrences in the NT — 2. Meaning — 3. The Gospels — 4. Paul — 5. Revelation

Lit.: BAGD s.v. — H. CONZELMANN, "Korinth und die Mädchen der Aphrodite," *idem, Theologie als Schriftauslegung* (1974) 152-66. — F. HAUCK and S. SCHULZ, *TDNT* VI, 579-95. — H. MERKEL, "Das Gleichnis von den 'ungleichen Söhnen' Mt 21,28-32," *NTS* 20 (1973/74) 254-61. — For further bibliography → πορνεία; see *TWNT* X, 1246f.

1. Πόρνη occurs 12 times in the NT, twice in reference to "the *harlot* Rahab" (Heb 11:31; Jas 2:25), 5 times in Revelation in reference to the "great harlot," the city of "Babylon," in Paul only in 1 Cor 6:15, 16, and 3 times in the Synoptics.

2. Πόρνη belongs etymologically to the vb. πέρνημι, "to buy," and thus fundamentally means "a purchased woman," i.e., "prostitute" (Germ. *Prostituierte*). (Germ. *Hure* originally designated the adulteress, though in today's usage it usually refers—mostly in a derogatory sense—to a woman who engages in arbitrary and unconditional extramarital sexual relations. Germ. *Dirne* formerly was a "corrupt woman," though it now refers only to a woman who prostitutes her body for hire.)

3. In a Matthean redactional saying (see Merkel 261)

Jesus complains of the hypocrisy of those who affirm God's will but do not act according to it (Matt 21:28ff.). In their own arrogance of faith, the Pharisees despise the tax collectors and *prostitutes* (vv. 31f.) because of their "impurity." When according to Luke 15:30 the "prodigal son" dissipates his money "with *prostitutes*" and his "righteous brother" notes it bitterly, here, too, we encounter the contempt of the establishment, those who are "moral" and righteous, for the "cheap woman."

4. In contrast, Paul is not concerned with contempt, but rather with condemnation in both a social and a religious sense.

In 1 Cor 5:9-11 he demands strict separation from the immoral man (→ πόρνος), in this case a Christian who has had sexual relations with his father's wife. The Corinthians should have nothing to do with brothers in the congregation who are guilty of immorality, greed, idolatry, etc., and should not even eat with them (v. 11, cf. v. 10). Though these phrases remain within the social realm, Paul addresses theological issues when he— again in a vice catalog—equates immoral men with idolaters, adulterers, drunkards, homosexuals, thieves, etc.; none of these will inherit the kingdom of God (6:9f.); similarly Eph 5:5; 1 Tim 1:10: they are condemned by the "law." Heb 13:4 formulates this more sharply: "God will judge the immoral and adulterous."

In 1 Cor 6:12-20 Paul demands that one have nothing to do with the πόρνη, and supports this with a theory peculiar to him. Under the slogan "all things are lawful" some circles in the Corinthian congregation supported sexual relations with the πόρνη. (It is reported that one thousand cult prostitutes were available in the temple of Aphrodite on Acrocorinth [see Conzelmann]). Paul answers: " 'All things are lawful for me,' but I will not be enslaved by anything" (v. 12b). He then compares human digestion with sexual practices and ascertains for the latter what amounts to a personal qualification, concluding: "The body is not meant for immorality, but for the Lord, and the Lord for the body" (v. 13). The body is the object of the resurrection action of God's power and thus as the expression of the personality belongs to membership in Christ. Sexual union with a cult prostitute amounts to becoming one body with her. Gen 2:24 is cited: "But he who is united to the Lord becomes one spirit with him" (v. 17). Hence "Christ's members" become members of the prostitute in sexual union with her (vv. 15f.). Paul views sexual union as a personal and total bonding. Body, spirit, and soul are a unity for him, and precisely this totality belongs to Christ by a person's faith in him. The human body, specifically that of the Christian, is a temple of the Holy Spirit "within you" (v. 19). Sexual intercourse with the cult prostitute is not merely a natural act, but concerns rather the whole human being and thus one's faith and Christ himself, especially considering the proximity of the act to idolatry. Paul's own positive statements concerning marriage (→ πορνεία 4.a) prove that this does not constitute a fundamental condemnation of sexuality or of sexual relations.

Heb 12:16 compares immoral and irreligious people with Esau, in accordance with tradition attested by Philo and the rabbinic literature, according to which Esau was the prototype of depravity, including sexual sins, even homosexuality (cf. Billerbeck III, 748; O. Michel, Heb [KEK] ad loc.).

5. Revelation 17–19 speaks of "Babylon," the "great *harlot*" (πόρνη μεγάλη, 17:1; 19:2; μήτηρ τῶν πορνῶν, 17:5; πόρνη, 17:15, 16), and of the judgment on this city. The designation on her forehead (exegetes mention that Roman prostitutes wrote their names on a headband) was a "mystery" (17:5). The μυστήριον points to "spiritual interpretation" (W. Bousset, *Rev* [KEK, ⁷1966] 404). The great demonic representation of the world metropolis is identified as Babylon, the city of exile and of alien gods. This alludes to the overwhelming natural power of sex and thus to the contrast with the law of God as the possibility of controlling what is natural as well as what is spiritual. Babylon is the city of nature gods, of arrogance, of pan-sexuality, and of idolatry—not unlike the modern big city. 17:1 introduces the judgment on this city. The woman is "the great city that has dominion over the kings of the earth" (v. 18). The ten horns and the beast will hate her "and make her desolate and naked, and devour her flesh and burn her up with fire" (v. 16). Then comes the cry of desolation (18:10): "Alas! alas! Great city, mighty city, Babylon! In one hour your judgment has come." For "all nations are drunk on the wine of her wild lasciviousness, earth's kings have committed immorality with her, and the merchants of the earth have grown rich with the wealth of her sensuality" (18:3). The judgment ends in 19:2. God is praised, "for he has judged the great *harlot* who corrupted the earth with her immorality."

The designation "harlot" for the great city "is first of all an expression of disgust for heathen idolatry" (E. Lohmeyer, *Rev* [HNT, ³1970] 140). It is disputed whether this city, "the mother of *harlots* and of earth's abominations," is to be identified with Rome (Bousset, *Rev* 404f., 410ff.) or in a general sense as an anti-divine power (Lohmeyer, *Rev* 140).

G. Fitzer

πόρνος, ου, ὁ *pornos* person who commits sexual immorality*

In lists of immoral people in 1 Cor 5:10, 11; 6:9; Eph 5:5; 1 Tim 1:10; Heb 12:16; 13:4; Rev 21:8; 22:15. 1 Cor 6:9 and Heb 13:4 differentiate between the *immoral* and adulterers (μοιχός). 1 Cor 5:9 recalls Paul's demand that one not associate with (συναναμίγνυσθαι) *immoral men*. F. Hauck and S. Schulz, *TDNT* VI, 579-95; H. Reisser, *DNTT* I, 497-501; → πόρνη 4, 5.

πόρρω *porrō* far, distant (adv.)*

Mark 7:6 par. Matt 15:8: "Their heart is far from me (πόρρω ἀπέχει ἀπ' ἐμοῦ)"; Luke 14:32: ἔτι αὐτοῦ πόρρω ὄντος, "while he is yet a great way off"; comparative πορρώτερον as an adv. in 24:28: "going *further*."

πόρρωθεν *porrōthen* from afar*

Heb 11:13: They saw the promises only *from afar*; Luke 17:12: οἱ ἔστησαν πόρρωθεν, "they stood *at a distance*"; similarly *Barn.* 9:1: οἱ πόρρωθεν, "those *in the distance*."

πορφύρα, ας, ἡ *porphyra* purple mollusk; purple (robe, garment)*

Πορφύρα designates purple dye, cloth, or garments, in the NT only cloth or garments. Luke 16:19, with βύσσος; Rev 18:12: purple garments with τὸ βύσσινον; Mark 15:17, 20: the purple garment that the soldiers put on Jesus.

πορφυρόπωλις, ιδος, ἡ *porphyropōlis* a woman dealer in purple cloth*

Acts 16:14: Lydia's was a πορφυρόπωλις, meaning probably that she sold purple wool. → Λυδία.

πορφυροῦς, 3 *porphyrous* purple*

John 19:2, 5: the ἱμάτιον πορφυροῦν that the soldiers put on Jesus (cf. Mark 15:17, 20: → πορφύρα); Rev 17:4; 18:6: subst. τὸ πορφυροῦν, the *scarlet robe*.

ποσάκις *posakis* how often*

Matt 23:37 par. Luke 13:34: "*How often* would I have gathered your children . . ."; Matt 18:21: "*How often* should I . . . forgive my brother?"

πόσις, εως, ἡ *posis* drinking (noun); drink, what is to be drunk*

Πόσις designates the act of drinking. Literal in Rom 14:17; Col 2:16, with βρῶσις, "eating." Only in John 6:55 does πόσις refer to what is to be drunk: "My blood is *drink* indeed." L. Goppelt, *TDNT* VI, 145-48; G. Graumann, *DNTT* II, 274-77.

πόσος, 3 *posos* how great? how much? pl.: how many?

Lit.: BAGD s.v. — LSJ s.v.

1. The correlative interrogative pron. πόσος occurs in direct and indirect questions (in the latter replacing indirect ὁπόσος; cf. Josephus *Ant.* xvi.351; xvii.30; see Moulton, *Grammar* III, 48) and in exclamations in the NT. There are 27 NT occurrences, most in the Synoptics, 1 in Acts (+ 22:28 v.l.), 4 in Paul (3 times in a πολλῷ μᾶλλον conclusion [→ 2.c]), and 2 in Hebrews (also in John 13:14 v.l.).

2.a) Sg. with a sg. noun following to refer to quantity: *how great(?)* (Matt 6:23; Mark 9:21: πόσος χρόνος, *how long?* cf. Sophocles *OT* 558). Without the accompanying noun in Luke 16:5, 7 (πόσον ὀφείλεις; *"How much* do you owe?"); Heb 10:29 (→ c).

Pl. with a pl. noun following to refer to number: *how many(?)* (Matt 15:34 par. Mark 8:5; Mark 6:38: *"How many* loaves have you?"; Luke 15:17: *"how many* of my father's hired servants"; Acts 21:20: *"how many* thousands there are among the Jews of those who have believed!"; cf. Josephus, *Ant.* vii.138; see also Matt 16:9, 10 par. Mark 8:19, 20). Without an accompanying noun in Matt 27:13 (πόσα σου καταμαρτυροῦσιν, *"how many things* they testify against you"); Mark 15:4 (πόσα σου κατηγοροῦσιν, *"how many* charges they bring against you," corresponding to v. 3: κατηγόρουν αὐτοῦ . . . πολλά).

b) In exclamations: Mark 15:4; Luke 15:17; Acts 21:20 (cf. → a); 2 Cor 7:11 (*"what* zeal it [the λυπηθῆναι κατὰ θεόν] has produced in you"); following the noun in Matt 6:23: τὸ σκότος πόσον, *"How great* is the darkness!"

c) As dat. of measure to answer "how much?" πόσῳ precedes a comparative in Heb 10:29 (πόσῳ χείρων τιμωρία, "how much worse punishment?"); Matt 12:12. With μᾶλλον in the *qal wāḥômer* conclusion (with πολλῷ): πόσῳ μᾶλλον (*"how much* more": Matt 7:11; 10:25; Luke 11:13; 12:24, 28; Rom 11:12, 24; Phlm 16; Heb 9:14; → μᾶλλον 3.a; πολύς 3.a).   M. Wolter

ποταμός, οῦ, ὁ *potamos* river, stream*

Rivers mentioned by name are the Jordan (Mark 1:5 par. Matt 3:6) and the Euphrates (Rev 9:14; 16:12). In the parable of the house upon the rock: Matt 7:25, 27 (οἱ ποταμοί = torrents) par. Luke 6:48, 49 (ὁ ποταμός = the [local] river). Sg. also in Acts 16:13 (a place of prayer at the river); Rev 12:15, 16; 22:1, 2. Pl. in John 7:38; 2 Cor 11:26 (danger from rivers); Rev 8:10; 16:4. John 7:38 presents as a scriptural passage: "Out of his heart will flow rivers of living water" (cf. R. Schnackenburg, *John* II [Eng. tr., 1982], who among others refers to Isa 12:3; Ezek 47:1-12). Rev 22:1 offers a parallel: Α ποταμός ὕδατος ζωῆς, *"river* of the water of life," flows in the heavenly Jerusalem (cf. Ezekiel 47; but also Gen 2:10). K. H. Rengstorf, *TDNT* VI, 595-607; *TWNT* X, 1247f. (bibliography); O. Böcher, *DNTT* III, 985-88.

ποταμοφόρητος, 2 *potamophorētos* swept away by a river*

Rev 12:15: ἵνα αὐτὴν ποταμοφόρητον ποιήσῃ, *"to sweep* her *away with the flood,"* i.e., to drown her. K. H. Rengstorf, *TDNT* VI, 607f.

ποταπός, 3 *potapos* of what kind*

Of people in Matt 8:27; Luke 7:39; 2 Pet 3:11; of things in Mark 13:1 (bis); Luke 1:29; 1 John 3:1. Spicq, *Notes* II, 725f.

ποταπῶς *potapōs* in what way

Adv. from ποταπός occurring in Acts 20:18 D.

ποτέ *pote* at some time or other; once*

An enclitic particle with temporal force. Referring to the past in John 9:13; Rom 7:9; 11:30; Gal 1:13, 23 (bis); 2:6; 1 Thess 2:5; Phlm 11; Eph 2:2, 3, 11, 13; 5:8, 29; Col 1:21; 3:7; Titus 3:3; Heb 1:5, 13; 1 Pet 2:10; 3:5, 20; 2 Pet 1:10, 21. Referring to the present in 1 Cor 9:7, to the future in Luke 22:32. Rom 1:10; Phil 4:10: ἤδη ποτέ, *"sometime* at last."

πότε *pote* when?*

The temporal adv. πότε usually occurs in direct questions, though also in indirect questions: Matt 24:3; 25:37, 38, 39, 44; Mark 13:4, 33, 35; Luke 12:36; 17:20; 21:7; John 6:25. Ἕως πότε, *how long,* in Matt 17:17 (bis); Mark 9:19 (bis); Luke 9:41; John 10:24; Rev 6:10.

πότερον *poteron* whether*

An interrogative adv. (BDF §64.6) occurring in disjunctive questions: πότερον — ἤ = *"whether*—or." John 7:17: "whether the teaching is from God or I am speaking on my own authority."

ποτήριον, ου, τό *potērion* drinking vessel, cup, goblet*

1. Occurrences and meaning — 2. Cups of suffering and cups of wrath — 3. Eucharistic cups

Lit.: O. BETZ, "Die paulinische Abendmahlstradition 1 Kor 10.11 und die Passahperikope Ex 11–13," Festgabe F. Lang, ed. O. Bayer and G.-U. Wanzeck (1978) 51-71. — G. BRAUMANN, "Leidenskelch und Todestaufe (Mc 10,38f.)," *ZNW* 56 (1965) 178-83. — H. A. BRONGERS, "Der Zornesbecher," *OTS* 15 (1969) 177-92. — D. COHN-SHERBOK, "A Jewish Note on τὸ ποτήριον τῆς εὐλογίας," *NTS* 27 (1980/81) 704-9. — A. FEUILLET, "La coupe et le baptême de la passion," *RB* 74 (1967) 356-91. — L. GOPPELT, *TDNT* VI, 135-60, esp. 148-58. — V. HOWARD, "Did Jesus Speak about His Own Death?" *CBQ* 39 (1977) 515-27. — R. LE DÉAUT, "Goûter le calice de la mort," *Bib* 43 (1962) 82-86. — H. PATSCH, *Abendmahl und historischer Jesus* (1972). — R. PESCH, *Das Abendmahl und Jesu Todesverständnis* (QD 80, 1978). — H. SCHÜRMANN, "Das apostolische Interesse am eucharistischen Kelch," *idem* II, 188-96. — G. THEISSEN, "Social Integration and Sacramental Activity," *idem, The Social Setting of Pauline Christianity* (1982) 145-74. — P. WOLF, *Liegt in den Logien von der "Todestaufe" (Mk 10,38f; Lk 12,49f) eine Spur des Todesverständnisses Jesu vor?* (Diss. Frankfurt, 1973). — For further bibliography see *TWNT* X, 1233.

1. The subst. ποτήριον, which corresponds with Heb. *kôs,* occurs 31 times in the NT, in the literal sense only in Mark 7:4; 9:41 par. Matt 10:42; Matt 23:25f. par. Luke

11:39. Otherwise it is metaphorical (Gospels, Revelation) or used as a metonym (the eucharist tradition in the Synoptics and Paul). Only Rev 17:4 mentions the material of a drinking vessel; nowhere does its form (see *BRL* 181, illustration 43) play a role.

2. The promise of a "*cup* of water" for bearing the name of Christ in Mark 9:41 reflects the climate of Christian persecution; Matthew makes this promise retroactive to the mission period of the disciples (10:42). In Matthew the Pharisaic custom of external cleansing of the drinking vessel (cf. Mark 7:4) is polemically countered by reference to the unrighteous content (23:25f.); Luke (11:39) already interprets this to refer to what is within a person (v. 40).

The logion concerning the cup of death (Mark 10:38a, 39a par. Matt 20:22f.), part of a pre-Markan composition and perceived by Mark as belonging to the theme of suffering *imitatio,* is comprehensible only against the background of OT and Jewish cup metaphors: The cup in or out of Yahweh's hand is an enduring image of judgment (e.g., Ps 75:9; Jer 25:15ff.; Hab 2:16); a cup can also acquire in a general fashion the meaning "fate, destiny" (Pss 11:6; 16:5; 4QpNah 4:6). This justifies the interpretation: "Are you able to accept the *fate of death* that God has determined for me?" If authentic material from tradition lies behind this symbolic expression, then Jesus was thinking of his own violent death. The image of the cup has the same meaning "fate of death" in Jesus' prayer in Gethsemane (Mark 14:36 par. Matt 26:39/Luke 22:42) and when Jesus restrains Peter at his arrest (John 18:11).

Revelation also refers back to the OT and Jewish imagery of Yahweh's judgmental wrath. In the passage about the harlot of Babylon the (golden) *cup* (17:4, following the model of Jer 51:7) appears in the semantic field of fornication, abomination, filth, and intoxicating wine (17:1f.; 18:3; cf. Jer 25:15, 27). Through this cup judgment is made according to deeds (18:6). It contains the fury of God's wrath (16:19) and is thus—without semantic model in the LXX—called "the *cup* of his anger" (14:10; Isa 51:17, 22; 1QpHab 11:14f.). God's "judgmental wrath," temporarily given over to the anti-Christian powers (cf. 13:7), will turn against those who previously possessed it and pay them back double (18:6ff.).

3. If, as is probable, one can assume a Passover framework for Jesus' words at the Last Supper, then the cup in Luke 22:17 is the first (Kiddush) cup over which the Seder is introduced with a benediction (*m. Pesaḥ.* 10:2), and the cup of the "interpetation" is the third cup (*m. Pesaḥ.* 10:7), the "consecrated cup" (Heb. *kôs šel beṟāḵâ, b. Ber.* 51a; *Jos. As.* 8:9[11]: ποτήριον εὐλογίας) after the main meal, over which Jesus gives thanks (Mark 14:23 par. Luke 22:10a/Matt 26:27/1 Cor 11:25a; cf. 10:16); → εὐλογέω 3. In the interpretation (made explicit

in Luke 22:20b par. 1 Cor 11:25b) the vessel is always a metonym for its contents, the wine.

In 1 Cor 10:16 Paul interprets the cup of blessing of the Last Supper as "communion" in the blood of Christ, i.e., actual participation in Christ's death. If this cup of blessing grants one a portion in Jesus' death ("for our sins," 15:3), then participation in the "cup of the Lord" excludes participation in the "cup of demons" (10:21). In ch. 11 Paul cites the words of the Last Supper as the ultimate authority in view of the social discrepancies in the Corinthian practice of the eucharist. Taking up the formulaic terms of the Last Supper, he differentiates the eucharistic meal— "eat this bread and drink this cup [i.e., its contents]" (vv. 26-28)—from the meal (eaten at home) whose purpose is to satisfy hunger; he characterizes the cup in v. 27 (as in 10:21) as the "cup of the Lord" and refers it to the blood, i.e., to the Lord's death (11:26). This representative atoning death in recalled and proclaimed in every celebration (→ ἀνάμνησις 2), so that whoever is not thinking of the Church as a whole (vv. 20-22, 33) receives the sacrament "in an unworthy manner" (v. 27) and thus "eats and drinks judgment upon himself" (v. 29).

H. Patsch

ποτίζω *potizō* give to drink, cause to drink; water (animals, plants)*

Mark 9:41 par. Matt 10:42: ποτίζω ποτήριον; Mark 15:36 par. used absolutely in Matt 27:48: ἐπότιζεν αὐτόν. Matt 25:35, 42 (ἐποτίσατέ με; cf. v. 37) and Rom 12:20 refer to giving thirsting persons something to drink. Luke 13:15 refers to *watering* livestock on the sabbath. 1 Cor 3:6-8 refers to the image of *watering* a plant. 3:2: "I *gave* you milk *to drink,* not solid food." The image of drinking of one Spirit (ἓν πνεῦμα ἐποτίσθημεν) in 1 Cor 12:13c presupposes that the Spirit can be "poured out" (cf. Acts 2:17; Joel 3:1 LXX). Paul is probably thinking more of baptism (see 1 Cor 12:13a; cf. G. J. Cuming *NTS* 27 [1980/81] 283-85) than of the eucharist (*contra* Calvin and others). Rev 14:8 refers to Babylon, "she who *made* all nations *drink* the wine of her impure passion." L. Goppelt, *TDNT* VI, 159f.; G. Braumann, *DNTT* II, 274-77; E. R. Rogers, "'Εποτίσθημεν Again," *NTS* 29 (1983) 139-42; Spicq, *Notes* Suppl. 566-69.

Ποτίολοι, ων *Potioloi* Puteoli*

The port city of Puteoli on the Gulf of Naples (modern Pozzuoli) is mentioned in Acts 28:13: Paul came ashore and stayed a week with the Christians there (v. 14). B. Andreae, *LAW* 2483.

πότος, ου, ὁ *potos* drinking (noun), drinking party*

Pl. in 1 Pet 4:3 in a vice catalog with κῶμοι, "revels."
L. Goppelt, *TDNT* VI, 145-48.

πού *pou* somewhere; approximately*

This enclitic adv. has a locative meaning in Heb 2:6; 4:4 (of quotations whose origin is not specified more closely). Acts 27:29: They feared that "we might run on the rocks *somewhere*." With the meaning *approximately* (in enumeration) in Rom 4:19: "because he was *about* a hundred years old."

ποῦ *pou* where? to what place?*

1. In the sense of *where(?)*:
a) in direct questions in Matt 2:2; 26:17; Mark 14:12, 14; Luke 8:25; 17:17, 37; 22:9, 11; John 1:38; 7:11, 35; 8:10 (v.l.); 8:19; 9:12; 11:34; 13:36; 16:5; Rom 3:27; 1 Cor 1:20 (ter); 12:17 (bis), 19; 15:55 (bis); Gal 4:15; 1 Pet 4:18; 2 Pet 3:4.
b) in indirect questions in Matt 2:4; 8:20; Mark 15:47; Luke 9:58; 12:17; John 1:39; 11:57; 20:2, 13, 15; Rev 2:13.

2. In the sense of *to what place(?)* (in the NT only in indirect questions): ποῦ ὑπάγει (-άγω, -άγεις), John 3:8; 8:14 (bis); 12:35; 14:5; 1 John 2:11. Heb 11:8: ποῦ ἔρχεται.

Πούδης, εντος *Poudēs* Pudens*

A Roman personal name. In Latin inscriptions *n* is frequently missing (cf. BDF §§41.2; 54). 2 Tim 4:21: an otherwise unknown Christian with this name.

πούς, ποδός, ὁ *pous* foot

1. Occurrences in the NT — 2. Literal usage — 3. Fig. for "human being" — 4. As a symbol of power

Lit.: BAGD s.v. — R. HENTSCHKE, *BHH* 505f. — B. KÖT-TING, *RAC* VIII, 722-43. — B. KÖTTING (and D. HALAMA), *RAC* VIII, 743-77. — K. WEISS, *TDNT* VI, 624-31. — For further bibliography see *TWNT* X, 1248.

1. There are 93 occurrences in the NT, 68 in the Gospels and Acts.

2. Used literally of a part of the body, sometimes also encompassing the leg: Mark 9:45a, b; Acts 16:24; 14:8: "could not use his *feet*"; with → κεφαλή in John 20:12; 1 Cor 12:21; with → χείρ in Matt 18:8a, b; 22:13 (cf. *1 Enoch* 10:4); Luke 24:39, 40; John 11:44: "hands and *feet* bound with bandages" (cf. J. Blinzler, *The Trial of Jesus* [1959] 264f.); Acts 21:11; 1 Cor 12:15. Of animals in Matt 7:6; Rev 13:2 (cf. Dan 7:5, 7).
"*Foot*washing" (as a sign of hospitality or as a servant's duty as in *Jos. As.* 7:1; 13:15[12]; *T. Abr.* 3:6f., 9;

6:13; cf. also Billerbeck II, 557; → νίπτω): John 13:5, 6, 8-10, 12, 14; 1 Tim 5:10; Luke 7:44a: "you gave me no water for my *feet*" (cf. Gen 24:32). At meals: Luke 7:38a: Jesus' *feet* (stretched out behind) as he sits at table; vv. 38c, 45: "kiss the *feet*" (→ καταφιλέω); v. 46 (cf. v. 38c); John 12:3a: "anoint the *feet*" (→ ἀλείφω). With → ὑπόδημα in Luke 15:22; Acts 7:33 (Exod 3:5); 13:25; cf. also Eph 6:15. Shaking off dust from the *feet* as a sign of judgment (cf. R. Pesch, *Mark* [HTKNT, ³1980] I, 329f.): Mark 6:11 par.; Luke 10:11; Acts 13:51.

Of upright posture, when revelation is received (as in Ezek 2:1 LXX; 4 Ezra 6:13; *2 Bar.* 13:2; *Jos. As.* 14:8[7], 11) in Acts 26:16; as an expression of life (as in Ezek 37:10; 4 Kgdms 13:21) in Rev 11:11; cf. also Acts 14:10.

Using Deut 2:5 LXX as a model, "not even a *foot's* length," Acts 7:5.

3. As in the OT, feet could represent the whole human being as regards his or her deeds or behavior (Luke 1:79; Acts 5:9; Rom 3:15 [cf. Isa 59:7; Prov 1:16]; 10:15 [cf. Isa 52:7]; Heb 12:13 [cf. Prov 4:26]). In Matt 4:6 par. the quotation from Ps 90:12b LXX refers in context to the endangering of the entire person.

4. The foot as a symbol of a person's power or authority is seen in "putting at (someone's) *feet*" (Matt 15:30; Acts 4:35, 37; 5:2). Pupils "sit at the *feet*" of the teacher (Luke 8:35; 10:39; Acts 22:3: παρὰ τοὺς πόδας Γαμαλιὴλ πεπαιδευμένος; cf. Billerbeck II, 763f.; C. Burchard, *ZNW* 61 [1970] 168).

Prostration (→ πίπτω) as the expression of obeisance (→ προσκυνέω) is seen in πεσὼν ἐπὶ τοὺς πόδας (Acts 10:25), προσκυνήσουσιν ἐνώπιον τῶν ποδῶν σου (Rev 3:9; cf. Isa 49:23), ἔμπροσθεν τῶν ποδῶν τοῦ ἀγγέλου (Rev 19:10; 22:8), and "they took hold of his *feet*" (Matt 28:9; cf. 2 Kgs 4:27). Prostration before a miracle worker (cf. G. Theissen, *The Miracle Stories of the Early Christian Tradition* [1983] 53) is specifically referred to in Mark 5:22 par.; 7:25 (προσέπεσεν πρὸς τοὺς πόδας αὐτοῦ; formally as in Esth 8:3 LXX); Luke 17:16; John 11:32. Prostration from fear during visions is seen in Rev 1:17 (cf. Dan 8:17f.; 4 Ezra 10:30; *Jos. As.* 14:10).

The *feet* of the powerful appearing one are referred to in a christophany (Rev 1:15; 2:18; cf. Dan 10:6) and an angelophany (Rev 10:1, 2).

Ps 109:1b LXX (cf. D. M. Hay, *Glory at the Right Hand* [SBLMS 18, 1973] 34-51; 122-29; 163ff.) is frequently quoted or otherwise used in early Christian literature both inside and outside the NT: ὑποπόδιον τῶν ποδῶν σου (or αὐτοῦ) (Luke 20:43; Acts 2:35; Heb 1:13; 10:13), similarly ὑποκάτω (cf. Ps 8:7b LXX) τῶν ποδῶν σου (Mark 12:36; Matt 22:44), ὑπὸ τοὺς πόδας (1 Cor 15:25). Ps 8:7b LXX (πάντα ὑπέταξας ὑποκάτω τῶν ποδῶν αὐτοῦ) is cited in Heb 2:8 and appears (with ὑπὸ τοὺς πόδας αὐτοῦ) in 1 Cor 15:27; Eph 1:22.

The eschatological defeat of Satan is referred to in Rom 16:20 with συντρίψει τὸν σατανᾶν ὑπὸ τοὺς πόδας ὑμῶν (cf. *T. Levi* 18:12; *T. Sim.* 6:6). The queen of heaven (Rev 12:1) has the moon "under her *feet*" just as her religio-historical model Isis has the globe (see M. Malaise, *Les conditions de pénétration et de diffusion des cultes égyptiens en Italie* [EPRO 22, 1972] 179f., 180 n.1). The earth as God's footstool (after the model of Isa 66:1 LXX) is mentioned in Matt 5:35; Acts 7:49 (quotation).   R. Bergmeier

πρᾶγμα, ατος, τό *pragma*   deed, event; matter; thing*

1. Occurrences and meanings — 2. *Deed, event* — 3. Other meanings in context

Lit.: BAGD s.v. — H.-C. HAHN, *DNTT* III, 1155-58. — C. MAURER, *TDNT* VI, 638-41. — MOULTON/MILLIGAN s.v. — E. REPO, *Der Begriff "Rhēma" im Biblisch-Griechischen* I (1951) 160f., 190f.

1. The subst. πρᾶγμα occurs 11 times in the NT, 4 of those in Paul and 3 in Hebrews and the others in Matt 18:19; Luke 1:1; Acts 5:4; Jas 3:16. It denotes the result of action (→ πράσσω), the *deed* or *event,* and also that which is to be done or is being done, the *matter, undertaking, business at hand.* Finally, πρᾶγμα can refer to the *matter of concern* in a general sense.

2. Πρᾶγμα refers to events in four NT occurrences. In Luke 1:1 pl. πράγματα is used of the Christ-event, about which the Evangelist's literary predecessors have already reported. In Acts 5:4 τὸ πρᾶγμα τοῦτο is *that which has occurred, this deed* (BAGD s.v. 1), what Ananias did. 2 Cor 7:11: "At every point you have proved yourselves guiltless in the *matter* (τῷ πράγματι)." Heb 6:18 speaks of "two unchangeable *things*" (God's promise and oath to Abraham) that prove God's dependability; here πρᾶγμα refers to "the word as occurrence, as event" (O. Michel, *Heb* [KEK, ¹³1975] ad loc.).

3. In its other NT occurrences πρᾶγμα does not imply that the action has come to completion or closure. As such it has different meanings in different contexts: *undertaking, business at hand* (Rom 16:2; 1 Thess 4:6), *matter, thing* (Matt 18:19; Heb 10:1; 11:1; cf. also 6:18 [→ 2]; Jas 3:16), *grievance, legal dispute* (1 Cor 6:1: πρᾶγμα ἔχω πρός τινα, "have a grievance against someone"; so also Xenophon *Mem.* ii.9.1; Josephus *Ap.* ii.177).   G. Schneider

πραγματεία, ας, ἡ *pragmateia*   pursuit, business*

2 Tim 2:4: αἱ τοῦ βίου πραγματεῖαι, "the *affairs* of civilian life." C. Maurer, *TDNT* VI, 640f.; Spicq, *Notes* II, 727-29.

πραγματεύομαι *pragmateuomai*   conduct business*

Luke 19:13: πραγματεύσασθε ἐν ᾧ ἔρχομαι, an order to the recipients of the ten pounds: "*Trade* with these till I come [again]." C. Maurer, *TDNT* VI, 641f.; Spicq, *Notes* II, 727-29.

πραγματία, ας, ἡ *pragmatia*   pursuit, business Alternate form of → πραγματεία.

πραιτώριον, ου, τό *praitōrion*   praetorium*

1. Occurrences and meanings — 2. The praetorium of Pilate in Jerusalem — 3. Phil 1:13; Acts 23:35

Lit.: BAGD s.v. — P. BENOIT, "Praetorium, Lithostroton and Gabbatha" (1952), *idem, Jesus and the Gospel* (1973) I, 167-88. — *idem,* "Le Prétoire de Pilate à l'époque byzantine," *RB* 91 (1984) 161-77. — J. BLINZLER, *Der Prozeß Jesu* (⁴1969) 253-59 (*The Trial of Jesus* [1959] 173-76). — R. ECKARDT, "Das Prätorium des Pilatus," *ZDPV* 34 (1911) 39-48. — KOPP, *Places* 366-73. — B. PIXNER, "Noch einmal das Prätorium, Versuch einer neuen Lösung," *ZDPV* 95 (1979) 56-86. — R. RIESNER, "Das Prätorium des Pilatus," *BK* 41 (1986) 34-37. — Schürer, *History* I, 361f. — L. H. VINCENT, "L'Antonia et le Prétoire," *RB* 42 (1933) 83-113. — For further bibliography see Blinzler.

1. Πραιτώριον is a Latin loanword (*praetorium*) and in the NT designates the residence of a Roman provincial governor (similarly *IG* XIV, 2548; ÄgU 288, 14; *Pap. Oxy.* 471, l. 110; *SIG* 880, 63). The *praetorium* was originally the tent in which the praetor lived, then it designated the praetorian guard or its barracks or the residence of a political official. In the NT πραιτώριον occurs in two contexts: in the Passion narrative (Mark 15:16 par. Matt 27:27; John 18:28a, b, 33; 19:9, → 2) and in the context of Paul's imprisonment (Phil 1:13; Acts 23:35, → 3).

2.a) According to Mark 15:16 the soldiers led Jesus, whom Pilate had given over for crucifixion (v. 15b), ἔσω τῆς αὐλῆς, ὅ ἐστιν πραιτώριον, "into the palace, that is, the *praetorium.*" There Jesus was mocked as "king of the Jews." Matt 27:27 omits reference to the αὐλή and speaks only of the πραιτώριον into which the soldiers brought Jesus. Mark 15:16b par. Matt 27:27b reports (hyperbolically?) that "the whole battalion" gathered together in the praetorium. John 18:28a tells that Jesus was led "to the *praetorium*" by Caiaphas, and 18:28b that the Jews who brought Jesus did not enter the praetorium "so that they might not be defiled" before the Passover meal. John knows of the praetorium from the Passion tradition. In John 18:33, after the proceedings "outside" (vv. 29-32), Pilate comes back "into the *praetorium,*" where he then questions Jesus himself. 19:9 reports that after the *Ecce homo* scene (vv. 4-8) Pilate again returns to the praetorium in order to question Jesus again.

b) The praetorium of Pilate was probably Herod's palace on the western hill of the city (so Schürer, Eckardt, Benoit, Kopp, and Blinzler), and not (as esp. Vincent asserts; Blinzler 174f. lists others who support this view) in the Tower of Antonia (northwest of the temple area). The identification with Herod's palace is supported by the Roman custom of taking over the residences of earlier local regents (→ 3.b). Furthermore, the reference to the crowd "going up" to Pilate (Mark 15:8: ἀναβὰς ὁ ὄχλος) better suits the topography if Herod's palace is assumed. Philo *Leg. Gai.* 306 calls Herod's palace the "house of the governors" (cf. further documentation in Benoit 156f.). In the 4th cent. pilgrims from Bordeaux asserted that the praetorium of Pilate lay in the western Tyropoeon Valley (cf. Kopp 371; Pixner).

3.a) Phil 1:13 tells why the situation of Paul as a captive "served to advance the gospel" (v. 12): "It has become known throughout the whole *praetorium* and to all the rest that my imprisonment is for Christ." Whether Paul composed Philippians in Caesarea (so, e.g., E. Lohmeyer, *Phil* [KEK, [14]1974] 3f.; cf. Acts 23:35) or in Ephesus (J. Gnilka, *Phil* [HTKNT] 24, 57f.), πραιτώριον refers to the official seat of the governor (with his officials), at which Paul's case (probably through the commencement of the trial) became public. Those who consider Rome the place of composition frequently interpret πραιτώριον as the praetorian guard or the imperial palace in Rome (Gnilka criticizes this view, 57f. with n.21).

b) Acts 23:35 tells of Paul being incarcerated in Jerusalem and taken to Caesarea to the governor Felix. On order of the governor he was to be "guarded in Herod's praetorium." Felix intended to try him when his accusers arrived. The πραιτώριον in Caesarea was another former palace of Herod the Great. Though it is not stated that Felix lived in the praetorium (E. Haenchen, *Acts* [Eng. tr., 1971] ad loc.), it is probably presupposed (cf. Schürer I, 361f.; II, 117; → 2.b).   G. Schneider

πράκτωρ, ορος, ὁ *praktōr* bailiff, constable*

The vocational designation for certain officials, esp. in finance. The πράκτωρ collected public debts, e.g., fines (*KP* IV, 1119). In Luke 12:58 (bis) πράκτωρ occurs with κρίτης: The πράκτωρ (*bailiff*) is under the judge and carries out his instructions. C. Maurer, *TDNT* VI, 642; Spicq, *Notes* II, 730-35.

πρᾶξις, εως, ἡ *praxis* activity, action, deed*

1. Occurrences — 2. Meanings in context — 3. The title of Acts

Lit.: H. C. HAHN, *DNTT* III, 1155-58. — C. MAURER, *TDNT* VI, 642-44. — G. SCHNEIDER, *Acts* (HTKNT, 1980) I, 73-76. — WIKENHAUSER, *Geschichtswert*, 94-104.

1. The subst. πρᾶξις occurs 6 times in the NT (→ 2) and also in the title of Acts: πράξεις (τῶν ἀποστόλων) (→ 3).

2. According to Matt 16:27 (cf. par. Mark) the Son of man "will repay [at the parousia] every person for *what he or she has done*" (cf. Ps 61:13 LXX; Prov 24:12: κατὰ τὰ ἔργα αὐτοῦ). Luke 23:51 (cf. par. Mark) reports that Joseph of Arimathea, as a member of the council, did not consent τῇ βουλῇ καὶ τῇ πράξει αὐτῶν (the Sanhedrin's decision against Jesus and its execution). Acts 19:18 reports that many in Ephesus who had recently become believers "confessed and divulged their [evil] *practices*."

In Rom 8:13; Col 3:9 the pl. also refers to evil *deeds* ("the *deeds* of the body" or "of the old nature"). Rom 12:4 compares the body and its parts and asserts that not all parts have the same *function* (οὐ τὴν αὐτὴν ἔχει πρᾶξιν).

3. The oldest witnesses to the Greek title of Acts as πράξεις (τῶν ἀποστόλων) are Irenaeus, Clement of Alexandria, Eusebius, and Origen (Tertullian and Cyprian call it *Acta*). Acts has had this title, therefore, though it is not original, since the 2nd cent.; this placed it into the category of contemporary πράξεις literature, which portrayed the great deeds of significant men (Wikenhauser). The analogy to the "deeds" of Jesus (Luke 1:1: πράγματα; Acts 1:1: ποιεῖν) probably influenced the choice of title. Nonetheless, the title "Acts of the Apostles" does not really correspond to the real theme and content of Acts (Schneider 74f.).   G. Schneider

πρασιά, ᾶς, ἡ *prasia* garden plot; section*

Fig. in Mark 6:40: ἀνέπεσαν πρασιαὶ πρασιαί (distributive doubling), "they sat down group by group," i.e., in ordered separation of groups by hundreds and fifties. R. Pesch, *Mark* (HTKNT) I, ad loc.

πράσσω *prassō* do, take care of, accomplish; behave, be situated*

1. Occurrences and meaning — 2. Paul — 3. Luke-Acts — 4. John and Ephesians

Lit.: G. EICHHOLZ, *Glaube und Werk bei Paulus und Jakobus* (TEH N.F. 88, 1961). — H. C. HAHN, *DNTT* III, 1155-58. — C. MAURER, *TDNT* VI, 632-44. — MOULTON/MILLIGAN s.v. — TRENCH, *Synonyms* 361-64.

1. The vb. πράσσω occurs 39 times in the NT, half in the Lukan literature (6 in the Gospel, 13 in Acts), 17 in the genuine Pauline Epistles, and in John 3:20; 5:29; Eph 6:21.

NT use of πράσσω is close to that of secular Greek (Maurer 633f.) and the LXX (*op. cit.* 634f.) in that πράσσω never has God as its subj. Hence it refers only to human actions, in contrast to → ποιέω, which, e.g., is used of God's creative activity. The general import of πράσσω is abstract and colorless. In the NT the word is found most where human action is judged negatively (cf. also → πρᾶξις 2).

2. In Paul οἱ πράσσοντες (Rom 1:32 bis) are Gentiles who have sunk into various iniquities. Rom 2:2, 3 speak in the same sense of τὰ τοιαῦτα πράσσοντες. Whoever (as a Jew?) "judges" the other, however, *is doing* the very same thing (2:1). 2:25 says to the Jew: "Circumcision indeed is of value if you practice (πράσσῃς) the law; but if you break the law, your circumcision becomes uncircumcision." In 7:15 mankind under the power of sin speaks: "For I *do* not *do* what I want . . ."; similarly v. 19: "For I do not do (ποιῶ!) the good I want, but the evil I do not want is what I *do* (πράσσω)." In 9:11 the objects of πράσσειν are ἀγαθόν and φαῦλον, referring to deeds that take from or add to a person's account. 13:4 speaks of God's wrath on the "wrong*doer*."

Πράσσω has various meanings outside Romans: 1 Thess 4:11: "*mind* your own affairs"; Gal 5:21: "those who *do* such things shall not inherit the kingdom of God"; 1 Cor 5:2: "he who *has done* this (ἔργον)"; 9:17: "for if I *do* this of my own will, I have a reward"; 2 Cor 5:10, of Christ's judgment seat, before which "each one may receive good or evil, according to what he *has done* in the body"; 12:21, of repentance from the ἀκαθαρσία, πορνεία, and ἀσέλγεια they *have practiced;* Phil 4:9, in the charge to *do* what the addressees have learned and seen in Paul.

3. In the Lukan literature the following trans. meanings occur: *accomplish/do* (Acts 5:35; 26:20, 26), of evil or negatively judged deeds (Luke 22:23; 23:41a, b; Acts 16:28; 19:36; 25:11, 25; 26:9, 31; pass. with dat. in Luke 23:15: οὐδὲν ἄξιον θανάτου ἐστὶν πεπραγμένον αὐτῷ ["by him"]; see BDF §191), *practice/engage in* (Acts 19:19: magic arts; cf. Moulton/Milligan), *collect* (taxes, Luke 3:13; 19:23).

Πράσσω occurs intrans. in the sense of *conduct oneself* in Acts 3:17; 17:7. On Acts 15:29 (εὖ πράξετε) see BDF §414.5; BAGD s.v. πράσσω 2b *(be well off).*

4. John 3:20: "Every one who *does* evil hates the light . . ." The same phrase, φαῦλα πράσσω (with Rom 9:11; 2 Cor 5:10; cf. Jas 3:16: πᾶν φαῦλον πρᾶγμα), also occurs in John 5:29, significantly with ἀγαθὰ ποιέω. Intrans. in Eph 6:21 (at the beginning of the conclusion to the letter): "Now that you also may know how I am, what I *am doing* (τί πράσσω), Tychicus will tell you everything. . . ."

G. Schneider

πραϋπαθία, ας, ἡ *praÿpathia* gentleness*

1 Tim 6:11: the final virtue in an enumeration of six (after ἀγάπη and ὑπομονή). The form πραϋπάθεια occurs

at times (Ign. *Trall.* 8.1). W. Michaelis, *TDNT* V, 939; W. Bauder, *DNTT* II, 256-59.

πραΰς, πραεῖα, πραΰ *praÿs* gentle, kind, mild → πραΰτης.

πραΰτης, ητος, ἡ *praÿtēs* kindness, modesty, mildness, gentleness*
πραΰς, πραεῖα, πραΰ *praÿs* gentle, kind, mild*

1. Occurrences in the NT — 2. Meaning — a) Semantic field — b) Prehistory — c) Context

Lit.: F. Böhl, "Die Demut (ˁnwh) als höchste der Tugenden. Bemerkungen zu Mt 5,3.5," *BZ* 20 (1976) 217-23. — H. Frankemölle, *Jahwebund und Kirche Christi* (1974) (on Matthew). — A. von Harnack, "'Sanftmut, Huld und Demut' in der alten Kirche" (FS J. Kaftan, 1920) 113-29. — F. Hauck and S. Schulz, *TDNT* VI, 645-51. — R. Leivestad, "'The Meekness and Gentleness of Christ' II Cor. X.1," *NTS* 12 (1965/66) 156-64. — T. Riise-Hansen, "Begrepene 'praytes' og 'parrhesia' i det nye testamente," *TTK* 15 (1944) 34-44. — H. Schlier, *Gal* (KEK, ⁴1965) 260f. — C. Spicq, "Bénignité, Mansuétude, Douceur, Clémence," *RB* 54 (1947) 321-39. — S. Wibbing, *Die Tugend- und Lasterkataloge im NT und ihre Traditionsgeschichte unter besonderer Berücksichtigung der Qumran-Texte* (1959). — A. Vögtle, *Die Tugend- und Lasterkataloge im NT* (1936), index s.v. — *idem, LTK* X, 399-401.

1. In the NT the adj. occurs 4 times, the noun 11 times (and its synonym πραϋπαθία once: 1 Tim 6:11). It is striking that in the Gospels only Matthew uses the adj. (3 times) and that the epistolary literature uses only the subst. (except in 1 Pet 3:4).

2.a) The meaning is determined first of all through the semantic field of virtues, itself structured by partial synonyms (→ c) and through antonyms and opposing terms such as rough, hard, violent, angry/anger, aggression, contentiousness, maliciousness (cf. Matt 11:28-30; Col 3:5, 8, 12; 2 Cor 10:1f.; Titus 3:2, among others).

b) Also significant to meaning is the word group's prior history. For Matt 21:5 the meaning is determined by the quotation of Zech 9:9 LXX with the post-exilic expectation of a Messiah who is not a Zealot, who renounces violence, and who in this sense is humble or gentle. The beatitude in Matt 5:5 derives from Ps 37:11 LXX (a wisdom psalm), as does Matt 11:29 in the call to those who labor and are heavy laden through reference to a model and vocabulary common in wisdom literature (cf. Sir 6:24-31; 24:3-22; 51:23-30). In epistolary parenetic-ethical passages the term occurs in Gal 5:23; Eph 4:2; Col 3:12; 2 Tim 2:25 in vice catalogs that themselves draw from early Hellenistic Jewish catalogs (Wibbing 118-23; on the status of scholarship see Vögtle, *LTK*). The prior history of these passages might also be signficant for the other NT occurrences, all of which stand in parenetic material. The later writings (2 Tim 2:25; Titus 3:2) betray the stylistic influence of diatribes and of popular or lay philosophical catalogs (Vögtle, *Tugend- und Lasterkataloge* 178-88; Wibbing 83f., 101-4).

c) Finally, meaning is determined by the context. Christology influenced by the OT characterizes Matthew (Frankemölle 7-83, 98f., 167-70, 183-85): Jesus is the "peaceful king" riding on an ass and a colt (21:5); he is the *gentle* and humble (→ ταπεινός) wisdom for "those who labor and are heavy laden," who find rest through the light yoke of Jesus' wisdom (11:29). The phrase "learn from me" (v. 29) has the same force as *imitatio* (cf. 9:13), the uniqueness of which is addressed in the psalm-like beatitudes (5:3-10; with the πραεῖς in v. 5 are also the poor in spirit, those who mourn, the merciful, etc.). Renunciation of violence and faithful trust in Yahweh characterize the πραεῖς (Böhl).

Paul, too, defends his own conduct in 2 Cor 10:1 by referring to the *"meekness* and gentleness (→ ἐπιείκεια) of Christ," through which his own weakness —against any Greek ideal of virtue or boldness (for criticism of Harnack and others cf. Leivestad 158ff.)— is christologically and ethically determined (similarly 1 Cor 4:21: "with love in a spirit of *gentleness*"). In the vice catalog in Gal 5:23 πραΰτης is characterized, along with love, peace, patience, faithfulness, etc., as "fruit of the Spirit" (similarly 6:1). This is in accord with Paul's pneuma-christology.

The Greek and Hellenistic concept of virtue already at work in Gal 5:23 (*contra* Hauck and Schulz 650, with Schlier 261) is strengthened in the catalogs of virtues in the deutero-Pauline Epistles (Eph 4:2f.: "lead a life . . . with all lowliness and *meekness,* with patience, forbearing one another in love"; Col 3:12f.: "compassion, kindness, lowliness, *meekness,* and patience"), in the Pastorals (2 Tim 2:25: kindly to every one, correcting opponents ἐν πραΰτητι; cf. Ign. *Trall.* 4:2; Titus 3:2: speak evil of no one, avoid quarreling, "be considerate and show πραΰτης toward all"), as well as in the later Epistles (1 Pet 3:4: in marriage women should be of a *gentle* and quiet spirit; 3:16: Christians should defend their faith with *gentleness* and reverence; Jas 1:21: receive God's word ἐν πραΰτητι without an angry tongue; according to 3:13 πραΰτης is the sign of appropriate conduct, as opposed to jealousy and contentiousness).

Nowhere do the NT authors allow πραΰτης and other ethical terms to be subsumed under the Greek idea of "virtue"; the theological and parenetic context prevents this, since as a gift of God πραΰτης is the characteristic Christian task and challenge. Πραΰτης is the courage necessary for service—renouncing violence and in faithful trust in Yahweh.   H. Frankemölle

πρέπω *prepō* be seemly, fitting, suitable*

Heb 7:26: "It *was fitting* that we should have such a high priest." Otherwise in the impersonal construction πρέπει (τινι), "it *is fitting* (for someone)" (Eph 5:3; 1 Tim 2:10; Titus 2:1; Heb 2:10), or πρέπον ἐστίν (Matt 3:15; 1 Cor 11:13). M. Pohlenz, NGWG.PH (1933) 53-92.

πρεσβεία, ας, ἡ *presbeia* embassy, legation → πρεσβεύω.

πρεσβεύω *presbeuō* be an ambassador*
πρεσβεία, ας, ἡ *presbeia* embassy, legation*

1. Occurrences in the NT — 2. Meaning — 3. Usage

Lit.: BAGD s.v. — G. BORNKAMM, *TDNT* VI, 681-83. — E. KÄSEMANN, "Some Thoughts on the Theme 'The Doctrine of Reconciliation in the NT," *The Future of Our Religious Past* (FS Bultmann, ed. J. M. Robinson, 1971) 49-64.

1. Vb. and noun occur a total of 4 times in the NT: πρεσβεύω once in Paul (2 Cor 5:20) and in Eph 6:20, πρεσβεία in Lukan parable material (Luke 14:32; 19:14).

2. Πρεσβεύω has an extensive prior history in classical and postclassical Greek (see BAGD, Bornkamm). It means *be an ambassador* or *envoy, function as an ambassador,* and retains this meaning in the NT. The noun has the same prior history and designates a *legation,* i.e., a group of persons who are to deliver a certain message or are commissioned with executing a certain task.

3. In 2 Cor 5:20 πρεσβεύω is used in an extremely decisive passage within Pauline theology, namely, in the context of the discussion of the work of reconciliation. God has reconciled the world to himself, and in this was not one who was passively reconciled, but rather the active reconciler (Conzelmann, *Theology* 208). Paul speaks as an ambassador of Christ and as such calls on the addressees on behalf of Christ to accept God's act of reconciliation in Christ (R. Bultmann, *2 Cor* [Eng. tr., 1985] 163).

In Eph 6:20 πρεσβεύω occurs in a request for prayer for the ambassador of the gospel who lies in chains (similarly Col 4:2-4). In comparison with 2 Cor 5:20 it is noteworthy that "Paul" here no longer speaks on behalf of the exalted Christ, but rather bears witness to the gospel. That is to say, ὑπὲρ οὗ πρεσβεύω is not to be translated "on behalf of whom . . . ," but "for whom I perform ambassadorship" (Bornkamm 682f.). In both cases the vb. expresses the official character of the Pauline message.

In the parable of war the unfortunate king who has underestimated his opponent sends an *embassy* before the battle and asks terms of peace (Luke 14:32). In the parable of entrusted money, which Luke, unlike Matthew, has enriched with a series of elements from the NT environment (Archelaus's ascension to power in 4 B.C.), the citizens send an *embassy* after the heir in order to prevent him from being crowned (Luke 19:14).   J. Rohde

πρεσβυτέριον, ου, τό *presbyterion* council of elders*

Lit.: B. Bonsack, "Der Presbyteros des dritten Briefs und der geliebte Jünger des Evangeliums nach Johannes," *ZNW* 79 (1988) 45-62. — G. Bornkamm, *TDNT* VI, 651-80. — M. M. Bourke, "Reflections on Church Order in the NT," *CBQ* 35 (1973) 323-45. — L. Coenen, *DNTT* I, 192-201, esp. 196, 199. — A. E. Harvey, "Elders," *JTS* 25 (1974) 318-32. — J. Jeremias, *Jerusalem in the Time of Jesus* (1969) 222-32. — *idem*, "ΠΡΕΣΒΥΤΕΡΙΟΝ außerchristlich bezeugt," *ZNW* 48 (1957) 127-32. — Leipoldt/Grundmann I, 143-291. — E. Lohse, *Die Ordination im Spätjudentum und im NT* (1951). — W. Michaelis, *Das Ältestenamt der christlichen Gemeinde . . .* (1953). — D. Powell, "Ordo Presbyterii," *JTS* 26 (1975) 289-328. — C. H. Roberts, "Elders," *JTS* 26 (1975) 403-5. — Schürer, *History* II, 199-218, 423-39. — G. Strecker, *1-3 John* (KEK) 22-26, 314-17. — For further bibliography → ἐπισκοπή; see BAGD s.v.; *TWNT* X, 1248f.

1. Πρεσβυτέριον occurs 3 times in the NT: twice in the Lukan literature and once in the Pastorals.

2. Luke 22:66; Acts 22:5 refer to the *council of elders* in Jerusalem, i.e., the Sanhedrin. 1 Tim 4:14 refers to a Christian congregational leader who already has a kind of ordained authority. Somewhat later Ignatius uses the term of a council convened to give counsel or representation to the bishop (*Eph.* 2:2; 20:2, and *passim*).

a) According to Luke 22:66 the presbyterium of the people assembled on the morning after Jesus' nocturnal arrest and consisted here apparently only of high priests and scribes (differently Luke 20:1, and correctly: high priests, scribes, and elders). Jesus was led into a full assembly of the Sanhedrin in order to be tried. It is uncertain whether Luke has a correct understanding of the circumstances at Jesus' time, since in Acts 5:21 he equates either the Sanhedrin with the Gerousia, or, following Roman circumstances, the council of elders with the Roman senate, and differentiates from this the council of judges, consisting of high priests and scribes (E. Preuschen, *Acts* [HNT] 31). According to Acts 22:5 Paul, in his own defense, calls on the high priest "and the whole *presbyterium*" to bear witness that until his conversion he conducted himself with rigorous exactitude according to the Pharisaic interpretation of the law.

b) In 1 Tim 4:14 members of a Christian *council of elders* are those who lay hands on Timothy in an ordination conferring the gift of grace (mediation of the Spirit to the apostolic pupil). But In 2 Tim 1:6 the apostle and in 1 Tim 5:22 the apostolic pupil are those who lay on hands. According to a different view (Jeremias, "ΠΡΕΣ-

BYTEPION"; cf. also G. Holtz, *Die Pastoralbriefe* [THKNT] 111f.), 1 Tim 4:14 refers to the laying on of hands that confers eldership.   J. Rohde

πρεσβύτερος, 3 *presbyteros* older; subst.: elder*

1. Occurrences in the NT — 2. Meanings — 3. Usage — a) Jewish *elders* — b) Christian *elders* — c) The twenty-four *elders* in Revelation — d) Older men

Lit.: → ἐπισκοπή, → πρεσβυτέριον.

1. All the writings of the NT except those of Paul use this word, for a total of 65 occurrences: 24 in the Synoptic Gospels, 1 in John, 17 in Acts, 5 in the Pastorals, 1 in Hebrews, 5 in the Catholic Epistles, and 12 in Revelation.

2. The NT uses πρεσβύτερος with three main and several secondary meanings, e.g., *members of the lay nobility,* as opposed to the high-priestly nobility among the members of the Sanhedrin, *elders* in the Jewish synagogue communities, Christian congregational *elders,* including members of the leadership council of the original community, *leaders* of Pauline Gentile mission congregations, the twenty-four heavenly *elders* of Revelation, and simply *those who are older.*

3. Πρεσβύτερος used substantively has an extensive prior history in classical Greece and in Hellenistic literature and in the OT and post-OT period (cf. G. Bornkamm, *TDNT* VI, 651-61; BAGD s.v.).

a) Jewish elders:

1) Those called *elders* as lay members of the Sanhedrin came from wealthy families who theologically followed the example of the Sadducean high-priestly nobility (Acts 23:1-10, 14). They play a role in the Synoptic Gospels in Jesus' trial, though the Synoptists do draw distinctions here. Above all, Matthew mentions as Jewish participants in the trial against Jesus in addition to the high priests also the *elders* (21:23; 26:3, 47; 27:1, 3, 12, 20; 28:12). Only in the first Passion prediction (16:21) and during the mockery at the cross (27:41) does Matthew also mention the scribes with them. In Mark and Luke all three groups are mentioned not only in the first Passion prediction (Mark 8:31; Luke 9:22), but also in connection with the question of authority (Mark 11:27; Luke 20:1). But at the sentencing only the high priests and scribes are mentioned, whereas those who arrest Jesus are sent by all three groups (Mark 14:43). In Luke 22:52 Jesus directly addresses chief priests, captains of the temple, and *elders* at his arrest. According to Matthew the scribes and *elders* gather with the high priest Caiaphas (26:57; similarly Mark 14:53; 15:1). Luke 22:54 also presupposes the presence of the *elders* with the high priest.

As part of the Sanhedrin the *elders* also played a role

in the persecutions of the apostles in Jerusalem (Acts 4:5, 8, 23). According to 6:12 Hellenistic Jews stir up the people, the scribes, and the *elders* against Stephen. The forty conspirators against Paul's life ask for help from the chief priests and *elders* in preparing a surprise attack (23:14). Ananias travels with a spokesman and some *elders* to the governor Felix in order to accuse Paul (24:1). The chief priests and *elders* ask the new governor Festus for judgment against Paul (25:15).

2) According to Luke 7:3 the centurion of Capernaum sends Jewish synagogue *elders* to Jesus with the request to heal his slave.

3) In connection with the dispute over cultic purity and impurity "the tradition of the πρεσβύτεροι" is mentioned as that which Jesus' disciples have violated. This refers to the Pharisaic scribes (the theological forefathers) who developed the Mosaic Torah casuistically in the pre-Christian centuries (Matt 15:2; Mark 7:3, 5).

4) The πρεσβύτεροι in Heb 11:12 are those mentioned in this chapter on the path of faith of those who went before, are the witnesses to the faith of the old covenant and thus members of past generations. Examples of these witnesses of faith from the past are then enumerated in 11:3ff.

b) Various groups of Christian elders can also be differentiated:

1) Luke describes the heads of the first Jerusalem church next to the apostles as elders. This group is for him probably analogous to the Sanhedrin of Judaism or, for the Gentile Christian readers of Acts, to the Gerousia of Hellenistic cities. In Acts 11:30 this governing body is the recipient of the collection from Antioch for Jerusalem. According to Acts 15:2, 4, 6, 22 the elders participate in the apostolic assembly, though the leading role remains with the apostles themselves (Peter is the speaker). In the text of the apostolic decree (15:23) and in reference to it as well (16:4) the elders are mentioned after the apostles. The ἐντολαὶ τῶν πρεσβυτέρων that according to 15:41 v.l. Paul and Silas deliver to the churches of Syria and Cilicia is the apostolic decree (15:23ff.). After Acts 16:4 the apostles are no longer mentioned, and Luke introduces the elders with James, the brother of Jesus, at their head as the new leadership of the Jerusalem church and as a kind of authoritative board for the Church at large (21:18).

2) Luke also mentions assemblies of elders as leaders of the Gentile Christian communities founded by Paul, analogous to the elders of the synagogue communities in Luke 7:3. These Christian elders were appointed with prayer and fasting by the founders of the congregations in every church (Acts 14:23). In Ephesus, too, a council of elders heads the church (20:17), and its task is compared to that of shepherds (20:28).

3) The same institution is found in the Pastorals and the Catholic Epistles. According to Titus 1:5 the apostolic pupil has, at the behest of the apostle Paul, appointed elders in the communities on Crete (the term is interchangeable with → ἐπίσκοπος in Titus 1:7). It is characteristic of elders who rule well that they are also active in preaching and teaching (1 Tim 5:17). They are to be protected against precipitous accusations (5:19). In 1 Pet 5:1ff. the author as a fellow elder (συμπρεσβύτερος) exhorts the other elders and instructs them concerning the conduct of the office of shepherd in the Christian community (cf. Acts 20:28). Jas 5:14 alludes to the existence of a council of elders whose members could be called to service on behalf of the sick.

4) The πρεσβύτερος occupies a unique position as the sender of 2 John (v. 1) and 3 John (v. 1). Although his identity remains unknown, he is probably not a member or head of a local council of elders, and πρεσβύτερος is likely the honorary name for a bearer and transmitter of the apostolic tradition of which Papias speaks (Eusebius *HE* iii.39.3f.; cf. Bornkamm 670; H. von Campenhausen, *Ecclesiastical Authority and Spiritual Power in the Church of the First Three Centuries* [1969] 121f., 162f.).

c) The twenty-four elders in Revelation are portrayed as heavenly beings. They are dressed in white robes, as are the innumerable martyrs from all the nations (7:9-17). Except in 5:5 and 7:13 they have representative (4:4; 7:11; 14:3) and cultic-worship functions (4:10; 5:6, 8, 11, 14; 11:16; 19:4).

d) Finally, πρεσβύτερος can be used simply of one who is older. Older men should not be rebuked, but rather exhorted in the appropriate manner (1 Tim 5:1, 2; cf. 1 Pet 5:5). In his Pentecostal prayer Peter quotes Joel 3:1 LXX and says in synonymous *parallelismus membrorum:* "Your young men will see visions, and your *old men* will dream dreams" (Acts 2:17b). John 8:9 probably refers to "older men," not to the elders of the Sanhedrin, since the adulteress was brought to Jesus by the scribes and Pharisees (8:3; cf. R. Schnackenburg, *John* [Eng. tr., 1982] II, 167). The brother of the prodigal son is described as *older* (ὁ υἱὸς πρεσβύτερος, Luke 15:25).

J. Rohde

πρεσβύτης, ου, ὁ   *presbytēs*   old man*

Luke 1:18, of Zechariah: "For I am an *old man,* and my wife is advanced in years"; Phlm 9, of Paul in his appeal to Philemon on behalf of Onesimus (v. 10); Titus 2:2, in the exhortation to *older men* (cf. v. 3: → πρεσβῦτις): They should be "temperate, serious, sensible. . . ." G. Bornkamm, *TDNT* VI, 683f.

πρεσβῦτις, ιδος, ἡ   *presbytis*   older woman*

Titus 2:3: "Bid the *older women* [cf. v. 2: → πρεσβύτης] likewise to be reverent in behavior, not to be slanderers. . . ."

πρηνής, 2 *prēnēs* forward, headlong*

Acts 1:18, of the fate of Judas: πρηνὴς γενόμενος, "falling *headlong*." K. Lake, *Beginnings* V, 22-30; G. Schneider, *Acts* [HTKNT] I, ad loc.; J. D. M. Derrett, *ZNW* 72 (1981) 132f.

πρίζω *prizō* saw apart, saw in two*

1st aor. pass. in Heb 11:37, the death of some of the witnesses of faith in former times: "They were stoned, they *were sawn in two,* they were killed with the sword. . . ." According to legend Isaiah met his death in this way (*Mart. Isa.* 5:1-6; Justin *Dial.* 120.

πρίν *prin* (adv.) earlier, before (adv.); before (prep.)*

1. As a temporal adv. in Mark 14:30, 72 par. Matt 26:34, 75/Luke 22:61: "*before* the cock crows"; Matt 1:18; Luke 2:26; John 4:49; 8:58; 14:29; Acts 2:20; 7:2; 25:16.

2. As prep. with gen. in textual variants of Matt 26:34; John 8:58. With acc. in Mark 15:42 v.l. (πρὶν σάββατον); John 11:55 v.l. (πρὶν τὸ πάσχα).

Πρίσκα, Πρίσκιλλα, ης *Priska, Priskilla* Prisca, Priscilla
→ ᾽Ακύλας.

πρό *pro* before; in front of, at*

Lit.: On preps. in general → ἀνά. — BAGD s.v. — BDF §213. — KÜHNER, *Grammatik* II/1, 454-56. — MAYSER, *Grammatik* II/2, 390-92. — B. REICKE, *TDNT* VI, 683-88. — L. RYDBECK, *Fachprosa, vermeintliche Volkssprache und NT* (1967) 62-77 (on John 12:1).

1. This prep. with gen. occurs 47 times in the NT. It does not occur in some of the shorter writings or in Revelation; in Mark it appears only in 1:2 in a quotation. It is usually used temporally (→ 2), less frequently spatially or fig. (→ 3).

2. Πρό means "before" in the comprehensive sense and refers to time and world at large wherever God's salvation plan is discussed, with phrases such as "*before* the foundation of the world" (John 17:24; Eph 1:4; 1 Pet 1:20) or "before the ages" (2 Tim 1:9; Titus 1:2; similarly 1 Cor 2:7; Jude 25; Col 1:17; John 17:5: πρὸ τοῦ followed by acc. with pres. inf.; elsewhere the inf. is aor.). These are theologically significant statements in that they refer to divine foreknowledge and action, whether to God's knowledge of what human beings need (Matt 6:8) and

the determination of Jesus' name even before his conception (Luke 2:21), or to Jesus' foreknowledge in his encounter with Nathanael (John 1:48) or his knowledge of his future suffering (13:19; Luke 22:15). John emphasizes the latter in 13:1 by associating it with a temporal determination that has already appeared in 11:55 and 12:1: "*before* the feast of the Passover." 12:1, in keeping with Hellenistic analogies, reads "six days *before* the Passover" (Reicke 686) or rather "six days earlier than the Passover" (Rydbeck 72-75); cf. Amos 1:1 LXX: πρὸ δύο ἐτῶν τοῦ σεισμοῦ; 4:7.

The reference point for "before" can also be the salvation-historical situation of the NT in relationship to the OT (Gal 3:23: "*before* faith came"; Matt 5:12: "for so they persecuted the prophets who were *before* you"; cf. John 10:8 v.l.), and equally the change in Paul's life, i.e., his conversion to Christianity (Rom 16:7) and call to be an apostle (Gal 1:17), which others before him (πρὸ ἐμοῦ) have already been. The significance of the historical moment comes to expression in a general fashion where Acts delimits the earlier insurrections, literally "*before* these days," from the events surrounding the apostles and Paul (5:36; 21:38).

References to the coming end involve πρό in Luke 21:12: "*before* all this"; Heb 11:5: "*before* he [Enoch] was taken"; in the comparison in Matt 24:38: "as in those days *before* the flood"; and in the phrase "*before* the time" (πρὸ καιροῦ, Matt 8:29; 1 Cor 4:5).

Other temporal references with πρό are: with substantives, Luke 11:38: "*before* dinner"; 2 Cor 12:2: "fourteen years *ago*"; 2 Tim 4:21: "*before* winter"; with a pron., John 5:7: "*before* me"; and with an inf., Acts 23:15: "*before* he comes near"; Gal 2:12.

3. Πρὸ προσώπου τινος in context has a temporal meaning, though it is formulated spatially: "*before* someone's) face/before (someone)." It is derived from Heb. *lipnê p-* and occurs in Matt 11:10 par. Mark 1:2/ Luke 7:27 (quoting Mal 3:1; Exod 23:20); Luke 1:76; 9:52; 10:1; Acts 13:24 (in the last passage with εἴσοδος ["*before* his coming"] so that it bears a temporal meaning). "*Before* the door" or "doors" is meant literally in Acts 12:6 (cf. v. 14), fig. in Jas 5:9. On the mention of "Zeus, whose temple was *in front of* the city," in Acts 14:13 (referring to the city patron, as possibly in D?) see Reicke 684.

Fig. πρό is used only as an expression of precedence: πρὸ πάντων, "*above* all/especially" (Jas 5:12; 1 Pet 4:8; cf. *Did.* 10:4).   W. Radl

προάγω *proagō* go before, lead the way, lead forward*

Lit.: E. L. BODE, *The First Easter Morning: The Gospel Accounts of the Women's Visit to the Tomb of Jesus* (AnBib 45,

1970) 31-37. — H. VON CAMPENHAUSEN, *Der Ablauf der Osterereignisse und das leere Grab* (SHAW, 1952/54; [3]1966). — C. F. EVANS, *Resurrection and the NT* (SBT 12, 1970) 78-81. — idem, "'I Will Go before You into Galilee,'" *JTS* 5 (1954) 3-18. — H. GRASS, *Ostergeschehen und Osterberichte* ([2]1962) 21, 113-27. — JEREMIAS, *Theology* 297. — G. KLEIN, "Die Verleugnung des Petrus. Eine traditionsgeschichtliche Untersuchung," *ZTK* 58 (1961) 285-328, esp. 296f. — E. LOHMEYER, *Galiläa und Jerusalem in den Evangelien* (FRLANT 52, 1936). — A. J. MALHERBE, "Through the Eye of the Needle: 'The Doctrine of Christ,'" *Restoration Quarterly* 6 (1962) 12-18. — E. MANI-CARDI, *Il cammino di Gesù nel Vangelo di Marco* (1981) 173-76. — W. MARXSEN, *Mark the Evangelist* (1969) 75-92, 111-16. — R. MCKINNIS, "An Analysis of Mark X 32-34," *NovT* 18 (1976) 81-100, esp. 82-86. — P. C. ODENKIRCHEN, "'Praecedam vos in Galilaeam' (Mt 26,32 cf. 28,7.10; Mc 14,28; 16,7 cf. Lc 24,6)," *VD* 46 (1968) 193-223. — K. L. SCHMIDT, *TDNT* I, 130f. — J. SCHREIBER, *Theologie des Vertrauens. Eine redaktionsgeschichtliche Untersuchung des Markus-Evangeliums* (1967). — R. H. STEIN, "A Short Note on Mark XIV 28 and XVI 7," *NTS* 20 (1973/74) 445-52. — B. STEINSEIFER, "Der Ort der Erscheinungen des Auferstandenen. Zur Frage alter galiläischer Ostertradition," *ZNW* 62 (1971) 232-65. — N. WIEDER, *The Judean Scrolls and Karaism* (1962) 1-51, esp. 30-48.

1. This vb. is found 20 times in the NT with 16 occurrences in the Gospels and Acts and 4 in the non-Pauline Epistles. The partc. occurs in the emphatically temporal sense of *preceding* in 1 Tim 1:18 (referring to the *earlier* prophetic predictions made to Timothy, probably at the time of his calling); 5:24 (referring to conspicuous sins that already during the lives of the sinners are *preceding* them to the heavenly judgment and thus mark them as already condemned); Heb 7:18 (referring to the *former* commandment, which God subsequently set aside). Προάγω is a legal term in Acts 12:6; 17:5; 25:26, where it means "lead before a legal body." In 2 John 9 the vb. is used of the heretic who *goes ahead* and leaves the christological confession behind (cf. Malherbe). In the remaining occurrences the spatial sense is dominant: *lead* (of the star that *leads* to where the child is, Matt 2:9; cf. Exod 13:21), *lead out* (of prison, Acts 16:30), *go before* or *precede* (the sinners and tax collectors precede "you" into the βασιλεία τοῦ θεοῦ, Matt 21:31).

2. The meaning *go before/lead* dominates in the Jesus tradition. In the transition to the third Passion prediction, Mark 10:32 emphasizes both Jesus' walking ahead of the disciples to Jerusalem into his suffering and, thereby, the implicit *imitatio* of the disciples (on redaction-critical interpretation of this verse cf. McKinnis; Schreiber 132; W. Grundmann, *Mark* [THKNT] 288; J. Gnilka, *Mark* [HTKNT] II, 95-97). The journey motif, according to which Jesus leads his disciples in a group to Jerusalem as the place of his completion, probably also affects Mark 11:9 par. Matt 21:9 (cf. Luke 18:39): After leaving Galilee Jesus goes to Jerusalem among a group of pilgrims. This journey into suffering is also the journey of the Son of man into heavenly glory, which is why it is not primarily subject to the earthly laws of space and time. Already the earthly Jesus knows of his journey to the resurrection and can participate in the mysterious possibilities of heavenly beings; cf. John 7:2-13, esp. v. 10: Jesus goes to Jerusalem from the perspective of his καιρός as his exaltation on the cross [ὡς] ἐν κρυπτῷ. In reverse fashion, the resurrected Jesus goes invisibly as a heavenly being before his disciples to Galilee (Mark 14:28 par. Matt 26:32), where they will see him when he appears again (Mark 16:7 par. Matt 28:7).

Scholarship vacillates between two interpretations of Mark 14:28; 16:7. On the one hand, a purely redaction-critical view interprets Jesus' journey to Galilee as a cipher for the mission to the Gentiles (Gnilka, *loc. cit.* 241ff.; Evans), as a situational reference on the part of Mark to the close parousia (Marxsen 82ff.), or as a general existential-theological reference (Schreiber 132). On the other hand, a "historical" interpretation postulates traditions of Galilean visions (epiphanies) in accordance with Matthew 28; John 21 at least as old as the Jerusalem Easter events (thus since Lohmeyer; cf. von Campenhausen, Stein; new material concerning Galilee = "land of Damascus" in Wieder) or in mutually exclusive competition with these events (so esp. Grass); Lohmeyer's interpretation with reference to the parousia has not gained acceptance.

One must recognize that Jesus as a charismatic exorcist belongs in religious history in the realm of pneumatic fringe experiences whose possibilities of expression also include mysterious changes of place, traffic with the heavenly world, and epiphanies of the glorified master from the heavenly world to his disciples. Mark 6:45ff. is, then, an example of one of the master's induced tests of his disciples, and 14:28; 16:7 are references to the victory over death and devil mediated to the disciple as part of the Galilean, charismatic master-disciple relationship, a victory effected by the master himself.

J.-A. Bühner

προαιρέομαι *proaireomai* (mid.)   choose for oneself, prefer*

2 Cor 9:7: καθὼς προήρηται τῇ καρδίᾳ, "as he *has made up* his mind [heart]."

προαιτιάομαι *proaitiaomai* accuse beforehand*

Rom 3:9, followed by acc. with inf.: "for we [i.e., I] *have already charged* that. . . ."

προακούω *proakouō* hear (of) beforehand*

Col 1:5: ἐλπίδα ἣν προηκούσατε, "the hope of which you *have heard before.*"

προαμαρτάνω *proamartanō* sin beforehand*

Pf. partc. in 2 Cor 12:21; 13:2: προημαρτηκότες, "those *who sinned before.*"

προαύλιον, ου, τό *proaulion* forecourt, gateway*

Mark 14:68: Peter went out (v. 66 from the → αὐλή) εἰς τὸ προαύλιον (cf. Matt 26:71: εἰς τὸν πυλῶνα).

προβαίνω *probainō* go ahead*

Literally in Mark 1:19 par. Matt 4:21 (προβάς). Fig. in Luke 1:7, 18: ἐν ταῖς ἡμέραις; 2:36: ἐν ἡμέραις πολλαῖς (of advanced age).

προβάλλω *proballō* put forward; put out*

Acts 19:33: προβαλόντων αὐτόν, Alexander, "whom the Jews had *put forward*"; Luke 21:30, of the emergence of plants: "as soon as [the trees] *come out in leaf*" (different in Mark 13:28). Spicq, *Notes* II, 743f.

προβατικός, 3 *probatikos* pertaining to sheep*

John 5:2: ἡ προβατική (*sc.* πύλη), the *Sheep Gate*: "Now there is in Jerusalem by the *Sheep Gate* a pool . . ."; → Βηθζαθά.

προβάτιον, ου τό *probation* lamb, small sheep Diminutive of → πρόβατον, "sheep," v.l. in John 21:16f. B C 565 pc. H. Preisker and S. Schulz, *TDNT* VI, 689-92.

πρόβατον, ου, τό *probaton* sheep*

1. Occurrences — 2. Literal usage — 3. A christological title? — 4. Fig. usage

Lit.: J. BOTTERWECK, "Hirt und Herde im AT und im Alten Orient," *Die Kirche und ihre Ämter und Stände* (Festgabe J. Kard, 1960) 339-52. — R. E. BROWN, " 'Other Sheep Not of This Fold': The Johannine Perspective on Christian Diversity in the Late First Century," *JBL* 97 (1978) 5-22. — J. H. FRIEDRICH, *Gott im Bruder? Eine methodenkritische Untersuchung von Redaktion, Überlieferung und Traditionen in Mt 25,31-46* (CTM A/7, 1977) 137-50. — F. HAHN, "Die Hirtenrede in Joh 10," FS Dinkler 185-200. — O. KEEL, "Tiere als Gefährten und Feinde des biblischen Menschen," *Heiliges Land* 7 (1979) 51-59. — O. KIEFER, *Die Hirtenrede* (SBS 23, 1967). — H. PREISKER and S. SCHULZ, *TDNT* VI, 689-92. — I. SEIBERT, *Hirt-Herde-König. Zur Herausbildung des Königtums in Mesopotamien* (SSA 53, 1969). — G. STEIN, "Das Tier in der Bibel. Der jüdische Mensch und sein Verhältnis zum Tier," *Judaica* 36 (1980) 14-26, 57-72. — W. TOOLEY, "The Shepherd and Sheep Image in the Teaching of Jesus," *NovT* 7 (1964/65) 15-25. — R. TUENTE, *DNTT* II, 412-14. — For further bibliography see *TWNT* X, 974f., 1244f., 1249.

1. 34 of the 39 NT occurrences are in the Gospels, esp. Matthew (11 occurrences) and John (19); Mark and Luke have 2 each. In the rest of the NT πρόβατον is rare, with one occurrence each in Acts, Romans, Hebrews, 1 Peter, and Revelation. Fig. usage predominates (25 of the occurrences); literal usage occurs only 13 times, once

as a symbol for Jesus' death. Πρόβατον frequently appears with the image of the shepherd (27 times, 15 of those in the shepherd discourse in John 10).

2. Jesus defends his sabbath healings with the symbol of the sheep that has fallen into a pit and must be rescued on the sabbath (Matt 12:11f.), a daily occurrence that was well known to his listeners.

Sheep were the most common animal in Palestine (cf. Job 1:3), and thus sheep-herding the most common occupation after agriculture. This is probably why πρόβατον, which actually means "small livestock," only occurs with the meaning "sheep" in the NT.

Luke 14:5; 13:15, which mention an ass or ox as the animal to be rescued, show that Matt 12:11f. is not intended figuratively. This is also the case in Matt 25:32f. (*contra* Preisker and Schulz 691f.; Jeremias, *Parables* 88, 206, and others; cf. Friedrich 143ff.), which shows the ease of separation at judgment by referring to the shepherd: Just as the shepherd separates the female from the male sheep at milking, so also will the judge separate the righteous from the unrighteous (Friedrich 150). The contrasting images of *sheep* and wolves are also meant literally (Matt 7:15 and 10:16), images juxtaposing the gentleness of sheep and the predatory nature of wolves. Matt 10:16 does, indeed, also contain metaphorical elements, as does Luke 15:4, 6 par. Matt 18:12, where πρόβατον is first meant literally. Other passages with literal usage are Rev 18:13 and John 2:14f. Sheep intended for sacrifice are mentioned in relation to the cleansing of the temple in John 2 and in Rom 8:36 and Acts 8:32 (both times as quotations from the LXX: Ps 43:23; Isa 53:7f.); like the LXX, the NT usually uses → ἀμνός for this meaning.

3. In Acts 8:32 Jesus is described as "a *sheep* led to slaughter," though significantly in a quotation (→ 2). This meaning occurs only here in the NT, where πρόβατον stands in synthetic parallelism with ἀμνός. No other passage really raises the issue of christological use of the word except Heb 13:20 (ὁ ποιμὴν τῶν προβάτων). Neither passage, however, uses πρόβατον as a title; only the symbol is intended. Otherwise → ἀμνός (2), "lamb," is used christologically.

4. In several occurrences one cannot easily discern whether a literal or fig. sense is intended. In the OT "shepherd" is a title for kings and esp. for God; thence πρόβατον became a symbol for the people or for those who need leadership.

The designation of the king as a "shepherd" also occurs often outside the Bible (cf. Seibert 1ff.; Botterweck 348ff.; Friedrich 146; → ποιμήν). God esp. is described as a shepherd (Ps 23:1; Isa 40:11; Ezek 34:12ff., etc.). "Sheep" refers then to the people (2 Sam 24:17), the people of God (Ps 74:1), or those led by others (cf. also Epictetus *Diss.* iii.22.35). The task of the shepherd in relation to the flock consists above all in caring for his charges, collecting the strays, protecting the sheep from danger, driving off threatening animals, and ministering to the weak.

Hence it is not altogether certain that Luke 15:4, 6 par. Matt 18:12 does not contain metaphorical elements (*contra* Tuente 412f.), as they became known later on the basis of harmonization with John 10, although this parable originally (as in Luke 15:8ff.) expressed the joy of God over the repentant sinner (in Luke) or the call "to the church leader to exercise faithful pastorship toward apostates" (in Matthew: Jeremias, *Parables* 40). Matt 10:16, too, where the contrast between sheep and wolves allows this image to be used, is already thinking of the disciples, i.e., πρόβατον is already a symbol for the threat to the dispersed Church. The same image occurs in Mark 14:27 par. Matt 26:31, where the context of the the image of the sheep and that of the shepherd is obvious, just as in Mark 6:34 par. Matt 9:36, where a simple comparison is used. In the other passages where Matthew uses πρόβατον he is thinking more of the people of Israel (10:6; 15:24).

1 Peter picks up the symbol of the dispersed sheep: 2:25, within the framework of the Isaiah-citations, quotes Isa 53:5, the image of the wandering sheep who have now turned to God, the Shepherd.

The great image of the good shepherd and the sheep in John 10, on the other hand, is christological and makes clear the close relationship between the sheep and their shepherd (vv. 1-4, 7ff., 11-13, 15f., 26f.). The sheep are those that belong to Jesus, "his own *sheep*" (v. 3), the ones belonging to him (v. 4), which are thus no longer lost but are the ones gathered in the "sheepfold" and protected by the shepherd, "his sheep." The resurrected Jesus entrusts this his congregation to Simon Peter at his calling (John 21:16f.) for loyal safekeeping (v. 15; ἀρνίον [→ ἀμνός 3] is used in the first exhortation to Peter). In both cases, however, the image of the shepherd is decisive, not that of the sheep.

All these texts using the image of shepherd and flock, of dispersion and gathering, contain "a significant potential for confidence, responsibility, and cohesion" (N. Brox, *1 Pet* [EKKNT] 139) as it is familiar to us esp. from Psalm 23. The sheep without a shepherd is lost (Mark 6:34 par.; Matt 12:11f.), needs protection (Luke 15:4; Matt 7:15; Matt 18:12 par.; John 20:11f.) and to be gathered in (Mark 14:27 par.; John 10:26f.). The uniqueness of the NT texts, however, is the supra-individual cohesion of the gathered sheep (esp. John 21:16f.; 1 Pet 2:25; John 10).   J. H. Friedrich

προβιβάζω *probibazō* lead forward, push into the foreground*

Matt 14:8: "*prompted (sent forward)* by her mother" (cf. par. Mark 6:24). Spicq, *Notes* II, 745.

προβλέπομαι *problepomai* (mid.) foresee*

Heb 11:40: God "*having foreseen* something better for us."

προγίνομαι *proginomai* happen earlier*

Rom 3:25: "because in his [God's] divine forebearance he had passed over *former* sins." → δικαιοσύνη 4.

προγινώσκω *proginōskō* know beforehand, have foreknowledge*
πρόγνωσις, εως, ἡ *prognōsis* foreknowledge*

Lit.: R. BULTMANN, *TDNT* I, 715f. — P. JACOBS and H. KRIENKE, *DNTT* I, 692f. — K. H. SCHELKLE, *1-2 Pet* (HTKNT, [3]1970) 20-25. — J. SCHMID, *LTK* X, 885-87. — S. SCHULZ, "Gottes Vorsehung bei Lukas," *ZNW* 54 (1963) 104-16. — For further bibliography see *TWNT* X, 1024f.

1. This compound vb. from → γινώσκω is used in the NT first of all of the divine *foreknowledge,* in relation to which the idea of election is always present. In the context of the theme "life in the Spirit as a position in hope" (8:18-30), Rom 8:29 emphasizes that the Christian lives in the knowledge that "those whom [God] *foreknew* he predestined to be conformed to his Son's image" and that "in everything God works for the good." "This 'knowledge' includes for Paul a recognition and appropriation . . ." (H. Schlier, *Rom* [HTKNT] 272). The same idea occurs in 11:2: God has not rejected Israel forever (v. 2a: "his people"), since he *foreknew* them (v. 2b). That is, he *knew* Israel *from the very beginning* and accepted it as his people.

Acts 26:5 speaks of human foreknowledge. In his defense before Agrippa and Festus (25:23–26:32) Paul briefly discusses his own life (vv. 4f.). All the Jews know about this (v. 4b), because they *have known* him *for a long time* (v. 5a), and they can testify to the veracity of his statement since they already knew of his life (cf. the intensification of the vb. by means of ἄνωθεν; cf. 22:3). 1 Pet 1:20 refers to Christ in a statement deriving from an earlier tradition and asserts that he *was destined* (by God, cf. the pass.) before the foundation of the world (cf. 2 Tim 1:9f.; Titus 1:2f.); this foreknowledge is not simply knowledge without participation, but rather a "creative willing" (Schelkle 50 n.3). The faithful, too, *know beforehand* that they are in danger of being carried away by the deception of lawless people and of losing their stability (2 Pet 3:17).

2. The noun **πρόγνωσις**, which in Jdt 9:6 refers to the predestining knowledge of God, expresses in Acts 2:23 God's *foreknowledge*, which is God's firm plan according to which the Israelites (v. 22) crucified and killed Jesus of Nazareth (cf. Luke 24:26f., 44-49; Acts 3:18;

13:27; 26:23). God's *foreknowledge,* established in his own decree (→ βουλή), reveals the Israelites as the actual guilty party in Jesus' death, whereas the ἄνομοι, the heathen Romans, are "merely instruments" and are thus exculpated (E. Haenchen, *Acts* [Eng. tr., 1971] 180). In the introduction to 1 Peter (1:1) the readers are addressed as "chosen" in accordance with God's *foreknowledge* (v. 2). This election is based on God's decree and obligates the chosen person to a responsibility that is manifested above all in obedience (v. 2b; → ὑπακοή 6).

A. Sand

πρόγνωσις, εως, ἡ *prognōsis* foreknowledge* → προγινώσκω (2).

πρόγονος, 2 *progonos* born earlier; subst.: ancestor*

The subst. οἱ πρόγονοι, *ancestors,* is used only in the Pastorals. 1 Tim 5:4, of active gratitude shown to (still living) *ancestors,* i.e., parents and grandparents; 2 Tim 1:3: "from [the time of] my *forefathers.*"

προγράφω *prographō* write beforehand/earlier; note ahead; write out publicly*

There are four occurrences in the NT. The literary meaning in Eph 3:3: καθὼς προέγραψα ἐν ὀλίγῳ, "as I *have written* to you *above/before,*" in reference to earlier statements in the same letter (e.g., 1:9ff.; 2:11ff.; hardly a reference by the pseudepigraphal author of Ephesians to letters of Paul accessible to him; see M. Dibelius and H. Greeven, *Eph* [HNT, ³1953] ad loc.; cf. further generally *Herm. Vis.* iv.3, 6; Ign. *Magn.* 6:1; Pap. Petrie III, 179; ÄgU 1107, 30); pass. in Rom 15:4: ὅσα γὰρ προεγράφη, "whatever *was written* in former days" (B lat have the simple vb. ἐγράφη), of "instruction" by scripture (specifically Ps 69:10); Jude 4: οἱ πάλαι προγεγραμμένοι εἰς τὸ κρίμα, *noted beforehand, entered into lists, predestined* (cf. Josephus *Ant.* xi.283; Lucian *Tim.* 51; Plutarch *Brut.* 27; on this point *1 Enoch* 81:4; 106:19; *2 Bar.* 24:1).

In Gal 3:1 οἷς κατ' ὀφθαλμοὺς Ἰησοῦς Χριστὸς προεγράφη ἐσταυρωμένος can be translated in one of two ways. The first is based on the sense "draw, paint" documented for the simple vb. γράφω: "before whose eyes Jesus Christ was portrayed as crucified." The second is based on a commonly occurring meaning for προγράφω, "proclaim publicly" (Aeschines ii.60f.; Plutarch *Cam.* 11; 1 Macc 10:36; Josephus *Ant.* x.254; see LSJ s.v. II.1), so that the clause refers to the public proclamation of the crucified Christ to the Galatians by Paul: "who was *publicly (clearly) placed* before you [before your very eyes]." The latter seems to be more likely, because Paul could

hardly be interested in a "portrayal" of the crucified Christ's sufferings, but only in the validity and indisputably public nature of the message of the cross, a message from which the Galatians were led astray by an incomprehensible "spell" (→ βασκαίνω); see esp. G. Schrenk, *TDNT* I, 770ff.; H. Schlier, *Gal* (KEK) ad loc.   H. Balz

πρόδηλος, 2 *prodēlos* conspicuous, evident, obvious*

1 Tim 5:24, 25, of *conspicuous* (among humans) sins (v. 24) and *conspicuous* good deeds (v. 25) as opposed to (momentarily) hidden ones that nonetheless are revealed at God's judgment; Heb 7:14: πρόδηλον (*sc.* ἐστίν) ὅτι, "for it is *evident/obvious* that. . . ."

προδίδωμι *prodidōmi* give beforehand, give in advance*

Rom 11:35 (cf. Isa 40:13f.; Job 41:2f.): τίς προέδωκεν αὐτῷ, "who *has given (beforehand)* to him [God] that he might be repaid?"; present in LXX Isa 40:14 א* A C probably as a v.l. from Rom 11:35. The meaning "betray, give over" occurs in Mark 14:10 D (in place of παραδίδωμι); *Mart. Pol.* 6:1f.; *Herm. Vis.* ii.2.2.

προδότης, ου, ὁ *prodotēs* traitor, betrayer*

Luke 6:16, of → Ἰούδας (6) → Ἰσκαριώθ, "who became a *traitor* (ὃς ἐγένετο προδότης)"; Acts 7:52: προδόται with φονεῖς; 2 Tim 3:4, in a vice catalog.

πρόδρομος, 2 *prodromos* going before; subst.: forerunner*

Heb 6:20: Jesus has gone into the inner shrine behind the curtain "as a *forerunner*" on our behalf (ὅπου πρόδρομος ὑπὲρ ἡμῶν εἰσῆλθεν Ἰησοῦς); cf. also John 14:2f. and the use of → ἀρχηγός (2) in Heb 2:10; 12:2. Πρόδρομος is used elsewhere of early ripe grapes (Num 13:20 LXX; Isa 28:4 LXX) or in a military sense of an advance guard or scouts (Wis 12:8; Polybius xii.20.7).

προεῖδον *proeidon* see in advance
2nd aor. of → προοράω.

προεῖπον *proeipon* foretell
2nd aor. of → προλέγω.

προελπίζω *proelpizō* hope in anticipation
→ ἐλπίζω 1, 4.

προενάρχομαι *proenarchomai* begin earlier*

2 Cor 8:6, of Titus: καθὼς προενήρξατο οὕτως καὶ ἐπιτελέσῃ, "as he *had already made a beginning* [in

Corinth, not in Macedonia, with the offering], so now also he should complete [with you] . . ."; v. 10: οἵτινες . . . προενήρξασθε ἀπὸ πέρυσι, "what a year ago *you began*" (see v. 11: νυνὶ . . . ἐπιτελέσατε . . . , ἡ προθυμία . . . τὸ ἐπιτελέσαι).

προεπαγγέλλομαι *proepangellomai* let be promised/announced beforehand*

Mid. in Rom 1:2, of God, who *let* his gospel *be promised beforehand* (προεπηγγείλατο) through his prophets (→ ἐπαγγελία 2, 4); pass. in 2 Cor 9:5: ἡ προεπηγγελμένη εὐλογία, "this gift you [the congregation] *have promised*" (of the offering collected in Corinth). J. Schniewind and G. Friedrich, *TDNT* II, 586.

προέρχομαι *proerchomai* go before; go further; arrive beforehand*

There are 9 occurrences in the NT, 5 of which are in the Synoptic Gospels and 3 in Acts. Προέρχομαι μικρόν, "*go* a little *farther*" (Mark 14:35 par. Matt 26:39); προέρχομαι ῥύμην μίαν, "*pass on* through one street" (Acts 12:10); *arrive earlier* (Mark 6:33, with acc. αὐτούς); *journey ahead* (absolute in Acts 20:5; with εἰς ὑμᾶς in 2 Cor 9:5); *go ahead* (ἐπὶ τὸ πλοῖον, Acts 20:13); *go before (someone), precede* (Luke 1:17: προέρχομαι ἐνώπιον αὐτοῦ, of John as the "predecessor" of God or of Jesus [cf. Mal 3:1]; 22:47, with acc. αὐτούς of Judas, who *went before* the crowd).

προετοιμάζω *proetoimazō* prepare beforehand, determine beforehand*

In the NT only with reference to the activity of God. Rom 9:23, of predestination to glory: προετοιμάζω εἰς δόξαν (opposite κατηρτισμένα εἰς ἀπώλειαν, v. 22), due to "the vessels of mercy" (→ σκεῦος); Eph 2:10, of the predestination or preparation of the faithful "for good works" (parallel to κτισθέντες), "that we should walk in them" (οἷς προητοίμασεν ὁ θεός, ἵνα . . .). → ἑτοιμάζω 3.

προευαγγελίζομαι *proeuangelizomai* proclaim the gospel in advance*

According to Gal 3:8 scripture "*preached the gospel beforehand* to Abraham" by allowing him to become a blessing to all nations (cf. Gen 12:3; 18:8); see further Rom 4:13ff.; Gal 3:15ff.; → ἐπαγγελία 4.a, b; εὐαγγέλιον 5. G. Friedrich, *TDNT* II, 737.

προέχω *proechō* be at/have an advantage; mid.: hold before oneself (as protection), throw up a defense*

In the NT only in Rom 3:9 (*lectio difficilior*): προεχόμεθα; οὐ πάντως. The mid. form is documented in

nonbiblical Greek with the meaning "throw up as a defense, hold in front as a defense" (*1 Enoch* 99:3; Thucydides i.140.4), but does not fit the context in Romans and would in any case require an acc. obj. Since a pass. rendering ("are we [Jews] excelled/surpassed?") makes no sense, the vb. is to be taken as a mid. form with an intrans. act. sense: "Do we *have an advantage?* Not at all" (cf. 3:1; see also the v.l. προκατέχομεν περισσόν in D* G latt and others; cf. *praecellimus eos?*). On the alternation between act. and mid. in the NT see BDF §316. BAGD s.v.; C. Maurer, *TDNT* VI, 692f.; U. Wilckens, *Rom* (EKKNT) I, ad loc.

προηγέομαι *proēgeomai* go before; excel, outdo*

Trans. in Rom 12:10: τῇ τιμῇ ἀλλήλους προηγούμενοι, probably to be translated analogously to Phil 2:3: "As regards honor *count* one another *higher* (than yourselves)." If the meaning specific to the compound itself is used, one could (with the Latin, Syriac, and Armenian versions) translate: "Outdo one another in showing honor." BAGD s.v.; BDF §150).

πρόθεσις, εως, ἡ *prothesis* offering, presentation; intention, resolve*

There are 12 occurrences in the NT. Mark 2:26 par. Matt 12:4/Luke 6:4 speaks of "the bread of the *presence*" (following 3 Kgdms 21:7) with ἄρτοι τῆς προθέσεως (literally "bread of the *presentation*"; Heb. *lehem hapānîm;* see Lev 24:5-9; → ἄρτος 4). Heb 9:2 mentions "the *presentation/laying out* of the twelve loaves" (ἡ πρόθεσις τῶν ἄρτων) next to the golden lampstand and the gilded table (Exod 25:23ff.; 37:10ff.; Lev 24:5ff.) among the inventory of the "outer tent" before the curtain, thus called the "holy place," though, significantly, the altar for incense is missing.

Elsewhere πρόθεσις means *intention, resolve:* Acts 11:23: πρόθεσις τῆς καρδίας, "*steadfast purpose* of the heart"; 27:13: τῆς προθέσεως κεκρατηκέναι, "that they had obtained their *purpose*"; 2 Tim 3:10: *purpose* in the sense of "Paul's" *predisposition/aim* (with διδασκαλία, ἀγωγή, πίστις, μακροθυμία, etc.).

Κατὰ πρόθεσιν in Rom 8:28 refers to God's *purpose /decree* in the sense of a divine decision for salvation that transcends history (cf. Heb. *ʿēṣâ* in Isa 5:19; 14:26; 25:1 [pl.]; 1QS 2:22f.; 3:6 and elsewhere; in the LXX, however, this is not rendered with πρόθεσις, but with terms from the stem βουλ-). (Προ- appears four times in Rom 8:28-30; cf. also 9:11; 1 Cor 8:3; see H. R. Balz, *Heilsvertrauen und Welterfahrung* [BEvT 59, 1971] 107f. with n.213 [bibliography]; similarly Eph 1:11 (four instances of προ- in vv. 9-12.) Rom 3:11: κατὰ πρόθεσιν τῶν αἰώνων, "according to his eternal [salvation] *purpose*";

2 Tim 1:9: κατὰ ἰδίαν πρόθεσιν καὶ χάριν, "according to his own *free purpose* and grace" (i.e., "not according to our works"); Rom 9:11: ἡ κατ' ἐκλογὴν πρόθεσις τοῦ θεοῦ, "God's *purpose* of election." Thus the word, used of God, always refers to God's free primal decision for salvation. C. Maurer, *TDNT* VIII, 164-67; P. Jacobs and H. Krienke, *DNTT* I, 696f.; U. Wilckens, *Rom* (EKKNT) II, on 8:28.

H. Balz

προθεσμία, ας, ἡ *prothesmia* appointed day/time*

The subst. adj. (*sc.* ἡμέρα) occurs in the NT only in Gal 4:2 in reference to putting an underage heir under a guardian "until the *date set* by the father" (ἄχρι τῆς προθεσμίας τοῦ πατρός). Προθεσμία is a t.t. of Hellenistic guardianship laws that refer to an appointed end of guardianship determined by the father (cf. H. Schlier, *Gal* [KEK] ad loc.). Paul, however, does not fully carry through the comparison, which—taken strictly—presupposes the father's death (4:1; cf. vv. 3-7). He merely wants to show that God has determined an end to the present enslavement (v. 3) of the heirs (of the promise) under the dominion of the στοιχεῖα τοῦ κόσμου (v. 5).

προθυμία, ας, ἡ *prothymia* readiness, goodwill, eagerness*

There are 5 occurrences in the NT, besides Acts 17:11 all in 2 Corinthians 8–9. Acts 17:11: μετὰ προθυμίας, "with *eagerness*" (cf. on this phrase Philo *Abr.* 246; *1 Clem.* 33:1). Paul emphasizes the *readiness/goodwill* of the Corinthians in relation to the offering: 2 Cor 8:11: προθυμία τοῦ θέλειν, "*readiness* in desiring" (that should be matched by completion of the offering out of "what they have"); according to v. 12 προθυμία also includes action, concretely the preparation and collection of money (εἰ γὰρ ἡ προθυμία πρόκειται); in 9:2 Paul praises the church's προθυμία, while according to 8:19 (πρὸς τὴν . . . προθυμίαν ἡμῶν) he sees his own work in this matter of the offering as occurring for the Lord's honor and as a demonstration of his own *goodwill* or *eagerness*, thus placing his own προθυμία next to that of the Corinthians. K. H. Rengstorf, *TDNT* VI, 697-700; Spicq, *Notes* II, 746-51.

πρόθυμος, 2 *prothymos* ready, willing, eager*

Mark 14:38 par. and Matt 26:41, in the words to Peter and the disciples in Gethsemane: "The spirit indeed is *willing* (τὸ μὲν πνεῦμα πρόθυμον), but the flesh is weak (ἀσθενής)." Σάρξ is used here of fundamental human frailty and πνεῦμα of willingness before God that cannot, however, accomplish anything without one's own engagement ("watch") and support from God ("pray"; cf. W. Schmithals, *Mark* [ÖTK] II, 638-40). K. H. Rengstorf, *TDNT* VI, 695f., overemphasizes the anthropologi-

cal dualism; the statement is a didactic maxim that can be fully explained neither from Ps 51:14 nor from the opposition between flesh and spirit in Qumran and Paul (only here in the Synoptic Gospels). The statement stands, rather, closer to, e.g., Rom 7:15, 22f.; 1 Pet 2:11. Its literal transposition into Pol. *Phil.* 7:2 suggests the language of edification (see also J. Gnilka, *Mark* [EKKNT] II, 262). Subst. in Rom 1:15: τὸ κατ' ἐμὲ πρόθυμον (v.l. -μος [adj.]), "so [here is] my *eagerness/concern*" (on κατ' ἐμέ as a circumlocution for the gen. → κατά 4.d; see BDF §224.1; §266.2). K. H. Rengstorf, *TDNT* VI, 694-97; Spicq, *Notes* II, 746-51.

προθύμως *prothymōs* eagerly, willingly*

1 Pet 5:2: μηδὲ αἰσχροκερδῶς ἀλλὰ προθύμως, "not for shameful gain, but *eagerly,*" of the pastoral task of the presbyters (parallel to μὴ ἀναγκαστῶς ἀλλὰ ἑκουσίως, and indeed surpassing this contrast in v. 2a; cf. L. Goppelt, *1 Pet* [KEK] ad loc., who also points out that in the Hellenistic environment the quality demanded of office-holders can be expressed by προθύμως; cf. *SIG* I, 493, 10; *OGIS* II, 737, 9; Spicq, *Notes* II, 750f.).

πρόϊμος, 2 *proïmos* early; subst.: early things, early fruits, early rain*

Jas 5:7: subst. πρόϊμον with ὄψιμον. The mss. add καρπός (א and others) or ὑετός (A P Ψ Koine). 5:7a (ἐκδέχεται τὸν . . . καρπόν) and the phrase ἕως λάβῃ (v. 7b) may refer to the *early rain* (in the autumn; cf. LXX Deut 11:14; Joel 2:23; Jer 5:24; also 4 Ezra 8:42). The farmer's patient and confident expectation regarding the fruit of the earth that receives the "*early* and late *rain*" (from God) is a symbol for trusting perseverance until the parousia of the Lord. On the word formation see BAGD s.v.; BDF §35; → ὄψιμος.

προϊνός, 2 *proïnos* early, in the morning
V.l. in Rev 2:28 A 046; 22:16 A in place of → πρωϊνός.

προΐστημι *proïstēmi* direct, be at the head of, manage; care for; apply oneself to*

There are 8 occurrences in the NT, all intrans., with 6 of those in the Pastorals. In the meaning *be at the head of/manage* the shading *care for* is always present; there is no difference in meaning between mid. and (intrans.) act.: 1 Tim 3:5; 5:17: καλῶς προΐστημι/προΐσταμαι τοῦ ἰδίου οἴκου, "how to *manage/take good care of* his own household"; children are mentioned separately in 3:12: τέκνων . . . καὶ τῶν ἰδίων οἴκων. This plays an important role in the "virtue catalog" of the ἐπίσκοποι (3:1ff.) and διάκονοι (3:8ff.; no parallels in the LXX, but several in Greek literature: Sophocles *Ant.* 661f.; Plutarch *Lyc.* 19; see further M. Dibelius and H. Conzelmann, *The Pas-*

toral Epistles [Hermeneia] on 1 Tim 3:4f.; N. Brox, *Die Pastoralbriefe* [RNT] ad loc.; H. Almquist, *Plutarch und das NT* [1946] 125; cf. also Pol. *Phil.* 11:2). It is similarly used (absolutely) of the office of the πρεσβύτεροι (καλῶς προεστῶτες) in 1 Tim. 5:17 (cf. *Herm. Vis.* ii.4.3).

It is used absolutely also by Paul: Rom 12:8: ὁ προϊστάμενος ἐν σπουδῇ, either *"he who is in an office of leadership,* [let him do it] with zeal" or (following the parallel partc. ὁ μεταδιδούς/ὁ ἐλεῶν) *"he who gives aid . . ."*; possibly a similar double meaning in 1 Thess 5:12: οἱ κοπιῶντες ἐν ὑμῖν καὶ προϊστάμενοι ὑμῶν . . . καὶ νουθετοῦντες ὑμᾶς, ". . . those who *care* for you [through tasks of leadership]"; the series of vbs. shows that Paul is not yet thinking of any actual office of "director" or "head" (→ πρεσβύτερος 3.b; → ἐπίσκοπος 2; see also Dibelius and Conzelmann, *Pastoral Epistles,* excursus on 1 Tim 3:7).

The meaning *apply oneself to* (προΐστασθαι καλῶν ἔργων) occurs in Titus 3:8, 14. BAGD s.v.; B. Reicke, *TDNT* VI, 700-703; L. Coenen, *DNTT* I, 192-94.

προκαλέω *prokaleō* call forth; mid.: challenge, provoke*

Mid. in Gal 5:26: ἀλλήλους προκαλούμενοι, *"provoking* one another" (with κενόδοξοι, φθονοῦντες) in the hostile sense. So also in Lucian *Symp.* 20; neutral in 2 Macc 8:11.

προκαταγγέλλω *prokatangellō* foretell, announce beforehand, promise*

Acts 3:18, of God's *foretelling* (προκατήγγειλεν) Christ's suffering through the prophets; 7:52, of the prophets as προκαταγγείλαντες. → καταγγέλλω 2.

προκαταρτίζω *prokatartizō* prepare beforehand, make ready*

2 Cor 9:5: *"arrange in advance* for this gift that you have promised" (ἵνα . . . προκαταρτίσωσιν τὴν προεπηγγελμένην εὐλογίαν ὑμῶν).

πρόκειμαι *prokeimai* lie before, lie in view, be at hand*

There are 5 occurrences in the NT, 3 of those in Hebrews. 2 Cor 8:12: εἰ ἡ προθυμία πρόκειται, "if the readiness *is there*"; Heb 6:18: ἡ προκειμένη ἐλπίς, "the hope *set before us*"; 12:1: ὁ προκείμενος ἡμῖν ἀγών, "the race that is [yet] *set before us*" (cf. 1 Cor 9:24ff.; Phil 1:30; 2:16; 2 Tim 4:7; Josephus *Ant.* xix.92; see esp. O. Michel, *Heb* [KEK] ad loc.). Jude 7: πρόκειμαι δεῖγμα, "as an example *before our eyes.*"

In Heb 12:2 ἀντὶ τῆς προκειμένης αὐτῷ χαρᾶς must in context refer to as "joy" the exaltation held out as a prospect by God to Christ (v. 2c) and thus with v. 1 refer to the ὑπομονή of Christ, who "for the sake of the joy *before him /placed before his eyes*" endured the cross and thus became the "pioneer and perfecter" of the faith and perseverance also demanded from the Church in its struggle; translating ἀντί as "instead" would disrupt the flow of vv. 1-3 (cf. vv. 5ff.) and also rob → χαρά (articular!) of its eschatological significance (for further suggestions for interpretation see esp. O. Michel, *Heb* ad loc.).

προκηρύσσω *prokēryssō* publicly/loudly proclaim; proclaim beforehand*

Acts 13:24, of John the Baptist, who "before Jesus' coming" (πρὸ προσώπου τῆς εἰσόδου αὐτοῦ) *announced beforehand* (or possibly *loudly proclaimed*) the baptism of repentance; on the first tr. cf. Josephus *Ant.* x.79; Pol. *Phil.* 6:3.

προκοπή, ῆς, ἡ *prokopē* progress, advancement → προκόπτω.

προκόπτω *prokoptō* go forward, advance*
προκοπή, ῆς, ἡ *prokopē* progress, advancement*

1. Occurrences in the NT — 2. Meaning — 3. Colloquial usage — 4. As a term for education

Lit.: Spicq, *Notes* II, 752-55. — G. STÄHLIN, *TDNT* VI, 703-19. — For further bibliography see *TWNT* X, 1249.

1. Of 9 occurrences in the NT (6 of the vb.: Gal 1:14; Rom 13:12; 2 Tim 2:16; 3:9, 13; Luke 2:52; 3 of the noun: Phil 1:12, 25; 1 Tim 4:15) 4 are in the Pastorals.

2. The vb. was originally a trans. navigational metaphor ("drive forward by means of blows"), but is only intrans. and colloquial in Hellenistic Greek, referring to different varieties of progress (synonymous with αὐξάνω, κραταιόω, περισσεύω, πληθύνω, προάγω, προβαίνω, and τελειόω). It is completely absent in the LXX (only 3 Macc 5:18 A, where it appears to be the result of a scribal error). It acquired a specialized meaning in the philosophical ethics of the Stoics (and in Philo) as a preferred word for the course of education.

The noun, first documented in Polybius, reflects both Hellenistic usages of the vb. There are 2 occurrences in the LXX: colloquial in 2 Macc 8:8: "success [in war]"; philosophical in Sir 51:17, where it is used absolutely as a *nomen resultantum* for "general progress in instruction."

3. Phil 1:12: Paul's incarceration served the *advancement* (the *growing acceptance*) of the gospel; Rom 13:12: The night *comes to an end* (cf. Josephus *B.J.* iv.298).

4. Paul reports in Gal 1:14 that he continually (impf.) *advanced spiritually and morally/educated himself* in Judaism. In Phil 1:25 he hopes he can still contribute something to the *further development (progress)* of the

congregation, namely, to their joy in the faith. The note in Luke 2:52 (cf. 1:80; 2:41) is a typical biographical recollection: With the help of wisdom Jesus *made progress* (following Sir 51:17) in both maturity (cf. Stählin 712f.; differently—despite the reference to Stählin—→ ἡλικία 2) and favor with God and people. According to 1 Tim 4:15 it is not Timothy's "advancement," but his *education* or *progress in instruction* that should become known (absolutely as *nomen resultantum*, as in the appropriately titled treatise by Epictetus [*Diss.* i.4]). This stands in conscious contrast to the ironically assumed self-designation of the false teachers in 2 Timothy (cf. 2 John 9): They are precisely not those who are "*far advanced*" or who "continually *perfect themselves*" (3:9)—or they are so only toward "ungodliness" (2:16) or "from bad to worse" (3:13, as in Josephus *Ant.* iv.59, on the band of Korah). One should not translate this term with *progress* or *progressively* in the contemporary sense, which refers to universal history, whereas the Hellenistic expression refers to individual history.
            W. Schenk

πρόκριμα, ατος, τό *prokrima* prejudgment*

1 Tim 5:21: χωρὶς προκρίματος, "without *favor/prejudgment*" (with μηδὲν . . . κατὰ πρόσκλισιν).

προκυρόω *prokyroō* validate beforehand, confirm legally*

Pass. in Gal 3:17: διαθήκη προκεκυρωμένη ὑπὸ τοῦ θεοῦ, "a covenant *previously ratified* [before the Mosaic law] by God" (the antonym is the legal t.t. → ἀκυρόω). J. Behm, *TDNT* III, 1100.

προλαμβάνω *prolambanō* take beforehand, anticipate; surprise*

Used temporally in Mark 14:8: προέλαβεν μυρίσαι, "she has anointed [my body] beforehand/in advance," i.e., without knowing it she has honored the dead while he is still alive. Temporal usage is probably also intended in 1 Cor 11:21: ἕκαστος τὸ ἴδιον δεῖπνον προλαμβάνει, "each one *goes ahead* [at the gathering for the Lord's Supper] with his own meal," i.e., before all have arrived, so that then (during the Lord's Supper itself) some are still "hungry" and some are already "drunk" (cf. 11:22 and esp. vv. 33f.: ἀλλήλους ἐκδέχεσθε. εἴ τις πεινᾷ ἐν οἴκῳ ἐσθιέτω, namely, in order then—at the "meal"—to be able to wait for the others and not shame those who depend on the communal meal). The meaning "consume" for προλαμβάνω here, while possible, is nonetheless weakly supported (BAGD s.v.; H. Conzelmann, *1 Cor* [Hermeneia] ad loc.); Paul would then be similarly criticizing "private" meals as a disruption of community fel-

lowship and as incurring guilt before the Kyrios; that would, however, fail to recognize that the Corinthians were endangering both the communal beginning *and* the communal completion of the meal itself (see esp. Bornkamm, *Aufsätze* II, 141-46; G. Theissen, *Studien zur Soziologie des Urchristentums* (WUNT 19, 1979) 293ff., esp. 300-302 [bibliography]).

Be surprised or *caught* is probably the meaning intended by the pass. in Gal 6:1: καὶ . . . ἔν τινι παραπτώματι, "even . . . in any [possibly grievous] trespass," though this may also be translated: "*to be surprised* by a trespass," though this is made less likely by the entire formulation of v. 1a (cf. H. Schlier, *Gal* [KEK, ¹⁴1971] ad loc.). G. Delling, *TDNT* IV, 14f.

προλέγω *prolegō* foretell, tell beforehand, say in advance, mention earlier*

There are 15 occurrences in the NT. *Tell beforehand:* Matt 24:25: Jesus as subj. with a contextually understood acc. obj.; Mark 13:23: Jesus as subj., πάντα as obj.; Acts 1:16: πληρωθῆναι τὴν γραφὴν ἣν προεῖπεν τὸ πνεῦμα τὸ ἅγιον; Rom 9:29: καθὼς προείρηκεν Ἡσαΐας (citing Isa 1:9); pass. in 2 Pet 3:2: τὰ προειρημένα ῥήματα ὑπὸ τῶν ἁγίων προφητῶν; cf. Jude 17: . . . ὑπὸ τῶν ἀποστόλων. Paul occasionally reminds his addressees of earlier statements: *say earlier, (already) said (once) earlier:* 2 Cor 13:2: προείρηκα καὶ προλέγω, "I proclaimed/warned before and *I am saying* [now again] *in advance*"; similarly Gal 5:21: ἃ προλέγω ὑμῖν καθὼς προεῖπον (in a warning spoken earlier during Paul's mission and now repeated with respect to the future threat to the congregation and the Church); 1 Thess 3:4: προελέγομεν ὑμῖν (at the establishment of the congregation); cf. 4:6: καθὼς καὶ προείπαμεν ὑμῖν καὶ διεμαρτυράμεθα. He also refers thus to earlier statements in the same letter: 2 Cor 7:3: προείρηκα γάρ (cf. 6:11f., possibly also 4:12); Heb 4:7: καθὼς προείρηται (referring to 3:15). In Gal 1:9 ὡς προειρήκαμεν καὶ ἄρτι πάλιν λέγω could refer to the immediately preceding curse (v. 8), but the strong προ- and emphatic ἄρτι πάλιν probably point to an earlier oral message, possibly during a second visit to Galatia (see H. Schlier, *Gal* [KEK] ad loc.).

προμαρτύρομαι *promartyromai* bear witness to beforehand*

1 Pet 1:11, of Christ's spirit, which *predicted beforehand* Christ's suffering and glorification (πνεῦμα . . . προμαρτυρόμενον). This statement is unique in the NT; προμαρτύρομαι occurs neither in the LXX nor in classical Greek. It is first documented in Pap. London IV, 1356, 32 (8th cent. A.D.). H. Strathmann, *TDNT* IV, 512.

προμελετάω *promeletaō* take care of beforehand, think about beforehand, prepare*

Luke 21:14 (cf. par. Mark 13:11: μὴ προμεριμνᾶτε; Matt 10:19: μὴ μεριμνήσητε): μὴ προμελετᾶν ἀπολογηθῆναι, "not to *meditate beforehand* how to conduct one's defense [at a trial]," probably not in the technical sense of "preparing" a speech or the like (as in Aristophanes *Ec.* 117; Plato *Sph.* 218d). The vb. does not occur in the LXX.

προμεριμνάω *promerimnaō* worry about beforehand*

Mark 13:11: μὴ προμεριμνᾶτε τί λαλήσητε, *"do not be anxious beforehand . . .";* → προμελετάω. This vb. does not occur in the LXX or in classical Greek.

προνοέω *pronoeō* worry, be concerned, take care → πρόνοια.

πρόνοια, ας, ἡ *pronoia* care, provision*
προνοέω *pronoeō* worry, be concerned, take care*

Lit.: BAGD s.v. — J. Behm, *TDNT* IV, 1009-16. — P. Jacobs and H. Krienke, *DNTT* I, 693-95.

1. Πρόνοια occurs in the NT only in Acts 24:2 and Rom 13:14. In the latter, πρόνοιαν ποιοῦμαι (cf. Dan 6:19; *Ep. Arist.* 80; Josephus *Ap.* i.9; *Vita* 62; Philo *Ebr.* 87) means the same as προνοέω. Προνοέω occurs in the mid. in Rom 12:17 and in the act. (also v.l. mid.) in 2 Cor 8:21 and 1 Tim 5:8.

2. In Greek philosophy (Xenophon *Mem.* i.4.6; Plato *Ti.* 30c; cf. already Herodotus iii.108.2), esp. in Stoicism (Zeno frag. 176; Chrysippus 962, 1118; Epictetus *Diss.,* index s.v. in the ed. by H. Schenkl [²1916]; Marcus Antonius ix.1.10) πρόνοια refers not only to human foreknowledge and care, but also to divine providence. The noun also has the latter sense in Hellenistic Judaism, e.g., in the LXX (Wis 14:3; 17:2; 3 Macc 4:21; 5:30; 4 Macc 13:19; 17:22), in Philo, who even wrote a book titled Περὶ προνοίας (cf. Seneca *De Providentia*), and in Josephus (*Ant.* i.225; xi.169; xiii.80). "Providence" in this sense can even be a metonym for God (Wis 17:2; 4 Macc 9:24; 17:22).

In the NT, on the other hand, both noun and vb. are used only of human beings. In Acts 24:2 the advocate for the Jews, Tertullus, extols in typical Hellenistic rhetorical language the *provisions* of the Roman official Felix. In Rom 13:14 Paul warns not only against false *concern* (so Behm 1012), but in general against *provision* or *care* for the "flesh," i.e., attention to the vainglorious nature of human beings (cf. H. Schlier, *Rom* [HTKNT] 400), since such *care and nurturing* leads basically to the ἐπιθυμίαι of human selfishness and reawakens "the baptized person's past" (Schlier, *Rom* 202). In Rom 12:17 and 2 Cor 8:21 Paul appears to alter the maxim in Prov 3:4 LXX, according to which

one should be *concerned* with what is good and honorable before God and people, first in a general imv., then in a statement addressing his own *provision* against suspicion involving the offering. In 1 Tim 5:8 *care/provision* for one's relatives is called for.

W. Radl

προοράω *prooraō* see in advance, foresee; mid.: have before one's eyes*

There are 4 occurrences in the NT. Acts 2:31: "David" (Ps 16:8-11) *foresaw* and spoke of Christ's resurrection (προϊδὼν ἐλάλησεν); similarly Gal 3:8: προϊδοῦσα ἡ γραφή (cf. also Philo *Imm.* 2.9; Josephus *B.J.* i.69). With the meaning *see* someone *previously,* i.e., in the past, in Acts 21:29: ἦσαν γὰρ προεωρακότες Τρόφιμον. Mid. in Acts 2:25, of "David": προορώμην τὸν κύριον ἐνώπιόν μου διὰ παντός (citing Ps 15:8 LXX), "I *saw* the Lord always *before me.*" W. Michaelis, *TDNT* V, 381f.

προορίζω *proorizō* predestine*

There are 6 occurrences in the NT, all referring to the predestination of events and peoples by God before all time or before their concrete historical time. Thus the vb. functions as an intensified form of the simple vb. → ὁρίζω. The gathering together of Jesus' adversaries occurred according to God's plan (Acts 4:28: ὅσα ἡ χείρ σου καὶ ἡ βουλὴ [σου] προώρισεν γενέσθαι); of the σοφία θεοῦ . . . , ἣν προώρισεν ὁ θεὸς πρὸ τῶν αἰώνων εἰς δόξαν ἡμῶν (1 Cor 2:7). Divine predestination aims at the concrete historical revelation of what was previously hidden and is thus spoken of by Paul in statements regarding salvation, i.e., doxologically; this is the case in reference to the predestination of the chosen to be conformed to the image of God's Son, i.e., to the eschatological destiny of suffering and glorification (Rom 8:29: οὓς προέγνω, καὶ προώρισεν; v. 30: οὓς δὲ προώρισεν, τούτους καὶ ἐκάλεσεν; → προγινώσκω; πρόθεσις; σύμμορφος, see H. R. Balz, *Heilsvertrauen und Welterfahrung* [BEvT 59, 1971], 108f.). Eph 1:5 is also concerned with the predestination of the faithful to salvation (προορίσας ἡμᾶς εἰς υἱοθεσίαν); so also 1:11 (προορισθέντες κατὰ πρόθεσιν). Προορίζω does not occur in the LXX, just as the simple form ὁρίζω does not occur there in the sense of "predestination/predetermination" by God. K. L. Schmidt, *TDNT* V, 456; P. Jacobs and H. Krienke, *DNTT* I, 695f.; → ὁρίζω (bibliography).

προπάσχω *propaschō* suffer previously*

1 Thess 2:2: προπαθόντες καὶ ὑβρισθέντες, "though we *had already* [before coming to you, 1:1] *suffered* and been shamefully treated [at Philippi]." Cf. Acts 16:20ff.

159

προπάτωρ, ορος, ὁ *propatōr* forefather, ancestor*

Rom 4:1, of Abraham: τὸν προπάτορα ἡμῶν κατὰ σάρκα. Paul speaks here first as a Jew of Abraham as the "physical/historical" (κατὰ σάρκα implies no negative evaluation) *forefather* of all Jews, since he will later present him as the real "father of all who believe without being circumcised" (4:11). On the text-critical and content problems in Rom 4:1f. see esp. U. Wilckens, *Rom* [EKKNT] ad loc.

προπέμπω *propempō* escort; equip (for further journeys), send out*

There are 9 occurrences in the NT. In Paul the vb. always has the meaning *equip for (further) journeys/send on one's way:* Rom 15:24: ἐλπίζω . . . ὑφ' ὑμῶν προπεμφθῆναι; 1 Cor 16:6: ἵνα ὑμεῖς με προπέμψητε; v. 11: προπέμψατε δὲ αὐτόν [Timothy] ἐν εἰρήνῃ; 2 Cor 1:16: ὑφ' ὑμῶν προπεμφθῆναι εἰς τὴν Ἰουδαίαν; similarly also Titus 3:13: σπουδαίως πρόπεμψον, ἵνα μηδὲν αὐτοῖς λείπῃ; 3 John 6: οὓς . . . προπέμψας ἀξίως τοῦ θεοῦ; Acts 15:3: προπεμφθέντες ὑπὸ τῆς ἐκκλησίας. With the meaning *escort/accompany* in Acts 20:38: εἰς τὸ πλοῖον; 21:5: προπεμπόντων ἡμᾶς πάντων . . . ἔξω τῆς πόλεως.

προπετής, 2 *propetēs* reckless, thoughtless*

Acts 19:36: μηδὲν προπετὲς πράσσειν, "do nothing *rash*"; 2 Tim 3:4, in a vice catalog: *thoughtless/reckless;* cf. Spicq, *Notes* II, 756f.: "unchecked or inconsiderate aggressiveness" (757).

προπορεύομαι *proporeuomai* go before*

Luke 1:76, of John the Baptist: προπορεύσῃ γὰρ ἐνώπιον (v.l. πρὸ προσώπου, as frequently in the LXX) κυρίου, "you *will go before* the Lord"; Acts 7:40: θεοὶ οἳ προπορεύσονται ἡμῶν, "gods *to go before* us" (cf. Exod 32:1, 23).

πρός *pros* with gen.: to the advantage of, for; with dat.: at, by, with; with acc.: to, toward, against; with reference to

1. Occurrences in the three cases — 2. With acc. as designation — a) of place — b) of time — c) of goal — d) of reference point

Lit.: On preps. in general → ἀνά. — BAGD s.v. — BDF §§239f. — M. J. HARRIS, *DNTT* III, 1204-6. — KÜHNER, *Grammatik* II/1, 515-21. — MAYSER, *Grammatik* II/2, 492-509. — MOULTON, *Grammar* III, 273f. — B. REICKE, *TDNT* VI, 720-25.

1. The prep. πρός has maintained its usage with all three cases in the NT, though it occurs with the gen. only in Acts 27:34: " . . . this contributes *to* your preserva-

tion." With the dat. it occurs 7 times, always with a local meaning (John 18:16: "Peter stood *at* the door"; similarly 20:11, 12 bis; Mark 5:11; Rev 1:13) and only in Luke 19:37 in the sense of attained locality: "as he was now coming *near/to* the descent of the Mount of Olives." Direction or inclination toward something or someone is usually indicated by πρός with the acc. This meaning occurs over 700 times in the NT (*VKGNT* II, 691) and in all the NT writings except Jude.

Πρός with acc. never occurs in Matthew or Mark after vbs. of speaking, however, other than in reciprocal usage, though it occurs in such contexts in the Lukan literature 149 times (100 in the Gospel, 49 in Acts), and elsewhere in the NT only in John (14 occurrences) and Hebrews (6) (J. Jeremias, *Die Sprache des Lukas-Evangeliums* [1980], 33). A characteristic phrase in Luke's Gospel is εἶπεν(-ον, -αν) δὲ πρός, sometimes with a following subj. (e.g., 9:13, 14, 50; 20:41 different from par. Mark; cf. Acts 9:15; H. Schürmann, *Jesu Abschiedsrede* [²1977] 121; on the Lukan redaction with vbs. of speaking cf. *idem, Der Paschamahlbericht* [²1968] 4f.).

2.a) Usually πρός refers to the location toward which something is moving or at which something already is: 1) Movement toward a geographical location, a thing, or a person: Matt 2:12: "not to return *to* Herod"; Mark 1:33, after a pf. pass. partc.: "gathered together *about/ before* the door"; after a subst. in Eph 2:18; 1 Thess 1:9; with vbs. of sending in Mark 12:2, 4, 6; with a vb. of leading in Luke 4:40. Speaking to an addressee (cf. → 1): a Hebraism in the almost adv. phrase στόμα πρὸς στόμα in 2 John 12 and 3 John 14: "talk with you face *to* face /in person" (BAGD s.v. III.1.e); reflexively in Mark 12:7: "they said *to* one another"; also of supplication (Acts 8:24) or of prayer in general (Rom 10:1).

2) Being and remaining: Matt 13:56, with εἶναι; Gal 2:5, with διαμένειν; reflexively in Luke 18:11: "prayed thus *with* himself"; with the art. in Mark 2:2: τὰ πρὸς τὴν θύραν "[the place] *about* the door"; with παρουσία in Phil 1:26, though this can, however, also mean "arrival." Mark 11:4 ("tied *at* the door"); 14:54 par. Luke 22:56 ("*at* the fire") may belong under 1) above.

b) Πρός is used temporally of: 1) approach toward a point in time (Luke 24:29: "it is *toward* evening") and 2) time itself (Heb 12:11: "*for* now") or its duration (12:10: "*for* a few days"; John 5:35; 2 Cor 7:8; Gal 2:5; Phlm 15, all πρὸς ὥραν, "*for/up to* an hour"; cf. 1 Thess 2:17: "[only] a short time").

c) Πρός can also designate goal, i.e., that toward which an action is directed: 1) The consciously sought goal of action can thus be expressed with a noun: Acts 3:10: "he sat *for* alms," i.e., "begging" (BAGD s.v. ἐλεημοσύνη); Rom 3:26; 1 Cor 7:35; or with an inf. (Matt 23:5; Acts 3:19).

2) The same holds for consequences or result, as in 1 Cor 14:26: "*for* edification"; Matt 5:28: "*to the end of* lustful desiring" (aor. inf.). Πρὸς φθόνον in Jas 5:4: should possibly (see Reicke 725) also be included here ("*to the point of* jealousy"), though the phrase is probably purely adv.: "jealously" (see BAGD s.v. III.6).

3) Πρός after adjectives and participles with nouns designates that for which someone or something is suited, ready, or useful: Titus 1:16; 3:1: "*for* every good work"; 1 Tim 4:8 (bis); 2 Tim 3:16 (4 occurrences of πρός with ὠφέλιμος).

d) The relationship described by πρός can be personal or simply one of reference.

1) The attitude toward persons is friendly (1 Thess 5:14: "patient *with* them all"; on the relationship with God cf. Rom 5:1; 2 Cor 3:4) or hostile (Luke 23:12: "*at* enmity with each other"; Eph 6:12: "contending *against* . . ." [πρός 6 times]).

2) The relationship with someone or something is of varying intensity. When according to Mark 12:12 par. Jesus tells a story *against/with a view to* someone, this implies that the person spoken of is to be moved or struck by the story (cf. 10:5 par.), and the parable πρὸς τὸ δεῖν προσεύχεσθαι is told "*to the effect* that they ought always to pray" (Luke 18:1). Τὰ πρός designates simply point of view in the sense of *as it concerns* (Rom 15:17; Heb 2:17; 5:1: "that which concerns God"; Luke 14:32; 19:42: "that which concerns peace/peace conditions"). In abbreviated interrogative sentences πρός refers to the person that is concerned about a matter (Matt 27:4; John 21:22: τί πρὸς ἡμᾶς/σε; "What is that *to* us?"). Finally, πρός can identify the standard to which one refers in a comparison (Gal 2:14: "*in accordance with* the truth of the gospel"; Rom 8:18: *comparing with;* 2 Cor 5:10).   W. Radl

προσάββατον, ου, τό *prosabbaton* day before the sabbath (Friday)*

In Mark 15:42 the day of → παρασκευή ("day of preparation") is additionally identified: ὅ ἐστιν προσάββατον, "that is, *the day before the sabbath/Friday*" (cf. Jdt 8:6; Ps 92:1 LXX; Josephus *Ant.* iii.255f.; Heb. ʿereḇ šabbāṯ, *m. Šabb.* 2:7; 19:1; see Billerbeck I, 1052f.).

προσαγορεύω *prosagoreuō* address, name (vb.), give a name to*

According to Heb 5:10 Christ *received* from God *the name* of high priest after the order of Melchizedek. This refers to a public proclamation like Ps 110:4. The author of Hebrews, following Heb 4:14f. and going beyond the text of Ps 109:4 LXX (ἱερεύς), speaks of the ἀρχιερεύς and thus prepares the way for the exposition in Heb 5:11ff.

προσάγω *prosagō* bring by, lead forth, bring to; intrans.: approach*

Luke 9:41: προσάγαγε, *bring here;* Acts 16:20: προσαγαγόντες αὐτοὺς τοῖς στρατηγοῖς, "they *brought* them *to* the magistrates"; pass. in Matt 18:24 v.l. Intrans. in Acts 27:27: ὑπενόουν . . . προσάγειν τινὰ αὐτοῖς χώραν, "they suspected that some land *was nearing* them." Fig. in 1 Pet 3:18, of Christ, who died for sins in order to *lead* the faithful to God (ἵνα ὑμᾶς προσαγάγῃ θεῷ; cf. also Rom 5:1f.; Eph 2:18; 3:12 [→ προσαγωγή]; Heb 10:22). This statement is probably influenced directly neither by the sacrificial (Exod 29:10) nor by the legal terminology (Exod 21:6) of the LXX, nor by the meaning "lead before" (to an audience before the king: Xenophon *Cyr.* i.3.8); see esp. L. Goppelt, *1 Pet* (KEK) on 3:18c with n.21. K. L. Schmidt, *TDNT* I, 131-33.

προσαγωγή, ῆς, ἡ *prosagōgē* access, approach*

Lit.: BAGD s.v. — LSJ s.v. προσαγωγεῖον. — MAYSER, *Grammatik* I/3, 20; II/1, 129; II/2, 40. — MOULTON/MILLIGAN s.v. — F. MUSSNER, *Christus, das All und die Kirche* (1955, ²1968) 102-4. — PREISIGKE, *Wörterbuch* II, 387. — K. L. SCHMIDT, *TDNT* I, 133f.

Προσαγωγή occurs in the NT only in Rom 5:2; Eph 2:18; 3:12. Although trans. usage is possible ("lead to"; → προσάγω), the meaning in these occurrences is probably intrans.: *access, approach* (see E. Käsemann, *Rom* [Eng. tr., 1980] 133). The point of departure recalls cultic circumstances: access to the temple, to the holy of holies (cf. Heb 10:19-22), and thence "to God" (cf. 1 Pet 3:18), "to the Father" (Eph 2:18), or as a preliminary stage to participation in God's glory: "this grace (χάρις) in which we [presently] stand" (Rom 5:2). Προσαγωγή is used absolutely in Eph 3:12: Christ (v. 11) embodies *access* to God (cf. vv. 17-19). This *access* comes by trust and is accompanied by candor (see J. Gnilka, *Eph* [HTKNT] 178). The three occurrences of the word agree that Christians (both Jewish and Gentile, in one Spirit, Eph 2:18) are those who have received (pf., Rom 5:2) this *access,* which is opened to us by (Eph 3:12: in) Christ. Rom 5:2 and Eph 3:12 (perhaps echoing Romans; see Gnilka, *Eph*) emphasize that this *access* has occurred "in faith" or has been acquired "through faith" (in Christ). Despite contradictory textual witnesses, in Rom 5:2 τῇ πίστει is probably authentic (see Käsemann, *Rom, contra* H. Schlier, *Rom* [HTKNT] 142, et al.; cf. *TCGNT* 511f.).   U. Borse

προσαιτέω *prosaiteō* beg*

John 9:8: ὁ καθήμενος καὶ προσαιτῶν, "who used to sit and *beg*," of a man who was blind from birth; cf. also the partc. προσαιτῶν in Mark 10:46 v.l. (in place of → προσαίτης) par. Luke 18:35 v.l. (in place of ἐπαιτῶν).

προσαίτης, ου, ὁ *prosaitēs* beggar*

Mark 10:46, of Bartimaeus, who sat by the road leading out of Jericho as a τυφλὸς προσαίτης; John 9:8, of a man blind from birth; → προσαιτέω. Jesus did not give alms to these blind beggars, but rather healed them and thus enabled them to lead new and independent lives (cf. also Matt 9:27ff.; 20:29ff.; Luke 16:3; 18:35; Acts 3:2ff.). Προσαίτης does not occur in the LXX (the vbs. do: προσαιτέω in Job 27:14 and ἐπαιτέω in Ps 108:10 LXX; Sir 40:28; cf. also 40:30; 37:11). *BL* 208; H. Peucker, *BHH* 236.

προσαναβαίνω *prosanabainō* climb/move up farther*

Luke 14:10: The host in the parable of the feast speaks to one who has seated himself at the lowest place: φίλε, προσανάβηθι ἀνώτερον, ". . . *go up higher* [to a place of honor at the table]."

προσαναλόω *prosanaloō* spend in addition to, expend*

Luke 8:43: ἰατροῖς προσαναλώσασα ὅλον τὸν βίον, "who had *spent* all her living upon physicians" (cf. Mark 5:26). It is probable that this phrase, omitted in p⁷⁵ B (D) and others, does belong to the original Lukan text; cf. *TCGNT* ad loc.

προσαναπληρόω *prosanaplēroō* fill up by adding to, supply what is lacking*

Occurs only in 2 Cor 9:12; 11:9 in the phrase προσαναπληρόω τὰ ὑστερήματα (9:12)/τὸ ὑστέρημα (11:9), *supply/fill out* the shortage *by adding what is missing/eliminate* the shortage (cf. also Aristotle *Pol.* 1256.b.3; Wis 19:4).

προσανατίθεμαι *prosanatithemai* impose/submit in addition (for oneself); confide/trust (in someone), take counsel with*

Only mid. in the NT: Gal 1:16: οὐ προσανεθέμην σαρκὶ καὶ αἵματι, "I *did* not *confer with* flesh and blood/*did* not *turn to* . . ." (J. Behm, *TDNT* I, 353f.: "did not expound it to men"); trans. in 2:6: ἐμοὶ γὰρ οἱ δοκοῦντες οὐδὲν προσανέθεντο, "those of repute *imposed* nothing *additional* on me [of themselves]" (cf. ἀναθέμην, "lay before," v. 2; also Acts 25:14; "lay/impose on [oneself]" in Xenophon *An.* ii.2.4; Lysias vii.19) as opposed to the παρείσακτοι ψευδάδελφοι (v. 4), who probably demanded "additional requirements" (see also Paul's separate report before the δοκοῦντες, v. 2), and with an eye toward the only "additional requirement," namely, support of the poor (v. 10; see esp. H. Schlier, *Gal* [KEK] ad loc. [bib-

liography]; cf. also Xenophon *Mem.* ii.1.8). Behm's suggested interpretation (353f.), "import, expound," appears too weak for the context, since it is a matter either of disputing additional requirements (as would be the case, e.g., in Acts 15:28f.) or at least of disputing additional theological aspects amplifying the Pauline mission to the Gentiles from the side of the Jerusalem representatives.

προσανέχω *prosanechō* proceed toward, approach

Acts 27:27 B²: προσανέχω . . . αὐτοῖς χώραν, "that land *was nearing* them" (in place of → προσάγω).

προσαπειλέομαι *prosapeileomai* threaten further, utter yet further threats*

Mid. and absolute in Acts 4:21: προσαπειλησάμενοι ἀπέλυσαν, "when they *had further threatened* them [Peter and John], they let them go."

προσαχέω *prosacheō* resound

Acts 27:17 B* gig s, of the rumble of the surf announcing the proximity of land (in place of → προσάγω).

προσδαπανάω *prosdapanaō* expend additionally, have additional costs*

Luke 10:35: ὅ τι ἂν προσδαπανήσῃς, "whatever *more* you *spend*."

προσδέομαι *prosdeomai* require (something) → δέομαι 3.

προσδέχομαι *prosdechomai* receive, accept; look for, expect*

1. Occurrences in the NT — 2. "Receive" — 3. "Accept" — 4. "Look/wait for"

Lit.: W. GRUNDMANN, *TDNT* II, 50-59. — E. HOFFMANN, *DNTT* II, 244ff. — H.-G. LINK, *DNTT* III, 744ff. — For further bibliography → δέχομαι.

1. The vb. προσδέχομαι occurs 14 times in the NT: 5 times in Luke, twice in Acts, twice in the genuine Pauline Epistles (Rom 16:2; Phil 2:29), twice in Hebrews, and in Mark 15:43; Titus 2:13; Jude 21.

2. Προσδέχομαι in the sense of *receive* (somebody) means "offer hospitality" to that person. The Pharisees and scribes criticize Jesus' keeping company with tax collectors and sinners and accuse him of *receiving* sinners and eating with them (Luke 15:2). Paul asks that the Romans *receive* Phoebe (Rom 16:2) and the Philippians to *receive* Epaphroditus (Phil 2:29) "in the Lord."

3. The meaning *accept* occurs twice, once in the sense

of passive acceptance and once in the sense of active concurrence. The addressees of Hebrews are exhorted to persevere and reminded that some of them suffered with those who were imprisoned and joyfully *accepted* the plundering of their property (Heb 10:34). Among the models of faith, some let themselves be tortured instead of *accepting* release, so that they might attain a better resurrection (11:35).

4. The meaning *expect* (or *wait/look for*) dominates in the NT. Three times this expectation is messianic: Simeon *waits for* Israel's consolation (Luke 2:25); Anna speaks of Jesus to all who *are looking for* Jerusalem's redemption (2:38). Joseph of Arimathea, a respected member of the Council, *is looking for* the kingdom of God (Mark 15:43 par. Luke 23:51). Jesus exhorts his disciples to be attentive and ready; they should be "like servants *waiting for* their master (Luke 12:36). More than forty men who have conspired against Paul keep ready and *await* word from the tribune to kill Paul (Acts 23:21). Paul confesses before the Roman governor that he *expects* the resurrection of both the just and the unjust (24:15). Titus 2:13 speaks of *awaiting* the blessed hope, the epiphany of the great God and Savior Jesus Christ. Jude 21 exhorts the readers to persevere in the love of God and *wait for* the mercy of Jesus Christ unto eternal life.

A. Palzkill

προσδίδωμι *prosdidōmi* give over, give (in addition to)
Luke 24:30 D in place of → ἐπιδίδωμι.

προσδοκάω *prosdokaō* expect, hope for, wait/look for*

There are 16 occurrences in the NT: 2 in Matthew, 6 in Luke, 5 in Acts, and 3 in 2 Peter. Expectation can be in the sense of (patient, long-enduring) hope or of fear. In an apocalyptic-eschatological sense of hopeful expectation of "he who is to come" in Matt 11:3 par. Luke 7:19, 20 (Q): σὺ εἶ ὁ ἐρχόμενος, ἢ ἕτερον προσδοκῶμεν; absolute in Luke 3:15: προσδοκῶντος τοῦ λαοῦ; of Christian hope in 2 Pet 3:12: προσδοκῶντες καὶ σπεύδοντες τὴν παρουσίαν, "*waiting for* and earnestly desiring the coming" (→ σπεύδω); 3:13: καινοὺς οὐρανοὺς καὶ γῆν καινὴν . . . προσδοκῶμεν; 3:14: ταῦτα προσδοκῶντες (cf. LXX Pss 103:27; 118:166; 2 Macc 7:14; 12:44; 15:8; *1 Clem.* 23:5; Ign. *Pol.* 3:2). Οὐ προσδοκάω emphasizes the moment of surprise in Matt 24:50 par. Luke 12:46. Of *waiting* a long time for someone who is late: Luke 1:21, for Zechariah; 8:40, for Jesus; cf. further Acts 10:24 (for Peter). Of a beggar in 3:5: προσδοκῶν . . . λαβεῖν, "*expecting* to receive something from them"; 27:33: προσδοκῶντες ἄσιτοι, "*wait in suspense* without eating*" (cf. v. 21), i.e., for fourteen days in an

apparently hopeless situation of distress at sea. With an element of fear or tension in Acts 28:6a, b: πολὺ προσδοκάω, "*wait* for a long time." C. Maurer, *TDNT* VI, 725ff.; E. Hoffmann, *DNTT* II, 244ff.

προσδοκία, ας ἡ *prosdokia* expectation*

Luke 21:26: φόβος καὶ προσδοκία τῶν ἐπερχομένων, "fear and *foreboding* of what is coming" (cf. Plutarch *Ant.* 75.4; Aristotle *EN* 1115a.9); Acts 12:11: πάσῃ ἡ προσδοκία τοῦ λαοῦ τῶν Ἰουδαίων, "all that the Jewish people were expecting" (of hostile expectations directed toward Peter). C. Maurer, *TDNT* VI, 725ff.

προσεάω *proseaō* permit to go farther*

Acts 27:7, of a difficult wind that did not *allow* the ship *to go on* (μὴ προσεῶντος). On the ship's route see E. Haenchen, *Acts* (Eng. tr., 1971) ad loc.

προσεγγίζω *prosengizō* approach, come near
Mark 2:4 v.l. in place of → προσφέρω; Acts 27:27 v.l in place of → προσάγω; 10:25 D.

προσεδρεύω *prosedreuō* sit upon, be upon
1 Cor 9:13 v.l. in place of → παρεδρεύω (obj.: τῷ θυσιαστηρίῳ).

προσεργάζομαι *prosergazomai* earn/make in addition*

Luke 19:16: "your pound *has made* ten pounds *more*" (προσηργάσατο), i.e., ten have been made from it (Matt 25:20: five).

προσέρχομαι *proserchomai* come to, approach, come near to*

1. Occurrences in the NT and basic meaning — 2. Approaching Jesus — 3. Jesus' approach — 4. Other usage in the Synoptic Gospels and Acts — 5. Cultic usage (esp. in Hebrews)

Lit.: J. R. EDWARDS, "The Use of Προσέρχομαι in the Gospel of Matthew," *JBL* 106 (1987) 65-74. — H. J. HELD, "Matthew as Interpreter of the Miracle Stories," G. Bornkamm, G. Barth, and H. J. Held, *Tradition and Interpretation in Matthew* (NTL, 1963) 165-299, esp. 226-28. — W. MUNDLE, *DNTT* II, 320-24. — J. SCHNEIDER, *TDNT* II, 683f.

1. Προσέρχομαι occurs 86 times in the NT, most frequently in Matthew (51 occurrences). The other occurrences are in Mark (5), Luke (10), Acts (10), Hebrews (7), and John 12:21; 1 Tim 6:3; 1 Pet 2:4. In most cases this vb. refers to approaching in a spatial sense. In Hebrews and 1 Pet 2:4 προσέρχομαι in the cultic sense means to "approach" or "come before" God.

2.a) People *approach* or *come to* Jesus for various

reasons (the disciples in Matt 5:1; 8:25 par. Luke 8:24; Matt 13:10, 36; Mark 6:35 par. Matt 14:15/Luke 9:12; Matt 15:12, 23; 17:19; 18:1, 21; 24:1, 3; 26:17; John's disciples in 9:14; 14:12; the rich young man in 19:16; the mother of Zebedee's sons in 20:20; the woman who wants to anoint Jesus in 26:7; the women after Jesus' resurrection in 28:9). People who seek healing for themselves or others *come to* Jesus (cf. Held 214-17: Matt 8:2: lepers; 8:5: the centurion's servant; 9:20 par. Luke 8:44: a sick woman; Matt 9:28: two blind men; 15:30: the lame, crippled, and dumb during the feeding; 17:14 par. Luke 9:42: the "somnambulistic" or possessed boy; Matt 21:14: the blind and lame during the temple scene). Cf. also Acts 28:9 (on Malta sick people come to Paul).

b) In other cases adversaries *come to* Jesus: Matt 8:19; Mark 12:28 (scribes); Mark 10:2 par. Matt 19:3; Luke 13:31 (Pharisees); Matt 22:23 par. Luke 20:27 (Sadducees); Matt 15:1 (Pharisees and scribes); 16:1 (Pharisees and Sadducees); 21:23 (high priests and elders).

c) Otherworldly powers also *come to* Jesus: during the temptation the devil (Matt 4:3) and angels (4:11). After the resurrection of Jesus an angel *came up* and rolled back the stone from the sepulcher (28:2).

3. Jesus himself *comes to* the disciples twice: after the transfiguration (17:7) and at his last commissioning (28:18). In like manner he *comes to* the sick (Mark 1:31) and the dead (Luke 7:14).

4.a) Προσέρχομαι is used 7 times in parables (Matt 13:27; 21:28, 30; 25:20, 22, 24; Luke 10:34). The collectors of the half-shekel tax *went up to* Peter to ask him a question (Matt 17:24).

b) In the Passion story the vb. occurs in Mark 14:45 par. Matt 26:49 (Judas *went up to* Jesus); Matt 26:50 (emissaries from the Council); 26:60a, b (false witnesses); 26:69, 73 (a maid and bystanders *came up to* Peter); 27:58 par. Luke 23:52 (Joseph of Arimathea *went to* Pilate); Luke 23:36 (soldiers *came up to* Jesus).

c) Προσέρχομαι occurs with κολλάομαι in Acts 8:29; 10:28. Besides 7:31 (Moses before the burning bush) and 12:13 (the maid came to the door) the vb. also occurs in 9:1; 18:2; 22:26, 27; 23:14 in reports about Paul. John 12:21 tells that some "Greeks" *came to* Philip and asked him, "Sir, we wish to see Jesus."

5. Προσέρχομαι is used cultically in 1 Pet 2:4 (*come to* Jesus, the "living stone") and in Heb 4:16 (*draw near to* the throne of grace); 7:25; 11:6 (*draw near to* God); 10:1, 22 (*draw near to* the sanctuary); 12:18, 22 (*come to* Mount Zion). 1 Tim 6:3 speaks of *turning to* the "sound words of our Lord Jesus Christ."   E. Palzkill

προσευχή, ῆς, ἡ *proseuchē* prayer; place of prayer
→ προσεύχομαι.

προσεύχομαι *proseuchomai* pray, request*
προσευχή, ῆς, ἡ *proseuchē* prayer; place of prayer (house of prayer, synagogue)*

1. NT occurrences and meanings — 2. NT usage — a) General usage and constructions — b) Intercessory prayer; the content of prayers — c) Synonyms and related terms — d) The Gospel of John and the Johannine Epistles — 3. Prayer in the Bible — a) Fundamental considerations — b) Faith and true prayer — 4.a) Paul — b) The post-Pauline Epistles — 5.a) Mark and Matthew — b) Luke-Acts — 6. Προσευχή = "place of prayer"

Lit.: J. B. BAUER and H. ZIMMERMANN, *SacVb* 679-86 . — BAGD s.v. — O. BAUERNFEIND, *RGG* II, 1218-21. — K. BERGER, *TRE* XII, 47-60. — W. BIEDER, "Gebetswirklichkeit und Gebetsmöglichkeit bei Paulus," *TZ* 4 (1948) 22-40. — S. H. BLANK, "Some Observations Concerning Biblical Prayer," *HUCA* 32 (1961) 75-90. — H. VON CAMPENHAUSEN, "Gebetserhörung in den überlieferten Jesusworten und in der Reflexion des Johannes," *idem, Urchristliches und Altkirchliches. Vorträge und Aufsätze* (1979) 162-81 (= *KD* 23 [1977] 157-71]). — D. COGGAN, *The Prayers of the NT* (1975). — G. DELLING, *Worship in the NT* (1962) 104-27. — A. DIETZEL, "Beten im Geist," *TZ* 13 (1957) 12-32. — idem, *Die Gründe der Erhörungsgewißheit nach dem NT* (Diss. Mainz, 1955). — F. V. FILSON, "Petition and Intercession," *Int* 8 (1954) 21-34. — E. FUCHS, "Gebet und Gebetssituation," *EvT* 29 (1969) 133-44. — R. GEBAUER, *Das Gebet bei Paulus. Forschungsgeschichtliche und exegetische Studien* (1989). — G. DE GENNARO, ed., *La preghiera nella Bibbia* (1983). — A. GONZALEZ, *DBSup* VII, 555-606. — H. GREEVEN, *Gebet und Eschatologie im NT* (NTF III/2, 1931). — A. HAMMAN, "La prière I," *Le NT* (1959). — idem, "La prière chrétienne et la prière païenne, formes et différences," *ANRW* XXIII/2 (1980) 1190-1247. — G. HARDER, *Paulus und das Gebet* (NTF I/10, 1936). — O. G. HARRIS, *Prayer in Luke-Acts* (Diss. Vanderbilt University, 1966). — idem, "Prayer in the Gospel of Luke," *SWJT* 10 (1967) 59-69. — J. HEINEMANN, *Prayer in the Talmud. Forms and Patterns* (1964; SJ 9, 1977). — M. HENGEL, "Proseuche und Synagoge. Jüdische Gemeinde, Gotteshaus und Gottesdienst in der Diaspora und in Palästina," FS Kuhn 157-84 (= *The Synagogue* [ed. J. Gutmann; 1975] 27-54). — J. HERRMANN and H. GREEVEN, *TDNT* II, 775-808, esp. 803-8. — J. JEREMIAS, "Daily Prayer in the Life of Jesus and the Primitive Church," *idem, The Prayers of Jesus* (1967) 66-81. — N. B. JOHNSON, *Prayer in the Apocrypha and Pseudepigrapha. A Study of the Jewish Concept of God* (JBL Monograph Series 2, 1948). — R. KERKHOFF, *Das unablässige Gebet* (1954). — L. KRINETZKI, *Israels Gebet im AT* (CiW VI/5a, 1965). — G. LATHROP, "The Prayers of Jesus and the Great Prayer of Church," *LQ* 26 (1974) 158-73. — F. LENTZEN-DEIS, "Beten kraft des Gebetes Jesu," *GuL* 48 (1975) 164-78. — J. MARTY, "Étude des textes cultuels de prière contenus dans le NT," *RHPR* 9 (1929) 234-68, 366-76. — J. J. MICHALCZYK, "The Experience of Prayer in Luke-Acts," *Review for Religious* 34 (1975) 789-801. — O. MICHEL and T. KLAUSER, *RAC* IX, 1-36. — J. M. NIELEN, *Gebet und Gottesdienst im NT* (²1963). — W. OTT, *Gebet und Heil. Die Bedeutung der Gebetsparänese in der lukanischen Theologie* (SANT 12, 1965). — O. H. PESCH, *Sprechender*

Glaube. Entwurf einer Theologie des Gebetes (1970). — *idem,*
Das Gebet (1972). — J. D. QUINN, "Apostolic Ministry and
Apostolic Prayer," *CBQ* 33 (1971) 479-91. — J. M. ROBINSON,
"Die Hodajot-Formel in Gebet und Hymnus des Frühchristen-
tums," FS Haenchen 194-235. — J. M. ROSS, *Terms for Prayer*
in the NT (Diss. Southern Baptist Theological Seminary, 1951).
— C. SCHNEIDER, "Paulus und das Gebet," *Angelos* IV (1932)
11-28. — H. SCHÖNWEISS, *DNTT* II, 861-64. — SCHÜRER, *His-*
tory II, 439-41. — H. SCHULTZE, "Gebet zwischen Zweifel und
Vertrauen," *EvT* 30 (1970) 133-48. — E. VON SEVERUS, *RAC*
VIII, 1134-1258. — R. L. SIMPSON, *The Interpretation of Prayer*
in the Early Church (1965). — T. C. G. THORNTON, " 'Continuing Steadfast in Prayer.' New Light on a NT Phrase," *ExpTim*
83 (1971/72) 23f. — L. VISCHER, "Das Gebet in der alten
Kirche," *EvT* 17 (1957) 531-46. — O. WEINREICH, "Gebet und
Wunder, I: Primitiver Gebetsegoismus," *Genethliakon* (FS
W. Schmid, 1929) 169-99. — G. WENZ, "Andacht und Zuver-
sicht. Dogmatische Überlegungen zum Gebet," *ZTK* 78 (1981)
465-90. — C. WESTERMANN, *RGG* II, 1213-17. — G. P. WILES,
Paul's Intercessory Prayers (SNTSMS, 1974). — R. ZORN, *Die*
Fürbitte im Spätjudentum und im NT (Diss. Göttingen, 1957).
— For further bibliography → εὔχομαι; see *TWNT* X, 1091-93;
BAGD s.v.

1. Προσεύχομαι occurs 85 times in the NT, with particular frequency in the Synoptic Gospels and Acts (60
occurrences total: 15 in Matthew, 10 in Mark, 19 in Luke,
and 16 in Acts), 12 occurrences in Paul (8 in 1 Cor 11:4f.,
13; 14:13-15), 7 in the deutero-Pauline Epistles, and 6 in
the Catholic Epistles (4 in Jas 5:13-18); it also occurs in
Matt 23:14 v.l. In 23 of the occurrences in the Gospels
it refers to prayer by the disciples or the Church, 22 times
to prayer by Jesus (10 of those occurrences in Luke, 6 in
Matthew, 5 in Mark).

The noun προσευχή is distributed differently; of its
36 occurrences (+ Matt 17:21 v.l.), 7 are in the Synoptic Gospels (2 are Lukan references to prayer by Jesus),
9 in Acts (2 as a designation for a *place of prayer:*
16:13, 16), 8 in Paul, 6 in the deutero-Pauline Epistles,
3 in the Catholic Epistles, and 3 in Revelation. Neither
the vb. nor the noun occurs in John or 1–3 John (→
2.d).

Προσεύχομαι occurs more frequently in the NT than
other terms for praying, requesting, etc. (εὔχομαι occurs
7 times, εὐχή 3 times, αἰτέω 70 times, ἐρωτάω 63 times,
προσκυνέω 60 times, εὐλογέω 42 times, εὐχαριστέω 38
times, and δέομαι 22 times). The simple vb. εὔχομαι is
quite common in classical Greek and occurs only slightly
less frequently in the LXX than the compound (as is the
case with εὐχή over against προσευχή); in the NT, however, it is to a large extent overshadowed by the compound. In extrabiblical Greek προσεύχομαι (like the
simple vb.) can mean "pray" and "vow/pledge" (e.g.,
Preisigke, *Sammelbuch* III 6713.10f.). In the LXX it is
usually the equivalent of the hithpael of *pll.* Προσευχή is
rare in extrabiblical Greek and usually stands for *t^epillāh*
in the LXX. Both words are used in the LXX only of

prayer directed to God (as opposed to → εὔχομαι [1],
which renders eleven Hebrew terms).

Similarly, in the NT προσεύχομαι exclusively means
pray, utter prayers, petition for someone or something;
προσευχή means *prayer, intercession,* and finally, as a
designation for the place where communal prayer takes
place, *place of prayer* (outside the NT also "house of
prayer, synagogue": → 6).

2.a) Προσεύχομαι is used in various constructions.
Usually (almost 50 times) it is used absolutely to mean
pray, utter prayers, worship (Matt 6:5 bis, 6 bis, 7, 9;
14:23; 19:13; 26:36, 39; Mark 1:35; 6:46; 11:25; 14:32;
Luke 1:10; 3:21; 5:16; 6:12; 9:28, 29; 11:1 bis, 2; 18:1,
10; 22:41; Acts 1:24; 6:6; 9:11, 40; 10:9, 30; 11:5; 12:12;
13:3; 14:23; 16:25; 20:36; 21:5; 22:17; 28:8; 1 Cor 11:4,
5; 14:14b; 1 Thess 5:17; 1 Tim 2:8; Jas 5:13, 18; Jude
20). The use of προσευχή also consistently presupposes
that the *prayer* is directed to God; only in Luke 6:12
(προσευχὴ τοῦ θεοῦ); Acts 12:5; Rom 15:30 (πρὸς τὸν
θεόν) is God specifically named as the one prayed to (cf.
also Acts 10:4, 31). Dat. θεῷ (θεοῖς, etc.)—frequently
seen in extrabiblical language—also recedes significantly, occurring only in 1 Cor 11:13 (τῷ θεῷ contextually
determined; cf. v. 12) and Matt 6:6b (τῷ πατρί σου; cf.
vv. 6c, 9). The LXX formulation προσεύχομαι πρὸς (τὸν)
θεόν/κύριον (Gen 20:17; 1 Kgdms 1:10 and *passim*) is
completely absent (its first occurrence in Christian literature is in *Herm. Vis.* i.1.9).

Occasionally the manner of praying is specified more
closely: by dat. γλώσσῃ, τῷ πνεύματι, τῷ νοΐ (1 Cor 14:14a,
15 bis); cf. ἐν πνεύματι ἁγίῳ (Jude 20), ἐν παντὶ καιρῷ ἐν
πνεύματι (Eph 6:18), προσευχῇ προσεύχομαι, *pray fervently*
(Jas 5:17; cf. also 1 Cor 11:5); by adverbs: ἐκτενέστερον
προσεύχομαι (Luke 22:44), ἀδιαλείπτως προσεύχομαι
(1 Thess 5:17), προσεύχομαι πάντοτε (2 Thess 1:11; cf.
Acts 12:5); by acc. neut. προφάσει μακρὰ προσεύχομαι, "for
a pretense *make long prayers*" (Mark 12:40 par. Luke
20:47/Matt 23:14 v.l.).

Circumstances are specified more closely: "stand and
pray" (Mark 11:25), "kneel down and *pray*" (Luke 22:41;
Acts 9:40; 20:36; 21:5; cf. Matt 26:39; Luke 22:46),
"*prayer* and fasting" (Matt 17:21 v.l.; Acts 13:3; 14:23;
cf. 1 Pet 4:7; 1 Cor 7:5).

The wording of prayers is introduced by (καὶ) λέγων
(Matt 26:39, 42 [44: εἴπων]; Luke 22:41f.; cf. further
Mark 14:35, 39; Luke 18:11; Acts 1:24 and esp. the
introduction to the Lord's Prayer, Matt 6:9ff.; Luke
11:2ff.). Named as the one prayed to are πάτερ (Matt 6:9;
26:39, 42; Luke 22:41f.), ὁ θεός (18:11), and σὺ κύριε
(Acts 1:24).

The time of prayer is specified in Acts 3:1; 10:9, 30
(see further → 3.b), as is the place of prayer in Matt 6:5f.
(synagogues, street corners, rooms); Luke 18:10; Acts 3:1

(temples); 10:9 (the housetop); 16:13 (at the riverside); this esp. includes the combination οἶκος προσευχῆς for the temple (Matt 21:13; Mark 11:17; Luke 19:46; cf. Isa 56:7; 60:7; 1 Macc 7:37).

Jesus usually prays alone: κατ' ἰδίαν (Matt 14:23 [in the hills]; cf. 26:36 [ἀπελθών], 39 [προελθὼν μικρόν], 42 [ἀπελθών], 44 [ἀφεὶς αὐτοὺς πάλιν ἀπελθών]; Mark 1:35 [ἀπῆλθεν εἰς ἔρημον τόπον]; 6:46 [ἀπῆλθεν εἰς τὸ ὄρος]; 14:32, 39; Luke 5:16 [ὑποχωρῶν ἐν ταῖς ἐρήμοις]; 6:12 [ὄρος]; 9:18 [κατὰ μόνας]; 9:28 [ὄρος]; 22:41 [ἀπεσπάσθη . . . ὡσεὶ λίθου βολήν]).

b) That prayer to God is *intercession* for certain people can be specified in prep. phrases: προσεύχεσθε περὶ τῶν ἐπηρεαζόντων ὑμᾶς (Luke 6:28, with εὐλογέω), προσεύχεσθε ὑπὲρ τῶν διωκόντων ὑμᾶς (Matt 5:44), other constructions with περί (Acts 8:15 [περὶ αὐτῶν]; 2 Thess 1:11; Col 1:3 [περὶ ὑμῶν]; 4:3; 1 Thess 5:25; 2 Thess 3:1; Heb 13:18 [περὶ ἡμῶν]) and with ὑπέρ (Col 1:9 [ὑπὲρ ὑμῶν]; Rom 15:30 [προσευχαὶ ὑπὲρ ἐμοῦ]), of intercessory prayer "over" a sick person (προσευξάσθωσαν ἐπ' αὐτόν) in Jas 5:14; cf. further Col 4:12; 1 Tim 2:1; Phlm 4:22; of intercessory prayer with laying on of hands in Matt 19:13; Acts 13:3; 14:23.

The content of a prayer can stand in the acc.: πάντα ὅσα προσεύχεσθε (Mark 11:24), τὸ γὰρ τί προσευξώμεθα (Rom 8:26), τοῦτο προσεύχομαι (Phil 1:9). It can also be expressed by an inf. (Luke 22:40; Jas 5:17 [τοῦ μὴ βρέξαι, with pleonastic τοῦ; see BDF §400.7), with ἵνα (Matt 24:20; 26:41; Mark 13:18; 14:38; Phil 1:9; Col 4:3; 2 Thess 1:11; 3:1), or with ὅπως (Acts 8:15; Jas 5:16 v.l.; see BDF §392.1.c).

c) Προσεύχομαι and προσευχή refer in a comprehensive fashion to the prayers of Jesus and to those of believers and the Church; in so doing they touch on various forms and aspects of prayer (worship, supplication, intercession, specific individual prayers, steadfast prayer, and liturgical prayer), with the specific sense disclosed from each context.

Προσεύχομαι is found with the vbs. ὑμνέω (Acts 16:25: προσευχόμενοι ὕμνουν τὸν θεόν), προφητεύω (1 Cor 11:4f.: προσευχόμενος [-ομένη] ἢ προφητεύων [-ουσα]), εὐχαριστέω (Col 1:3: εὐχαριστοῦμεν . . . προσευχόμενοι; cf. further Eph 1:16; Phlm 4), αἰτέω (Mark 11:24: προσεύχεσθε καὶ αἰτεῖσθε; par. Matt 21:22: αἰτήσητε ἐν τῇ προσευχῇ; cf. Col 1:9; see also → αἰτέω 3, 4).

Προσευχή occurs esp. with the nouns νηστεία (Matt 17:21 v.l. par. Mark 9:29 v.l.; cf. Acts 13:3; 14:23; 1 Pet 4:7), διδαχὴ τῶν ἀποστόλων, κοινωνία, κλάσις τοῦ ἄρτου (Acts 2:42), διακονία τοῦ λόγου (6:4), ἐλεημοσύναι (10:4, 31), δέησις (Eph 6:18; 1 Tim 5:5; Jas 5:16f.), δέησις μετὰ εὐχαριστίας (Phil 4:6; cf. Col 4:2; Eph 1:16), δεήσεις, ἐντεύξεις, εὐχαριστίαι (1 Tim 2:1). Other constructions are "be steadfast (προσκαρτερέω) in *prayer*" (Acts 1:14; 2:42; 6:4; Rom 12:12; Col 4:2 [with γρηγορέω]), "that your *prayers* may not be hindered (μὴ ἐγκόπτεσθαι)"

(1 Pet 3:7), "remember (someone) in (one's) *prayers* (μνείαν ποιέομαι)," sometimes after εὐχαριστέω (Rom 1:10; Eph 1:16; 1 Thess 1:2; Phlm 4), and προσευχαὶ τῶν ἁγίων (Rev 5:8; 8:3, 4).

Compared to the synonyms (→ 1), προσεύχομαι and προσευχή are characterized above all by referring to prayer to God in the comprehensive sense, and never to requests of daily life. Since the elements of praise (Acts 16:25), request (Mark 11:24 par.; Eph 6:18; Col 1:9; 1 Tim 2:1; 5:5), and esp. of thanksgiving (Eph 1:16; Phil 4:6; Col 1:3; 4:2; 1 Thess 1:2; 1 Tim 2:1; Phlm 4) can be underscored by means of additional terms (see above), προσεύχομαι and προσευχή emerge as the fundamental NT terms for prayer (on John → d); they express the encounter between the believer and God, an encounter that manifests itself in individual acts of prayer and supplication (in Jas 5:16f. δέησις is used with προσευχῇ προσεύχομαι; cf. also Mark 13:18; Phlm 22) and in an ongoing, communal attitude and behavior influenced by prayer.

On the other hand, e.g., → αἰτέω (4) occurs with the meaning "(immodest) demand" in both a secular and religious sense (though never of prayers by Jesus, and never in Paul as a term for prayer); → ἐρωτάω (3), in addition to the common general use, is used in John for Jesus' prayers (in 1 John 5:16 also for the Church's intercessory prayer); → εὐλογέω (3) and → εὐχαριστέω (2, 3) refer with few exceptions (→ εὐχαριστέω 1) to prayer of praise and thanksgiving; → κράζω (3) is used of loud calling and (in Paul) the cry of the Church inspired by the Spirit; → δέομαι (2) can mean "request" as well as "pray, intercede" in a general sense, while δέησις can refer to regular prayer and specific individual requests (cf. also Herrmann and Greeven 806-8).

d. In John and 1–3 John προσεύχομαι, εὔχομαι, and προσευχή are missing for understandable theological reasons. The terms for prayer in John are above all προσκυνέω (11 occurrences, referring to the prayer of believers in 4:22, 23, 24; 9:38, elsewhere to the cultic prayer of Jews and Samaritans), αἰτέω (9 occurrences in the mouths of believers, 6 times in reference to intercessory prayer "in the name [ἐν τῷ ὀνόματι] of Jesus"), εὐχαριστέω (3 times of Jesus' prayer of thanksgiving, 2 of those referring to thanksgiving over bread), and finally ἐρωτάω, which is reserved for Jesus' requests on behalf of his followers (6 occurrences; cf. esp. αἰτέομαι [referring to the request of the disciples] with ἐρωτάω [for the request of Jesus] in 16:26). Furthermore, Jesus "speaks" (λέγω) to his Father in heaven (11:41f.; 12:27; 17:1). He stands in an enduring and intimate relationship to the "Father" (10:30; 14:9) and does not need—in contrast to the Synoptic Gospels (→2.a, 5)—any regular or pious pattern of prayer as would be expressed by προσεύχομαι and προσευχή. His prayers to the Father mediate rather this oneness with God also to his disciples (14:16; 17:9, 15, 20), who, far from traditional cultic prayer, "worship what they know," namely, "the Father in spirit and truth" (4:22-24; see von Campenhausen 170-77).

3.a) Prayer in the Bible is the expression of the believer's experience of proximity to God and dependence on God; thus it also constitutes worship in the real sense. Through praise, thanksgiving, lament, and request believers witness that they live from the goodness of God the Creator and Savior. Their call to God responds to their experience of God's words and actions (see Lentzen-Deis 165-68). Prayer is thus more than an inward, meditative process. It flows from the human "heart" (cf. Pss 13:6; 19:15; 33:21; 57:8; Rom 8:27; Gal 4:6; 2 Tim 2:22), expresses itself in speaking, calling, crying, rejoicing, lamenting, and pleading, and encompasses—esp. in the activity of prostration and proskynesis (→ προσκυνέω 3) —the entire person (cf. Gen 24:26ff.; 34:8ff.; 1 Kgs 8:54; Ps 29:2; Isa 1:15-17; Matt 26:39; Eph 3:14; also 1 Tim 2:8). Prayers were spoken in situations of distress (1 Kgs 19:4; Pss 6:7ff.; 118:25; 142:2ff.) as well as of joy (Exod 15:1; 1 Sam 25:32ff.; Ps 22:23ff.), in daily life (Gen 24:12ff.; 2 Kgs 20:2f.; Ps 55:18) and in the cult or at holy places (Gen 12:8; 13:4; 1 Sam 1:3, 10ff.; Ps 134:2; Isa 56:7). Special forms of prayer are confession of sins (Josh 7:19; 2 Sam 24:10; Dan 9:3f.) and intercession (e.g., through prophets: Amos 7:2f., 5f.; Jer 37:3; prophetic intercession can be prohibited or rejected by God: Jer 7:16; 11:14; Ezek 9:8ff.; 11:13ff.; cf. further Gen 18:23ff.; 20:7; Jer 15:1; 29:7; Neh 1:4ff.). Prayers express trust in the God who answers prayers (Ps 65:3; cf. 3:5; 18:7; Jer 29:12-14) and can be reminders to God of his salvation deeds and promises (Exod 32:11ff.; Deut 9:26ff.; Ps 77:1ff.).

b. These concerns overshadow the usual widespread goals of prayer such as attempts to influence the deity or requests for well-being or prosperity (see Weinreich; von Severus 1134ff.), goals also criticized in Greek philosophy as inappropriate (Plato *Phdr.* 279b, c; *Euthphr.* 14b; see also Philo *Spec. Leg.* i.24).

In Greek tradition prayer as supplication to the gods predominates; nothing should be undertaken without invoking the gods with sacrifice and prayer (Homer *Il.* vi.308ff.; viii.236ff.; Plato *Ti.* 27c), and true prayer directs itself toward divine and spiritual things (Xenophon *Mem.* i.3.2; Diodorus Siculus x.9.7; cf. further Herrmann and Greeven 778-84; Delling 112-14). The prayer of the primitive Christian Church, however, lives by unqualified trust in the salvation given by God through Christ. This faith finds expression before God and in the community of believers in prayer, and at the same time prayer supports and strengthens that faith. Primitive Christian prayer owes its character to the prayer of Jesus and his salvation work. Just as believers picked up Jesus' cry "Abba" (ἀββά 3, 4), so also they learned to pray in the name of Jesus Christ and to address God with reference to him (John 14:13; 15:16; Rom 1:8; 7:25; 2 Cor 1:20; Eph 5:20; Col 3:17). In so doing they prayed not from their own power, but rather by the power of God's Spirit dwelling in them (Eph 3:20; cf. Bieder, Dietzel); the Spirit reassures them that they are God's children (Rom

8:15f.; Gal 4:6), answers their "groaning" for redemption (Rom 8:23), and with its own "sighs too deep for words" intercedes with God on their behalf (8:26f.; see H. Balz, *Heilsvertrauen und Welterfahrung* [1971] 72ff.).

According to earliest Christian tradition Jesus prayed (Mark 1:35; 14:32ff.; Matt 11:25-27 par.; 14:23; Luke 3:21; Heb 5:7; → 2.a) and taught his disciples how to pray (Mark 11:24f. par.; 14:38 par.; Matt 5:44 par.; 6:5ff.; 7:7ff.; Luke 11:1ff.; 18:1ff.; cf., however, Luke 5:33-35). He differentiated sharply between true prayer and external false prayer (Matt 6:5, 7; Mark 12:38-40 par.) and promised that the prayers of the faithful would be answered by God (Matt 6:8, 14; 7:7ff. par.; Mark 11:23ff. par.). The praise and requests of the Lord's Prayer constitute true prayer (Matt 6:9-13 par.), esp. the request for forgiveness (6:14f.), which corresponds to one's own readiness to forgive (cf. also Luke 18:13f.; Jas 4:2ff.), and the (Lukan) request for the Spirit of God (Luke 11:13). Prayer implies submission to God's will (Mark 14:35f. par.; Rom 1:10ff.; 2 Cor 12:8f.) and at the same time is the expression of trust in the help of God that extends even into daily life (Matt 6:32 par.; Mark 13:18 par.; Phil 4:6; thanksgiving at meals: Acts 27:35; Rom 14:7; 1 Cor 10:30; 1 Tim 4:3-5; see also Mark 5:41 par.; 14:22f. par.; Luke 24:30; mission and travel plans: Rom 1:10ff.; Col 4:3; suffering and disease: Jas 5:13ff.).

True prayer is heard above all in the congregational assembly (cf. 1 Cor 11:4ff.; 14:13ff.; Rom 15:6; Acts 1:14; 2:42, 46f.; 12:5, 12; see Nielen 145ff.) and characterizes the entire life of the faithful (Luke 18:1, 7; 1 Thess 5:17; Eph 6:18; Col 4:2; 1 Tim 2:8; 5:5) as well as that of the apostle (Rom 1:9f.; 1 Thess 1:2; 3:9; Phlm 4), and expresses itself esp. in thanksgiving (→ 2.c; Rom 1:8; 6:17; 7:25; 1 Cor 1:4f.; 14:16; 2 Cor 4:15; Phil 4:6; Col 1:3; 4:2; 1 Tim 2:1; Rev 11:17f.) and intercession (→ 2.b; for the individual church or congregation: Rom 1:10; Eph 1:16; Phil 1:9; Col 1:3, 9; 4:12; 1 Thess 1:2f.; 3:9ff.; for the apostle: Rom 15:30; Phil 1:19; Col 4:3f.; 1 Thess 5:25; 2 Thess 3:1; Phlm 22; also Heb 13:18; for an individual: Phlm 4; for all people and those in high positions: 1 Tim 2:1f.; for the ill: Jas 5:14ff.; for enemies: Matt 5:44 par.; for Israel: Rom 10:1; cf. 9:3f.). Yet even if prayer is possible for all believers in all places (cf. John 4:20ff.), certain prerequisites are nonetheless mentioned (faith: Mark 11:24f.; Jas 1:5-7; 5:15; willingness to forgive: Matt 5:23f.; 6:14f.; Mark 11:25; holiness and love: 1 Tim 2:8; 1 Pet 3:17; sobriety: 4:7; cf. also 1 Cor 14:15).

Like Jesus, believers pray to God; if, however, true prayer is made in the name of Jesus and for the sake of Christ (see above; cf. esp. 2 Cor 1:20), then prayers can also be made directly to the exalted one (John 14:14; 1 Cor 16:22; Rev 22:20; 2 Cor 12:8; Acts 7:59f.; cf. 1 Cor 1:2; Phil 2:10; Rev 5:8, 14; see also Nielen 163ff.; Delling 117ff.).

Times of prayer are mentioned in Acts 3:1; 10:9, 30 (the sixth and ninth hours); Mark 1:35; Luke 6:12 (night; cf. also 1 Cor 7:5; Eph 6:18; Col 4:2; 1 Tim 5:5). Actions of prayer are mentioned in Acts 7:60; 20:36; 21:5; Eph 3:14 (proskynesis; → 2.a; 3.a); 1 Tim 2:8 (uplifted hands); Mark 11:25 (standing); and John 11:41 (Jesus lifts up his eyes to heaven).

4.a) In Paul προσεύχομαι and προσευχή are used of the gift inspired by the Spirit within believers to call on God steadfastly (Rom 1:9f.; 12:12; 1 Thess 1:2; Phlm 4) and with joyous confidence in salvation (Phil 4:4-6; 1 Thess 5:17), with praise, thanksgiving, and in intercession. Prayer uttered in the congregation of believers is a particular expression of enrichment, not, as one might expect, of dependence on God; it releases believers from all anxiety concerning their own situation if they but let their requests be made known "in every respect" (ἐν παντί, Phil 4:6) before God in prayer (see Greeven 140ff.). The frequently occurring pl. προσευχαί (Rom 1:10; 15:30; 1 Thess 1:2; Phlm 4:22) refers to the natural, self-evident nature of prayer as pointedly as do parenetic exhortations to prayer (Rom 12:12; Phil 4:6; 1 Thess 5:17, 25).

Believers need not be anxious concerning the correct language in which to pray to God, since in their own groaning for redemption (Rom 8:23) they sense that the Spirit himself is at work and inspires within them true prayer (v. 26: καθὸ δεῖ refers not to occasional "weakness in prayer" or anything similar, but rather to the fundamental appropriateness of prayer that the believers can entrust to the work of the Spirit; → 3.b; see also Greeven 152ff., 167f.; Ott 140f.). Nonetheless, with respect to "the other person" (1 Cor 14:17) it is not enough simply to give oneself over to the ecstatic prayer of glossolalia, in which the νοῦς remains unfruitful (v. 14). Prayer attains its goal in the spiritually inspired person's attentiveness to God and to the congregation, not in the rapture of inspiration (v. 15). Hence Paul is concerned primarily with intercession, something he does for the churches (μνείαν ὑμῶν ποιοῦμαι ἐπὶ τῶν προσευχῶν μου, Rom 1:9f.; cf. 1 Thess 1:2; Phlm 4; Phil 1:9) and in like manner expects from them (Rom 15:30; 1 Thess 5:25; Phlm 22); intercessory prayer is, after all, nothing other than a sharing of the struggle the apostle has to wage (συναγωνίσασθαί μοι, Rom 15:30; cf. Ott 142).

Paul counters ascetic impulses among the Corinthians by asserting that prayer and marital status are not mutually exclusive; each should be accorded its own place and time (1 Cor 7:5). He does warn female ecstatics, however, in regard to prayer in the worship service not to put their own understanding of God's immediacy and their knowledge of the fundamental equality of all in the Church above the traditional (Jewish) custom of wearing a veil or other headcovering, since precisely this custom shows

that one recognizes and appreciates the differences between women and men set by God (11:4, 5, 13; see Nielen 287ff.; von Severus 1181f.; → ἐξουσία 4; κεφαλή 3.c).

b) The post-Pauline Epistles show that prayer increasingly becomes a comprehensive and determining (πᾶς etc.: Eph 6:18; Col 1:3; 4:12; 2 Thess 1:11; 1 Tim 2:1, 8) life expression of the early Christian Church, a sign of piety in a world hostile to those concerned with salvation (1 Tim 2:1ff.) and a sign of trust in the helping nearness of God (cf. Jas 5:13ff.; Jude 20). Prayer parenesis addresses above all the prerequisites for proper prayer: "being watchful" (Col 4:2) and recognition of (weaker) women by men (1 Pet 3:7: εἰς τὸ μὴ ἐγκόπτεσθαι τὰς προσευχὰς ὑμῶν). 1 Tim 2:8ff. warns both men and women that neither anger nor quarreling nor unseemly behavior is compatible with prayer in the congregation; rather, one owes God "in every place . . . holy hands" (v. 8; cf. also Jas 5:26: faith and forgiveness of sins), just as prayer in the larger sense presupposes lucidity and sobriety (1 Pet 4:7). Steadfast prayer is emphasized in Eph 6:18 (ἐν παντὶ καιρῷ); Col 4:2 (προσκαρτερεῖτε); 1 Tim 5:5 (referring to widows: νυκτὸς καὶ ἡμέρας).

Prayer is above all intercession "for all the saints and also for me" (Eph 6:18f.; cf. Col 4:3; 2 Thess 3:1; Heb 13:18: for the ill [and sinners]; Jas 5:14ff.; indeed, ὑπὲρ πάντων ἀνθρώπων, 1 Tim 2:1ff.: δεήσεις προσευχαὶ ἐντεύξεις εὐχαριστίαι [v. 1] emphasizes the disposition, common to all expressions of prayer, toward the salvation of all human beings; see von Severus 1183f.); similarly, the "apostle" prays for the Church (Eph 1:16: εὐχαριστῶν ὑπὲρ ὑμῶν . . . ἐπὶ τῶν προσευχῶν μου; cf. Col 1:3, 9; 2 Thess 1:11; and esp. the image of Paul as stuggling in prayer for the Church, Col 4:12: πάντοτε ἀγωνιζόμενος ὑπὲρ ὑμῶν ἐν ταῖς προσευχαῖς).

5.a) According to Mark Jesus prays in solitary settings (1:35; 6:46; 14:32ff. [on v. 38 cf. Col 4:2]); he teaches his disciples about the relationship between prayer, faith, confidence in being answered, and the willingness to forgive (11:24f.) and simultaneously sharply criticizes misuse of prayer as a public demonstration of piety (12:40). No particular theological agenda can be discerned; the Markan Jesus does, indeed, call for prayer (9:29; cf. also 11:17; 13:18; 14:38) and in his own hour of distress entrusts his fate to the Father (in three prayers: 14:35, 39, 41). But he is not a teacher of prayer in the real sense (the tradition of the Lord's Prayer is absent).

In the Markan passages that Matthew uses, he emphasizes the same fundamental elements: prayers of Jesus (14:23; 19:13 [without par.]; 26:36ff. [Mark 1:35 is missing]), answer to prayers (21:22; cf. 7:11; 18:19f.), the call to prayer (24:20; 26:41). Jesus' criticism of prayer is summarized in 6:5ff. (Mark 12:40 is missing) and combined with a didactic exposition of prayer that keeps Christian prayer far from any elements of "hypocrisy" (6:5f.) and of "Gentile" invocation of God (vv. 7f.); it is rather the call to the Father manifested in the Lord's Prayer, a Father who is loving (vv. 9-13) and who already knows the needs of his faithful (v. 8). Prayer for those who persecute the Church (5:44 [Q]: ὑπὲρ τῶν διωκόντων ὑμᾶς; cf. Rom 12:14) is, as the antithetical relationship between 5:43 and 44 shows, characterized by the commandment of love for one's enemy and is not developed into any real didactic exposition concerning true intercession.

b) Luke, on the other hand, uses προσεύχομαι and προσευχή with striking frequency of the prayers of Jesus (3:21; 5:16; 6:12; 9:18, 28f.; 11:1; 22:41ff.), even if he does omit or rearrange several Markan passages (Mark 1:35; 6:46; 14:32). Jesus prays at decisive junctures in the Gospel: after his baptism by John (Luke 3:21), before the calling of the Twelve (6:12), before Peter's confession (9:18), and before the Transfiguration (9:28f.). He demonstrates thereby in a special way his close relationship to the Father and thus becomes both a model and a teacher of prayer for the disciples, one who molds them into a praying community (over against the followers of the Baptist: 11:1; cf. 5:33-35). His prayer struggle on the Mount of Olives teaches the disciples by example about overcoming temptation in prayer (22:40ff.), just as on the cross he does not die the death of a forsaken person (Mark 15:34), but rather that of one submitting in prayer to God's will (23:46, citing Ps 30:6 LXX; cf. Acts 7:59f.; see Ott 97f.). Characteristic Lukan elements are the request for the Spirit (11:2 v.l. [see Greeven 73ff.]; 11:13 [differing from Matt 7:11]; cf. Acts 4:31; 8:15) and for deliverance from temptation (22:40) and Jesus' intercession for the disciples' faith (cf. 22:32: δέομαι). Accordingly, the Lukan Jesus teaches his disciples in parables (11:5ff.; 18:1ff.) and in a narrative example (18:9ff.) to pray with confidence (11:13), at all times and steadfastly (18:1; cf. 21:36; → 4.b), and as sinners dependent only on God's mercy (18:13f.). The Church will stand fast in constant prayer during the time between Jesus and the judgment of the Son of man (18:8; 21:36).

Acts develops further the ideas established in the Gospel of Luke. True to the commissioning of its Lord, the church in Jerusalem from the very beginning holds fast to prayer (ἦσαν προσκαρτεροῦντες ὁμοθυμαδὸν τῇ προσευχῇ, 1:14; 2:42 [pl. probably in reference to regular prayers]; cf. 2:46: καθ᾽ ἡμέραν τε προσκαρτεροῦντες ὁμοθυμαδὸν ἐν τῷ ἱερῷ; 6:4: προσευχή and διακονία τοῦ λόγου as tasks of the Twelve; see further 3:1; 12:5, 12; 20:36; 21:5). Prayer accompanies important decisions in the development of the Church's life, i.e., the choice of a twelfth apostle (1:24), the appointment of the Seven amid prayer and the laying on of hands (6:6), Peter and John's request for the Spirit for Samaria (8:15), Peter's vision (10:9), and the mission of

Paul and Barnabas to Antioch (13:3: νηστεύσαντες καὶ προσευξάμενοι καὶ ἐπιθέντες τὰς χεῖρας αὐτοῖς ἀπέλυσαν; cf. further 14:23; 20:36). Like Peter (3:1; 9:40; 10:9; 11:15), Paul esp. is portrayed as one who prays (9:11; 16:25; 20:36; 21:5; 22:17; 28:8). The God-fearing centurion Cornelius distinguishes himself by steadfast prayer (προσευχαὶ καὶ ἐλεημοσύναι, 10:4 [cf. Did. 15:4]; see further 10:2, 30), so that God answers him and finally leads him to faith (10:4, 31; cf. the similar situation of Paul in 9:11). Prayer is part of miraculous rescues (12:5, 12; 16:25) and leads to a healing (28:8; cf. Jas 5:14ff.) and the raising of a dead person (9:40). Hence in prayer the Church knows itself (in an exemplary fashion; see Greeven 117ff.) to be bound to God and subject to his guidance. Prayer is, to be sure, no longer primarily (as in Paul → 4.a) the expression of faith rendering thanks for Christ's salvation work, but is rather a manifestation of the *praxis pietatis,* the inheritance of Jewish piety, of a Church that knows itself to be both guided and encouraged by Jesus himself in prayer for salvation (see Ott 124ff., 137ff.).

6. In Acts 16:13, 16 προσευχή (only in biblical and early Christian usage [see, however, 3 Macc 7:20]) is to be understand locally as a reference to the *place of prayer* of the Jews in Philippi, which Paul and his followers anticipate finding and do, indeed, find outside the city at a river (the Gangites; perhaps for ritual washings; see K. H. Rengstorf, *TDNT* VI, 602f.; W. Schrage, *TDNT* VII, 814f.). Προσευχή was in common use in Diaspora Judaism from the 3rd cent. B.C., and esp. in the period of early Roman emperors, as a designation for synagogues, as shown by Philo's use (*Leg. Gai.* 20, 23, 43; *Flacc.* 41 and *passim*) and numerous inscriptions (see Hengel; BAGD s.v. 2). Since Luke elsewhere always uses the (Palestinian) term συναγωγή (19 times, 16 of those referring to a synagogue building), he might have taken προσευχή in 16:13, 16 from a source document; in any case he was doubtlessly thinking of a *place of prayer* in the open, possibly one frequented only by women.

H. Balz

προσέχω *prosechō* turn one's attention to; be concerned about; pay attention to, heed, be careful of; occupy oneself with*

This vb. occurs 24 times in the NT, 10 of those in the Gospels (6 in Matthew, 4 in Luke), 6 in Acts, and 4 in 1 Timothy; it does not occur in Paul, Mark, or John and is always act.

Frequently (always in the Gospels) προσέχω has the meaning *watch out/be on guard,* 7 times (all in the Gospels) with the prep. ἀπό (cf. BDF §149): Matt 7:15: ἀπὸ τῶν ψευδοπροφητῶν; 10:17: ἀπὸ τῶν ἀνθρώπων; 16:6, 11: ἀπὸ τῆς ζύμης τῶν Φαρισαίων καὶ Σαδδουκαίων (cf. v. 12); with reflexive pron. in Luke 12:1: προσέχετε ἑαυτοῖς ἀπὸ τῆς ζύμης; 20:46: ἀπὸ τῶν γραμματέων; without ἀπὸ and with reflexive pron. in the same meaning in 17:3: *be on (one's) guard/pay attention (to oneself)* (προσέχετε ἑαυτοῖς); similarly with μήποτε in 21:34; Acts 5:35: προσέχετε ἑαυτοῖς ἐπὶ τοῖς ἀνθρώποις τούτοις τί μέλλετε πράσσειν, probably "*take care* what you do with these people"; without reflexive pron. and with inf. (with μή) in Matt 6:1: "*beware lest*. . . ."

Otherwise the meaning *pay attention to, follow, listen to* (with dat.) predominates: Acts 8:6: τοῖς λεγομένοις (cf. 16:14); 8:10: ᾧ προσεῖχον πάντες, "they all *gave heed* to him"; v. 11: προσεῖχον δὲ αὐτῷ, "they *gave heed* to him"; 1 Tim 1:4: προσέχω μύθοις . . . , "*be addicted to/give oneself over to* myths"; cf. 4:1: πνεύμασιν πλάνοις . . .; Titus 1:14: Ἰουδαϊκοῖς μύθοις . . .; positively in Heb 2:1: προσέχω τοῖς ἀκουσθεῖσιν, "*pay closer attention* to what we have heard/to what God has let us hear" (namely, the gospel of Christ; cf. 1:2ff.); 2 Pet 1:19, of the salvation proclamations of the prophets (προφητικὸς λόγος), which the believers irrevocably possess through the eyewitness testimony of God to his Son (1:16-18; cf. Matt 17:5 par.): ᾧ καλῶς ποιεῖτε προσέχοντες, "You will do well *to pay attention to* this."

Προσέχω also means *apply oneself to, look after, observe:* 1 Tim 4:13: τῇ ἀναγνώσει . . .; Heb 7:13: *occupy oneself with, engage in* τῷ θυσιαστηρίῳ, "at the altar" (of Christ's descent from the tribe of Judah rather than Levi; see also v. 14); negatively in the sense "not *addicted to*" in 1 Tim 3:8 (οἴνῳ πολλῷ); Acts 20:28: *watch out for, take care of* (ἑαυτοῖς καὶ παντὶ τῷ ποιμνίῳ).

προσηλόω *proseloō* nail to, nail securely*

Col 2:14, fig. of the "bond of guilt" (→ χειρόγραφον) that God, with the death of Christ on the cross, "set aside, nailing it to the cross" (προσηλώσας αὐτὸ τῷ σταυρῷ; cf. also John 20:25). The basis for the imagery might be the inscription on the cross with its designation of the guilt of the person crucified (see M. Dibelius and H. Greeven, *Col* [HNT] ad loc.; cf. Mark 15:26). What is meant here is that the "document" is completely suspended, i.e., human subjection to sin is eliminated before God (see E. Lohse, *Col* [Hermeneia] ad loc. [bibliography]; on this discussion see esp. E. Schweizer, *Col* [Eng. tr., 1982] ad loc.).

προσήλυτος, ου, ὁ *proselytos* proselyte, convert to Judaism*

1. Occurrences in the NT — 2. Origin and Jewish usage — 3.a) Matt 23:15 — b) Occurrences in Acts

Lit.: B. J. BAMBERGER, *Proselytism in the Talmudic Period* (1939). — BAGD s.v. — S. BIALOBLOCKI, *Die Beziehungen des Judentums zu Proselyten und Proselytentum* (1930). — BILLERBECK I, 924-31; II, 715-23; IV, 353-414. — BOUSSET/GRESSMANN 76-86. — W. G. BRAUDE, *Jewish Proselyting in the First Five Centuries of the Common Era* (1940). — H. CONZEL-MANN, *Heiden—Juden—Christen* (BHT 62, 1981) 18-21. — P. DALBERT, *Die Theologie der hellenistisch-jüdischen Missionsliteratur unter Ausschluß von Philo und Josephus* (1954). — *idem, BHH* 1515. — F. M. DERWACTER, *Preparing the Way for Paul. The Proselyte Movement in Later Judaism* (1930). — HARNACK, *Mission* I, 1-18. — J. JEREMIAS, *Jesus' Promise to the Nations* (1958). — *idem, Jerusalem at the Time of Jesus* (1969), index s.v. proselyte. — H. G. KIPPENBERG, *KP* IV, 1187. — K. G. KUHN, *TDNT* VI, 727-44. — K. G. KUHN and H. STEGEMANN, *PW* IX, 1248-83. — K. LAKE, "Proselytes and God-fearers," *Beginnings* V, 74-96. — E. LERLE, *Proselytenwerbung und Urchristentum* (1960). — N. LEVISON, "The Proselyte in Biblical and Early Post-Biblical Judaism," *SJT* 10 (1957) 45-56. — J. A. LOADER, "An Explanation of the Term *prosēlutos*," *NovT* 15 (1973) 270-77. — J. NOLLAND, "Uncircumcised Proselytes?" *JSJ* 12 (1981) 173-94. — A. PAUL, *DBSup* VIII, 1353-56. — M. H. POPE, *IDB* III, 921-31. — PREISKER, *Zeitgeschichte* 290-93. — REICKE, *NT Era,* index s.v. — L. SCHIFFMANN, *Who Was a Jew? Rabbinic and Halakhic Perspectives on the Jewish-Christian Schism* (1985) 19-39, 82-90. — H. J. SCHOEPS, *Paul: The Theology of the Apostle in the Light of Jewish Religious History* (1961) 221-29. — T. R. SCHREINER, *ISBE* III, 1005-11. — SCHÜRER, *History* III, 150-76. — M. SIMON, *Verus Israel* (Eng. tr., 1986). — *idem,* "Sur les débuts du prosélytisme juif," *Hommages à André Dupont-Sommer* (ed. A. Caquot and M. Philonenko; 1971) 509-20. — S. ZEITLIN, "Proselytes and Proselytism during the Second Commonwealth and Early Tannaitic Period," *Harry Austryn Wolfson Jubilee Volume* (1965) II, 871-81 (= *idem, Studies in the Early History of Judaism* II [1974] 407-17). — For further bibliography see *TWNT* X, 1249; Kuhn *(TDNT);* Kuhn and Stegemann (PW).

1. Προσήλυτος occurs 4 times in the NT (Matt 23:15; Acts 2:11; 6:5; 13:43) and is used consistently there in accordance with the usage of Hellenistic Judaism as a t.t. for a Gentile who has converted to Judaism.

2. As a technical designation for "men and women who—without descending from Jewish parentage—have become members of the Jewish cultic community or have *joined* it on the basis of a legally binding acceptance process" (Kuhn and Stegemann 1249) this term is documented only in Jewish and Christian literature and probably originated in the Hellenistic Diaspora. (Attempts at etymological derivation from Semitic roots [e.g., Loader 270ff.: *qrb*] are as unpersuasive as reference to a supposed parallel in the cult of Isis: *advena,* Apuleius *Met.* xi.26; so R. Reitzenstein, *Hellenistic Mystery Religions* [1978] 19f., 238; BAGD s.v.). The term served to differentiate actual converts from mere sympathizers, the "God-fearers" (σεβόμενος [τὸν θεόν]; → σέβομαι).

The precise technical usage was anticipated by a semitechnical usage seen in the LXX, which with striking consistency employs προσήλυτος (which is derived from the stem -ελυ-) for 71 of 92 MT occurrences of the Hebrew personal-legal term *gēr,* which designates an alien who has settled in the land of Israel (cf. R. Martin-Achard, *THAT* I, 409-12; D. Kellermann, *TDOT* II, 439-49). Usually, however, the LXX renders *gēr* differently (with γειώρας, ξένος, or πάροικος) where the context makes understanding *gēr* as a religious term problematic (cf. Kuhn 731).

Philo knows προσήλυτος as a t.t. (*Som.* ii.273; *Spec. Leg.* i.51, 308), but generally prefers expressions such as ἔπηλυς

(*Flacc.* 54; *Exsec.* 152) or ἐπήλυτος (*Virt.* 104; *Spec. Leg.* i.52f.). Josephus completely avoids this Jewish Greek neologism (probably, like Philo, out of consideration for his Greek readers), though his use of the pf. partc. προσεληλυθυῖα of a female convert (*Ant.* xiv.110) does document his acquaintance with both the term and the concept. The word is also documented in inscriptions from Jerusalem and Italy (cf. *CIJ,* index s.v.; Kuhn and Stegemann 1264-67, 1272).

Alongside this use of προσήλυτος in the Hellenistic realm, Heb. *gēr,* as well, became a t.t. in Palestine for proselytes (Billerbeck II, 715-23; Kuhn 734-42; Kuhn and Stegemann 1251-53), a process that was not without influence in the rabbinic interpretation of OT occurrences of the word. On the expansion and historical significance of the Jewish mission, the process for acceptance of converts, their legal and social position, and the controversial evaluation of proselytism in rabbinic discussion, see Kuhn 737-42; Kuhn and Stegemann 1254-80 (bibliography).

3.a) Jesus' cry of woe against the scribes and Pharisees "who cross sea and land to make a single *proselyte*" (Matt 23:15) does not condemn Jewish mission activity as such (*contra* H. J. Holtzmann, *Die Synoptiker* [HKNT, [3]1902] 279; E. Lohmeyer, *Matt* [KEK] 343, and others). It is, rather, aimed at the results of these efforts in its reference to "what comes of this when the Pharisees—ὑποκριταί, as Jesus characterizes them—engage in this kind of mission" (Kuhn and Stegemann 1280; similarly A. Schlatter, *Der Evangelist Matthäus* [[6]1963] 675; Jeremias, *Promise* 17 n.4; Lerle 64, and others), namely, one who is "twice as much a child of hell" as those who have persuaded him to convert. This criticism is probably based less on the possibility, utilized by many proselytes, of annuling a marriage entered into before conversion (*contra* Lerle 65; P. Bonnard, *Matt* [CNT] 338 n.1) than on the zeal of converts (T. Zahn, *Matt* [KNT] I, 644, and others), which leads them into legalistic misunderstandings and failure to recognize God's will.

This passage presupposes the Pharisaic movement's generally positive posture regarding mission activity before the change in attitude on proselytizing that came after the catastrophe of A.D. 70. One must admittedly keep in mind that the polemic character and hyperbolic formulation of this statement relativize to a large extent its value as a source on the scope and intensity of Pharisaic propaganda.

b) The naming of "both Jews and *proselytes*" in Acts 2:11 does not expand the "list of nations" by distinguishing groups; "the phrase . . . covers *all* the preceding groups with respect to religious affiliation" (E. Haenchen, *Acts* [Eng. tr., 1971] 171), namely, Jews by birth and by conversion, thus encompassing Judaism in its totality both geographically and with regard to ancestry.

The characterization of Nicolaus as a "*proselyte* of Antioch" (Acts 6:5) justifies the conclusion that the rest of those named in the list of seven "Hellenists" were Jews by birth.

Since Luke elsewhere always distinguishes proselytes and "God-fearers" (→ σέβομαι), we should probably assume that the combination "God-fearing proselytes," which appears only in Acts 13:43, came about through the insertion of a gloss (i.e., προσηλύτων; see E. Haenchen, *Acts* 413 n.5). Despite consistent technical use of σεβόμενος in Acts (13:50; 16:14; 17:4, 17; 18:7) the possibility cannot be excluded that this is simply a case of "careless expression" (H. Conzelmann, *Acts* [Hermeneia] 106).   H. Kuhli

πρόσθεσις, εως, ἡ *prosthesis* addition; distribution (?)

Ms. D has in Mark 2:26; Matt 12:4; Luke 6:4 the phrase ἄρτοι τῆς προσθέσεως (instead of → πρόθεσις). The meaning "distribution" or even "laying out" or the like is not documented elsewhere; cf. possibly Ezek 47:13 LXX; also Lev 24:9.

πρόσκαιρος, 2 *proskairos* lasting only a time, momentary, transitory*

There are 4 occurrences in the NT. In the allegorical interpretation of the parable of the fourfold sowing, one person is described as a πρόσκαιρος, i.e., a person *of the moment, of inconstancy,* who has no roots in himself and thus makes precipitous decisions from which he then falls away with equal ease, since they are not grounded in deep conviction (Matt 13:21 [cf. vv. 5f.] par. Mark 4:17 [cf. vv. 5f.]). The adj. is used in a similarly critical fashion in Heb 11:25 in the story of Moses, who rejected the chance "to enjoy the *fleeting/momentary* pleasures of sin (πρόσκαιρον ἔχειν ἁμαρτίας ἀπόλαυσιν)," namely, the aristocratic life of a "son of Pharaoh's daughter" (v. 24; cf. Exod 2:11ff.; Josephus *Ant.* ii.51: πρόσκαιρος τῆς ἐπιθυμίας ἡδονή).

In 2 Cor 4:18 the word is used eschatologically: τὰ γὰρ βλεπόμενα πρόσκαιρα τὰ δὲ μὴ βλεπόμενα αἰώνια (cf. *OGIS* II, 669, 14). "The things that are seen" (cf. Wis 13:7), in contrast to what is invisible and eternal, are bound to a specific finite time. The maxim in v. 18b (H. Windisch, *2 Cor* [KEK] ad loc., lists analogies in content from Hellenistic literature) picks up the contrast from v. 17 (→ παραυτίκα → ἐλαφρόν/αἰώνιον βάρος), and thus additionally supports the insight that the present tribulations of the faithful (in this world) lose their importance in comparison to the expected eternal glory, which is already experienced in daily renewal (v. 16). Πρόσκαιρος here thus means *valid for a certain time, transient, temporal.* Hence the θλίψεις (sufferings) themselves, as visible and transitory experiences, guide one to pay attention to what is invisible and eternal (v. 18a): What is seen becomes reason for hoping in what is unseen, and present experience of suffering becomes a confirmation of hope in the eternal glory (cf. 4:10-12; Rom 5:3; 8:18, 24f.); → καιρός 3; → αἰώνιος 2. G. Delling, *TDNT* III, 463f.   H. Balz

προσκαλέομαι *proskaleomai* summon (to oneself), invite, call*

This vb. occurs 29 times in the NT (always mid.); 6 of those occurrences are in Matthew, 9 in Mark, 4 in Luke, 9 in Acts; 1 in Jas 5:14. In the Gospels the literal sense *summon, call to oneself* predominates and usually has as its subj. Jesus, who *calls* or *summons* his disciples (usually προσκαλεσάμενος; Matt 10:1; 15:32; 20:25; Mark 6:7; 8:1; 10:42; 12:43), the people (ὄχλος: Matt 15:10; Mark 7:14; 8:34; cf. 3:13), a child (Matt 18:2; Luke 15:26; cf. 18:16), or the scribes (Mark 3:23). Only 4 times in the Gospels is there another subj. (Matt 18:32: the servant's master; Mark 15:44: Pilate [*have someone summoned*]; Luke 7:18: John the Baptist; 16:5: a steward; cf. further Acts 6:2: the Twelve; 13:7: Sergius Paulus [*have someone summoned*]; 23:17, 18: Paul; 23:23: a tribune; Jas 5:14: a sick person calling for τοὺς πρεσβυτέρους). Acts 5:40 is probably employing the vb. as a t.t. *summon* to a court proceeding (προσκαλεσάμενοι τοὺς ἀποστόλους).

Acts 2:39 refers in a fig. sense to the *call* to God of those who live "far off" (probably Gentiles; cf. Joel 3:5; Isa 57:19). Acts 13:2 refers thus to a call by the Holy Spirit (τὸ πνεῦμα τὸ ἅγιον) to a certain task (ἔργον); cf. 16:10, with inf. εὐαγγελίσασθαι. K. L. Schmidt, *TDNT* III, 500f.; L. Coenen, *DNTT* I, 271, 274.

προσκαρτερέω *proskartereō* hold fast to, endure in, stand perpetually ready, persevere in*

There are 10 occurrences in the NT, 6 of them in Acts. Under the influence of the simple form → καρτερέω ("be strong/steadfast"), the compound vb. also often has the secondary meaning of decisive or unflinching perseverance. This becomes esp. clear in προσκαρτερέω τῇ προσευχῇ (Acts 1:14, with adv. ὁμοθυμαδόν; 6:4: τῇ προσευχῇ καὶ τῇ διακονίᾳ; Rom 12:12, with τῇ θλίψει ὑπομένοντες; Col 4:2) and similarly in προσκαρτεροῦντες τῇ διδαχῇ τῶν ἀποστόλων καὶ τῇ κοινωνίᾳ, τῇ κλάσει τοῦ ἄρτου καὶ ταῖς προσευχαῖς (Acts 2:42). In these instances προσκαρτερέω emphasizes the persistent and submissive *perseverance* and *tenaciousness* of a self-enclosed group collectively oriented toward specific goals; this also includes Acts 2:46: καθ᾽ ἡμέραν προσκαρτεροῦντες ὁμοθυμαδὸν ἐν τῷ ἱερῷ, "day by day *abiding* together in the temple."

Of individuals in Acts 8:13: Σίμων . . . ἦν προσκαρτερῶν τῷ Φιλίππῳ, "he *held fast/tenaciously to* Philip"; 10:7: οἱ προσκαρτεροῦντες αὐτῷ, of the soldiers who were *assigned* to Cornelius or who *held true* to him (Spicq, *Notes* II, 758: "attached to his service"; E. Haenchen, *Acts* [Eng. tr., 1971] ad loc.: "orderlies"). Mark 3:9 and Rom 13:6 use προσκαρτερέω in a more general fashion: ἵνα πλοιάριον προσκαρτερῇ αὐτῷ, "that a boat *be*

ready for them" (Mark 3:9); λειτουργοὶ γὰρ θεοῦ εἰσιν εἰς αὐτὸ τοῦτο προσκαρτεροῦντες, "they are servants of God when they *persistently/eagerly attend to this* [collection of taxes]" (Rom 13:6; cf. also Pap. London III, 904, 26f.; further documentation in Spicq, *Notes* II, 758f. with n.3; on this discussion see E. Käsemann, *Rom* [Eng. tr., 1980] ad loc.). W. Grundmann, *TDNT* III, 618f.

προσκαρτέρησις, εως, ἡ *proskarterēsis* perseverance*

Eph 6:18: ἐν πάσῃ προσκαρτερήσει, "with all *perseverance,*" of persistent and enduring prayer. W. Grundmann, *TDNT* III, 619f.; Spicq, *Notes* II, 760f.

προσκεφάλαιον, ου, τό *proskephalaion* cushion, pillow*

Mark 4:38: Jesus slept in the stern of the ship "on a *cushion*" (ἐπὶ τὸ προσκεφάλαιον καθεύδων). Cf. Ezek 13:18, 20.

προσκληρόομαι *prosklēroomai* fall to (by lot); pass.: be bequeathed (by God)*

Pass. in Acts 17:4: προσεκληρώθησαν τῷ Παύλῳ, "they *were given/assigned to* Paul" (cf. Philo *Leg. Gai.* 68); W. Foerster, *TDNT* III, 765f., prefers the tr. "attach oneself to."

πρόσκλησις, εως, ἡ *prosklēsis* invitation; preference, favor*

1 Tim 5:21 v.l. in place of → πρόσκλισις.

προσκλίνομαι *prosklinomai* incline toward, join, follow*

Pass. in Acts 5:36, of Theudas, "whom a number of men, about four hundred, *joined* (προσεκλίθη)."

πρόσκλισις, εως, ἡ *prosklisis* inclination, favor*

1 Tim 5:21: μηδὲν ποιῶν κατὰ πρόσκλισιν, "do nothing from *inclination,*" i.e., from partiality or favor toward certain people (parallel to χωρὶς προκρίματος).

προσκολλάομαι *proskollaomai* adhere to, be inseparably bound to, join with devotion*

Pass. in Eph 5:31: ἄνθρωπος . . . προσκολληθήσεται πρὸς τὴν γυναῖκα αὐτοῦ, "the man *will be joined fast/ inseparably bound* to his wife" (citing Gen 2:24 LXX; Heb. *dābaq*); Mark 10:7 ℵ B Ψ, and others; Matt 19:5 ℵ C K L, and others. On the use of both the compound and simple vb. in reference to marital or sexual relations in general cf. 3 Kgdms 11:2; Sir 19:2; 1 Esdr 4:20; 1 Cor

6:16 (but see also v. 17); Pap. London V, 1731, 16 (κολλᾶσθαι ἑτέρῳ ἀνδρί); also Gen 34:3 (MT: *dābaq;* LXX: προσέσχεν τῇ ψυχῇ). K. L. Schmidt, *TDNT* III, 823; H. Seebass, *DNTT* II, 348-50; → κολλάω.

πρόσκομμα, ατος, τό *proskomma* offense, stumbling*

There are 6 occurrences in the NT, other than 1 Pet 2:8 all in Paul. *Nomen actionis* in the phrase λίθος προσκόμματος, "stumbling stone" (i.e., "stone *over which one stumbles*," or *"onto which one falls"*: genitive of quality), in Rom 9:32, 33 (with πέτρα σκανδάλου, citing Isa 8:14; 28:16); 1 Pet 2:8 (with κεφαλὴ γωνίας [→ γωνία 3.a, b; Ps 117:22 LXX] and πέτρα σκανδάλου). According to the MT of Isa 8:14 God himself will become "a stone of offense" (Heb. *negep,* "offense"; elsewhere usually *môqeš,* "trap, snare"), but the LXX inserts negatives, resulting in a statement of salvation. Paul, on the other hand, reverses the salvation statement of Isa 28:16 by understanding the "precious cornerstone" (λίθος πολυτελὴς ἐκλεκτὸς ἀκρογωνιαῖος) to be laid for Zion as, instead, a "stumbling stone"; the salvation proclamation has, indeed, been fulfilled, but initially against Israel, which has stumbled over Christ. 1 Pet 2:6-8 combines the two passages from Isaiah with Ps 117:22 LXX: For believers Christ is the true cornerstone, while nonbelievers ("the builders who rejected the stone," 1 Pet 2:7/Ps 117:22 LXX) stumble over him, in accordance with God's will. What happened with Israel repeats itself in the foundering of the world on Christ, so that only believers remain as the "living stones" for building the "spiritual house" (1 Pet 2:5) and as a "holy nation" (v. 9).

Elsewhere πρόσκομμα refers to occasions for *offense* or for stumbling in faith or conscience. The freedom of the strong can become an offense to the weak and subject them to unwarranted human prejudice. Therefore, the Church's criterion should not be whether one's opinion is right or wrong, but τὸ μὴ τιθέναι πρόσκομμα τῷ ἀδελφῷ ἢ σκάνδαλον, "never to put a *stumbling block* or hindrance in the way of a brother" (Rom 14:13); similarly 1 Cor 8:9: μή πως ἡ ἐξουσία ὑμῶν αὕτη πρόσκομμα γένηται τοῖς ἀσθενέσιν. The freedom of the strong can seduce the weak into a freedom that their conscience cannot answer; as a result they stumble over the γνῶσις of the strong, and pneumatic freedom becomes sin against one's brother and against Christ (8:12: ἁμαρτάνετε). Rom 14:20 is concerned with such *taking offense:* "Indeed everything is clean, ἀλλὰ κακὸν τῷ ἀνθρώπῳ τῷ διὰ προσκόμματος ἐσθίοντι (for him who eats it with *offense*)." Here, too, the offense of the strong toward the weak consists in their seducing them into attitudes and actions that cannot be supported by the latter's conscience and faith; they thus fall back into the old contradiction between faith and action and thus into sin (cf. 14:21, 23). G. Stählin, *TDNT* VI, 745-58; *TWNT* X, 1250 (bibliography); J. Guhrt, *DNTT* II, 705-7; → σκανδαλίζω; σκάνδαλον.

H. Balz

προσκοπή, ῆς, ἡ *proskopē* (occasion for) offense*

2 Cor 6:3: μηδεμίαν ἐν μηδενὶ διδόντες προσκοπήν, "we put no *occasion for offense/stumbling* in anyone's way"; → πρόσκομμα.

προσκόπτω *proskoptō* strike; take offense at*

There are 8 occurrences in the NT, in Paul only Rom 9:32; 14:21, both times (as also in 1 Pet 2:8) with the noun → πρόσκομμα. In the literal sense *strike* in Matt 4:6 par. Luke 4:11: μήποτε προσκόψῃς πρὸς λίθον τὸν πόδα σου (citing Ps 90:12 LXX), representing a protected life; used absolutely, *stumble* in John 11:9, 10: (οὐ) προσκόπτει; with dat. in Matt 7:27, of storm winds that *beat* against a house (προσέκοψαν τῇ οἰκίᾳ ἐκείνῃ).

Fig. in Rom 9:32, of Israel *taking offense* at/stumbling over Christ (προσέκοψαν, citing Isa 8:14); similarly 1 Pet 2:8, of Israel, as nonbelievers in general, οἳ προσκόπτουσιν τῷ λόγῳ ἀπειθοῦντες, "they *take offense/stumble* [on the λίθος προσκόμματος, v. 8a] because they do not obey the word" (→ πρόσκομμα).

Take offense/stumble in Rom 14:21 with regard to the strong being considerate toward the weak. Paul advises his readers to refrain from anything (such as eating meat or drinking wine) that might be an offense or stumbling block to one's brother: ἐν ᾧ ὁ ἀδελφός σου προσκόπτει (replaced by λυπεῖται in ℵ* P; προσκόπτει ἢ σκανδαλίζεται ἢ ἀσθενεῖ in p[46vid] ℵ[2] B D F Koine, etc.). Such offense or stumbling affects the conscience and thus ultimately the eschatological existence of one's brother, his salvation before God (cf. 1 Cor 8:7ff.; 10:23ff.; → πρόσκομμα). G. Stählin, *TDNT* VI, 745-58; J. Guhrt, *DNTT* II, 705-7; → σκανδαλίζω; σκάνδαλον.

προσκυλίω *proskyliō* roll up to*

Mark 15:46 par. Matt 27:60: προσεκύλισεν λίθον μέγαν ἐπὶ τὴν θύραν/τῇ θύρᾳ τοῦ μνημείου, "he *rolled* a great stone *against* the door of the tomb" (this part of the account omitted in Luke 23:53; see, however, the additions in mss.; esp. D; cf. further 24:2!).

προσκυνέω *proskyneō* worship (vb.), do homage*

1. Occurrences — 2. Usage — 3. Meaning — a) Matthew and Mark — b) Luke-Acts — c) John — d) Revelation — e) Other occurrences — 4. Theological significance

Lit.: J. B. Bauer and H. Zimmermann, *SacVb* 9-15. — N. Füglister, *BL* 71. — H. Greeven, *TDNT* VI, 758-66 (older literature). — J. Hasenfuss and F. Mussner, *LTK* I, 498-500.

— F. HEILER, *RGG* I, 356f. — K. P. JÖRNS, *Das hymnische Evangelium* (1971) 33f., 83, 97, 151. — G. LOHFINK, *Die Himmelfahrt Jesu* (1971) 171-74, 253f. — idem, "Gab es im Gottesdienst der neutestamentlichen Gemeinden eine Anbetung Christi?" *BZ* 18 (1974) 161-79. — B. A. MASTIN, "Daniel 2:46 and the Hellenistic World," *ZAW* 85 (1973) 80-93. — C. F. D. MOULE, *The Origin of Christology* (1971) 175f. — R. PESCH, "Der Gottessohn im matthäischen Evangelienprolog," *Bib* 48 (1967) 395-420, esp. 414f. — R. SCHNACKENBURG, "Worship in Spirit and Truth," idem II, 85-114. — For further bibliography see *TWNT* X, 1250.

1. Of 60 occurrences in the NT, Matthew has 13, Mark 2, Luke 3, John 11, Acts 4, 1 Corinthians 1, Hebrews 2, and Revelation 24. The centers of gravity for the use of προσκυνέω are thus in Matthew, John, and Revelation.

2.a) Προσκυνέω is used without an obj. as a t.t. for participation in temple worship (in Jerusalem or on Mount Gerizim; John 4:20a, b; 12:20; Acts 8:27; 24:11; Rev 11:1) and as a t.t. for Jewish pilgrimage to Jerusalem. The one to whom such worship is directed can be designated by dat., acc., ἔμπροσθεν (Rev 19:10a; 22:8), or ἐνώπιον (Luke 4:7; Rev 3:9; 15:4); no difference in meaning is discernible among the various constructions.

b) Προσκυνέω is used frequently with πίπτω, "fall down" (Matt 2:11; 4:9; 18:26; Acts 10:25; 1 Cor 14:25; Rev 4:10; 5:14; 7:11; 11:16; 19:4, 10a; 22:8), or similar expressions (τίθημι τὰ γόνατα in Mark 15:19; κρατέω τοὺς πόδας in Matt 28:9). This suggests that homage expressed by προσκυνέω also occurs generally with prostration.

c) Use of προσκυνέω with (προσ-)ἔρχομαι is common (Matt 2:2, 8; 8:2; 9:18; 15:25; 20:20; 28:9; Acts 8:27). This manner of expression has cultic shading (→ ἔρχομαι).

3. Whereas in extrabiblical Greek the meaning of προσκυνέω extends from worship to simple appreciation, the religious meaning of the word is maintained in the NT.

a) Matthew uses προσκυνέω in 8:2; 9:18; 14:33; 15:25; 20:20 (in contrast to the corresponding passages in Mark) of the behavior of those coming to Jesus. In a reverse fashion Matt 27:29 does not pick up the mocking gesture mentioned in Mark 15:19, and the demonic gesture of submission in Mark 5:6 is absent from Matthew. In Matt 14:33 homage is directed expressly to the Son of God, in 28:9, 17 to the resurrected Christ, and in 2:2, 8 to the newborn Messiah. In Matthew προσκυνέω thus expresses the trusting homage of one who sees God reflected in Jesus, and the term thus has the sense of worshipful reverence. In 4:9f., therefore, the tempter's insistence that Jesus fall down and worship him is countered by the assertion that God alone is worthy of such worship (4:10, citing Deut 6:13). By using προσκυνέω Matthew thus allows the Christ's glory to shine behind the earthly Jesus,

the glory of the Christ who is exalted to the right hand of God; thus also the fullness and authority of God's power is seen (cf. 28:18). In 18:26 the Evangelist sees God himself standing behind the merciful king, so that there, too, more is intended than merely the gesture of supplication of a subject facing his lord.

b) Luke-Acts reserves προσκυνέω for God and the exalted Lord. Satan's claim that Jesus should worship him is rejected (Luke 4:7f., citing Deut 6:13). Acts 7:43 bases Israel's exile to Babylon on guilt that it incurred by *worshipping* images. When Cornelius throws himself down before Peter (10:25), the apostle restrains him by pointing out that he, Peter, is also only a man. What never happens in Luke's Gospel to Jesus before the cross does occur in 24:52 before the Lord ascends into heaven: The disciples *worship* him.

c) John 4:20-24 deals with the question of the legitimate place to *worship* God. Jesus declares the alternative "Jerusalem or Gerizim" posed by the Samaritan woman at Jacob's well (v. 20a, b) to be outdated (vv. 21, 23a, b). Though the Jews' worship is, indeed, put before that of the Samaritans (v. 22a, b), this difference is overcome because "now" "the true worshipers *worship* the Father in spirit and truth" (v. 23a). This does not constitute a rejection of worship at specific places; it is not a matter of the "inwardness" of worship. "Spirit" is the opposite of "flesh," of powerless and selfish human existence. Worship "in spirit" is worship within the liberated human situation newly disclosed by God. It happens in the "truth" that has come through Christ (1:17). Indeed, Christ *is* the "truth" (14:6). God's Spirit leads into "truth" (16:13). Worship "in spirit and truth" (so also 4:24a, b) is worship made possible by Jesus Christ and realized in the believer by the Holy Spirit. Fellowship with Jesus leads to correct worship of the Father—without rejecting preferred places of worship. In 9:38 προσκυνέω is used of an expression of faith in the Son of man Jesus as a response to the experience of divine power in healing (cf. v. 33).

d) The use of προσκυνέω in Revelation has two centers of gravity: the worship of God and the Lamb in the heavenly liturgy (4:10; 5:14; 7:11; 11:16; 19:4) and the worship of the dragon, the "beast from the sea," and his image on earth (13:4 bis, 8, 12, 15; 19:20; cf. 20:4), worship described as a distortion of the heavenly liturgy (cf. 13:1-8; 5:6-14). This anti-divine cult leads to ruin (14:9, 11; 16:2; 19:19-21), rejection of it to life (20:4). Only worship of God allows one to come through judgment by God (14:7). When at the end all nations worship the victorious God (15:4), the heavenly worship will fill the New Creation. Only God and the Lamb are worthy of worship, so the angels ward off any homage to themselves (19:10b; 22:8f.). Only blasphemers throw themselves down before demons and idols (9:20).

Rev 3:9 occupies a special position. The resurrected Lord assures the church in Philadelphia that he will make their adversaries come and bow down before their feet in homage by showing these adversaries that he, the Lord himself, stands behind this church. Προσκυνέω is used here of homage before humans, in reference to the Christ standing behind them. 3:11 suggests that this disclosure before the adversaries is expected to take place at Christ's parousia.

e) In 1 Cor 14:25 προσκυνέω is used of worship of God in the Christian worship service. Prostration appears to have been a common gesture of worship, at least in the church at Corinth. Heb 1:6 (citing Deut 32:43 LXX) emphasizes the position of the Son of God over all creation. The homage of the angels demonstrates his divine honor. In 11:21 (citing Gen 47:31 LXX) the meaning of προσκυνέω is unclear: Is the author thinking of a gesture of worship?

4. The use of προσκυνέω in the NT is based on that of the OT, with a stronger concentration of the meaning in the direction of worship. What is new in the NT is that now the exalted Christ emerges next to God as the one worshipped (esp. noticeable, e.g., in Rev 5:13f.; Luke 24:52). The exalted Lord is not simply viewed as being of equal stature with God: The Lamb does not sit on a second throne next to God, but stands rather among the elders (Rev 5:6) and receives the scroll with the seven seals from God's hand (5:7). Matthew (with John), however, interprets prostration before Jesus, on the basis of the tradition before him, as worshipful homage based on Jesus' dignity as God's Son. Such worshipful homage of Christ is in the NT not exclusively directed toward him; it is worship directed toward the God who reveals himself in Jesus Christ. It is difficult to be sure that this development over against the OT in the 1st cent. really corresponded to actual worship of Jesus Christ expressed through prostration in the Christian worship service; certain elements point to this (cf. Rev 5:8, where "the prayers of the saints" are offered to the Lamb). In Revelation the heavenly liturgy is portrayed with elements of the Christian worship service (cf. G. Delling, *NovT* 3 [1959] 107-37; J. J. O'Rourke, *CBQ* 30 [1968] 399-409; Jörns; P. Prigent, *RSR* 60 [1972] 165-72; Lohfink, *BZ* 18); this prostration before God *and the Lamb* might also be taken from the congregational worship service.   J. M. Nützel

προσκυνητής, οῦ, ὁ *proskynētēs* worshiper, one who prays*

John 4:23: οἱ ἀληθινοὶ προσκυνηταὶ προσκυνήσουσιν, "the true *worshipers* will worship in spirit and truth," in a context characterized by the vb. → προσκυνέω (vv. 20 bis, 21, 22 bis, 23 bis, 24 bis). The noun is otherwise

documented only in post-NT literature (*OGIS* I, 262, 21). H. Greeven, *TDNT* VI, 766; *TWNT* X, 1250 (bibliography); Schnackenburg II, 85-114.

προσλαλέω *proslaleō* speak to/with, address*

Acts 13:43: προσλαλοῦντες αὐτοῖς ἔπειθον, "they *spoke to* them and urged them"; 28:20: ὑμᾶς ἰδεῖν καὶ προσλαλῆσαι, "to see you and *speak with* you."

προσλαμβάνομαι *proslambanomai* receive, take aside, take*

There are 12 occurrences in the NT (all mid., as also [except in Wis 17:10] in the LXX), 5 of those in Acts and 4 in Romans. *Take/receive* someone: Acts 18:26; 28:2 (into houses); Phlm 17 (cf. v. 12 ℵ² C*/² D Koine, etc.). In Rom 14:1, 3; 15:7 (bis) that God has *received* believers (ὁ θεὸς/Χριστὸς [. . .] προσελάβετο) is the reason for also *accepting/welcoming* one another (esp. "the weak": προσλαμβάνεσθε . . . ἀσθενοῦντα/ἀλλήλους; cf. also Pss 26:10 LXX; 64:5 LXX; *1 Clem.* 49:6). Other meanings are: *take* someone *aside,* Mark 8:32 par. Matt 16:22 (not in Luke): προσλαβόμενος ὁ Πέτρος αὐτόν (sc. Jesus); *take along,* Acts 17:5: ἄνδρας τινὰς πονηρούς; *take* (food) *in,* 27:33: μηθέν; 27:36: τροφῆς (partitive genitive). G. Delling, *TDNT* IV, 15; B. Siede, *DNTT* III, 750f.

προσλέγω *proslegō* reply, respond

Mark 16:14 W (in the Freer logion).

πρόσλημψις, εως, ἡ *proslēmpsis* acceptance*

Rom 11:15, of Israel's *acceptance* (possibly *reacceptance*) by God as the goal of the history of God with mankind (opposite: → ἀποβολὴ αὐτῶν). On the orthography see BDF §101 s.v. λαμβάνειν.

προσμένω *prosmenō* remain at/with; persevere with*

There are 7 occurrences in the NT. Literal: *stay with* Jesus, Mark 8:2 par. Matt 15:32; *remain there,* 1 Tim 1:3: ἐν Ἐφέσῳ; Acts 18:18: ἔτι προσμείνας ἡμέρας ἱκανάς (sc. in Corinth). Fig.: Acts 11:23: προσμένω τῷ κυρίῳ, "remain true to the Lord"; 13:43: τῇ χάριτι τοῦ θεοῦ; 1 Tim 5:5: ταῖς δεήσεσιν καὶ ταῖς προσευχαῖς, "continue in supplications and prayers." F. Hauck, *TDNT* IV, 579.

προσορμίζομαι *prosormizomai* come into the harbor, dock, land*

Mark 6:53: ἦλθον εἰς Γεννησαρὲτ καὶ προσωρμίσθησαν, "came and *moored to the shore/docked*" (aor. pass.).

προσοφείλω *prosopheilō* owe additionally*

Phlm 19: ὅτι καὶ σεαυτόν μοι προσοφείλεις, "to say nothing of the fact that you *owe* me even your very self." The prep. prefix προς- is probably best explained from the context (v. 18). Paul intends to accept responsibility for the debts of the runaway slave Onesimus (εἰ δέ τι . . . ὀφείλει, τοῦτο ἐμοὶ ἐλλόγα, v. 18), not to mention that actually Philemon is responsible for them (ἵνα μὴ λέγω σοι, v. 19) and—in addition to this assumption of debt —even owes Paul "his own self"; v. 19 is to be understood as a parenthetical statement (cf. BDF §495 n.1). See further LSJ s.v.; *contra* P. Stuhlmacher, *Phlm* (EKKNT) ad loc.

προσοχθίζω *prosochthizō* be provoked/indignant /angry*

Heb 3:10, of God's *anger* at those of the wilderness generation (προσώχθισα τῇ γενεᾷ ταύτῃ, citing Ps 94:10 LXX); προσοχθίζω occurs again in the subsequent interpretation of the quotation (Ps 94:7-11 LXX) in Heb 3:17 (τίσιν δὲ προσώχθισεν . . . ; "with whom *was he provoked*?"); cf. also *Herm. Sim.* ix.7.6 (used absolutely).

πρόσπεινος, 2 *prospeinos* hungry*

Acts 10:10: ἐγένετο πρόσπεινος, "he became hungry."

προσπήγνυμι *prospēgnymi* fasten, nail on*

Absolute in Acts 2:23: τοῦτον . . . προσπήξαντες ἀνείλατε, "you nailed him to the cross and killed him."

προσπίπτω *prospiptō* fall down before, fall at the feet of; fall upon, strike against*

There are 8 occurrences in the NT, 7 with the meaning *fall down:* with dat. in Mark 3:11: προσπίπτω αὐτῷ (unclean spirits falling before Jesus); 5:33 par. Luke 8:47: τρέμουσα προσπίπτω (a healed woman falls before Jesus); Luke 8:28 (a possessed person falls before Jesus); 5:8: προσπίπτω τοῖς γόνασιν Ἰησοῦ (Peter falls before Jesus); with prep. in Mark 7:25: προσπίπτω πρὸς τοὺς πόδας αὐτοῦ (the Syrophoenician woman falls before Jesus); Acts 16:29: ἔντρομος γενόμενος προσέπεσεν (the jailer falls before Paul and Silas [dat.]). In contrast to προσκυνέω, προσπίπτω is not used in the NT as a t.t. for gestures of prayer and reverence, but rather of surprise and sudden dismay. Some spoken words or a specific action always precedes, and the act of falling down is normally followed—usually immediately—by a request or word of confession.

The literal sense *strike against* in Matt 7:25, with dat., of storms beating against a house: προσέπεσαν τῇ οἰκίᾳ ἐκείνῃ (on conjectured προσέπαισαν see BAGD s.v. προσ-

παίω; BDF §202 s.v. προσ-; par. Luke 6:48f. has → προσρήγνυμι; cf. also Matt 7:27 v.l. [in place of → προσκόπτω]).

προσποιέομαι *prospoieomai* pretend, give the appearance (of)*

Luke 24:28, of the (unrecognized) resurrected Lord: προσεποιήσατο πορρώτερον πορεύεσθαι, "he *appeared* to be going further." John 8:6 K pm: μὴ προσποιούμενος, "without giving the appearance."

προσπορεύομαι *prosporeuomai* approach, come toward*

Mark 10:35: James and John *come forward to* Jesus (with a personal request; προσπορεύονται αὐτῷ).

προσρήγνυμι *prosrēgnymi* strike, break; intrans.: break against*

With dat. in Luke 6:48, 49: προσέρηξεν ὁ ποταμός (τῇ οἰκίᾳ), "the stream *struck against* the house" or "*broke against* the house"; cf. Matt 7:27 v.l.; → προσπίπτω. On the word formation see BDF §101 s.v. ῥηγνύναι. Pass. "break/founder on" in *Barn.* 3:6.

προστάσσω *prostassō* command, order, determine*

There are 7 occurrences in the NT. Of the sacrifice for cleansing of leprosy commanded by Moses in Mark 1:44 par. Matt 8:4/Luke 5:14: ἃ (ὃ/καθὼς) προσέταξεν Μωϋσῆς (cf. Lev 14:2ff.); with dat. of person, *command, commission* in Matt 1:24: ὡς προσέταξεν αὐτῷ ὁ ἄγγελος κυρίου; pass. in Acts 10:33: πάντα τὰ προστεταγμένα σοι ὑπὸ τοῦ κυρίου; cf. v. 48: προσέταξεν with acc. and inf., "he [Peter] *commanded*." Προστεταγμένοι καιροί in Acts 17:26 are "periods *allotted/determined* [by God]," probably meaning seasons (cf. 14:17; Pss 74:17; 104:19; Wis 7:18; Philo *Spec. Leg.* ii.56f.; the moment that the periods of days and years were determined is emphasized in *Pss. Sol.* 18:10; *1 Enoch* 2:1; 82:7ff.; esp. *1 Clem.* 20:1-12 [within the praise of God's creation deeds; 8 formulations with the stem ταγ-], esp. vv. 2, 4, 9); an interpretation referring to historical periods is also possible (cf. Luke 21:24; → καιρός 6). On this discussion see H. Conzelmann, *Acts* (Hermeneia) ad loc.; E. Haenchen, *Acts* (Eng. tr., 1971) ad loc.; G. Delling, *TDNT* VIII, 37ff.

προστάτις, ιδος, ἡ *prostatis* protectress, helper, assistant*

Rom 16:2: Phoebe, as deaconess of the church at Cenchreae, has already become "a helper of many and of myself [Paul] as well (προστάτις πολλῶν)." The fem. form of προστάτης ("chief, patron"), which occurs only here in the NT, is probably not to be understood in the technical sense of a leadership function (on this see BAGD s.v.; cf. E. Käsemann, *Rom* [Eng. tr., 1980] ad loc.), but refers rather to Phoebe's support of strangers and the poor, just as προστάτις originally referred to a woman "who looks after the legal protection of strangers and freedmen" (O. Michel, *Rom* [KEK] ad loc.; B. Reicke, *TDNT* VI, 703; F. W. Beare, *BHH* 1463; G. Theissen, *The Social Setting of Pauline Christianity: Essays on Corinth* (1982) 88f.; G. Lohfink, *Diakonie* 11 (1980) 385-400, esp. 389-91.

προστίθημι *prostithēmi* add to; increase; proceed [to]*

There are 18 occurrences in the NT. The word is esp. common in Luke's writings (7 occurrences in the Gospel, 6 in Acts); Paul has it only in Gal 3:19.

The basic meaning *add to* predominates: Act. with acc. obj. in Matt 6:27 par. Luke 12:25: ἐπὶ τὴν ἡλικίαν αὐτοῦ πῆχυν (ἕνα). Pass. in Matt 6:33 par. Luke 12:31: *be given to* (by God) (ταῦτα [πάντα]); Gal 3:19: (ὁ νόμος) προσετέθη, "the law *was added* [to the promise to Abraham]"; Heb 12:19: παρῃτήσαντο μὴ προστεθῆναι αὐτοῖς λόγον, "they entreated that no further messages *be spoken/directed* to them" (→ παραιτέομαι); of people *added* in Acts 2:41: προσετέθησαν . . . ψυχαὶ ὡσεὶ τρισχίλιαι; v. 47: τοὺς σῳζομένους . . . ἐπὶ τὸ αὐτό; 5:14: πιστεύοντες τῷ κυρίῳ; 11:24: ὄχλος ἱκανὸς τῷ κυρίῳ; of death in 13:36: Δαυὶδ . . . προσετέθη πρὸς τοὺς πατέρας αὐτοῦ, "David *was gathered* to his fathers." Pass., used absolutely, in Mark 4:24 (redactional): καὶ προστεθήσεται ὑμῖν, "[still more] *will be given* to you" (cf. v. 25), a reference to God's goodness, which is never exhausted for believers. With acc. obj. and ἐπί in Luke 3:20: προσέθηκεν καὶ τοῦτο ἐπὶ πᾶσιν, "he *added* this to them all" (cf. BDF §461.2).

With an inf. following προστίθημι means "*continue/proceed* to . . .": Luke 20:11, 12: προσέθετο . . . πέμψαι (cf. par. Mark 12:4f.: πάλιν ἀπέστειλεν); Acts 12:3: προσέθετο συλλαβεῖν . . ., "he *proceeded* to arrest Peter also." The construction is probably a Hebraism from Heb. *wayyôsep lᵉ* (see BDF §§392.2; 435.a); cf. also Luke 19:11: προσθεὶς εἶπεν παραβολήν, "he *proceeded* to tell a parable" (after a word of salvation in vv. 9f.; cf. BDF §435; *contra* BAGD s.v. 1.c). Προστίθημι occurs in Luke 17:5 with the meaning *increase* (πρόσθες ἡμῖν πίστιν). C. Maurer, *TDNT* VIII, 168f.

προστρέχω *prostrechō* run to*

In the NT only partc. (except aor. ind. προσέδραμεν in John 20:16 v.l.): Mark 9:15: προστρέχοντες; 2nd aor. προσδραμών in 10:17; Acts 8:30.

προσφάγιον, ου, τό *prosphagion* relish; fish (noun)*

John 21:5: μή τι προσφάγιον ἔχετε; "do you not have anything *to eat* with the bread / any *fish?*" (cf. v. 6). According to Hesychius προσφάγιον (from προς- and φαγεῖν) means the same as ὄψον, which like → ὀψάριον often referred to fish; cf. also Pap. Oxy. no. 498, ll. 33, 39: ἄρτον ἕνα καὶ προσφάγιον.

πρόσφατος, 2 *prosphatos* fresh, new*

Heb 10:21: ὁδὸς πρόσφατος καὶ ζῶσα, "a *new* and living way," of the new immediate access to God disclosed through Christ "through the curtain"; cf. also Eccl 1:9; Ps 80:10 LXX. C. Maurer, *TDNT* VI, 766f.

προσφάτως *prosphatōs* shortly before, recently*

Acts 18:2: προσφάτως ἐληλυθώς, "*recently* come"; cf. *Mart. Pol.* 4.

προσφέρω *prospherō* bring to, offer (vb.)

1. Occurrences in the NT — 2. With personal obj. — 3. With things as obj. — 4. Of offerings

Lit.: J. JEREMIAS, *Abba* (1966) 103-7, 311-23, 326-28. — J. KÜHLEWEIN, *THAT* II, 674-81. — K. Weiss, *TDNT* IX, 65-68. — For further bibliography see *TWNT* X, 1289.

1. Of the 47 occurrences in the NT, 20 are in Hebrews, the rest in the Gospels and Acts: 15 in Matthew (including 18:24, which has v.l. προσάγω), 3 in Mark (+ v.l. in 10:13 [the second occurrence in the verse]: *TCGNT* 105), 4 in Luke, 3 in Acts, and 2 in John.

2. The use of προσφέρω in Mark 2:4 of the *bringing* of the sick (or of children in Mark 10:13 par. Luke 18:15) to Jesus is picked up in a stereotypical phrase in Matthew (redactional), from his first summaries in 4:24; 8:16 and further in 9:2, 32; 12:22; 14:35; 17:16. Luke 23:14 has Pilate use it in a reprimanding, critical sense: They *dragged* Jesus to him. In Matt 18:24, too, it is not a matter of leading the accused before the court: The term is used rather in the sense common since Thucydides in the pass. with dat.: "A person *met* him/introduced himself to him." This might also be the sense in Matt 19:13 in the redactional alteration into pass.: A group of children *met* him. In Heb 12:7 the pass. qualifies God's actions: "He *is treating* you (in discipline) as sons."

3. Consistent with Matthew's principle of treating subsequent passages similarly, Matt 22:19; 25:30 speak of *offering* money contributions (so also Acts 8:18). In Matt 2:11 προσφέρω refers to the *offering* of gifts of adoration. Since Matthew repeats this same syntagma in 5:23, 24 and subsequently in 8:4 (in a redactional expan-

sion of Mark 1:44 par. Luke 5:14), and since in neither instance is a priest addressed, here too the vb. refers not to the sacrificial offering itself, but rather "can only refer to the handing of the offering to the priest" (Weiss 66, *contra* Jeremias 103f.; cf. already Lev 8:18, 22 and *passim*). Luke 23:36 (par. John 19:29) refers to the *offering* of vinegar at the crucifixion in a manner recalling the use of προσφέρω from Hippocrates and Plato onward of both offering food and drink and, reflexively, *taking* medicine.

4. Acts 7:42, citing an altered form of Amos 5:25, picks up the cultic usage influenced by the LXX (above all in Leviticus, Numbers, Ezekiel 43ff. [over 80 occurrences, though never, significantly, in Philo]), where it refers to presentation of offerings: In the desert Israel brought offerings not to God, but to "the host of heaven." In Acts 21:26 Paul pays the expenses of poor Nazarites for the *offering* of a sacrifice. Abel, as the first witness of the fundamental virtue of steadfastness and hope, *offered* God a sacrifice oriented toward the new aeon (Heb 11:4); the testing of Abraham at the *offering* of Isaac was similarly exemplary because of the same basic virtue (11:17a; pf. of abiding example; see BDF §342.5), since he *was prepared to offer* his only son as a sacrifice (11:17b: conative impf.).

Over against these offerings stand the old regular *burnt offerings* of the Levites, which are oriented toward the old aeon and for which Hebrews uses προσφέρω 11 times (with what is offered indicated in 5:1; 8:3a, b, 4; 9:7, 9; 10:1, 8, 11; anaphoric absolute in 5:3; 10:2). The reference to sin in 5:1, 3; 9:7 (ὑπέρ or περί with gen.; so also with synonym → ἀναφέρω in 7:27) is not final ("for removal, atonement") but causal ("because of the presence of" [or final "to reveal sins"]), since according to the whole disposition of Hebrews (10:1-4, 11; cf. 7:11, 18; 9:8-10) atonement of sins was not actually accomplished during the old aeon; sacrifice was intended rather to create consciousness of sin.

Hence the old sacrificial service is countered with increasing intensity by use of προσφέρω (5 times) of Jesus' *self-offering* as that which discloses access to the new aeon and as the only offering that effects atonement (2:16f.; 9:15; cf. 9:14, 25, 28; 10:12; hence 5:7 is also thinking specifically of Jesus' death, since every sacrificial slaughtering was accompanied constitutively by prayers; in Sir 46:16 any sacrificial activity already counts as an expression of prayer; this semantic element of the hopeful request for the end of the old aeon and the establishment of the new is thus also seen in Hebrews 9–10, as in 7:27b; 11:4, 17).

The anti-Judaism of Hebrews is eclipsed only by the bitter insinuation in John 16:2: In a unique and erroneous statement it asserts that the Jews believed they were *offering* service to God with the feared and deadly persecutions of Christians following their expulsion from synagogues.

W. Schenk

προσφιλής, 2 *prosphilēs* pleasing, lovely*

Phil 4:8: ὅσα προσφιλῆ, ὅσα εὔφημα, "whatever is *lovely,* whatever is gracious," concluding a series of positive predicates that are to characterize the behavior of the Church; cf. also *Diog.* 11:2.

προσφορά, ᾶς, ἡ *prosphora* sacrificial offering/ gift*

1. Occurrences in the NT — 2. Sacrificial offering — 3. Christological usage

Lit.: → προσφέρω.

Of the 9 NT occurrences 5 are in Hebrews 10. The term also occurs twice in Acts and once each in Romans and Ephesians. It occurs 14 times in the LXX (9 of those in Sirach), always, except in 1 Esdr 5:51; Sir 46:16, as *nomen actionis:* "sacrificial gift."

2. In Rom 15:16, in a unique ad hoc metaphor, Paul speaks of himself as priest of the Messiah Jesus, and describes his leading the Gentiles to God as his *offering* (the Gentiles themselves are not the offering), a statement that, considering that the Jewish temple was still standing, signified a clear separation. In contrast, in Acts 21:26 Luke has Paul follow the advice of James and the elders and make an *offering* in the temple (cognate acc. as in Dan 4:34), which is emphatically underscored by the reminder in 24:17 *(nomen actionis: sacrificial offerings)*.

3. The redundant style of Ephesians christologically addends to the old, noncultic formula of self-sacrifice for the death of Jesus (Gal 2:20) the hendiadys of the atonement cult as *offering* and sacrifice (προσφορά καὶ θυσία). Heb 10:5, 8 (pl.) takes the same hendiadys from Ps 39:7 LXX and has Jesus utter it when he comes into the old aeon, indicating that the levitical *burnt offerings (nomen actionis)* were not at all commensurate with God's salvation plan. Only Jesus' unique *self-offering* accomplishes this (10:10, 14): He gives up his body as that part of the old aeon taken on in his incarnation, thus giving up the old aeon itself and opening up access to the new age. The summary exegetical conclusion in 10:18 asserts that there can be no more *sin offerings;* this is a fundamental statement and refers both to levitical offerings—which according to the disposition of Hebrews in any case serve only to elicit a consciousness of sin and not at all to atone for sin—and to the exclusion of any future possibility of atonement, since only Jesus' own self-offering *as* access to the new aeon has effected such atonement.

W. Schenk

προσφωνέω *prosphōneō* call out; call to oneself*

This vb. occurs 7 times in the NT. *To call to,* with dat.: Matt 11:16: τοῖς ἑτέροις; par. Luke 7:32: ἀλλήλοις; Luke 23:20: αὐτοῖς (absolute in TR); Acts 22:2: ὅτι τῇ Ἑβραΐδι διαλέκτῳ προσεφώνει αὐτοῖς; without dat. in 21:40. *Call to oneself,* with acc.: Luke 6:13; 13:12; Acts 11:2 D.

προσχαίρω *proschairō* be glad

Mark 9:15 D it: προσχαίροντες in place of προστρέχοντες.

πρόσχυσις, εως, ἡ *proschysis* sprinkling; smearing*

Heb 11:28: ἡ πρόσχυσις τοῦ αἵματος, "the *sprinkling* [of the doorposts and lintel] with the blood [of the Passover lamb]," of the exodus event (Exod 12:7, 13f., 22ff.). This noun does not occur in the LXX; the vb. προσχέω occurs only in reference to the sprinkling of the altar with the blood of the sacrifice (Exod 24:6; 29:16, and *passim*).

προσψαύω *prospsauō* touch*

Luke 11:46, of the teachers of the law who load people with heavy burdens: ἑνὶ τῶν δακτύλων ὑμῶν οὐ προσψαύετε τοῖς φορτίοις, "and you yourselves do not *touch* the burdens with one of your fingers."

προσωπολημπτέω *prosōpolēmpteō* judge a person by appearances*

This vb. is documented only in Christian writers and is used of prejudicial partiality for the greater at the expense of the lesser. Absolute in Jas 2:9: εἰ δὲ προσωπολημπτεῖτε, ἁμαρτίαν ἐργάζεσθε. Cf. esp. Lev 19:15: οὐ λήμψῃ πρόσωπον πτωχοῦ οὐδὲ θαυμάσεις πρόσωπον δυνάστου. Cf. further λαμβάνω πρόσωπον in Luke 20:21; Gal 2:6; *Barn.* 19:4; *Did.* 4:3; similarly Gen 19:21; Deut 1:17; 10:17; 16:19; Sir 35:13; Mark 12:14 par. Matt 22:16; Jude 16; → προσωπολημψία. E. Lohse, *TDNT* VI, 780f.

προσωπολήμπτης, ου, ὁ *prosōpolēmptēs* one who shows partiality or judges according to appearances*

Acts 10:34: οὐκ ἔστιν προσωπολήμπτης ὁ θεός, "God shows no partiality," i.e., does not give Jews precedence over Gentiles; cf. Deut 10:17; Rom 2:11; → προσωπολημψία.

προσωπολημψία, ας, ἡ *prosōpolēmpsia* partiality*

1. Occurrences in the NT — 2. Field of meaning; combinations and traditions — 3. Typical genres — 4. Characteristics of NT usage

Lit.: → πρόσωπον.

1. Προσωπολημψία occurs 4 times in the NT: Rom 2:11; Eph 6:9; Col 3:25; Jas 2:1.

2. The phrase πρόσωπον λαμβάνω (cf. LXX Ps 81:2; Sir 4:22; 35:13; Mal 1:8) and words derived from it— προσωπολημψία, → προσωπολημπτέω, → προσωπολήμπτης, and → ἀπροσωπολήμπτως—are modeled after Heb. *nāśā' pānîm* (lift up, as a sign of appreciation, the face of one who has prostrated himself in greeting). The derived words are documented only in Christian writings (and in *T. Job* 4:8: ἀπροσωπόλημπτος; 43:13: προσωπολημψία). Together with the phrases λαμβάνω (βλέπω, θαυμάζω) πρόσωπον (Matt 22:16; Mark 12:14; Luke 20:21; Gal 2:6; Jude 16) they constitute the heart of a semantic field, which in what follows will be presented according to its various forms and typical associations (→ 3).

The action described by this word group is always regarded negatively. Warnings are given against it, and it is not considered a factor in God's judgment (cf. the negative statements in *m. 'Abot* 4:22; *Jub.* 33:18). The origin of the idea is the warning against partiality in judgment (Lev 19:15; Mal 2:9; Sir 4:22, 27; *Did.* 4:3; *Barn.* 19:4; Pol. *Phil.* 6:1). Luke 20:21 uses it fig. of the teacher's response (of partiality in one's behavior toward people in general: *1 Clem.* 1:3; cf. 1 Tim 5:21f.).

When God's judgment is spoken of (2 Chr 19:6f. speaks of human judgment in the light of divine judgment), fixed combinations of terms are used:

a) With "truly/truth" (*1 Enoch* 63:8; *T. Job* 4:8-11; 43:13; 2 Esdr 4:35-39), "righteous" (*Jub.* 5:16; 21:4; *T. Job* 43:13; 4:8-11; *2 Bar.* 44:4; 2 Esdr 4:38f.; *Pss. Sol.* 2:17f.; *Did.* 4:3), "judge" (*Pss. Sol.* 2:17f.; *Jub.* 5:16; 33:18; *Barn.* 4:12; *Did.* 4:3), "(righteous) judgment" (*2 Enoch* 46:3 [longer recension]; *Apoc. Paul* 14; *Jub.* 21:4; *2 Bar.* 13:8), "deeds/works" (*1 Enoch* 63:8; Rom 2:10f.; Acts 10:34; *Barn.* 4:12), "reward according to works" (*T. Job* 4:8; Sir 35:13, 15; *Pss. Sol.* 2:16-18; Ethiopic 2 Esdras [G. Dillman, *Veteris Testamenti Aithiopici* V, 182]; Rom 2:10f.; 1 Pet 1:17; *Apoc. Paul* 14; Syriac *Hist. Imag.* 205; Arabic [Karshuni] *Apocalypse of Peter* [ed. A. Mingana, 1931] II, 216), "each/all" (*Jub.* 5:16; 1 Pet 1:17; *Barn.* 4:12; *Jub.* 21:4; *T. Job* 43:13), "sins" (*1 Enoch* 63:8; *Pss. Sol.* 2:16-18), "receive for what one has done" (Col 3:24f.; *Barn.* 4:12).

b) Parallel associations occurring often: acceptance of bribes (Deut 10:17; 2 Chr 19:7; *Jub.* 5:16; 21:4; 33:18;

Sir 35:14f.; *m. 'Abot* 4:22), delay (*1 Enoch* 63:8), forgetting (*m. 'Abot* 4:22), sacrifice (Sir 35:15; *Jub.* 33:13, 18; Syriac *Hist. Imag.* 205), remorse and intercession (Arabic *Apocryphal Gospel of John* [ed. G. Galbiati, 1957] 37:104), concealment (*2 Enoch* 46:3), God's intervention for widows or orphans or even the suspension of these privileges (Sir 35:15-17).

c) The suspension of social distinctions is typical: between great and small (*Jub.* 5:15), slaves and free (Col 3:24f.; Eph 6:8f.; Syriac *Hist. Imag.* 205), poor and rich (inscription from the tomb of Petosiris I: F. W. von Bissing, *Altägyptische Lebensweisheit* [1955] 147f.; Ethiopic 2 Esdras V, 182; Jas 2:1, 9; Syriac *Hist. Imag.* 205), lesser and higher placed (Lev 19:15; inscription from the tomb of Petosiris III: E. Otto, *Die biographischen Inschriften der ägyptischen Spätzeit* [1954] 181), and Jews and Gentiles (Rom 2:10f.; Acts 10:34).

3. Typical genres are:
a) Enumeration of attributes of God in the style of ecphrasis (Deut 10:17; Sir 35:13ff.; *T. Job 43:13; m. 'Abot* 4:22; *Jub.* 21:4; Acts 10:34; cf. *Apostolic Constitutions* vii.35),

b) portrayals of God's historical judgments (*Bib. Ant.* 20:4; Sir 35:15; *Jub.* 5:13-16; 21:4; 30:16; 33:18; *T. Job* 4:8; *2 Bar.* 44:4ff.; 13:9f.; *Pss. Sol.* 2:17f.),

c) portrayals of God's eschatological judgment (*2 Enoch* 46:3; 1 Pet 1:17; *Barn.* 4:12; *T. Job* 4:8; Arabic *Apocryphal Gospel of John* 37:104; Arabic [Karshuni] *Apocalypse of Peter* II, 216), whereby two groups are distinguished (Rom 2:9-11; *Barn.* 4:12),

d) portrayals of individual judgment (*Apoc. Paul* 14),

e) motivation of individual exhortations (Sir 35:6-15; *Jub.* 30:16; 33:18; Col 3:24f.; Eph 6:8f.; *Barn.* 4:12),

f) (eschatological) admonitions or as titles of parenetic texts or testaments (*Jub.* 21:4; *2 Bar.* 44:4ff.; 1 Pet 1:17; *Bib. Ant.* 20:4; Arabic *Apocryphal Gospel of John* 37:104), and

g) first-person address by the condemned (*1 Enoch* 63:8).

4. NT usage is characterized by:
a) circumlocution by means of synonymous phrases for just compensation (Col 3:25 [cf. 3:24; 4:1]; Eph 6:9 [cf. v. 8]) and

b) transferal of statements originally referring to God's judgment onto events of the mission or the Church (Gal 2:6: the standard for Paul's evaluation of the Jerusalem authorities; Acts 10:34: the reason for admitting Gentiles), which shows that God's ultimate standards are already being applied in the present. K. Berger

πρόσωπον, ου, τό *prosōpon* surface, face

1. NT occurrences and general usage — 2. "Visible appearance" — 3. "Fall on one's face" — 4. Transfiguration of one's face — 5. Christ's face — 6. Prep. phrases — 7. "See someone's face"

Lit.: E. LOHSE, *TDNT* VI, 768-80, esp. 768. — F. NÖTSCHER and T. KLAUSER, *RAC* I, 437-40. — L. VON ROMPAY, "The Rendering of πρόσωπον λαμβάνειν and Related Expressions in the Early Oriental Versions of the NT," *OBL* 6-7 (1975/76) 569-77. — O. WISCHMEYER, *Der höchste Weg. Das 13. Kapitel des 1. Korintherbriefs* (1981), 136f., 170. — For further bibliography see *TWNT* X, 1250.

1. Πρόσωπον occurs 76 times in the NT; it does not occur in John and Romans, but is found with striking frequency in 2 Corinthians (12 occurrences) and once in Hebrews. In several occurrences it refers simply to the earth's *surface* (Luke 21:35; Acts 17:26) or to the human *face* (Matt 6:16f.; 26:67; Mark 14:65; Jas 1:23).

2. The visible and given world is not unproblematic: It needs to be interpreted and evaluated. E.g., one must interpret the sky (Matt 16:3; Luke 12:56). Or one counters the merely external but obvious world with the dimension that, though invisible, is nonetheless more valuable and, indeed, alone decisive (2 Cor 10:1, 7; the contrast of outer vs. inner [= heart] is seen in 1 Thess 2:17a; 2 Cor 5:12).

3. The fixed phrase "fall on one's *face*" is used of reaction to epiphanies (Luke 5:12; 17:16; Matt 17:6; 26:39; 1 Cor 14:25: the experience of God's presence in the congregation; Luke 24:5: at the discovery of the empty tomb) or the vision of God's throne (Rev 7:11; 11:16). Here and in what follows it is in a person's face that the relationship between two parties expresses itself in a decisive way.

4. In 2 Corinthians 3, as in Exod 34:30 and broader Jewish tradition, the transfiguration of Moses' face is discussed. According to Paul, however, Moses did not conceal his face to save Israel from having to see its brightness and splendor, but rather to prevent the transitory nature of that splendor from being revealed (3:7, 13). But just as Israel could not see Moses, so also could it not subsequently see Scripture properly, though now admittedly because it carries a veil over its own mind (3:15). For Christians, however, that veil has fallen, and they can see the splendor and are thus themselves transformed.

This tradition of the transfigured face is expanded beyond Moses: The face of God's emissaries is transfigured as they execute their commission, which is viewed as a sign of legitimacy (Stephen in Acts 6:15; Jesus in Matt 17:2; Luke 9:29; Daniel in Hippolytus *In Dan.* iii.7.5; Abraham in Philo *Virt.* 217; Hananiah in Syriac *Acts of Philip* [ed. W. Wright, 1871/1968] 84; cf. *Acts of Paul and Thecla* 3). The same is also applied to angels (Rev 10:1).

5. 2 Corinthians offers a different understanding of the face of Christ. As God's likeness, Christ possesses glory (4:4, 6); this glory is mediated in the gospel or as knowledge in the sense of illumination to human beings; it penetrates into hearts, and does so ἐν προσώπῳ Χρισ-

τοῦ, i.e., Christ is the center of this event, the decisive partner in relationship to God and human beings. Hence Paul can also say that he has forgiven the congregation ἐν προσώπῳ Χριστοῦ (2:10).

6. In prep. phrases the *face* is the central factor of a scene taking place within its horizon. Here there is a relationship between the turning of the face and the direction of an action: The action turns away from that center or takes place "before it": In every case the face itself is decisive for the locative orientation of the action. The authority of the person from whose perspective or toward whom an activity is oriented is thus established spatially and effective. Thus quite straightforwardly in Acts 5:41; 7:45. Esp., however:

a) Disaster proceeds outward from the Lord's *presence (= face):* 2 Thess 1:9; 1 Pet 3:12; Rev 6:16.

b) One flees from another's *presence* because one expects disaster from the turning of the face (and thus from the direction of the gaze: Rev 12:14; 6:16; cf. also Acts 7:45). Such flight from someone's presence can thus be the simple reaction to superior power (Rev 20:11).

c) The coming of salvation from God's *presence* is a metaphor for the origin of a dynamic process or subject-object relationship effected or prompted by God (Acts 3:20, though not to be understood in the sense of any preexistence of salvation).

d) Authoritative commissioning occurs "before one's face" (in quotations: Mark 1:2 par.; elsewhere: Luke 9:52; 10:1; "going before the Lord" in Luke 1:76 is to be interpreted similarly). In Acts 13:24 ("before the *presence /face* of his coming") Luke may have misunderstood a Semitism.

e) The direction that the *face* is turned indicates the direction of the central figure itself (Luke 9:51, 53; cf. 2 Sam 17:11).

f) What occurs κατὰ πρόσωπον, "in the presence of (someone)," is clear, open, and obviously visible so that that person can take notice of it (Luke 2:31). What is public is spoken of in this way (Gal 2:11; 2 Cor 8:24) frequently with directly forensic implications (Acts 3:13; 25:16; 2 Cor 8:24 with εἰς).

g) In 2 Cor 1:11 ἐκ προσώπων refers to the origin of an action. Despite the pl. form (which carries particular rhetorical weight here), this is not a matter of "persons" (πρόσωπον acquires this meaning only gradually during the course of the history of dogma, and above all at the beginning of the 19th cent. the concept of person is given its present connotations); the reference is, rather, to the many who are the origin or source of gratitude (here, too, it is a matter of the direction or disposition of various— in this case many—centers).

7. To "see" someone's face means to have contact with that person. The decisive poles of relationship

(countenance and seeing) thus metaphorically represent the entire relationship (so in Acts 20:25, 38; visit: 1 Thess 2:17; 3:10; not yet "known": Gal 1:22; Col 2:1). This also refers to contact with God either through the cult or by eschatological fellowship with God:

a) The cultic sense (Isa 1:12; Pss 11:7; 16:11; 17:15; 24:6; 42:3; 95:2; *y. Ḥag.* 1.76a.35; *Deut. Rab.* 7:2 [204a]; rabbinic literature often avoids anthropomorphism by altering this to "allow his presence/face to be seen") is seen in Heb 9:24 (the high priest Christ intercedes before God) and probably also in Matt 18:10 (the contact the "little ones'" angels have with God is probably to be understood as intercession; cf. also 2 Esdr 7:98; *Midr. Ps.* 11:7; *2 Enoch* 21:1; 22:6).

b) Eschatological fellowship with God is, admittedly, also thought of in terms of the cult (in the heavenly sanctuary: *Jub.* 1:28; *Sib. Or.* v.426f.; *2 Enoch* 67:2; 2 Esdr 7:87, 91, 98; *T. Zeb.* 9:8; *b. Menaḥ.* 43b; *b. Soṭa* 42a; *b. B. Bat.* 10a). This sense is intended in the NT in 1 Cor 13:12, which portrays the entire relationship to God ("face to face") such that both "poles" of contact are turned toward one another (the tr. "person to person" implies more than is intended). One cannot differentiate Rev 22:4 (seeing God's *face*) from 1 Cor 13:12 by suggesting that in the former God is an object, while in the latter Paul is concerned merely with modality; this is to think too much from a modern perspective; both senses are always implied together.   K. Berger

προτάσσω *protassō* predetermine, determine beforehand

Acts 17:26 D* pc bo: προτεταγμένοι καιροί in place of προστεταγμένοι καιροί (→ προστάσσω).

προτείνω *proteinō* stretch out, extend*

Acts 22:25, of Paul, whom they "stretched out [and bound to the whipping post or bench] with thongs" like a criminal (ὡς προέτειναν αὐτὸν τοῖς ἱμᾶσιν [final dative]). → ἱμάς.

πρότερος, 3 *proteros* earlier*

1. NT occurrences and usage — 2. The Fourth Gospel — 3. The Pauline corpus — 4. Hebrews — 5. 1 Pet 1:14

Lit.: BAGD s.v. — BDF §62.

1. Πρότερος occurs in the NT only in the temporal sense. It appears in Eph 4:22 as a fem. adj. ("the *former* manner of life"). In 10 other occurrences neut. πρότερον is an adv. meaning *earlier, previously, before* (though used as an adj. in Heb 10:32: "the *former* days"; 1 Pet 1:14: "your *former* desires"); both with art. (John 6:62; 7:50; 9:8; Gal 4:13; 1 Tim 1:13) and anarthrous (2 Cor

1:15; Heb 4:6; 7:27; 10:32; 1 Pet 1:14). Πρότερος does not occur in the Synoptic Gospels, Acts, or Revelation, perhaps because the older meaning of πρότερος ("the first of two") was taken over by → πρῶτος (so, e.g., Matt 21:28; Rev 20:5; 21:1). Nonetheless, πρότερος as an adjectivally intensified adv. in the NT has not entirely lost its reference to temporal contrast, though such contrast must for the most part be inferred from the context.

2. The Fourth Gospel uses πρότερος consistently as an articular adv. In the Son of man saying in John 6:62 *before* refers to the Christ's preexistence, mentioned here in the context of his ascension. 7:50 refers to Nicodemus, who has already sought out Jesus *(once) before*. In 9:8 τὸ πρότερον means *formerly/at one time*.

3. The adv. appears with the art. in Gal 4:13 and refers there to Paul's preaching of the gospel *the first time*. In 2 Cor 1:15 the adv. is anarthrous; Paul changed his travel itinerary: He *first/earlier* wanted to come to the addressees, but "then" went to Macedonia. Πρότερος appears as an adj. (→ 1) in the post-Pauline Eph 4:22, which calls for a radical change from one's *"former* manner of life" (v. 22) corresponding to the putting on of the new nature (v. 24). In 1 Tim 1:13 πρότερος stands in "Paul's confession": "though I *formerly* blasphemed him [i.e., Christ]."

4. Hebrews uses the adv. consistently without the art. (4:6; 7:27; 10:32). The temporal contrast comes to expression esp. in 7:27: The high priests brought sacrifices *first* for their own sins and "then" for those of the people.

5. 1 Pet 1:14 uses the adv. without the art. The admonition seeks to erase the earlier ignorance in order to address the necessary present yearning for salvation of Christians (vv. 15f.). Here πρότερον maintains the element of temporal tension.

H. Langkammer

προτίθεμαι *protithemai* display/exhibit publicly; plan, determine beforehand*

This term is used only in the mid. in the NT. Rom 3:25 contains a formulation probably borrowed by Paul referring to Christ's atoning death (ὃν προέθετο ὁ θεὸς ἱλαστήριον). The context (cf. 3:21) addresses God's activity in Christ, and thus the translation suggested is "whom God put forward/displayed as an expiation by his blood." This is also supported by the construction of the relative clause with double acc. but without any complementary vb., such as would be required by a (linguistically possible) statement about divine predetermination; cf. C. Maurer, *TDNT* VIII, 165f.; E. Käsemann, *Rom* (Eng. tr., 1980) ad loc.; D. Zeller, *TP* 43 (1968) 57f. This corresponds to the cultic use of προτίθεμαι in the LXX to refer to the public display of the "bread of presentation," cf. Exod 29:23; 40:4; see U. Wilckens, *Rom*

(EKKNT) I, ad loc. with n.537; cf. also the subst. → πρόθεσις.

In Rom 1:13 προτίθεμαι refers to Paul's intentions (πολλάκις προεθέμην ἐλθεῖν); in Eph 1:9 it refers to God's activity on behalf of the faithful, the purpose that he *determined beforehand* (ἣν προέθετο ἐν αὐτῷ, cf. vv. 5, 11; cf. also *Diog.* 9:2. C. Maurer, *TDNT* VIII, 164-67; P. Jacobs and H. Krienke, *DNTT* I, 696f.

προτρέπομαι *protrepomai* encourage, challenge, urge*

Absolute in Acts 18:27: προτρεψάμενοι . . . ἔγραψαν, either "they encouraged [Apollos] and wrote . . ." or "they wrote to the disciples [in Corinth], *encouraging* them to receive him [Apollos]." The first tr. would require αὐτόν as the obj. of προτρέπομαι; cf. esp. Spicq, *Notes* II, 762-64, who refers to the "official" character of the word in certain invitations.

προτρέχω *protrechō* run ahead*

Luke 19:4, of Zacchaeus: προδραμὼν εἰς τὸ ἔμπροσθεν, "he *ran on ahead*"; John 20:4, of the "other disciple": προέδραμεν τάχιον τοῦ Πέτρου, he *"outran* Peter," i.e., he "passed" him.

προϋπάρχω *proÿparchō* exist beforehand*

Luke 23:12, of Herod (Antipas) and Pilate, who "before this [the trial of Jesus] *had been*" at enmity with each other" (προϋπῆρχον); Acts 8:9, of Simon (the magician): προϋπῆρχεν . . . μαγεύων, "who had *previously* practiced magic."

πρόφασις, εως, ἡ *prophasis* pretext, excuse; (valid) excuse*

There are 6 occurrences in the NT, 5 of them dat. προφάσει (1 Thess 2:5 with ἐν): *by subterfuge, for deception* (Mark 12:40 par. Luke 20:47/Matt 23:14 v.l.; Acts 27:30, with ὡς, "as if," "under pretense"; Phil 1:18, in contrast to ἀληθείᾳ; 1 Thess 2:5: ἐν προφάσει πλεονεξίας, "under a *cloak/pretense* for greed"). In John 15:22: *excuse/basis for excuse*. BAGD s.v.; C. Schäublin, *MH* 28 (1971) 133-44; Spicq, *Notes* II, 765-67.

προφέρω *propherō* produce, bring out*

Luke 6:45 (bis): προφέρει τὸ ἀγαθόν/τὸ πονηρόν, what is in the heart comes forth.

προφητεία, ας, ἡ *prophēteia* prophetic activity; gift of prophecy; prophecy
→ προφητεύω.

προφητεύω *prophēteuō* prophesy

προφητεία, ας, ἡ *prophēteia* prophetic activity; gift of prophecy; prophecy

1. Occurrences in the NT and basic meaning — 2. Shades of meaning.

Lit.: → προφήτης; further: N. BROX, "Προφητεία im ersten Timotheusbrief," *BZ* 20 (1976) 229-32.

1. The vb. occurs 11 times in Paul (all in 1 Corinthians), 9 times in the Gospels, 4 times in Acts, twice in Revelation, and in 1 Pet 1:10 and Jude 14. The noun occurs 7 times in Paul, 7 times in Revelation, twice each in 1 Timothy and 2 Peter, and in the Gospels only in Matt 13:14. Of these 28 and 19 occurrences, 19 and 16 refer to the activity of NT prophetic figures, the others to OT prophetic figures. The basic meaning is that of prophetic activity, though in individual instances it can acquire various shades of meaning.

2. The vb. has the meaning *prophesy,* i.e., proclaim some future event before its occurrence with its salvation-historical implications, with the following subjects: Isaiah in Mark 7:6 par. Matt 15:7; "all the prophets and the law" in Matt 11:13; the OT prophets in 1 Pet 1:10 (see Brox, *1 Pet* [EKKNT] 69), Enoch in Jude 14, Zechariah in Luke 1:67, the high priest in John 11:51, John in Rev 10:11.

Paul uses the noun of *the gift* (charism, Rom 12:6) *of prophecy* (1 Thess 5:20; 1 Cor 12:10; 13:2, 8) or *prophetic utterance* (1 Cor 14:6, 22). Such prophetic activity serves the "upbuilding, encouragement, and consolation" of the congregation (1 Cor 14:3, 31).

In Mark 14:65 par. imv. προφήτευσον is used to challenge Jesus to guess who has struck him. The deeper meaning is that Jesus, who in the opinion of his adversaries falsely claims prophetic authority, is challenged by them to act as a prophet (Schneider 101f.; Schnider 157f.).

Matt 7:22 castigates prophets who prophesy in Jesus' name without keeping God's law. In Acts, Luke attributes prophetic powers to the church in Jerusalem (2:17, 18), to John's disciples in Ephesus (19:6), and to Philip's daughters (21:9).

According to 1 Tim 1:18; 4:14 the bestowal of ecclesiastical office is accompanied by prophetic utterances by Church prophets (Brox, *Pastoralbriefen* ad loc.). 2 Pet 1:20f. admonishes the readers not to interpret scriptural prophecy individually. Revelation characterizes its author's activity as prophetic (19:10) and his work as a book of prophecy (1:3; 22:7, 10, 18, 19).   F. Schnider

προφήτης, ου, ὁ *prophētēs* prophet

1. NT occurrences — 2. OT prophets in the NT — 3. John the Baptist — 4. Jesus — 5. Early Christian prophets

Lit.: D. E. AUNE, *Prophecy in Early Christianity and the Ancient Mediterranean World* (1983). — *idem,* "The Use of προφήτης in Josephus," *JBL* 101 (1982) 419-21. — K. BERGER, "Zu den sogenannten Sätzen heiligen Rechts," *NTS* 17 (1970/71) 10-40. — *idem,* "Die sogennanten 'Sätze heiligen Rechts' im NT," *TZ* 28 (1972) 305-30. — *idem, Die Auferstehung des Propheten und die Erhöhung des Menschensohnes* (SUNT 13, 1976). — N. BROX, *Die Pastoralbriefe* (RNT 7, 1969) 118, 180. — *idem, 1 Pet* (EKKNT, 1979) 69. — BULTMANN, *History* 125-30. — U. BUSSE, *Die Wunder des Propheten Jesus. Die Rezeption, Komposition und Interpretation der Wundertradition im Evangelium des Lukas* (FzB 24, 1977). — H. VON CAMPEN-HAUSEN, *Ecclesiastical Authority and Spiritual Power in the Church of the First Three Centuries* (1969). — F. CHRIST, *Jesus Sophia* (ATANT 57, 1970). — E. COTHENET, *DBS* VIII, 1222-1337. — G. DAUTZENBERG, *Urchristliche Prophetie. Ihre Erforschung, ihre Voraussetzung im Judentum und ihre Struktur im ersten Korintherbrief* (BWANT 104, 1975). — *idem,* "Zur urchristlichen Prophetie," *BZ* 22 (1978) 125-32. — G. FRIEDRICH, *TDNT* VI, 828-61. — F. GILS, *Jésus Prophète d'après les Évangiles Synoptiques* (1957). — H. GREEVEN, "Propheten, Lehrer, Vorsteher bei Paulus," *ZNW* 44 (1952/53) 1-43. — HAHN, *Titles* 352-88. — HARNACK, *Mission,* I, 408-17. — G. F. HAWTHORNE, "The Role of Christian Prophets in the Gospel Tradition," FS Ellis 119-33. — M. HENGEL, *The Charismatic Leader and His Followers* (1981). — D. HILL, *NT Prophecy* (1979). — E. KÄSEMANN, *NT Questions of Today* (1969) 67-107. — W. A. MEEKS, *The Prophet-King* (1967). — U. MAUSER, *Gottesbild und Menschwerdung. Eine Untersuchung zur Einheit des A und NT* (1971). — R. MEYER, *TDNT* VI, 812-28. — A. MORENO, "Apóstoles y profetas (1 Co 12,28)," *La vie de la Parole* (FS P. Grelot, 1987) 381-95. — U. B. MÜLLER, *Prophetie und Predigt im NT. Formgeschichtliche Untersuchungen zur urchristlichen Prophetie* (SNT 10, 1975). — *idem,* "Vision und Botschaft. Erwägungen zur prophetischen Struktur der Verkündigung Jesu," *ZTK* 74 (1977) 416-48. — F. MUSSNER, "Ursprünge und Entfaltung der neutestamentlichen Sohneschristologie," *Grundfragen der Christologie heute* (QD 72, 1975) 77-113. — G. NEBE, *Prophetische Züge im Bilde Jesu bei Lukas* (BWANT 127, 1989). — F. NEUGEBAUER, "Geistsprüche und Jesuslogien," *ZNW* 53 (1962) 218-28. — J. PANAGOPOULOS, ed., *Prophetic Vocation in the NT and Today* (NovTSup 45, 1977). — H. PATSCH, "Die Prophetie des Agabus," *TZ* 28 (1972) 228-32. — C. PERROT, " 'Un prophète comme l'un des prophètes' (Mc 6:15)," *De la Tôrah au Messie* (FS H. Cazelles, 1981) 417-23. — W. ROTH-FUCHS, *Die Erfüllungszitate des Matthäus* (1969). — A. SATAKE, *Die Gemeindeordnung in der Johannesapokalypse* (WMANT 21, 1966). — P. SCHÄFER, *Die Vorstellung vom heiligen Geist in der rabbinischen Literatur* (SANT 28, 1972). — R. SCHNACK-ENBURG, "Die Erwartung des 'Propheten' nach dem NT und den Qumran-Texten," *SE* I, 622-39. — G. SCHNEIDER, *Verleugnung, Verspottung und Verhör Jesu nach Lk 22,54-71* (SANT 22, 1969) 101f. — F. SCHNIDER, *Jesus der Prophet* (OBO 2, 1973). — H. SCHÜRMANN, "Die Symbolhandlungen Jesu als eschatologische Erfüllungszeichen," *BibLeb* 11 (1970) 29-41, 73-78. — E. SCHWEIZER, *Church Order in the NT* (1961). — *idem,* "Observance of the Law and Charismatic Activity in Matthew," *NTS* 16 (1969/70) 213-30. — O. H. STECK, *Israel und das gewaltsame Geschick der Propheten* (WMANT 23, 1967). — K. STEN-DAHL, *The School of St. Matthew and Its Use of the OT* (²1967). — G. STRECKER, *Der Weg der Gerechtigkeit* (FRLANT 82,

[3]1971). — W. TRILLING, "Die Täufertradition bei Matthäus," *BZ* 3 (1959) 271-89. — For further bibliography see *TWNT* X, 1250-54.

1. Προφήτης occurs 144 times in the NT, most frequently in Luke-Acts (29 occurrences in the Gospel, 30 in Acts) and Matthew (37 occurrences). It occurs 14 times in John, 10 times in Paul (Romans, 1 Corinthians, and 1 Thessalonians), 8 times in Revelation, and 6 times in Mark. It is also found in isolated instances in Ephesians, Titus, Hebrews, James, and 1–2 Peter. Of the 144 occurrences, 123 refer to OT prophets and 21 to NT prophets.

2. Among the OT prophets Isaiah, Jeremiah, Daniel, Joel, and Jonah are mentioned by name in the NT. The writings of Hosea, Amos, Micah, Habakkuk, and Zechariah are mentioned without the prophet's name (cf. Friedrich 831f.). Samuel (Acts 3:24), David (2:30), Elisha (Luke 4:27), Balaam (2 Pet 2:16), and Anna (Luke 2:36: προφῆτις) are also identified in the NT as prophets. According to Titus 1:12 the Gentile poet Epimenides is a prophet of the Cretans.

As a rule the NT sees in the OT prophets persons through whom God spoke (διὰ στόματος πάντων τῶν προφητῶν, Acts 3:18; cf. v. 21). Some passages summarize the entire OT revelation with the formula "the law and the prophets" (Matt 5:17; 7:12; 11:13; 22:40; Luke 16:16; 24:27, 44; Rom 3:21, and *passim*). According to Heb 1:1 God spoke to the fathers ἐν τοῖς προφήταις; ἐν here is analogous to Heb. instrumental *b*[e]. The prophets are an instrument of God through whom he has revealed himself to mankind. The origin of prophecy is not human will; "but persons moved by the Holy Spirit spoke from God" (2 Pet 1:21). Nonetheless, prophecy, too, needs human inquiry. According to 1 Pet 1:10 the prophets themselves reflected in the spirit of the preexistent Christ on how their own prophecies revealed something of the Christ-event. The Son of God himself, however, finally made that prophetic word more sure (2 Pet 1:19).

The NT understands the prefix προ- in προφήτης not only instrumentally, but also temporally. The prophets predicted. God himself proclaimed the gospel beforehand through his prophets in the holy Scriptures (προ-επαγγέλλομαι, Rom 1:1f.; cf. 9:29; 2 Pet 3:2; Acts 3:18; 7:52; 1 Pet 1:11). The proclamation of all the prophets from Samuel onward directs itself toward the Christ-event (Acts 3:24), and in the foreground of those prophecies stand Christ's suffering, death, and resurrection (cf. Friedrich 833). Hence "from the law of Moses and the prophets" one can attempt to win the Jews to Jesus (Acts 28:23). The prophetic utterances are an authority that legitimizes and molds the proclamation.

Matt 1:22f.; 2:5f., 15, 17f., 23 and similar passages are known as formula quotations (Germ. *Reflexionszitate*) and are typically introduced by the citation formula "All this took place to fulfill . . ." (Stendahl 39ff.; Strecker 49ff.). Matthew relates certain details of Jesus' life and then reflects on them with an appropriate OT quotation. Since the prophets are recognized as an absolute authority, the OT quotation confirms that Jesus is the Messiah.

The NT often refers to the persecution and violent deaths of the prophets, usually to explain opposition to Jesus or his disciples (Mark 12:1-9 par.; Luke 6:22 par. Matt 5:12; Luke 11:47f. par. Matt 23:30f.; Luke 13:33f.; Acts 7:52; 1 Thess 2:15f.; Rom 11:3).

3. Q portrays John the Baptist (→ Ἰωάννης 2) as a prophet of the law in Israel (Luke 3:7-9 par. Matt 3:7, 10, 12). John's baptism proclaims that God's work regarding the messianic period has commenced (Luke 3:11 par. Matt 3:11). Accordingly, the preacher of penitence and prophet of the law, as precursor, is subordinated to Jesus (Luke 7:24-35 par. Matt 11:7-19). The Baptist's own stature ("more than a prophet," Luke 7:26 par. Matt 11:9) derives from that of Jesus, and thus in the Lukan childhood stories this precursor is called "the *prophet* of the Most High" (Luke 1:76), while Jesus is called "the Son of the Most High" (1:32, 35).

For Mark this prophet with the camel's hair coat and leather belt (Mark 1:6) is a precursor of and thus subordinated to Jesus (1:2-8), and his violent prophetic ending (6:14-29) anticipates Jesus' own fate (9:11-13; cf. also 11:32 with 12:12).

Although Matthew equates John with Jesus as regards proclamation and prophetic activity (cf. Matt 3:2 with 4:17 and 3:10 with 7:19; see Trilling), by identifying him with Elijah he does nonetheless also subordinate him to the Messiah Jesus (11:14; 17:13).

Luke illustrates the activity of the prophet John by portraying him as an itinerant preacher (Luke 3:3), a teacher of prayer (11:1), and a proclaimer of ethical demands (3:10-14). Considered from the perspective of salvation history, the Baptist belongs to the period of "the law and prophets" (16:16).

John denies explicitly that the Baptist is the Christ, Elijah, or the eschatological prophet (John 1:21, 25). He is "the voice of one crying in the wilderness" (1:23), and both he and his baptism witness for Jesus so that the people may believe in him (1:7f., 15, 19, 32-34; 3:26, 28f.; 5:33).

4. In the Synoptic tradition Jesus is described several times as a prophet, though the term is used of Jesus with various nuances.

According to Mark 6:14-16 par.; 8:27-30 par. the people considered Jesus a prophet (on prophetic expectations at the time of Jesus cf. Meyer; Schäfer). As suggested by the other opinions offered by the people (the Baptist raised, Elijah), this implies an eschatological prophetic figure (explicitly in Luke 9:8, 19; Matt 16:14; cf. Hahn, *Titles* 192; Schnider 181-87).

In Matt 21:11 the "Lord" (21:3), "king" (v. 5), and "Son of David" (v. 9) who enters Jerusalem is identified by the people as "the prophet Jesus from Nazareth of Galilee." According to Matt 21:46 the high priests and Pharisees fear the crowd "because they consider him a prophet."

Luke 7:16 understands Jesus' raising of the young man of Nain as the work of a prophet, and 7:39 considers Jesus' miraculous prescience to be a prophetic gift. Finally, 24:19 summarizes Jesus' entire presence and demeanor as that of "a prophet mighty in deed and word before God and all the people." All these statements reflect the Lukan understanding and conception of the eschatological prophet (cf. Busse).

In Acts Peter (3:22) and Stephen (7:37) portray the exalted Christ as the "prophet like Moses" promised in Deut 18:15, 18, which was interpreted by the Samaritans (cf. Meeks 250-54) and in Qumran (1QS 9:9-11; 4QTestim 5:8) as the promise of an eschatological prophet (cf. also *T. Levi* 8:15). Acts and probably also Mark 9:7 par. (ἀκούετε αὐτοῦ alludes to Deut 18:15 LXX: αὐτοῦ ἀκούσεσθε) see this promise as fulfilled in Jesus. In Stephen's speech the understanding of Jesus as "the prophet like Moses" also plays a part in the Christ-Moses typology, through which Jesus' activity for Israel and Israel's resistance to Jesus are underscored.

John employs the idea of the prophet Jesus as a conscious illustrative device in the service of his overall christological agenda. In the narrative of Jesus' encounter with the Samaritan woman (John 4:1-42) Jesus' prophetic gift of miraculous prescience (4:16-19) is the expression of a deeper knowledge to which he as God's self-revelation has access (4:26; cf. 7:28f.). Recognition of Jesus as a prophet thus anticipates his free self-revelation as the world's savior (4:26, 39-42). In John, Jesus' healing of the blind (9:1-41) is not only a powerful demonstration of the prophet Jesus (v. 17), but also the expression of his self-revelation as the light of the world (9:5, 39; cf. 8:12). In his own confession to Jesus the prophet even a man blind from birth can be summoned by Jesus (9:39) and led by Jesus' self-revelation (vv. 35-37) to believing adoration (v. 38). In the story of the miraculous feeding John shows that Jesus' powerful deed of increasing the bread does not lead the people to belief in him as the bread of life (6:35f.); rather, the people misunderstand the eschatological prophet and savior Jesus by seeking to use him for their own purposes (6:14f.; cf. 6:26).

Jesus' prophetic works challenge one to take a stand. It causes a rift in the people (John 7:40-43) and among the officials (vv. 50-52). Some consider Jesus a deceiver and false prophet (7:47; 8:48; 9:16, 24); others regard him as the prophet of God (4:19; 7:40; 9:17). Recognition

that Jesus is a prophet thus does not fully exhaust the mystery of his personality, though it does constitute a kind of incremental comprehension of who he is. Jesus not only fulfills the expectation of an eschatological prophet, but also the revelation of God in person, and as such eclipses all prophets of salvation history (8:48-58).

Along with the direct (titular) prophet-christology the NT also offers an indirect prophet-christology constituted by traditions assignable to the realm of prophetic tradition. These include baptism as the authorization of one's calling, criticism of the cult, instructions for one's followers, admonitions and cries of woe, symbolic actions, the gift of the Spirit, and the fate of violent death. Comparisons between the Jesus tradition and the OT prophets, however, also disclose the "limits" of any NT prophet-christology and its "opening" to a christology of the Son (cf. Hengel, Mauser, Mussner, Schnider).

5. According to the NT evidence various primitive Christian communities had persons described as *prophets*. In 1 Cor 12:28f.; Eph 4:11 they are mentioned with apostles and teachers, in Luke 11:49; Eph 2:20; 3:5 with apostles, in Acts 13:1 with teachers, and in Rev 18:20 with saints and apostles. This suggests that the prophets occupied a certain position in their communities. Because of the lack of source material, however, it is difficult to describe that position more closely.

Scholars have tried to gain more insight into NT prophecy first by identifying forms of prophetic speech (Germ. *prophetische Redegattungen*) in the NT and then by determining the settings in NT prophetic circles of these forms (cf. Bultmann, Käsemann, Satake, Müller [*Prophetie*]). But the method for determining concrete historical circumstances from prophetic speech forms has not yet been clarified and has accordingly led to quite different conceptions of primitive Christian prophecy (for criticisms see Neugebauer; Schweizer, "Observance" 226; Berger, "'Sätze'"; Cothenet 1285f.; Dautzenberg, *Prophetie*). Therefore, it is better to examine the statements on NT prophecy with regard to redactional context rather than the history of the forms.

According to 1 Cor 14:3, 31 Paul expects from prophets the "upbuilding, encouragement, and consolation" of the congregation and the persuasion of outsiders (vv. 24f.). Hence prophetic speech should take place quite apart from any ecstatic disposition and proceed rather in an ordered manner (vv. 29-32), in comprehensible and rational language (vv. 15f.), and according to the proportion of faith (Rom 12:6). The prophets he thus speaks of were probably members of the local congregation (von Campenhausen 60f.; Greeven 9), not itinerant prophets (*contra* Harnack).

Matt 10:41; 23:34 and the warning against false prophets (Matt 7:15, 22f., but cf. Luke 13:26; Mark 13:22 par.) indicate the presence of Christian prophets in the Syria-Palestine area.

Acts views the emergence of prophets as a sign of the eschatological pouring out of the Spirit. Basically, all Christians have the gift of prophecy (2:17-21; 19:6).

Prophets who are specifically mentioned and sometimes named (in Antioch, 13:1f.; in Jerusalem, 11:27f.; 15:22, 32; the four daughters of Philip, 21:9) illustrate the activity of the Spirit in the time of the Church. Some of these were leaders in the congregations (13:1-3; 11:27; 15:22, 32).

According to Eph 2:20; 3:5; 4:11 the apostles and early Christian prophets, as the authoritative proclaimers of the mystery of the universal Church of Jews and Gentiles, are the basis of the post-apostolic Church.

Revelation mentions early Christian prophets in 10:7 (alone); 11:18; 16:6; 18:24 (with "the saints"); and 18:20 (with the apostles and saints). The author of Revelation calls himself one of the prophets (22:9: σύνδουλος . . . τῶν προφητῶν), but then claims special authority for himself (vv. 18f.).

F. Schnider

προφητικός, 3 *prophētikos* prophetic*

In Rom 16:26 γραφαὶ προφητικαί probably does not refer to OT prophecy (cf., however, 1:2), and also not specifically to early Christian prophecy, but rather in the larger sense to the *prophetic* (i.e., Spirit-induced) chracter of early Christian writings (cf. also Eph 3:5), viewed here through the eyes of a post-Pauline generation fundamentally as the relevation of God (φανερωθέντος δὲ νῦν; cf. further E. Käsemann, *Rom* [Eng. tr., 1980] ad loc.). In 2 Pet 1:19 ὁ προφητικὸς λόγος is "scriptural prophecy" (cf. 1:20f.; 2:1; 3:2). *2 Clem.* 11:2 cites an (unknown) "prophetic utterance." → προφητεύω.

προφῆτις, ιδος, ἡ *prophētis* prophetess*

Luke 2:36, of the *prophetess* Anna; Rev 2:20, of a woman from Thyatira called Jezebel (cf. 1 Kgs 16:31; 21:5ff., 23ff.; 2 Kgs 9:22) who "calls herself a *prophetess*" (ἡ λέγουσα ἑαυτὴν προφῆτιν) but deceives members of the Church and seduces them to practice immorality (cf. Acts 21:9; 1 Cor 11:5; 14:34; 1 Tim 2:12); on the name and position of this "prophetess" see Rev 2:14f.; → Ἰεζάβελ.

προφθάνω *prophthanō* come before*

With a partc. in Matt 17:25: προέφθασεν . . . λέγων, "he *spoke to him first,* saying"; with an inf. in *2 Clem.* 8:2; cf. BDF §414.4.

προχειρίζομαι *procheirizomai* choose, appoint, designate beforehand*

There are 3 occurrences of this vb. in Acts, all mid. and pass.; on the meaning cf. the adj. πρόχειρος, "at hand." Twice it refers to God's choice of Paul: Acts 22:14: ὁ θεὸς . . . προεχειρίσατό σε (spoken by Ananias); 26:16:

ὤφθην σοι, προχειρίσασθαί σε ὑπηρέτην (spoken by the exalted Lord). Here the vb. probably emphasizes the persuasive character of divine appointment.

The vb. is pass. in 3:20: ὁ προκεχειρισμένος ὑμῖν Χριστὸς Ἰησοῦς, "the Christ *appointed* for you, [namely,] Jesus" (on the idea of predestination [and proclamation beforehand] in this passage cf. vv. 13, 17f., 21, 24-26; 4:28; 10:41). In this context χριστός here is a designation for the Messiah, which is suggested as well by the dat. of advantage ὑμῖν (cf. Josh 3:12).

The vb. occurs neither in Philo nor in Josephus, nor in extrabiblical early Christian writings. G. Lohfink, "Christologie und Geschichtsbild in Apg 3,19-21," *BZ* 13 (1969) 223-41, esp. 235f.; W. Michaelis, *TDNT* VI, 862-64; Spicq, *Notes* II, 768-70.

προχειροτονέω *procheirotoneō* choose or select beforehand*

Acts 10:41: μάρτυρες οἱ προκεχειροτονημένοι ὑπὸ τοῦ θεοῦ, "witnesses *chosen* by God *beforehand,*" namely, to testify to Christ's resurrection and appearances (cf. 1:22f.; Luke 24:36ff.).

Πρόχορος, ου *Prochoros* Prochorus*

A member of the circle of the Seven around the Hellenist Stephen (Acts 6:5; the meaning of the Greek name is "dance leader").

πρύμνα, ης, ἡ *prymna* stern, afterdeck*

Mark 4:28, of Jesus sleeping during a nocturnal storm "in the [elevated] *stern* (ἐν τῇ πρύμνῃ) on a cushion"; Acts 27:29: ἐκ πρύμνης, "from the *stern*"; 27:41: ἡ πρῶρα . . . ἡ πρύμνα, "the bow . . . the *stern.*"

πρωΐ *prōi* early (adv.), early in the morning*

This adv. occurs 12 times in the NT, though only in Matthew, Mark, John, and Acts. It means *early in the morning* (ὀψίας γενομένης . . . πρωΐ) in Matt 16:3 (with C D L W Θ f¹ Koine latt, etc.); 21:18; Mark 11:20; 16:9. Special combinations are: ἅμα πρωΐ, "early in the morning" (Matt 20:1), πρωΐ ἔννυχα λίαν, "*in the early morning* when it was still dark/night" (Mark 1:35), ἢ ὀψὲ ἢ μεσονύκτιον ἢ ἀλεκτοροφωνίας ἢ πρωΐ, "in the evening or at midnight, at cockcrow or *in the morning,*" referring to the division of night into four watches of three hours each (13:35), εὐθὺς πρωΐ, "as soon as it was *morning*" (15:1), λίαν πρωΐ, "very early *in the morning*" (16:2), ἦν δὲ πρωΐ (subst. adv. [cf. BDF §434], John 18:28), πρωΐ σκοτίας ἔτι οὔσης, "*early,* while it was still dark" (20:1), ἀπὸ πρωΐ ἕως ἑσπέρας, "from *morning* till evening" (Acts 28:23), cf. further εὐθὺς ἐπὶ τὸ πρωΐ, "just toward morning" (Mark 15:1 v.l.) and τὸ πρωΐ (Acts 5:21 D).

πρωΐα, ας, ἡ *prōia* morning*

In the NT only in the phrase πρωΐας δὲ (ἤδη) γενομένης, "when *morning* came/when it had become *morning*" (Matt 27:1; John 21:4; cf. πρωΐας in Matt 21:18 v.l.).

πρώϊμος, 2 *prōimos* early

Variant spelling of → πρόϊμος (antonym of → ὄψιμος), probably not influenced by πρό (= "early in the year"), but rather by → πρωϊνός, though the two words are differentiated in the LXX; cf. BAGD s.v. πρόϊμος; BDF §35.1.

πρωϊνός, 3 *prōinos* early, belonging to the morning*

The adj. occurs in the NT in the phrase ὁ ἀστὴρ ὁ πρωϊνός, "the *morning* star [i.e., Venus]": in Rev 2:28 perhaps as a sign of dominion (Isa 14:12; Ezek 32:7) or (as in 2 Pet 1:19: φωσφόρος) as a sign of the day (of salvation) after the dark night; in Rev 22:16 as a designation for the eschatological Christ from the root of David (cf. Isa 9:1; 11:1, 10; 60:1; Num 24:17; CD 7:18f.; Ign. *Eph.* 19:2).

πρῷρα, ης, ἡ *prōra* foreship, bow*

Acts 27:30: ἐκ πρῴρης, "from the *bow*" (cf. ἐκ πρύμνης, v. 29); v. 41: ἡ πρῷρα . . . ἡ πρύμνα.

πρωτεύω *prōteuō* be first, occupy first place*

Col 1:18, of Christ, who as the ἀρχή and πρωτότοκος ἐκ νεκρῶν "is preeminent in all things" (ἵνα γένηται ἐν πᾶσιν αὐτὸς πρωτεύων; cf. τὰ πάντα, vv. 16f., 20). Πρωτεύω takes up → πρωτότοκος (vv. 15, 18) and πρὸ πάντων (v. 17a) and emphasizes the comprehensive *prae* of the mediator of creation and salvation. W. Michaelis, *TDNT* VI, 881f.

πρωτοκαθεδρία, ας, ἡ *prōtokathedria* place of honor; best seat (in a synagogue)*

Πρωτοκαθεδρία is not documented in non-Christian writings. In the NT it occurs 4 times in Jesus' criticism of the scribes and Pharisees, who prefer places of honor both during meals and in the synagogue (Mark 12:39 par. Matt 23:6/Luke 20:46: [τὰς (Matthew) πρωτοκαθεδρίας ἐν ταῖς συναγωγαῖς [with → πρωτοκλισία]; sg. in Luke 11:43). As a rule the learned sat in the synagogues not with the congregation (in the center of the room), but rather before the Torah shrine on a platform facing the people, or on benches at the side walls (cf. Billerbeck I,

915f.; W. Grundmann, *Mark* [THKNT] on 12:39). This does not refer to the → καθέδρα Μωϋσέως (Matt 23:2) but to elevated seats visible to all and sought for reasons of prestige. W. Michaelis, *TDNT* VI, 870f.

πρωτοκλισία, ας, ἡ *prōtoklisia* place of honor, first seat (at a meal)*

This word, documented only infrequently in Greek, occurs 4 times in the NT. In Mark 12:39 par. Matt 23:6/ Luke 20:46 it is used of the scribes, who preferred seats of honor in the synagogues (→ πρωτοκαθεδρία) and during meals or banquets (τὴν πρωτοκλισίαν [Matt]/ πρωτοκλισίας [Mark/Luke] ἐν τοῖς δείπνοις). It must be recalled that people reclined at table (→ ἀνακλίνω; κατακλίνω). In Luke 14:7 (pl.) it refers generally to invited guests; in the parable in 14:8 (sg.) it refers to a wedding feast; the sg. is contrasted to the ἔσχατος τόπος (vv. 9f.). During the time of Jesus places of honor at a meal were assigned according to reputation and rank (about A.D. 300, according to *b. B. Bat.* 120a, according to age). The places of honor were located at the head or the middle of the table (specifics in Billerbeck IV, 618), probably near the host or other dignitaries. Cf. also Matt 10:37 par. W. Michaelis, *TDNT* VI, 870f.

πρωτόμαρτυς, υρος, ὁ *prōtomartys* first witness; first martyr (?)

Acts 22:20 v.l. in place of → μάρτυς. On the question of martyrological interpretation see BAGD s.v. μάρτυς 3 (with older bibliography); E. Haenchen, *Acts* (Eng. tr., 1971) ad loc.; → μάρτυς 4, 5.

πρῶτον *prōton* first of all, before all; above all

1. Occurrences and meanings — 2. Temporal precondition — 3. Temporal priority

Lit.: BAGD s.v. πρῶτος 2. — W. MICHAELIS, *TDNT* VI, 868-70. — D. ZELLER, *Juden und Heiden in der Mission des Paulus* (1973) 141-45, 149-51 (on Rom 1:16; 2:9, 10).

1. Πρῶτον is the neut. of → πρῶτος and is used as an adv. in the sense of *first, earlier,* primarily in the temporal sense, though also referring to sequence in enumerations (cf. Rom 1:8; 3:2; 1 Cor 12:28) and priority or rank (e.g., 2 Cor 8:5; 1 Tim 2:1; BAGD). The adv. occurs 60 times in the NT. Comparison with πρῶτος shows that πρῶτον predominates in John and Romans, then recedes in Hebrews (only in 7:2), and is completely absent in Revelation. It is most common in Matthew (8 occurrences), Mark (7), Luke (10), John (8), Acts (5), and Romans (6). The adv. occurs with the art. in the NT (τὸ πρῶτον, "the first time") only in John 10:40; 19:39 and with the meaning *at first* only in John 12:16.

2. Πρῶτον in the sense of a (necessary) precondition often occurs in relation to eschatological fulfillment. Thus Mark 9:11f., e.g., says that Elijah had to "come first." The context alludes to the eschatological end. Luke 17:25 speaks of the suffering and rejection of the Son of man and emphasizes even more strongly the necessity (δεῖ) of the events. Luke 21:9 speaks of the events preceding the end; they are necessary and predetermined in God's salvation plan (δεῖ), though they do not yet announce a near end. 2 Thess 2:3f. similarly portrays the necessity of the falling away from God and of the appearance of the adversary. Only then can Christ's eschatological victory take place, though its date as yet remains unknown.

Πρῶτον also appears in the sense of a precondition in the Synoptic eschatological discourse in Mark 13:10. "The gospel must first be preached to all nations" before the end. Par. Matt 24:14 substitutes καὶ τότε for πρῶτον: "and [only] then the end will come." This temporal element is esp. noticeable in Matthew. Hence the worldwide proclamation of the gospel is a condition for the advent of the end.

In Jesus' ethical demands πρῶτον appears in the sense of a precondition without any reference to a clear eschatological demarcation: so Matt 5:24 in the saying about reconciliation and Matt 7:5 par. Luke 6:42 in the saying concerning judgment of one's brother. Πρῶτον also appears in Jesus' wisdom sayings: so Luke 14:28 in a proverb concerning the figuring of costs beforehand, v. 31 in a reflection on strategy, and Matt 6:33. The eschatological viewpoint is missing, and πρῶτον (in the sense of first of all, above all) refers to the search for the kingdom of God. Everything else is brought into abrupt contrast, and thus in Matt 6:33 πρῶτον designates exclusive value or priority.

Such preconditions, however, can also prove to be negative and detrimental if they issue from human beings instead of from God. This is the case, e.g., with those who first wish to bury their father and take leave before following Jesus (Matt 8:21 par. Luke 9:59; Luke 9:61).

3. Πρῶτον appears in the sense of temporal priority in Rom 1:16. The addressees of the gospel were first Jews. But Greeks (Gentiles) are placed on an equal salvation-historical level with παντὶ τῷ πιστεύοντι. Thus Paul declares: Ἰουδαίῳ τε πρῶτον καὶ Ἕλληνι. Πρῶτον demonstrates here a "nuance of rank" (Zeller 142) and should therefore not be translated "and then to the Greeks" but "also to the Greeks." Temporal priority is, however, maintained (cf. Acts 3:26; 13:46). In Rom 2:1-11 Paul twice emphasizes this priority, both in the prediction of tribulation (v. 9) and in the blessing (v. 10).

Πρῶτον occupies a unique position in 1 Pet 4:17. Judgment begins "first with us," i.e., with the community of believers, those who have heeded God's salvation message. But this appears to refer neither to a specific time nor to any sort of priority; it emphasizes rather that both believers and nonbelievers are subject to judgment. Πρῶτον here suggests an element of privilege. In spite of judgment in the larger sense, which is painted in somber colors, believers can still be saved. This statement becomes understandable when one considers the overall concerns of 1 Peter.

H. Langkammer

πρῶτος, 3 prōtos first, earliest

1. Occurrences in the NT and range of meanings — 2. Temporal (and numerical) meaning — 3. Rank among persons — 4. Spatial meaning — 5. Exclusivity

Lit.: BAGD s.v. 1. — W. MICHAELIS, *TDNT* VI, 865-68. — MOULTON/MILLIGAN s.v.

1. Πρῶτος occurs 96 times in the NT (including the variant readings in John 5:4; 8:7). In addition to this the adv. → πρῶτον (from the neut. form of πρῶτος) occurs 60 times. Πρῶτος is esp. common in the Gospels (17 occurrences in Matthew, 10 in Mark, 10 in Luke, and 5 in John in addition to the variant readings mentioned), Acts (18 occurrences), Hebrews (9), and Revelation (18).

Πρῶτος functions as the superlative of πρό and designates the *first* of several or the *first* of two. It can also have the meaning of πρότερος (→ 2 on Acts 1:1).

From the time of Homer πρῶτος was used primarily in a three senses. The temporal meaning was most common, then that of rank or degree, and finally the rare spatial meaning. In the LXX, e.g., where πρῶτος occurs about 240 times, one-third of the occurrences are temporal. In Philo the sense of exclusivity also appears when he speaks of God as πρῶτος θεός (e.g., *Migr.* 181; *Abr.* 115).

2. In the NT the temporal meaning appears to predominate, though even it can have variations of nuance. The formulation "on the *first* day of Unleavened Bread" (Mark 14:12 par. Matt 26:17) would have to be considered a purely numerical specification referring to Nisan 14, the day on which the leavening was brought out of the house in the morning, although Nisan 15 was the first real day of celebration. Only in Mark 16:9 does πρῶτος refer to Easter as the *first* day of the week (cf. Matt 28:1 par. Luke 24:1: μία σαββάτων, see further John 20:1; Acts 20:7; 1 Cor 16:2). In Acts 1:1 πρῶτος is used in the sense of πρότερος (πρῶτος λόγος; BAGD s.v. 1.b). Rev 2:4f. is an example of temporal juxtaposition. The "*first* love" and the "*first* works" (in the sense of "earlier") are contrasted with present circumstances. The "original" enthusiasm of Christian life had been extinguished.

Temporal juxtaposition can also develop into general juxtaposition so that the temporal motif loses significance. Thus Hebrews contrasts the "*first* covenant" (8:7, 13; 9:1, 15, 18) with the "new (καινή)" (8:8, 13; 9:15; cf.

12:24: νέα διαθήκη). Heb 8:7 designates the new covenant as δευτέρα (cf. 10:9), but never does Hebrews use the phrase παλαιὰ διαθήκη, probably because πρῶτος could also convey the connotation of παλαιός, "old, aged, former, etc." (cf. 8:13). Hebrews also justifies the theological sense of this juxtaposition, e.g., in a general sense in 8:7, and in 9:1-10 on the basis of the incompleteness of the OT ritual procedures, and then in 9:11 contrasts those procedures with the deed of the only possible mediator of the new covenant (9:15a).

Πρῶτος can also contain the idea of a temporal differentiation. 1 Tim 5:12, e.g., speaks of a "violation of the *first* pledge." The contrast is already expressed in 5:8: disowning one's faith is worse than lack of faith (ἀπιστία).

Πρῶτος usually fixes a point of time in the past. But there are instances where this interest in the past recedes and is directed toward the future. Hence in Rev 21:1, e.g., the "*first* heaven" and the "*first* earth" refer to what was and is transitory. The eschatological perspective is important in 21:6: The seer-prophet is interested in the "new." This eschatological circle of references also includes eschatological judgment sayings of Jesus: Matt 12:45b compares a man's last situation with his *first* situation (τῶν πρώτων). The first were bad, and the last will be incomparably worse (cf. Luke 11:26; Matt 27:64; 2 Pet 2:20; Rev 2:19). The "first" are associated with "that generation" which has not accepted Christ. Here πρῶτος becomes more a present reference point than a reference to the past.

Πρῶτος can also indicate a general change of disposition: In 1 Cor 15:45 Adam is "the *first* man," Christ the δεύτερος ἄνθρωπος. Adam is from the earth, Christ from heaven. The abrupt contrast is maintained while the temporal motif recedes. In the context of this juxtaposition πρῶτος does not, of course, refer to temporal sequence, something the apostle's later exposition makes clear. As Paul discusses in the section on the resurrection of the body, Adam secures the earthly creation (v. 47), while Christ is the model of the heavenly person (v. 48).

3. The perspective of rank and priority manifests itself primarily in the juxtaposition of πρῶτος and ἔσχατος, though in Mark 10:44 the key term ἔσχατος is not actually used. Jesus is addressing the disciples concerning rank. Contrasts to πρῶτος are διάκονος and δοῦλος (Mark 10:43f. par. Matt 20:26f.). Whoever strives for rank and preeminence should first perform service, as does the Son of man (Mark 10:45). Here, too, the temporal element recedes.

In Mark 10:31, e.g., we see a transition from rank to revaluation: "But many that are *first* will be last, and the last *first.*" This total role reversal implies in this judgment statement a reordering of values (cf. Matt 20:16; Luke

13:30). In such juxtaposition, however, πρῶτος maintains its value despite the consciously intended tension. The juxtaposed elements are to be viewed from the perspective of a reversal of their rank. Hence in Mark 12:29-31, e.g., the *first* commandment (v. 29) together with the "second" (v. 31) are juxtaposed with all the others as the ἐντολὴ πρώτη πάντων (v. 28; cf. Matt 22:36: ἐντολὴ μεγάλη). In Mark 6:21; Luke 19:47; Acts 13:50; 25:2; 28:17 (οἱ) πρῶτοι appears without any contrasting elements as a collective designation of honor regarding the "leading men." On Acts 28:7 (πρῶτος of the island of Malta) see Wikenhauser, *Geschichtswert* 343-46.

4. Heb 9:2, 6, 8 (the description of the tabernacle) is the only real NT occurrence of the rare spatial meaning of πρῶτος. It refers here to a spatial division in which each room has its own purpose, though even here the motif of priority can be sensed. The priests had access to the "first/outer" tent, but only the high priest went into the second. Ἡ πρώτη σκηνή is the less important place.

5. Πρῶτος indicates exclusivity in Rev 1:17; 2:8; 22:13 (as in Philo, though without any closer specification): "the *first* and the last." Πρῶτος stands here neither in a comparison nor in any tension with the "last." Both predicates refer to Christ, to his eternal dominion over everyone and everything. Ὁ πρῶτος stresses his preexistence and asserts that he is the primal cause of everything, since everything has its beginning in him; ὁ ἔσχατος emphasizes perfection in Christ, who is himself without end. One might thus speak of two mutually inclusive predicates of exclusivity.   H. Langkammer

πρωτοστάτης, ου, ὁ *prōtostatēs* leader, ringleader*

Acts 24:5: Tertullus accuses Paul of being the πρωτοστάτης τῆς τῶν Ναζωραίων αἱρέσεως, "*ringleader* of the sect of the Nazarenes.*" Paul is thus suspected of being an agitator.

πρωτοτόκια, ων, τά *prōtotokia* birthright, right of primogeniture*

Heb 12:16, of Esau: ὃς . . . ἀπέδετο τὰ πρωτοτόκια ἑαυτοῦ, "who sold his *birthright* for a single meal" (cf. Gen 25:33f.). BDF §120.1; W. Michaelis, *TDNT* VI, 874-76.

πρωτότοκος, 2 *prōtotokos* firstborn*

1. Occurrences in the NT — 2. Meaning outside the NT — 3. Christ as πρωτότοκος and Christians as firstborn — a) Luke 2:7 — b) Col 1:15 — c) Col 1:18 — d) Rom 8:29 — e) Rev 1:5 — f) Heb 1:6 — g) Summary of

christological usage — h) Heb 12:23: "the assembly of the firstborn"

Lit.: K. H. BARTELS, *DNTT* I, 667-69. — C. BURGER, *Schöpfung und Versöhnung. Studien zum liturgischen Gut im Kolosserbrief und Epheserbrief* (WMANT 40, 1975) 38-53. — J.-B. FREY, "La signification du terme πρωτότοκος d'après une inscription juive," *Bib* 11 (1930) 373-90. — J. GNILKA, *Col* (HTKNT, 1980) 51-87. — A. HOCKEL, *Christus der Erstgeborene* (1965) (on Col 1:15). — W. MICHAELIS, *TDNT* VI, 871-82. — J. MILGROM, *IDBSup* 337f.

1. The adj. πρωτότοκος occurs 8 times in the NT. Only Luke 2:7 uses it adjectivally (of Jesus: "she gave birth to her *firstborn* son"). Otherwise it is always subst. (of Christ in Rom 8:29; Col 1:15, 18; Heb 1:6; Rev 1:5; of others in Heb 11:28 [τὰ πρωτότοκα, "the *firstborn*" of the Israelites] and 12:23 [ἐκκλησία πρωτοτόκων, referring to Christians]).

2. A Jewish tomb inscription from Tell el-Yehudieh (Leontopolis) of *ca.* 5 B.C. is considered the oldest documentation of πρωτότοκος used of human beings in the pass. sense: "In the labors of the birth of my firstborn child fate led me to the end of my life" (Preisigke, *Sammelbuch* 6647, 6). The other rare occurrences speak mainly of animals and come from the 4th cent. A.D. Πρωτότοκος has thus a general meaning related to the extrabiblical term πρωτόγονος.

Πρωτότοκος occurs about 130 times in the LXX, usually rendering *bᵉkôr (bᵉkōr)*, "firstborn" (cf. M. Tsevat, *TDOT* II, 121-27). In the OT the religious reference to "first *production*" predominates. For fruits the LXX uses πρωτογέν(ν)ημα. God has special rights of ownership over every firstborn; it should be sanctified to the Lord (Exod 22:28f.; 34:19; Num 18:15ff.; Deut 15:19ff.). In such cases the emphasis is on both πρo- and -τοκος, though it can be weighted toward πρo-. In Exod 4:22, e.g., υἱὸς πρωτότοκός μου Ἰσραήλ expresses the unique relationship between Israel and Yahweh. It is this sense that the OT knows God as Israel's "Father" (e.g., Jer 31:9). Ps 88:28 LXX speaks similarly of the (messianic) king: It is not the relationship between the king as πρωτότοκος and the "kings of the earth" that stands in the foreground, but rather his relationship with God, whose elect and beloved the king is. This accent manifests itself even more sharply in *Pss. Sol.* 13:9; 18:4; 2 Esdr 6:58 in the equation of firstborn, only begotten, chosen one, and beloved.

3.a) In the NT πρωτότοκος appears first in Luke 2:7. The paronomastic use of τίκτω makes it clear that a natural birth is spoken of. The newborn is called πρωτότοκος, thus emphasizing -τοκος. The prefix, however, also appears to be emphasized. As the firstborn Jesus was dedicated to God in a special way (Exod 13:12; 34:19; cf. Luke 2:23 with Exod 13:12 and the motif of spiritual umbrage in Luke 1:35). In relation to the angel's promise (Luke 1:32f.) and the Bethlehem motif (2:1-5) πρωτότοκος becomes a reference to the child as the firstborn of the line of David. Hence in 2:7 πρωτότοκος identifies Jesus as the firstborn dedicated to God and characterized as the messianic heir.

b) Col 1:15 probably distributes emphasis similarly.

Gen. πάσης κτίσεως is dependent on πρωτότοκος and makes it clear that the *firstborn* stands in a relationship to creation as its mediator. Hence this is not a matter of a purely temporal priority of the preexistent Christ, but rather of a superiority in essence. This unique position also seems to be at issue in v. 17a, suggesting an emphasis on πρo-. Is there also a specific relationship to God? Since Col 1:15-18a(-20) must be considered an older Christ-hymn, one perhaps cannot refer to the phrase "beloved Son" in v. 13b, even though the author of the Epistle does thus refer to the Father-Son relationship. One must also consider whether the hymn did not originally have a title similar to v. 13b. In any case, Christ, as the mediator of creation, is not a part of creation himself, but stands rather in a unique relationship to God, the "invisible." Hence in 1:15 one should not overlook the accentuation of the second part of πρωτότοκος.

c) Πρωτότοκος in v. 18a must be viewed differently. Here it is first asserted that Christ is "the beginning" of a new series (cf. 1 Cor 15:20, 23; Acts 3:15; 5:31). As such he is the "*firstborn* from the dead" (cf. Acts 26:23). Νεκροί refers to all those who because of the sin of Adam are subject to death. The resurrection overcomes death once and for all. Though this also implies temporal priority, it probably refers first to the resurrection of Christ as the basis for the general resurrection.

d) The phrase "*firstborn* among many brethren" (Rom 8:29) occurs in Paul's portrayal of the line of development determined by God along which the path of salvation for Christians proceeds, specifically in regard to their coming to be conformed to "the image of his Son." Paul is thinking of the perfected fellowship with Christ that is based on his resurrection, commences with the general resurrection at the last judgment, and issues in being conformed (cf. 1 John 3:2) to the image of the exalted and transfigured Christ. In this eschatological υἱοθεσία (cf. Rom 8:23) Christ is the πρωτότοκος of his brethren. Despite this conformity to the Son's image, Christ as God's "Son" remains above the other brethren in majesty and rank. He is God's "proto-image," as it were, according to which Christians' new and final form of existence is modelled. In Rom 8:29 this relationship of πρωτότοκος to God is maintained, though the πρo- is strongly emphasized.

e) Rev 1:5 thinks of the resurrection in calling Christ "the *firstborn* of the dead." The following phrase, "ruler of kings on earth," alludes to Ps 88:28b LXX, and the introductory phrase, "faithful witness," to Ps 88:38 LXX. Ps 88:28a LXX also contains the title πρωτότοκος in the utterance of David: "You are my Father, my God." It is certain that Rev 1:5 is asserting a unique position of precedence for the resurrected Christ. Yet, like Rom 8:29, πρωτότοκος is also connected to "his Father," and the resonance of this connection is heard in v. 6. Hence here, too, the emphasis of -τοκος is not completely suspended, particularly since the dependence on Psalm 88 cannot be overlooked.

f) Heb 1:6 is the only text about Christ as πρωτότοκος that does not offer additional exposition or interpretation. Christ is solemnly proclaimed as the Son with an allusion to Ps 2:7. Since by the procreation of the Son (v. 5) is probably meant the resurrection (cf. Acts 13:33), the bringing of the *firstborn* into the world likely does not refer to the incarnation, but rather to the parousia. His filial rights as Son guarantee to Christ the rights of primogeniture promised to him as a member of the line of David (2 Sam 7:14) and (v. 6b) the angels' adoration (cf. Deut 32:43 LXX; Ps 96:7 LXX). Here the Son's unique relationship to God is esp. emphasized.

g) In summary we can see that even where the first part of the compound πρωτότοκος is emphasized, the Son motif more or less always resonates as well, and thus the unique relationship between the πρωτότοκος and God is maintained. It does not, to be sure, ever lead, as in Judaism of the time, to a complete identification of πρωτότοκος with μονογενής. But the motif of the Son is probably determinative for πρωτότοκος (which is taken from the LXX) to the extent it is applied to Christ. Thus the relationship Christ as πρωτότοκος has to God is established differently than in the OT (LXX): In the OT it is established through προ-, in the NT (except in Luke 2:7) it is established through -τοκος. Προ- takes the Son as the point of departure, who as -τοκος stands close to God. In the OT προ- takes God as the point of departure, so that a -τοκος could arise in the first place. One should not overlook this fundamental difference.

h) Heb 12:23 speaks in a liturgical manner of "the assembly of the *firstborn* enrolled in heaven." It does not appear likely that these "firstborn" are angels, since angels were mentioned already in 12:22. Enrollment in heaven applies otherwise only to human beings who are destined for eternal life (Exod 32:32; Dan 12:1). These "firstborn" cannot be the OT people of God or the witnesses of faith in Hebrews 11, since the author considers the NT conception of salvation to be incomparably superior to that of the OT. Besides this, the author is addressing the NT community and is portraying their access to God. All the members of the "firstborn" are already in heaven. The addressees "come" to this as well (προσέρχομαι, v. 22). Hence πρωτότοκος cannot refer to the congregation addressed by the Epistle. Accordingly, a comprehensive vision of the eschatological heavenly liturgy appears to be portrayed, and "the assembly of the *firstborn*" refers to all those who through the blood of the mediator of the new covenant have already attained access to God. The Epistle's addressees are to participate in the heavenly festal gathering with this assembly.

H. Langkammer

πρώτως *prōtōs* for the first time*

According to Acts 11:26 "in Antioch the disciples were called Χριστιανοί *for the first time*"; → Χριστιανός.

πταίω *ptaiō* stumble; make a blunder/mistake; be ruined*

The 5 NT occurrences are all intrans. and are all used fig. in the sense "err or sin": absolute in Rom 11:11, of (stubborn) Israel: μὴ ἔπταισαν ἵνα πέσωσιν; "have they stumbled so as to fall into ruin?" (cf. ἀποβολὴ . . . πρόσλημψις, v. 15); Jas 2:10: πταίσῃ ἐν ἑνί, *"fail in one point"* (opposed to ὅλον τὸν νόμον τηρεῖν); 3:2a: πολλὰ γὰρ πταίομεν ἅπαντες, "for we all *make many mistakes*"; v. 2b: ἐν λόγῳ οὐ πταίει, *"make no mistakes* in what one says"; with the meaning *stumble/fall* in 2 Pet 1:10: οὐ μὴ πταίσητέ ποτε (cf. Vg.: *non peccabitis aliquando*) the tr. "run into misfortune" (Germ. *ins Unglück geraten* in W. Bauer, *Griechisch-deutsches Wörterbuch zu den Schriften des NT* [⁴1952-⁶1988] s.v.) unjustifiably weakens the statement; cf. W. Schrage, *2 Pet* (NTD) ad loc. K. L. Schmidt, *TDNT* VI, 883f.

πτέρνα, ης, ἡ *pterna* heel*

John 13:18: ἐπαίρω τὴν πτέρνην ἐπί τινα, "lift one's *heel* against another," i.e., in order to kick him; cf. Ps 41:10 (Ps 40:10 LXX, however, has μεγαλύνω πτερνισμόν).

πτερύγιον, ου, τό *pterygion* summit, pinnacle*

This diminutive of → πτέρυξ, "wing," occurs in Matt 4:5 par. Luke 4:9 in relation to Jesus' temptation in the temple: καὶ ἔστησεν αὐτὸν ἐπὶ τὸ πτερύγιον τοῦ ἱεροῦ. Πτερύγιον designates generally the most extreme edge or extremity; in reference to buildings that would be a tower, roof ridge, pinnacle, etc. (cf. LSJ s.v.). In this instance one might think of (1) a protruding rampart corner of the temple square (e.g., the southeast corner, which protrudes high over the Kidron Valley: G. Dalman, *Sacred Sites and Ways* [1935] 296f.), (2) the roof pinnacle of the "royal hall" at the south end of the temple square (Josephus *Ant.* xv.412 emphasizes its dizzying height), (3) a gate structure with a three-cornered, wing-like design (J. Jeremias, *ZDPV* 59 [1936] 195-208; criticized in BAGD s.v.; see, however, also E. Lohmeyer, *Matt* [KEK] 54 with n.1), (4) a balcony on the outer side of the temple wall (A. Schlatter, *Matt* [⁶1963] on 4:5; cf. *b. Pesaḥ.* 35b), or possibly (5) the roof of the temple building (*b. Ta'an.* 29a *Bar.; Pesiq. Rabbati* 36 [162a]). It is not possible to determine the exact location (on the whole question see Billerbeck I, 150f.; for comprehensive discussion and criticism of the views listed here see N. Hyldahl, *ST* 15 [1961] 113-27). According to Hegesippus (apud Eusebius *HE* ii.23.11f.) James fell from the πτερύγιον τοῦ ναοῦ (on the suggestion that being thrown from a height was a form of stoning see Hyldahl 121ff.). G. Schrenk, *TDNT* III, 236; *BL* 1931.

                                    H. Balz

πτέρυξ, υγος, ἡ *pteryx* wing*

There are 5 occurrences in the NT, all pl. Of the *wings* of a bird or hen as a place of protection for its young in Matt 23:37 par. Luke 13:34: ὑπὸ τὰς πτέρυγας; Rev 4:8: the four creatures have six *wings* each (cf. Isa 6:2); 9:9: ἡ φωνὴ τῶν πτερύγων, "the noise of the [locusts'] *wings*"; 12:14: the "two *wings*" (δύο πτέρυγες) of the great eagle (cf. *T. Mos.* 10:8; Deut 32:11; Isa 40:31).

πτηνός, 3 (2) *ptēnos* winged; subst.: bird*

Neut. pl. subst. πτηνά in 1 Cor 15:39: *birds* (with ἄνθρωποι, κτήνη, and ἰχθύες; cf. Gen 1:26, 28; Rom 1:23).

πτοέομαι *ptoeomai* be frightened, be terrified*

Only pass. in the NT: Luke 21:9: μὴ πτοηθῆτε, "do not be terrified"; 24:37: πτοηθέντες δὲ καὶ ἔμφοβοι γενόμενοι, "but they were *startled* and frightened"; 12:4 𝔭⁴⁵ 700 (in place of φοβέομαι).

πτόησις, εως, ἡ *ptoēsis* the act of terrifying, intimidation; fear, terror*

1 Pet 3:6, in the exhortation to Christian women married to non-Christian men: μὴ φοβούμεναι μηδεμίαν πτόησιν, "fear no *intimidation* [from the men]" (cf. in contrast ἐν φόβῳ, of fear of God, 3:2; see also Prov 3:24f. LXX). A pass. rendering is also possible: "fear no *terror*" (πτόησιν would then be cognate acc.; cf. also 3:14; Mark 4:41; BDF §153.1), though this accommodates the context less persuasively. See L. Goppelt, *1 Pet* (KEK) ad loc.

Πτολεμαΐς, ΐδος *Ptolemaïs* Ptolemais*

A Phoenician port city at the north end of the Bay of Acre on the site of the OT (and modern) city of Acco, destroyed in 312 B.C. by Ptolemy I and rebuilt as a Hellenistic city with the new name Πτολεμαΐς by Ptolemy II (*Ep. Arist.* 115; 1 Macc 5:15; 10:51ff.). In 65 B.C. Ptolemais became Roman. Herod built a gymnasium there (Josephus *B.J.* i.422); Claudius settled a colony of veterans there (*Colonia Claudia Caesaris Ptolemais:* Pliny *HN* v.17.75). During the Jewish War two thousand Jews were allegedly slain in Ptolemais (Josephus *B.J.* ii.477).

According to Acts 21:7 Paul came to Ptolemais by sea from Tyre at the end of the "third missionary journey" and found Christians there, with whom he spent a day.

O. Crusius, PW I, 1171-73; Abel, *Géographie* II, 235-37; A. van den Born, *BL* 42; K. Elliger, *BHH* 55f.; M. S. Enslin, *BHH* 1530; R. Fellmann, *LAW* 2480f.; H. G. Kippenberg, *KP* IV, 1233f.

πτύον, ου, τό *ptyon* winnowing shovel*

Matt 3:12 par. Luke 3:17: οὗ τὸ πτύον ἐν τῇ χειρὶ αὐτοῦ, referring to the *winnowing shovel* of "him who is coming" predicted by John the Baptist. This one will (soon, since the shovel is already in his hands) clear his threshing floor by throwing the threshed wheat into the air against the wind so that chaff and grain are separated (cf. Isa 30:24). The symbol of the πτύον is also used of the punishing God (cf. Jer 15:7) or the final judge. According to Egyptian portrayals, in this "casting" of grain two wooden boards were used: They were first held together and then separated in the air. See *BHH* 32f. plate 1a; P. H. Menoud, *BHH* 2192.

πτύρομαι *ptyromai* be frightened, let oneself be intimidated*

Pass. in Phil 1:28: μὴ πτυρόμενοι ἐν μηδενί, "not *frightened* in anything" (parallel to μιᾷ ψυχῇ συναθλοῦντες, v. 27).

πτύσμα, ατος, τό *ptysma* spittle*

According to John 9:6 Jesus used his spittle to heal a blind man on the sabbath: ἔπτυσεν χαμαὶ καὶ ἐποίησεν πηλὸν ἐκ τοῦ πτύσματος καὶ ἐπέχρισεν . . . ἐπὶ τοὺς ὀφθαλμούς. Both the healing itself and the mixing and kneading of "paste" were transgressions against the sabbath (*m. Šabb.* 7:2; 24:3; *y. Šabb.* 14:14d; see Billerbeck II, 530). In antiquity spittle was generally regarded as a healing substance (esp. for blindness), though not in the OT (Tacitus *Hist.* iv.81; Dio Cassius lxvi.8; *b. B. Bat.* 126b; *y. Sota* 1:16d; *'Abot. R. Nat.* 36; cf. Billerbeck II, 15-17). Its apotropaic effects against demons might also play a role; → πτύω. BAGD s.v. (bibliography); H. Aschermann, *BHH* 1826; O. Böcher, *Dämonenfurcht und Dämonenabwehr* (BWANT 90, 1970) 218-20, index s.v. Speichel.

πτύσσω *ptyssō* fold, roll up*

Luke 4:20: πτύξας τὸ βιβλίον, "*after he* [Jesus] *had rolled up* the book/scroll"; → βιβλίον 2.

πτύω *ptyō* spit, spit out*

In the NT only in the context of Jesus' healings: absolute in Mark 7:33: πτύσας ἥψατο τῆς γλώσσης αὐτοῦ, "he *spat* and touched his [the deaf mute's] tongue [with spittle]"; 8:23: πτύσας εἰς τὰ ὄμματα αὐτοῦ, "he *spat* on his eyes"; John 9:6: ἔπτυσεν χαμαί, "he *spat* on the ground." The vb. is always found with terms for other healing procedures, such as "putting his fingers in his ears," "laying on hands," or "taking the sick person aside"; in Mark 8:23 the healing is effected by the action (and its repetition), and in 7:33 and John 9:6 by the action together with the following words or commission by Jesus (v. 7). → πτύσμα.

πτῶμα, ατος, τό *ptōma* fall (noun); that which has fallen, corpse*

This noun occurs 7 times in the NT, always with the meaning *corpse* (so in the LXX only in Judg 14:8): Matt 14:12 (v.l. σῶμα Koine, etc.) par. Mark 6:29: ἦραν τὸ πτῶμα (of John); Matt 24:28, in imagery of *carrion:* ὅπου ἐὰν ᾖ τὸ πτῶμα (cf. par. Luke 17:37: τὸ σῶμα); Mark 15:45: Jesus' *corpse* (v.l. σῶμα A C W Koine, etc.); Rev 11:8f. (ter): the *corpses* of the two witnesses (vv. 8, 9a sg.; v. 9b pl.). W. Michaelis, *TDNT* VI, 166f.

πτῶσις, εως, ἡ *ptōsis* collapse (noun), falling down*

The meaning *fall, falling down* predominates with πτῶσις, which occurs only rarely in the LXX, though more commonly than → πτῶμα. Matt 7:27, of the *collapse* of a house (cf. par. Luke 6:49: ῥῆγμα); Luke 2:34: Christ is set εἰς πτῶσιν καὶ ἀνάστασιν πολλῶν ἐν τῷ Ἰσραήλ, "for the *fall* and rising of many in Israel" (cf. Isa 8:14f.; 28:16; → ἀνάστασις 2).

πτωχεία, ας, ἡ *ptōcheia* poverty → πτωχός.

πτωχεύω *ptōcheuō* become poor → πτωχός (1 and 4).

πτωχός, 3 *ptōchos* poor*
πτωχεία, ας, ἡ *ptōcheia* poverty*
πτωχεύω *ptōcheuō* become poor*

1. Occurrences in the NT — 2. The influence of the OT and Jewish writings — 3. The Gospels — a) Luke 6:20 par. Matt 5:3; Luke 7:22 par. Matt 11:5 — b) Mark 10:17-22 par. — c) Mark 12:41-44 par. — d) Mark 14:3-9 par. — e) Luke 14:12-14, 21; 16:20, 22; 19:8 — 4. Paul — 5. James — 6. Revelation

Lit.: B. ANTONINI, A. M. BELLIA, et al., *Evangelizare pauperibus. Atti della XXIV settimana Biblica (1976)* (1978). — J. BOTTERWECK, *TDOT* I, 27-41. — H. BRAUN, *Spätjüdisch-häretischer und frühchristlicher Radikalismus* (BHT 24, [2]1969) esp. I, 77-80; II, 73-80. — A. CRONBACH, "The Social Ideas of the Apocrypha and Pseudepigrapha," *HUCA* 18 (1944) 119-56. — DUPONT, *Béatitudes.* — J. DUPONT, "Les πτωχοὶ τὶ πνεύματι

de Matthieu 5,3 et les 'nwj rwch de Qumran," FS Schmid (1963) 53-64. — H.-H. ESSER and C. BROWN, *DNTT* II, 821-29. — D. FLUSSER, "Blessed Are the Poor in Spirit . . . ," *IEJ* 10 (1960) 1-13. — A. GELIN, *Les Pauvres de Yahvé* ([3]1956). — A. GEORGE, *DBSup* VII, 387-406.— D. GEORGI, *Die Geschichte der Kollekte des Paulus für Jerusalem* (1965). — E. GERSTENBERGER, *THAT* I, 20-25. — J. G. GOURBILLON, *Der Gott der Armen im Alten und Neuen Testament* (1961). — P. GRELOT, "La pauvreté dans l'Écriture Sainte," *Christus* 8 (1961) 306-30. — F. HAUCK and E. BAMMEL, *TDNT* VI, 885-915. — K. HOLL, "Der Kirchenbegriff des Paulus in seinem Verhältnis zu dem der Urgemeinde," *idem, Gesammelte Aufsätze* (1928) II, 44-67. — T. HOYT, *The Poor in Luke-Acts* (Diss. Duke University, Durham, NC, 1975). — J. JOCZ, "God's 'Poor' People," *Judaica* 28 (1972) 7-29. — H.-J. KANDLER, "Die Bedeutung der Armut im Schrifttum von Chirbet Qumran," *Judaica* 13 (1957) 193-209. — L. E. KECK, "The Poor among the Saints in the NT," *ZNW* 56 (1965) 100-129. — *idem,* "The Poor among the Saints in Jewish Christianity and Qumran," *ZNW* 57 (1966) 54-78. — L. E. KECK, J. MAIER, and D. MICHEL, *TRE* IV, 72-85. — G. KRETSCHMAR, "Ein Beitrag zur Frage nach dem Ursprung frühchristlicher Askese," *ZTK* 61 (1964) 27-67. — E. KUTSCH, *RGG* I, 622-24. — S. LÉGASSE, "Les pauvres en esprit et les 'volontaires' de Qumran," *NTS* 8 (1961/62) 336-45. — J. LEIPOLDT, "Jesus und die Armen," *NKZ* 28 (1917) 784-810. — E. LOHSE, "Das Evangelium für die Armen," *ZNW* 72 (1981) 51-64. — J. MAIER, *Die Texte vom Toten Meer* (1960) II, 83-87. — R. MARTIN-ACHARD, *THAT* I, 341-50. — F. MUSSNER, *Jas* (HTKNT, [3]1975) 76-84. — K. F. NICKLE, *The Collection* (1966). — W. SATTLER, "Die Anawim im Zeitalter Jesu Christi," *Festgabe für Adolf Jülicher* (1927) 1-15. — J. SCHMID, *LTK* I, 878-81. — L. SCHOTTROFF and W. STEGEMANN, *The God of the Lowly. Socio-Historical Interpretations of the Bible* (1984). — *idem, Jesus and the Hope of the Poor* (1986). — M. SCHWANTES, *Das Recht der Armen* (BEvT 4, 1977). — W. STEGEMANN, *The Gospel of the Poor* (1984). — G. THEISSEN, *The Social Setting of Pauline Christianity* (1982). — P. TRUMMER, "Was heißt 'Armut um des Evangeliums willen'?" *idem, Aufsätze zum NT* (1987) 7-37. — F. ZEHRER, "Arm und Reich in der Botschaft Jesu," *BiLi* 36 (1962/63) 148-63. — For further bibliography → πλούσιος; see *TWNT* X, 1254-56.

1. Of these three words, the adj. occurs most frequently in the NT: 34 times, with 20 in the Synoptics and the other occurrences distributed in John (4), Paul (4), James (4), and Revelation (2). The noun occurs twice in 2 Corinthians and once in Revelation. The one NT occurrence of the vb. is in 2 Corinthians. The word group is entirely absent from the Epistles of John, Acts, and the Pauline antilegomena.

2. In Greek πτωχός (in contrast to → πένης, which designates dearth of possessions) designates the person wholly without possessions who must acquire the necessities of life through petition, hence those "poor as beggars." In the NT, however, one must consider above all the semantic components influenced by the OT and Jewish history of the idea. The following elements are important: According to OT and broader oriental understanding the poor person stands under the special protection of the deity. The poor (Heb. *dal, 'ebyôn*) person is one deprived of his inherited rights (land! cf. the social criticism of the older prophets). Since the land itself stands under Yahweh's legal possession

and has been given by him to the whole people, enduring poverty in Israel is not really allowed (covenantal law). Deuteronomy, according to which there should be no poor people in Israel, makes comprehensive provisions for the poor. Esp. in the Psalms the poor (*'ānî*, *'ebyôn*) person, who in crying out in his own defense is simultaneously pleading God's case, becomes the self-identification of the person in prayer; this religious component dominates the concept of the *'ᵃnāwîm*, the "humble pious ones." The tribulations of the exile resulted in the entire people collectively appearing as the poor (*'ᵃnîyîm*, *'ᵃnāwîm*, *'ebyônîm*), to whom is given God's saving promise (deutero- and trito-Isaiah). In early Judaism the concept in this eschatological shading served above all opposition groups (the idea of the "remnant") in formulating their own self-understanding as an collective elect (cf. Qumran). The conceptual proximity to "righteous" and "holy" is characteristic (cf. *Psalms of Solomon*).

The understanding of the poor (*rāš*) in the wisdom literature is less theological. In the rabbinic literature, too, any intimations of an ideology of the poor remain on the fringes, though almsgiving for the poor does occupy an important position (cf. Billerbeck IV/1, 536-58).

3.a) Luke 6:20 par. is based on a saying of Jesus: "Blessed are the *poor*, for theirs is the kingdom of God" (on the reconstruction of this text see Schulz, *Q* 76f.). The context in Luke 6:21 suggests that actual poor people are meant. The blessing follows the line of OT and Jewish thinking, according to which the poor stand under God's special protection, though it hardly intends to carry forth the prophetic social criticism directly. It is, rather, a proclamation that exposes the insufficiency of any earthly system of values for the presently commencing eschatological events. Against the background of Judaism of the time it is noteworthy that in this salvation proclamation Jesus neither mentions conditions (as is usually the case in apocalyptic blessings; cf. E. Schweizer, *NTS* 19 [1972/73] 121-26) nor does he qualify the poor religiously (cf., e.g., the "poor" as "those who keep the law": 1QpHab 12:2ff.; 4QpPsᵃ 2:9ff.; cf. *T. Jud.* 25:4). This complete lack of conditions manifests itself in an exemplary fashion in this offer of salvation, by which God through Jesus' proclamation overcomes Israel's failure to keep the law, a failure that cannot be lessened by recourse to any previous salvation identity or titles (→ μετάνοια 4).

Hence Jesus can understand his entire proclamation, with reference to Isa 61:1f., as good news for the *poor*: so Luke 7:22 par. With this "application of the typology 'poor' to the elected collective" (Maier, *TRE* IV, 81), which was common from the time of the exile, Jesus is nonetheless not establishing any sort of "remnant Israel," but rather includes all Israel in its complete dependence on God's salvation activity.

The logia source takes up both of these sayings of Jesus. The redactional fourth blessing in Luke 6:22f. par. (second person!) suggests the agenda of identifying one's own group with the "poor."

In Luke this blessing of the *poor* then directs itself in

6:20 straightforwardly (second person) to the disciples or the Church, to whom eschatological consolation is given in time of tribulation. It is not, however, a matter of simple consolation; rather, salvation is already historically and visibly given in view of the time of Jesus himself, who proclaimed the good news to the *poor* (7:22). The allusion to Isa 61:1 in 7:22 can thus be used in Luke 4:18f. to characterize Jesus' entire ministry.

Matthew interprets the poor in the first blessing (5:3) as "*poor* in spirit." This expression (as in 1QH 14:3; 1QM 14:7; cf. 1QH 18:14f.) might be influenced by Isa 61:1; 66:2 (Maier, *Texte* II, 85). It refers to those who know themselves to be completely dependent on God's mercy. Matthew thereby takes the edge off Jesus' blessing, but at the same time secures it against the misinterpretation that external poverty by itself guarantees salvation. Matthew's interpretation articulates precisely the attitude already indirectly addressed in the saying of Jesus (Q) taken up in 11:5.

b) The exhortation in Mark 10:21 expands the demand Jesus makes of some of those called to follow him to leave their possessions; it now demands that they sell their possessions and give the proceeds to the *poor* (alluding to the traditional Jewish idea that alms secure a treasure in heaven). The goal here is to clarify paradigmatically (following or *imitatio* becomes a paradigm for faith in the post-Easter community) just how radically and definitively one's decision of faith in Jesus will tear one away from other commitments and to show what one must be prepared to do in a given concrete case, or just how difficult it is for a rich person to realize such an exclusive commitment to Jesus.

Luke 18:22 underscores the radical nature of this demand by emphasizing "sell *all* that you have and distribute to the poor."

Matt 19:21 requires only the sale of one's possessions (τὰ ὑπάρχοντα; cf. K. Bornhäuser, *Der Christ und seine Habe nach dem NT* [1936] 30-43). "If you would be perfect," on the other hand, represents no restriction regarding "a higher stage of morality" (so E. Bammel, *TDNT* VI, 903; but cf. Matt 5:48!).

c) The story of the *poor* widow (Mark 12:41-44 par.) shows that the value of a gift depends on its significance for the giver (vv. 42, 43 par. Luke 21:[2]3).

d) Mark 14:7 (par. Matt 26:11; John 12:8) does not mean to "depreciate almsgiving" (*contra* E. Bammel, *TDNT* VI, 903), but rather to protect anointing from misinterpretation as a violation of the unquestioned obligation to care for the *poor* (Mark 14:5; Matt 26:9; John 12:5) and to confirm it as a duty of love in view of the burial of Jesus, which was also understood as a duty of love (cf. Billerbeck IV/1, 578ff.; Mark 14:8 par.). The redactional insertion in Mark 14:7b questions the sincerity of the objection in v. 5 and seeks to counter any sense that service to Christ and service to the poor are opposed to each other (on the subsequent history of the passage cf. R. Storch, FS Jeremias [1970] 247-58). In John 12:6 Judas Iscariot is the one who objects, and he uses care for the *poor* only as a pretext. The mention of Judas's money box furnishes the prerequisite for the later misunderstanding that Jesus had commissioned him to give something to the *poor* (13:29).

e) Luke 14:12-14 (material from Jewish Christian tradition reworked by Luke) questions the idea of works done for the sake of what others might do in return. It is because they are not able to return favors that "the *poor,* maimed, lame, and blind" should be invited (v. 13). It is questionable whether the criticism implied in this tradition, i.e., of the custom of denying access to certain people because of their defects (cf. 2 Kgs 5:8; 1QSa 2:2-10), is still at work here in Luke. In any case he maintains this perspective in that in the parable of the banquet (14:21) he again mentions "the *poor,* maimed, blind, and lame," now as a metaphor (for sinners and tax collectors?), in the course of a universally expanding salvation history.

The parable of *poor* (16:20, 22) Lazarus (= Eleazar: "God has helped," possibly a reference to a religious understanding of the poor) and the rich man illustrates the Lukan understanding of the abrupt contrast in 6:20, 24 (→ πλούσιος). Zacchaeus, who according to 19:8 (redactional?) wants to give half his goods to the *poor* (cf. the rabbinic maximum percentage of twenty percent: Billerbeck IV/1, 547), is an example of correct dealing with fortune.

4. In Rom 15:26 ("the *poor* among the saints at Jerusalem") one can no longer really decide whether "saints" is epexegetical or partitive gen. But absolute use of "poor" in Gal 2:10 does suggest that the term was a self-designation of the primitive community in Jerusalem (Holl 59; Georgi 23; E. Bammel, *TDNT* VI, 909). One should not, however, understand this as an honorific title that makes a claim to be God's eschatological people *over against* the rest of Israel. Rather, recalling Jesus' own understanding of his mission (→ 3.a.1), it is a confession *in view of* Israel that with the events occurring in and around Jesus God's eschatological work with Israel has commenced.

The collections with which Paul responds to the levies in Gal 2:10 (eagerly!) are not a sign of any legal subordination of the mission churches. Even from the perspective of Jerusalem such levies probably had theological motives in addition to their social motives: The collections aided the understanding of the mission to the Gentiles as part of the eschatological events concerning Israel (in the sense of the trito-Isaianic pilgrimage of nations? [Isa 60:5, 11; 61:6, etc.]; Acts 24:16f. appears to exclude the

conclusion that "the collection has partly come into the hands of the Jewish leaders" and is "designed to alleviate the widespread suffering in the primitive church" [*contra* Bammel, *TDNT* VI, 909]).

In 2 Corinthians 8 Paul solicits generous participation in the collection by referring to the exemplary behavior of the Macedonian churches (in view of their own profound *poverty* [v. 2]). The antithesis with which v. 9 develops the idea of Christ's self-effacement is characterized by this context: He who was rich became *poor* for your sake (ἐπτώχευσεν) so that you might become rich through his *poverty.* The apostle is himself characterized by a similar antithesis, since he who is *poor* nonetheless makes many others rich (2 Cor 6:10). The charactization of the pseudo-divine elements in Gal 4:9 (with language borrowed from Jewish mission polemics) as "weak and *poor*" underscores their inability to make salvation available.

5. The "case" mentioned in Jas 2:2, namely, that in the church assembly the well-to-do rather than the *poor* get the better seats, is hardly a documentation of actual practice. It belongs rather to the rhetorical style of the Epistle (cf. M. Dibelius and H. Greeven, *Jas* [Hermeneia] 130-32). James is attacking a status-oriented model of interaction that has arisen (again) in the Church and is irreconcilable with faith (2:1). The supporting arguments in 2:5-13 are of varying theological importance.

James 2:5 varies the theme of blessing (→ 3.a): "Has not God chosen those whom the world regards as *poor* (πτωχοὶ τῷ κόσμῳ) to be rich in faith and heirs of the kingdom that he has promised to those who love him?" The eschatological promise of salvation in the blessing is developed according to both its future and present (rich in faith) dimensions. The reference to love as the human characteristic corresponding to the divine act of election does soften the paradox of the original blessing, but it is theologically appropriate: God's election cannot be coerced through (external) poverty, and yet his freedom shows itself precisely in the election of the poor. Hence any dishonoring of the *poor* (2:6) is also to be disqualified theologically.

6. Revelation always uses "poor" and "poverty" in opposition to → πλούσιος (7). The literal sense is intended in 2:9, where the *poverty* of the church in Smyrna is mentioned, and in 13:16, where in an enumeration of social classes "the rich and the *poor*" are mentioned with others. The usage is fig. in 3:17: The church in Laodicea, which thinks itself rich and prosperous, is characterized as "wretched, pitiable, *poor,* blind, and naked" (the last three adjectives anticipate v. 18).   H. Merklein

πυγμή, ῆς, ἡ *pygmē* fist*

Mark 7:3, in an enigmatic passage about the Jews: ἐὰν

μὴ πυγμῇ νίψωνται τὰς χεῖρας οὐκ ἐσθίουσιν (πυγμή is omitted in Δ syrˢ copˢᵃ and replaced by πυκνά, "frequently" [adv. neut. pl.], in ℵ W Vg, etc. [cf. Luke 5:33]). Suggested interpretations are, e.g.: a) washing or drying of the fist in the other cupped hand, b) washing of hands up to the wrist or elbow, and c) washing with a handful of water (cf. Lat. *pugnus/pugillus* as a common unit of measurement); on these interpretations see BAGD s.v.; K. L. Schmidt, *TDNT* VI, 915-17; M. Hengel, *ZNW* 60 (1969) 182-98; J. Gnilka, *Mark* (EKKNT) I, ad loc.

Jewish tradition requires the rinsing or washing of hands. The rinsing of someone else's hands with water from one's own cupped hands (or with two handfuls of water: S. M. Reynolds, *ZNW* 62 [1971] 295f.) is rejected in *m. Yad.* 1:2; *t. Yad.* 2:7. According to *m. Yad.* 2:3; *t. Yad.* 2:4; *b. Soṭa* 4b *Bar.* the hands become impure up to the wrist and so must be cleansed to the wrist (*contra y. Ber.* 8:12a; *b. Ḥul.* 106a *Bar.*). Since a rinsing of only the fist is excluded (the entire hand including the wrist must be rinsed), Mark 7:3 must refer either to rinsing the hands with a handful of water (in which case *m. Yad.* 1:2 and the parallel passages are objecting from a later perspective to a custom widespread during Jesus' time: so Hengel 195f., who postulates a Latinism in Mark; *contra* Hengel, Reynolds considers πυγμῇ dat. of relation: "with cupped hand"; cf. *idem, JBL* 85 [1966] 87), or to rinsing the hands up to the wrist. Both interpretations, however, run into linguistic problems (see on this esp. Reynolds). The idea of mistranslation from Aramaic (e.g., Schmidt 916; P. R. Weis, *NTS* 3 [1956/57] 233-36) does not do justice to the expository character of the Markan parenthesis (vv. 3f.). See also Billerbeck I, 695-704; W. D. McHardy, *ExpTim* 87 (1975/76) 119; J. M. Ross, *ExpTim* 87 (1975/76) 374f.

H. Balz

πύθων, ωνος, ὁ *pythōn* soothsayer; ventriloquist; python*

According to Acts 16:16 Paul and Silas met a "[Gentile] slave girl who had a spirit *of divination*" (παιδίσκη ἔχουσα πνεῦμα πύθωνα). Πύθων is in apposition to πνεῦμα (𝔭⁴⁵ Koine, etc., alleviate the difficulty with πνεῦμα πύθωνος; cf. BDF §242). Πύθων is the name of the serpent or dragon that guarded the Delphic oracle and was said to have been slain by Apollo (Strabo ix.3.12). In the Roman period πύθων was used of ventriloquists (= ἐγγαστρίμυθος, Plutarch *De Def. Orac.* 9 [*Moralia* 414E]). Suidas s.v., on the other hand, speaks of πνεῦμα πύθωνος. Origen, *De. Prin.* iii.3.5, describes the python as a demon. Hence Luke is trying to make it clear that a soothsaying demon is speaking from within the slave girl (with loud crying; cf. Acts 16:17; Mark 5:7 par., etc.); → μαντεύομαι. BAGD s.v.; W. Foerster, *TDNT* VI, 917-20; *KP* 1280.

πυκνός, 3 *pyknos* frequent(ly), often*

Neut. used as adv. in Luke 5:33; Mark 7:3 v.l.: νηστεύω πυκνά, "fast *often*"; comparative πυκνότερον as adv. in Acts 24:26: *more often, more frequently;* adjectival in 1 Tim 5:23: πυκναὶ ἀσθένειαι, "*frequent* ailments."

πυκτεύω *pykteuō* fight with fists, be a fistfighter, box*

Fig. in 1 Cor 9:26: οὕτως πυκτεύω ὡς οὐκ ἀέρα δέρων, "I do not *box* as one beating the air." Characteristically, Paul is not interested in the contrast between a serious struggle with an adversary and mere "shadow-boxing"; he does not wish to beat others, but is interested rather in his own full engagement as an apostle against his own body (v. 27). K. L. Schmidt, *TDNT* VI, 916f.

πύλη, ης, ἡ *pulē* gate, door, portal*

1. Meaning and occurrences — 2. Literal usage — a) Luke 7:12 — b) Acts 9:24 — c) Acts 16:13 — d) Heb 13:12 —e) Acts 3:1-10 — f) Acts 12:10 — 3. The Gates of Hades — 4. Fig. usage (Matt 7:13f.)

Lit.: L. DELEKAT and B. REICKE, *BHH* 2009-11. — W. ELLIGER, *Paulus in Griechenland* (SBS 92/93, 1978). — S. GERO, "The Gates or the Bars of Hades? A Note on Matt 16:18," *NTS* 27 (1980/81) 411-14. — H. HOMMEL, "Die Tore des Hades," *ZNW* 80 (1989) 124f. — J. JEREMIAS, *TDNT* VI, 921-28. — R. KRATZ, *Rettungswunder. Motiv-, traditions- und formkritische Aufarbeitung einer biblischen Gattung* (1979). — J. MARCUS, "The Gates of Hades and the Keys of the Kingdom (Matt 16:18-19)," *CBQ* 50 (1988) 443-55. — E. STAUFFER, "Das Tor des Nikanor," *ZNW* 44 (1952/53) 44-66. — For further bibliography → θύρα.

1. In contrast to θύρα (door) πύλη refers apparently to a larger *gate* or *gate complex* (esp. pl.), though it can also be used as a synonym of θύρα (cf. Acts 3:2, 10; Matt 7:13f., though cf. Luke 13:23f.) and less often of → πυλών (which usually refers to a gate complex or gateway; cf. esp. Acts 12:13f.). Πύλη is used of *city gates* in Luke 7:12 (Nain); Acts 9:24 (Damascus); 16:13 (Philippi); Heb 13:12 (Jerusalem), of a *temple gate* in Acts 3:10 (cf. 3:2), of a prison gate in Acts 12:10, and of the *Gates* of Hades in Matt 16:18; fig. usage occurs in Matt 7:13a, b, 14.

2.a) Jesus encounters a funeral procession before the *gate*, i.e., outside the city of Nain (Luke 7:12). Hellenistic stories of raising of the dead usually have the thaumaturge encounter the funeral procession (cf. Philostratus, *VA* iv.45), while in Jewish stories the miracle worker is usually called to the dead person (cf. 1 Kgs 17:17-24; 2 Kgs 4:18-37; Acts 9:36-42).

b) According to Acts 9:24 the city gates of Damascus were guarded day and night so that Paul could not escape.

c) Acts 16:13 probably refers to the western "Krenides Gate" in Philippi leading out to the fertile plain. On a sabbath Paul went through this gate with his companions to reach a Jewish place of prayer by the river. Elliger (47-50; bibliography) suggests, however, that what is intended is a colossal arched gate that has been discovered farther to the west and that presumably marked the western border of the territory of the Roman colony from the time of Augustus. It is unlikely, however, that πύλη would be used by itself for such an arch or that the law stipulating that cultic places of unofficial religions must lie outside the pomerium would be applied in this case. It remains doubtful whether either the gate or the river mentioned by Luke can be located more specifically.

d) In Heb 13:12 ἔξω τῆς πύλης is probably used *pars pro toto* to mean "outside the city." Executions—including that of Jesus— took place outside city gates. Hebrews uses the image within the framework of its "theology of sacrifice" "to illustrate the complete separation of Christianity from Judaism" (Jeremias, *TDNT* VI, 921f.).

e) Acts 3:1-10 mentions the "Beautiful *Gate*" of the Jerusalem temple in the story of the healing of a lame man. The lame beggar is sitting in a propitious position (cf. Mark 10:46): At the hour of prayer the temple is frequented by generous worshipers. The "Beautiful Gate" —the exact identity of which is difficult to ascertain— is usually identified as the "Nicanor Gate," which separated the Women's Court on its west side from the inner Court of the Israelites (cf. Stauffer; on other suggestions see G. Schneider, *Acts* [HTKNT] I, ad loc., with further bibliography).

f) In the narrative of the miraculous opening of the prison door and liberation of Peter (Acts 12:1-19) πύλη is used of the gate leading from the prison into the city (v. 10; the semantically more significant term is θύρα, v. 6). The attribute "iron" underscores the stability of the gate structure and thus throws the "automatic" opening before the angel and Peter into even sharper relief (cf. Kratz 459-73). This liberation miracle leads into a charmingly contrasting episode: Peter, having just reached freedom through the prison gate, stands before yet another closed gate (θύρα τοῦ πυλῶνος, v. 13; → πυλών).

3. Antiquity thought of heaven and the underworld as realms separate from earth and closed off by strong gates preventing unauthorized persons from entering. The gates of heaven can be opened before the epiphany of heavenly beings, in prayer, or through magic; the gates of the underworld prevent those incarcerated from escaping, and are opened only through violence—e.g., to superior deities—or in exceptional cases. According to primarily late canonical and apocryphal texts (1 Pet 3:19; Rev 1:18; *Acts Pil.* 17ff.; also in eastern iconography) the resurrected Christ (in the framework of the idea of the *de-scensus*) breaks open the gates of the underworld. But according to Matt 16:18 "the *Gates* of Hades" (*pars pro toto*) are unable to overcome the Church, which rests on a foundation of rock (cf. Kratz 407-30).

4. Matt 7:13f. speaks in antithetical parallelism of the ethical choice facing human behavior by means of the metaphor of two gates and two paths. The wide *gate* and easy way lead to destruction (v. 13b), while the narrow *gate* and hard way, i.e., the more difficult conditions, lead to salvation and life (vv. 13a, 14); the dimensions of both alternatives are in agreement with their different outcomes.

R. Kratz

πυλών, ῶνος, ὁ *pylōn* gate, portal; gate complex*

Πυλών occurs 18 times in the NT, 5 times in Acts and 11 in Revelation 21–22. In contrast to → πύλη, πυλών usually refers to a gate structure or complex or an entrance hall; accordingly, it is not used fig. in the NT. Luke 16:20 refers to the *gate* of wealthy homes: πρὸς τὸν πυλῶνα; Acts 14:13 probably refers to the *gate complex* of a temple of Zeus: ἐπὶ τοὺς πυλῶνας; 12:13 (similarly v. 14 bis) refers to a *vestibule* or *gateway:* ἡ θύρα τοῦ πυλῶνος; probably so also 10:17: ἐπὶ τὸν πυλῶνα; Matt 26:71: the *porch/entrance* of the high priest's palace (v. 58), which Peter reaches from the inner court (ἐξελθὼν εἰς τὸν πυλῶνα, "he went out [from the court] to the *porch*"); Rev 21:12 (bis), 15, 21 (bis), 25; 22:14 refer to the twelve gates of the heavenly Jerusalem, three of which face each of the four points of the compass (21:13: 4 occurrences; cf. Ezek 48:30ff.). J. Jeremias, *TDNT* VI, 921-28, esp. 922.

πυνθάνομαι *pynthanomai* inquire, ask, find out*

Πυνθάνομαι occurs 12 times in the NT, including 7 times in Acts. With indirect question following, meaning *inquire* in Matt 2:4: πυνθάνομαι παρά τινος ποῦ . . .; Luke 15:26: πυνθάνομαι τί ἂν εἴη ταῦτα; similarly 18:36; John 13:24: πυνθάνομαι τίς ἂν εἴη; cf. Acts 21:33. With direct question following, meaning *inquire* in the sense of "interrogate," Acts 4:7; *want to know*, 10:29; *inquire*, 23:19; πυνθάνομαι εἰ, "*inquire* whether," in 10:18; πυνθάνομαι ὅτι, "*find out/learn* that," in 23:34. With acc. obj., meaning *ask about,* in John 4:52; Acts 23:20: τὶ ἀκριβέστερον πυνθάνομαι, "*inquire* somewhat more closely."

πῦρ, ός, τό *pyr* fire*

1. Occurrences in the NT — 2. Meaning — 3. Fire as a part of daily life — 4. Fire as a symbol or in comparisons — 5. Heavenly fire — a) Fire in the heavenly realm — b) Fire coming from the heavenly realm to earth — 6. The fire of hell

Lit.: P. A. AMIET, et al., *Le feu dans le Proche-Orient Antique* (1973). — K. BERGER, "Hellenistisch-heidnische Prodigien und die Vorzeichen in der jüdischen und christlichen Apokalyptik," *ANRW* (1980) II/23/2, 1428-69. — J. BERGMAN, J. KRECHER, and V. HAMP, *TDOT* II, 418-28. — H. BIETENHARD, *DNTT* I, 653-58. — J. DANIÉLOU, *RAC* VII, 786-90. — M. DELCOURT, *Pyrrhos et Pyrrha* (1965). — G. DELLING, "Βάπτισμα βαπτισθῆναι," *idem, Studien zum NT und zum hellenistischen Judentum* (1970) 236-56. — J. D. M. DERRETT, "Salted with fire. Studies in texts: Mark 9:42-50," *Theology* 76 (1973) 364-68. — J. D. G. DUNN, "Spirit-and-fire baptism," *NovT* 14 (1972) 81-92. — A. FRIDRICHSEN, "Würzung mit Feuer," *SO* 4 (1926) 36-38. — T. F. GLASSON, "Water, Wind and Fire (Luke III.16) and Orphic Initiation," *NTS* 3 (1956/57) 69-71. — J. GNILKA, *Ist 1 Kor 3,10-15 ein Schriftzeugnis für das Fegfeuer?* (1955). — J. GOETTMANN, "Le feu du ciel sur la terre," *BVC* 33 (1960) 48-61. — I. GRUENWALD, *Apocalyptic and Merkavah Mysticism* (1980). — J. JEREMIAS, *Unknown Sayings of Jesus* (1957) 54-56. — F. LANG, *Das Feuer im Sprachgebrauch der Bibel* (Diss. Tübingen, 1950). — *idem, TDNT* VI, 928-48. — *idem,* "Erwägungen zur eschatologischen Verkündigung Johannes des Täufers," FS Conzelmann 459-73. — R. MAYER, *Die biblische Vorstellung vom Weltenbrand* (1956). — J. MICHL, "Gerichtsfeuer und Purgatorium. Zu 1 Kor 3,12-25," *SPCIC 1961* (AnBib 17-18, 1963) I, 395-401. — P. D. MILLER, "Fire in the Mythology of Canaan and Israel," *CBQ* 27 (1965) 256-61. — F. MORENZ, "Feurige Kohlen auf das Haupt," *TLZ* 78 (1953) 187-92. — J. MORGENSTERN, *The Fire Upon the Altar* (1963). — A. G. PATZJA, "Did John the Baptist Preach a Baptism of Fire and the Holy Spirit?" *EvQ* 40 (1968) 21-27. — E. PAX, *Epiphaneia* (1955). — E. T. SANDERS, "Pyrhōsis and the First Epistle of Peter 4:2," *HTR* 60 (1967) 501. — P. SCHÄFER, "Engel und Menschen in der Hekhalot-Literatur," *Kairos* 22 (1980) 201-25. — W. SPEYER, "Die Zeugungskraft des himmlischen Feuers in Antike und Urchristentum," *AuA* 24 (1978) 57-75. — *idem, RAC* X, 1107-72. — F. STOLZ, *THAT* I, 242-46. — H. ZIMMERMANN, "'Mit Feuer gesalzen werden.' Eine Studie zu Mk 9,49," *TQ* 139 (1959) 28-39. — For further bibliography see Lang (older works); *TWNT* X, 1256f.

1. The 73 NT occurrences have a clear center of gravity in Revelation (26 occurrences) and the Synoptic Gospels (12 in Matthew; 6 in Mark; 7 in Luke); πῦρ also occurs with relative frequency in Hebrews (5 times). It occurs only 4 times in the Pauline letters (Rom 12:20 [quotation]; 1 Cor 3:13 bis, 15), once in John, 4 times in Acts, once in 2 Thessalonians, and more frequently in the Catholic Epistles (3 times in James, once each in 1–2 Peter, twice in Jude). The word usually appears in the NT in eschatological contexts.

2. The meaning *fire* applies to all these occurrences; concerning the various aspects → 3-6. In the LXX πῦρ is almost without exception the tr. of Heb. *'ēš* or Aram. *nûr.*

3. a) Fire is among the necessities of daily life (cf. Sir 39:26f.); its function in village life is essential, but it is dangerous (Mark 9:22 [with ὕδατα] par. Matt 17:15 [with ὕδωρ]). It is used both for watch fires (→ φῶς, Luke 22:56) and for warmth (22:55; cf. Acts 28:2f., 5). b) It is also used for destruction in war (Rev 17:16 [cf. Jer 41:22 LXX = MT 34:22]; 18:8) and c) as an instrument of torture or death (the power of fire extinguished through faith, Heb 11:34; cf. Dan 3:17; 1 Macc 2:59 [ἐκ φλογός]; *1 Clem.* 45:7).

4. In several passages the common use of fire in the crafts and agriculture is the basis of fig. and symbolic language:

a) 1 Pet 1:7 uses the common metaphor of refinement of gold (cf. Prov 17:3; 27:21; Zech 13:9; Mal 3:3; Wis 3:6; Sir 2:5; 1QH 5:16): Πειρασμός proves the genuineness (→ δοκίμιον) of faith, which is more precious than gold, which is perishable, even though it is refined by fire. According to Rev 3:18 the Laodicean church is advised to buy gold refined by fire. "Refined gold is . . . a symbol for that which has withstood and continues to withstand all tests" (H. Kraft, *Rev* [HNT] 85).

b) The use of fire in agricultural life figures in judgment sayings, e.g., in John the Baptist's proclamation: "Every tree not bearing good fruit is cut down and thrown into the fire" (Matt 3:10 par. Luke 3:9 [Q]; cf. Matt 7:19). Matt 3:12 par. Luke 3:17 (Q) shows that what is meant is eschatological destruction: The coming one "will gather his wheat into the granary, but will burn the chaff with unquenchable fire." The elements of gathering and destroying are also seen in Matt 3:11 par. Luke 3:16 in a juxtaposition of baptism by the Holy Spirit and by fire, i.e., eschatological purification and renewal through the Spirit (cf. 1QS 4:21) and judgment of annihilation for those who do not change (see Lang, "Erwägungen" 466-73; Delling 249). Just as weeds are burned, so also at the end of time the angels sent by the Son of man will gather in evildoers and throw them into the furnace of fire (→ κάμινος: Matt 13:40, 42); cf. burning of branches pruned from the vine (John 15:6). Poison generated by the rusting of gold and silver (on the difficulties associated with this idea see M. Dibelius, *Jas* [Hermeneia] 236f.) becomes a witness against the rich and devours their flesh like fire (Jas 5:3; cf. Jdt 16:17; Isa 66:24). Just as a small fire ignites a great forest, so also is the effect of the tongue ruinous; it is itself a fire (Jas 3:5f.; → γλῶσσα 4; Dibelius, *Jas* 190-203).

5. Heavenly fire is viewed from two perspectives: a) as an attribute of the heavenly realm, i.e., of 1) God, 2) the exalted Christ, 3) angels, and 4) the heavenly cult, and b) as that which comes to earth 1) to save or 2) to destroy. Thus fire is both a characteristic and an instrument of divine judgment.

a) 1) God is himself a devouring fire (Heb 12:29, quoting Deut 4:24; cf. Deut 9:3; Isa 33:14). Elements of theophany—lightning, voices, and thunder— issue from his throne, and seven torches burn before it (Rev 4:5; cf.

2 Bar. 21:6; *1 Enoch* 14:22; streams of fire [Dan 7:10] from the throne: *1 Enoch* 14:19; *3 Enoch* 19:33; see Gruenwald 35f.).

2) In a vision the seer John sees Christ with divine characteristics from Dan 7:9f. In Dan 7:9 the throne is like fiery flames (ὡσεὶ φλὸξ πυρός; see also *1 Enoch* 14:19). But in Rev 1:14 (cf. 2:18; 19:12) it is Christ's eyes that are like a flame of fire (cf. Dan 10:6: λαμπάδες πυρός, of an angel; *2 Enoch* 1:5).

3) According to Heb 1:7 (quoting Ps 103:4 LXX) God makes his servants (angels) "flames of fire" (πυρὸς φλόγα; LXX: πῦρ φλέγον; this reverses what is in MT, where God makes flames of fire into his servants; cf. 2 Esdr 8:21; on rabbinic use of this Psalm verse see Billerbeck III, 678f.; further 1QH 1:10ff.; on the close relationship between angels and fire see Schäfer 202 [*Hekalot Rabbati* 17:8]; Gruenwald 43f.; *2 Bar.* 21:6). In accordance with the idea that certain angels control natural phenomena (*Jub* 2:2; cf. *1 Enoch* 60:12-20), Rev 14:18 asserts that an angel has power over fire (16:5: over water; 7:1: four angels over the four winds; cf. also 9:11, 14; cf. Billerbeck III, 820; Gabriel is the "prince of fire" in *b. Pesaḥ.* 118a). In Rev 10:1 a mighty angel displays the attributes of divine presence (cloud [Exod 13:21]; rainbow [Ezek 1:28]; sun [cf. Rev 1:16; Exod 34:33, 35]) and has feet (legs) like pillars of fire (cf. Exod 13:21: ἐν στύλῳ πυρός).

4) Fire in the heavenly cult is seen where the sea of glass (Rev 4:6) is mingled with fire (15:2). In Rev 8:5 an angel throws fire from the heavenly altar to the earth, resulting in thunder, voices, lightning, and earthquake. This passage provides the transition from the fire of the heavenly world to those passages speaking of the appearance of this fire on earth—primarily for judgment, but also for salvation.

b) 1) Fire is a symbol for God's presence in blessing in the two great OT divine epiphanies. Exod 3:1ff. is referred to in Acts 7:30: An angel appeared to Moses (LXX ἄγγελος κυρίου, Exod 3:2) in a flame in a bush (LXX ἐκ βάτου, 3:2). Exodus 19 (Deut 4:11; 5:22) is referred to in Heb 12:18, though in antithesis: The locus of divine encounter is *not* "what may be touched," i.e., a mountain, or "a blazing fire" (κεκαυμένον πῦρ; cf. Deut 4:11; 5:23; 9:15: τὸ ὄρος ἐκαίετο πυρί; cf. the continuation of the series of OT epiphanies in Heb 12:18-21 and the antithesis in vv. 22-24; see O. Michel, *Heb* [KEK] 460ff.).

According to Acts 2 (see Speyer, "Zeugungskraft" 68) and in analogy to Num 11:25, the Spirit came over the gathering of apostles at Pentecost, rested on each individual in the form of tongues of fire (Acts 2:3), and entered each one (v. 4). Either the tongues of fire are divided, or one is to understand that the tongues of fire distribute themselves on the individuals (so H. Conzelmann, *Acts* [Hermeneia] 14; concerning tongues of fire see Isa 5:24 MT; *1 Enoch* 14:15; 71:5; 1Q29 1:3; 2:3).

2) Fire as a component of theophanies is used esp. common in judgment sayings, after the model of OT and apocalyptic usage (→ 4.b).

In history fire can fall on a village and consume it (Luke 9:54; cf. 2 Kgs 1:10, 12, 14; on the inauthentic reference to Elijah cf. 1 Kgs 18:38; Sir 48:1). Luke 17:29 alludes to the OT judgment of destruction (cf. Gen 19:24).

Fire is also the preferred instrument of eschatological judgment. According to 1 Cor 3:13 the fire of judgment will show whether the foundation of the Church was laid properly. If an individual's work is burned up, he will be saved, but only as one who barely escapes fire (v. 15; see BAGD 730).

According to Rom 12:20 one heaps burning coals on one's enemy's head by renouncing revenge and thus leaving retribution to God (v. 19; cf. Deut 32:35) and by practicing love of enemy (quoting Prov 25:21f. LXX). It is not clear whether this speaks of a punishment and penitential rite or conjures future judgment by fire on the enemy (see also → ἄνθραξ). Acts 2:19 quotes Joel 3:1-5: Blood, fire, and smoke announce the last days, so that such characteristics of theophanies become anticipatory signs (on fire as *prodigium* see Berger 1437 n.31 and more generally 1436-38). Jesus and his angels appear at judgment in flaming fire (2 Thess 1:7).

Luke 12:49 is also difficult: "I came to throw *fire* on the earth, and would that it were already kindled!" Fire here in the Lukan context is probably the "fire of discord" (so Lang, *TDNT* VI, 942), but this would not be so in the original setting of the saying: If v. 49 is taken with v. 50 (see Delling 245-47), both allude to an event connected with Jesus' ministry: v. 50 to his death (cf. Mark 10:38), v. 49 to the judgment of God (v. 49b divine passive?). The Lukan context suggests that Jesus' ministry effects division (vv. 51-53).

The eschatological judgment connected with Jesus is probably also intended in the agraphon "Whoever is near me is near the fire, whoever is far from me is far from the kingdom" (on the text in Didymus and Origen as well as *Gos. Thom.* 82, see Jeremias 54-56).

Mark 9:49 probably also refers to purification through judgment: "For everyone will be salted with *fire*." This is probably not an allusion to use of fire and salt during amputations (see Derrett 364-68). More likely it alludes to the cleansing power of fire and salt. If ἁλισθήσεται is to be understood as divine passive, then it is clear through whom judgment will occur.

Revelation variously portrays the judgments preceding the epiphany of Christ (19:11ff.). Again, fire, often accompanied by or mixed with other instruments of judgment, always plays a destructive role. An angel throws fire from the heavenly altar onto the earth (8:5); during the trumpet judgments hail and fire mixed with blood fall from heaven (v. 7; fire and hail in Exod 9:23-25; fire and blood in Joel 3:3)—but the beast (13:13) is also able to make fire come down from heaven (cf. Elijah in 1 Kgs 18:38) and deceive people; a great mountain burning with fire is thrown into the sea (Rev 8:8; cf. Jer 51:25 LXX; *1 Enoch* 18:13; 21:3). Fire and smoke and sulphur issue from the mouths of horses in 9:17f. (see Job 41:10-12). At the bowl judgments, too, people are scorched with fire (Rev 16:8). The two witnesses (11:3) protect themselves with fire that consumes their foes (cf. 2 Kgs 1:9-12, 14) coming from their mouths (Rev 11:5; see Jer 5:14; fire from God's mouth, 2 Sam 22:9). Finally, the armies of Gog and Magog are consumed by fire from heaven (Rev 20:9, quoting 2 Kgs 1:10, 12, 14; cf. Ezek 38:22).

According to Heb 10:27 nothing remains for deliberate sinners other than the terrible prospect of judgment and the "fury of *fire*" (cf. Isa 26:11 LXX; Zeph 1:18). According to 2 Pet 3:7, by the same word that effected both creation and the flood the present heavens and earth are stored up for fire (cf. v. 10). This is the only NT instance of the idea of world conflagration, which is documented in Zoroastrianism, Judaism (*Sib. Or.* iii.84; iv.172, and elsewhere; 1QH 3:29ff.; see Mayer), Greek thought (Plato *Ti.* 22c), and esp. in Stoicism (see Hengel, *Judaism* I, 191, 200f., 214, 236). In 2 Pet 3:7, however, divine judgment rather than periodic natural events are intended.

6. Finally, the fire of hell is an instrument of the power of divine judgment. The most influential passage for this idea was Isa 66:24. → Γέεννα (2) is called γέεννα τοῦ πυρός (Matt 5:22; 18:9), "unquenchable fire" (Mark 9:48 [cf. vv. 43, 45]; Matt 3:12 par. Luke 3:17), or "eternal fire" (Matt 18:8; 25:41). Judgment by fire is frequently contrasted to possession of ζωή (Mark 9:43; Matt 18:8f.) or to entrance into the βασιλεία τοῦ θεοῦ (Mark 9:47; cf. Matt 13:41-43, 50). Sodom and Gomorrah suffer eternal fire (cf. Gen 18:20f.; 19:1ff.; Isa 1:9; Jer 23:14; Ezek 16:48ff.; *Jub.* 16:5; 2 Macc 2:5; *T. Naph.* 3:4; 4:1; *T. Ash.* 7:1; Matt 10:15; 11:24; Rom 9:29) because of immoral behavior with angels (Jude 7). Jude 23 calls on the readers to snatch doubters out of the fire (of judgment).

One variation of the portrayal of eternal eschatological judgment as a particular place of punishment is the lake of fire in Revelation. It is called simply λίμνη τοῦ πυρός (20:14, 15), λίμνη τοῦ πυρὸς καὶ θείου (20:10; cf. 21:8), or λίμνη τοῦ πυρὸς τῆς καιομένης ἐν θείῳ (19:20). The beast and the false prophet are thrown into this lake (19:20), as are the διάβολος (20:10), θάνατος and ᾅδης (v. 14), and finally anyone whose name is not written in the book of life (20:15; cf. 14:10). Death in the lake of fire is the "second death," i.e., eternal death (20:14).

H. Lichtenberger

πυρά, ᾶς, ἡ *pyra* woodpile, place where a fire is made*

Πυρά refers basically to the place where fire is made or to burning or combustible material piled up: Acts 28:2: ἅπτω πυράν, "kindle a *pile of wood*/[camp]fire"; 28:3: ἐπὶ τὴν πυράν, "on the *fire.*" Concerning the "funeral pyre" of martyrs cf. *Mart. Pol.* 13:2f.

πύργος, ου, ὁ *pyrgos* tower*

Mark 12:1 par. Matt 21:33: ᾠκοδόμησεν πύργον, of a *watchtower* in a vineyard (cf. Isa 5:2; 2 Chr 26:10; Billerbeck I, 868f.; Isa 1:8, e.g., speaks only of a watchman's booth); Luke 13:4: ὁ πύργος ἐν τῷ Σιλωάμ, probably a *tower* on the wall (cf. Josephus *B.J.* 145) that collapsed and buried eighteen persons (on this formulation cf. Josephus *B.J.* v.292; see further Spicq, *Notes* II, 776 with n.2). Luke 14:28 (πύργον οἰκοδομῆσαι) refers to a more elaborate fortified structure (cf. v. 29) with an unspecified purpose (on interpretation of it as a "farm building" see BAGD s.v. 2; W. Michaelis, *TDNT* VI, 955: "out-building"). W. Michaelis, *TDNT* VI, 953-56; D. Sperber, "On the *pyrgos* as a farm building," *Association for Jewish Studies Review* 1 (1976) 359-61; Spicq, *Notes* II, 774-79.

πυρέσσω *pyressō* suffer with a fever*

Mark 1:30 par. Matt 8:14, of Simon Peter's mother-in-law, who "lay sick with a *fever*" (πυρέσσουσα). The vb. does not occur in the LXX; → πυρετός. K. Weiss, *TDNT* VI, 956-59.

πυρετός, οῦ, ὁ *pyretos* fever*

Πυρετός occurs 6 times in the NT. Luke 4:38, of Simon's mother-in-law: συνεχομένη πυρετῷ μεγάλῳ, "she was ill with a high *fever*" (cf. Mark 1:30 par. Matt 8:14); Luke is probably making the customary medical differentiation between πυρετὸς μέγας and μικρός (see BAGD s.v.). Mark 1:31 par. Matt 8:15: ἀφῆκεν αὐτὴν ὁ πυρετός; par. Luke 4:39, ἐπετίμησεν τῷ πυρετῷ καὶ ἀφῆκεν αὐτήν, clearly identifies the healing as an exorcism. Acts 28:8: συνέχομαι (cf. Luke 4:38) πυρετοῖς καὶ δυσεντερίῳ, "lay sick with *fever* and dysentery." John 4:52: ἀφῆκεν αὐτὸν ὁ πυρετός. K. Weiss, *TDNT* VI, 956-59.

πύρινος, 2 *pyrinos* fiery, like fire, red*

Rev 9:17: The demonic horses and riders of the sixth trumpet vision wear "breastplates *of fire,* sapphire, and sulphur" (θώρακας πυρίνους . . .). This juxtaposition suggests that the emphasis is on color, hence "*fire red,* dark red [or "smoke blue": cf. v. 18], and sulphur yellow" (cf. Job 41:10ff.). This may be a reference to the various colors of the flames that according to Rev 9:18 issue from the mouths of the horses: fire, smoke, and sulphur. F. Lang, *TDNT* VI, 951f.

πυρόομαι *pyroomai* burn, be inflamed/red hot*

Πυρόομαι occurs 6 times in the NT, always pass. Literal usage: Eph 6:16: "the *flaming* darts (τὰ βέλη [τὰ] πεπυρωμένα) of the evil one"; 2 Pet 3:12, of the originally Persian and Stoic idea of the world conflagration at the end of time (only here in the NT): οὐρανοὶ πυρούμενοι λυθήσονται, "the heavens will be dissolved *by burning*" (cf. vv. 7, 10; opposite: καινοὶ οὐρανοί, v. 13; cf. also Zeph 1:18; 3:8; *2 Bar.* 31:5; *1 Enoch* 83:3f.; → πῦρ 5.b.2); *burn/purify through fire* (referring to metals) in Rev 1:15: ἐν καμίνῳ πεπυρωμένης, "refined as in a furnace" (the grammatically incorrect gen. is corrected in mss. to dat. or nom.); 3:18: χρυσίον πεπυρομένον, "gold *refined by fire*" (i.e., pure gold as a portrayal of salvation; cf. Ps 17:31 LXX). Only fig. in Paul: 1 Cor 7:9: πυροῦσθαι, *be aflame* with passion (cf. Sir 23:16); 2 Cor 11:29: οὐκ ἐγὼ πυροῦμαι, "I do not *burn*," i.e., with anger at those who deceive the Church and in burning love for the Church. BAGD s.v.; F. Lang, *TDNT* VI, 948-50.

πυρράζω *pyrrazō* be (fiery) red*

Matt 16:2, 3: πυρράζει ὁ οὐρανός, of the red color of the evening or morning sky as a proven sign of the coming weather. Not in א B X, etc.

Πύρρος, ου *Pyrros* Pyrrhus*

The father of Sopater of Beroea, one of Paul's seven companions on his return journey from Greece to Jerusalem (Acts 20:4).

πυρρός, 3 *pyrros* fiery red*

Rev 6:4: ἵππος πυρρός, "a *bright red* horse" (the second of four horses colored white, red, black, and pale respectively: vv. 1-8; cf. Zech 1:8; 6:1-3; the four basic colors in antiquity were τὸ λευκόν, μέλαν, ἐρυθρόν, χλωρόν [Theophrastus *Sens.* 13:73ff.]); Rev 12:3: δράκων μέγας πυρρός, "a great *red* dragon," the adversary of the woman (cf. Isa 14:29; 27:1; H. Kraft, *Rev* [HNT] ad loc.). F. Lang, *TDNT* VI, 952.

πύρωσις, εως, ἡ *pyrōsis* fire; burning; heat*

Rev 18:9, 18, of the eschatological burning of "Babylon": ὁ καπνὸς τῆς πυρώσεως αὐτῆς, "the smoke of her *burning*" (cf. v. 8); 1 Pet 4:12, of refinement of metals in fire as a portrayal of the testing of faith through suffering, which is actually the suffering of Christ (v. 13): ἡ ἐν ὑμῖν πύρωσις πρὸς πειρασμὸν ὑμῖν γινομένη, "the *fiery*

ordeal that comes on you to prove you." F. Lang, *TDNT* VI, 950f.

πωλέω *pōleō* sell*

There are 22 occurrences in the NT: 17 in the Gospels, 3 in Acts, and 1 each in 1 Cor 10:25; Rev 13:17. Act. in Mark 10:21: ὅσα ἔχεις; par. Matt 19:21: σοῦ τὰ ὑπάρχοντα; par. Luke 18:22: πάντα ὅσα ἔχεις; Matt 13:44: πάντα ὅσα ἔχει; Luke 12:33: τὰ ὑπάρχοντα; 22:36: τὸ ἱμάτιον; Acts 5:1: κτῆμα; with an obj. implied by the context in Acts 4:34, 37. Subst. partc. οἱ πωλοῦντες of *those who buy* or *sell:* Mark 11:15 (bis) par. Matt 21:12 (bis): the dealers in the temple (with ἀγοράζοντες; cf. Luke 19:45; John 2:14, 16; a general reference in Matt 25:9). Absolute in Matt 21:12a; 25:9; Mark 11:15a; Luke 19:45; Luke 17:28 (ἐπώλουν with ἠγόραζον and other daily activities in Sodom at the time of Lot); Rev 13:17: ἀγοράσαι ἢ πωλῆσαι. Pass. in Matt 10:29 par. Luke 12:6: δύο or πέντε στρουθία; 1 Cor 10:25: πᾶν τὸ ἐν μακέλλῳ πωλούμενον, "everything sold in the meat market."

πῶλος, ου, ὁ *pōlos* young animal, colt; young donkey; foal of an ass*

There are 12 occurrences in the NT, 11 of them in Mark 11 par., 1 in John 12:15. Πῶλος is a designation for a certain animal, but also means more generally *young animal, colt* (of the particular animal); thus with ὄνος, the foal of an ass, Matt 21:2, 5 (ἐπὶ ὄνον καὶ ἐπὶ πῶλον υἱὸν ὑποζυγίου), 7 (cf. Zech 9:9 LXX: ἐπὶ ὑποζύγιον καὶ πῶλον νέον); John 12:15: ἐπὶ πῶλον ὄνου (cf. v. 14: ὀνάριον). In all the other references to the animal that Jesus' rode into Jerusalem (Mark 11:2, 4, 5, 7 par. Luke 19:30, 33 bis, 35) πῶλος stands alone without any further identification. W. Bauer (BAGD; *JBL* 72 [1953] 220-29) prefers the meaning "horse" (cf. πῶλος = ἵππος in Pseudo-Callisthenes ii.14.2; 15.9). Since, however, in the LXX πῶλος as the tr. of *'ayir* can mean "ass's colt" without any further specification (Gen 49:11; Judg 10:4; 12:14; also Zech 9:9; cf. further O. Michel, *TDNT* VI, 960), and since the narratives in Mark and Luke probably also presuppose Zech 9:9 (possibly also Gen 49:11), our passages probably also refer to the *foal of an ass.* O. Michel, *TDNT* VI, 959-61; *idem, NTS* 6 (1959/60) 81f.; R. Bartnicki, *NovT* 18 (1976) 161-66; *TWNT* X, 1257 (bibliography).

πώποτε *pōpote* at any time, ever*

This adv. occurs 6 times in the NT, 5 of those in John and 1 John, always with a negative particle: Luke 19:30; John 1:18; 8:33; 1 John 4:12: οὐδεὶς πώποτε, "no one *ever*"; John 5:37: οὔτε . . . πώποτε; 6:35: οὐ μὴ διψήσει πώποτε, "he shall *never [not ever]* thirst."

πωρόω *pōroō* harden, make stubborn*

The vb. occurs 5 times in the NT, always fig., and 4 times pass. in the sense of *to be obtuse,* referring to the human "heart" (3 times) or human "senses" (once). The vb. does not occur with this meaning in the LXX.

Two occurrences in Mark refer to Jesus' disciples, who even at the miraculous feeding are incapable of trusting faith; 6:52: ἦν αὐτῶν ἡ καρδία πεπωρωμένη; 8:17: πεπωρωμένην ἔχετε τὴν καρδίαν ὑμῶν (cf. v. 18; Jer 5:21; Ezek 12:2). The context of the latter passage (cf. 8:21) suggests that hardening of the heart is to be understood as lack of understanding. It expresses, therefore, human dependence on the faith mediated by Christ: Only from the perspective of the cross does the meaning of Christ's deeds become clear. The prophetic statement of hardening (Isa 6:9-11) is taken up in John 12:40 so that God is the direct cause of the people's inability to believe: ἐπώρωσεν αὐτῶν τὴν καρδίαν (Isa 6:10 LXX: ἐπαχύνθη γὰρ ἡ καρδία τοῦ λαοῦ τούτου).

Paul's use of the vb. is concerned with the hardening of "Israel" in the face of God's eschatological offer of salvation, in which only a "remnant" now participates, so that someday all of Israel may be won (Rom 11:7: οἱ δὲ λοιποὶ ἐπωρώθησαν, quoting Deut 29:3; Isa 29:10; cf. further Rom 11:5, 11f.). Here, too, hardening is understood in a profound sense as God's work with the goal of winning the Gentiles and ultimately "all" Israel to salvation. Similarly 2 Cor 3:14: ἐπωρώθη τὰ νοήματα αὐτῶν. → πώρωσις, → παχύνω. K. L. Schmidt, *TZ* 1 (1945) 1-17; K. L. Schmidt and M.A. Schmidt, *TDNT* V, 1025-28; *TWNT* X, 1226 (bibliography); J. Gnilka, *Die Verstockung Israels* (1961); U. Becker, *DNTT* II, 153-56.

πώρωσις, εως, ἡ *pōrōsis* stubbornness, hardening*

There are 3 occurrences in the NT, all, as with the vb. → πωρόω, fig. Mark 3:5: πώρωσις τῆς καρδίας (of the Pharisees); Rom 11:25: πώρωσις ἀπὸ μέρους τῷ Ἰσραὴλ γέγονεν (cf. vv. 4f., 7 [→ πωρόω], 11f.); Eph 4:18, of the Gentiles, who are excluded from the life of God διὰ τὴν πώρωσιν τῆς καρδίας αὐτῶν, referring above all to their manner of life (cf. vv. 17, 19ff.; Rom 1:21ff.). K. L. and M. A. Schmidt, *TDNT* V, 1025-28; U. Becker, *DNTT* II, 153-56.

πώς *pōs* somehow, perhaps*

This enclitic particle occurs 15 times in the NT (never in the Gospels), always with the particles εἰ (4 times) or μή (11 times). Εἴ πως, "somehow," in Acts 27:12; Rom 1:10; 11:14; Phil 3:11. μή πως (→ μήπως), "lest somehow," in 1 Cor 8:9; 9:27; 2 Cor 2:7; 9:4; "that *perhaps*" (after φοβέομαι) in 11:3; 12:20 (bis); Gal 4:11; similarly Rom 11:21 (where an expression of worry is implied; μή

πως omitted in א A B C, etc.) and 1 Thess 3:5: "for fear that *somehow.*" As the introduction to an indirect question in Gal 2:2: "lest *somehow.*"

πῶς *pōs* how?, in what way?; but how! never, impossible; in what sense?; that (conj.)*

1. Occurrences in the NT — 2. Modal usage — 3. *What?* — 4. Expression of amazement and surprise — 5. Exclamation — 6. Disapproval — 7. Congruity — 8. Rhetorical questions — 9. Indirect questions

Lit.: BAGD s.v. — BEYER, *Syntax* 126. — BDF §§106; 436. — LSJ s.v. — H. JUNGVIK, "Zum Gebrauch einiger Adverbien im NT," *Eranos. Acta Philologica Suecana* 62 (1964) 29-39, esp. 31f.

1. Πῶς occurs 103 times in the NT (not including Mark 8:21 v.l.; *ca.* 130 occurrences in the LXX). It occurs frequently in John, which has 20 occurrences (none with subjunc. or opt.), 14 of those in rhetorical questions expressing incomprehension (in direct questions only in 9:10, 19, 26; in indirect questions only in vv. 15, 21), and in Mark (14 occurrences, 7 in indirect questions, 4 in rhetorical questions). Of 14 occurrences in Matthew 10 are in rhetorical questions (only 3 in indirect questions, all in traditional material). The word occurs 16 times in Luke's Gospel (7 times in indirect questions, 5 in rhetorical questions) and 9 times in Acts (7 in indirect questions, only once [8:31] in a rhetorical question [the only occurrence with opt.]). Of 22 occurrences in Paul, 8 are in Romans (all in rhetorical questions, except in 4:10), 9 in 1 Corinthians (5 in rhetorical questions, 4 in indirect questions); it occurs in rhetorical questions in Gal 2:14; 4:9; 2 Cor 3:8 and in indirect questions in 1 Thess 1:9; 4:1. Further occurrences in indirect questions are in Col 4:6 par. Eph 5:15; 2 Thess 3:7; 1 Tim 3:15; Rev 3:3; in rhetorical questions in 1 Tim 3:5; Heb 2:3; 1 John 3:17 (and 4:20 v.l.).

2. The adv. interrogative particle with ind. is clearly modal: *in what way? how?* in Rom 4:10a (cf. the development in v. 10b); Luke 8:18; John 9:10, 19, 26 (cf. vv. 15, 21 in indirect questions, v. 16 in a rhetorical question: *impossibly/not possible*—so also perhaps v. 10 as an expression of incomprehension); Matt 22:12 is uncertain (→ 5); similarly Luke 1:34 (cf. v. 37: *impossible*); 1 Cor 15:35b (a rhetorical question quoting the Corinthian false teachers; possibly also modal in view of the Pauline parallel question in v. 35c if ποίῳ is synonymous).

3. In Hellenistic Greek πῶς is also used in place of the neut. interrogative pron. τί, *what?* (see Ljungvik): so Mark 4:30b (with subjunc. [cf. the second question in v. 30c], probably influenced by Latin ablative sg. *a quo,*

which can also mean "how? in what way?"); Luke 10:26 (despite BAGD not modal); but not the indirect question in Luke 8:18 (*contra* BDF §436), since it is a summarizing conclusion (vv. 12-15 is concerned with the *how* of the hearing). The meaning *what?* is clearly intended in Acts 2:8 (cf. the obj. in v. 11b) and in the indirect questions in 1 Cor 3:10 (cf. v. 12); Col 4:6 (recalling concretely the content of the writing; cf. v. 3: τὸ μυστήριον); Mark 5:16; Rev 3:3.

4. Πῶς as an interrogative expressing amazement (*I do not understand how; how is it possible that*) is difficult to distinguish from its use in rhetorical questions (*it is impossible that*): Matt 21:20 (considering the following adv. → 5); possibly also as connotation in Luke 1:34 (→ 2); Acts 2:8 (→ 3; Mark 4:40 v.l., since it never occurs with a negation in Mark: see *TCGNT* 84).

5. On that basis πῶς is used as an exclamatory particle in expressions of amazement (instead of ὡς: BDF §436): *how very . . . !:* Mark 10:23 (par. Luke 18:24: adv. for intensification is considered good Greek [Kühner, *Grammatik* II/1, 663]); Mark 10:24 (with adj.); Luke 12:50; John 11:36; possibly also Matt 21:20 (LSJ; Moule, *Idiom-Book* 132 with note on 207; → 4).

6. Wherever the question more strongly suggests disapproval (*how can you say? with what right?*) it is difficult to distinguish the usage from → 4 and → 8: Mark 12:35 par. Luke 20:41; Matt 7:4 par. Luke 6:42; Matt 22:12; Luke 12:56 (note voc.).

7. Similarly, questions of objective congruity are hardly distinguishable from → 8 (*with what right, in what sense, how?*): BDF §442.8): Mark 9:12 ("If Elijah does come first to restore all things, *how* then is it written . . . ?"); Matt 22:43; 26:54 (with deliberative subjunc. instead of classical fut.: *impossible*).

8. The rhetorical question with πῶς always asks about compatibility and always presupposes its answer—*impossible*—as self-evident. Thus it is typically employed in the course of argumentation, e.g., as an apodosis that is the logical conclusion after a conditional or causal protasis: Gal 2:14: "Since [not "if": εἰ with ind. of actual case] you . . . then you cannot possibly . . ."; 4:9 (after causal partc.); 1 Cor 14:7, 9, 16; 15:12; Rom 3:6; 6:2; with reversed order of clauses (and thus with deliberative subjunc.) in Rom 10:14a, b, c, 15. With normal clausal sequence with the negative in the apodosis (2 Cor 3:8; Rom 8:32) the sense is *quite surely, certainly* (Kühner, *Grammatik* II/2, 522 n.9)—probably also in the only similar passage in Matthew (16:11: not in the sense of οὔπω). A simple apodosis occurs in 1 Tim 3:5 (a parenthetical proverb); Heb 2:3; 1 John 3:17; Matt 12:26 par. Luke 11:18 (abbreviated in Mark 3:23); Matt 22:45; John 3:12; 5:47; 6:42 (abbreviated in v. 52); 8:33; 14:5, 9. Reversed clausal order is seen in Matt 12:29, 34 (repeated in 23:33 in abbreviated form with subjunc.); Acts 8:31; John 3:4 (repeated in abbreviated form in v. 9); 4:9; 5:44; 7:15. The conclusion particle is amplified in the stylistically good Greek syntagm καὶ πῶς (*totally impossible, completely out of the question:* Kühner, *Grammatik* II/2, 518 n.5; BDF §442.5): Mark 4:13 (with fut., as in classical Greek; cf. Luke 1:34; Matt 7:4; 12:26); 9:12; Luke 20:44; John 12:34 (and 14:5, 9 v.l.).

9. Of the 37 occurrences of the (metalinguistic) indirect question 4 imply the sense of *what* (→ 3). After vbs. of perceiving, knowing, and saying πῶς usually means *how* (used in place of ὅπως): 1 Thess 4:1 (with anaphoric art. giving πῶς the value of a noun; par. Eph 5:15; 1 Tim 3:15 as a reflection of the letter up to that point); Luke 12:11 (par. Matt 10:19; 1 Cor 7:32, 33, 34 with deliberative subjunc.); 12:27 (par. Matt 6:28); Mark 11:18 (with subjunc., par. 14:1, 11; Luke 22:2, 4 with anaphoric art. as in Acts 4:21: Kühner, *Grammatik* II/1, 625f.); Acts 15:36; 20:18. Further, πῶς is used with increasing frequency in place of ὅτι (*that;* cf. Acts 9:27b, d with 27c; Moulton, *Grammar* III, 137 n.2; BDF §396): 1 Thess 1:9 (par. Luke 8:36; Acts 11:13); Mark 2:26 (par. Matt 12:4); 12:26, 41; Luke 14:7; Acts 12:17; 2 Thess 3:7.

W. Schenk

P ϱ

'Pαάβ, 'Pαχάβ *Rhaáb, Rhachab* Rahab*

The name of the "harlot Rahab" (Heb. *rāḥāḇ*) who according to Josh 2:1ff. hid two Israelite spies on the roof of her house in Jericho and thus according to 6:17, 22f., 25 was spared when the city was destroyed. The name occurs 3 times in the NT. The form 'Pαάβ (cf. BDF §39.3; Josephus *Ant.* 5:8: 'Pαάβη, v.l. 'Pαχάβη) occurs in Heb 11:31, where Rahab's actions in Jericho are reckoned to her as faith (πίστει 'Pαάβ ἡ πόρνη οὐ συναπώλετο; cf. Josh 2:9ff.), and in Jas 2:25, where her deed counts as a work of faith ('Pαάβ ἡ πόρνη οὐκ ἐξ ἔργων ἐδικαιώθη[;]). The form 'Pαχάβ occurs in the genealogy of Jesus in Matt 1:5, where Rahab is mentioned as the mother of Boaz and thus as the great-grandmother of Jesse, David's father (rabbinic texts know her as Joshua's wife, ancestress of priests and prophets, and a proselyte [*Mek. Exod.* 18:1; *Sipre Num.* 78 on 10:29). G. Kittel, *TDNT* III, 1-3, esp. 3; K. Elliger, *BHH* 1547; A. van den Born, *BL* 1442; J. D. Quinn, *Bib* 62 (1981) 225-28; R. E. Brown, *Bib* 63 (1982) 79f.

ῥαββί *rhabbi* rabbi, my master*
ῥαββουνί *rhabbouni* my master*

1. Occurrences in the NT — 2. Meaning and Jewish background — 3. Mark and Matthew — 4. John

Lit.: DALMAN, *Words* 324f., 331-40. — J. W. DOEVE, *BHH* 1541-45. — J. DONALDSON, "The Title Rabbi in the Gospels . . . ," *JQR* 63 (1972/73) 287-91. — B. GERHARDSSON, *Memory and Manuscript* (ASNU 22, 1961) 324-35. — GOPPELT, *Theology*, I, 163-65. — HAHN, *Titles* 73-89. — M. HENGEL, *The Charismatic Leader and His Followers* (1981) 42-57. — E. LOHSE, *TDNT* VI, 961-65. — R. RIESNER, *Jesus als Lehrer* (WUNT II/7, 1981) 266-76. — H. P. RÜGER, *TRE* III, 608. — A. SCHULZ, *Nachfolgen und Nachahmen* (SANT 6, 1962) 21-49. — H. SHANKS, "Is the Title 'Rabbi' Anachronistic in the Gospels?" *JQR* 53 (1962/63) 337-45. — idem, "Origins of the Title 'Rabbi,'" *JQR* 59 (1968/69) 152-57. — S. ZEITLIN, "The Title Rabbi in the Gospels is Anachronistic," *JQR* 59 (1968/69) 158-60. — For further bibiography see *TWNT* X, 1257.

1. 'Pαββί occurs in the NT only in the Gospels of Matthew, Mark, and John. The 15 occurrences are found in Mark 9:5 (voc. ῥαββί is replaced by κύριε in par. Matt 17:4 and by ἐπίστατα in par. Luke 9:33); 11:21 (not in par. Matt 21:20); 14:45 par. Matt 26:49; Matt 23:7, 8 (M); 26:25 (M; cf. Mark); John 1:38, 49; 3:2, 26; 4:31; 6:25; 9:2; 11:8. John 1:38 translates voc. ῥαββί with διδάσκαλε (cf. 3:2); Matt 23:8 also shows that διδάσκαλος is an equivalent term. 'Pαββί is used primarily of Jesus (except in Matt 23:7, 8; John 3:26).

The form ῥαββουνί occurs only as an address for Jesus in Mark 10:51 (by the blind man; replaced by κύριε [!] in par. Matt 20:33 and Luke 18:41) and John 20:16 (by Mary Magdalene for the resurrected Jesus). It is amplified in John 20:16 by διδάσκαλε. The "Western" text (D it) has κύριε ῥαββί in Mark 10:51 instead of ῥαββουνί.

2. In Judaism at the time of Jesus voc. *rabbi*, "my master" (transliterated as ῥαββί) was the form of address for scholars or the learned (Dalman 331, with reference to Matt 23:7). *Rab* was frequently the designation for teachers (of the law; Dalman 333); the original meaning was "great one." *Rabbān* is also derived from *rab*. Palestinian Aramaic preferred the ending *-ôn* instead of *-ān* and thus generated the form *rabbôn*, from which Gk. ῥαββουνί, *my master,* resulted (Dalman 324).

Concerning the possible "anachronistic" usage of the title ῥαββί in the Gospels see the discussion between Shanks, Zeitlin, and Donaldson. The Gospel tradition is consistent with the meaning of the terms in Judaism in interpreting ῥαββί and ῥαββουνί with "teacher" or "lord" (→ 1). Judaism of Jesus' time did not yet restrict the address "rabbi" to educated and ordained scholars. Neglect of this fact has led to interpretations of the relationship between Jesus and his disciples that too schematically follow the analogy of the relation of "teacher of the law" to "students of the law" (see Hengel; → ἀκολουθέω 4). Hahn (75) refers to findings suggesting that in the Gospels the address "rabbi" "is brought only secondarily into connection with the idea of discipleship" (Mark 10:51f.).

3. The tradition's inclination either to suppress this title (Matthew) or to avoid it completely (Luke) suggests

that ῥαββί really was applied to Jesus during his earthly ministry (→ 1). Voc. διδάσκαλε, found frequently in all the Gospels except John (Mark 4:38; 9:17, 38; 10:17, 20, 35 and *passim*), in many instances probably renders an original ῥαββί (→ διδάσκω 4.a).

Ῥαββί already belongs to the pre-Markan tradition, but "there is no evidence of the word in the logia-source [Q]" (Hahn 74). In Mark ῥαββί is used of Jesus by Peter (9:5; 11:21) and Judas (14:45). When the blind beggar of Jericho addresses Jesus with ῥαββουνί (10:51), Mark probably simply follows the narrative as it was transmitted, though the form does show within the context of Mark's Gospel the wider gulf between Jesus and someone not belonging to the circle of the Twelve.

Matthew generally limits use of ῥαββί. Scribes and Pharisees in Judaism like to be addressed with ῥαββί (Matt 23:7). Jesus' disciples, however, should not allow themselves to be thus addressed, since Jesus is their only teacher and they are brothers (23:8). Only the betrayer Judas uses the address ῥαββί of Jesus (26:25, 49).

4. In the Fourth Gospel the address ῥαββί is translated by "teacher" when it first appears (John 1:38) and is used of Jesus by former disciples of John the Baptist. John's disciples use it of John himself in 3:26. The address "rabbi" in 1:49 introduces Nathanael's confession of Jesus as Son of God. Nicodemus combines the address with the words "We know that you are a teacher come from God" (3:2). Jesus' disciples also use the address "rabbi" in 4:31; 9:2; 11:8 of their master, and the people use it in 6:25. This address is commensurate with the relationship between the μαθηταί and their teacher (cf. 1:38; 3:25f.; 4:31; 9:2; 11:8). Ῥαββουνί is documented only in reference to the resurrected Jesus (20:16), where it is intended to eclipse voc. κύριε (v. 15), with which the erroneously identified gardener is addressed (cf. also τὸν κύριον in v. 18 and the confession of Thomas in 20:28). John avoids voc. διδάσκαλε (except in the translations in 1:38 and 20:16; cf., however, the "Synoptic" passage 8:4 [v.l.]).

G. Schneider

ῥαββουνί *rhabbouni* my master
→ ῥαββί.

ῥαβδίζω *rhabdizō* deliver blows with a stick, beat with a rod, flog*

This vb. occurs twice in the NT and refers to the Roman punishment of scourging *(verberatio)*, which could be used both for chastisement and for torture during interrogation (though not with Roman citizens; cf. → μαστιγόω). According to Acts 16:22 Paul and Silas were condemned to (public) scourging by the Roman magistrates for inciting a public disturbance (ἐκέλευον ῥαβδίζειν; cf. v. 23: πολλάς τε ἐπιθέντες αὐτοῖς πληγάς; vv. 35,

38: the ῥαβδοῦχοι, "lictors," who carried bundles of fasces; v. 37). According to 2 Cor 11:25 Paul suffered this punishment three times (τρὶς ἐρραβδίσθην, in addition to five scourgings in synagogues, v. 24). C. Schneider, *TDNT* V, 970f.

ῥάβδος, ου, ἡ *rhabdos* stick, staff, rod*

Ῥάβδος appears 12 times in the NT, including 4 times each in Hebrews and Revelation.

According to Matt 10:10 par. Luke 9:3 (Q) the disciples sent out by Jesus are not allowed to take a *staff* (μηδὲ ῥάβδον, Matthew; μήτε ῥάβδον, Luke); cf., however, Mark 6:8 (εἰ μὴ ῥάβδον μόνον), where *staff* and sandals are the only equipment allowed the messengers. Whereas the Markan version can be understood as a means of reducing weight (see J. Gnilka, *Mark* [EKKNT] I, ad loc.), the abrupt prohibition of any equipment in Q might be emphasizing the difference between early Christian messengers and itinerant Cynic preachers, for whom a "stave, satchel, and a single philosopher's cloak" were characteristic (cf. M. Hengel, *The Charismatic Leader and his Followers* [1981] 28; J. D. Crossan, *Biblical Research* 36 [1991] 4-9).

1 Cor 4:21 refers (ironically) to the *rod* as an instrument of chastisement: ἐν ῥάβδῳ ἔλθω πρὸς ὑμᾶς; (opposite: ἐν ἀγάπῃ, thinking perhaps of the → παιδαγωγός [v. 15], who often employed the rod).

Heb 1:8 (bis) refers to the *scepter* of God in the hand of the Son as ruler (ῥάβδος τῆς εὐθύτητος /τῆς βασιλείας, quoting Ps 44:7 LXX). 9:4 mentions "the budding *rod* of Aaron" in the ark (ἡ ῥάβδος ᾿Ααρὼν ἡ βλαστήσασα; cf. Num 17:14ff., esp. v. 25; see further C. Schneider, *TDNT* VI, 969f.). 11:21 refers to the *staff* over which Jacob, dying, bowed (to God; τὸ ἄκρον τῆς ῥάβδου αὐτοῦ, "the head of his *staff*") as a sign of humility (cf. Gen 47:31 LXX, which departs from MT: *rō᾿š hammiṭṭâ*, "the head of his bed").

Rev 11:1 refers to the "measuring rod like a *staff*" (→ κάλαμος ὅμοιος ῥάβδῳ; cf. Ezek 40:3). Revelation also mentions the (iron shepherd's) *rod* as a sign of eschatological dominion over the nations (ποιμαίνω . . . ἐν ῥάβδῳ σιδηρᾷ, Ps 2:9 LXX), which will be in the hands of both Christ (Rev 12:5; 19:15) and "the one who conquers" (2:27); cf. *Pss. Sol.* 17:24; Isa 11:4. C. Schneider, *TDNT* VI, 966-70.

ῥαβδοῦχος, ου, ὁ *rhabdouchos* lictor, policeman, constable*

Acts 16:35, 38 refers to the Roman lictors in Philippi. Lictors are always mentioned in connection with their "magistrates" or *duumviri*. The title is an administrative t.t. (cf. Polybius v.26.10). As a rule the στρατηγοί of a city had two lictors. → ῥαβδίζω; C. Schneider, *TDNT* VI, 971.

ῥαβιθά *rhabitha* girl

Mark 5:41 D ῥαββὶ θαβιτά (in place of ταλιθά) can be traced back to fem. ῥαβιθά from Aram. *rabîtā'*, "girl"; cf. H. P. Rüger, *TRE* III, 609.

Ῥαγαύ *Rhagau* Reu*

The father of Serug and son of Peleg (Gen 11:18-21; Heb. *rᵉ'û*) in the genealogy of Jesus (Luke 3:35).

ῥᾳδιούργημα, ατος, τό *rhadiourgēma* wantonness, deception, wrongdoing*

Acts 18:14: ῥᾳδιούργημα πονηρόν after ἀδίκημα as a transgression requiring legal redress: "vicious *crime.*"

ῥᾳδιουργία, ας, ἡ *rhadiourgia* wantonness, deception, wickedness*

Acts 13:10, of the magician Elymas, who is "full of all deceit and *villainy*" (παντὸς δόλου καὶ πάσης ῥᾳδιουργίας); opposite: δικαιοσύνη.

ῥαίνω *rhainō* sprinkle

Acts 19:13 v.l.: pass. ἱμάτιον ῥεραντισμένον αἵματι in place of βεβαμμένον (from βάπτω, cf. → βαπτίζω 9).

Ῥαιφάν *Rhaiphan* Rephan*

Lit.: W. BAUDISSIN, *RE* XVI, 639-49. — K.-H. BERNHARDT, *BHH* 300, 1622. — A. VAN DEN BORN, *BL* 1492. — E. HAENCHEN, *Acts* (Eng. tr., 1971), on 7:43. — J. NELIS, *BL* 942. — G. SCHNEIDER, *Acts* (HTKNT) ad loc.

According to Acts 7:43 (𝔭⁷⁴ ℵᶜ A, etc.), following Amos 5:26 LXX, the name of a heathen deity whose constellation helped guide the Israelites in the wilderness. The form of the name varies in the mss. of both the LXX and the NT ('Ρομφάν/μ, 'Ρεμφάν/μ, 'Ρεφά, and similarly) and deviates from the MT *(kîyûn)*. The name in Amos 5:26 is based on the name of the Akkadian celestial god *kêwān* (= Saturn), which is probably read by the Masoretes with the vowels of *šiqqûṣ*, "abomination," and rendered by the LXX with 'Ραιφάν (instead of Καιφάν).

ῥακά *rhaka* buffoon, empty-head, fool*

Matt 5:22: a term of contempt (v.l. ῥαχά ℵ* D W) that can probably be derived from Aram. *rêqā'*, "empty, frivolous" (probably not from ῥάκος, "rags, raggedy person"). *Rêqā'* is a Jewish term of abuse (cf. *b. Ber.* 32b; *b. Sanh.* 100a) that also appears in a Zenon papyrus from 257 B.C. as a Greek loanword ('Αντίοχον τὸν ῥαχᾶν, Preisigke, *Sammelbuch* 7638, 7). The word usually carries with it the idea of emptiness or lack of insight, as it does in its interpretation by the Church fathers, and is

probably hardly to be distinguished from the following word, μωρέ (→ μωρία 3). Billerbeck I, 278f.; G. Dalman, *Jesus-Jeschua* (1922; 1967) 68-71; BAGD s.v. (bibliography); J. Jeremias, *TDNT* VI, 973-76; *TWNT* X, 1257 (bibliography); R. A. Guelich, *ZNW* 64 (1973) 39-52; H. P. Rüger, *TRE* III, 608.

ῥάκος, ου, τό *rhakos* piece of cloth, patch*

Mark 2:21 par. Matt 9:16: ἐπίβλημα ῥάκους ἀγνάφου, "a patch from a *piece of* unshrunk *cloth,*" in Jesus' admonition not to use the "new" (God's new dominion) as a patch for the "old," since the new eclipses ("tears away from") the old; cf. further Luke 5:36; *Gos. Thom.* 47; Sir 9:10. F. Hahn, *EvT* 31 (1971) 357-75.

Ῥαμά *Rhama* Ramah*

A city (Heb. *rāmâ*) in the area of the tribe of Benjamin (Josh 18:25) 8 km. north of Jerusalem near the border between Judah and Israel (modern *er-Râm;* cf. further Judg 19:13; 1 Kgs 15:17ff.; Isa 10:29; Hos 5:8). According to Jer 31:15 Rachel, as Benjamin's mother (cf. Gen 35:16-20), weeps in Ramah over the abduction of her children. Rachel's grave (Gen 35:19: between Bethel and Ephrath; 1 Sam 10:2: on the border between Benjamin and Ephraim) came to be associated with Bethlehem (cf. Gen 48:7; *Jub.* 32:34; also Mic 5:2: "Bethlehem-Ephrathah"; the domed structure of Rachel's tomb erected during the Crusades lies north of Bethlehem today). So also Matt 2:18, following Jer 31:15, associates Rachel's lament with the murder of male children in Bethlehem: φωνὴ ἐν 'Ραμὰ ἠκούσθη. . . . Kopp, *Places* 9, 31f., 36f.; K. Elliger, *BHH* 1547f.; A. van den Born and H. Haag, *BL* 1444, 1445f.

ῥαντίζω *rhantizō* besprinkle, cleanse by sprinkling; mid.: cleanse oneself*

All 4 NT occurrences of ῥαντίζω are in Hebrews 9–10. 3 refer to cultic sprinkling of human beings or objects with blood or cleansing water for the purpose of purification and expiation (Num 19:1ff.; Lev 14:4-7; etc.) and 1 refers fig. to the "sprinkling" of hearts (Heb 10:22).

Heb 9:13 speaks of the "blood of goats and bulls" (cf. Lev 4:6, 17; 16:14f., 18f.) and the "ashes of a red heifer" (cf. Num 19:2ff., 9, 17ff.) used for sprinkling defiled persons: τὸ αἷμα τράγων καὶ ταύρων καὶ σποδὸς δαμάλεως ῥαντίζουσα τοὺς κεκοινωμένους. According to Num 19:17ff. the ashes of the red heifer, as an ingredient of the water of purification, represents the heifer itself. The context in Hebrews is concerned with atonement during the great day of reconciliation (cf. Heb 9:7, 12, 14), which is expanded here to include the water of purification of Numbers 19. This combination allows the reader to view the sprinkling of cultic objects in the sanctuary according to Lev 16:14f., 18f. together with the cleansing of human beings according to Lev 14:1ff.; Num 19:11ff. (after leprosy and contact with a corpse) and then to juxtapose these means of expiation—which effect only purification of the flesh—with the blood of Christ, which purifies one's conscience from dead works and thus renders true service to God possible (Heb 9:14).

Similarly, Heb 9:15ff. looks at the ratification of the Sinai covenant together with the ratification of the new covenant, both of which occurred by the spilling of blood. According to 9:19, 21 Moses at Sinai sprinkled "both the book itself [of the covenant] and all the people" (αὐτό τε τὸ βιβλίον καὶ πάντα τὸν λαὸν ἐρράντισεν, v. 19) as well as "both the tent and all the vessels used in worship" "in the same way with blood" (τῷ αἵματι ὁμοίως ἐρράντισεν, v. 21). In Exod 24:3-8, however, the book and the cultic objects are not sprinkled (cf. Lev 16:14ff.; Num 19:4), like the τράγοι ("ram"; cf. Lev 16:5ff.; mentioned with the μόσχοι, as well as the ὕδωρ, ἔριον κόκκινος, and ὕσσωπος (cf. Lev 14:4ff.; Num 19:6)—all mentioned in Heb 9:19 (μόσχων καὶ τῶν τράγων omitted in 𝔓⁴⁶ ℵ² K L, etc.).

The author of Hebrews is concerned primarily with juxtaposing the αἷμα τῆς διαθήκης (Exod 24:8, cited in Heb 9:20) and the ultimate atonement of Christ's sacrificial death, which eclipses and suspends all the purification and expiation activities of the old covenant. Hence only a fig. use of ῥαντίζω—mediated through baptism—conveys the salvation meaning of Christ's death for believers, "whose hearts *are sprinkled clean* [with the blood of Christ] (ἐρραντισμένοι τὰς καρδίας) from an evil conscience" (10:22; cf. also Ps 51:9; Ezek 36:25; 1QS 4:21; → ῥαντισμός, Heb 12:24).

The mid. form of ῥαντίζω refers to purification cleansings in Mark 7:4 ℵ B, etc. (in place of βαπτίζομαι; → βαπτίζω 9). C.-H. Hunzinger, *TDNT* VI, 976-84; *TWNT* X, 1257 (bibliography); G. R. Beasley-Murray, *DNTT* I, 224f.

             H. Balz

ῥαντισμός, οῦ, ὁ *rhantismos* sprinkling*

According to Heb 12:24 believers have come "to the *sprinkled* blood [of Jesus] (αἵματι ῥαντισμοῦ)" that speaks more than the blood of Abel, namely, of forgiveness rather than reprisal. The phrase may be modeled on the OT ὕδωρ ῥαντισμοῦ (cf. Num 19:9, 13) and thus fundamentally (summarizing Heb 9:1ff.) expresses the superiority of Jesus' atonement death over the old covenant's means of atonement (→ ῥαντίζω).

In 1 Pet 1:2 the phrase εἰς ῥαντισμὸν αἵματος Ἰησοῦ Χριστοῦ relates life characterized by the Spirit and obedience to the atoning death of Jesus Christ. The juxaposition of ὑπακοή and ῥαντισμός and the prep. εἰς specifying the goal suggest a life enduring in obedience and in the

reconciliation of the new covenant through the death of Christ (cf. Heb 9:14; 12:24), and refer less likely to baptism as a one-time event at which one accepts the atonement effected by Jesus' death (cf. also *Barn.* 5:1; 8:3). L. Goppelt, *1 Pet* (KEK) 83f., referring to 1QS 3:6-8, assumes the influence in 1 Pet 1:2 of a baptismal catechism in which baptism is interpreted as "a call into the condition of salvation," and considers it less a reflection on individual "acts of baptismal rites" (84). Ῥαντισμός is not documented in extrabiblical writings. C.-H. Hunzinger, *TDNT* VI, 976-84; *TWNT* X, 1257 (bibliography); G. R. Beasley-Murray, *DNTT* I, 224f.   H. Balz

ῥαπίζω *rhapizō* beat (with a staff or rod); slap*

In Matt 26:67, as in most uses of the vb. in Greek literature, ῥαπίζω probably refers to blows with a staff or rod (absolute οἱ δὲ ἐράπισαν after → ἐμπτύω and → κολαφίζω). The context (v. 68: → παίω; cf. Luke 22:64) suggests that these blows were an expression of dishonorable chastisement, and thus that were likely to the face (cf. Billerbeck I, 1024f.; Josephus *Ant.* viii.408 [ῥαπίζω as the rendering of πατάσσω ἐπὶ τὴν σιαγόνα, 3 Kgdms 22:24]; Hos 11:4; Isa 50:6). Matt 5:39 clearly intends a blow to the cheek with the hand (or possibly with the back of the hand as a sign of particular dishonor: cf. *m. B. Qam.* 8:6; Billerbeck I, 342f.; perhaps, however, in view of Matt 5:29f.; 6:3 δεξιός is used here without any special significance).

ῥάπισμα, ατος, τό *rhapisma* blow, slap, cuff*

Mark 14:65: ῥαπίσμασιν λαμβάνω, a vernacular expression meaning "greet someone with a *slap*" (cf. Lat. *verberibus accipere;* BDF §§5.3; 198.3; → λαμβάνω 3.c); John 18:22: δίδωμι ῥάπισμα; 19:3: δίδωμι ῥαπίσματα, "*strike/slap* in the face"; cf. *Barn.* 5:14; *Diog.* 1:4; → ῥαπίζω.

ῥάσσω *rhassō* strike; drag to and fro; throw down

Mark 9:18 D in place of the Ionic form → ῥήσσω, which is also used in Koine and has perhaps "merged" with → ῥήγνυμι (BDF §101).

ῥαφίς, ίδος, ἡ *rhaphis* needle*
βελόνη, ης, ἡ *belonē* needle*
τρῆμα, ατος, τό *trēma* opening, hole; eye of a needle*
τρυμαλιά, ᾶς, ἡ *trymalia* hole; eye of a needle*
τρύπημα, ατος, τό *trypēma* drilled hole; eye of a needle*

1. Occurrences and meanings — 2. "Eye of a needle" in Jewish proverbs — 3. Mark 10:25 par. Matthew/Luke

Lit.: E. BEST, "The Camel and the Needle's Eye (Mk 10:25)," *ExpTim* 82 (1970/71) 83-89. — S. LÉGASSE, *L'appel du riche (Marc 10,17-31 par.)* (1966). — R. LEHMANN and K. L. SCHMIDT, "Zum Gleichnis vom Kamel und Nadelöhr und Verwandtes," *TBl* 11 (1932) 336-40. — O. MICHEL, *TDNT* III, 592-94. — P. S. MINEAR, "The Needle's Eye," *JBL* 61 (1942) 157-69. — G. SCHNEIDER, *Luke* (ÖTK, 1977) II, 370f. — N. WALTER, "Zur Analyse von Mc 10,17-31," *ZNW* 53 (1962) 206-18. — For further bibliography → κάμηλος.

1. These five words occur in the following NT passages: ῥαφίς in Mark 10:25 par. Matt 19:24 (eye of a *needle*); βελόνη in Luke 18:25, but cf. Mark 10:25 (eye of a *needle*); τρῆμα in Luke 18:25 par. Matt 19:24 B ℵ* (*eye* of a needle); τρυμαλιά in Mark 10:25 par. Matt 19:24 C Θ al (*eye* of a needle); τρύπημα in Matt 19:24, but cf. Mark 10:25 (*eye* of a needle). Βελόνη and τρῆμα, both used in Luke, correspond more closely to classical usage than do the other three words.

2. Rabbinic Judaism speaks proverbially of "the eye of a needle" as the smallest possible opening (J. N. Sepp, *ZDPV* 14 [1891] 30-34): "Make me an opening for repentance as big as the eye of a needle" (*Midr. Cant.* 5:2). That which is impossible is likened to the elephant that is unable to pass through the eye of a needle (*b. Ber.* 55b; *b. B. Meṣ.* 38b). The camel was considered the largest animal in Palestine (→ κάμηλος 2.b; cf. Matt 23:24: camel and gnat).

3. Mark 10:25 par. is an entry-saying that speaks of the impossibility of a rich man (→ πλούσιος 2) entering the kingdom of God. The sense of this radical (and authentic) saying of Jesus lies not in any theoretical reflection, but rather in the address to the rich. The "narrow gate" in the entry-saying in Matt 7:13f. par. Luke 13:23f. is comparable (see Schulz, *Q* 309-12) and is characteristically formulated in the imv. (cf. also Jeremias, *Parables* 195). Attempts to relate the "eye of the needle" in the saying to one of the narrow gates of Jerusalem (this interpretation reported by Paschasius Radbertus [9th cent.], *PL* CXX, 665) arises from the desire to attribute to Jesus a "dogmatic" manner of speaking and have him speak of the difficulty (not the impossibility!) of a rich man entering the kingdom (cf. Mark 10:23 par.: δυσκόλως).   G. Schneider

ῥαχά *rhacha* buffoon, empty-head, fool
In Matt 5:22 ℵ* D W as a different transliteration of Aram. *rêqā';* → ῥακά.

῾Ραχάβ *Rhachab* Rahab
→ ῾Ραάβ.

῾Ραχήλ *Rhachēl* Rachel*

In Matt 2:18 the lament of Rachel (Heb. *rāḥēl*) over the dispersal of her children (i.e., the tribe of Benjamin;

Jer 31:15 [38:15 LXX]) is related to murder of male children in Bethlehem by Herod the Great: ῾Ραχὴλ κλαίουσα τὰ τέκνα αὐτῆς. Bethlehem was already known in early Jewish tradition as the location of Rachel's grave (cf. Gen 35:19; Ruth 4:11; → ῾Ραμά), while in Jer 31:15 Ramah in Benjamin is presupposed. According to Gen 29:6ff.; 30:6ff., 22ff.; 35:16ff. Rachel was Laban's daughter and Jacob's second wife. Through the slave Bilhah she became the mother of Dan and Naphtali and was herself the mother of Joseph and Benjamin, at whose birth she died. K. Cramer and K. Elliger, *BHH* 1548f.; A. van den Born and H. Haag, *BL* 1444.

῾Ρεβέκκα, ας *Rhebekka* Rebecca*

In Rom 9:10 Paul mentions Rebecca (Heb. *ribqâ*) after Sarah (v. 9) as further proof that from the beginning God's promise was not bound to physical lineage and thus to membership in the people of Israel, since Rebecca had conceived two sons by Isaac (῾Ρεβέκκα ἐξ ἑνὸς κοίτην ἔχουσα, Ἰσαὰκ τοῦ πατρὸς ἡμῶν; cf. Gen 25:21ff.), the twins Esau and Jacob, of whom according to God's will the firstborn had to serve the younger (Rom 9:11-13, quoting Gen 25:23; Mal 1:2f.; cf. further Gen 27:5ff., 42ff.). K. Cramer, *BHH* 1558; *BL* 1449.

ῥέδη, ης, ἡ *rhedē* (four-wheeled) wagon, carriage*

Rev 18:13, in an enumeration of the riches of "Babylon" modeled on Ezek 27:12ff.: καὶ ἵππων καὶ ῥεδῶν καὶ σωμάτων (gen. dependent on γόμος, "cargo" [Rev 18:11]), "of horses, *wagons,* and slaves." Cf. H. Kraft, *Rev* (HNT) ad loc. ῾Ρέδη is a Latinism (BDF §5.1).

῾Ρεμφά(-άμ, -άν), ῾Ρεφά, ῾Ρομφά(-άν) *Rhempha(m/n), Rhepha, Rhompha(n)* Rephan, Rompha
Variant forms and spellings of the name of the deity → ῾Ραιφάν in Acts 7:43.

ῥέω *rheō* flow (vb.)*

Fig. in John 7:38: ποταμοὶ . . . ῥεύσουσιν ὕδατος ζῶντος, "rivers of living water *shall flow*." On the suggested scriptural references for v. 38 see R. Schnackenburg, *John* II (Eng. tr., 1982) ad loc. Though 4:14 may suggest a reference here to the believer as a "spring of water," the context (see esp. 7:37, 39) also suggests that Christ is referred to. The metaphor probably alludes to the drawing of water from the Pool of Siloam during the Feast of Tabernacles and refers according to v. 39 to the (future) reception of the Spirit. On the problems involved with interpretations that go farther see esp. L. Goppelt, *TDNT* VIII, 326f.; F. Hahn, FS Dahl 51-70; J. Becker, *John* (ÖTK) I, ad loc. (bibliography).

Ῥήγιον, ου   *Rhēgion* Rhegium*

A trade city (modern Reggio di Calabria) in Bruttium (modern Calabria) in southern Italy on the Straits of Messina, opposite the Sicilian city of Messina. Paul touched on Rhegium during his sea journey to Rome from Syracuse (Acts 28:13: κατηντήσαμεν εἰς Ῥήγιον). B. Andreae, *LAW* 2611; W. Bieder, *BHH* 1572; *BL* 1475; E. T. Salmon, *OCD* 920.

ῥῆγμα, ατος, τό   *rhēgma* ruin, collapse, fissure*

Luke 6:49: ῥῆγμα τῆς οἰκίας ἐκείνης, the *collapse* of a house (cf. Matt 7:27: → πτῶσις); on the otherwise rare reference of this word to the collapse of a house cf. LXX Amos 6:11 A (B: ῥάγμα).

ῥήγνυμι   *rhēgnymi* tear to pieces; let break forth, turn loose*

Ῥήγνυμι occurs in the NT in the pres. pass. (Matt 9:17), fut. act. (Mark 2:22; Luke 5:37), and 1st aor. act. (Matt 7:6; Gal 4:27). The secondary form ῥήσσω appears in textual variants (Matt 9:17 D; Luke 5:6 D), representing a retroformation from the fut. ῥήξω (see BDF §73; cf. LSJ s.v.). In contrast, the older epic vb. → ῥήσσω lies behind Mark 9:18 par. Luke 9:42 (see BDF §101).

Mark 2:22 par. Matt 9:17 (pass.)/Luke 5:37, of new wine that *bursts* old wineskins; fig. in Matt 7:6, of unpredictable animals (swine) that *tear* people *apart (with their teeth):* μήποτε . . . ῥήξωσιν ὑμᾶς; because they cannot eat the pearls thrown to them); absolute in Gal 4:27: ῥῆξον καὶ βόησον, "let your voice break forth and shout" (quoting Isa 54:1 LXX; Heb. *pāṣaḥ,* "rejoice"); cf. *2 Clem.* 2:1.

ῥῆμα, ατος, τό   *rhēma* word; thing*

1. Occurrences — 2. Usage — 3. Meanings — 4. Luke-Acts and John

Lit.: J. BARR, *The Semantics of Biblical Language* (1961) 129-40. — BAGD s.v. — O. BETZ, *DNTT* III, 1119-23. — T. Boman, *Hebrew Thought Compared with Greek* (1960) 58-69. — BULTMANN, *Theology* II, 59-69. — C. BURCHARD, "A Note on Ῥῆμα in *Jos. As.* 17:1f.; Luke 2:15, 17; Acts 10:37," *NovT* 27 (1985) 281-95. — A. DEBRUNNER, H. KLEINKNECHT, O. PROCKSCH, and G. KITTEL, *TDNT* IV, 69-143. — E. REPO, *Der Begriff "Rhēma" im Biblisch-Griechischen* (2 volumes, 1951, 1954). — H. SCHLIER, *HTG* II, 845-67. — For further bibliography see Schlier; *TWNT* X, 1157-60.

1. Λόγος occurs 330 times in the NT, while ῥῆμα, which often means the same thing, occurs only 68 times. Of these, 33 are in Luke-Acts, 12 are in John, and fewer are in Matthew (5), Mark (2), or the genuine Pauline

Epistles (4 in Romans 10; 2 in 2 Corinthians), and none at all, e.g., in the Pastorals or Revelation.

2. Ῥῆμα usually refers to that which is spoken and appears with the vb. λαλέω (Matt 12:36; John 6:63; 8:20, and *passim*; with λέγω only in John 14:10; ἀπαγγέλλω in Acts 16:38, ἀποφθέγγομαι in 26:25, and other vbs.). In individual instances it is also that which is possessed (John 6:68) or given (17:8). It can also be that which is remembered, with (ἀνα-)/(ὑπο-)μιμνῄσκω (Matt 26:75 par. Mark 14:72/Luke 22:61; Luke 24:8; Acts 11:16; 2 Pet 3:2; Jude 17; cf. συν-/διατηρέω in Luke 2:19, 51; οἶδα in Acts 10:37), that which is perceived by the senses (with ἀκούω in John 8:47; 12:47; Acts 10:22; 2 Cor 12:4; ἐνωτίζομαι in Acts 2:14; γεύομαι in Heb 6:5; εἶδον in Luke 2:15), that which is understood or not understood (Mark 9:32 par. Luke 9:45 bis; Luke 2:50; 18:34; 20:26; 24:11), and in individual instances that which is received (John 12:48; Eph 6:17) or believed (John 5:47).

Subjects of vbs. that have ῥῆμα as their obj. are: prophets (2 Pet 3:2), angels (Luke 2:17), Jesus (Matt 27:14 and *passim*), the apostles (Acts 5:20, 32; Jude 17), Peter (Acts 10:44; 11:14), Stephen (6:11, 13), Paul (and Barnabas; 13:42; 26:25; 28:25), the police in Philippi (16:38), human beings in general (Matt 12:36), shepherds (Luke 2:15), Mary (2:19, 51), the disciples (Mark 9:32 par.; Luke 18:34; 20:26; 24:11), Peter (Matt 26:75 par.; Acts 11:16), the women at the tomb (Luke 24:8), a believer (John 8:47; 12:47, 48), the Jews (Acts 2:14), Cornelius (10:22), and Paul (2 Cor 12:4).

Ῥῆμα as the subj. is always found with intrans. vbs.: with γίνομαι (Luke 3:2; cf. 2:15; Acts 10:36), ἐξέρχομαι (Rom 10:18; cf. Matt 4:4: ἐκπορεύομαι), ἐγγύς εἰμι (Rom 10:8a), μένω (John 15:7; 1 Pet 1:25a), φαίνομαι κτλ. (Luke 24:11), and ἀδυνατέω (1:38). In these cases ῥῆμα is that which comes from God. In accordance with this genitives with ῥῆμα indicating the creator or originator are only θεός (Luke 3:2; John 3:34; 8:47; Eph 6:17; Heb 6:5; 11:3; cf. John 10:21), κύριος (Luke 22:61; Acts 11:16; 1 Pet 1:25a), Ἰησοῦς (Matt 26:75), Χριστός (Rom 10:17), or a pron. (for Jesus in Luke 5:5; 7:1; 20:26; 24:8; John 12:48; 15:7; cf. Heb 1:3; the angels in Luke 1:38; Peter in Acts 2:14; the messengers in Rom 10:18). Obj. genitives with ῥῆμα are ζωή (Acts 5:20), ἀλήθεια καὶ σωφροσύνη (26:25), and πίστις (Rom 10:8b).

3. Ῥῆμα has two fundamental meanings: *word* and *thing*. It thus corresponds to Heb. *dābār,* for which it often serves as a tr. in the LXX. And just as in the LXX it is usually clear which meaning is intended (cf. Gen 22:1 [after these things"] with 47:30 ["according to your word"]), so also in almost all NT occurrences.

In Matt 27:14, e.g., it is clear that Jesus did not "answer" "even to a single word." The etymological similarity between ῥῆμα and ἐρῶ, ἐρρέθην and εἴρηκα (no pres.) clearly influences its meaning; it contains or refers to what is *said,* and this is where the meaning of ῥῆμα coincides in part with that of λόγος. Both can refer to sayings of Jesus, as they do together in Luke 9:44, 45 (cf. Mark 10:22 with 14:72; Matt 26:1: πάντες οἱ λόγοι οὗτοι; Luke 7:1: πάντα τὰ ῥήματα αὐτοῦ), or to the entirety of his message (Matt 24:35: οἱ λόγοι μου; John 15:7: τὰ ῥήματά μου; cf. 17:8 with v. 14). Classical Greek λόγος implies "the connected rational element in speech . . . in contrast to ῥῆμα as the individual and more emotional expression or saying, though this does, of course, fall into a pattern, so that the fact of speech is the essential thing" (Kleinknecht 79); but in NT Greek this distinction is relativized (cf. Heb 12:19). The NT speaks concretely of a ῥῆμα in prophecies (Luke 9:45 bis), in commissions (5:5), in threats (Acts 6:13), in didactic sayings (10:22), in the message of salvation in general (1 Pet 1:25b: τὸ ῥῆμα τὸ εὐαγγελισθὲν εἰς ὑμᾶς; cf. Rom 10:8), and perhaps in the baptismal formula (Eph 5:26).

Clear examples of the meaning *thing/matter* are in Luke 1:37 ("With God nothing will be impossible"); Matt 18:16; 2 Cor 13:1 ([legal] *matter/case*), the last two OT citations (Gen 18:14; Deut 19:15). As the dir. obj. of (δια-)λαλέω (Luke 1:65; Acts 13:42), τὰ ῥήματα ταῦτα could refer to the spoken words, though the context suggests that *events* are meant, and that ῥῆμα, esp. in Acts 13:42, refers here as little as in Luke 2:15, 19, 51 only to what was previously *said* (on λαλέω with the acc. of thing cf. Acts 2:11). In Acts 10:37 τὸ γενόμενον ῥῆμα is not the λόγος of v. 36, but rather the *events* of vv. 38f.

4. a) Besides the citation of Deut 19:15, only in Luke-Acts do both meanings of ῥῆμα occur.

1) Ῥῆμα in the sense of *word* is in Luke usually that with which the persons addressed are concerned when trying unsuccessfully to understand (Luke 2:50; 9:45), when failing to recognize (24:11), when remembering (22:61; 24:8), and when acting accordingly (1:38; 2:29 with κατά, 5:5 with ἐπί). In Acts, on the other hand, except in 11:16 and 16:38, ῥῆμα is used of the word spoken by the witnesses for Jesus. Ῥῆμα as the word of God appears only before the appearance of Jesus, after Simeon (Luke 2:29) only with John as the last prophet (3:2) in the formula of the prophetic tradition (see P. K. D. Neumann, "Das Wort, das geschehen ist . . . ," *VT* 23 [1973] 171-217): ἐγένετο ῥῆμα θεοῦ.

2) Ῥῆμα meaning *thing* also occurs in Luke only in the prehistories (1:37, 65; 2:15, 19, 51). In addition, Acts also looks back at *events* (5:32; 10:37; 13:42).

b) John always uses ῥῆμα in a collective sense of Jesus' words, including in the sense that he speaks God's words (3:34; 8:47), which he receives and passes on (17:8). Furthermore, Jesus' words are also his works, and ῥήματα and ἔργα alternate with one another (14:10; 17:4

with v. 8), as do λαλέω and (ἔργα) ποιέω (8:28, 38; 15:22 with v. 24) and ἀκούω and ὁράω (8:38). Accordingly, the ῥήματα are intended fundamentally as sayings about Jesus himself, i.e., not as christological instruction but as self-mediation: "His word is identical with himself" (Bultmann II, 63).

W. Radl

Ῥησά *Rhēsa* Rhesa*

The son of Zerubbabel and father of Joanna in the genealogy of Jesus according to Luke 3:27.

ῥήσσω *rhēssō* strike; drag to and fro; throw down

Ῥήσσω is used in Ionic and Koine Greek instead of ῥάσσω. It is used of a demon's power over a boy in Mark 9:18 (ῥήσσει αὐτόν) par. Luke 9:42 (ἔρρηξεν αὐτόν, with συνεσπάραξεν); cf. Mark 9:18 D (→ ῥάσσω). On the relationship between ῥήσσω (already considered a part of older epic style) to → ῥήγνυμι see BDF §101; BAGD s.v. προσρήσσω.

ῥήτωρ, ορος, ὁ *rhētōr* orator, advocate, attorney*

According to Acts 24:1 Tertullus accompanies the high priest Ananias to Caesarea as a *advocate/spokesman before the law* in Paul's trial (cf. Pap. Oxy. no. 37, l. 4).

ῥητῶς *rhētōs* expressly, specifically*

1 Tim 4:1: τὸ δὲ πνεῦμα ῥητῶς λέγει, "now the Spirit *expressly* says" (namely, through prophets in the Church; cf. Justin *Apol.* I, 63.10); see also 2 Tim 3:1ff.; 4:3ff. Ῥητῶς also appears in prophecies in Justin *Apol.* I, 35.10; 63.10.

ῥίζα, ης, ἡ *rhiza* root; shoot*

1. Occurrences in the NT — 2. Synoptics — 3. The metaphor of the olive tree in Romans — 4. The "root" of David's line — 5. "Root" in parenesis

Lit.: A. T. HANSON, *Studies in Paul's Technique and Theology* (1974), 105-25. — C. MAURER, *TDNT* VI, 985-91. — D. ZELLER, *Juden und Heiden in der Mission des Paulus* (1973) 215-18; 238-45 (on 3).

1. The noun ῥίζα occurs 17 times in the NT: 3 times in Matthew, 3 in Mark, 2 in Luke, 5 in Romans, 2 in Acts, and once each in 1 Tim 6:10 and Heb 12:15. In most occurrences ῥίζα is used either metaphorically or in parables.

2. The metaphor of the axe that "even now is laid to the root of the trees" (Matt 3:10 par. Luke 3:9) announces the imminent judgment that will separate trees bearing good fruit from those that do not. Whoever bears no "fruit of conversion" is cut down and thrown into the fire, i.e., is condemned.

The parable of the seeds (Mark 4:6 par. Matt 13:6; cf. Luke 8:6, where ῥίζα is replaced by ἰκμάς) shows that the *root,* which needs good soil, gives the plant water. Without this root the plant withers away. The interpretation of the parable (Mark 4:17 par. Matt 13:21/Luke 8:13) refers the condition of having *roots* to human beings. "By leaving out ἐν ἑαυτοῖς Luke emphasizes more strongly than Mark or Matthew the fact that what matters is not man himself but his rooting in the soil outside" (Maurer 988).

In the story of the withered fig tree (Mark 11:20; cf. Matt 21:20) ῥίζα is meant literally, not metaphorically. The disciples saw that the fig tree cursed by Jesus was withered away from its *roots* (ἐκ ῥιζῶν).

3. In Rom 11:13-24 Paul characterizes the relationship between the Jews and the Gentile Christians in the metaphor of the olive tree. Ῥίζα occurs here four times. In v. 16 it refers to the patriarchs of Israel. If the root (the patriarchs) is holy, then so are the branches. Paul places the Gentile Christians into context with Israel and admonishes them not to boast concerning the fallen Jews or to give up on them. Some branches (i.e., unbelieving Jews) have broken off from the wild olive tree (v. 17a), and in their place the Gentile Christians were grafted as wild shoots. These wild branches thus shared the richness of the *root* of the olive tree (v. 17b). Paul makes it clear to the Gentile Christians that their election is no reason to boast over the broken branches. The Gentile Christians are not the ones supporting the *root:* The *root* (= the patriarchs) supports them (v. 18). This means that the origin of Gentile Christianity, too, was established in the "fathers" of Israel. The patriarchs are the rich *root* (v. 17b) for both Jews and Gentiles, for they receive the promises fulfilled in Christ.

Hanson emphatically asserts that here as in Rom 15:12 Paul uses ῥίζα to refer to Christ (cf. esp. 117, 119, 125). We must agree with Maurer, however, that "the metaphor must not be over-expressed to the point of equating the holy root with Christ as in patristic exegesis and K. Barth" (989 n.22).

4. Rom 15:12 expressly cites Isa 11:10 (ἡ ῥίζα τοῦ Ἰεσσαί; cf. also Isa 11:1): "Jesse's *root* will come, he who rises to rule the Gentiles. In him the Gentiles will place their hope." For Paul this prophetic pronouncement has been fulfilled in Christ. Rev 5:5 and 22:16 assert that the messianic promises are fulfilled in "the *root* of David": The *root* of David has conquered (5:5) and is the bright morning star (22:16). In these three passages, then, ῥίζα refers to the (Davidic) Messiah.

5. 1 Tim 6:10 warns against greed, the "*root* of all evils"; many have fallen prey to this craving and "wandered from the faith and pierced their hearts with many pangs."

Heb 12:15 warns against squandering God's grace—

so that no "*root* of bitterness spring up and cause trouble, and by it the many become defiled."

A. Palzkill

ῥιζόω *rhizoō*   cause to take root; pass.: be rooted or firmly established*

In the NT only pass. pf. partc., used fig.: Eph 3:17: ἐν ἀγάπῃ ἐρριζωμένοι, "being rooted in love" (with τεθεμελιωμένοι); Col 2:7: ἐρριζωμένοι καὶ ἐποικοδομούμενοι ἐν αὐτῷ, "rooted and built up in him [Christ, as foundation]"; → ῥίζα. C. Maurer, *TDNT* VI, 990f.

ῥιπή, ῆς, ἡ *rhipē*   throwing, rapid movement*

1 Cor 15:52: ἐν ῥιπῇ ὀφθαλμοῦ, of the shortest possible time necessary to "cast" a glance: "in the *twinkling* of an eye" (immediately after ἐν ἀτόμῳ, "in a moment"); 𝔓⁴⁶ D* F G and others read → ῥοπή, "downward movement, twinkling."

ῥιπίζω *rhipizō*   swing, move back and forth*

In Jas 1:6 the doubter is compared with the waves of the sea, "that are driven and *tossed by the wind*" (κλύδων . . . ἀνεμιζόμενος καὶ ῥιπιζόμενος); cf. Philo *Gig.* 51; *Migr.* 148; Dio Chrysostom *Or.* 32.23. Comparisons with the sea are popular in diatribe.

ῥιπτέω *rhipteō*   throw, throw off*

Alternate form of → ῥίπτω occurring in the NT only in Acts 22:23: ῥιπτούντων τὰ ἱμάτια. Since ῥιπτέω does not mean "tear to pieces," Job 2:12, e.g. (ῥήξαντες . . . τὴν . . . στολήν, as a sign of lament), cannot be considered a parallel passage; rather, the clause in Acts 22:23 is to be understood (with Exod 32:19; Deut 9:17, 21; 4 Kgdms 7:15; and esp. Plato *R.* v.474a: ῥίψαντας τὰ ἱμάτια) as "*casting off* their garments" as a sign of excitement or indignation (in reaction to Paul's blasphemy). One may also compare this to the Roman custom of *iactatio togarum* (cf. Ovid *Am.* ii.2.74), so that it may refer to a "*waving* of garments" (cf. Acts 13:51; 14:14; 18:6). H. J. Cadbury (*Beginnings* V, 269-77) suggests an apotropaic rite; cf., however, E. Haenchen, *Acts* (Eng. tr., 1971) ad loc. Further documentation in H. Conzelmann, *Acts* (Hermeneia) ad loc.; Spicq, *Notes* II, 782f.

ῥίπτω *rhiptō*   throw, throw to the ground, cast down*

Ῥίπτω occurs 7 times in the NT: pass. in Matt 9:36, of the crowds "harassed and *[lying] helpless*": ἐσκυλμένοι καὶ ἐρριμμένοι; cf. also Jer 14:16): act. in 15:30: *put down* (sick people at Jesus' feet); 27:5: *throw* (ῥίψας τὰ ἀργύρια εἰς τὸν ναόν); Luke 4:35: *throw down* (ῥῖψαν αὐτὸν τὸ δαιμόνιον); 17:2: "*be cast* into the sea" (ἔρριπται εἰς τὴν θάλασσαν, metaphorical); Acts 27:19: *throw overboard, cast out* (the ship's tackle); 27:29 (four anchors). The fig. meaning of ῥίπτω as "reject, cast out" (cf. Jer 7:15; Ps 30:23 LXX) does not occur in the NT. BAGD s.v.; W. Bieder, *TDNT* VI, 991-93; Spicq, *Notes* II, 780-83.

Ῥοβοάμ *Rhoboam* Rehoboam*

The son of Solomon and father of Abijah in the genealogy of Jesus according to Matt 1:7 (bis); Luke 3:23ff. D (cf. 1 Kgs 11:43; 12:1ff.; 14:21ff.; 1 Chr 3:10; 2 Chr 9:31ff.). After Solomon Rehoboam carried on the royal line of David in Judah, while Israel made Jeroboam (from Ephraim, 1 Kgs 11:26) king in the north. A. Jepsen, *BHH* 1572; A. van den Born, *BL* 1482.

Ῥόδη, ης *Rhodē* Rhoda*

The common name of a slave (= "rose") in the house of Mary, the mother of John Mark, in Jerusalem: παιδίσκη . . . ὀνόματι Ῥόδη, Acts 12:13. She is mentioned in vv. 13-15 as the first witness of Peter's miraculous liberation from prison, though "in her joy she did not open the gate" (ὑπακοῦσαι, v. 13). E. Haenchen, *Acts* (Eng. tr., 1971) ad loc.

Ῥόδος, ου *Rhodos* Rhodes*

The southernmost island of the Sporades in the Aegean off the southwest coast of Asia Minor. Paul reached Rhodes during his last journey to Jerusalem coming from Miletus by way of Cos (Acts 21:1: ἤλθομεν . . . εἰς τὴν Ῥόδον, in a "we"-narrative). There were Jews living on Rhodes (1 Macc 15:23). In the 1st cent. B.C. Rhodes belonged for a time to the Roman province of Asia, though it otherwise remained a free city. W. E. Gerber, *BHH* 1596; G. T. Griffith, *OCD* 923; *BL* 1475; E. Meyer, *KP* IV, 1421-23.

ῥοιζηδόν *rhoizēdon* with (loud) hissing, with roaring speed*

In 2 Pet 3:10 (οἱ οὐρανοὶ ῥοιζηδὸν παρελεύσονται) the power and speed with which the heavens and earth will pass away at the end is expressed by the noise with which a strongly thrown object cuts through the air (cf. LSJ s.v. ῥοιζαῖος). Possibly also "with a din."

Ῥομφά(ν) *Rhompha(n)* Rompha
Alternate form of the name of the deity → Ῥαιφάν in Acts 7:43 ℵ* B.

ῥομφαία, ας, ἡ *rhomphaia* sword*

Ῥομφαία occurs 7 times in the NT, 6 of those in Revelation and once in Luke 2:35 (over 230 occurrences in the LXX). Luke 2:35 refers to the *sword* that will pierce

through Mary's soul (σοῦ . . . τὴν ψυχὴν διελεύσεται ῥομφαία) as a metaphor for violent pain (cf. *Sib. Or.* iii.315). Rev 1:16; 2:12 refer to the "two-edged *sword*" (ῥομφαία δίστομος ὀξεῖα) issuing from the mouth of the exalted Christ, as a portrayal of his power through the word (cf. Isa 11:4; 49:2; *Pss. Sol.* 17:24, 35f.; 2 Thess 2:8); cf. further ῥομφαία τοῦ στόματος in 2:16; similarly 19:15, 21; 6:8 refers to the comprehensive annihilating power of the "fourth rider" (ἐν ῥομφαίᾳ καὶ ἐν λιμῷ καὶ ἐν θανάτῳ; cf. Ezek 14:21; see also → μάχαιρα in Rev 6:4 as a metonym for war). W. Michaelis, *TDNT* VI, 993-98.

ῥοπή, ῆς, ἡ *rhopē* downward movement, inclination, twinkling

1 Cor 15:52 p⁴⁶ D* F G, etc., in place of → ῥιπή. Ῥοπή by itself can mean "moment" (Wis 18:12; 3 Macc 5:49; *Ep. Arist.* 90).

Ῥουβήν *Rhoubēn* Reuben*

In Rev 7:5 the "tribe of Reuben" (φυλὴ Ῥουβήν, Heb. *re'ûbēn*, eldest son of Jacob and Leah, Gen 29:32) is mentioned in an enumeration of the twelve tribes (in second position despite his being the first son), from which twelve thousand members are "sealed" (cf. Ezek 9:4, 6), i.e., spared destruction. L. Pap, *BHH* 1623; A. van den Born, *BL* 1493f.

Ῥούθ *Rhouth* Ruth*

The Moabite Ruth (Heb. *rût*) is mentioned in the genealogy of Jesus according to Matt 1:5 as the wife of Boaz and mother of Obed, and as one of the non-Jewish women in Jesus' ancestry (cf. G. Kittel, *TDNT* III, 1-3). Ruth came to Bethlehem from Moab and was considered the great-grandmother of David (Ruth 1:4, 7, 19, 22; 4:5ff., 11f., 21f.). H. W. Hertzberg, *BHH* 1630f.; W. Dommershausen, *BL* 1495f.

Ῥοῦφος, ου *Rhouphos* Rufus*

1. Mark 15:21: a son of Simon of Cyrene mentioned with his brother Alexander. 2. In Rom 16:13 Paul greets Ῥοῦφος ὁ ἐκλεκτὸς ἐν κυρίῳ along with his mother (καὶ ἡ μήτηρ αὐτοῦ καὶ ἐμοῦ). The identity of these two people cannot be established, since one can at most surmise that the Rufus mentioned in Mark 15:21 lived in Rome. B. Reicke, *BHH* 1624.

ῥύμη, ης, ἡ *rhymē* lane, street*

Matt 6:2: the "hypocrites" sound trumpets when giving alms ἐν ταῖς συναγωγαῖς καὶ ταῖς ῥύμαις; Luke 14:21: εἰς τὰς πλατείας καὶ ῥύμας τῆς πόλεως, "to the streets and *lanes*"; Acts 9:11: ἡ ῥύμη ἡ καλουμένη Εὐθεῖα, "the *street* called Straight" in Damascus, an opulent street running through the city from east to west; 12:10: Peter and the angel "pass through one *street*" (προέρχομαι ῥύμην μίαν).

ῥύομαι *rhyomai* save, rescue*

1. Occurrences in the NT — 2. Meanings — 3. Contexts — 4. Usage

Lit.: R. Batey, "So All Israel Will Be Saved," *Int* 20 (1966) 218-28. — U. Bergmann, *Rettung und Befreiung* (Diss. Heidelberg, 1961). — *idem, THAT* II, 96-99. — N. A. Dahl, "The Messiahship of Jesus in Paul," *idem, The Crucified Messiah and Other Essays* (1974) 37-47, 170-72. — E. Grässer, *Das Problem der Parusieverzögerung in den synoptischen Evangelien und in der Apostelgeschichte* (²1960) 104f. — F. J. C. Iturbe, " 'Et sic omnis Israel salvus fieret' Rom 11,26," *SPCIC 1961* (AnBib 17-18, 1963) I, 329-40. — W. Kasch, *TDNT* VI, 998-1003. — K. G. Kuhn, "Πειρασμός —ἁμαρτία —σάρξ im NT und die damit zusammenhängenden Vorstellungen," *ZTK* 49 (1952) 200-222. — U. Luz, *Das Geschichtsverständnis des Paulus* (1968) 286-300. — G. Riese, *Die alttestamentlichen Zitate im Römerbrief* (Diss. Munich, 1977). — J. Schneider and C. Brown, *DNTT* III, 200-205. — E. W. Smith, "The Form and Religious Background of Romans 7:24-25a," *NovT* 13 (1971) 127-35. — P. Stuhlmacher, "Zur Interpretation von Röm 11,25-32," *Probleme biblischer Theologie* (FS G. von Rad, 1971) 555-70. — D. Zeller, *Juden und Heiden in der Mission des Paulus* (²1973). — For further bibliography see the commentaries, esp. on Rom 7:24; 11:26.

1. With only 17 occurrences, ῥύομαι appears much less frequently than → σῴζω. There are 3 occurrences in the Gospels (Matt 6:13; 27:43; Luke 1:74), 3 in Romans, 3 in 2 Cor 1:10; 3 in 2 Timothy, 2 in 2 Peter, and single occurrences in Col 1:13; 1 Thess 1:10; and 2 Thess 3:2. The background of several of these occurrences is OT usage, either by way of quotation, as in Matt 27:43 (Ps 21:9 LXX; cf. Wis 2:18-20); Rom 11:26 (Isa 59:20), unambiguous borrowing, as in Luke 1:74 (Ps 96:10 LXX; Mic 4:10); 2 Thess 3:2 (Isa 25:4 LXX); 2 Tim 3:11 (Ps 33:20 LXX; cf. *Pss. Sol.* 4:23); 2 Tim 4:17 (1 Macc 2:60; cf. Dan 6:21 LXX, Theodotion; 6:28 Theodotion; Ps 21:21f. LXX), or possible borrowing, as in 2 Cor 1:10 (Ps 55:14 LXX; Job 5:20).

2. In the NT mid. deponent ῥύομαι always means *save, rescue*. The relationship with σῴζω emerges in Rom 11:26 and 2 Tim 4:18— and in 2 Pet 2:7, since the rescue of Lot, described in Gen 19:17 (19), 20, 22 with forms of σῴζω (see also *1 Clem.* 11:1) is described with ἐρρύσατο, as in Wis 10:6; see further Luke 1:74 in context (cf. vv. 69, 71, 77).

In the LXX ῥύομαι most frequently translates the hiphil of *nṣl* (81 times, also twice the [Aramaic] aphel and 4 times the niphal of the vb.), and much less often *g'l* (12 times, almost all in deutero-Isaiah), the piel of *plṭ* (10 times), the hiphil of *yšʿ* (7

times), the piel of *mlṭ* Piel (6 times), and the niphal of the same vb. (twice), among others.

3. The subject of ῥύομαι in the NT (as is usually the case in the OT) is God (also as Kyrios in 2 Timothy) or Jesus/Christ, participially as ὁ ῥυόμενος (Rom 11:26; 1 Thess 1:10). The vb. is pass. in Luke 1:74; Rom 15:31; 2 Thess 3:2; 2 Tim 4:17. Rescue takes place "from (ἀπό) evil" (Matt 6:13), "from unbelievers" (Rom 15:31), "from wicked and evil people" (2 Thess 3:2), and "from every evil" (2 Tim 4:18). Where ἀπό is used the focus may be on a future situation, from which rescue occurs, while if the situation is past or present ἐκ is used: "from the hands of our enemies" (Luke 1:74; see also Josephus *Vita* 83), "from this body of death" (Rom 7:24), "from so deadly a peril" (2 Cor 1:10), "from the dominion of darkness" (Col 1:13), "from all persecutions" (2 Tim 3:11), "from the lion's mouth" (metaphorical in 2 Tim 4:17), and "from trial" (2 Pet 2:9).

4. Ῥύομαι is used in the NT, therefore, of rescue or deliverance from enemies, mortal danger, perils and persecutions; from the danger of sin and helplessness before sin, death, and other anti-divine powers; and from temptation and judgment. The decisive feature of all rescue is that it can and does occur only through God or Jesus.

a) Israel's deliverance from enemies (→ ἐχθρός 2) is spoken of in the larger context of salvation (Luke 1:74; see vv. 68-79).

b) Deliverance from mortal danger and persecution: The crucified Jesus is mocked, and God, in whom he trusts, should rescue him to verify his claim to be God's Son (Matt 27:43). This mockery is sharpened all the more when Jesus' adversaries cite Ps 21:9 LXX and Wis 2:18, passages promising deliverance by God. Paul requests prayers that he be delivered from unbelievers in Judea (Rom 15:31); God has delivered Paul from mortal danger (actually "death," see vv. 8f.; from persecutions in 2 Tim 3:11; cf. *Pss. Sol.* 13:4) and will continue to offer deliverance (2 Cor 1:10; see H. Lietzmann, *2 Cor* [HNT] 101 ad loc.). As in 2 Cor 1:11, so also in 2 Thess 3:2, appeal is made to intercessory prayer for deliverance. Deserted by everyone at his trial, Paul is *rescued* "from the lion's mouth" by the Kyrios (God, 2 Tim 4:17; cf. Dan 6:21, 28 Theodotion; 1 Macc 2:60; the same metaphor in Ps 22:21f.; cf. 1QH 5:7, 13f.; *Jos. As.* 12:11).

c) Rescue from the might of anti-divine powers is seen in the deliverance from the dominion of darkness and transferal to the kingdom of the beloved Son (of God), "in whom we have redemption, the forgiveness of sins" (Col 1:13).

All Israel will be rescued and its sins forgiven when "the Deliverer will come from Zion" (Rom 11:26). The saving (σῴζω) of "all Israel" (Rom 11:26a) occurs according to the citation from Isa 59:20 (Rom 11:26f. with Isa 27:9; also interpreted in rabbinic writings as a messianic text: cf. *b. Sanh.* 98a) through the coming (ἥξει) of the Deliverer (ὁ ῥυόμενος) from Zion (ἐκ Σιών, LXX: ἕνεκεν Σιών, MT: *lᵉṣiyyôn*). This probably refers to the eschatological parousia of the exalted Christ from the heavenly Jerusalem (cf. Gal 4:26; Stuhlmacher 560f.; E. Käsemann, *Rom* [Eng. tr., 1980] 314; O. Michel, *Rom* [KEK] 356; H. Schlier, *Rom* [HTKNT] 341; U. Wilckens, *Rom* [EKKNT] II, 256: parousia, though Zion = center of Israel) rather than to the historical Jesus or to the christological events in general (Luz 295; see also Zeller 260).

d) Deliverance from sin and temptation: God rescued "righteous Lot, greatly distressed by the licentiousness of the wicked" (→ 2; 2 Pet 2:7; cf. *Did.* 5:2; *T. Reu.* 4:10). "The Lord knows how to rescue the godly" from such πειρασμός (cf. 1 Tim 6:9) that characterizes their situation in this world (2 Pet 2:9).

To the petition for preservation from or in the eschatological πειρασμός, the Matthean version of the Lord's Prayer (Matt 6:13 par. Luke 11:4; cf. Rev 3:10) adds "but *deliver* us from evil" (→ πονηρός 4.c). It is disputed whether this continuation maintains the eschatological aspect of the sixth petition or is asking generally for deliverance from everything evil (cf. 2 Tim 4:18; see Grässer 104f.); Kuhn 220f. suspends the alternatives. The background of Matt 6:13b may be the seventh of the Eighteen Benedictions (deliver *[gā'al]* from peril; see further Billerbeck I, 422f.).

e) Deliverance from sin and death: The cry of prayer in Rom 7:24 poses irrevocably and uniquely the question of deliverance from sin and death. Parallels in form (LXX Pss 13:7; 52:7; cf. Lam 2:13) and content from Jewish (see Billerbeck III, 239f.; *Jos. As.* 6:2ff.) and Hellenistic (see Smith 127-35) sources only serve to illustrate the radical nature of the Pauline view of the hopelessness of the human condition without Christ (answered in Rom 7:25a; 8:1ff.).

f) Deliverance from judgment: Jesus, raised from the dead and expected from heaven, will deliver us from the (judgment) wrath to come (1 Thess 1:10).

H. Lichtenberger

ῥυπαίνομαι *rhypainomai* (pass.) become dirty/defiled*

Fig. in Rev 22:11: ὁ ῥυπαρὸς ῥυπανθήτω ἔτι, "let the filthy still be filthy [in view of the near end]" (in contrast: ὁ ἅγιος ἁγιασθήτω ἔτι; cf. also Ezek 3:27; Dan 12:10); the ultimate separation of the saved from the condemned has thus already taken place for the seer.

ῥυπαρεύομαι *rhypareuomai* (pass.) become dirty/defiled

Rev 22:11 Koine (not documented in any other writings) in place of → ῥυπαίνομαι.

ῥυπαρία, ας, ἡ *rhyparia* dirt; impurity of thoughts, baseness*

Fig. in Jas 1:21: ἀποθέμενοι πᾶσαν ῥυπαρίαν καὶ περισσείαν κακίας, "put away all *filthiness* and rank growth of wickedness" so that meekness might result (ἐν πραΰτητι) and instead of ungodly anger (v. 20) the saving word might dwell in the heart (v. 21b). The phrase is probably borrowed from baptismal parenesis.

ῥυπαρός, 3 *rhyparos* dirty, unclean, defiled*

Literal in Jas 2:2, of the poor man who "in *shabby* clothing (ἐν ῥυπαρᾷ ἐσθῆτι) comes into the assembly" (in contrast to the rich: χρυσοδακτύλιος ἐν ἐσθῆτι λαμπρᾷ; cf. Zech 3:3f.; Philo *Jos.* 105). Fig. in Rev 22:11: ὁ ῥυπαρός, of "the filthy person" (in contrast to ὁ ἅγιος) as a sign of ultimate condemnation; cf. Ign. *Eph.* 16:2; → ῥυπαίνομαι.

ῥύπος, ου, ὁ *rhypos* dirt, uncleanness*

Literal in 1 Pet 3:21, of baptism, which does not remove *dirt* from the body (= flesh; οὐ σαρκὸς ἀπόθεσις ῥύπου), but rather appeals to God for a clear conscience, i.e., places the baptized person into a state of complete dependence on deliverance by God (v. 21a). The parenthesis in v. 21 seeks to preclude any misunderstanding of baptism as a cleansing effective in and of itself (cf., e.g., Eph 5:26) and emphasizes rather the newly established relationship with God. Therefore the fig. sense of "defilement in this (old) life" also resonates in this literal usage of the word (cf. also *Barn.* 11:11; *1 Clem.* 17:4; see further L. Goppelt, *1 Pet* [KEK] ad loc.).

ῥυπόομαι *rhypoomai* (mid.) defile oneself
Rev 22:11 TR in place of → ῥυπαίνομαι.

ῥύσις, εως, ἡ *rhysis* flowing, flow (noun)*

In the NT only in the phrase ῥύσις (τοῦ) αἵματος, "*flow* of blood" (Mark 5:25 par. Luke 8:43, 44; cf. πηγὴ τοῦ αἵματος in Mark 5:29; Matt 9:20 uses αἱμορροοῦσα); cf. Lev 15:2ff.

ῥυτίς, ίδος, ἡ *rhytis* wrinkle, fold; blemish*

Eph 5:27, in the metaphor of the ἐκκλησία as Christ's bride, which he has made to be "without spot or *wrinkle* or any such thing (μὴ ἔχουσαν σπίλον ἢ ῥυτίδα ἢ τι τῶν τοιούτων)" so that it is ἁγία καὶ ἄμωμος (cf. also v. 26). The metaphor portrays the complete love and care that Christ gives his Church, which is to be reflected in the love that husbands have for their wives.

Ῥωμαϊκός, 3   *Rhōmaikos*   Roman, Latin

Luke 23:38 ℵ* A C³ D Koine, etc., add (cf. John 19:20) that the inscription on the cross was written in Greek, Latin (γράμμασιν . . . Ῥωμαϊκοῖς), and Hebrew letters.

Ῥωμαῖος, 3   *Rhōmaios*   Roman (adj. and noun), Roman citizen*

Lit.: H. CONZELMANN, *Acts* (Hermeneia), on 16:37. — E. HAENCHEN, *Acts* (Eng. tr., 1971), on 22:22ff. — G. LINDESKOG and B. REICKE, *BHH* 1610f. — W. STEGEMANN, "War der Apostel Paulus ein römischer Bürger?" *ZNW* 78 (1987) 200-229. — L. WENGER, *RAC* II, 778-86, esp. 778f., 782ff. — For further bibliography see Conzelmann.

Ῥωμαῖος occurs 12 times in the NT, 11 times in Acts and in John 11:48. It is adjectival in Acts 16:37; 22:25 and otherwise substantival, with the art. (οἱ Ῥωμαῖοι) in John 11:48; Acts 2:10; 28:17.

In John 11:48 members of the Sanhedrin do not want to give the *Romans* (as a world political power) any reason to intervene politically in Jerusalem (ἐλεύσονται οἱ Ῥωμαῖοι καὶ ἀροῦσιν . . .). According to Acts 28:17 Paul fell "into the hands of the *Romans*" because of charges brought by the Jews (παρεδόθην εἰς τὰς χεῖρας τῶν Ῥωμαίων) even though they already had recognized his innocence (cf. 25:18ff.; 26:31f.). Hence Christ's fate repeats itself in Paul. The phrase ἔθος Ῥωμαίοις (25:16) refers to legal right recognized by the Romans giving every accused person the opportunity to defend himself (cf. Justinian *Digest* xlviii.17.1; Appian *BC* iii.54.222).

In Acts 2:10, on the other hand, οἱ ἐπιδημοῦντες Ῥωμαῖοι in the "list of nations" (vv. 9-11) are Jews *from Rome* who lived as foreigners in Jerusalem and whose language is presupposed to be Latin. The superscription of Romans, πρὸς Ῥωμαίους, refers to *Christians in Rome*.

The other occurrences refer to persons of Roman citizenship, such as the inhabitants of the Roman colony Philippi in Acts 16:21. Paul himself possesses Roman citizenship (sg. in 22:25, 26, 27, 29; 23:27; pl. [Paul and Silas] in 16:37, 38). As a *civis Romanus* (by birth) he could not be beaten (16:37f.; 22:24ff.; → μαστιγόω) and was legally entitled to standard trial procedure (16:37; 22:25).   H. Balz

Ῥωμαϊστί   *Rhōmaisti*   in Latin (adv.)*

John 19:20, referring to the inscription on Jesus' cross: ἦν γεγραμμένον Ἐβραϊστί, Ῥωμαϊστί, Ἑλληνιστί. John (in contrast to Mark 15:26 par.) mentions the three languages (national, administrative, and commercial), probably as a reference to the universal kingship of Jesus. Multilingual inscriptions were, however, common; see T. F. Regard, *RAr* 5/28 (1928) 95-105.

Ῥώμη, ης   *Rhōmē*   Rome*

Lit.: C. ANDRESEN, *LAW* 2633-70, esp. 2668ff. — R. E. BROWN and J. P. MEIER, *Antioch and Rome* (1983) 87-216. — H. CANCIK, *BL* 1482-88. — G. DELLING, *BHH* 1606-9. — M. DIBELIUS, *Rom und die Christen im 1. Jahrhundert* (1942). — J. B. FREY, "Le Judaisme à Rome aux premiers temps de l'église," *Bib* 12 (1931) 129-56. — R. GROSS, *KP* IV, 1441-51. — S. L. GUTERMANN, *Religious Toleration and Persecution in Ancient Rome* (1954). — H. KOESTER, *History, Culture, and Religion of the Hellenistic Age (Introduction to the NT* I, 1982). — P. LAMPE, *Die stadtrömischen Christen in den ersten beiden Jahrhunderten* (WUNT II/18, 1987). — R. PENNA, "Les Juifs à Rome au temps de l'apôtre Paul," *NTS* 28 (1982) 321-47. — C. SAULNIER, "Rome et la Bible," *DBSup* X, 863-1008. — W. WIEFEL, "Die jüdische Gemeinschaft im antiken Rom und die Anfänge des römischen Christentums," *Judaica* 26 (1970) 65-88. — U. WILCKENS, *Rom* (EKKNT) I, 33-42. — For further bibliography see Cancik.

Rome is mentioned 8 times in the NT: 5 times in Acts, twice in Romans, and in 2 Tim 1:17. The reference is always to the city of Rome: as the location of a Christian church (Rom 1:7: πᾶσιν τοῖς οὖσιν ἐν Ῥώμῃ; v. 15: ὑμῖν τοῖς ἐν Ῥώμῃ), as the place where "Paul" was chained (2 Tim 1:17), as the place from which "Jews" were expelled under Claudius (Acts 18:2: χωρίζεσθαι πάντας τοὺς Ἰουδαίους ἀπὸ τῆς Ῥώμης; → Ἀκύλας 2; → Κλαύδιος 1), and as the center of the Roman Empire and the goal of the Pauline missionary activity after its beginnings in Jerusalem (19:21: δεῖ με καὶ Ῥώμην ἰδεῖν [i.e., after his visit to Jerusalem]; 23:11: ὡς . . . εἰς Ἰερουσαλήμ, οὕτω σε δεῖ καὶ εἰς Ῥώμην μαρτυρῆσαι; cf. Rom 15:19; on Paul's arrival in Rome cf. Acts 28:14, 16).

Rome is also mentioned in 1 Pet 5:13 v.l. (in place of Βαβυλών) and in numerous mss. (usually Koine) in subscriptions to Galatians, Ephesians, Philippians, Colossians, 2 Thessalonians (6 614 pc), 2 Timothy, Philemon, and Hebrews (A P).

In Romans Paul turns his attention to a church that is already large and significant and has close connections with the churches in Greece and Asia Minor through various personal contacts (Rom 16:1ff.), though nothing is now known about its initial founding and establishment. In any case, Aquila and Prisca might have come to Corinth as Christians from Rome during the time of the edict of Claudius (A.D. 49/50, Acts 18:2; see above). Jews had dwelled in Rome since the 2nd cent. B.C. and their numbers increased greatly because Jewish slaves were brought in after Pompey's conquest of Palestine (63 B.C.). In the 1st cent. A.D. many Jews (as freedmen) acquired Roman citizenship, and from the time of Caesar Jews enjoyed special privileges, though they had to endure both persecutions and, periodically, expulsion from Rome (e.g., under Tiberius, A.D. 19; by Sejanus [cf. Philo *Leg. Gai.* 24]; the expulsion rescinded A.D. 32 [cf. *Leg. Gai.* 161]). The unrest under Claudius may have been connected with the founding of Christian communities. In any case, under Nero the Christian church in Rome reached proportions that made it appear suspect to the Emperor (Tacitus *Ann.* xv.44; Suetonius *Nero* xvi.2).

According to Acts 28:16ff., 30 Paul endured house arrest in Rome at the end of his missionary career and preached to both Jews and Christians, while his own concerns centered on winning the Roman church for his mission to Spain (Rom 15:22ff.). Luke, on the other hand, is concerned with forging a bridge between Jerusalem as the place where the gospel began and Rome as the center of the Empire.

H. Balz

ῥώννυμαι *rhōnnymai* (pass.) be strong, feel well*

The imv. pf. pass. form ἔρρωσθε, *"fare well,"* common in Hellenistic epistolary conclusions, occurs in the NT in Acts 15:29 (the conclusion to the Jerusalem letter taking the "apostolic decree" to the church at Antioch); cf. further 23:30 v.l.; 2 Macc 11:21, 33; *Ep. Arist.* 40, 46; Ign. *Eph.* 21:2; *Magn.* 15; *Phld.* 11:2; *Pol.* 8:3.

Σ σ

σαβαχθανι *sabachthani* you have forsaken me
→ ελωι

σαβαώθ *sabaōth* Sabaoth*

Σαβαώθ is the Greek transliteration of Heb. pl. *ṣᵉḇāʾôt̲*, "armies, hosts"; it occurs over 60 times in the LXX in the phrase κύριος σαβαώθ as the tr. of the divine name *yhwh (ᵉlōhê) ṣᵉḇāʾôt̲*, "Lord of the heavenly hosts/Lord of power" (absent in Ezekiel, Joel, Obadiah, and Jonah; the LXX also has κύριος ὁ θεὸς ὁ παντοκράτωρ in Hos 12:6; Amos 3:13; κύριος ὁ θεὸς δυνάμεων in Ps 79:8, 15). In the NT σαβαώθ occurs only in Rom 9:29 (κύριος σαβαώθ, quoting Isa 1:9) and Jas 5:4 (κύριος σαβαώθ, quoting Isa 5:9; cf. Ps 18:7 LXX); see also *1 Clem* 34:6 (quoting Isa 6:3); → παντοκράτωρ 1, 3. F. Hesse, *BHH* 2205; P. van Imschoot, *BL* 684; A. S. van der Woude, *THAT* II, 498-507.

σαββατισμός, οῦ, ὁ *sabbatismos* sabbath observance; sabbath rest*

Lit.: E. GRÄSSER, *Heb* (EKKNT, 1990) I, 216-20. — O. HOFIUS, *Katapausis* (1970) 102-15. — E. LOHSE, *TDNT* VII, 34f. — G. VON RAD, "Es ist noch eine Ruhe vorhanden dem Volke Gottes," *idem, Gesammelte Studien zum AT* (1958) I, 101-8.

1. The NT offers in Heb 4:9 the oldest documentation of the noun σαββατισμός, which occurs several times in post-NT early Christian writings independently of Heb 4:9 (e.g., Justin *Dial.* 23:3; Origen *Orat.* 27:16; Epiphanius *Haer.* xxx.2.2; lxvi.85.9; *Acts (Martyrdom) of Peter and Paul* 1; *Apostolic Constitutions* ii.36.2; pseudo-Macarius (Symeon) *Homily* 12.2.4 [ed. H. Berthold, GCS; Eng. tr., A. J. Mason, 1921]). At present, σαββατισμός has been documented in non-Christian writings only in Plutarch *Superst.* 3 (*Moralia* 166a).

The noun is derived from the vb. σαββατίζω, which in the the LXX appears as the tr. of Heb. *šabbāt̲*. The vb. means: a) "celebrate/observe the sabbath" (Exod 16:30; Lev 23:32; 2 Macc 6:6; so also Ign. *Magn.* 9:1; Pap. Oxy. 1, l. 2; Justin

Dial. 10:1 and *passim*), b) "observe (sabbath) rest" (Lev 26:34f.; 2 Chr 36:21; 1 Esdr 1:55).

Accordingly, the subst. means *sabbath observance* (thus in the non-NT passages mentioned) and *sabbath rest* (thus the understanding of σαββατισμός in Heb 4:9 by Origen *Cels.* v.59; *Selecta in Exod* on 16:23 [*PG* XII, 289b]).

2. In Heb 4:9 σαββατισμός encompasses both *sabbath rest* and (cultic) *sabbath observance*. The word is neither identical in meaning nor interchangeable with → κατάπαυσις (3:11, 18; 4:1, 3, 5, 10f.); it designates more closely what the people of God should expect when they enter the κατάπαυσις of God (cf. 4:9 with v. 6a). Just as God rested on the seventh day of creation from all his works, so also will believers find the eternal sabbath rest on the day of the completion of salvation in God's "place of rest" (see 4:10). Quietistic or mystic elements have nothing to do with this expectation. The statement in Heb 4:9f. remains dependent on a Jewish sabbath theology that associates the idea of sabbath rest with ideas of worship and praise of God (*Jub.* 2:21; 50:9; *Bib. Ant.* 11:8; 2 Macc 8:27; cf. also *1 Enoch* 41:7). Accordingly, the author of Hebrews understands by σαββατισμός the eternal sabbath celebration of salvation, i.e., the perfected community's worship before God's throne.   O. Hofius

σάββατον, ου, τό *sabbaton* sabbath; week

1. Origin, meaning, and occurrences in the NT — 2. Jesus' sabbath observance — 3. The sabbath conflicts in the Gospels — 4. Other occurrences

Lit.: S. BACCHIOCCHI, *Un esame dei testi biblici e patristici allo scopo d'accertare il tempo e le cause del sorgere della domenica come giorno del Signore* (Diss. Rome, 1974) — *idem, Anti-Judaism and the Origin of Sunday* (1975). — *idem, From Sabbath to Sunday. A Historical Investigation of the Rise of Sunday Observance in Early Christianity* (1977). — W. BISHAI, "Sabbath Observance from Coptic Sources," *AUSS* 1 (1963) 25-31. — J. BRIEND, *DBSup* X, 1132-70. — H. BRAUN, *Spätjüdisch-häretischer und frühchristlicher Radikalismus* (²1969) I, 116-20; II, 69-73. — D. A. CARSON, ed., *From Sabbath to Lord's*

Day (1982). — C. Dietzfelbinger, "Vom Sinn der Sabbatheilungen Jesu," *EvT* 38 (1978) 281-98. — J. FRANCKE, *Van sabbat naar zondag. De rustdag in Oud en NT* (1973). — T. FRIEDMAN, "The Sabbath: Anticipation of Redemption," *Judaism* 16 (1967) 443-52; 18 (1968) 225-27. — J. GNILKA, *Mark* (EKKNT, 1978) I, 118-32. — J. GRAY, "The Day of Yahweh in Cultic Experience and Eschatological Prospect," *SEÅ* 39 (1974) 5-37. — W. GRIMM, *Der Ruhetag. Sinngehalte einer fast vergessenen Gottesgabe* (ANTJ 4, 1980). — G. VAN GRONINGEN, ed., *The Sabbath-Sunday Problem. A Symposium* (1968). — F. HAHN, "Schabbat und Sonntag," *EvT* 46 (1986) 495-507. — O. HOFIUS, *Katapausis. Die Vorstellung vom endzeitlichen Ruheort im Hebräerbrief* (WUNT 11, 1970). — K. HRUBY, "La célébration du sabbat d'après les sources juives," *OrSyr* 7 (1962) 435-62; 8 (1963) 55-79. — J. JEREMIAS, *Unknown Sayings of Jesus* (1957) 49-54. — K. KERTELGE, *Die Wunder Jesu im Markus-Evangelium* (SANT 23, 1970) 82-85. — N. LEE, *The Covenantal Sabbath. The Weekly Sabbath Scripturally and Historically Considered* (1972). — E. LOHSE, *TDNT* VII, 1-35. — R. S. McCONNELL, *Law and Prophecy in Matthew's Gospel* (1969) 66-72. — J. MORGENSTERN, *IDB* IV, 135-41. — J. NELIS and H. HAAG, *BL* 1498-1501. — R. NORTH, *NCE* XII, 778-82. — F. NÖTSCHER, *LTK* IX, 188-90. — R. PESCH, *Mark* (HTKNT, 1976) I, 178-97. — J. ROLOFF, *Das Kerygma und der irdische Jesus* (1970) 52-88. — W. RORDORF, *Sunday. The History of the Day of Rest and Worship in the Earliest Centuries of the Christian Church* (1968). — idem, *Sabbat und Sonntag in der alten Kirche* (1972). — idem, "Ursprung und Bedeutung der Sonntagsfeier im frühen Christentum," *Liturgisches Jahrbuch* 31 (1981) 145-58. — J. SCHARBERT, "Biblischer Sabbat und modernes Wochenende," *Die alttestamentliche Botschaft als Wegweisung* (FS H. Reinelt, 1990) 285-306. — B. E. SHAFER, *IDBSup* 760-62. — W. H. SHEA, "The Sabbath in the Epistle of Barnabas," *AUSS* 4 (1966) 149-75. — O. SKRZYPCZAC, *Enciclopedia della Bibbia* VI (1971) 9-15. — F. STOLZ, *THAT* II, 863-69. — W. STOTT, *DNTT* III, 405-15. — K. A. STRAND, ed., *The Sabbath in Scripture and History* (1982). — idem, "Some Notes on the Sabbath Fast in Early Christianity," *AUSS* 3 (1965) 167-74. — idem, *Essays on the Sabbath in Early Christianity, with a Source Collection on the Sabbath Fast* (1972). — M. F. UNGER, "The Significance of the Sabbath," *BSac* 123 (1966) 53-57. — A. VERHEUL, "Du sabbat au Jour du Seigneur," *QLP* 51 (1970) 3-37. — For further bibliography see Gnilka 118, 124; Nötscher; Pesch 186f., 196f.

1. The sanctification of the seventh day of the week (the sabbath) was the source of decisive religious behavior and customs in Israel. Genuine analogies and a possible origin have not yet been discovered, and the etymology of σάββατον (Heb. *šabbāt*) is disputed. The sabbath serves as a day of rest (excessively interpreted both at the time of the NT and subsequently) and of worship (in the temple and synagogue). After the exile sabbath and circumcision were the distinguishing features of Israel. The significance of the sabbath is seen in statements asserting, e.g., that it should be observed even in hell (*b. Sanh.* 65b; *Gen. Rab.* 11[8b]; Billerbeck IV, 1082f.), or that the Messiah would appear if Israel would keep but two sabbaths correctly (Simeon ben Yoḥai, *ca.* 150: *b. Šabb.* 118b *Bar.*).

NT usage of the word is in accord with Jewish usage. Of 68 NT occurrences (11 in Matthew, 12 in Mark, 20 in Luke, 10 in Acts, 13 in John, also in 1 Cor 16:2; Col 2:16) 24 are pl. Both in sg. and pl. σάββατον invariably

refers to the sabbath or, according to the context, the week. ἡ ἑβδόμη, "the seventh (day)," is also used of the sabbath (Heb 4:4).

2. The NT presupposes that Jesus participated in the sabbath worship. Mark 1:21-28 has Jesus' ministry commence on the sabbath with teaching ("as one who had authority") and exorcism. The healing of Peter's mother-in-law rounds out (presumably redactionally) this first sabbath in Jesus' ministry (1:29-31). Luke 4:31 does not quite maintain this prominent position of the sabbath at the beginning of Jesus' ministry, since the scene in the synagogue in Nazareth precedes this passage (4:16-30). Both Mark 6:2 (cf. Luke 4:16) and Luke 13:10 speak of Jesus' participation in sabbath worship (which was, in any case, open to any Israelite).

3. The disputes spoken of in the Gospels between Jesus and others concerning behavior on the sabbath are of great significance. They concern both a) what may be done, i.e., plucking grain on the sabbath (Mark 2:23-28) and b) what may be left undone, in the five stories of healings on the sabbath, which form-critically are explained on the basis of Mark 3:1-6 (par.; see Luke 13:10-17; 14:1-6; John 5:1-18; 9:1-38).

a) According to Mark 2:23 par. Matt 12:1/Luke 6:1 the disciples are guilty of pilfering (though permitted according to Deut 23:25), and that, to be sure, on the sabbath. The Pharisees declare that this is prohibited (Mark 2:24 par. Matt 12:2/Luke 6:2; also meant as a transgression against where one may go on the sabbath? cf. *Jub.* 50:12). Plucking grain is interpreted as reaping, and rubbing the grains as threshing; reaping and threshing, however, are among the thirty-nine classes of work prohibited on the sabbath (*m. Šabb.* 7:2).

Jesus' response points to the example of David fleeing before Saul to the high priest Ahimelech (incorrectly called Abiathar in Mark 2:26; the parallels omit the name altogether, probably consciously), thereby countering the charge of sabbath transgression by asserting that he himself stands above the sabbath commandment. (One factor here may be the occasional rabbinic conjecture that David's eating the consecrated bread—according to rabbinic judgment done because of the life-threatening situation [cf. Billerbeck I, 618f.]—took place on the sabbath; this is probably a play on the typology David—Jesus: "Something greater than David is here.") Mark 2:26 emphasizes that David also gave the bread to those who were with him, and v. 27 asserts that the sabbath was made for mankind, not mankind for the sabbath.

Various Jewish formal parallels exist for the latter assertion (cf. in addition to Exod 23:12 and Deut 5:14f. above all 1 Macc 2:39-42; 5:19!; *2 Bar.* 14:18; cf. *T. Mos.* 1:12; 2 Esdr 6:55-59; 7:11; *Jub.* 1:27, 29; CD 12:15;

m. Yoma 8:6 ["only if life is in danger"]; similarly *b. Yoma* 85a, b; *m. Šabb.* 18:3; *Mek. Exod.* 31:13 ["the sabbath is given to you, and not you to the sabbath," R. Simeon ben Menasya, *ca.* 180]; Josephus *Ant.* xii.276; M. Ernst, *Die Worte Jesu im Markus-Evangelium* [Diss. Salzburg, 1975]). In context this assertion presupposes that Jesus' interpretation of the understanding of the sabbath commandment is the deciding factor. On the other hand, exact observance of the sabbath commandment can also serve the interests of (dependent!) human beings.

Perhaps the parallels in Matthew and Luke do not include this sentence because of such difficulties in its interpretation. It is usually assumed that the omission simply emphasizes Jesus' authority all the more, while the establishment of the assertion as an ethical norm is no longer of concern. In any case, Mark 2:27 presupposes an understanding influenced by reason (and is thus definitely related to a statement such as 12:17 par.). Perhaps the presence of ἐγένετο alludes to the creation order.

All three Synoptics offer the conclusion that "the Son of man is lord even of the sabbath" (Mark 2:28 par. Matt 12:8/Luke 6:5). This can be understood both as spoken by Jesus and as arising in the Christian community (of the Evangelist). The assumption is, again: If every person, "then certainly the Son of man"; or "the Son of man" represents here (in accordance with Dan 7:21f., 27) (Jesus' new) people of the saints. Finally, this sentence may also have been a v.l. to Mark 2:27 if "Son of man" originally meant merely "man." In the present redactional context in all three Synoptics, however, this is an unequivocal christological assertion: The appropriate understanding of the sabbath is up to Jesus; his authority is greater even than that of David, for himself and his followers, though according to the formulation here Jesus exercises it only for his followers.

This conclusion has occasioned the oft expressed (though not persuasive) assumption on the part of form-critical scholarship that subsequent emancipation from the law in the Church influenced or even generated the material of tradition (Jesus now as the Church's teacher). Present discussion generally considers either vv. 25f. and 28 to be additions, or vv. 23-26 to be the original unit and vv. 27f. the addition.

Matthew adds the argument that the priests in the temple (Num 28:9; on the laying out of the bread of the Presence cf. Lev 24:8f.) "profane" the sabbath in the execution of their duties and are guiltless (Matt 12:5). "Something greater [or v.l. "someone greater"] than the temple is here" (v. 6): Jesus liberates people to do works of mercy (v. 7; cf. Hos 6:6). Matthew is probably orienting the pericope toward the theme of rest effected by Jesus (11:28-30). On the Matthean argumentation cf. *b. Šabb.* 132b and *passim.* "Temple service overrides the sabbath" (Billerbeck I, 620-22).

In this context the v.l. in Luke 6:4 D with an agraphon of Jesus is noteworthy: Jesus saw a man working on the sabbath and told him: "Man, if you know what you are doing, you are blessed; if not, you are cursed and a transgressor against the law." This saying presupposes an element of (unspecified) insight enabling one to transgress against the sabbath commandment without sinning. The source and character of this agraphon are disputed (whether it is genuinely from Jesus or of gnostic origin), and its historicity problematic (despite Jeremias).

b) The classic narrative of healing on the sabbath is that concerning the man with the withered hand (Mark 3:1-6 par.). Jesus is in the synagogue on the sabbath (Mark 3:2 par. Matt 12:10/Luke 6:7). He is being watched (inquisitorial tactics? cf. E. Stauffer, *Jesus, Gestalt und Geschichte* [1957] 69). "Mortal danger" overrides the sabbath (*m. Yoma* 8:6; see above), but this is not such a situation, so that such a healing on the sabbath would violate the sabbath.

Mark 3:4 par. Matt 12:12/Luke 6:9 reduces the problem to whether healing (doing something unequivocally good) may be left undone on the sabbath. The parallel statement "to save a life or to kill" is formulated either in ignorance of the rabbinic legal situation or as its conscious radicalization (if the latter, it means that not providing needed aid is akin to allowing a person in mortal danger to die). Ψυχή might be an allusion to Gen 2:7 (G. Dautzenberg, *Sein Leben bewahren* [1966] 160).

Luke 13:10-17, possibly dependent on this tradition, tells of the healing in the synagogue service of a woman crippled for eighteen years. Jesus is not asked to do so, but he heals through words and the laying on of hands. The synagogue ruler becomes indignant because of this healing on the sabbath (v. 14). Jesus argues in response that one also unties the knot in order to lead his ox or ass to water on the sabbath (v. 15). This sentence is often considered the point of departure for this story (which overlooks the central significance of "to untie" in v. 16; cf. Roloff 67-69). The Halakah in this case is disputed. Positively one can say that a daughter of Abraham must be loosed from this bond also, even on the sabbath (Luke 13:16).

Luke 14:1-6 tells of the healing of a man with dropsy (which he might have, according to rabbinic opinion [Billerbeck II, 203f.], because of immorality). Here Luke presents the account in such a way that Jesus, on his own initiative, inquires whether healing on the sabbath is permitted (v. 3). One positive argument is that one immediately pulls out an ass or (even) an ox that has fallen into a well on the sabbath (an Aramaic play on words may be at work here: *bᵉrāʾ*/son—*bᵉʿîrāʾ*/ox— *bêrāʾ*/well; Black, *Approach* 168f.; a mistranslation is also possible: son/ass). Matt 12:11 employs the same argument in relation to the healing of the man with a withered hand ("a *single* sheep"). Here, too, the Halakic rules make it unclear whether the assertions of the two Evangelists stand up to rabbinic interpretation (cf. CD 11:13f.: prohibited!). In any case, for Jesus such deliverance is a matter of course (e.g., Braun, *Qumran* I, 26).

Basically the modern sabbath disputes concern whether Jesus suspended the sabbath (e.g., Rordorf, *Sunday* 295f.) or interpreted it anew (e.g., Bacchiocchi, *From Sabbath* 304).

John offers (as a variation of Mark 2:1-12 par.?) the story of the healing at the pool called Bethzatha/Bethesda of a man lame for thirty-eight years (John 5:1-9 [-18]). In contrast to the formal Synoptic parallels this healing took place on a sabbath (v. 9, presumably a redactional motif). Thus did Jesus cause indignation (vv. 10, 16). According to 5:17 Jesus argues that "my Father is working up to now" (C. Maurer, "Steckt hinter Joh 5,17 ein Übersetzungsfehler?" *WuD* 5 [1957] 130-40 believes this reflects a tr. error: "still"), "and I am working also." This is a variation of the Jewish (rabbinic and Philonic) conception of the working rest of God. Thus Jesus not only broke (regularly: impf.) the sabbath, but also made himself equal to God (v. 18).

The argument concerning circumcision is also mentioned in reference to the healing of the lame man (John 7:22f.). Moses prescribed circumcision, which actually came not from Moses but from the fathers, for the sabbath (Lev 12:3), and thus the law of Moses cannot be broken through circumcision on the sabbath. Circumcision is considered a healing of a man; how, then, can the healing of the *whole* man on the sabbath be reason for anger (cf. *t. Šabb.* 15:16; *b. Yoma* 85b: "because of one member he overrides the sabbath," though as grounding the principle that "a life in danger overrides the sabbath"; Billerbeck II, 488)?

The healing of a blind man (John 9:1-7) is also said to have taken place on a sabbath (9:14, redactional?). Here, as in ch. 5 (according to 5:10 the only objection is to the carrying of the pallet, which Jesus had ordered; to be sure, the order "rise" in v. 12 can also refer to the healing), the objection is not to the healing itself, but at first to the making of the clay with which Jesus anointed the man's eyes (9:15f.). To be sure, the continuation of the story does not insist on this at all, since Jesus is guilty from the beginning (v. 24).

4. The religious significance of the sabbath is also seen in John 19:31: The "high sabbath" should not be defiled by Jesus left hanging on the cross. Matt 24:20 shows Jewish Christian influence in its wish that the flight not take place in winter or on a sabbath (cf. in contrast the council of conscience in 1 Macc 2:41; hardly because the persons fleeing would be noticed as Christians, *contra* W. Grundmann, *Matt* [THKNT] 506). Mark 16:1 par. Matt 28:1 (cf. Luke 23:54, 56) presupposes observance of sabbath rest (the women who want to anoint Jesus).

Acts tells of several visits with preaching in the synagogue by Paul and his companions on the sabbath (Acts 13:14; 17:2, "as was his custom"; 18:4). On a sabbath Paul finds pious women (open to Judaism) at a place of prayer by a river (16:13). The holy Scriptures (the prophets) are read on the sabbath (13:27), whereby Moses is preached (15:21). 13:42, 44 also speak of visits to the synagogue on the sabbath.

Questions concerning the sabbath also play a role in the religious disputes in the church at Colossae (Col 2:16). Like festivals and new moons sabbath observance is only a shadow of what is to come (2:17; cf. the similar argument in Gal 4:9f.).

Σάββατον also means *week* (Luke 18:12). Ἡ πρώτη (Mark 16:9), μία σαββάτου (1 Cor 16:2), or σαββάτων (Matt 28:1b; Mark 16:2; Luke 24:1; John 20:1, 19; Acts 20:7) is the first day of the *week*, i.e., Sunday. That the women went to Jesus' tomb on the first day of the week, found it empty, and then received the explanation that it was empty because of the resurrection (Mark 16:2 par. Matt 28:1/Luke 24:1/John 20:1) may be one reason Sunday serves as the assembly day of the Christian service (1 Cor 16:2: opportunity to put aside or collect money for the offering; Acts 20:7: breaking bread, Paul's talk). On the development toward the Christian Sunday → ἡμέρα 2.d, κύριος 12.

W. Beilner

σαγήνη, ης, ἡ   *sagēnē*   dragnet*

Matt 13:47 (M) mentions a (drag-)net in a parable of the kingdom of heaven (σαγήνη βληθεῖσα εἰς τὴν θάλασσαν). A dragnet is larger and more complex than a casting net (→ ἀμφίβληστρον) and after being cast "is drawn onto land in a large circle by ropes" (C. Edlund, *BHH* 483) so that many and various fish can be caught in it. Dalman, *Arbeit* VI, 348-50.

Σαδδουκαῖος, ου, ὁ   *Saddoukaios*   Sadducee*

1. Occurrences in the NT — 2. Jewish sources — 3. Significance for the story of Jesus

Lit.: E. BAMMEL, "Sadduzäer und Sadokiden," *ETL* 55 (1979) 107-15. — G. BAUMBACH, *Jesus von Nazareth im Lichte der jüdischen Gruppenbildung* (1971) 49-71 (= *Kairos* 13 [1971] 17-37). — idem, "Der sadduzäische Konservativismus," Maier /Schreiner 201-13. — P. GEOLTRAIN, *BHH* 1639f. — J. JEREMIAS, *Jerusalem in the Time of Jesus* (1969) 228ff. — J. LE MOYNE, *Les Sadducéens* (1972). — J. MAIER, *Geschichte der jüdischen Religion* (1972) 43-48. — R. MEYER, *TDNT* VII, 35-54. — K. MÜLLER, "Jesus und die Sadduzäer," *Biblische Randbemerkungen* (FS R. Schnackenburg, 1974) 3-24. — SCHÜRER, *History* II, 381-88, 404-14. — O. SCHWANKL, *Die Sadduzäerfrage (Mk 12,18-27 parr)* (BBB 66, 1987). — M. SIMON, *DBSup* X, 1545-56. — idem, *Jewish Sects at the Time of Jesus* (1967), esp. 22-27. — For further bibliography see *TWNT* X, 1159f.

1. Of the 14 occurrences in the NT 9 are in the Synoptic Gospels (7 of those in Matthew) and 5 in Acts. The Sadducees almost always play the role of those denying the resurrection (cf. Mark 12:18[ff.] par. Matt 22:23, 34 /Luke 20:27; Acts 4:1f.; 23:6-8). According to Acts 23:8 they also rejected popular belief in angels and spirits, and according to 5:17 they were identical with the ruling class of high priests. Only Matthew considers the Sadducees and Pharisees together (cf. 3:7; 16:1, 6, 11, 12).

2. According to Josephus the Sadducees were one of the four Jewish "schools of philosophy" and were distinguished from the Pharisees, Essenes, and Zealots by their strong emphasis on the personal responsibility of each individual and through their doctrine of imminent restitution whereby reward and punishment appear in exact correspondence to a person's actions in this life (*B.J.* ii.164f.; *Ant.* xiii.173). They thus represented the older, pre-Pharisaic position (cf. Exod 20:5f.; 34:7) and on the basis of this strictly conservative attitude rejected as innovations the Pharisaic doctrines of predestination, resurrection of the dead and judgment in the afterlife, and the oral Torah. On this basis both Josephus and rabbinic writers equate the Sadducees with the "Epicureans" (cf. *Ant.* x.277ff.; *m. Sanh.* 10:1). Because of their rigid adherence to the written Torah they were on the one hand "more heartless in judgment than any other Jews" (*Ant.* xx.199), yet on the other hand more generous and open regarding the cultural achievements of Hellenism. Socially the Sadducees included the small upper class (cf. *Ant.* xiii.298; xviii.17) that as the priestly nobility set the tone for society. As their name shows, they understood themselves to be the successors of the legitimate high-priestly line of Zadokites (cf. 1 Chr 5:27ff.; 24:1ff.). They probably constituted themselves as the party of the Jerusalem priestly nobility in the 2nd cent. B.C. (cf. Josephus *Ant.* xiii.171ff., 288ff.) and took over the national ideology of the Hasmonean temple state.

3. The Sadducees were of decisive importance in the condemnation and death of Jesus, since at that time only Sadducees and Romans had the power to implement legal decisions. Since no political-revolutionary messianic claims can be documented for Jesus, the Romans can only be viewed as those who carried out the decision of the Jewish priestly hierarchy reigning in Judea A.D. 6-41 (cf. Josephus *Ant.* xx.251). The Sadducees probably interpreted Jesus' critical comments concerning rules of cultic purity (cf. Mark 7:15 par.) and the temple (cf. Mark 14:58 par.) as transgressing against the reigning religio-political structure of Judea and thus against the Romans as the "protectors of the law" (Josephus *B.J.* iv.184). On this basis, then, they managed to get Jesus crucified as a rebel or agitator.

G. Baumbach

Σαδώκ *Sadōk* Zadok*

The name (Heb. *ṣādôq*) of the son of Azor and father of Achim in the genealogy of Jesus according to Matt 1:14 (bis); Luke 3:23ff. D. This sequence is not documented in the OT.

σαίνω *sainō* upset, shake; pass.: be shaken, stagger*

1 Thess 3:3: τὸ μηδένα σαίνεσθαι, "that no one *be shaken/waver.*" The meaning "deceive" (Aeschylus *Th.* 383) fits the context less persuasively (cf. στηρίξαι, v. 2; ἐν ταῖς θλίψεσιν, v. 3; Vg. *ut nemo moveatur;* Hesychius [s.v. σαίνεται]: κινεῖται, σαλεύεται, ταράττεται; so also older Greek interpreters). F. Lang, *TDNT* VII, 54-56; BAGD s.v. (bibliography).

σάκκος, ου, ὁ *sakkos* sack, (mourning) sackcloth/garment*

Σάκκος is a Semitic loanword (cf. Heb. *śaq*) referring to a coarse, rough-linen material or a garment made of it. Such garments are mentioned in ancient writings, esp. the OT, as indicating mourning or penitence, being dark in color and distinguished from normal comfortable clothing by its coarse weave (cf. Isa 3:24; 50:3; Jer 6:26; Jonah 3:5; 2 Sam 21:10; 1 Kgs 20:31, and *passim*). *Sackcloth* probably consisted of coarse material girded around the loins (Isa 22:12; Jer 4:8) enabling the mourners to beat themselves on their bare chest (Isa 32:11f.; → κόπτω). Other acts of self-humiliation accompanied this, such as sprinkling oneself with ash (→ σποδός), cutting one's hair, and the like (Isa 58:5; Jer 48:37; Amos 8:10). Prophets could also wear *sackcloth* as a sign of lamentation and penitence (cf. Isa 20:2; Bar 4:20; Dan 9:3; see also G. Stählin, *TDNT* VII, 61-63 with n.48).

In the NT σάκκος occurs once in a metaphor for the eclipse of the son: μέλας ὡς σάκκος τρίχινος, "black as *sackcloth*" (Rev 6:12; cf. Isa 50:3). In Rev 11:3 it is used of the clothing of the two witnesses: προφητεύσουσιν . . . περιβεβλημένοι σάκκους (cf. v. 10: οἱ δύο προφῆται); *sackcloth* characterizes them as prophets commissioned to give the call to penitence. Matt 11:21 par. Luke 10:13 (Q), probably alluding to Jonah 3:4ff. (cf. Matt 12:41 par.), expresses the anticipated conversion of the Galilean cities through the traditional gestures of mourning and penitence: πάλαι ἂν ἐν σάκκῳ καὶ σποδῷ (Luke: καθήμενοι) μετενόησαν "[Tyre and Sidon] would have repented long ago [sitting] in *sackcloth* and ashes" (cf. Dan 9:3; Esth 4:1f.; on "sitting in sackcloth and ashes" see Isa 58:5; Esth 4:3; see further Josephus *Ant.* xx.123; *Barn.* 7:5; *TDNT* VII, 62 with n.47f.). BAGD s.v. (Greek parallels); G. Stählin, *TDNT* VII, 56-64; G. Fohrer, *BHH* 1638.

H. Balz

Σαλά *Sala* Shelah*

The name Σαλά (Heb. *šelaḥ*) occurs twice in the genealogy of Jesus in Luke 3:32, 35. In v. 35 it refers to *Shelah,* the son of Cainan and father of Eber (cf. Gen 10:24 LXX; 11:13-15 LXX; 1 Chr 1:18 A; it can vary in the MT, where Arphaxad [Arpachshad] is considered the father of Shelah). Luke 3:32 also mentions a Σαλά as the son of Nahshon and father of Boaz. According to 1 Chr 2:11; Ruth 4:20f. (as in Matt 1:4f.), however, the name should be Salmon (so also as an assimilation in some Lukan mss.: א² A D L, etc., and Koine).

Σαλαθιήλ *Salathiēl* Shealtiel, Salathiel*

The name (Heb. *š^ealtî'ēl*) of the father of Zerubbabel (cf. 1 Chr 3:19; 2 Esdr 3:2; 5:2; 22:1; Hag 1:1) in the genealogy of Jesus according to Matt 1:12 (bis); Luke 3:27. According to Matt 1:12a he is the son of Jechoniah (cf. 1 Chr 3:17), according to Luke 3:27 the son of Neri (a name not documented in the OT).

Σαλαμίς, ῖνος *Salamis* Salamis*

A large port city on the east coast of Cyprus, important for trade with Syria. Salamis was the first mission stop for Paul and his companions Barnabas and John Mark on the "first missionary journey" coming from Antioch to Cyprus by way of Seleucia: καὶ γενόμενοι ἐν Σαλαμῖνι κατήγγελον . . . ἐν ταῖς συναγωγαῖς τῶν Ἰουδαίων (Acts 13:5). During the time of the Ptolemies Salamis was the seat of the governor of Cyprus, though it then lost this function in the Roman period to the city of Paphos (cf. 13:6ff.). P. Bratsiotis, *BHH* 1645f.; E. Meyer, *KP* IV, 1505f.

Σαλείμ *Saleim* Salim*

According to John 3:23 John the Baptist (after his activity at Bethany on the other side of the Jordan; cf. 1:28; 3:26) baptized in the vicinity of Salim (ἦν . . . ὁ Ἰωάννης βαπτίζων ἐν Αἰνὼν ἐγγὺς τοῦ Σαλείμ; *NTG* and others read Σαλίμ, cf. also BDF §38). According to Eusebius *Onom.* 40:2f. Aenon near Salim is located ca. 12 km. south of Scythopolis (Beth-Shean) in northern Samaria. Another place called Salim is situated today *ca.* 6 km. east of Neapolis (Shechem; cf. Jdt 4:4: Σαλημ). Jesus or his disciples, on the other hand, baptized in Judea (John 3:22; 4:2f.). BAGD s.v. Σαλίμ; Kopp, *Places* 129-37; B. Reicke, *BHH* 1648; R. Schnackenburg, *John* (Eng. tr., 1982) I, ad loc.

σαλεύω *saleuō* shake, cause to sway; pass.: sway back and forth, waver*

Σαλεύω occurs 15 times in the NT, esp. in Luke's writings (4 times each in Luke and Acts). Literal in Matt 11:7 par. Luke 7:24: "a reed *shaken* by the wind" (κάλαμος ὑπὸ ἀνέμου σαλευόμενος); Luke 6:38: a measuring vessel whose contents are well *shaken* (μέτρον σεσαλευμένον); 6:48: *shaking* a house (σαλεῦσαι); cf. Acts 16:26: the foundations of the prison *were shaken* (σαλευ-

θῆναι) in an earthquake; 4:31: the *shaking* of a place (ἐσαλεύθη ὁ τόπος) as a sign of the answering of prayers and the coming of the Spirit (cf. also John 12:28-30; Amos 9:5; Mic 1:4; Hab 3:6, and *passim* of the power of God's word and actions; Isa 6:4; Exod 19:18; Josephus *Ant.* vii.76f. of God's presence; Virgil *Aen.* iii.89f. speaks of quaking as a sign of answered prayers). Cf. the shaking of the powers in the heavens (eclipse of the sun and moon and falling of the stars) as signs of the commencing last judgment and transformation of the cosmos: αἱ δυνάμεις αἱ ἐν τοῖς οὐρανοῖς/τῶν οὐρανῶν σαλευθήσονται (Mark 13:25 par. Matt 24:29/Luke 21:26; cf. Isa 13:10; 34:4; Ezek 32:7f.; Joel 2:10; 4:15f.; *1 Enoch* 102:2).

In Heb 12:26f. (3 occurrences), too, the shaking of the earth by God's word (v. 26a; cf. Exod 19:18; Pss 68:9; 114:7) and the shaking (σείω) of heaven and earth "yet once more" (for the end; Heb 12:26b, quoting Hag 2:6, 21 LXX) is a sign of the all-transforming power of God's word, so that at the end "what is shaken" (τὰ σαλευόμενα, Heb 12:27a) and thus the created and visible world— earth and heaven—is removed so that "what cannot be shaken" (τὰ μὴ σαλευόμενα, v. 27b), i.e., God's kingdom, may endure forever (cf. v. 28: βασιλεία ἀσάλευτος). This contrast (cf. also 11:1, 3) also appears in Philo (see G. Bertram, *TDNT* VII, 67f.), though in Hebrews it is eschatologically focussed on the power and legitimacy of God's kingdom that is superior to all creation and has already been received by the faithful.

All other NT occurrences use σαλεύω fig.: ἵνα μὴ σαλευθῶ, "that I may not *be shaken*" (Acts 2:25, quoting Ps 15:8 LXX); cf. 2 Thess 2:2: σαλευθῆναι ἀπὸ τοῦ νοός, "not to be quickly *shaken* in mind"; σαλεύοντες καὶ ταράσσοντες τοὺς ὄχλους, "*stirring up* and exciting the crowds" (Acts 17:13). G. Bertram, *TDNT* VII, 65-71; J. W. Thompson, *JBL* 94 (1975) 580-87.

H. Balz

Σαλήμ *Salēm* Salem*

In Heb 7:1 Melchizedek is called "king of Salem" (βασιλεὺς Σαλήμ; cf. Gen 14:8: *šālēm*), which v. 2 then interprets as "king of peace" (βασιλεὺς Σαλήμ, ὅ ἐστιν βασιλεὺς εἰρήνης; cf. Heb. *šālam, šālôm;* the same interpretation appears in Philo *All.* iii.79: Μελχισεδὲκ βασιλέα τῆς εἰρήνης—Σαλήμ τοῦτο γὰρ ἑρμηνεύεται). According to OT and Jewish tradition Salem is an abbreviated form of "Jerusalem": In Ps 76:3 Salem is mentioned with Zion; Josephus *Ant.* i.180 understands Salem (Σολυμᾶ) as an older name for what later became Jerusalem; cf. 1QapGen 22:13; Ps 110:4. Others think of → Σαλείμ or Σαλημ (the latter in Jdt 4:4). See further G. Fohrer and E. Lohse, *TDNT* VII, 299f.; Kopp, *Places* 129-37, 283f.; A. van den Born and W. Baier, *BL* 1506; K. Elliger, *BHH* 1647f.

Σαλίμ *Salim* Salim

Variant spelling of → Σαλείμ (John 3:23) in various mss. and editions.

Σαλμών *Salmōn* Salmon*

Σαλμών appears in the genealogy of Jesus according to Matthew as the son of Nahshon (1:4) and father of Boaz (1:5; cf. 1 Chr 2:11; Ruth 4:20f.; Luke 3:32 TR in place of → Σαλά; Heb. *śalmôn*).

Σαλμώνη, ης *Salmōnē* Salmone*

A promontory on the northeast corner of Crete, occurring in this form only in Acts 27:7 (elsewhere Σαλμώνιον and similarly). Because of unfavorable winds, Paul's ship sailed around Crete on the southern side of the island ("under the lee"), just as he had previously done off Cyprus (v. 4); the ship changed course "off Salmone" (κατὰ Σαλμώνην). H. Conzelmann, *Acts* (Hermeneia) ad loc.

σάλος, ου, ὁ *salos* wavering, shaking*

Luke 21:25: the "roaring of the sea and the waves" (ἦχος θαλάσσης καὶ σάλου; cf. Jonah 1:15; Ps 88:10 LXX; see also 45:4; 64:8; 92:1ff.), part of the terrifying events of the end (cf. also Mark 13:24f. par.; Isa 13:10; 24:19f.; 34:4; 2 Esdr 5:1ff.; 6:13ff.; *1 Enoch* 91:16; *Sib. Or.* iii.675ff.). → σαλεύω.

σάλπιγξ, ιγγος, ἡ *salpinx* trumpet*

1. Occurrences in the NT — 2. Meaning — 3. NT usage — 4. Σαλπίζω

Lit.: B. BAYER, *EncJud* XII, 554-66, esp. 563, 565. — BILLERBECK I, 387f., 959f.; III, 481, 635; IV/1, 536ff. — D. A. FOXVOG and A. D. KILMER, *ISBE* III, 439f., 446. — G. FRIEDRICH, *TDNT* VII, 71-88. — P. GRADENWITZ, *The Music of Israel. Its Rise and Growth through 500* (1949), index s.v. trumpet. — K.-E. GRÖZINGER, *Musik und Gesang in der Theologie der frühen jüdischen Literatur* (1982). — W. HARNISCH, *Eschatologische Existenz* (FRLANT 110, 1973) 19-51. — E. KOLARI, *Musikinstrumente und ihre Verwendung im AT* (1974) 49-51. — H. KRAFT, *Rev* (HNT, 1974) 133f. — A. L. LEWIS, *EncJud* XIV, 1442-47. — B. REICKE, *BHH* 1481. — H. P. RÜGER, *BRL* 235. — H. SEIDEL, "Horn und Trompete im alten Israel unter Berücksichtigung der 'Kriegsrolle' von Qumran," *Wissenschaftliche Zeitschrift der Karl-Marx-Universität Leipzig. Gesellschafts- und sprachwissenschaftliche Reihe* 6 (1956/57) 589-99. — A. SENDREY, *David's Harp: The Story of Music in Biblical Times* (1964) 121-28. — *idem, Music in Ancient Israel* (1969) 332-65. — G. WALLIS, *BHH* 1258-62, 1480f. — Y. YADIN, *The Scroll of the War of the Sons of Light against the Sons of Darkness* (1962) 87-113. — For further bibliography see Friedrich.

1. All but 2 of the 11 NT occurrences of σάλπιγξ are in eschatological passages (Matt 24:31; 1 Cor 15:52; 1 Thess 4:16; 6 occurrences in Revelation), where the sounding of the σάλπιγξ opens the eschatological events. The exceptions are Heb 12:19 (a theophany) and 1 Cor 14:8 (a metaphor).

2. The σάλπιγξ is a long, straight metal wind instrument with a bell and a mouthpiece (cf. Josephus *Ant.* iii.291; see also the portrayal on the Arch of Titus) capable of producing only a few natural tones that could be articulated loudly and distinctly (see Sendrey 334f.).

In the LXX σάλπιγξ translates Heb. *šôpār* (*ca.* 40 times), *hªṣoṣᵉrâ* (*ca.* 20 times), *qeren* (9 times), and occasionally *yôḇēl*, *tāqôʿa*, and *tᵉrûʿâ*. In the NT σάλπιγξ probably refers (with Exod 19:16, 19; 20:18 MT *qôl [haš-]šôpār*) to the shofar, preferably the curved horn of a ram or ibex (Heb 12:19, probably also in 1 Cor 15:52; 1 Thess 4:16; Matt 6:2; 24:31; see Billerbeck I, 959f.; III, 635). The use of σάλπιγξ in the NT is determined by OT usage. In times of war, horns (1 Sam 13:3; Job 39:24f.; 2 Sam 2:28) and trumpets (Num 10:9; 2 Chr 20:28) are blown. 1QM prescribes precisely differentiated trumpet signals for military actions (see Yadin 87-113; Seidel 597ff.). In cultic use the σάλπιγξ is blown during the sacrifice at festival times (Num 10:10; cf. 2 Chr 29:27f.; 2 Chr 5:13f. [MT variously "trumpets"]), at the year of release, and on the Day of Atonement (Lev 25:9; MT *šôpār*). According to the LXX the σάλπιγξ sounds at the theophany in Exod 19:16ff., probably as a portrayal of the divine voice, and at the eschatological appearance of Yahweh (Isa 27:13; Zech 9:14 [MT variously *šôpār*]).

The *šôpār* continues to play a role in the Jewish cult today (see Lewis; Sendrey 353-65); the trumpet ceased to be used after the end of the temple cult (see Friedrich 83f.; Sendrey 342-52). The trumpet has special significance in NT usage as an eschatological signal (e.g., as in 2 Esdr 6:23; *Apoc. Abr.* 31:1; *Sib. Or.* iv.174), in portrayals of judgment (as in *Sib. Or.* viii.239; cf. *Apoc. Mos.* 22; see, however, 37), and as a signal of the beginning of the time of salvation (*Pss. Sol.* 11:1; tenth of the Eighteen Benedictions [*šôpār*]).

In the NT the σάλπιγξ is a signal instrument rather than a musical instrument (though → σαλπιστής in Rev 18:22 may refer to a musician).

3. a) The σάλπιγξ as an eschatological instrument for signaling brings together elements of theophany with eschatological elements. Various aspects come to expression. At the sound of "God's trumpet" (after the "cry of command, with the archangel's call") the Kyrios will descend from heaven to raise the dead and carry up the living (1 Thess 4:16; cf. *Did.* 16:6). The transformation of believers will take place at the sounding of "the last trumpet" (1 Cor 15:52). The coming Son of man will send out his angels "with a loud trumpet call" (μετὰ σάλπιγγος μεγάλης) to gather his elect (Matt 24:31; see Billerbeck I, 959f.). The phrase σάλπιγξ μεγάλη is related to φωνὴ μεγάλη ὡς σάλπιγγος in Rev 1:10 as the designation for particular loudness; in 4:1, too, Christ's voice is compared with the sound of a trumpet. Both passages clearly manifest elements of theophany (cf. Exod 19:16, 19; 20:18). The seven angels in Rev 8:2 are given trum-

pets (cf. v. 6) to open the judgments (cf. *Apoc. Mos.* 22; also Rev 8:13; 9:14).

b) Heb 12:19 uses elements of OT theophanies (σάλπιγγος ἦχος; cf. Exod 19:16, 19; 20:18) to indicate the newness of the encounter with God in Christ.

c) Speaking in tongues without interpretation is compared with (among other musical examples) an indistinct signal from a war bugle (1 Cor 14:8; distinct signals, e.g., 1QM 2:15ff.; 7:13ff.; 8:1ff.).

4. The vb. **σαλπίζω**, *to trumpet, sound the trumpet**, occurs 12 times in the NT, except in Matt 6:2 always in eschatological contexts (10 times in Revelation; once in 1 Cor 15:52); in the LXX it almost always translates *tāqaʿ* (39 times), rarely *hᵃṣoṣer* (6 times) or *rûʿa*.

Just who sounds the "last trumpet" in 1 Cor 15:52 (→ 3.a) is unclear. Rev 8:6, 7, 8, 10, 12, 13; 9:1, 13; 10:7 portray the sequential trumpets of the seven trumpeting angels as anticipating the judgments coming upon the earth; when the seventh angel sounds his trumpet, God and his Christ assume dominion over the world (11:15).

Matt 6:2 mentions an enigmatic custom of announcing almsgiving by "trumpeting," i.e., perhaps by blowing on the shofar. Such public ostentation is contrasted with the secret almsgiving that the Father, who sees in secret, will reward (see Billerbeck I, 388; IV/1, 536ff.; Friedrich 85f.).

H. Lichtenberger

σαλπίζω *salpizō* trumpet (vb.), sound a trumpet
→ σάλπιγξ 4.

σαλπιστής, οῦ, ὁ *salpistēs* trumpeter*

Rev 18:22: φωνὴ . . . σαλπιστῶν οὐ μὴ ἀκουσθῇ, "the sound of *trumpeters* shall be heard no more" in "Babylon" at the end of time. Σαλπιστής refers to trumpeters (with "singers, minstrels, and flute players") as a musician (at festivals), whereas → σάλπιγξ is usually used in the NT to refer to a signalling trumpet.

Σαλώμη, ης *Salōmē* Salome*

Mark 15:40; 16:1 mention Salome (with Mary Magdalene and Mary the mother of James the younger and of Joses) among the Galilean followers of Jesus who were in Jerusalem and witnessed Jesus' crucifixion and the empty tomb on Easter Sunday. Matt 27:56 mentions, in addition to Mary Magdalene and Mary the mother of James and Joseph, a third woman, the unnamed mother of the sons of Zebedee. Therefore, the conclusion is drawn that Salome was Zebedee's wife (see also Matt 20:20). She is also occasionally identified with the sister of Jesus' mother (John 19:25; cf. J. Blinzler, *Die Brüder und Schwestern Jesu* [SBS 21, 1967] 113f. with n.11). Salome also appears in apocryphal Gospels (*Gos. Thom.*

61; *Prot. Jas.* 19:3; 20:1ff.; esp. often in *Gos. Eg.*, cf. Hennecke/Schneemelcher I, 166-69, 172f., 177f., generally 426ff.; see also Zahn, *Kanon* VI, 340f.).

Salome is also the name of the daughter of Herodias mentioned, but not by name, in Mark 6:22ff.; Matt 14:6ff. At the time of the story in the Gospels Herodias was the wife of Herod Antipas, but Salome was the offspring of her first marriage to Herod, the son of the Boethusian Mariamne (who is called Philip in Mark 6:17), and came to be the wife of the tetrarch Philip (mentioned in Luke 3:1; cf. further Josephus *Ant.* xviii.136f.; → Ἡρῳδιάς). C. E. B. Cranfield, *BHH* 1650f.; A. van den Born, *BL* 1507; J. Mehlmann, *RCB* N.F. 1 (1964) 196-208.

Σαμάρεια (Σαμαρία), ας, ἡ *Samareia (Samaria)* Samaria*
Σαμαρίτης, ου, ὁ *Samaritēs* Samaritan*
Σαμαρῖτις, ιδος, ἡ *Samaritis* Samaritan woman; adj.: Samaritan*

1. Occurrences in the NT — 2. The history of Samaria — 3. Luke — 4. John — 5. Acts

Lit.: R. BACH and C. COLPE, *RGG* V, 1350-55. — A. D. CROWN, ed., *The Samaritans* (1989). — R. BERGMEIER, "Zur Frühdatierung samaritanischer Theologumena," *JSJ* 5 (1974) 121-53. — G. BOUWMAN, "Samaria im lukanischen Doppelwerk," *Theologie aus dem Norden* (ed. A. Fuchs; 1977) 118-41. — J. BOWMAN, *The Samaritan Problem. Studies in the Relationship of Samaritanism, Judaism, and Early Christianity* (1975). — J. JEREMIAS, *TDNT* VII, 88-94. — J. KILGALLEN, *The Stephen Speech* (1976). — H. G. KIPPENBERG, *Garizim und Synagoge* (1971). — S. LOWY, *The Principles of Samaritan Bible Exegesis* (1977). — J. MACDONALD, *The Theology of the Samaritans* (1964). — L. A. MAYER and D. BROADRIBB, *Bibliography of the Samaritans* (1964). — R. PUMMER, "The Present State of Samaritan Studies," *JSS* 21 (1976) 39-61; 22 (1977) 27-47. — J. D. PURVIS, "The Fourth Gospel and the Samaritans," *NovT* 17 (1975) 161-98. — E. RICHARD, "Acts 7: An Investigation of the Samaritan Evidence," *CBQ* 39 (1977) 190-208. — G. SCHNEIDER, "Stephanus, die Hellenisten und Samaria," *Les Actes des Apôtres* (ed. J. Kremer; 1979) 215-40. — N. SCHUR, *History of the Samaritans* (1989). — G. S. SLOYAN, "The Samaritans in the NT," *Horizons* 10 (1983) 7-21. — For further bibliography see *TWNT* X, 1260.

1. Σαμάρεια as the designation of the region of *Samaria* (→ 2) occurs 11 times in the NT: Luke 17:11; John 4:4, 5, 7; Acts 1:8; 8:1, 5, 9, 14; 9:31; 15:3. The words derived from Σαμάρεια, namely, Σαμαρίτης (Matt 10:5; Luke 9:52; 10:33; 17:16; John 4:9, 39, 40; 8:48; Acts 8:25) and Σαμαρῖτις (John 4:9a, b: "Samaritan woman") refer to the inhabitants, esp. in the sense of affiliation with the religious community of Samaria.

Mark never mentions the Samaritans, and Matthew mentions them only once (and negatively, at that: 10:5), but the Lukan writings (Luke 9:51-56; 10:30-37; 17:11-19; Acts 1:8; 8:1-25; 9:31; 15:3) and John (4:4-42) are greatly interested in them. In general the Gospels reflect the hostility between Jews and Samaritans. On the Jewish side the word Σαμαρίτης is used as an insult and equated with "possessed person" (John 8:48). The Jewish scribe in Luke 10:37 avoids uttering the word "Samaritan" and instead uses a circumlocution. Jesus himself calls the Samaritan leper an ἀλλογενής (17:18), and the disciples are astonished that Jesus speaks with a Samaritan woman (John 4:27), while for her part the woman is astonished that he asks her for a drink (4:9). In Matt 10:5f. Jesus forbids going among Samaritans and Gentiles. On the Samaritan side Jesus is refused quarters there (Luke 9:52f.), whereupon the sons of Zebedee want to bid fire come down on the inhospitable village. One must thus ask to what extent the reports of Jesus' mission work in Samaria (→ 3, 4) have been colored by later developments.

2. The city of Samaria owes its significance to the decision by Omri (878/77-871/70 B.C.) to erect his residence there (1 Kgs 16:24). After a three-year siege Samaria fell in 722/21 B.C. to the Assyrians, who made it the capital of the province, deported its inhabitants, and replaced them with Assyrian settlers from Cuthah and other places (cf. 2 Kgs 17:24, 30). Josephus (*Ant.* IX, 288) and the Mishnah thus call the Samaritans Cutheans. After Cyrus conquered Babylon in 539 B.C. he allowed the Jews living there to return to Palestine. When the Samaritans wanted to participate in the building of the temple in Jerusalem, Zerubbabel rebuffed their offer (Ezra 4:2f.). It was probably at this time that the Samaritans erected their own cult center on Mt. Gerizim. The real schism came, according to Josephus (*Ant.* xi.324), in 332 B.C., when a Macedonian military colony was established under Alexander the Great through which the city of Samaria was gradually Hellenized. This development continued during the period of the Ptolemies and Seleucids and reached its zenith under Herod the Great, who expanded the city and renamed it Sebaste in honor of Emperor Augustus (*Augustus* = σεβαστός). After that the name Samaria was reserved for the region or district, as is the case throughout the NT.

"Samaritans" (Vg. *Samaritani;* LXX and NT Σαμαρῖται; Josephus also uses Σαμαρεῖς; Heb. *šômᵉrônî*) is today used only of adherents of the distinct religious observance that developed from the schism. Since the canonical divisions of the Prophets and the Writings had not yet been collected at the time of the division from Judaism, the Samaritans did not take them over. The textual transmission of the Samaritan Pentateuch went its own way and deviates from the MT in about six thousand instances. The community numbers only a few hundred members today.

3. All three pericopes in Luke taking place in Samaria are exclusive to this Gospel and reflect its interest in despised and rejected persons. According to Luke, Jesus' final journey to Jerusalem passed through Samaria. This Samaritan journey must, however, be a fiction, since it is not possible that Jesus was invited to eat with the Pharisees (11:37; 14:1) and enter a synagogue (13:10) in Samaria (Bultmann, *History* 363).

4. John 4:4-42 uses the encounter of Jesus with a "Samaritan woman" to trace the Samaritan mission back to Jesus. The ἄλλοι (v. 38) are the "Hellenists," who labored with the difficult work of the initial proclamation, whereas the apostles then merely entered into that labor (cf. Acts 8:14).

5. Acts reports programmatically the promise of the resurrected Christ that the disciples will be his witnesses, among other places, also "in Samaria" (1:8). According to 8:4-25 Philip, one of the Hellenists scattered by persecution after Stephen's execution, proclaimed Christ in Samaria. This story shrinks to a very brief notice if one considers that the narrative of Simon the magician has been woven into it through a redactional procedure typical for Luke (K. Löning, Schreiner/Dautzenberg 205-9). The high point of the pericope is the baptism of the magician (v. 13); since, however, Justin, an inhabitant of Samaria, states that around the middle of the 2nd cent. Simon was revered as the highest god by almost all Samaritans (*Apol.* i.26.3; *Dial.* 120.6), one should not overestimate the success of Christian missionary activity in Samaria.

Many authors see traces of Samaritan theology in the extensive speech of Stephen (Acts 7). Although these so-called Samaritanisms also occur in isolated instances elsewhere (Schneider), this accumulation in Acts 7 remains unexplained. It is also peculiar in a Christian apology that the name of Jesus does not occur at all and that the figure of Moses occupies the most prominent position.

G. Bouwman

Σαμαρία, ας *Samaria* Samaria
Alternate spelling of → Σαμάρεια (cf. BDF §38).

Σαμαρίτης, ου, ὁ *Samaritēs* Samaritan
→ Σαμάρεια.

Σαμαρῖτις, ιδος, ἡ *Samaritis* Samaritan woman; adj.: Samaritan
→ Σαμάρεια.

Σαμοθρᾴκη, ης *Samothrakē* Samothrace*

An island in the northeastern Aegean; according to Acts 16:11 Paul reached it on his "second missionary journey" coming from Troas (εὐθυδρομήσαμεν εἰς Σαμοθρᾴκην) and set out the following day for Neapolis. K. Fredrich, PW IA, 2224-26; K. Lehmann, *Samothrace* (1955); C. von Gablenz, *BHH* 1663; *BL* 1516; E. Mensching, *LAW* 2697.

Σάμος, ου *Samos* Samos*

An island (with a city of the same name) in the Aegean Sea off the west coast of Asia Minor, southwest of Ephesus. According to Acts 20:15 Paul touched on Samos (παρεβάλομεν εἰς Σάμον) at the end of his "third missionary journey" on the way back to Jerusalem from Macedonia by way of Troas, Assos, Mitylene, Chios, Miletus, etc. (D Koine, etc., add: καὶ μείναντες ἐν Τρωγυλλίῳ [the orthography is inconsistent] and are thinking of Paul staying on the coastal promontory across from Samos). Samos was an independent (from 19 B.C.) trade and cultural center (home of Pythagoras) with a Jewish community (1 Macc 15:23) and port of call on the sea route from the Hellespont to Syria. L. Bürchner, PW IA, 2162-2218; F. V. Filson, BHH 1663; BL 1516; E. Mensching, LAW 2696f.

Σαμουήλ *Samouēl* Samuel*

Samuel (Heb. *šᵉmû'ēl*) is mentioned 3 times in the NT. Acts 3:24 refers to him as the first of the prophets (πάντες δὲ οἱ προφῆται ἀπὸ Σαμουήλ), and in 13:20 he concludes the period of the judges and begins that of the prophets (ἔδωκεν κριτὰς ἕως Σαμουὴλ [τοῦ] προφήτου). Heb 11:32 mentions him among the "cloud of witnesses" (12:1) after the ("great") judges and David (as king) as "forefather" of the prophets (περὶ Δαυίδ τε καὶ τῶν προφητῶν).

Samuel was the son of Elkanah and Hannah (1 Sam 1:20) from Ramah in Ephraim (1:1; according to 1 Chr 6:12 he was a Levite). Tradition portrays him functioning as a priest (1 Sam 2:35ff.; 7:7ff.), judge (7:3ff., 15ff.; 8:1ff.), and prophet (9:9ff.; 10:1ff.; 15:10ff.; 19:18ff.). He participated decisively in the establishment of monarchy in Israel (8:4ff.; 10:1ff.; 12:19ff.) and above all established the ascendancy of David (16:1ff.; 19:18ff.). Sir 46:13 considers Samuel a Nazirite, prophet, judge, and priest; cf. Σαμουὴλ ὁ προφήτης, 1 Esdr 1:18. In Jer 15:1 Samuel stands next to Moses; cf. Ps 99:6. H. J. Stoebe, BHH 1663f. (bibliography); M. Rehm, BL 1516f.

Σαμφουριν *Samphourin* Sepphoris

The place name Sepphoris has been inserted into John 11:54 D (Arabic Ṣaffûriyeh, 6 km. north of Nazareth): ἀπῆλθεν . . . εἰς τὴν χώραν Σαμφουριν. This information cannot be reconciled geographically with the presumed location for → Ἐφραίμ (v. 54c). G. Dalman, *Sacred Sites and Ways* (1935) 219.

Σαμψών *Sampsōn* Samson*

Heb 11:32 mentions Samson (Heb. *šimšôn;* cf. Judges 13–16) among the "witnesses of faith" from the "great" judges (before Jephthah!). On the orthography cf. BDF §39.8. E. Jenni, BHH 1799f.; L. Thum, BL 1593f.

σανδάλιον, ου, τό *sandalion* sandal*

According to Mark 6:9 the "Twelve" sent out by Jesus (v. 7) are to wear *sandals* (ἀλλὰ ὑποδεδεμένοι σανδάλια) and are allowed to have a staff (v. 8), but no other equipment or provisions (cf., however, Luke 9:3 par. Matt 10:9f.; Luke 10:4; 22:35, where even staff and sandals are disallowed; → ῥάβδος). Sandals (like the staff) were customary for foot journeys in Palestine (cf. also → ὑπόδημα, Mark 1:7 par.; John 1:27) and are necessary for covering longer distances by land (according to Amos 2:6; 8:6 the needy could end up in slavery for a debt as small as a pair of sandals; according to *b. Taʿan.* 13a regulations for going without shoes [during mourning and fasting] applied only to the area within the city limits; cf. further Billerbeck I, 566-69). Hence there is no real theological relationship between Mark 6:9 and Exod 12:11. In addition to sandals, sturdier enclosed shoes were also known and considered more sophisticated (cf. Ezek 16:10). According to Acts 12:8 the angel tells Peter, who is freed from prison, to "put on your sandals" (ὑπόδησαι τὰ σανδάλιά σου). A. Oepke, *TDNT* V, 310-12; G. Fohrer, BHH 1738; A. van den Born and W. Baier, BL 1520f.

σανίς, ίδος, ἡ *sanis* (thick) board, plank*

Acts 27:44, of those shipwrecked with Paul making their way to land "on *planks*" (ἐπὶ σανίσιν, with ἐπί τινων τῶν ἀπὸ τοῦ πλοίου, which is probably to be understood in the neutral sense as other debris from the ship); cf. Ezek 27:5; see E. Haenchen, *Acts* (Eng. tr., 1971) ad loc.; Spicq, *Notes* II, 786.

Σαούλ *Saoul* Saul
→ Σαῦλος.

σαπρός, 3 *sapros* rotten, decayed; unuseable, bad*

Σαπρός occurs 8 times in the NT, outside the Synoptic Gospels only in Eph 4:29. It is not found in the LXX. The literal meaning is found in metaphors and parables of Jesus, e.g., referring to "*rotten/worthless* fish," which are thrown back into the water (τὰ δὲ σαπρὰ ἔξω ἔβαλον; in contrast: συνέλεξαν τὰ καλὰ εἰς ἄγγη; Matt 13:48). Matthew also refers to "*bad/worthless* trees," which bear only "*evil* fruit" (cf. Ezek 17:9): σαπρὸν δένδρον καρποὺς πονηρούς (7:17); οὐδὲ δένδρον σαπρὸν καρποὺς καλούς (v. 18); δένδρον σαπρὸν καὶ τὸν καρπὸν αὐτοῦ σαπρόν (12:33); οὐ . . . δένδρον καλὸν ποιοῦν καρπὸν σαπρόν, οὐδὲ πάλιν δένδρον σαπρὸν . . . καρπὸν καλόν (Luke 6:43). The alternating synonyms (σαπρός/πονηρός, οὐ[δὲ] σαπρός/καλός) show that σαπρός here carries the meaning *rotten* already in the general sense of *worthless, bad* (cf. *Herm. Sim.* ii.3f.; the fish are still caught in the net, and the tree still bears fruit).

The term is used in a clearly fig. sense in Eph 4:29: πᾶς λόγος σαπρός . . . μὴ ἐκπορευέσθω, "let no *evil* talk/*rotten* word come out of your mouths" (contrasted to εἴ τις ἀγαθὸς πρὸς οἰκοδομὴν τῆς χρείας . . .); cf. 5:4. BAGD s.v.; O. Bauernfeind, *TDNT* VII, 94-97.

Σάπφιρα, ης *Sapphira* Sapphira
→ ʼΑνανίας 1.

σάπφιρος, ου, ἡ *sapphiros* sapphire*

Rev 21:19, referring to the twelve jewels in the foundation of the heavenly Jerusalem: ὁ δεύτερος [θεμέλιος] σάπφιρος (cf. Exod 28:17-20; 39:10-13; Ezek 28:13; Isa 54:11f.; Tob 13:16f.), a transparent blue stone, probably lapis lazuli; see further Exod 24:10; Job 28:6, 16; Sir 32:5; 43:19. W. Frerichs, *BHH* 362-65, esp. 363; A. van den Born, *BL* 1523; R. G. Bullard, *ISBE* IV, 629.

σαργάνη, ης, ἡ *sarganē* basket*

Paul reports in 2 Cor 11:33 that he was "let down in a *basket* through a window in the wall" of Damascus (ἐν σαργάνῃ ἐχαλάσθην); cf. Acts 9:25 (ἐν σπυρίδι), which mentions persecution by Jews as the reason for the flight from Damascus, whereas Paul himself speaks of being pursued by the governor under the Nabatean king Aretas (IV; → ʼΑρέτας); cf. also Josh 2:15; 1 Sam 19:12. Spicq, *Notes* II, 787f.

Σάρδεις, εων *Sardeis* Sardis*

Sardis, situated *ca.* 80 km. east of Smyrna, was well known in the 6th cent. B.C. as the beautiful capital of Lydia, but was destroyed in A.D. 17 by an earthquake, then rebuilt under Tiberius. According to Rev 1:11 it is the location of one of the seven churches to which the seer's book is to be sent (εἰς Σάρδεις). 3:1 addresses "the angel of the church in Sardis" (τῷ ἀγγέλῳ τῆς ἐν Σάρδεσιν ἐκκλησίας γράψον); cf. v. 4: ὀλίγα ὀνόματα ἐν Σάρδεσιν. The church in Sardis is reprimanded because, though it has the reputation of being alive, it is "dead" in its works (v. 1); it is exhorted to repent and to "wake up" (v. 3). This admonition, however, concerns only part (though the majority) of the church, since some "have not soiled their garments" (v. 4). M. Rissi, *BHH* 1670f.; A. van den Born and H. Haag, *BL* 1524; P. Hommel, *LAW* 2700f.; C. J. Hemer, *NTS* 19 (1972/73) 94-97.

σάρδινος, ου, ὁ *sardinos* carnelian
Rev 4:3 TR (as a late form) in place of → σάρδιον.

σάρδιον, ου, τό *sardion* carnelian*

In Rev 4:3 the seer speaks of the appearance of the one seated on the throne in heaven: ὅμοιος ὁράσει λίθῳ ἰάσπιδι καὶ σαρδίῳ, "in appearance like jasper and *carnelian*" (cf. also Ezek 1:26-28). 21:20 mentions carnelian as the sixth of the jewels in the foundation of the heavenly Jerusalem: ὁ ἕκτος σάρδιον (cf. Exod 28:17-20; 39:10-13; Isa 54:11f.; Tob 13:16f.). Σάρδιον is a reddish gem (cf. further LXX Exod 25:7; 35:9; Prov 25:11f.; Ezek 28:13) deriving its name from its source in Sardis. W. Frerichs, *BHH* 362-65, esp. 363; R. G. Bullard, *ISBE* IV, 626.

σαρδόνυξ, υχος, ὁ *sardonyx* sardonyx*

According to Rev 21:20 the fifth of the twelve jewels in the foundation of the heavenly Jerusalem is sardonyx: ὁ πέμπτος σαρδόνυξ (cf. ὀνύχιος in LXX Exod 28:20; 39:13; Ezek 28:13; ὄνυξ in Job 28:16, and *passim*). Sardonyx is a reddish-white or brownish-white striped onyx stone. W. Frerichs, *BHH* 362-65, esp. 363; R. G. Bullard, *ISBE* IV, 628.

Σάρεπτα, ων *Sarepta* Zarephath*

According to Luke 4:26 Jesus mentions in his synagogue sermon in Nazareth the sending of the prophet Elijah to the widow of Zarephath in Sidon, where he raised her dead son (ἐπέμφθη Ἠλίας . . . εἰς Σάρεπτα τῆς Σιδωνίας πρὸς γυναῖκα χήραν; cf. 1 Kgs 17:7ff., esp. v. 9) and uses it as testimony that prophets are not accepted in their own countries (Luke 4:24) and that God is turning his attention to others (i.e., the Gentiles); cf. the example of Elisha in v. 27 (2 Kgs 5:1ff.).

Zarephath was a Phoenician coastal city between Tyre and Sidon (Heb. *ṣārᵉpaṯ;* gen. pl. Σαρεπτων in Obad 20) now known as Ṣarafand (on orthography and declension see BDF §§39.2; 56.2). K. Elliger, *BHH* 2204; A. van den Born, *BL* 1524; G. Schneider, *Luke* (ÖTK) I, ad loc. (bibliography on 4:16ff.).

σαρκικός, 3 *sarkikos* belonging to the realm of the flesh, fleshly*
σάρκινος, 3 *sarkinos* made of flesh, fleshly*

Lit.: E. BRANDENBURGER, *Fleisch und Geist. Paulus und die dualistische Weisheit* (WMANT 29, 1968) 42-58. — R. JEWETT, *Paul's Anthropological Terms* (AGJU 10, 1971) 49-166. — M. C. PARSONS, "Σαρκινός, σαρκικός in codices F and G," *NTS* 34 (1988) 151-55. — A. SAND, *Der Begriff "Fleisch" in den paulinischen Hauptbriefen* (BU 2, 1967) 183-217. — E. SCHWEIZER, *TDNT* VII, 143f. — H. SEEBASS and A. C. THISELTON, *DNTT* I, 671-82. — SPICQ, *Notes* Suppl., 600-602. — For further bibliography see *TWNT* X, 1260f.

1. a) **Σαρκικός** is rare in secular Greek (Robertson, *Grammar* 158f.; LSJ 1584); it means *made of* (the sub-

stance) *flesh* or *fleshly*. Of the 7 NT occurrences 6 are in Paul and 1 in 1 Peter.

In 1 Cor 3:3 (bis) "to be *of the flesh*" actually means the same as κατὰ ἄνθρωπον περιπατεῖν. The adj. has a fig. sense determined by the contrasting πνευματικός: The spiritual person no longer lives in a *fleshly*, i.e., merely worldly existence. Σαρκικός is used substantively in 1 Cor 9:11 of *material goods* to which Paul can lay claim. It is not used here negatively (*contra* Schweizer 144) or in the sense of Gnostic physical dualism (*contra* Jewett 125); it refers rather to temporal things necessary for securing one's material (earthly) existence. The adj. has the same meaning in Rom 15:27: The believers in Macedonia and Achaia feel obligated to make contributions of *material goods* to the saints in Jerusalem. *Earthly* wisdom (2 Cor 1:12) is the imperfect wisdom of those still living in the old aeon and thus without God's grace (v. 12c). In 2 Cor 10:4 the adj. interprets the phrase κατὰ σάρκα (vv. 2, 3) and refers to the struggle (in apostolic activity) with powerless worldly weapons that are useless against the mighty weapons of the *militia Christi* (v. 4b; cf. 2 Cor 6:7; Rom 6:13; 13:12).

b) The v.l. in 1 Cor 3:3 (bis); 2 Cor 1:12 is an assimilation by the Western Text to σάρκινος, which Paul does not really distinguish from σαρκικός. The superficial replacement of the more pointed ἄνθρωποι by σαρκικοί in 1 Cor 3:4 in ℵ[2] Ψ Majority Text and elsewhere is an accommodation to 3:1-3.

c) 1 Pet 2:11 speaks of the passions *of the flesh* "without any significant anthropological, philosophical, or soteriological implications" (N. Brox, *1 Pet* [EKKNT] 112). It refers thus to desires of the *senses* conflicting with the will of the inner person (ψυχή).

2. a) Σάρκινος, which in secular Greek speaks of "flesh" as a substance (the distinction between the two adjs. is not consistently followed), occurs 3 times in Paul and once in Hebrews. *Those of the flesh* (1 Cor 3:1, subst.) are those who have not yet come of age in Christ and are not yet ready for the solid food (of faith). In 2 Cor 3:3 σάρκινος is used of the heart *of flesh* (cf. Ezek 11:19; 36:26 LXX), a metaphor for the person oriented toward God from within the vital center of his heart. The "I" in Rom 7:14 considers himself *carnal;* the statement is interpreted more specifically through the phrase "sold under sin," i.e., controlled by the power of sin. This addresses the person who, left to his own devices, suffers the contradiction between what he wants and what he actually does; this is not, however, an instance of Gnostic dualism (*contra* Jewett 155).

b) On the v.l. σαρκικός in Rom 7:14 (ℵ[2], Majority Text) and 1 Cor 3:1 (Western Text, Majority Text) → 1.b.

c) In Heb 7:16 the ἐντολὴ σαρκίνη is the *"physical law"* belonging to the material realm and lacking the power of indestructible life; it refers not to a commandment inclined toward sin, but rather to one restricted in

its positive efficacy (the v.l. σαρκικός [cf. *NTG* ad loc.] is again an accommodation to σαρκικός without any particular emphasis).

A. Sand

σάρκινος, 3 *sarkinos* made of flesh, fleshly → σαρκικός 2.

σάρξ, σαρκός, ἡ *sarx* flesh

1. Occurrences and meaning — 2. Usage — 3. Paul — 4. The deutero-Pauline writings — 5. The Synoptics and Acts — 6. John and 1–2 John — 7. Other NT writings

Lit.: P. BONNARD, "La chair dans le johannisme, et au-delà," *idem, Anamnesis* (1980) 187-93. — E. BRANDENBURGER, *Fleisch und Geist. Paulus und die dualistische Weisheit* (WMANT 29, 1968) 42-58. — H. CLAVIER, *BHH* 485f. — P. VAN IMSCHOOT, *BL* 482-86. — R. JEWETT, *Paul's Anthropological Terms* (AGJU 10, 1971). — O. KUSS, *Rom* (1959) 506-40. — C. H. LINDIJER, *Het Begrip Sarx bij Paulus* (1952). — D. LYS, "L'arrière-plan et les connotations vétérotestamentaires de *sarx* et de *sōma*," *VT* 36 (1986) 163-204. — A. SAND, *Der Begriff "Fleisch" in den paulinischen Hauptbriefen* (BU 2, 1967). — E. SCHWEIZER, F. BAUMGÄRTEL, and R. MEYER, *TDNT* VII, 98-151. — H. SEEBASS and A. C. THISELTON, *DNTT* I, 671-82. — SPICQ, *Notes* Suppl., 591-600. — W. D. STACEY, *The Pauline View of Man* (1956). — For further bibliography see Jewett; Sand; *TWNT* X, 1260f.

1. This noun occurs 147 times in the NT (only 8 times pl., the balance sg.) and is among words with the largest NT frequency (among the anthropological terms σάρξ stands in third position behind ἄνθρωπος and καρδία). It is one of Paul's favorite words (72 occurrences, 26 of those in Romans, 18 in Galatians) and is also common in the post-Pauline tradition (25 occurrences, including the Pastorals and Hebrews). It occurs only once each in 1 Timothy, Philemon, James, and 2 John. 1/2 Thessalonians, 2 Timothy, Titus, and 3 John do not use the word.

The range of meaning extends from the substance *flesh* (both human and animal), to the human body, to the entire person, and to all humankind. This variety is already seen in the LXX, where σάρξ translates Heb. *bśr* (*ca.* 265 times), though where the reference is to flesh as food, the LXX usually uses κρέας, which occurs in the NT twice with the same meaning (Rom 14:21; 1 Cor 8:13). The NT reflects and maintains the OT view of the human being as an undivided whole almost without exception (far from any notions of dichotomous, trichotomous, or dualistic perspectives such as those in Greek philosophy, Hellenism, and Gnosticism). This is shown *inter alia* by the infrequent occurrence of the pl. (Jas 5:3; Rev 17:16; 19:18 [5 occurrences], 21, where the reference within the context of judgments is to the eating of human *flesh*).

2. An examination of the use of σάρξ must be based not on its use with other terms (*flesh* and *blood*, in the *flesh*, according to the *flesh*) but on objective criteria, since some word combinations can have widely diverging meanings in different contexts. (1) Σάρξ refers, first, to the bodily substance, the *flesh* of circumcision, then the human body itself (frequently with a closer qualification, e.g., ἀσθένεια), and finally the whole person or humanity (in the universal sense: all of humanity; in the partial sense: the people Israel, σάρξ referring to physical lineage and expressing genealogical membership in Israel). (2) In a further group σάρξ refers to earthly and natural existence and then to the *merely* worldly existence of human beings (κατὰ σάρκα in combination with a vb.). (3) Finally, and esp. in Paul, σάρξ implies a theological understanding of mankind subject to the power of sin. The theological implications emerge above all from use with ἁμαρτία, νόμος, and θάνατος and from the contrast σάρξ —πνεῦμα. Here statements about *flesh* come into direct contact with those about anti-divine powers of perdition.

3. a) 1 Cor 15:39 speaks of the substance *flesh;* πᾶσα σάρξ refers not to all humanity, but rather to various *kinds of flesh* (human beings, livestock, birds, fish). Paul means the same when he speaks of the "thorn in the *flesh*" (2 Cor 12:7) to express that he is a person plagued by the body. Circumcision is performed "in the *flesh*" (Gal 6:12, 13; Phil 3:3, 4; Rom 2:28). Σάρξ has an unspecific meaning in these OT-influenced passages; only from the context do we discover that Paul rejects circumcision "in the flesh."

Flesh is also a term—again under OT influence—for the human body (1 Cor 6:16; cf. 2 Cor 7:5; Eph 5:31) as well as for the whole person. Other substantives specify more closely that the person in view is threatened and endangered: Reference is made to weakness (Gal 4:13; Rom 6:19), troubles (1 Cor 7:28), destruction (1 Cor 5:5), and defilement (2 Cor 7:1) of the *flesh*. Qualified by an adj. the human being is portrayed as mortal *flesh* (2 Cor 4:11), though flesh to which even now the life of Jesus is revealed. "All *flesh*" refers, as in the OT, to all human beings, all humanity (Gal 2:16; Rom 3:20; both influenced by Ps 142:2 LXX: πᾶς ζῶν). Paul twice uses the phrase "*flesh* and blood" (1 Cor 15:50; Gal 1:16; cf. Sir 14:18; 17:31; *1 Enoch* 15:4-6), referring thus to those who are excluded from the kingdom of God or whose authority is insufficient.

In the genealogical sense *flesh* refers to the people of Israel, to whom a person belongs through conception and birth (Gal 4:23, esp. vv. 23, 29; Rom 9:3; 11:14) and whose members are τέκνα τῆς σαρκός and thus not true children of Abraham (Rom 9:8; cf. 4:1: Abraham is the forefather "according to the *flesh*" [κατὰ σάρκα refers to the subj., not to the vb.; cf. Kuss 179f.]). "Israel according

to the *flesh*" (1 Cor 10:18) is not characterized by the use of further terms as belonging to the realm of the σάρξ that now lies behind Paul (*contra* Weiss, *1 Cor* [KEK] 260), but rather as the "historical Israel" (H. Conzelmann, *1 Cor* [Hermeneia] 172 n.29); Rom 1:3 and 9:5 confirm this understanding when they speak of Christ "according to the *flesh*" in view of his earthly and historical manner of existence (in Rom 9:5 the decisive contrasting term πνεῦμα is admittedly missing as compared with 1:3).

Life "in the *flesh*" (Gal 2:20; 2 Cor 10:3 bis; Phil 1:22, 24; Phlm 16) expresses the normal manner of earthly existence (without any special qualification). Although the phrase sounds slightly Hellenistic, in substance it nonetheless agrees with the OT view of human beings, since according to Greek understanding the soul can indeed be in the body, but not the human being "in the *flesh*."

b) The close relationship between flesh and world (and thus the emphasis on a merely worldly existence) is addressed in 1 Cor 1:26 in the reference to those who are "wise according to the *flesh*." Such wisdom is not yet "sinful-human, sinful-worldly" (*contra* Lindijer 151); only when such wisdom seduces one to depend on it in a fashion counter to the call from God is it rejected as wisdom of this world (cf. → σαρκικός, 1 Cor 9:11; 2 Cor 1:12; Rom 15:27). Κατὰ σάρκα in combination with a vb. characterizes human behavior as a purely worldly activity and perspective (2 Cor 1:17; 5:16 bis; 10:2, 3; 11:18 [in this sense also Gal 3:3, σαρκί]); such behavior is preliminary and not yet focused on what is really of value. Only activity and judgment within the Lord or the Spirit effects salvation.

c) Paul's statements using σάρξ of human beings subject to the all-encompassing power of sin are esp. important (Rom 7:5 [14], 18, 25; 8:5 bis, 6, 7, 8). Mankind so considered is bound to a sinful existence hostile to God and is incapable of attaining redemption on its own. But Jesus' death and resurrection robs sin of its power. God sent his Son "in the likeness of sinful *flesh*" for the sake of sin and in order to condemn sin "in the *flesh*," i.e., in precisely the "place" where it set up its power: in the worldly-physical sphere to which all human beings belong without exception (8:3). Because of this, however, human beings, though living "in the *flesh*," are no longer condemned to live "according to the *flesh*"; this existence hostile to God is suspended (Rom 8:4, 9, 10, 12, 13). But only in obedience to God's Spirit is it possible to perform works of the Spirit instead of those of the *flesh* (Gal 5:13, 16, 17, 19, 24; 6:8).

4. The post-Pauline tradition to a large extent follows Paul's understanding of mankind while setting its own new emphases. Col 2:1 uses σάρξ in the sense of "visible

corporeality" (Schweizer 136); the use of κατὰ σάρκα in 3:22 also corresponds to Pauline usage: The (worldly) master exercises his lordship in the earthly-worldly realm (so also in Eph 6:5). According to Col 1:24 Paul suffers in his own earthly-physical existence what is lacking in Christ's afflictions (cf. 2 Cor 4:11; Gal 6:17). The "indulgence of the flesh" in Col 2:23 (a difficult phrase; cf. BAGD s.v. πλησμονή) probably refers to the oversatiation of a person not oriented toward the order of God (on the attempts at syntactical correction see J. Ernst, Col [RNT] 213f.). The "uncircumcision of the *flesh*" in Col 2:13 characterizes as dead that person who, though he may not have sinned by trusting in the *flesh,* did so through his licentiousness (cf. the catalog of vices in 3:5); he must receive the true circumcision, i.e., the putting off of the "body of *flesh*" (of sinful existence; 2:11; cf. Eph 2:11). Hellenistic influence is apparent in Col 1:22; 2:11, 18; both the earthly body (1:22, of Jesus; 2:11) and human understanding (2:18) acquire through the gen. construction the accent of emphatically physical corporeality or perspective (cf. Sir 23:17; 1QpHab 9:2). The designation of the wife as σάρξ (Eph 5:29; or σῶμα, v. 28) is traditional; what is new is the transferal of this notion to the Christian community in v. 32. The "passions of our *flesh*" (2:3) belong to the time of death (vv. 1, 2) when demonic powers controlled the "desires of the *flesh*"; the partition into σάρξ and διάνοια does not yet represent a genuinely Hellenistic perspective, since even in the OT (Num 15:39 LXX) such distorted perspective of thought is emphasized. "Blood and *flesh*" (reversed order; cf. Heb 2:14) refer to the two fundamental substances of the human body distinguishing it from incorporeal spirits (Eph 6:12). 1 Tim 3:16 is reminiscent of Rom 8:3 and Eph 2:14, though the decisive difference is that the appearance of Christ "in the *flesh*" already in and of itself has revelatory significance.

5. The OT formula πᾶσα σάρξ also occurs (apart from OT quotations in Mark 10:8a par. Matt 19:5b: Gen 2:24; Luke 3:6: Isa 40:5) in Mark 13:20 par. Matt 24:22: No human being could be saved in judgment if the Lord did not shorten the days. "*Flesh* and blood" (Matt 16:17) follows OT terminology and refers to those incapable of proclaiming what alone is of value. Σάρξ and πνεῦμα stand over against one another in Mark 14:38 par. Matt 26:41; one cannot, however, speak of "anthropological dualism" (*contra* Schweizer 124; H. Braun, *Spätjüdisch-häretischer und frühchristlicher Radikalismus* [1957] II, 115 n.4 views the passage as a secondary parenetic insertion); the weakness of the σάρξ and the willing spirit correspond rather to the OT understanding of the conflict between good and evil in human beings (cf. Ps 50:14 LXX). "*Flesh* and bones" (Luke 24:39) refer to the actual corporeality (appearance in person) of the resurrected

Jesus in contrast to an incorporeal and unreal spirit. Acts cites the OT twice with the phrase πᾶσα σάρξ, "all human beings" (2:17: Joel 3:1 LXX; 2:26: Ps 15:9 LXX). Acts 2:31 concludes from the incorruptibility of Jesus' σάρξ that of the human σάρξ (cf. 2:26f.); this refers to the resurrection body of Jesus (ψυχή in v. 27 is not repeated in v. 31).

6. a) The Gospel of John, in which σάρξ appears with relative infrequency (13 times), uses this term in a unique fashion. The phrase "all flesh" (John 17:2) is traditional: The Father gives the Son sovereignty over all mankind. In 8:15 the formula κατὰ σάρκα is used with the art.; judgment "according to the *flesh*" is another expression for human incomprehension (cf. v. 14) and refers to judgment according to (superficial) appearances (cf. also 7:24), which cannot recognize who Jesus truly is. Similarly 3:6: Whoever is born "of the *flesh*" is (only) *flesh,* i.e., belongs (only) to the worldly sphere having no part in the kingdom of God. Only through birth within the πνεῦμα does one come into the kingdom of God. *Flesh,* however, does not characterize human beings as subject to the power of sin; a person becomes sinful only by rejecting πίστις. The meaning is similar in 6:63; the contrast between σάρξ and πνεῦμα is not that found in Paul, but expresses rather that the understanding of Jesus' speech (v. 60) is possible only in the Spirit. In the Johannine prologue *flesh* (1:13) refers to physical lineage (cf. the interpretative αἷμα and θέλημα ἀνδρός)— contrasted with birth from God. Σάρξ is thus thought of as having a will—as does a human being: The birth willed by the physical human being corresponds to the conception desired by the person. 1:14 asserts that, like every person, the Logos, too, took on physical form; it chose the same earthly existence that every human being has, it set up its tent, and it dwelled among us.

Probably an ecclesiastical redactor inserted John 6:51c-58 into the speech about the bread of life (ch. 6). The appearance of σάρξ 6 times (4 times with αἷμα) suggests a cultic act (the celebration of the eucharist) as the setting of this interpolation. The vivid, perhaps anti-Docetic report (σῶμα in the Synoptics is replaced by σάρξ) interprets the living bread eaten in faith as the *flesh* and blood of Jesus eaten at the eucharist. The transition in v. 51c suggests a misunderstanding among the listeners that the interpolation seeks to remove: Eating the *flesh* and blood of the Son of man also gives eternal life. The stronger expression τρώγω, "to chew," need not be viewed as a strengthening of the possible anti-Docetic posture, as comparison with 13:18 shows: There ἐσθίω from Ps 40:10 LXX is also replaced by τρώγω (cf. also Matt 24:38 with Luke 17:27).

b) According to 1 John 4:2 (some mss. repeat ἐν σαρκί in v. 3) and 2 John 7 the confession that Jesus came "in the *flesh*," i.e., as a human being, separates the true believers from the prophets of lies. Faith (or its absence) is now revealed not only in relation to God, but also in relation to the one sent by God. 1 John 2:16 interprets the "lust of the *flesh*" more closely by referring to the "lust of the eyes": The person is completely oriented toward the world from which physical desire and visual lust come; he loves it and is thus completely subject to it.

7.a) In Heb 5:7 σάρξ is used of Jesus' earthly existence; the "days of his *flesh*" are his days on earth. During this time he took on "blood and *flesh*" (2:14b; → 4), as does every person (v. 14a). This comparison prohibits the assertion that "the 'substantial' character . . . is now much more prominent" (*contra* Schweizer 141). The "fathers of our *flesh*" (12:9) are our earthly fathers to whom we were obedient. "Regulations (δικαίωμα) of the *flesh*" (9:10) are cultic requirements of the law (food, drink, and purity regulations) that only effect a preliminary "purification of the *flesh*" (9:13), i.e., of the external person. In contrast, Christ's blood purifies the human conscience (v. 14). This dichotomous-sounding statement corresponds to early Christian tradition (Mark 7:15 par. Matt 15:11; cf. Heb 10:22).

According to Heb 10:20 entry into the sanctuary is gained "through the *flesh*" of Jesus; this text does, however, present some difficulties.

Is σάρξ here a metaphorical designation for Jesus' *death?* Vv. 5 and 10 show that σῶμα would have to be used. Is διά locative (with the "curtain") or instrumental (with σάρξ)? Or does διά even have a consistent meaning here? Σάρξ could refer to human nature; then the question arises whether this nature must be destroyed (as the curtain was torn) to open access to the sanctuary; "nature," however, is not really an adequate rendering of σάρξ. The excellent attestation of the text here makes it impossible to assume the presence of a later gloss that might be eliminated. The context suggests the direction our solution must take: Jesus' blood was spilled at the cross (v. 19); thus the death on the cross made access to the sanctuary possible. This led through the curtain, and this symbolic event is then interpreted concretely through the term *flesh:* Jesus opened the way once and for all through (instrumental) the sacrifice of the "body of flesh" in death.

b) 1 Pet 1:24 (quoting Isa 40:6 LXX) uses πᾶσα σάρξ in accord with OT usage to mean "every *person*," "*everyone.*" 3:18 speaks of Christ, who suffered (the v.l. ἀπέθανεν, while well attested, is not the preferred reading; cf. *NTG²⁶* and *UBSGNT* with *NTG²⁵*) and was killed in the *flesh* (cf. 1:18f.; 2:24). Σάρξ refers to "the mortal human condition" (L. Goppelt, *1 Pet* [KEK] 245 with n.27) or *earthly existence* in general (but not to the body as a soteriological category, *contra* N. Brox, *1 Pet* [EKKNT] 168; K. H. Schelkle, *1 Pet* [HTKNT] 103f., is ambiguous) contrasted with pneumatic existence (cf. Rom 1:3f.). This contrast is also a factor in the difficult text 1 Pet 4:6, though in reference to the dead: They receive the good news that though in their *earthly existence* they will be judged as humans, they will then live in the spirit like God (cf. Rom 8:27; 2 Cor 7:9, 10, 11).

In 1 Pet 4:1a, too, σαρκί (dat. of respect, as in 3:18) refers to earthly existence characterized by πάσχειν as the sphere in which Jesus' Passion was manifested historically (cf. 3:18a; there as always in 1 Peter ἁμαρτία is pl.). The statement in 4:1b can best be described (with Goppelt, *1 Pet* 268) as a general parenthetical justification; it refers in a general sense to the human σάρξ as the "place" where sin rules, but where a person through suffering (probably threats, persecution, and mortal suffering, not bodily harm [*contra* Brox, *1 Pet* 181]) has ceased from sin (cf. Rom 7:6; BAGD s.v. 2) so as for the rest of the *earthly* time no longer to live by human passions (4:2).

The "dirt of the *flesh*" (3:21) is contrasted with the good conscience (cf. Heb 9:10f.; the contrast is not, however, strictly carried through): baptism does not effect an *external and physical* cleansing, but rather "a promise to God for a good conscience" (ἐπερώτημα, literally "question, appeal," is to be rendered here "promise, vow"; → ἐπερώτημα). The background here is the determination of a person according to (unimportant) external and (decisive) internal criteria.

The statements concerning σάρξ in 1 Peter stand fully within early Christian tradition and also take up in part Paul's anthropological-theological conception, though no longer with his linguistic exactitude and conceptual consistency; this becomes esp. clear in the new understanding of sin.

c) According to Jude 7 Sodom and Gomorrah (and the surrounding cities) indulged in "unnatural *flesh*." This probably refers to sexual lust; the perjorative sense is expressed esp. through ἕτερος and suggests perverted desires. The historical perspective recalls particularly Gen 19:4-25: Like the cities mentioned there, the false teachers in Jude engage in fornication with unnatural *flesh* (v. 8). V. 23 is probably to be interpreted in this way as well. 2 Pet 2:10 picks up Jude 7, though without the adj. ἕτερος; instead, it adds "the lust of defiling passions," thereby rejecting the σάρξ, the human *body,* as an object of sexual gratification (cf. also 2:18).   A. Sand

Σαρούχ *Sarouch* (Serug)
TR form of → Σερούχ.

σαρόω *saroō* sweep (clean)*

Matt 12:44 par. Luke 11:25 with κοσμέω; Luke 15:8, in the parable of the lost drachmas.

Σάρρα, ας *Sarra* Sarah*

The wife of Abraham (Gen 17:15 LXX and *passim*) and mother of Isaac (Rom 4:19; 9:9; Heb 11:11). The parenesis for wives refers to Sarah, who obeyed Abraham and called him "lord" (1 Pet 3:6; cf. Gen 18:12).

Σαρών, ῶνος, ὁ *Sarōn* Sharon*

Acts 9:35 mentions with the inhabitants of Lod (Lydda) also those of the plain of *Sharon:* "they turned to the Lord." Σαρών is the transliteration of Heb. *šārôn* (e.g., Isa 33:9) and refers to the Palestinian coastal plain approximately between Joppa (Japho, so AV) and Caesarea or Mt. Carmel. H. Haag, *LTK* IX, 333.

σατάν, ὁ *satan* Satan

The indeclinable name σατάν appears in 2 Cor 12:7 ℵ² Aᶜ D² Ψ Koine syʰ (transliteration of Heb. *śāṭān*) as a variant of → σατανᾶς.

σατανᾶς, ᾶ, ὁ *satanas* Satan*

1. Religious-historical considerations — 2. Occurrences in the NT — 3. The NT understanding of σατανᾶς — 4. Σατανᾶς in the eschatological drama — 5. Jesus and σατανᾶς

Lit.: H. BIETENHARD, J. S. WRIGHT, and C. BROWN, *DNTT* III, 468-76. — O. BÖCHER, *Das NT und die dämonischen Mächte* (SBS 58, 1972). — W. FOERSTER, *TDNT* VI, 151-63. — H. HAAG, *Teufelsglaube* (²1980). — M. LIMBECK, "Die Wurzeln der biblischen Auffassung vom Teufel und den Dämonen," *Concilium* (German) 11 (1975) 161-68. — B. NOACK, *Satanás und Sotería. Untersuchungen zur neutestamentlichen Dämonologie* (1948). — FR. BRUNO DE JÉSUS-MARIE, ed., *Satan* (Eng. tr., 1951). — S. VOLLENWEIDER, " 'Ich sah den Satan wie einen Blitz vom Himmel fallen' (Lk 10,18)," *ZNW* 79 (1988) 187-203. — For further bibliography → δαιμόνιον; διάβολος; see also *TWNT* X, 1261f.

1. The biblical writings derive their designation for the adversary of humans (1 Sam 29:4; 1 Kgs 5:18, and *passim*) and supernatural adversary of God and accuser of humans from Heb. *śṭn*, "show enmity, accuse" (*haśśāṭān*, Job 1:6-12; 2:1-7; Zech 3:1f.; *śāṭān*, 1 Chr 21:1; LXX: διάβολος). In its Greek transliteration (σατανᾶς [Aram. *sāṭānā'*], Sir 21:27; *T. Dan* 3:6; 5:6; 6:1; *T. Gad* 4:7; *T. Ash.* 6:4 v.l.) the original appellative became the direct proper name of the anti-divine power. Heb. *maśṭēmâ* ("enmity," Hos 9:7f.) is related to the same root; Satan is the "angel of enmity" (1QM 13:11; CD 16:5; cf. 1QS 3:23). In *Jubilees* Mastema is the name of "the chief of the Spirits" (*Jub.* 10:8; 11:5, 11; 17:16, and *passim*). Judaism in antiquity considered Satan/Mastema to be the incarnation of the principle of hostility to both God and mankind and the regent of all evil spirits (→ δαιμόνιον 2).

2. Σατανᾶς occurs 36 times in the NT, almost exactly as often as the synonym → διάβολος (34 occurrences). Of the 15 Synoptic occurrences, 10 are in the pericopes Mark 1:12f. par.; 3:22-27 par.; and 8:31-33 par. There are 10 occurrences in the Pauline writings, 8 in Revelation, 2 in Acts, and only 1 in John, apparently in a set phrase (13:27; cf. Luke 22:3). That σατανᾶς and διάβολος are synonymous is shown by comparison of Mark 1:13 (σατανᾶς) with par. Matt 4:1/Luke 4:2 (διάβολος), and of

Mark 4:15 (σατανᾶς) with par. Luke 8:12 (διάβολος). Other synonyms include → ἐχθρός and → πονηρός. Σατανᾶς almost always appears with the art. (without art.: voc. in Mark 3:23; Luke 22:3; 2 Cor 12:7); 2 Cor 12:7 offers a v.l. with the indeclinable secondary form Σατάν.

3. Satan, identical with the snake in the fall of Adam and Eve (Rev 12:9; 20:2 with Gen 3:1-15), reigns over an empire of self-enclosed, anti-divine power (Mark 3:23 bis; 3:26 par. Matt 12:26 bis/Luke 11:18). In accord with OT and Jewish demonogony (*1 Enoch* 6–11; 15:3-12; *Jub.* 5:1-10, and *passim*; → δαιμόνιον 2), Satan, with his "angels" (2 Cor 12:7), is traced back to the fall of angels in Gen 6:1-4 (Luke 10:18; Rev 12:7-9). His realm is that of darkness (Acts 26:18; 2 Cor 11:14), and to him are subordinated the spirits of disease (Luke 13:16; 2 Cor 12:7; 1 Thess 2:18 [?]; 1 Tim 1:20) and death (1 Cor 5:5; cf. 15:26; Heb 2:14). As the chief spirit or demon he is equated with Zeus, the highest god of the Gentiles (Rev 2:13 bis). Satan is held responsible for worship of idols, for false teaching (Rev 2:24), and for the rejection of Jesus by the Jews (Rev 2:9; 3:9).

Above all, however, Satan is the tempter (cf. Job 1:6-12; 2:1-7) and seducer (Matt 4:10 par. Mark 1:13; Matt 16:23 par. Mark 8:33; Luke 22:31; 1 Cor 7:5; cf. 2 Cor 2:11). He is the originator of both sin and wickedness (Mark 4:15; Luke 22:3 par. John 13:27; Acts 5:3; 1 Tim 5:15; cf. Matt 16:23 par. Mark 8:33).

4. According to the portrayals of older Jewish and early Christian apocalyptic writings the original fall of Satan and his demons (according to Gen 6:1-4) will be repeated at the end of time (cf. Luke 10:18; Rev 12:7-9). After a thousand years σατανᾶς will be loosed from his prison for the final battle (Rev 20:7) and will lend his power to the ἄνομος (2 Thess 2:9). Rom 16:20 promises God's quick victory over Satan (cf. Gen 3:15; *T. Levi* 18:12). The devil (διάβολος) and his angels will meet an end in eternal fire (Matt 25:41; Rev 20:10).

5. With these statements concerning σατανᾶς and the διάβολος as the prince of demons, the NT stays within the context of OT and Jewish dualism and hopes for an eschatological defeat of this adversary. Jesus, however, appeared in order to destroy the work of the devil (1 John 3:8c); his victory over the demons means the end of Satan's kingdom and the beginning of God's (Matt 12:28 par. Luke 11:20).

O. Böcher

σάτον, ου, τό *saton* seah, measure*

A Hebrew *sᵉ'â* is a dry volume measure for grain (Aram. *sā'ṭā'*). Matt 13:33 par. Luke 13:21 refers to "three *measures* of meal" in the parable of the leaven. Billerbeck I, 669f. figures one seah to 13.131 liters. A. Segrè, *JBL* 64 (1945) 357-75; H. Chantraine, *KP* IV, 1563; E. M. Cook, *ISBE* IV, 1050f.

Σαῦλος, ου *Saulos* Saul*
Σαούλ *Saoul* Saul*

Lit.: H. J. CADBURY, *The Book of Acts in History* (1955) 69ff.
— H. CONZELMANN, *Acts* (Hermeneia), on 13:9. — E. HAEN-CHEN, *Acts* (Eng. tr., 1971), on 13:9. — G. A. HARRER, "Saul who also is called Paul," *HTR* 33 (1940) 19-34. — K. LÖNING, *Die Saulustradition in der Apostelgeschichte* (NTAbh 9, 1973). — For further bibliography → Παῦλος.

1. Paul is mentioned by his Jewish name (Heb. *šā'ûl*) 22 times in the NT, all in Acts. 15 times the Grecized form Σαῦλος appears (all between Acts 7:58 and 13:9). 8 times the indeclinable form Σαούλ appears (all voc. and all in narrative of his conversion: 9:4 bis, 17; 22:7 bis, 13; 26:14 bis; in 26:14 with Ἑβραΐς διάλεκτος) and is to be understood as a literary archaism. Acts 13:21 mentions the first Israelite king Σαούλ, son of Kish (cf. 1 Sam 9ff.; 1 Chr 8:33; 10:1ff.; 1 Macc 4:30; *1 Clem.* 4:13) and attributes to him a reign of forty years (as does Josephus *Ant.* vi.378; according to x.143 only twenty years).

2. The Grecized form of the name (Σαῦλος) was common in the Hellenistic age (several occurrences in Josephus) and might have been given to Paul by his parents (→ Παῦλος 2). In general Luke's narrative first uses this form (and in Acts 22:7 D; 26:14 v.l. it replaces the archaizing form) since it would be more accessible to the Hellenistic reader (7:58; 8:1, 3; 9:1, 8, 11, 22, 24; 11:25, 30; 12:25; 13:1, 2, 7, 9; but 𝔭45 always has Σαούλ: see Harrer 24f.). Esp. the archaizing form reveals the Lukan intention of introducing Paul as a good Jew and in this way corresponds to the broader Lukan portrait of Paul.

But from Acts 13:9 (Σαῦλος δέ, ὁ καὶ Παῦλος) on Saul is referred to in narrative by his Roman name. One may assume (with Harrer) that Paul also carried the similar-sounding Roman name (perhaps as a *cognomen* in addition to the Jewish name as *signum* or supernomen) from birth (cf. his Roman citizenship: 22:28). Nonetheless, a literary agenda stands behind the change in Acts 13:9: The excellent Jew Saul becomes Paul, the missionary to the Gentiles! This agenda is cleverly worked into an episode telling about a Roman official with this name (→ Σέργιος Παῦλος; the change is not, however, to be associated with the name of the Roman proconsul; cf. Haenchen).

Can the name Saul ever have been present in pre-Lukan tradition? The only possibilities would be the baptism story in Acts 9 (according to Löning) and the reports in Acts 11:30 (the collection) and 13:1 (the list of co-workers). In the second and third of these Paul is already mentioned as an Antiochian coworker in the service of a Hellenistic mission community. The baptism story, too, as the report of the conversion of a great man, was probably related only on the basis of more extensive successes. As his letters attest, Paul was probably known only by his Roman name (→ Παῦλος 1, 2), so that one should reject the possibility of a genuine Saul tradition. In a skillful literary manner Luke has woven his own personal knowledge into the form of an illuminating and convincing portrayal.

G. Schille

σβέννυμι *sbennymi* extinguish*

Literally, of the extinguishing of a fire in Heb 11:34; Eph 6:16 (flaming darts); Matt 12:20 (a smoldering wick). Pass., *to go out,* in Matt 25:8 (lamps); Mark 9:48; 9:44, 46 v.l. (the fire of hell is not *quenched;* Isa 66:24). Fig., *quench, suppress,* in 1 Thess 5:19: "Do not *quench* the Spirit." F. Lang, *TDNT* VII, 165-68; Spicq, *Notes* II, 789f.

σεαυτοῦ, ῆς *seautou* yourself*

The second person sg. reflexive pron. occurs in the NT (BDF §283):
a) gen. (σεαυτοῦ) in John 1:22; 8:13; 18:34; Acts 26:1; 2 Tim 4:11,
b) dat. σεαυτῷ, *to/for yourself,* in John 17:5 ("in *thy* own presence"); Acts 9:34 *("your own");* 16:28; Rom 2:5; 1 Tim 4:16a, and
c) acc. σεαυτόν in Mark 1:44 par. Matt 8:4/Luke 5:14; Mark 15:30 par. Matt 27:40/Luke 23:37; Matt 4:6 par. Luke 4:9; Matt 8:4 (cf. Mark 1:44); Luke 4:23; 23:39; John 7:4; 8:53; 10:33; 14:22; 21:18; Rom 2:1, 19, 21; 14:22; Gal 6:1; Phlm 19; 1 Tim 4:7, 16b; 5:22; 2 Tim 2:15; Titus 2:7. The commandment to love one's neighbor ὡς σεαυτόν (Lev 19:18) occurs in Mark 12:31 par. Matt 22:39/Luke 10:27; Matt 19:19; Rom 13:9; Gal 5:14; Jas 2:8.

σεβάζομαι *sebazomai* show religious reverence, worship*

Rom 1:25, of Gentiles who *worshiped* and served the creature rather than the Creator (ἐσεβάσθησαν καὶ ἐλάτρευσαν). W. Foerster, *TDNT* VII, 172f.; W. Günther, *DNTT* II, 91-94.

σέβασμα, ατος, τό *sebasma* object of worship; sanctuary*

Acts 17:23, of *objects of worship* in Athens; 2 Thess 2:4, with θεός. W. Foerster, *TDNT* VII, 173f.; W. Günther, *DNTT* II, 91-94.

Σεβαστός, 3 *Sebastos* revered, worthy of reverence; Augustus*

In all NT occurrences (3, all in Acts) Σεβαστός represents Lat. *Augustus,* the designation for the Roman

emperor (cf. Pausanias iii.11.4). In Acts 25:21, 25 ὁ Σεβαστός = "His (imperial) *Majesty."* 27:1 mentions the →
σπεῖρα Σεβαστή, the *"Augustan (i.e., imperial)* Cohort"
(cohors Augusta). Augusta as a designation for an auxiliary guard is documented elsewhere; cf. E. Haenchen,
Acts (Eng. tr., 1971) ad loc. H. Dieckmann, *ZKT* 43
(1919) 213-34; W. Foerster, *TDNT* VII, 174f.

σέβομαι *sebomai* worship, revere*

The mid. of σέβω is always associated God or a deity
in the NT. The one worshipped is acc. in Mark 7:7 par.
Matt 15:9 (Isa 29:13); Acts 18:13; 19:27. The expression
σεβόμενος τὸν θεόν, *"worshiper* of God," is used of a
Gentile sympathetic to the synagogue who does not, however, observe the Torah in its entirety and who above all
does not submit to circumcision (Josephus *Ant.* xiv.110;
Acts 16:14; 18:7). Σεβόμενοι used absolutely means the
same thing (13:50; 17:4, 17). The meaning of σεβόμενοι
προσήλυτοι (13:43) is difficult to ascertain. Σεβόμενοι
here is probably not used as a t.t. Schürer, *History* III,
150-76; W. Foerster, *TDNT* VII, 168-72; W. Günther,
DNTT II, 91-94.

σειρά, ᾶς, ἡ *seira* cord, chain*

2 Pet 2:4: God kept the fallen angels captive "with
the *chains* of nether gloom" in the underworld (σειραῖς
ζόφου); → ταρταρόω; σειρός; σιρός.

σειρός, οῦ, ὁ *seiros* pit, cavern*

2 Pet 2:4 v.l. (A B C): "in gloomy *pits."* ℵ has the
better orthography with → σιρός. In any case, → σειρά
is probably to be preferred (with 𝔭⁷² Koine vg sy).
TCGNT ad loc.

σεισμός, οῦ, ὁ *seismos* earthquake; shaking*
σείω *seiō* shake, cause to quake; pass.: tremble*

1. Meaning — 2. The earthquake motif in Matthew —
3. Earthquake as a topos in stories of miraculous deliverance — 4. Earthquake as an apocalyptic sign

Lit.: R. BAUCKHAM, "The Eschatological Earthquake in the
Apocalypse of John," *NovT* 19 (1977) 224-33. — G. BORN-
KAMM, *TDNT* VII, 196-200. — A. HERMANN, *RAC* V, 1070-1114.
— J. JEREMIAS, *Theophanie. Die Geschichte einer alttesta-
mentlichen Gattung* (WMANT 10, 1965). — R. KRATZ, *Aufer-
weckung als Befreiung. Eine Studie zur Passions- und
Auferstehungstheologie des Matthäus* (SBS 65, 1973). — idem,
Rettungswunder (1979). — M. RIEBL, *Auferstehung Jesu in der
Stunde seines Todes? Zur Botschaft von Mt 27,51b-53* (SBB,
1978).

1. Earthquakes are among those natural phenomena perceived as numinous in antiquity. People both stood in reverent
awe before them in recognition of the superiority of the divine

and also shrank back full of fear in recognition of their own
nothingness; this ambivalent character should thus always be
kept in mind. We can easily understand how earthquakes appear
among the earliest motifs underscoring the appearance of deities.
The Greco-Hellenistic world usually considered earthquakes as
an expression of divine wrath and a bad omen (Poseidon, Mars,
and others)—doubtlessly because of the experience of the destructive effects of earthquakes—and also as the background of
the birth and death of gods and divine persons.

In the OT earthquake is a basic motif in portrayals of
theophanies (cf. Judg 5:4f.) showing the reaction of nature to
Yahweh's coming (cf. Ps 68:8f.; Mic 1:3f.; Isa 63:19). This motif
was variously illuminated and expanded and appeared with other
motifs, such as fire, storm, lightning, thunder, and darkness (Ps
18:8-16). Both parts of the originally two-part theophany portrayals, Yahweh's coming and nature's reaction, later appeared
independently, extracted from their original setting, which was
the victory songs of the wars of Yahweh. Hence we later find
statements about nature's reaction most frequently in hymns to
Yahweh and in prophetic proclamation of judgment and salvation. The mutual influence of the tradition of the "day of
Yahweh" and the theophany tradition explains the presence of
theophany motifs in the former (cf. Amos 8:9f.; Joel 2:10). As
was the case with the original coming of Yahweh, so also the
eschatological appearance of God (for judgment) is underscored
by accompanying cosmic events (an expansion to include God's
representative, the Messiah, is not that remote). In early Jewish
and "intertestamental" writings earthquakes and related motifs
usually appear in apocalyptic texts as announcements of
catastrophe and chaos before the end.

2. Matthew refers to earthquake in a manner evoking
the OT theophany motif; thereby, in critical passages in
his Gospel, he transfers an essential and primally characteristic cosmic phenomenon associated with the epiphany
of Yahweh quite consciously to the Kyrios Jesus, thus
portraying him in the role and function of Yahweh as the
master of the cosmos and natural forces. In one especially
impressive example of his miraculous powers ("and behold!") Matthew portrays Jesus as outdoing other miracle
workers (8:24; esp. in the story of Jonah) as master, like
Yahweh, over the forces of chaos, sea, and storm; as
during God's original creation, so now these forces are
vanquished anew by the Son of God (cf. the collective
conclusions in 8:27; 14:33).

We see equally conscious literary structuring when
the redactor uses the strikingly appropriate theophany
motif to mark obviously decisive passages in the Gospel,
such as Jesus' messianic entry into Jerusalem (21:10) and
his death there (27:51), and thus both the beginning (cf.
16:21) and the end of the Passion story. Matthew has
already given the answer to the collective question "Who
is this?" (21:10) through his presentation of the entry
pericope (the influence of Zechariah on the context is
significant): Jesus is the Son of David, the prophet, the
king who enters his city while nonetheless submitting
humbly to the Father's will in the Passion. In him the
promises are fulfilled. At Jesus' death (27:51) Matthew

takes up and accents anew an apocalyptically colored theophany tradition: God himself confirms with signs the true Son of God as the bringer of salvation, in contrast, as it were, to the unanswered demands for signs by the "tempters" beneath the cross. That the centurion and the guards confirm these signs by referring precisely to the earthquake (27:54) shows its dominant position. Finally, Matt 28:2 underscores Jesus' resurrection as the ultimate conquest of death's sovereignty, and thus as the high point of the Gospel, with the earthquake motif (again emphasized by "and behold!"). Jesus' death and resurrection are brought into a salvation-historical context by means of precise motif parallels: "In Jesus' death and resurrection a theophany occurs—an act of God whose effects are accessible to human experience"—"theophany as Christophany" (Riebl 78). Cf. → 3.

3. The earthquake as a miraculous agent of the loosing of bonds or liberation appears within the framework of the mission-theologically oriented genre of miraculous door-openings and deliverance (along with self-liberation and the intervention of a heavenly being), e.g., with Paul and Silas in Acts 16:26. The deity manifests its power to its adversaries and intervenes in favor of its proclaimers. In Matt 28:2 (apparently composed by the Matthean redactor) the earthquake and other pertinent motifs from the Matthean tomb stories (27:62–28:15) signal the presence of the genre of "miraculous deliverance," though here admittedly with multi-layered meanings. It provides the background for the angel's descent, underscores the miraculous door-opening, and accompanies the indirectly expressed (undescribed) liberation of Jesus from the tomb. The determining factor is the theological agenda Matthew carries through his Gospel by means of the earthquake motif (→ 2). The guards' reaction to the angelophany (28:4; the vb. σείω is transferred here to human emotions) comes from the pre-Matthean apologetic tradition of miraculous deliverances (27:62-66; 28:11-15): In deliverance miracles the guards, as adversaries, are excluded from the miraculous events; the consequences of this for the continuation of the legend in 28:11ff. are that the Jews' story is rendered laughable.

4. In the Synoptic apocalypse (Mark 13:8 par. 24:7/ Luke 21:11) earthquakes within the framework of a pre-Markan tradition belong to a series of eschatological horrors marking the beginning of the cosmic woes (in the Synoptic Gospels this constitutes a correction of the interpretation of the Jewish war as the final catastrophe); the same is true of Rev 6:12 at the opening of the sixth seal—the original meaning of the theophany motif is still discernible: the mighty approach of God, annihilation of enemies, wrath, and punishment. Rev 6:13 compares the falling of the stars with the shedding of fruit by the fig tree "shaken by a gale" (σειομένη). After the opening of

the seventh seal thunder, lightning, and earthquake all result from the angel throwing the censer onto the earth (8:5). The conclusion of the second "woe" (11:13) and the emptying of the seventh bowl (16:18) both result in cosmic disturbances of catastrophic proportions. Act. σείω in Heb 12:26 (following Hag 2:6f.) belongs here as well. The appearance of the ark of the covenant in Rev 11:19 is accompanied by the purest theophany motifs.

R. Kratz

σείω *seiō* shake, cause to quake; pass.: tremble → σεισμός.

Σεκοῦνδος, ου *Sekoundos* Secundus*

Transliteration of the Latin personal name *Secundus*. Acts 20:4 mentions with Aristarchus another companion of Paul named Secundus, both from Thessalonica.

Σελεύκεια, ας *Seleukeia* Seleucia*

The name of the port city of Syrian Antioch at the mouth of the Orontes River, established *ca.* 300 B.C. by Seleucus Nicator. R. Fellmann, *LAW* 2758, 2761; E. Olshausen, *KP* V, 85. Acts 13:4 reports that Barnabas and Paul sailed from Seleucia to Cyprus.

σελήνη, ης, ἡ *selēnē* moon*

As in Greek culture and Judaism, the moon is frequently mentioned in the NT together with the sun and the stars (Luke 21:25; 1 Cor 15:41; Rev 6:12; 8:12) or just the sun (Rev 12:1; 21:23). The lunar eclipse is among the eschatological afflictions (Mark 13:24 par. Matt 24:29). Acts 2:20a speaks of the transformation of the moon "into blood" before the "day of the Lord" as predicted by Joel 3:4 LXX. M. Eliade, *RGG* IV, 1094-97; J. Nelis, *BL* 1165-67 (bibliography).

σεληνιάζομαι *selēniazomai* be moonstruck*

Along with demoniacs and paralytics Matt 4:24 mentions those who are *moonstruck*. The healing story in 17:15 says that "he [the son] *is moonstruck* [i.e., epileptic] and suffers terribly."

Σεμεΐν *Semeïn* Semein*

A name in the genealogy of Jesus in Luke 3:26, son of Josech. Heb. *šim'î* appears several times in the OT (e.g., Exod 6:17; Num 3:18).

σεμίδαλις, εως, ἡ *semidalis* fine flour*

Rev 18:13, with wine, oil, and wheat. The word is also documented in Hellenistic Jewish writings and as a loanword in rabbinic writings. See also *Barn.* 2:5 (Isa 1:13 LXX).

σεμνός, 3 *semnos* honorable, respectable
→ σεμνότης.

σεμνότης, ητος, ἡ *semnotēs* respectfulness, dignity*
σεμνός, 3 *semnos* honorable, respectable*

1. Occurrences in the NT — 2. Meaning — 3. Phil 4:8 — 4. The Pastorals

Lit.: W. FOERSTER, *TDNT* VII, 191-96. — J. GNILKA, *Phil* (HTKNT, 1968) 6-11, 218-23. — G. LOHFINK, "Paulinische Theologie in der Rezeption der Pastoralbriefe," *Paulus in den neutestamentlichen Spätschriften* (QD 89, ed. K. Kertelge; 1981) 70-121, esp. 79-86, 106-14. — A. VÖGTLE, *Die Tugend- und Lasterkataloge im NT* (1936), index s.v. — For further bibliography → εὐσέβεια.

1. Words from this group appear in the NT only in Phil 4:8 (ὅσα σεμνά) and two of the Pastorals (adj. in 1 Tim 3:8, 11; Titus 2:2; noun in 1 Tim 2:2; 3:4; Titus 2:7).

2. These words refer to that which is worthy of reverence, that which is exalted as part of the divine realm (the numinous), both things (with aesthetic overtones) and what is within human relationships (that which commands respect). What is thought of exactly is determined by what is referred to, be it vocations (e.g., rulers), classes (e.g., women), and accepted values (e.g., of the Stoics). The personal relationship between human beings and God in biblical religion prevents Hellenistic Judaism from using these terms in the religious sense to any great extent, and this extends to the NT as well (in the LXX only in Proverbs, 2 and 4 Maccabees; in Philo esp. of the dignity of the Torah).

3. Phil 4:8f. ("whatever is true, whatever is *honorable,* whatever is just . . . think about these things") occupies a special position within the genuine Pauline letters in both form and content (on the catalog of virtues in v. 8 see Vögtle 178-88). In view of the possibility considered by Gnilka (219) that letter fragment B ends at 4:1, his "reflections" justifying the addition of vv. 8f. actually suggest far more strongly that those two verses are an insertion by the redactor of the Philippian letter collection. This would explain not only the similarity of v. 9a to the Pastorals (Lohfink 85), but also the use of σεμνός in v. 8, as in 1 Timothy and Titus.

4. The Pastorals prescribe respectful behavior in the catolog of duties of the ἐπίσκοπος (1 Tim 3:4, regarding the management of his "household" or as an educational ideal), of the διάκονοι (v. 8), of women (v. 11; on their identity see N. Brox, *Die Pastoralbriefe* [RNT] 154f.), and of elderly men (Titus 2:2). These requirements are based on the goal, valid for all Christians, of a life ἐν πάσῃ εὐσεβείᾳ καὶ σεμνότητι (1 Tim 2:2), which will also influence non-Christians. The exhortation to teach in such a way as to show integrity and dignity, virtues in which the addressee should be a model (Titus 2:7), underscores this from the opposite perspective.   P. Fiedler

Σέργιος, ου *Sergios* Sergius*

This Roman gentilic name refers in the NT to the proconsul of Cyprus, *Sergius* Paulus (Acts 13:7). On documentation of this name in inscriptions see BAGD s.v.; E. Haenchen, *Acts* (Eng. tr., 1971) 86 n.2. → Παῦλος 6; Σαῦλος 2.

Σερούχ *Serouch* Serug*

An indeclinable personal name in the genealogy of Jesus in Luke 3:35 (cf. Gen 11:20-23; 1 Chr 1:26 LXX).

Σήθ *Sēth* Seth*

The indeclinable personal name of a son of Adam; father of Enosh (Luke 3:38; cf. Gen 4:25f.; 5:3-8 LXX). A. F. J. Klijn, *Seth in Jewish, Christian and Gnostic Literature* (1977).

Σήμ *Sēm* Shem*

The indeclinable personal name of a son of Noah (Luke 3:36; cf. Gen 5:32; 9:26f.).

σημαίνω *sēmainō* make known, report; foretell*

The general meaning *make known/public* occurs in Acts 25:27 (τὰς αἰτίας) and Rev 1:1 ("to his servant John"). In Acts 11:28 the vb. appears with acc. and inf. (so also Josephus *Ant.* vi.50; viii.409): Agabus "*foretold* by the Spirit that there would be a great famine over all the world." In John 12:33; 18:32; 21:19 it appears with an indirect question in Jesus' predictions of his own death.

σημεῖον, ου, τό *sēmeion* distinguishing mark, sign; miracle*

1. Occurrences in the NT — 2. The Gospels and Acts — 3. The Epistles — 4. Revelation

Lit.: O. BETZ, "Das Problem des Wunders bei Flavius Josephus im Vergleich zum Wunderproblem bei den Rabbinen und im Johannesevangelium," *Josephus-Studien* (FS O. Michel, 1974) 23-44. — O. BETZ and W. GRIMM, *Wesen und Wirklichkeit der Wunder Jesu* (1977). — W. J. BITTNER, *Jesu Zeichen im*

Johannesevangelium. Die Messias-Erkenntnis im Johannesevangelium vor ihrem jüdischen Hintergrund (WUNT II/26, 1987). — W. D. DENNISON, "Miracles as 'Signs.' Their Significance for Apologetics," *BTB* 6 (1976) 190-202. — R. FORMESYN, "Le sèmeion johannique et le sèmeion hellénistique," *ETL* 38 (1962) 856-94. — B. GERHARDSSON, *The Mighty Acts of Jesus According to Matthew* (1979), esp. 12-15. — R. GLÖCKNER, *Neutestamentliche Wundergeschichten und das Lob der Wundertaten Gottes in den Psalmen* (1983). — H. C. KEE, *Miracle in the Early Christian World* (1983). — R. LATOURELLE, *The Miracles of Jesus and the Theology of Miracles* (1988). — X. LÉON-DUFOUR, "Autour du ΣΗΜΕΙΟΝ johannique," FS Schürmann 363-78. — H. VON LIPS, "Anthropologie und Wunder im Johannesevangelium," *EvT* 50 (1990) 296-311. — E. LOHSE, "Miracles in the Fourth Gospel," *What About the NT?* (FS C. Evans, 1975) 64-75. — H. VAN DER LOOS, *The Miracles of Jesus* (NovTSup 9, 1965). — W. NICOL, *The Sēmeia in the Fourth Gospel* (NovTSup 32, 1972). — H. REMUS, "Does Terminology distinguish Early Christian from Pagan Miracles?" *JBL* 101 (1982) 531-51. — K. H. RENGSTORF, *TDNT* VII, 200-269. — SPICQ, *Notes* II, 796-801. — F. STOLZ, "Zeichen und Wunder," *ZTK* 69 (1972) 125-44. — M. TRAUTMANN, *Zeichenhafte Handlungen Jesu. Ein Beitrag zur Frage nach dem geschichtlichen Jesus* (FzB 37, 1980). — M. WHITTAKER, " 'Signs and Wonders': The Pagan Background," *SE* V (1968) 155-58. — W. WILKENS, *Zeichen und Werke* (ATANT 55, 1969). — For further bibliography see *TWNT* X, 1262f.

1. The noun σημεῖον occurs 77 times in the NT, esp. in the historical writings (13 times in Matthew, 7 in Mark [including 16:17, 20], 10 in Luke, 17 in John, 13 in Acts), with 10 occurrences in the Epistles and 7 in Revelation. In the LXX σημεῖον almost always translates Heb. *'ōt* (Aram. *'āt*); its usage has influenced that of the NT, as seen in a phrase taken over from the OT, σημεῖα καὶ τέρατα (*'ōtōt ûmôp̄ᵉtîm*, e.g., Exod 7:3; Deut 4:32; 6:22, esp. in Deuteronomy and the Deuteronomic and Priestly Codes; cf. Mark 13:22; John 4:48; Acts 4:30; 14:3; 15:12; cf. also 2:19, 43; 5:12; 2 Thess 2:9; Rom 15:19; 2 Cor 12:12).

2. a) In the Gospels and Acts σημεῖον is used of 1) a (visible) *sign* by which a person is recognized, as with the (previously agreed upon) kiss of the betrayer giving Jesus away to the temple guard (Matt 26:48), or the manger designating the newborn savior (Luke 2:12; on the phrase "and this will be a *sign* for you" cf. 1Q27 I 1:5; Exod 3:12; 1 Sam 2:34; 14:10), or 2) a warning *omen,* sent by God and usually of a cosmic nature, that announces the end of history (Mark 13:4; Luke 21:7) or the advent of the Son of man and the fulfillment of the aeon (Matt 24:3). As with the "footprints of the Messiah" (*m. Soṭa* 9:15), the latter includes the chaos of war, famine, and epidemics and earthquakes, "terrors and great *signs* from heaven" (Luke 21:11), and "*signs* in sun, moon, and stars" (21:25). Here the influence of the OT is important (cf. Isa 13:10; 34:4 in Mark 13:24f. par. and Joel 3:3, quoted in Acts 2:19). Phenomena accompanying

the "day of Yahweh" are to serve in a parenetic and legal sense as warning signs to the generation of the end time. Nonetheless, these "*signs* of the times" are not understood (Matt 16:3). The high point of the parousia is the appearance of the "sign of the Son of man in heaven" (24:30), referring to the fulfillment, visible to all, of the advent and enthronement of the eschatological judge seen by Daniel in his night visions (Dan 7:13f.; Zech 12:10-14. Jesus himself is set by God "for a *sign* that is spoken against" in Israel; his mission will reveal what is in human hearts, and these hearts will decide their own eschatological fates.

b) In contrast to Jesus' healing miracles, which as powerful works (δυνάμεις = *gᵉbûrôt*) reveal the beneficial righteousness of divine sovereignty and presuppose faith, σημεῖον refers to miracles confirming the claim of a savior or prophet sent by God; they are meant to awaken faith (cf. Exod 4:1-9) and are demanded or prompted rather than requested.

The transformation miracle with the staff-snake is an example here (Exod 3:12; 4:1-5; 7:8ff.); the Egyptian plagues are also signs pointing to God (Exod 7:3; 10:2; Deut 7:19; 26:8; cf. Acts 7:36). Before the Jewish war prophets appeared promising "*signs* of freedom" (Josephus *B.J.* ii.259; *Ant.* xx.168) with the intention of proving that God was with them. The salient symbolic feature of these promised miracles was their coincidence with the deeds of Moses or Joshua (cf. *Ant.* xx.97 with Josh 3:7; xx.169f. with Josh 6:8ff.). Josephus does, however, condemn these men as swindlers and seducers (*Ant.* xx.167; *B.J.* ii.259-61). These legitimizing signs are ambiguous.

Mark 13:22 and Matt 24:24 warn against false prophets and messiahs: They will perform great signs and miracles in order to deceive even the elect if possible (cf. Deut 13:1-4). Their stage is the desert (Matt 24:26; cf. *B.J.* ii.259).

Jesus emphatically rejects the demand that he perform a "*sign* from heaven" (i.e., from God; Mark 8:11f.; Matt 16:1; Luke 11:16; cf. Matt 12:38); the demand simply reveals a perverted generation's lack of faith (Mark 8:12; Matt 16:4; 12:39). According to Matt 12:39; 16:4; Luke 11:29 t' is generation will receive only the "*sign* of the prophet Jonah," meaning (according to Q) Jonah's successful call to repentance in the Gentile city of Nineveh; so also should Israel be guided to repentance through Jesus' preaching (Matt 12:41; Luke 11:32). According to Matt 12:40 the miraculous rescue by the fish is to be this "*sign* of Jonah" pointing to the Son of man and his own sojourn "in the heart of the earth," i.e., to Jesus' death and resurrection. Perhaps this interpretation is also valid for Luke 11:30 (Jonah became a sign to Nineveh) and the Gospel of John, where the raising of Lazarus on the fourth day (11:39) stands in place of the sign of Jonah. Finally, Herod Antipas tried in vain to evoke a (confirming) sign from Jesus (Luke 23:8).

The devil's demands in Matt 4:1-11 par. are also to be understood as demands for signs, as is the challenge to Jesus to climb down from the cross (Mark 15:30 par.). Although miracles such as the calming of the storm, walking on water, or multiplying the bread could evoke the impression of confirming signs because of their relationship to Exodus 14–16, they are portrayed as acts of helping mercy (Mark 4:38f.; 6:34, 50f.).

According to the inauthentic conclusion to Mark the resurrected Jesus promises to believers the power to perform miracles as reported of the disciples and manifested in the charismatics of the Church (16:17; cf. Luke 10:17-19; 1 Cor 12:4ff., 28ff.). Such miracles are called "signs" because they confirm the proclamation visibly (Mark 16:20).

c) Although John also recognizes the problems inherent in signs and in the demand for signs (2:18, 23; 4:48; 6:2, 14, 30), he nonetheless calls miracles σημεῖα because through them Jesus manifests his glory and reveals his mission as the Son of God (2:11; 20:30f.). Whereas the Baptist performs no signs (10:41), many great signs charactize Jesus' activity (3:2; 7:31; 9:16; 11:47; 12:37); the appearances of the resurrected Jesus are to be understood similarly (20:30). The Johannine miracles point beyond themselves to the eschatological Savior (6:14; 7:31; 12:18) and provoke faith in him (2:11, 23; 4:53; 9:35; 11:47f.; 20:30f.). But this faith can remain superficial and egocentric (4:48; 6:14, 30) or can be rejected (12:37, 39); and signs cannot always defeat the conviction that Jesus is a deceiver (11:47f., following Deut 13:1-4); thus what the sign signifies is overlooked, namely, that the miracle is a work of God, whose "arm" becomes effective through Christ (12:37f., quoting Isa 53:1; cf. 5:20, 36; 9:3f.; 17:4). Apart from the passages that interpret the signs, the confirming power of the signs in John is amplified by characteristics of each, the purpose of which is to eclipse the classical examples of the miracles of Moses, Elijah, and Elisha (cf. 2:1-11; 4:46-54; 5:1-7 with 1 Kings 17; 2 Kings 5, John 6:9 with 2 Kgs 4:42f., John 6:31 with Exod 16:4, 13-15). The (interrupted) enumeration of signs begun in John 2:11; 4:54 recalls the first two miracles of Moses (Exod 4:8) and Elijah (1 Kings 17). Viewed from this perspective these signs concur with the Johannine theology, disclose no lacunae, and betray nothing of the use of a primitive "signs source" aiming to eclipse or outdo Hellenistic miracle workers.

d) Although Acts also understands the miracles of Jesus and the apostles as confirming signs, the term δυνάμεις, which is actually more appropriate for those of Jesus, can also appear in addition to σημεῖα καὶ τέρατα (2:22; 8:13). The frequently used phrase "signs and wonders" obscures the distinction between the two expressions, since the sequence "wonders and signs" is also possible (2:22, 43; 6:8; 7:36). Jesus was "attested" to the Jews "by God with mighty works and wonders and signs which God did through him in their midst" (2:22). The revelatory and instrumental character of these signs is grounded in the idea of mission, oriented toward Moses, and designed for continuity: Moses "performed wonders and signs in Egypt and at the Red Sea, and in the wilderness," thus pointing to a coming prophet equal to himself (7:36f.): Because God is to empower and send this prophet (Deut 18:15), God is also the source of the signs that legitimize Jesus. Signs and wonders are performed by the apostles (2:43; 5:12), by the "deacon" Stephen (6:8), by Philip (8:6, 13), and by Paul and Barnabas (14:3; 15:12). Although God himself is also acting in the apostolic signs (15:12), according to 4:30 they are performed "through the name of Jesus" (cf. 3:6 and t. Ḥul. 2:21ff.), who as the exalted Christ heals through his messengers (9:34) and thus himself confirms the truth of the word proclaiming him (14:3).

These signs stand in the service of the word: The healing of the lame man (3:1-8), even according to the admission of the adversaries, is a sign manifest to all the inhabitants of Jerusalem (4:16), prompting the question concerning the veracity of the proclamation. The signs seek to lead others to faith (8:6; cf. 9:35, 42) and defeat the magic of Simon Magus (8:13). They are not, however, mere demonstrative miracles like the triumphs of Moses and Aaron over the Egyptian magicians (cf. Exod 7:1-13), nor are they chastizing miracles (Acts 5:1-11 is not a σημεῖον), but rather healings as with Jesus (4:22; 9:32-42). Indeed, the "wonders (τέρατα) in heaven above" in 2:19 cited from Joel 3:3 are complemented by—in a phrase added to the citation—"σημεῖα on earth below," i.e., probably the miracles of Jesus and the apostles. The "signs and wonders" mentioned in 15:12 could refer to Paul and Barnabas's missionary successes among the Gentiles.

3. a) For Paul a σημεῖον can be an (external) *sign* such as his own signature at the conclusion of a letter (2 Thess 3:17). The "*sign* of circumcision" is, however, also a "seal of the righteousness of faith" that made Abraham the father of believing Gentiles (Rom 4:11).

b) Speaking in tongues is a "*sign* for unbelievers" (1 Cor 14:22) to the extent they do not recognize it as communication prompted by God (cf. Isa 28:11 in v. 21) and reveal through their mockery their own stubbornness and hopelessness.

c) Finally, a σημεῖον can be for Paul a *miracle* visibly disclosing the coming redemption and the activity of God. Paul considers the "demand for *signs*" to be a salient feature of Jewish eschatological expectation (1 Cor 1:22); for the acceptance of the proclamation of the cross it constitutes a hindrance equally as strong as the love of wisdom among the Greeks (cf. Mark 8:11f.). In 2 Cor 12:12, however, Paul refers to the "*signs* of a true apostle" performed through him in Corinth "in all patience, with *signs,* wonders, and mighty works"; they show that he is not inferior to the "superlative apostles." Such self-evaluation and measurement, however, is foolish (v. 11), since these signs were performed through the apostle by Christ with the power of the Spirit; they witness to the truth of the gospel and legitimize its proclaimer. The signs of the apostle are not only charismatic miracles, but also missionary successes visible in the life of the congregation (cf. 2 Cor 3:2).

The coming of the Antichrist will be accompanied by miracles, which Paul, following Deut 13:1-4, calls "pretended *signs* and wonders" (2 Thess 2:9). Church divisions necessitated as a test of faith doubtlessly also possess eschatologically symbolic character (1 Cor 11:18f.).

According to Heb 2:4 the proclamation of Jesus and that of his initial listeners was witnessed "by *signs* and wonders, and various miracles and by gifts of the Holy Spirit" (cf. Acts 2:22).

4. The seer of the Apocalypse views apocalyptic signs as incisive, symbolically intended scenes in heaven that merge into dramatic events: the female figure on the crescent moon (12:1), her adversary, the dragon (12:3), and the angels with the seven bowls (15:1). These signs also include the miraculous deeds with which the false prophet of the end time seduces people to worship the "beast" (13:13, 14; 19:20). The spirits issuing from this beast also perform signs through which they goad the kings of the world into the eschatological battle (16:14).

O. Betz

σημειόομαι *sēmeioomai* take notice*

The mid. form σημειόομαι can mean both *mark* (*OGIS* 629, 168; *1 Clem.* 43:1) and *take note* (of someone). It occurs in 2 Thess 3:14 in the exhortation to *note* that person who refuses to obey the (apostolic) words in the letter, and to have nothing to do with such a person. K. H. Rengstorf, *TDNT* VII, 265f.

σήμερον *sēmeron* today

1. Occurrences in the NT — 2. Meanings — 3. Luke — 4. Hebrews

Lit.: E. Fuchs, *TDNT* VII, 269-75. — P. Grelot, " 'Aujourd'hui tu seras avec moi dans le Paradis' (Luc XXIII 43)," *RB* 74 (1967) 194-214. — M. Rese, "Einige Überlegungen zu Lk XIII 31-33," *Jésus aux origines de la christologie* (ed. J. Dupont, et al.; 1975) 201-25. — H. Zimmermann, *Das Bekenntnis der Hoffnung* (1977) 129-37. — For further bibliography see *TWNT* X, 1263.

1. Σήμερον occurs 41 times in the NT, 20 times in Luke-Acts alone. Other significant multiple occurrences are in Matthew and Hebrews (8 times each). Paul uses the word 3 times, and Mark and James once each.

2. Commensurate with the biblical understanding of time, this adv. has a purely temporal sense only in its peripheral occurrences as a temporally neutral delimitation of a specific *today* (Matt 16:3; 21:28; 27:19; Acts 4:9; 19:40; 20:26; 22:3; 24:21; 26:2, 29; 27:33). Most of the occurrences follow the sense that Gerhard von Rad ascertained for the "endless variations played upon the word 'today'" in Deuteronomy (von Rad, *Theology* I, 231). Faith should learn from the examples of what is most transitory (Matt 6:30 par. Luke 12:28) so that it suffices to request only what is necessary for *today* (Matt 6:11), an idea actually made less rigorous in Luke 11:3. The prediction of Peter's denial (Mark 14:30) is interested less in the date of the denial itself than in the relationship between Peter's apparently flawless behavior (14:29, 31) and his denial. Paul interprets the OT prediction (Isa 29:10) with the well-known addition, taken from the LXX, ἕως τῆς σήμερον ἡμέρας as judgment (Rom 11:8). He understands Exod 35:35f. similarly in 2 Cor 3:14, 15.

3. The repeated Lukan insertion of σήμερον into his Gospel, which encompasses the story of Jesus from its beginning (2:11) and end (23:43), is without analogy. Through his presence Jesus confirms the fulfillment of the promise (4:21). 5:26; 19:5, 9; 23:43 show who profits by this presence. Σήμερον emphasizes the paradoxical (5:26) truth of the advent of salvation within time (2:11) just as strongly as it underscores how its ultimate presence eclipses all temporal standards (23:43). 13:33 (Lukan invention) underscores "that Jesus' path encompasses not only the salvation activity occurring 'today and tomorrow,' but also the Passion in Jerusalem (G. Schneider, *Luke* [ÖTK] II, 310).

4. Framed by the double citation of Ps 2:7 (Heb 1:5; 5:5), σήμερον in Ps 95:7, quoted in Heb 3:7, 15; 4:7, occupies a central position. In the first part of the exegesis of Ps 95:7-11 in Heb 3:7–4:11 σήμερον (3:15) underscores the admonition not to be like the wilderness generation (Numbers 14) and throw away *today* by falling away from God (3:12). In 4:7 σήμερον then serves to emphasize a *today* made new by God, the still valid promise of → κατάπαυσις (2). "Today" experiences "its limits" on the day of Christ's advent (Zimmermann 137). Heb 13:8 ("yesterday, *today,* and forever") is the christological center of the letter's concluding parenesis; its scope ranges from the recollection of the example of the leaders (13:7) to the "city that is to come" (13:14).

M. Völkel

σημιχίνθιον, ου, τό *sēmikinthion* apron
A secondary form of → σιμιχίνθιον assimilated to Lat. *semicinctium* (BDF §§5.1; 41.1).

σήπω *sēpō* cause to rot; rot*

In the NT—as frequently elsewhere—σήπω has the intrans. meaning *rot/decay.* Jas 5:2 uses it of the treasures of the rich: ὁ πλοῦτος ὑμῶν σέσηπεν. O. Bauernfeind, *TDNT* VII, 94-97.

σηρικός, 3 *sērikos* silken
A secondary form of → σιρικός. BDF §§41.1; 42.4.

σής, σητός, ὁ *sēs* moth*

Luke 12:33 par. Matt 19:20, of the moth whose larvae devour clothing. O. Bauernfeind, *TDNT* VII, 275-78; Schulz, *Q* 142-45; G. Schwarz, *Biblische Notizen* 14 (1981) 46-49.

σητόβρωτος, 2 *sētobrōtos* moth-eaten*

Jas 5:2, of the ἱμάτια of the rich (cf. Job 13:28 LXX). O. Bauernfeind, *TDNT* VII, 275-78.

σθενόω *sthenoō* strengthen*

Fut. σθενώσει in 1 Pet 5:10 in the series "[God himself] will restore, establish, *strengthen,* and settle you."

σιαγών, όνος, ἡ *siagōn* cheek*

Matt 5:39 par. Luke 6:29, in Jesus' demand that one renounce revenge. Only Matthew speaks specifically of the "right" cheek; a slap on the right cheek with the back of the right hand was considered esp. contemptuous (Jeremias, *Theology* 239). Schulz, *Q* 120-27.

σιαίνομαι *siainomai* be disgusted/annoyed
1 Thess 3:3 F G in place of pass. σαίνομαι (→ σαίνω).

σιγάω *sigaō* be or fall silent; keep secret, concealed*
σιγή, ῆς, ἡ *sigē* silence, stillness*

1. Occurrences — 2. Meaning — 3. Usage

Lit.: BAGD s.v. — G. DAUTZENBERG, *Urchristliche Prophetie* (BWANT 104, 1975) 253-90. — L. M. DEWAILLY, "Mystère et silence dans Rom XVI,25," *NTS* 14 (1967/68) 111-18. — G. FITZER, *Das Weib schweige in der Gemeinde* (TEH 110, 1963). — H. KRAFT, *Rev* (HNT, 1974) 132f.

1. The vb. σιγάω, already relatively rare in the LXX with at most 19 occurrences, occurs 10 times in the NT and is limited to Luke-Acts (6 occurrences; Luke 18:39 instead of σιωπάω in par. Mark 10:48), 1 Corinthians 14, and Rom 16:25. Σιγή occurs (as in the LXX) only twice (Acts 21:40; Rev 8:1).

2. Σιγάω means *keep silent or still,* including in the sense of *hold one's tongue* (BAGD) or *say nothing to*

anyone (Luke 9:36). It can also refer to the end of a speech: *stop speaking,* though in the NT clearly only in the pres. imv. in 1 Cor 14:30; in the other instances where *fall silent/stop speaking* must be the tr. (Luke 18:39; 20:26[?]; Acts 15:13), this meaning is indicated by the ingressive aor. The trans. meaning *keep secret* occurs in the NT only in Rom 16:25. Σιγή refers to *silence, stillness.*

3. Σιγάω and σιγή occur in four different contexts and corresponding textual types.

a) In the stories of the activity of Jesus and the apostles the narrative texts in Luke and Acts report the silence or "falling silent" of the disciples (Luke 9:36), of Jesus' adversaries (20:26), of the assembled congregation (Acts 12:17), of the apostolic assembly (15:12, 13), and of the people (21:40) and the corresponding demand the crowd makes of the the blind man (Luke 18:39). In Acts σιγάω or σιγή occurs within the context of important speeches in situations decisive for Peter, Paul, or the early Church (cf. Acts 15: speech in vv. 7-11, σιγάω in v. 12, speech summary in v. 12, σιγάω in v. 13, speech in vv. 13-21).

b) Paul establishes order in the congregational assembly in 1 Corinthians: The person speaking in tongues "is to *keep silence* [i.e., speaking in tongues is to cease] if there is no one to interpret" (1 Cor 14:28). And if a prophet is speaking when a revelation comes to another, the first should *be silent* (and sit down, v. 30).

One cannot view as genuinely Pauline the stipulation that "the women should *keep silence* in the churches" (v. 34a). This entire section (vv. 33b-36) contradicts the situation presupposed in 11:5, particularly, however—with its isolated and static standardization—the argumentative context and "theological agenda in chs. 12 and 14" (Dautzenberg 265). On the other hand, it is related conceptually, stylistically, and in content with 1 Tim 2:11f. and can easily be extracted from its present context. We are thus dealing here with an interpolation, albeit an extremely early one, since it is attested by all the extant mss. (even if vv. 34f. in D F G and others follow v. 40).

c) The concluding doxology in Romans speaks of God's resolution. The occasion for this praise is the revelation of "the mystery *kept secret* for long ages" (16:25). It is not directed in any esoteric fashion only to a small circle of the elect, but rather to all people.

d) A "*silence* in heaven for about half an hour" is part of the vision of the apocalyptic seer (Rev 8:1). At the opening of the seventh seal the original locus of the theophany, the series of cosmic events, is interrupted, and a stillness descends similar to that after God's appearance in 1 Kgs 19:11f., where stillness followed upon storm, earthquake, and fire (cf. Kraft).

W. Radl

σιγή, ῆς, ἡ *sigē* silence, stillness
→ σιγάω.

σίδηρος, ου, ὁ *sidēros* iron (noun)*

In Rev 18:12 with χαλκός ("bronze").

σιδηροῦς, 3 *sidērous* iron (adj.)*

Acts 12:10: an *iron* prison gate; Rev 9:9: *iron* breastplates. In the sense of "hard, merciless" (after the model of Ps 2:9 LXX) in the phrase "with a rod of *iron*" (Rev 2:27; 12:5; 19:15; → ῥάβδος).

Σιδών, ῶνος *Sidōn* Sidon*

An ancient Phoenician city often mentioned (almost formulaically) with Tyre (Mark 3:8 par. Luke 6:17; Mark 7:31; Matt 11:21, 22 par. Luke 10:13, 14; Matt 15:21 [but cf. par. Mark]). Only Acts 27:3 mentions Sidon alone: On the journey to Rome Paul is permitted to seek out "friends" in Sidon. A. H. M. Jones, *OCD* 986; L. Grollenberg, *LTK* IX, 734f.; M. Liverani, *ISBE* IV, 500-502; W. Röllig, *LAW* 2793f.; H. Weippert, *BRL* 296-98.

Σιδώνιος, 3 *Sidōnios* Sidonian, from Sidon; subst.: Sidonian*

Luke 4:26: "Zarephath, in the *Sidonian* country." Χώρας is to be understood with gen. τῆς Σιδωνίας (cf. 3 Kgdms 17:9). Acts 12:20 mentions the *Sidonians* together with the people of Tyre. → Σιδών.

σικάριος, ου, ὁ *sikarios* assassin, dagger carrier*

In Acts 21:38 this Latin loanword (*sicarius*, from *sica*, "dagger") is used in the pl. of a group of anti-Roman Jewish rebels who do not shrink from political murder (Josephus *B.J.* ii.254-57; *Ant.* xx.186). Schürer, *History* I, 463; II, 602f.; D. M. Rhoads, *Israel in Revolution 6-74 C.E.* (1976) 111-22; O. Betz, *TDNT* VII, 278-82; *TWNT* X, 1264 (bibliography); K. Schubert, *Die jüdischen Religionsparteien in neutestamentlicher Zeit* (1970) 66-70; M. Hengel, *The Zealots* (1989), esp. 46-53.

σίκερα, τό *sikera* strong drink*

This indeclinable noun (found also in the LXX) occurs in the NT only in Luke 1:15b (cf. Judg 13:4 A) in the announcement of the angel concerning John the Baptist: "He shall drink neither wine nor *strong drink*." Billerbeck II, 79f.

Σιλᾶς, ᾶ *Silas* Silas*
Σιλουανός, οῦ *Silouanos* Silvanus*

1. The relationship of the two names — 2. The Epistles — 3. Acts

Lit.: J. H. ELLIOTT, "Peter, Silvanus and Mark in I Peter and Acts," FS Rengstorf (1980) 250-67. — L. GOPPELT, *1 Pet* (KEK, 1978), esp. 347-49. — B. N. KAYE, "Acts' Portrait of Silas," *NovT* 21 (1979) 13-26. — O. Michel, *BHH* 1793. — W.-H. OLLROG, *Paulus und seine Mitarbeiter* (WMANT 50, 1979) 17-20. — L. RADERMACHER, "Der erste Petrusbrief und Silvanus," *ZNW* 25 (1926) 287-99. — E. G. SELWYN, *1 Pet* ([2]1947) 9-17, 60-63. — A. STEGMANN, *Silvanus als Missionär und "Hagiograph"* (1917). — A. WAINWRIGHT, "Where Did Silas Go? (and What Was His Connection with Galatians?)," *JSNT* 8 (1980) 66-70. — A. WIKENHAUSER, *LTK* IX, 753.

1. The name Σιλᾶς occurs in the NT 13 times in Acts (it occurs several times as a Semitic name in Josephus). It derives perhaps from an Aramaic form of the name "Saul." The name Σιλουανός occurs only in the Pauline writings (2 Cor 1:19; 1 Thess 1:1; further 2 Thess 1:1) and in 1 Pet 5:12. It derives from the Latin name *Silvanus* and is also documented in Josephus (*Ant.* xx.14) and rabbinic writings. The two names refer in the NT to the same person (*contra*, e.g., Radermacher 295), who perhaps used both names (a Semitic name and a Latin name). It is also possible that the Semitic name was both Grecized *(Silas)* and Latinized *(Silvanus);* cf. BDF §125.2.

2. According to 1 Thess 1:1 Silvanus is coauthor of the Pauline letter to Thessalonica along with Timothy. 2 Thess 1:1 repeats this information verbatim (cf. W. Trilling, *2 Thess* [EKKNT]), whereas Paul himself varies the prescripts to his letters. Our information says that Silvanus accompanied Paul only on the "second missionary journey"; if 2 Thessalonians were a genuine Pauline letter, it would, therefore, have to have been written shortly after 1 Thessalonians. Silvanus and Timothy are mentioned in 1 Thessalonians as coauthors probably not only as Paul's colleagues, but also as cofounders of the church in Thessalonica (cf. Acts 17:1-9).

2 Cor 1:19 should be evaluated similarly: Silvanus and Timothy together with Paul began preaching Christ in Corinth (cf. Acts 18:5).

Silvanus is also mentioned in the pseudonymous 1 Peter, this time together with "Peter": "By Silvanus, a faithful brother as I regard him, I have written briefly to you" (5:12, at the beginning of the letter's conclusion). Here Silvanus, a (well-known!) leading personality of the first Christian generation, is presented as the one who delivered the letter (not amanuensis or secretary; cf. N. Brox, *1 Pet* [EKKNT] 241-43). Silvanus was not the letter's author (*contra* Selwyn); see Brox, *1 Pet* 242. Perhaps there was a tradition linking Silvanus/Silas with the person of Peter. Cf. also *The Teaching of Silvanus* (*NHC* vii.4), which might be classified as Christian wisdom literature.

3. Acts first mentions *Silas* with Judas Barsabbas in

the narrative of the "apostolic assembly." Both are introduced as "leading men" of the (Jewish Christian) Jerusalem church (15:22) who are to take the "apostolic" letter to Antioch (vv. 23, 27, 30). 15:32 mentions the prophetic gifts of the two messengers who strengthened the Christians in Antioch (v. 32) before returning to Jerusalem (v. 33). After the contention between Paul and Barnabas concerning John Mark (15:37-39) Paul took Silas with him on the "second journey" (v. 40; v. 34 v.l. seeks to explain that Silas was able to go with Paul from Antioch). From 15:40 to 18:5 Silas is mentioned by name nine times. From 16:3 on he (along with Timothy) is Paul's companion on the first journey to Europe. In Philippi Silas is accused along with Paul before the city magistrates and thrown into prison (16:19, 25). The two attain freedom by means of a miracle and convert the jailer (vv. 26-34). 17:4 mentions the missionary success of Paul and Silas in Thessalonica, v. 10 their journey to Beroea. While Silas and Timothy remain in Beroea, Paul goes to Athens (vv. 14f.). After Paul journeyed from Athens to Corinth (18:1), his two companions followed from Beroea (v. 5). The participation of Silas in the founding of the churches at Thessalonica and Corinth is attested by genuine Pauline letters (→ 2).   G. Schneider

Σιλβανός, οῦ *Silbanos* Silvanus

V.l. in p⁴⁶ and others in 2 Cor 1:19 (in place of → Σιλουανός).

Σιλουανός, οῦ *Silouanos* Silvanus
→ Σιλᾶς.

Σιλωάμ, ὁ *Silōam* Siloam*

An indeclinable name referring to several water systems in Jerusalem and derived from Heb. *šlḥ*, "send." The Hebrew name *šilō(a)ḥ* referred originally to the water supply system originating at the Gihon spring, then to the pool into which it emptied. Ἡ κολυμβήθρα τοῦ Σιλωάμ in John 9:7 refers to the pool and is translated with ἀπεσταλμένος; cf. 9:11: "Go to Siloam and wash." Ὁ πύργος ἐν τῷ Σιλωάμ (Luke 13:4) is "the tower in Siloam," probably part of the city wall. Kopp, *Places* 314-20; H. Haag, *LTK* V, 904f.; D. Adan, *IEJ* 29 (1979) 92-100.

Σιμαίας, ου *Simaias* Simaias

A personal name in 2 Tim 4:19 v.l. (181 pc): the son of Aquila.

σιμικίνθιον, ου, τό *simikinthion* apron, loincloth*

The *apron* of the kind worn by workmen (Lat. *semicinctium*). Acts 19:12 reports that those in Ephesus took σουδάρια (handkerchiefs) and σιμικίνθια from Paul's body to the sick in order to heal them. E. Haenchen, *Acts* (Eng. tr., 1971) 562, translates: "handkerchiefs."

Σίμων, ος *Simōn* Simon

1. The name Simon — 2. Simon Peter — 3. Simon the Zealot — 4. Simon the brother of Jesus — 5. Simon of Cyrene — 6. Simon the father of Judas — 7. Simon the leper — 8. Simon the pharisee — 9. Simon the tanner — 10. Simon Magus

Lit.: J. BLINZLER, "Simon der Apostel, Simon der Herrenbruder und Bischof Symeon von Jerusalem," *Passauer Studien* (FS S. K. Landersdorfer, 1953) 25-55. — J. D. M. DERRETT, "Simon Magus (Act 8,9-24)," *ZNW* 73 (1982) 52-68. — J. A. FITZMYER, "The Name Simon," *idem, Essays on the Semitic Background of the NT* (1971) 105-12.
On 2 → Πέτρος; on 3–9 see below at the end of each section.
On Simon Magus: R. P. CASEY, *Beginnings* V, 151-63. — N. ADLER, *LTK* IX, 768f. — H. CONZELMANN, *Acts* (Hermeneia) 63. — E. HAENCHEN, "Simon Magus in der Apostelgeschichte," *Gnosis und NT* (ed. K. W. Tröger; 1973) 267-79. — K. BEYSCHLAG, *Simon Magus und die christliche Gnosis* (1974). — G. LÜDEMANN, *Untersuchungen zur simonianischen Gnosis* (1975). — K. RUDOLPH, *Gnosis: The Nature and History of Gnosticism* (1983) 294-98 and index s.v. — *idem, TRu* 42 (1977) 279-359. — G. SCHNEIDER, *Acts* (HTKNT) 481-95. — For further bibliography see Schneider.

1. The name Simon was popular both among Greeks and Jews (BAGD s.v.; Fitzmyer). In Judaism Σίμων is documented among other places also in the LXX (esp. 1–2 Maccabees), the *Epistle of Aristeas*, and Josephus.

2. Simon Peter probably acquired the name Simon in Hellenistically influenced Bethsaida (his brother Andrew [Mark 1:16] also had a "Greek" name). Σίμων was considered the equivalent of the Hebrew patriarchal name Symeon (→ Συμεών in Acts 15:14; 2 Pet 1:1). Σίμων is used of Peter 50 times in the NT (5 times in Matthew, 7 in Mark, 12 in Luke, 22 in John, 4 in Acts); → Πέτρος.

3. The apostolic catalog mentions another disciple with the name Simon (Mark 3:18 par. Matt 10:4), Σίμων ὁ → Καναναῖος (in next-to-last position, before Judas Iscariot). The Lukan parallels (Luke 6:15; Acts 1:13) call him "Simon the Zealot"; → ζηλωτής 3. J. Blinzler, *LTK* IX, 772f.; J.-A. Morin, *RB* 80 (1973) 332-58.

4. Mark 6:3 par. Matt 13:55 mentions among Jesus' brothers, with Judas, one named Simon (Mark places him in final position, Matthew in next-to-last position). J. Blinzler, *LTK* IX, 765.

5. Simon of Cyrene (→ Κυρηναῖος) is mentioned in the Synoptic Passion story as the one compelled to carry Jesus' cross (Mark 15:21 par. Matt 27:32/Luke 23:26). Only Mark mentions in this context his two sons Alexander and Rufus. J. Blinzler, *LTK* IX, 768.

6. The Fourth Gospel mentions Simon Iscariot as the father of Judas Iscariot (John 6:71; 13:2, 26; cf. 12:4 v.l.); → Ἰσκαριώθ. J. Blinzler, *LTK* IX, 767f.

7. Mark 14:3 par. Matt 26:6 mentions "Simon the leper (ὁ λεπρός)" who lived in Bethany. Before the Passion Jesus was anointed by a woman while a guest in Simon's house. J. Blinzler, *LTK* IX, 764.

8. According to Luke 7:40, 43, 44, a Pharisee named Simon was the host who critically observed the anointing of Jesus by a sinful woman. J. Blinzler, *LTK* IX, 770f.

9. A tanner named Simon from Japho (Joppa) is mentioned in Acts 9:43; 10:6, 17, 32b. Simon Peter was his guest until the messengers of Cornelius brought Peter to Caesarea. E. Haenchen, *Acts* (Eng. tr., 1971) 340, 347.

10. Acts 8:9, 13, 18, 24 tells of a magician/sorcerer (v. 9: μαγεύων) named Simon who lived in Samaria. He came to the Christian faith through Philip and was baptized (v. 13). When he saw that Peter and John could give the Holy Spirit through the laying on of hands he offered to buy such power with money (vv. 18f.). Peter cursed the magician and demanded that he repent (vv. 20-23). Simon then begged the intercession of the apostle (v. 24). Questions concerning the religious-historical evaluation of Simon Magus (the father of Gnosticism?) can hardly be answered with any certainty now.   G. Schneider

Σινᾶ *Sina* Sinai*

The LXX translates the name of Mount *Sinai* with indeclinable Σινᾶ (Exod 16:1; Deut 33:2, and elsewhere). Sinai is the mountain associated with the giving of the law; Acts 7:30 speaks of the wilderness "of Mount Sinai" and locates the divine revelation to Moses there (Exod 3:2). Acts 7:38 uses the LXX phrase ὁ ὄρος Σινᾶ in the context of the giving of the law.

Gal 4:24, 25 distinguishes between the two διαθῆκαι "The one from Mount Sinai bears children for slavery" and is represented by → Ἁγάρ (v. 24). This allegorical interpretation is then explained in v. 25: Hagar is the designation for "Mount Sinai in Arabia." Cf. F. Mussner, *TQ* 135 (1955) 55-60; F. Pastor Ramos, *EstBib* 34 (1975) 113-19; C. K. Barrett, FS Käsemann 1-16 (= Barrett, *Essays on Paul* [1982] 154-70); E. Lohse, *TDNT* VII, 282-87; *TWNT* X, 1264 (bibliography).

σίναπι, εως, τό *sinapi* mustard*

1. Occurrences in the NT — 2. The parable of the mustard seed — 3. The saying about the power of faith

Lit.: E. HAENCHEN, *Der Weg Jesu* (²1968) 180-86. — C.-H. HUNZINGER, *TDNT* VII, 287-91, 758. — JEREMIAS, *Parables* 146-49. — JÜLICHER II, 569-81. — F. KOGLER, *Das Doppelgleichnis*

vom Senfkorn und vom Sauerteig in seiner traditionsgeschichtlichen Entwicklung (FzB 59, 1988). — O. KUSS, "Zum Sinngehalt des Doppelgleichnisses vom Senfkorn und Sauerteig" (1959), *idem* I, 85-97. — R. LAUFEN, "ΒΑΣΙΛΕΙΑ und ΕΚΚΛΗΣΙΑ. Eine traditions- und redaktionsgeschichtliche Untersuchung des Gleichnisses vom Senfkorn," FS Zimmermann 105-40. — G. PACE, "La senapa del Vangelo," *BeO* 22 (1980) 119-23. — J. SCHMID, *Matthäus und Lukas* (BibS[F] 23/2-4, 1930) 102-4, 299-301. — G. SCHNEIDER, *Luke* (ÖTK, 1977) 301-3. — SCHULZ, *Q* 298-309, 465-68. — H. ZIMMERMANN, *Neutestamentliche Methodenlehre* (1976) 123-27. — P. ZINGG, *Das Wachsen der Kirche* (1974) 100-115. — J. ZMIJEWSKI, "Der Glaube und seine Macht," FS Zimmermann 81-103 (on Matt 17:20; 21:21; Mark 11:23; Luke 17:6).

1. Σίναπι occurs 5 times in the NT, all in the Synoptic Gospels: Mark 4:31 par. Matt 13:31/Luke 13:19, in the parable of the mustard seed; Matt 17:20 par. Luke 17:6, in the saying concerning the power of faith. In both instances "the stress is on the smallness of the grain of mustard-seed, which was proverbial in Palestine" (Hunzinger 289).

2. The parable of the mustard seed (Mark 4:30-32 par. Matt 13:31f./Luke 13:18f.) constitutes in Matthew and Luke a unit with the parable of the leaven (Matt 13:33 par. Luke 13:20f.). Both come from Q and were originally transmitted separately, as shown by Mark 4:30-32 and confirmed by *Gos. Thom.* 20, 96.

Mark and Matthew's version are based on a contrasting parable, while Luke maintains the Q form of a growth parable. "Since, however, both forms of the parable conclude by illustrating the *size* of the fully grown mustard shrub with the biblical-proverbial 'dwelling of the birds of the air,' the Q form is probably secondary to the Markan form" (Schneider 303, *contra* Jülicher 571; Schulz 300 n.288; Zingg 102; Laufen 114 is undecided). The contrast between the smallness of the mustard seed and the largeness of the mustard plant stands at the center in Mark. The focus is not on the process of growth; rather, the smallness of the beginning and largeness of the end are contrasted by juxtaposition. Although this aspect of contrast is not suppressed in Luke, that of growth stands in the foreground: A tree emerges from the seed. The smallness of the beginning of God's kingdom is followed inexorably by its greatness at completion. "Behind the parable there clearly lies the claim that the βασιλεία is already present in sign in the contemporary work of Jesus, even though it is now concealed and inconspicuous" (Hunzinger 291).

3. The saying of Jesus about the power of faith appears in three different versions (Mark 11:23 par. Matt 21:21; Matt 17:20; Luke 17:6). The various contexts are secondary, since originally the logion was transmitted separately. The Lukan version is probably original. The assertion is that even faith as tiny as a mustard seed suffices to

uproot a tree as large as a mulberry (not, as in Luke 19:4, a sycamore fig; cf. Hunzinger 758) and plant it in the sea. "The question of more or less faith is set aside [in the Lukan context] by the radical question whether there is faith or unbelief" (Hunzinger 290; cf. Schneider 348). Matt 17:20 places "faith as a grain of mustard seed" over the → ὀλιγοπιστία of the disciples.

E. Palzkill

σινδών, όνος, ἡ *sindōn* linen; shirt*

In the Passion narrative σινδών refers to the *linen shroud* used to wrap the body of Jesus (Mark 15:46 bis par. Matt 27:59/Luke 23:53). In Mark 14:51, 52 σινδών refers to the *linen cloth* of the young man who wanted to follow Jesus, who was clothed only in this linen, but then ran away without it. J. Blinzler, *VD* 34 (1956) 112f.; R. E. Brown, "Brief Observations on the Shroud of Turin," *BTB* 14 (1984) 145-48.

σινιάζω *siniazō* shake in a sieve, sift*

Fig. in Luke 22:31: Satan demanded "to *sift* [the disciples] like wheat," referring particularly to the trial that Jesus' Passion was for the disciples. E. Fuchs, *TDNT* VII, 291f.

σιρικός, 3 *sirikos* silken, silk (adj.)*

Variation in orthography in the older textual witnesses (uncials) for the customary → σηρικός. Rev 18:12: τὸ σιρικόν, *silken* wares.

σιρός, οῦ, ὁ *siros* pit, cave
2 Pet 2:4 ℵ (in place of → σειρά or → σειρός).

σιτευτός, 3 *siteutos* fattened*

Luke 15:23, 27, 30: ὁ μόσχος ὁ σιτευτός, "the *fattened* calf" (cf. Judg 6:28 A; Jer 26:21 LXX).

σιτίον, ου, τό *sition* food*

The diminutive form of σῖτος appears in Acts 7:12 in the pl. and refers to food (from grain); cf. also *Diog.* 6:9.

σιτιστός, 3 *sitistos* fattened*

Matt 22:4: pl. subst., of *fattened* livestock.

σιτομέτριον, ου, τό *sitometrion* measured ration of grain*

Luke 12:42: τὸ σιτομέτριον δίδωμι, "give the *portion of food*."

σῖτος, ου, ὁ *sitos* wheat; grain*

Matt 13:25, 29, of *wheat* among which weeds were sown; Matt 3:12; 13:30; Luke 3:17; 12:18, of the gathering of grain (wheat) into the granary; cf. further Mark 4:28; Luke 16:7; John 12:24; 1 Cor 15:37; Rev 6:6; 18:13; Luke 22:31: the disciples are to be sifted "like *wheat*"; Acts 27:38, of wheat as cargo on a ship. G. Ürögdi, *KP* V, 217-19.

Σιχάρ *Sichar* Sychar
A secondary form of → Συχάρ used in John 4:5 69 vg^{ww}.

Σιών *Siōn* Zion*

1. Occurrences in the NT — 2. OT and later tradition — 3. NT usage

Lit.: R. BACH, *BHH* 2224f. — W. BAIER, *BL* 1600f. — G. FOHRER and E. LOHSE, *TDNT* VII, 292-338, esp. 327ff. — H. GESE, "Der Davidsbund und die Zionserwählung," *idem, Vom Sinai zum Zion* (BEvT 64, 1974) 113-29. — *idem, Essays on Biblical Theology* (1981), index s.v. — KOPP, *Places* 323-34, 403f. — E. OTTO, *Jerusalem—die Geschichten der Heiligen Stadt* (Urban-Taschenbücher 308, 1980) 184-88. — N. W. PORTEOUS, "Jerusalem — Zion: The Growth of a Symbol," *Verbannung und Heimkehr* (FS W. Rudolph, 1961) 235-52. — VON RAD, *Theology* II, 155-69, 292-97. — W. SCHMAUCH, *Orte der Offenbarung und der Offenbarungsort im NT* (1956) 55-57, 114-21. — J. SCHREINER, *Sion—Jerusalem, Jahwes Königssitz* (SANT 7, 1963). — H. SCHULZ, *DNTT* II, 324-30. — F. STOLZ, *THAT* II, 543-51. — S. ZIMMER, *Zion als Tochter, Frau und Mutter* (Diss. Munich, 1959). — For further bibliography → Ἱεροσόλυμα; see also *TWNT* X, 1264f.

1. The name Σιών appears 7 times in the NT (Ἱεροσόλυμα/Ἱερουσαλήμ in contrast appears 139 times), 5 times in OT quotations or allusions: θυγάτηρ Σιών (Matt 21:5; John 12:15; cf. Zech 9:9; Isa 62:11), τίθημι ἐν Σιὼν λίθον (Rom 9:33; 1 Pet 2:6; cf. Isa 8:14; 28:16), ἥξει ἐκ Σιὼν ὁ ῥυόμενος (Rom 11:26; cf. Isa 59:20; Ps 13:7 LXX). Only Heb 12:22 (προσεληλύθατε Σιὼν ὄρει) and Rev 14:1 (ἐπὶ τὸ ὄρος Σιών) are freely formulated (cf., however, Joel 3:5; Isa 4:5).

2. In the topographical sense Σιών (Heb. ṣiyyôn, uncertain etymology; cf. Fohrer 294f.) originally designated the southeast hill of Jerusalem, the site of an ancient Canaanite settlement (occasionally called "Jebus/the Jebusite city," Josh 15:8; 18:28; Judg 19:10f.; 1 Chr 11:4) conquered by David and then called "the city of David" (2 Sam 5:6-9; 1 Kgs 8:1; 1 Chr 11:5-7; 2 Chr 5:2). David resided there in a fortress (1 Chr 11:7). The older, real name of the Canaanite settlement (and the city-state associated with it), "Jerusalem," was then also used for the city area expanded beyond the city of David after David's death (1 Kgs 9:15; 11:42; cf. the construction of the temple and palace under Solomon on the summit of Ophel situated to the north of Zion and somewhat higher: 1 Kgs 3:1; 8:1ff.; also Mic 4:8).

Zion receded as a topographical term, but was again used frequently in a later period, and then (often poetically) with an expanded meaning, referring to the Temple Mount or to the entire city of Jerusalem, particularly in the prophets (and among them esp. Isaiah, Jeremiah, Joel, Micah, and Zechariah— not in Ezekiel, Hosea, Nahum, Habakkuk, Haggai, or Malachi) and in the Psalms and Lamentations. "Zion" thus refers over 40 times to all Jerusalem (cf. Mic 3:10, 12), it is God's sanctuary (Ps 20:3), his holy mount and residence (Joel 2:1; 4:17, 21; Pss 9:12; 65:2; 76:3; 87:1ff.; 99:2), his city (Isa 60:14; Ps 48:3); Zion is also a term for Israel (Isa 46:13; 51:16; 59:20; Ps 149:2; Lam 1:17) or Judah (Jer 14:19). Particularly in the post-exilic period Jerusalem is often called "Zion" as the city of anticipated salvation (cf. 2 Kgs 19:31; Isa 18:7; 24:23; 35:10; 49:14ff.; 52:1, 8; 59:20; 62:1; 66:8; Zech 1:14ff.; 2:10; 8:3; 9:9; Ps 102:17) to which the nations will flow together (cf. Isa 2:2-4; 18:7; Ps 102:23; also 2 Bar. 68:5; Sib. Or. v.251f.) and from which God will carry out his judgment (Joel 4:16ff.). While the name "Jerusalem" can represent both the political and eschatological aspects of the city, the name "Zion" evokes, particularly after the exile, the aspect of salvation more strongly: Zion is above all the locus of the Temple Mount or of the Temple itself and its cult, the seat of God, the symbol of Israel, and finally the object of eschatological hope.

During the Jewish and Christian period Zion (along with the city of David) was thought to be located on the southwest hill of Jerusalem (cf. Josephus B.J. v.137). There the basilica ʿΑγία Σιών was erected around the middle of the 4th cent. and there, later, tradition located the sites of Jesus' Last Supper, of the assembly of the primitive Church (Acts 1:13), of the events of Pentecost, and of Stephen's and David's tombs (see further Kopp, Otto). In actual fact tradition does provide evidence that one (or the) center of the primitive Jerusalem church might have been located here (Otto 160-86; W. Baier, BL 299f.).

3. In the NT the name Σιών plays a subordinate role in relation to "Jerusalem." Matt 21:5 and John 12:15 insert into the narrative of Jesus' entry into Jerusalem a reference to Zech 9:9 addressed to the city (and its inhabitants: θυγάτηρ Σιών; cf. Isa 1:8; 10:32; 62:11; Jer 4:31; Zech 2:11 [θυγάτερ Βαβυλῶνος], 14; Lam 2:8) as the Israel of the promises (see also Mic 4:8; Zeph 3:14). In Rom 9:33 and 1 Pet 2:6 Σιών (as already in Isa 28:16) as the center of Israel stands for Israel itself (→ 2; cf. Rom 9:31; 1 Pet 2:8-10); similarly in Rom 11:26 Σιών (as already in Isa 59:20) refers not to Jerusalem as a city but to Israel as God's people (in contrast to Gentile Christians), though Paul replaces lᵉṣîyyôn/ἕνεκεν Σιών (Isa 59:20) with ἐκ Σιών.

Heb 12:22, in a rhetorically structured context (A. Strobel, Heb [NTD] ad loc.) and for the sake of contrasting typology, juxtaposes Mt. Sinai (vv. 18ff.) and ὄρος Σιώς, i.e., the πόλις θεοῦ ζῶντος, Ἰερουσαλὴμ ἐπουράνιος. Believers have access to a superior and enduring revelation, namely, Zion as the living God's heavenly residence, which is not a place of fear (as is Sinai; cf. Exod 20:19; Deut 5:23), but rather of the eschatological festal gathering of the assembly and of the new covenant (Heb 12:23f.). Just as Israel came from Sinai, so also believers on their own journey come from

Zion and the heavenly Jerusalem (cf. vv. 25ff.) and are simultaneously still on their way to this goal (cf. 13:14; → Ἰεροσόλυμα 4). Σιών (with "Jerusalem") is a metaphor for eschatological and heavenly salvation.

According to Rev 14:1 the seer sees the "lamb" and with it the 144,000 (God's eschatological people) on ὄρος Σιών, where they are protected from persecution and suffering (cf. ch. 13) and can at the same time hear and learn the "new song" sung in heaven (14:3). Zion is thus where the pious are delivered in time of persecution (cf. 7:1ff.; also Joel 3:5; Ps 125:1). The Messiah's appearance is also anticipated from Zion (cf. 2 Esdr 13:6f., 12, 35f.); it is contrasted with Armageddon, where the enemies of the pious assemble (Rev 16:16). At the end the seer views those rescued on Zion in the heavenly Jerusalem itself (22:3f.; cf. 3:12): He probably thinks of the saving mount Zion as a (still earthly?) prefiguration of the heavenly Jerusalem.

H. Balz

σιωπάω *siōpaō* be silent, become silent*

1. Σιωπάω occurs in the NT only in the Synoptics (10 occurrences, 5 of those in Mark). It has approximately the same meaning as → σιγάω, though it is only intrans. and designates perhaps—beyond mere cessation of speaking—total silence.

2. Jesus' Passion is the most important context in which σιωπάω appears. His silence, usually described by a negative with ἀποκρίνομαι (Mark 14:61; 15:5 par. Matt 27:[12]14; Luke 23:9) or ἀπόκρισις (John 19:9), allows him to appear in the role of the suffering righteous person (cf. Isa 53:7; Pss 37:14-16; 38:9f. LXX). The supplementary use of σιωπάω in Mark 14:61 amplifies this "kerygmatization of the narrative" (R. Pesch, Mark [HTKNT] II, 436); par. Matt 26:63 has σιωπάω alone.

Σιωπάω is also used of the surprised silence of both the adversaries (Mark 3:4) and the disciples (9:34) of Jesus, who usually embarrasses them with a question: οἱ δὲ ἐσιώπων. He silences the storm and sea with a command reminiscent of an exorcism (4:39; cf. 1:25). Just as Jesus "imperiously" rebukes the forces of nature, so also the crowd rebukes the blind (variously ἐπιτιμάω): He (they) should cease crying (10:48 par. Matt 20:31). The Pharisees demand that Jesus silence his disciples' praise (Luke 19:39: ἐπιτίμησον); yet in their place (and in actual fact: cf. Hab 2:11) the stones, i.e., the ruins of Jerusalem, would cry out (19:40). So also Paul will not be intimidated in Corinth (Acts 18:9). In Luke 1:20 σιωπάω refers to silence as punishment (μὴ δυνάμενος λαλῆσαι ἄχρι; cf. Acts 13:11: ἔσῃ τυφλὸς μὴ βλέπων . . . ἄχρι . . .), perhaps (Luke 1:62!) also deafness (so J. G. Anderson, "A New Translation of Luke 1:20," BT 20 [1969] 21-24).

W. Radl

σιωπῇ *siōpē* silently, secretly

The dat. of σιωπή, "silence," was used as an adv. from Homer on. John 11:28 D lat sy^s in place of λάθρᾳ.

σκανδαλίζω *skandalizō* give offense; pass.: reject faith, fall away from faith*

1. Occurrences and meaning — 2. Pass. use — 3. Act. use

Lit.: → σκάνδαλον.

1. Σκανδαλίζω occurs 29 times in the NT, 26 of those in the Gospels (14 in Matthew, 8 in Mark, 2 in Luke, 2 in John) and 3 in the Pauline Epistles. The pre-Christian vb., occurring with fig. meaning only in the LXX, refers to the offense that results in the loss of salvation. Depending on whether or not a person already believes, it refers either to a falling away from or a rejection of faith.

2. a) In the pass. σκανδαλίζω frequently means that a person "does not come to faith." Hence Jesus' relatives *take offense* at him (Mark 6:3 par. Matt 13:57), so that he wonders about their lack of faith (Mark 6:6a) or because of that lack of faith cannot perform many mighty works (Matt 13:58). According to Matt 15:12 the Pharisees *take offense* because Jesus exposes their purity regulations as superficial (15:3-11). In the blessing in connection with the Baptist's inquiry (Matt 11:6 par. Luke 7:23), those are counted as blessed who do not *take offense* at Jesus, i.e., who believe in him.

b) In the pass. σκανδαλίζω more often means, however, "fall away from faith." In the interpretation of the parable of the sower (Mark 4:13-20 par. Matt 13:18-23) those identified with the seeds sown on rocky ground, i.e., those "with no root in themselves," the inconstant ones, go astray to their own ruin when persecuted on account of the word, i.e., they fall away from faith (Mark 4:17 par. Matt 13:21). The Lukan parallel reads appropriately ἀφίστανται (8:13). In Matt 24:10 Jesus predicts that in the end time many will fall away. The result is that they will hate one another, wickedness will be multiplied, and love will grow cold. Yet whoever endures in love until the end will be saved (vv. 11, 13).

Mark 14:27 par. Matt 26:31 shows that such falling away from faith can be merely temporary, since even the disciples will *fall away*. Peter vehemently rejects Jesus' prediction and insists he will under no circumstances go astray (Mark 14:29 par. Matt 26:33b, c). In the Johannine farewell address (John 16:1) σκανδαλίζω does not only imply an "endangering of faith" (*contra* R. Schnackenburg, *John* [Eng. tr., 1982] III, 121), but rather "falling away from faith" entirely, from which the disciples and Christians are to be kept (Stählin, *TDNT* VII, 357; J. Becker, *John* [ÖTK] 493). The actual addressees here

are Jewish Christians (vv. 2-4a). In 2 Cor 11:29 Paul's enumeration of his tribulations and troubles reaches its climax in the rhetorical question, "Who is weak, and I am not weak? Who is *made to fall,* and I am not indignant?" Because Paul also understands σκανδαλίζομαι in the sense of a falling away from faith, he cannot feel solidarity with the person taking offense, as he does with the "weak," but can only express his concern.

3. In the act. σκανδαλίζω means "cause someone to fall away from (or reject) faith," as in the saying of Jesus about the person who "*causes* one of these little ones who believe in me *to sin [stumble]*" (Mark 9:42 par. Matt 18:6 /Luke 17:2). The Christian is enjoined to reject anything that might be an obstacle to faith, as emphasized in Mark 9:43, 45, 47 in metaphorical, hyperbolic language (*contra* Stählin, *TDNT* 352f.): Hand, foot, and eye—in Jewish understanding the loci of lust or sinful desires—must be given up if they threaten to become the cause of loss of faith and thus of salvation. This probably does not refer to self-chastisement as a means of passing judgment (*contra* R. Pesch, *Mark* [HTKNT] II, 115), but underscores rather the seriousness of conviction within which one must persevere if one wishes to enter (eternal) life or the kingdom of God.

Matt 5:29, 30 (Q) also issues an exhortation to decisive action. In relation to adultery the right eye and right hand—the most important members—should be discarded if they are a cause of sin. This challenge is motivated by the threat of eschatological judgment.

Matt 18:8, 9 apparently personifies both hand and foot, which are to be cut off, and the eye, which is to be plucked out, if any of these things causes one to sin or stumble. The reference is to Christians whom the Church should exclude for its own protection (cf. 18:15-18). Jesus justifies his decision to pay the temple tax—even though he actually is free from it—by explaining that he does not wish to *give offense* (Matt 17:27). That is, he wants to prevent the tax collectors from having any reason not to believe in him.

The Johannine speech about the living bread (John 6:51c-59) causes many disciples of Jesus, including Christians in the (Johannine) community, to murmur and take offense at Jesus (6:61), i.e., not to believe (v. 64), since their belief was not "by the Father" (v. 65). According to 1 Cor 8:9 a Christian's freedom regarding eating food offered to idols reaches its limit when it becomes a stumbling block to one's brother (πρόσκομμα). Hence Paul emphasizes that he will never again eat meat if by doing so he causes his brother to fall and thus to lose salvation (σκανδαλίζω, v. 13a, b), since otherwise that weaker brother is destroyed by the knowledge of the "stronger" (v. 11). Whoever sins against his brothers sins also against Christ (v. 12).   H. Giesen

σκάνδαλον, ου, τό *skandalon* enticement to unbelief, cause of salvation's loss, seduction*

1. Occurrences and meaning — 2. Matthew — 3. The rest of the NT

Lit.: H. GIESEN, *Christliches Handeln. Eine redaktionskritische Untersuchung zum* δικαιοσύνη-Begriff *im Matthäusevangelium* (EHS 23/181, 1982) 210-16. — A. HUMBERT, "Essai d'une Théologie du Scandale dans les Synoptiques," *Bib* 35 (1954) 1-28. — H.-S. LIE, *Der Begriff Skandalon im NT und der Wiederkehrgedanke bei Laotse* (EHS 23/24, 1973) 12-122. — J. MATEOS, "Analisis semantico de los Lexemas ΣΚΑΝΔΑΛΙΖΩ ΣΚΑΝΔΑΛΟΝ," *Filologia Neotestamentaria* 2 (1989) 57-92. — K. MÜLLER, *Anstoß und Gericht. Eine Studie zum jüdischen Hintergrund des paulinischen Skandalon-Begriffs* (SANT 19, 1969). — G. STÄHLIN, *Skandalon. Untersuchungen zur Geschichte eines biblischen Begriffs* (BFCT 2/24, 1930). — idem, *TDNT* VI, 339-58. — For further bibliography see *TWNT* X, 1265.

1. Σκάνδαλον occurs 15 times in the NT: 5 times in Matthew, 6 times in the Pauline Epistles, and once each in Luke, 1 Peter, 1 John, and Revelation. It occurs only rarely in extrabiblical writings, and in the NT (as in the LXX, where it usually translates *môqēš* and *mikšôl*) it is used figuratively as a t.t., sometimes in personifications. The original meaning, "trip-stick of a trap," is not documented in literature.

2. Matt 13:41 personifies πάντα τὰ σκάνδαλα (*contra* Lie 44) by identifying the phrase with the "evildoers" (*contra* Stählin, *Skandalon* 147, 149). This citation of Zeph 1:3 is modeled on a text related to the Symmachus recension: σκάνδαλα σὺν τοῖς ἀσεβέσιν. The σκάνδαλα originate with the devil (vv. 38f.); thus they will not pass judgment (v. 42). They are countered by the δίκαιοι (v. 43), the "sons of the kingdom" (v. 38) who owe their existence to the Son of man (v. 37) and will participate in the kingdom of the Father (v. 43). The σκάνδαλα are clearly characterized as eschatological demonic figures and are themselves the cause of their own loss of salvation.

According to Matt 16:23 Peter becomes the personified temptation of Jesus by trying to seduce him, as does Satan (cf. 4:10), into avoiding the way of suffering predestined for him by the Father (v. 22). Within the context of the protection of the "little ones" in the Church, i.e., probably the "weak ones" (18:6-10), Jesus utters an eschatological threat ("woe!") against the world (alienated from God) because of *temptations to sin* (v. 7a); though he allows that such *temptations* must come (v. 7b), he finally hurls an eschatological "woe!" against the person by whom the *temptation* comes (v. 7c). Σκάνδαλον is used here of the temptation to fall away from faith. The parallel, Luke 17:1, like Matt 18:7b, also underscores that such *temptations* are unavoidable; none-

theless, the person by whom they come receives the eschatological "woe!" that already places him under divine judgment.

3. The Pauline Epistles speak frequently of the crucified Christ as a σκάνδαλον. In the course of justifying his thesis that Christ's cross would be robbed of its power were he to preach the gospel with eloquent wisdom (1 Cor 1:17), Paul shows that proclamation of the crucified Messiah is a σκάνδαλον to Jews leading to eschatological ruin, and folly (μωρία, v. 23) to the Gentiles also bringing disaster. Jews and Gentiles, by accepting in faith the folly of the proclamation (of the cross; v. 21), not relying on their own accomplishments (v. 22), and showing themselves to be called (by God), experience the crucified Messiah as the power of God that raises the dead (v. 24; cf. v. 18b) and the wisdom of God (v. 24) that makes foolish the world's wisdom (v. 20d). In Gal 5:11 circumcision (law) and the "*stumbling block* of the cross"—probably as in 1 Cor 1:23 the only source of salvation—stand over against one another. If Paul were still preaching circumcision, he would be robbing the cross of its eschatological-critical power.

According to the hybrid citation in Rom 9:33 (Isa 28:16; 8:14) God caused Israel to stumble on Christ. Nonetheless, rejection of Christ by Israel, which pursued righteousness based on the law (v. 31) instead of allowing it to be given through faith in Christ (vv. 30, 32, 33), stands in the foreground. That is why Christ is a "stumbling stone" (λίθος προσκόμματος) for Israel and "a stone that will make them stumble" (πέτρα σκανδάλου), leading to a rejection of faith. 1 Pet 2:8 uses the same hybrid citation to threaten unbelievers for the sake of strengthening believers in persevering in their decision for Christ.

According to Rom 11:9 (quoting Ps 68:23 LXX) the sacrificial cult will become a *pitfall* of ruin for the Jews; for the "[feast] table" is not merely the communion of fellowship (so, e.g., H. Schlier, *Rom* [HTKNT] 325), but rather an object from which Israel expects salvation. Rabbinic tradition understands the "table" as an altar with the power of atonement (cf. also 1 Cor 10:21; also Müller 23-27).

In Rom 14:13 Paul admonishes the "strong," whose position he fundamentally shares (v. 14), not to cause the "weak" any *stumbling block to faith* through eating habits, as shown by the hendiadys πρόσκομμα ἢ σκάνδαλον, though also by v. 15c (ἀπόλλυμι). In Rom 16:17 the σκάνδαλα are the various satanic activities of the false teachers who endanger the salvation of Church members, who are being seduced into falling away from correct teaching; such teachers also threaten both the unity and very existence of the Church. Similarly, in Rev 2:14 σκάνδαλον refers to a *stumbling block* to faith in the context of false teaching.

According to 1 John 2:10 there is no *cause for stumbling or sin* in a believer who loves his brother (not: "in the realm of light," *contra* R. Schnackenburg, *1–3 John* [HTKNT] 115), i.e., no cause for unbelief and thus a loss of salvation. The theme of the incapacity of the Christian for sin is touched on here (cf. esp. 3:9).   H. Giesen

σκάπτω *skaptō* dig; dig around*

Luke 16:3, in a proverbial phrase: "I am not strong enough to *dig*"; 6:48, with βαθύνω (cf., however, Matt 7:24); 13:8: *digging around* a fig tree.

Σκαριώθ *Skariōth* Iscariot

V.l. of D in Mark 3:19; John 6:71. Elsewhere (Matt 10:4; 26:14; Mark 14:10) D reads Σκαριώτης. → Ἰσκαριώθ.

σκάφη, ης, ἡ *skaphē* boat*

The lifeboat (skiff) on a larger ship (Acts 27:16, 30, 32).

σκέλος, ους, τό *skelos* thigh*

John 19:31, 32, 33, in reference to the *crurifragium*, the breaking of Jesus' leg bones in order to hasten death.

σκέπασμα, ατος, τό *skepasma* covering*

This noun can refer to either *clothing* or a *house*. 1 Tim 6:8: "But if we have food and *clothing,* with these we shall be content."

Σκευᾶς, ᾶ *Skeuas* Sceva*

A personal name corresponding to Lat. *Scaeva.* According to Acts 19:14 a Jewish high priest had this name. B. A. Mastin, *JTS* 27 (1976) 405-12.

σκευή, ῆς, ἡ *skeuē* equipment, gear*

Acts 27:19, of the (expendable) *equipment* of the ship that the sailors threw into the sea. E. Haenchen, *Acts* (Eng. tr., 1971) ad loc.

σκεῦος, ους, τό *skeuos* object, vessel, instrument*

1. Occurrences in the NT, basic meanings — 2. Literal use — 3. Metaphorical and fig. use

Lit.: BAGD s.v. — LSJ s.v. — C. MAURER, *TDNT* VII, 358-67. — PREISIGKE, *Wörterbuch* II, 468f. — J. WHITTON, "A Neglected Meaning for σκεῦος in 1 Thess 4:4," *NTS* 28 (1982) 142f.

1. Σκεῦος occurs 23 times in the NT, equally dis-

tributed in twelve of the NT writings. Compared with secular Greek usage (known from the classical period, common in papyri) and the LXX (usually translating Heb. *kᵉlî*), NT usage betrays neither a significant change in meaning nor a narrowing to any one identifiable meaning. Σκεῦος invariably refers to objects of all kinds and can also be used metaphorically.

2. In Mark 11:16 σκεῦος means quite generally "anything" ("any vessel," according to Maurer 362) if the passage protests against the profanation of the temple building by its use as a shortcut (for porters?). If on the other hand Mark is involved in criticism of the cult itself, σκεῦος—as frequently in the LXX—is to be understood as (any kind of) cultic vessel or object (cf. R. Pesch, *Mark* [HTKNT] II, 198; J. Gnilka, *Mark* [EKKNT] II, 129; according to J. M. Ford, *Bib* 57 [1976] 249-53, "money bag"). In any case, the σκεύη τῆς λειτουργίας in Heb 9:21 are "equipment of the cult" (cf. Exod 40:9; Lev 8:11). In Acts 27:17 the reference is to an object belonging to a ship's equipment—probably an anchor (cf. Pap. Zenon 6.10; Preisigke, *Sammelbuch* III, 6712). Pl. τὰ σκεύη often refers collectively to one's *goods* or *possessions,* as in Mark 3:27 par. Matt 12:29/Luke 17:31 (here probably *household items;* cf. Lysias xix.31).

More frequently the meaning is *vessel.* A *vessel* filled with vinegar stood under the cross (John 19:29), and an unidentified *vessel* replaces the Markan "bushel" in Luke 8:16 (par. Mark 4:21: μόδιος). Peter saw a *vessel* that was difficult to describe ("like a great sheet"; cf. the v.l. documenting incomprehension here) in his vision (Acts 10:11, 16; 11:5). Rev 18:12, recalling Ezek 27:12ff., enumerates *vessels* made of precious materials, and 2 Tim 2:20 distinguishes between *vessels* of precious materials and those of inferior materials and between their respective uses.

3. The NT uses σκεῦος metaphorically or figuratively several times. According to "the one who conquers" (Rev 2:27, quoting Ps 2:9; cf. also *Pss. Sol.* 17:23), the ἔθνη are given over like breakable "earthen *pots*" (τὰ σκεύη τὰ κεραμικά) to those reigning with Christ in the end time. One metaphor common both in Hellenistic and Jewish tradition is that of the human person or the human body as a vessel, often an unsuitable vessel (Artemidoros Daldianus v.25; Seneca *Marc.* 10.13; Epictetus *Diss.* iii. 24.33; 1QH 4:9; *b. Taʿan.* 7a). This lies behind both the parenesis in 1 Thess 4:4 (each should τὸ ἑαυτοῦ σκεῦος κτᾶσθαι ἐν ἁγιασμῷ καὶ τιμῇ, "possess his *body* in holiness and honor"; cf. O. Merk, *Handeln aus Glauben* [1968] 46f.; J. Whitton, *NTS* 28 [1982] 142f.) and the metaphor in 2 Cor 4:7 of the gospel (of the διακονία τῆς δόξης according to R. Bultmann, *2 Cor* [Eng. tr., 1985] 112) as the treasure "in earthen (ὀστρακίνοις) *vessels*" (referring to the weak and unimpressive corporeality of the gospel's

proclaimers, Paul and his companions; cf. 1 Cor 1:26–2:5). In the household code in 1 Pet 2:18–3:12, following rabbinic language (Billerbeck III, 632f.), the woman is described as the weaker *vessel* (3:7); the suggestion is repeatedly made to understand σκεῦος as "woman" also in 1 Thess 4:4 (see Maurer 365-67).

An OT motif (cf. esp. Isa 29:16; Wis 15:7) lies behind the metaphor of the potter in Rom 9:20-24, which demonstrates God's freedom in both wrath and mercy. Two separate groups of human beings are juxtaposed here: unbelieving Jews and God's people composed of Jews and Gentiles. They are contrasted as ὃ μὲν εἰς τιμὴν σκεῦος, ὃ δὲ εἰς ἀτιμίαν (σκεῦος), "one *vessel* for beauty, and another for menial use" (v. 21) and as σκεύη ὀργῆς . . . εἰς ἀπώλειαν and σκεύη ἐλέους . . . εἰς δόξαν, "vessels of wrath made for destruction, vessels of mercy made for glory" (vv. 22f.), i.e., as works always subject to the free power of their creator (cf. U. Wilckens, *Rom* [EKKNT] II, 198-206 ad loc.; A. T. Hanson, *TS* 32 [1981] 433-43). This metaphor is picked up in 2 Tim 2:20 and parenetically transferred into a polemic against heresy: Whoever distances himself from heretical practices becomes a σκεῦος εἰς τιμήν, but the heretics are (σκεύη) εἰς ἀτιμίαν. Finally, in the metaphorical designation of Paul as σκεῦος ἐκλογῆς (Acts 9:15) the instrumental character of σκεῦος predominates; Paul is an *instrument* selected for a certain purpose (namely, for mission work; concerning human beings as the instruments of others cf. also Polybius frag. xiii.5.7; xv.25.1).

E. Plümacher

σκηνή, ῆς, ἡ *skēnē* tent, booth*

1. Occurrences and meaning — 2. The σκηναί at the Transfiguration — 3. The eternal habitations (Luke 16:9) — 4. The heavenly tent in Hebrews and Revelation

Lit.: A. ALT, "Zelte und Hütten," *Alttestamentliche Studien* (FS F. Nötscher; BBB 1, 1950) 16-25. — T. FISCHER, *Die himmlischen Wohnungen. Untersuchungen zu Joh 14,2f* (EHS 23/38, 1975) 115-229. — K. GOLDAMMER, "Elemente des Sc amanismus im AT," *Ex Orbe Religionum* (Studia G. Widengren, 1972) II, 266-85. — O. HOFIUS, *Katapausis* (WUNT 11, 1970) 59-74. — *idem, Der Vorhang vor dem Thron Gottes* (WUNT 14, 1972) 50-73. — *idem,* "Das 'erste' und das 'zweite' Zelt," *ZNW* 61 (1970) 271-77. — W. Michaelis, *TDNT* VII, 368-81. — J. M. NÜTZEL, *Die Verklärungserzählung im Markusevangelium* (FzB 6, 1973) 122-41. — For further bibliography see *TWNT* X, 1265f.

1. Σκηνή occurs 20 times in the NT, 10 of those in Hebrews. In the LXX it translates words for several types of shelter that (from a cultural-historical perspective) fall "beneath" that provided by a house (cf. Heb 11:9: Abraham's faith is manifested by his "dwelling" in tents, whereby he remains open to God's promise); it refers esp. to the *tent* and *booth* (on the cultural and historical dis-

tinctions cf. Alt). Σκηνή is particularly the designation for the tabernacle of levitical sacrificial worship (Heb 13:10; Acts 7:43, of a Gentile sacrificial tent). On this basis Hebrews and Revelation penetrate through to the inherent level of the heavenly tabernacle (cf. also Acts 7:44). The rebuilding of the "dwelling of David" (Acts 15:16)— originally the splendid royal tabernacle in the field— refers in Luke to the messianic renewal of God's people and the gathering of the nations.

2. In Mark 9:5 par. Matt 17:4/Luke 9:33, does Peter want to hold fast to the heavenly glory, and is his suggestion to build booths an allusion to the Feast of Tabernacles? (Cf. Nützel 126-34; Michaelis 379-81 on the discussion.) The reference to the biblically central scene at Sinai is unmistakable: Through these booths, analogous to the tabernacles, the heavenly glory will have a locus for appearance (on the phrase "booths of heavenly glory" cf. A. Jellinek, *Beth ha Midrasch* [³1967] V, 179, ll. 5f.). In religious history both the σκηναί and the Mosaic tent recall shamanistic temple yurts (cf. Goldammer 272, who also illuminates other motifs).

3. The "eternal habitations" in Luke 16:9 correspond to the dwelling in σκηναί of the righteous (*T. Abr.*, recension A, ch. 20), of the martyrs (*Mart. Andr.* [Coptic Papyrus Utrecht 1, pp. 13f.]), and of the eschatologically renewed Israel (2 Esdr 2:11). Jewish tradition also speaks of baldachins and heavenly dwellings (cf. Fischer, esp. 227f.; Billerbeck II, 221; Levy II, 92; Jellinek, *Beth ha Midrasch* II, 52; III, 133; V, 42, 45, 47); on this complex cf. also John 14:2 and → σκῆνος.

4. Heb 8:2, 5 concludes from the derivation of the tabernacle from a heavenly prototype according to Exod 25:40 that there is "a true tent (tabernacle)," i.e., a place for the cult, in heaven set up by God himself (on this set of ideas cf. Hofius, *Vorhang* 4-19). The identifying features of the heavenly sanctuary over against the earthly one of the old covenant are, first, it is ἐν τοῖς οὐρανοῖς (it belongs to the celestial world), indeed, its holy of holies is in οὐρανός (9:24; on the distinction in Hebrews between σκηνή, the sanctuary in its totality, and τὰ ἅγια, the holy of holies in the σκηνή, cf. Hofius, *Vorhang* 56-73, esp. 71), i.e., it is in the highest heaven, so that God's residence is cultically qualified (cf. Hofius 70f.); second, it is "true," i.e., it qualifies history as both heavenly and eschatological; third, it is greater and more perfect and thus corresponds to its heavenly purpose (9:11). In contrast, the earthly sanctuary is merely a shadow-copy to which one looks back from an eschatological perspective (8:5; 9:11).

The distinction between a "first" and "second" tent so decisive for the context of Hebrews 9 (vv. 2, 3, 6, 21) is reflected philologically and technically in the distinction between a πρῶτον and a δεύτερον οἶκος in Josephus *B.J.* v.193ff. (cf. Hofius, "Zelt" 274f.). This refers to the first and second part of the tent and thus to the separation of the sanctuary from the holy of holies. Recalling the closed access to the holy of holies in the earthly cultic tent, Christ entered once and for all through the heavenly sanctuary into the holy of holies by means of his own blood, and now is seated there at God's right hand (9:8-10; 8:1): His crucifixion thus becomes an eschatological heavenly event. This cosmological doctrine of the tent in Hebrews is not influenced by Gnosticism; it serves rather, in the sense of Jewish cult apocalyptic, to interpret christology and the doctrine of reconciliation from within the heavenly and eschatological dimension—two categories that in the NT period manifest almost exclusively cultic characteristics.

This is also true of the temple doctrine of Revelation. The heavenly sanctuary is the origin of salvation history (15:5ff. and elsewhere)—hence also the blasphemy of the beast is directed against the heavenly sanctuary (13:6) —and eschatological salvation means the completion of the previously cultically circumscribed salvation gifts (21:3-8; 21:23–22:4; cf. Heb 8:2). The christological background for the teaching regarding Christ as high priest in Hebrews (and as the lamb in Revelation) lies in the early Christian tradition of the Son and the Son of man (cf. O. Michel, *Heb* [KEK] 143ff.): The Son belongs in the house of the Father; as this is expressed cultic-apocalyptically, he belongs in the heavenly tent.

J.-A. Bühner

σκηνοπηγία, ας, ἡ   *skēnopēgia*   Feast of Tabernacles*

Σκηνοπηγία derives from σκηνή and πήγνυμι, and thus means the setting up of a tent and thence the *Feast of Tabernacles*, e.g., Deut 16:16 (and elsewhere in the LXX): ἡ ἑορτὴ τῆς σκηνοπηγίας. This feast is celebrated between the fifteenth and twentieth days of the month of Tishri. Billerbeck II, 774-812. In the NT it is mentioned in John 7:2 (and 5:1 v.l.): "the Jews' feast ἡ σκηνοπηγία." W. Michaelis, *TDNT* VII, 390-92; S. Safrai, in *The Jewish People in the First Century* II (Compendia 1/2, 1976) 812f., 894-96.

σκηνοποιός, οῦ, ὁ   *skēnopoios*   tentmaker*

Acts 18:3, of Aquila and Priscilla, with whom Paul stayed and worked in Corinth, "because he was of the same trade . . . for by trade they were tentmakers." Cf. 1 Cor 4:12; 1 Thess 2:9. Billerbeck II, 745-47; W. Michaelis, *TDNT* VII, 393-94; R. F. Hock, *JBL* 97 (1978) 555-64; *idem, CBQ* 41 (1979) 438-50; *idem, The Social Context of Paul's Ministry: Tentmaking and Apostleship*

(1980); P. Lampe, "Paulus— Zeltmacher," *BZ* 31 (1987) 256-61.

σκῆνος, ους, τό   *skēnos*   tent; body*

Lit.: E. E. ELLIS, "2 Corinthians 5:1-10 in Pauline Eschatology," *NTS* 6 (1959/60) 211-24, esp. 216-19. — F. G. LANG, *2 Kor 5,1-10 in der neueren Forschung* (BGBE 16, 1973) 132-34, 178-85. — W. MICHAELIS, *TDNT* VII, 381-83. — O. MICHEL, "'Ein Bau von Gott.' Fragen zu 2 Kor 5,1," *Wort und Wirklichkeit* (FS E. L. Rapp, 1976) I, 85-89. — For further bibliography see *TWNT* X, 1265f.

Σκῆνος occurs in the NT only in 2 Cor 5:1, 4. Since the basic meaning *tent* hardly comes through, one must assume that the real meaning of the word in this context is *body* (Michaelis 382f.). But Paul himself emphasizes the idea of construction, and for that reason one may not take the question of individual corporeality and the fate of the individual body as the basis for exegesis (as do Ellis and Lang).

One must differentiate between three concentric conceptual circles: 1) The juxtaposition of the earthly tent and the edifice of God in heaven not made by hands corresponds to biblical temple doctrine (→ σκηνή), just as the expectation of being clothed is based on the apocalyptic hope of Zion's transformation (5:4; cf. Isa 2:2; *1 Enoch* 90:28f.; 2 Esdr 10:25ff.). 2) In Qumran (1QS 4:20) and in the NT details about the temple's construction are transferred to the community of faith (1 Cor 3:9; 14:5). 3) The statement about the construction of the individual body is based on these two corporate perspectives (cf. 1QH 7:4, 8; see Michel 87f.). The individual level is thus carried by a cultic ontology taken up by Paul, one transformed, however, into a new ecclesiology by the revelation of Christ: The σῶμα Χριστοῦ constitutes a heavenly-earthly realm of salvation in which the community of those with spiritual gifts participate and into which they will someday enter completely.

In this entire complex σκῆνος interprets transitory earthly-corporeal existence as the shadow and prefiguration of the heavenly-eschatological manner of existence of the redeemed community of God. Both correspondence and distinctions are interwoven, as in aspects of the christological doctrine of the cross and exaltation, but not extrapolated in a linear, historical fashion.

J.-A. Bühner

σκηνόω   *skēnoō*   dwell in a tent; be cultically present*

Lit.: H. GESE, "The Prologue to John's Gospel," *idem, Essays on Biblical Theology* (1981) 167-222. — W. Michaelis, *TDNT* VII, 385-86. — For further bibliography → σκηνή; σκῆνος; see also *TWNT* X, 1265f.

Σκηνόω appears only in John 1:14 and 4 times in

Revelation. The meaning *dwell in a tent* is determined by the traditio-historical precedence of the OT, as is the meaning of → σκηνή. In the OT *šākan* (cf. rabbinic *š^ekînâ*) is used of God's revelation as an "indwelling" in a "tent" (cf. Gese 204).

Thus John 1:14 understands the incarnation of the Logos not merely as the eschatological fulfillment of prophetic logos-revelation, but rather as the transcendence of the doctrine of God's earthly-cultic presence (for the analogous interpretation in the wisdom tradition cf. Sir 24:8): God's revealed glory (on δόξα, χάρις, and ἀλήθεια as divine predicates cf. Gese 204f.) finds its eschatological form in an earthly, historically limited life. Σκηνόω thus does not emphasize the temporary change of location of the heavenly λόγος; rather, the actual incarnation discloses its eschatological form of revelation: The earthly Jesus, whom the Gospel of John also identifies in a summary focussed on the cross as the "lamb of God" (1:29, 36), reveals the form of the Logos and thus of God (cf. 12:45; 14:9) once and for all, including in the heavenly-eschatological dimension (cf. Rev 19:13; 21:22f., 27; 22:1, 3). Ἐσκήνωσεν ἐν ἡμῖν stands over against the existence of the μονογενὴς θεός at the breast of the Father in a relationship of correspondence and identity expressed in a weakened form of the analogous difference inherent in the relationships οἰκία τοῦ σκήνους and οἰκοδομὴ ἐκ θεοῦ (2 Cor 5:1; cf. E. Haenchen, *John* [Hermeneia] 119).

In addition to the eschatological and enduring cultic dwelling of God (and of the lamb, Rev 21:3, 22) *with* mankind apart from any temple, Revelation also knows of the throne of God *over* the martyrs who have been glorified in heavenly holiness (7:15). In 12:12 (and probably also in 13:6) σκηνόω is used of heavenly participation in the glory of God's σκηνή by those who have been transformed (cf. E. Lohmeyer, *Rev* [HNT] 72, 104, 166).

J.-A. Bühner

σκήνωμα, ατος, τό *skēnōma* tent, dwelling*

Acts 7:46 (Ps 131:5 LXX): the temple as God's *habitation* (on textual criticism see G. Schneider, *Acts* [HTKNT] I, 466f.); 2 Pet 1:13, 14, of the human body: "to be in this *body*" (v. 13), i.e., "to live," and "putting off this *body*" (v. 14), i.e., death. W. Michaelis, *TDNT* VII, 383f.

σκιά, ᾶς, ἡ *skia* shadow; shadowy copy*

1. Occurrences in the NT — 2. Shadow — 3. Shadowy copy

Lit.: H. C. HAHN, *DNTT* III, 553-56. — S. SCHULZ, *TDNT* VII, 394-400. — For further bibliography see *TWNT* X, 1266.

1. The noun σκιά occurs 7 times in the NT: 4 times with the basic meaning *shadow* (Mark 4:32; Acts 5:15 literally, Matt 4:16 and Luke 1:79 fig.) and 3 times with the meaning *shadowy copy* (Col 2:17; Heb 8:5; 10:1).

2. Σκιὰ θανάτου, "*shadow* of death," in Matt 4:16 (citing Isa 9:1) refers to the alienation of God from the Gentiles, to whom the messianic savior promised in Isa 9:1ff. appears in Jesus. In Luke 1:78f., equally messianic and dependent on the OT texts Num 24:17; Isa 9:1; Mal 3:20; and Ps 106:10, 14 LXX, σκιὰ θανάτου is a metaphor for subjection to sin and death: Jesus, the "light dawning upon us from on high," brings forgiveness and peace to those lost in sin (v. 77).

Σκιὰ θανάτου occurs several times in the LXX and renders Heb. *ṣlmwt,* which was probably originally read *ṣalmût* (or *ṣalmôt*) = "darkness, gloom." The Masoretic pointing *ṣalmāwet* understands the word—as does the LXX and Targum (*ṭûlā' d^emôṭā'*)—as a compound of *ṣēl* ("shadow") and *māwet* ("death").

3. Σκιά can refer to the *shadow* of an object and hence a mere "copy" in contrast to the reality or true and essential being. Philo uses the contrasting pair σκιά/σῶμα, i.e., "copy" and "prototype" (e.g., *Migr.* 12; *Her.* 72; cf. *Conf.* 190).

In the NT this usage appears in Col 2:17. The false teachers of Colossae demand adherence to the OT food and festival regulations, which they regarded as necessary for salvation (v. 16). The author of the letter counters this by emphasizing that these regulations are "only a *shadowy copy* of what is to come [according to the OT]; but the substance [of salvation] belongs [only] to Christ." The author is unmoved by the question of the extent to which the regulations are "a copy of what is to come." He is concerned only with the assertion that the δόγματα completely lack what is reality in Christ, and are thus meaningless for the believer in Christ (→ δόγμα 4).

Hebrews 8:5 (cf. 9:23f.) describes the tent-sanctuary erected by Moses (→ σκηνή 4) as a mere "copy" (→ ὑπόδειγμα) and "shadow" (σκιά) of the "pattern" mentioned in Exod 25:40 (→ τύπος), i.e., of the heavenly sanctuary (Heb 8:2; 9:11). Analogously, according to 10:1 the sacrificial cult prescribed by the Torah of Sinai represents merely a *shadow* (σκιά) pointing toward the "true form" (→ εἰκών 4) of the eschatological atonement events corresponding to God's salvation will. This means that the rites performed in the earthly sanctuary could not and were not intended to effect atonement and forgiveness of sins (7:11, 19a; 9:6ff.; 10:1ff., 11); their significance consisted in revealing human sinfulness, the alienation of the sinner from God, and the necessity of atonement and the removal of sins (10:1ff.). The saving atonement has been realized in the unique and once-for-all self-sacrifice of the high priest Jesus, who offered his own blood in the heavenly holy of holies before God

(8:1f.; 9:11ff.; 10:10ff., 19ff.). Now that the "reality" of salvation has appeared in Christ, the time of the "copies" is over (8:13; 10:8f., 18).

            O. Hofius

σκιρτάω *skirtaō* spring, leap, jump*

Luke 6:23, of *leaping* as an expression of joy (cf., however, par. Matt 5:12); Luke 1:41, 44, of the (joyous) movements of the child in the womb (cf. v. 15: from the womb onward John is "filled with the Holy Spirit"). G. Fitzer, *TDNT* VII, 401f.

σκληροκαρδία, ας, ἡ *sklērokardia* hardness of heart*
σκληρός, 3 *sklēros* hard, rough*
σκληρότης, ητος, ἡ *sklērotēs* hardness, stubbornness*

1. Occurrences in the NT — 2. Meanings — 3. Σκληροκαρδία and σκληρότης — 4. Σκληρός

Lit.: U. BECKER, *DNTT* II, 153-56. — J. BEHM, *TDNT* III, 613f. — K. BERGER, "Hartherzigkeit und Gottes Gesetz. Die Vorgeschichte des antijüdischen Vorwurfs in Mc 10,5," *ZNW* 61 (1970) 1-47. — idem, *Die Gesetzesauslegung Jesu* (WMANT 40, 1972) 508-75, 579. — K. L. and M. A. SCHMIDT, *TDNT* V, 1028-31. — G. SCHNEIDER, "Jesu Wort über die Ehescheidung in der Überlieferung des NT," *TTZ* 80 (1971) 65-87. — A. S. VAN DER WOUDE, *THAT* II, 689-92. — For further bibliography see the commentaries; → πωρόω.

1. Σκληροκαρδία appears in Mark 10:5 par. Matt 19:8 and Mark 16:14, σκληρότης only in Rom 2:5. The adj. σκληρός is used of a person in Matt 25:24 and in 4 other instances (Acts 26:14; John 6:60; Jude 15; Jas 3:4) in a neutral technical sense.

2. The adj. is used in both secular and biblical writings both literally and figuratively, particularly with reference to divine will. Here the fig. meaning of σκληρότης (already in classical Greek) and σκληροκαρδία (only in the biblical realm) is determined. Use in the NT is determined entirely from OT and early Jewish statements. Recalling such adj. constructions as σκληρὸς τὴν καρδίαν (Prov 28:14) or σκληροκάρδιοι (Ezek 3:7), the LXX uses the neologism σκληροκαρδία in the demand (Deut 10:16; Jer 4:4) to circumcise "the foreskin of your heart" (so MT). The rebuke of "foreskin [uncircumcision] of the heart" is a topos of the deuteronomistic-prophetic (and, dependent on it, of early Jewish) conversion and repentance preaching: Israel "stubbornly" refuses to listen to God. The NT "Christianizes" this rebuke by directing it, in the manner of Jewish intramural polemics (esp. from Qumran), against "the Jews" (Mark 10:5 par.); so also in the hendiadys in Rom 2:5 ("by your hard and impenitent heart"); cf. Acts 7:51, where uncircumcision in heart and ears metaphorically underscores the rebuke of dis-obedience, i.e., refusal to believe (in *T. Sim.* 6:2 σκληροτραχηλία is parallel to σκληροκαρδία). This anti-Jewish usage, which is analogous to other "stubbornness sayings" in the NT, is continued in the early Church—in contrast to Christian intramural parenetic use (as witnessed by Mark 16:14).

3. In the dispute concerning divorce (Mark 10:2-9) Jesus' prohibition, despite the objection presented by Deut 24:1-4, is defended by the assertion that regulation concerning the divorce certificate is discredited as an accommodation (on the use of πρός see Berger, *Gesetzesauslegung* 541f. n.1; → πρός 2.d) to Israel's disobedience to God, disobedience continuing unbroken from the beginning (v. 5: "for your *hardness of heart*"). The same objection in Matt 19:8 (on the restructuring of the Markan-material in Matt 19:3-9 see Schneider 82f.) addresses the practice of divorce ἐπὶ πορνείᾳ.

Rom 2:5 focuses on the rebuke of hardness of heart that, according to Paul's understanding of Christ, applies automatically to Jews who do not believe in Christ (and who are thus not prepared to repent), and relates it to the inevitability of judgment. Mark 16:14 attacks Christian unbelief despite previous resurrection witnesses.

4. When "many of Jesus' disciples" describe his speech regarding the bread of life as *hard* (John 6:60), the motif of unbelief is resonant, just as it is in Jude 15 (the *harsh* things said by the ungodly; see [Greek] *1 Enoch* 1:9) and probably also in Christ's words to the the persecutor Paul (Acts 26:14). The adj. is used without religious implications in Matt 25:24 ("a *hard* man"); Jas 3:4 ("*hard [strong]* winds").

            P. Fiedler

σκληρός, 3 *sklēros* hard, rough
→ σκληροκαρδία (4).

σκληρότης, ητος, ἡ *sklērotēs* hardness, stubbornness
→ σκληροκαρδία.

σκληροτράχηλος, 2 *sklērotrachēlos* stiff-necked, stubborn*

Acts 7:51, at the conclusion of Stephen's speech: "you *stiff-necked* people, uncircumcised in heart and ears" (cf. Deut 9:6, 13 and elsewhere in the LXX); cf. → σκληροκαρδία 2. K. L. and M. A. Schmidt, *TDNT* V, 1029; U. Becker, *DNTT* II, 153, 155.

σκληρύνω *sklērynō* harden, make stubborn*

Act. with God as subj. in Rom 9:18: *harden the heart* (of someone); with human beings as subj. in Heb 3:8, 15; 4:7: *harden* one's heart. Pass. in Acts 19:9; Heb 3:13:

become stubborn, unyielding. K. L. and M. A. Schmidt, *TDNT* V, 1030f.; U. Becker, *DNTT* II, 153-56.

σκολιός, 3 *skolios* crooked*

Literal (with antonym εὐθύς) in Luke 3:5; fig. *(crooked, false)* in Acts 2:40; Phil 2:15: "this *crooked* generation"; 1 Pet 2:18: *perverse* δεσπόται, to whom (just as to the "kind") obedience is due. G. Bertram, *TDNT* VII, 403-8.

σκόλοψ, οπος, ὁ *skolops* stake, splinter, thorn*

This noun is used esp. of (various) irritating foreign bodies (BAGD s.v.). Paul alludes to his own malady in 2 Cor 12:7: "A *thorn* was given me in the flesh" (σκόλοψ τῇ σαρκί). The more specific significance of this σκόλοψ cannot be determined with certainty. G. Delling, *TDNT* VII, 409-13; *TWNT* X, 1266 (bibliography); D. M. Park, *NovT* 22 (1980) 179-83 (with the interpretation *stake*).

σκοπέω *skopeō* look out, watch out for*

With acc. obj. in Paul (Rom 16:17; 2 Cor 4:18; Gal 6:1; Phil 2:4; 3:17). In Gal 6:1 a μή clause follows σκοπῶν σεαυτόν: *"Look to* yourself, lest . . ."* Luke 11:35 uses the vb. without an acc. obj., though with a μή clause in the ind. *(be careful, lest . . .)*. E. Fuchs, *TDNT* VII, 414-16.

σκοπός, οῦ, ὁ *skopos* goal*

Phil 3:14: κατὰ σκοπὸν διώκω, "press on toward the *goal*." E. Fuchs, *TDNT* VII, 413f.; W. Bauder and H. G. Link, *DNTT* II, 52; R. Alpers-Gölz, *Der Begriff σκοπός in der Stoa und seine Vorgeschichte* (1976).

σκορπίζω *skorpizō* scatter; distribute*

John 10:12, of a wolf that *scatters* the sheep; Matt 12:30 par. Luke 11:23 probably also intends this metaphor of a flock being gathered (συνάγω) or *scattered* (σκορπίζω). Pass. in John 16:32: *be scattered,* in Jesus' prediction of the disciples' flight. The meaning *distribute* occurs in 2 Cor 9:9: God *distributed/gave* to the poor (Ps 111:9 LXX). O. Michel *TDNT* VII, 418-22.

σκορπίος, ου, ὁ *skorpios* scorpion*

In similes in Rev 9:3, 5, 10; Luke 10:19: scorpions mentioned with serpents; 11:12: scorpions, after v. 11 has already mentioned serpents.

σκοτεινός, 3 *skoteinos* gloomy, dark*

With the contrasting term φωτεινός in Matt 6:23 par. Luke 11:34, 36. H. Conzelmann, *TDNT* VII, 441; F. Hahn, FS Schmid (1973) 107-38.

σκοτία, ας, ἡ *skotia* darkness*

In the proper sense in Matt 10:27 par. Luke 12:3 (metaphorical); John 6:17; 20:1. In an extended sense, of darkness of the spirit or soul in Matt 4:16 v.l. and frequently in John (1:5a, b; 8:12; 12:35a, b, 46) and 1 John (1:5; 2:8, 9, 11a, b, c). H. Conzelmann, *TDNT* VII, 423-45; H. C. Hahn, *DNTT*, I, 421-25.

σκοτίζομαι *skotizomai* be or become dark, be darkened*

Pass. and literal in Mark 13:24 par. Matt 24:29; Luke 23:45 TR; Acts 8:12; metaphorically of darkening of the heart in Rom 1:21, of the eyes in 11:10 (Ps 68:24 LXX). H. Conzelmann, *TDNT* VII, 423-45.

σκοτόομαι *skotoomai* become dark, darken*

Rev 9:2: the darkening of the sun and air (cf. Job 3:9); 16:9: the kingdom of the "beast"; metaphorical in Eph 4:18: ἐσκοτωμένος τῇ διανοίᾳ. H. Conzelmann, *TDNT* VII, 440, 442.

σκότος, ους, τό *skotos* darkness, gloom*

1. Occurrences in the NT and meaning — 2.a) The Pauline corpus — b) The Gospels and Acts

Lit.: H. CONZELMANN, *TDNT* VII, 423-45. — H. C. HAHN, *DNTT* I, 421-25. — L. R. STACHOWIAK, "Die Antithese Licht—Finsternis. Ein Thema der paulinischen Paränese," *TQ* 143 (1963) 385-422. — For further bibliography see *TWNT* X, 1266.

1. The noun σκότος occurs 31 times in the NT, distributed over 15 different NT documents (John often uses → σκοτία instead of σκότος). Σκότος means *darkness, gloom* and is used in both literal and metaphorical senses, esp. in the Pauline corpus.

2.a) The Pauline writings frequently use σκότος within light-*darkness* symbolism (φῶς—σκότος); in 1 Cor 4:5, e.g., in an enumeration of the duties of the teachers of the gospel, judgment is portrayed as the illumination of what is now hidden in darkness. This light-darkness symbolism also plays a role in 2 Cor 4:6, where Paul describes his own conversion as "one element of that event parallel to creation" (R. Bultmann, *2 Cor* [Eng. tr., 1985] 109): Creation (cf. Gen 1:3; Ps 112:4) and the events of salvation are parallel. In 2 Cor 6:14 (the authenticity of the parenetic section 6:14–7:1 is disputed) φῶς and δικαιοσύνη on the one hand, and σκότος and ἀνομία on the other are related to one another. In the eschatological parenesis in 1 Thess 5:1-11 Paul uses the contrast between light and darkness (v. 5) to describe the two kinds of existence of Christians. V. 4 exhorts Christians not to remain in darkness. Similarly, Rom 13:12 (also parenetic) exhorts its readers to cast off the ἔργα τοῦ σκότους (so also Eph 5:11; cf. also 1 John 1:6, which speaks of walking in darkness). In Rom 2:19 the phrase οἱ ἐν σκότει refers to those without any real knowledge of God.

Within the deutero-Pauline letters Col 1:13 juxtaposes the realms of light and darkness using typical conversion terminology (so also frequently in the Qumran writings: 1QM 1:1, 5, 11; 1QS 1:9; 1QS 2:5, etc.): The Church confesses that a change of sovereignty has occurred: God has delivered its members from the dominion of darkness and transferred them to the kingdom of the Son of his love (cf. 1 Pet 2:9: a calling from darkness into the light). The same terminology used in Col 1:12-14 also appears in Acts 26:18. Eph 5:8 no longers speaks of the antithesis between two realms; rather, the believers are themselves those who were *darkness* and are now light (parenetic: ἦτε γάρ ποτε σκότος, νῦν δὲ φῶς ἐν κυρίῳ), with the conclusion drawn: "Walk as children of light" (cf. 1 Thess 5:4f.; 1 John 1:6). In Eph 6:12 the phrase οἱ κοσμοκράτορες τοῦ σκότους is used of the "world rulers" over whom Christ has already triumphed, but who nonetheless still threaten the lives of believers.

b) Σκότος is used literally of the *eclipse* (of the sun) descending on the earth at the hour of Jesus' crucifixion (Mark 15:33 par. Matt 27:45/Luke 23:44). This darkness is considered an apocalyptic sign anticipating the day of God (cf. Amos 8:9).

Only Matthew uses the phrase εἰς τὸ σκότος τὸ ἐξώτερον (Matt 8:12; 22:13; 25:30). The guest without a wedding garment (22:13) and the worthless servant (25:30) are cast "into the *darkness* outside/into the outermost *darkness*." Here σκότος refers to the eschatological place of punishment (with the same sense in ὁ ζόφος τοῦ σκότους, 2 Pet 2:17; Jude 13). Matt 4:16 and Luke 1:79 both quote Isaiah (cf. Isa 9:2; 42:7), but while the LXX has the fut., Matthew uses the pf.: The prophet's promise has been fulfilled; the people have seen a great light. Σκότος appears further in Matt 6:23 (bis); Luke 11:35; 22:53; Acts 13:11. Peter's Pentecost sermon uses words of the prophet Joel (Acts 2:20: Joel 2:31; cf. 2:10; Isa 13:10): "The sun will be turned into darkness and the moon into blood."

In the Gospel of John σκότος occurs only in 3:19 (→ 1); the antithesis between φῶς and σκότος has theological significance for John (→ σκοτία). This is not, however, any form of cosmological dualism (as is encountered in Gnosticism), but rather a dualism of conviction and decision. Only through the coming of the light—i.e., of him who reveals the light—into the world are human deeds (3:19, 20, 21) revealed as darkness; people have closed themselves off from the light. W. Hackenberg

σκύβαλον, ου, τό *skybalon* refuse, rubbish*

Phil 3:8: πάντα ἡγέομαι σκύβαλα, "I count all things as *refuse*." M. Dibelius, *Phil* [HNT] ad loc.; F. Lang, *TDNT* VII, 445-47; Spicq, *Notes* II, 802-4.

Σκύθης, ου, ὁ *Skythēs* Scythian*

In Hellenism the Scythian was considered the quintessential barbarian. Col 3:11, with βάρβαρος. T. Hermann, *TBl* 9 (1930) 106f.; O. Michel, *TDNT* VII, 447-50; T. T. Rice, *OCD* 968; K. Schefold, *LAW* 2819-21.

σκυθρωπός, (3) 2 *skythrōpos* with a dismal look, with a sad gaze*

This adj. is documented from the time of Aeschylus, including in the LXX and in Hellenistic Judaism. Matt 6:16, of the dismal look accompanying fasting; Luke 24:17, of the sad gaze of the disciples in Emmaus. W. Bieder, *TDNT* VII, 450f.

σκύλλω *skyllō* act.: tire, worry; pass.: trouble oneself*

Act. in Mark 5:35 par. Luke 8:49; pass. in Matt 9:36; Pass. in the sense of *trouble oneself* only in Luke 7:6.

σκῦλον, ου, τό *skylon* booty*

Luke 11:22: σκῦλα διαδίδωμι, "divide the *spoil*."

σκωληκόβρωτος, 2 *skōlēkobrotos* eaten by worms*

Acts 12:23, of Herod Agrippa's sudden fatal illness (cf. Josephus *Ant.* xix.346-50). F. Lang, *TDNT* VII, 456f.; Spicq, *Notes* II, 805f.

σκώληξ, ηκος, ὁ *skōlēx* worm*

Mark 9:48 (Isa 66:24), of the insatiable worms that torment the damned; similarly in 9:44, 46 v.l. F. Lang, *TDNT* VII, 452-56.

σμαράγδινος, 3 *smaragdinos* emerald (adj.)*

Rev 4:3: "an emerald-looking rainbow."

σμάραγδος, ου, ὁ *smaragdos* emerald (noun)*

Rev 21:19 mentions the translucent, light-green jewel among the materials in the foundations of the new Jerusalem. O. Böcher, *Kirche und Bibel* (FS E. Schick, 1979) 19-32.

σμῆγμα, ατος, τό *smēgma* salve
John 19:39 v.l. in place of → σμίγμα or → μίγμα.

σμίγμα, ατος, τό *smigma* salve
John 19:39 v.l. (Ψ 892ˢ pc) in place of → μίγμα.

σμύρνα, ης, ἡ *smyrna* myrrh*

The resin of a shrub indigenous to southern Arabia. Matt 2:11, of a precious gift with gold and frankincense; John 19:39: used with aloe (→ ἀλόη) at the burial of Jesus. W. Michaelis, *TDNT* VII, 457f.

Σμύρνα, ης *Smyrna* Smyrna*

In the NT only Rev 1:11; 2:8 mention this commercial city on the west coast of Asia Minor, though Ignatius of Antioch mentions it more frequently. C. J. Cadoux, *Ancient Smyrna* (1938); B. Kötting, *LTK* IX, 839f.; E. Meyer, *LAW* 2822.

Σμυρναῖος, 3 *Smyrnaios* coming from Smyrna

Subst. (ὁ Σμυρναῖος) pl. in Rev 2:8 TR.

σμυρνίζω *smyrnizō* treat with myrrh*

On the cross Jesus was given "wine *mingled with myrrh*" (Mark 15:23). W. Michaelis, *TDNT* VII, 458f.

Σόδομα, ων, (τά) *Sodoma* Sodom*
Γόμορρα, ων, τά *Gomorra* Gomorrah*

The city Σόδομα, which God destroyed with fire and brimstone because of its sinfulness, is mentioned frequently in the NT with Γόμορρα, which was destroyed with it (Gen 19:1-29; Matt 10:15; Rom 9:29; 2 Pet 2:6; Jude 7; Mark 6:11 TR). Sodom is also mentioned alone (Matt 11:23, 24 par. Luke 10:12; Luke 17:29). Rev 11:8 mentions Sodom with Αἴγυπτος, asserting that "spiritually (πνευματικῶς)" Jerusalem is called "*Sodom* and Egypt." Σόδομα is neut. pl. Γόμορρα is fem. sg. (2 Pet 2:6: ἡ Γόμορρα) or more often, by assimilation to Σόδομα, neut. pl. (BDF §57). H. Junker, *LTK* IX, 845f.; A. van den Born, *BL* 613, 1609.

Σολομών, ῶνος *Solomōn* Solomon*

1. Occurrences in the NT — 2. The δόξα of Solomon — 3. The σοφία of Solomon — 4. The στοά of Solomon

Lit.: A. VAN DEN BORN and W. BAIER, *BL* 1507-10. — J. BOWMAN, "Solomon and Jesus," *Abr-Nahrain* 23 (1984/85) 1-13. — J. BRIEND, et al., *DBSup* XI, 431-85 (on the NT: J. Brière, 480-85). — A. JEPSEN, *BHH* 1651-53. — E. LOHSE, *TDNT* VII, 459-65. — K. PREISENDANZ, PW Suppl. VIII (1956) 660-704. — M. REHM, *LTK* IX, 272-74.

1. The NT almost always uses the form Σολομών, -ῶνος (so also Josephus). The form Σολομῶν, -ῶντος appears only in Acts 3:11; 5:12. The most common form of the name in the LXX is Σαλωμών.

The 12 occurrences of the name in the NT are distributed among Matthew (5 occurrences), Luke (3), John (1), and Acts (3). Solomon, the son and successor of David (Matt 1:6, 7), was considered a lover of splendor (Matt 6:29 par. Luke 12:27) and a wise man (Matt 12:42 par. Luke 11:31). He constructed the first temple in Jerusalem (Acts 7:47).

2. Matt 6:29 par. Luke 12:27 assert concerning the "lilies of the field" that "even Solomon in all his glory (δόξα) was not arrayed like one of these." This proverb from the logia source (Q) refers to those of little faith (ὀλιγόπιστοι) who doubt God's care (Matt 6:30; Luke 12:28). Cf. Schulz, *Q* 149-57. On the "glory" of Solomon see 2 Chr 9:13-28; further Lohse 461f.

3. Solomon was proverbially wise (cf. 1 Kgs 5:9-14; 2 Chr 9:1-12; Prov 1:1; 10:1; 25:1; see also Lohse 462f.). Matt 12:42 par. Luke 11:31 recalls the "queen of the South" who came to Jerusalem "to hear Solomon's wisdom" (cf. 2 Chr 9:1-12). Jesus, as the spokesman of wisdom, adds: "And behold, something greater than Solomon is here." In this saying the present generation, which rejects Jesus, is shamed by the Gentile queen. Cf. Schulz, *Q* 250-57.

4. The "portico of Solomon," a columned hall in the eastern part of the Herodian temple, is traced back to King Solomon (Josephus *Ant.* xx.221; *B.J.* v.185). John 10:23 mentions Jesus walking (περιπατέω) "in the temple, in the portico of Solomon." This scene, in which Jesus is questioned concerning his messiahship (10:22-30), takes place during the feast of the dedication of the temple in winter (Hanukkah).

Acts 3:11 reports that all the people ran together to Solomon's portico after Peter and John healed the lame man. Here Peter gave the "temple address" (3:12-26). 5:12 relates that the entire early Jerusalem church came together in Solomon's portico. According to the transition summary the portico of Solomon was the locus of the "teaching of the apostles." On the topography see Kopp, *Places* 286f.; G. Schneider, *Acts* (HTKNT) I, 303f.

G. Schneider

σορός, οῦ, ἡ *soros* coffin, bier*

Luke 7:14: Jesus "came and touched the *bier*." This noun occurs only rarely in Hellenistic Jewish writings (Gen 50:26 LXX; *T. Reu.* 7:2).

σός, σή, σόν   *sos, sē, son*   your

The second person sg. possessive adj. (BDF §285) carries more emphasis than gen. σοῦ and σεαυτοῦ or expresses a contrast. It rarely occurs in the NT outside the Gospels (8 occurrences in Matthew, 2 in Mark, 4 in Luke, 7 in John) and Acts (3 occurrences); it occurs only 3 times in Paul. It is used adj. with a noun (Matt 7:3, 22 ter; 13:27; 24:3; Mark 2:18; Luke 5:33; 22:42; John 4:42; 18:35; Acts 5:4; 24:2, 4; 1 Cor 8:11; 14:16; Phlm 14) and subst. with the art. (οἱ σοί, *your friends,* Mark 5:19; τὸ σόν, *what is yours,* Matt 20:14; 25:25; τὰ σά, *what is yours,* Luke 6:30; John 17:10b).

σουδάριον, ου, τό   *soudarion*   handkerchief*

This Latin loanword *(sudarium)* referring to a handkerchief is mentioned in Luke 19:20 as used to hold money and in John 11:44 and 20:7 as the head *cloth* of a corpse. Acts 19:12: Paul's σουδάρια and σιμικίνθια. R. Robert, "Le 'suaire' johannique," *RevThom* 97 (1989) 599-608.

Σουσάννα, ης (ας)   *Sousanna*   Susanna*

A fem. proper name used in Luke 8:3 of one of Jesus' female Galilean disciples with Mary Magdalene and Joanna.

σοφία, ας, ἡ   *sophia*   wisdom*

1. Occurrences in the NT — 2. Semantic field and meanings — 3. Theological usage — a) General usage in the early Church — b) James — c) Paul — d) Q

Lit.: R. Baumann, *Mitte und Norm des Christlichen. Eine Auslegung von 1 Kor 1,1–3,4* (NTAbh 55, 1968). — F. Christ, *Jesus Sophia* (ATANT 57, 1970). — H. Conzelmann, *IDBSup* 956-60. — G. Fohrer and U. Wilckens, *TDNT* VII, 465-528. — J. Goetzmann, *DNTT* III, 1026-33. — H. Koester, "One Jesus and Four Primitive Gospels," *idem* and J. M. Robinson, *Trajectories through Early Christianity* (1971) 158-204. — H. von Lips, *Weisheitliche Traditionen im NT* (WMANT 64, 1990). — B. L. Mack, *Logos und Sophia* (SUNT 10, 1973). — H. Merklein, "Zur Entstehung der urchristlichen Aussage vom präexistenten Sohn Gottes," *Zur Geschichte des Urchristentums* (ed. G. Dautzenberg et al.; QD 87, 1979) 33-62. — H. P. Müller and M. Krause, *TDOT* IV, 364-85. — A. Polag, *Die Christologie der Logienquelle* (WMANT 45, 1977). — K.-G. Sandelin, *Die Auseinandersetzung mit der Weisheit in 1 Kor 15* (Meddelanden fran Stiftelsen for Åbo Akademi Forskningsinstitut 12, 1976). — H. M. Schenke, "Die Tendenz der Weisheit zur Gnosis," *Gnosis* (FS H. Jonas, 1978) 144-57. — G. Schimanowski, *Die jüdischen Voraussetzungen der urchristlichen Präexistenzchristologie* (WUNT II/17, 1985). — Schulz, *Q* 224-28, 336-45. — E. Schweizer, *TDNT* IX, 661-63. — H. Weder, *Das Kreuz Jesu bei Paulus* (FRLANT 125, 1981) 121-75. — U. Wilckens, *Weisheit und Torheit* (BHT 26, 1959). — *idem,* "Zu 1 Kor 2,1-16," FS Dinkler 501-37. — M. Winter,

Pneumatiker und Psychiker in Korinth (MTSt 12, 1975). — For further bibliography see *TWNT* X, 1266-69; Weder; Wilckens, *Weisheit.*

1. The noun σοφία occurs 51 times in the NT, most frequently in Paul (19 times), and there almost always critically of the language of his Corinthian adversaries (16 occurrences in 1 Corinthians 1–3). The same is true of → σοφός. Use of σοφία in the deutero-Pauline writings Colossians and Ephesians (9 occurrences) and in the Lukan writings (6 occurrences in the Gospel, 4 in Acts) is noteworthy. James and Revelation follow with 4 occurrences each, Matthew with 3, and Mark and 2 Peter with 1 each. On the whole this constitutes a low frequency of occurrence.

2. In the NT σοφία has a uniquely colorful spectrum of meanings whose elements cannot always be sharply distinguished.

1) Σοφία can be used of the personal character trait of *wisdom,* i.e., *wisdom* as a spiritual or intellectual capacity of human beings (Luke 2:52) and, at its highest potential, of God (Rom 11:33). "Wise" refers to human *wisdom* (1 Cor 1:19: ἡ σοφία τῶν σοφῶν); it stands next to σύνεσις (1:9), γνῶσις (Col 2:3), φρόνησις (Eph 1:17f.), and belongs together as a trait with "understanding" (ἐπιστήμων, Jas 3:13) and "sensible" (φρόνιμος, 1 Cor 4:10), and its opposite is μωρός (3:18). Practical behavior is often determinative (Col 4:5: ἐν σοφίᾳ περιπατέω; cf. Jas 3:13-15). Such σοφία is often viewed as a natural gift (Luke 2:40, 52; Acts 7:10: χάρις), and this provides the transition to the next meaning, which is:

2) σοφία as a special spiritual (pneumatic) gift bestowed on individual Christians, and thus associated with πνεῦμα (Acts 6:3, 10: πνεῦμα καὶ σοφία), ἀποκάλυψις (Eph 1:17); cf. σοφία πνευματική (Col 1:9).

3) Since wisdom manifests itself esp. in language, σοφία is used of *wisdom* manifested in word and writing, which is often almost identical with the wisdom tradition. "Moses was instructed in all the σοφία of the Egyptians" (Acts 7:22), and Paul speaks "God's *wisdom,*" whereas the new wise men in Corinth probably want to impart a σοφία originating with cosmic-pneumatic powers (1 Cor 2:6f.). Wisdom expressed verbally is a gift of the Spirit (λόγος σοφίας, 1 Cor 12:8). A transition to → 1) exists wherever σοφία λόγου also designates certain behavior or an erroneous kind of eloquent wisdom (1:17, → 3.c).

4) These first three meanings are closely related to σοφία as the name of a personified figure of revelation, namely, the heavenly *wisdom* of the OT and Jewish tradition that emerges clearly first in Proverbs 8 (→ 3.c). This figure is the source of worldly wisdom, e.g., of kings (vv. 15f.), and of wisdom as the unique gift of the Spirit (→ 3.c on 1 Cor 1:21). Its voice is heard in certain wisdom sayings passed down by tradition (Luke 11:49). In the

NT Christ has taken the place of this figure, though only Luke 7:35 par. uses the title *"wisdom* of God."

On the whole σοφία is always religiously oriented. It is noteworthy that all the occurrences are in the context of profound crisis. The human wisdom that is normally judged positively in and of itself has failed before God's wisdom and has proven itself folly in the face of the Christ-event. The spiritual (pneumatic) gift of wisdom and wisdom teaching appear ambivalent and in need of critical integration into the revelation of Christ. God's wisdom in person was refused and rejected. After passing through judgment it emerges as new and true, namely, genuinely life-giving wisdom in Christ (1 Cor 1:30; Col 2:3).

3.a) Wherever the NT affirms human σοφία, such wisdom has always come in a special way from God. Such is the case with the young Jesus: He was "filled with *wisdom,* and God's favor was on him"; "Jesus increased in *wisdom,* maturity, and favor with God and mankind" (Luke 2:40, 52; cf. the implied OT horizon, 1 Sam 2:26: the child Samuel). Solomon was considered extraordinarily wise, though Jesus eclipsed even his wisdom (Matt 12:42; Luke 11:31). Jesus' wisdom as a teacher, together with his mighty deeds, astonishes those around him, and the Gospel writers see a suggestion of the christological mystery (Mark 6:2; Matt 13:54; cf. Luke 4:21-23; John 7:15f.). In all this Jesus' wisdom is not some esoteric secret; rather, he is open to tradition, teaches "what is new and what is old" (Matt 13:52), and addresses the intellect of his listeners with persuasive power to give them insight (φρόνιμος) in their comprehension of the eschatological hour of decision. Accordingly, early Church paraclesis exhorts its listeners to acquire a new worldly wisdom illuminated by the insights of faith and nurtured by the indwelling Spirit of Christ: "Conduct yourselves wisely toward outsiders," making the most of the time of mission activity, speaking graciously and yet confidently (Col 3:16; 4:5-6).

b) James offers a unique picture, a thoroughly paracletic and strongly wisdom-oriented writing. In a beautifully formed saying 1:5 picks up the saying of Jesus in Matt 7:7 par. Luke 11:9 and alters it comprehensively (as does Luke 11:13: request for the Holy Spirit) into a petition for *wisdom,* conceived as the basic power supporting the believer's life, inaccessible to human beings, coming "from above" (Jas 1:17f.). The sinner can be sure this fundamental request will be granted by God, since God "gives to all generously and without reproach" (1:5). The substance of this σοφία is God's perfect will, the will of his salvation (1:18; 2:5), and his instructions for life (1:25: "the perfect law of liberty"). Whoever makes this request becomes a listener and receives through the vivifying word, itself grounded firmly in the Church (1:17-

21), precisely by accepting that word and acting according to it (1:21b-25). Like all early Church paraclesis, James, too, develops this salvation doctrine only on occasion (e.g., 2:14-26); usually he merely evokes it with brief references, though for just this reason such references do carry some weight. It is esp. true of Christian teachers (3:13) that wisdom from God is true only if it is genuinely lived.

James includes in his admonition the example of a different wisdom, one that is only superficially σοφία, and characterizes it (3:15) as earthly (ἐπίγειος), unspiritual (ψυχική), and devilish (δαιμονιώδης). This striking characterization is not adequately explained as an expression for Gnostic-heretical influences. The concern is, rather, with the constant threat that the life of faith will be emptied and alienated into hypocritical superficiality. Such fascinating wisdom, full of pious enthusiasm and righteousness (cf. knowledge on the part of demons, 2:19), James considers undermined by sin itself, motivated by unholy impulses and selfish ambition (3:14, 16), emerging from "your passions, which are at war in your members" (4:1). Such godless, merely earthly, all-too-human (ἐπίγειος, ψυχική, 3:15) behavior in reality makes room for the world (4:4), the devil (4:7), and his demons.

True wisdom from God is "pure" of all selfish ambition, and thus "sincere" (ἀνυπόκριτος), and "undivided," without duplicity and wavering (ἀδιάκριτος, 3:17). Its content is characterized by "meekness" (πραΰτης, 3:13; 1:21), a goodness capable of enduring tribulation without anger. This must include the capability and willingness to accept criticism: Σοφία makes one compliant, "open to reason" (εὐπειθής), "gentle" (ἐπιεικής), and for precisely that reason "peaceable" (εἰρηνικός). Whoever lives this wisdom from above will create peace, being filled with this new life from God, particularly with mercy (3:17).

c) Apart from Rom 11:33; 1 Cor 12:8 Paul's references to σοφία are in the context of the Corinthian discussion, including 2 Cor 1:12: Paul does not live and work in "earthly *wisdom*" (σοφία σαρκική).

Paul opens the discussion with a critical treatment of the term σοφία λόγου. An irresistibly powerful "wisdom of words" was considered the distinguishing feature of spiritual wisdom (so Acts 6:3, 10; cf. 9:22; 18:24-28; 19:8 [πείθων]; Luke 21:15). Hence it was a serious matter that the Corinthians saw none of this in Paul. His response is that σοφία λόγου "empties" Christ's cross and takes away the saving "power of God" from God's deed in the event of the cross (1 Cor 1:17f.). Just what Paul means here has long been disputed.

The decisive point of departure must be Paul's reference to his own proclamation as μωρία, "folly" (the antithesis σοφία—μωρία should be considered Pauline). He certainly does not mean it lacks cogency or even rhetorical polish; 1:21 is itself rhetorically splendid. Paul himself characterizes this folly as *God's* foolishness and "God's weakness" (1:25). A powerless God would be an absurdity, but Paul teaches that precisely this weakness of God possesses superior power (ἰσχυρότερον), i.e., the saving power of God's self-sacrificing love in Christ (cf. Rom 5:5, 8; 8:32, 35-38; 1 Cor 8:2f.; 13, and elsewhere). From this perspective the message of the cross acquires the form of a solicitous request of God (2 Cor 5:14f., 19-20); beguiling exhibitions of power oriented to religious wisdom easily destroy such a message, even if the cross as a transition stage continues to have a part in the drama of redemption (Weder 132). Paul, as God's messenger, recognizes in reverent awe ("in fear and trembling," 1 Cor 2:3) that he is bound to this "mystery of God." Hence he decided (ἔκρινα) to appear in Corinth "in weakness" (2:2f.; cf. 1 Thess 2:8), not "in plausible words of *wisdom*" (2:2-4) or "in lofty words of *wisdom*" (2:1), since that would be to build on sand and to abandon the revelation that did not come to Paul through human cleverness (2:13). Human wisdom, even that of Paul himself, cannot ground faith; "God's power" is needed for that (2:5).

With all this, however, Paul is, indeed, presenting wisdom! But it is the wisdom of the cross. It illuminates God's way in the inconspicuous and sometimes embarrassing (1 Cor 1:28) missionary events of the early Church. This happens in a concentrated fashion in 1:18-21 and 2:6-8: In the cross of Christ God has completed the world's judgment, the world's end. The prophecy has been fulfilled asserting that God "will destroy the wisdom of the wise" and "make them foolish" (citations from Isa 29:14; 19:11f.), because such wisdom has failed. But at the same time God offers rescue. "For since, in God's *wisdom*, the world did not know God through *wisdom*, it pleased God through the folly of what we preach to save those who believe" (1:21). Paul skillfully varies the substance of σοφία here. He speaks of God's wisdom, in the sense derived from OT and Jewish tradition, as the mediator from the beginning of God's creative saving power. To this is opposed a human wisdom, to which was disclosed that saving recognition of God. But this human wisdom missed the mark and, according to Rom 1:18, willfully suppressed it (cf. Sandelin, Weder). The highest goal of all philosophy of Paul's time was knowledge of the divine. But God has now undercut that entire undertaking. Instead of such knowledge God now offers the foolishness of the message of love from the cross as the way to salvation, a path of knowledge inaccessible through human devices. Wise men of the old kind will not find here the wisdom or exhibitions of divine power they seek (1 Cor 1:22); they are in fact noticeable by their absence (1:20). Only God's call and election opens the way, and God begins with the fools and the lowly in order to shame the wise and to save all (1:26-29).

In 1 Cor 2:6-8 Paul goes even further. "The *wisdom* of this age's rulers," of the cosmic powers in the background, has also been undercut on the cross. They alternate between accusation and deception. In their high estimate of glossolalia ("tongues of angels," 13:1) the Corinthian pneumatics appear to enjoy contact with heavenly power. In Galatia and Colossae, as in Hellenistic Jewish Alexandria, one expected participation in spiritual power from angelic powers. That, however, is a power of seduction, and a different pneuma (2 Cor 11:2-4, 13; cf. "the spirit of the world," 1 Cor 2:12). Spirit now stands against spirit. Following this, and speaking in completely different terms, Paul gives an example of the self-adulation of the Corinthian pneumatics and of their "*wisdom* for the mature" (2:6). Τέλειος here is a concept from the mysteries that has already become a shared image or metaphor, though it is not yet thought of in Gnostic terms. A pronounced claim of religious power has been made in the name of the power of pneuma, radical like certain anthropological and ethical assertions in Corinth (e.g., 6:12a), razor-sharp in judgment. Paul's theology of the cross changes this entirely: Whoever does not perceive God in the word of the cross is spiritually empty and ψυχικός. The self-confidence of these wise men, however, is a revival of the older form of worldly wisdom that they think they are defeating on its own turf.

According to 1 Cor 2:8 these powers have deprived themselves of their own power, though not by allowing the Redeemer to pass by unrecognized in the cosmos, but by bringing Jesus to the cross as keepers of the accusing Torah (cf. Gal 3:13). God's wisdom, hidden beneath foolishness, the "hidden *wisdom* of God" (2:7), and God's path—disclosed in 1:21—were and still are hidden from the angelic powers; before all time began God predestined this wisdom for the eschatological generation of his people. Apocalyptic expectation is now fulfilled. Believers on earth already participate in the heavenly divine glory. The designation "Lord of glory" (2:8) already carries christological coloring, but can also be illuminated from the perspective of the apocalyptic tradition (Baumann 222-25); for Paul it stands for the crucified one. Recognition of him is first and last not a matter of high-flying and profound wisdom, but of faith. In Paul theology follows faith and can never overtake it. Whoever has Christ in faith also has "the power of God and the *wisdom* of God" (1:24, 30) in its fullness. No theology can measure its depth (Rom 11:33). But faith knows the full depth of the deity (1 Cor 2:10-12) by being encompassed by God's unfathomable love (8:3). Whoever stands fast in the faith of the cross is truly "mature" or "perfect" (cf. Phil 3:12-15) and "wise" (1 Cor 3:18) and will remain so as long as "God's secret *wisdom*" (2:7) illuminating the cross does not become a stumbling block for him, but rather grounds him even more deeply in faith.

d) The personified "wisdom of God" is already addressed in the Corinthian discussion, and in the confession quoted in 1 Cor 8:6 Paul has already transferred its functions to Christ. This occurs elsewhere in 1 Corinthians as well (Sandelin, et al.). In the NT, however, apart from the title Logos in John 1, the name "wisdom of God" is associated with Jesus only in a few sayings from Q. The particular tradition-historical questions are difficult to answer, though these christological predicates may extend back into a relatively early period.

Luke 7:35 par. concludes a two-part unit of tradition concerning the rejection of Jesus and John by "this generation" with a remark about wisdom: "Yet *wisdom* is justified by all her children" ("by her deeds" in Matt 11:19).

Luke 11:49 concludes a series of cries of "woe" over the Pharisees (vv. 42-44) and teachers (vv. 46-48) with a word of judgment to "this generation" (v. 50): "Therefore also God's *wisdom* said, 'I will send them prophets and apostles. . . .' " With the rejection of these messengers of God the measure of sin will then be full for all generations and reckoned to this one. In the parallel tradition, Matt 23:34-36, this saying attributed to "wisdom" has become a saying of Jesus. In both instances the OT and early Jewish tradition of personified wisdom is thrown into clear relief.

This is also true in other Synoptic texts: Jesus' cry of exaltation (Matt 11:25-26 par.) and the following cry of the Savior (vv. 28-30 par.) as well as the Jerusalem passage (Matt 23:27-39 par.). "Jesus, as the spokesman and mediator of wisdom, appears, above and beyond that, also as wisdom itself" (Christ 153). It is disputed whether early Gnostic influence is present here. In any case, the formerly mythological elements come from the OT and early Jewish tradition, though there is a tendency toward Gnosticism. The main theological motivation behind this christological outline is a confession, with elements critical of the Torah, of the saving wisdom of God in the Christ-event (Merklein).   H. Hegermann

σοφίζω *sophizō* make wise, instruct in wisdom; mid.: devise slyly or craftily*

In 2 Tim 3:15 σοφίζω is associated with the Scriptures, which have power "to *instruct* you for salvation." 2 Pet 1:16: σεσοφισμένοι μῦθοι, "*cleverly devised* myths" or "*ingeniously reasoned* myths." U. Wilckens, *TDNT* VII, 527f.

σοφός, 3 *sophos* wise, learned*

1. Occurrences in the NT — 2. Meaning and usage — 3. Theological usage in 1 Corinthians 1–3

Lit.: → σοφία, also: E. E. ELLIS, " 'Wisdom' and 'Knowl-

edge' in I Corinthians," *idem, Prophecy and Hermeneutic in Early Christianity* (1978) 45-62. — HENGEL, *Judaism* 153-75, 255-314. — J. M. ROBINSON, "Logoi Sophon: On the Gattung of Q," *idem* and H. Koester, *Trajectories through Early Christianity* (1971) 71-113. — K.-G. SANDELIN, *Die Auseinandersetzung mit der Weisheit in 1 Kor 15* (Meddelanden fran Stiftelsen for Åbo Akademi Forskningsinstitut 12, 1976) 137-45, 147-53. — *idem, Wisdom as Nourisher: A Study of an OT Theme, Its Development within Early Judaism and Its Impact on Early Christianity* (1986). — H. STADELMANN, *Ben Sira als Schriftgelehrter* (WUNT II/6, 1980) 4-26, 177-270. — For further bibliography see *TWNT* X, 1266-69.

1. Of the 20 NT occurrences of σοφός 10 are in the specifically focused context of 1 Corinthians 1–3 (1:19, 20, 25, 26, 27; 3:10, 18 bis, 19, 20), which also indirectly influences the 4 other Pauline occurrences (1 Cor 6:5; Rom 1:14, 22; 16:19). There are 2 deutero-Pauline occurrences (Rom 16:27; Eph 5:15), 3 in the Synoptics, 2 of those in Q (a wisdom-oriented thanksgiving in Matt 11:25 par. Luke 10:21) and 1 in probably redactional material in Matt 23:24 (σοφός does not occur in par. Luke 11:49), and 1 in Jas 3:13.

2. In adj. usage σοφός is used of the "experience" or "technical understanding" of a master builder (1 Cor 3:10) and of the understanding of what is ethically right in daily life (Rom 16:19: σοφὸς εἶναι εἰς τὸ ἀγαθόν; cf. subst. in Eph 5:15: "Look carefully then how you walk, not as unwise people but as *wise*"). Similarly, σοφός also refers to the ability to smooth over worldly disputes within a congregation (1 Cor 6:5). It is never used in the NT in the genuinely philosophical sense. Superior and comprehensive knowledge is attributed to God: he is extraordinarily wise in the execution of his will (1:25; 3:19) and ultimately "alone is *wise*" (Rom 16:27).

These texts are close to those that use σοφός subst. in the sense of the Greco-Hellenistic ideal of education (Rom 1:14, 22) or of the religious tradition of Israel. Both lines converge in Jewish Hellenism and are criticized together in the NT: Eschatological election will not include the wise and understanding among the Jews (Matt 11:25 par.), the Jewish scribes (1 Cor 1:20), nor the *wise* among the Greeks, the "debaters" (συζητητής, v. 20), nor the "influential" and "highly regarded" (v. 26). Yet Paul, as the messenger of the saving gospel, is "under obligation" precisely to the *wise* as well (Rom 1:14), those who became guilty before other human beings in their own specialty, namely, "claiming to be *wise*," and yet failing to recognize the knowledge of God that is accessible in creation (1:22; cf. v. 25 and 2:17-24 on Jewish σοφός). The foolishness of the gospel will make fools of them and in just that way will also make them wise (1 Cor 3:18). Accordingly, Paul frequently defines σοφός more closely: the σοφός of this age (1:20), in this age (3:18), "σοφός according to worldly standards (κατὰ σάρκα)"

(1:26), and inserts σοφός thus into an antithetical dialectic: σοφός—μωρός, variously interpreted also as ἀσθενής—ἰσχυρός (1:25, 26-28; 3:18; completely different in Rom 16:19: σοφός—ἀκέραιος).

3. In Corinth the new "wise ones" (1 Cor 3:18) understand themselves to be simultaneously "prophets," "pneumatics," and "mature" (14:37; 2:6, 13, 15); contrasting concepts are "unspiritual" ("psychic," 2:14) and νήπιος ("immature, not of age," 3:1). A new, primitive Christian understanding of the wise person emerges here as also in churches in the Synoptic tradition (Matt 23:34 par.; cf. further Jas 3:13): The mediator of revelation sent by Christ, by the wisdom of God, prophetically and spiritually empowered, surpasses and suspends all previous wise persons, be they priestly (Sirach [cf. Hengel, Stadelmann], Qumran), apocalyptic (Daniel, *1 Enoch*), or Alexandrian Jewish (Wisdom, Philo). Here a counterfeiting of the kerygma of Christ threatens to turn it into dualistic wisdom, into "gnosis"; all four Gospels oppose this, though Paul does so most of all. Jewish wise men such as Aristobulus or Philo believed themselves capable of surpassing all the wise men of the world, including Plato, with "Moses," i.e., with the Torah revelation (cf. *JSHRZ* III/2, 273-76; Philo *Spec. Leg.* 165f.; see Hengel 312), but the cross has put an end to this competition.

Paul warns against the self-deception of believing one can have Christ and simultaneously groom oneself as a wise man with reputation and superiority, as a "σοφός in this age" (1 Cor 3:18). Here Christians, too, are overtaken by the judgment of God, "who catches the wise" and exposes their futility (vv. 19, 20). In 1 Corinthians Paul develops this rather extensively (→ σοφία 3.c). On the path of God's foolish wisdom the true σοφός is a humble servant and helper (3:5; 2 Cor 1:24; "we are weak, but you are strong," 1 Cor 4:10) and, in the world's eyes, the ultimate fool, "the offscouring of all things" (4:13).

H. Hegermann

Σπανία, ας *Spania* Spain*

In Rom 15:24, 28 Paul focuses on *Spain* as a goal. Rome is to serve him as a kind of "bridgehead." On Spain see H. Rix, *LAW* 2848-52 (bibliography); R. Grosse, *KP* II, 1185-89; H. Volkmann, *KP* V, 1606f.; M. I. Henderson, *OCD* 1005f. On the question whether Paul ever reached Spain, see the older works cited in BAGD s.v.

σπάομαι *spaomai* pull, draw*

Mid. in Mark 14:47; Acts 16:27: σπάομαι τὴν μάχαιραν; "draw one's sword" (so also in the LXX and Josephus).

σπαράσσω *sparassō* pull to and fro, tear, convulse*

Of an "unclean spirit" that *convulses* the possessed person in Mark 1:26; 9:26; Luke 9:39.

σπαργανόω *sparganoō* wrap in swaddling cloths*

Mary "wrapped her newborn son in swaddling cloths and laid him in a manger" (Luke 2:7); pass. in 2:12 as a sign of the child the shepherds are to find.

σπαταλάω *spatalaō* indulge, live luxuriously*

1 Tim 5:6, of widows: "she who *is self-indulgent* is dead even while she lives"; Jas 5:5, in the judgment against the rich: "You *have lived* on the earth in luxury (ἐτρυφήσατε) and *pleasure* (ἐσπαταλήσατε)."

σπεῖρα, ης, ἡ *speira* cohort, troop*

1. Occurrences in the NT and general meaning — 2. The Passion narrative — 3. Acts

Lit.: BAGD s.v. — J. BLINZLER, *Der Prozeß Jesu* (⁴1969) 90-98. — T. R. S. BROUGHTON, "The Roman Army," *Beginnings* V, 427-45. — C. CICHORIUS, PW IV, 231-356. — P. WINTER, *On the Trial of Jesus* (1961) 44-50.

1. This military t.t. is documented from the time of Polybius and occurs in the LXX (Jdt 14:11; 2 Macc 8:23; 12:20, 22) and Josephus. It is used to translate Lat. *cohors* (Polybius xi.23.1), *manipulus* (Polybius vi.24.5, etc.), and other words. The *cohors* was one-tenth of a legion (→ λεγιών 1) and thus comprised about 500 men.

2. In the Passion narrative σπεῖρα occurs in Mark 15:16 par. Matt 27:27 and John 18:3, 12. According to Mark and Matthew Pilate's guard called together "the whole *cohort*" before mocking and mistreating Jesus. John 18:3 relates that Judas procured (λαβών) "the σπεῖρα and some officers from the chief priests and the Pharisees." This *band* (so RSV) that is to arrest Jesus is equipped with torches, lanterns, and weapons, but is not a Roman "cohort" (so Blinzler 94f.; *contra* Winter 44f.). John 18:12 mentions the same σπεῖρα along with the χιλίαρχος ("captain") and the "officers of the Jews" at the arrest of Jesus. If the fourth Evangelist considers this σπεῖρα a contingent of Roman troops, he is guilty of historical error (Blinzler).

3. Acts 10:1 introduces the centurion Cornelius as stationed in Caesarea and belonging to the "Italian *Cohort.*" 21:31 speaks of the "tribune of the *cohort*" in Jerusalem; this refers to the Roman occupation of the Tower of Antonia. 27:1 introduces the centurion Julius, who belonged to the "Augustan *Cohort.*" Σεβαστή (*[cohors] Augusta*) is a frequently documented honorary predicate referring to auxiliary troops.   G. Schneider

σπείρω *speirō* sow*

1. Occurrences in the NT and meaning — 2.a) Paul — b) The Gospels

Lit.: G. QUELL and S. SCHULZ, *TDNT* VII, 536-47, esp. 546. — For further bibliography → σπέρμα; see also *TWNT* X, 1270.

1. This vb. occurs 52 times in the NT; it occurs esp. often in Matthew (17 times) and Mark (12 times), and 14 times in the Pauline writings (elsewhere in the NT only in Jas 3:18). Σπείρω means to *sow* (seed) and is used both literally (esp. in the Gospels) and figuatively (esp. in Paul; cf. BAGD s.v.). The compound ἐπισπείρω appears only in Matt 13:25. Σπείρω is frequently used in conjunction with θερίζω (this image of sowing and reaping originated in wisdom literature).

2.a) Paul uses σπείρω 6 times in 1 Cor 15:36-44 alone. In his dispute with the false teachers in Corinth Paul uses the metaphor common in early Christianity of grain (i.e., wheat; → σπέρμα 1; cf. John 12:24; *1 Clem.* 24:4f.) to show the continuity within the discontinuity between present and future life. He uses the vb. literally in vv. 36f., and the metaphor emerges in vv. 42ff. Σπείρω and ἐγείρω are juxtaposed in four contrasting pairs. The impersonal contrasting pairs (σπείρεται) merge in v. 44 into the central assertion: Σπείρεται σῶμα ψυχικόν, ἐγείρεται σῶμα πνευματικόν. Here σῶμα refers to the concrete manner of existence of human beings, qualified as either earthly or heavenly.

Paul frequently employs the metaphor of sowing and reaping, e.g., in 1 Cor 9:11, where σπείρω refers to mission activity (cf. also 2 Cor 9:6, 10, where the focus is on the church's gift of love). In Gal 6:7f. the metaphor serves the eschatological motivation of believers' behavior: Whoever sows σάρξ will reap φθορά, but whoever sows πνεῦμα will reap ζωὴ αἰώνιος.

b) The Gospels usually use σπείρω literally, as in the parables of the sower (Matt 13:3, 4, 18, 19, 20, 22, 23 par. Mark 4:3, 4, 14, 15, 16, 18, 20 par. Luke 8:5 ter), the weeds among the wheat (Matt 13:24, 27, 37, 39), the mustard seed (Matt 13:31 par. Mark 4:31, 32), and the entrusted talents (Matt 25:24, 26 par. Luke 19:21, 22), and in the image of the birds of the air (Matt 6:26 par. Luke 12:24). In the allegorical interpretations (not original parts of the parables) of the parables of the sower (Matt 13:18ff. par.) and of the weeds among the wheat (Matt 13:27ff.) the literal use flows into the figurative. The interpretation presupposes the metaphor common in Judaism of God's planting (cf. Matt 15:13). The original metaphor of sowing is concerned with the coming of the kingdom of God, but in the interpretation the conduct of believers is the focus.

The image of sowing and reaping (→ a) occurs in Matt 25:24, 26 par. Luke 19:21f. In John 4:36f. this image is set in a proverb; in the eschaton sowing and reaping occur simultaneously (cf. R. Bultmann, *John* [Eng. tr., 1971] ad loc.).
W. Hackenberg

σπεκουλάτωρ, ορος, ὁ *spekoulatōr* executioner*

This Latin loanword *(speculator)* originally referred to a *scout,* then also to a *courier.* Mark 6:27 uses it of an *executioner* (so also, e.g., Seneca *Ben.* iii.25; *Ira* i.18.4). Schürer, *History* I, 371f.; A. R. Neumann, *KP* V, 300f.; Spicq, *Notes* II, 730-37; A. N. Sherwin-White, *Roman Society and Roman Law in the NT* (1963) 124.

σπένδομαι *spendomai* be offered*

In the NT only the pass. of σπένδω ("offer a libation") occurs: Phil 2:17: "Even if I *am to be poured as a libation. . . .*" 2 Tim 4:6 picks up this topos: "I am already on the point of *being poured as a libation.*" A. Citron, *Semantische Untersuchung zu* σπένδεσθαι—σπένδειν—εὔχεσθαι (1965); O. Michel, *TDNT* VII, 528-36.

σπέρμα, ατος, τό *sperma* seed; descendants*

1. Seeds of plants — 2. Sperm — 3. Descendants

Lit.: General: BAGD s.v. — H. D. PREUSS, *TDOT* IV, 143-62. — G. QUELL and S. SCHULZ, *TDNT* VII, 536-47. — C. WESTERMANN, *BHH* 1661f.
On 1: G BARTH, "Auseinandersetzungen um die Kirchenzucht im Umkreis des Matthäusevangeliums," *ZNW* 69 (1978) 158-77. — H. BRAUN, "Das 'Stirb und werde' in der Antike und im NT," *idem, Gesammelte Studien zum NT und seiner Umwelt* (³1971) 136-58. — J. D. CROSSAN, "The Seed Parables of Jesus," *JBL* 92 (1973) 245-66. — M. E. DAHL, *The Resurrection of the Body* (1962) 121-25. — J. JEREMIAS, "Die Deutung des Gleichnisses vom Unkraut unter dem Weizen," FS Cullmann (1962) 59-63. — idem, *Parables* 81-84, 146-53, 224f. — O. KUSS, "Zum Sinngehalt des Doppelgleichnisses vom Senfkorn und Sauerteig," *Bib* 40 (1959) 641-53. — R. MORISETTE, "La condition de ressuscité," *Bib* 53 (1972) 208-28. — K. USANI, "How are the Dead Raised?" *Bib* 57 (1976) 468-93.
On 2: R. E. BROWN, *1 John* (AB, 1982) 408-11. — K. WENGST, *Häresie und Orthodoxie im Spiegel des ersten Johannesbriefes* (1976) 44-46.
On 3: K. BERGER, "Abraham in den paulinischen Hauptbriefen," *MTZ* 17 (1966) 47-89. — C. DIETZFELBINGER, *Paulus und das AT* (1961) 19-23, 27, 31. — T. B. DOZEMAN, "*Sperma Abraam* in John 8 and Related Literature: Cosmology and Judgement," *CBQ* 42 (1980) 342-58. — G. KLEIN, "Röm 4 und die Idee der Heilsgeschichte," *idem, Rekonstruktion und Interpretation* (1969) 145-69, esp. 158-62. — idem, "Exegetische Probleme in Röm 3,21–4,25," *ibid.* 170-79. — H. MERKLEIN, "Die Auferweckung Jesu und die Anfänge der Christologie," *ZNW* 72 (1981) 1-26, esp. 13-16. — F. MUSSNER, "Wer ist 'der ganze Samen' in Röm 4,16?" FS Zimmermann 213-17. — H. SCHLIER, "Zu Röm 1,3f," FS Cullmann (1972) 207-18. — A. VÖGTLE, "Mythos und Botschaft in Apk 12," FS Kuhn 395-415. — For further bibliography see *TWNT* X, 1270.

1. According to Matt 13:24, 27, 37f. the good *seed* grows along with the weeds until the harvest. The main focus of this parable is Jesus' refusal to separate out the community of the holy remnant—as did other Jewish groups (*Gos. Thom.* 57). The pre-Matthean allegorical interpretation distinguishes the sons of the kingdom of the Son of man from the sons of the evil one (vv. 37-39) and warns against the desire to separate good and evil by human standards. Finally, the Matthean redactor uses the contrasting fate of weeds and wheat to warn against false security concerning one's own salvation (vv. 40-43).

In the parable in Mark 4:31 par. Matt 13:32 (*Gos. Thom.* 20) the fate of the tiny mustard seed—proverbially the smallest discernible of all *seeds* (Billerbeck I, 669)—testifies to God's miraculous power, which even now, unseen, is at work in Jesus, preparing the completion of the kingdom.

In 1 Cor 15:38 Paul employs the ancient example of the wheat seed (cf. John 12:24; *1 Clem.* 24:5; *b. Sanh.* 90b; *b. Ketub.* 111b) to demonstrate in the death of seeds the necessity of dying as a precondition for resurrection (re-embodiment!) by God.

2. 1 John 3:9, using an ontological citation from its Gnostic adversaries, refers to God's *sperm;* in the context of the metaphor of procreation by God for the sake of being a child of God 1 John refers metaphorically to the Spirit (3:24; 4:13) or to the event of the word itself (1:10; 2:14; Jas 1:18, 21; 1 Pet 1:23), whereby God gives to the reborn person the possibility of life in righteousness and brotherly love in the form of the inability to sin (God's sperm characterizes one's actions).

3. Mark 12:19, 20, 21, 22 par. Matt 22:24f./Luke 20:28 quote Gen 38:8 as amplification of the law of levirate marriage (Deut 25:5-10). In Heb 11:11, in the stories of the heroes of faith, the male function of procreating *descendants* is transferred to Sarah, the infertile ancestress of Israel, as a result of her exemplary power of faith. 11:18 recalls the courage in faith of Abraham, who risked the promise of descendants by sacrificing Isaac (citing Gen 21:12 LXX; so also Rom 9:7). Rev 12:17 uses σπέρμα fig.: The Messiah Jesus and those Christians prepared for martyrdom as his siblings (cf. Rom 8:29; Heb 2:11f.) are counted together as descendants of the woman, i.e., of Christ's Church as the antitypical fulfillment of Eve (Gen 3:15).

The t.t. "seed of Abraham" (→ Ἀβραάμ 2) is theologically significant:

a) as a designation for Israel in its empirical existence as the chosen carrier of the promise (Luke 1:55; Acts 7:5f.; Rom 4:13, 16; Gal 3:16; 2 Cor 11:22), whereby Paul distinguishes between authentic and inauthentic descendants (Rom 9:7f.), or speaks of Jewish Christians as the holy remnant of the Jewish people of God, a remnant that does not exclude itself from salvation by refusing to believe (Rom 9:29, quoting Isa 1:9 LXX: descendants that make new life possible);

b) particularly as a designation for the people of God constituted by faith in Christ and composed of both Jews and Gentiles; here the advantage of being Abraham's descendants (cf. John 8:33, 37) is secularized, or the Gentiles are brought into Israel's election (Rom 4:16, 18; 9:7; Gal 3:29; Heb 2:16);

c) as a designation for Jesus as the promised Messiah (Acts 3:25; Gal 3:16, 19), though there is no early rabbinic parallel for such messianic interpretation; and

d) as a designation for Paul as a member of the chosen people (a characteristic feature of an apostle?) and as a living example of God's plan of salvation for Israel (Rom 11:1; 2 Cor 11:22).

The formula referring to Jesus as "descended from David" (→ υἱός 6) originated in Jewish Christian circles and is of particular christological significance; it is more than a biographical reference, since it confesses faith in the resurrected Jesus as the Messiah promised in Nathan's prophecy (2 Sam 7:12, and elsewhere; Rom 1:3; 2 Tim 2:8; John 7:42; Acts 13:23 [alluding to 2 Sam 22:51 LXX]). Concerning this biographical tradition cf. Matt 1:16, 20; Mark 12:35ff. par.; Luke 1:27; 2:4, 11; 3:31; Rev 5:5; 22:16.

U. Kellermann

σπερμολόγος, ου, ὁ *spermologos* gossip, babbler*

Acts 17:18, in the question of an Athenian philosopher concerning Paul: "What would this *babbler* say?" The adj. σπερμολόγος means "picking up seeds." Used subst., it refers to the rook (the Old Word crow; so Aristophanes, Aristotle), then—figuratively—to a *babbler* (so, e.g., Demosthenes *Or.* xviii.127; Dionysius of Halicarnassus *Antiquitates Romanae* xix.5.3; Philo *Leg. Gai.* 203). Wettstein, *NT* ad loc.; Spicq, *Notes* II, 807f.

σπεύδω *speudō* hurry; trans.: hasten, strive for*

Σπεύδω is intrans. in the NT only in the Lukan writings (Luke 2:16; 19:5, 6; Acts 20:16; 22:18) and always in combination with another vb. (Acts 20:16 with inf.). It is trans. only in 2 Pet 3:12: "waiting for and *earnestly desiring* (προσδοκῶντας καὶ σπεύδοντας) the coming of the day of God."

σπήλαιον, ου, τό *spēlaion* cave, den*

Of a *den* as a hiding place for robbers (Mark 11:17 par. Matt 21:13/Luke 19:46; cf. Jer 7:11), of a refuge during persecution and danger (Heb 11:38; Rev 6:15), of a tomb (John 11:38; cf. *T. Reu.* 7:2).

σπιλάς, άδος, ἡ   *spilas*   rock in the sea, reef; blemish*

Metaphorical in Jude 12: at feasts the libertines are σπιλάδες. The meaning *blemishes* fits the context (see also 2 Pet 2:13) better than *reefs*. K. H. Schelkle, *Jude* (HTNKT) ad loc.; Spicq, *Notes* II, 809-11. → σπίλος; σπιλόω.

σπίλος, ου, ὁ   *spilos*   stain, blemish*

Eph 5:27, with ῥυτίς: the Church without "*spot or wrinkle*"; 2 Pet 2:13, with μῶρος: "*blots and blemishes*," of libertine false teachers.

σπιλόω   *spiloō*   stain, soil*

Metaphorical in Jas 3:6; Jude 23.

σπλαγχνίζομαι   *splanchnizomai*   have pity*

1. Occurrences in the NT — 2. Meaning — 3. Jesus' parables — 4. Jesus as the representative of God's compassion

Lit.: → σπλάγχνον; also: G. SELLIN, "Lukas als Gleichniserzähler (II)," *ZNW* 66 (1975) 19-60, esp. 26f., 49f.

1. This pass. deponent vb. occurs in the NT only in the Synoptic Gospels, 12 times altogether, 4 of those in Mark, 5 in Matthew (3 from Mark, 1 in M, 1 redactional), and 3 in Luke (L).

2. The act. vb. (2 Macc 6:8), like σπλαγχνεύω, means "partake of sacrifices" (→ σπλάγχνον 2). The particular meaning of the deponent vb. derives from the special meaning "pity, compassion" of the noun and usually specified more closely by synonyms (→ σπλάγχνον 3.c). It occurs once in the LXX (Prov 17:5), 6 times in *T. Zeb.* (see H. Köster, *TDNT* VII, 551f.), and *T. Abr.* (B) 12. Symmachus (1 Kgs 23:21; Ezek 24:21) probably already presupposes NT usage (or that of *T. Zeb.*).

3. Σπλαγχνίζομαι appears in 3 parables of Jesus: Matt 18:23ff. (v. 27), with contrasting → ὀργίζομαι (v. 34), with the evil servant's master as subj.; Luke 15:11ff. (v. 20), with the lost son's father as subj. (here the older son provides the contrast with his "anger" at the father's behavior, v. 28); in the exemplary story of the Good Samaritan (Luke 10:30ff.) ἐσπλαγχνίσθη represents the decisive motive behind the Samaritan's compassionate behavior toward the victim. Whereas Matt 18:23ff. and Luke 15:11ff. clearly portray God's behavior toward human beings, Luke 10:30ff. apparently portrays the Samaritan as one who "gauges" God's own compassion and thus does God's will. Any allegorical interpretation of the Samaritan using σπλαγχνίζομαι as a point of departure to refer to Jesus misses the mark (Sellin 25-27).

4. The occurrences in Mark, Matthew (other than

18:27), and Luke 7:13 portray Jesus as one who compassionately takes an interest in those in need and helps them.

Mark 6:34, probably as a result of the redactor's hand, introduces the story of the feeding of the five thousand with a clear allusion to Ezekiel 34, so that Jesus appears as the compassionate (and eschatological) representative of God himself. In 8:2 (the feeding of the four thousand) Mark has Jesus himself speak the words "I *have compassion* on the crowd." Matthew uses both Markan passages (Matt 9:36 and 14:14a, repeated in 15:32) and in 20:34 redactionally adds (to Mark 10:52) "out of compassion" as a motive for the healing of the blind man. This is consistent with Luke 7:13 (Jesus' compassion on a dead man's mother) and with the motivation in Mark 1:41 (healing of a leper) and 9:22 (the father of the epileptic cries "Have pity"), though the vb. does not appear in the Synoptic parallels to these Markan passages (is it perhaps a later addition to the canonical Markan text?).

The association of the vb. with Jesus thus represents a "messianic" characterization of Jesus (so Köster, *TDNT* VII, 554f.) that admittedly is atypical of Jewish messianic expectations. In the OT (Psalms, deutero-Isaiah) it is rather God himself who compassionately turns his attention to the humble and lowly. In *T. Zeb.* 8:1 (cf. 8:2) the σπλαγχνίζεσθαι of God becomes an eschatological statement (cf. also *T. Abr.*[B] 12 as well as the specific usage in the *Shepherd of Hermas;* see Köster 558). This primitive Christian application of the vb. to Jesus thus allows him—as the "Son"—to act in the role of God himself as eschatological Savior.

                                    N. Walter

σπλάγχνον, ου, τό   *splanchnon*   pl.: inner organs; "heart," inner yearning, compassion*

1. Occurrences in the NT — 2. The physical sense — 3. Of emotion

Lit.: T. KOEHLER, *DBSup* X, 1313-28. — H. KÖSTER, *TDNT* VII, 548-59. — E. C. B. MACLAURIN, "The Semitic Background of Use of 'en splanchnois,' " *PEQ* 103 (1971) 42-45. — M. J. J. MENKEN, "The Position of σπλαγχνίζεσθαι and σπλάγχνα in the Gospel of Luke," *NovT* 30 (1988) 107-14. — Spicq, *Notes* II, 812-15. — H. J. STOEBE, *THAT* II, 761-68.

1. Only the pl. of σπλάγχνον occurs in the NT (as almost always in Greek literature as well). It occurs once in Luke (1:78) and in Acts (1:18), 8 times in the Pauline Epistles (twice each in 2 Corinthians and Philippians; 3 times in Philemon [!]; once in Colossians), and once in 1 John (3:17).

2. In the physical sense τὰ σπλάγχνα are the *inner organs* of human beings and animals, the latter esp. in regard to their use in the sacrificial cult (thence derivatives in the LXX). In the NT itself this meaning is seen

only once, and then in a general sense: When Judas took his own life "all his *bowels* gushed out" (Acts 1:18; cf. 4 Macc 5:30; 10:8; 11:19).

3. The extended sense emerges from the presupposition that the σπλάγχνα were the seat of feelings.

a) Older Greek literature viewed the σπλάγχνα particularly as the seat of violent, aggressive feelings. Only in the Hellenistic period were the σπλάγχνα considered the place where one "becomes weak, soft" (so Sir 30:7; Wis 10:5c; *Jos. As.* 6:1) or experiences dejection (*Pss. Sol.* 2:14); they are also the seat of natural maternal love (4 Macc 14:13; 15:23, 29), as well as of affection in the larger sense.

b) Paul's usage derives from these considerations. One's positive inclination toward others, the inner yearning for communion with beloved friends is located in the σπλάγχνα. 2 Cor 7:15 speaks of Titus's *heartfelt affection* for the Corinthians. In Phil 1:8 Paul speaks of his own yearning for the Philippians "with the σπλάγχνα of Christ Jesus": It is, as it were, the *heart* of the Kyrios himself that "speaks" in Paul's heart and yearns for fellowship with his brethren; that is how Paul describes the depth of his yearning.

In Philemon Paul's emotional participation in the fate of the slave Onesimus, who was sent back to his master, is shown in the three occurrences of τὰ σπλάγχνα. Philemon is praised because his manner (or some specific action?) "refreshes" the σπλάγχνα (the *hearts*) of the saints (v. 7); Paul hopes the same will be the case now (v. 20). He calls Onesimus "my very *heart*" (v. 12: τὰ ἐμὰ σπλάγχνα; similarly Philo regarding Jacob and his favorite, Joseph [*Jos.* 25]); cf. Phlm 10.

Only Paul's use of the term in 2 Cor 6:12 is relatively neutral. Literally: "You are not short of space in us, but rather in your own *hearts,*" i.e., not I, but you are taking poor care of yourselves, are not doing yourselves any good. Yet most exegetes understand this passage to mean "it is not that I am hard-hearted (closed off) toward you, but rather that you are toward me."

c) The meaning *pity, compassion, mercy* occurs in the NT (apart from 1 John 3:17) only in combination with synonyms (attributive or in parataxis).

A secular occurrence from 5 B.C. (ÄgU IV, 1139, 17) cannot be interpreted with certainty (Köster 549 n.11). This meaning probably developed under the influence of Heb. *raḥᵃmîm* (Mac-Laurin), which itself derives more strongly than does the Greek from the meaning "womb" (Stoebe). In the LXX this meaning "compassion" does not yet occur (except in Prov 12:10), though it does in *T. 12 Patr.,* esp. *T. Zeb.* 7–8 (see Köster 551f.).

In the benediction in Luke 1:78 God's saving eschatological appearance is traced back to the "*compassionate* heart (σπλάγχνα ἐλέους) of our God" (cf. *T. Zeb.* 8:2a; Pr Man 7). In Phil 2:1 Paul exhorts the Philippians to seek harmony with reference to the σπλάγχνα καὶ οἰκτιρμοί. Here he is either appealing to his readers' predisposition to sympathy (R. Bultmann, *TDNT* V, 161) or introducing his own *heartfelt sympathy* for them or (generally) God's *compassion* as a supporting argument. In the catalog of

characteristics of loving conduct (Col 3:12ff.) the very highest is σπλάγχνα οἰκτιρμοῦ ("compassion *coming from the heart*"), next to → χρηστότης and others. Τὰ σπλάγχνα appears in 1 John 3:17 without any further or more specific interpretation, though it is clearly used in the sense of that particular compassionate disposition ideally characterizing the Christian heart, a disposition that always is prepared to realize itself in tangible acts of compassion.

N. Walter

σπόγγος, ου, ὁ *spongos* sponge*

Mark 15:36: the *sponge* full of vinegar given to the crucified Jesus; so also Matt 27:48; John 19:29.

σποδός, οῦ, ἡ *spodos* ashes*

Matt 11:21 par. Luke 10:13, in the common phrase "in sackcloth and *ashes*" as an expression of penitence; Heb 9:13, of the *ashes* of the red heifer (Num 19:9; cf. also *Barn.* 8:1).

σπορά, ᾶς, ἡ *spora* seed*

Σπορά originally referred to the activity of sowing, then also to *that which has been sowed, the seed* (1 Pet 1:23). S. Schulz, *TDNT* VII, 537, 546.

σπόριμος, 2 *sporimos* sown; subst.: grain*

Only subst. τὰ σπόριμα occurs in the NT (Mark 2:23 par. Matt 12:1/Luke 6:1): One sabbath Jesus went through the *grainfields*. S. Schulz, *TDNT* VII, 538, 547.

σπόρος, ου, ὁ *sporos* seed*

Mark 4:26f.; Luke 8:5, 11, in the parable of the sower: "to scatter *seed* on the ground" (Mark 4:26); "to sow (σπείρω) *seed*" (Luke 8:5, like Deut 11:10 LXX). 2 Cor 9:10: "He who supplies *seed* to the sower and bread for food will provide and multiply your *seed* and increase the harvest of your righteousness": ὁ σπόρος ὑμῶν is a metaphor for resources distributed to those in need. S. Schulz, *TDNT* VII, 537, 546f.

σπουδάζω *spoudazō* hurry, make every effort*

With inf. in Gal 2:10; 1 Thess 2:17; Eph 4:3; 2 Tim 2:15; 4:9, 21; Titus 3:12; Heb 4:11; 2 Pet 1:10, 15; 3:14. Of these, the imv. is used in 2 Tim 2:15; 4:9, 21; Titus 3:12; 2 Pet 1:10; 3:14, and the imperatival partc. in Eph 4:3. Aor. subjunc. occurs in Heb 4:11. G. Harder, *TDNT* VII, 559-68; Spicq, *Notes* II, 816-25.

σπουδαῖος, 3 *spoudaios* eager, industrious*

2 Cor 8:22a, with ἐν πολλοῖς πολλάκις; vv. 17, 22b: comparative σπουδαιότεϱος, *very earnest.* G. Harder, *TDNT* VII, 559-68; Spicq, *Notes* II, 816-25.

σπουδαίως *spoudaiōs* hurriedly, eagerly*

Luke 7:4: παϱακαλέω σπουδαίως, "they besought him *earnestly*"; 2 Tim 1:17; Titus 3:13: *eagerly;* comparative in Phil 2:28: "I am *especially eager* to send him [Epaphroditus]." Spicq, *Notes* II, 818.

σπουδή, ῆς, ἡ *spoudē* haste, eagerness*

The 12 occurrences of this noun are distributed over both meanings: *haste* (Mark 6:25; Luke 1:39) and *eagerness* (Rom 12:8, 11; 2 Cor 7:11, 12; 8:7, 8, 16; Heb 6:11; 2 Pet 1:5; Jude 3). G. Harder, *TDNT* VII, 559-68; Spicq, *Notes* II, 816-25.

σπυϱίς, ίδος, ἡ *spyris* basket*

Mark 8:8, 20 par. Matt 15:37 and 16:10: the baskets at the miraculous feeding; Acts 9:25: Paul was let down over the wall out of the city of Damascus in a basket; cf. 2 Cor 11:32f. Spicq, *Notes* II, 787f.

στάδιον, ου, τό *stadion* stade; stadium, arena*

Στάδιον refers first to a unit of measurement = 600 Greek feet or 192 m. (Matt 14:24; Luke 24:13; John 6:19; 11:18; Rev 14:20; 21:16). It also occurs with the meaning *arena/racetrack* (documented since Pindar) in 1 Cor 9:24 (also *Mart. Pol.* 6:2; 8:3, and elsewhere); → ἀγών 4.

στάμνος, ου, ἡ *stamnos* jar*

Heb 9:4: the earthen vessel holding the manna (Exod 16:33 LXX).

στασιαστής, οῦ, ὁ *stasiastēs* rebel*

Mark 15:7: Barabbas was imprisoned with the *rebels* who had committed murder. Spicq, *Notes* II, 826-28.

στάσις, εως, ἡ *stasis* existence; uprising; strife*

The meaning *existence* occurs only in Heb 9:8 ("still *standing*"). Στάσις occurs in the sense of *insurrection* in Mark 15:7 par. Luke 23:19, 25; Acts 19:40. The meaning *strife/riot* occurs in Acts 15:2; 23:7, 10; 24:5. G. Delling, *TDNT* VII, 568-71; Spicq, *Notes* II, 826-28.

στατήρ, ῆϱος, ὁ *statēr* stater*

The στατήϱ is a silver coin (shekel) worth four drach-

mas (→ δϱαχμή 2; Matt 17:27; 26:15 v.l. [D al]). E. Klostermann, *Matt* (HNT) 147.

σταυϱός, οῦ, ὁ *stauros* cross*

1. Occurrences in the NT; terminology and archaeology of crucifixion — 2. Literal usage, esp. in the Gospels — 3. Metaphorical usage — 4. As a key word for specific theological motifs in the Pauline corpus — a) The authentic letters — b) The deutero-Pauline letters

Lit.: R. S. Barbour, "Wisdom and the Cross in 1 Corinthians 1 and 2," FS Dinkler 57-71. — BAGD s.v. — E. Benz, *Der gekreuzigte Gerechte bei Plato, im NT und in der alten Kirche* (AAWLM.G 1950, 12; 1950). — J. Blinzler, *Der Prozeß Jesu* (⁴1969) (cf. *The Trial of Jesus* [1959]). — E. Brandenburger, "Σταυϱός, Kreuzigung Jesu und Kreuzestheologie," *WuD* 10 (1969) 17-43. — H. Cohn, *The Trial and Death of Jesus* (1972). — G. Delling, *Der Kreuzestod Jesu in der urchristlichen Verkündigung* (1972). — W. Dietrich, "Kreuzesverkündigung, Kreuzeswort und Kreuzesepigraph: Randbemerkungen zum 'Kreuz Christi' bei Paulus," FS Rengstorf (1973) 214-31. — E. Dinkler, "Comments on the History of the Symbol of the Cross," *JTC* 1 (1965) 124-47. — *idem,* "Kreuzzeichen und Kreuz —Tav, Chi und Stauros," *idem, Signum Crucis* (1967) 26-54. — *idem,* "Jesu Wort vom Kreuztragen," *ibid.,* 77-98. — E. E. Ellis, "Christ Crucified," *idem, Prophecy and Hermeneutic in Early Christianity* (WUNT 18, 1978) 72-79. — D. Flusser, "Der Gekreuzigte und die Juden," *FrRu* 28 (1976) 152-57. — G. Friedrich, *Die Verkündigung des Todes Jesu im NT* (²1985). — O. Genest, "L'interprétation de la mort de Jésus en situation discursive. Un cas-type: L'articulation des figures de cette mort en 1–2 Corinthiens," *NTS* 34 (1988) 506-35. — J. B. Green, *The Death of Jesus: Tradition and Interpretation in the Passion Narrative* (WUNT II/33, 1988). — D. J. Halperin, "Crucifixion, the Nahum Pesher, and the Rabbinic Penalty of Strangulation," *JJS* 32 (1981) 32-46. — E. Haulotte, "Du récit quadriforme de la Passion au concept du Croix," *RSR* 73 (1985) 187-228. — M. Hengel, *Crucifixion: In the Ancient World and the Folly of the Message of the Cross* (1977). — H. M. Jackson, "The Death of Jesus in Mark and the Miracle from the Cross," *NTS* 33 (1987) 16-37. — E. Käsemann, "The Saving Significance of the Death of Jesus in Paul," *idem, Perspectives on Paul* (1971) 32-59. — H.-W. Kuhn, "Jesus als Gekreuzigter in der frühchristlichen Verkündigung bis zur Mitte des 2. Jahrhunderts," *ZTK* 72 (1975) 1-46. — *idem,* "Der Gekreuzigte von Giv'at ha-Mivtar. Bilanz einer Entdeckung," FS Dinkler 303-34, with illustrations 14-17. — *idem,* "Die Kreuzesstrafe während der frühen Kaiserzeit. Ihre Wirklichkeit und Wertung in der Umwelt des Urchristentums," *ANRW* II/25 (1982) 648-793. — *idem, TRE* XIX, 713-25. — LSJ 1635. — U. Luz, "Theologia crucis als Mitte der Theologie im NT," *EvT* 34 (1974) 116-41. — W. Michaelis, "Zeichen, Siegel, Kreuz," *TZ* 12 (1956) 505-25. — P. S. Minear, "The Crucified World: The Enigma of Gal 6:14," FS Dinkler 395-407. — L. Morris, *The Cross in the NT* (1965). — F.-J. Ortkemper, *Das Kreuz in der Verkündigung des Apostels Paulus* (SBS 24, ²1968). — J. Schneider, *TDNT* VII, 572-84. — W. Schrage, "Das Verständnis des Todes Jesu Christi im NT," *Das Kreuz Jesu Christi als Grund des Heils* (ed. E. Bizer, et al; ³1969) 49-90. — *idem,* " '. . . den Juden ein Skandalon'? Der Anstoß des Kreuzes nach 1 Kor 1,23," *Gottes*

Augapfel. Beiträge zur Erneuerung des Verhältnisses von Christen und Juden (ed. E. Brocke and J. Seim; 1988) 59-76. — idem, "Leid, Kreuz und Eschaton. Die Peristasenkataloge als Merkmale paulinischer theologia crucis und Eschatologie," EvT 34 (1974) 141-75. — P. STUHLMACHER, "Eighteen Theses on Paul's Theology of the Cross," idem, Reconciliation, Law, and Righteousness (1986) 155-68. — W. VOGLER, "Jesu Tod— Gottes Tat? Bemerkungen zur frühchristlichen Interpretation des Todes Jesu," TLZ 113 (1988) 481-92. — H.-R. WEBER, The Cross: Tradition and Interpretation (1979). — H. WEDER, Das Kreuz Jesu bei Paulus. Ein Versuch, über den Geschichtsbezug des christlichen Glaubens nachzudenken (FRLANT 125, 1981). — For further bibliography → κρεμάννυμι; ξύλον; see also Kuhn, "Kreuzesstrafe"; TWNT X, 1270f.

1. This noun occurs 27 times in the NT: 16 times in the four Gospels, 10 times in the Pauline corpus, and once in Heb 12:2. It designates an upright stake and in all these occurrences refers to what at that time was a uniquely Roman means of execution.

The Romans used crucifixion as a form of punishment more frequently after the Punic Wars. Constantine abolished it after 320 as an insult to the cross of Christ. According to extant witnesses for the period of early Christianity it was a means of execution particularly in Rome and Italy for slaves and freedmen, and in Palestine esp. for rebels. From the beginning of Roman rule until shortly before the outbreak of the Jewish War in A.D. 66 all witnesses to executions by crucifixion in Palestine —as far as can be determined—refer to rebels and rebel sympathizers crucified by the Romans. Therefore, Jesus was almost certainly executed by the Romans as a political agitator (though he doubtlessly did not present himself as such). The crucifixion of Jesus probably followed the crucifixion procedure apparently common at that time (cf. for Palestine also the find at Giv'at ha-Mivtar), i.e., on a stake with a horizontal crosspiece, and probably on a crux commissa (a t-shaped cross). In addition to the noun σταυρός, which refers to the "cross" in other texts of the period, the NT also occasionally uses → ξύλον (3.a) for "cross" under certain circumstances (always in Acts).

2. Used literally, σταυρός always refers in the NT to the cross of Jesus (and otherwise in the NT always refers to Jesus' crucifixion), though the Gospels also mention the simultaneous crucifixion of two "robbers" and mention crucifixion in the broader sense in Jesus' accusations against the Jewish authorities (→ σταυρόω 2.a; συσταυρόω 1).

The literal sense occurs in the Synoptics in only two contexts: the carrying of the cross to the place of execution by Simon of Cyrene (Mark 15:21 par. Matt 27:32/ Luke 23:26; cf. patibulum ferat per urbem, deinde adfigatur cruci, pseudo[?]-Plautus Carbbonaria [apud Nonius Marcellus 221]; see esp. Plutarch De sera numinis vindicta 9); the phrase used is αἴρειν τὸν σταυρὸν αὐτοῦ, "to take up and carry his [Jesus'] cross" (thus Mark and Matthew; αἴρω τὸν σταυρόν is not documented in extrabiblical writings), or φέρειν τὸν σταυρόν, "to carry the cross" (thus Luke; the phrase also occurs in Chariton iv.2.7). John 19:17 portrays the situation differently;

Jesus goes out "bearing his own cross" (ἑαυτῷ; cf. Blinzler 363f. n.32; with βαστάζω also in Chariton iv.2.7; 3.10; Artemidorus Daldianus ii.56). In the the other Synoptic context, the mocking of Jesus on the cross, σταυρός appears only in the first two Gospels (Mark 15:30, 32 par. Matt 27:40, 42), each time in the challenge to "come down from the cross" (καταβαίνειν ἀπὸ τοῦ σταυροῦ). On the question of a Markan theology of the cross → σταυρόω 2.a.

In John σταυρός occurs in three further instances in the Passion Narrative. 19:19 reports that the inscription is put "on the cross" (ἐπὶ τοῦ σταυροῦ), which is presupposed by Matt 27:37; Luke 23:38, whereas Mark 15:26 speaks only of an "inscription"; an inscription on a cross cannot be documented in extrabiblical writings (cf. Kuhn, "Jesus" 5f. n.14). According to John 19:25 women stood "by the cross" (παρὰ τῷ σταυρῷ), first and foremost Jesus' mother. Finally, according to 19:31 Jesus and the robbers were not to remain on their crosses on the ("great"?) sabbath (μὴ μείνῃ ἐπὶ τοῦ σταυροῦ τὰ σώματα, alluding to Deut 21:23). On the Johannine theology of the cross → σταυρόω 2.a.

Outside the Gospels σταυρός is used literally in the strict sense only in two instances. Paul probably adds to the hymn in Phil 2:6-11 "even death on a cross" to the phrase "unto death" (θανάτου δὲ σταυροῦ, v. 8; so common scholarly opinion), as an antithesis against his adversaries (→ 4.a on 3:18; on the theological significance of the insertion see Weder 209-17). This Pauline context is thus the first to associate the servant Jesus (v. 7) with the crucifixion of slaves, which was customary during the Roman period.

Heb 12:2 asserts that Jesus "endured the cross (σταυρός) for [because of προ-, ἀντί is not "instead of"] the joy that was set before him, despising the [accompanying] shame (αἰσχύνη)."

The "shame" associated with the manner of Jesus' death is also mentioned in Heb 6:6 (παραδειγματίζω with → ἀνασταυρόω) and 11:26; 13:13 (ὀνειδισμός; on 13:13 → 3). In 11:26 (ὀνειδισμὸς τοῦ Χριστοῦ) the author shows that the shame of crucifixion is to be understood primarily from the perspective of the OT idea of the shame of the anointed one (Ps 88:51f. LXX; cf. Ps 68:10 LXX), but since 12:2 uses αἰσχ-, which is found in texts of the time that refer to the shame of crucifixion (cf., e.g., αἴσχιστος, Achilles Tatius ii.37.3), the ancient evaluation of crucifixion also plays a role here (cf. also καταισχύνω, 1 Cor 1:27; the paradox in 1 Cor 2:8; and δειγματίζω, Col 2:1).

3. Jesus' saying concerning bearing one's cross in following him is well documented. Q offers the oldest version, which is negative: "Whoever does not take [or receive] his cross and follow me is not worthy of me" (Matt 10:38; the phrase with λαμβάνω is not documented in extra-Christian writings) or "[not] to bear one's own cross" (Luke 14:27, with βαστάζω as in John 19:17; →

2). Mark 8:34 offers a positive variation: "take up [and bear] one's cross and follow me" (with αἴρω as in Mark 15:21 par. Matt 27:32; → 2). From that point the saying appears a second time in the first and third Gospels (Matt 16:24 par. Luke 9:23 [also with αἴρω]); it appears yet again with αἴρω in Mark 10:21 v.l. It appears also in *Gos. Thom.* 55 in a negative variation (probably with βαστάζω). John 12:26 deviates far from these examples (no mention of bearing one's cross), and probably also Heb 13:13 (τὸν ὀνειδισμὸν αὐτοῦ φέρειν; → 2 on 12:2 and on φέρω in Luke 13:26).

Dinkler's interpretation of the saying ("Jesu Wort" 77ff.) in the variation with λαμβάνω is improbable. He asserts that it is an authentic saying of Jesus that refers to an eschatological marking (as in Ezek 9:4ff.) with the "mark" of God (Heb. *tāw*, i.e., first, "sign" and, second, in paleo-Hebrew in the form of a lying or standing cross): The original sense would be λαμβάνειν τὸ σημεῖον αὐτοῦ (cf. *Pss. Sol.* 15:6).

This saying is intended to point to a following or *imitatio* in suffering (cf., aside from the juxtaposition of bearing [taking] one's cross and succession in Q and Mark, the addendum "as I" in *Gos. Thom.*), not to a one-time martyrdom (Jeremias, *Theology* 242). It is metaphorical (this is made esp. clear by "daily" in Luke 9:23), since it cannot be saying that each follower should expect crucifixion nor, esp., that each will literally go to his own place of execution with the crosspiece on his shoulders. The saying reflects on Jesus' death (and only as such was it comprehensible), since "cross" and particularly "bear one's cross" in the metaphorical sense cannot be presupposed in Semitic usage during this period (just as it cannot be presupposed for Greek usage).

Col 2:14 uses σταυρός in a metaphorical phrase, though again with clear reference to Jesus' historical death on the cross. According to the tradition that this passage has presumably assimilated, God nailed to the cross the "bond" of our trespasses "that stood against us," with the author of Colossians probably adding "with its legal demands (→ δόγμα 4)": God thus completely canceled our trespasses through Jesus' death on the cross. The (actually un-Pauline) assertion is thus that Jesus' death on the cross effects the forgiveness of sins (cf. v. 13), and the passage presupposes the common practice of nailing the condemned one to the cross (see Kuhn, "Der Gekreuzigte" 328f.) rather than (*contra* Michaelis 523, et al.) the nailing to the cross of an inscription announcing one's guilt (→ 2 on John 19:19; Philo *Post.* 61; *Som.* ii.213 uses προσηλόω in the first sense and also fig.).

According to this passage God "made a public example of the principalities and powers" (ἐδειγμάτισεν ἐν παρρησίᾳ; cf. the juxtaposition of ἀνασταυρόω and παραδειγματίζω in Heb 6:6) "and triumphed over them" (v. 15), which can be understood as a paradoxical reversal of the shame of the crucifixion (→ 2 on Heb 12:2).

4. Paul's references to the *cross* ("of Christ," or similar-

ly) are the oldest literary witnesses to the crucifixion of Jesus, but in them the noun refers to more than just the means of execution: It is a catch-word (and simultaneously the historical basis) for certain theological motifs (noun and vb. "are used primarily as theological concepts," Ellis 72) and therefore a cipher (see Brandenburger, Σταυρός 35; Kuhn, "Jesus" 29; cf. also the classification in BAGD). The substance of this agenda focuses on Jesus' historical death precisely as death on a cross.

a) Except for Phil 2:8, the authentic Pauline Epistles use σταυρός as an abbreviation for certain aspects of the salvation event, namely, the "stumbling block" that the crucified Jesus presents to Jewish thinking and the "folly" the "Greeks" or "Gentiles" see in God's salvation activity in the cross (cf. 1 Cor 1:22f.). In the three contexts in Galatians and 1 Corinthians 1–2 in which Paul uses particularly the catch-words "cross" or "crucify" (see Kuhn, "Jesus" 27-41), the noun appears in the phrases "the cross of Christ and the law" (Galatians) and "the cross of Christ and wisdom" (1 Corinthians 1–2). In Gal 5:11 "the stumbling block" (the tr. "offense" psychologizes too one-sidedly) that the cross means to some (τὸ σκάνδαλον τοῦ σταυροῦ; note how Paul already uses the phrase absolutely), in contrast to the Jewish use of σκάνδαλον, is not only a "stumbling block" that leads to a loss of salvation, but also, positively, that which can very well effect salvation (see K. Müller, *Anstoß und Gericht* [1969]); the formulation indicates this: "In that case the stumbling block of the cross has been removed" (a conceptual parallel to καταργέω is κενόω in 1 Cor 1:17; both vbs. occur in Rom 4:14).

The use of *cross* in this instance—addressing the opposition of Jewish Christians in the Galatian church—acknowledges that an understanding of Deut 21:23 (also present in early Judaism) considered the crucified Christ to be cursed by the law, and that precisely by his acceptance of this curse believers in him are freed from the law as a means to salvation (literally "from the curse of the law," Gal 3:13; → κρεμάννυμι 2). From the perspective of this curse Jesus, precisely as one crucified, is a σκάνδαλον "to Jews," as Paul later writes in 1 Cor 1:23.

Σταυρός occurs twice more in Paul's conclusion to Galatians. As 6:12 (cf. 5:11) makes apparent, Christians could be "persecuted for the *cross* of Christ" (dat. of cause). Paul's Jewish Christian adversaries wished to save Gentile Christians from this by having them submit to circumcision. Paul accuses his adversaries of boasting because of such circumcision of Gentile Christians (6:13) and says of himself in 6:14 that he does not glory "except in the cross of our Lord Jesus Christ."

According to 1 Cor 1:17f. "Christ's cross" would be robbed of its effect, more specifically "emptied" (cf. above on Gal 5:11), if the apostle's own activity associated itself with "eloquent wisdom." The repetition of the art. in ὁ λόγος ὁ τοῦ σταυροῦ (1:18; missing above all in 𝔭⁴⁶ and B) places the emphasis on gen. τοῦ σταυροῦ (cf. Kühner, *Grammatik* II/1, 617) and refers anaphorically to the full phrase with τοῦ Χριστοῦ (v. 17; BDF §271): "the word, precisely this word of the cross."

This refers to the proclamation of that Jesus who through his death in time and history humbled himself precisely on the cross (on the paradox in 1 Cor 2:8 → σταυρόω 2.c) and who, according to 1:26–2:5, turned his attention to the weak while "shaming the wise" and the "strong" (on καταισχύνω in 1:27 → 2 [on Heb 12:2]) and cutting off any possibility of salvation as a *fait accompli* ("already"; cf. 4:8), something Paul thus emphasizes against this Corinthian wisdom christologically, sociologically, and eschatologically. Precisely this proclamation of the cross is δύναμις θεοῦ for the believers (see also v. 24; the same holds true of the "gospel" in Rom 1:16).

In Philippians Paul seems to be dealing with adversaries related in some respects to those of 1 Corinthians. He calls them (3:18) "enemies of Christ's cross" (→ 2 on 2:8). In contrast to his statements about the death, dying, and sacrifice of Jesus (e.g., 1 Cor 15:3-5), Paul's statements about the cross are almost never directly associated with any assertions about the resurrection (on the exception in 2 Cor 13:4 → σταυρόω 2.c), though they do presuppose it. The Pauline theology of the cross thus appears to be from the apostle himself, apparently with no predecessor in earlier tradition (at most a line of tradition might exist between Gal 3:13 and the contrast schema in Acts 5:30 and 10:39; → ξύλον 3.a).

b) The author of Colossians has inserted the phrase "by the blood of his [death on the] *cross*" into the Christ-hymn he received from tradition (1:20). The hymn refers to the cosmic reconciliation God has effected through Christ, and this added phrase is un-Pauline and contaminates the Pauline theology of the cross by interpreting Jesus' death as a blood sacrifice (→ αἷμα 6; crucifixion was not a particularly bloody way to die, *contra* Hengel, *Crucifixion* 31; see Kuhn, "Kreuzesstrafe" 695f.). On Col 2:14 → 3. The author of Ephesians has amplified a Christ-hymn (2:16) that speaks of the reconciliation of Gentiles and Jews to one another "in one body" and "to God" *through the cross* (ἐν αὐτῷ refers in the present context more to the *cross* than to Christ [in contrast v. 1]); the context concerning the law is noteworthy (v. 15).

The mention of "comprehending" the "breadth and length and height and depth" (Eph 3:18)—at least as understood by the author of Ephesians—is probably also a reference to the cross of Christ understood cosmically (cf. *Mart. Andr.* Prius 14 [Hennecke/Schneemelcher II, 418f.]; *Acts Pet.* 38[9] [Hennecke/Schneemelcher II, 320]), which the author of the letter interprets as "knowledge" of the loving sacrifice of Christ on the cross (v. 19; cf. 5:2, 25).

                                 H.-W. Kuhn

σταυρόω *stauroō* crucify*

1. Occurrences in the NT; terminology of crucifixion —

2. Literal usage — a) Gospels — b) Acts — c) Paul — d) Revelation — 3. Fig. usage

Lit.: → σταυρός.

1. Σταυρόω occurs 46 times in the NT, 35 times in the Gospels (10 times in Matthew, 8 in Mark, 6 in Luke, 11 in John), twice in Acts, 8 times in Paul, and once in Rev 11:8. The vb., which in and of itself means "drive in stakes," is used in the NT in the literal sense only of execution by crucifixion, almost always referring to the crucifixion of Jesus (the only exception being the reference to the two robbers crucified with him; cf. further Matt 23:34). Paul's fig. use of the vb. in Galatians is based on the crucifixion of Jesus.

On the archaeology of crucifixion → σταυρός 1. Of vbs. characteristically used of crucifixion in the first century and a half after Christ the NT uses, almost exclusively, σταυρόω, which Josephus also uses several times. In 4 instances the NT uses → κρεμάννυμι (2) of crucifixion, as frequently in Plutarch and Appian, but in 3 of those instances citing Deut 21:23. → Ἀνασταυρόω, common esp. in Josephus and also in Plutarch, occurs only in Heb 6:6 (fig.), and προσηλόω, occasionally found in Philo, Josephus, and Plutarch, occurs only in Col 2:14 (also fig.; → σταυρός 3); ἀνασκολοπίζω, which appears several times in Philo, does not occur at all in the NT. The NT also uses → συσταυρόω and προσπήγνυμι (the latter only in Acts 2:23).

2. a) The following occurrences of the vb. refer to the crucifixion of Jesus: Jesus' prediction of his own death (Matt 20:19; 26:2); the two angels' recollection of this prediction at the tomb (Luke 24:7); the demand of the "crowd," of "the Jewish authorities," of both together, and of "the Jews" (Mark 15:13f. par. Matt 27:22f./Luke 23:21, 23; John 19:6a, 15a); Pilate's words (John 19:6b, 10, 15b); the handing-over of Jesus to be crucified (Mark 15:15 par. Matt 27:26; John 19:16); the statement that Jesus was led away to be crucified (Mark 15:20 par. Matt 27:31); the portrayal of the crucifixion itself (Mark 15:24f. par. Matt 27:35/Luke 23:33; John 19:18, 23); the identification of the place where he was crucified (John 19:20, 41); and the recollection of the two disciples going to Emmaus (Luke 24:20). Jesus is called the ἐσταυρωμένος by the angel in the account of the empty tomb (Mark 16:6 par. Matt 28:5): The pf. is used (instead of the expected aor.) probably, given the context of the Markan Passion theology, as in Paul (→ c), to characterize Jesus as he who remains the crucified one (cf. Delling 72).

One can speak of a Markan theology of the cross in that Mark starts off Jesus' path to the Passion—not geographically, but theologically—with Jesus' first prediction of suffering and resurrection, and then begins the actual journey to the cross with Jesus' remarks about bearing one's cross and following him (8:34).

The Johannine theology of the cross cannot be subsumed under the rubric of the word-group σταυρ-; it requires rather an understanding of the death of Jesus (precisely) on the cross as ὑψωθῆναι (3:14; 12:32, 34; cf. 8:28).

Reference is also made to the simultaneous crucifixion of the two "robbers" (→ συσταυρόω 1; Mark 15:27 par. Matt 27:38 [cf. Luke 23:33 par. John 19:18]).

Jesus himself refers to crucifixion in his prediction that prophets, wise men, and scribes will suffer a violent fate in Israel (Matt 23:34; the reference is to Jesus' death: This passage does not document a historical use of crucifixion by Jewish authorities any more than any other NT passage).

b) Peter refers to crucifixion in his sermons in Acts 2:36; 4:10 in what is known as the contrast schema, the origin of which is still disputed, and in a statement concerning Jesus' resurrection (or similarly; other vbs. are used for the execution of Jesus on a cross in 2:23; 5:30; 10:39; cf. 13:29 [D* adds σταυρόω]; 3:15 only uses "kill").

c) Within the Pauline conceptual context of "cross of Christ and the law" (→ σταυρός 4.a) Gal 3:1 (at the beginning of the theological part of the letter, 3:1–5:12, which also ends with a statement about the cross in 5:11) says that Jesus Christ "was proclaimed/set forth publicly [so LSJ s.v. προγράφω II.1; literally: *written in*]" before the Galatians precisely "as crucified" (the "bewitching" by the adversaries constitutes the contrasting element). Paul is referring to his own proclamation of the salvation that God gives independently of the Torah (this cannot possibly refer to any description of the sufferings of the crucified Jesus; the tr. "described/portrayed before your eyes" is thus incorrect; → προγράφω).

The Pauline conceptual context "cross of Christ and wisdom" can be comprehended precisely by the paradoxical juxtaposition of ὁ κύριος τῆς δόξης and σταυρόω in 1 Cor 2:8 (→ σταυρός 4.a). Demonic powers (→ ἄρχων 2.c) have given over the "Lord of glory" to the reality of this punishment of the cross (→ σταυρός 2). A corrective to the christology of Paul's adversaries is also intended when the apostle claims to know only Jesus Christ, "and him [namely] crucified," as he says in 2:2, as opposed to "lofty words" and "eloquent wisdom" (cf. 1:17; 2:1), terms with which Paul apparently characterizes the theology and conduct of his adversaries (→ σταυρός 4.a). Such "wisdom of words," which for Paul contradicts Jesus as crucified, brings the apostle within the context of 1:23 into contact with Greek thought (on the crucified Christ, who is also called a σκάνδαλον "to Jews" here, → σταυρός 4.a). The NT refers to Jesus as the *crucified one* with the pf. partc.—apparently to express enduring validity (→ 2.a)—a total of 5 times (besides 1 Cor 1:23; 2:2 also Gal 3:1; Mark 16:6 par. Matt 28:5). In the face of divisions within the Corinthian church Paul asks in 1 Cor 1:13 whether he, Paul, *was crucified* for them (the soteriological ὑπέρ or something similar appears in the con-

text of Paul's statements about the cross only here and in Gal 3:13). In 2 Cor 13:4 the conceptual context of cross and wisdom intersects that of the relationship between "weakness" and divine "power" (verbatim also in 1 Cor 2:3-5; 2 Cor 12:9f.; on 2 Cor 13:4 → σταυρός 4.a).

d) Rev 11:8 refers to Jerusalem as "Sodom and Egypt, where their [namely, the two witnesses of God] Lord *was crucified*" (just as they, too, were killed there).

3. Within the conceptual context of Pauline theology of the cross dealing with the new existence of the believers, σταυρόω and → συσταυρόω (2) are used metaphorically—σταυρόω twice in Galatians. (Non-Christian uses for "crucify" used metaphorically in the NT period can be found in Philo, who thus uses προσηλόω [→ σταυρός 3 on Col 2:14] and κρεμάννυμι [see esp. *Prov.* ii (Armenian) = Eusebius *PE* viii.14.24f.]). In Gal 5:24 Paul speaks of those belonging to Christ as those who have "*crucified* the flesh with its passions and desires." In 6:14b Paul asserts that through the cross of Christ "the world *has been crucified*" for the person who believes ("to me," dat. of advantage; the κόσμος is already replaced by the καινὴ κτίσις, v. 15b) and the "[old] person" has suffered this death "to the detriment of the [power-wielding] world" (dat. of disadvantage). Therefore, "neither circumcision nor uncircumcision" counts for anything, since they are merely external characteristics of the old person (v. 15a; note the chiastic sequence: v. 14bα = v. 15b; v. 14bβ = v. 15a). The corresponding occurrences of → συσταυρόω (2) show that this metaphorical usage is to interpreted christologically.

The background in the history of religions of these statements about crucifying/killing (the flesh, etc.) is disclosed by texts from Philo to the Gnostics that are characterized by dualistic wisdom-oriented thinking; such texts speak of the "killing" of the body or of the flesh (cf. Rom 8:13), e.g., Philo *Ebr.* 69f. (see E. Brandenburger, *Fleisch und Geist* [1968] 216-21).

H.-W. Kuhn

σταφυλή, ῆς, ἡ *staphylē* grape*

Matt 7:16 par. Luke 6:44: One does not gather *grapes* from thorns; Rev 14:18: the angel's command is to "put in your sickle, and gather the clusters of the vine of the earth, for its *grapes* are ripe."

στάχυς, υος, ὁ *stachys* ear of grain*

Mark 2:23 par. Matt 12:1/Luke 6:1: Jesus' disciples plucking *ears of grain* (→ τίλλω); Mark 4:28 (bis), in series: blade (χόρτος), *ear,* "grain (σῖτος) in the *ear*."

Στάχυς, υος *Stachys* Stachys*

In Rom 16:9 Paul greets *Stachys* (τὸν ἀγαπητόν μου) with Urbanus. This name appears several times, e.g., in

Pap. Zenon; *IG* III, 1080 l. 37; 1095, 19; XII, 3 ll. 624, 749; *CIL* VI, 8607.

στέγη, ης, ἡ *stegē*   roof*

Mark 2:4: the removal of a roof; Matt 8:8 par. Luke 7:6: the centurion says to Jesus, "Lord, I am not worthy to have you come under my *roof* [i.e., into my house]."

στέγω *stegō*   pass over in silence; endure*

1 Cor 13:7: "love *covers* all things," i.e., all unpleasantness from other people ("with the cloak of love"); 9:12: "*enduring* anything" (this meaning could also apply in 13:7); absolute in 1 Thess 3:1, 5: μηκέτι στέγων, "when I could *bear it* no longer." W. Kasch, *TDNT* VII, 585-87; Spicq, *Notes* II, 829f.

στεῖρα, ας *steira*   barren, infertile*

Of a woman incapable of conceiving or bearing children (Luke 1:7, 36; Heb 11:11). On the blessing of the barren (Luke 23:29; Gal 4:27) cf. Isa 54:1; *2 Clem.* 2:1.

στέλλομαι *stellomai*   withdraw, avoid*

The mid. form of στέλλω means *withdraw* (from someone; 2 Thess 3:6); also *avoid, shy away from* (2 Cor 8:20 with τοῦτο: "*avoid* this").

στέμμα, ατος, τό *stemma*   wreath, flower garland*

Acts 14:13, of the priest of Zeus in Lystra who "brought oxen and *garlands* to the gates" to offer as sacrifice to Zeus. Sacrificial animals were decorated with garlands; see K. Baus, *Der Kranz in Antike und Christentum* (1940) 7-17.

στεναγμός, οῦ, ὁ *stenagmos*   sigh, groan (noun) → στενάζω.

στενάζω *stenazō*   sigh, groan (vb.)*
στεναγμός, οῦ, ὁ *stenagmos*   sigh, groan (noun)*

1. Occurrences in the NT — 2. LXX — 3. General use in the NT — 4. Paul

Lit.: H. R. BALZ, *Heilsvertrauen und Welterfahrung* (BEvT 59, 1971) 52-54, 57, 77f., 91f. — P. BENOIT, "We Too Groan Inwardly As We Wait for Our Bodies to Be Set Free," *idem, Jesus and the Gospel* (1973) 40-50. — E. KÄSEMANN, "The Cry for Liberty in the Worship of the Church," *idem, Pauline Perspectives* (1971) 122-37. — J. L. NELSON, *The Groaning of Creation: An Exegetical Study of Romans 8:18* (Diss. Union Theol. Seminary, Richmond, VA, 1969). — J. SCHNEIDER, *TDNT* VII, 600-603. — A. VÖGTLE, *Das NT und die Zukunft des Kosmos* (1970) 197-208. — R. WONNEBERGER, "Der Beitrag der generativen Syntax zur Exegese. Ein Beispiel (2. Kor 5,2f.)—neun

Thesen," *Bijdr.* 36 (1975) 312-17. — For further bibliography see Balz.

1. This vb. occurs 6 times in the NT, 3 of those in Paul in eschatological contexts (Rom 8:23 [cf. the compound συστενάζω in v. 22]; 2 Cor 5:2, 4) and the others in Mark 7:34; Heb 13:17; Jas 5:9. Paul uses the noun, also in an eschatological context (Rom 8:26), and it also occurs in an OT citation in Acts 7:34 (cf. Exod 2:24; 6:4; → 3).

2. The LXX uses στενάζω (30 occurrences) and στεναγμός (27 occurrences) to render 15 different Hebrew equivalents. Both vb. and noun are usually used metonymically as strong expressions for human lament and powerless suffering in situations that people cannot change on their own (cf. Job 23:2; 30:25; Ps 30:11 LXX; Jer 4:31). They are also used of prayer to God and characterize not the content of prayer so much as its profundity and intensity (the στεναγμός of the people in Egypt, Exod 2:24; 6:5; cf. further Ps 78:11 LXX; Tob 3:1 ℵ). God answers such prayer, since it constitutes a cry of extreme distress (cf. Philo *Det.* 92–94; *Migr.* 15; *All.* iii.211ff.; *Imm.* 115). The pious can expect deliverance from tribulation into the salvation of God, where ὀδύνη, λύπη, and στεναγμός no longer exist (Isa 35:10; 51:11; cf. also Rev 21:4: πένθος, κραυγή, πόνος).

3. Acts 7:34 is concerned with such στεναγμός to God (cf. Exod 3:7 LXX: κραυγή, see → 1). God saw the ill-treatment of his people in Egypt and heard their *groaning*. Mark 7:34 (found only in Mark) should probably be understood similarly: Before healing the deaf man "Jesus looked up to heaven and *sighed* [ἐστέναξεν; cf. also 6:41; John 11:41]." The methods of magic have an echo here in that *sighing* can be a sign of the (healing) power secured by the healer and concentrated in him (cf. *PGM* II, 13, 945; see also Dibelius, *Tradition* 85f. with n.2; Schneider 603). The actual meaning may be, however, that Jesus, as the representative of the sick person and for his sake, presents that person's suffering to God with extraordinary personal empathy.

A different sense is intended in (μὴ) στενάζοντες (in contrast to μετὰ χαρᾶς) in Heb 13:17: the justified worry and disappointment on the part of church leaders over the Christians for whom they are responsible (cf. O. Michel, *Heb* [KEK] ad loc.). Jas 5:9 also intends a different sense for the vb.: it does not befit Christians to *grumble* or inwardly complain about one another (indeed, this constitutes "judgment" of the other person: 4:11f.; cf. 1 Pet 4:9); the Judge (who is coming soon) will judge those who in their hearts elevate themselves above their brethren (cf. 4:12; 2:13).

4. Paul uses στενάζω in Rom 8:23; 2 Cor 5:2, 4 as a powerful metaphor for the dejection and powerless yearning of believers in their present suffering (ὄντες ἐν τῷ σκήνει, 2 Cor 5:4). Through the Spirit, however, and on the basis of their promised adoption as sons (Rom 8:23), they know about their predestined eschatological salvation. This knowledge (οἴδαμεν, 2 Cor 5:1; ἐν τούτῳ, v. 2;

cf. Wonneberger) enables them to know that their lives under the conditions of this world are merely preliminary and "alienated." Their *groaning* expresses their eager expectation and longing (ἀπεκδεχόμενοι, Rom 8:23; ἐπιποθοῦντες, 2 Cor 5:2) for the final fulfillment of the promised salvation already given to them in faith; such "groaning" is the existential-corporeal expression (cf. καὶ αὐτοὶ ἐν ἑαυτοῖς στενάζομεν, Rom 8:23) of their eschatological existence. In it they become aware of their own destiny in salvation, just as in the "groaning in travail" of all of creation (πᾶσα ἡ κτίσις συστενάζει καὶ συνωδίνει ἄχρι τοῦ νῦν, 8:22) they see its destiny in the freedom of God's children (cf. R. Bultmann, *2 Cor* [Eng. tr., 1985] on 5:2; Balz 52ff.).

Rom 8:26 is unique in the NT in speaking of an intercessory prayer offered by the Spirit on behalf of believers "with *sighs* too deep for words" (στεναγμοῖς ἀλαλήτοις). This statement might refer in general to the believers' prayers, which lack the articulation appropriate to the salvation of God (see, e.g., U. Wilckens, *Rom* [EKKNT] II, ad loc.), so that the Spirit steps in for them as intercessor and mediator of prayer. But the theological train of thought in vv. 18ff. seems to suggest rather that Paul refers here to glossolalia, mentioning it after the "groaning" of creation and that of believers (8:19ff., 23ff.) as a third "groaning" (namely, of the Spirit itself; cf. 1 Cor 14:2ff., esp. v. 14), that which shows even now that God's future salvation already has dominion over the sufferings of the present age (cf. Käsemann; *idem, Rom* [Eng. tr., 1980] 240-43; Balz 77ff. [bibliography, other occurrences]; H. Paulsen, *Überlieferung und Auslegung in Röm 8* [WMANT 43, 1974] 122f.; viewed differently by P. von der Osten-Sacken, *Röm 8 als Beispiel paulinischer Soteriologie* [FRLANT 112, 1975] 272ff.).

H. Balz

στενός, 3 *stenos* narrow*

Matt 7:13, 14: the *narrow* πύλη (θύρα in Luke 13:24; see Schulz, *Q* 309-12); Matt 7:14 v.l.: the *narrow* way. G. Bertram, *TDNT* VII, 604-6.

στενοχωρέω *stenochōreō* crowd, confine*

Στενοχωρέω (like → στενοχωρία) occurs in the NT only in the genuine Pauline letters. Pass. twice in 2 Cor 6:12: "You are not *restricted* by us [i.e., the apostle], but you are *restricted* in your own affections"; pass. also in 4:8: "We are afflicted (θλιβόμενοι) in every way, but not *pushed into a corner* (στενοχωρούμενοι)." G. Bertram, *TDNT* VII, 606ff.; R. Schippers, *DNTT* II, 807-9.

στενοχωρία, ας, ἡ *stenochōria* narrowness; distress, anxiety*

With → θλῖψις in Rom 2:9; 8:35; in the latter passage the enumeration continues with διωγμός and other terms; pl. in 2 Cor 6:4; 12:10 in the "catalog of sufferings." Cf. → στενοχωρέω. G. Bertram, *TDNT* VII, 606ff.

στερεός, 3 *stereos* firm, solid; steadfast*

Literal in 2 Tim 2:19 (θεμέλιος); Heb 5:12, 14 (τροφή); fig. in 1 Pet 5:9 (στερεοὶ τῇ πίστει). G. Bertram, *TDNT* VII, 609-14.

στερεόω *stereoō* make strong/firm; secure*

Pass. in the literal sense *(become strong)* in Acts 3:7, in reference to the lame man: His lame feet and ankles *were made [became] strong;* act. in the same narrative: Christ's name *made* this lame man *strong* (v. 16); pass. used fig. in 16:5: "So the churches *were strengthened* [impf.] in the faith." G. Bertram, *TDNT* VII, 613.

στερέωμα, ατος, τό *stereōma* firmness, strength*

Col 2:5: στερέωμα τῆς εἰς Χριστὸν πίστεως ὑμῶν: The author of the letter rejoices at the "firmness of your faith in Christ." Cf. Acts 16:5 (στερεόω); 1 Pet 5:9 (στερεός). G. Bertram, *TDNT* VII, 614.

Στεφανᾶς, ᾶ *Stephanas* Stephanas*

This personal name, which occurs elsewhere as well (*CIG* II, 3378; Preisigke, *Sammelbuch* 361 l. 10), refers in 1 Cor 1:16 to a member of the church at Corinth. Paul baptized Stephanas and his household as "the first converts in Achaia" (16:15). 16:17 mentions that Stephanas came with others to Paul (in Ephesus). Cf. the subscription of 1 Corinthians.

στέφανος, ου, ὁ *stephanos* wreath, crown*
στεφανόω *stephanoō* crown (vb.), adorn*

1. Occurrences in the NT and general meaning — 2. In the Pauline and post-Pauline Epistles — 3. James and Revelation — 4. The Passion narrative

Lit.: K. BAUS, *Der Kranz in Antike und Christentum* (Theophaneia 2, 1940). — A. J. BREKELMANS, *Martyrerkranz* (AnGr 150, 1965). — O. BRONEER, "The Apostle Paul and the Isthmian Games," *BA* 25 (1962) 2-31. — *idem,* "The Isthmian Victory Crown," *AJA* 66 (1962) 259-63. — O. FIEBIGER, PW IV, 1636-43. — R. GANSZYNIEC, PW XI, 1588-1607. — W. GRUNDMANN, *TDNT* VII, 615-36. — C. MEISTER, *BHH* 999f. — For further bibliography see *TWNT* X, 1271.

1. The noun occurs 18 times in the NT, 3 of those in Paul, 3 in the post-Pauline Epistles, 8 in Revelation, and 4 in the Gospels. The vb. occurs only in 2 Tim 2:5; Heb 2:7, 9.

Στέφανος encompasses the meanings of both "wreath"

and "crown," though the latter also corresponds to διάδημα, the bejeweled diadem. Wreaths appear as expressions of joy and of religious consecration in all public and private celebrations of the Greeks and Romans. Accordingly, in the first centuries Christians perceived their use as heathen and either avoided or rejected it. They then limited themselves to using the word fig. for their expectations of the eschaton and of life after death. The OT shows similar reservations concerning the wreath. The most significant uses of the wreath in the public life of antiquity were the Olympic laurel and the victory wreath of the Roman conqueror. NT use of the word and image is influenced by both these instances; Revelation also uses the wreath as a sign of royal sovereignty.

2. The apostle Paul often compares Christian life with races in the stadium or with self-sacrificial training for competition (1 Cor 9:24-26; Gal 2:2; 5:7; Phil 2:1; 3:12-14). The goal—eternal life—is the "imperishable wreath"; it corresponds to the "perishable" wreath attained by the victor in athletic competition (1 Cor 9:25). The use of the image in 1 Pet 5:4 reflects Paul's usage. 1 Thess 2:19 and Phil 4:1 use it similarly; both passages understand the Church itself as an honorific distinction for the apostle. (Any interpretation of Phil 4:1 should bear in mind that the apostle thinks he is near the end of his life; in antiquity the mystagogue crowned himself with a wreath when, during the initiation into the mysteries, he experienced the anticipation of his own death and drew near to his god during the mystery celebration itself.) Athletic competition also serves as the metaphor in 2 Timothy; in 2:5 the author asserts that one must fight "fairly" (νομίμως, less colorfully in 4:7: καλῶς, "well") in order to receive the "crown of righteousness" from the "righteous judge" (4:8). "Righteousness" in this context should not be understood in the Pauline fashion, since it refers here to the reward one can legitimately claim for a certain accomplishment, and not to righteousness effected and bequeathed by God.

3. The two references to the wreath or crown "of life" (Jas 1:12; Rev 2:10) are directed to the person who overcomes in the eschatological trial (of faith). In the open letter of Revelation "he who conquers" (→ νικάω 4) is understood as the vanquisher of death standing in the succession of Christ, one who will receive the crown of life as the victory prize, or who already possesses it, though it may still be lost again (3:11). The "elders" wear a similar crown (4:4); they are the great prophets God sent to the Jews, who slew them. Their crowns, however, must also be considered signs of sovereignty, since these prophets were called to be coregents as a reward for their loyalty to God; this is also expressed by the thrones on which they are seated. Accordingly, they cast their crowns

down in order to worship God (and the Lamb) at his exaltation (4:10).

The crown also appears as a sign of sovereignty on the head of the angel who appears in human form (Rev 14:14) and whose task is the execution of world judgment. For this reason many consider the angel to be one form of the appearance of Christ; in that case the crown would have to be interpreted as a sign of victory. The characteristic form of Christ in Revelation, however, is the slaughtered lamb, which wears no crown, whereas its adversaries (12:3; 13:1) are adorned with diadems and thereby identified as the prince of this world and his copy.

Originally the crowns on the heads of the locust-horses (Rev 9:7) were also signs of sovereignty, since the conception of this vision was influenced by the idea of the kings from the north or from the underworld. The "crown of twelve stars" adorning the heavenly woman (12:1) shows first the cosmic significance of this portent viewed in heaven. It, too, can be viewed as a crown of sovereignty, since the woman—the Church—as the mother of the Messiah is also the mother of a king. The crown worn by the rider of the white horse (6:2), however, is clearly a victory wreath and serves to designate victory as the task of this rider. The riders together symbolize a lost war and its consequences, and the victory by the first rider begins the horrors of the end time. This disaster has absolutely nothing to do with the victorious "Word of God" in 19:11ff. (13) (→ ἵππος 2).

4. A unique sign of sovereignty is the "crown of thorns" that the Roman soldiers place on Christ's head to mock him as king of the Jews (Matt 27:29; Mark 15:17; John 19:2, 5), which has become among Christians a symbol, not only, like the cross, of Christ's suffering, but also of his kingship (see Grundmann 632, 635; cf. also Heb 2:7, 9 [citing Ps 8:6 LXX]).

H. Kraft

Στέφανος, ου *Stephanos* Stephen*

Lit.: J. BIHLER, "Der Stephanusbericht (Apg 6,8-15 und 7,54–8,2)," *BZ* 3 (1959) 252-70. — idem, *Die Stephanusgeschichte im Zusammenhang der Apostelgeschichte* (1963). — F. F. BRUCE, *Peter, Stephen, James, and John* (1979) 49-85. — O. CULLMANN, *The Johannine Circle* (1976) 39-53. — W. FOERSTER, "Stephanus und die Urgemeinde," *Dienst unter dem Wort* (FS H. Schreiner, 1953) 9-30. — M. HENGEL, *Between Jesus and Paul* (1983) 1-29, 133-56. — J. KILGALLEN, *The Stephen Speech* (AnBib 67, 1976). — M. H. SCHARLEMANN, *Stephen: A Singular Saint* (AnBib 34, 1968). — G. SCHNEIDER, "Stephanus, die Hellenisten und Samaria," *Les Actes des Apôtres* (ed. J. Kremer; 1979) 215-40. — idem, *Acts* (HTKNT, 1980) 405-80. — M. SIMON, *St. Stephen and the Hellenists in the Primitive Church* (1958). — O. H. STECK, *Israel und das gewaltsame Geschick der Propheten* (WMANT 23, 1967) 265-69 (on 3). — U. WILCKENS, *Die Missionsreden der Apostelgeschichte* (WMANT 5, ³1974) 208-24 (on 3). — For further bibliography

→ Ἑλληνιστής; see also Schneider, *Acts*. On Stephen's speech (Acts 7:2-53) see Schneider, *Acts* I, 441f.

1. In the NT only Acts mentions the first Christian martyr, Stephen (6:5, 8, 9; 7:59; 8:2; 11:19; 22:20). The Greek name Στέφανος appears in Plato and Demosthenes, in inscriptions and papyri (Moulton/Milligan s.v.), and in Josephus *B.J.* ii.228. In Acts Stephen is the first of the seven chosen to solve the conflict between "Hellenists" and "Hebrews" in the primitive Church; 6:5 calls him "a man full of faith and of the Holy Spirit." Although according to 6:2 the seven were chosen for table service (welfare for the poor), Stephen appears publicly as a speaker (6:9-14; 7:2-53), and the second of the seven, Philip, as a missionary (8:4-40). Stephen was perhaps the primary theological representative of the Christian "Hellenists" (→ Ἑλληνιστής), though the speech attributed to him (7:2-53) was not given in the situation presented in the passage (→ 3). The conflict between the "Hellenists" and the "Hebrews" probably presupposed more profound theological differences than those suggested in 6:1-6.

2. Acts places Stephen's speech within the report of his martyrdom (6:8-15; 7:54-60; 8:1-3). The report itself suggests that the features recalling an assembly of the Sanhedrin probably came about by assimilation to the trial of Jesus. The original martyrdom report more likely told of tumultuous lynch-mob justice (H. Conzelmann, *Acts* [Hermeneia] 61; Schneider, *Acts* I, 432-34). The reasons given for the violent measures taken against Stephen are: his great wonders and signs (6:8), the inability of Hellenistic Jews to withstand his wisdom in disputation (vv. 9f.), and the charge that he blasphemed against Moses and God (v. 11). False witnesses make this last charge more specific by asserting that Stephen spoke blasphemous words against the temple and the law (vv. 14f.). After Stephen confesses to seeing Jesus standing at God's right hand (7:55f.), he is cast out of the city and stoned (vv. 57-60). Devout men bury him and lament his death (8:2), and his death is the catalyst for a persecution causing the "Hellenists" to leave Jerusalem (8:1b; 11:19). Finally, these "Hellenists," as missionaries to the Gentiles (11:20), become a historical bridge between Jerusalem and the later mission work of Paul (13:1-4). Acts 22:20 calls Stephen a μάρτυς of Jesus Christ and looks back on his martyrdom. But in this reference → μάρτυς (2) is not yet a designation for Christian blood martyrdom, since Stephen is a "witness" on the basis of his proclamation.

3. The speech attributed to Stephen (Acts 7:2-53) does not record what was actually spoken in the situation. Rather, it is a secondary insertion into the framework of the narrative and has been thoroughly reworked by the author of Acts. The author does, however, make use of a traditional speech, which already had a longer history within tradition (Schneider, *Acts* I, 441-69). The earliest stratum represented in the present text was probably a historical survey from Abraham through Moses up to the building of the temple (approximately vv. 2b-48a). Its intention—in the synagogues of the Jewish Diaspora— could have been to emphasize that neither God's presence nor his activity on behalf of his people was restricted to Palestine. This basic outline of Israel's history was reworked by "Hellenistic" Christians (in Palestine) to produce a "Deuteronomistic" conversion sermon. As part of this reworking the polemical passages (vv. 35, 37, 39-42a, 51-53) were added. Luke was probably the first to insert the two Scripture citations in vv. 42b-43 and vv. 48b-50. According to this hypothesis, Luke might have acquired the prototype of his speech of Stephen from within the circles of Christian "Hellenists" (Steck 268f.; Wilckens 219).

G. Schneider

στεφανόω *stephanoō* crown, adorn
→ στέφανος.

στῆθος, ους, τό *stēthos* breast*

Rev 15:6: the seven angels "robed in pure bright linen, and their *breasts* (τὰ στήθη) girded with golden girdles"; John 13:25 and 21:20: "lying close to the *breast* of Jesus"; Luke 18:13; 23:48: τύπτω τὸ στῆθος (αὐτοῦ), "beat [one's own] *breast*" as a sign of grief or remorse.

στήκω *stēkō* stand*

Στήκω is a Hellenistic pres. formation from the pf. of the vb. → ἵστημι, ἕστηκα, whose meaning *stand* it thus shares. This synonymity becomes clear, e.g., in Mark 3:31 par.: Mark uses στήκω, while Matthew and Luke use the pf. of ἵστημι (cf. also Mark 11:25 with Matt 6:5). At times the textual tradition fluctuates between the two vbs. (John 1:26; 8:44 [cf. BDF §§14; 73]; see also Rev 12:4 [the LXX already reflects this situation as well: Exod 14:13]). The majority of NT occurrences are in Paul, who uses this vb. and the pf. of ἵστημι of Christian existence (→ ἵστημι 3); in so doing he almost always uses στήκω in the imv. (1 Cor 16:13; Gal 5:1; Phil 1:27; 4:1; 1 Thess 3:8; 2 Thess 2:15; ind. in Rom 14:4). For bibliography see → ἵστημι.

M. Wolter

στηριγμός, οῦ, ὁ *stērigmos* firmness, stability*

2 Pet 3:17b: "lose one's *stability*," i.e., one's firm grip. The Church is warned not to allow itself to be carried away "by the error of lawless men" (v. 17). G. Harder, *TDNT* VII, 657.

στηρίζω *stērizō* fix firmly, strengthen*

1. Occurrences in the NT and meanings — 2. Luke — 3. The Pauline corpus — 4. The Catholic Epistles and Revelation

Lit.: G. HARDER, *TDNT* VII, 653-57. — G. SCHNEIDER, " 'Stärke deine Brüder!' (Lk 22,32)," *Catholica* 30 (1976) 200-206. — J. STARCY, "Obfirmavit faciem suam ut iret Jerusalem," *RSR* 39 (1951/52) 197-202 (on Luke 9:51). — P. D. M. TURNER, "Two Septuagintalisms with στηρίζειν," *VT* 28 (1978) 481f.

1. The vb. στηρίζω occurs 13 times in the NT, 3 of those in Luke, 6 in the Pauline corpus, 3 in the Catholic Epistles, and 1 in Rev 3:2. It is noteworthy that the compound → ἐπιστηρίζω occurs only in Acts (4 times), always fig. (14:22; 15:32, 41; 18:23). Acts also uses στερεόω (3 times, fig. in 16:5), which occurs nowhere else in the NT.

2. Luke 9:51, at the beginning of the "journey narrative," makes a significant statement that evokes the language of similar OT formulations (Jer 3:12; 21:10; Ezek 6:2, and elsewhere): "When the days drew near for him to be received up, he *set* his face [resolutely] to go to Jerusalem." Στηρίζω refers here to Jesus' "unalterable purpose" (Harder 656). He submits resolutely to the realization of the divine plan (cf. Luke 9:22). 16:26 also uses στηρίζω literally: "Between us and you a great chasm *has been fixed* [ἐστήρικται, pf. pass.]." According to 22:32 Jesus gives Simon Peter the task of *strengthening* his brethren. This fixes the (post-)Easter task of Peter as that of strengthening Christians in their faith; cf. 24:33f.

3. The Pauline corpus use στηρίζω only fig. in the sense of *strengthen, establish firmly, make firm.* The vb. is used with these acc. objects: ὑμᾶς (Rom 16:25; 1 Thess 3:2; 2 Thess 3:3), ὑμῶν τὰς καρδίας (1 Thess 3:13; 2 Thess 2:17). It is pass. in Rom 1:11, where Paul wishes to impart to the addressees a spiritual gift "to *strengthen* you." All these passages are concerned with strengthening the churches—through Timothy (1 Thess 3:2) or through God (Rom 1:11; 16:25; 1 Thess 3:13; through Christ and God in 2 Thess 2:17; 3:3).

4. According to 2 Pet 1:12 (pass.) such strengthening or securing of the Church is established in truth; cf. v. 10: "Be the more zealous to confirm (βέβαιος) your call and election." See also 3:17 with the admonition not to lose one's "stability" (στηριγμός) because of false teaching. Cf. further → ἀστήρικτος (2:14; 3:16).

Jas 5:8 advises patience regarding the parousia: "*Establish* your hearts." 1 Pet 5:10 attributes the strengthening of the addressees to God: "The God of all grace . . . will himself restore, establish (στηρίξει), strengthen (σθενώσει), and settle (θεμελιώσει) you." Rev 3:2 exhorts the church at Sardis: "Awake, and *strengthen* what remains and is on the point of death."

G. Schneider

στιβάς, άδος, ἡ *stibas* leafy branches*

In Mark 11:8b στιβάς probably refers to bundles of leafy branches. This noun is not documented in Hellenistic Jewish writings, though it does occur as a loanword in the rabbinic literature. The story of Jesus' entry into Jerusalem reports that many people spread their garments on the road and "others spread *leafy branches* that they had cut from the fields" (v. 8). The parallel Matt 21:8 interprets this quite specifically ("others cut branches [κλάδους] from trees"), while Luke 19:36 omits the information in Mark 11:8b entirely. R. Pesch, *Mark* (HTKNT) II, ad loc., interprets στιβάς as bundles of branches from olive trees.

στίγμα, ατος, τό *stigma* brand, mark*

1. Meaning — 2. Branding and tattooing in the NT world — 3. Gal 6:17

Lit.: O. BETZ, *TDNT* VII, 657-64. — U. BORSE, "Die Wundmale und der Todesbescheid," *BZ* 14 (1970) 88-111. — T. GÜTTGEMANNS, *Der leidende Apostel und sein Herr* (FRLANT 90, 1966) 126-35 (on discussion of Gal 6:17). — W. KLASSEN, "Short Comments: Gal 6:17," *ExpTim* 81 (1969/70) 378. — F. MUSSNER, *Gal* (HTKNT, 1974) 418-20. — For further bibliography see Güttgemanns.

1. Στίγμα, occurring in the NT only in Gal 6:17, originally meant *prick, point* (cf. στιγμή); it then referred to a physical *blemish* or *mark* caused, e.g., by branding or tattooing.

2. a) It was quite common for animals to be branded (with signs or letters, also σφραγίς, χαρακτήρ) for the sake of identification. Identification of slaves with brands was an established custom only in the Orient (Code of Hammurabi §146, cf. §226f. [*ANET* 172, 176]; cf. also Exod 21:5f.; Deut 15:16f.). In the Greco-Roman world such identification was used only on slaves who had committed a particularly serious crime or had tried to escape and on military deserters or forced laborers. In these instances, then, such marks did not designate any sort of social standing, but rather were signs of particular dishonor, and whenever possible the person thus marked tried to render the marks unrecognizable. Only in the post-NT period are such στίγματα documented as a "normal" means of identification of slaves or recruits in the Roman army. Already Pseudo-Phocylides 225, however, presupposes that such identification of slaves with στίγματα was common, though he prohibits it in deference to the human dignity even of slaves.

b) Oriental religions document the custom of particularly pious individuals marking themselves to indicate belonging to a certain deity, just as they also referred to themselves as "slaves" of the deity. Tattoos were thus a kind of confessional sign and talisman. Corresponding (metaphorical) expressions are not alien to the OT (Isa 44:5; 49:16).

c) Judaism in the Hellenistic period viewed circumcision as

a confessional sign that excluded religious tattooing (3 Macc 2:29f.; cf. Lev 19:28). Cf. in Revelation the juxtaposition of the heavenly "seal" for the pious (7:2f.) and the "mark" that the servants of the "beast" sear onto their hands or foreheads (14:9-11, etc.).

3.a) Exegesis of Gal 6:17 must ignore the religious-psychopathic phenomenon of "stigmata" that is evoked by—and that receives its terminological designation from—meditative reflection on Gal 6:17. It must also not think of scars resulting from previous wounds and coinciding by chance with the five wounds of the cross, or any other special relationship between Paul's στίγματα and the body of the crucified Jesus: Nowhere does Paul offer any evidence suggesting reflection on the Passion of Jesus oriented in this way. Nor are interpretations probable that suggest Paul was tattooed at baptism with the sign χ for χ(ριστός) (E. Dinkler, *Signum Crucis* [1967] 93) or with an abbreviated form of Jesus' name (so F. J. Dölger, *Sphragis* [1911] 51).

b) Scholars today widely assume that Paul is speaking of scars resulting from events such as those mentioned in 1 Cor 15:32 or 2 Cor 11:23-27 and esp. 1:8f. (Borse 99ff.: when Galatians is written the scars are in part still "fresh"). When Paul calls such scars received in the service of his Lord στίγματα τοῦ Ἰησοῦ, he might have been thinking as much of the forced branding of the slave as of pious self-marking (tattooing) as an expression of belonging to a cultic "lord"; his own self-designation as δοῦλος Χριστοῦ Ἰησοῦ (Rom 1:1, etc.; cf. Gal 1:10) agrees in both respects (*contra* Borse 94f.). In any case, Paul understands these scars as enduring signs that he belongs to Jesus, signs making him independent of other people and unassailable. In the postscript written in his own hand Paul thus asserts that these marks of his relationship to his Lord's suffering really ought to spare him any further "troubles" from the Galatians (i.e., questioning of his apostolic authority? cf. chs. 1–2).

Neither the word στίγμα nor anything else in Gal 6:17 justifies the assertion that Paul saw his own body as the " 'locus' of the epiphany and presence of the earthly Jesus as Lord" (Güttgemanns 134). The overall context in Galatians, however (esp. 5:1-11; 6:12-15), does permit the conclusion that Paul views his στίγματα as a counter to the circumcision advocated by his adversaries in Galatia, which he considers merely a sign of renewed enslavement to the law, whereas his own marks of suffering identify him as a free person in Christ (cf. Betz 663f.).

N. Walter

στιγμή, ῆς, ἡ *stigmē* point, moment*

Luke 4:5 (cf. par. Matthew) uses this term in reference to time: The devil shows Jesus all the kingdoms of the world ἐν στιγμῇ χρόνου.

στίλβω *stilbō* shine, gleam*

Mark 9:3, in the story of the Transfiguration: Jesus' garments became στίλβοντα λευκὰ λίαν (Matt 17:2: λευκὰ ὡς τὸ φῶς). G. Fitzer, *TDNT* VII, 665f.

στοά, ᾶς, ἡ *stoa* columned portico, colonnade*

John 10:23; Acts 3:11; 5:12: the "*portico* of Solomon"; John 5:2: the five *porticos* of the Bethesda complex (→ Βηθζαθά 1).

στοιβάς, άδος, ἡ *stoibas* leafy branches
TR spelling of → στιβάς (Mark 11:8).

Στοϊκός, 3 *Stoikos* Stoic*

The spelling of this adj. should actually be Στωϊκός (BDF §35.1). Acts 17:18 mentions with Epicureans "*Stoic* philosophers" with whom Paul disputed in Athens. M. Pohlenz, *Die Stoa* (2 vols.; [4]1970); J. Rief, *LTK* IX, 1088-90; G. Patzig, *RGG* VI, 382-86; H. Dörrie, *KP* V, 376-78; K. von Fritz, *OCD* 1015f.; P. P. Hallie, *EncPh* VIII, 19-22 (bibliography); H. Koester, *History, Culture, and Religion of the Hellenistic Age* (Introduction to the NT I; 1982) 147-53 (bibliography).

στοιχεῖον, ου, τό *stoicheion* foundation, element*

1. Occurrences in the NT — 2. Hellenistic usage — 3. The Pauline corpus — 4. 2 Pet 3:10, 12 — 5. Heb 5:12

Lit.: BAGD s.v. — H. D. BETZ, *Gal* (Hermeneia) 204f., 215-17. — J. BLINZLER, "Lexikalisches zu dem Terminus τὰ στοιχεῖα τοῦ κόσμου bei Paulus," *SPCIC 1961* (AnBib 17/18, 1963) II, 429-43. — G. DELLING, *TDNT* VII, 670-87. — J. GNILKA, *Col* (HTKNT, 1980) 121-27, 156f. — E. LOHSE, *Col and Phlm* (Hermeneia) 96-99, 122f. — W. SCHWABE, "*Mischung*" *und* "*Element*" *im Griechischen bis Platon* (Archiv für Begriffsgeschichte 3, 1980) 254-61. — E. SCHWEIZER, "Die Elemente der Welt," *idem, Beiträge zur Theologie des NT* (1970) 147-63. — *idem,* "Slaves of the Elements and Worshippers of Angels: Gal 4:3, 9 and Col 2:8, 18, 20," *JBL* 107 (1988) 455-68. — P. VIELHAUER, "Gesetzesdienst und Stoicheiadienst im Galaterbrief," FS Käsemann 543-55. — For further bibliography see *TWNT* X, 1271f.

1. Στοιχεῖον occurs 4 times in the Pauline corpus, twice in 2 Peter, and once in Hebrews, always pl.

2. Στοιχεῖον refers to "that which belongs to a series," in linguistic theory the individual constituent parts of a syllable or word, its "smallest constituent parts," in music the individual tone. This leads to the meanings "principles of something" (Xenophon *Mem.* ii.1.1; Plutarch *Lib. Educ.* 16 [*Moralia* 12c]) and "principles of a science or art" (of music: Plato *Tht.* 206b; of mathematics: Euclid *Elementa*).

This expression played a significant role in the cosmology of antiquity. Plato was already familiar with the designation, later common in Stoic philosophy, of the four (Empedoclean) "[proto-]elements of the cosmos" (earth, water, air, and fire) as στοιχεῖα (cf. *Ti.* 48b; Zeno of Citium (apud Diogenes Laertius vii.136f.); similarly Philo *Her.* 140; *Cher.* 127). The celestial bodies also belong to the realm of the elements (Philo *Spec. Leg.* ii.255; Wis 13:2), though they were probably called στοιχεῖα only after the NT (Blinzler 432ff.; Delling 681-83; cf., however, Lohse 99 n.41). Philo (*Spec. Leg.* 255f.; *Vit. Cont.* 3-5: differentiation between cults of the elements and of the celestial bodies!) and Wis 13:1-11, among others, already show that the elements were worshipped in Hellenistic syncretism; just how far their deification went, however, is unclear (cf. Delling 673-75, 676-81).

3. It is much disputed whether the στοιχεῖα τοῦ κόσμου (Gal 4:3, 9) are to be understood within this syncretistic context, and resolution of the question depends on whether Paul has picked up a catchword used by his Galatian adversaries. If this is the case, then the false teachers demonstrate not only a Judaizing tendency (cf. 5:1-4), but also a Hellenistic syncretistic tendency that included worship of the *cosmic elements,* esp. observance (4:10) of special dates and festivals (cf. Schweizer, "Elemente" 162).

More likely Paul uses this term, known to him from (Stoic) popular philosophy, on his own initiative to designate collectively both the Jewish Torah, which the false teachers understood as a path to salvation and advised the Galatians to follow at least in part (5:3), and the previous Gentile piety of the Galatians (4:3f., 8f.). He considered both to be manifestations of that power presently enslaving human beings (4:3, 5, 8f.), a power that nonetheless appears "beggarly" compared to the υἱοθεσία (v. 5); such power was the basis of human religious existence before Christ (Delling 685; cf. Vielhauer).

In contrast, the mention of the *elemental spirits* in Col 2:8, 20 undoubtedly does make use of the terminology of the false teachers in Colossae, in whose mystery-oriented (?—cf. v. 18) φιλοσοφία such spirits might have played a significant role. This philosophy amplified the traditional Christian message with its own παράδοσις (v. 8) and regarded these spirits as powers capable of preventing a person from attaining the fullness of salvation (cf. v. 9), if that person did not submit to them by following certain religious practices (such as worship of angels, partial renunciation of food, etc.: vv. 16-18; cf. the neo-Pythagorean text in Diels, *Fragmente* I, 448, l. 33-451, l. 19; Schweizer, "Elemente" 160ff.). Over against these assertions the author of Colossians, using Pauline formulations (cf. v. 20 ["if with Christ you died to the elemental spirits of the universe"] with Rom 7:4, 6; Gal 2:19), emphasizes the invalidity of such regulations generated by worship of στοιχεῖα for the Christian who is removed from that world.

4. According to Stoic doctrine the *elements* will perish in the final conflagration (Diogenes Laertius vii.134). 2 Pet 3:10, 12 uses this image to portray the apocalyptic events on the "[judgment] day of the Lord."

5. Heb 5:12 (cf. 6:1) speaks of the "first *principles* (στοιχεῖα τῆς ἀρχῆς) of God's word," i.e., of Christianity (cf. O. Michel, *Heb* [KEK] 235f.), which the letter's recipients need to learn anew; the reference is to the repetition of catechism instruction.

E. Plümacher

στοιχέω *stoicheō* be in line, agree, accord*

Lit.: BAGD s.v. — G. DELLING, *TDNT* VII, 666-69. — LSJ s.v.

1. This vb. occurs in the NT in Acts 21:24 and in Paul's letters (4 times).

Στοιχέω might be derived from military terminology: The fighting power of the hoplite phalanx depended on the individual soldier "being [firmly] in line (στοῖχος)" (cf. Xenophon *Cyr.* vi.3.34; Lycurgus *Leocrates* 77). Στοιχέω then came to mean fig. "agree, be in accord" (cf. Musonius 102.9 [τῷ λόγῳ] and the terminology of honorific inscriptions [Delling 667]). The NT takes this usage as its point of departure.

2. When the Lukan Paul endorses cultic vows, this shows that he, too, to the extent that he observes the law, *stands as one (agrees)* with Jews who faithfully keep the law (Acts 21:24; cf. *SIG* II, 708, 5). Rom 4:12 speaks of *falling* into the line of footprints (τοῖς ἴχνεσιν) of Abraham's faith (cf. O. Stumpff, *TDNT* III, 403; the meaning frequently attributed to στοιχέω esp. here and in Acts 21:24, namely, "walk," is nowhere documented: Delling 668f.).

In Gal 5:25 Paul concludes the parenesis following a catalog of vices and virtues (vv. 19-22) with this gnomic statement: Εἰ ζῶμεν πνεύματι, πνεύματι καὶ στοιχῶμεν, "If we live by the Spirit, let us also *be in accord with* the Spirit" (see H. D. Betz, *Gal* [Hermeneia] 293f.). The benediction at the end of this same letter is directed to those who *agree* (6:16) with the κανών defined in 6:15. Στοιχέω also appears in Phil 3:16, again in a concluding passage, this time at the end of a dispute with church members who consider themselves sure of their own spiritual maturity: Only (πλήν) one should *hold true to, stay in agreement with* what has been (spiritually) attained.

E. Plümacher

στολή, ῆς, ἡ *stolē* robe*

Στολή refers esp. to a long, flowing robe. Luke 15:22: "the best *robe*"; fig. in Rev 7:14; 22:14: washing of *robes.* The στολὴ λευκή is associated with angels (Mark 16:5) and with transformed believers (Rev 6:11; 7:9, 13). Mark 12:38 par. Luke 20:46: scribes who like to walk about in long *robes*. U. Wilckens, *TDNT* VII, 687-91; for further bibliography see *TWNT* X, 1272.

στόμα, ατος, τό *stoma* mouth

1. Occurrences in the NT — 2. Meaning — 3. Use in various genres

Lit.: BAGD s.v. — K. WEISS, *TDNT* VII, 692-701. — M. WILCOX, *The Semitisms of Acts* (1965) 74-76.

1. Στόμα occurs 78 times in the NT, with noticeably high frequency in Revelation (22 occurrences), Matthew (11), Luke (9), and Acts (12); it occurs once in John and not at all in Mark.

2. Στόμα usually refers to the *mouth* as the organ of speech. God's word usually comes from his *mouth* (Matt 4:4), and he speaks (in a Hebraism: cf. BDF §217) "by the *mouth* of all the prophets" (Acts 3:18). The Holy Spirit speaks "by David's *mouth*" (1:16); God speaks by (or in) the Holy Spirit by David's *mouth:* διὰ πνεύματος ἁγίου στόματος Δαυίδ (4:25; on this "bombastic construction" see G. Schneider, *Acts* [HTKNT] I, 357). Jesus "opens his *mouth*" to preach (Matt 5:2 and elsewhere), and "gracious words come out of his *mouth*" (Luke 4:22). Zechariah's *mouth* "is opened," i.e., he is able to speak again (1:64). Paul is "struck on the *mouth*" because he has said something unacceptable (Acts 23:2). The phrase στόμα πρὸς στόμα (2 John 12; 3 John 14) refers to "face to face" discussion (→ πρός 2.a).

a) Στόμα can even refer to speech itself, e.g., "the *evidence* of two or three witnesses" (Matt 18:16; 2 Cor 13:1 = Deut 19:15) or the "clever response" (στόμα καὶ σοφία) given before authorities by persecuted Christians (Luke 21:15). Στόμα also appears as a reference to the organ used for eating (Matt 15:11a, 17; Acts 11:8) and drinking (John 19:29; Rev 3:16).
Στόμα refers further to the *mouths* of animals, e.g., of fish (Matt 17:27) and horses (Jas 3:3; Rev 9:17, 18, 19), as well as the *jaws* of lions (2 Tim 4:17; Heb 11:33). Στόμα refers fig. to the *gaping abyss* of the earth (Rev 12:16a) and the *edge* or *sharpness* of the devouring sword (Luke 21:24; Heb 11:34).

3. Στόμα appears in the most diverse genres. Some examples:
a) The narrative reports of the Gospels and Acts use στόμα in the context of miracles (Matt 17:27; Luke 1:64), suffering (John 19:29; Acts 23:2), and esp. preaching (Luke 4:22; Acts 15:7). The solemn introductory phrase about the opening of the mouth underscores the significance of this last example: ἀνοίγω τὸ στόμα (Matt 5:2; Acts 8:35; 10:34; 18:14; cf. the prediction in Matt 13:35 = Ps 77:2 LXX).
b) Στόμα appears in legal regulations concerning state-

ments by witnesses (Matt 18:16; 2 Cor 13:1) and confessions at a trial (Luke 19:22; 22:71), as well as verbal transgressions (11:54) or cultic transgressions (Acts 11:8).
c) Concrete commandments specify the kinds of things that do not belong in the mouths of Christians (Eph 4:29; Col 3:8; Jas 3:10: ἐκ τοῦ στόματος; 1 Pet 2:22: ἐν τῷ στόματι; cf. Rev 14:5).
d) The polemic against false teachers uses στόμα in its accusation against them (Jude 16).
e) In a confession one speaks aloud (Rom 10:9, 10: [ἐν τῷ] στόματι) what the heart believes (cf. also v. 8).
f) In Revelation στόμα is associated almost exclusively with apocalyptic notions. In fantastically depicted scenes the mouth or maw is usually the source from which—in addition to haughty and blasphemous words (13:5, 6)—threatening and destructive things issue or break forth (ἐκπορεύομαι: 1:16; 9:17, 18; 11:5; 19:15; ἐξέρχομαι: 19:21): the sword of Christ (1:16; 2:16; 19:15, 21), the fire of the two witnesses (11:5), fire, smoke, and sulphur from the horses (9:17, 18, 19), water from the serpent (12:15, 16b), and froglike demonic spirits (16:13 ter).

W. Radl

στόμαχος, ου, ὁ *stomachos* stomach*

1 Tim 5:23, in advising "Timothy" to drink a little wine "for the sake of your *stomach* and your frequent ailments." This is a rejection of rigorous asceticism; cf. N. Brox, *Die Pastoralbriefe* (RNT) ad loc.; Spicq, *Notes* II, 831-34.

στρατεία, ας, ἡ *strateia* military campaign, warfare*

Fig. in 2 Cor 10:4: "weapons of our *warfare*"; similarly in 1 Tim 1:18, of "the good *warfare*." O. Bauernfeind, *TDNT* VII, 701-13.

στράτευμα, ατος, τό *strateuma* army; pl.: troops*

Sg. in Rev 19:19b and, referring to a small group of soldiers, in Acts 23:10, 27. Pl. in Rev 19:14, 19a: *armies;* Matt 22:7; Luke 23:11; Rev 9:16: *troops*. O. Bauernfeind, *TDNT* VII, 701-13.

στρατεύομαι *strateuomai* carry out a (military) campaign; engage in military service, be a soldier*

Literal in Luke 3:14: στρατευόμενοι, *soldiers;* 1 Cor 9:7; 2 Tim 2:4. Fig. in 2 Cor 10:3, of apostolic activity; 1 Tim 1:18: τὴν καλὴν στρατείαν; of the struggles of human passions in Jas 4:1; 1 Pet 2:11. O. Bauernfeind, *TDNT* VII, 701-13.

στρατηγός, οῦ, ὁ *stratēgos* military leader; prae-tor, magistrate*

Pl. in Acts 16:20, 22, 35, 36, 38, of the *magistrates* of the Roman colony of Philippi (Wikenhauser, *Geschichtswert* 346f.); 4:1; 5:24: the στρατηγὸς τοῦ ἱεροῦ, the *captain* of the Jerusalem temple; Ὁ στρατηγός absolute in 5:26; so also in Josephus (*B.J.* 294; *Ant.* xx.131); pl. in Luke 22:4, 52: "*captains* of the temple." Schürer, *History* II, 277-79; W. Schwahn, PW Suppl. VI, 1071-1158; O. Bauernfeind, *TDNT* VII, 701-13; H. Volkmann, *KP* V, 388-91.

στρατιά, ᾶς, ἡ *stratia* army*

Luke 2:13: "the heavenly *host*" (a LXX expression; cf. Billerbeck II, 116f.); Acts 7:42, of the stars as the "*host* of heaven" (cf. 2 Chr 33:3, 5; Jer 8:2 LXX). O. Bauernfeind, *TDNT* VII, 701-13.

στρατιώτης, ου, ὁ *stratiōtēs* soldier*

Literal *soldiers* in Mark 15:16 par. Matt 27:27; Matt 8:9 par. Luke 7:8; Matt 28:12; Luke 23:36; John 19:2, 23 (bis), 24, 32, 34; Acts 10:7; 12:4, 6, 18; 21:32 (bis), 35; 23:23, 31; 27:31, 32, 42; 28:16. Fig. in 2 Tim 2:3 in the challenge to "Timothy" to take his share of suffering with the letter's author, "Paul," "as a good *soldier* of Christ Jesus"; cf. 1 Tim 1:18. O. Bauernfeind, *TDNT* VII, 701-13.

στρατολογέω *stratologeō* gather an army, recruit soldiers*

2 Tim 2:4, referring to the στρατευόμενος, whose aim is to satisfy the *one who enlisted him*. O. Bauernfeind, *TDNT* VII, 701-13; Spicq, *Notes* II, 835.

στρατοπεδάρχης, ου, ὁ *stratopedarchēs* camp commander

Acts 28:16 TR. Other textual witnesses read here στρατοπέδαρχος (ου, ὁ); *TCGNT* ad loc. Wikenhauser, *Geschichtswert* 358f.

στρατόπεδον, ου, τό *stratopedon* camp; army*

Στρατόπεδον can be used specifically of a Roman *legion* (Polybius Frag. i.16.2, and elsewhere; ÄgU 362.xi.15), and this may be the case in Luke 21:20 (cf. par. Mark 13:14): Jerusalem "surrounded by *armies/legions*." O. Bauernfeind, *TDNT* VII, 704f.

στρεβλόω *strebloō* turn, twist*

With the acc. in the sense of *distort* so that a false meaning results. So 2 Pet 3:16, in reference to the Pauline letters "in which there are some things hard to understand (δυσνόητά τινα), which the ignorant and unstable *twist* to their own destruction." A. Vögtle, FS Mussner 223-39.

στρέφω *strephō* turn, turn around*

1. NT occurrences and usage — 2. As a Lukan narrative signal — 3. Of inner conversion

Lit.: G. BERTRAM, *TDNT* VII, 714f. — J. DUPONT, "ἐὰν μὴ στραφῆτε καὶ γένησθε ὡς τὰ παιδία," FS Black (1969) 50-60. — For further bibliography see *TWNT* X, 1272.

1. Of the 21 NT occurrences of the simple vb. (LXX *ca.* 50 occurrences, *ca.* 40 of those from the MT), 10 are Lukan (7 in the Gospel, 3 in Acts). The 6 occurrences in Matthew are not parallel with any in Luke. Mark never uses στρέφω, John uses it 4 times, Revelation once. The vb. occurs in words of Jesus only in Matthew (3 times: 5:39 [probably Q]; 7:6; 18:3 [redactional]).

The act. appears only 4 times, 3 of those unequivocally trans.: *(directly) turning* the other cheek (Matt 5:39); *bringing back* the pieces of silver (27:3); *turning* water into blood (Rev 11:6, in an allusion to the Egyptian plagues in place of the compound μεταστρέφω in Pss 77:44; 104:29 LXX). The act. in Acts 7:42 might be intrans. ("God *turned away*"), since it is in direct antithesis to v. 39. The other 17 occurrences of the vb. use the pass. reflexively.

2. Luke standardizes the pass. by using it in all 7 occurrences in his Gospel (7:9, 44; 9:55; 10:23; 14:25; 22:61; 23:28 [10:22 is considered a later addition to v. 23; see *TCGNT* 152]), always the aor. partc. (στραφείς), always with Jesus as the subj. (the compound ὑποστρέφω, on the other hand, is usually used of the reaction of his followers as a "doxology indicator"), and always at the beginning of the sentence. A statement by Jesus usually follows (only metalinguistically reported in 9:55; 22:61 reports a glance or look—though even this evokes the recollection of a "word of the Lord"). This expression functions to signal a high point and refers to a *direct act of turning* that throws the following statement into emphatic relief. The influence of this usage can be seen where the vb. is taken up programmatically at the beginning of the second main part of Acts (13:46: "Behold, we *turn* to the Gentiles"; cf. 18:6; 28:28).

In Matthew 9:22; 16:23 the partc. also is used with Jesus as subj. (Mark differs redactionally in both instances: → ἐπιστρέφω), but the partc. follows the subj. In John 1:38 the partc. also appears at the beginning of a sentence with Jesus as subj. (who *turns*; finite vb. in 20:14, of Mary) and 20:16 as a new action (from the perspective of the gesture of warding off in v. 17): *turning* to him.

3. Στρέφω is used of *conversion* in John 12:40 (citing Isa 6:10; Mark 4:12 has ἐπιστρέφω, but John avoids compounds) and Matt 18:3 (v. 4 uses → ταπεινόω synonymously). It is used negatively in Acts 7:39: "they [our fathers] *turned* to Egypt [in their attitudes]" (which v. 40 then specifies more concretely); Matt 7:6 uses it similarly in an allegorical context (referring to "dogs" and "swine") as a conditional aor. partc. with a future element: *when they have fallen away again.* 　　　　W. Schenk

στρηνιάω *strēniaō* lead a luxurious life*

Rev 18:7, 9, with πορνεύω of the great "Babylon." → στρῆνος.

στρῆνος, ους, τό *strēnos* opulence, luxury*

"The merchants of the earth have grown rich with the *wealth* of her [Babylon's] wantonness" (Rev 18:3; → στρηνιάω).

στρουθίον, ου, τό *strouthion* sparrow*

As an example of a worthless object of commerce (Matt 10:29, 31 par. Luke 12:6, 7). G. Grimme, *BZ* 23 (1935) 260-62; O. Bauernfeind, *TDNT* VII, 730-32; Schulz, *Q* 157-64.

στρωννύω, στρώννυμι *strōnnyō, strōnnymi* spread out*

At Jesus' entry into Jerusalem many people *spread* their garments on the road (as a carpet, Mark 11:8 par. Matt 21:8a, b; cf. 4 Kgdms 9:13). Imv. στρῶσον σεαυτῷ (*sc.* τὴν κλίνην) in Acts 9:34 means "make your bed." Ἀνάγαιον ἐστρωμένον (Mark 14:15 par. Luke 22:12) is hardly "paved upper room" (*contra* BAGD s.v.), but more likely "an upper room that has been *fitted out* [with carpets and cushions]" (cf. Dalman, *Arbeit* VII, 185).

στυγητός, 3 *stygētos* hated, detestable*

We once lived "in malice and envy, *hated* by people and hating one another" (Titus 3:3).

στυγνάζω *stygnazō* be shocked; become sad*

Mark 10:22, of a person: ἐπὶ τῷ λόγῳ, "*his countenance fell*/he *was sad* at that saying"; Matt 16:3, of the appearance of heaven: πυρράζει στυγνάζων ὁ οὐρανός, "the sky is red and *gloomy*," a sign of stormy weather.

στῦλος, ου, ὁ *stylos* column, pillar*

Lit.: R. D. Aus, "Three Pillars and Three Patriarchs: A Proposal Concerning Gal 2:9," *ZNW* 70 (1979) 252-61. — C. K. Barrett, "Paul and the 'Pillar' Apostles," FS de Zwaan 1-19.

— A. Jaubert, "L'image de la colonne," *SPCIC 1961* (AnBib 17-18, 1963) II, 101-8. — H. Kraft, *Die Entstehung des Christentums* (1981) 124-39. — U. Wilckens, *TDNT* VII, 732-36. — R. H. Wilkinson, "The ΣΤΥΛΟΣ of Revelation 3:12 and Ancient Coronation Rites," *JBL* 107 (1988) 498-501. — For further bibliography see *TWNT* X, 1272f.

1. Στῦλος occurs 4 times in the NT (Gal 2:9; 1 Tim 3:15; Rev 3:12; 10:1), always fig. or metaphorically. It occurs in connection with the temple structure in Rev 3:12 (στῦλος ἐν τῷ ναῷ τοῦ θεοῦ); similarly in 1 Tim 3:15, where the ἐκκλησία as στῦλος καὶ ἑδραίωμα τῆς ἀληθείας is equated with the οἶκος θεοῦ (cf. Eph 2:19ff.). Gal 2:9 (οἱ δοκοῦντες στῦλοι εἶναι) might also presuppose such an understanding (cf. *1 Clem.* 5:2; see Barrett 12ff.; Wilckens 734f.). On the other hand, Exod 13:21f. resonates in Rev 10:1 (οἱ πόδες αὐτοῦ ὡς στῦλοι πυρός).

2. In the NT στῦλος is used of a "pedestal" for the Holy Spirit serving to make it visible and to mediate its effects. In 1 Tim 3:15 the congregation itself is the *pillar* of the Spirit, and the Spirit is called "truth" because of its revelatory function. The early Church referred to those occupying its leading spiritual offices with the honorific title *pillars* as prophets perpetually filled with the Spirit and capable of mediating that Spirit (Gal 2:9). Since the first Christians read the OT as a prophecy of their present eschatological existence (1 Cor 10:6, 11), they understood Jer 1:18 (MT; Aquila and Symmachus: στῦλος σιδεροῦς) as an announcement of the establishment of a prophetic office leading from the end time into the kingdom of God (Kraft 126). Rev 3:12 uses στῦλος similarly: The Holy Spirit will take its place forever, in the manner of a statue, upon him who conquers ("God" here is God in the form of the Holy Spirit; in a slightly altered form of this image he resides in the new city of God). In Rev 10:1 an angel of cosmic proportions appears to the seer; its task is to mediate to him the as yet unrevealed announcement of the raising of the dead. With its cloudlike garments and its legs like *pillars* of fire this angel recalls the form in which God guided his people during the wilderness wanderings (cf. Exod 13:21f.). 　　　H. Kraft

Στωϊκός, 3 *Stōikos* Stoic

Στωϊκός in Acts 17:18 is the more correct, though probably not original, spelling, in contrast to → Στοϊκός (B al, *UBSGNT* and *NTG*; see BDF §35.1), which is assimilated to στοά; Passow II, 1578 considers it a poetic abbreviation.

σύ *sy* you

Lit.: BAGD s.v. — BDF §§277.1; 279; 281; 284. — Kühner, *Grammatik* II/1, 555-60. — Mayser, *Grammatik* II/1, 62-65.

1. The second person sg. personal pron. occurs a total

of 1066 times in the NT, mainly in the narrative writings, then less often in the Epistles (only once in Philippians) except for Philemon (20 times), 3 John (10 times), and the Pastorals (41 times). The otherwise enclitic oblique cases σου, σοι, and σε are accented when used emphatically (including after preps. except πρός in Matt 14:28), but the nom. appears only accented and emphasized (174 times, though also pleonastically in Mark 14:68), most often in the Passion narratives, in John (61 times), and in Romans (12 times).

2. Theological significance must be attributed to the frequent use of the nom. for identification by σὺ εἶ with a title or name: σὺ εἶ ὁ χριστός (ὁ υἱὸς . . . ; Mark 8:29 par.; 14:61 par.; Luke 23:39; John 10:24; 11:27), etc. This construction also occurs without a name: εἰ σὺ εἶ, "if it is *you*" (Matt 14:28), in interrogatives: σὺ τίς εἶ; σὺ Ἠλίας εἶ; . . . (John 1:19, 21 bis).

Nom. σύ is also used emphatically in combination with a voc.: "*you*, O Bethlehem" (Matt 2:6); "*you*, Capernaum" (Matt 11:23; Luke 10:15); "*you*, child" (Luke 1:76), with a noun and partc. ("*you*, a Jew/although *you* are a Jew," John 4:9; Gal 2:14), to contrast persons (e.g., "I—*you*," Matt 3:14), esp. in the emphatic phrases καὶ σύ ("*you* also," Mark 14:67 par.; Luke 10:37; 19:19, 42; John 7:52; Acts 25:10; Gal 6:1; 2 Tim 4:15) and σὺ δέ ("but as for *you*," Luke 9:60; 16:7, 25; Rom 11:17, 20; 14:10; 1 Tim 6:11; 2 Tim 3:10, 14; 4:5; Titus 2:1; Heb 1:11, 12; Jas 4:12). The clause σὺ λέγεις/εἶπας (Mark 15:2 par.; Matt 26:25, 64; John 18:37) is not intended as an evasion or denial (so BAGD 226, 469), but as an affirmation; → εἶπον.   W. Radl

συγγένεια, ας, ἡ *syngeneia* kin, relatives*

The NT invariably uses this noun concretely of one's "relatives" (Luke 1:61; Acts 7:3, 14). W. Michaelis, *TDNT* VII, 736-42; for further bibliography see *TWNT* X, 1273.

συγγενεύς, έως, ὁ *syngeneus* relative*

Συγγενεύς (a later variation of συγγενής, so also 1 Macc 10:89 A) occurs in Mark 6:4 and Luke 2:44: ἐν τοῖς συγγενεῦσιν. On this dat. construction see BDF §47.4; Mayser, *Grammatik* I/2, 57.

συγγενής, 2 *syngenēs* related*

Συγγενής is subst. in all its NT occurrences. It is used in the sense of *relative* in the sg. (John 18:26 [masc.]; Luke 1:36 TR [fem.]) and pl. (οἱ συγγενεῖς, Luke 1:58; 14:12; 21:16; Acts 10:24). It is also used in the sense of *countryman/one from the same people* (Rom 9:3; 16:7,

11, 21). W. Michaelis, *TDNT* VII, 736-42; Spicq, *Notes* II, 836-39.

συγγενίς, ίδος, ἡ *syngenis* (female) relative*

The fem. form of → συγγενής occurs in the NT only in Luke 1:36 in reference to Elizabeth, Mary's *kinswoman*.

συγγνώμη, ης, ἡ *syngnōmē* concession*

1 Cor 7:6, in contrast to ἐπιταγή: "I say this by way of *concession,* not command." N. Baumert, *Ehelosigkeit und Ehe im Herrn. Eine Neuinterpretation von 1 Kor 7* (FzB 47, 1984) 359-63; R. Bultmann, *TDNT* I, 716f.; K. Metzler, *Der griechische Begriff des Verzeihens. Untersucht am Wortstamm συγγνώμη von den ersten Belegen bis zum vierten Jahrhundert n. Chr.* WUNT II/144, 1991.

συγκάθημαι *synkathēmai* sit together*

Mark 14:54, of Peter (and the guards) in the courtyard of the high priest; Acts 26:30: οἱ συγκαθήμενοι αὐτοῖς, of those who heard Paul's defense while *sitting together* with Agrippa, Bernice, and Festus.

συγκαθίζω *synkathizō* cause to sit down with; intrans.: sit down together with others*

Trans. in Eph 2:6: God made us *sit down with* Christ in heaven; intrans. in Luke 22:55.

συγκακοπαθέω *synkakopatheō* suffer together with*

2 Tim 1:8; 2:3, imv. in the challenge to suffer for the gospel along with the imprisoned "Paul." W. Michaelis, *TDNT* V, 936f.

συγκακουχέομαι *synkakoucheomai* be mistreated with*

Heb 11:25, of Moses, who chose to "*share ill-treatment* with God's people rather than enjoy the fleeting pleasures of sin."

συγκαλέω *synkaleō* call together; mid.: call to oneself*

Act. in Mark 15:16; Luke 15:6, 9; Acts 5:21; mid. in Luke 9:1; 23:13; Acts 10:24; 28:17. K. L. Schmidt, *TDNT* III, 496f.

συγκαλύπτω *synkalyptō* cover up completely*

"Nothing *is covered up* that will not be revealed"

(Luke 12:2; simple vb. in par. Matt 10:26). W. Kasch, *TDNT* VII, 743.

συγκάμπτω *synkamptō* bend*

Rom 11:10, quoting Ps 68:24 LXX: "*Bend* their backs forever."

συγκαταβαίνω *synkatabainō* go down with someone*

Acts 25:5: *going down* from Jerusalem to Caesarea Maritima; cf. ἀναβαίνω (v. 1), of the journey in the opposite direction.

συγκατάθεσις, εως, ἡ *synkatathesis* agreement*

2 Cor 6:16: τίς συγκατάθεσις ναῷ θεοῦ μετὰ εἰδώλων; "What agreement has God's temple with idols?"

συγκατανεύω *synkataneuō* consent, agree

Acts 18:27 D. On this "Western" reading see *TCGNT* ad loc. (467f.).

συγκατατίθεμαι *synkatatithemai* consent, agree to*

With dat. in Luke 23:51: Joseph of Arimathea did not *consent* to the Sanhedrin's decision against Jesus (→ Ἰωσήφ 6). Also as v.l in D (Acts 4:18; 15:12).

συγκαταψηφίζομαι *synkatapsēphizomai* be chosen together with*

Acts 1:26, of Matthias, who "*was enrolled with* the eleven apostles." G. Braumann, *TDNT* IX, 604-7.

σύγκειμαι *synkeimai* recline together
Matt 9:10 D in place of → συνανάκειμαι.

συγκεράννυμι *synkerannymi* mix together, unite*

Only fig. in the NT: 1 Cor 12:24: τὸ σῶμα, unite the body together into an organism; Heb 4:2: the message of the gospel is united with the listeners through faith (instrumental dat.).

συγκινέω *synkineō* stir up, set into motion*

Acts 6:12, with acc.: "*stir up* the people."

συγκλείω *synkleiō* enclose simultaneously, close together*

Literal in Luke 5:6, of catching fish in a net; fig. in Rom 11:32: God *has consigned* all to disobedience; Gal

3:22, 23: Scripture *has consigned* all things to (the power of) sin. O. Michel, *TDNT* VII, 744-47.

συγκληρονόμος, 2 *synklēronomos* inheriting together*

Rom 8:17: "heirs of God, *fellow heirs* with Christ"; Eph 3:6: the Gentiles are *fellow heirs* as well as σύσσωμα and συμμέτοχα of the promise; with obj. gen. of the thing in Heb 11:9; 1 Pet 3:7. W. Grundmann, *TDNT* VII, 787; W. Mundle, *DNTT* II, 295-304; R. Schnackenburg, *Eph* (EKKNT) 135f.

συγκοινωνέω *synkoinōneō* participate/take part in together*

Eph 5:11; Rev 18:4, of co-perpetrators; of helping empathy in Phil 4:14. F. Hauck, *TDNT* III, 797-809; J. Schattenmann, *DNTT* I, 639-44.

συγκοινωνός, οῦ, ὁ *synkoinōnos* fellow participant, partner*

With obj. gen. (of that in which one participates with others) in Rom 11:17; Phil 1:7; with personal gen. in 1 Cor 9:23; Rev 1:9. F. Hauck, *TDNT* III, 797-809; F. Schattenmann, *DNTT* I, 639-44.

συγκομίζω *synkomizō* bring in; bury*

Acts 8:2: *bury* (Sophocles *Aj.* 1048), of Stephen's burial.

συγκρίνω *synkrinō* compare; interpret*

To be translated *compare* in 2 Cor 10:12a, b. In 1 Cor 2:13 *compare* is less likely than *interpret/explain;* cf. H. Conzelmann, *1 Cor* (KEK, ²1981) 78 n.7; G. Dautzenberg, *Urchristliche Prophetie* (1975) 138-40; F. Büchsel, *TDNT* III, 953.

συγκύπτω *synkyptō* bend over; be completely bent /humpbacked*

Luke 13:11, of a woman whose back was *bent over* because of illness and who could no longer fully straighten herself (ἀνακύπτω). W. Grundmann, *Luke* (THKNT) ad loc.; G. Schwarz, *Biblische Notizen* 15 (1981) 47.

συγκυρία, ας, ἡ *synkyria* coincidence, chance*

Luke 10:31: κατὰ συγκυρίαν, "by chance."

συγχαίρω *synchairō* rejoice with; congratulate*

Luke 1:58; 15:6, 9; 1 Cor 12:26; 13:6; Phil 2:17, 18.

The meaning *congratulate* is possible in Luke 1:58; Phil 2:17f. H. Conzelmann, *TDNT* IX, 359-76.

συγχέω *syncheō* confuse, stir up*

The Jews from Asia *"stirred up* all the crowd" when they saw Paul in the temple (Acts 21:27).

συγχράομαι *synchraomai* have dealings with, associate with*

John 4:9, in the narrator's commentary: "For Jews *have no dealings* with Samaritans."

συγχύννω *synchynnō* confuse, stir up*

4 occurrences in Acts: act. in 9:22; pass. in 2:6; 19:32 (cf. → σύγχυσις in v. 29); 21:31 (cf. → συγχέω in v. 27).

σύγχυσις, εως, ἡ *synchysis* confusion*

"So the city [Ephesus] was filled with *confusion*" (Acts 19:29). Cf. → συγχύννω in v. 32.

συζάω *syzaō* live with*

Rom 6:8, of the life of believers together with Christ. The Corinthians are in Paul's heart εἰς τὸ συναποθανεῖν καὶ συζῆν, "to die together and to *live together*" (2 Cor 7:3). Christians die and live with their Lord (2 Tim 2:11; cf. Rom 6:8).

συζεύγνυμι *syzeugnymi* yoke together*

Mark 10:9 par. Matt 19:6, in the conclusion: "what therefore God has *joined together*, let no person put asunder."

συζητέω *syzēteō* consider, dispute, reflect on*

Lit.: J. SCHNEIDER, *TDNT* VII, 747f.

1. Συζητέω occurs 10 times in the NT, 6 times in Mark, the rest in the Lukan writings (twice each in the Gospel and Acts). The vb. means: a) *investigate together* or *consider, discuss* (περί τινος), b) *dispute* (τινί, though also πρός τινα), and c) *meditate/reflect* (περί τινος).

2. The NT uses συζητέω of both simple *pondering* and vehement *disputes*. One of Jesus' miracles in Capernaum aroused such astonishment among the people that they *"questioned* among themselves" what it all meant (Mark 1:27). This refers to simple questioning of one another and collective *discussion*. According to Mark 9:10 the disciples *consider together* what Jesus' words concerning the resurrection of the dead mean. The Emmaus disciples (Luke 24:15) *discuss* what happened in the preceding days. The sense of Luke 22:23 is ambivalent: Though the

disciples' response to Jesus' prediction that one of them will betray him could be simple "questioning," the context suggests a *dispute* or *argument* (cf. 22:24ff.).

Mark 8:11 clearly refers to a dispute among adversaries. The Pharisees *argue* with Jesus and demand unequivocal signs from him, something the Evangelist describes as a testing of Jesus (πειράζοντες αὐτόν). 9:14, 16 also refers to a critical argument: scribes *argue* with the disciples concerning their failure to heal an epileptic boy, a criticism apparently supported by the crowd (vv. 17f.). The serious dispute between Jesus and the Sadducees (12:18-27) is characterized in 12:28 as a συζητεῖν.

Acts 6:9 and 9:29 use the vb. in an unequivocally hostile sense. The Hellenistic Jews who *dispute* with Stephen bring about his arrest and death (6:9ff.) since they cannot stand up to him in disputation. The same seriousness characterizes συζητέω in 9:29: Paul disputes (frequently: impf.) with the same adversaries as Stephen, and they react in the same way as in the story of Stephen: "with a threat against his life" (E. Haenchen, *Acts* [Eng. tr., 1971] 333).

                                                             E. Larsson

συζήτησις, εως, ἡ *syzētēsis* dispute (noun)
Acts 15:2, 7; 28:29 TR. J. Schneider, *TDNT* VII, 748.

συζητητής, οῦ, ὁ *syzētētēs* disputant*

1 Cor 1:20 asks: "Where is the *debater* of this age?" Cf. Ign. *Eph.* 18:1, which cites 1 Cor 1:20 in part. J. Schneider, *TDNT* VII, 748.

σύζυγος, 2 *syzygos* in the same yoke*

Phil 4:3 addresses a γνήσιε σύζυγε, "true *yokefellow*." Σύζυγος has as yet not been documented as a proper name, and just whom Paul is addressing here cannot be determined with any certainty. G. Delling, *TDNT* VII, 748ff.; BAGD s.v.

συζωοποιέω *syzōopoieō* make alive together with*

Col 2:13 par. Eph 2:5: God *has made* Christians *alive together with* Christ. The context indicates that the reference is to resurrection from the death of sin (νεκροὺς . . . τοῖς παραπτώμασιν).

συκάμινος, ου, ἡ *sykaminos* mulberry tree*

In Luke 17:6 Jesus uses this term in a saying concerning faith, which he likens to a mustard seed, which is capable of rooting up a tree as large as a συκάμινος and planting it in the sea. C.-H. Hunzinger, *TDNT* VII, 758 (cf. 287-91); G. Schneider, *Luke* (ÖTK) II, 347f.

συκῆ, ῆς, ἡ *sykē* fig tree*

Mark 11:13, 20, 21 par. Matt 21:19 (bis), 20, 21, in the pericope of the cursing of the fig tree; in parables in Mark 13:28 par. Matt 24:32/Luke 21:29; Luke 13:6, 7. According to John 1:48, 50 Jesus saw Nathanael "under the *fig tree*." Jas 3:12 asks whether a *fig tree* can yield olives (cf. Matt 7:16b). Rev 6:13 (cf. Isa 34:4) uses the simile "as the *fig tree* sheds its winter fruit." C.-H. Hunzinger, *TDNT* VII, 751-57; for further bibliography see *TWNT* X, 1273.

συκομορέα, ας, ἡ *sykomorea* sycamore-fig tree*

Luke 19:4: Zacchaeus climbed into a *sycamore fig tree* so he could see Jesus. C.-H. Hunzinger, *TDNT* VII, 758.

σῦκον, ου, τό *sykon* fig*

The fruit of the fig tree (→ συκῆ; Mark 11:13; Matt 7:16 par. Luke 6:44). Jas 3:12 asks whether a grapevine can yield *figs*. C.-H. Hunzinger, *TDNT* VII, 751-55.

συκοφαντέω *sykophanteō* accuse falsely, slander; extort*

The two meanings of this vb. are documented in the NT only in Luke 3:14; 19:8. In the first passage it refers to the Baptist's exhortation to the soldiers not to *trick/oppress* anyone *by false accusation*. 19:8 describes Zacchaeus's confession: "If I have *defrauded* any one of anything." E. Nestle, *ZNW* 4 (1903) 271f.; C.-H. Hunzinger, *TDNT* VII, 759.

συλαγωγέω *sylagōgeō* carry off as booty, rob*

Fig. in Col 2:8 of the carrying off of truth into the slavery of error.

συλάω *sylaō* rob*

In 2 Cor 11:8 Paul uses a metaphorical phrase to express how he put up with support by other churches: "I *robbed* other churches. . . ." Spicq, *Notes* II, 840f.

συλλαλέω *syllaleō* converse with*

With dat. of the person in Mark 9:4 par. Luke 9:30; Luke 22:4; with μετά τινος in Matt 17:3 (cf. par. Mark 9:4); Acts 25:12; with πρός in Luke 4:36.

συλλαμβάνω *syllambanō* seize, apprehend; conceive, become pregnant; assist*

1. The act. is divided into two basic meanings:
a) *seize, apprehend*, esp. of a person's arrest (Mark

14:48 par. Matt 26:55; Luke 22:54; John 18:12; Acts 1:16, of Jesus; Acts 12:3; pass. in 23:27). Luke 5:9 of catching fish; and
b) *conceive*, of a woman becoming pregnant (Luke 1:24, 31, 36; pass. in 2:21); fig. in Jas 1:15, of ἐπιθυμία that then gives birth to sin.

2. Pass.:
a) with the same meaning as act. (→ 1.a) in Acts 26:21: *seize, grasp* (cf. *Mart. Pol.* 6:1).
b) with dat. in Luke 5:7; Phil 4:3: *grasp together,* i.e., *assist, aid.* G. Delling, *TDNT* VII, 759-62.

συλλέγω *syllegō* gather, collect*

Matt 7:16 par. Luke 6:44: *gather* grapes from thorns; Matt 13:28, 29, 30, 40: *gather* weeds or (v. 41) σκάνδαλα out of the kingdom of the Son of man; 13:48: *collect* the good fish out of the net.

συλλογίζομαι *syllogizomai* discuss, consider, figure*

Luke 20:5 (par. Mark 11:31: διαλογίζομαι): συλλογίζομαι πρὸς ἑαυτόν, "*discuss* something with one another" (so also Plutarch *Pomp.* 60.3). I. H. Marshall, *Luke* (NIGTC) ad loc.; G. Mussies, *Miscellanea Neotestamentica* (NovTSup 47/48, 1978) II, 59-76.

συλλυπέομαι *syllypeomai* feel sympathy*

The pass. of συλλυπέω (cf. Isa 51:19 LXX) occurs in the NT only in Mark 3:5: Jesus "*grieved* [for the sick man] because of their [the Pharisees'] hardness of heart." R. Bultmann, *TDNT* IV, 323f.

συμβαίνω *symbainō* happen; encounter, meet*

Συμβαίνει τί τινι in Mark 10:32, of Jesus' fate; in Acts 20:19, of what the Jews did to Paul; in 1 Cor 10:11, of what happened to the Israelites in the wilderness (τυπικῶς: as a warning to us!); 1 Pet 4:12; 2 Pet 2:22; with inf. in Acts 21:35: "*It happened* that he [Paul] was actually carried by the soldiers because of the violence of the crowd." Τὸ συμβεβηκός τινι, "what *happened* to someone," in Acts 3:10; τὰ συμβεβηκότα, *events,* in Luke 24:14.

συμβάλλω *symballō* converse; grasp the true sense; meet with; mid.: be of use/assistance*

Lit.: W. C. VAN UNNIK, "Die rechte Bedeutung des Wortes treffen. Lukas II 19," *Sparsa collecta* (1973) I, 72-91.

1. The vb. συμβάλλω (basic meaning: "throw together"/"bring together" [trans.] or "meet" [intrans.]) occurs in the NT exclusively in the Lukan writings: twice in the Gospel (2:19; 14:31 + v.l. 11:53 D) and 4 times in Acts

(4:15; 17:18; 18:27; 20:14). Luke uses the act. both trans. (→ 2.a, b) and intrans. (→ 2.c), the mid. only in the intrans. sense (→ 2.d).

2. a) In Acts 4:15; 17:18 συμβάλλω is used absolutely for συμβάλλω λόγους (Euripides *IA* 830), "have a conversation/converse." Συμβάλλω πρὸς ἀλλήλους (4:15) suggests the tr. "*confer* with one another." Συμβάλλω τινί (17:18) means either "*converse* with someone" (as in Plutarch *Apophthegmata Laconica, Callicratidas* 2 [= *Moralia* 222D]) or more sharply "*get into an argument* with someone" (as in Luke 11:53 D).

Acts 17:18 could also intend the intrans. sense "come into contact with someone"; cf. Epictetus *Diss.* iv.12.7; Iamblichus *VP* ii.12; Pap. Fayûm 129, 2.

b) Luke 2:19, which is attributable to the Lukan redaction, is difficult to evaluate. (The common tr. "ponder /consider" is not documented elsewhere— including in the extra-NT passages cited by BAGD s.v. 1.a.β. It is questionable whether Herodotus vii.24 [mid.!] can be considered a witness.) Since the overall context of v. 19 concerns extraordinary and mysterious occurrences, the vb. might mean *grasp the true sense, hit upon the right meaning* (as in Euripides *Med.* 675; *IT* 55; Josephus *Ant.* ii.72; *B.J.* iii.352; Philostratus *VA* iv.43; see further Wettstein, *NT* I, 663f. as well as comments by van Unnik). In contrast to the πάντες of v. 18, who can only "wonder" at what the shepherds told them, Mary knows the true significance "of all these things" (πάντα τὰ ῥήματα ταῦτα). She recognizes in the miraculous appearance of the angel and its message (vv. 9-14) a confirmation of the promise she herself has already received from the angel (1:26ff.).

c) In Acts 20:14 συμβάλλω τινί means "*meet with* someone" (as in Josephus *Ant.* i.219; vi.56, 275; vii.224). In Luke 14:31 συμβάλλω τινὶ εἰς πόλεμον means "wage warfare with someone" (cf. συμβάλλω τινὶ εἰς μάχην, Josephus *Ant.* xii.222, 342; *B.J.* i.191).

d) Mid. συμβάλλομαί τινι in Acts 18:27 means "*be of use to* someone/*help* someone" (Epictetus *Diss.* iii.22.78).

O. Hofius

συμβασιλεύω *symbasileuō* rule with someone*

1 Cor 4:8, in the rejection of the Corinthians' assertion that they already reign with Christ (H. Conzelmann, *1 Cor* [Hermeneia] ad loc.); fut. in 2 Tim 2:12, of Christians reigning with Christ: συμβασιλεύσομεν with συζήσομεν. H. Kleinknecht, *TDNT* I, 591.

συμβιβάζω *symbibazō* bring together; conclude; prove; enlighten*

Col 2:19; Eph 4:16, of the body, which is *held together* by its joints and ligaments; fig. in Col 2:2: *unite;* Acts 16:10: *conclude/infer;* 9:22: *prove;* 1 Cor 2:16 and

Acts 19:33: *enlighten/instruct.* G. Delling, *TDNT* VII, 763-66.

συμβουλεύω *symbouleuō* give advice; mid.: consult together, agree*

Act. with dat. of the person in John 18:14; Rev 3:18. Mid. with a ἵνα clause in Matt 26:4 (so also John 11:53 TR); with final inf. in Acts 9:23.

συμβούλιον, ου, τό *symboulion* decision, plan; council*

1. Occurrences in the NT — 2. Mark and Matthew — 3. Acts 25:12

Lit.: BAGD s.v. — BDF §5.3. — MOULTON/MILLIGAN s.v. (on Acts 25:12). — G. SCHNEIDER, *Verleugnung, Verspottung und Verhör Jesu nach Lk 22:54-71* (SANT 22, 1969) 108 (on Mark 15:1 par. Matt 27:1).

1. Συμβούλιον occurs 8 times in the NT, 5 of those in Matthew, the others in Mark 3:6; 15:1; Acts 25:12. It refers to *advice* and its results, *decision.* The latter sense dominates in the NT.

2. Συμβούλιον λαμβάνω is a Latinism *(consilium capere),* "take counsel" (so Matt 12:14; 22:15; 27:1, 7; 28:12). Συμβούλιον δίδωμι (Mark 3:6) and συμβούλιον ποιέω (Mark 15:1) are to be translated similarly. In contrast, συμβούλιον ἑτοιμάζω (Mark 15:1 ℵ C L 892 pc) means "*form* a plan." In Mark and Matthew it is always Jesus' adversaries who are thus said to proceed in consultation against him and form plans (Mark 3:6 par. Matt 12:14: the Pharisees [as in Matt 22:15]; Mark 15:1 par. Matt 27:1: the groups within the Sanhedrin [cf. Matt 27:7; 28:12]).

3. In Acts 25:12 the συμβούλιον is the advisory body, the *council/assembly* as a body: Festus conferred "with his *council.*" Cf. E. Haenchen, *Acts* (Eng. tr., 1971) ad loc. This meaning—seen only here in the NT—has parallels elsewhere (4 Macc 17:17; Josephus *Ant.* xiv.192; xvi.163; cf. Moulton/Milligan s.v.).

G. Schneider

σύμβουλος, ου, ὁ *symboulos* adviser, counselor*

Rom 11:34, in a question (Isa 40:13 LXX): "Who has known the Lord's mind or has been his *counselor?*" G. Bornkamm, "The Praise of God (Romans 11.33-36)," *idem, Early Christian Experience* (1969) 105-11.

Συμεών *Symeōn* Symeon, Simeon*

1. The name Simeon/Symeon — 2. Persons with this name in the NT — a) The patriarch — b) In Jesus'

genealogy — c) The man in the temple — d) Symeon Niger — e) Simon Peter

Lit.: BDF §53.2 — J. Blinzler, *LTK* IX, 761f. (on 2.c). — S. Lösch, "Der Kämmerer der Königin Kandake (Apg. 8:27)," *TQ* 111 (1930) (511 on 2.d). — Moulton/Milligan s.v. — J. Winandy, "La prophétie de Syméon (Lc, II, 34-35)," *RB* 72 (1965) 321-51 (on 2.c).

1. Συμεών is the transliteration of the Hebrew personal name *šim^eʿ ôn*. While the name is indeclinable in the NT, it is declined in Josephus *B.J.* iv.159; *Ant.* xii.265 (-ῶνος). The 7 NT occurrences of this name refer to five different people (→ 2.a-e).

2.a) The patriarch Simeon is mentioned in Rev 7:7 as the ancestor of the eponymous tribe (cf. Jdt 6:15).

b) The genealogy of Jesus in Luke 3:30 mentions a Simeon, the son of Judah and father of Levi.

c) Luke 2:25, 34 tells of an old man named Simeon who lived in Jerusalem. In the temple he acknowledges Jesus prophetically as the Messiah (2:29-32, 34f.).

d) According to Acts 13:1, Symeon "who was called Niger" (Lat. *niger* = "the black one") belonged to the teachers and prophets in the church at Antioch.

e) Acts 15:14 and 2 Pet 1:1 use the name Συμεών to refer to Simon Peter. The "Hebraic" sounding name is likely intended to add a more formal tone (BDF). In Acts 15:14 the name is probably not an indication of a source using the form Συμεών (with Conzelmann, *Acts* [Hermeneia] ad loc.; *contra* R. Pesch, FS Mussner 119).

         .G. Schneider

συμμαθητής, οῦ, ὁ *symmathētēs* fellow disciple*

John 11:16: the *fellow disciples* of Thomas, a disciple of Jesus. K. H. Rengstorf, *TDNT* IV, 460.

συμμαρτυρέω *symmartyreō* bear witness in support of*

In the NT σύν in συμμαρτυρέω serves only to intensify, so that συμμαρτυρέω means simply *confirm/witness to.* Rom 2:15; 9:1, of the confirming witness of the → συνείδησις (3.b); 8:16, of the witness of the πνεῦμα. H. Strathmann, *TDNT* IV, 508-10.

συμμερίζομαι *symmerizomai* share with*

1 Cor 9:13: συμμερίζομαι τῷ θυσιαστηρίῳ, "*share* at the altar [in the sacrificial offerings]."

συμμέτοχος, 2 *symmetochos* sharing with*

Eph 3:6: the Gentiles are fellow heirs and *fellow partakers* of the promise; 5:7 warns against being *associates*

of the sons of disobedience (v. 6). H. Hanse, *TDNT* II, 830-32.

συμμιμητής, οῦ, ὁ *symmimētēs* fellow imitator*

Phil 3:17, in the exhortation to join in *imitating* Paul, i.e., to imitate his example. W. Michaelis, *TDNT* IV, 659-74.

συμμορφίζω *symmorphizō* give the same form*

Pass. in Phil 3:10: συμμορφιζόμενος τῷ θανάτῳ αὐτοῦ, "*formed like* his [Christ's] death." G. Braumann, *DNTT*, I, 705-8.

σύμμορφος, 2 *symmorphos* having the same form*

Lit.: H. R. Balz, *Heilsvertrauen und Welterfahrung* (BEvT 59, 1971) 109-15 — C. K. Barrett, *Rom* (BNTC/HNTC, 1962) 169-71. — W. Grundmann, *TDNT* VII, 766-97, esp. 787f., 792. — J. Jervell, *Imago Dei* (FRLANT 76, 1960) 271-81. — E. Käsemann, *Rom* (Eng. tr., 1980) 242-45. — J. Kürzinger, "Συμμόρφους τῆς εἰκόνος τοῦ υἱοῦ αὐτοῦ (Röm 8,29)," *BZ* 2 (1958) 294-99. — H. Lausberg, *Handbuch der literarischen Rhetorik* (1960) §623. — P. von der Osten-Sacken, *Römer 8 als Beispiel paulinischer Soteriologie* (FRLANT 112, 1975) 67-76. — H. Paulsen, *Überlieferung und Auslegung in Römer 8* (WMANT 43, 1974) 133-77.

1. Σύμμορφος is analogous to adjs. such as σύγγονος ("sharing the same γένος" = "related by blood"), σύγκληρος ("sharing the same κλῆρος" = "bordering, neigboring"), σύμβωμος and σύνναος ("sharing the same altar/temple"), and is derived from the noun → μορφή. The adj. connects persons having the same μορφή. Rom 8:29 uses it with gen. (BDF §§182; 194) and Phil 3:21 with dat. (BDF §194).

2. In Rom 8:29 Paul constructs a rhetorically polished *gradatio* (often called the "golden chain" and considered pre-Pauline) in four members: v . . . w/w . . . x/x . . . y /y . . . z; at the beginning of each successive syntactical unit he repeats the vb. from the previous one (on this rhetorical figure see Demosthenes *Cor.* 179 [in Lausberg]). In an insertion interrupting this sequence (von der Osten-Sacken 68; Paulsen 136) Paul asserts that believers, who are elect according to God's salvation purpose, are also predestined "to be *conformed* to the image of his Son." This conformity with Christ is not yet realized in its ultimate form (*contra* Käsemann 245: an "enthusiastic baptismal tradition" that overlooks the eschatological reservation), but must be understood rather in the context of Rom 8:18-30 as an eschatological assertion. Barrett (170) interprets it in a purely futuristic sense: We will be conformed to the image of the resurrected Christ in his δόξα, just as at present we are conformed to his death (cf. Phil 3:10: συμμορφιζόμενοι).

Since the overall context of Rom 8:18-30 addresses the theme of future glory, much suggests that Paul expects this conformity to the image of Christ in his δόξα to take place in the future.

The eschatological statement in Phil 3:21 is also formulated on the basis of tradition. At the parousia Christ will transfigure the earthly body of Christians to be like (σύμμορφος) his own glorious (heavenly) body (→ μετασχηματίζω in the same verse).

The question remains open whether the event described here as "conformity" to Christ should be understood as a transfiguration of being and essence, or as a change of that particular form (→ μορφή 4) which constitutes one's identity.   W. Pöhlmann

συμμορφόω *symmorphoō* give the same form
Phil 3:10 TR in place of → συμμορφίζω.

συμπαθέω *sympatheō* sympathize with*

With dat. of thing (ταῖς ἀσθενείαις ἡμῶν) in Heb 4:15; with dat. of person (τοῖς δεσμίοις) in 10:34. W. Michaelis, *TDNT* V, 935f.; Spicq, *Notes* II, 842f.

συμπαθής, 2 *sympathēs* sympathetic*

In second position in a five-item catalog of virtues in 1 Pet 3:8. W. Michaelis, *TDNT* V, 935f.; Spicq, *Notes* II, 842f.

συμπαραγίνομαι *symparaginomai* come together*

Luke 23:48, of the ὄχλοι who came to the θεωρία (Jesus' crucifixion).

συμπαρακαλέω *symparakaleō* encourage/console together*

Paul wishes to see the Christians in Rome so that he and they "can *be mutually encouraged* by each other's faith" (Rom 1:12).

συμπαραλαμβάνω *symparalambanō* take/bring along*

With acc. of the person in Acts 12:25; 15:37, 38; Gal 2:1. In all instances the reference is to travelling companions of Paul (and Barnabas).

συμπαραμένω *symparamenō* stay to help/support
Phil 1:25 TR in place of → παραμένω.

συμπάρειμι *sympareimi* be present with*

Acts 25:24, with dat.: "*be present* with someone."

συμπάσχω *sympaschō* suffer with*

Rom 8:17: *suffer with* Christ; 1 Cor 12:26, metaphorically of the body, in which all members *suffer together*. W. Michaelis, *TDNT* V, 925f.

συμπέμπω *sympempō* send with*

2 Cor 8:22 (τινά τινι); 8:18 (τινὰ μετά τινος).

συμπεριέχω *symperiechō* stand around, surround

Luke 12:1 D: πολλῶν δὲ ὄχλων συμπεριεχόντων κύκλῳ. E. Klostermann, *Luke* (HNT) ad loc.

συμπεριλαμβάνω *symperilambanō* embrace*

Acts 20:10: Paul bends over the young man who fell to his death and *embraces* him (acc. of the person is understood). Cf. Xenophon *An.* vii.4.10 (περιλαβὼν τὸν παῖδα).

συμπίνω *sympinō* drink together*

Acts 10:41, with → συνεσθίω: After Christ's resurrection the apostles, as his witnesses, "ate and *drank* with him," i.e., took a meal with him.

συμπίπτω *sympiptō* collapse*

Luke 6:49 (cf. par. Matt 7:27: ἔπεσεν): συνέπεσεν (ἡ οἰκία).

συμπληρόω *symplēroō* fill completely; pass.: become completely full*

Luke 8:23, of a ship that becomes completely filled with water during a storm; pass. in Luke 9:51; Acts 2:1, referring fig. to time. G. Delling, *TDNT* VI, 308f.

συμπνίγω *sympnigō* choke, press upon*

Mark 4:7: plants choked by weeds; corresponding metaphorical usage occurs in Mark 4:19 par. Matt 13:22 /Luke 8:14. Luke 8:42, of the ὄχλοι that *press around* Jesus. H. Bietenhard, *TDNT* VI, 455-58.

συμπολίτης, ου, ὁ *sympolitēs* fellow citizen*

Fig. in Eph 2:19, of the Gentiles, who as Christians become "*fellow citizens* with the saints." H. Volkmann, *KP* V, 447-49.

συμπορεύομαι *symporeuomai* journey together; come together*

Luke 7:11; 14:25; 24:15, of a shared journey/trip (with dat. of the person). The Lukan writings in general understand Christian existence as a journey with Jesus. Mark 10:1, of the crowds who *come together* to Jesus (with πρός τινα).

συμποσία, ας, ἡ *symposia* common meal

Instead of pl. συμπόσια (→ συμπόσιον) Mark 6:39 D reads κατὰ τὴν συμποσίαν. BDF §158.

συμπόσιον, ου, τό *symposion* group of people eating*

In Mark 6:39 (bis) the pl. is repeated to give a distributive sense (BDF 493.2): divided by *various eating groups* or according to *eating groups*. Συμπόσιον originally referred to a drinking party or banquet. The meaning *group of people eating* also occurs in Plutarch *Sept. Sap.* 157d; *Quaest. Conv.* 704d. W. H. Gross, *KP* V, 449f.

συμπρεσβύτερος, ου, ὁ *sympresbyteros* fellow elder*

In 1 Pet 5:1 the author ("Peter"), as a *"fellow elder* and witness of Christ's sufferings," exhorts the elders (πρεσβύτεροι) of the church to "tend God's flock" properly (vv. 2f.). G. Bornkamm, *TDNT* VI, 654; N. Brox, *1 Pet* (EKKNT) 228f.

συμφέρω *sympherō* bring together; assist, help; be advantageous, useful*

1. Occurrences in the NT — 2. Grammatical peculiarities — 3. Primary considerations regarding meaning

Lit.: BAGD s.v. — BDF index s.v. — K. WEISS, *TDNT* IX, 69-78.

1. Συμφέρω occurs 15 times in the NT, slightly more frequently in the narrative writings (9 times in the Gospels and Acts), though with no less significance in the epistolary literature (5 occurrences in Paul, 1 in Hebrews). On secular, OT, and Jewish usage cf. Weiss 69-75.

2. Συμφέρω can appear in various constructions with its intrans. meaning *be useful, advantageous:* absolute in 1 Cor 6:12; 10:23: οὐ πάντα συμφέρει; 2 Cor 12:1: οὐ συμφέρον; with dat. of the person benefited in 2 Cor 8:10 (cf. also Matt 5:29, 30, etc.; frequently documented in classical Greek and papyri: Mayser, *Grammatik* II/2, 265). The direction and goal of the advantage or benefit is indicated by a ἵνα clause in Matt 5:29, 30; 18:6; John 11:50; 16:7; by an inf. in Matt 19:10; by acc. with inf. in John 18:14. Subst. partc. in Acts 20:20 (pl.); 1 Cor 12:7 (sg.); Heb 12:10 (sg. with prep.): *something useful* or *beneficial* (cf. Mayser, *Grammatik* II/1, 2; II/2, index [623]).

3. The most significant connotations of συμφέρω in both the Gospels and the Epistles are found in the meaning *be useful/advantageous.*

a) Matthew uses συμφέρω in exaggerated figures of speech (5:29, 30: mutilation of the body; 18:6: drowning with a millstone fastened round the neck) to throw the irreplaceable value (συμφέρει with personal dat.) of eternal salvation into relief over against earthly advantages. 19:10 can be understood in a similarly radical fashion of figurative exaggeration (cf. 19:12: mutilation of the body): Jesus' unequivocal stance (no more divorce!) is contrasted with human excuses (then better no marriage at all!). The difference is that in the first case it is a genuinely "spiritual" advantage or benefit, in the second merely an "earthly-human" one—despite the apparent posture of renunciation on the part of the disciples.

b) Whereas Matthew is inclined to introduce συμφέρω in the context of Church problems, John's use is more christocentric. The benefit of Jesus' death is at first perceived, according to the suggestion of Caiaphas, as being done with a bothersome rebel (11:50; cf. 18:14). This is then interpreted from a soteriological perspective and seen to be at work in gathering God's dispersed people (11:51f.). 16:7 sees the future value of Christ's return to the Father: It is what precipitates the sending of the Paraclete and its inaugurating activity in the community of disciples (16:8).

c) Paul focuses on advantage for the Church and its growth. Freedom misused for the sake of one's own advantage (1 Cor 6:12; 10:23, probably referring to libertine slogans—"all things are allowed"; Paul counters vehemently with "but not all things are *helpful*") helps the Church as little as does egocentric charismatic activity (12:7). This includes also the apostle's advice to bring to a conclusion the collection for the Jerusalem church (2 Cor 8:10), as well as the Lukan reference (Acts 20:20) to the profitable, obvious effects of the Pauline proclamation; in contrast, Paul's own boasting in the ironic fashion of fool's talk is of no use at all (2 Cor 12:1), unless it serves to irritate his adversaries and shake up the congregation (12:11).

d) Heb 12:10 speaks of the instructional benefit of the present tribulations for a person's maturing process toward sanctification and righteousness. In Acts 19:19 συμφέρω is used literally: Magic books are *brought together* to be burned.

e) In summary, NT use of συμφέρω places not human-earthly benefit and personal advantage in the conceptual foreground, but rather the welfare and growth of the Church (Matthew, Paul). These goals in their own turn are based on the salvation work of Jesus Christ and the Paraclete (John).

A. Kretzer

σύμφημι *symphēmi* agree, admit*

Rom 7:16: σύμφημι τῷ νόμῳ ὅτι καλός, "I *agree* that the law is good," namely, if I do what I do not want and thus am made aware of the failure of my own actions.

σύμφορος, 2 *symphoros* beneficial, advantageous; subst.: benefit, advantage*

1 Cor 7:35 uses the subst. in the sense of "furtherance": τό τινος σύμφορον: someone's *benefit, advantage;* 10:33: "my own *advantage*" (in contrast to ἀλλὰ τὸ πολλῶν); → συμφέρω 3.c.

συμφορτίζω *symphortizō* burden together
Pass. in Phil 3:10 v.l.: συμφορτιζόμενος τῷ θανάτῳ αὐτοῦ instead of συμμορφιζόμενος κτλ.

συμφυλέτης, ου, ὁ *symphyletēs* compatriot, fellow countryman*

1 Thess 2:14: pl. "your own *countrymen*," speaking of persecutions of the church in Thessalonica by its Macedonian fellow citizens.

σύμφυτος, 2 *symphytos* grown together, belonging together, united*

According to Rom 6:5 those who have been baptized "have been *united* with him [Christ] in a death like his" (σύμφυτοι γεγόναμεν τῷ ὁμοιώματι τοῦ θανάτου αὐτοῦ; associative dat.; see, however, BDF §194) will also be united with him in a resurrection like his. The verbal adj. σύμφυτος (from → συμφύω, "grow up with, be grown together/united with") encompasses the meanings *grown together, fused, united,* and also *inborn, innate.*

Paul explains v. 4 in v. 5 (γάρ). He focuses on the unbreakable relationship between believers and Christ's death and resurrection effected by baptism, which itself can be understood as the realization of the death (of the old person, vv. 6f.) and of the life from God (vv. 4c, 8-11). Within the context of the σύν-statements in vv. 1-11 σύμφυτος emphasizes esp. the indivisible, eternally valid, and as it were organic fusion of believers with the salvation event in Christ (cf. Aristotle *Pol.* ii.4.6, 1262b; Plato *Phdr.* 246d; *R.* 588d; Plutarch *Lyc.* 25.5; Theophrastus *CP* v.5.2; see esp. Spicq, *Notes* II, 844-46). F. Mussner, *TTZ* 63 (1954) 257-65; W. Grundmann, *TDNT* VII, 786, 790f.; Kuss I, 151-61; U. Wilckens, *Rom* (EKKNT) II, ad loc.; → ὁμοίωμα 2.b.

συμφύω *symphyō* grow together, grow up together*

Luke 8:7, of thorns that *grew together* with the sown seeds and choked them: συμφυεῖσαι (2nd aor. pass. partc.) αἱ ἄκανθαι (cf. par. Mark 4:7/Matt 13:7: ἀνέβησαν). Spicq, *Notes* II, 844-46.

συμφωνέω *symphōneō* agree, come to agreement, be in accord with*

There are 6 occurrences in the NT, 4 referring to agreement between persons: Matt 18:19: "If two of you *agree*" about the content of common prayer, God will answer such prayer (because the Church "on earth" is guaranteed the promise of the presence of Christ, vv. 18, 20); 20:2, of a contractual agreement about wages (one denarius) for a day's work (with μετά and gen.); so also 20:13 (with dat.); impersonal pass. in Acts 5:9: τί ὅτι συνεφωνήθη (D: συνεφώνησεν) ὑμῖν, "How is it that you *have agreed* together . . ." (cf. Lat. *convenit inter vos;* BDF §§202 s.v. συν-; 409.3). Luke 5:36, of things *matching;* Acts 15:15, of words *agreeing.* O. Betz, *TDNT* IX, 304-9; Spicq, *Notes* II, 847-50.

συμφώνησις, εως, ἡ *symphōnēsis* agreement*

2 Cor 6:15: τίς δὲ συμφώνησις Χριστοῦ πρὸς Βελιάρ; "what *accord* has Christ with Beliar?" Συμφώνησις is parallel here to μετοχή, κοινωνία (v. 14), μερίς (v. 15), and συγκατάθεσις (v. 15) in a series of rhetorical and antithetically formulated questions. The word is hardly used in classical and Hellenistic texts or in the papyri. Spicq, *Notes* II, 847-50.

συμφωνία, ας, ἡ *symphōnia* (musical) harmony; music*

Luke 15:25: συμφωνία καὶ χοροί, "*music and dancing*" as expressions of joyous celebration. Συμφωνία probably refers here to the collective playing of various instruments (cf. Pap. Oxy. no. 1275, ll. 9, 12; Pollux *Onomasticon* iv.83, 107; Philo *Sacr.* 74), though it can also refer to the music of single instruments (cf. Dan 3:5, 15 LXX) such as the double flute (cf. Billerbeck IV, 396, 400: a loanword in rabbinic writings [*m. Kelim* 11:6]), the shepherd's flute, or the bagpipe; see further BAGD s.v. (bibliography); O. Betz, *TDNT* IX, 307f. (bibliography); Spicq, *Notes* II, 847f.

σύμφωνος, 2 *symphōnos* in agreement, harmonious*

Subst. in 1 Cor 7:5: ἐκ συμφώνου, "by [mutual] *agreement/arrangement*," a phrase that occurs frequently in the papyri in reference to contractual arrangements (cf. O. Betz, *TDNT* IX, 305, 308; Spicq, *Notes* II, 850), though Paul uses it of the mutual dependence of husband and wife.

συμψηφίζω *sympsēphizō* count up, compute*

Acts 19:19: συνεψήφισαν τὰς τιμὰς αὐτῶν, "they *counted* the value of them [the magic books]"; pass. in 1:26 D: "be *counted among*" (in place of συγκαταψηφίζομαι). G. Braumann, *TDNT* IX, 604-7.

σύμψυχος, 2 *sympsychos* harmonious, in full accord, of one mind*

Phil 2:2, in a parenetic context with τὸ αὐτὸ φρονῆτε, τὴν αὐτὴν ἀγάπην ἔχοντες . . . τὸ ἓν φρονοῦντες. E. Lohmeyer, *Phil* (KEK) ad loc.: "*one* heart and soul"; differently A. Fridrichsen, *Philologische Wochenschrift* 58 (1938) 910-12: "from the bottom of one's soul." In this context, however, σύμψυχος refers to the unity of the Church in feeling as well as in thought and action.

σύν *syn* (together) with*

1. Differences in meaning from μετά; NT occurrences — 2. As an expression of mutuality — 3. Other usage — 4. Σὺν Χριστῷ and similar expressions in Paul

Lit.: On preps. in general → ἀνά. — BAGD s.v. — BDF §221. — W. GRUNDMANN, *TDNT* VII, 766-97. — KÜHNER, *Grammatik* II/1, 466f. — LSJ s.v. — MAYSER, *Grammatik* II/2, 398-401. — SCHWYZER, *Grammatik* II, 487-91.
On 4: J. DUPONT, Σὺν Χριστῷ. *L'union avec le Christ suivant Saint Paul* (1952). — M. J. HARRIS, *DNTT* III, 1207. — O. KUSS, *Rom* (²1963), excursus "Mit Christus," 319-81. — E. LOHMEYER, "Σὺν Χριστῷ," *Festgabe A. Deissmann* (1927) 218-57. — G. OTTO, *Die mit σύν verbundenen Formulierungen im paulinischen Schrifttum* (Diss. Berlin, 1952). — R. SCHNACKENBURG, *Das Heilsgeschehen bei der Taufe nach dem Apostel Paulus* (MTS I/1, 1950), excursus "Die Herkunft der Formel σὺν Χριστῷ," 167-75. — For further bibliography see *TWNT* X, 1273.

1. In contrast to μετά with the gen., which originally had a locative sense ("in the middle of, among," which is why Homer usually uses it with locative dat.), σύν refers to association or accompaniment, as a rule among persons, and is thus used with the associative dat. This distinction, however, had already disappeared by the classical period, and the choice of σύν or μετά usually became a matter of style. On the whole use of σύν recedes (exceptions include Xenophon and, probably because of Ionic influence, the Ptolemaic papyri). Like the NT the LXX overwhelmingly prefers μετά.

In the NT there are only 127 occurrences of σύν, over against 346 for → μετά with gen. These 127 occurrences are found almost exclusively in Luke-Acts (23 in the Gospel, 52 in Acts) and Paul (37). The rest are in Matthew (4 occurrences), Mark (6), John (3), James (1), and 2 Peter (1). Σύν does not occur at all in 2 Thessalonians, the Pastorals, Hebrews, 1 Peter, 1–3 John, or Revelation. Compounds with σύν- are distributed similarly: Of 94 σύν- compounds in the NT, 78 are in Luke-Acts and 46 occur only there.

2. Σύν refers to mutuality of being or doing: spend time "*with* the disciples" (Acts 14:28); Mary remained *with* Elizabeth three months (Luke 1:56); go or come *with* someone (John 21:3, etc.); pray *together with* someone (Acts 20:36); serve *with* someone (Phil 2:22); sell something *with* someone (Acts 5:1); die *with* someone (Matt

26:35; cf. 27:38). Εἶναι σύν τινι means "to be together *with* someone" or to accompany that person (Luke 7:12; 8:38; 24:44): be among someone's followers (22:56; Acts 4:13); take sides *with* one or another position (Acts 14:4). Οἱ σύν τινι (ὄντες) frequently refers to a person's "companions" or "attendants": Τίτος ὁ σὺν ἐμοί, "Titus, my *companion*" (Gal 2:3); οἱ σὺν ἐμοὶ ἀδελφοί, "the brothers who are *with* me" (Phil 4:21; cf. Rom 16:14f.; Gal 1:2).

Σύν can also be used of spiritual companionship: "I am *with* you in spirit" (Col 2:5). In 1 Cor 15:10b, "the grace of God which is *with* me," the phrase common in Greek literature, σὺν θεῷ (θεοῖς), "with the *help* of God (or of the gods)," is reversed, i.e., God, not the human person, initiates the action (cf. v. 10a, the apostolic blessing formulas, and the OT Yahweh assurances: "I am *with* you" and similar phrases, always with μετά). The classical formulation has no real parallel in the NT; 1 Cor 5:4 (σὺν τῇ δυνάμει τοῦ κυρίου ἡμῶν Ἰησοῦ, "*together with* the power of our Lord Jesus") is at most only a formal parallel.

3.a) A person (or group of persons) can be added with σύν so that he or she is included in the preceding (broader) category (cf., e.g., Herodotus viii.113): "the chief priests and the scribes *with* the elders" (Luke 20:1; cf. Mark 15:1); Herod mocked Jesus "*with* his soldiers" (Luke 23:11); "to all the saints in Philippi *with* the bishops and deacons" (Phil 1:1); "to him *and* to all who were in his house" (Acts 16:32; cf. 10:2; 14:5; "*with* John" in 3:4 is probably a later insertion). The reference can also be to things: τὸ ἐμὸν σὺν τόκῳ, "my own [money] *with* interest" (Matt 25:27; cf. Demosthenes *Or.* 28.13); they let the paralyzed man down "*with* his bed" (Luke 5:19); the sun rose "*with* its scorching heat" (σὺν τῷ καύσωνι, Jas 1:11).

b) Σύν serves rarely as a summarizing element: σὺν πάσῃ κακίᾳ, "*with* all malice" (Eph 4:31); σὺν πᾶσιν τούτοις, "*besides* all this" (Luke 24:21).

c) Acts 7:35, σὺν χειρὶ ἀγγέλου, sent "*by* the angel's hand," is a solemn, Hebraic circumlocution for a simple prep. expression evoked by the elevated style of the passage.

4. In contrast to the more common ἐν Χριστῷ (→ ἐν 2.d.2) σὺν Χριστῷ occurs only 12 times in the Pauline letters, always in a context speaking of the future and usually in opposition to the death of Jesus or of the person. The phrase thus does not refer primarily to any active life "in" or "by" Christ, but rather to future communion with Christ: 2 Cor 13:4b: "for we are weak *in* him (ἐν αὐτῷ), but we shall live *with* him (σὺν αὐτῷ)." The oldest occurrences are still close to Jewish apocalyptic (Lohmeyer 234ff.) and are in 1 Thessalonians (e.g., "and so we shall always be *with* the Lord," 4:17). The apostle's wish to depart this life and "be *with* Christ" (Phil 1:23) already shows the intimacy of communion with

Christ characteristic of Paul: This communion is to be expected right after the death of the individual, and not just after eschatological awakening.

The formula recalling Jesus' death and/or resurrection shows the specifically Pauline understanding of this phrase: Christ dies "so that we . . . might live *with* him" (1 Thess 5:10); he who raised Jesus will also raise us "*with* Jesus" (σὺν Ἰησοῦ, 2 Cor 4:14); Jesus died and was raised, and God will in the same manner "through Jesus" bring "*with* him those who have fallen asleep" (1 Thess 4:14).

Other passages focus less on eschatological communion with Christ than on participation in his death and resurrection as effected, according to Pauline understanding, through baptism: "If we have died *with* Christ we believe that we shall also live *with* him" (Rom 6:8; cf. 1 Thess 5:10; 2 Cor 4:14). This participation is thought of in analogy to the cultic events of the mystery religions and is expressed in a plethora of σύν-compounds: συναποθνῄσκω, "die *with*" (2 Tim 2:11); συμπάσχω, "suffer *with*" (Rom 8:17); συσταυρόομαι, "be crucified *with*" (6:6; Gal 2:19); συνθάπτομαι, "be buried *with*" (Rom 6:4; Col 2:12); συνεγείρω, "be raised up *with*" (Eph 2:6); συζωοποιέω, "make alive together *with*" (2:5; Col 2:13); συζάω, "live *with*" (Rom 6:8; 2 Tim 2:11), and others.

The use of "with Christ" in Colossians shows a close relationship between eschatological hope and the conduct of one's life here and now. Just as death "*with* Christ" delivers one from the elements of this world (2:20), so "being raised *with* Christ" obligates one to strive for "the things that are above" (τὰ ἄνω). Now life "*together with* Christ" is hidden in God, but after the parousia "you also will appear *with* him in glory" (3:1-4). Sacramental acts (cf. also 2:13), ethical obligation, and eschatological expectation of communion mutually permeate one another here.   W. Elliger

συνάγω *synagō* gather in, collect; receive as a guest

1. The semantic problem — 2. Considerations from tradition history — 3. Use in the NT

Lit.: K. BERGER, "Volksversammlung und Gemeinde Gottes. Zu den Anfängen der christlichen Verwendung von 'ekklesia,'" *ZTK* 73 (1976) 167-207. — J. FRIEDRICH, *Gott im Bruder?* (1977) 20f. (on Matthew). — P. HOFFMANN, *Die Toten in Christus* (²1969) 212-18 (on 1 Thessalonians). — P. G. MÜLLER, *XPI-ΣTOΣ APXHΓOΣ* (1973) 313-16. — W. SCHRAGE, " 'Ekklesia' und 'Synagoge.' Zum Ursprung des urchristlichen Kirchenbegriffs," *ZTK* 60 (1963) 178-202. — W. THÜSING, *Per Christum in Deum* (²1969) 202f. (on 1 Thessalonians). — For further bibliography → συναγωγή.

1. Like the simple vb. → ἄγω, the compound with συν- has no technical meaning. The compound combines the simple vb. and the prep. (→ σύν) in their respective basic meanings. Con-

text, particularly any contrasting terms, offers criteria for appropriate exegesis. Vb. and prep. can also appear separately, e.g., 1 Thess 4:14: "God will bring with him those who have fallen asleep" (ἄξει σὺν αὐτῷ)—at the resurrection of the dead (v. 16) on the basis on the resurrection of Jesus (v. 14b: ἀνέστη). It is uncertain whether Paul refers here to the "author (→ ἀρχηγός) of life" (Acts 3:15) or the "first fruits (→ ἀπαρχή) of those who have fallen asleep" (1 Cor 15:20; so Müller). In any case, there is no t.t. in 1 Thess 4:14 (Hoffmann).

2. In secular Greek the vb. is documented in the pass. in commercial usage in the sense of "yield as a total sum" and in the trans. act. with the meaning "collect" in the life of Greek associations (*SIG* s.v.; Preisigke, *Wörterbuch* s.v.; so also LXX and Josephus [BAGD s.v.]). The meaning in these cases, as in the NT, depends on factors of content and context (*contra* Berger 203 n.163, who asserts that συνάγω ἐκκλησίαν is a t.t. for the gathering together of an assembly; the twenty-six temporally and geographically diverse occurrences in *SIG* do not suggest this conclusion; ἐκκλησίαν is the obj. in four instances). Influence on NT usage cannot be documented. The nontechnical character of the vb. is also evident in the Gospels, since, of the 5 occurrences in Mark, Luke does not carry over even one, and Matthew only one (Matt 13:2). Neither does the usage in Q (Luke 3:17 par. Matt 3:12; Luke 11:23 par. Matt 12:30; cf. also Matt 24:28 with Luke 17:37 with the doubling of the prep. in → ἐπισυνάγω) constitute anything resembling a genuine tradition.

The majority of the 59 occurrences of συνάγω are in Matthew (24) and the Lukan writings (6 in Luke, 11 in Acts). While the vb. is evenly distributed in Mark (5 times), John (7), and Revelation (5), it is strikingly rare in Paul (only 1 Cor 5:4). On the whole the contextual evidence reveals a lack of theological connotations, and the NT documentation can thus be presented on the basis of objective categories, since individual writings do not suggest any linguistic peculiarities.

3. In addition to collecting or gathering of objects (→ a), the vb. also refers to the uniting or assembling of people (→ b). It also occurs in the unique meaning *receive (as a guest)* (→ c).

a) Collecting or gathering things: wheat (Matt 3:12 par. Luke 3:17), provisions (Matt 6:26), weeds (Matt 13:30), fish (Matt 13:47), crops (Luke 12:17, 18), possessions (15:13), fragments of bread (John 6:12, 13), and vines (15:6). Sowing and *gathering in* the harvest is used as a metaphor (Matt 25:24, 26; John 4:36: gathering fruit for eternal life). Metaphorical use of the vbs. *gather in* and "scatter" also occurs in a saying of Jesus: "He who does not *gather* with me scatters" (Luke 11:23 par. Matt 12:30); the opposition of the two actions excludes any neutral response to Jesus.

b) The majority of occurrences are used of the assembling, uniting, and bringing together of persons (high priests and scribes, everyone, kings, children of God, and others) or of a collective body (Sanhedrin, cohort, city, church [only in Acts 14:27]; according to Acts 11:26 Paul and Barnabas *met with* the church for collective work); act., pass., and reflexive *(assemble together)* forms are used interchangeably. No distinctions are made regarding Jewish or Christian persons or institutions. The vb. displays no specific ecclesiastical character either in Acts 14:27 or 1 Cor 5:4 ("when you are *assembled*"), nor any traditional, technical, or eschatological character in Matt 25:32; John 11:52; Rev 19:17 (*contra* Schrage 185f.). On συνήχθη (John 18:2) see H. Reynen, *BZ* 5 (1961) 86-90.

c) The special meaning *receive (as a guest)* (Matt 25:35, 38, 43) emerges from the contrast "stranger/homeless" on the one hand, and *receive* (*sc.* into one's home) on the other (on this addition cf. Deut 22:2; Judg 19:18; 2 Kgs 11:27, though the author may well consciously formulate it thus on the basis of similarity to the LXX).

H. Frankemölle

συναγωγή, ῆς, ἡ *synagōgē* assembly, congregation; place of assembly; synagogue (building)
ἐπισυναγωγή, ῆς, ἡ *episynagōgē* assembly, gathering*

1. Occurrences and meanings in the NT — 2. The semantic field — 3. Considerations from tradition history (OT and Judaism) — 4. Archaeological and literary witnesses — 5. NT situations and loci — a) Mark — b) Luke-Acts — c) Matthew — d) The remaining NT writings

Lit.: G. BAUMBACH, " 'Volk Gottes' im Frühjudentum. Eine Untersuchung der 'ekklesiologischen' Typen des Frühjudentums," *Kairos* 21 (1979) 30-47. — BILLERBECK IV / 1, 115-52. — H. CONZELMANN, *The Theology of Luke* (1982). — I. ELBOGEN, *Der jüdische Gottesdienst in seiner geschichtlichen Entwicklung* (1962 = ³1931). — H. FRANKEMÖLLE, *Jahwebund und Kirche Christi* (1974) (on Matthew). — K. GALLING, "Erwägungen zur antiken Synagoge," *ZDPV* 72 (1956) 163-78. — J. GNILKA, *Mark* (EKKNT, 1978) I. — J. G. GRIFFITHS, "Egypt and the Rise of the Synagogue," *JTS* 38 (1987) 1-15. — J. GUTMANN, ed., *The Synagogue: Studies in Origin, Archeology, and Architecture* (1975). — F. HAHN, *Mission in the NT* (1965). — M. HENGEL, "Proseuche und Synagoge. Jüdische Gemeinde, Gotteshaus und Gottesdienst in der Diaspora und in Palästina," FS Kuhn 157-84. — K. HRUBY, *Die Synagoge. Geschichtliche Entwicklung einer Institution* (1971). — F. HÜTTENMEISTER and G. REEG, *Die antiken Synagogen in Israel* (1977) I-II. — H. KASTING, *Die Anfänge der urchristlichen Mission* (1969). — H. G. KIPPENBERG, *Garizim und Synagoge. Traditionsgeschichtliche Untersuchungen zur samaritanischen Religion der aramäischen Periode* (1971) 145-71. — A. T. KRAABEL, "The Diaspora Synagogue," *ANRW* II/19, 1 (1979) 477-510. — C. H. KRAELING, *The Synagogue* (1956). — S. KRAUSS, *Synagogale Altertümer* (1966 = 1922). — idem, *PW* IV A (1932) 1284-

1316. — W. S. LASOR and T. C. ESKENAZI, *ISBE* IV, 676-84. — L. I. LEVINE, ed., *Ancient Synagogues Revealed* (1981). — H. MERKLEIN, "Die Ekklesia Gottes. Der Kirchenbegriff bei Paulus und in Jerusalem," *BZ* 23 (1979) 48-70. — L. ROST, *Die Vorstufen von Kirche und Synagoge im AT. Eine wortgeschichtliche Untersuchung* (1938). — S. SAFRAI, "The Synagogue," *The Jewish People in the First Century* (Compendia 1, ed. S. Safrai and S. Stern; 1976) II, 908-44. — W. SCHRAGE, *TDNT* VII, 798-841. — SCHÜRER, *History* II, 423-54. — I. SONNE, *IDB* IV, 476-91. — G. STEMBERGER, *Das klassische Judentum. Kultur und Geschichte der rabbinischen Zeit* (1979) 92-109. — K. STENDAHL, *RGG* III, 1297-1304. — P. STUHLMACHER, *Gerechtigkeit Gottes bei Paulus* (1965) 210-17. — J. WEINGREEN, "The Origin of the Synagogue," *idem, From the Bible to the Mishna* (1976). — E. ZIEBARTH, *Das griechische Vereinswesen* (1969 = 1896). — For further bibliography → συνάγω; see also *TWNT* X, 1273f.

1. Of the 56 occurrences of συναγωγή in the NT 8 are in Mark, 9 in Matthew, 34 in Luke-Acts (15 in the Gospel, 19 in Acts), 2 in John, 1 in James, and 2 in Revelation. It is striking that Paul does not use the word, nor (probably) does Q (Matt 6:2, 5 and 9:35 are exclusively Matthean; 23:34, *contra* Luke 11:49 [where συναγωγή is missing], is redactional). Markan usage has strongly affected the tradition; of the 8 Markan occurrences, Matthew takes over 5 and omits Mark 1:21, 23, 29; Luke takes over all but Mark 1:21. Mark has also determined the meaning: Without exception συναγωγή refers to the *synagogue building/synagogue.* Ἐπισυναγωγή is semantically hardly distinguishable (*contra* Schrage 841f., who asserts an "eschatological orientation" for the entire NT on the basis of the one eschatological occurrence in 2 Macc 2:7f.) and occurs only in 2 Thess 2:1 and Heb 10:25.

Συναγωγή in the sense of a Jewish *assembly* occurs only in Acts 13:43 and in the sense of Christian assembly only in Jas 2:2 (so also ἐπισυναγωγή in Heb 10:25). Acts 9:2 speaks fig. of *"synagogues [congregations]* in Damascus" (cf. also 6:9). In Rev 2:9 and 3:9 "pseudo-Jews" who persecute the Christian communities in Smyrna and Philadelphia are polemically called "συναγωγή [= congregation] of Satan" instead of συναγωγή κυρίου (cf. Num 16:3; 20:4; 27:17; Josh 22:16; Ps 73:2 LXX); but no consensus exists concerning whether, given the designation "those who say that they are Jews and are not," this refers to members of the Jewish nation or to syncretistic Christians (→ Ἰουδαῖος 7). Only 2 Thess 2:1 speaks in the context of the parousia of the ἐπισυναγωγή, i.e., the *assembling* of Christians with Christ.

Despite the predominant technical meaning (συναγωγή as a building), the openness and flexibility with which the term is used in other NT occurrences is striking. Surprisingly, this openness is carried over into the post-NT period, when even a Christian building for worship can be called συναγωγή, and συναγωγή is frequently documented as a self-designation for Christians (on these occurrences see Schrage 841). This post-NT usage (e.g., Ign. *Pol.* 4:2; *Herm. Man.* xi.9, 13f.) reflects both NT and pre-NT usage (→ 3). The development in use of the word is influenced by geographic, political, religious (relationships between Diaspora and homeland, between Jews and Christians), and other factors.

2. In a given semantic field individual terms can overlap in meaning or mutually complement one another and thus give shape to and make distinctions within a concept. This is the case with → ἱερόν (temple, temple complex), ναός (temple edifice: O. Michel, *TDNT* IV, 882f.), ὁ ἅγιος τόπος (holy place, etc.: H. Köster, *TDNT* VIII, 204f.), and οἶκος τοῦ θεοῦ (house of God, etc.: Michel, 121f.) and also with the semantic field including → ἐκκλησία (assembly of the political commmunity, congregation of God in LXX and NT), συναγωγή, προσευχή (prayer, place of prayer, synagogue: H. Greeven, *TDNT* II, 808; cf. Acts 16:13, 16 in a "we"-narrative), and words documented variously outside the NT (προσευκτήριον, σαββατεῖον [building], and συναγώγιον [assembly, congregation]; see Schürer 424-27, 439f. for references). The metonymy *assembly = place of assembly = building* seen in regard to συναγωγή and προσευχή is common in Greek (cf. ἀγών for assembly and place of assembly, προσβολή for docking, place for docking, harbor). Both the history of these NT terms and their identity within the given semantic field obfuscate any sharply defined limits of meaning.

3. The LXX always uses συναγωγή to translate Heb. *ʿēḏâ* (a more recent term is *kᵉneseṯ;* Aram. *kᵉništāʾ*), whereas qāhāl (*qᵉhal yhwh*) is rendered both with συναγωγή and ἐκκλησία. Since this occurs consistently within individual books, the preference of the translator was apparently the determining factor (Schrage 802). On the basis of this linguistic history and under the influence of the LXX (where συναγωγή encompassed two Hebrew terms), συναγωγή would naturally have suggested itself as a self-designation for Christian congregation—if contemporary Judaism had not already fixed the primary meaning as locative, "house of meeting" (exceptions [→ 1] confirm the rule; cf. Schrage 807f.).

Therefore, contemporary Jewish practice was the nontheological reason that Christian groups chose ἐκκλησία as their self-designation; this choice cannot be explained (as by Rost, K. L. Schmidt [*TDNT* III, 514, 516f.], and others) from the LXX or as an anti-synagogical and anti-salvation-historical choice (on criticism cf. Frankemölle 224f.; Berger 184f.; Merklein 58ff.). One must also reject derivation from apocalyptic writings suggesting an understanding of ἐκκλησία as "eschatological company of God" (Stendahl 1299; Stuhlmacher 210f.), since a single occurrence of *qᵉhal ʾēl* (1QM 4:10; possibly also a corrected passage in 1QSᵃ 1:25) cannot constitute the basis of an entire tradition history for ἐκκλησία (why not for συναγωγή? cf. Baumbach 40f., who asserts that *ʿēḏâ* is a preferred word in 1QSᵃ and 1QM with theological significance there, whereas qāhāl in 1QM refers four times to the military company of the enemy and only once to the *qᵉhal ʾēl* [4:10]).

The fundamental decision of the early Jerusalem church and the Hellenists against συναγωγή and for ἐκκλησία might have been determined primarily on the basis of contemporary usage

(συναγωγή as a building), along with secondary theological considerations (Frankemölle 225; Merklein 59). Since ἐκκλησία τοῦ θεοῦ/κυρίου (cf. συναγωγή κυρίου, Num 16:3; 20:4; 27:17; 31:16, and elsewhere) as the designation for a group is documented in the earliest documents of the NT (1 Thess 2:14; Gal 1:13, and elsewhere), use of ἐκκλησία in the NT must address the problem of continuity evoked by the polarity Israel—Church (*contra* Schrage and Berger 199; with Merklein 64; Stuhlmacher 211 n.2). Συναγωγή could not perform this function for Christians in spite of its weighty theological history in the LXX.

4. According to Acts 15:21 "Moses has had in every city those who preach him, for he is read every sabbath in the *synagogues.*" Hence the synagogue must already have existed for a long time. With this "proof" of age Luke is part of a long tradition (on Ps 74:8 and Ezek 11:16 cf. Galling); Philo, Josephus, and later Jewish writings also trace the synagogue back to Moses (documentation in Schürer 427, esp. n.6).

The origins of the synagogue are, however, shrouded in mystery. Even today questions remain concerning when, where, and under what historical circumstances the institution of the synagogue came into existence. As a rule its origin is associated with the Babylonian Exile, when there was no temple. According to 1 Kgs 8:46-50 gatherings took place during the Exile in which the people prayed toward Jerusalem; according to Ezra 7:25 Artaxerxes II mandated instruction in the law. In the place of an original connection with the temple cult (so Krauss), the thesis of an origin of the συναγωγή independent of the temple has become generally accepted (beginning with Elbogen); Hengel (180f.) suggests that in Palestine itself both aspects came into play: The secular designation συναγωγή might have been chosen out of consideration for the temple. It is certain, however, that the synagogue in the Diaspora is clearly older than in Palestine.

In the Hellenistic period one must accordingly differentiate between terms used in the home country (συναγωγή) and those used in the Diaspora, esp. Egypt (προσευχή). Προσευχή (taken over from the LXX and meaning "prayer"; cf. Isa 56:7: "house of prayer") as a reference to the building itself is attested in inscriptions and papyrus documents from the 3rd cent. B.C. on; συναγωγή does not appear as such a designation (on the confirmation of Schürer's thesis [439f.] and the suspicion of Schrage 817f. n.119, cf. Hengel, who has well known and more thorough witnesses, two from the 3rd cent.). There is no evidence of any technical difference between συναγωγή and προσευχή (Krauss 1288). The designation of Palestinian synagogues as συναγωγή by Philo (in *Omn. Prob. Lib.* 81 the Palestinian Essenes mention the συναγωγή) or Josephus can be explained on the basis of the writer's perspective or traced back to Judaizing groups (Hengel 169, 177). The metonymy from assembly/congregation to edifice can be documented in both instances. The assertion that transferal of the Palestinian term *(bêt) kᵉneseṯ* = συναγωγή occurred only in Palestine (Hengel 170 n.53) seems somewhat one-sided in view of attestation of συναγωγή in Cyrenaica (cf. Hengel 182) and for → ἀρχισυνάγωγος not only in Palestine, but also in Egypt, Asia Minor, Greece, Italy, and Cyrenaica (documentation in Schürer 433ff.; Schrage 844-47; criticism also from Berger 184 n.93). Consideration of the semantic field might disclose necessary distinctions between the individual terms.

The displacement of the original expression in the Diaspora by the Palestinian designation came about because: 1) within the Diaspora itself assemblies and groups based on nationality increasingly became private religious groups (Hengel 171) after the model of Hellenistic associations, and 2) the political (Hasmoneans, Herod) and theological influence of Palestine increased.

The oldest archaeological evidence of a συναγωγή in Palestine is the Theodotus inscription from Jerusalem (before A.D. 70) commemorating the founding of a synagogue "for reading the law and teaching the commandments," combined with housing accommodations and a water system. The oldest synagogue excavated thus far (1st cent. B.C.) is on the island of Delos; it was a remodeled residence, and this may have been common practice, including among the Christian "house churches" (cf. the "house church" and synagogue in Dura-Europas on the Euphrates). Literary attestation of synagogues from the Hellenistic period is found wherever Jews lived in the Roman or Parthian empires. In Palestine they are attested by Josephus, the Mishnah, and particularly by the NT. There is both archaeological and literary evidence for the existence of several synagogues even in smaller towns (480 [or 394] synagogues are said to have been destroyed in Jerusalem in A.D. 70). Samaritan synagogues should be mentioned with Jewish synagogues (despite Schrage; cf. Kippenberg; for a comprehensive study of all the synagogues cf. Hüttenmeister and Reeg, with maps).

There was no need in pre-Maccabean Judea for synagogues because of the relatively small area and the existence of the temple. Only the emergence of the Pharisees and the conquest of Judea in 104-103 B.C. strengthened the emergence of synagogues, even in Jerusalem. It was particularly in the Hellenized border communities (Lydda, Caesarea, Dora, Tiberias) that Jews first organized themselves into synagogues based on nationality. Synagogues were extraordinarily useful as meeting houses, esp. during the Judaizing of Galilee. They served as town halls, legal buildings, repositories for lost items, collection rooms, and schools, though their primary function, esp. after the destruction of the temple, was study of the Torah, prayer, and thus cultivation of individual piety (Schrage 821-26). The NT reflects this plurality of uses.

5. Because of the Palestinian provenance of the NT tradition the term συναγωγή predominates in the NT, in the Gospels esp. because of the location of Jesus' ministry. The Gospel writers presuppose that Galilee at the time of Jesus was completely Jewish and that the villages therefore had synagogues. Synagogues are mentioned in Capernaum (Mark 1:21; Luke 4:33; 7:5; John 6:59) and Nazareth (Luke 4:16). According to Matt 4:23; 9:35 Galilee even had what could be called a network of synagogues, and according to Luke 4:44 Jesus also preached in the synagogues of Judea. Jerusalem had several synagogues (Acts 24:12), probably organized according to nationality (6:9).

a) Mark associates not only Jesus' preaching and teaching activity with the synagogues (1:21, 39; 6:2), but also his healing activity (1:23ff., 39; 3:1ff.); although healing in synagogues is not documented in Jewish writings, it is not singled out as being esp. problematic in the NT disputes. Mark's summary in 1:39 ("He went through all Galilee, preaching in their synagogues and casting out demons") particularly places Jesus' mission activity in a

specific setting (Gnilka 78, 89), but any historical inquiry back to the actual situation of Jesus is extraordinarily difficult, so that one cannot decide in each instance whether the synagogue as setting really belongs to the original narrative material. Indeed, a schematization and concentration of Jesus' activity on the sabbath and in the synagogues is unmistakable in Mark. This stands at odds historically with the variable itinerancy of Jesus in Q, where the word συναγωγή makes no appearance. Historically, it is probably not the case that Jesus' ministry took place primarily on the sabbath and in synagogues (contra Schrage 831f.); as an itinerant prophet Jesus addressed people in the context of their own lives.

According to Mark 13:9 the disciples will be given up to local councils, beaten in synagogues (for Jewish parallels cf. Macc 3:12; m. Šebu. 4:10), and dragged before Gentile governors and kings. The transparency of their situation and the reworking of it in light of persecution by Jews is still disputed with regard to ch. 13. Christians are persecuted as apostates because of their confession of Christ (cf. 2 Cor 11:24f.). The reference to the synagogue is a part of the Markan thesis (cf. Hahn 111-20), according to which Jesus' ministry is "first" (7:27a) directed to Israel, though even so it already reaches out to Gentiles (3:7f.; 5:1-20; 7:24, 31; 8:13ff.), whereas parts of Israel reject Jesus (3:6, 22-30; 4:11f.). For Mark this offer to the synagogue is forfeited with the cross.

b) Luke carries through this Markan understanding in his own two-volume work. Acts 13:46 provides the key: "It was necessary" for the gospel to be proclaimed "first" to the Jews; since they reject it, the Gentiles now hear it (cf. 3:26). On the basis of this understanding of salvation history, which is developed narratively in Luke and Acts, Jesus' ministry is limited—more than in Mark—to Israel, specifically to Galilee (on the passages that do not fit this pattern see Hahn 128-36), since only Acts (after chs. 8–12) has a universal orientation. Accordingly, Jesus and the early Church are focused on the temple in Jerusalem (Luke 2:22-52; 19:28ff.; Acts 1:12–8:1). Therefore, when the proclamation of the gospel "first" to the Jews is mentioned, there is no mention of any activity in synagogues (so Acts 8:4f., 40; 9:32, 43; 11:19).

But in the Galilean period Jesus, "as his custom was," goes to the synagogue on the sabbath (4:16; cf. the verbatim par. in Acts 17:2 referring to Paul). The programmatic appearance in the synagogue in Nazareth (Luke 4:16ff.) and even more the summary description of Jesus' teaching in the synagogues of Galilee (4:15; in v. 44 surprisingly expanded to include the synagogues of Judea and attested in narration in 4:33; 6:6; 13:10; cf. also Jesus' contacts with persons associated with synagogues in 7:5; 8:41) characterize the Lukan agenda. This is also outlined in a schematic structure (initial success, conflict, expulsion; cf. with Luke 4:16-30: Acts 9:20ff.;

13:44ff.; 14:1ff., etc.). Israel is from the very beginning the divided people of God (→ λαός 3.c). Luke has systematized and constructed a typology for Jesus' contact with the synagogue—*contra* Mark (Conzelmann 31, 190). Parallel to this, the motif of synagogue contact is in Acts (according to the scheme just mentioned) applied to the missionary activity in the Diaspora (after 13:5), so that Luke transfers Palestinian terminology to the meeting houses of the Diaspora (Schürer 439ff.) and also passes into tradition the Palestinian form of the synagogue worship service (Luke 4:16ff.; Acts 13:14ff.: Hengel 181 n.102). This scheme serves to clarify both the cleft in the people of God and the relationship between Israel and the Church.

The extent to which this literary scheme is a reworking of historical recollection must remain an open question, even if the existence of synagogues in Damascus, Salamis on Cyprus, Antioch, Thessalonica, Beroea, Athens, Corinth, and Ephesus, and several in Jerusalem (Acts 6:9; 24:12) is factual. The "God-fearers," those sympathetic to the synagogues, were an interesting target group for Christian mission activity. Considering, however, that according to Luke only the Pauline mission strategy takes synagogues into consideration (synagogues are not mentioned in regard to the other apostles and missionaries), the question arises whether this does not primarily reflect the Lukan understanding of Paul. Paul docs, to be sure, mention the salvation-historical "first" (cf. Rom 1:16); yet he never mentions the συναγωγή and offers no personal evidence that he as the "apostle to the Gentiles" (Rom 11:13; cf. Gal 1:15f.) ever viewed synagogues as a point of departure for his own mission activity.

Conflicts between the early Church and Hellenistic synagogues organized according to nationality (from Cilicia and Asia, with Alexandrians, Freedmen, and Cyrenians: Acts 6:9) are already reflected in the Gospels (Luke 12:11; 21:12 par. Mark 13:9: courts of the synagogues; cf. Acts 6:9f.).

c) Despite constant emphasis on continuity with the history of the Jewish faith, Matthew emphasizes most strongly the distance between Church and synagogue by using αὐτῶν with συναγωγή (so 4:23 [par. Mark 1:39]; 9:35; 10:17; 12:9; exceptions are indirect mentions of synagogues in 6:2, 5; 23:6). In 23:34 Matthew has Jesus speak with exaggerated directness of "your synagogues"; "*their* synagogues" in 13:54 is in tension with the identification of Nazareth as "*his own* country." Unlike Mark's eschatological speech (Mark 13:9), Matthew's commissioning speech in 10:17 already presupposes being delivered up to councils and flogged in "their synagogues." For Matthew Church and synagogue belong to two different worlds and are entirely separate. Like Jesus, Christians are killed, crucified, and persecuted from city to city (23:34, 37). The christologically based ἐκκλησία (16:18; cf. 18:17) stands as an independent entity over against the συναγωγή.

d) In John συναγωγή (6:59; 18:20), neutral in and of itself, nonetheless stands in an unequivocally negative semantic field characterized by → ἀποσυνάγωγος (9:22; 12:42; 16:2) and "the" Ἰουδαῖοι as sons of the devil (8:44, contextually determined: Ἰουδαῖοι is also used neutrally and positively). Rev 2:9; 3:9 ("synagogues of Satan") is also characterized by this anti-Jewish tendency; this is probably more a reworking of material on the basis of local tensions with synagogues rather than with synagogues in general.

Post-NT neutral or positive use of συναγωγή for Christian congregations (→ 1) must be evaluated with regard to temporal and geographical factors (the actual relationship between church and synagogue in the particular location). Christianity did not everywhere stand in a relationship of genuine tension with Judaism, and this is reflected in usage of the word.   H. Frankemölle

συναγωνίζομαι *synagōnizomai* fight together, assist in battle*

Rom 15:30: Paul asks the Romans to "*strive together* with me (συναγωνίσασθαί μοι)" in the struggle awaiting him in Jerusalem. → ἀγών 1, 4.

συναθλέω *synathleō* fight together, assist in battle*

Phil 1:27: The church is to *strive side by side* with one mind for the faith of the gospel (συναθλοῦντες τῇ πίστει [dat. of advantage] τοῦ εὐαγγελίου); 4:3: ἐν τῷ εὐαγγελίῳ συνήθλησάν μοι, "they *have labored side by side* with me in the gospel." The gospel itself leads its witnesses into this battle, since it elicits both opposition and persecution; it thus requires of believers mutual assistance, steadfastness, and willingness to suffer; cf. 2 Tim 2:5; Heb 10:32f.; Ign. *Pol.* 1:3; 3:1; *1 Clem.* 5:1. E. Stauffer, *TDNT* I, 167f.

συναθροίζω *synathroizō* gather, assemble*

Pf. pass. partc. in Acts 12:12: *(having) gathered together;* cf. Luke 24:33 v.l.; act. in Acts 19:25.

συναίρω *synairō* suspend, cancel*

In the NT only in Matthew in the phrase (also common in the papyri) συναίρω λόγον, *settle accounts* (18:23, 24 [λόγον supplied from v. 23]; 25:19). The expression is taken from the language of commerce. Spicq, *Notes* II, 851.

συναιχμάλωτος, ου, ὁ *synaichmalōtos* fellow prisoner*

In Rom 16:7 (Andronicus and Junias); Phlm 23 (Epaphras); and Col 4:10 (Aristarchus) Pauline colleagues are referred to as *fellow prisoners*. The noun evokes less the idea of normal imprisonment (→ δεσμός) than military usage, namely, "prisoners of war," which Paul and his colleagues become in the battle for the gospel (cf. → συστρατιώτης, Phil 2:25; Phlm 2; → ἀγών; πανοπλία). Nonetheless, συναιχμάλωτος does not refer fig. to any "inner struggle" (*contra* G. Kittel, *TDNT* I, 196f.), but rather literally to actual imprisonment.

συνακολουθέω *synakoloutheō* accompany → ἀκολουθέω 5.

συναλίζομαι *synalizomai* eat salt together; share table fellowship, eat together*

Acts 1:4: συναλιζόμενος παρήγγειλεν αὐτοῖς, "*at the meal* he gave them charge." This tr. is suggested by the sg. form and the attestation of the partc. in most older versions (Latin, Syriac, Armenian, Ethiopian, Coptic; Vg.: *convescens*), even if συναλίζομαι is not documented with this meaning before the end of the 2nd cent. It is significant, however, that συναλίζομαι in Manetho *Apostelesmatica* v.339; *Ps.-Clem. Rec.* vii.2; *Hom.* xiii.4 is used of the eucharist. In ancient custom salt and table fellowship were associated (Plutarch *Moralia* 684e; Archilochus 95 [E. Diehl, *Anthologia* II, 239]; Demosthenes *Or.* 19.189; Libanius *Decl.* iv.29 [ed. R. Förster, V, 246]; Origen *Cels.* ii.21). On table fellowship with the resurrected Jesus cf. Acts 10:41; Luke 24:30f., 42f.; see further BAGD s.v. 1; E. Haenchen, *Acts* (Eng. tr., 1971) ad loc. (both with bibliography).

Another possibility for συναλίζω would be "assemble" (pass.: "come together"), though then the pl. would have to be used (see further BAGD s.v. 2). Several minuscules read deponent συναυλιζόμενος, "spend the night with, stay with" (BAGD s.v. 3), of which συναλίζομαι could be an orthographic variation. See K. Lake and H. J. Cadbury, *Beginnings* IV, 5; G. Schneider, *Acts* (HTKNT) ad loc.; on the whole question *TCGNT* ad loc.

συναλλάσσω *synallassō* reconcile*

Acts 7:26, referring to Moses and his Israelite brethren: συνήλλασσεν αὐτοὺς εἰς εἰρήνην, "he [Moses] *tried to reconcile* them," conative impf.; cf. BAGD §326; Exod 2:13f.

συναναβαίνω *synanabainō* go/come up together*

In the NT of persons who *came up with* Jesus to Jerusalem: Mark 15:41: many other women (αἱ συναναβᾶσαι); Acts 13:31, more generally: the disciples from Galilee (τοῖς συναναβᾶσιν). → ἀναβαίνω.

συνανάκειμαι *synanakeimai* recline together at table, eat together*

In the NT this term, like → ἀνάκειμαι, only occurs in the Gospels. Those eating were served while reclining on cushions. Mark 2:15 par. Matt 9:10 refers to a group of tax collectors and sinners who *were eating together* with Jesus and the disciples (συνανέκειντο τῷ Ἰησοῦ καὶ τοῖς μαθηταῖς αὐτοῦ) and were thus fully accepted into table fellowship. The subst. partc. οἱ συνανακείμενοι refers to *those together at table* (Mark 6:22 par. Matt 14:9; Luke 7:49; 14:10, 15). F. Büchsel, *TDNT* III, 654f.; B. Reicke, *BHH* 1991-93.

συναναμ(ε)ίγνυμαι *synanam(e)ignymai* mix together; pass.: mingle/associate with*

In the NT this vb. is used only by Paul and in 2 Thessalonians and refers in every instance to association of believers with those who have fallen away from faith in Christ, which is warned against: 1 Cor 5:9: μὴ συναναμίγνυσθαι πόρνοις; v. 11: μὴ συναναμίγνυσθαι ἐάν τις ἀδελφὸς ὀνομαζόμενος ἢ πόρνος . . .; cf. 2 Thess 3:14, referring to any member of the congregation who does not obey the apostolic message: τοῦτον σημειοῦσθε, μὴ συναναμίγνυσθαι αὐτῷ.

Such association, i.e., table fellowship (cf. the parallel term → συνεσθίω, 1 Cor 5:11; Gal 2:12), with "sinners" destroys the purity of the community (cf. the metaphor of the leavening, 1 Cor 5:6-8). But this does not mean that believers are to avoid any association with "sinners of this world"; they judge "sinners" among themselves, but God will judge those "outside" (vv. 11-13, cf. vv. 1-5). According to 2 Thess 3:14 such exclusion aims at "conversion" (ἵνα ἐντραπῇ; cf. 1 Cor 5:5). The Jewish idea of keeping God's people pure by prohibiting marriage with Gentiles (Hos 7:8 LXX; *Ep. Arist.* 142), however, is not a factor for Paul (cf. 1 Cor 7:12ff.). Cf. further 11:31f.; 16:22; Matt 18:15ff.; *Did.* 10:6; 14:2; 15:3; 1QS 6:24ff.; 8:16ff. On orthography cf. BDF §23; the phonetic spelling -μίγνυμαι occurs in numerous old mss. H. Greeven, *TDNT* VII, 852-55.

συναναπαύομαι *synanapauomai* rest together, rest in someone's company*

Rom 15:32: Paul wishes to *rest/be refreshed* in the company of the Romans after his visit to Jerusalem (ἵνα . . . συναναπαύσωμαι ὑμῖν), God willing. → ἀνάπαυσις.

συναναστρέφομαι *synanastrephomai* associate with, go about with

Acts 10:41 D² gig p sy^h adds καὶ συνανεστράφημεν after συνεφάγομεν καὶ συνεπίομεν αὐτῷ; D* reads συνεστράφημεν (D also adds → συστρέφω in 11:28; 16:39; 17:5); see *TCGNT*.

συναντάω *synantaō* come toward, encounter*

Literal in Luke 9:37; 22:10: *come toward;* Acts 10:25: *go toward;* Heb 7:1, 10: *encounter.* Fig. in Acts 20:22: τὰ συναντήσοντά μοι, "what *shall befall* me."

συνάντησις, εως, ἡ *synantēsis* encounter, meeting

Matt 8:34 C L W Koine, etc.; John 12:13 D G L, etc.: εἰς συνάντησιν (instead of ὑπάντησιν), "toward" (with dat.).

συναντιλαμβάνομαι *synantilambanomai* undertake together, take part with, assist*

This double compound, common in Hellenistic Greek, refers to support or assistance through cooperation (συν-) and simultaneously representative (-αντι-) aid. Luke 10:40: Mary should *help* her sister Martha with serving; Rom 8:26: "the Spirit *helps* us in our weakness" (συναντιλαμβάνεται τῇ ἀσθενείᾳ [v.l.: gen.] ἡμῶν), i.e., it helps believers who are unable to pray appropriately to God by interceding—though not without their participation— with a prayer that God will hear; cf. Num 11:17; Ps 88:22 LXX. G. Delling, *TDNT* I, 376; H. R. Balz, *Heilsvertrauen und Welterfahrung* (1971) 71f.

συναπάγομαι *synapagomai* be carried away, be drawn along*

In the NT only pass.: Rom 12:16: τοῖς ταπεινοῖς συναπαγόμενοι, "let yourselves *be drawn down* to/by the lowly" (opposed to: τὰ ὑψηλὰ φρονοῦντες). Arrogant self-assertion and haughtiness are countered by the humility of love. Dat. τοῖς ταπεινοῖς can be either neut. or masc. If the latter, then "fellowship with the lowly and oppressed" is esp. emphasized (E. Käsemann, *Rom* [Eng. tr., 1980] 347-48 [bibliography]; cf. BAGD s.v. [bibliography]). In any case, Paul seeks to "orient" the church toward the lowly (Käsemann 347; cf. v. 16c). The vb. also occurs with the meaning *be carried away* in Gal 2:13 (referring to Peter); 2 Pet 3:17.

συναποθνήσκω *synapothnẹ̄skō* die with*

Of the close relationship between apostle and congregation in Mark 14:31: συναποθανεῖν σοι (par. Matt 26:35: σὺν σοὶ ἀποθανεῖν; cf. John 11:16); 2 Cor 7:3: εἰς τὸ συναποθανεῖν καὶ συζῆν (cf. Heliodorus *Aethiopica* x.19.2; Nicolaus of Damascus frag. 80 [*FGH* IIA, 379]; see also G. Stählin, FS Braun 503-21; J. Lambrecht, *Bijdr.* 37 [1976] 234-51). Used christologically in the hymn in 2 Tim 2:11: εἰ γὰρ συναπεθάνομεν, καὶ συζήσομεν· εἰ ὑπομένομεν, καὶ συμβασιλεύσομεν. . . . "Dying with Christ" corresponds to participation in the life of Christ (cf. Rom 6:4-11; 8:17; 2 Cor 4:10; → σύν 4). But in 2 Tim 2:11 συναποθνήσκω refers not to baptism (as in Rom 6:4ff.) but to the apostle's suffering and martyrdom: His steadfastness leads him (and his congregation) to (future) life. W. Grundmann, *TDNT* VII, 786, 793f.; N. Brox, *Die Pastoralbriefe* (RNT) on 2 Tim 2:11; Spicq, *Notes* II, 852f.

συναπόλλυμαι *synapollymai* perish with, die together*

Mid. in Heb 11:31, of Rahab, who "by faith *did* not *perish* with those who were disobedient" (συναπώλετο); cf. Josh 2:8ff.; 6:17, 22ff.

συναποστέλλω *synapostellō* send at the same time, send together with*

2 Cor 12:18, of an ἀδελφός whom Paul *sent with* (συναπέστειλα) Titus to Corinth to organize the collection (cf. 8:6, 18f.; this probably does not refer to the [further] ἀδελφός of 8:22f.); see also R. Bultmann, *2 Cor* (Eng. tr., 1985) ad loc.

συναρμολογέω *synarmologeō* fit/join together, unite*

This compound is documented only in Christian writings and, like the simple vb., belongs to the language of building construction: *fit together (stones;* cf. ἀρμός, "joint"). According to Eph 2:21 (πᾶσα οἰκοδομὴ συναρμολογουμένη) in Christ "the whole structure [of the Church of Jews and Gentiles] *is joined together into a whole*" so that Christ constitutes the "cornerstone" (→ γωνία 3.c). He alone establishes the Church's unity, i.e., its unity within multiplicity; he alone maintains its connection with the "saints and members of the household of God" (v. 19, i.e., Jewish Christians). This building metaphor is also conceived dynamically, since the edifice joined together by Christ continues to grow (particularly now, with the addition of those who were Gentiles) toward its goal of being a ναὸς ἅγιος ἐν κυρίῳ (v. 21b) or a κατοικητήριον τοῦ θεοῦ ἐν πνεύματι (v. 22; see also. → οἰκοδομή 3.a).

Eph 4:16 transfers this metaphor of fitting together to the body of Christ (ἐξ οὗ πᾶν τὸ σῶμα συναρμολογούμενον καὶ συμβιβαζόμενον). Here the unity of Christ's body— on the basis of the parenetic context (cf. 4:1)—is established first by the cooperation of all members, each according to its own purpose. But the foundation still resides in Christ, who is the head of the body (v. 15) and who through the interrelationship of the members effects its growth into the οἰκοδομὴ ἑαυτοῦ ἐν ἀγάπῃ (v. 16b). C. Maurer, *TDNT* VII, 855f.; → οἰκοδομή (bibliography).

συναρπάζω *synarpazō* seize violently, grab, drag away
→ ἁρπάζω 4.

συναυλίζομαι *synaulizomai* sleep together; recline together; be with
Acts 1:4 v.l. for → συναλίζομαι (cf. Xenophon *Cyr.* i.2.15, etc.).

συναυξάνομαι *synauxanomai* increase together, grow together*

Matt 13:30 (M): the weeds and wheat allowed to *grow together* until the harvest (ἄφετε συναυξάνεσθαι ἀμφότερα).

σύνδεσμος, ου, ὁ *syndesmos* bond, shackle
→ δεσμός 5.

συνδέω *syndeō* bind together (with someone), shackle together*

In the NT only pass.: fig. in Heb 13:3: ὡς συνδεδεμένοι, "as though [you were] *shackled with them*," of concern for imprisoned church members (δέσμιοι), whose fate the believers should bear together in their φιλαδελφία (13:1); cf. 10:34; 11:36.

συνδοξάζω *syndoxazō* glorify together*

Pass. in Rom 8:17 of the *glorification* of believers *with* Christ, which will follow from their present communion with his suffering and reveal itself eschatologically (εἴπερ συμπάσχομεν ἵνα καὶ συνδοξασθῶμεν; cf. 8:18, 19, 21, 30). G. Kittel, *TDNT* II, 253f.

σύνδουλος, ου, ὁ *syndoulos* fellow slave
→ δουλεύω.

συνδρομή, ῆς, ἡ *syndromē* running together (noun), mob*

Acts 21:30: συνδρομὴ τοῦ λαοῦ, "a *running together* of people," i.e., "a *mob*."

συνεγείρω *synegeirō* awaken together, cause to rise up together*

Ephesians and Colossians use this compound vb. of believers' participation, effected by God, in Christ's resurrection. Eph 2:6: καὶ συνήγειρεν καὶ συνεκάθισεν ἐν τοῖς ἐπουρανίοις (cf. v. 5: ὄντας ἡμᾶς νεκροὺς . . . συνεζωοποίησεν τῷ Χριστῷ). Rom 6:4ff. understands the new life of believers under grace as participation in the reality of Christ's resurrection. But the aor. in Eph 2:6 goes beyond Paul and emphasizes the present realization of the salvation event (cf., however, 2 Cor 4:14, though also, e.g., Ign. *Pol.* 6:1).

Similarly Col 2:12: ἐν ᾧ [= Christ] καὶ συνηγέρθητε; 3:1: συνηγέρθητε τῷ Χριστῷ. According to vv. 13ff. resurrection with Christ liberates believers from sin and from subjection to the principalities and powers. Nonetheless, this does not constitute a suspension of eschatological hope, since they seek "the things that are above" (3:1), and their life is "[still] hidden with Christ in God" (vv. 3f.). W. Grundmann, *TDNT* VII, 786f., 792f.; P. Siber, *Mit Christus leben* (ATANT 61, 1971) 191-213; H. Conzelmann, *Eph* (NTD); E. Schweizer, *Col* (Eng. tr., 1982) (bibliography); → ἐγείρω 1.

συνέδριον, ου, τό *synedrion* Sanhedrin*

1. Occurrences in the NT and meaning — 2. History — 3. In sayings of Jesus — 4. In the Passion narrative — 5. Acts

Lit. (general): BAGD s.v. — H. BELLEN, *KP* V, 455f. — E. LOHSE, *TDNT* VII, 860-71. — F. POLAND, PW II/8, 1333-53. — H. J. SCHOEPS, *BHH* 740f.

On 1: F. E. MEYER, "Einige Bemerkungen zur Bedeutung des Terminus 'Synhedrion' in den Schriften des NT," *NTS* 14 (1967 /68) 545-51.

On 2: S. B. HOENIG, *The Great Sanhedrin* (1953). — J. JEREMIAS, *Jerusalem at the Time of Jesus* (1969). — S. KRAUSS, "Sanhedrin-Makkōt," *Die Mischna* (1933) IV/4-5, 19-51. — H. MANTEL, *Studies in the History of the Sanhedrin* (1961). — REICKE, *NT Era* 142-52. — E. RIVKIN, "Beth Din, Boulé, Sanhedrin: A Tragedy of Errors," *HUCA* 46 (1975) 181-99. — S. SAFRAI, "Jewish Self-Government," *The Jewish People in the First Century* (Compendia 1, ed. S. Safrai and M Stern; 1974) I, 379-419. — SCHÜRER, *History* II, 199-226. — G. STEMBERGER, *Das klassische Judentum* (1979) 54-60. — S. ZEITLIN, "The Political Synedrion and the Religious Sanhedrin," *JQR* 36 (1945/46) 109-40. — idem, "Synedrion in the Greek Literature, the Gospels and the Institution of the Sanhedrin," *JQR* 37 (1946 /47) 189-98. — R. A. GUELICH, "Matt 5:22: Its Meaning and Integrity," *ZNW* 64 (1973) 39-52. — D. R. A. HARE, *The Theme of Jewish Persecution of Christians in the Gospel of St. Matthew* (SNTSMS 6, 1967) 96ff. — M. WEISE, "Mt 5:21f.—ein Zeugnis sakraler Rechtsprechung in der Urgemeinde," *ZNW* 49 (1958) 116-23. — H. T. WREGE, *Die Überlieferungsgeschichte der Bergpredigt* (1968) 59ff.

On 4: J. BLINZLER, *Der Prozeß Jesu* (⁴1969) 129-259 (cf.

idem, *The Trial of Jesus* [1959]). — idem, "Das Synedrium von Jerusalem und die Strafprozeßordnung der Mischna," *ZNW* 52 (1961) 54-65. — idem, "Zum Prozeß Jesu," *Aus der Welt und Umwelt des NT* (1969) 124-46. — S. G. F. BRANDON, *The Trial of Jesus of Nazareth* (1968). — T. A. BURKILL, "The Competence of the Sanhedrin," *VC* 10 (1956) 80-96. — idem, "The Trial of Jesus," *VC* 12 (1958) 1-18. — D. R. CATCHPOLE, "The Problem of the Historicity of the Sanhedrin Trial," *The Trial of Jesus* (FS C. F. D. Moule, 1970) 47-65. — W. GRUNDMANN, "The Decision of the Supreme Court to Put Jesus to Death (John 11:47-57) in Its "Context: Tradition and Redaction in the Gospel of John," *Jesus and the Politics of His Day* (ed. E. Bammel and C. F. D. Moule; 1984) 295-318. — G. HAUFE, "Der Prozeß Jesu im Lichte der gegenwärtigen Forschung," *ZdZ* 22 (1968) 93-101. — J. JEREMIAS, "Zur Geschichtlichkeit des Verhörs Jesu vor dem Hohen Rat," *ZNW* 43 (1950/51) 145-50. — G. D. KILPATRICK, *The Trial of Jesus* (1953) — S. LÉGASSE, "Jésus devant le Sanhedrin," *RTL* 5 (1974) 170-97. — H. LIETZMANN, "Der Prozeß Jesu," Lietzmann II, 251-63. — idem, "Bemerkungen zum Prozeß Jesu," *ibid.* 264-76. — G. LINDESKOG, "Der Prozeß Jesu im jüdisch-christlichen Religionsgespräch," FS Michel 325-36. — R. PESCH, *Mark* (HTKNT, 1977) II, 404-24. — G. SCHNEIDER, "Gab es eine vorsynoptische Szene 'Jesus vor dem Synedrium'?" *NovT* 12 (1970) 22-39. — idem, "Jesus vor dem Synedrium," *BibLeb* 11 (1970) 1-15. — E. STAUFFER, *Jerusalem und Rom* (1957) 67-73, 120-22. — A. STROBEL, *Die Stunde der Wahrheit* (1980). — P. WINTER, *On the Trial of Jesus* (²1974). — idem, "The Trial of Jesus and the Competence of the Sanhedrin," *NTS* 10 (1963/64) 494-99. — idem, "The Marcan Account of Jesus' Trial by the Sanhedrin," *JTS* 14 (1963) 94-102. — idem, "Zum Prozeß Jesu," *Antijudaismus im NT?* (ed. W. P. Eckert, N. P. Levinson, and M. Stöhr; 1967) 95-104. — For further bibliography see Blinzler; Lohse; Pesch; *TWNT* X, 1274.

1. Συνέδριον (Aram. *sanhedrîn*, a loanword from Greek; Heb. *bēṭ dîn haggāḏōl*) occurs 22 times in the NT (3 each in Matthew and Mark, once each in Luke and John; 14 times in Acts) and refers to the highest Jewish legal and administrative body, situated in Jerusalem. In John 11:47 the Sanhedrin is called the "assembly," Acts 4:15 mentions the assembly room, and Luke 22:66 mentions the assembly house of the Sanhedrin.

2. A decree of Antiochus III (223-187 B.C.) calls the aristocratic senate of priests and elders the γερουσία (Josephus *Ant.* xii.138, 142; cf. Acts 5:21). The t.t. "Sanhedrin" appeared at the time of Hyrcanus II (63-40 B.C., Josephus *Ant.* xiv.167ff.) and became common during the Herodian period. Rabbinic witnesses cite Num 11:16 to support their assertion that the Sanhedrin consisted of 70 + 1 members (with the high priest presiding). Its three factions were the sadducean aristocracy of priests and laymen, and, from the time of Alexandra (75-67 B.C., Josephus Ant. xiii.408ff.), primarily pharisaic scribes. It met according to Josephus in the βουλή (*B.J.* v.144) or the βουλευτήριον (vi.354) of the upper city, according to the Mishnah in the inner forecourt of the temple, and according to the Talmud later in the *ḥānûṭ* (bazaar).

The powers of the Sanhedrin originally included both civil and cultic interpretation and application of the laws of the Torah, decisions concerning war and peace, legal jurisdiction in the courts, temple supervision, and decisions concerning religious practice (calendar, feasts). The significance of the Sanhedrin was diminished during the period of the Hasmoneans, and Herod made the Sanhedrin subservient by liquidating his opponents among its members (Josephus *Ant.* xiv.175; cf. xv.173; Matt 2:4ff.), reserving the *ius gladii* for himself. Although the Sadducees were the dominant faction in the Roman period, important decisions could not be made without the support of the Pharisees (Josephus *Ant.* xviii.17). After A.D. 6 the Sanhedrin also acquired jurisdiction and police powers in Judea and Jerusalem. In A.D. 6-66, however, the *ius gladii* resided with the Romans (cf. *Meg. Taʿan.* 6; John 18:31; Josephus *B.J.* ii.117; *Ant.* xx.200ff.; *m. Sanh.* 7:2; cf. *y. Sanh.* 1:18a[42]; 7:24b[48]; this point is still disputed in scholarship). Executions by the Sanhedrin, excepting punishment for unauthorized entrance into the temple (Josephus *B.J.* vi.125f.), went beyond the Sanhedrin's actual competence (Acts 7:54ff.; Josephus *Ant.* xx.200ff.) or were a sign of Jewish autonomy at the time of Agrippa (*m. Sanh.* 7:2; Acts 12:2).

The assembly of scholars at Jamnia (after A.D. 70), with powers limited to religious matters and dependent on Jewish recognition, viewed itself as the Sanhedrin's successor. Procedural details are described in the Mishnah tractate *Sanhedrin*. According to the Mishnah, small sanhedrins were formed both in the smaller Palestinian locales and in the provinces of the Diaspora on the model of the Great Sanhedrin (cf. Billerbeck II, 816f.)

3. Mark 13:9 par. Matt 10:17, reflecting Jewish Christian missionary experience, predicts that the disciples will be given up to *synagogue courts*. The shocking and forensically impractical assertion concerning holy law in Matt 5:22 places insults to one's brother along with murder under the jurisdiction of the *court of the Jerusalem Sanhedrin* (the climax in this particular context) or of the Christian congregational council.

4. Although the Synoptic Gospels make the Sanhedrin responsible for Jesus' death, the t.t. appears only rarely in the Passion Narrative. Mark 14:55 par. Matt 26:59 mentions the Sanhedrin in the context of the search for witnesses and the interrogation of Jesus for the sake of establishing a crime meriting capital punishment (cf. Mark 14:64; Matt 26:66). In Mark 15:1 the tautology (omitted by Matthew) "the whole Sanhedrin," mentioned after the enumeration of its constituent factions, summarizes and underscores the Markan point, namely, that the highest Jewish authority issues the accusation. Luke 22:66 alters this to read "and they led him into their Sanhedrin" (i.e., into their assembly building). Luke changes the (Markan) nocturnal assembly into a custody hearing in the palace of the high priest, while the trial itself, following the Sanhedrin scenes in Acts and Mishnaic law, takes place in the morning and issues no formal judgment. John 11:47 places the decision for capital punishment in an *assembly* prior to the Jerusalem period, and has no specifically Jewish trial later.

The historical question of the function and competence of the Sanhedrin is implied in any legal-historical discussion of the *ius gladii* of the Sanhedrin and is important in Christian-Jewish dialogues concerning Jesus' death (which have often been anti-Semitic and more recently are directed toward understanding Jesus more as a part of the Jewish people) and in tradition-historical questions (pre-Markan Passion narrative? Lukan special source?). The question of Jewish responsibility for Jesus' death can hardly be answered, given the Gospels' tendency to portray the trial as a prototype of the christological dispute between Church and synagogue and to lay the lion's share of the blame at the feet of the Jews. One cannot necesarily judge the oldest tradition historically on the basis of Mishnaic law or of some postulated earlier Sadducean law and attempt to elim-inate possible irregularities (the noctural assembly, proceedings on a day of preparation, a single hearing, and that in the palace of the high priest, the ambiguity of blasphemy).

The occasion of a Roman trial involving capital punishment makes it conceivable that the events precipitated by Judas' betrayal, within the temporal context of the Passover Feast, put pressure on the Sanhedrin, which had already decided on capital punishment for Jesus because of his criticism of the temple. Accordingly, the Sanhedrin either acted according to the demands of the moment (Billerbeck II, 821f.) and convened a special sitting, or, on the basis of the accusation that Jesus was inciting the people, held a legal noctural hearing with only one sitting (*t. Sanh.* 10:11) and decided on execution on the day of preparation of a pilgrimage festival, in accordance with *m. Sanh.* 11:4; *t. Sanh.* 11:7 (Strobel). The Sanhedrin likely established the blasphemy of inciting the people (Jesus' claim to be the Son of man; cf. John 11:48) and then left it to Pilate to draw the (false) conclusion of political high treason.

5. In Acts the Sanhedrin appears as a *religious council in the temple* and divided, in a simplified manner, be-tween Sadducees who are hostile to Christians and Pharisees who are not (5:34; 23:6). The reports intend to show an increase in the persecutions of the early Church by the Sanhedrin (5:21, 27, 41; 6:12, 15; 22:30; 23:1, 15, 20, 28; 24:20), something Luke probably concludes both from his own contemporary experience (persecution by Agrippa; execution of James) and from Paul's biography. The convening of the Sanhedrin by the Roman tribune (22:30) is historical unthinkable. See also B. Reicke, "Judeo-Christianity and the Jewish Establishment," *Jesus and the Politics of His Day* (ed. E. Bammel and C. F. D. Moule; 1984) 145-52.

U. Kellermann

(συνέδριος)/σύνεδρος, ου, ὁ *synedr(i)os* mem-ber of a council

In Acts 5:35 D inserts πρὸς τοὺς ἄρχοντας καὶ τοὺς συνεδρίους after πρὸς αὐτούς. Συνέδριος is an incorrect spelling (cf. συνέδριον, v. 34) of σύνεδρος. *TCGNT* ad loc.

συνείδησις, εως, ἡ *syneidēsis* consciousness, con-science, conviction

1. Occurrences in the NT — 2. Usage outside the NT; derivation — 3. Paul — 4. The rest of the NT

Lit.: J. BLÜHDORN, ed., *Das Gewissen in der Diskussion* (1976). — C. BROWN, *DNTT* I, 351-53. — BULTMANN, *Theology* I, 216-20. — H. CHADWICK, *RAC* X, 1025-1107. — H.-J. ECK-STEIN, *Der Begriff Syneidesis bei Paulus. Eine neutestamentlich-exegetische Untersuchung zum "Gewissensbegriff"* (WUNT II/10, 1983). — J. M. ESPY, "Paul's 'Robust Conscience' Re-examined," *NTS* 31 (1985) 161-88. — P. W. GOOCH, " 'Con-science' in 1 Corinthians 8 and 10," *NTS* 33 (1987) 244-54. — H. C. HAHN, *DNTT* I, 348-51. — R. JEWETT, *Paul's Anthropo-logical Terms* (1971) 402-46. — M. KÄHLER, *Das Gewissen* (1878; 1967). — D. E. MARIETTA, JR., *The NT Concept of Con-science* (Diss. Vanderbilt, 1959). — C. MAURER, *TDNT* VII, 898-919. — C. A. PIERCE, *Conscience in the NT* (1955). — SPICQ, *Notes* II, 854-58. — *idem, SacVb* 131-34. — J. STELZENBERGER, *Syneidesis im NT* (1961). — J. STĘPIEN, " 'Syneidesis.' La con-science dans l'anthropologie de Saint-Paul," *RHPR* 60 (1980) 1-20. — R. T. WALLIS, et al., *The Idea of Conscience in Philo of Alexandria* (1975). — For further bibliography see Chadwick; Maurer; *DNTT* I, 353; *TWNT* X, 1274f.

1. Συνείδησις occurs 30 times in the NT, 14 of those in Paul, and not at all in the Gospels (except in one reading in John 8:9, a secondary passage). This statistical evidence suggests that Paul first introduced συνείδησις into Christian writing (→ 3.c).

2. Συνείδησις (or τὸ συνειδός, which does not occur in the NT) does not correspond to any Hebrew term and occurs in the LXX only in isolated instances (Eccl 10:20; Wis 17:11; Sir 42:18). Indeed, the word is rare before 200 B.C., though subse-quently it occurs frequently in secular Greek (e.g., Plutarch), in Hellenistic Jewish writing (Philo and Josephus), and in authors of the Roman period (e.g., Cicero and Seneca) in the tr. *con-scientia*. It possibly is of popular derivation and might have been quite common in popular Hellenistic philosophy. Συνείδησις, following the basic meaning of the vb. σύνοιδα, means "human knowledge of something." It also refers to "moral conscious-ness" (usually of a bad deed).

3. a) Συνείδησις appears in 1 Corinthians in Paul's response to the Corinthians' inquiry concerning eating food offered to idols (chs. 8–10, introduced by περί in 8:1). The authors of the Corinthians' letter (referred to in scholarship as the "strong," οἱ δυνατοί, even though that term does not occur until Rom 15:1) believed that one was allowed to eat food offered to idols (εἰδωλόθυτον). Other Corinthians (the "weak," cf. 1 Cor 8:9) were un-certain. Paul basically agrees with the fundamental prin-ciples expressed in the Corinthians' letter (cf. 8:1, 4; 10:23), but then makes any individual decision dependent on the situation: The weak lack the knowledge (γνῶσις) possessed by the letter's authors, namely, that "an idol has no real existence" (8:4), and thus by habit (from before their conversion) attribute special significance to such food. After eating such food, their conscience, being weak, is defiled (v. 7). Their συνείδησις would not be edified or strengthened if they saw the "strong" eating food offered to idols (v. 10; perhaps the letter's authors advocated the opposite opinion). Rather, they would take

offense and be ruined by the freedom of the "strong" (v. 11). Eating food offered to idols in such a situation would be a sin "against Christ," who (also) died for the weak (vv. 11ff.).

In 10:23ff. Paul returns to the theme of "meat offered to idols" and uses συνείδησις 4 times. He offers two guidelines (again dependent on the situation): The Corinthians a) can buy anything in the market without raising questions διὰ τὴν συνείδησιν (10:25f.) and b) may, if they want, accept invitations into the houses of un- believers and eat anything without raising questions διὰ τὴν συνείδησιν (v. 27). If, however, someone (probably a guest who is not a believer, since ἱερόθυτον [v. 28] is the correct term for meat offered in sacrifice) points out to them that the meat has been offered, then "for the sake of the one who pointed this out, and διὰ τὴν συνείδησιν," the Corinthians should not eat it (v. 28). The reference here is apparently not to the συνείδησις of the weak, but rather to that of the guest who is not a believer; in that person's opinion (as well as that of the weak [8:7]) eating meat offered to idols created a bond between the one who ate and the demons. Although according to Paul Chris- tians are fundamentally free and thus not subject to judg- ment by the συνείδησις of others (10:29), the demonstra- tive gesture of not eating in this situation is required, since otherwise the judgment of the nonbeliever's συνείδησις might interpret such eating as an acknowl- edgement of idols.

In 1 Corinthians, then, συνείδησις refers to active and discerning (self-)awareness (cf. Maurer 914), con- viction generated by a specific standard demanding cer- tain behavior. It is assumed to be a universally human phenomenon. Although it can err, it is precisely in such instances that it is of significance for the behavior of Christians by its very actuality (cf. the two cases in 8:7-13 and 10:28-30).

It may be that the Corinthians were the ones to initiate use of συνείδησις in the context of these questions con- cerning meat offered to idols (so Pierce, Maurer, and many others). This is suggested by Paul's surprisingly frequent use of the word in chs. 8 and 10, its absence in 1 Thessalonians, his use of διὰ τὴν συνείδησιν as a fixed phrase, and its absence in the further development of 1 Corinthians 8 and 10 in Romans 14–15 and its replace- ment there by πίστις (14:1). This attractive conjecture, however, must remain just a conjecture, since the Hel- lenistic Jew Paul more likely acquired the word directly from Hellenistic popular philosophy (→ 2).

b) The other Pauline occurrences can be understood against the background of 1 Corinthians 8 and 10. 2 Cor 1:12 speaks of the witness of the συνείδησις concerning the integrity of Paul's conduct, 4:2 of the apostle's abil- ity to commend himself to every συνείδησις before God, and 5:11 of the fact that in their own συνείδησις the

Corinthians know who Paul really is. In all three in- stances συνείδησις refers to a judgment, and 4:2 shows anew that συνείδησις is regarded as a universally human phenomenon.

Rom 2:15 and 9:1, like 2 Cor 1:12, introduce the idea of the witness of the συνείδησις. Rom 2:15 again under- scores the role of συνείδησις of judgment, esp. moral judgment, and appears to specify more closely the activ- ity of the συνείδησις as both accusing and excusing thoughts. In this way it shows that the Gentiles already know of the Torah. But this should not be misunderstood in the sense of a natural theology: the working of the συνείδησις described by Paul remains preliminary and is deciphered first only on judgment day (v. 16).

The fixed phrase διὰ τὴν συνείδησιν (three occur- rences in 1 Cor 10:25-28) appears in Rom 13:5: One ought to be subject to the governing authorities (ἐξουσία) not only because of wrath, which the government authori- ties represent before evildoers, but also διὰ τὴν συνείδη- σιν. Συνείδησις here is the inner authority that recognizes the necessity of obedience.

c) In sum, συνείδησις does not play a central role in Pauline anthropology (unlike πνεῦμα, σάρξ, καρδία, σῶμα). Neither is it central to Paul in ethical thinking, since he never invokes it as a moral principle and is far removed from any idealistic understanding of συνείδησις as the voice of God. Indeed, the notion of pangs of conscience is fundamentally alien to him (cf. K. Stendahl, "The Apostle Paul and the Introspective Conscience of the West," *HTR* 56 [1963] 199-215 = *idem, Paul Among Jews and Gentiles and Other Essays* [1976] 78-96). He probably acquired the term directly from Hellenistic popular philosophy (less likely from the Corinthian Christians) and variously placed it into a new context (→ a, b) without altering its fundamental meaning (→ 2).

4. In other NT writings συνείδησις is characterized as ἀγαθή (Acts 23:1; 1 Tim 1:5, 19; 1 Pet 3:16, 21), καθαρά (1 Tim 3:9; 2 Tim 1:3), καλή (Heb 13:18; cf. 9:9, 14), ἀπρόσκοπος (Acts 24:16), and πονηρά (Heb 10:22), and is thus clearly thought of as having fixed attributes. In contrast to Paul's usage, discussion of συνείδησις thus acquires central significance in the post-Pauline writings and, again unlike Paul, has a firm orientation toward a single morality that does not include choices. This can only be understood as "a sign of the transformation of an unbroken eschatological understanding of the world into a view which must reckon with the fact that, for the time being, the world is going to remain as it is (and that Christians are to exist within it)" (M. Dibelius and H. Conzelmann, *The Pastoral Epistles* [Hermeneia, 1972] 20).

If this usage of συνείδησις reflects a development

within the Church away from Paul, then 2 post-Pauline occurrences of the word used absolutely reflect an independent recollection of the Hellenistic usage seen in Paul: Heb 10:2 ("*consciousness* of sin"; cf. Philo *Det.* 146) and 1 Pet 2:19 ("*knowledge* of God"; *contra* L. Goppelt, *1 Pet* [KEK] 194ff.).   G. Lüdemann

συνεῖδον *syneidon* become aware of, realize 2nd aor. of → συνοράω.

σύνειμι (I) *syneimi* be with*

Compound of → εἰμί: Luke 9:18: συνῆσαν αὐτῷ, "they *were with* him"; Acts 22:11: οἱ συνόντες, "those with [me]."

σύνειμι (II) *syneimi* come together*

Compound of εἶμι ("go, come"): Luke 8:4: συνιόντος δὲ ὄχλου πολλοῦ, "*when* a great crowd of people *had come together.*"

συνεισέρχομαι *syneiserchomai* enter together*

John 6:22: Jesus *had* not *entered* the boat *with* his disciples (οὐ συνεισῆλθεν . . . εἰς τὸ πλοῖον); 18:15: συνεισῆλθεν . . . εἰς τὴν αὐλήν.

συνέκδημος, ου, ὁ *synekdēmos* traveling companion*

Acts 19:29: Paul's *traveling companions* in Ephesus; 2 Cor 8:19: Paul's (official) *traveling companion* appointed by the (Macedonian) churches to assist with the collection (cf. 8:18; 12:18), probably as both an aid and a trustee (working with yet another brother [8:22; both referred as ἀπόστολοι ἐκκλησιῶν in v. 23] and Titus [vv. 6, 16; Paul's συνεργός, v. 23).

συνεκλεκτός, 3 *syneklektos* chosen together with*

1 Pet 5:13: ἡ ἐν Βαβυλῶνι (v.l. adds ἐκκλησία) συνεκλεκτή, "*the lady* [i.e., church] *elect with* [you] in Babylon [= Rome]"; cf. the reference to the addressees as ἐκλεκτοί, 1:1; 2 John 1:13: ἐκλεκτὴ κυρία and ἡ ἀδελφὴ ἡ ἐκλεκτή as designations for churches; → ἐκλεκτός 5.

συνεκπορεύομαι *synekporeuomai* go out with

Acts 3:11 D and elsewhere. On the topographical problems associated with this v.l. see *TCGNT* ad loc.

συνελαύνω *synelaunō* drive, force

Acts 7:26 v.l. (συνήλασεν) in place of συναλλάσσω.

συνεπιμαρτυρέω *synepimartyreō* testify at the same time, attest additionally*

Heb 2:4, of God, who *also [at the same time] attested* salvation in Christ (συνεπιμαρτυροῦντος τοῦ θεοῦ); cf. *1 Clem.* 23:5; 43:1; *Ep. Arist.* 191. H. Strathmann, *TDNT* IV, 510.

συνεπίσκοπος, ου, ὁ *synepiskopos* fellow bishop Phil 1:1 B² K 33, etc., in place of σὺν ἐπισκόποις.

συνεπιτίθεμαι *synepitithemai* join in attacking, participate, attack together*

Mid., used absolutely, in Acts 24:9: συνεπέθεντο δὲ καὶ οἱ Ἰουδαῖοι, "but the Jews also *joined in the attack/ supported* [*the charge;* cf. vv. 2, 8]."

συνέπομαι *synepomai* follow with, be among someone's following*

Acts 20:4, of Paul's companions during his final journey from Greece to Jerusalem (συνείπετο δὲ αὐτῷ . . .).

συνεργέω *synergeō* work together with, cooperate, assist
→ συνεργός.

συνεργός, 2 *synergos* fellow worker*
συνεργέω *synergeō* work together with, cooperate, assist*

1. Occurrences in the NT and extra-Pauline meaning — 2. Paul's use — 3. Historical considerations

Lit.: G. BERTRAM, *TDNT* II, 635-55; VII, 871-76. — H. CONZELMANN, *History of Primitive Christianity* (1973) 160f. — E. E. ELLIS, "Paul and His Co-Workers," *NTS* 17 (1970/71) 437-52 (= *idem, Prophecy and Hermeneutic in Early Christianity* [WUNT 18, 1978] 3-22). — E. LOHSE, "Die Mitarbeiter des Apostels Paulus im Kolosserbrief," FS Stählin 189-94. — W.-H. OLLROG, *Paulus und seine Mitarbeiter* (WMANT 50, 1979). — G. SCHILLE, *Die urchristliche Kollegialmission* (ATANT 48, 1967) 25-109. — For further bibliography see *TWNT* X, 1274.

1. This adj. occurs, always subst., 13 times in the NT, 11 of those in Paul's letters, and in Col 4:11; 3 John 8. The vb. occurs 3 times in Paul and in Mark 16:20; Jas 2:22. The word group is common in secular Greek and designates there the "working together or cooperation" of various circumstances. In reference to persons it designates a person's (or god's) "support, assistance, concern" for another. This meaning occurs 4 times in the NT, apart from Rom 8:28 only in the extra-Pauline writings: the vb. in Jas 2:22: "faith *was active together* with his works"; Rom 8:28: "for those who love God everything *works together* for good"; Mark 16:20: "God *assisted*

them"; the noun in 3 John 8: *"fellow workers* for the truth."

2. In all other Pauline occurrences (and in Col 4:11, which is influenced by Paul) συνεργός and συνεργέω have a different and specific meaning, which does not occur again in post-Pauline writings. They identify a person who is active with and like Paul as a representative of God in the mission "work" (→ ἔργον [4]; 1 Cor 3:12-14; Phil 2:30) of proclamation. The συνεργός is thus Paul's *fellow worker, fellow missionary, mission colleague:* "In the service of God we are *fellow workers*" (1 Cor 3:9)— not synergistically "God's fellow workers," as the context clearly shows by emphasizing God's origination of the mission work, the responsibility of each worker's work, and the examination of the work of each before God (vv. 5-15). The συνεργός is also not Paul's "helper," "companion," or "servant," as the word has repeatedly been mistranslated.

Thus Timothy is commended as the *"fellow worker* of [appointed by] God in the gospel" (1 Thess 3:2; the v.l. διάκονος, emphasizing even more strongly the idea of commissioning, is virtually identical in meaning). Titus is described as "my friend and *fellow worker* as regards you" (2 Cor 8:23; a distinction is made between personal and objective designations). The Jewish Christians greeted in Colossae are called *"fellow workers* for God's kingdom" (Col 4:11), and in this sense Paul is himself only a *"fellow worker* in the service of your joy" (2 Cor 1:24) and offers exhortation only "as *one who works together*" (6:1), i.e., as one standing along with and not over the women and men working together with him in missionary activity "in Jesus Christ" (Rom 16:3, 9, 21; Phlm 1, 24).

Being a fellow worker or missionary colleague, however, means accepting work, toil, struggle, and renunciation. Paul calls Epaphroditus of Philippi "my brother and *fellow worker* and fellow soldier" (Phil 2:25). Euodia, Syntyche (4:2), and "Clement and the rest of my *fellow workers*" are Paul's "comrades in the struggle for the gospel" (4:3). The Corinthians are called upon to show proper respect "to every *fellow worker* and laborer in the mission" (pleonastic, 1 Cor 16:16).

3. The position of Paul's fellow workers has barely been examined for its possible value in Pauline exegesis and the history of the Pauline mission. Paul explicitly calls no less than sixteen persons "fellow workers," and his usage, along with circumstantial evidence, suggests that he would have so identified another twenty to twenty-five women and men. Acts and the Pastorals have picked up this evidence and added another fifteen names. Paul's association with so many fellow workers has no parallel in early Christian missionary activity.

With Barnabas, later with Silvanus and Timothy, and finally with Timothy alone, i.e., in the sense of the OT principle that something should be attested by two or three witnesses (Deut

17:6, and elsewhere; cf. Mark 6:7; Acts 1:23, etc.), Paul undertook missionary journeys, during which he proclaimed the kingdom of Christ and founded churches. Because of this association and to the extent that Pauline letters are extant for this period, these fellow workers appear in the epistolary prescripts: As partners they share responsibility for the Pauline missionary activity. Paul met some of these fellow workers more or less by chance. Each worked independently for a while with the others (e.g., Apollos, Prisca, and Aquila), though they were always of one mind. Titus was particularly significant for the Pauline missions, since he assisted Paul in the organization of the collection in the Gentile churches for the Jewish Christian "poor" in Jerusalem (2 Cor 8:6, 10, 16f.; 12:17f.).

The overwhelming majority of Paul's fellow workers came from his own, still young churches. As delegates and representatives of their churches (ὑπὲρ ὑμῶν, Col 1:7; 4:12f.; cf. Phlm 13) they worked for a time with Paul himself in mission activity, thus making up a "lack" in their own churches (1 Cor 16:17; Phil 2:30), and then returned to those churches (1 Cor 16:15-18; Phil 2:25-30; Col 1:7f.; 4:12f.; Phlm 13). These churches were present in Paul's missionary work through the representation of these "messengers of the churches" (ἀπόστολοι ἐκκλησιῶν, 2 Cor 8:23; cf. Phil 2:25) and declared thereby, as members of Christ's body, their own co-responsibility for building the kingdom of God.

W.-H. Ollrog

συνέρχομαι *synerchomai* come together, assemble, gather*

The vb. occurs 30 times in the NT, esp. in Acts (16 occurrences) and 1 Corinthians (7, 5 of those in ch. 11 [vv. 17, 18, 20, 33, 34], the other 2 in 14:23, 26); it does not otherwise occur in Paul.

Συνέρχομαι means generally *come together, assemble, gather together:* Mark 3:20: ὄχλος; Luke 5:15: ὄχλοι πολλοί; John 18:20: πάντες οἱ Ἰουδαῖοι; Acts 2:6; 5:16: τὸ πλῆθος; 10:27: πολλοί; 16:13: γυναῖκες; 19:32: οἱ πλείους; 28:17: οἱ ὄντες τῶν Ἰουδαίων πρῶτοι; Mark 14:53 and Acts 22:30: the Sanhedrin; Acts 1:6: the disciples; 25:17: *assembling* at one place (συνέρχομαι ἐνθάδε).

The vb. is also used with the dat. to mean *coming/going with* someone or *accompanying* someone: Luke 23:55: the women together with Jesus; Acts 1:21: one disciple together with the eleven; cf. further John 11:33; Acts 10:23, 45; 11:12; 21:16: σὺν ἡμῖν; fig. in 15:38: "*go to work together* with (συνέρχομαι . . . εἰς τὸ ἔργον)"; 9:39: *meet* with someone, *come to* someone. Of sexual or marital relations in Matt 1:18: πρὶν ἢ συνελθεῖν αὐτούς; 1 Cor 7:5 v.l.: ἐπὶ τὸ αὐτὸ συνέρχομαι; cf. Prov 5:20; Wis 7:2; Philo *Virt.* 40, 111; Josephus *Ant.* vii.168; in the papyri συνέρχομαι (πρὸς γάμον) means "marry" (Preisigke, *Wörterbuch* II s.v.).

In Paul συνέρχομαι (only in 1 Corinthians) is a t.t. for the gathering/assembling of the congregation: 1 Cor 11:18: συνέρχομαι ἐν ἐκκλησίᾳ, "*come together* in a congregational gathering"; 14:23: ἐὰν . . . συνέλθῃ ἡ ἐκκλησία ὅλη ἐπὶ τὸ αὐτό, "when the whole church *assembles* [in one place]" (cf. 11:20; *Barn.* 4:10); 14:26: ὅταν συνέρχησθε. The purpose of the assembly can be indicated with final εἰς: 11:33: εἰς τὸ φαγεῖν; v. 34: μὴ εἰς κρίμα; so also can the unintended result: v. 17: οὐκ εἰς τὸ κρεῖσσον ἀλλὰ εἰς τὸ ἧσσον συνέρχεσθε. J. Schneider, *TDNT* II, 684.   H. Balz

συνεσθίω *synesthiō* eat together*

This vb. occurs 5 times in the NT: Luke 15:2, of the Jesus eating with sinners: συνεσθίει αὐτοῖς; Acts 10:41, of the "witnesses" eating with the resurrected Christ: συνεφάγομεν καὶ συνεπίομεν αὐτῷ (cf. 1:4: συναλίζομαι); 11:3, of Peter eating with the uncircumcised (with Gentiles in Gal 2:12). According to 1 Cor 5:11 the Corinthians should refuse table fellowship with those members of the congregation who have regressed into behavior not in keeping with Christian principles (μηδὲ συνεσθίειν), an exhortation to be understood in the broadest sense and not just of the eucharist (cf. 5:9: μὴ συναναμίγνυσθαι). V. Parkin, "Συνεσθίειν in the NT," *SE* IIIB (1964) 250-53; F. Mussner, " 'Das Wesen des Christentums ist συνεσθίειν.' Ein authentischer Kommentar," *Mysterium der Gnade* (FS J. Auer, 1975) 92-102; H. Wagenhammer, " 'Das Wesen des Christentums ist συνεσθίειν.' Bemerkungen zu einem Programmwort," FS Mussner 494-507.

σύνεσις, εως, ἡ *synesis* understanding, insight, faculty of comprehension*

This noun occurs 7 times in the NT and appears frequently in the LXX, esp. in the wisdom literature (e.g., Ps 110:10 LXX; Prov 2:1ff.; Sir 5:10; 34:11). It usually refers to (God-given) insight into God's activity and will.

Mark 12:33 picks up the three expressions in the Shema (Deut 6:5 LXX: καρδία, ψυχή, δύναμις) and replaces them with καρδία, σύνεσις, and ἰσχύς, so that, in view of Mark 12:30, σύνεσις replaces ψυχή and διάνοια. Vv. 30 and 33 betray the influence of Hellenistic language (see Bornkamm, *Aufsätze* III, 40f.); σύνεσις refers along with καρδία and ἰσχύς to the totality of the human being in willing, judgment, and action.

Luke 2:47 uses σύνεσις in the sense of *understanding* or *powers of reasoning.* 1 Cor 1:19 (ἡ σύνεσις τῶν συνετῶν, quoting Isa 29:14) refers critically to "the cleverness of the clever," which is based on the σοφία τοῦ κόσμου (v. 20) and is thus subject to God's judgment and condemnation: It cannot understand the word of the cross.

Σύνεσις is used otherwise of the *insight* of believers. Eph 3:4: σύνεσις ἐν τῷ μυστηρίῳ τοῦ Χριστοῦ, "into the mystery of Christ," received through revelation (cf. v. 3); 2 Tim 2:7: σύνεσις ἐν πᾶσιν, "*proper understanding* in

everything"; Col 1:9: πᾶσα σοφία καὶ σύνεσις πνευματική, "all spiritual wisdom and *insight,*" referring to knowledge of God's will (σύνεσις also appears with σοφία in Deut 4:6; Dan 2:20; Josephus *Ant.* viii.24; cf. also Eph 1:8). In Col 2:2 the phrase πλοῦτος τῆς πληροφορίας τῆς συνέσεως, "riches of the fullness of *understanding*" (similar to Eph 3:4, above) is used of "knowledge of God's mystery, of Christ." Only this understanding of the salvation significance of Christ (in contrast to false teaching, Col 2:8) constitutes, along with ἀγάπη, the correct posture of the believer; it resides in the καρδία. H. Conzelmann, *TDNT* VII, 888-96; J. Goetzmann, *DNTT* III, 130-33.

H. Balz

συνετός, 3 *synetos* insightful, intelligent, smart*

In Matt 11:25 par. Luke 10:21 συνετοί (with σοφοί) refers to the *smart people* (of the world): It is not to them that revelation is given, but rather to the νήπιοι. The term is used similarly in 1 Cor 1:19: → σύνεσις τῶν συνετῶν with σοφία τῶν σοφῶν (quoting Isa 29:14 LXX). Acts 13:7 uses συνετός in a positive sense of Sergius Paulus, who was considered an ἀνὴρ συνετός, "an insightful, intelligent man," i.e., he wanted to hear the message of Paul and Barnabas. H. Conzelmann, *TDNT* VII, 888-96; J. Goetzmann, *DNTT* III, 130-33.

συνευδοκέω *syneudokeō* be pleased with, agree, consent, be willing*

6 occurrences in the NT: Luke 11:48: τοῖς ἔργοις τῶν πατέρων, "*consent to*"; Acts 8:1; 22:20: *be in agreement with* (the killing of Stephen); Rom 1:32: *approve, applaud;* 1 Cor 7:12, 13, of a spouse who is not a believer: συνευδοκέω οἰκεῖν μετά τινος, "*wish to [continue to] live* with," though this presupposes that the spouse who is the believer first expresses this wish to remain together (cf. vv. 15f.).

συνευωχέομαι *syneuōcheomai* feast/carouse together*

2 Pet 2:13, of false teachers who *feast together/carouse* with Christians (in broad daylight). Some mss. (A^c B Ψ, etc.) read ἐν ταῖς ἀγάπαις (instead of ἐν ταῖς ἀπάταις), thus thinking of the communal meal also mentioned in Jude 12: οἱ ἐν ταῖς ἀγάπαις ὑμῶν . . . συνευωχούμενοι ὑμῖν. Cf. W. Schrage, *2 Pet/Jude* (NTD) ad loc.

συνεφίστημι *synephistēmi* rise up simultaneously, join in attacking*

Acts 16:22, with κατά and gen. of the ὄχλος that *joined* (with the owners of the slave girl with a spirit of divination) *the attack* against Paul and Silas.

συνέχω *synechō* hold together, enclose; hold prisoner; seize, press hard, dominate*

Lit.: BAGD s.v. — H. Köster, *TDNT* VII, 877-85.

1. Συνέχω occurs 12 times in the NT, and is a preferred term in the Lukan writings (6 times in the Gospel, 3 in Acts); it also occurs twice in Paul and once in Matthew. On secular, OT, and Jewish usage cf. Köster 877-82.

2. As relatively rare as συνέχω is in the NT, its meaning and intentions can be strikingly diverse and variable.

a) Luke uses the vb. with Jesus as its obj. in the sense *press in on, enclose* in 8:45 and with a negative polemical focus in 22:63 (in the Passion narrative). He uses it with hostile elaboration and emphasis of Jerusalem's destruction in 19:43. Acts 7:57 represents the borderline of literal and fig. usage: Stephen's adversaries *press their hands against* their ears, both so that they will not have to hear (literally) and to represent stubbornness (fig.).

b) Συνέχω can function as a t.t. in the portrayal of certain symptoms of illness that control and oppress a person (Luke 4:38; Acts 28:8; Matt 4:24) and in a portrayal of great fear (Luke 8:37).

c) In a comprehensive sense Paul is *dominated/occupied*—by his task as proclaimer of the word (Acts 18:5), as one *compelled* by his love for Christ (2 Cor 5:14), and as one *hard pressed* between being with the Lord and being with the Church (Phil 1:23).

d) Luke 12:50 speaks metaphorically of Jesus' *distress* (συνέχομαι) with respect to the baptism to be completed in him and thus brings to expression both his radical commitment to his calling, alluding thereby to his martyrdom (so Köster 884f.), and his human distress and anxiety at the fate awaiting him (a possible tr. is "I am very depressed"). These two aspects, considered also from the perspective of the word's meaning, need not exclude one another: Jesus' mission demands his full concentration and makes a total claim on him and is, therefore, naturally associated with human anxiety and limitations (cf. 8:37).
A. Kretzer

συνήδομαι *synēdomai* rejoice with, joyfully agree, congratulate; rejoice completely*

In Rom 7:22 συνήδομαι τῷ νόμῳ either amplifies the statement and means "I *rejoice completely in* the law in my inmost self (κατὰ τὸν ἔσω ἄνθρωπον)," or, more likely, in view of σύμφημι in v. 16, "I *joyfully agree with* the law. . . ."

συνήθεια, ας, ἡ *synētheia* habit, custom*

John 18:39: *custom* (on the question of the Passover amnesty see R. Schnackenburg, *John* [Eng. tr., 1982] 251-53); 1 Cor 11:16: τοιαύτην συνήθειαν ἔξω, "recognize such practice"; 8:7: συνήθεια τοῦ εἰδώλου, "*a situation of being accustomed* to idols."

συνηλικιώτης, ου, ὁ *synēlikiōtēs* person of one's own age, contemporary*

In Gal 1:14 Paul looks back on his earlier life before his calling (*ca.* twenty years previous), a time in which through his particular zeal he advanced far beyond "many *my own age*" in Judaism.

συνθάπτω *synthaptō* bury with, bury together*

Only fig. in the NT. According to Rom 6:4 Christians are buried with Christ through baptism into his death (συνετάφημεν οὖν αὐτῷ), referring to the ultimate death to sin (cf. v. 2: ἀπεθάνομεν τῇ ἁμαρτίᾳ), which is confirmed by burial (cf. 1 Cor 15:4) and simultaneously allows Christians, through the newness of their own lives, to participate in Christ's resurrection from the dead (→ σύμφυτος; συναποθνήσκω; σύν 4). According to Col 2:12 to be baptized is to be buried and raised with Christ through faith in the power of God, who raised Christ from the dead (cf. v. 20; see E. Schweizer, *Col* [Eng. tr., 1982] ad loc.; → συνεγείρω). W. Grundmann, *TDNT* VII, 786, 790f., 792f.; for further bibliography see *TWNT* X, 1273.

συνθλάω *synthlaō* crush together, smash, shatter*

Luke 20:18a: Every person who falls against the cornerstone (i.e., Christ, v. 17; cf. Ps 118:22; possibly also: who stumbles against or falls over the cornerstone —cf. Isa 8:14f.) *will be broken to pieces/shattered* (συνθλασθήσεται; probably secondary from Luke in Matt 21:44 ℵ B C L W, etc.). This image of falling against the stone and the stone itself falling (Luke 20:18b; cf. Dan 2:35f., 45f.) could be connected to a Jewish proverb that influenced, e.g., *Midr. Esth.* 7:10 on 3:6: "If the stone falls on the pot, woe to the pot! If the pot falls on the stone, woe to the pot! Either way, woe to the pot!" (see J. Jeremias, *TDNT* IV, 275ff.). But it may also associate the image of the (hostile) attack against the cornerstone with the falling of the stone in accordance with Daniel 2.

συνθλίβω *synthlibō* press together, press (around), press about*

Mark 5:24, 31, of the ὄχλος (πολύς) that *pressed around* Jesus/*pushed up to* Jesus (acc.).

συνθρύπτω *synthryptō* break into pieces, pulverize; soften, wear down*

Fig. in Acts 21:13: συνθρύπτω τὴν καρδίαν, "*soften/ wear down* [someone's] heart," i.e., "pressure [someone] hard for a decision"; another possibility is *"break* [someone's] heart" through grief (cf. κλαίοντες).

συνίημι *syniēmi* understand, comprehend, grasp*

1. Συνίημι occurs 26 times in the NT, 18 of those in the Gospels (9 in Matthew, 5 in Mark, 4 in Luke, none in John), 4 in Acts; in the Epistles it occurs twice in Romans and once each in 2 Cor 10:12 and Eph 5:17.

Only in Acts 7:25a does συνίημι occur unequivocally according to the athematic conjugation in -ίημι (inf. συνιέναι), with deviations in mss. also in Luke 24:45; cf. Matt 13:19, 23 (partc. συνιείς); 2 Cor 10:12 (ind. συνιᾶσιν) and elsewhere. These are joined by forms of the newer conjugation in -ίω, e.g., Matt 13:13 (ind. συνίουσιν); Rom 3:11 (partc. συνίων). Both conjugations include ind. (or imv.) συνίετε (Matt 15:10; Mark 8:17, 21; Eph 5:17) and subjunc. συνίωσιν (or συνιῶσιν, Mark 4:12; Luke 8:10); cf. further BAGD s.v. (bibliography); BDF §94; H. Conzelmann, *TDNT* VII, 892f.

Συνίημι originally meant "bring together" (Homer *Il.* i.8), but in the NT is used only fig. Only rarely does συνίημι refer generally to *understanding* or *insight* (Acts 7:25 bis; 2 Cor 10:12 [omitted in D* F G, etc.]). Rather, it almost always refers to God's word or to Jesus' message and actions. OT tradition echoes in quotations and allusions (Isa 6:9f. in Mark 4:12 par.; cf. 8:17, 21; Acts 28:26f.; Isa 52:15 LXX in Rom 15:21; Ps 13:2 LXX in Rom 3:11).

2. In the Synoptic tradition the idea of prophetic obscurity (Isa 6:9f.) plays an important role. Just as God himself withheld understanding and insight from his people (ἀκούσετε καὶ οὐ μὴ συνῆτε, v. 9; μήποτε τῇ καρδίᾳ συνῶσιν, v. 10) in order to make possible a completely new beginning, so also does Jesus, according to Mark 4:12 (redactional), speak to outsiders in "parables" in order to make it impossible for them to understand (the mystery of the kingdom of God) in spite of their hearing of it (ἵνα . . . ἀκούοντες ἀκούωσιν καὶ μὴ συνιῶσιν). What has become known as the Markan "parable theory" belongs in this context of the Markan understanding of the "messianic secret"; with the aid of the citation from Isaiah it traces Jesus' own people's rejection of his message back to God's will (see further W. Marxsen, *ZTK* 52 [1955] 255-71; G. Haufe, *EvT* 32 [1972] 413-21; H. Räisänen, *Die Parabeltheorie im Markusevangelium* [1973]; P. Lampe, *ZNW* 65 [1974] 140-50; J. Gnilka, *Mark* [EKKNT] I, ad loc. [bibliography]).

An idea corresponding to this basic Markan notion is also found in the statements about the lack of understanding among the disciples. According to 6:52 (redactional) the disciples' astonishment (at Jesus' walking on the water and calming of the storm) is an expression of their hardened hearts and lack of understanding in view of the miracle of the bread: οὐ γὰρ συνῆκαν ἐπὶ τοῖς ἄρτοις (cf. 8:17: οὔπω νοεῖτε οὐδὲ συνίετε; the allusion to Isa 6:9f.

or Jer 5:21 in Mark 8:18; 8:21: οὔπω συνίετε;). Only from the perspective of the cross and resurrection do the disciples comprehend in faith.

Matthew strengthens the Markan statements about the puzzling and difficult parables (addressed to the people) by going beyond Mark (cf. Mark 4:12 [συνίημι] with Matt 13:13 [συνίημι]) and citing Isa 6:9f. LXX once more in full (συνίημι, Matt 13:14, 15). He also inserts, again going beyond Mark, συνίημι into the parable of the sower (vv. 19, 23), thus emphasizing even more sharply what is said about "hearing" and *understanding* or *not understanding*. Hence while outsiders do not receive the mystery of God's kingdom (vv. 11f., 34), the disciples do manage to break through to an appropriate understanding (cf. v. 51: συνήκατε ταῦτα πάντα; λέγουσιν αὐτῷ· ναί).

Matthew omits Mark 6:52 and speaks instead of the disciples' worshipping and confession of the Son of God (Matt 14:33). Mark 8:17, 21 is similarly altered. In both passages Matthew omits the Markan συνίημι and its attendant mention of the disciples' failure to understand (see Matt 16:9, 11), and then in conclusion (unlike Mark) has the disciples finally comprehend the meaning of Jesus' words: τότε συνῆκαν . . . (16:12; cf. 17:13: τότε συνῆκαν οἱ μαθηταί). In contrast to the people at large, the disciples are thus not unremittingly threatened by stubbornness and lack of understanding, but rather at most by → ὀλιγοπιστία (2), lack of trust, something they can, however, overcome through their Lord's help.

Luke 8:9, 10 incorporates Mark 4:11f. in a weakened and abbreviated form. The disciples' lack of understanding (in the Markan view) refers from the perspective of Luke 18:34 to the suffering of the Son of man according to Scripture (καὶ αὐτοὶ οὐδὲν τούτων συνῆκαν); it is the resurrected Jesus himself who first opens the disciples' minds to the significance τοῦ συνιέναι τὰς γραφάς (24:45). Jesus' own → σύνεσις (2:47; cf. v. 52) is contrasted with the lack of understanding on the part of his parents, to whom Jesus nonetheless subordinates himself (v. 51). This OT motif of obscurity also appears in Acts 28:26, 27 (citing Isa 6:9f.), referring to the Roman Jews' rejection of the Pauline proclamation; this opens up once and for all to the Gentiles the path to salvation (28:28).

Paul understands insight (into God's salvation plan) as a gift bestowed by the salvation proclamation itself precisely on those who have not (yet) heard of God (οἷ οὐκ ἀκηκόασιν συνήσουσιν, Rom 15:21, quoting Isa 52:15 LXX). No one is "righteous" on his own initiative and power, nor does anyone *understand* (οὐκ ἔστιν δίκαιος οὐδὲ εἷς, οὐκ ἔστιν ὁ συνίων, Rom 3:10f.; citing Ps 13:2 LXX).

Jesus' (enlightening) instruction of the people concerning purity and impurity employs the term συνίημι together with ἀκούω (Mark 7:14 par. Matt 15:10; cf. also 13:19, 23). Eph 5:17 contrasts συνίετε τί τὸ θέλημα τοῦ θεοῦ with μὴ γίνεσθε ἄφρονες. BAGD s.v.; G. Barth in Barth, G. Bornkamm, and H. J. Held, *Tradition and Interpretation in Matthew* (1963) 105-12; H. Conzelmann, *TDNT* VII, 888-96.   H. Balz

συνίστημι, συνιστάνω *synistēmi, synistanō* put together, fit together; introduce, make known, display, prove to be; come together, hold together, unite; be composed of, consist of, have existence in*

1. Occurrences in the NT — 2. Forms and syntax — 3. Exegetical considerations

Lit.: BAGD s.v. — BDF index s.v. — W. KASCH, *TDNT* VII, 896-98. — H. SCHLIER, *Rom* (HTKNT, 1977) (on 3:5; 5:8).

1. Συνίστημι occurs 16 times in the NT: 14 times in the Pauline corpus (9 of those in 2 Corinthians), and once each in Luke and 2 Peter.

2. It is grammatically striking that "συνίστημι offers the only correctly constructed athematic present forms in NT usage" (Kasch 896). Whereas in koine Greek as a whole μι- vbs. generally recede, συνίστημι is an exception, in that it consistently has a present form with no variable vowel.

In the meaning *prove to be* συνίστημι can be used with a double acc. (Gal 2:18) or with dat. of respect and acc. with inf. (2 Cor 7:11). The various trans. (e.g., Rom 16:1) or intrans. (e.g., Luke 9:32) meanings of συνίστημι emerge from their respective contexts and are to be rendered accordingly.

3.a) In the first significant set of occurrences in Paul συνίστημι means *commend (oneself)* and is used in the context of his apostolic service in disputation with his adversaries. With this meaning συνίστημι can be used both positively and negatively or even in an ambiguously ironic sense. Paul positively commends himself to every person's conscience (2 Cor 4:2), gives the church the opportunity to commend him (5:12), and proves himself a servant of God (6:4). His commendation of Phoebe (Rom 16:1) can also be understood positively. In contrast, Paul deals negatively with proclaimers who commend or praise themselves (2 Cor 10:12) with no consideration for the one genuine commendation by the Lord himself (v. 18). The reference to the apostle's repeated and apparently aggressive self-commendation (3:1) should probably be understood as an ambiguously ironic statement, since this commendation should in reality be issued by the church itself (12:11) on the basis of his publicly evident achievements (v. 12). Paul's use of συνίστημι in this sense is a masterful display of his rhetorical and stylistic talents.

b) In a second field of meaning συνίστημι is a significant term in Paul's theology of justification and the law.

Rom 3:5 reveals "that God's covenantal loyalty is not only not abrogated by the disloyalty 'of a few,' but rather is brought all the more clearly into focus by proving to be unshakable. . . . Our own unrighteousness reveals God's righteousness" (Schlier 94). 5:8 then offers the reason for this: God demonstrated his love for us "in that while we were still sinners Christ died for us." Precisely this is "the astonishing and unique element in Christ's death. . . . God's love for us is love for sinners" (Schlier 154).

Gal 2:18 belongs to this context as well. Here Paul puts his own theological reflection into practice and evaluates it with respect to table fellowship with the Gentile Christians in Antioch: Anyone persuaded of justification by faith in Jesus Christ (2:16) can never return to Jewish observance of the law, since whoever sets up the law again (which Paul himself has torn down) shows himself to be a sinner and presents himself as a transgressor against the law by subjecting himself to its power anew (cf. Rom 4:15). Συνίστημι in this context is an essential christological and soteriological term in Pauline theology. Its point of departure God posits only in Jesus Christ, but its goal is the person himself, his deliverance and justification, revealed in Jesus Christ. "What the term denotes here is thus close to φανερόω and might be rendered 'to bring to light' " (Kasch 898).

c) Col 1:17, within the hymn in 1:15-20, shows Christ to be the one in whom creation *has its existence* (συνέστηκεν; cf. the pf. as "continuance of completed action," BDF §340). Stoic and Hellenistically influenced cosmology that understands the world as divided into constituent individual elements probably has influenced both this passage and 2 Pet 3:5: The earth *has its existence* through water "as a means of creation and a primal element" (Kasch 897).

Luke 9:32 uses συνίστημι initially in the locative sense: Moses and Elijah *stand together* with the transfigured Jesus. This locative association, however, can also point to a more profound existential meaning in the sense of common mission and prophetic destiny (cf. v. 31: the conversation concerning Jesus' fate with a focus on "fulfillment").   A. Kretzer

συνοδεύω *synodeuō* go with, travel together, accompany*

Acts 9:7: οἱ συνοδεύοντες αὐτῷ, "those traveling with him." Fig. in *Barn.* 1:4.

συνοδία, ας, ἡ *synodia* group of travelers, traveling company*

Luke 2:44: ἐν τῇ συνοδίᾳ, referring concretely to a *group of pilgrims/travelers.*

σύνοιδα *synoida* know, be conscious of*

Lit.: → συνείδησις.

The vb. σύνοιδα appears twice in the NT, once used reflexively (1 Cor 4:4) and once nonreflexively (Acts 5:2). It is a genuinely Greek vb. and means *have knowledge of something* or, reflexively, *be conscious of something* (cf. Plato *Ap.* 21b: οὔτε μέγα οὔτε σμικρὸν σύνοιδα ἐμαυτῷ σοφὸς ὤν [further parallels in Wettstein, *NT,* on 1 Cor 4:4]). Σύνοιδα also occurs in isolated instances in the LXX; cf. Job 27:6: οὐ γὰρ σύνοιδα ἐμαυτῷ ἄτοπα πράξας.

In Acts 5:2 σύνοιδα refers to Sapphira's guilty complicity (i.e., knowledge) regarding her husband Ananias's sale of a piece of property (συνειδυίης καὶ τῆς γυναικός).

In 1 Cor 4:4 Paul emphasizes over against his Corinthian critics that he is not aware of any transgression on his part (οὐδὲν γὰρ ἐμαυτῷ σύνοιδα). He has just declared (4:3) that it means nothing to him to be judged either by the Corinthians or any other human authority. Nonetheless, he is not justified merely by not being aware of any transgression. Rather, it is the Kyrios who will judge him in time (4:5). Paul's use of σύνοιδα is identical with his use of → συνείδησις (3). Humans are capable of judging, i.e., of accusing or acquitting, but Paul considers such judgments preliminary at best, since only that judgment attending the advent of the Kyrios will disclose a person's hidden motives (cf. the parallel to 1 Cor 4:5 in Rom 2:16). Hence the Pauline use of σύνοιδα in 1 Cor 4:4 emphatically shows that συνείδησις and σύνοιδα have no independent terminological significance within Pauline anthropology. The apostle picked up this terminology and interpreted it from the perspective of his eschatology.

                                   G. Lüdemann

συνοικέω *synoikeō* live or dwell together, have marital relations*

1 Pet 3:7, of *marital cohabitation/relations* between men and women (συνοικοῦντες; א*: συνομιλοῦντες); cf. Herodotus i.93; Sir 25:8.

συνοικοδομέω *synoikodomeō* build together → οἰκοδομή 5.c.

συνομιλέω *synomileō* associate with, converse with*

Acts 10:27: συνομιλῶν αὐτῷ, "in *conversation with* him"; more generally "associate with" in 1 Pet 3:7 א*.

συνομορέω *synomoreō* be next door to, border*

Acts 18:7, of the house of Titius Justus in Corinth,

"which *was next door* to the synagogue (ἣν συνομοροῦσα τῇ συναγωγῇ)."

συνοράω *synoraō* perceive, become aware of, make clear to oneself*

Acts 12:12: συνιδών, *when he realized [this]/when he became aware [of it]* (cf. vv. 9, 11); 14:6: συνιδόντες, *when they noticed/learned of* it.

συνορία, ας, ἡ *synoria* neighboring area
Matt 4:24 v.l. in place of → Συρία (2).

συνοχή, ῆς, ἡ *synochē* prison; anxiety, distress*

This word occurs in the NT only with the meaning *anxiety/distress.* Luke 21:25: συνοχὴ ἐθνῶν, "anxiety among the nations" (cf. Ps 65:8f.); 2 Cor 2:4: συνοχὴ καρδίας, *"anguish* of heart" (with πολλὴ θλῖψις and διὰ πολλῶν δακρύων).

συνταράσσω *syntarassō* confuse, disturb
Luke 9:42 D in place of → σπαράσσω.

συντάσσω *syntassō* organize, direct*

In the NT only 2 Matthean occurrences relating Jesus' giving specific instructions: 21:6: καθὼς συνέταξεν (v.l. προσέταξεν) αὐτοῖς ὁ Ἰησοῦς (cf. 26:19: ὡς συνέταξεν); 27:10: καθὰ συνέταξέν μοι κύριος (citing Exod 9:12; 37:20 LXX, etc.; allusions to Zech 11:12f.; Jer 18:2f.; 32:7-9).

συντέλεια, ας, ἡ *synteleia* completion, end, end time*

6 occurrences in the NT, 5 of those in Matthew, all in the apocalyptic phrase συντέλεια (τοῦ) αἰῶνος, "the *end* of this world/age." Matt 13:39, 40, 49 interpret the parables of the weeds among the wheat and of the fishnet; 24:3 uses συντέλεια with → παρουσία (cf. → συντελέω in Mark 13:4); Matt 28:20 uses it in the promise of the resurrected Jesus to the disciples. In Heb 9:26b the phrase ἅπαξ ἐπὶ συντελείᾳ τῶν αἰώνων refers to Christ's unique final appearance "at the *end* of the age." The salvation event itself is thus already a sign of the end time, a time in which believers already live (→ ἅπαξ 3; αἰών 4.c); these eschatological events are juxtaposed with the extended periods since the creation of the world (v. 26a). Cf. further συντέλεια τοῦ αἰῶνος (*T. Benj.* 11:2), τῶν αἰώνων (*T. Levi* 10:2), συντέλεια used absolutely with συντέλεια καιροῦ or καιρῶν (Dan 9:27 LXX and Theodotion); καιρὸς συντελείας (*T. Zeb.* 9:9); ἡμέραι τῆς συντελείας (*Herm. Sim.* ix.12.3). G. Delling, *TDNT* VIII, 64-66.

συντελέω *synteleō* complete, finish, fulfill*

6 occurrences in the NT. Luke 4:13: πάντα πειρασμόν, *finish, bring to an end* (cf. Matt 7:28 Koine); Heb 8:8: *fulfill, execute* (διαθήκην καινήν, by God; cf. Jer 31:31-33; also 41:8, 15 LXX [διαθήκην]).

Rom 9:28: λόγον γὰρ συντελῶν καὶ συντέμνων ποιήσει κύριος (citing Isa 10:22 LXX; cf. 28:22 LXX; Dan 5:27 LXX), "the Lord will accomplish his word by *fulfilling/ executing* and curtailing." That is, he will fulfill it only for the "remnant" (cf. Rom 9:27; H. Schlier, *Rom* [HTKNT] ad loc.; U. Wilckens, *Rom* [EKKNT] II, ad loc.). If one understands λόγος as "event" or "reckoning" (differently → λόγος 4.c; see, however, E. Käsemann, *Rom* [Eng. tr., 1980] 272ff.), then συντελέω yields the meaning "carry through" or "conclude."

Pass. in Luke 4:2, of time *coming to an end* (ἡμέραι); Acts 21:27, with μέλλω; Mark 13:4, in an apocalyptic context: *be completed, come to an end* (ὅταν μέλλη ταῦτα συντελεῖσθαι πάντα; cf. Matt 24:3: παρουσία καὶ συντέλεια τοῦ αἰῶνος; Luke 21:7: ὅταν μέλλη ταῦτα γίνεσθαι). BAGD s.v.; G. Delling, *TDNT* VIII, 62-64.

συντέμνω *syntemnō* abbreviate, shorten, limit*

Rom 9:28, with → συντελέω (quoting Isa 10:22 LXX; cf. 28:22 LXX; Dan 5:27 LXX) of God's promise (λόγος) that God will carry out while simultaneously "fulfilling" (συντελῶν) and *curtailing/limiting* (συντέμνων). The limitation can refer either to the scope of the promise for Israel or to the "diminishing" of Israel itself (down to a "remnant"; cf. Rom 9:27/Isa 10:22). The rendering of λόγος with "event, reckoning" is less persuasive; thereby συντέμνω would mean "conclude quickly" (cf. Isa 28:22: συντετελεσμένα καὶ συντετμημένα πράγματα). BAGD s.v.

συντεχνίτης, ου, ὁ *syntechnitēs* one who practices the same trade

Acts 19:25 D syᵖ, ʰ sa replaces ἐργάται with τεχνῖται and then picks it up again with ἄνδρες συντεχνῖται.

συντηρέω *syntēreō* preserve, keep, protect; keep in one's memory*

Act. in Mark 6:20: Herod (Antipas) *kept* John the Baptist *safe* (from the plots of Herodias, v. 19), i.e., "he *protected* him (συνετήρει αὐτόν)" during his incarceration; Luke 2:19: Mary *kept in her memory* the angel's words delivered by the shepherds (πάντα συνετήρει τὰ ῥήματα ταῦτα); cf. Sir 39:2; Dan 7:28 Theodotion. Pass. in Matt 9:17: *be preserved;* Luke 5:38 v.l. (in contrast to ἀπόλλυμι).

συντίθεμαι *syntithemai* reach/conclude an agreement, decide*

The NT uses only the mid. form of this vb., always in reference to *decisions or resolutions* of Jewish groups or councils: Luke 22:5 (the high priests and captains of the temple together with Judas); John 9:22 (οἱ Ἰουδαῖοι); Acts 23:20 (οἱ Ἰουδαῖοι).

συντόμως *syntomōs* briefly, shortly; immediately*

Acts 24:4: ἀκοῦσαί σε ἡμῶν συντόμως, "that you may hear us [our charges] *briefly*"; with the meaning *immediately* in Mark 16:8 v.l. (the short conclusion).

συντρέχω *syntrechō* run with*

Mark 6:33 and Acts 3:11, of the running together of the people; fig. in 1 Pet 4:4: μὴ συντρεχόντων ὑμῶν, "that you not now *go along with them/plunge with them* into the same wild profligacy."

συντρίβω *syntribō* grind down, break, shatter*

7 occurrences in the NT. Mark 5:4, of *grinding through/rubbing through* foot chains; 14:3, of *breaking* an alabaster jar; cf. Rev 2:27 (τὰ σκεύη τὰ κεραμικά; cf. Ps 2:9; *Pss. Sol.* 17:23).

John 19:36, of the *crurifragium*: ὀστοῦν οὐ συντριβήσεται αὐτοῦ. According to 19:31 the Jews ask, because of the coming great sabbath, that the crucified men's legs be broken to hasten their deaths; since Jesus had already died, his legs (alone) were not broken (v. 33). For John this proves that Jesus is the true Passover lamb whose bones, according to Exod 12:10 LXX; 12:46; Num 9:12, should not be broken. The same applies according to Ps 34:20 to the believer protected by the Lord; Jesus thus also dies as a righteous person; cf. further 1 Cor 5:7; Luke 23:47; *Gos. Pet.* 4:14; Lactantius *Divinae Institutiones* iv.26.32f.

Luke 9:39, of the effect of an evil spirit on a possessed person: *mistreat, oppress;* Rom 16:20: "God . . . *will crush* Satan under your feet" (cf. Mal 3:21). The image of the *"shattered/crushed* reed (κάλαμον συντετριμμένον)" (Matt 12:20) comes from Isa 42:3 (LXX: κάλαμον τεθλασμένον, originally probably the bruised reed that indicated the death sentence but was not entirely broken, i.e., the sentence was not carried out) and refers generally to believers who, having been broken and shattered (cf. Pss 50:19 LXX; 146:3 LXX; Isa 57:15; 61:1) or oppressed (cf. Isa 66:2 Theodotion) experience consolation and salvation; cf. also Luke 4:18 v.l.; *Barn.* 2:10; *1 Clem.* 18:17; 52:4. BAGD s.v.; G. Bertram, *TDNT* VII, 919-25.

σύντριμμα, ατος, τό *syntrimma* destruction, ruin*

Rom 3:16, with ταλαιπωρία ("misery"), of the effects of the actions of sinful people on themselves and others (cf. Isa 59:7).

σύντροφος, 2 *syntrophos* brought up together, intimate*

Acts 13:1 refers to → Μαναήν as a σύντροφος of the tetrarch Herod (Antipas): *intimate friend, friend from youth* (subst.; cf. 2 Macc 9:29)

συντυγχάνω *syntynchanō* come together with*

Luke 8:19, of Jesus' mother and brothers: οὐκ ἠδύναντο συντυχεῖν αὐτῷ, "they could not *reach* him [i.e., *come together with* him]."

Συντύχη, ης *Syntyche* Syntyche*

A Christian woman in Philippi. Paul admonishes her and → Εὐοδία: τὸ αὐτὸ φρονεῖν (Phil 4:2). According to v. 3 the two have "labored for the gospel" with Paul and others. R. Knippenberg, *BHH* 1918.

συνυποκρίνομαι *synypokrinomai* be hypocritical together*

Gal 2:13 speaks of other Christian Jews who *were hypocritical together* with Peter, namely, who gave up their previous table fellowship with Gentile Christians after the arrival of the emissaries from James, specifically out of fear of the Jews (v. 12), not out of conviction (cf. → ὑπόκρισις, v. 13). U. Wilckens, *TDNT* VIII, 568f.

συνυπουργέω *synypourgeō* support together*

2 Cor 1:11: συνυπουργούντων καὶ ὑμῶν ὑπὲρ ἡμῶν τῇ δεήσει. Ὑπὲρ can be taken with συνυπουργέω: "by *interceding for our support* through prayer"; or συνυπουργέω can be taken absolutely: "to which you also *together provide assistance* through your intercession for us."

συνωδίνω *synōdinō* suffer agony or pain together*

According to Rom 8:22 all creation until the present has been characterized by a common groaning and by agony and pain: πᾶσα ἡ κτίσις συστενάζει καὶ συνωδίνει (v.l. ὀδυνεῖ) ἄχρι τοῦ νῦν. Συν- here refers to creation in its entirety. The idea behind this is the apocalyptic image of the sufferings or agony of the messianic time that are signs anticipating the coming new age (cf. 2 Esdr 4:27, 40ff.; 5:50ff.; *Mek. Exod.* 16:29; *b. Sanh.* 98b, etc.; in the OT: Isa 26:17f.; Mic 4:9f.; in the NT: Mark 13:8 par.; John 16:21f.). Paul's focus here is creation subjected to

mortality and therefore looking toward future deliverance. On the usage here cf. further Heraclitus *Quaestiones Homericae* 39 (ed. F. Oelmann, et al. [1910] 58); Diodorus Siculus v.5.1. H. R. Balz, *Heilsvertrauen und Welterfahrung* (BEvT 59, 1971) 52-54; G. Bertram, *TDNT* IX, 667-74.

συνωμοσία, ας, ἡ *synōmosia* conspiracy*

Acts 23:13, of a Jewish conspiracy against Paul (cf. v. 12: συστροφή, ἀναθεματίζω).

Σύρα, ας, ἡ *Syra* Syrian woman
Mark 7:26 v.l.: Σύρα Φοινικίσσα in place of → Συροφοινίκισσα.

Συρακοῦσαι, ῶν *Syrakousai* Syracuse*

Syracuse, the port city on the east coast of Sicily, is mentioned in Acts 28:12. Coming from Malta, Paul reached Syracuse aboard an Alexandrian ship (→ Διόσκουροι; παράσημος) and stayed there three days before continuing on to Rhegium (→ Ῥήγιον). Syracuse was an ancient Greek colony conquered by the Romans in 212 B.C. W. Bieder, *BHH* 1918; A. van den Born, *BL* 1694f.; H.-P. Drögemüller, *KP* V, 460-69; A. G. Woodhead, *OCD* 1030.

Συρία, ας *Syria* Syria*

Lit.: BAGD s.v. — A. VAN DEN BORN, *BL* 1695f. — E. HONIGMANN, PW IV/A, 1549-1727. — A. H. M. JONES and H. SEYRIG, *OCD* 1030f. — B. REICKE, *BHH* 1919-22. — W. RÖLLIG, *KP* V, 469-73. — W. STROTHMANN, *LAW* 2966-68. — E. WIRTH, *Syrien. Eine geographische Landeskunde* (1971). — For further bibliography see BAGD; van den Born; Reicke; Jones and Seyrig.

1. The NT mentions Syria 8 times (5 times in Acts, once each in Matthew 4:24, Luke 2:2, and Gal 1:21).

In the Hellenistic period the name Συρία was used in a broad sense of the area from the Euphrates west to the Mediterranean Sea, bordered in the north by the Taurus Mountains and in the south by Palestine. The name referred originally to the Assyrian Empire (Herodotus vii.63). The LXX and Vg. use Συρία/*Syria* to refer to Aram, i.e., the inland country east and northeast of the Anti-Lebanon Range. Under the Persians the fifth satrapy of Trans-Euphrates or Syria encompassed the actual area of Syria (see above) including Palestine. During the period of the Diadoches Syria was subject to the Seleucids, and in 64 B.C. Pompey made Syria a Roman province (an imperial province from 27 B.C.) encompassing Syria, Phoenicia, eastern Cilicia, and in the south Samaria, Idumea, Judea (after A.D. 6), and later Galilee, with Antioch as its capital (→ Ἀντιόχεια 1). Syria and Palestine had close connections during the Hellenistic period. After Herod Archelaus was deposed (A.D. 6-7) a census was conducted in Syria and Judea under the Syrian governor → Κυρήνιος (Luke 2:2; cf. Josephus *Ant.* xvii.355; xviii.1-5; see below). A great many Jews lived in Syria, particularly in Antioch and Damascus (→ Δαμασκός), and an emphatically Hellenistic Judaism emerged in both cities at an early period (cf. Acts 9:2; 11:19ff.).

2. Luke 2:2 associates Publius Sulpicius Quirinius (→ Κυρήνιος) as the ἡγεμονεύων τῆς Συρίας with the first → ἀπογραφή (3) of the whole world (v. 1) (→ κῆνσος 2); this reference is to the Roman province. Otherwise the NT uses Συρία as a geographical term. According to Acts 15:23 the letter of the Jerusalem church is directed to Gentile Christians κατὰ τὴν ᾿Αντιόχειαν καὶ Συρίαν καὶ Κιλικίαν (cf. Συρία καὶ Κιλικία, v. 41). In Paul's journeys Syria was the first stop on his return trip to Palestine (14:26; 18:18; 20:3; 21:3) and is visited as he sets out again (18:22). Paul himself mentions that after his first stay in → ᾿Αραβία (2) and → Δαμασκός (Gal 1:17), and after his first visit to Jerusalem (vv. 18-20) he went to Syria and Cilicia (v. 21).

In Matt 4:24 ὅλη ἡ Συρία probably refers to the area bordering Galilee immediately to the north (and east; cf. → Δεκάπολις and Transjordan in 4:25; see further Mark 1:28 [ὅλη ἡ περίχωρος τῆς Γαλιλαίας, corresponding to the v.l. συνορία instead of Συρία, Matt 4:24]; Mark 3:7f.: Galilee, Judea, Jerusalem, and Idumea mentioned with Transjordan, Tyre, and Sidon). This Matthean emphasis on Jesus' early "success" in Syria might be a reference to the home area of the Evangelist and his church. Syria is also mentioned in Ign. *Eph.* 21:2; *Magn.* 14; *Pol.* 7:1; *Rom* 2:2; *Smyrn.* 11:1; *Trall.* 13:1.   H. Balz

Σύρος, ου, ὁ *Syros* the Syrian*

In a citation from 4 Kgdms 5:1ff. Luke 4:27 mentions → Ναιμὰν ὁ Σύρος, a non-Israelite whom Elisha healed of leprosy. Luke picks up the usage of the LXX, according to which Συρία correponds to Heb. ᾿^arām; → Συρία 1.

Συροφοινίκισσα, ης, ἡ *Syrophoinikissa* Syro-Phoenician woman*

Mark 7:26 identifies a woman whose daughter Jesus heals in the region of Tyre (v. 24) as → Ἑλληνίς, Συροφοινίκισσα τῷ γένει, referring thereby to her Hellenistic-Gentile origin in Phoenicia, the coastal area of the Roman province Syria, which was often called "Syro-Phoenicia" to distinguish it from the former colony of Phoenicia at Carthage ("Libo-Phoenicia"; cf. Diodorus Siculus xix.93.7 with xx.55.4; Justin *Dial.* 78). Matthew, on the other hand, because it is focused on Syria, uses the older name → Χαναναία (15:22; cf. Gen 10:19; 12:6; Josh 5:12 and elsewhere). BAGD s.v.; B. Reicke, *BHH* 1922; T. A. Burkill, *ZNW* 57 (1966) 23-37; A. Dermience, *RTL* 8 (1977) 15-29; G. Theissen, "Lokal- und

Sozialkolorit in der Geschichte von der syrophönikischen Frau (Mk 7,24-30)," *ZNW* 75 (1984) 202-25.

συρρήγνυμι *syrrēgnymi* collide, crash together Luke 6:49 D in place of προσρήγνυμι.

Σύρτις, εως *Syrtis* Syrtis*

A large gulf on the north coast of Africa south and southeast of Sicily. The eastern part of the gulf, "Greater Syrtis" (now called the Gulf of Sidra or Gulf of Benghazi) is between Benghazi and Leptis Major, toward Cyrenaica; the eastern part, "Lesser Syrtis" (now called the Gulf of Gabes/Qabis), is toward Numidia/Tunisia. According to Acts 27:17 the ship's crew feared between blown by the storm into the Syrtis, which was generally avoided because of its shifting sandbars and unpredictable currents (Strabo xvii.3.20; Lucan *Bellum Civile [Pharsalia]* ix.303ff.; Josephus *B.J.* ii.381). Since the island → Καῦδα is mentioned shortly before this incident (Acts 27:16), this particular reference is probably to the eastern, or Greater Syrtis. B. Reicke, *BHH* 1922-24; A. van den Born, *BL* 1696; H. Gärtner, *KP* V, 475.

σύρω *syrō* pull, drag; sweep away, drag away*

John 21:8 refers to a boat *dragging* a net full of fish (σύροντες τὸ δίκτυον; see R. Schnackenburg, *John* III [Eng. tr., 1982] 354-57). According to Rev 12:4 the dragon's tail *sweeps away* (σύρει) a third of the stars of heaven (cf. Dan 8:10). Acts 8:3 refers to a violent *dragging away* of men and women (ἄνδρας καὶ γυναῖκας); 14:19 (τὸν Παῦλον); 17:6 (᾿Ιάσονα καί τινας ἀδελφούς).

συσπαράσσω *sysparassō* tear about, convulse*

Mark 9:20 (πνεῦμα) and Luke 9:42 (δαιμόνιον) refer to a demon that violently *convulses* a sick boy when Jesus encounters him (epilepsy; variously synonymous with → ῥήσσω [Mark 9:18/Luke 9:42]).

σύσσημον, ου, τό *syssēmon* previously arranged signal, identifying sign*

Mark 14:44: Judas's kiss as a *prearranged sign* (δεδώκει . . . σύσσημον αὐτοῖς); the meaning "signal" occurs in Ign. *Smyrn.* 1:2 (citing Isa 5:26).

σύσσωμος, 2 *syssōmos* belonging to the same body, incorporated along with*

Eph 3:6: the Gentiles through Christ become "fellow heirs and *members of the same body* (σύσσωμα) [of Christ] and partakers of the promise." This adj., like συγκληρονόμος and συμμέτοχος, is an artificial construction attested only in Christian writings; cf. 2:16, 19 (συμπολῖται); 4:4ff. E. Schweizer, *TDNT* VII, 1080.

συστασιαστής, οῦ, ὁ *systasiastēs* fellow insurrectionist

Mark 15:7 A Koine in place of → στασιαστής.

συστατικός, 3 *systatikos* introducing, commending, serving to commend*

According to 2 Cor 3:1 Paul needs no "letter of recommendation" (συστατικαὶ ἐπιστολαί) either to or from the church, since the Corinthian church itself is his → ἐπιστολή (3) (v. 2; cf. 4:2). Συστατικὴ ἐπιστολή is a frequently used t.t. for letters of reference given to travelers or emissaries (cf. Pap. Oxy. no. 1634, l. 20; Diogenes Laertius viii.87; Epictetus *Diss.* ii.3.1; see Spicq, *Notes* II, 864f.). Paul himself used the form indicated by the term in his own letters (Rom 16:1f., for Phoebe; 1 Cor 4:17; 16:10f.; Phil 2:19-23, for Timothy; 2 Cor 8:16ff., for Titus and his companions; see further Acts 15:25-27; 18:27; Col 4:7-10; Phlm 12, 17). The missionaries working against Paul in Corinth based their own authority on letters of recommendation (from unknown sources) and were referred or recommended further by the church, whereas Paul invokes his own "commendation" by the Kyrios (cf. 2 Cor 10:12, 18). W. Baird, *JBL* 80 (1961) 166-72.

συσταυρόω *systauroō* crucify together with*

Lit.: BAGD s.v. — E. BRANDENBURGER, *Fleisch und Geist. Paulus und die dualistische Weisheit* (1968) 216-21. — *idem*, *DNTT* I, 400f. — *idem*, "Σταυρός, Kreuzigung Jesu und Kreuzestheologie," *WuD* 10 (1969) 17-43, esp. 40f. — W. GRUNDMANN, *TDNT* VII, 786, 791f. — H.-W. KUHN, "Jesus als Gekreuzigter in der frühchristlichen Verkündigung bis zur Mitte des 2. Jahrhunderts," *ZTK* 72 (1975) 1-46, esp. 37-39. — LSJ s.v. συσταυρόομαι. — *ThGL* s.v. — H. WEDER, *Das Kreuz Jesu bei Paulus* (FRLANT 125, 1981) 175-82.

1. This vb. is attested only in Christian writings. In the Gospels it is always pass. and always refers to the two men crucified with Jesus. In Mark 15:32 par. Matt 27:44 (with σύν) they revile Jesus; in John 19:32 (with simple dat.) their lower legs are broken in order to hasten their death (cf. *Gos. Pet.* 4:14).

2. The overall Pauline context, which views the crucified Jesus together with the new existence of believers, is also found (apart from Gal 5:24; 6:14; → σταυρόω 3) in Gal 2:19, where (as in 6:13) it is directly associated with the theme of the Torah, where Paul also speaks of the crucified Jesus (→ σταυρός 4.a, σταυρόω 2.c): "Through the law I died to the law so that I might live for God. I *have been crucified with* Christ." Paul also

picks up this idea in Rom 6:6, where the context in the history of religions, which speaks of "killing" the body (or similar phrases; cf. 8:13), is even more easily recognizable (→ σταυρόω 3): "Our old self *was crucified with* him so that the sinful body might be destroyed, and we might no longer serve sin."

H.-W. Kuhn

συστέλλω *systellō* press or draw together; wrap or cover up*

1 Cor 7:29: ὁ καιρὸς συνεσταλμένος ἐστίν, "the time [remaining until the parousia] is *compressed/very short.*" In the context of vv. 26, 28, 31 this refers to the final time remaining for this world before the end, an end in which believers are to prove themselves. This does not necessarily presuppose that Paul is thinking of any God limiting the tribulations facing the pious (cf. Mark 13:20; → καιρός 3). He is not offering that kind of consolation, but is emphasizing rather that one should concentrate on what is essential and on one's eschatological freedom within the structures of this world, which will not last much longer (vv. 29b-31). As a rule συστέλλω emphasizes the element of *shrinking* or *diminishing* (Diodorus Siculus iii.39; Josephus *Ant.* xvi; Sir 4:31; Acts 27:15 v.l.), though it can also refer to a *compression/crowding* or *brevity* (Diodorus Siculus iv.20; Hippocrates *Art.* 50; cf. συνεσταλμένως ζῇ, Plutarch *Apophth. Lac. Alcamenes* 3 [*Moralia* 216F]). The substance of Rom 13:11-14 and 1 Thess 5:6 also suggests this interpretation (cf. 2 Esdr 4:26, 45, 50ff.). Paul's eschatological admonition here is thus that the congregation not be confused in their own eschatological awareness by worries concerning the order and structure of this world, which is itself about to end.

Acts 5:6 says before the burial of Ananias: συνέστειλαν αὐτόν (cf. 5:10 D [sy^p]: συστείλαντες ἐξήνεγκαν). Συστέλλω here can mean "collect together, pack up" (cf. Psellus 50.31) or, more likely, *wrap up, cover up* (cf. Euripides *Tr.* 378; Lucian *Im.* 7; Plutarch *Galba* 18; so also the Syrian and Coptic versions; Vg., on the other hand, uses *amoverunt*). The corpse was *covered* and then taken out. BAGD s.v.; K. H. Rengstorf, *TDNT* VII, 596f.

H. Balz

συστενάζω *systenazō* groan together, sigh together*

Rom 8:22: πᾶσα ἡ κτίσις συστενάζει καὶ συνωδίνει ἄχρι τοῦ νῦν. Paul uses συστενάζω as a powerful metaphor for the yearning of creation in its entirety (συν-)·for liberation to "the glorious freedom of God's children" (v. 21, cf. v. 19). The "groaning" of the κτίσις corresponds to that of believers (v. 23) and of the Spirit (v. 26; → στενάζω; συνωδίνω). The basis of creation's continuing enslavement to transitoriness and mortality is the "fall" of mankind (cf. Gen 3:17; Isa 24:1ff., 20; 2 Esdr 4:26ff.; *Gen. Rab.* 2 [3b]; 5 [4d]; 12 [8d]), through which creation —"unwillingly" (οὐχ ἑκοῦσα, Rom 8:20)—was drawn into the fate of alienation from God. Therefore it longs (→ ἀποκαραδοκία, → ἀπεκδέχομαι, v. 19) for the fulfillment of its own real destiny through the renewal of mankind. J. Schneider, *TDNT* VII, 600-603; H. R. Balz, *Heilsvertrauen und Welterfahrung* (1971) 36-54.

συστοιχέω *systoicheō* stand in the same line; correspond*

This word is used both generally in the military sense (Polybius x.23.7: "keep in line or file") and esp. in a logical-conceptual sense (Aristotle *Metaph.* x.9.1066a). According to Gal 4:25 Hagar (the παιδίσκη, vv. 22f.; the Sinai Covenant of servility, vv. 24f.) *stands* ("allegorically," v. 24) *in the same line* with the νῦν Ἰερουσαλήμ (→ Ἰεροσόλυμα 4), which submits to slavery to the law. The reference is thus to a typology evoking positively the correspondence between the descendants of Sarah, the "free" woman (ἐλευθέρα) according to the promise, and the ἄνω Ἰερουσαλήμ as the mother of the free (4:22f., 26-31). G. Delling, *TDNT* VII, 669.

συστρατιώτης, ου, ὁ *systratiōtēs* fellow soldier, comrade*

Only fig. in the NT. Phil 2:25, of Epaphroditus (with ἀδελφός, συνεργός) as a term of honor (cf. vv. 29f.); Phlm 2, of Archippus. This usage presupposes the metaphor of the struggle of faith on behalf of the gospel in a world hostile to God (cf. Phil 1:27-30; 3:18; 4:3; Rom 13:12; 2 Cor 6:7; 10:3-6; 1 Thess 5:8; Col 2:1; Eph 6:10ff.; → ἀγών [4]; πανοπλία). According to Suetonius (*Divus Iulius* 67) Caesar honored his own troops by addressing them as *commilitones* (cf. Polyaenus *Stratagems* viii.23.22: συστρατιῶται). On fig. usage cf. esp. Philo *Decal.* 53; *Ebr.* 75f.; *All.* iii.14. O. Bauernfeind, *TDNT* VII, 710f.

συστρέφω *systrephō* gather up; pass.: come together, assemble*

Acts 28:3: Paul *gathers up* a bundle of sticks; pass. in Matt 17:22: συστρεφομένων αὐτῶν, *"when they were together"* (ἀναστρεφομένων in C D L Koine, etc.). Συστρέφω is an (added) v.l. in D(*) in Acts 10:41; 11:28; 16:39; 17:5; → συναναστρέφομαι.

συστροφή, ῆς, ἡ *systrophē* unlawful assembly, mob; plot*

Acts 19:40: περὶ τῆς συστροφῆς ταύτης, "because of this *mob*" (cf. στάσις in the same verse); 23:12: *plot*,

conspiracy (cf. ἀναθεματίζω in the same verse and → συνωμοσία in v. 13).

συσχηματίζομαι *syschēmatizomai* be formed on the model of, take on the form of something, conform to*

Rom 12:2: μὴ συσχηματίζεσθε τῷ αἰῶνι τούτῳ, "do not *be conformed* to this world" (in the sense of a regression or lapse back into the ways of the world; cf. E. Käsemann, *Rom* [Eng. tr., 1980] 329-31; contrasted with μεταμορφοῦσθε); 1 Pet 1:14: "by not living *according to* your earlier passions."

Συχάρ *Sychar* Sychar*

John 4:5 refers to Sychar as πόλις τῆς Σαμαρείας λεγομένη Συχάρ near Jacob's field and well (vv. 5f.), and as the home of the Samaritan woman (vv. 7, 28-30, 39). According to Jerome *Quaestiones in Genesin* 66.6; *Epistula* 108.13 Sychar is a corruption of → Συχέμ (Sichem also appears in sy[s, c]). Jerome's information, however, can be traced to the mention of Sichem in Gen 33:18-20; 35:4; 48:22; Josh 24:32 in connection with Jacob's field. Since during the time of Jesus and the fourth Gospel Sichem had long been destroyed (128 B.C. by John Hyrcanus I; Flavia Neapolis [Nâblus] was founded nearby by Vespasian in A.D. 72), Sychar should probably be identified with the larger Samaritan settlement closest to the well during the period in question. Even if tradition correctly locates Jacob's well in *bîr yaʿqûb*, directly east of the village Balâṭah, Sychar is more likely located at the village ʿAskar situated *ca.* 1 km. northeast along the road from Judea to Galilee (on the southeastern slope of Mount Ebal; John 4:3), since the date of the founding of Balâṭah is uncertain and a larger settlement (πόλις) is presupposed not far from the well (vv. 28-31). ʿAskar might have been built at the location of the older Sychar and possibly even preserved some of the older name. BAGD s.v. (bibliography); K. Elliger, *BHH* 1896; A. van den Born, *BL* 1582 (bibliography); Kopp, *Places* 155-66; M. Delcor, *ZDPV* 78 (1962) 34-48; R. Schnackenburg, *John* I (Eng. tr., 1982) ad loc.

H. Balz

Συχέμ *Sychem* Shechem*

Συχέμ, from Heb. *šᵉ̱kem,* "back, shoulder," is the Grecized name of an ancient Canaanite city situated in the Ephraim mountain range in the narrow sloping valley between Mount Gerizim and Mount Ebal (hence the name). The OT mentions it in Gen 12:6; 48:22; Josh 24:1, and elsewhere (LXX: Συχέμ and Σίκιμα; → Συχάρ). Shechem was mentioned already in 1900 B.C. and played a significant role in the patriarchal period (Abraham: Gen 12:6; Jacob: 33:18f.; 48:22 [property of Jacob and Joseph]; Joseph: 37:14; Josh 24:32 [the tomb of Joseph]; see further

Genesis 34). For a long time it was the center of the tribal confederacy (Josh 24:1ff.; 1 Kings 12; first capital of the Northern Kingdom, 12:25). After its destruction by the Assyrians (724 /23) Shechem flourished again only in the late post-exilic period under the Samaritans (→ Σαμάρεια 2), probably after the annexation of Samaria under Alexander the Great in 331 B.C. The Samaritans founded their own center with a sanctuary on Mount Gerizim (cf. the polemic against Shechem in Sir 50:26; 2 Chr 13:4-12). Under Antiochus IV Epiphanes the temple on Mount Gerizim was transformed into a temple of Ζεὺς Ξένιος (2 Macc 6:2). John Hyrcanus I destroyed the city and temple in 128 B.C. (Josephus *Ant.* xiii.255). Until the founding of the colony *Flavia Neapolis* (present-day Nâblus) west of Shechem by Vespasian in A.D. 72, → Συχάρ probably assumed the role of Shechem. Tell Balâṭah, 1.5 km. southeast of Nâblus, shows the former location of Shechem.

Acts 7:16 mentions Shechem twice as the location of the tomb of Jacob and his sons, which Abraham had bought from the sons of Hamor. This confuses Abraham's purchase of the cave of Machpelah (Gen 23:1ff., 16ff.; according to 25:9; 49:30ff.; 50:13f. also the tomb of Abraham and Jacob) with Jacob's purchase of property at Shechem (33:18f.). According to Josh 24:32, however, Joseph was buried on Jacob's property at Shechem; see also E. Haenchen, *Acts* (Eng. tr., 1971) ad loc.

Acts 7:16b 𝔭⁷⁴ D Ψ Koine vg (τοῦ Συχέμ) presupposes the personal name Shechem (Hamor as the father of Shechem, Gen 33:19) instead of the place name Shechem. BAGD s.v.; K. Elliger, *BHH* 1781-83 (bibliography); H. Haag, *BL* 1582-84 (bibliography, including excavation reports); Kopp, *Places* 158-65; G. E. Wright, *EAEHL* 1083-94 (bibliography, including excavation reports).   H. Balz

σφαγή, ῆς, ἡ *sphagē* slaughter (noun)*

Σφαγή occurs twice in quotations from the OT with → πρόβατον (2, 3): Acts 8:32 quotes Isa 53:7 (ὡς πρόβατον ἐπὶ σφαγὴν ἤχθη) and interprets it in connection with Jesus' suffering and death. In Rom 8:36 Paul uses the metaphor of the "sheep for the *slaughter*" (πρόβατα σφαγῆς, quoting Ps 43:23 LXX; cf. further Jer 12:3; Zech 11:4, 7) to refer to believers who live through trials and tribulations for Christ's sake (Rom 8:35-37). As in the OT, this metaphor emphasizes that "sheep to be slaughtered," in contrast to "sheep for wool," are fed and allowed to graze only for the sake of being slaughtered; they endure this difficult death (Jer 12:3) without complaint or resistance (Isa 53:7), indeed even without suspecting (Jer 11:19 [Aquila and Symmachus: εἰς σφαγήν]).

Jas 5:5 uses σφαγή in charges against the rich: ἐθρέψατε τὰς καρδίας ὑμῶν (v.l.: ὡς) ἐν ἡμέρᾳ σφαγῆς, "you have fattened your hearts on the day of *slaughter*." In view of vv. 3b-4, 6 the ἡμέρα σφαγῆς does not refer to the "day of *slaughter*" as a day of rejoicing for the rich, but either to the day of slaughtering the poor and pious

(cf. Rev 6:9; 18:24; *1 Enoch* 100:7), or the day of the last judgment, in accord with the apocalyptic context (cf. Jas 5:1, 3; also Jer 12:3; 46:10; Isa 34:2, 6; Zeph 1:17; Rev 19:17f.; *1 Enoch* 94:7). The latter view emphasizes esp. the connection with Jas 5:3b (ἐθησαυρίσατε ἐν ἐσχάταις ἡμέραις), and thinks of judgment as imminent or already underway (cf. vv. 8f.); otherwise the reference would be to a past "day of misfortune" for the poor that left the rich untouched or was even caused by them. Cf. M. Dibelius, *Jas* (Hermeneia, 1976) ad loc.; W. Schrage, *Jas* (NTD) ad loc.; O. Michel, *TDNT* VII, 935-38.

H. Balz

σφάγιον, ου, τό *sphagion* (slain) sacrificial offering*

Acts 7:42b (μὴ σφάγια καὶ θυσίας προσηνέγκατέ μοι[;]) interprets Amos 5:25 (counter to the original sense) as saying that during forty years in the wilderness Israel offered its "*slain beasts* and [other] sacrifices" (the Hebrew text refers to "food offerings": zᵉḇāḥîm ûminḥâ) not to God, but to idols (cf. Acts 7:42a, 43; → θυσία 1).

σφάζω *sphazō* slaughter (vb.)*

There are 10 occurrences in the NT: 2 in 1 John 3:12 and 8 in Revelation. In every NT occurrence σφάζω refers either directly or figuratively to the violent killing of human beings.

1 John 3:12 uses it as a powerful expression for the fratricide committed by Cain: ἔσφαξεν τὸν ἀδελφὸν αὐτοῦ /ἔσφαξεν αὐτόν, *he slaughtered* him (cf. Gen 4:8 LXX: ἀπέκτεινεν αὐτόν; 4 Kgdms 10:7; on the other hand, Jer 52:10 LXX also uses σφάζω in reference to human beings).

In Rev 5:6, 12; 13:8 Christ is called (τὸ) ἀρνίον (τὸ/ ὡς) ἐσφαγμένον (cf. 5:9: ἐσφάγης). This emphasizes both the helplessness of the crucified Christ (cf. Isa 53:7) and the majesty of the exalted Christ (cf. on Rev 5:6: Deut 33:17; Zech 4:10). Rev 5:1 refers to the enthronement of the "Lamb," whereby the visionary ὡς (v. 6) introduces the christological interpretation central to the message of Revelation (→ ἀμνός 2, 3; → σφαγή). 6:9 calls Christian martyrs ἐσφαγμένοι (cf. 18:24). 6:4 speaks in a general sense of killing in war. According to 13:3a one of the seven heads of the beast from the sea (cf. v. 1) is ὡς ἐσφαγμένον εἰς θάνατον, "as if mortally *wounded*" (cf. ἡ πληγὴ τοῦ θανάτου, v. 3b; similarly v. 14); the wound heals, however (vv. 3b, 14), so that it appears as a counterpart to the suffering and resurrected Christ, eliciting both wonder and worship (vv. 3c-4, 11ff.). This is probably an allusion to the legend of *Nero redux* or *redivivus* (cf. Suetonius *Caes.* vi.57; Tacitus *Hist.* ii.8; *Sib. Or.* iv.119ff., 137ff.; v.143ff., 361ff.; see O. Michel, *TDNT*

VII, 934f.; E. Lohse, *Rev* [NTD] on 13:3). H. Kraft (*Rev* [HNT] ad loc.) interprets this as an allusion to the murder of Domitian. O. Michel, *TDNT* VII, 925-35.

σφάλλω *sphallō* cause to fall; pass.: fall, stumble
Matt 15:14 v.l.: ὁδηγῶν σφαλήσεται, "in leading, he will stumble," in place of ἐὰν ὁδηγῇ.

σφόδρα *sphodra* very much, extremely, greatly*

Σφόδρα, an adv. form of σφοδρός, occurs 11 times in the NT, 5 of those in Matthew. It does not occur in the Epistles. It appears with the adj. μέγας (as a circumlocution for the superlative form, which recedes significantly in the NT) in Matt 2:10 ("*very* great joy"); Mark 16:4; Rev 16:21; with πλούσιος in Luke 18:23. It is used with the vb. φοβέομαι in Matt 17:6, 27:54 ("be filled with *great* fear"); with ἐκπλήσσομαι in 19:25 ("be *greatly* astonished"), with λυπέομαι in 17:23; 18:31; 26:22 ("be *greatly* distressed"), and with πληθύνομαι in Acts 6:7 ("*greatly* increase/multiply").

σφοδρῶς *sphodrōs* very (much), violently*

Σφοδρῶς, an adv. form of σφοδρός, occurs in the NT only in Acts 27:18: σφοδρῶς δὲ χειμαζομένων ἡμῶν, "we were *violently* pressed by the storm."

σφραγίζω *sphragizō* seal, secure, confirm, attest*

Lit.: → σφραγίς.

1. This vb., attested from Aeschylus *Eu.* 828, occurs 15 times in the NT, 8 of those in Revelation. Like the noun → σφραγίς, it is used both literally and figuratively.

According to Dan 6:17 a large stone was laid across the opening of the lions' den and sealed, a fountain can be sealed (Cant 4:12), and purchase and marriage contracts are sealed (Jer 39:10f., 25, 44 LXX; Tob 7:14). The guilt of Israel's enemies lies hidden with God, sealed up in his storeroom (Deut 32:34). Sins (like money in a bag) can be sealed up (Job 14:17). God himself seals up stars and people (9:7; 37:7). A revelation remains sealed up and thus hidden or secret (Dan 12:9; cf. also 12:4).

2. In the NT σφραγίζω is used literally in Matt 27:66 (guards secure Jesus' tomb "*by sealing* the stone"; cf. Dan 6:17) and Rev 20:3 (the pit into which the devil is cast is closed and sealed). Rom 15:28, on the other hand, where Paul urgently speaks of concluding the collection for the Jerusalem poor, probably is not referring to literal sealing (as, e.g., in Tob 9:5); σφραγίζω here is intended more in the sense of *dependably confirming/attesting* (cf. BAGD s.v. 2.d; Fitzer, 948; O. Michel, *Rom* [KEK] ad loc.). This is also the meaning intended in John: "Whoever receives his [Jesus'] testimony *has attested/ set his seal* to this, [namely,] that God is true" (3:33). In

a reverse fashion, God the Father has *legally authorized /attested/confirmed* the Son of man (6:27). In 2 Cor 1:22 Paul asserts that God "*has put his seal* on us and given us his Spirit in our hearts as a guarantee." The context of this much-discussed assertion and its variation in Eph 1:13 and 4:30 ("you *have been sealed* by the Holy Spirit [for the day of redemption]") refers to Christian baptism, which makes the baptized person a possession of God. Was it already associated in early Christian times with a sealing for Christ (i.e., with the sign of the cross as a [Heb.] *tāw* or [Greek] X: so Dinkler, "Taufterminologie" *passim,* esp. 109-13; "Jesu Wort" 93f.)?

Revelation, in addition to 20:3 (see above), has 7 further occurrences of σφραγίζω. 5 of those (7:3, 4 bis, 5, 8) are in the context of the seal of God (→ σφραγίς 4.b), and the other two speak of (not) sealing the revelation itself: According to 22:10 the seer should not *seal* the words of the prophecy, i.e., keep them concealed or secret; in 10:4, on the other hand, he is virtually ordered to do so: "*Seal up* [i.e., close and do not reveal] what the seven thunders have said."

T. Schramm

σφραγίς, ῖδος, ἡ *sphragis* seal (noun)*

1. Occurrences in the NT and meaning — 2. Seals in antiquity — 3. The LXX — 4. The NT — a) The Pauline corpus — b) Revelation

Lit.: J. DIEHL, *Sphragis* (1938). — E. DINKLER, "Die Taufterminologie in 2 Kor 1,21f," idem, *Signum Crucis. Aufsätze zum NT und zur christlichen Archäologie* (1967) 99-117. — idem, "Jesu Wort vom Kreuztragen," *ibid.* 77-98. — idem, *RGG* VI, 1366f. — F. DÖLGER, *Sphragis* (1911). — G. FITZER, *TDNT* VII, 939-53. — W. HEITMÜLLER, "Σφραγίς," *Neutestamentliche Studien* (FS G. Heinrici, 1914) 40-59. — H. VON LIPS, *Glaube —Gemeinde—Amt* (1979) 100f. — G. SAUER, *BHH* 1786-90. — R. SCHIPPERS, *DNTT* III, 497-501. — L. WENGER, PW IIA, 2361-2448. — For further bibliography see *TWNT* X, 1275f.

1. Σφραγίς occurs 16 times in the NT: Paul uses it in Rom 4:11 and 1 Cor 9:2; it occurs further in 2 Tim 2:19, and 13 times in Revelation. The noun is attested from the 6th cent. B.C. and refers both to the instrument with which one seals (e.g., a cylinder seal, signet ring, or stone; cf. Sauer for particulars) and to the seal impression itself (*sigillum,* from *signum*) as a sign of attestation.

2. Seals were quite commonly used in antiquity in both private and public life and were of great legal significance (cf. Wenger; Fitzer 939-43). Objects, animals (including sacrificial animals), human beings, specifically slaves, were identified and protected as the property of their owner by means of a sign, image, letter, or word(s), or by a combination of these (Heitmüller 45ff.). An analogy in religious life was the sealing or marking of participants in the mystery cults as a means of religious stigmatization (→ στίγμα 2.b; Dölger 39ff.). On contracts, testaments, and documents in general seals functioned, with or in place of signatures, to attest the contents of documents

and guarantee their integrity or secrecy. Accordingly, one could speak fig. of sealing one's mouth or of sealing words (cf. Diogenes Laertius i.58; Theognis *Elegiacus* i.178; Timotheus *Persae* 159f.).

3. Σφραγίς occurs *ca.* 25 times in the LXX, always, except in Exod 35:22, translating *ḥôṯām*. It is used both literally and figuratively. A master workman produces seals (Sir 38:27; cf. 45:11f.). Jezebel writes letters in the name of Ahab and seals them with his seal (3 Kgdms 21:8). According to Bel and the Dragon the temple door is shut and sealed with the king's signet; the next morning the integrity of the seal is examined. A money bag can also be secured with seals (Tob 9:5; cf. 4 Kgdms 22:4). Wisdom recommends locking things where there are many hands and using a good seal if a wife is evil (Sir 42:6). The preciousness of the signet(-ring) is made clear by similes such as Sir 17:22 ("A man's almsgiving is like a signet with the Lord, and he will keep a person's kindness like the apple of his eye"); Cant 8:6 ("Set me as a seal on your heart, as a seal on your arm"); Sir 49:11 (Zerubbabel was "like a signet ring on the right hand"; cf. Hag 2:23). Σφραγίς is used fig. in the wisdom "prayer for self-control" in Sir 22:27 ("Who will set a guard before my mouth, an artful seal before my lips, so that I . . . do not fall and my tongue does not plunge me into ruin").

In Jewish writings fig. use of σφραγίς is developed further, esp. in Philo (Fitzer 946f.). The interpretation of circumcision as a covenantal seal and the "seal of Abraham" is particularly significant (Dölger 51ff.; O. Michel, *Rom* [KEK] on 4:11). The idea of the marking of the righteous with God's name is related, though σφραγίς is not used in connection with it; cf. among others Gen 4:15; Exod 28:36; Isa 44:5; Lev 19:28; Ezek 9:4ff.; CD 19:10-12; esp. *Pss. Sol.* 15:6-9: "For God's mark is on the righteous for their salvation. Famine and sword and death shall be far from the righteous; for they will retreat from the devout like those pursued by famines." Those marked are thereby identified as God's possession, and they stand under his protection (Dölger 55ff.; Dinkler, "Jesu Wort" 85ff.).

4. a) According to 1 Cor 9:2 the church in Corinth is for Paul the *seal* (i.e., legal attestation or attesting sign) of his apostleship. In the face of polemical challenges (cf. 2 Cor 3:2; 11f.) this seal shows him, as it would for any person carrying such a seal, to be authorized and legally empowered.

In Rom 4:9-12 Paul is intent on proving that Abraham is the father of all believers, both uncircumcised and circumcised. In the covenant of Gen 15:6ff. faith is reckoned as righteousness—long before circumcision (17:10ff.). Abraham thus received circumcision—Paul is consciously formulating here: "the sign of circumcision" —"as a *seal* [i.e., attestation/confirmation] of the righteousness of faith reckoned to him while he was still uncircumcised" (Rom 4:11). It is disputed whether "with the word σφραγίς Paul is thinking of baptism and thus interpreting Abraham's circumcision as a proleptic 'seal of the righteousness of faith'" (U. Wilckens, *Rom* [EKKNT] I, 266f., q.v. for information concerning the status of this discussion).

In the somewhat ambiguous metaphor in 2 Tim 2:19

σφραγίς is probably to be understood as a *seal* or *inscription* (cf. Fitzer 948f.; N. Brox, *Die Pastoralbriefe* [RNT] 249; von Lips 100f.). In the face of heretical threats to the Church's faith the author assures his readers: "God's firm foundation stands and bears this *inscription:* 'The Lord knows those who are his' [Num 16:5], and 'Let everyone who names the Lord's name depart from iniquity' [cf. Isa 26:13]." This is hardly to be taken as an allusion to baptism (*contra* V. Hasler, *Die Briefe an Timotheus und Titus* [ZBK] 69f.).

b) 11 of the 13 occurrences of σφραγίς in Revelation concern "the scroll, written within and on the back, sealed with seven *seals,*" in the right hand of the one seated on the throne (5:1). The apocalypse reveals secret and thus sealed knowledge; only the Lamb can disclose it and open the seals (vv. 2, 5, 9). This recalls Roman legal practice, according to which a testament was secured with seven seals (Fitzer 951), though it is altered here: In the interest of portraying a gradual step-by-step revelation of the end events the seals are opened one at a time (6:1, 3, 5, 7, 9, 12; 8:1).

Rev 7:2 and 9:4, with allusions to Ezek 9:4ff. and *Pss. Sol.* 15:6-9 (→ 3), speak of the "*seal* of the living God" with which the other angel "seals the servants of our God on their foreheads," twelve thousand from each of the twelve tribes, as protection against the four angels sent for destruction at the judgment of the end time. This "*seal* of God" is God's name and/or Christ's name (14:1; 3:12; 22:4); it is a sign of possession and protection (analogous to the tattooing of slaves or sealing in the mystery cults). Consistent with this, those who are subservient to the world carry the name and mark of the beast on their foreheads or hands (13:16; 14:9; 20:4; cf. W. Bousset, *Rev* [KEK] 281; Dölger 55ff.; Dinkler, "Jesu Wort" 92f.).

T. Schramm

σφυδρόν, οῦ, τό *sphydron* ankle*

Acts 3:7: ἐστερεώθησαν . . . τὰ σφυδρά, "the [feet and] *ankles* [of the lame man] were made strong"; v.l. τὰ σφυρά, "the heels/ankles."

σφυρόν, οῦ, τό *sphyron* heal, ankle
Acts 3:7 ℵ² B² D E Ψ Koine in place of → σφυδρόν.

σχεδόν *schedon* almost, nearly*

In the NT always with πᾶς: Acts 13:44; 19:26; Heb 9:22.

σχῆμα, ατος, τό *schēma* form, appearance, deportment*

1. Occurrences in the NT — 2. Phil 2:7 — 3. 1 Cor 7:31

Lit.: BAGD s.v. — J. F. COLLANGE, *Phil* (Eng. tr., 1979) 103f. 93. — CREMER / KÖGEL 465-67. — J. GNILKA, *Phil* (HTKNT, 1968) 121. — E. KÄSEMANN, "A Critical Analysis of Philippians 2:5-11," *JTC* 5 (1968) 45-88. — J. B. LIGHTFOOT, *Phil* ([12]1913) 127-33. — E. LOHMEYER, *Kyrios Jesus. Eine Untersuchung zu Phil 2:5-11* ([2]1961) 37f. — R. P. MARTIN, *Carmen Christi. Philippians ii.5-11 in Recent Interpretation and in the Setting of Early Christian Worship* (SNTSMS 4, 1967) 207. — *PGL* s.v. — J. SCHNEIDER, *TDNT* VII, 954-58.

1. Σχῆμα occurs twice in the NT: 1 Cor 7:31 and Phil 2:7.

2. In the pre-Pauline Christ-hymn in Phil 2:6-11 the earthly existence of the incarnate Son of God is described in three participial clauses (vv. 7f.: μορφὴν δούλου λαβών /ἐν ὁμοιώματι ἀνθρώπων γενόμενος /σχήματι εὑρεθεὶς ὡς ἄνθρωπος), each of which in its own way (→ μορφή [2]; ὁμοίωμα [3.a]) expresses hymnically the reality of Christ's incarnation. Σχῆμα here refers to the *(external) appearance* of the incarnate (i.e., human) Son of God.

The distinction in meaning between μορφή and σχῆμα should not be fixed to any extreme contrast (e.g., "intrinsic being" vs. "outward appearance," "essence" vs. "accidence" [Lightfoot 133], "nature" vs. "history" [Lohmeyer]). Σχῆμα refers neither to purely external appearance in contrast to essential nature (Lightfoot 133: "the externals of the human nature") nor to "the essence of the particular historical activity of a person" in contrast to his natural features (Lohmeyer 38). It refers, rather, to the specific appearance unique to one person and unalterably associated with him. Σχήματι εὑρεθεὶς ὡς ἄνθρωπος thus means: *"With respect to his appearance* he was found to be a man." Σχήματι here is understood as dat. of respect (BDF §197; Moulton, *Grammar* III, 220).

3. In 1 Cor 7:31 the apostle places the ethical behavior of Christians under the eschatological reservation. He argues from the perspective of the immediately anticipated end of the world to justify saying: παράγει γὰρ τὸ σχῆμα τοῦ κόσμου τούτου, "the world *in its present form*" (BAGD) "is passing away." Hence Christians should make use of this world and its possibilities only as an interim and should encounter it only with the attitude of ὡς μή. When the world in its specific present form passes away, there is no essence remaining at its core or anything of that nature. According to Paul's apocalyptic expectations concerning the end one must reckon with the world's total destruction; τὸ σχῆμα τοῦ κόσμου τούτου thus means the present and visible world as a whole (so also Käsemann 69).   W. Pöhlmann

σχίζω *schizō* split, tear (vb.)*
σχίσμα, ατος, τό *schisma* rip, tear; division, dissension*

1. Occurrences in the NT — 2. Literal usage — 3. Fig. usage

Lit.: BAGD s.v. — C. MAURER, *TDNT* VII, 959-64. — M. MEINERTZ, "Σχίσμα und αἵρεσις im NT," *BZ* 1 (1957) 114-18.

1. The vb. occurs 11 times in the NT (also in the LXX, e.g., Exod 14:21, referring to water), in all four Gospels and in Acts. The noun (which does not occur in the LXX, which has σχισμή 3 times) occurs in Mark 2:21 par. Matt 9:16 and 3 times each (and with the same meaning, → 3) in John and 1 Corinthians.

2. In their literal meanings these words refer both to natural and supernatural events.

a) In regard to the former reference is made to ordinary woven or sewn objects that should not be torn or cut apart, i.e., damaged. According to John 19:24 the soldiers would rather "not *tear*" Jesus' "seamless tunic" (v. 23) and so "cast lots for it" (in accord with the citation from Ps 21:19 LXX). According to 21:11 the disciples catch 153 fish; "and the net *was not torn* (ἐσχίσθη) even though there were so many." In Mark 2:21 par. Matt 9:16 Jesus explains the difference between his disciples' fasting and that of John the Baptist's disciples by pointing out the incompatibility of the old situation with the new; his parable shows that a piece of unshrunk cloth (Luke 5:36a: a piece *cut* from a new garment) is incompatible with an old garment: "A worse *tear*" would result (Mark par. Matthew), quite aside from the fact that the new garment would be *torn,* and the two pieces would not match, as Luke emphasizes (Luke 5:36b), already thinking of the distinction between synagogue and Church.

b) In regard to supernatural events reference is made not to secular objects of daily use but to heaven, earth, and the temple, the rending of which serve to reveal the significance of Jesus' person or his death. At his baptism he sees "the heavens *torn open*" (Mark 1:10; par. Matthew/Luke: ἀνοίγω; cf. Isa 63:19 [MT: *qāraʿ*; LXX: ἀνοίγω]). The opening of (the vault of) heaven precedes a divine epiphany (cf. 3 Macc 6:18; *Jos. As.* 14:2; see R. Pesch, *Mark* [HTKNT] I, 90f.)—"the Spirit descends upon him like a dove" and "a voice comes from heaven" saying: "You are my Son. . . ."

Mark 15:38 describes the direct results of Jesus' death (in v. 37): "And the curtain of the temple *was torn* in two (ἐσχίσθη εἰς δύο) from top to bottom." This is followed by the declaration of the Roman centurion. The sign in v. 38 can be interpreted negatively (for the temple and Israel) or positively (for the Gentiles and the world). Comparison with 1:10 shows that in both instances God's dwelling opens, and a confession or declaration concerning the Son of God follows, at the beginning of Mark from heaven itself and at the end—at the opening of the temple—from the mouth of a Gentile. Without this paradox the tearing of the curtain of the temple (Luke 23:45) is just an anticipatory sign of Jesus' death, along with the solar eclipse (v. 44; cf. Joel 3:3f.); in Matt 27:51 in any case it is one of its direct effects, though it occurs with the earthquake (v. 51b), during which rocks *are split* (v. 51c), as if creation were being torn asunder.

3. Fig. usage includes the reference to the division or polarization generated among the Jews by Jesus' person (σχίσμα: John 7:43; 9:16; 10:19), to the opposing parties generated by Paul and Barnabas' activity in Iconium and by Paul's defense before the Sanhedrin (ἐσχίσθη τὸ πλῆθος: Acts 14:4; 23:7), to dissension in the Corinthian church, with groups (1 Cor 1:10) claiming different sources of authority (v. 12; on the kind and number of these "parties" see H. Conzelmann, *1 Cor* [Hermeneia] 33f.), to lack of unity concerning the eucharist (11:18, with αἱρέσεις in v. 19), and to disunity among charismatics (12:25).   W. Radl

σχίσμα, ατος, τό *schisma* rip, tear; division, dissension
→ σχίζω.

σχοινίον, ου, τό *schoinion* cord (made of rushes), rope, line*

John 2:15: Jesus made a whip "of cords" (ἐκ σχοινίων); Acts 27:32: τὰ σχοινία τῆς σκάφης, "the boat's *ropes/mooring ropes*." T. Drew-Bear, *Glotta* 50 (1972) 223f.

σχολάζω *scholazō* have time for, devote oneself to; stand empty, be unused*

Matt 12:44, of a house: εὑρίσκει σχολάζοντα, "he [the unclean spirit] finds it *empty/unoccupied*"; Luke 11:25 v.l. 1 Cor 7:5: σχολάζω τῇ προσευχῇ, "*devote oneself* to prayer" (cf. Ign. *Pol.* 1:3: προσευχαῖς; 7:3: θεῷ; Lucian *Macr.* 4; *VH* ii.15: φιλοσοφίᾳ . . .). Σχολάζω used absolutely or with inf., gen., or prep. (ἀπό) refers to passivity or rest (of things or persons), but with dat. (or prep., πρός and others) it refers to devotion to and free time (for things or persons); over against the element of leisure that of intensive and undivided devotion predominates (cf. οὐ μέλλω θεῷ σχολάζειν, εἰ μὴ πρότερον ἀπαρτίσω τὸν υἱόν μου, Preisigke, *Sammelbuch* I, 4515).

σχολή, ῆς, ἡ *scholē* school, place of learning*

According to Acts 19:9 Paul went after his expulsion from the synagogue in Ephesus to the σχολὴ Τυράννου, probably a kind of *auditorium* or *instruction hall,* not a private synagogue or assembly room of a Gentile cultic group (cf. αἱ σχολαὶ τῶν φιλοσόφων, Plutarch *Per.* 35;

Rect. Rat. 12 [*Moralia* 43F]; σχολὴν ἔχειν, Epictetus *Diss.* iii.21.11). Billerbeck II, 751; E. Haenchen, *Acts* (Eng. tr., 1971) ad loc.

σῴζω *sōzō* rescue, save, preserve, help*

1. Occurrences in the NT — 2. Usage — a) Mortal danger and death — b) Disease and possession — c) Guilt (sin) and alienation from God — d) Eternal ruin — 3. Characteristic use — a) Paul — b) Luke

Lit.: → σωτήρ and see also: F. BOVON, "Le salut dans les écrits de Luc," *RTP* 23 (1973) 296-307. — C. BROWN, *DNTT* III, 205-13. — G. DAUTZENBERG, *Sein Leben bewahren* (1966) 51-67, 154-68. — J. DÍAZ Y DÍAZ, *Die Wortgruppe* σῴζειν, σωτηρία, σωτήρ in den neutestamentlichen Briefen (Diss. Heidelberg, 1965) 5-73. — A. GEORGE, "Le vocabulaire de salut," *idem, Études sur l'oeuvre de Luc* (1978) 307-20. S. LYONNET and L. SABOURIN, *Sin, Redemption, and Sacrifice* (1970) 63-78. — D. MEEKS et al., *DBSup* XI, 486-740. — J. I. PACKER, "The Way of Salvation," *Bibliotheca Sacra* 129 (1972) 195-205, 291-306. — J. SCHNEIDER, *DNTT* III, 214-16. — W. SCHRAGE, "Heil und Heilung im NT," *EvT* 46 (1986) 197-214. — SPICQ, *Notes* Suppl. 629-36. — F. STOLZ, *THAT* I, 785-90. — B. H. THROCKMORTON, "Σῴζειν, σωτηρία in Luke-Acts," *SE* VI (1973) 515-26. — W. C. VAN UNNIK, "L'usage de σῴζειν 'sauver' et des dérivés dans les évangiles synoptiques," *idem, Sparsa Collecta* (1973) I, 16-34. — W. WAGNER, "Über ΣΩZEIN und seine Derivate im NT," *ZNW* 6 (1905) 205-35. — K. WURM, *Rechtfertigung und Heil. Eine Untersuchung zur Theologie des Lukas unter dem Aspekt "Lukas und Paulus"* (Diss. Heidelberg, 1978) 127-39.

1. The LXX usually uses this frequently occurring vb. to render *yāša'*. It occurs 106 times in the NT and is distributed fairly evenly in the various writings. It does, however, occur only 6 times in John (compared to 15 in Mark, including 16:16), and not at all in 1–3 John, Revelation, or some of the other letters (Galatians, Philippians, Philemon, Colossians, 2 Peter).

2. In the NT the initiator of saving and helping action is often God, usually mentioned only indirectly through the divine passive (cf., however, 1 Cor 1:21; 2 Tim 1:9; 4:18; Titus 3:5; Jas 4:12), or Jesus, in isolated instances also Paul (Rom 11:14; 1 Cor 9:22; 10:33; 1 Thess 2:16), another Christian (general in Jas 5:20; one's spouse in 1 Cor 7:16 bis; Timothy in 1 Tim 4:16), or the Church (Jude 23). Subjects of σῴζω also include faith itself (→ 2.b, c; also Jas 2:14; cf. Eph 2:8) or "the prayer of faith" (Jas 5:15: ἡ εὐχὴ τῆς πίστεως), the received word (1:21), and baptism (1 Pet 3:21). Those who are said to be saved are, in addition to other individual persons (→ esp. 2.a, b), also Jesus himself (→ 2.a) and his disciples, Israel (Rom 9:27; 11:14, 26; Jude 5; the Jews in John 5:34), Gentiles (e.g., 1 Thess 2:16), all people (e.g., 1 Tim 2:4), and "the world" (John 3:17; 12:47). That from which one is saved (ἀπό in Matt 1:21; Acts 2:40; Rom 5:9; ἐκ in John 12:27; Heb 5:7; Jas 5:20; Jude 23) include mortal

danger, death, disease, possession, sin and alienation from God, and eternal ruin.

a) Acts 27:20, 31 speaks of rescue from disaster at sea: Paul is ultimately responsible for all *being saved* (27:44, with διασῴζω; cf. v. 43; 28:1, 4). Jesus' disciples and Peter, despite the presence of their "Lord," fear perishing in the storm on the sea and so cry out for his saving help: κύριε, σῶσον (Matt 8:25; 14:30)—a cry that appears clearly stylized when compared with Mark 4:38. Jesus himself, in the face of death, asks the "Father" for deliverance "from this hour" (John 12:27). It is God "who is able to *save/preserve* him from death (ἐκ θανάτου, Heb 5:7)," though certainly in a manner different from that thought of by those who mock him at the cross. They challenge him ironically as the one who would destroy and rebuild the temple (Mark 15:30 par. Matt 27:40), as the Son of God (Matt 27:40), God's anointed, the king of the Jews, and the Messiah (Luke 23:35, 37, 39), to *save* himself (and those crucified with him: v. 39). They remind Jesus of the earlier power through which he *saved* others, and mock him because he now "cannot *save* himself" (Mark 15:31 par. Matt 27:42; cf. Luke 23:35), and because Elijah does not "come and *save* him" (Matt 27:49).

The apocalyptic idea of the terrible tribulations and disasters of the end time foresees a shortening of that time, without which no one *would be saved/would survive* (Mark 13:20 par. Matt 24:22). Deliverance from mortal danger finally also includes liberation "from the land of Egypt" (Jude 5); this is juxtaposed with the destruction of those Israelites who did not believe, the condemnation of the guilty angels, and the destruction of Sodom and Gomorrah (vv. 5-7). Only Luke 8:50 uses σῴζω in connection with raising of the dead. Admittedly the girl in the story died only a short time before, and according to Jesus' own words was merely sleeping (v. 52; cf. John 11:11f.); in any case, he set out "in order to *save* her life" (Mark 5:23: ἵνα σωθῇ καὶ ζήσῃ).

b) In the Gospels it is usually the sick who experience Jesus' help described by σῴζω. In the story of the dying girl Jesus also encounters a woman suffering from a flow of blood for twelve years. She is confident that if she merely touches Jesus' garment she *will be healed* (σωθή- σομαι: Mark 5:28 par. Matt 9:21; Luke omits the sentence). Indeed, she *is healed* in this way—as are many others later (Mark 6:56: ἐσῴζοντο)—and is *"made well* from that hour on"* (Matt 9:22: ἐσώθη) because of her faith. "Your faith *has made you well*," Jesus says to her (Mark 5:34 par. Matt 9:22/Luke 8:48). And he adds: "Go in peace" (Mark 5:34 par. Luke 8:48). This shows that Jesus' σῴζειν effects not only physical *healing,* but well-being in a broader sense. This is also the case in the healing of the blind man, who follows Jesus, and of the leper, who gratefully returns; to them, too, Jesus speaks

(formulaic) words concerning their own saving faith (Mark 10:52 par. Luke 18:42 or Luke 17:19). It is thus understandable that healings (from illness) can be described with σῴζω, just as can the deliverance of a possessed person from his demons (Luke 8:36).

Mark 3:1-6 par. Luke 6:6-11 sets a different accent in its description of the healing of the withered hand. Here, in a dispute setting, the conflict concerning the sabbath commandment is reduced to whether one is allowed "to *save* a person or to kill" on the sabbath, i.e., to *help* him or to allow him to die (v. 4 par. Luke 6:9; cf. Dautzenberg 156).

If one considers these healings in the Synoptics with those in Acts by Peter and Paul (4:9; 14:9), one sees that, except for the summary report in Mark 6:56, σῴζειν always reestablishes a person's integrity by removing from him chronic impairment: blood flow, blindness, leprosy, lameness, or possession (cf. in contrast Matt 8:7, 8 par. Luke 7:3, 7 with θεραπεύω/διασῴζω or ἰάομαι). Things stand a bit differently in John 11:12 and Jas 5:15.

c) Sin has profoundly alienated human beings from their own creaturely essence and thus also from the Creator. Just as he frees the individual from debt (Luke 7:41f., 48), thus *saving* him (v. 50), so also does "God with us" (Matt 1:23) *save* the entire people "from their sins" (v. 21). Christ "came into the world to *save* sinners" (1 Tim 1:15), i.e., to seek those alienated from God and bring them home (Luke 19:10; cf. 15:3-7, 8-10, 24, 32). Deliverance in the sense of homecoming also means change and conversion. This is Jesus' goal for his Jewish listeners (John 5:34) and Paul's hope for Israel (Rom 9:27; 11:14, 26).

As the "apostle to the Gentiles" (11:13f.) Paul works toward what he sees as his principal task, namely, "by all means to *save* some" (ἵνα πάντως τινὰς σώσω, 1 Cor 9:22 [cf. Rom 11:14]). The context indicates that Paul refers here (and similarly in 10:33) not to eternal salvation, but rather to conversion to faith in Christ: In 9:19-23 Paul shows how he seeks to "win" (κερδαίνω: vv. 19, 20 bis, 21, 22) both Jews and Gentiles, both strong and weak. Such "saving" is made possible not only by missionary proclamation (1 Thess 2:16), but also by marriage of a nonbeliever with a believer (1 Cor 7:16 bis).

The post-Pauline Epistles also speak of present salvation within faith. According to 1 Tim 2:4 (cf. John 10:9) σωθῆναι refers to knowledge of the truth, and σῴζω is used in the aor. in 2 Tim 1:9 and Titus 3:5. Whereas in Paul's letters God as the ultimate initator is concealed behind pass. forms, these three post-Pauline references speak expressly of God's intention or deed. Saving takes place "by grace" (pf. pass. partc. in Eph 2:5, 8), concretely in purifying baptism (Titus 3:5), and in the new ark (1 Pet 3:21).

Luke equates σωθῆναι and baptism with believing

acceptance of the word (Luke 8:12); he mentions both together in Acts 2:40, 41; 11:14, 15f. (with 10:47f.); 16:30, 31-33. Deliverance "from this crooked generation" (2:40) consists according to 2:47 of acceptance of those who "let themselves be saved" (cf. imv. in 2:40) into the new community. In 15:1, 11, too, the dispute—at least initially—focuses on whether circumcision or grace establishes membership in the Church. In 2:21 and 4:12, on the other hand, that ultimate deliverance (in the name of Jesus) resulting from present salvation stands in the foreground.

d) Future eternal salvation by and with God is clearly the reference where σωθῆναι is described as deliverance "into the kingdom of heaven" (2 Tim 4:18) or as "entry into the kingdom of God" (Mark 10:25, 26 par. Matt 19:24, 25/Luke 18:25, 26; cf. Luke 13:23; Mark 16:16). This is also the case where σῴζω is used in the context of judgment (Rom 5:9, 10; 1 Cor 3:15; 5:5; Heb 7:25; Jas 4:12; 1 Pet 4:18), expresses deliverance from "fire" (Jude 23) or rescue of the ψυχή from death (Jas 1:21; 5:20), or is the opposite of total "destruction" (1 Cor 1:18, 21; 2 Cor 2:15; 2 Thess 2:10). The almost formulaic contrast of σῴζω and ἀπόλλυμι (cf. also Matt 8:25; Luke 6:9; 19:10; Jas 4:12) also characterizes this saying by Jesus: "Whoever gives up his life" will gain salvation beyond death—he will "*save* (σῴζω) it"; but "whoever would *save* (σῴζω) his life will lose it" (Mark 8:35 bis par. Matt 16:25/Luke 9:24 bis; cf. Mark 8:36 par.: κερδαίνω—ζημιόομαι). Concerning steadfastness in faith, "he who endures to the end," even to death, "will be *saved*," i.e., eternally rewarded (Mark 13:13 par. Matt 24:13 and 10:22; cf. Luke 21:19: κτήσασθε τὰς ψυχὰς ὑμῶν, "you will gain your lives"). On the basis of certain prerequisites σῴζω in Rom 10:9, 13; 1 Tim 2:15 promises salvation. The pres. form in 1 Cor 15:2 probably also refers to future salvation, since it apparently views in one's (present) steadfastness regarding the gospel the conditions for being saved (in the future).

3. a) It is characteristic of Paul's use of σῴζω that the vb. refers either to present missionary efforts by the apostle or other Christians or to God's future decision. In regard to the former it concerns membership in the Church and thus in Christ; in regard to the latter it concerns one's eternal destiny, salvation with God. Deliverance can thus mean the same thing as justification and reconciliation; Paul can also, however, juxtapose these, as shown by Rom 5:9, 10: δικαιωθέντες νῦν σωθησόμεθα and καταλλαγέντες — σωθησόμεθα ἐν τῇ ζωῇ αὐτοῦ. Ultimate deliverance, however, is given only in judgment (1 Cor 3:15; 5:5); in faith and baptism, however, a person can already participate in divine salvation: According to Rom 8:24 we "*are saved* in hope (τῇ ἐλπίδι ἐσώθημεν)": Through Christ God has ended our hopeless

condition (cf. 1 Thess 4:13) and in Christ has given us life in hope.

b) Luke demonstrates the enormous range of meaning of σῴζω. He uses it of rescue from death, i.e., from mortal danger (Luke 23:35, 37, 39; Acts 27:20, 31) or from death that has already occurred (Luke 8:50), of the fundamental element of help in Jesus' healing deeds (6:9; 8:48; 17:19; 18:42; 23:35) and in those of the apostles (Acts 4:9; 14:9), including the liberation of a possessed person (Luke 8:36). He also uses it of forgiveness of particular sinners (7:50; 19:10) and of collective forgiveness for the people (Acts 2:40). The goal of activity described by σῴζω is salvation within the Church mediated by faith and baptism, which includes the mediation of the Spirit (2:38) and elicits rejoicing (2:46; 16:34; → ἀγαλλιάω), as well as eternal life itself (Luke 9:24 bis; 13:23; 18:26). On the whole one can say that with the exception of this latter case deliverance (saving) and salvation according to Luke occur—in various ways— in the activity of Jesus and his Church. Indeed, Luke even associates what both he and the prophets understand as ultimate deliverance in "the name of the Lord" (Acts 2:21; cf. 4:12) with the present time of the Church, and does so by referring the appropriate citation from Joel (3:5) as an eschatological promise to the sending of the Spirit at Pentecost (Acts 2:16f.).

W. Radl

σῶμα, ατος, τό *sōma* body

1. Meaning in Greek — 2. OT and early Judaism — 3. NT (except Paul) — 4. Σῶμα as corporeality — 5. Resurrection of the σῶμα — 6. "Body of Christ" as the crucifixion body, the eucharistic offering, and the Church — 7. Pre-Pauline analogies — 8. Body of Christ and people of God — 9. Expansion of the term in Colossians and Ephesians — 10. Σῶμα in Gnosticism

Lit.: G. BOF, "Il σῶμα quale principio della sessualità in Paolo," *BeO* 19 (1977) 69-76. — CONZELMANN, *Theology* 176-98. — B. DAINES, "Paul's Use of the Analogy of the Body of Christ," *EvQ* 50 (1978) 71-78. — G. DALMAN, *Jesus-Jeshua: Studies in the Gospels* (1929) 141-45. — E. E. ELLIS, "*Sōma* in First Corinthians," *Int* 44 (1990) 132-44. — J. ERNST, *Pleroma und Pleroma Christi* (BU 5, 1970), esp. 154-90. — K. M. FISCHER, *Tendenz und Absicht des Epheserbriefs* (FRLANT 111, 1973) 48-78. — J. GNILKA, *Col* (HTKNT, 1980) 67-70, 128-34, 148, 152f., 167f. — R. H. GUNDRY, *Sōma in Biblical Theology, with Emphasis on Pauline Anthropology* (SNTSMS 29, 1976). — F. HAHN, K. KERTELGE, and R. SCHNACKENBURG, *Einheit der Kirche* (1979), esp. 35-46, 63-67, 73-78, 98-108. — D. J. HARRINGTON, *God's People in Christ* (1980). — S. HEINE, *Leibhafter Glaube. Ein Beitrag zum Verständnis der theologischen Konzeption des Paulus* (1976). — A. E. HILL, "The Temple of Asclepius: An Alternative Source for Paul's *Body* Theology?" *JBL* 99 (1980) 437-39. — E. KÄSEMANN, "Aspekte der Kirche," idem, *Kirchliche Konflikte* (1982) I, 7-36, esp. 8-12. — idem,

"The Theological Problem Presented by the Motif of the Body of Christ," *idem, Perspectives on Paul* (1971) 102-21. — G. W. KNIGHT, "The Church of the NT," *Presbyterion* 3 (1977) 30-36. — E. LOHSE, "Christusherrschaft und Kirche im Kolosserbrief," *idem, Einheit des NT* (²1976) 263-66. — *idem, Grundriß der neutestamentlichen Theologie* (²1979) 88f., 101-3. — G. LUEDEMANN, *Paul, Apostle to the Gentiles* (1984) 243f. — U. LUZ, *Das Geschichtsverständnis des Paulus* (BEvT 49, 1968) 212f. — W. A. MEEKS, "In One Body," FS Dahl 201-21. — P. MÜLLER, *Der Soma-Begriff bei Paulus* (1988). — R. PESCH, *Das Abendmahl und Jesu Todesverständnis* (QD 80, 1978) 190-93. — L. RAMAROSON, " 'L'Église, Corps du Christ' dans les écrits pauliniens," *ScEs* 30 (1978) 129-41. — B. R. REICHENBACH, "Resurrection of the Body, Re-Creation, and Interim Existence," *JTSA* 21 (1977) 33-42. — H. W. ROBINSON, "The Hebrew Conception of Corporate Personality," *Werden und Wesen des AT* (BZAW 66, ed. J. Hempel; 1936) 49-62. — J. A. T. ROBINSON, *The Body* (²1977). — SCHELKLE, *Theology* IV, 29-32, 160f. — H. SCHLIER, "Fragmente über die Taufe," Schlier IV, 134-50, esp. 142-50. — *idem, Grundzüge einer paulinischen Theologie* (1978) 97-106, 194-200. — *idem,* "Über das Prinzip der kirchlichen Einheit im NT," Schlier IV, 179-200. — *idem,* "Über den Heiligen Geist nach dem NT," Schlier IV, 151-64, esp. 157f. — R. SCHNACKENBURG, *Eph* (Eng. tr., 1991), esp. 298-302. — H.-H. SCHREY, *TRE* XX, 638-43. — E. SCHWEIZER, *Col* (Eng. tr., 1982) 163f., 182-86, 262f. — *idem,* "Die Leiblichkeit des Menschen. Leben—Tod—Auferstehung," *idem, Beiträge zur Theologie des NT* (1970) 165-82. — *idem, TDNT* VII, 1024-94. — H.-F. WEISS, " 'Volk Gottes' und 'Leib Christi,' " *TLZ* 102 (1977) 411-20. — U. WILCKENS, "Eucharistie und Einheit der Kirche," *KD* 25 (1979) 73-77. — G. S. WORGUL, "People of God, Body of Christ: Pauline Ecclesiological Contrasts," *BTB* 12 (1982) 24-28. — J. A. ZIESLER, "Σῶμα in the Septuagint," *NovT* 25 (1983) 133-45. — For further bibliography see *TWNT* X, 1276-78.

1. Σῶμα is a quintessentially Greek term. In Homer it designates only "corpse." The Greeks did not differentiate linguistically between "body," i.e., visible matter pertaining to a particular entity (e.g., of animate or inanimate beings), and "body" as the vessel of the (human) soul with its attendant implications of feelings, sentiments, and life in its nonphysical aspects. Σῶμα can thus refer to a celestial body or any other inanimate object, and then later to a slave, and not merely to the animal or human body as vessel of a spirit. Thus Plato and his school could understand the body as that which falls away with death and liberates the soul, as the soul's tomb (*Grg.* 493a), its prison (*Cra.* 400b, c), and its dead shell (*Phdr.* 250c; *Phd.* 66b). Aristotle viewed the body as the material from which the soul fashions the human being as its work of art (*De An.* ii.1-2.412a19ff.); the Stoics, following Aristotle, conceived the soul in a quite modern fashion as bodily, and human beings accordingly as a unity of body and soul (Zeno Eleaticus *Frag.* 135 and *passim*). A "good and beautiful" life and—as its climax—an equally beautiful death bring this divine work of art to completion. Here the human being in particular is an individual, and one speaks of a city with ten thousand "bodies" the way later generations would speak of ten thousand "souls."

"Body" can also be used of an ordered whole, e.g., that of a people, an army, or a herd. In this sense the cosmos itself is a divinely ordered and governed body whose head is Zeus, heaven, the Spirit, or perhaps even the Logos (Cornutus *Theol. Graec.*

20; Orphica *Frag.* 21a; Diodorus Siculus i.11.5f.; Philo *Som.* i.144; *Quaest. Ex.* ii.117, if this is not a Christian interpolation). Life is then unity with nature, and death a natural completion. This, too, the Stoics incorporated into their own thought. Democritus (*Frag.* 34) already conceived the human body as a microcosm; after all, the same Greek words refer respectively to wind and breath, to the rounded vault of heaven and the skull, to the celestial supports and the cervical vertebra, and to the vault of heaven and the palate.

2. The OT views this complex completely differently and has no word for "body" in this sense. The human being does not *have* flesh and soul; rather, a person *is* both, transitory and mortal and yet alive (cf. also E. Jacob, *TDNT* IX, 622-31). Only as such a unity does a person exist at all; thus it is quite alien to the OT to distinguish between body and soul in the fashion of Plato (→ 1). Neither does it make sense to separate out the individual person with his or her individual body from the whole of the people (as does Aristotle [→ 1]). When a person is singled out, this results from God's call to service for the people, not from any physical singularity. From this perspective it is virtually impossible to view the human being as does Democritus (→ 1) —as a self-contained work of art, as a world unto itself. This is why death can be conceived neither as the liberation of the soul, nor as the completion of a beautiful life, nor as a purely natural end, all of which softens death's hard edges. Only God is stronger than death, though there is still no talk of life after death: "My flesh and my heart may fail, but God is my rock forever" (Ps 73:26).

Aramaic popular usage at the time of Jesus picked up the word *gûpâ* (used biblically in one instance of "corpse," 1 Chr 10:12), probably under Greek influence, to refer to "body" also in the sense of the ego, the person (cf. Billerbeck II, 492), of the whole or the torso as opposed to the members or head (Billerbeck IV, 63 [*m. Pesaḥ.* 10:3]; III, 446 [*t. Taʿan* 2:5]), or even in the sense of the material form in contrast to the soul (Billerbeck I, 654f. [*Lev. Rab.* 34] and *passim*); cf. also *gešēm*, body, in Dan 4:30.

3. The NT was written by Israelites, or at least by persons familiar with Israel's Bible. The non-Pauline writings speak often of the dead body (or of the body destined for death, Mark 14:8). This body can, however, be raised (Matt 27:52; Acts 9:40; John 2:21) and is thus the vessel of the person, not material separate from it. As in Greek and Aramaic, it represents the whole over against the parts (Matt 5:29f.; 6:22f.; Jas 3:2f., 6); the body and soul (i.e., the vital power maintained by eating and drinking) are the two inseparable aspects of the human being (Matt 6:25). The body is the actual ego, or person, from which a member can be separated, but which a member can also influence. The assertion that people can kill only the (earthly) body does not presuppose a soul that survives outside the body; rather, it presupposes God, who governs body *and* soul beyond death as well (Matt 10:28).

At the eucharist the statement "this is my *body*" was originally separated from the reference to the cup by the whole meal itself (so also at Jewish banquets or the

Passover meal, and still in 1 Cor 11:25a). The intended meaning was presumably "this is my person—the guarantee of my actual presence" (→ 2). The reference to the cup, which probably originally read "this is the [new?] covenant in my blood" (1 Cor 11:25), was gradually assimilated to the first statement ("this is my blood," Mark 14:24). Otherwise "flesh," not "body," would have to appear next to "blood" ("body" normally is never used together with "blood"); also, liturgical development follows increasingly parallel assimilation, not the reverse—modern texts are more strongly harmonized than any NT text. The form of Mark 14:24 then placed the otherwise rare concept of the sacrifice of the body (and blood) into the foreground (Heb 10:5, 10; 1 Pet 2:24). In a way alien to the Greek (4 Macc 10:4; 13:13; *1 Enoch* 108:8f.; Josephus *B.J.* vii.352-55; cf. Wis 9:15), this meant the complete sacrifice of one's self, and not just of some external husk that otherwise burdens the soul.

4. Paul, too, can speak of the sacrifice of the body, though he is not thinking of death (except in 1 Cor 13:3), but rather of putting one's body at the disposal of the Lord here on earth. This is appropriate service to God understandable to all (Rom 12:1), just as Paul himself practices in a radical fashion (1 Cor 9:27). The body—not the soul—is the temple of the Holy Spirit (1 Cor 6:19f.). It is on this body, on "mortal flesh," that Jesus' cross manifests itself, which it does so concretely that one can see the scars (probably from scourging; 2 Cor 4:10f.; Gal 6:17).

Paul emphasizes to the Corinthians the corporeality of life in faith, something for which we all must answer some day (2 Cor 5:10). The body is more than some neutral digestive and reproductive entity (1 Cor 6:13). It always belongs here or there, it is a "[bodily] member of Christ" or "of a prostitute" (v. 15); it always belongs to someone—to sin and death or to Christ (Rom 6:6; 7:24; also 8:13 without the final clause). This shows that the body is the place where the transition from indicative to imperative particularly takes place. Because Christ has purchased it, it can no longer belong to the prostitute. Because God's mercy stands over it, it should be put into service (Rom 12:1). Because through baptism we are dead to sin and alive to God, sin should no longer rule in our "mortal bodies" (Rom 6:11f. = in "us," v. 13). Paul conceives this unity of the body with Christ so strongly that not only does "the body belong to the Lord" but "the Lord belongs to the body" (1 Cor 6:13).

5. The significance of the resurrection of the "body" thus becomes understandable (1 Cor 15:35-44). The body, from head to foot, is all of my own person and distinguishes it from others. This includes what Luke 10:20 (cf. Isa 43:1) expresses in its reference to "name": Resurrection concerns "me" and is not a dissolution of my person into some general or collective element. "We," "our mortal bodies," are raised (1 Cor 6:14; Rom 8:11).

The other aspect, however, is decisive. With its eyes, ears, hands, and feet, the body is a means of communication opening me to others. As a body, I am thus indissolubly bound to Christ. This is why it is precisely the body that is raised, though admittedly such that it is transfigured and is no longer "flesh and blood." No imagery can adequately express this total otherness, so Paul not only distinguishes between seed and plant, human being and animal, earthly and celestial, but also refers to the infinite distinctions among plants, animals, and celestial bodies. What finally touches on the reality of this transformation is only the assertion that it is no longer the "soul" but rather the "Spirit" of God that creates, molds, and defines the new body (1 Cor 15:35-44, 50f.; Phil 3:21). Thus Paul can say that we will move from our (earthly) body, not into "nakedness," into a soul liberated from material substance, but rather into new "clothing," which is still a bodily housing for us (2 Cor 5:1-3, 8). In 2 Cor 12:2f. Paul reckons with the possibility of a person leaving the body while being carried away to the "third heaven"; it is unimportant to him whether it happened just that way. In any case, the life of resurrection is bodily, a life in fellowship with the Lord and one's fellow Christians established already before death itself, a fellowship finding its fulfillment in an inconceivable openness to the Lord (and to those similarly resurrected?).

6. This implication of church clarifies the term "body of Christ." It is (a) Jesus' body sacrificed on the cross for the community of believers (Rom 7:4; Col 1:22). In the eucharist (b) this "body for you" is bequeathed to that church; the emphasis here, however (as is the case with the blood, which is not equated with the body), is on Jesus' own activity "for you," not on the substance itself (1 Cor 11:24f.). It is manifested in the attendant blessing bequeathing fellowship with Christ and his deed (10:16). Here Paul reverses the liturgical sequence to accommodate it to his own apparently original interpretation: When the bread joins the church itself with Christ's body, which was sacrificed for its people, then they themselves become (c) *one* body, namely, the body of Christ. As 10:1-13 and 15:29 show, the Corinthians were sacramentalists and did indeed believe this. They forgot, however, that this is a reality of event, not of substance—indeed of a relationship, not of material; in short, it is a reality of life, not of inert physical disposition, and is a reality intent on shaping the church itself and on establishing Christ's rule. Hence according to 11:27, those who celebrate the eucharist "in an unworthy manner" (i.e., such that they eat and drink what was intended for the poorest members of the church, so that the latter must be fed with the sacrament alone, vv. 21, 33), by transgressing

against their brothers and sisters also transgress against him who has sacrificed "body and blood" for them. The similarly constructed sentence in 8:11f. says the same thing.

7. In what sense is the Church the body of Christ? Various linguistic possibilities made this new concept easier for Paul to express. The Greek understanding of the body as a unified whole (→ 1) created the oft-repeated fable that allegedly hindered the revolution of the workers against the upper classes: The members of the body rebelled against the inactive stomach, only to discover that they perished without it. Paul uses the body in a similar parable (1 Cor 12:14-26), though for him it is more than a metaphor. It is the body of Christ; indeed, Christ himself *is* the body into which all members are baptized (vv. 27, 12f.). The Greek understanding of the cosmic body representing the unity of God and world, as opposed to Gnostic-dualistic alienation, doubtless also played a role (→ 1, 9). It makes it possible to conceive an organic unity not only as a "body" but at the same time as a world permeated by God's providence. Cosmic elements, however, appear first only in Colossians and Ephesians, and the body of Christ is always the Church, never the world.

John 15:1 asserts that Christ is the vine in which the believers live as his branches. In the OT the vine is Israel, conceived in contemporary Judaism as a cosmic quantity extending from heaven to the nether world (*Bib. Ant.* 12:8f., simultaneously conceived as a temple edifice). A basis for this understanding is already found in Ps 79:12 LXX, where the Greek text of v. 16 equates the vine Israel and the Son of man. Behind John 1:51 stands a tradition viewing the Son of man as the new Jacob-Israel. Hence this understanding of Jacob-Israel encompassing the fate of the entire people (*Jub.* 2:23f.; 19:27-29; similarly of Adam: Wis 10:1, 4; 2 Esdr 7:118; *2 Bar.* 54:15, 19; as a cosmic entity: Billerbeck IV, 946f.) could be transferred in a pre-Johannine phase to the Son of man, who determines the life of the church. In John 15 the historical-temporal dimension is admittedly altered into a spatial dimension, just as in the post-Johannine tradition the temporal-future aspects in Christ are almost always spatially present in Christ, indeed in the believers themselves. Paul, too, juxtaposes the temporal understanding of the "present" Jerusalem with the spatial understanding of the Jerusalem "above" (Gal 4:25f.). The assertion concerning the branches living in the vine Christ runs perfectly parallel to that concerning the members living in the body of Christ, except that the eschatological Adam (Heb. "first man" and "humankind") replaces the eschatological Israel (1 Cor 15:22, 45). This is the universal expansion by the apostle to the Gentiles. It resonates in the Qumran belief that Adam's glory will be eschatologically reestablished in the Qumran community (1QS 4:23; CD 3:20; 1QH 17:15; 4QpPs^a 3:1f.).

8. This transposition into the spatial expresses linguistically that for both Paul and John the present connection with Christ through the Spirit is decisive. The Church *is* in Christ *one* person (Gal 3:28), *is* the body of Christ,

and only secondarily also a collection of members (1 Cor 12:27). V. 12 comes close to identifying the Church with the perpetually living Christ (cf. 1:13); the body is thus not formed first only by its constituent parts; the believers are baptized into that body. The linguistically possible tr. "so that it comes to be" or "baptized unto it" is precluded by v. 12. This is also why Paul never speaks of fellowship of God or Christ with the individual, but rather always with the church. Wherever Paul has to speak of the individual (who goes to the prostitute), he strikingly avoids the form "*one* body" (6:16f.). Nonetheless what has already been asserted (→ 6) continues to hold true: The body of Christ always remains grounded in the one-time historical event of the cross. Eph 2:16 does not even make clear whether it is the body on the cross, i.e., Jesus' "blood" and "flesh" (vv. 13f.), or the body identified with the church that reconciles them, so inseparable are the two. Paul can thus also use temporal-historical language to speak of the people of God (admittedly only in citations, Rom 9:25f.; cf. 15:10) or even of Israel (only Gal 6:16, of the church of Jesus, unless this is a reference to a special Jewish Christian group), i.e., of those who "follow in Abraham's footsteps" and are his children, who were always there in some fashion throughout history (Rom 4:9-25; 9:7-13; 11:1-5; Gal 3:6-29).

9. Col 1:18 spoke in the original hymnic form of Christ as the head of the world body (only here does it read "of the body" as opposed to "of his body," cf. → 1). The letter's author, however, refers this to the Church (also in 1:24; 3:15). According to 2:10 (cf. v. 15) and Eph 1:22f. (cf. v. 10), Christ is indeed the head *over* everything, but *for* the Church, which alone is "his body." Yet this identification of Christ as the head (differently in 1 Cor 12:21) also unequivocally emphasizes his counterpart in the Church and thereby also the latter's responsibility. Through its own and the apostle's proclamation it is to grow out into the world itself (Col 1:23; 2:19; Eph 3:10; 4:12, 16). The Christ preached by them is not some mysterious cosmic power, though he is the power of the Spirit in their proclamation, that he might "fill" all things (Eph 1:23; 4:10), e.g., also their marriages. There is indeed talk of the man as the head of the woman (Eph 5:23 as well as 1 Cor 11:3), but Christ as the head, manifested in love of his "body," also characterizes this relationship between men and their wives, who are "their own bodies," or even "themselves" (Eph 5:28). This formulation no longer describes the blood bond, and certainly not any privilege of possession, as does the traditional formulation of the wife as the man's "own flesh" (Sir 25:26; *Life of Adam and Eve* 3), but rather a complete unity.

10. In Gnosticism "body" in the sense of a whole encompassing the redeemed does not appear before Mani (*ca.* A.D. 250) except in writings clearly dependent on Paul (*1 Clem.* 37:5; 38:1;

46:7; Pol. *Phil.* 11:4; *2 Clem.* 14:2-4; Ign. *Smyrn.* 1:2; 11:2; cf. *Eph.* 4:2; 20:1; *Trall.* 11:2; Justin *Dial.* 42:3). The Greek formula referring to the world body appears in *Corp. Herm.* 4:1f.; cf. 2:2-6; 8:3 (11:19); similarly in Hippolytus *Haer.* vii.23.3; 24.1f., referring to Basilides. This can also be used of the unity of the world or of God (Tatian *Or. Graec.* 12:2; Athenagoras *Suppl.* 8:1). The only pre-Manichaean attestations appear to be in Clement of Alexandria *Excerpta ex Theodoto* 42:2ff. and *Interpretation of Knowledge* (*NHC* XI, 1). The former speaks of the "body of Jesus," referring perhaps only to Jesus' earthly body, perhaps to the body surrounded by the "angels" of believers, which for that reason is "of the same essence as the Church." The latter speaks formulaically of the Church as the "single body" (17:15); at the same time, however, it speaks of the head that on the cross draws the members (of the Logos) to itself. Both these examples are clearly Christian-influenced language. Otherwise one encounters only expositions about "members" that are sometimes evil powers, sometimes the believers (*Pistis Sophia* 98:242f.; 101:254; *Thund.* 17:18f., 22; *Odes Sol.* 17:15, where the Savior is the head of his members). This, too, is a relatively sparse collection, and almost certainly Christian-influenced. All this makes it extremely unlikely that Paul's understanding of the "body of Christ" can be traced back to a Gnostic model.

E. Schweizer

σωματικός, 3 *sōmatikos* bodily, corporeal*

1 Tim 4:8: ἡ σωματικὴ γυμνασία, "training *only for the body*" (in contrast to εὐσέβεια). According to Luke 3:22, at Jesus' baptism the Holy Spirit "descended upon him in *bodily* form (σωματικῷ εἴδει, redactional), as a dove" (par. Matt 3:16/Mark 1:10 has only ὡσεὶ [ὡς] περιστερά); Luke is concerned with showing that this descent of the Spirit upon Jesus could be perceived by witnesses (cf. Luke 3:21), whereas according to Mark and Matthew only Jesus saw the Spirit coming from heaven as a dove (just as according to Mark 1:10 only he saw the heavens opened); cf. Acts 2:2-4; → περιστερά 2.

σωματικῶς *sōmatikōs* corporeally, bodily*

Lit.: A. ANWANDER, "Zu Kol 2,9," *BZ* 9 (1965) 278-80. — J. ERNST, *Pleroma und Pleroma Christi* (BU 5, 1970) 94-105. — C. F. D. MOULE, *Col and Phlm* (CGTC, 1957). — E. SCHWEIZER, *TDNT* VII, 1075-77. — SPICQ, *Notes* II, 866.

Col 2:9 speaks of the → πλήρωμα (3.b) τῆς θεότητος, which dwells (κατοικεῖ . . . σωματικῶς, cf. 1:18-20) *bodily*, i.e., in tangible and perceivable form (cf. Philo *Her.* 84; *OGIS* II, no. 664, 17; Pap. Fayûm 21, 10; Pap. Flor. 51, 5) in Christ (as the earthly and exalted one). This refers to God's full and exclusive presence in Christ in the sense of the incarnation and the dominion of the exalted one, which makes every other kind of worship and knowledge of God futile and deceptive (2:8). Exegetical history has also understood σωματικῶς in the sense of "completely" (Jerome), "really, actually" (Augustine), or "essentially, in essence" (Greek fathers)

of the third and fourth centuries; see E. Lohse, *Col and Phlm* [Hermeneia] ad loc.; E. Schweizer, *Col* [Eng. tr., 1982] ad loc.). This already betrays, however, a later Christian agenda. The discussion in Colossians emphasizes the corporeality and concreteness of God's presence in Christ and then also in his → σῶμα (9), the Church.

Σώπατρος, ου *Sōpatros* Sopater*

Σώπατρος, the son of Pyrrhus, a Christian from Beroea, one of the seven companions on Paul's final journey from Greece to Jerusalem (Acts 20:4; v.l. → Σωσίπατρος, cf. Rom 16:21; Sopater is occasionally equated [linguistically correctly] with Sosipater; cf. H. Lietzmann, *Rom* [HNT] on 16:21). W. Bieder, *BHH* 1824; A. van den Born, *BL* 1618.

σωρεύω *sōreuō* gather up, heap up, fill up*

Rom 12:20, in a metaphor: *heap* burning coals on someone's head (citing Prov 25:22; → ἄνθραξ); pass. and fig. in 2 Tim 3:6: γυναικάρια σεσωρευμένα ἁμαρτίαις, "women *full* of sin."

Σωσθένης, ους *Sōsthenēs* Sosthenes*

Acts 18:17 mentions the → ἀρχισυνάγωγος Sosthenes in Corinth. After Paul is acquitted by Gallio, Sosthenes is beaten before the tribunal by the angry Jewish mob, perhaps because he made the unsuccessful accusation against Paul. Since in 18:8 → Κρίσπος appears as another ruler of the synagogue, one who was converted with the rest of his household and is also mentioned in 1 Cor 1:14, Σωσθένης ὁ ἀδελφός mentioned in 1 Cor 1:1 as coauthor has often been identified as the (assumed to be converted) ruler of the synagogue mentioned in Acts 18:17. In that case he then would have accompanied Paul from Corinth to Ephesus. No additional information, however, supports this hypothesis. Σωσθένης is also mentioned in the postscript to 1 Corinthians (minuscule 104). C. Colpe, *BHH* 1824; A. van den Born, *BL* 1620.

Σωσίπατρος, ου *Sōsipatros* Sosipater*

According to Rom 16:21 the Jewish Christian Sosipater, together with other Jewish Christians (οἱ συγγενεῖς μου), greets the Christian church in Rome. An identification of Sosipater with → Σώπατρος might be supported by the assertion in Acts 20:4 that Sopater briefly spent time with Paul after the composition of the letter to the Romans. B. Reicke, *BHH* 1824.

σωτήρ, ῆρος, ὁ *sōtēr* deliverer, savior*

1. Occurrences in the NT — 2. Origin — 3. Meaning

Lit.: C. ANDRESEN, RAC VI, 54-219. — P. S. BERGE, "Our Great God and Saviour": A Study of Soter as a Christological Title in Titus 2:11-14 (Diss. Union Theological Seminary, Richmond, 1973). — O. CULLMANN, The Christology of the NT (1959) 238-45. — D. CUSS, Imperial Cult and Honorary Terms in the NT (1974). — G. DAUTZENBERG, "Σωτηρία, ψυχῶν (1 Petr 1,9)," BZ 8 (1964) 262-76. — F. J. DÖLGER, "Der Heiland," AuC 6 (1950) 241-72. — F. DORNSEIFF, PW II/5, 1211-21. — A. FEUILLET, Christologie paulinienne et tradition biblique (1973). — W. FOERSTER and G. FOHRER, TDNT VII, 965-1024. — A. GEORGE, "L'emploi chez Luc du vocabulaire de salut," NTS 23 (1976/77) 308-20. — R. GLÖCKNER, Die Verkündigung des Heils beim Evangelisten Lukas (1976), esp. 96-154. — H. HAERENS, "Σωτήρ et σωτηρία," Studia Hellenistica 5 (1948) 57-68. — HAHN, Titles 51f. (n. 136), 82 (120 n. 113), 256f. (273 n. 107), 260. — H. KASPER, Griechische Soter-Vorstellungen und ihre Übernahme in das politische Leben Roms (Diss. Mainz, 1959). — E. LARSSON, TRE XIV, 616-22. — H. LINSSEN, "Θεὸς σωτήρ," Jahrbuch für Liturgiewissenschaft 8 (1928) 1-75. — S. LYONNET, De vocabulario redemptionis (1960). — K. PRÜMM, "Herrscherkult und NT," Bib 9 (1928) 3-25, 129-42, 289-301. — J. T. ROSS, The Conception of σωτηρία in the NT (1947). — J. SALGUERO, "Concetto biblico di salvezza-liberazione," Ang 53 (1976) 11-55. — J. SCHARBERT, Heilsmittler im AT und im Alten Orient (1964). — W. STAERK, Soter. Die biblische Erlösererwartung als religionsgeschichtliches Problem (2 vols.; 1933-38). — G. VOSS, Die Christologie der lukanischen Schriften in Grundzügen (1965) 45-60. — For further bibliography see TWNT X, 1276.

1. In the NT σωτήρ is used 8 times of God (Luke 1:47; then in later Epistles 1 Tim 1:1; 2:3; 4:10; Titus 1:3; 2:10; 3:4; Jude 25). It is used 17 times of Christ. Except in Phil 3:20, later texts use σωτήρ formulaically (Luke 2:11; John 4:42; Acts 5:31; 13:23; Eph 5:23; 2 Tim 1:10; Titus 1:4; 2:13; 3:6; 2 Pet 1:1, 11; 2:20; 3:2, 18; 1 John 4:14). The tr. varies between Rescuer, which emphasizes more the negative, and Savior, which highlights the positive, particularly with an eschatological emphasis.

2. Anyone who saves or delivers (→ σῴζω) can be called a deliverer or rescuer (σωτήρ). In secular Greek usage the gods are deliverers both as helpers of human beings and as protectors of collective entities (e.g., cities); this is the case with Zeus, Apollo, Poseidon, the Dioscuri Castor and Pollux, Heracles, Asclepius as the helper of the sick, and Serapis; it is true also for philosophers (Dio Chrysostom Or. 32.8) and statesmen (Thucydides v.11.1; Plutarch Cor. 11, also in inscriptions and elsewhere). In the Hellenistic ruler cult θεὸς σωτήρ is attested in writings and inscriptions as a title of the Ptolemies and Seleucids. Inscriptions in the eastern part of the Empire called Pompey "Soter and Founder," Caesar "Soter of the World," and Augustus "Soter of Humankind." Hadrian had the title σωτήρ τοῦ κόσμου.

The LXX uses σωτήρ to translate various Hebrew words and is occasionally used in reference to human beings (Judg 3:9; 12:3; 2 Esdr 19:27); σωτήρ frequently refers to God, as in Isa 12:2; Bar 4:22; Ps 23:5; Mic 7:7; Hab 3:18; Judg 9:11; Esth 5:1; Sir 51:8; Wis 16:7; 1 Macc 4:30; 3 Macc 6:29. In the Psalms of Solomon God is σωτήρ as Savior of the righteous (3:6; 8:33; 16:4) as well as of Israel (17:3), to whom he will send the Messiah. God is the Creator and σωτήρ (Sib. Or. iii.35). Philo

often calls God the σωτήρ. The Qumran scrolls also express this confidence. God was Israel's helper in its past history (1QM 10:4; 14:4; 18:7). Now he delivers the poor and the pious (1QH 2:32, 35; 5:18; 1QM 14:10; 1QS 10:17) as well as the entire community, who collectively are "the people of God's salvation" (1QM 1:12; 14:5). In contrast, the Messiah is never unequivocally called σωτήρ in the LXX; Zech 9:9; Isa 49:6; 4 Ezra 13:26 can at most be understood as allusions.

3. In the NT the use of σωτήρ for God is influenced first by the OT; this is the case in Luke 1:47 (Hab 3:18), which is part of a psalm influenced largely by the OT. The repeated reference in the Pastorals to God as σωτήρ probably follows Hellenistic Jewish usage. When the text emphasizes that God is the Deliverer of all people (1 Tim 4:10; Titus 2:10f.), this is perhaps a reaction against Gnostic thought that divides people into the chosen and the rejected; similarly, 1 Tim 1:1 and Titus 1:3 teach the universality of salvation. The doxology in Jude 25 calls the one God σωτήρ, and the addition "through Jesus Christ" establishes the relationship to the latter; the context determines whether he is understood as the mediator either of redemption or of the glorification of God.

Phil 3:20 is the earliest NT text referring to Christ as σωτήρ. The title is not attributed to the historical Christ, however, but to Christ as the anticipated eschatological perfecter. Paul probably is not making this statement in any emphatically elevated dogmatic sense (e.g., as a contrast to the imperial cult), but rather as a parallel construction to his own frequent statements about the σῴζειν and σωτηρία through Christ. Eph 5:23 (post-Pauline), which explains σωτήρ functionally, might be using a previously established fixed title. As the head of the body, which is the Church, Christ is its Savior. He gives himself up for the Church in order to "sanctify" it, i.e., to lead it out of the world and into God's kingdom (Eph 5:2, 25f.). According to Eph 2:5, 8, too, the Church is already saved. Here salvation is not anticipated eschatologically but is already present.

In the (post-Pauline) Pastorals σωτήρ is already a fixed title for Christ. "The grace given ages ago is now manifested through the appearance of our Savior Christ Jesus" (2 Tim 1:10). Here as in further texts (Titus 1:4; 2:13; 3:6) σωτήρ appears in the context of words adopted from Hellenistic Christian language, particularly relating to the imperial cult (ἐπιφάνεια, μέγας θεός, φιλανθρωπία). Since the LXX never refers to the Messiah as σωτήρ, the usage in the Pastorals probably echoes Hellenistic cultic language.

Σωτήρ is repeatedly used of Christ in 2 Peter, a pseudepigraphon from ca. A.D. 100. This would suggest that christology had already developed to an advanced stage and become fixed. Σωτήρ has become an ecclesiastical honorific title for Christ and is associated with the attribution of deity (1:1: "in the righteousness of our God and *Savior* Jesus Christ"). Of equal value in this regard is v. 11: "the eternal kingdom of our Lord and *Savior* Jesus Christ"; similarly 2:20; 3:2, 18. Whereas NT doxologies are normally addressed to God, here (3:18) it is to "our Lord and *Savior* Jesus Christ."

In Luke 2:11, too, σωτήρ in reference to Christ represents later christology. The angel's words summarize the Church's christological confession: "For to you is born this day in the city of David a *Savior,* who is Christ the Lord." The apostolic proclamation (Acts 5:31) uses (as Rom 1:4 already does as well) the symbol of Christ's death and exaltation ("God exalted him at his right hand as Leader and *Savior*"). Yet another part of the confession (Rom 1:3) resonates in Paul's proclamation in Acts 13:23: "From the line of David God has brought to Israel a *Savior,* Jesus, as he promised." Σωτήρ summarizes Christ's entire ministry and purpose.

According to John 4 the revelation of Jesus is completed in the Samaritans' confession: "We know that this is in truth the *Savior* of the world" (v. 42). Everything until now has been preliminary, but now there is absolute fulfillment and completion. Although the title σωτὴρ τοῦ κόσμου was generated by the (Greco-Roman) proclamation of Caesar, the fourth Gospel probably is not using it in any polemical or antithetical fashion against the imperial cult. It suggested itself naturally to the writer of John, since it emphatically proclaims redemption encompassing the entire world (1:1; 3:16f.; 6:33). 1 John 4:14 repeats the title: "The Father has sent his Son as the *Savior* of the world." The context emphasizes both the universality and the certainty of redemption. Just like the Gospel of John, so also is 1 John (2:2; 4:9) focused on the whole world.   K. H. Schelkle

σωτηρία, ας, ἡ   *sōtēria*   deliverance, salvation*

1. Occurrences in the NT — 2. Origin — 3. Meaning in the NT

Lit.: → σωτήρ.

1. In the NT σωτηρία occurs often in the epistolary writings (14 times in Paul, 4 in the deutero-Pauline writings, 7 in Hebrews, 6 in the Catholic Epistles), 3 times in Revelation, 4 in Luke, 6 in Acts, and once each in John (4:22) and Mark (16:8 v.l.).

2. The word and concept σωτηρία in the NT derive first from the LXX, where it is the Hellenistic representation for various Hebrew words. In both places σωτηρία refers to "help, deliverance, salvation" through people or circumstances, though it is ultimately deliverance by God. Σωτηρία can refer to God's activity in the larger sense, but without overlooking his individual deeds. It refers to liberation from evil powers, and in the ultimate sense deliverance in the decisive final judgment and accordingly eschatological salvation for the world (Jdt 8:17; Wis 16:6; 18:7; Sir 16:1; 1 Macc 5:62). The later parts of the OT finally arrive

at this latter assertion (e.g., Isa 49:6 [= Luke 2:32; Acts 13:47]). The servant of God will be "a light to the nations"; "God's *salvation* will reach to the end of the earth." Apocalyptic writing intensifies the word's eschatological import (*T. Jud.* 22:2; *T. Naph.* 8:2; *T. Gad* 4:7; 5:7; 8:4; *T. Benj.* 9:2). 1QM 1:5; 13:13; 1QH 15:16 are comparable, affirming that those delivered may view God's salvation. The community is "the people of God's *salvation*" (1QM 1:12; 4:5); God gives eternal salvation (1QM 18:9).

Like → σῴζω, σωτηρία is common in extrabiblical secular Greek. Deliverance can come from human beings or from natural circumstances, and σωτηρία can refer to "welfare, well-being" in the larger sense. In the religious realm σωτηρία is deliverance by the gods from all sorts of danger, and finally also from the power of death (*Corp. Herm.* 7:1f.). In mystery religions the μύστης receives a portion of the god's salvation. (Firmicus Maternus *Errore Profanarum Religionum* 22:1: "Be confident, initiates [μύσ(τ)αι]! Since the god is saved, so also will salvation come to us from these tribulations.") Here, however, the god's suffering and salvation are not the cause of the redemption of the μύσται but only their model.

3. The initial OT coloring of σωτηρία in the NT becomes clear in the many OT citations (so Luke 1:69; Acts 13:47; 2 Cor 6:2a; Phil 1:19; 1 Thess 5:8; Heb 5:9). Acts 7:25 and 27:34 use σωτηρία to mean *deliverance* in the secular-historical sense. According to the OT parallels Ps 18:3 and 1 Sam 2:10, σωτηρία in Luke 1:69 and (in accordance with Ps 106:10) in Luke 1:71 refers first of all to messianic deliverance from the hands of national enemies. In Luke 1:77 σωτηρία is the redemption of the people from sin. This is probably also true, at least in an initial sense, in 19:9. In any event, σωτηρία refers to deliverance from present distress in 2 Cor 1:6 and Phil 1:19.

Otherwise σωτηρία regularly refers to *salvation* in the supernatural-eschatological sense. Among these texts those of Paul are the most significant. "The gospel is the power of God for *salvation* to every one who believes" (Rom 1:16). Σωτηρία here is the eschatological salvation of the whole world. Israel is included in this σωτηρία (10:1), as are the other nations (11:11). Salvation consists in the righteousness effected by God (10:10). 13:11 speaks of "our *salvation,*" which is nearer to us now than when we first came to faith. In the occurrences in 2 Corinthians 1, where Paul reports with much agitation how he has just been delivered from mortal danger (v. 10), σωτηρία likely refers to the present time, though time that admittedly comes to its ultimate goal only in the future. The apostle's present afflictions happen "for the comfort and *salvation*" of the whole church (v. 6). Paul interprets a line from Isa 49:8 ("on the day of salvation I helped you") thus: "Behold, now is the day of *salvation*" (1 Cor 6:2b). Godly grief produces "repentance that leads to *salvation*" (7:10). This salvation is already present now and will be fulfilled eschatologically at the end.

In Philippians Paul speaks of the present peril of imprisonment, though he knows (1:19) that it "will turn out for *deliverance*" (cf. Job 13:16 LXX). "Salvation" refers to deliverance from pressing circumstances, but also to the ultimate, eschatological experience. The steadfastness uniting the Philippian church with the apostle is "a clear omen of *salvation* from God" for them (1:28), at the same time throwing its eschatological completion into relief. For now, in the apostle's absence, the church should labor for its own "*salvation* with fear and trembling" (2:12f.). In 1 Thess 5:8f. Paul explains the basis, substance, and goal of σωτηρία: By dying for our sake, Christ has obtained salvation, for which God has destined us. Paul uses the Christian trio faith, hope, and love in a metaphor of outfitting for battle. The hope of salvation should be like a helmet.

Eph 1:13 describes coming to faith. In Christ you "have heard the word of truth, the gospel of your *salvation*." Just as the word mediates the truth it teaches, so the gospel not only proclaims salvation but also effects it. Coming to faith is completed in being sealed by the Holy Spirit. The hymnic style of the letter to the Ephesians requires solemn, probably preformulated and fixed, declarations. Perhaps Rom 1:16 plays a part here. The same is true of 2 Thess 2:13: "God chose you from the beginning [as the first ones?] for *salvation*, through sanctification by the Spirit and belief in the truth," a verse that incorporates the earlier 1 Thess 5:9. This election is a NT certainty (Rom 8:29f.; Eph 1:4) and finds its goal in deliverance, or salvation, which from all eternity God wills and plans to grant. In its execution God's deed through his sanctifying Spirit is united with the obedience of faith on the part of the redeemed believer.

These already represent formulaic declarations (1 Pet 1:22f.; 2 Pet 1:12). The concept of σωτηρία in 2 Tim 2:10 is also formulaic: "Therefore I endure everything for the sake of the elect, that they also may obtain the *salvation* that in Christ Jesus goes with eternal glory." The apostle's suffering becomes a blessing for the church (2 Cor 1:6). Christ obtained and gives salvation, which is eternal glory. The holy Scriptures "are able to instruct for *salvation* through faith in Christ Jesus" (2 Tim 3:15). 2 Tim 3:16 describes the value, dignity, and efficaciousness of the holy Scriptures, expressing at the same time the early Jewish high estimation of Scripture. They instruct and equip one for every good work and finally lead to salvation, a goal attained by faith in Jesus Christ.

Σωτηρία is an important word in Hebrews. The present crisis is characterized by sin (1:3; 2:17) and death (2:14f.; 9:27f.). Salvation was promised to the first covenant (9:1) and was realized in God's work of salvation through Jesus Christ (5:9; 9:12). Those called are sanctified in faith (3:1), which will be perfected in Christ's second appearance for salvation in the eternal

inheritance (9:15; 12:22f.). The will of God's grace addresses human beings. Angels are sent to serve those who are to obtain salvation (1:14). Salvation is offered in the present hour of the world, and those who neglect it will be subject to judgment (2:3). God has already made the "pioneer of *salvation*" perfect through suffering (v. 10), who thus becomes the initiator of salvation as the eternal high priest for all who obey him (5:9f.). Although the letter issues a firm warning, it is convinced that the listeners "preserve the better things and *salvation*" (6:9). Christ will appear a second time without sin for the salvation of those who await him, a promise that summarizes the entire eschatological gift (9:28). Among the witnesses of faith the letter mentions "Noah, who constructed an ark for the *saving* of his household" (11:7). In this case σωτηρία was something accomplished in a particular historical time.

1 Peter gives various emphases to σωτηρία. Salvation is prepared "to be revealed now in the last time" (1:5). Perfection is near, and expectation is still intense. Salvation is already present as a guarantee to each individual, for now "you are carrying the goal of your faith, the *salvation* of your souls" (v. 9). The prophets foretold salvation, and the angels long to look at it (vv. 10-12), statements that signify its greatness. The newly baptized should "grow up to *salvation*" (2:2). Such a goal is our "imperishable heavenly inheritance" (1:4).

The beloved should understand the postponement of the parousia "as *salvation*," since this grants time and opportunity for others to obtain salvation (2 Pet 3:15). Salvation is also grace and perfection in a larger sense, and thus Jude intends to write "of your common *salvation*" (v. 3). This letter emphasizes the universality of salvation. Unlike the mystery religions, which grant it to a few initiates, or Gnosticism, which limits it to the special elect, salvation here is given to the world and will appear as deliverance in the final judgment (v. 23).

In Revelation σωτηρία refers to the deliverance of the Church by God and the Lamb from the enduring tribulations. In heaven that salvation is bequeathed them in the praise spoken after the preservation of the people of God (7:10). "The *salvation* and the power and the kingdom of our God" is the cry after the war in heaven and the vanquishing of the dragon by Michael and his angels (12:10). This heavenly victory cry resounds as well after the fall of Babylon (19:1).

We next mention texts from Luke-Acts, though one should ask to what extent they express later theological interpretation. In visiting Zacchaeus, Jesus comments, "Today *salvation* has come to this house" (Luke 19:9). Although Zacchaeus is a sinner, Jesus overcomes evil through his word and deeds, and thus salvation is a present reality for the entire house. Acts uses → σῴζω and σωτηρία quite often. In 7:25 σωτηρία refers to the possibility that Moses would deliver the people of Israel. Acts 27:34 uses the term in its secular sense in referring to Paul's *rescue* from the shipwreck. Otherwise the word always carries the more profound idea of eschatological salvation. Σωτηρία is proclaimed (4:12) as the word of salvation (13:26, 47; modeled after Isa 49:6, which also appears in Luke 2:32). Salvation is simultaneously experienced in the forgiveness of sins. Though now is the time to seize it, it will also be fulfilled in the future (4:12). The proclamation is the way of salvation (16:17).

In John 4:22 Christ says: "*Salvation* is from the Jews." Though the Messiah will arise from Israel, he brings about worship of the Father in spirit and truth everywhere (v. 23). Some commentators dispute the originality of this statement about salvation from the Jews and identify it as a later editorial gloss. It contradicts the overall judgment of the Gospel of John about the unbelief of the Jews (8:17, 41-45; 10:34; 13:33; so R. Bultmann, *John* [Eng. tr., 1971] 189f. n. 6). John does, however, also mention believing Jews (2:23; 8:31; 10:21; 11:45; 12:9-11; cf. Rom 9:4f. Thus this statement about "salvation from the Jews" is indeed possible (see H. Thyen, "Das Heil kommt von den Juden," FS Bornkamm 163-84).

K. H. Schelkle

σωτήριον, ου, τό *sōtērion* salvation, deliverance → σωτήριος.

σωτήριος, 2 *sōtērios* salutary, bringing salvation*
σωτήριον, ου, τό *sōtērion* salvation, deliverance*

1. Occurrences in the NT — 2. Origin — Meaning

Lit.: → σωτήρ. See also H. J. HAUSER, *Strukturen der Abschlußerzählung der Apostelgeschichte (Apg 28:16-31)* (AnBib 86, 1979), esp. 119-24.

1. The adj. σωτήριος occurs in Titus 2:11. Neut. subst. τὸ σωτήριον occurs in Luke 2:30; 3:6; Acts 28:28; Eph 6:17.

2. Σωτήριος is used in Greek within the whole range of → σῴζω. In the LXX, where it occurs frequently, it refers to "that which brings salvation/deliverance," though particularly "peace offering"; thus also Sir 35:1; 47:2; 1 Macc 4:56. In the *T. 12 Patr.* σωτήριος primarily refers simply to God's salvation; thus *T. Benj.* 9:2; *T. Dan* 5:10; *T. Sim.* 7:1.

3. In the NT σωτήριος occurs in Luke's introduction, which uses also the related words → σωτήρ and → σωτηρία. Simeon says in the psalm in Luke 2:30: "My eyes have seen your *salvation*." That salvation is the Messiah appearing in the child. Isa 40:5 lies behind this statement: "God's salvation was sent to the nations," a passage cited in Luke 3:6 and resonating in Acts 28:28. Isa 59:17 ("helmet of salvation") plays a role in 1 Thess 5:8 ("put on the breastplate of faith and love"), where

salvation is the content of hope, and Eph 6:17 ("take the helmet of *salvation*"), where salvation—as in 1:13—is understood as present. This distinction probably corresponds to that between the authentic Pauline Epistles and the deutero-Pauline; in the former the eschaton is yet future, in the latter already fulfilled. This is true in any case of Titus 2:11: "For the grace of God *for the salvation* (ἡ χάρις τοῦ θεοῦ σωτήριος) of all men has appeared." This grace guides us in ethical behavior as described in the code in v. 12. "Thus we await the blessed hope and appearance of the glory of our great God and Savior (σωτῆρος) Jesus Christ" (v. 13).

K. H. Schelkle

σωφρονέω *sōphroneō* be reasonable, be sensible; be of sound mind
→ σωφροσύνη.

σωφρονίζω *sōphronizō* bring one to one's senses; urge
→ σωφροσύνη.

σωφρονισμός, οῦ, ὁ *sōphronismos* admonition; self-discipline
→ σωφροσύνη.

σωφρόνως *sōphronōs* soberly, sensibly, in a disciplined fashion
→ σωφροσύνη.

σωφροσύνη, ης, ἡ *sōphrosynē* reasonableness; decency*
σωφρονέω *sōphroneō* be reasonable, be sensible; be of sound mind*
σωφρονίζω *sōphronizō* bring one to one's senses; urge*
σωφρονισμός, οῦ, ὁ *sōphronismos* admonition; self-discipline*
σωφρόνως *sōphronōs* soberly, sensibly, in a disciplined fashion*
σώφρων, 2 *sōphrōn* sensible; self-controlled*

1. Occurrences in the NT and etymology — 2. Soundness of mind — 3. Self-control and moderation — 4. Reasonableness, decency

Lit.: U. LUCK, *TDNT* VII, 1097-1104. — H. F. NORTH, *Sophrosyne* (1966). — SPICQ, *Notes* II, 867-74. — A. VÖGTLE, *Die Tugend- und Lasterkataloge im NT* (1936), index s.v. — S. WIBBING, *Die Tugend- und Lasterkataloge im NT* (1959). — For further bibliography see Luck.

1. The words in this group occur a total of 16 times in the NT, 10 of these in the Pastorals alone, where they are prominent in the lists of class obligations. The group derives from the adj. σώφρων, which contains the roots

σῶς and φρήν and is influenced by Greek thought. Its wide-ranging meaning can be grasped best by noting terms that contrast with it (μανία, ὕβρις, ἀκολασία; → 2-4).

2. The basic meaning *of sound mind* appears in Mark 5:15 par. Luke 8:35 in the vb. σωφρονέω, *be in one's right mind, be normal*—in contrast to the mania of the possessed man described in 5:3-5. In Acts 26:25 Paul, employing a topos of apologetic speech (cf. *Acta Appiani*, Pap. Oxy. no. 33, ll. 10ff. [σωφρονίζειν]; Justin *Apol.* 13:2ff.) against the charge of μανία, asserts that his words show σωφροσύνη. In 2 Cor 5:13 σωφρονέω is contrasted with ecstasy (→ ἐξίστημι 3).

3. Similar to the opposition between σωφρονέω and μαίνομαι (cf. BAGD 802), the contrast with ὕβρις is also introduced. Rom 12:3 employs wordplay in warning μὴ ὑπερφρονεῖν παρ᾽ ὃ δεῖ φρονεῖν, ἀλλὰ φρονεῖν εἰς τὸ σωφρονεῖν; i.e., do not strive after what is not seemly, but rather after *moderation* and *self-control*. Instead of striving after the more striking gifts of grace that others may have received, the Romans should each do what is appropriate for himself or herself, an old definition of σωφροσύνη (Plato *Chrm.* 161b; cf. 1 Thess 4:11). The specifically Christian element here is that hubris has a corrective in the measure (→ μέτρον) of faith assigned by God and is overcome through the renewal of the νοῦς (Rom 12:2).

4. In the eclectic philosophical tradition (see North) that the NT encountered, in part through Diaspora Judaism, σωφροσύνη refers to the dominion of the νοῦς over the lower impulses as one of the four cardinal virtues countering licentiousness (see Vögtle 58-72; Wibbing 15-33). It is demanded in regents' codes and instructions for vocational obligations (see Vögtle 73-81). Thus the bishop must be *sensible* (1 Tim 3:2; Titus 1:8: σώφρων in stereotypical combination with κόσμιος and δίκαιος). One can expect this character trait from elders (Titus 2:2: σώφρων associated here as elsewhere with σεμνός), though the young also should *control themselves* (v. 6: σωφρονέω). Older women should urge younger women to be thus (vv. 4f.; the factitive vb. σωφρονίζω here is weakened to *admonish*). Applied to women here, σώφρων (v. 5) along with ἀγνός is used to mean *modest, chaste*. Similarly, σωφροσύνη refers to feminine *decency* in 1 Tim 2:9 (here used in parallel with αἰδώς, referring to self-adornment) and in v. 15 (in view of one's life as a mother).

We must go beyond admonitions, however. The question remains as to the source of the standards of Christian σωφροσύνη. Is it from laws? From the faculty of reason oriented toward nature (Greek philosophy)? From wisdom gained from the Torah (Diaspora Judaism)? In addition to two other traditional virtues, Titus 2:12 mentions a *reasonable* life (adv. σωφρόνως) consisting in the renunciation of worldly passions, a matter in which the grace of God, having appeared in Christ, instructs us. 2 Tim 1:7 even speaks of the God-given spirit of *self-control* (σωφρονισμός, here meant not as an activity but as the result of σωφρονίζω). Thus even if the Pastorals adopt a Hellenistic ideal, they do allude to its salvation-historical relevance. Both Philo (cf. *All.* i.63ff.) and the Wisdom of Solomon (8:7; 9:11) also recognize that the traditional virtues originate in divine wisdom.

Titus 2:12f. shows that such self-control and reasonableness do not mean mere accommodation to one's civic environment, but are coupled rather with anticipation of the parousia. This eschatological context becomes more pronounced in 1 Pet 4:7, which, in view of the nearness of the end, exhorts readers to *keep sober/sensible* (aor. of σωφρονέω; note also → νήφω, with the related νηφάλιος in 1 Tim 3:2 and Titus 2:2, in proximity to σώφρων; cf. *Sib. Or.* 3:41: ἐκνῆψαι καὶ σώφρονα πρὸς νοῦν ἐλθεῖν). This attitude refers to the separation from human desires (cf. 1 Pet 1:13f.; 2:11; 4:2ff.) while focusing on God's coming world. This is not a criticism of "eschatological frenzy" (*contra* Luck 1102; Spicq 867f.).

D. Zeller

σώφρων, 2 *sōphrōn* sensible; self-controlled → σωφροσύνη.

T τ

ταβέρνα, ας, ἡ *taberna* shop; tavern, inn*

This loanword (from Lat. *taberna*) occurs in Acts 28:15 in the place name → Τρεῖς ταβέρναι. *Taberna* refers to a shop or (frequently) a tavern or inn (esp. along the larger highways), often with the implication of a dubious reputation. T. Kleberg, *Hôtels, restaurants, et cabarets dans l'antiquité romaine* (BEURU 61, 1957) 19ff., 29ff., 63ff.; W. H. Gross, *KP* V, 478f.

Ταβιθά *Tabitha* Tabitha*

Lit.: W. BIEDER, *BHH* 1923. — BILLERBECK II, 694. — A. VAN DEN BORN, *BL* 1697. — E. HAENCHEN, *Acts* (Eng. tr., 1971) ad loc. — H. P. RÜGER, *TRE* III, 609.

Acts 9:36, 40 mentions the female disciple Tabitha from Joppa, who distinguished herself through good works on behalf of the poor (v. 36) and widows (v. 39) and who was raised from the dead by Peter (vv. 38-41). The command "Tabitha, ἀνάστηθι" (v. 40) is closely related to Mark 5:41 (→ ταλιθα κουμ, v.l. ταβιθα, θαβιτα, *tabea;* cf. E. Nestle, "Schila et Tabitha," *ZNW* 9 [1910] 240). Ταβιθά derives from Aram. *ṭabyeṭaʾ, ṭebîṭāʾ,* "gazelle"; hence the name is also rendered thus in Greek by → Δορκάς, vv. 36, 39, probably already in the tradition used by Luke.

τάγμα, ατος, τό *tagma* order, arrangement*

Lit.: BAGD s.v. — J. BAUMGARTEN, *Paulus und die Apokalyptik* (WMANT 44, 1975) 99-106. — K. BROCKELMANN, *Lexicon Syriacum* (1966) 816, s.v. *tgmʾ.* — H. CONZELMANN, *1 Cor* (Hermeneia) 270f. — G. DELLING, *TDNT* VIII, 31f. — F. FROITZHEIM, *Christologie und Eschatologie bei Paulus* (FzB 35, 1979) 145-49. — H. LIETZMANN and W. G. KÜMMEL, *1-2 Cor* (HNT, ⁵1969) 80f. — LSJ s.v. — U. LUZ, *Das Geschichtsverständnis des Paulus* (BEvT 49, 1968) 339-58. — *PGL* s.v. — H.-H. SCHADE, *Apokalyptische Christologie bei Paulus* (GTA 18, 1981) 36f., 95-98, 202f. — E. SCHENDEL, *Herrschaft und Unterwerfung Christi* (BGBE 12, 1971) 10-12. — VOLZ, *Eschatologie* 256. — H.-A. WILCKE, *Das Problem eines messianischen Zwischenreichs bei Paulus* (ATANT 51, 1967) 76-85.

Τάγμα occurs in the NT only in 1 Cor 15:23: ἕκαστος δὲ ἐν τῷ ἰδίῳ τάγματι.

a) The interpretation of vv. 23f. as three *groups* of the resurrection (BAGD, Lietzmann and Kümmel) is precluded because of the meaning of → τέλος. Wilcke 83f. (cf. Schendel 10ff.) interprets contrary to this view. V. 23 allegedly refers to v. 22: Every person belongs either to the *group* represented by Adam or to that constituted by Christ. This understanding falters theologically because Paul views all Christians as being affected by Adam's fate of mortality in their earthly existence, and it falters syntactically by starting an incomplete independent clause with ἀπαρχὴ Χριστός. Elsewhere τάγμα is used other than for "group" (see the dictionaries). Like → τάξις (cf. *1 Enoch* [Greek] 2:1), τάγμα refers to the result of → τάσσω and acquires the locative sense "rank, position" (cf. *1 Clem.* 37:3; 41:1) and the temporal sense "sequence" (cf. *Herm. Sim.* viii.8.2ff.). "It is clear that Paul intends a temporal sequence with the terms ἀπαρχή—ἔπειτα—εἶτα" (Luz 341).

b) This means that in 1 Cor 15:23 τάγμα refers to the fixed sequence of the last things: "Each in his own *turn*" is raised, thus "Christ as the first fruits, then at his coming the Christians." The problem with this passage is that this apocalyptic schema of stages does not correspond to the Pauline doctrine of resurrection. Christ has already risen, and though Paul associates the overcoming of death with the τέλος, he does not include the general resurrection.

R. Bergmeier

τακτός, 3 *taktos* fixed, determined*

Acts 12:21: τακτῇ ἡμέρᾳ, "on the *appointed* day."

ταλαιπωρέω *talaipōreō* be depressed, feel miserable; lament*

Jas 4:9 admonishes sinners and "those of double mind" (v. 8): ταλαιπωρήσατε, *lament, mourn* (over your misery; followed by πενθήσατε καὶ κλαύσατε); according to vv. 9b, 10 this is referring to an expression of repentance and humility. The context demands that ταλαιπωρέω cannot (as is usually the case elsewhere) be understood only intrans. as a designation of a miserable condition (Josephus *Ap.* i.237; *Herm. Vis.* iii.7.1); M. Dibelius, *Jas* (Eng. tr., 1976) ad loc.; Spicq, *Notes* II, 875.

ταλαιπωρία, ας, ἡ *talaipōria* misery, distress*

Rom 3:16: → σύντριμμα καὶ ταλαιπωρία, "ruin and *misery*" (citing Ps 13:3 LXX; Isa 59:7 LXX) as the result of the actions of sinful people (cf. ἡ ταλαιπωρία τῶν πτωχῶν, *1 Clem.* 15:6 [citing Ps 11:6 LXX]). Αἱ ταλαιπωρίαι . . . αἱ ἐπερχόμεναι in Jas 5:1 refers to the eschatological *miseries* that will come upon the rich; their wealth and misuse of power (vv. 2ff.) will subject them to judgment and ruin (cf. Isa 13:6; Jer 5:26ff.; Amos 5:7ff.; Mic 2:4; *1 Enoch* 94:8f.; 97:8ff.; Rev 3:17). Spicq, *Notes* II, 875.

ταλαίπωρος, 2 *talaipōros* miserable, afflicted, wretched*

Rom 7:24, in the outcry of the person enslaved under the law and sin: ταλαίπωρος ἐγὼ ἄνθρωπος, "*wretched* man that I am!" Ταλαίπωρος identifies the condition as simultaneously unhappy and lamentable (τί γὰρ εἰμί; ταλαίπωρον ἀνθρωπάριον, of those who live only a superficial and earthly existence far from the divine: Epictetus *Diss.* i.3.5; cf. iii.26.3; iv.6.18; *Jos. As.* 6:5, 7; *T. Abr.* [B] 10; Wis 3:11; *1 Clem.* 23:3; *2 Clem.* 11:1f.). Rev 3:17 mentions rich people (in Laodicea) who in truth are *wretched* because they lack the wealth (v. 18) that counts before God (ταλαίπωρος with ἐλεεινός, πτωχός, τυφλός, γυμνός); cf. Wis 13:10; Jas 5:1. Spicq, *Notes* II, 876f.

ταλαντιαῖος, 3 *talantiaios* weighing one talent, "heavy as a hundredweight"*

Rev 16:21: χάλαζα μεγάλη ὡς ταλαντιαία, "great hailstones, heavy as talents/as a hundredweight" (cf. Exod 9:22ff.). One talent in Israel probably weighed *ca.* 34 kg., and in Roman areas *ca.* 41 kg.; → τάλαντον 1.

τάλαντον, ου, τό *talanton* talent*

Lit.: BAGD s.v. — H. CHANTRAINE, *KP* V, 502f.

1. In Greek τάλαντον first refers to "scale" (related to τάλας, "supporting, bearing"), then also "that which has been weighed /the weight." The division of the talent into sixty minas, which was also customary in Greece, points to Mesopotamia as its place of origin. The talent is the largest unit of weight, coming in bars weighing thirty to forty kg., approximately what a single person can carry (comparable to the Eng. "hundredweight"). In the LXX τάλαντον translates Heb. *kikkār* ("circle"). Solomon received 666 talents in one year (1 Kgs 10:14), and King Omri bought the hill of Samaria for two talents of silver (1 Kgs 16:24). In the Hel-

lenistic period Jonathan requested tax privileges from King Demetrius II and promised in return three hundred talents (1 Macc 11:28). Roughly speaking, we might compare one talent with the modern "million."

2. This order of magnitude must be kept in mind when Matt 18:24 speaks of the man relieved of a debt of ten thousand talents. Matt 25:15-28 tells of a royal fortune divided into portions of five talents (vv. 15, 16, 20 bis), two talents (vv. 15, 22 bis), and one talent (vv. 24, 25, 28). The first two portions are doubled (vv. 20, 22, 28). This parable is the source of the present-day meaning of Eng. "talent" in reference to mental ability, first used in this sense probably by Paracelsus (1537). Luke 19:13-25, the parallel to Matthew 25, divides (more realistically) ten minas among ten servants. Rev 16:21 reflects the original meaning of τάλαντον as a unit of weight: hailstones heavy as a hundredweight (literally "heavy as talents"; → ταλαντιαῖος) fall from heaven.   B. Schwank

ταλιθα *talitha* girl, little girl*

According to Mark 5:41 Jesus speaks to the "sleeping" daughter of Jairus, the ruler of the synagogue: ταλιθα → κουμ (Aramaic), which is then translated: "Little girl, I say to you, arise" (ὅ ἐστιν μεθερμηνευόμενον· τὸ κοράσιον, σοὶ λέγω, ἔγειρε, cf. also Luke 8:54; different in Matt 9:25). Ταλιθα is the Greek transliteration of Aram. *ṭalyeṭā'* or *ṭelîṭā'* (*Tg. Yer. I* Gen 34:4). Mss. sometimes have ταβιθα instead of ταλιθα (W and others, cf. Acts 9:36, 40), ῥαββι θαβιτα (D, from ῥαβιθα as a result of dittography [= Aram. *reḇîṭā'*, "girl," *Tg. Yer. I* Gen 24:16]), and *tabea acultha (cumhi)* (e, explanation disputed). C. E. B. Cranfield, *BHH* 1928; *TCGNT* ad loc.; H. P. Rüger, *TRE* III, 609.

ταμεῖον (ταμιεῖον), ου, τό *tameion (tamieion)* storeroom, chamber, (hidden) room*

The Hellenistic contraction ταμεῖον for the older ταμιεῖον (thus in only a few mss.) appears in all 4 NT occurrences (see further BAGD s.v.; BDF §31.2). Ταμεῖον occurs as a loanword in rabbinic texts (*ṭamyôn*). In Luke 12:24 it clearly refers to a *storeroom* (with → ἀποθήκη, "silo, barn"; cf. also Deut 28:8); otherwise, depending on the context, it refers generally to a room within a house that can be closed off and remain invisible from the outside (cf. Gen 43:30 LXX; 3 Kgdms 22:25; Isa 26:20 LXX; Sir 29:12 [treasury]). Matt 6:6 refers to prayer in the *(hidden) room* (cf. κλείσας τὴν θύραν, ἐν τῷ κρυπτῷ; cf. further 4 Kgdms 4:33 [οἶκος]; *T. Jos.* 3:3: εἰσερχόμενος εἰς τὸ ταμεῖον κλαίων προσηυχόμην Κυρίῳ); Matt 24:26 and Luke 12:3 both emphasize the element of concealment, Matthew contrasting *inner rooms* and the desert, Luke *private rooms* (in which one exchanges secrets) and housetops. (On housetops as public places, cf. Isa 15:3; 22:1; a parallel here is the contrast between σκοτία and φῶς, Luke 12:3.)

ταμιεῖον, ου, τό *tamieion* storeroom, chamber, (hidden) room
Uncontracted older form of Hellenistic → ταμεῖον.

τάξις, εως, ἡ *taxis* order, sequence; kind*

1. Occurrences in the NT — 2. Order, sequence — 3. Condition, kind, manner

1. Τάξις occurs 9 times in the NT, 6 of these in Hebrews (*contra* G. Delling, *TDNT* VIII, 27 n. 1).

2. It refers to *order* within the congregation—parenetically in 1 Cor 14:40: κατὰ τάξιν (cf. *T. Naph.* 2:9: ἐν τάξει; see further H. Conzelmann, *1 Cor* [Hermeneia] 247 n. 63); Col 2:5: the *well-ordered situation.* Luke 1:8 refers to the *sequence/turn* of service of the priestly → ἐφημερία.

3. Τάξις refers also to a particular *condition, nature, manner* (cf. *Ep. Arist.* 69; 2 Macc 9:18; Plutarch *Pel.*: ἐν παροιμίας τάξει): following Ps 109:4 LXX, "according to the *nature* of Melchizedek," Heb 5:6, 10; 6:20; 7:11c, 17 is interpreted by κατὰ τὴν ὁμοιότητα Μελχισέδεκ in 7:15, in contrast to κατὰ τὴν τάξιν ᾿Ααρών in 7:11d; cf. P. Ellingworth, "Just like Melchizedek," *BT* 28 (1977) 236-39. W. R. G. Loader, *Sohn und Hoherpriester* (WMANT 53, 1981), interprets the alternative *ways* of functioning as a priest, established either through → νόμος (4.b) or through → ὁρκωμοσία, in the sense of an old and new *order,* qualified by mortality on the one hand, and indestructible life on the other (143ff.; cf. also 212ff., 220ff., 243ff.).   R. Bergmeier

ταπεινός, 3 *tapeinos* lowly, of low position, insignificant; humble*

Lit.: DUPONT, *Béatitudes* III, 521-37. — H.-H. ESSER, *DNTT* II, 259-64. — W. GRUNDMANN, *TDNT* VIII, 1-26. — S. LÉGASSE, *Jésus et l'enfant* (ÉBib, 1969) 223-31. — R. LEIVESTAD, "Ταπεινός —ταπεινόφρων," *NovT* 8 (1966) 36-47. — S. REHRL, *Das Problem der Demut in der profan-griechischen Literatur im Vergleich zu LXX und NT* (1961). — Spicq, *Notes* II, 878-80. — For further bibliography see *TWNT* X, 1278.

1. Ταπεινός occurs 8 times in the NT: once each in Matthew and Luke, and 6 times in the Epistles. It is translated *small, insignificant, lowly, weak* (→ 2) and, in certain contexts, *humble* (→ 3).

2. In the Magnificat the ταπεινοί are the *lowly* (RSV "those of low degree," Luke 1:52), as opposed to the mighty. OT promises of God's eschatological deeds (Ps 147:6; Job 5:11; 12:19; 1 Sam 2:7) begin to be fulfilled

when God puts down the mighty from their thrones and exalts the lowly. In Jas 1:9 the brother who is ταπεινός is clearly *lowly* in a social sense, being juxtaposed with one who is rich; this insignificant brother should boast in his "exaltation"—understood in a spiritual sense. 2 Cor 7:6 also uses the term in an ethically neutral sense; God, who comforts the *lowly/downcast* (Isa 49:13), also comforts Paul and his companions with the arrival of Titus in Macedonia (v. 5). To the charge that he is quite different, namely, ταπεινός, when he is present than when absent (2 Cor 10:1b), Paul responds not by arguing ironically (*contra* Rehrl 174; R. Bultmann, *2 Cor* [Eng. tr., 1985] 183) but by paradoxically making a virtue out of his lowliness, for precisely in his lowliness and weakness (v. 10) does God's power become manifest (12:9; 11:30). This is a consequence of the continuation of Christ's own "weakness," who now "lives by the power of God" (13:3f.; 10:1a).

In Rom 12:16 the gender of pl. ταπεινοῖς is disputed: is it to be understood as neut. or as masc.? The neut. is suggested by the juxtaposition of τὰ ὑψηλά (so H. Schlier, *Rom* [HTKNT] 380). Since ταπεινός—in reference to things—almost of necessity implies a derogatory value judgment (Leivestad 45f.: "earthly," "worldly"), this analysis contradicts Pauline theology (cf. v. 2). The masc. is suggested by the use of the adj. elsewhere in the NT, by the vb. → συναπάγομαι, which here (*contra* Grundmann 20 n. 56) does not refer to "be carried away (in ecstatic rapture)" but rather "allow oneself to be drawn down to, associate with" (BAGD 784), mid. "stoop" (E. Käsemann, *Rom* [Eng. tr., 1980] 348), and by the two other admonitions: to be of one mind together (v. 16a), and not to consider oneself wise (v. 16c; citing Prov 3:7). The believers are urged not to be conceited but to turn their attention to the insignificant ones in the church.

3. Only in 1 Pet 5:5c and Jas 4:6b (citing Prov 3:34 LXX) are the ταπεινοί the *humble* who are confronted with the proud. In the cry of rejoicing in Matt 11:29 the qualification τῇ καρδίᾳ is not intended as an intensification of the humble condition; rather, it delimits the area in which Jesus is lowly and gives to ταπεινός in combination with πραΰς the sense of *humble* (Leivestad 44f.).   H. Giesen

ταπεινοφροσύνη, ης, ἡ *tapeinophrosynē* humility, modesty*
ταπεινόφρων, 2 *tapeinophrōn* humble, modest*

1. Occurrences in the NT — 2. Noun — 3. Adj.

Lit.: J. DUPONT, *Paulus an die Seelsorger* (1966) 25-42. — F. O. FRANCIS, "Humility and Angelic Worship in Col 2:18," *ST* 16 (1962) 109-34. — N. KEHL, "Erniedrigung und Erhöhung in Qumran und Kolossä," *ZKT* 91 (1969) 364-94. — K. THIEME, "Die ΤΑΠΕΙΝΟΦΡΟΣΥΝΗ Philipper 2 und Römer 12," *ZNW*

8 (1907) 9-33. — K. Wengst, *Humility: Solidarity of the Humiliated* (1988). — *idem*, " '. . . einander durch Demut für vorzüglicher halten. . . .' Zum Begriff der 'Demut' bei Paulus und in paulinischer Tradition," FS Greeven 428-39. — C. Wolff, "Niedrigkeit und Verzicht in Wort und Weg Jesu und in der apostolischen Existenz des Paulus," *NTS* 34 (1988) 183-96. — For further bibliography → ταπεινός.

1. The noun ταπεινοφροσύνη occurs 7 times in the NT: in Acts 20:19 and 6 times in the Epistles. This word, which does not occur in the LXX, has become the t.t. for Christian *humility*. The adj. occurs only in 1 Pet 3:8 (and Prov 29:23 LXX).

2. In his farewell address in Miletus (Acts 20:18-35) "Paul" speaks of the character of his service as an example for church officeholders. One can "serve the Lord" only "in all *humility*" (v. 19), i.e., in selflessness and renunciation of any will to rule, or (positively) in goodness and with understanding. The apostle's "tears" underscore this as an expression of his pastoral labor and his trials and persecution at the hands of the Jews. Christian humility as service to the Lord is always simultaneously service to the community of believers, articulated here as pastoral care.

According to Phil 2:3 ταπεινοφροσύνη is the fundamental attitude of Christians in view of the unity of the church. It stands over against any attitude of selfishness and conceit, which disrupts and destroys church life. *Humility* counts others better than oneself—regardless of social standing. Those who are humble seek not their own advantage but the opportunity to serve others (v. 4). Christian humility is grounded in the self-humiliation of Christ (cf. vv. 5, 6-11, esp. v. 8).

The admonitions to various social groups (1 Pet 5:1-5) conclude with the exhortation to everyone to practice ταπεινοφροσύνη. This is grounded in Prov 3:34 LXX (v. 5c). In 1 Pet 5:5b, as in Phil 2:3, ταπεινοφροσύνη is the fundamental attitude of Christians in their relationships with one another and with their fellow human beings. In Col 3:12 ταπεινοφροσύνη is one of five virtues Christians should express in their own actions. This is possible on the basis of God's elect love, which each Christian experiences in baptism (v. 11). Here, too, ταπεινοφροσύνη also serves the church, since the demand is made of Christians to accept one another and—when necessary—to make reconciliation with one another (v. 13). Eph 4:2 reduces the virtues from Col 3:12 to three. Here, too, *humility* should manifest itself in Christians' love for one another.

In Col 2:18, 23, too, it appears more appropriate to take one's cue from the general usage of this term within the NT and to understand ταπεινοφροσύνη here as *humility* (against the views of most authors). Humility is doubtless perverted whenever heretics take pleasure in it (θέλω

ἐν as a Septuagintism), are puffed up without reason as a result of their own fleshly mind (ὑπὸ τοῦ νοὸς τῆς σαρκός, v. 18), i.e., are without love (cf. 1 Cor 13:4), and are separated from Christ, their head (Col. 2:19a). Such humility is not, however, to be identified with the heretics' fasting exercises (*contra* Francis 114-19; Kehl 368, 370f.; E. Schweizer, *Col* [Eng. tr., 1982] 159) or with their cultic practice generally (*contra* Grundmann 22; J. Gnilka, *Col* [HTKNT] 149). Neither does the word refer to angels, even though the cult of angels is mentioned with it (v. 18); and it does not suggest the Greek understanding of ταπεινοφροσύνη as "servility, dependence, abject fawning" (*contra* Gnilka 149) but refers rather to the selfless love that Col 2:18 denies the heretic.

According to v. 23 the heretics do indeed have the reputation of wisdom because of their self-chosen cult, their self-abasement, and their severity to the body, but all that is of no value (τιμή here refers to "value," not "honor," with Schweizer, *Col.* 169, and *contra* Gnilka, *Col.* 161) and only serves the indulgence of the flesh, i.e., religiously inspired egoism, which excludes humility. If one allows ταπεινοφροσύνη to maintain its positive sense, the contrasting character of these statements—which are full of sarcasm—comes through quite clearly.

3. Like the noun, the adj. **ταπεινόφρων** appears in the context of Christian Church life. The goal of all admonitions to Christians (1 Pet 2:3–3:7) is that the community of believers maintain a peaceful, harmonious life characterized by brotherly love (3:8). Christians should renounce any superiority and revenge and with a *modest, humble* disposition be prepared for service.   H. Giesen

ταπεινόφρων, 2 *tapeinophrōn* humble, modest → ταπεινοφροσύνη 1, 3.

ταπεινόω *tapeinoō* make low, humble (vb.)*
ταπείνωσις, εως, ἡ *tapeinōsis* humiliation, humility, lowliness*

1. Occurrences in the NT — 2. Luke 3:5 — 3. "All who humble themselves . . ." — 4. Phil 2:8 — 5. Paul — 6. Ταπείνωσις

Lit.: → ταπεινός. On Phil 2:8 see also: W. Grundmann, "Der Weg des Kyrios Jesus Christus. Erwägungen zum Christushymnus Phil 2:6-11 und der damit verbundenen Konzeption im NT," *idem, Wandlungen im Verständnis des Heils* (1980) 9-24. — G. Howard, "Phil 2:6-11 and the Human Christ," *CBQ* 40 (1978) 368-87.

1. The vb. occurs 14 times in the NT, 8 of these in Matthew and Luke and 6 in the Epistles. It usually has a fig. meaning, particularly when, together with the reflexive pron. or in the mid., it describes appropriate human conduct before God. The noun, too, which is used

only 4 times in the NT, can refer to *humility* before God, though it is also used in the sense of *humiliation.*

2. John the Baptist challenges his listeners, through his message of conversion and salvation (Luke 3:3) corresponding to Isa 40:3-5 LXX, to ready themselves for God's salvation (v. 6) by preparing the way of the Lord and making his paths straight (v. 4). The decisive feature, however, must be performed by God himself, for every valley will be filled (by him) and every mountain *made low* (by him; passivum divinum), i.e., leveled (v. 5). Eschatological salvation thus commences with God's own actions.

3. The assertion "All who exalt themselves *will be humbled,* and all who *humble themselves* will be exalted" occurs 3 times in the Jesus tradition. The pass. speaks variously of God's eschatological action. In Matt 23:12 the saying appears in the context of a warning against Pharisaic activity. Humbling oneself is the same as being a servant (v. 11), and God exalts such a person. All who seek to enhance their own reputation, however (vv. 5-10), God will humble, i.e., they will not pass judgment. In Luke 14:11 this same logion concludes the admonishment to the guest to take the place of honor only when it is offered by one's host (vv. 8-10; cf. Prov 25:6f.). This narrative becomes a metaphor for God's salvation activity. According to the exemplary story of the Pharisee and the tax collector in the temple (Luke 18:9-13), this same saying (v. 14) explains why the latter goes home justified, whereas the former does not. God is already acting on behalf of the humble, just as he otherwise brings people low.

According to Matt 18:4 the person who *humbles himself* like the child whom Jesus symbolically places in the midst of the disciples (vv. 1f.) will be the greatest in the kingdom of heaven, for which self-humility is the prerequisite (v. 3). Both Jas 4:10 and 1 Pet 5:6 exhort Christians to *humble themselves* (aor. imv. pass.) so that God may exalt them.

4. In Phil 2:8 the vb. is used with the reflexive pron. and refers to Jesus' free decision to become a human being, which includes the path to death. In the death on the cross Jesus' self-humiliation proves to be efficacious for salvation. It is not a model to be imitated by Christians but rather the basis for Christian humility (v. 3).

5. In Phil 4:12 ταπεινοῦσθαι is to be translated *to be abased* in the sense of "to live with renunciation," as the contrast with περισσεύειν shows. In 2 Cor 11:7 Paul views the source of his own independence in self-abasement, which consists in the renunciation of the support actually due him from the church (1 Cor 9:4-7). When in 2 Cor 12:21 he fears God will humble him upon his arrival, he is probably thinking of the abuses he might find in Corinth (vv. 20, 21b). Paul feels responsible for

the congregation, which is also why he can be proud of them (1:14). In his failure in this respect Paul apparently recognizes that conversion depends ultimately on God (v. 21b). Rather than be resigned, however, he is determined to conduct a trial in the church (13:1-3). This does not, however, constitute the apostle's humiliation, since in any case such an interpretation depends on textual conjectures (negation of ταπεινόω; *contra* R. Bultmann, *2 Cor* [Eng. tr., 1985] 238f.).

6. In the Magnificat the *lowliness* of the handmaiden, whom God has regarded mercifully (Luke 1:48), is not the shame of infertility as in 1 Sam 1:11 (Hannah's prayer; cf. Luke 1:25); it recalls Mary's self-designation as "handmaid of the Lord" (v. 38), whom God chose in her lowly estate (cf. vv. 52f.). According to Acts 8:32f. the Ethiopian minister is reading from the fourth Servant song (Isa 57:3f. LXX) when Philip comes upon him. The *humiliation* in which judgment was suspended (v. 33) likely refers not only to Jesus' death but also to his life and ministry, since Philip uses the text as an occasion to proclaim the message of Jesus himself, and not merely of his death (v. 35).

According to Phil 3:21 the "the body of our lowliness," i.e., of our earthly existence limited by death, will be transfigured into the form of Christ's glorious body, i.e., into our new existence "in heaven" (v. 20). The *humiliation* in which the rich should boast (according to Jas 1:10) is hardly their "subjection to death" (vv. 10c, 11; *contra* W. Grundmann, *TDNT* VIII, 21; Esser 263; F. Mussner, *Jas* [HTKNT] 74), unless one understands this exhortation ironically (as does Rehrl 189). Rather, the subjection to death common to all human beings should motivate the rich to become aware now of their own lowliness before God and not to depend on their wealth (cf. W. Schrage, *Jas* [NTD 10] 18).   H. Giesen

ταπείνωσις, εως, ἡ *tapeinōsis* humiliation, humility, lowliness
→ ταπεινόω 1, 6.

ταράσσω *tarassō* stir up; confuse, trouble, disturb*

Ταράσσω occurs 18 times in the NT, 11 of which are in the Gospels (6 in John); it occurs in Paul only in Gal 1:7 and 5:10. The literal meaning is intended only in John 5:7 in reference to the waters of the pool of Bethesda: ὅταν ταραχθῇ τὸ ὕδωρ, *be stirred up/move;* cf. 5:4 v.l.: ἄγγελος . . . ἐταράσσετο τὸ ὕδωρ. Otherwise the term is always used fig. of *confuse, stir up* people (τὸν ὄχλον, Acts 17:8; τοὺς ὄχλους, v. 13) or *disturb/cause restlessness* (by words and false teaching), referring to Jewish Christians in Jerusalem (ἐτάραξαν ὑμᾶς λόγοις, 15:24; cf.

οἱ ταράσσοντες ὑμᾶς, Gal. 1:7; ὁ δὲ ταράσσων ὑμᾶς, 5:10, which doubtless is a generic sg.).

The vb. is pass. in 1 Pet 3:14: μὴ φοβηθῆτε μηδὲ ταραχθῆτε, "have not fear, nor *let yourselves be confused*" (cf. Isa 8:12 LXX; also *T. Job* 46:3). The pass., which expresses the reaction of *being startled, terrified* because of extraordinary phenomena, appears in Matt 14:26: ἐταράχθησαν λέγοντες ὅτι φάντασμά ἐστιν (cf. Mark 6:50); Matt 2:3: Ἡρῴδης ἐταράχθη; Luke 1:12: ἐταράχθη Ζαχαρίας; 24:38: τί τεταραγμένοι ἐστέ; "Why are you *troubled?*" (cf. πτοηθέντες, ἔμφοβοι in v. 37).

In John ταράσσω occurs with the special meaning *inner agitation, emotion, distress* on the part of Jesus. John 11:33: ἐνεβριμήσατο τῷ πνεύματι καὶ ἐτάραξεν ἑαυτόν, "he was deeply moved in his spirit [cf. ἐν ἑαυτῷ, v. 38] and *was distressed*" (cf. Mark 1:43; see R. Schnackenburg, *John* II [Eng. tr., 1979] ad loc.); John 12:27: ἡ ψυχή μου τετάρακται, "my soul *is troubled*" (cf. Gen 41:8 LXX; Ps 6:4 LXX; *T. Dan* 4:7b; Matt 26:38); John 13:21: Ἰησοῦς ἐταράχθη τῷ πνεύματι. Jesus' condition of being troubled and disturbed in view of his coming suffering is for John a sign of the humanity of the Son of God, who obediently bends to the Father's will. Jesus exhorted his disciples, "Let not your hearts *be troubled*" (μὴ ταρασσέσθω ὑμῶν ἡ καρδία, 14:1, 27; cf. also Pss 54:5; 108:22 LXX; *T. Dan* 4:7a). Spicq, *Notes* II, 881-85.

H. Balz

ταραχή, ῆς, ἡ *tarachē* tumult, disturbance

John 5:4 v.l.: ταραχὴ τοῦ ὕδατος, of the "*disturbance /troubling* of the waters" in the pool of Bethesda, cf. → ταράσσω (v. 7); Mark 13:8 v.l.: *tumultuous events/ disturbance.*

τάραχος, ου, ὁ *tarachos* excitement, disturbance, distress*

Acts 12:18: τάραχος οὐκ ὀλίγος, "no small *excitement /agitation*"; 19:23: τάραχος οὐκ ὀλίγος περὶ τῆς ὁδοῦ, "no small *unrest/tumult* because of the Way [i.e., the Christian proclamation]."

Ταρσεύς, έως, ὁ *Tarseus* (a person) from Tarsus → Ταρσός.

Ταρσός, οῦ *Tarsos* Tarsus*
Ταρσεύς, έως, ὁ *Tarseus* (a person) from Tarsus*

Lit.: H. Böhlig, *Die Geisteskultur von Tarsos im augusteischen Zeitalter* (1913). — H. Goldman, *Excavations at Gözlü Kule, Tarsus* (3 vols.; 1950-63). —E. Haenchen, *Acts* (Eng. tr., 1971) on Acts 22:3. — A. H. M. Jones, *The Cities of the Eastern Roman Provinces* ([2]1971) 192ff. — D. Magie, *Roman Rule in Asia Minor* (1950) II, 1146ff. — W. M. Ramsay, *The Cities of St. Paul* (1907) 85-244. — W. Ruge, PW IVA/2, 2413-39. — W. C.

van Unnik, *Tarsus or Jerusalem: The City of Paul's Youth* (1952) (= *idem, Sparsa Collecta* [1973] I, 259-320). — *idem, Sparsa Collecta* I, 321-27. — H.-E. Wilhelm, *BHH* 1933.

Tarsus, under Caesar known briefly as Juliopolis, from 64 B.C. was the capital of the Roman province Cilicia and had a history traceable back to the Assyrian period. Even before Alexander the Great, it was the capital city of an independent kingdom. Strabo xiv.5.9 calls it a city of scholars, Diodorus Siculus xiv.20.2 "the largest of the cities in Cilicia." The proper noun Ταρσός is additionally attested in Dio Chrysostom *Or.* 16[33].17; 17[34].46; Arrian *Anabasis* ii.4.7; and in Josephus and inscriptions. The phrase Ταρσὸς τῆς Κιλικίας (Acts 22:3) was common (Diodorus Siculus xx.108.2; Xenophon Ephesius ii.13.5; Josephus *Ant.* ix.208).

Luke calls Ταρσός "a city not undistinguished" (Acts 21:39) and mentions it several times (9:30; 11:25), since it was Paul's birthplace (22:3; from here also incorporated into 21:39 D). Paul is twice called "a man of *Tarsus*" (9:11; 21:39), again a form common at the time (Apollodorus of Athens [*FGH* 244, frag. 55]; Strabo xiv.5.14; Arrian *Anabasis* ii.4.7; Plutarch *Mar.* 46.2 and elsewhere; 2 Macc 4:30; inscriptions). According to the Lukan portrayal Paul's early period in Tarsus was probably limited to the first few months of life or even only to his birth, since Acts 22:3 attributes a Hellenistic schema to the course of Paul's youth (birth, upbringing [i.e., the first three years under his mother's care], education [i.e., by his father and teachers]), suggesting that from his young childhood Paul was brought up in Jerusalem (van Unnik). This may be the source of the Lukan portrayal (→ Παῦλος 4) that views Paul as a pupil of Rabbi Gamaliel (Acts 22:3) and presupposes that Paul has relatives in Jerusalem (23:16).

G. Schille

ταρταρόω *tartaroō* cast into Tartarus/hell, imprison in hell*

2 Pet 2:4, of fallen angels, whom God did not spare but "*imprisoned* in pits of gloom *in hell* (σειραῖς ζόφου ταρταρώσας)" (cf. Gen 6:1-4; Isa 24:21f.; Job 41:24 LXX; *1 Enoch* 10:4ff., 11ff.; 12:4ff.; 91:15; *Sib. Or.* ii.302; Jude 6; Rev 20:1-3). In Greek mythology Tartarus is the place of punishment of the Titans and of disobedient gods and is conceived as a gloomy place deep under the earth (cf. Hesiod *Th.* 720ff.; Homer *Il.* 14.279f.), occasionally also as the deepest place in Hades (→ ᾅδης). This conception also influenced Jewish apocalyptic thought. BAGD s.v.; H. von Geisau, *KP* V, 530f.

τάσσω *tassō* fix, appoint, determine, order*

Lit.: R. Bergmeier, "Loyalität als Gegenstand paulinischer Paraklese," *Theokratia* I (ed. K. H. Rengstorf; 1970) 51-63. — G. Delling, *TDNT* VIII, 27-31. — J. Friedrich, W. Pöhlmann, and P. Stuhlmacher, "Zur historischen Situation und Intention von Röm 13,1-7," *ZTK* 73 (1976) 131-66. — W. Schrage, *Die Christen und der Staat nach dem NT* (1971) 14-28, 50-62. — U. Wilckens, "Römer 13,1-7," idem, *Rechtfertigung als Freiheit* (1974) 203-45.

1. Τάσσω occurs 8 times in the NT (5 times in the Lukan writings) and is used in a way commensurate with general Greek usage (cf. BAGD s.v.; Delling).

2. a) *Fix, order, determine, appoint:* Acts 28:23: "*appoint* a day" (mid. as in Polybius iii.99.1; 2 Macc 14:21). According to Rom 13:1b Paul shares the common conviction of contemporary Judaism that → ἐξουσία (3) is bestowed by God (cf. Wilckens 223-26; Friedrich, Pöhlmann, and Stuhlmacher 145); he concludes: "Those [powers] that exist *have been instituted* by God" (13:1c). This theological use of τάσσω is used of *institute, appoint* (cf. 2 Sam 7:11) and corresponds to legal-political usage (cf., e.g., Tob 1:21; 2 Macc 8:22); see Bergmeier 60f.; → διατάσσω 5.

Τάσσω is also used with preps. 1 Cor 16:15: "they *have placed themselves* in the service of the saints," in the sense of "take on the responsibility/service" (cf. ἑαυτοὺς ἐπὶ τὴν διακονίαν τάττουσιν ταύτην, Plato *R.* 371c); Luke 7:8: "someone *set* under the power of command" (cf. τοῖς ὑπὸ τὴν αὐτῶν βασιλείαν τασσομένοις, *OGIS* I, 56, 13). The expression "*ordained* to eternal life" (Acts 13:48) is also attested in rabbinic writings (see Billerbeck II, 726f.), though it does not refer to the predestination of the individual, but rather to the election of the totality of the saved, cf. *1 Clem.* 58:2: οὗτος ἐνται γμένος καὶ ἐλλόγιμος ἔσται εἰς τὸν ἀριθμὸν τῶν σῳζομένων (see R. Bergmeier, *Glaube als Gabe nach Johannes* [BWANT 112, 1980] 60f.).

b) When it refers to *order, direct,* τάσσω is used with the acc. and inf. (BDF §409): in the sense of *determine/ arrange* (Acts 15:2); "all that *is appointed/determined* for you to do" (22:10; cf. Thucydides iii.22: οἷς ἐτέτακτο παραβοηθεῖν). Matt 28:16 uses the term in a fashion analogous to the formula for the carrying out of orders (cf. Matt 21:6 and elsewhere), though here it has been editorially altered beyond tradition (cf. εἰς τὴν Γαλιλαίαν, 28:7, 10 par. Mark 16:7): "to the mountain to which Jesus *had directed/sent* them" (cf. J. Lange, *Das Erscheinen des Auferstandenen im Evangelium nach Matthäus* [FzB 11, 1973] 436ff., 448ff.).   R. Bergmeier

ταῦρος, ου, ὁ *tauros* bull, ox*

Matt 22:4 mentions the slaughter of "*oxen* and fattened calves" (ταῦροι καὶ σιτιστά) for a royal wedding feast (cf. Prov 9:2; *b. Ketub.* 3b, 4a). Acts 14:13 mentions *oxen* as sacrificial beasts (for Zeus); see further Heb 9:13 (αἷμα τράγων καὶ ταύρων) and 10:4 (cf. Isa 1:11; Lev 16:2ff., 14ff.), referring to the levitical atonement sacri-

fices eclipsed and supplanted by the αἷμα τοῦ Χριστοῦ (9:14), since they produce only cultic purity and do not cleanse one from sin. K.-H. Bernhardt, *BHH* 1870f.; M. Weippert, *BL* 1647f.

ταὐτά *tauta* the same

This instance of crasis (ταὐτά for τὰ αὐτά) occurs in the NT only as a textual variant in Luke 6:23, 26; 17:30 in the combination κατὰ ταὐτά. See BDF §18.

ταφή, ῆς, ἡ *taphē* burial; burial place*

Matt 27:7: ταφὴ τοῖς ξένοις, "*burial place* for strangers" (of the potter's field/field of blood; → κεραμεύς).

τάφος, ου, ὁ *taphos* grave, tomb*

1. Occurrences in the NT — 2. The woes in Matt 23:27, 29 — 3. Jesus' tomb according to Matthew — 4. Rom 3:13

Lit.: C. Andresen, *RGG* II, 1816f. — J. Blinzler, "Die Grablegung Jesu in historischer Sicht," *Resurrexit* (ed. E. Dhanis; 1974) 56-107. — I. Broer, *Die Urgemeinde und das Grab Jesu* (SANT 31, 1972). — H. von Campenhausen, *Der Ablauf der Osterereignisse und das leere Grab* (SHAW 1952/4, [3]1966). — W. L. Craig, "The Historicity of the Empty Tomb of Jesus," *NTS* 31 (1985) 39-67. — J. Jeremias, *Heiligengräber in Jesu Umwelt* (*Mt 23,29; Lk 11,47*) (1958). — L. A. Keck, "The Function of Rom 3:10-18," FS Dahl 141-57. — R. Kratz, *Auferweckung als Befreiung* (SBS 65, 1973) on Matt 27:62–28:15. — A. Kuschke, *BRL* 122-29. — T. R. W. Longstaff, "The Women at the Tomb: Matt 28:1 Reexamined," *NTS* 27 (1980/81) 277-82. — F. Neirynck, "John and the Synoptics: The Empty Tomb Stories," *NTS* 30 (1984) 161-87. — J. Nelis, *BL* 638-42. — L. Oberlinner, "Die Verkündigung der Auferweckung Jesu im geöffneten und leeren Grab," *ZNW* 73 (1982) 159-82. — L. Schenke, *Auferstehungsverkündigung und leeres Grab* (SBS 33, [2]1969). — For further bibliography → θάπτω.

1. The noun τάφος occurs 7 times in the NT, 6 of these in Matthew. Rom 3:13 uses τάφος in a scriptural citation. Apart from the woes uttered against the scribes and Pharisees (Matt 23:27, 29), which come from Q (cf. Luke 11:44, 47), Matthew mentions only Jesus' tomb (27:61, 64, 66; 28:1). In the woes Luke reads τὰ μνημεῖα in both instances instead of the pl. of τάφος. Matthew might have replaced μνημεῖον with τάφος (Schulz, *Q* 105, 108). The Lukan parallel to Matt 27:61 uses τὸ μνημεῖον instead of ὁ τάφος (Luke 23:55, dependent on Mark 15:46). Here, too, Matthew uses the catchword τάφος on his own initiative. Τάφος is attested since Homer (*Od.* 4.547; 20.307 and elsewhere, referring to "burial, burial service"; cf. → θάπτω); in all NT occurrences, however, it refers to *tomb*. Only in Rom 3:13 is it used fig.

2. The woes against the scribes and Pharisees in Matt

23:27, 29 are constructed parallel. In both instances Jesus calls them ὑποκριταί, and a ὅτι clause then explicates their "hypocrisy" (and justifies the woes). V. 27b: "You are like whitewashed *tombs*"; v. 29b: "for you build the *tombs* of the prophets and adorn the monuments of the righteous." In the first instance the pretense consists in the tombs' appearing beautiful on the outside while abounding with impurity on the inside (v. 27c, d): Those criticized by Jesus appear to be righteous on the outside, though they are inwardly full of "hypocrisy and lawlessness" (v. 28). In the second cry of woe, Jesus contrasts the care given to the tombs of the prophets and saints (v. 29b) with the hypocrisy of the scribes and Pharisees: they are actually of one mind with their fathers, who murdered the prophets (vv. 30f.). See Schulz, *Q* 105f., 108-10.

3. Only Matthew calls Jesus' tomb a τάφος. In 27:61 (different in Mark 15:47) he speaks of the women "sitting opposite the *tomb*" after Jesus' burial (v. 60: in a tomb hewn in the rock). In the section exclusive to Matthew concerning the tomb guards (27:62-66), v. 64 reports that the chief priests and Pharisees petitioned Pilate "to secure the *tomb* until the third day." Thus commences the Matthean portrayal of the resurrection of Jesus, following the model of deliverance miracles (Kratz 60). Pilate puts a guard at their disposal, and "they made the *tomb* secure" by sealing it with a stone and posting a guard in front (v. 66). On Easter Sunday the two women come "to see the *tomb*" (28:1). Matthew probably assimilated the information in 27:61 and 28:1 to Jewish burial customs (Longstaff).

4. Rom 3:13a ("their throat is an open *grave*") stands in a collection of biblical quotations (vv. 10b-18) Paul has probably taken from a testimonium (or florilegium). Formally this is a "message of judgment" (E. Käsemann, *Rom* [Eng. tr., 1980] 85f.). Although a convincing analysis of the structure of this collection is not possible, it is nonetheless clear that with vv. 13f. "sins of the word are especially stressed" (Käsemann 86) and that v. 13a, b finds its biblical parallel in Ps 5:10 LXX (v. 13c cites Ps 139:4 LXX). Jer 5:16 calls the mouth of slanderers "an open tomb." Rom 3:13 appears to reflect Jewish hatred of the gospel (Käsemann 86f.).   G. Schneider

τάχα *tacha* perhaps, possibly, probably*

Τάχα occurs in the NT with the ind., otherwise usually with ἄν and opt. Rom 5:7: τάχα τις καὶ τολμᾷ, "*perhaps* one will even dare"; Phlm 15: *perhaps/possibly*. BAGD s.v.; BDF §385.

ταχέως *tacheōs* fast, quickly; soon, too quickly*

Ταχέως occurs 15 times in the NT (though not in Matthew or Mark), 10 times in the positive degree

ταχέως; 4 times in the comparative τάχιον, *faster, right away;* and only in Acts 17:15 in the superlative (ὡς) τάχιστα, *fast/as fast as possible.* Ταχέως usually occurs with vbs. of motion: ἐξέρχομαι ταχέως (Luke 14:21); ταχέως ἀνίστημι καὶ ἐξέρχομαι (John 11:31; cf. v. 29); esp. in organizational messages in letters: ταχέως ἔρχομαι (1 Cor 4:19; Phil 2:24; 2 Tim 4:9, v.l. τάχιον); ταχέως πέμπω (Phil 2:19); ταχέως γράφω (Luke 16:6). It refers to *all too quickly, hastily, frivolously* in Gal 1:6 (ὅτι οὕτως ταχέως μετατίθεσθε); 2 Thess 2:2 (εἰς τὸ μὴ ταχέως σαλευθῆναι); 1 Tim 5:22 (χεῖρας ταχέως μηδενὶ ἐπιτίθει).

The comparative τάχιον has an intensifying effect only in John 20:4 (προέδραμεν τάχιον τοῦ Πέτρου, "he ran *faster* than Peter") and Heb 13:19 (ἵνα τάχιον ἀποκατασταθῶ ὑμῖν, "that I may be restored to you *faster/as soon as possible*"). Otherwise it corresponds to an intensified positive: John 13:27 (ὃ ποιεῖς ποίησον τάχιον, "what you are going to do, do *quickly/right away*"); Heb 13:23 (ἐὰν τάχιον ἔρχηται, "if he comes *very soon/right away*"); cf. 1 Tim 3:14 v.l.; 2 Tim 4:9 v.l.; see BDF §§61, 244.

The superlative phrase ὡς τάχιστα, *as fast as possible* (Acts 17:15), derives from literary language (Josephus *Vita* 16; BDF §60). BAGD s.v.

ταχινός, 3 *tachinos* imminent, near*

2 Pet 1:14: ταχινή ἐστιν ἡ ἀπόθεσις, "the putting off of my body *will soon occur*"; 2:1: ταχινὴ ἀπώλεια, "*swift /sudden* destruction."

τάχιον *tachion* faster; soon, right away
→ ταχέως.

τάχιστα *tachista* fastest, most quickly
→ ταχέως.

τάχος, ους, τό *tachos* quickness, haste, speed*

In the NT only in the combination ἐν τάχει, *immediately, without delay* (Acts 12:7; 22:18; cf. 10:33 D; 17:15 D); *soon* (Luke 18:8; Acts 25:4; Rom 16:20; 1 Tim 3:14 [v.l. τάχιον]; Rev 1:1 and 22:6: ἃ δεῖ γενέσθαι ἐν τάχει, "what must *soon/in a short time* take place" [cf. Dan 2:28f.; 2:45 Theodotion; Mark 13:7 par.]).

ταχύ *tachy* quickly, soon, right away
Neut. sg. of → ταχύς, used as an adv.

ταχύς, 3 *tachys* fast, swift*

This word occurs as an adj. only in Jas 1:19: ταχὺς εἰς τὸ ἀκοῦσαι, "*quick* to hear." It appears otherwise (12 times) in the neut. sg. as the adv. ταχύ: *soon, in a short time,* or *immediately thereafter* (Mark 9:39); *right away, quickly, immediately, without delay* (Matt 5:25; 28:7, 8 ["depart *quickly*"; cf. Mark 16:8 TR: ταχὺ ἔφυγον]; Luke 15:22; John 11:29 [cf. v. 31]). It occurs 6 times in Revelation in the phrase ἔρχομαι ταχύ (2:16; 3:11; 11:14; 22:7, 12, 20; also 2:5 Koine and elsewhere) as a word of both consolation and admonition.

τέ *te* and

1. Occurrences in the NT — 2. Τέ alone — 3. Τὲ (. . .) καί — 4. Ambiguous occurrences — 5. Τὲ . . . τέ — 6. Τέ with ἔτι or γάρ

Lit.: BAGD s.v. — BDF §§443f. — KÜHNER, *Grammatik* II /2, 241-45. — MAYSER, *Grammatik* II/3, 155-66. — MORGEN-THALER, *Statistik* 148. — MOULTON, *Grammar* III, 338f. — RADERMACHER, *Grammatik* 5f. — VKGNT II s.v.

1. The coordinating conj. τέ, an enclitic always used in postpositive position, functions either independently or in combination with καί or—rarely—with other connectives, or it appears with a second τέ in the sense of *both . . . and.*

Τέ occurs 215 times in the NT, 151 of which (i.e., 70 percent) are in Acts (an unusually high frequency, not just by NT standards), 20 in Hebrews, 18 in Romans, and 9 in Luke. It does not occur in Mark, Galatians, Colossians, 1–2 Thessalonians, 1–2 Timothy, Titus, Philemon, 1–2 Peter, or 1–3 John. (These enormous differences in statistical occurrence are explained by differing treatments of the tradition, in which in several instances τέ and δέ appear to have been exchanged; examples in BDF §443.) In view of the statistical findings and to avoid distorting the overall picture, Acts is treated separately in the sections below.

2. Τέ occurs as an independent particle (aside from Acts) only rarely in the NT (13 times). It usually connects two verbal statements, including participles (Matt 27:48; 28:12; Rom 16:26; Heb 1:3), infs. (Eph 3:19), and finite vbs. (John 4:42; 6:18; Rom 2:19; Heb 12:2; Jude 6). Only in 1 Cor 4:21, Heb 6:5, and 9:1 does it connect two nouns.

In contrast, in half the instances in Acts (i.e., *ca.* 75 times, and indeed *ca.* 95 times if one includes the instances under → 4), τέ is used independently, in the majority of instances as a connective for two finite vbs. 12:17 is typical: διηγήσατο . . . εἶπέν τε, "he told them . . . *and* said." In a striking number of instances the first of two elements joined with τέ is a predicative partc., e.g., 12:12: συνιδών τε ἦλθεν, "*and* when he realized this, he went."

In isolated instances τέ is also used to connect two participles (only 2:33; 5:19; 10:22; 20:11; 27:20; 28:23), infs. (only 11:26; 15:5, 39; 19:12; 20:35; 23:10, 24; 27:21b), or nouns (only 9:15; 24:5; 26:4), and in 1:15 and 4:13 also to introduce a parenthetical comment. In

these cases τέ is probably often merely a stylistic variation of the much more frequent καί, though τέ sometimes does show a closer connection between two statements than does καί.

3. By far the most frequent usage of τέ in the NT (not counting Acts) is in combination with καί. When used together, these two conjunctions signal a closer connection between two sentence parts than either particle can alone, for which English has no simple equivalent.

Τέ and καί appear together when the first of the two connected items consists of only one word (e.g., Heb 11:32: Δαυίδ τε καὶ Σαμουήλ). Otherwise they are most often separated by at least one element of the first item (e.g., Luke 2:16: τήν τε Μαριὰμ καὶ τὸν Ἰωσήφ).

Examples such as Plato *Phd.* 58c show that this rule is not inflexible: μεταξὺ τῆς δίκης τε καὶ τοῦ θανάτου, and Acts 14:5 and 26:20. The rule, however, perhaps helps to analyze the use of πάντων in Rev 19:18. There the pronoun is likely not a modifier of the following word ἐλευθέρων but stands in apposition to what follows ("of all men—both free and slaves"; otherwise one would expect the sequence to be πάντων τε ἐλευθέρων καὶ . . .). Rom 1:16 and 2:9, 10 are a special case; the adv. πρῶτον is inserted between the connected sentence members (e.g., Rom 1:16: Ἰουδαίῳ τε πρῶτον καὶ Ἕλληνι), which on the basis of its own position manifests a particular affinity with Ἰουδαῖος.

As a rule, τὲ (. . .) καί connects nouns or adjs., rarely nominal forms of a vb. (only Heb 2:11; 6:4; Luke 12:45). The occurrence of τὲ . . . καί connecting finite vb. forms (Luke 24:20), also a rarity outside the NT, is thus questionable (*contra* BDF §443.1).

That τὲ (. . .) καί connects elements more closely than καί alone can be seen in the following examples, where a) further sentence members are coordinated to the two elements connected by τὲ (. . .) καί, b) a synonymous or contrasting conceptual pair is coordinated, c) the unity of the conceptual pair is expressed through a more general term either preceding or following, or d) the unity is expressed by other words.

a) Luke 2:16: τήν τε Μαριὰμ καὶ τὸν Ἰωσήφ καὶ τὸ βρέφος, the parents as a couple with the child; cf. also Heb 9:2; Luke 12:45; 1 Cor 1:30; Heb 2:4; 6:19; 11:32; Rev 19:18.

b) Heb 5:7: δεήσεις τε καὶ ἱκετηρίας, synonyms; Heb 5:14: καλοῦ τε καὶ κακοῦ, antonyms; cf. Matt 22:10; Luke 12:45; 22:66; Rom 1:12, 14 (bis); 3:9, etc.

c) Matt 22:10: πάντας . . . , πονηρούς τε καὶ ἀγαθούς, where the word pair stands in apposition to πάντας; cf. Luke 22:66; John 2:15; 1 Cor 1:24, 30, etc.; the comprehensive term follows the pair, e.g., in Rom 3:9; 10:12; Heb 2:11.

d) Luke 23:12: ἐγένοντο δὲ φίλοι ὅ τε Ἡρῴδης καὶ ὁ Πιλᾶτος, where τε . . . καί expands φίλοι.

In Acts τέ is connected with καί at least 40 times, 22 of these in the form τὲ καί. In two of the latter, the first item joined has several constituent parts, thus breaking the rule discussed above. Τὲ (. . .) καί almost exclusively connects information about persons or places, and only

τεκνογονία

once each joins infs. (1:1), temporal information (9:24), abstract nouns (26:3), advs. (26:22), things (21:5), and scriptural information (28:23). Hence the use of τέ (. . .) καί is more limited in Acts than in the rest of the NT and in some instances appears to be formulaic, e.g., in the more frequent combination (varying only in case) ἄνδρες τε καὶ γυναῖκες (5:14; 8:12; 9:2; 22:4).

4. The function of τέ is not clear in all cases. In Luke 21:11 τέ can be a connective between vv. 10 and 11 or between σεισμοί and λιμοί (cf. BDF §443.1); similarly Luke 24:20; on Heb 6:4 cf. O. Michel, *Heb* [KEK] 241.

In Acts there are over 20 cases in which it is uncertain whether τέ is connected with a preceding clause or—in the case of asyndetic clausal addition—whether it is in construction with a following καί or even τέ (→ 5). Since in all significant instances the relevant preceding and following elements are finite vb. forms, if one considers the findings under → 3 (i.e., that τὲ [. . .] καί connects only nominal forms), one can probably safely assume that the author did not perceive or employ τὲ (. . .) καί with vbs. as creating a functional unity.

Acts contains some complicated cases. In the sequence μέλλειν τε καὶ καθαιρεῖσθαι in 19:27, τέ establishes the connection with a preceding λογισθῆναι, καθαιρεῖσθαι is dependent on μέλλειν, and accordingly καί is to be translated "also." In 9:18, 29 τὲ καί stands between predicates, and yet they function separately; it would be contrary to Lukan style, however, to analyze the first of the two predicates as standing in an asyndetic relation to the preceding material. Further examples: 2:43, 46; 6:12; 7:26; 8:28; 9:3; 13:4, 11; 14:21; 16:3, 34; 19:6; 21:30; 22:7, 23; 25:2; 26:10f.; 24:23 (with infs.).

5. The connection of two sentence elements with τὲ . . . τέ in the sense of *both . . . and* is rare in other prose as well, and the NT offers only the following examples: Rom 14:8: ἐάν τε γάρ . . . ἐάν τε, "*[both]* if . . . *and* if"; ἐάν τε οὖν . . . ἐάν τε, "so then, *[both]* whether . . . *or* whether [both if . . . and if]"; Acts 26:16: μάρτυρα ὧν τε εἶδες ὧν τε ὀφθήσομαί σοι, "witness *both* to the things that you have seen *and* to those that I will show to you"; also 26:10.

Rom 1:26f. is not without ambiguity, since the equality of the second member is already unusually emphasized by ὁμοίως and καί. In Acts 2:46, 17:4, 27:3, and Heb 6:2 considerations of content suggest that the τὲ . . . τέ construction signifies only a simple enumeration joined with *and*.

6. Τέ appears to function only for intensification of other connectives when it follows ἔτι in Luke 14:26 and Acts 21:28, and when it precedes γάρ in Rom 7:7 and 2 Cor 10:8. On words with the suffix -τε such as ὥστε, οὔτε, μήτε, εἴτε, → s.v.   K.-H. Pridik

τεῖχος, ους, τό *teichos* wall; city wall*

Τεῖχος occurs in Acts 9:25 and 2 Cor 11:33 (variously διὰ τοῦ τείχους) in reference to the *city wall* of Damascus, through which Paul was lowered (through a window, 2 Cor 11:33) in a basket. Heb 11:30 mentions τὰ τείχη Ἰεριχώ (Josh 6:14ff.). Rev 21:12 speaks of the *city wall* of the heavenly Jerusalem, which is a great, high wall with twelve gates (v. 12; cf. Ezek 48:30ff.) and twelve foundation stones (v. 14); it measures 144 cubits (vv. 15, 17; cf. Ezek 40:3ff.), its substructure is made of jasper (v. 18), and its foundations are adorned with precious jewels (v. 19; cf. Isa 54:11f.; Tob 13:17). D. Georgi, FS Bornkamm 351-72.

τεκμήριον, ου, τό *tekmērion* proof*

Τεκμήριον, in contrast to μαρτύριον and similar terms (→ μαρτυρία), refers to evidential proof credible on its own merits (cf. Thucydides ii.39; Plato *Lg.* x.886d and elsewhere); so also Acts 1:3: ἐν πολλοῖς τεκμηρίοις, of the appearances and activity of the resurrected Jesus during the "forty days" between resurrection and ascension. D. L. Mealand, "The Phrase 'Many Proofs' in Acts 1:3, and in Hellenistic Writers," *ZNW* 80 (1989) 134f.

τεκνίον, ου, τό *teknion* little child*

The diminutive form of → τέκνον occurs in the NT only in the voc. pl. τεκνία and only in John and 1 John as an endearing address used by Jesus for his disciples (John 13:33) or by the author of 1 John for his congregation (2:1, 12, 28; 3:7, 18; 4:4; 5:21). Cf. in contrast τέκνα τοῦ θεοῦ (John 1:12; 11:52; 1 John 3:1, 2, 10; 5:2).

τεκνογονέω *teknogoneō* bear or beget children*

1 Tim 5:14: younger widows not enrolled in the "list of widows" (vv. 9ff., → χήρα) should remarry, *bear children,* and take care of their households.

τεκνογονία, ας, ἡ *teknogonia* childbearing (noun)*

According to 1 Tim 2:15 in its interpretation of Gen 3:16, *bearing children/motherhood* is the special task of women, including according to v. 15b a life in faith (possibly a reference to the rearing of children in faith; cf. *b. Ber.* 17a): σωθήσεται δὲ διὰ τῆς τεκνογονίας. The background is probably the Jewish view that to endure the pains of childbirth suspends the curse in Gen 3:16. In anti-Gnostic polemic, both men (1 Tim 2:8) and women (vv. 9ff.) are directed toward the God-given orders of life and living together. (On the Gnostic hostility toward marriage, cf. Irenaeus *Haer.* i.24.3: *nubere autem et generare a Satana dicunt esse;* 1 Tim 4:3: κωλυόντων γαμεῖν). M. Dibelius and H. Conzelmann, *Pastoral Epistles* (Hermeneia) ad loc.

(excursus); A. Kassing, *LuM* 23 (1958) 39-63; N. Brox, *Die Pastoralbriefe* (RNT) ad loc.

τέκνον, ου, τό *teknon* child*

1. Occurrences in the NT and meaning — 2. Hebraisms involving τέκνον — 3. Τέκνον and one's parents — 4. Spiritual children in the faith — 5. Children of God — a) Paul — b) John and 1 John

Lit.: O. BAUERNFEIND, *RGG* II, 1798-1800. — O. BETZ, "Die Geburt der Gemeinde durch den Lehrer," *NTS* 3 (1956/57) 314-26 (on 1QH 3:1ff.). — BILLERBECK I, 219f., 371-74. — J. BLINZLER, "Kind und Königreich Gottes (Mk 10,14f.)," *idem, Aus Welt und Umwelt des NT* (1969) 41-53. — *idem, LTK* VI, 148f. — G. BRAUMANN, *DNTT* I, 285-87. — B. BYRNE, *"Sons of God"— "Seed of Abraham": A Study of the Idea of the Sonship of God of All Christians in Paul against the Jewish Background* (AnBib 83, 1979). — G. DELLING, "Lexikalisches zu τέκνον" (1964), *idem, Studien zum NT und zum hellenistischen Judentum* (1970) 270-80. — *idem,* "Die 'Söhne (Kinder) Gottes' im NT," FS Schürmann 615-31. — A. DUPREZ, "Note sur le rôle de l'Esprit-Saint dans la filiation du chrétien," *RSR* 52 (1964) 421-31 (on Gal 4:6). — W. GRUNDMANN, *Die Gotteskindschaft in der Geschichte Jesu und ihre religionsgeschichtlichen Voraussetzungen* (1938). — G. HAUFE, "Das Kind im NT," *TLZ* 104 (1979) 625-38. — J. JEREMIAS, *Infant Baptism in the First Four Centuries* (1960). — *idem, The Origins of Infant Baptism* (1963). — *idem, Theology,* 178-203. — G. KLEIN, "Jesus und die Kinder. Bibelarbeit über Mk 10,13-16," *idem, Ärgernisse* (1970) 58-81. — S. LÉGASSE, *Jésus et l'enfant* (ÉBib, 1969), index s.v. (353). — A. OEPKE, *TDNT* V, 616-54. — E. PAX, *LTK* IV, 1114-16. — R. SCHNACKENBURG, *1–3 John* (HTKNT, ⁵1975) 175-83. — H.-H. SCHROEDER, *Eltern und Kinder in der Verkündigung Jesu* (TF 53, 1972). — W. TWISSELMANN, *Die Gotteskindschaft der Christen nach dem NT* (1939). — M. VELLANICKAL, *The Divine Sonship of Christians in the Johannine Writings* (AnBib 72, 1977).

1. Τέκνον occurs 99 times in the NT. It is esp. common in Matthew (14 times) and Luke (14 times) but appears not at all in Hebrews, James, or Jude. Τέκνον is etymologically related to → τίκτω ("bear/beget") and refers to the *child* in relationship to its parents. In addition to the literal meaning (→ 3), its fig. use also occurs quite frequently (→ 4 and 5).

2. In several cases, τέκνον appears in a Hebraistic phrase. As in the LXX, a city's inhabitants are referred to as its τέκνα (Matt 23:37 par. Luke 13:34; Luke 19:44; Gal 4:25). The connection between a group of people and an abstract reality or quality is expressed by τέκνα with gen. (Eph 2:3 [ὀργῆς]; 5:8 [φωτός]; 1 Pet 1:14 [ὑπακοῆς]; 2 Pet 2:14 [κατάρας]); see Radermacher, *Grammatik* 28. Cf. also Luke 7:35 (par. Matt 11:19 C Koine D): τέκνα of wisdom.

3. In the following instances τέκνον is used in its literal sense of a child in relationship with its father and mother (Mark 12:19; 13:12a par. Matt 10:21a; Luke 1:7; Acts

7:5; Rev 12:4; the pl. is used in Matt 7:11; 10:21b; 15:26; 18:25; 19:29; 22:24; Mark 7:27 bis; 10:29, 30; 13:12b; Luke 1:17; 11:13; 14:26; 18:29; 20:31; 23:28; Acts 21:5, 21; 1 Cor 7:14; 2 Cor 12:14a, b; 1 Thess 2:7, 11 [metaphorically]; 1 Tim 3:4, 12; 5:4; Titus 1:6). Of significance regarding the question of early Christian infant baptism is 1 Cor 7:14: The children of Christian parents are "holy" (and not "unclean").

The "household codes" in Col 3:20, 21 and Eph 6:1, 4 address or otherwise mention *children.* According to the context, τέκνον also more specifically refers to the *son* (Matt 21:28a; Phil 2:22; Rev 12:5). The voc. τέκνον also addresses the son (Matt 21:28b; Luke 2:48; 15:31; 16:25).

The pl. of τέκνον refers in a larger sense to someone's *descendants* (Matt 2:18; 27:25; Acts 2:39; 13:33; Gal 4:27, 31). This might also be the sense intended in Rom 9:8a (τὰ τέκνα τῆς σαρκός), 9:8b, and Gal 4:28 ([τῆς] ἐπαγγελίας; cf. also → 2). "*Children* of the devil" in 1 John 3:10 are contrasted with "*children* of God" (→ 5.b); cf. Acts 13:10.

4. The transition to fig. usage can be seen when Jesus addresses an adult as *my child [son]* (Mark 2:5 par. Matt 9:2). The relationship to one's teacher or apostle is described as being a (spiritual) child in the faith (1 Cor 4:14, 17; 2 Cor 6:13; Gal 4:19; Phlm 10; 1 Tim 1:2; 2 Tim 1:2; Titus 1:4; 3 John 4). This is also expressed in the voc. τέκνον (1 Tim 1:18; 2 Tim 2:1; pl.: Mark 10:24). The adherents of false teaching are called its *children* (Rev 2:23), as are the members of a church (2 John 1, 4, 13). In the context of children of faith, τέκνον expresses the analogy between child and procreator (Matt 3:9 par. Luke 3:8 ["*children* to Abraham"]; John 8:39 ["Abraham's *children*"]; cf. Rom 9:7; 1 Pet 3:6).

5. a) Paul associates the idea of Christians as God's children with that of their adoption by God. When one cries out in the Spirit "Abba! Father!" this shows the believers that they are "God's *children*" (Rom 8:16); as children they are also heirs, i.e., fellow heirs of Christ (v. 17). For Paul τέκνα θεοῦ is synonymous with υἱοὶ θεοῦ (cf. vv. 14, 19). The slavery of φθορά is juxtaposed with the "freedom of the glory of the *children* of God" (v. 21). Our future adoption as sons will effect the "redemption of our bodies" (v. 23). Not all descendants are Abraham's *children* (9:7), it is not the "*children* of flesh" who are the "*children* of God" (v. 8a), but rather the "*children* of the promise" (v. 8b). 9:26 cites Hos 2:1 LXX and thus establishes scripturally this condition of being a child of God. Paul does, however, prefer the expression υἱοὶ (τοῦ) θεοῦ (Rom 9:26; 2 Cor 6:18, with θυγατέρες; Gal 3:26; 4:6, 7). In Phil 2:15 he exhorts his listeners as "God's *children*" to live unblemished lives amid a perverse generation. The

parenesis in Eph 5:1 challenges Christians as "[God's] beloved *children*" to be "imitators of God."

The background of this early Christian talk of being children of God is essentially Jesus' own proclamation of God the Father, something discernible in Matt 5:45 par. Luke 6:35. Here such sonship is admittedly conceived quite strictly as a position to be attained in the future, a status to be conferred at the eschaton on the imitators of God's generous and forgiving goodness. Matt 5:9 also preserves this future eschatological character in saying that the peacemakers will be called "sons of God." The idea prevalent in Greek religion that all human beings are by nature children of God is just as alien to the gospel as it is to the OT. See J. Schmid, *Matt* (RNT) 111f.; Oepke 651; G. Delling, FS Dahl 18-28.

b) "Johannine" theology establishes the condition of believers as God's children with reference to their having been begotten by God (John 1:12f.). One encounters only the term τέκνον in this context, and not also υἱός, which is reserved for christological statements. Those born of God have received the ἐξουσία "to become *children* of God" (v. 12). Faith and sonship stand in eschatological tension. According to 11:52 Jesus' death occurred "not for the people alone, but also in order to gather into one the scattered *children* of God." In contrast to 1:12, which speaks of the power of believers to *become* God's children, their status as children of God is already taken for granted here: "The children of God here are those who are called and chosen by faith in Christ"—a "predestinarian view" (R. Schnackenburg, *John* II [Eng. tr., 1979] 350).

1 John speaks frequently of being "born of God" (2:29; 3:9; 4:7; 5:1, 4, 18). A person becomes a "*child* of God" by being born of God (3:1f., 10; 5:2). 3:9f. alternates between the terms "one born of God" and "*child* of God." The latter is no mere honorific title. 5:1f. shows "that the author is serious in his comparison with natural procreation; at the same time, it is clear that this manner of speech is only intended as an analogy or metaphor: the child of God *is* not the seed of God; rather, God's seed *remains in him*" (Schnackenburg, *1–John* 175). The antithetical expression "*children* of the devil" (3:10) should also warn against any "naturalistic" misinterpretation of such procreation by God.   G. Schneider

τεκνοτροφέω *teknotropheō* bring up children*

One of the prerequisites for admission to the status of widowhood is to have brought up children (εἰ ἐτεκνοτρόφησεν, 1 Tim 5:10).

τέκτων, ονος, ὁ *tektōn* (building) worker, carpenter*

Lit.: BAGD s.v. — R. A. BATEY, "Is Not This the Carpenter?"

NTS 30 (1984) 249-58 (esp. n. 2). — P. H. FURFEY, "Christ as Tektôn," *CBQ* 17 (1955) 324-35. — H. HÖPFL, "Nonne Hic Est Fabri Filius?" *Bib* 4 (1923) 41-55. — R. KNIERIM, *BHH* 2241.

Τέκτων refers to "one who makes, produces" (Latin *faber*), esp. when referring to woodworking (cf. Homer *Il.* 6.315; Plato *R.* x.597d; Josephus *Ant.* xv.390; τέκτων ξύλων καὶ τέκτων λίθων, 2 Kgdms 5:11; cf. 1 Chr 22:15; τέκτων καὶ ἀρχιτέκτων, Sir 38:27). According to Matt 13:55 Jesus is called ὁ τοῦ τέκτονος υἱός, and according to Mark 6:3, in contrast, ὁ τέκτων, ὁ υἱὸς τῆς Μαρίας (v.l. τοῦ τέκτονος υἱὸς καὶ τῆς Μαρίας; syr^pal omits ὁ τέκτων; cf. *TCGNT* ad loc.). These alterations and assimilations of the Markan statement to Matt 13:55 show that referring to Jesus himself as a worker was soon perceived as being offensive; cf. also Origen *Cels.* vi.34, 36, according to which Celsus uses this tradition against Jesus, whereupon Origen responds that nowhere in the Gospels is Jesus himself portrayed as a worker. Jewish society, however, by no means considered practicing a trade as a workman to be any sort of personal blemish; quite the contrary, it was one of the duties of a father to teach his son a trade (*t. Qidd.* 1:11; Billerbeck II, 10f.; on Matt 13:55 see *b. Sanh.* 106a, b). One can assume that Jesus and his father Joseph were *building workmen/carpenters*. In both occurrences the term ὁ τέκτων functions to present Jesus as the well-known fellow citizen in his home village, not to denigrate his lineage.

τέλειος, 3 *teleios* perfect, complete; adult*

1. Occurrences in the NT — 2. Range of meaning — 3.a) Matthew — b) 1 Cor 2:6 — c) Eph 4:13 — d) James

Lit.: G. BARTH, "Matthew's Understanding of the Law," in G. BORNKAMM, G. BARTH, and H. J. HELD, *Tradition and Interpretation in Matthew* (1963) 95-105. — A. BAUMANN, *Mitte und Norm des Christlichen* (1968) 193-96. — H. BRAUN, *Spätjüdisch-häretischer und frühchristlicher Radikalismus* (2 vols.; 1969), s.v. τάμîm and τέλειος. — H. BRUPPACHER, "Was sagte Jesus in Mt 5,48?" *ZNW* 58 (1967) 145. — G. DELLING, *TDNT* VIII, 67-78. — M. DIBELIUS, *Jas* (Hermeneia) 116-20. — J. DUPONT, "L'appel à imiter Dieu en Mt 5,48 et Luc 6,36," *RivB* 14 (1966) 137-58. — R. FABRIS, *Legge della libertà in Giacomo* (1977). — H. FRANKEMÖLLE, *Jahwebund und Kirche Christi* (1974) 286-93. — G. GERLEMAN, *THAT* II, 919-35, esp. 920f., 926f. — H. HÜBNER, *Das Gesetz in der synoptischen Tradition* (1973) 110-12. — K. KOCH, *THAT* II, 1045-51. — J. KÜNZEL, *Studien zum Gemeindeverständnis des Matthäusevangeliums* (1978) 218-50. — G. MIEGGE, *Il Sermone sul monte* (1970) 158-61. — P. J. DU PLESSIS, *Τέλειος: The Idea of Perfection in the NT* (1959). — R. REITZENSTEIN, *Hellenistic Mystery-Religions* (1978) 426-36. — B. RIGAUX, "Révélation des mystères et la perfection à Qumran et dans le NT," *NTS* 4 (1957 /58) 237-62. — L. SABOURIN, "Why Is God Called 'Perfect' in Mt 5,48?" *BZ* 24 (1980) 266-68. — W. SCHMITHALS, *Gnosticism in Corinth* (1971) 151-55. — R. SCHNACKENBURG, "Christian Perfection according to Matthew," Schnackenburg I, 158-89. —

W. Trilling, *Das wahre Israel* (^{3}1964) 192-96. — M. Winter, *Pneumatiker und Psychiker in Korinth* (1975). — Y. S. Yang, *Vollkommenheit nach paulinischem und konfuzianischem Verständnis. Ein Vergleich der Begriffe "téleios" bei Paulus und "Chéng" beim Verfasser des Buches "Chung-Yung"* (Diss. St. Ottilien, 1984). — E. Yarnold, "Τέλειος in St. Matthew's Gospel," *SE* IV (1968) 269-73. — J. Zmijewski, "Christliche 'Vollkommenheit.' Erwägungen zur Theologie des Jakobusbriefes," *SNTU* 5 (1980) 50-78. — For further bibliography → τέλος; see further *TWNT* X, 1279.

1. The 20 occurrences of τέλειος in the NT are distributed as follows: 3 in Matthew, 1 in Romans, 3 in 1 Corinthians, 1 in Ephesians, 1 in Philippians, 2 in Colossians, 2 in Hebrews, 5 in James, 1 in 1 Peter (adv.), 1 in 1 John.

2. In classical and Hellenistic Greek τέλειος refers to *perfect, without defect* (of sacrificial animals), *complete, fully developed, adult*.

Plato considers a person who has moved from corporeal existence to the world of ideas by recollection of his or her being to be τέλειος (*Phdr.* 249c). According to Aristotle "perfect virtue" (ἡ τελεία ἀρετή), which is realized in choice, includes practical reason (φρόνησις) and natural inclination to good (*MM* ii.3.1200a). That which is consistently chosen on its own merits is "simply perfect" (ἁπλῶς τέλειον), i.e., happiness or blessedness (εὐδαιμονία, *EN* i.7.1097a; → τέλος 2). For the Stoics the "complete person" is one who both has and realizes all virtues (von Arnim, *Fragmenta* III, 73, no. 299). For Philo the τέλειον ἀγαθόν is the highest form of ethical life (ἀγαθότης), in which all individual virtues are put into practice (*Migr.* 36f.); admittedly, the patriarchs are portrayed in Stoic terminology as "perfected ones" (*Abr.* 52ff.) in order to present the Mosaic law to readers schooled in Stoic thought (Winter 102f.; on Philo in general see *Abr.* 98-157). Philo also speaks of God as τὸ τέλειον (*Gig.* 45). In the *Corpus Hermeticum* those baptized with the νοῦς have become τέλειοι ἄνθρωποι, who in contrast to the λογικοί participate in gnosis (iv.4; cf. Reitzenstein 431f.).

Of the 91 occurrences of *tāmîm* in the OT, the LXX translates only 4 with τέλειος: Gen 6:9: Noah is τέλειος, *blameless,* an ἄνθρωπος δίκαιος; Exod 12:5: the Passover lamb is *without blemish;* Deut 18:13: by avoiding pagan cults, "You shall be [cultically] *pure/blameless* before your God" (cf. MT: "You should belong *wholly to [tāmîm tihyeh ʿim]* Yahweh, your God"); 2 Kgdms 22:26: μετὰ ἀνδρὸς τελείου. Of the 28 occurrences of *šālēm*, the LXX renders only 5 with τέλειος (the idiom τέλειος τῇ καρδίᾳ in 3 Kgdms 8:61; 11:4; 15:3, 14; 1 Chr 28:9).

Τέλειος is used in a threefold fashion in the NT:

a) as an adj. referring to people or God: *(the) complete /mature ones* (1 Cor 2:6; Heb 5:14; perhaps also Phil 3:15; Col 4:12 [is the intention here to distinguish between less perfect Christians, or is the word used ironically?]); *perfect,* of God (only Matt 5:48) and human beings (Matt 5:48; 19:21; Col 1:28; Jas 1:4; 3:2); *mature* (1 Cor 14:20, contrasted with παιδίον); on Eph 4:13 → 3.c.;

b) as the neut. subst. τὸ τέλειον, that which is *perfect* (Rom 12:2, with ethical reference; 1 Cor 13:10, with eschatological reference);

c) as an adj. modifying various terms: the "greater and more *perfect* tent" (Heb 9:11); "*perfect* work" (Jas 1:4); every "*perfect* gift" (v. 17); the "*perfect* law of freedom" (v. 25); "*perfect* love" (1 John 4:18).

3.a) Since τέλειος in Matthew is always redactional, it carries theological significance despite occurring only 3 times. In 5:48 the redactor uses it twice to replace οἰκτίρμων (Luke 6:36: Q) as a conclusion to the preceding antitheses and as the sum of fulfillment of the law (cf. 5:17; see W. Grundmann, *Matt* [THKNT] 179f. and *passim; contra* Delling 74 n. 35). Barth (97ff.) draws attention to the analogous use of *tāmîm* in 1QS and τέλειος in Matthew, though at the same time he correctly points out that Matthew does not use τέλειος as does the Qumran sect, namely, in a quantitative, extensive sense (as regards obedience to the Torah), but rather in an intensive sense (Braun II, 43 n. 1). Whereas the Qumran writings are concerned with correct, flawless fulfillment of the entire Torah, τέλειος in Matt 5:48 refers to a deepening of the law that culminates in the renunciation of vengeance on the one hand, and love of one's enemies on the other (Hübner 111), and in 19:21 in the renunciation of possessions by the rich. Neither 5:48 nor 19:21 makes legal demands.

b) When in 1 Cor 2:6 Paul addresses Christians as *complete/mature,* i.e., as "perfected pneumatics" (H. Lietzmann and W. G. Kümmel, *1-2 Cor* [HNT] 11) or "a higher class of believer" (H. Conzelmann, *1 Cor* [Hermeneia] 60), to whom he may presume to offer the proclamation of *his* wisdom (→ σοφία 3.c), he is responding to the Gnostic terminology prevalent in the church. (Because of 3:1, should we see in 2:6 an ironic undertone?) Since, however, the content of this wisdom ultimately consists in the cross of Christ proclaimed to *everyone,* Paul effectively bypasses any fundamental distinction between the *perfect* and the *imperfect* (cf. Winter 218: Paul cannot portray the esoteric wisdom announced in 2:6 with any consistency, since for all practical purposes he refers sophia to the proclamation of the cross meant for all Christians).

c) The meaning of εἰς ἄνδρα τέλειον in Eph 4:13 is disputed because of variously interpreted religio-historical presuppositions.

According to the view that considers the Gnostic savior-myth to be the background of this passage, Christ as the *perfect* man is the anthropos conceived as the highest pinnacle of his pleroma (→ πλήρωμα 3.b; so, e.g., earlier H. Schlier, *Christus und die Kirche im Epheserbrief* [1930] 27f.). F. Mussner represents the completely opposite view that the body of Christ (→ σῶμα 9) is in no way to be taken as a cosmic entity (*Christus, das All und die Kirche* [^{2}1968]). Among others, C. Colpe, who notes Philo's influence (FS Jeremias [1960] 172-87), and E. Schweizer, who cites the influence of Greek thought (*Neot* [1963] 293-316), mediate between this latter untenable view and that of Schlier. J. Gnilka understands ἀνὴρ τέλειος as a *grown* man: the church as an organism is involved in a process of growth that leads to adulthood, or the mature man (*Eph* [HTKNT] 215).

The thesis has by no means been refuted that the author of Ephesians is using Gnostic terminology in an anti-Gnostic argument. It does, however, need more detailed explication in view of the attempts of Colpe and others to show the indebtedness of the argument to contemporary influences.

d) Τέλειος is a key word in James. This parenetic letter challenges Christians to be *perfect* (1:4: τέλειοι used with ὁλόκληροι), either through the *"perfect* work" of steadfastness in temptation (v. 4) or through control over what one says (3:2). This result is made possible because every *"perfect* gift" comes from God (1:17)—above all, the *"perfect* law of freedom" (v. 25; → νόμος 4.b). Although this phrase may well betray Stoic influence (Stoic parallels are cited in Dibelius and in K. Niederwimmer, *Der Begriff der Freiheit im NT* [1966] 37ff.), James ultimately stands within the Jewish tradition of the law. As in Rom 13:8-10 (not Gal 5:14, → νόμος 4.b), the law is understood from the perspective of the commandment to love (2:8). It is striking how unaffectedly James understands originally cultic terms such as τέλειος in an exclusively ethical fashion (see H.-M. Schenke and K. M. Fischer, *Einleitung in die Schriften des NT* [1979] II, 232).

The problem lies in the precise determination of the relationship between the OT law and that of James. Is the attribute τέλειος added from the perspective of the "incomplete" law of the old covenant (F. Mussner, *Jas* [HTKNT] 109)? Or, following Fabris, is the *perfect* law as the "implanted word" (1:21) the law promised by Jeremiah and Ezekiel that God puts into every person's heart, in which case James would be of particular importance for a comprehensive biblical theology (Fabris 238f.: "The point of mediation between the two Testaments is constituted by the prophecy of law and Spirit being placed in the heart")? According to James, however, the *perfect* law is a law of freedom, not because God has put it into the Christian's heart, thus liberating that person for love, but because the *perfect* law itself can make a person who accepts it free to do deeds of love (→ ἐλευθερία 6). Such an understanding of the law is not mediated christologically and must be evaluated from the specific perspective of christology.

H. Hübner

τελειότης, ητος, ἡ *teleiotēs* perfection, completeness*

Col 3:14 speaks of → ἀγάπη (3.c) as the σύνδεσμος (→ δεσμός 5) τῆς τελειότητος, "bond of *perfection,*" an obj. gen. encompassing the previously enumerated individual Christian virtues and bringing them to perfection /completion; cf. BAGD s.v. σύνδεσμος ("bond of perfect unity"). The gen. could also be interpreted qualitatively (i.e., "the *perfect* bond"), which would change nothing in the relationship of ἀγάπη ἐπὶ πᾶσιν δὲ τούτοις (v. 14a). On this formulation cf. Plato *Plt.* 47.310a (ξύνδεσμος ἀρετῆς); *Lg.* xxi.5.921c (τῆς πόλεως σύνδεσμος, of the

νόμος). Τελειότης in Col 3:14 hardly refers to the "completeness" of the church (*contra* G. Delling, *TDNT* VIII, 79); instead, the context (vv. 12ff.) suggests the effects the parenesis has on the believers.

Heb 6:1 contrasts τελειότης with the "elementary doctrines of Christ" and refers to *completeness/perfection* in the sense of "maturity" or of "adulthood" in faith as the goal of the mature church, which is no longer in the initial situation of a young missionary church (cf. 5:11-14; see further 1 Cor 3:1ff.).

τελειόω *teleioō* complete (vb.)*

1. Occurrences in the NT — 2. Meaning — 3.a) The Johannine writings — b) Hebrews

Lit.: G. DELLING, *TDNT* VIII, 79-84. — J. D. M. DERRETT, "The Lucan Christ and Jerusalem: τελειοῦμαι (Lk 13:32)," *ZNW* 75 (1984) 36-43. — M. DIBELIUS, "Der himmlische Kultus nach dem Hebräerbrief," *idem, Botschaft* II, 160-76. — E. KÄSEMANN, *The Wandering People of God* (1984) 133-44. — O. MICHEL, *Heb* (KEK, ⁷1975) 144-46, 223-29, and *passim.* — A. VAN-HOYE, "L'oeuvre du Christ, don du Père (Jn. 5,36 et 17,4)," *RSR* 48 (1960) 377-419. — A. WIKGREN, "Patterns of Perfection in the Epistle to the Hebrews," *NTS* 6 (1959/60) 159-67. — For further bibliography → τέλος; τελέω.

1. Of the 23 occurrences of τελειόω in the NT, 9 are found in the Johannine writings (5 in John, 4 in 1 John), 9 in Hebrews, 2 in Luke, and 1 each in Acts, Philippians, and James.

2. Τελειόω as a causative vb. (with virtually the same meaning as → τελέω) is used of *complete* (metaphorically, Acts 20:24: "one's course"), *bring to an end* (e.g., Luke 2:43: "the days"), *place in a certain (final) condition* and thus *make complete/perfect* (→ 3), but also to *fulfill* (Scripture). The pass. τῇ τρίτῃ τελειοῦμαι (Luke 13:32) is translated "on the third day *I will reach my goal*" (BAGD s.v. 1), though it probably also implies "I *will come to the conclusion* (of my entire ministry)" (W. Grundmann, *Luke* [THKNT] 289); Jas 2:22: ἐκ τῶν ἔργων . . . ἐτελειώθη, faith "*reached completeness* on the basis of works"; Phil 3:12: οὐχ ὅτι . . . ἤδη τετελείωμαι, "not as if I already *had reached my goal.*"

3.a) John 4:34 is characteristic of Johannine christology. Jesus' entire being is involved in doing the Father's will and thus in *carrying out* his work, i.e., the work (→ ἔργον 3) the Father has commissioned him to do (R. Bultmann, *John* [Eng. tr., 1971] 194 n. 3: "τελειοῦν does not have to mean bringing something to a finish which has already been begun"; Delling 81: "carrying out the work of salvation"; differently R. Schnackenburg, *John* I [Eng. tr., 1968] 447: "bring to completion the work begun by the Father"). By *completing* the work commissioned him by the Father (17:4; "the event of the cross has also to be included in this work," Schnackenburg, *John* III [Eng. tr., 1982] 197), he has glorified the Father. 5:36 focuses more on the individual works, without losing sight of the "whole of Jesus' activity" (Bultmann, *John* 265f.). The works the Father commissioned Jesus to do show that Jesus is sent by the Father. The unity of the Father and Son is to be a model for those who believe in the Son (17:20), that they "may be *perfectly one*" (ἵνα ὦσιν τετελειωμένοι εἰς ἕν, v. 23). The phrase ἵνα τελειωθῇ ἡ γραφή (19:28) is synonymous with ἵνα ἡ γραφὴ πληρωθῇ, "that the Scripture be fulfilled" (19:24, → πληρόω 3.a).

1 John is combating enthusiastic Gnostics who claim among other things both to know and to love God. The criterion for knowledge of God, however, is brotherly love (which they do not practice). In a unique way in 2:3f. the author presents the idea that genuine knowledge of God can be recognized only in such brotherly love (cf. 4:20f. with 2:3ff.); only in the person who keeps God's word, i.e., the commandment of love, "has God's love *reached its goal* [*is perfected*, RSV; *comes to entirety*, Delling 81]" (ἡ ἀγάπη τοῦ θεοῦ τετελείωται, 2:5). Τοῦ θεοῦ here is clearly a subj. gen. (R. Bultmann, *1–3 John* [Hermeneia, 1973] 25; H. Balz, *1 John* [NTD] 176; Delling 81f.; differently → ἀγάπη 3.d; unclear: R. Schnackenburg, *1–3 John* [HTKNT] 103: "not to be understood simply as 'love toward God' [obj. gen.] . . . an expression for that which inheres in the Christian as divine essence"), as shown by the parallels 4:12 ("his love *attains its goal* in us" [RSV "is perfected"], τετελειωμένη ἐστίν; cf. Balz, *1 John* 171) and 4:17 (τετελείωται ἡ ἀγάπη μεθ' ἡμῶν). Precisely in our love for one another, however, does God's love attain its goal (v. 12). In v. 18, however, the subj. of οὐ τετελείωται ἐν τῇ ἀγάπῃ is the person who still fears. In all four instances τελειόω thus has an essential connection with ἀγάπη.

b) In the letter to the Hebrews τελειόω has a cultic sense. (Cf. the LXX cultic idiom τὰς χεῖρας τελειόω, which should probably be interpreted with Delling 81 as making someone "able to practice the cultus," thus referring to the OT priestly ordination. See also M. Noth, *Exod* [Eng. tr., 1962] 230f.: "The expression 'fill the hand', which outside the OT is in evidence in so early a source as the cuneiform texts of Mari, originally referred to the payment of certain fees for the performance of certain offices. In the OT the expression is applied specially to priests and has the formal meaning of instituting a priest in his office, perhaps with the passage of time losing its reference to its original etymological significance.") Together with other typical expressions from the OT cult (προσφέρω, "offer"; θυσία, "sacrifice"; προσέρχομαι, "approach [the Deity]"; νόμος, here, the OT "cultic law"), τελειόω nonetheless points beyond cultic thinking as such, for the law (→ νόμος 4.b) and the regularly occurring offerings that it requires cannot *make*

the cultic participants *perfect*, i.e., they cannot "put someone in the position in which he can come, or stand, before God" (Delling 82; 7:19; 9:9; 10:1). By his "single offering" (προσφορά, 10:14; cf. 10:1), however, the high priest Christ was able to do this.

Jesus himself, however, also attained perfection. It pleased God to *make him perfect* (2:10) through suffering as the pioneer of salvation. As he was crowned with glory and honor because of the suffering of death (v. 9), so he leads many sons to glory (if ἀγαγών refers to Jesus [Käsemann 144] and not to God [Michel 147f.]). The Son, perfected in glory by God, himself perfects the sons in glory. Similarly 5:8f.: He who learned obedience through his suffering became, as the *perfecter* (RSV "being made perfect"; τελειωθείς), the source of eternal salvation for all who obey him (see also 7:28).

The differing translations of 2:10 emerge in part from different evaluations of the religio-historical background. According to Käsemann the Gnostic redeemer myth is the major influence. Esp. O. Hofius (*Katapausis* [1970]; *Der Vorhang vor dem Thron Gottes* [1972]) has presented cogent counterarguments. The hypothesis of the letter's Gnostic conception, or of its anti-Gnostic conception couched in Gnostic terminology, has by no means been persuasively refuted (on the discussion of this question, which is central to any understanding of τελειόω, see Michel 225ff.; H.-M. Schenke and K. M. Fischer, *Einleitung in die Schriften des NT* [1979] II, 263ff. [with Hofius, *contra* Käsemann]).

How can one reconcile Jesus' being made perfect by God through his suffering and yet, as the preexistent Christ, being already the reflection (→ ἀπαύγασμα 2) of the divine glory (1:3), one who continues in this majesty yesterday, today, and forever (13:8) and as such makes the sons perfect? According to Fischer, we cannot logically integrate the two statements of enthronement-christology and preexistence-christology (Schenke and Fischer, *Einleitung* II, 252f.). The same holds true for the use of τελειόω. One might consider whether this terminological incompatibility might be explained through the incorporation of elements of the Gnostic myth and their subsequent resynthesis, admittedly with anti-Gnostic tendencies.

The statement concerning "the spirits of just men made *perfect*" (12:23) is difficult to assess. Is it to be understood eschatologically (God's judgment over them has already been made; cf. the rabbinic manner of speech regarding the "perfect righteous ones" [gᵉmûrîm ṣaddîqîm])? Or is the meaning soteriological (deceased *perfected ones;* 2:10; 5:9; cf. Michel 467)? The context might suggest the latter. 11:40 says unequivocally that the witnesses of faith of the old covenant "are not to *be made perfect* apart from us" (cf. further E. Grässer, "Exegese nach Auschwitz? Kritische Anmerkungen zur hermeneutischen Bedeutung des Holocaust am Beispiel von Hebr 11," *KD* 27 [1981] 152-63).   H. Hübner

τελείως *teleiōs* fully, perfectly, completely*

In 1 Pet 1:13 τελείως might modify νήφοντες ("be

completely sober"; cf. also 4:7; 1 Thess 5:6), or as suggested by the context (1 Pet 1:3-12, 14ff.) it should be taken with ἐλπίσατε, yielding the eschatological sense "Set your hope *completely* upon the grace that is coming to you at the (future) revelation of Jesus Christ" (cf. 1:3-5, 7; 4:13; *Did.* 10:6). As this world nears its end, one should live only in terms of the grace guaranteed to be revealed in its full power in the future.

τελείωσις, εως, ἡ *teleiōsis* perfection, fulfillment*

Luke 1:45 speaks of the *fulfillment/carrying out* of divine promises; Heb 7:11 mentions *perfection* in the sense of the perfect priestly service that was unattainable through the levitical priesthood (cf. τελείωσις [Heb. *millu'îm*] as a cultic t.t. in the LXX: Exod 29:26, 27, 31; Lev 8:28, and elsewhere); → τελειόω 3.b. G. Delling, *TDNT* VIII, 84-86.

τελειωτής, οῦ, ὁ *teleiōtēs* perfecter*

Heb 12:2 calls Jesus ὁ τῆς πίστεως ἀρχηγὸς καὶ τελειωτής. In him the faith of the "cloud of witnesses" (12:1; cf. 11:1ff.) becomes manifest (ἀφορῶντες, 12:2), both in its origin (ἀρχηγός) and in its completion. Τελειωτής is attested only in Christian writings. G. Delling, *TDNT* VIII, 86f.

τελεσφορέω *telesphoreō* bear ripe fruit, mature (vb.)*

Luke 8:14 refers to the seed that falls among the thorns; it is like those who hear the word but are "choked" by their own ends: οὐ τελεσφοροῦσιν (cf. καρποφορέω, v. 15; see also Mark 4:19; Matt 13:22: ἄκαρπος γίνεται).

τελευτάω *teleutaō* end, come to an end; die*

Τελευτάω occurs 13 times in the NT, always intrans. It refers to the death of a person in Matt 2:19; 9:18; 22:25; Luke 7:2 (ἤμελλεν τελευτᾶν); John 11:39; Acts 2:29 (ἐτελεύτησεν καὶ ἐτάφη); 7:15; Heb 11:22 (τελευτῶν, "as he lay dying"; cf. Gen 50:24). The Heb. formula *môt yûmāt* (Exod 21:17; Lev 20:9) is rendered in Mark 7:10 par. Matt 15:4 by θανάτῳ τελευτάτω, "*let* him surely *die/* be punished by death." Mark 9:48 (cf. vv. 44, 46 v.l.) refers to the unending torment of those cast into hell: ὅπου ὁ σκώληξ αὐτῶν οὐ τελευτᾷ, "where the [gnawing] worm *does* not *die/end.*"

τελευτή, ῆς, ἡ *teleutē* end; end of life, death*

Matt 2:15: ἕως τῆς τελευτῆς Ἡρῴδου; cf. v. 19. Τελευτή is a frequently used euphemism for death.

τελέω *teleō* complete, fulfill; carry out, pay out*

1. Occurrences in the NT — 2. Meaning and idioms — 3.a) Matthew 10:23 — b) John

Lit.: E. BAMMEL, "Mt 10,23," *ST* 15 (1961) 79-92. — G. DELLING, *TDNT* VIII, 57-61. — H. FRANKEMÖLLE, *Jahwebund und Kirche Christi* (1974) 130-35. — E. GRÄSSER, *Das Problem der Parusieverzögerung in den synoptischen Evangelien und in der Apostelgeschichte* ([2]1960) 137-41. — W. G. KÜMMEL, "Die Naherwartung in der Verkündigung Jesu," Kümmel I, 457-70, esp. 465-69. — idem, *Promise and Fulfillment: The Eschatological Message of Jesus* (1957) 61-66. — H. SCHÜRMANN, "Zur Traditions- und Redaktionsgeschichte von Mt 10,23," Schürmann I, 150-56. — A. SCHWEITZER, *Das Abendmahl im Zusammenhang mit dem Leben Jesu und in der Geschichte des Urchristentums.* II: *Das Messianitäts- und Leidensgeheimnis* (1901). — For further bibliography → τέλος; τελειόω; τέλειος.

1. Τελέω occurs 28 times in the NT, most often in Matthew (7 times) and Revelation (8 times). It appears 5 times in the Lukan writings (4 in Luke, 1 in Acts), twice each in John and Romans, and only once each in 2 Corinthians, Galatians, 2 Timothy, and James.

2. Τελέω, often indistinguishable from → τελειόω, refers to *bring to an end, complete* (a race, 2 Tim 4:7; a testimony, Rev 11:7). The pass. refers to a certain period of time that will *come to an end:* ἄχρι (ὅταν) τελεσθῇ τὰ χίλια ἔτη, "till the thousand years *were ended*" (Rev 20:3, 5, 7 [→ χίλιοι]). Rev 15:1 refers to God's wrath (a bit differently, Delling 59: "The wrath of God is 'executed'"), and v. 8 refers to the seven plagues. The pass. can also be used of *be ended/completed, come to completion,* of Jesus' baptism unto death (Luke 12:50); power in weakness (2 Cor 12:9; RSV "make perfect"); God's mystery (Rev 10:7; Delling 59: God's secret plan is "fulfilled"; E. Lohmeyer, *Rev* [HNT] 86: "The aor. ἐτελέσθη effectively posits as already completed that which only . . . is intended for the future").

Τελέω is largely synonymous with → πληρόω. The act. voice refers to *fulfill,* used of everything written about Jesus (Acts 13:29) and of the law (Rom 2:27; Jas 2:8; see also Luke 2:39). The pass. *be fulfilled* is virtually identical with πληρωθῆναι: everything written about the Son of man *will be fulfilled* (τελεσθήσεται, Luke 18:31; similarly 22:37; Rev 17:17). Ἐπιθυμίαν σαρκὸς οὐ μὴ τελέσητε (Gal 5:16) can be translated in a way that expresses the active character of the passions: "Do not *allow* the desires of the flesh to *attain their goal.*" In Matt 17:24 and Rom 13:6 τελέω refers to "*pay* [taxes]."

For Matthew the phrase καὶ ἐγένετο ὅτε ἐτέλεσεν ὁ Ἰησοῦς, "And when Jesus *finished* [these sayings, parables, etc.]" (7:28; 11:1; 13:53; 19:1; 26:1), is idiomatic. This usage is actually a Septuagintism (LXX καὶ ἐγένετο

for Heb. *way^ehî;* see Beyer, *Syntax* 31 with n. 5; →
γίνομαι 2.b; differently Delling 60 n. 22).

3. a) The discussion surrounding Matt 10:23 has been
generated above all by A. Schweitzer, whose understanding of
Jesus stems from this verse. In his view, Jesus assumes that the
Son of man will come before the disciples have fulfilled their
missionary task; when they return, however, Jesus decides to
bring the kingdom of God into existence forcibly through his
own suffering. Schweitzer erred in attributing the entire farewell
discourse to the historical Jesus, since 10:23 has been inserted
redactionally into a discourse composed of various elements
from tradition.

Any interpretation of οὐ μὴ τελέσητε in Matt 10:23
must distinguish between its meaning respectively in the
present context and in the original logion. Matthew understood v. 23b from the perspective of v. 23a; i.e., in
their flight from persecution the disciples still find towns
of refuge in Israel before the Son of man comes (v. 23a
and b as a unified "apocalyptic word of consolation").
Yet v. 23b (despite Schürmann 151 n. 6, who attributes
10:23 to Q—a highly unlikely hypothesis) is an originally independent logion in which οὐ μὴ τελέσητε τὰς
πόλεις τοῦ Ἰσραὴλ ἕως . . . can only mean "*You will* not
conclude (the missionary task to) the cities of Israel
before . . ." (Kümmel, *Promise* 62; *idem,* "Naherwartung" 466f.; Grässer 137).

Frankemölle (132f.) considers Matthew to be the probable
source of 10:23. In contrast, P. Vielhauer (*Aufsätze zum NT*
[1965] 64 n. 43) and Schürmann, on the basis of his Q-hypothe-
sis, both support the original unity of 10:23a-b. Bammel,
R. Schnackenburg (*God's Rule and Kingdom* [1963] 247f.), and
others contest the idea that the logion refers to missionary activity. According to G. Strecker, the reference is not to Palestinian cities but to cities inhabited by Jews all over the world (*Der
Weg der Gerechtigkeit* [³1971] 41f.). The question of authenticity is disputed even by those who consider 10:23b to be an
originally independent, individual logion. For example, Kümmel
("Naherwartung" 467f.) considers it authentic, Grässer (137f.)
inauthentic.

b) Τελέω occurs in John only in 19:28, 30 in the
form τετέλεσται. In v. 30 Jesus' last words are "it is
completed/brought to an end" (R. Bultmann, *John*
[Eng. tr., 1971] 673f. n. 6), for he knows that everything, i.e., all the work the Father commissioned him
to do, is brought to its conclusion (v. 28). On the one
hand, these words reflect 13:1 (here, as in 19:28, note
εἰδώς): Jesus loves his own "up to the end, to the last"
(εἰς τέλος; Bultmann, *John,* 487 ["which means at the
same time, right to its completion"] with n. 6;
R. Schnackenburg, *John* III [Eng. tr., 1982] 283). On
the other hand, 13:31f. and 17:1ff. should also be considered: Father and Son are glorified in the completed
work (→ δοξάζω 3). Τετέλεσται is accordingly a significant expression of the theological intentions of the
Evangelist, who views Jesus' death as God's victory.

H. Hübner

τέλος, ους, τό *telos* conclusion, goal, end; customs,
tax

1. Occurrences in the NT — 2. Range of meaning — 3.
Τέλος as an eschatological term — a) End of the world
and death of the individual — b) Rom 10:4

Lit.: R. BADENAS, *Christ the End of the Law: Romans 10:4
in Pauline Perspective* (1985). — R. BRING, *Christus und das
Gesetz* (1969) 35-72. — G. DELLING, *TDNT* VIII, 49-57. —
idem, "Telos-Aussagen in der griechischen Philosophie," *idem,
Studien zum NT und zum hellenistischen Judentum* (1970) 17-31.
— *idem,* "Zur paulinischen Teleologie," *idem, Studien zum NT*
311-17. — F. FLÜCKIGER, "Christus des Gesetzes τέλος," *TZ* 11
(1955) 153-57. — H. HÜBNER, *Law in Paul's Thought* (1984).
— W. C. LINSS, "Exegesis of *telos* in Romans 10:4," *BR* 33
(1988) 5-12. — U. LUZ, *Das Geschichtsverständnis des Paulus*
(1968) 139-45. — F. NÖTSCHER, *Zur Terminologie der Qumran-
Texte* (1956) 167-69. — H. RÄISÄNEN, *Paul and the Law* (1983)
53-56. — R. SCHIPPERS, *DNTT* II, 59-65. — P. STUHLMACHER,
"'The End of the Law': On the Origins and Beginning of Pauline
Theology," idem, *Reconciliation, Law, and Righteousness*
(1986) 134-54. — N. WIEDER, "The Term *qs* in the Dead Sea
Scrolls and in Hebrew Liturgical Poetry," *JJS* 5 (1954) 22-31.
— H. A. WILCKE, *Das Problem eines messianischen Zwischen-
reiches bei Paulus* (1967) 87-92. — For further bibliography →
τέλειος; see further *TDNT* VIII, 50 n. 3; *TWNT* X, 1278f.

1. Τέλος occurs 40 times in the NT, 13 of these in the
Synoptic Gospels, 1 in John, 14 in the Pauline corpus (13
in the authentic letters), 4 each in Hebrews and 1 Peter,
1 in James, and 3 in Revelation.

2. Τέλος, a word with uncertain etymology (see Frisk,
Wörterbuch II, 872f.), manifests a wide range of meaning
both in classical Greek and in the LXX and NT, ranging
from *completion, conclusion, goal* to *end, end of the
world, death.* Only peripherally does τέλος refer to *tax*
(Matt 17:25; Rom 13:7). The NT contains no examples
of its use to refer to "office, administration, host,
division" or "initiation (into the mysteries)."

Particularly since Plato the causal view of natural events is
replaced by the teleological, though the use of τέλος is not critical
in this shift (e.g., *Mx.* 249a: ἀνδρὸς τέλος, "maturity of man-
hood"). In his own teleological thinking, Aristotle understands
τέλος as one of the four causes (τὸ οὗ ἕνεκα, "the because of
which"), almost identical with nature (φύσις, *Ph.* ii.2.194a). In
his ethics he defines "the highest good" (τἀγαθὸν καὶ τὸ ἄριστον
[*EN* i.2.1094a]) as the "goal of our actions" (τέλος τῶν πρακτῶν).
Shortly thereafter he mentions happiness (εὐδαιμονία) as the τῶν
πρακτῶν τέλος (i.7.1097b); for human beings this consists primarily in a life according to reason (x.7.1178a).

The Stoics use τέλος particularly as a concept of ethics. It is
defined, e.g., as οὗ ἕνεκα πάντα πράττεται καθηκόντως, as ὁ κατ'
ἀρετὴν βίος, or—particularly characteristic of the Stoics—as τὸ
ὁμολογουμένως τῇ φύσει ζῆν (von Arnim, *Fragmenta* III, 3, no.
2; 6, no. 16; 69, no. 280). Philo considers the Stoic τέλος as τὸ
κατ' ἀρετὴν βιοῦν given in the Mosaic law (*Virt.* 15).

Whereas in Greek philosophy, as in classical Greek
in general, τέλος is increasingly and predominantly used

of *finality,* not for *end* (see also LSJ s.v.), it is striking that precisely in theologically decisive passages in the NT (→ 3) τέλος does not refer to *completion* or anything similar, but rather *end.* It is not surprising, then, that the attempt is repeatedly made to translate τέλος in Rom 10:4 (→ 3.b) as *completion* instead of *end* (admittedly more from dogmatic prejudice than from philological considerations).

Τέλος refers to *conclusion, goal* in 1 Tim 1:5 ("the *goal* of our proclamation is love") and 1 Pet 1:9 ("the *goal* [RSV *outcome*] of faith [is] the salvation of your souls"). In Rom 6:21f. τέλος intends neither finality nor simply the ascertainment of an end; rather, it expresses a *consecutive* line of thinking, i.e., the *result* emerging necessarily from a certain manner of existence: death and eternal life as the *ultimate destiny* following existence under sin or under righteousness; see also 2 Cor 11:15 and Phil 3:19. On the religio-historical background of the majesty formula "I am . . . the beginning and the *end*" (Rev 21:6 [referring to God] and 22:13 [referring to Christ]); see E. Lohmeyer, *Rev* (HNT) 168, 179.

Of the prep. phrases with τέλος occurring frequently in the LXX and also found in the NT, note esp. εἰς (τὸ) τέλος, "to the *end*," though also "completely, totally" (in 1 Thess 2:16, God's eschatological wrath has come upon the Jew "completely"; differently Mark 13:13, → 3.a). (Εἰς τὸ τέλος renders Heb. *lamᵉnaṣṣēaḥ,* which is "basically still unexplained" [so H. J. Kraus, *Psalms 1–59* (Eng. tr., 1988) 29] in the superscriptions to fifty-five psalms and leaves its meaning obscure.) Note also ἄχρι τέλους (Heb 6:11) and μέχρι τέλους (3:14), "until the *end*"; ἕως τέλους, "fully" (2 Cor 1:13; probably different in 1 Cor 1:8: "to the *end of the world,*" so H. Conzelmann, *1 Cor* [Hermeneia] 28; according to Delling, *TDNT* VIII, 56: "fully"). Τὸ τέλος, "finally" (1 Pet 3:8), is an adv. adj.

3. Consistent with the fundamental message of the NT, τέλος is largely used in an eschatological sense, referring either to the *end of the world,* to the "martyr's death" amid apocalyptic tribulations, or to the "*end* of the law" during the end time inaugurated by Christ.

a) One basic meaning of τέλος in the NT is *end of the world* (Mark 13:7 par. Matt 24:6/Luke 21:9; Matt 24:14 [redactional]; 1 Cor 10:11 [pl.]; 15:24 [see Wilcke 91f.]; 1 Pet 4:7; Rev 2:26 [cf. also from Qumran *haqqēṣ hā'aḥᵃrôn,* 1QpHab 7:7 and elsewhere]). Despite the proximity of Mark 13:7, τέλος in v. 13 (as already in the preceding tradition behind it) probably refers (at least primarily) to the *death* of the person who endures (W. Grundmann, *Mark* [THKNT] 355; E. Schweizer, *Mark* [Eng. tr., 1970] 272; R. Pesch, *Mark* [HTKNT] II, 287; highly unlikely is the view of J. Gnilka, *Mark* [EKKNT] II, 192, that the individual already attains the longed-for end through violent death). Matthew takes

over Mark 13:13 both in the commissioning speech (10:22) and in the eschatological speech (24:13). It is questionable whether he understands 24:13 as "holding out . . . in the face of false teachers" (so E. Schweizer, *Matt* [Eng. tr., 1975] 451f.).

b) Rom 10:4 is esp. disputed. "For every believer, Christ is the τέλος of the law (→ νόμος 4.b) for the attainment of righteousness (→ δικαιοσύνη 4) that is valid before God." Is this a reference to the "end" of the law, or to its "completion"? Since in Romans Paul evaluates the Mosaic law more positively than in Galatians, one is tempted to accept the second meaning here (so, e.g., though without the idea of a development of Pauline theology, P. von der Osten-Sacken, *Römer 8 als Beispiel paulinischer Soteriologie* [1975] 250ff.).

Yet the context unequivocally precludes this understanding. (Note the juxtaposition of justification by the law and by faith in 10:5ff. to justify the assertion in 10:4. C. E. B. Cranfield, *Rom* [ICC] II, 515ff., can interpret τέλος as the "goal of the law" only by means of an arbitrary christological exegesis of 10:5 dependent on K. Barth.) The translation must remain "*end* of the law" (E. Käsemann, *Rom* [Eng. tr., 1980] 279ff.; according to U. Wilckens, *Rom* [EKKNT] II, 222f., Christ is the *end* of the law because, as a power himself, he suspends the power of the law that curses the sinner, and he is simultaneously the *goal* of the law). One can perhaps differentiate between these two ideas: Christ is the *end* of the law that is misused for the sake of self-justification (Hübner, 148f.; cf. Bultmann, *Theology* 263), though not the end of the law as a personal challenge (cf. Rom 13:8-10). The fulfillment of the law (→ πλήρωμα 3.a; → πληρόω 3.b) through love is not exactly the same as justification.

In 2 Corinthians, composed shortly before Romans, τέλος refers to *end* in the context of the assertions concerning the lapsed Mosaic dispensation. Moses veils his face so that the Israelites cannot see the *end* of the dispensation both given and ending (→ καταργέω 3) with the law (3:13).

H. Hübner

τελώνης, ου, ὁ *telōnēs* revenue officer, tax collector

1. Occurrences in the NT — 2. Tax collectors in antiquity — 3. Jesus and the tax collectors — 4. The tradition of tax collectors in the Gospels

Lit.: H. BRAUN, "Gott, die Eröffnung des Lebens für die Nonkonformisten," FS Fuchs 97-101. — P. FIEDLER, *Jesus und die Sünder* (1976). — J. FRICKEL, "Die Zöllner, Vorbild der Demut und wahrer Gottesverehrung," *Pietas* (FS B. Kötting; 1980) 369-80. — J. GIBSON, "Hoi telōnai kai hai pornai," *JTS* 32 (1981) 429-33. — E. GRÄSSER, "Der Mensch Jesus als Thema der Theologie," FS Kümmel (1975) 129-50. — F. HERREN-BRÜCK, *Jesus und die Zöllner* (WUNT II/41, 1990). — *idem,* "Wer waren die 'Zöllner'?" ZNW 72 (1981) 178-94. — *idem,*

"Zum Vorwurf der Kollaboration des Zöllners mit Rom," *ZNW* 78 (1987) 186-99. — O. HOFIUS, *Jesu Tischgemeinschaft mit den Sündern* (1967). — H. MERKLEIN, "Dieser ging als Gerechter nach Hause . . . ," *BK* 32 (1977) 34-42. — O. MICHEL, *TDNT* VIII, 88-105. — F. SCHNIDER, "Ausschließen und ausgeschlossen werden (Lk 18,10-14a)," *BZ* 24 (1980) 42-56. — L. SCHOTTROFF and W. STEGEMANN, *Jesus and the Hope of the Poor* (1986). — W. STENGER, *"Gebt dem Kaiser, was des Kaisers ist . . . !" Eine sozialgeschichtliche Untersuchung zur Besteuerung Palästinas in neutestamentlicher Zeit* (1988). — P. STUHLMACHER, "The New Righteousness in the Proclamation of Jesus," *idem, Reconciliation, Law, and Righteousness* (1986) 30-49. — M. TRAUTMANN, *Zeichenhafte Handlungen Jesu* (1980). — M. VÖLKEL, "Freund der Zöllner und Sünder," *ZNW* 69 (1978) 1-10. — H. YOUTIE, "Publicans and Sinners (1937)," *ZPE* 1 (1967) 1-20.

1. Τελώνης occurs in the NT only in the Synoptics (3 times in Mark, 8 in Matthew, and 10 in Luke).

2. The usual translation of τελώνης as *tax collector* limits the term too much. Τελώνης "denotes a person who purchases from the state the rights to official taxes and dues . . . and who collects these from the people who owe them" (Michel 89).

The yearly leasing to private citizens of the right to make collections, practiced in the Greek city-states, was taken over from the Hellenistic kingdoms of the Diadochs. The one holding the lease had to pay the sum required during the course of the year and could keep any excess collected; if there was a deficit, this person, with any guarantors, was responsible to make it up. This system of leasing the right to make collections also developed in the Roman republic. Beginning at the end of the third century B.C., a separate leasing class arose, the *ordo publicanorum*, belonging to the nobility. An enormous amount of capital was needed to purchase the tax lease of an entire region, and to this purpose special leasing companies were formed (*societas publicanorum*). A customs officer (*portitor*) collected the dues.

The usual assumption is that the Romans introduced this tax system into Palestine; the Synoptic τελώνης would thus have been an employee of a Roman tax leasing company (so recently Michel 97f.; Schottroff and Stegemann 7ff.). Yet esp. the analogy with neighboring Egypt suggests that in Palestine—except for the years 63–44 B.C.—the Hellenistic system of small tax collectors was maintained till the end of the first century A.D. (Youtie, Herrenbrück).

Hence the τελώνης at the time of Jesus was a well-to-do Jew who had paid for the privilege to collect individual fees (market duties, tolls) or taxes (on businesses, houses, and consumers). Hellenistic writings take an extremely negative view of the τελώνης. Already in the first post-Christian century rabbinic writings betray an unbridgeable gulf between Pharisees and tax collectors (Herrenbrück 199-211); a τελώνης who wanted to join a Pharisee guild had to give up his profession and pay just compensation to all those he cheated.

3. Several old traditions mention the special attention Jesus showed tax collectors:

a) Mark 2:14 (with J. Gnilka, *Mark* [EKKNT] I, 104, *contra* R. Pesch, *Mark* [HTKNT] I, 164, to be viewed as a pre-Markan passage) mentions the calling of a tax collector by the name of Levi into Jesus' following. An apothegmatic dispute (vv. 15-17) tells of Jesus' eating with "sinful *tax collectors*" and of the offense taken by the Pharisaic scribes. The metaphor of the physician and the sick (v. 17a) implies a christological claim that the logion in v. 17b then explicates. At none of these levels of tradition is the reference to "earthly-secular association" (Braun 99), since eating together "does not bind people together among themselves, but rather before and with God" (Hofius 11; cf. Grässer 137ff.).

b) In a christologically altered saying, the logia source transmits the defamatory assertion that Jesus was a "crony of tax collectors and sinners" (Matt 11:19 par. Luke 7:34).

c) The parable of the Pharisee and tax collector (Luke 18:10-14a) formulates the antithesis to the Pharisaic ideal by having a sinful τελώνης be accepted by God, while the correct Pharisee is rejected.

These older elements of tradition come together into a consistent picture. Like Matt 20:1-15 and Luke 15:11-32, they show that in Jesus' proclamation, "God is far more interested in being graciously generous than in calculating each person's degree of righteousness" (Stuhlmacher 33). Jesus shows in word and deed that God's salvation is open to all who allow it to be given.

4. The Synoptics have reworked this theme with different emphases.

a) Mark probably took the dispute in 2:1–3:5 from an older collection in which the story of the banquet with tax collectors addressed the issue of eating between Jewish Christians and Gentile Christians (H. W. Kuhn, *Ältere Sammlungen im Markusevangelium* [1971] 91ff.). By inserting the calling as a prelude, he historicized the incident, so that it now becomes an example of Jesus' conflict with the scribes and Pharisees that leads to the cross.

b) The Matthean community likewise fails to express any positive interest in the τελώνης. According to Matt 5:46 Christian love of one's enemy should transcend the mutual love allegedly also practiced by tax collectors. According to 18:17 the person unwilling to repent is equated with "a tax collector and Gentile." Although the parable of the unequal sons (21:28-32) does culminate in the assertion that tax collectors and harlots would enter the kingdom of heaven before the Jewish representatives, since they had believed John the Baptist (vv. 31b, 32), the context suggests that Matthew is "less interested in the faith of sinners . . . than in the conclusion official Judaism should draw from the story" (R. Hummel, *Die Auseinandersetzung zwischen Kirche und Judentum im Matthäusevangelium* [²1966] 24). The replacement of the name Levi by that of Matthew, known from the list of apostles (Matt 9:9; cf. 10:3, → Μαθθαῖος), might be the result of Matthew's having a limited role within the circle of the Twelve (R. Pesch, "Lévi—Matthäus," *ZNW* 59 [1968] 40-56). Matthew's justification of Jesus' attention to tax collectors with a reference to Hos 6:6 (9:13a) christologically epigrammatizes the narrative by making Jesus the fulfiller of Scripture.

c) Luke portrays the tax collectors in a positive light. They are baptized by John (3:12; 7:29f.) and are among Jesus' listeners (15:1f.), which brings them into an antagonistic position over against the Pharisees. Luke sees in them an example of willingness to repent (5:32; cf. 15:7, 10); he thus makes the tradition appropriately relevant for this period of the Church's development.   H. Merkel

τελώνιον, ου, τό *telōnion*   tax office, customs house*

Mark 2:14 par. Matt 9:9/Luke 5:27: καθήμενος ἐπὶ τὸ τελώνιον, "sitting at the *tax office.*"

τέρας, ατος, τό *teras*   miracle, wonder, miraculous sign, portent*

1. Occurrences in the NT and Greek usage — 2. NT usage

1. Τέρας occurs 16 times in the NT, always pl. τέρατα and always with σημεῖα (occasionally also with δυνάμεις). Cf. the OT phrase *'ōṯōṯ ûmôp̄ᵉṯîm* (Exod 7:3 and elsewhere; → σημεῖον 1).

In Greek τέρας can refer esp. to the overwhelming or shocking character of an event that happens παρὰ φύσιν (cf. Suidas s.v. τέρας) and to incomprehensible things in the larger sense (Plato *Tht.* 163d, 164b), which can, however, also be traced back to the gods (Homer *Il.* 4.398; 12.209). In the LXX τέρας as the translation of *môp̄ēṯ* refers to God's astonishing and miraculous deeds (Ps 104:5 LXX, used with τὰ θαυμάσια, ὧν ἐποίησεν, and τὰ κρίματα; cf. Exod 4:21; Isa 20:3; Ezek 12:6, 11, and elsewhere). Accordingly, in Josephus (*Ant.* ii.286; *B.J.* vi.291, 295) and Philo (*Vit. Mos.* i.80, 90) the τέρατα can lead to the recognition of God's power. In the LXX phrase σημεῖα καὶ τέρατα, which is used esp. in the context of the Exodus event (Deut 11:3; 34:11; Jer 39:20 [LXX]; Ps 134:9 [LXX]), the theological emphasis is on τέρας, which emphasizes the sovereignty and uniqueness of God's actions (cf. also Deut 28:46; Dan 4:37 [LXX]; see K. H. Rengstorf, *TDNT* VIII, 119f., 122f.).

2. Τέρας occurs in the Gospels only in Mark 13:22 par. Matt 24:24, referring to the sensational "[great] signs and *wonders*" performed by the seducers of the last days (cf. 2 Thess 2:9; Deut 13:2ff.), and in John 4:48 in Jesus' criticism of the insistence on confirmatory *miraculous* signs (cf. 2:23-25; 6:14f.). The Gospels probably do not use τέρας to refer to Jesus' own deeds because in the LXX it refers to God's mighty deeds and in secular Greek emphasizes the miraculous and unnatural elements of an event (→ 1); cf. K. Kertelge, *Die Wunder Jesu im Markusevangelium* (SANT 23, 1970) 28f.; → δύναμις 6, θαυμαστός 3, σημεῖον 2.

Use of the term in Acts (9 occurrences: 4 times σημεῖα καὶ τέρατα, 5 times τέρατα καὶ σημεῖα), however, follows the OT quite closely. It always refers to the "signs and *wonders*" that God performed (ποιήσας, 7:36) during the Exodus from Egypt and that according to Joel 3:3 LXX "shall be" in the last days (δώσω, 2:19; Luke adds σημεῖα). God's σημεῖα καὶ τέρατα "happen" διὰ τοῦ ὀνόματος . . . Ἰησοῦ (4:30: γίνεσθαι) and διὰ τῶν ἀποστόλων (πολλὰ . . . τέρατα καὶ σημεῖα . . . ἐγίνετο, 2:43) or διὰ τῶν χειρῶν τῶν ἀποστόλων (ἐγίνετο σημεῖα καὶ τέρατα πολλά, 5:12); cf. 14:3 referring to the κύριος (διδοὺς σημεῖα καὶ τέρατα γίνεσθαι διὰ τῶν χειρῶν αὐτῶν); 15:12: ὅσα ἐποίησεν ὁ θεὸς σημεῖα καὶ τέρατα . . . δι' αὐτῶν.

Accordingly, Jesus' own deeds are actually confirming evidences of God's activity: Ἰησοῦν . . . ἀποδεδειγμένον ἀπὸ τοῦ θεοῦ εἰς ὑμᾶς δυνάμεσι καὶ τέρασι καὶ σημείοις οἷς ἐποίησεν δι' αὐτοῦ ὁ θεός (2:22). Only of Stephen is it said that he ἐποίει τέρατα καὶ σημεῖα μεγάλα (6:8), but here, too, the initiating power does not come from him, but rather from God (he is πλήρης χάριτος καὶ δυνάμεως). Hence through τέρατα Luke interprets Jesus and his messengers as eschatological representatives of God's power of salvation; he emphasizes esp. that God's mighty deeds were done "among the people" (2:22; 4:30f.; 5:12; 6:8; ἐν τοῖς ἔθνεσιν, 15:12), as a witness for, but also against, them (cf. also Exod 11:10; Deut 6:22; 7:19; 29:3).

The σημεῖα καὶ τέρατα of the apostle Paul attest God's δύναμις effective through Christ and the Spirit (Rom 15:19; 2 Cor 12:12, pass. κατειργάσθη). Paul is probably thinking of gifts of the Spirit and healings, areas in which he is the equal of his critics. In Heb 2:4 σημεῖα καὶ τέρατα refer to God's deeds among the believers (along with δυνάμεις and πνεύματος ἁγίου μερισμοί); through them and the proclamation of the Lord and his followers, God testifies to his salvation (on this formulation cf. Acts 14:3 [μαρτυρέω ἐπί/συνεπιμαρτυρέω]). K. H. Rengstorf, *TDNT* VIII, 113-26; *TWNT* X, 1280 (bibliography); G. Delling, *Studien zum NT und zum hellenistischen Judentum* (1970) 146ff.; O. Hofius, *DNTT* II, 633.   H. Balz

Τέρτιος, ου *Tertios*   Tertius*

According to Rom 16:22 Tertius (i.e., "the third" according to birth) greets the church as the writer to whom Paul dictated the letter to the Romans: Ἀσπάζομαι (first person sg. only here) ὑμᾶς ἐγὼ Τέρτιος ὁ γράψας τὴν ἐπιστολὴν ἐν κυρίῳ. Tertius is also mentioned in the postscript to Romans (minuscule 337). He was a Christian (ἐν κυρίῳ) and probably lived in Corinth, as did Paul's fellow workers and friends mentioned in vv. 21-23. Paul dictated other letters to a secretary (cf. 1 Cor 16:21; Gal 6:11; see also 2 Thess 3:17; Col 4:18), as was the custom with official letters and occasionally also with private ones (Billerbeck III, 319; O. Roller, *Das Formular der paulinischen Briefe* [1933] 11ff.). It is unusual, however, that the scribe also greets the congregation; thus he does not see himself merely as a nameless amanuensis (cf. Roller 513 n. 141). Since names such as Τέρτιος and Κούαρτος (Rom 16:23) also appear frequently elsewhere as Roman names of slaves and freedmen, it is conceivable that Tertius became a Christian while still a slave, and now, like Quartus, is considered an ἀδελφός (v. 23); he might also have been a native of Rome and thus already acquainted with the addressees.

Τέρτουλλος, ου *Tertoullos* Tertullus

According to the postscript to Philemon (minuscule 42 [390]) Onesimus suffered martyrdom in Rome during the time of the eparch Tertullus. T. Zahn, *Introduction to the NT* (1909) I, 458 n. 7; *TCGNT* ad loc.

Τέρτυλλος *Tertyllos* Tertullus*

Tertullus appears in Acts 24:1, 2 as the name of the attorney (→ ῥήτωρ) whom the Jewish delegation of the high priest Ananias brought along to Caesarea from Jerusalem in order to present charges (vv. 2-8) against Paul before Felix. Luke effectively stylizes his words into a prototypical trial speech ("a masterpiece . . . of lesser rhetorical art," Lösch 317) but discloses little of the actual relationship between the Sanhedrin and the governor. S. Lösch, *TQ* 112 (1931) 295-319; E. Haenchen, *Acts* (Eng. tr., 1971) on 24:1ff.

τέσσαρες, 2 *tessares* four*

This number occurs 40 times in the NT: 6 times in the Gospels, 6 in Acts, and 28 in Revelation. Of these, τέσσαρες appears as part of the following larger numbers: *24* (→ εἴκοσι 2; Rev 4:4 bis, 10; 5:8; 11:16; 19:4); *84* (Luke 2:37); *144* (cubits; Rev 21:17); *144,000* ("sealed," or marked by the name of the Lamb and his Father, i.e., 12,000 from each tribe; Rev 7:4; 14:1, 3).

Four is a popular small whole number esp. suited for spatial organization (four winds, four corners, four sides, four city quarters, four corners of the earth [Akkadian title of pomp: "king of the four corners of the earth"]). It also plays a part in temporal information (a fever lasting four days is dangerous; the soul departs the body on the fourth day after death) and in general concepts (four virtues or emotions: Aeschylus *Th.* 610; Diogenes Laertius vii.110; four epochs of the world: Hesiod *Op.* 109ff.; four elements: Empedocles *Frag.* 6 [I, 311]; the Pythagoreans engaged in numerical speculation concerning the τετρακτύς, or 10, the sum of the first four numbers, cf. Hierocles Platonicus *In Carmen Aureum* 20 [130.16f.]; Sextus Empiricus *Adversus Mathematicos* iv.3); for further documentation and details see H. Balz, *TDNT* VIII, 128f. For this reason the number four refers in a general sense to something self-enclosed and ordered, and

to totality or universality; only rarely is it used as a sacred number (Hierocles Platonicus, loc. cit.: ἡ τέτρας, θεὸς νοητός).

In the OT the number four occurs with similar meaning referring to the totality of creation and of historical events. There are four rivers in paradise (Gen 2:10ff.); four winds, or heavenly regions (Dan 11:4; Ps 107:3; cf. Isa 11:12; Jer 49:36); four borders of the land of Israel (Ezek 7:2); four horns (Zech 1:18), four smiths (v. 20), four chariots (6:1) with four differently colored horses (vv. 2f.), and four regions of the earth (vv. 5ff.); four creatures in Ezekiel's theophany vision (variously four faces of a man, lion, ox, and eagle) with four wings each and four wheels on the chariot (Ezek 1:5ff.); four winds and four beasts (Dan 7:2ff.; cf. 7:17; 8:8, 22; 11:4); four corresponding kingdoms (Dan 2:31ff.; cf. 2 Esdr 11:39f.; 12:11f.). The four-cornered sacrificial altar is also of significance (Exod 27:1f.; cf. Ezek 40:41f.; 43:16f., 20).

2. In the NT τέσσαρες is used in a general fashion, of four daughters (Acts 21:9), four Nazirites (v. 23), four porters (on the four corners of the stretcher, Mark 2:3), similarly four corners of a sheet (Acts 10:11; 11:5); four anchors let out from the stern provide a particularly effective mooring (Acts 27:29). Roman military organization manifests itself in Acts 12:4, according to which Peter is guarded by "four squads of soldiers" (of four soldiers each, τέσσαρσιν τετραδίοις); the squads are thus relieved every three hours. The division of Jesus' garments into "four parts" (John 19:23) also presupposes a retinue of four soldiers. According to John 11:17 Lazarus "had already been in the tomb four days" (cf. v. 39) and thus unequivocally dead according to human standards. In Mark 13:27 par. Matt 24:31 the "four winds" represent the totality of the earth (cf. Dan 7:2; 11:4; Ps 107:3; see also 2 Esdr 13:5; *1 Enoch* 18:2f., where the four winds carry both the earth and heaven).

Τέσσαρες plays a special role in Revelation as an expression of totality. The tradition of the four creatures around God's throne chariot is taken up several times (τέσσαρα ζῷα, Rev 4:6, 8; 5:6, 8, 14; 6:1, 6; 7:11; 14:3; 15:7; 19:4). According to 4:7 they are no longer (as in Ezek 1:6, 10) the faces of four creatures but four different creatures: lion, ox, eagle, and man; they surround God's throne and serve his glorification (6:8: they repeat the Sanctus day and night, cf. Isa 6:3; Rev 19:4). Perhaps one should intepret this complex as portraying the mighty zodiac figures of the ancient Babylonian astral myth, which originally supported the vault of heaven on its four ends but have now been taken into God's service once and for all. Commensurate with this idea, according to 7:1 (ter) four angels stand at the "four corners of the earth" (cf. 20:8) as guardians over the four winds (cf. 7:2). According to 9:13 a voice sounds from the "four horns [τέσσαρες omitted in 𝔭⁴⁷ ℵ¹ A and elsewhere] of the golden altar" (cf. Exod 27:1f.; 30:2f.; see above); in 9:14f. four angels of destruction are loosed who are bound (differently than in 7:1f.) at the Euphrates. There

351

are also four horses (6:1-8; cf. Zech 1:8ff.; 6:1ff.), whose appearance is associated with the first four seals and the cries of the four creatures (6:1).

Irenaeus (*Haer.* iii.11.8) explains the number four in the Gospels with reference to the expansion of the church into the four regions of the world; he views the Gospels as the four pillars of the church and identifies the Evangelists with the four creatures (see above); this view was taken up by Augustine *De Consensu Evangelistarum* i.1.3; 6.9. H. Balz, *TDNT* VIII, 127-35; E. D. Schmitz, *DNTT* II, 688f.   H. Balz

τεσσαρεσκαιδέκατος, 3 *tessareskaidekatos* fourteenth*

Acts 27:27: "the *fourteenth* night," corresponding to v. 33: "the *fourteenth* day."

τέσσερες, 2 *tesseres* four

Ionic form of → τέσσαρες. Because of general mixing of forms esp. the neut. τέσσερα occurs in NT mss.; see H. Balz, *TDNT* VIII, 127f.

τεσσεράκοντα *tesserakonta* forty*

1. Of the 22 occurrences of τεσσεράκοντα in the NT, 8 are in Acts and 6 in Revelation. It also occurs in numerical combination in John 2:20: τεσσεράκοντα καὶ ἓξ ἔτη, referring to the time it took to build the (Herodian) temple (cf. Josephus *Ant.* xv.380: building commenced probably 20/19 B.C.); "42 months" for the destruction of Jerusalem (Rev 11:2; similarly 13:5; cf. 11:3; 12:6, 14; Dan 7:25; 12:7, 12); "144 cubits" (Rev 21:17); "144,000 sealed" (7:4; cf. 14:1, 3); → τέσσαρες.

Forty is an important round number, esp. in connection with periods of time. Forty days was the length of a period of fasting (Diogenes Laertius viii.40; Porphyry *Vita Pythagorae* 57) and of rain (Pseudo-Callisthenes iii.26.7; cf. Gen 7:4, 12, 17; 8:6); Moses spent forty days and nights on the mountain (Exod 24:18; Deut 9:9, and elsewhere), and Elijah in the desert (1 Kgs 19:8); forty days of penitence were made for Nineveh (Jonah 3:4); after the birth of a male child the mother is unclean for forty days (Lev 12:3f.; other references to forty days appear in 1 Sam 17:16; Ezek 4:6). Forty lashes are the measure of punishment, which may not be exceeded (Deut 25:3).

The period of forty years is applied in a general sense to the stages of life and is considered the period in which one generation lives and works: forty years as the age of maturity for certain tasks (Aristotle *Athenian Constitution* 29; Porphyry *Vita Pythagorae* 9) and as the age for marriage (Gen 25:20; 26:34; cf. further Josh 14:7; 2 Sam 2:10); 120 years as the span of life (Gen 6:3; Deut 34:7). Forty years were spent in the wilderness (Exod 16:35; Num 14:33; Deut 2:7; 29:5; Josh 5:6). This same period determines the framework of Judges (3:11, 30; 5:31; 8:28; 13:1) and is the length of the reigns of David (2 Sam 5:4f.; 1 Kgs 2:11), Solomon (1 Kgs 11:42), Jehoash (2 Kgs 12:2), and Saul (Josephus *Ant.* vi.378). At the age of forty a rabbinic student may make independent decisions (*b. Soṭa* 22a; *b. ʾAbod. Zar.* 19b). Forty years is also the messianic interim (*Pesiqta Rabbati*

1 [4a]; *b. Sanh.* 99a; cf. also CD 20:15; 1QM 2:6, 9; *Apoc. Elijah* [Hebrew] 6:5). Forty days of writing or teaching occur before the rapture of "Ezra" (2 Esdr 14:23, 36, 42, 44, 49) and of "Baruch" (*2 Bar.* 76:2-4).

2. Forty occurs as a general round number in Acts 4:22 (sick for more than forty years); 23:13, 21 (forty conspirators); 2 Cor 11:24 might be the oldest attestation of the elimination of the *fortieth* lash.

The *forty* days of temptation in the desert (Mark 1:13 par. Matt 4:2 [forty days and forty nights]/Luke 4:2), which invokes OT motifs (→ 1), emphasizes the time of Jesus' testing and obedience before the commencement of his ministry; it is a time of nearness to God (Mark) and of corresponding affinity to Moses (Matthew, also Luke; cf. Exod 24:18; 34:28; Deut 9:9, 11, 18; 10:10). The *forty* days of Jesus' epiphanies before the ascension (Acts 1:3) are to be understood as a typical period, not an exact interval (cf. 13:31: ἡμέρας πλείους); the writer's concern is for the salvation gift of the earthly presence of the resurrected Jesus and for the reliable instruction of the disciples (λέγων τὰ περὶ τῆς βασιλείας τοῦ θεοῦ, 1:3), cf. the statements about Ezra and Baruch (→ 1). On "forty days" in the Gospels see A. Schneider, *Gesammelte Aufsätze* (1963) 17-34.

Israel's forty years in the wilderness are considered to be a time of salvation during which the fathers admittedly tempted and provoked God (Heb 3:10 [citing Ps 94:10 LXX], 17 [cf. Exod 17:2ff.; Num 14:26ff.]; Acts 7:42 [citing Amos 5:25 LXX; → σφάγιον]; cf. also Acts 13:18). 13:21 attributes a forty-year reign to Saul (differently 1 Sam 13:1: two years; cf., however, Josephus *Ant.* vi.378; → 1), probably as a period of peace granted by God. Following tradition (cf. Exod 7:7; Deut 8:2; 34:7; *Sifre Deut.* 357 on 34:7), a life span of three times *forty* years is assumed for Moses (Acts 7:23, 30, 36). R. Poelman, *Times of Grace: The Sign of Forty in the Bible* (1964); H. Balz, *TDNT* VIII, 135-39 (bibliography).   H. Balz

τεσσερακονταετής, 2 *tesserakontaetēs* forty-year (adj.)*

Acts 7:23: τεσσερακονταετὴς χρόνος, referring to Moses' mature years (cf. Exod 2:11 LXX: μέγας γενόμενος); 13:18: ὡς τεσσερακονταετῆ χρόνον, referring to Israel's wanderings in the wilderness. → τεσσεράκοντα.

τεταρταῖος, 3 *tetartaios* four-day; happening on the fourth day*

John 11:39, referring to Lazarus: τεταρταῖος γάρ ἐστιν, "he is [already dead] *four days*"; cf. 11:17. → τέσσαρες.

τέταρτος, 3 *tetartos* fourth*

Τέταρτος occurs 10 times in the NT: in Mark 6:48; Matt 14:25: referring to the *fourth* watch; Acts 10:30: ἀπὸ τετάρτης ἡμέρας μέχρι ταύτης τῆς ὥρας, "it is now the *fourth* day to the hour" (D: ἀπὸ τῆς τρίτης ἡμέρας . . .). Otherwise it occurs only in Revelation, in 4:7 and 6:7: τὸ τέταρτον ζῷον; 6:7: σφραγὶς ἡ τετάρτη; 8:12 and 16:8: ὁ τέταρτος ἄγγελος; 21:19: ὁ τέταρτος (θεμέλιος); 6:8: τὸ τέταρτον τῆς γῆς, "[a] fourth of the earth" (cf. Ezek 5:12). → τέσσαρες.

τετρααρχέω *tetraarcheō* be tetrarch, rule as tetrarch*

This vb. occurs three times in Luke 3:1 (in each case τετρααρχοῦντος with gen.), referring to two of Herod's sons who *were tetrarchs* of Galilee (Antipas) and of Ituraea and Trachonitis (Philip), and also to Lysanias as the tetrarch of Abilene. On the orthography see BDF §124. Luke perhaps has consciously juxtaposed four rulers in 3:1 (three tetrarchs and the Roman governor), though he does appear to have a precise acquaintance with the title "tetrarch"; → τετραάρχης.

τετραάρχης, ου, ὁ *tetraarchēs* tetrarch*

Τετραάρχης originally referred to the ruler of a fourth of a previously undivided region. It was then the title of a regent dependent on a more powerful ruler, or of a ruler who administered a small part of a larger kingdom, often in the sense of a governor. Whereas Herod (the Great) was himself originally a tetrarch (after 42 B.C., then after 40 [37] B.C. a king), after his death in 4 B.C. his sons Antipas and Philip became tetrarchs of Galilee and Perea or Trachonitis, Batanea, and Gaulanitis, and his son Archelaus ethnarch of Judea and Samaria (Matt 2:22: βασιλεύει).

In the NT only Antipas is referred to as → Ἡρῴδης (2) ὁ τετραάρχης (Matt 14:1; Luke 3:19; 9:7), probably in order to distinguish him from his father → Ἡρῴδης (1) (Matt 2:1, 3; Luke 1:5: βασιλεύς). Acts 13:1 perhaps intends to distinguish him from → Ἡρῴδης (3) (12:1; → Ἀγρίππας 1). BAGD s.v. τετραάρχης; E. Trocmé, *BHH* 1956f.

τετράγωνος, 2 *tetragōnos* four-square, four-cornered*

Rev 21:16 speaks of the heavenly Jerusalem: ἡ πόλις τετράγωνος κεῖται (cf. Ezek 48:8ff., 30ff.; also 43:16). The context suggests that the reference to a square and a cube intends to express totality or completeness; cf. Ennius *Annales* 158: *Roma quadrata;* Herodotus i.178

(Babylon as a square with 120 stades per side). H. Kraft, *Rev* (HNT) ad loc.

τετράδιον, ου, τό *tetradion* squad of four soldiers*

Acts 12:4: Peter was guarded in prison by four *squads of four men each* (commensurate with the Roman military procedure of relieving each squad after three hours; cf. also the four watches); Philo *Flacc.* 111.

τετρακισχίλιοι, 3 *tetrakischilioi* four thousand*

This number appears in the story of the miraculous feeding of the four thousand: Matt 15:38 (τετρακισχίλιοι ἄνδρες χωρὶς γυναικῶν καὶ παιδίων); 16:10; Mark 8:9 (ὡς τετρακισχίλιοι), v. 20. Acts 21:38: τετρακισχίλιοι ἄνδρες τῶν σικαρίων (cf. Josephus *B.J.* ii.254ff.).

τετρακόσιοι, 3 *tetrakosioi* four hundred*

Acts 5:36 speaks of the followers of Theudas: ἀνδρῶν ἀριθμὸς ὡς τετρακοσίων, → Θευδᾶς. 7:6 refers to the Egyptian enslavement of Israel: ἔτη τετρακόσια (citing Gen 15:13). Acts 13:19 mentions the period "about *450* years" from the sojourn in Egypt to the beginning of the time of the judges (probably 400 years in Egypt [7:6], 40 years in the wilderness [13:18], and 10 years territorial annexation; the mss. D^2 E Ψ and Koine alter the passage such that the 450 years refer to the time of the judges up to Samuel, corresponding to the sum of the years given in Judges, including 1 Sam 4:18 according to the Hebrew text; cf. E. Haenchen, *Acts* [Eng. tr., 1971] ad loc.). According to Gal 3:17 the law originated *430* years after the promise to Abraham; thus it cannot make the promise void (cf. also Exod 12:40f.).

τετράμηνος, 2 *tetramēnos* lasting four months*

Subst. in John 4:35: τετράμηνος, as the shortest period of time between sowing and harvesting (TR τετράμηνον).

τετραπλοῦς, 3 *tetraplous* fourfold*

Luke 19:8 refers to Zacchaeus's *fourfold* restitution, a quantity considered generous enough in every respect (cf. Exod 21:37; 2 Sam 12:6; Plato *Lg.* ix.878c; see Billerbeck II, 249-51; Spicq, *Notes* II, 886f.).

τετράπους, 2 *tetrapous* four-footed, four-legged*

In the NT this term always occurs as the neut. pl. subst. τὰ τετράποδα (always with ἑρπετά and πετεινά, cf. Gen 1:24-26; 6:20) referring to "*four-legged* animals." Acts 10:12: πάντα τὰ τετράποδα (cf. Lev 11; Deut 14:3ff.); 11:6 (with τὰ θηρία, cf. Gen 1:24); on Rom 1:23 cf. Deut 4:15ff.; Ps 106:20; Jer 2:11; Wis 12:24.

τετραρχέω *tetrarcheō* be tetrarch, rule as tetrarch
Classical orthography (which avoided hiatus in compounds) of → τετρααρχέω (so in Hellenistic and NT Greek; cf. BDF §§17, 124; Moulton, *Grammar* II, 62f., 91f.).

τετράρχης, ου, ὁ *tetrarchēs* tetrarch
Classical orthography of → τετρααρχης. → τετραρχέω.

τεφρόω *tephroō* reduce to ashes, cover with ashes*

2 Pet 2:6 uses τεφρώσας in a reference to God, who *turned* the cities of Sodom and Gomorrah *to ashes* (Gen 19:24ff.; cf. Philo *Ebr.* 223).

τέχνη, ης, ἡ *technē* art, trade*

Acts 17:29: χάραγμα τέχνης καὶ ἐνθυμήσεως ἀνθρώπου, "a work of human *art/craftsmanship* and reflection," which does not conform to the ways of God (cf. 19:26; Deut 4:38; Isa 40:18; 44:9ff.; Jer 10:1ff.; Wis 13:10). According to Acts 18:3 Aquila and Priscilla were σκηνοποιοὶ τῇ τέχνῃ, "tentmakers *by trade/vocation*" (cf. → ὁμότεχνος, → σκηνοποιός). Rev 18:22 asserts that "no craftsman of any *craft*" (πᾶς τεχνίτης πάσης τέχνης) will be found in Babylon (i.e., Rome).

τεχνίτης, ου, ὁ *technitēs* artisan, craftsman*

The pl. refers to silversmiths in Acts 19:24, 38 (cf. 19:25 D among others [instead of ἐργάται]); the sg. is used in a general sense in Rev 18:22 (→ τέχνη). Heb 11:10 refers to God as the τεχνίτης καὶ δημιουργός, "*builder/architect* and maker" of the heavenly Jerusalem (cf. 11:16; 12:22; Rev 21:10; Wis 13:1ff.; Philo *Mut.* 29f.; → δημιουργός); on the Logos as τεχνίτης καὶ δημιουργὸς τῶν ὅλων, cf. *Diog.* 7:2.

τήκομαι *tēkomai* melt; pass away*

2 Pet 3:12 uses the pass. to refer to the day of God, because of which the "cosmic elements *are dissolved*" (στοιχεῖα καυσούμενα τήκεται; cf. 3:10; *1 Enoch* 1:6; *T. Levi* 4:1; *2 Clem.* 16:3; Diogenes Laertius vii.134 addresses the Stoic idea of the world conflagration; → στοιχεῖον 2, 4).

τηλαυγῶς *tēlaugōs* very plainly, clearly*

This adv., from τηλαυγής, "far-shining, plain," occurs in Mark 8:25: ἐνέβλεπεν τηλαυγῶς ἅπαντα, "he [the healed blind man] could see everything *quite clearly*" (v.l. δηλαυγῶς).

τηλικοῦτος, αὕτη, οὗτο *tēlikoutos* so great, so important, so powerful*

Jas 3:4: τὰ πλοῖα τηλικαῦτα ὄντα, "the ships are *so great* [in contrast to ἐλάχιστον]"; 2 Cor 1:10: τηλικοῦτος θάνατος, "*such great* danger of death" (RSV "so deadly a peril"; cf. vv. 8f.); Heb 2:3: τηλικαύτη σωτηρία, "*such a great* salvation"; Rev 16:18 (pleonastic): σεισμὸς . . . μέγας . . . τηλικοῦτος σεισμὸς οὕτω μέγας, "a great earthquake . . . *so great* an earthquake, so powerful" (Dan 12:1).

τηρέω *tēreō* guard, preserve; hold fast to, keep, follow

1. Occurrences in the LXX and the NT — 2. Guard — 3. Preserve, maintain — 4. Keep in unblemished condition — 5. Keep, follow

Lit.: R. KRATZ, *Auferweckung als Befreiung* (SBS 65, 1973). — idem, *Rettungswunder. Motiv-, traditions-, und formkritische Aufarbeitung einer biblischen Gattung* (1979). — H. RIESENFELD, *TDNT* VIII, 140-46. — H. G. SCHÜTZ, *DNTT* II, 132f.

1. Like φυλάσσω, τηρέω in the LXX usually translates *šāmar* and, like the synonym, to a large extent covers the field of meaning of the Hebrew equivalent; whereas φυλάσσω clearly predominates in the LXX, in the NT τηρέω is about twice as common (70 occurrences). It occurs most frequently in John (18 times) and Revelation (11 times), but not at all in Mark, Luke, or Hebrews.

2. Τηρέω is used with its literal meaning—to *guard* (prisoners)—most often in Acts (24:23; 25:4, 21), among other places in the context of the tradition of miraculous deliverance (12:5, 6; 16:23). The presence of guards in the Matthean tomb stories (Matt 28:4) also evokes features of this genre (cf. Kratz, *Auferweckung, Rettungswunder*). The redactional introduction of the guards beneath the cross (Matt 27:26, 54) probably derives from the apologetic intentions of the Matthean Passion narratives (witnessing by Gentiles); the redactor additionally wants to make parallel the events surrounding the death and resurrection (cf. 27:51-54 with 28:2-4) and to apostrophize both death and resurrection as theophanies.

3. Τηρέω with following temporal information is used for "*preserve/keep* until" the appropriate time (John 2:10: keep the good wine until last; 12:7: save the anointing oil until the day of burial). As a rule, such keeping is viewed from the perspective of "until the eschaton," both in the positive sense of keeping the heavenly inheritance (1 Pet 1:4) and keeping the good people for Christ (Jude 1) and in the negative sense of keeping the unrighteous (2 Pet 2:9), the fallen angels (v. 4; Jude 6b), heaven and earth (for judgment, 2 Pet 3:7), and the false teachers (for

eternal damnation). In a reverse fashion, the darkness can also be lifted for the false teachers (v. 17).

4. From the perspective of keeping or preserving the unblemished nature of a person or a condition, τηρέω refers to ethical objectives such as purity (1 Tim 5:22), being undefiled (Jas 1:27), and the chasteness of a virgin (1 Cor 7:37); hence one can also say of the angels that they have not kept their → ἀρχή (3.c) (Jude 6a). The common expression "*keep* the faith" (2 Tim 4:7) in its present context exhibits a theological character. From prison "Paul" admonishes the church at Ephesus to maintain unity (Eph 4:3). Rev 16:15 uses the term metaphorically.

Personal objs. include the disciples or Christians. In the Johannine farewell speech Jesus asks the Father to *keep* the disciples, to *guard* them from the evil one (John 17:11, 12, 15). According to 1 John 5:18 the Son of God guarantees protection from the evil one. In 1 Thess 5:23 and Jude 1 such keeping has eschatological reference.

5. Like → φυλάσσω, about half the occurrences of τηρέω are used for *keep/follow* (the law, commandments). According to Matt 23:3 Jesus challenges the disciples to do and *follow* what the Pharisees and scribes say, but not to copy their actions. In John 9:16 the Pharisees on their part charge Jesus with not *keeping* the sabbath. Conservative early Christians from Pharisaic circles want to obligate converted Gentiles to keep the Mosaic law (Acts 15:5), a point of contention addressed by the apostolic council in Jerusalem. There is some question whether in Matt 19:17 the insistence that the rich young man keep the commandments already has the "new righteousness" in view. Finally, Jas 2:10 addresses the question of keeping the whole law. As a rule, however, such references are to *keeping* the commandments (the word) of Jesus, which are qualified by "love" (cf. John 14 *passim;* 1 John 2:3-5). The Father's love comes through the Son to the Church. Just as Jesus keeps the Father's word (John 8:55; 15:10), so also should the disciples keep his commandments so that their own words are then kept (15:20). 1 John addresses similar issues.

The open letters to the churches (Rev 2:26; 3:3, 8, 10) hold out the prospect of eschatological reward for steadfast keeping of the commandments. Matt 28:20 (like 1 Tim 6:14) attributes a normative character with eschatological consequences to Christian instruction based on Jesus' commandments.   R. Kratz

τήρησις, εως, ἡ *tērēsis* custody, imprisonment; prison; observance, keeping, fulfilling*

Acts 4:3: ἔθεντο εἰς τήρησιν, *custody, imprisonment;* 5:18: ἔθεντο . . . ἐν τηρήσει δημοσίᾳ, more likely *prison.* According to 1 Cor 7:19 only the τήρησις ἐντολῶν θεοῦ counts before God, the "*fulfilling/keeping* of God's commandments" (cf. Wis 6:18; Sir 32:23; cf. also Gal 5:6; 6:15). H. Riesenfeld, *TDNT* VIII, 146.

Τιβεριάς, άδος *Tiberias* Tiberias*

Lit.: ABEL, *Géographie* II, 483f. — BAGD s.v. — BILLERBECK II, 467-77. — A. VAN DEN BORN and H. HAAG, *BL* 1750f. — M. S. ENSLIN, *BHH* 1982f. — H. G. KIPPENBERG, *KP* V, 812. — KOPP, *Places* 225-30.

The city founded by Herod Antipas in A.D. 26-27 on the west coast of the Sea of Galilee (as the capital of his region in place of Sepphoris), in honor of the emperor Tiberius (Josephus *Ant.* xviii.36ff.). In the NT only John mentions the city.

According to John 6:23 boats from Tiberias (ἐκ Τιβεριάδος) come near the place where Jesus fed the five thousand on the other side; in 21:1 the Sea of Galilee (or Gennesaret, → Γεννησαρέτ) is called θάλασσα τῆς Τιβεριάδος, recalling the rather unusual way 6:1 introduces it: πέραν τῆς θαλάσσης τῆς Γαλιλαίας τῆς Τιβεριάδος (v.l.: . . . θαλάσσης τῆς Γαλιλαίας εἰς τὰ μέρη τῆς Τιβεριάδος, see R. Schnackenburg, *John* II [Eng. tr., 1979], ad loc.). From the perspective of the redactional formulation in 21:1 one might also understand the mention of Tiberias in 6:1, 23 as a redactional insertion; this would explain both the lack of clarity in 6:23 (ἐγγύς can also refer to Tiberias) and the uncertainty of the textual interpretation of 6:1 by copyists (see Schnackenburg, *John*). The name "Sea of Tiberias" also occurs elsewhere (with λίμνη in Pausanias v.7.4; Josephus *B.J.* iii.57; iv.456). Jesus himself apparently avoided using "Tiberias."

Since Tiberias was situated over a burial ground and was thus considered unclean by pious Jews, Herod had to populate the city by coercion and also bring in foreign settlers. Initially the Hellenistic element predominated (under a Hellenistic administration), and only later was Tiberias pronounced ceremonially clean (*y. Šeb.* 9:38d). Although Tiberias took part in the Jewish War, Vespasian spared the city (Josephus *B.J.* iii.443ff.). Because of the redaction of the Mishna in Tiberias (*ca.* A.D. 200, under Yehuda Ha-Nasi) and the transferal there about the same time of the rabbinic patriarchate from Sepphoris, Tiberias became the Palestinian center for rabbinic teaching and one of the Jews' four sacred sites in Palestine. (Later, *ca.* A.D. 400, the Palestinian Talmud was codified in Tiberias, and a Masoretic school arose there.)

Τιβέριος, ου *Tiberios* Tiberius*

Lit.: BAGD s.v. (bibliography). — J. P. V. D. BALSDON, *OCD* 1071f. — A. VAN DEN BORN, *BL* 1751. — K. CHRIST, *LAW* 3083f. — R. HANSLIK and A. LIPPOLD, *KP* V, 814-18. — G. MAYEDA, *BHH* 1983f.

Luke 3:1 dates the appearance of John the Baptist in the fifteenth year of the reign of the Roman emperor *Tiberius* (ἐν ἔτει δὲ πεντεκαιδεκάτῳ τῆς ἡγεμονίας Τιβερίου Καίσαρος), thus in the period A.D. 28/29. (Tiberius, as the adopted son and successor of Augustus Caesar, was emperor from August 19, A.D. 14, till March 16, 37.) The NT also refers elsewhere to Tiberius with the title → Καῖσαρ (bibliography). Tiberius was considered to be a just emperor who to a large extent brought peace to the provinces and above all was tolerant toward the Jews (Josephus *Ant.* xviii.65ff.; Philo *Leg. Gai.* 160f.).

τίθημι *tithēmi*   put, place, lay

1. Occurrences in the NT — 2. General usage in Greek — 3. LXX — 4. NT — a) General usage — b) Lukan peculiarities — c) Johannine peculiarities

Lit.: BAGD s.v. — J. JEREMIAS, *Die Sprache des Lukasevangeliums* (KEK Sonderband, 1980). — C. MAURER, *TDNT* VIII, 152-68. — T. SCHRAMM, *Der Markusstoff bei Lukas* (SNTSMS 14, 1971). — A. J. SIMONIS, *Die Hirtenrede im Johannesevangelium* (1967) 264-76. — For further bibliography see *TWNT* X, 1280f.

1. Τίθημι occurs 100 times in the NT, 39 of these in the Lukan corpus, 18 in John, and 16 in the Pauline corpus.

2. This vb. occurs frequently in secular Greek since Homer and is used in both local and metaphoric senses with a wide range of meanings determined by the context. It occurs in the language of commerce, the military, sports, law (e.g., "*set* a law," Sophocles *El.* 580), philosophy ("*recognize* a premise/*posit* a thesis," Plato *Phd.* 79a, 100a), and religion (the gods "*set* valid ordinances," Homer *Od.* 8.465; human beings "*make* votive offerings to the deity," *Od.* 12.347; on this complex see Maurer 152f. for numerous examples).

3. On the whole, the use of τίθημι in the LXX corresponds to that of secular Greek (Maurer 153f.). Special OT phrases with τίθημι include "*put* one's life at stake" (Judg 12:3; 1 Kgdms 19:5; 28:21; Job 13:14); "*turn* one's attention to something" (Ps 47:14 LXX and elsewhere); "*bear* something in mind" (e.g., 2 Kgdms 19:20); and "*take* into one's heart" (Ezek 14:3, 4, 7).
In more than a fourth of the OT occurrences God is the subject of τίθημι. The order for creation *is set* by him, as are both salvation and judgment. He *sets* the stars (Gen 1:17), just as he *gathers* the primal waters and oceans into their boundaries (Ps 32:7 LXX; Job 38:10); it is God who *makes* Abraham the father of many nations (Gen 17:5f.) and Jacob's descendants as numerous as the sand of the sea (32:13). He *makes* David king and *establishes* his throne forever and will *place* his enemies under his feet as his footstool (Pss 88:28, 30; 109:1 LXX). He *appoints* both prophet (Jer 1:5) and servant (Isa 49:2) to their service and *determines* salvation and judgment both of the individual and of the nation as a whole (e.g., Pss 11:6; 20:10; 65:9; 89:8 LXX; Amos 8:10; Mic 1:7; 4:7; Ezek 37:14).

4. Except for some peculiarities in the term's use in

Luke (→ b) and the Johannine writings (→ c), NT authors follow the usage in Greek at large and in the LXX (→ a).

a) Accordingly, one reads that a light "*is* not *put* under a bushel, but rather on a stand" (Mark 4:21 par.); the sick *are laid down* in the marketplaces (6:56); wine *is served* (John 2:10); a corpse *is laid* in the tomb (Mark 6:29; 15:46f.; John 19:41f.; 20:2, 13, 15). One can *put aside* (i.e., invest) money (so that it works, Luke 19:21f.); contributions *are put aside* for the collection (1 Cor 16:2). As founder of the church at Corinth, Paul *laid* a foundation (3:10f.); free of charge he *proclaims (lays forth)* the gospel (9:18).
Concerning God's activity: "He *sets up* the word of reconciliation for us" (2 Cor 5:19 [mid.]), for he "has not *destined* us for wrath, but rather to obtain salvation" (1 Thess 5:9 [mid.]); he *appoints* the members of the congregation just as he did the apostle (1 Cor 12:18, 28; 1 Tim 1:12; 2:7; 2 Tim 1:11). Citations also mention God's salvation works as his *positing/setting* (the mediation of the Spirit, the submission of enemies, the illumination of Gentiles, etc.; cf. Matt 12:18 [Isa 42:1]; Matt 22:44 par.; Acts 2:34f.; 1 Cor 15:25; Heb 1:13 [Ps 109:1 LXX]; Acts 13:47 [Isa 49:6]; Rom 4:17 [Gen 17:5]; Rom 9:33 [Isa 28:16]).

b) Except for Mark 15:19, the "firmly fixed and yet nonclassical phrase" τίθημι τὰ γόνατα (cf. Lat. *genua ponere*), "kneel down [*bend* one's knee]," occurs only in Luke (and in 4 of the 5 instances in combination with → προσεύχομαι 2.a; Luke 22:41; Acts 7:60; 9:40; 20:36; 21:5 [cf. Jeremias 294]). Also, only Luke, after the model of his source's Semitisms (Schramm 79ff.), uses the phrases τίθημι ἐν καρδίᾳ, "take to heart/pay attention to" (Luke 1:66 [mid.]; 21:14; Acts 5:4 [mid.]), and τίθεμαι εἰς τὰ ὦτα, "listen to/impress upon one's memory" (Luke 9:44). Cf. also Acts 1:7; 19:21 (Jeremias 71).

c) In the Johannine writings the phrase τίθημι τὴν ψυχήν μου ὑπέρ τινος occurs (John 10:11, 15, 17, 18a, b; 13:37, 38; 15:13; 1 John 3:16 bis). It expresses—probably also in John 10:11, 15 (*contra* R. Bultmann, *John* [Eng. tr., 1971] 371f. n. 5; cf. the thorough discussion in Simonis 264ff.)—more than the OT "parallels" do (see Judg 12:3; 1 Kgdms 19:5; 28:21; Job 13:14); it is used for not merely "*put* one's life at stake/risk one's life" but rather "*sacrifice* one's life." In Johannine usage the Greek phrase is theologically filled and defined from the perspective of Isa 53:10 (cf. Mark 10:45 par.: δοῦναι τὴν ψυχὴν αὐτοῦ λύτρον ἀντὶ πολλῶν, "sacrifice his life as a ransom for the many"; cf. Maurer 155f.).   T. Schramm

τίκτω *tiktō*   bear, bring forth*

Τίκτω occurs 18 times in the NT: 4 times in Matthew, 5 in Luke, 5 in Revelation, and otherwise only in John 16:21; Gal 4:27; Heb 6:7; Jas 1:15. The pres. τίκτω υἱόν, *"bear* a son," occurs in Matt 1:25; Luke 1:31; 2:7; Rev 12:5; and the fut. τέξεται υἱόν in Matt 1:21, 23 (cf. Isa 7:14 LXX). Other objs. appear in Rev 12:4b (τίκτω τὸ τέκνον) and v. 13 (τίκτω τὸν ἄρσενα). It occurs absolutely in Luke 1:57 (ἐπλήσθη ὁ χρόνος τοῦ τεκεῖν αὐτήν), cf. 2:6; John 16:21; Gal 4:27 (citing Isa 54:1 LXX); Rev 12:2, 4a. The pass. occurs in Matt 2:2 (ὁ τεχθεὶς βασιλεὺς τῶν Ἰουδαίων, the *newborn/just born* king of the Jews) and Luke 2:11 (ἐτέχθη ὑμῖν σήμερον σωτήρ). The term is used fig. and metaphorically in Heb 6:7 (γῆ . . . τίκτουσα βοτάνην εὔθετον, cf. Aeschylus *Ch.* 124) and Jas 1:15 (ἡ ἐπιθυμία συλλαβοῦσα τίκτει ἁμαρτίαν, cf. φιλεῖ δὲ τίκτειν ὕβρις . . . ὕβριν, Aeschylus *A.* 7.764ff.).

τίλλω *tillō* pluck, pick*

This vb. occurs in Mark 2:23 par. Matt 12:1/Luke 6:1: τίλλω (τοὺς) στάχυας, *"pluck/pick* [the] ears of grain"; Luke adds ψώχοντες ταῖς χερσίν. Τίλλω is used of *pluck /pick* in a general sense, with various objs. (e.g., hair: Homer *Il.* 22.78, 406; Ezra 9:3; wings: Dan 7:4 LXX; leaves: Plutarch *Themistocles* 13 [*Moralia* 185e]). Spicq, *Notes* II, 888f., working from papyri and the Lukan version, deduces the meaning "pick out the grains," though this can hardly be correct, since → ψώχω refers in Luke to the grinding of the plucked ears of grain, which shows that the grains themselves are edible. According to Deut 23:25 LXX one was allowed to gather ears of grain by hand in someone else's field (συλλέξεις). As a secondary part of the work of harvesting, the plucking of ears of grain (in an expansion of the prohibition of plowing and harvesting according to Exod 34:21) was not permitted on the sabbath, according to rabbinic opinion (*y. Šabb.* 7:9b; *t. Šabb.* 9:17; cf. *m. 'Ed.* 2:6). Dalman, *Arbeit* II, 339; BAGD s.v.

Τιμαῖος, ου *Timaios* Timaeus*

Mark 10:46: Timaeus is the name of the blind beggar's father; → Βαρτιμαῖος.

τιμάω *timaō* estimate; honor

1. Occurrences in the NT — 2. Meanings — 3. John

Lit.: H. KRÄMER, "Eine Anmerkung zum Verständnis von Mt 15,6a," *WuD* 16 (1981) 67-70. — J. SCHNEIDER, *TDNT* VIII, 178f. — C. WESTERMANN, *THAT* I, 794-812, esp. 794-98, 801f. — For further bibliography → τιμή.

1. Of the 21 occurrences of τιμάω, 16 are found in the Gospels alone (6 in Matthew, 3 in Mark, 1 in Luke, 6 in John), 1 each in Acts, Ephesians, 1 Timothy, and 2 in 1 Peter. Of the 10 occurrences in the Synoptic Gospels, 7 appear in OT citations. Of these, 5 are in the fourth commandment (Roman Catholic/Lutheran numbering:

Mark 7:10 par. Matt 15:4 [v. 6 refers to v. 4]; Mark 10:19 par. Matt 19:19/Luke 18:20 [also Eph 6:2]) and 2 in Isa 29:13 LXX (with minor deviation from LXX; Mark 7:6 par. Matt 15:8). On the alleged Jeremiah citation Zech 11:13 in Matt 27:9, which has 2 occurrences of τιμάω, → τιμή 2. Hence in the Synoptic Gospels every occurrence of τιμάω is either an OT citation or an allusion to one.

2. Τιμάω, a denominative vb. from → τιμή, is used either for *estimate/set a price or value* (Matt 27:9: τὴν τιμὴν τοῦ τετιμημένου [*sc.* ἀγροῦ] ὃν ἐτιμήσαντο, "the price for the field whose price they had *estimated/set*"; see BAGD s.v. 1) or for *honor,* with objs. variously God (Mark 7:6 par.), father and mother (→ 1), "us" (Acts 28:10), widows (1 Tim 5:3), everyone (1 Pet 2:17a), and the emperor (v. 17d).

3. John 5:23, with its four occurrences of τιμάω, expresses the center of Johannine theology: All should *honor* the Son as they *honor* the Father (see R. Schnackenburg, *John* II [Eng. tr., 1979] 108: "the definition of a duty"), because the Father has given all judgment, and thus his divine authority, over to the Son (v. 22). Like vv. 19f., "v. 22 asserts equality of the working of the Father and the Son" (R. Bultmann, *John* [Eng. tr., 1971] 256). Thus whoever does not *honor* the Son does not *honor* the Father (v. 23b). It is Jesus himself, however, who *honors* the Father (8:49). The Father will *honor* whoever serves Jesus (12:26).   H. Hübner

τιμή, ῆς, ἡ *timē* price, value; honor*

1. Occurrences in the NT — 2. Range of meaning — 3.a) Τιμὴ καὶ δόξα — b) 1 Cor 6:20; 7:23 — c) Col 2:23

Lit.: S. AALEN, *DNTT* II, 48-51. — R. DEICHGRÄBER, *Gotteshymnus und Christushymnus* (1967) 28f. — DEISSMANN, *Light* 319-30. — W. ELERT, "Redemptio ab hostibus," *TLZ* 72 (1947) 265-70. — K.-P. JÖRNS, *Das hymnische Evangelium* (1971) 32f., 36-38, 52-55. — B. REICKE, "Zum sprachlichen Verständnis von Kol 2,23," *ST* 6 (1952) 39-52. — J. SCHNEIDER, *TDNT* VIII, 169-78. — G. SCHÖLLGEN, "Die διπλῆ τιμή von 1 Tim 5,17," *ZNW* 80 (1989) 232-39. — C. WESTERMANN, *THAT* I, 794-812. — For further bibliography → δόξα.

1. Of the 41 occurrences of τιμή, only 3 are in the Gospels (2 in Matthew and 1 in John). In contrast, it appears 6 times in Acts, 26 times in the Epistles (11 times in Paul), and 6 times in Revelation.

2. Since Homer τιμή encompasses the range of meaning "estimation, price, value, honor," as well as "compensation, penalty, punishment" (Frisk, *Wörterbuch* II, 901). The former group approximately covers the meanings found in the NT.

In Acts τιμή usually refers to *price* (with gen. of price or value in 7:16: buy for the *price* of a sum of silver), *proceeds* (4:34; 5:2f.: from the sale of a piece of property), or *value* (19:19: books of magic with a *value* of fifty thousand pieces of silver). Only in 28:10 is it used for *honor*: πολλαῖς τιμαῖς ἐτίμησαν ἡμᾶς, "they showed us great *honor[s]*." In Matt 27:6 τιμὴ αἵματος is usually rendered appropriately as "blood *money.*" The alleged Jeremiah citation (see Zech 11:13) in Matt 27:9—τὴν τιμὴν τοῦ τετιμημένου (*sc.* ἀγροῦ) ὃν ἐτιμήσαντο, "the *price* for the field whose price they had set" (see BAGD s.v. τιμάω 1)—occurs neither in the LXX nor in the MT (on this problem see E. Klostermann, *Matt* [HNT] 218f.; K. Stendahl, *The School of St. Matthew* [²1968] 120-26; G. Strecker, *Der Weg der Gerechtigkeit* [³1971] 76-82: τιμή was already present in the tradition; R. H. Gundry, *The Use of the OT in St. Matthew's Gospel* [1975] 122-27). The Pauline phrase ἠγοράσθητε τιμῆς is of particular theological significance: "you were bought *at a high price* [or: *for cash*]" (1 Cor 6:20; 7:23; → 3.b).

Honor is paid to God (1 Tim 1:17 and elsewhere, → 3.a) or to Jesus (Heb 5:4; 2 Pet 1:17, and elsewhere, → 3.a), and to human beings (John 4:44 [honor in the sense of *recognition*]; Rom 2:7, 10 [τιμή with δόξα in the eschatological sense]; 12:10; 13:7 [hence all occurrences in Romans refer to *honor*]; 1 Tim 6:1 [slaves to their masters]; 1 Pet 1:7 [τιμή with δόξα, again in the eschatological sense]; 2:7; 3:7 [husbands to their wives]), and also to certain parts of the human body (1 Cor 12:23f.; see H. Conzelmann, *1 Cor* [Hermeneia] 214f.). Rom 9:21 (εἰς τιμὴν σκεῦος, "*honorable* vessel," in contrast to εἰς ἀτιμίαν) and probably also 2 Tim 2:20f. in its subsequent interpretation both refer to human beings, Romans in a "predestinarian" context, 2 Timothy in a parenetic context (polemic against heretics).

1 Thess 4:4 is disputed: "each one should possess his → σκεῦος in holiness and *honor.*" This can be interpreted either "hold one's own body in *honor*" or, more likely, "live with one's wife in *honor*" (so C. Maurer, *TDNT* VII, 365-67); cf. 1 Pet 3:7. The intepretation of διπλῆς τιμῆς in 1 Tim 5:17 is also disputed. It can refer either to double *compensation* for those who discharge their leadership office well (J. Jeremias, *Die Briefe an Timotheus und Titus* [NTD 9] 41; M. Dibelius and H. Conzelmann, *Pastoral Epistles* [Hermeneia] 77f.; Schneider 177: "more likely") or to double *honor* (W. Michaelis, *Das Ältestenamt der christlichen Gemeinde im Lichte der Heiligen Schrift* [1953] 112-19).

3. a) The combination of τιμή and → δόξα, "*honor* and glory," occurs occasionally in the LXX, though probably not yet as an idiomatically fixed hendiadys (for God, e.g.: Ps 8:6; 95:7 LXX; for Aaron: Exod 28:2; or for human beings in general: Ps 8:6). It does function as such a phrase, however, in the NT, particularly in doxological and hymnic texts praising God (1 Tim 1:17; cf. 6:16 with κράτος αἰώνιον instead of δόξα; Rev 4:11 [see also v. 9];

5:13; 7:12) or the "Lamb" (Rev 5:12f.). The stereotypical phrase τιμὴ καὶ δόξα occurs in the hymns of Revelation along with other honorific predicates whose choice is variously determined by the context (Jörns 33 and elsewhere). Rev 21:26 ("they will bring into it the glory and the *honor* of the nations") stands within an extremely free paraphrase above all of Isaiah 60 (see W. Bousset, *Rev* [KEK]; E. Lohmeyer, *Rev* [HNT]; H. Kraft, *Rev* [HNT] ad loc.).

Heb 2:7, 9 cites Ps 8:6 LXX and refers it to the suffering Jesus (→ τελειόω 3.b; on the possible differences between τιμή and δόξα in Heb 3:3 see O. Michel, *Heb* [KEK] 176: Τιμή is only a part of the δόξα). While Heb 2:7, 9 stands in the larger context of Ps 2:7 (cf. Heb 1:5; see also 5:4 along with 5:5), in 2 Pet 1:17 the reception of "*honor* and glory" is established through the transfiguration and the voice from heaven commensurate with Ps 2:7 (K. H. Schelkle, *1–2 Peter* [HTKNT] 198f.; for a different interpretation see p. 198 n. 3). On Rom 2:7, 10 and 1 Pet 1:7, → 2.

b) The tr. of τιμῆς ἠγοράσθητε (1 Cor 6:20; 7:23) as "you were bought *at a high price*" takes as its model the Vg. (*pretio magno*). The objection has been repeatedly raised, however, that the concern is not with how high the price might be, and thus the tr. is suggested "you were bought *for cash [payment]*" (H. Lietzmann and W. G. Kümmel, *1–2 Cor* [HNT] 28f.; H. Conzelmann, *1 Cor* [Hermeneia] 113 with n. 44). According to F. Büchsel, "The rather abrupt way in which the phrase is introduced in both cases shows that it is a kind of slogan of Paul's. . . . Intentionally it is not said who has bought them, or from whom they are bought, or at what cost" (*TDNT* I, 125). Gal 3:13 and 4:5 (with ἐξαγοράζω), however, show that at the very least the price was indeed high —namely, the sacrifice of Jesus under the curse of the law. (We may accept this conclusion, even if between Galatians and 1 Corinthians a certain shift in emphasis in the image and idea has taken place.) To that extent one is thus justified in translating τιμῆς in these verses *at a high price/expensively.*

It is also disputed whether the idea of the *sacral* purchase of a slave's freedom by the deity lies behind 1 Cor 6:20; 7:23 (cf. Deissmann 324f.: ἐπρίατο ὁ ᾿Απόλλων ὁ Πύθιος παρὰ . . . ἐπ᾿ ἐλευθερίᾳ σῶμ[α] γυναικεῖον . . . τιμᾶς ἀργυρίου μνᾶν τριῶν καὶ ἡμιμναῖου). Conzelmann's objection (*1 Cor* 113) that ἀγοράζειν means "buy in the market" and thus "does not fit in with the texts from Delphi" is inconclusive, since Paul did not necessarily borrow from this terminology. Büchsel (*TDNT* I, 125) and others might be correct in asserting that the reference to "the usual [vs. sacral] manumission of slaves" suffices to explain the passage, as in their isolated interpretation of 1 Corinthians 6 and 7. Büchsel, however, does admit that in Galatians 3 and 4 this idea "corresponds to the contemporary practice of sacral manumission" (126). This is of significance for 1 Corinthians particularly if, as is probably the case, it was written after Galatians. Further objections *contra* Deissmann (→

ἐξαγοράζω), considering Paul's well-known inappropriate comparisons, are not convincing, though they should be carefully considered.

c) According to G. Bornkamm Col 2:23 can "hardly be translated with any certainty" (*Aufsätze* I, 151; similarly E. Schweizer, *Col* [Eng. tr., 1982] 168: "almost impossible to translate"). It is clear, however, that the deutero-Pauline author—quite in the theological tradition of Paul—wants to expose the real roots of the cult of asceticism (on the worship of cosmic elements, → στοιχεῖον 3) and thus of all religions based on cultic self-redemption. The term τιμή may even have been a "catchword from the false teachings" in Colossae (E. Lohse, *Col and Phlm* [Hermeneia] 124; one cannot determine with any certainty whether τιμή here is additionally a t.t. for deification within the mystery cults; cf. Bornkamm, *Aufsätze* I, 151; Lohse 127; cf. R. Reitzenstein, *Hellenistic Mystery-Religions* [1978] 320-22). In any case, the form of *honor* sought in physical asceticism ultimately serves—admittedly unconsciously—the satisfaction of the flesh and thus leads to dishonor (an idea at least distantly related to Rom 1:21ff., → ἀτιμία 3), for asceticism as a sacrilegious means of control over God and as unadmitted self-idolatry denies God the honor due him. Not to honor God means to dishonor oneself. E. Lohmeyer thus speaks justifiably of Col 2:23 as the "ironic response" to the Colossian philosophy (*Col* [KEK] 129).   H. Hübner

τίμιος, 3 *timios* honored, respected; costly, valuable*

Lit.: → τιμή.

1. Of the 13 occurrences of τίμιος in the NT, 2 are in Acts, 5 in the Epistles (1 each in 1 Corinthians, Hebrews, James, 1 Peter, and 2 Peter), and 6 in Revelation.

2. The adj. τίμιος, derived from → τιμή, is translated *honored, respected* (a teacher of the law: Acts 5:34), *honorable* (marriage: Heb 13:4), *precious, costly, valuable* (stone[s]: 1 Cor 3:12; Rev 17:4; 18:12, 16; 21:11, 19; wood: Rev 18:12; fruit of the earth: Jas 5:7). Greater theological significance can be attributed to 1 Pet 1:19 (in the Pauline tradition, → τιμή 3.b): "you were ransomed (→ λύτρον 5) . . . by the *precious* blood of Christ," and 2 Pet 1:4: "*precious* and very great promises" granted by God.

Acts 20:24 is linguistically dense: οὐδενὸς λόγου ποιοῦμαι τὴν ψυχὴν τιμίαν ἐμαυτῷ ὡς τελειῶσαι τὸν δρόμον μου. Do we have here, as H. Conzelmann (*Acts* [Hermeneia] 174) suggests, "a mixture of the two expressions οὐδενὸς λόγου ποιοῦμαι, 'I have regard for nothing,' and 'I do not consider my life precious'"? The sense, however, is clear: "I do not account my life *of any value,* if only I may accomplish my course."   H. Hübner

τιμιότης, ητος, ἡ *timiotēs* costliness; fortune, wealth*

Rev 18:19 uses ἡ τιμιότης in an abstract sense for the *fullness of costly things* or *wealth* in Babylon (i.e., Rome); cf. Ezek 26:12; 27:9ff., 33.

Τιμόθεος, ου *Timotheos* Timothy*

1. Authentic attestation (Pauline letters) — 2. Colossians, 2 Thessalonians, Pastorals, Hebrews — 3. Acts — 4. Extrabiblical writings

Lit.: BAGD s.v. — N. BROX, "Zu den persönlichen Notizen der Pastoralbriefe," *BZ* 13 (1969) 76-94. — S. J. D. COHEN, "Was Timothy Jewish (Acts 16:1-3)? Patristic Exegesis, Rabbinic Law, and Matrilineal Descent," *JBL* 105 (1986) 251-68. — H. C. KEE, *IDB* IV, 650f. — W.-H. OLLROG, *Paulus und seine Mitarbeiter* (1979), index s.v. (273). — H. OPITZ, *BHH* 1988f. — W. STENGER, "Timotheus und Titus als literarische Gestalten," *Kairos* 16 (1974) 252-67. — P. TRUMMER, *Die Paulustradition der Pastoralbriefe* (1978) 76ff., 113ff. — K. WEGENAST, *KP* V, 851f.

1. Timothy ("one who honors God") is a common Greek name. The NT information about Timothy comes from different groups of writings and thus may not simply be added together.

Only the clearly genuine Pauline letters are an authentic source concerning Timothy. 2 Cor 1:1, Phil 1:1, and Phlm 1 (Col 1:1) mention Timothy as the single coauthor, while 1 Thess 1:1 (2 Thess 1:1) mentions him together with Silvanus (Silas, → Σιλᾶς). Paul refers to Timothy as his "brother" (2 Cor 1:1; 1 Thess 3:2; cf. also Col 1:1), "fellow worker" (1 Thess 3:2; Rom 16:21), and "beloved and faithful child in the Lord" (1 Cor 4:17). Together with Paul, Timothy fulfills an important function in the proclamation (2 Cor 1:19) and discharges his own tasks as well. He strengthens a distressed congregation and calms the apostle with his good news (1 Thess 3:1-6). 1 Cor 4:17 and 16:10f. commend Timothy for his missionary work in Corinth, and at the same time Paul defends him. This support—and the special function of Titus (mentioned in 2 Corinthians)— does not permit the conclusion that Timothy was not up to the task (*contra* Kee 650f.), since even Paul himself had difficulties with this congregation. In any case, Phil 2:19-22 offers the most glowing reference for Timothy: Paul has "no other like-minded one (ἰσόψυχον)" who will genuinely (γνησίως) concern himself with the affairs of the church and who has served with Paul in the gospel "as a son with a father." The final authentic attestation is Timothy's greeting in Rom 16:21.

2. Col 1:1 and 2 Thess 1:1 offer nothing new over against the clearly genuine letters concerning Timothy's identity and function. The picture presented by the Pas-

torals, on the other hand, initially appears quite different. Timothy as the "legitimate child in the faith" (1 Tim 1:2) and "beloved child" (2 Tim 1:2) is the addressee of two letters, the transmission of the proclamation is entrusted to him (1 Tim 1:18; 6:20), and throughout he is addressed in the second person in these letters. Closer examination, however, discloses that the Pastorals are doubly pseudonymous, i.e., the addressees are also fictionalized (Stenger 253). Apparently such concrete and endearing details concerning Timothy as the names of his grandmother Lois and his mother Eunice (2 Tim 1:5), his early instruction in the holy Scriptures (3:15), his ordination by Paul (1:6—differently in 1 Tim 4:14), his weak stomach (1 Tim 5:23), etc. offer no dependable information about Timothy but may be considered fictitious epistolary topoi for post-Pauline officeholders in general. The somewhat loosely addended conclusion to Hebrews occupies a special position here. Timothy, who according to 13:23 has just been released, represents a nominal if indirect possible connection between Hebrews and the Pauline tradition.

3. Acts reports more thoroughly and dependably about Timothy, without conforming to the Pauline letters. Timothy, the son of a Jewish Chistian mother and a Gentile father (Acts 16:1) from Lycaonia (probably Lystra), is chosen by Paul as a companion upon recommendation by the Christians there, and he is circumcised out of consideration for the Jews living there (vv. 2f.), which appears noticeably at odds with both Gal 2:3 on the one hand and 2 Tim 1:5 on the other. Amid the difficulties generated by the mission in Greece, Silas and Timothy at first remain in Beroea (17:14). According to vv. 15f. Paul, who in the meantime had arrived in Athens, requests they come as soon as possible; they join him, however, only in Corinth (18:5). According to 19:22 Timothy, together with Erastus, prepares Paul's farewell visit to Macedonia and then joins the large following accompanying Paul on his final journey to Jerusalem (20:4).

4. The postbiblical tradition (e.g., Eusebius *HE* iii.4.5), which makes Timothy the first bishop of Ephesus, offers almost no information beyond that in the NT.   P. Trummer

Τίμων, ωνος *Timōn* Timon*

Timon, a common personal name in Greek, appears in Acts 6:5 as the name of one of the seven included with the Hellenist Stephen.

τιμωρέω *timōreō* punish, chastise*

The act. occurs in Acts 26:11 and probably refers to the synagogue punishment of scourging: τιμωρῶν αὐτούς; the pass. occurs in 22:5: ἵνα τιμωρηθῶσιν. See also Billerbeck IV, 329ff.

τιμωρία, ας, ἡ *timōria* punishment, chastisement*

Heb 10:29: ἀξιόομαι τιμωρίας, "incur *punishment*" (cf. Diodorus Siculus i.96.5). BAGD s.v.

τίνω *tinō* pay, settle up*

2 Thess 1:9 uses the combination δίκην τίνω, "*pay* [as] punishment," common since Sophocles.

τίς, τί *tis, ti* who? what? which?

1. Occurrences in the NT — 2. Usage — 3. Syntactic position

Lit.: O. Bächli, " 'Was habe ich mit Dir zu schaffen?' Eine formelhafte Frage im AT und NT," *TZ* 33 (1977) 69-80. — BAGD s.v. — BDF, index s.v. — G. Braumann, "Wozu (Mark 15:34)," FS Rengstorf (1973) 155-65. — R. Bultmann, *Der Stil der paulinischen Predigt und die kynisch-stoische Diatribe* (FRLANT 13, 1910 = 1984). — J. C. Hawkins, *Horae synopticae* (²1909 = 1968). — J. Jeremias, *Die Sprache des Lukasevangeliums* (KEK Sonderband, 1980). — Johannessohn, *Präpositionen*, index s.v. — Kühner, *Grammatik* II/2, 632, 705f. (indices). — W. Larfeld, *Die neutestamentlichen Evangelien nach ihrer Eigenart und Abhängigkeit untersucht* (1925). — LSJ s.v. τις, τι B. — Mayser, *Grammatik*, index s.v. — H. R. Moeller and A. Kramer, "An Overlooked Structural Pattern in NT Greek," *NovT* 5 (1962) 25-35. — Moulton / Milligan s.v. — H. Rix, *Historische Grammatik des Griechischen. Laut- und Formenlehre* (1976) 186-88. — Schwyzer, *Grammatik* I, 615f. — Sophocles, *Lexicon* s.v. — G. R. Stanton, "Quid ergo Athenis et Hierosolymis? Quid mihi tecum est? And τί ἐμοὶ καὶ σοί;" *RMP* 116 (1973) 84-90. — Zerwick, *Biblical Greek* §221.

1. The (in)direct interrogative pron. (on etymological considerations see Schwyzer and recently Rix; attested since Homer *Il.*) occurs 555 times in the NT, overwhelmingly in the nom. or acc. sg. neut. (340 times) and in the nom. sg. masc./fem. (146 times; for additional information on frequency see *VKGNT* II, 396, or the *Computer-Konkordanz* [1980] appendix 60*f.). The Attic oblique cases τοῦ and τῷ (vs. τίνος and τίνι) occur neither in the NT nor in papyri (see Mayser I/2, 70). Τίς occurs esp. frequently in the Synoptic Gospels (91 times in Matthew, 72 in Mark, 114 in Luke) and in the Pauline corpus (107 times, 43 in Romans alone), but does not occur at all in Titus, Philemon, 2 Peter, 2–3 John, or Jude. The indefinite → τις occurs as a v.l. in Rom 8:24 (τις, τί καί in the text of *NTG*); Heb 3:16; Jas 3:13 (εἴ τις); cf. also Mark 5:31 *contra* Luke 8:46, and Mark 11:3 par. Luke 19:31 *contra* Matt 21:3. The interrogative pron. always has the acute accent on the first syllable.

2. Τίς is used subst. and, less frequently (see BAGD s.v. 2), adj. in a) direct and b) indirect questions (*who, what, which*) and c) as a substitute for the rel. pron. In a) and, less frequently, in b) it can also be used as a substitute for → ποῖος (as pred. nom.; see BAGD s.v. 1aβ,

1bβ) or together with ποῖος (as adj.; see BDF §298.2; note v.l. Mark 4:30 [omitted in *NTG*]; Acts 7:49; cf. also Matt 5:46f. *contra* Luke 6:32f.). Τίς also can substitute for πότερος (see BAGD s.v. 1aγ, 1bγ; BDF §298.1). In some cases the neut. τί functions as a pred. nom. with a pl. or a personal subj. (i.e., one that is not neut. gender; see BAGD s.v. 1bδ; also Acts 13:25 [v.l. τίνα]; 17:20 [v.l.]; 1 Cor 3:5 bis [v.l. τίς]; further classical examples in LSJ s.v. I.2). Particles such as → ἄρα (1.a.1) can also accompany it. On γάρ and οὖν, → a.1.

a) In direct questions:

1) Τίς usually occurs with the ind. (e.g., of the gnomic fut., see BDF §349.1; the copula can also be omitted, see §127.3 and Jeremias on Luke 24:17), in fixed phrases such as the following: τίς ἐξ ὑμῶν . . . ; (introduction to parables and metaphors instead of a conditional clause, see Jeremias on Luke 11:5 and 22:23; also with ἄνθρωπος, e.g., Luke 15:4 *contra* Matt 18:12 [τίνι ἀνθρώπῳ], or without ἐξ, see BAGD s.v. 1aα; BDF §164.1); τίς οἶδεν, εἰ and similar phrases (→ εἰ 2.c); τίς (. . .) οὗτος . . . ; (referring to Jesus, see Jeremias on Luke 7:49); τί ἐμοὶ καὶ σοί; and similar expressions (in addition to BAGD s.v. 1bε, see also Sophocles s.v. 1; Bächli [emphasis on the OT] 77-80; Stanton 87-90; LSJ s.v. I.8.c); τί σοὶ (ὑμῖν) δοκεῖ; (Matthean prefatory question; overview in Hawkins 8.33, cf. also Larfeld 295; occurs outside Matthew only in John 11:56); τί γάρ; (Rom 3:3; Phil 1:18; cf. Kühner II/2, 337); τί οὖν; or more fully τί οὖν ἐροῦμεν; → οὖν; → λέγω 3 (short questions raising objections or prolonging a discussion; in addition to BAGD s.v. 1bε, see generally Bultmann 13f., 53, 101; also occurs without οὖν, see BDF §366.2). The NT does not attest, e.g., τί δέ; (see LSJ s.v. I.8.f.). For examples of questions expecting a negative response, see BAGD s.v. 1aα and LSJ s.v. I.5.

Prep. phrases commonly include τίς (see BAGD s.v. 1bα), with διὰ τί; occurring esp. frequently (*why;* also Mark 7:5; ellipsis in Rom 9:32; 2 Cor 11:11). In an adv. meaning τί; also occurs alone (v.l. for διὰ τί, Luke 24:38; cf. also Mark 11:3 with Luke 19:31), similarly τί ὅτι; (see BDF § 299.3). A virtual synonym is εἰς τί; (Matt 14:31; Matt 26:8 par. Mark 14:4; Mark 15:34 [see Braumann] *contra* Matt 27:46 [differently Acts 19:3]). Further examples of prep. phrases are in BAGD s.v. 1bα, including κατὰ τί; (*by what?* Luke 1:18, see BAGD s.v. κατά 5aδ). On LXX usage see Johannessohn; on classical usage LSJ s.v. I.8.h. Τί introduces an exclamation (*what!*) in Matt 7:14 (*NTG* ὅτι) and Luke 12:49 (BDF §299; BAGD s.v. 3b; Sophocles s.v. 5).

2) Τίς can also occur with the deliberative subjunc. (though less than 35 occurrences, including with θέλω inserted in Matt 20:32 par. Mark 10:51/Luke 18:41; Matt 27:17, 21; Mark 10:36; 15:12), almost always subst. (adj. in Matt 19:16 *contra* Mark 10:17; Mark 4:30) and neut.

(τίς [= πότερος] only in Matt 27:17, 21). It appears, e.g., in the phrases τί ποιήσω; in Matt 20:32 par. Mark 10:51 /Luke 18:41; Matt 27:22 par. Mark 15:12; Mark 10:17 *contra* Matt 19:16 (see above)/Luke 18:18 (τί ποιήσας; cf. Luke 10:25 and Jeremias ad loc.; Kühner II/2, 100; LSJ s.v. II.2); Mark 10:36; Luke 12:17; 16:3; 20:13; Acts 22:10 (pl. in Luke 3:10, 12, 14; Acts 2:37; 4:16; pres. in John 6:28) and in τίνι ὁμοιώσω; in Mark 11:16 par. Luke 7:31; Luke 13:18b, 20.

3) It occurs with the potential opt. only in Acts 17:18, where τί is used subst.

b) In indirect questions:

1) Τίς appears most often with the ind. (→ a.1), esp. after → οἶδα 3.f.1 (24 times, see also *VKGNT* I s.v. [b]; adj. in 1 Thess 4:2), γινώσκω (12 times, see also *VKGNT* I s.v. [b]; with subst. question in Acts 22:30; thorough documentation of occurrences in Hawkins 47; see generally BDF §267), → ἀκούω 5.e (in Matt 21:16; Luke 18:6, and 7 times in Revelation), and λέγω (Matt 22:17; Matt 24:3 par. Mark 13:4; Luke 20:2 [*NTG* punctuates as a direct question]; Acts 24:20).

2) It occurs 25 times with the deliberative subjunc. (→ a.2; with subst. question in Rom 8:26; → b.1), exclusively subst. and almost always neut. (τίς in Luke 12:5; paratactic τίς τί in Mark 15:24; cf. Luke 19:15 [v.l., though in the text of *NTG;* with ind.], see BAGD s.v. 1c). It appears, e.g., after ἔχω (Matt 15:32 par. Mark 8:2; Mark 6:36 [v.l. omitted in *NTG*]; 8:1; Acts 25:26; see also the first papyrus example cited in Moulton/Milligan s.v. 2) and μεριμνάω (Matt 6:25 par. Luke 12:22; Matt 10:19 par. Mark 13:11 [προ-]/Luke 12:11).

3) Τίς appears also with the potential (→ a.3) or oblique opt. (8 times in Luke and Acts, also John 13:24 [*NTG* v.l.]; Acts 17:20 [v.l.]; with subst. question in Luke 1:62; 9:46; 22:23; → b.1; see Hawkins 22, 46f. and esp. Jeremias on Luke 1:62). It is usually subst. (pred. nom. in Luke 8:9; Acts 10:17); 4 times it appears after πυνθάνομαι (Luke 15:26; 18:36; John 13:24 [different in *NTG*]; Acts 21:33), and twice after διαπορέω (Acts 5:24; 10:17).

c) Τίς is also used as a substitute for the rel. pron. (v.l. Mark 14:36; John 13:18; 16:18; cf. also Matt 10:19 *contra* Luke 12:12; Matt 12:3 *contra* Luke 6:3; Mark 9:6 *contra* Luke 9:33; a few examples from papyri in Moulton/Milligan s.v. 2 and Mayser II/1, 80; classical examples also in LSJ s.v. II.b and d; see also BAGD s.v. 1aδ; BDF §298.4; Zerwick §221). Τί occurs subst. in Mark 4:24; 14:36; Luke 17:8 (with subjunc.) and with a rel. pron in 1 Tim 1:7 (after νοέω also in Mark 13:14 [v.l.]). Τίς is adj. in 1 Cor 15:2 (cf. H. Conzelmann, *1 Cor* [Hermeneia] on the tr. of the passage). *NTG* punctuates Acts 13:25 and Jas 3:13 as direct questions.

3. Syntactically, τίς appears overwhelmingly in the initial position (note anaphora, e.g., in Rom 8:33-35;

2 Cor 6:14-16; examples from Epictetus in Bultmann 17, 40, 71). Exceptions include, e.g., σὺ τίς εἶ; (see BDF §475; also John 1:22 [v.l.]; 21:12; pl. in Acts 19:15) and σὺ τί λέγεις; (Mark 14:68; John 8:5; 9:17 [v.l.]). The occurrence in final position in John 21:21 is unique (epiphoric; cf. Epictetus *Diss.* iv.1.102, cited in Bultmann 24). On the position (and function) of the acc. forms in certain inf. constructions see Moeller and Kramer 31, 35 (7 examples).   A. Horstmann

τις, τι   *tis, ti*   anyone, anything; someone, something

1. Occurrences in the NT — 2. Variations in meaning — 3. Usage — 4. Syntactic postion

Lit.: → τίς, τί. See also: BEYER, *Syntax* 76ff., 109f., 226-32. — KÜHNER, *Grammatik* I/1, 345f. — G. MUSSIES, *The Morphology of Koine Greek as Used in the Apocalypse of St. John* (NovTSup 27, 1971). — T. SCHRAMM, *Der Markus-Stoff bei Lukas* (SNTSMS 14, 1971). — J. WACKERNAGEL, *Vorlesungen über Syntax* (²1957) II, 114-19. — ZERWICK, *Biblical Greek* §9.

1. The indefinite pron. τις, attested since Homer *Il.*, occurs 526 times in the NT, overwhelmingly in the nom. masc./fem. (sg. 238 times, pl. 76 times) and in the nom. or acc. neut. sg. (95 times). For other frequency information see *VKGNT* II, 396, or the *Computer-Konkordanz* (1980) appendix 58*f. The Attic oblique forms του and τῳ (vs. τινος and τινι) do not occur in the NT, though του does occur in isolated instances in the papyri (see Mayser I/2, 70). (On etymological considerations → τίς, τί 1; comparative linguistic considerations appear in Wackernagel. On the ancient discussion concerning whether to classify it as a noun or a pron., see Apollonius Dyscolus *De Pronominibus* 27.1–28.9.)

Τις occurs in all NT writings, with particularly high frequency in the two Lukan works (80 times in Luke, 115 in Acts) and the Pauline corpus (157 times, 55 in 1 Corinthians alone). The interrogative pron. → τίς occurs as a v.l. in Heb 5:12; 1 Pet 5:8 (including with an inf.; see Mayser II/3, 54; Sophocles s.v. 3; LSJ s.v II.a). As an enclitic, this pron. takes the acute accent only if an additional enclitic follows (e.g., 1 Cor 10:19). In such cases, the two-syllable forms are accented on the final syllable (e.g., Luke 19:8; Gal 1:7), as they are when they follow a word accented with an acute on the penult (e.g. Mark 7:2; Acts 25:13) and when they appear in initial position (→ 4), thus always distinguishing themselves from the corresponding interrogative forms.

2. Τις usually indicates a) something indefinite or undetermined: *(any)one, anything; someone, something;* pl. *some* (see BAGD s.v. 1aα; 1bα; 2aα, γ; 2c, d); negated *no one, nothing* (see BAGD s.v. 1aγ, 1bβ, 2aγ). It often corresponds to the indefinite art. in English *(a, an)*. Τις can also b) designate *a certain [per-*

son] (with or without giving the name, see BAGD s.v. 1aβ, 2aβ; BDF §301.1), as well as c) refer to something or someone *important* (see BAGD s.v. 1aζ; BDF §301; see also LSJ s.v. II.5).

3. Τις is used a) subst. and b) adj.

a) Τις is used subst. (its only usage in Revelation; see Mussies 183).

1) Τις and τινες occur as subj., esp. in conditional clauses (11 of the 12 occurrences in Revelation [13:17 not cited in Mussies]; thus εἴ τις 12 times in 1 Corinthians, as anaphora in 2 Cor 11:20, ἐάν τις 18 times in John, εἴ τινες only in Rom 11:17; Gal 1:7; 1 Pet 3:1; see generally Beyer 76 n. 1; 78 nn. 1, 2; 226-32). Εἴ τις can correspond to ὅς (cf. Mark 4:23 with v. 9) or ὅστις (v.l. Mark 8:34; 1 Cor 7:13 [ἥτις in the text of *NTG*]; 1 Pet 3:1); similarly ἐάν τις (v.l. ὅς [ἐ]άν in John 8:51; 16:23; Eph 6:8; 1 John 5:14). The pron. often follows a negation (οὐ . . . τις/μή [. . .] τις = [οὐ . . .] οὐδείς/[μὴ . . .] μηδείς; cf. Matt 22:46 with Mark 12:34; → 2.a; see BDF §431; Beyer 109f.; papyri examples in Mayser II/2, 567; classical examples also in Diels, *Fragmente,* index s.v.).

A partitive gen. often expands an indefinite pron., as does (less often) ἐκ (usually coming after the pron., e.g., Matt 16:28 par. Mark 9:1/Luke 9:27, where a rel. clause follows; preceding a rel. clause in John 6:64) or ἐν (see BAGD s.v. 1aα, 1bα; BDF §164; → τίς 2.a.1) or occasionally also a partc. (after τινες in Mark 14:57; Acts 15:1; with the art. in Gal 1:7; see BDF §412.4; after τις in 1 Cor 6:1; with art. in Col 2:8).

2) Τι occurs only 14 times in the nom., 6 of these in the phrase εἶναί τι (→ 2.c; referring to persons in 1 Cor 3:7; Gal 2:6; 6:3; to things in 1 Cor 10:19 bis; Gal 6:15).

3) The oblique cases are used particularly as objs. (τι at least 80 times, e.g., in the phrase ἔχειν τι κατά τινος in Matt 5:23; cf. Mark 11:25; πρός τινα in Acts 24:19; paratactic τινός τι in Luke 19:8; → τίς 2.b.2; see also LSJ s.v. III.2.d), following a prep. (e.g., πρός in Luke 18:9; Acts 19:38; 24:12; Col 3:13), and in the acc. with inf. (e.g., Acts 5:36; → 2.c; 3.a.2; parallels in Moulton/Milligan s.v.; similarly adj. in Acts 8:9). On constructions with oblique cases, → 1; on preceding negation cf. Matt 8:28 with Mark 5:4, and Luke 8:51 with Mark 5:37. See BAGD s.v. 1bβ; on partitive gen. see also BAGD s.v. 1bα; on following partc. see BAGD s.v. 1aδ.

b) In adj. use (papyri examples in Mayser II/2, 84f.) τις appears in all genders (see BAGD s.v. 2.a), esp. in the Lukan corpus (see Jeremias on Luke 1:5) in the following combinations:

1) With a noun, e.g., in the combinations ἄνθρωπός τις (on the introduction to parables and miracle stories, see Jeremias on Luke 10:30; cf. also Schramm 155f.) and ἀνήρ τις (see Jeremias on Luke 10:30); also with pl. (see BAGD s.v. 2d); on Phil 2:1 see Zerwick §9.

Τίτιος

Τίτος

2) With a neut. adj., e.g., μικρόν τι in 2 Cor 11:1, 16; περισσοτερόν τι in Luke 12:4 and 2 Cor 10:8.

3) With a personal name (→ 2.b; see LSJ s.v. II.6; e.g., Luke 23:26; Acts 9:43; 10:5, 6; 19:14; 21:16; 22:12; 24:1; 25:19).

4) With a numeral: εἷς τις, adj., only in Mark 14:51 (v.l.; see BAGD s.v. εἷς 3c; on τις as a substitute for the Markan εἷς in Luke, see Jeremias on Luke 1:5; cf. also Luke 9:57 *contra* Matt 8:19); δύο τινές in Luke 7:18; Acts 23:23 (see BAGD s.v. 2bα; LSJ s.v. II.8).

4. Τις occurs relatively rarely in the initial position (see classical examples in Kühner I/1, 345f.; see also LSJ s.v. III.1.a). There are several examples, however, of initial τινὲς δέ (Matt 27:47; Luke 6:2; 11:15; John 7:44; 11:37, 46; 13:29 v.l.; Acts 17:34 [adj.]; 19:31; 24:19 [adj.]; 1 Cor 8:7; 15:6). It also is first when it appears with correlatives (papyri examples in Mayser II/1, 57; classical examples also in LSJ s.v. III.1.b), e.g., τινὲς μέν . . . τινὲς δέ in Phil 1:15 (see BAGD s.v. 1aε). See also Acts 17:18, as well as the unique construction in 1 Tim 5:24: τινῶν . . . τισὶν δέ.

The pron. is in second position in καί τινες (Mark 8:3; 11:5; 14:57; 15:35; Luke 19:39; Acts 10:23; 15:1; 17:4). This position is possible also after other particles, e.g., εἰ or ἐάν (→ 3.a.1), less frequently ἵνα (Mark 9:30; 11:16; John 2:25; 6:50; 13:29; 15:13; 16:30; Rom 1:11, 13; 1 John 2:27), and in isolated instances after ὡς (2 Pet 3:9), καθώς (anaphora in 1 Cor 10:8f.), or καθάπερ (1 Cor 10:10). A rel. pron. precedes it in 1 Tim 1:6, 19; 6:10, 21 (variously referring to a following partc.); on preceding negation → 3.a.1/3.

Τις appears in third position only if the negation follows the particle. It occurs esp. frequently after δέ, in isolated instances after γάρ (Acts 19:24; 1 Cor 8:10; 1 Tim 5:15), and after ἄν only in Acts 2:45 = 4:35 (classical examples of τις after εἰ, δέ, γάρ, ἄν in Diels, *Fragmente*, index s.v.).

The position at or near the beginning of the sentence (see BDF §473.1) results in τις also occurring before a noun, even with separation or dislocation (see BDF §§301, 473.1; classical examples in Kühner II/1, 665f.), or before a vb. (e.g., Luke 19:8; → 3.a.3). Otherwise the word order frequently varies both in the mss. (e.g., Acts 23:23; → 3.b.4) and in reliable texts (cf., e.g., Luke 10:38 with 17:12). The attributive position between art. and noun in 2 Tim 2:18 is unique. On the position (and function) of the acc. sg. τινα in the inf. constructions in Acts 5:36 or 8:9 (→ 3.a.3), see Moeller and Kramer 31, 35 (→ τίς 3).

A. Horstmann

Τίτιος, ου   *Titios*   Titius*

The name of Titius, a worshiper of God (σεβόμενος τὸν θεόν, → σέβομαι), occurs in Acts 18:7 with the surname → Ἰοῦστος ("the just one"). His house (οἰκία) in Corinth was next door (→ συνομορέω) to the synagogue. Because of the opposition of the Jews (v. 6) Paul moved from the synagogue (v. 4) into the house of the "Gentile" (v. 6) Titius Justus. The mss. ℵ E and others read the name as → Τίτος Ἰοῦστος and thus probably equate Titius with Paul's disciple → Τίτος, who is otherwise not mentioned in Acts; in A B² D* Ψ Koine P he is called simply Ἰοῦστος. E. J. Goodspeed ("Gaius Titius Justus," *JBL* 69 [1950] 382f.) identifies him with the Corinthian → Γάϊος (3) (Τίτιος) in Rom 16:23. J. Mánek, *BHH* 916; BAGD s.v.; E. Haenchen, *Acts* (Eng. tr., 1971) ad loc.

τίτλος, ου, ὁ   *titlos*   inscription, notice*

John 19:19, 20 refers to the inscription on the cross (→ ἐπιγραφή) as a τίτλος (from Lat. *titulus*). According to Roman custom a tablet indicating the nature of the offense was often carried before a condemned man or hung around his neck (Suetonius *Caligula* 32; *Domitian* 10; cf. Dio Cassius liv.3); in Jesus' case it was fastened to the top of his cross. According to John 19:19f. it carried the inscription written in three languages ("Hebrew [i.e., Aramaic], Latin, and Greek," cf. Luke 23:38 v.l.): Ἰησοῦς ὁ Ναζωραῖος ὁ βασιλεὺς τῶν Ἰουδαίων (cf. Mark 15:26 par.; → βασιλεύς 4). G. Delling, *BHH* 1005; J. de Fraine, *BL* 993; BAGD s.v.

Τίτος, ου   *Titos*   Titus*

1. Titus in Galatians and 2 Corinthians — 2. Titus in the Pastorals

Lit.: BAGD s.v. — C. K. BARRETT, "Titus," FS Black (1969) 1-14 (= *idem, Essays on Paul* [1982] 118-31). — B. HOLMBERG, *Paul and Power* (CB.NT 11, 1978) 60-62. — A. JÜLICHER, *RE* XIX, 798-800. — W. H. OLLROG, *Paulus und seine Mitarbeiter* (WMANT 50, 1979) 33-37 and index s.v. — H. OPITZ, *BHH* 1994. — J. REUSS, *BL* 1318. — A. SUHL, *Paulus und seine Briefe* (SNT 11, 1975), index s.v.

1. Titus was one of Paul's fellow workers; he is mentioned only in the Pauline corpus itself, and by Paul himself only in 2 Corinthians (9 times, 6 of these in chs. 8f.) and Gal 2:1, 3, otherwise in 2 Tim 4:10; Titus 1:4; cf. also the postscript to 2 Corinthians Koine (ἐγράφη ἀπὸ Φιλίππων διὰ Τίτου καὶ Λουκᾶ) and to Titus (πρὸς Τίτον . . .).

Titus was a Gentile Christian (Ἕλλην, Gal 2:3) whom Paul took along to the apostolic council in Jerusalem as a representative of the Antiochian Christians together with Barnabas (συμπαραλαβὼν καὶ Τίτον, v. 1), though without having to circumcise him there (v. 3).

Titus later played an important role in Paul's disputes with the church in Corinth. After experiencing serious insults and offenses during an "interim visit" to the congregation (2 Cor 2:5-8; 7:12; 12:20f.; 13:2), Paul wrote

363

a letter to Corinth "with many tears" (2:4) after his return to Ephesus and sent Titus (probably carrying the letter) to reestablish peace with the church. From Ephesus Paul then went to Troas, found that Titus had not yet returned there from Corinth (vv. 12f.), and so continued on to Macedonia to meet him (v. 13). There he was comforted by the coming of Titus (παρεκάλεσεν ἡμᾶς ὁ θεὸς ἐν τῇ παρουσίᾳ Τίτου, 7:6), who had in the meantime won the Corinthian church back for the apostle and therewith also the apostle back for the church (vv. 5ff., 13, 14).

From Macedonia Paul then sent Titus to Corinth again to conclude the work of collection that Paul himself had begun earlier (καθὼς προενήρξατο, 8:6; cf. v. 10; 9:2; ἵνα . . . καὶ ἐπιτελέσῃ . . . τὴν χάριν ταύτην, 8:6). Since the beginning of the collection is dated "a year ago" (ἀπὸ πέρυσι, 8:10; 9:2), Titus might have paid his first visit to Corinth even before the delivery of the "letter of tears" (cf. 1 Cor 16:1-4), a visit Paul does not specifically mention.

Titus's third visit to the church (2 Cor. 8:16, 23; together with a delegate from the Greek churches [vv. 18f.] and an additional brother [vv. 22-24]) serves to conclude Paul's commissioned collection appropriately, something for which Paul also petitions Titus according to 12:18 (bis; if ch. 12 is actually a part of the "letter of tears," v. 18 would have to refer to a previous visit by Titus, and thus to the beginning of the collection activity presupposed in 8:6, 10; 9:2).

2. According to 2 Tim 4:10 Titus later engaged in mission activity in Dalmatia. Titus 1:4 refers to him as γνήσιον τέκνον and (v. 5) as "Paul's" representative in Crete authorized to appoint elders and solidify the organization of the churches. According to tradition, after Paul's death Titus returned to Crete, where he became a bishop and lived to an old age (Eusebius *HE* iii.6.6). On Acts 18:7 v.l. → Τίτιος.   H. Balz

τοιγαροῦν *toigaroun* for that reason, then, therefore*

Τοιγαροῦν introduces an inference from a preceding statement (1 Thess 4:8; cf. v. 7). In Heb 12:1 it introduces an exhortation (on the basis of ch. 11).

τοίνυν *toinyn* so, thus, for that reason, therefore*

Τοίνυν is an inferential particle that in Luke 20:25 (with imv.) and Heb 13:13 (with hortatory subjunc.) stands at the beginning of the sentence and introduces an exhortation. In 1 Cor 9:26 (with ind.; cf. Jas 2:24 Koine with ind.) it appears in the second position (as in classical usage) and introduces an assertion.

τοιόσδε, 3 *toiosde* such as this, of this kind, such (a one)*

2 Pet 1:17: φωνὴ . . . τοιάδε, "a voice *of this kind*" (referring to the citation following in v. 17b and to the uniqueness of the divine call itself).

τοιοῦτος, αὕτη, οὗτο(ν) *toioutos* such as this, of such a kind, such (a one)*

The correlative adj. τοιοῦτος occurs 57 times in the NT; it is actually used correlatively, however, in only a few instances: τοιούτους ὁποῖος καὶ ἐγώ εἰμι, "*such* as I am" (Acts 26:29; cf. Lat. *qualiscumque*); οἷος . . . τοιοῦτοι (1 Cor 15:48 bis; 2 Cor 10:11b; BDF § 304).

Τοιοῦτος is often used as an adj. without the art. with nouns that also lack articles (Matt 9:8; 18:5; Mark 4:33; John 9:16; Acts 16:24; 1 Cor 11:16; 2 Cor 3:4, 12; Heb 7:26; 12:3; 13:16; Jas 4:16; see BDF §274) and often is specified more closely by a rel. clause (1 Cor 5:1; Heb 8:1). With nouns accompanied by the art. it is used attributively (Mark 9:37; 2 Cor 12:3) or predicatively (Mark 6:2). Mark 13:19 sounds like a Semitism: θλῖψις οἵα οὐ γέγονεν τοιαύτη, "tribulation as has not occurred *in this way*" (cf. Exod 9:18; see BDF §297). In John 4:23 τοιοῦτος occurs predicatively in a double acc. with a partc. (τοιούτους ζητεῖ τοὺς προσκυνοῦντας αὐτόν, "he seeks *such persons/persons of that kind* [cf. v. 23a] who worship him"); τοιοῦτος ὢν ὡς in Phlm 9 is translated "since I am *the sort of person* as/*in my position* as."

Otherwise τοιοῦτος is used subst. Without the art. it occurs only as neut. pl.: τοιαῦτα, *such things* (Mark 7:13: παρόμοια τοιαῦτα, "*such things* as that"; Luke 9:9; Heb 11:14); otherwise with the art.: τὰ τοιαῦτα, *things of that sort, such things* (Acts 19:25; Rom 1:32: οἱ τὰ τοιαῦτα πράσσοντες; 2:2, 3; Gal 5:21; Eph 5:27: ἤ τι τῶν τοιούτων, "or *any such thing*"; 1 Cor 7:15: ἐν τοῖς τοιούτοις, "in *such cases*"). It refers also to persons: ὁ τοιοῦτος, *such a person, one like that* (occasionally corresponding to οὗτος, see BDF §304; Matt 19:14; Mark 10:14; Luke 18:16; [John 8:5]; Acts 22:22; Rom 16:18; 1 Cor 5:5 *[this man]*; 5:11; 7:28; 16:16, 18; 2 Cor 2:6, 7 *[this man]*; 10:11a; 11:13; 12:2, 5 *[this man]*; Gal 5:23; 6:1; Phil 2:29; 2 Thess 3:12; Titus 3:1; 3 John 8).

τοῖχος, ου, ὁ *toichos* wall*

Acts 23:3: τοῖχε κεκονιαμένε, "you whitewashed *wall*," an invective Paul directs against the high priest Ananias (probably a common insult, here likely alluding to Ezek 13:10-12 and asserting that the members of the Sanhedrin and the high priest are like a cracked wall that can hide its fragility only by its whitewash). J. Schneider, *TDNT* III, 827.

τόκος, ου, ὁ *tokos* interest (on money)*

Matt 25:27 par. Luke 19:23: σὺν τόκῳ, "with *interest*" (from the money changer/banker), used here as a metaphor for fruitfulness; cf. also Exod 22:24; Deut 23:20f.; Ezek 18:17; Prov 28:8.

τολμάω *tolmaō* dare, trust oneself, have the courage; take upon oneself, presume, bring oneself*

1. Occurrences in the NT — 2. Basic meanings — 3. Paul

Lit.: H. D. Betz, *Der Apostel Paulus und die sokratische Tradition* (BHT 45, 1972) 67f. — G. Fitzer, *TDNT* VIII, 181-86. — J. Zmijewski, *Der Stil der paulinischen "Narrenrede"* (BBB 52, 1978) 232-35.

1. Τολμάω occurs 16 times in the NT, 8 of these in Paul (4 times in 2 Corinthians) and usually with a following inf. It refers to courage or (with negation) fear (in Phil 1:14 note the correspondence between τολμάω and ἀφόβως).

2. In the Gospels τολμάω is used without negation only in Mark 15:43: "Joseph of Arimathea went *courageously* (τολμήσας εἰσῆλθεν) to Pilate and asked for the body of Jesus" (see BDF §414; cf. also Plutarch *Cam.* 22.6; *Demetr.* 44). Paul equates τολμάω with boldness in the rhetorical question in 1 Cor 6:1: "*Does* any one of you *dare* go to law before the unrighteous?"

Used with negation (*not trusting oneself, not daring, not having the courage*), τολμάω in Acts 5:13 describes the fear of the other Christians before the inhabitants of Jerusalem, or in 7:32 Moses' fear before the divine δόξα. A series of disputes in Mark 12:34 par. Matt 22:46/Luke 20:40 concludes redactionally with "And after that no one *dared* to ask him any question." The force of Jesus' own answers here discourages any further questions from his listeners (cf. Matt 22:46: "And no one was able to answer him"). John 21:12 is analogous: Recognizing Jesus' presence, the disciples *dared not* ask about his identity. In both instances οὐ τολμάω expresses the respectful fear of persons over against one who is superior. The polemic in Jude 9 reflects a similar shyness; in contrast to adversaries who revile the angelic powers (v. 8), even the archangel Michael himself *did not dare* revile the devil (cf. the parallel in 2 Pet 2:10f., where the revilers are called "bold, willful people" [→ τολμητής]). Paul uses οὐ τολμάω rhetorically in reference to himself (Rom 15:18; 2 Cor 10:12 [ironically, cf. 10:2; 11:21; → 3.a]) as an expression of his apostolic modesty.

3. a) Paul uses τολμάω absolutely in a dispute with his adversaries in 2 Corinthians (10:2; 11:21 bis). The background here is their objection that Paul in his personal presence, in contrast to themselves (and also to his own letters from a distance), is humble (→ ταπεινός) and weak

(→ ἀσθενής 2.b and 4; cf. 10:1, 10). Paul counters this charge in 10:2 with an admonition to the Corinthians to watch out, lest during his time in Corinth he would have to prove his courage (θαρρέω) and assurance (πεποίθησις, as in Phil 1:14, issuing from τολμάω) through bold and aggressive behavior toward his revilers (τολμάω ἐπί τινα; with this meaning also *1 Enoch* [Greek] 7:4; cf. also *Jos. As.* 28:7[5] [= Batiffol 83, l. 6]; Pap. Leipzig 39.8).

The context in 2 Cor 11:21 suggests that Paul is boasting about personal merits and accomplishments (→ καυχάομαι 3). Paul, in the role of the fool, competes in such boasting with his adversaries (see 11:17, 23; 12:11; → ἀφροσύνη 3.d) and in no way lags behind them (see also 12:11b): "Whatever any one *presumes* for himself . . . I *presume* for myself as well" (i.e., "Whatever they are, so too am I," see H. Windisch, *2 Cor* [KEK] 350; cf. Zmijewski; Betz regards τολμάω as "rhetorical-Sophist terminology" [67]). It is entirely possible that Paul here repeats a catchword used against him by his adversaries.

b) In Rom 5:7b τολμάω is almost synonymous with → ὑπομένω (see F. Field, *Notes on the Translation of the NT* [1899] 155; for examples from outside the NT see Fitzer 181): "Perhaps one *might take it upon oneself* to die for the good" (τολμάω ἀποθνῄσκειν ὑπέρ τινος also in Euripides *Alc.* 644; *IA* 1389; Demosthenes *Or.* 26.23; Plato *Smp.* 180a, and elsewhere; esp. frequent in Isocrates *Panegyricus* 77; *To Philip* 55; *Archidamus* 94; *On Peace* 143).

M. Wolter

τολμηρός, 3 *tolmēros* bold, audacious*

Rom 15:15, using the comparative as an adv.: τολμηρότερον (A B al read τολμηροτέρως) δὲ ἔγραψα ὑμῖν, "but I have written to you *very boldly*." G. Fitzer, *TDNT* VIII, 186.

τολμητής, οῦ, ὁ *tolmētēs* daredevil, audacious person*

2 Pet 2:10, in reference to false teachers: τολμηταὶ αὐθάδεις, "*bold,* arrogant *people.*" G. Fitzer, *TDNT* VIII, 185.

τομός, 3 *tomos* cutting, sharp*

In Heb 4:12 the comparative τομώτερος refers metaphorically to "the word of God."

τόξον, ου, τό *toxon* bow (of an archer)*

Rev 6:2: The rider on the white horse "had a *bow.*"

τοπάζιον, ου, τό *topazion* topaz*

In antiquity topaz was often made into seals and gems. Rev 21:20 mentions it as a precious stone.

τόπος, ου, ὁ *topos* place, position, location

1. Occurrences in the NT — 2. Τόπος as designation of place — 3. Fig. usage

Lit.: BAGD s.v. — H. CONZELMANN, "Miszelle zu Apk 18,17," *ZNW* 66 (1975) 288-90. — H. KÖSTER, *TDNT* VIII, 187-208.

1. Τόπος occurs 95 times in the NT, 56 of which are in the Gospels (10 in Matthew, 10 in Mark, 19 in Luke, 17 in John), 18 in Acts, 8 in Revelation, and only 13 in all the Epistles together (3 in Romans, 3 in Hebrews, 2 in 1 Corinthians, and 1 each in 2 Corinthians, Ephesians, 1 Thessalonians, 1 Timothy, and 2 Peter). The word occurs primarily in the narrative writings, and there most frequently in Luke.

2. Τόπος refers to *place* or *locale* in a variety of ways.

a) Τόπος occurs in the Passion story along with specific mention of the *place name*. The place of Jesus' crucifixion is the τόπος Golgotha (Mark 15:22 par.; John 19:17). The Hebrew name is either subsequently explained in Greek as Κρανίου Τόπος (Mark 15:22; Matt 27:33) or added to the preceding Greek translation (John 19:17). In the style of the LXX, Luke 23:33 writes only ἐπὶ τὸν τόπον τὸν καλούμενον Κρανίον. This precise designation must go back to the oldest transmitted tradition. The Lukan formulation has its secular counterpart in Acts 27:8: εἰς τόπον τινὰ καλούμενον Καλοὺς λιμένας.

b) Τόπος refers to *places visited* by the disciples or Paul, such as the unspecified Palestinian locales into which Jesus sends his disciples (Mark 6:11; Luke 10:1), certain cities in Asia Minor (Derbe, Lystra, Iconium; out of consideration for their inhabitants Paul has the Gentile Christian Timothy circumcised, Acts 16:3 [historically disputed]), and unnamed ports along the province of Asia mentioned in the account of the captive apostle's journey to Rome (Acts 27:2).

c) Τόπος refers to a *specific locale,* either a named inhabited plain (Gennesaret, Matt 14:35) or a place described in further detail with an adj. or rel. clause: ἔρημος τόπος as a "lonely/desolate *place*" to which Jesus withdraws alone or with his disciples (Mark 1:35 par.; 1:45; 6:31f.); τόπος πεδινός, "level *place*" at which the disciples and people hear what is known as Jesus' Sermon on the Plain (Luke 6:17); ἄνυδροι τόποι, "waterless *places*" through which the exorcised unclean spirit passes (Matt 12:43); τραχεῖς τόποι, "rocky *places*" in the sea, i.e., a reef (Acts 27:29); τόπος διθάλασσος, probably a shoal just offshore against which the ship with the captive apostle runs aground (v. 41).

Formulations with rel. clauses and ὁ τόπος ὅπου follow the pattern of Hebraisms. Such structures refer to the place of Jesus' burial (Mark 16:6 par.) and in John often to an important place connected with the story of Jesus

or John the Baptist; the reader is explicitly reminded of such places by repeated references (6:23; 10:40; 11:30; 19:20, 41). Τόπος can also refer to the setting of the current action; as such it thus serves to connect locales within a narrative and can be translated simply *there* (Luke 10:32; 19:5; 22:40; John 5:13; 6:10).

d) Τόπος can refer to a *specific building,* such as the house in which the Jerusalem congregation assembles for prayer (Acts 4:31). Following Jewish usage, the temple is called τόπος ἅγιος or τόπος οὗτος. The mysterious allusion in Matt 24:15 (cf. Mark 13:14) refers to the temple, and Stephen and Paul are accused of speaking and teaching against it (Acts 6:13, 14; 21:28). Two OT citations in Stephen's speech also speak of the temple as τόπος (7:7, 49). With the phrase ὁ τόπος οὗτος Luke apparently is drawing upon Jeremiah's temple criticism (cf. Köster 197f.; see also → ναός 6). In John 4:20 the temple or Jerusalem appears as ὁ τόπος ὅπου προσκυνεῖν δεῖ, which now, however, is eschatologically superseded. In juxtaposing τόπος and ἔθνος, John 11:48 might also be referring to the temple.

e) Τόπος refers to the *specific place* of persons or things. There is no place in the inn for the newborn baby Jesus (Luke 2:7), and no place at the feast table for additional guests (14:22). Τόπος also refers to the ἔσχατος τόπος for the prudent guest in contrast to the place of honor (vv. 9f.). Occasionally the thing concerned appears in gen. with τόπος: e.g., the sword's sheath (Matt 26:52: ὁ τόπος αὐτῆς) or the position of the nails in the crucified Jesus (John 20:25b: ὁ τόπος τῶν ἥλων [text uncertain]).

The mythical language of Revelation is intended to express theological assertions. Removal from traditional places announces eschatological judgment, as with the lampstand of the disobedient church (2:5) and with every mountain and island in the context of the eschatological convulsions of the cosmos (6:14). In contrast, the woman, i.e., the Church, has her own place in the desert prepared by God for her protection during the period of tribulation in the last days (12:6, 14). The destruction of the very existence of those without a τόπος during those last days is expressed by the phrase borrowed from Dan 2:35: καὶ τόπος οὐχ εὑρέθη αὐτοῖς. Such will it be for the dragon expelled from heaven (12:8) and for sky and earth in their flight from the countenance of God (20:11).

Outside Revelation τόπος refers only occasionally and with edifying intentions to the heavenly place of the Church (John 14:2f.) or to the place of torment for the rich (Luke 16:28). In the case of Judas (Acts 1:25), his τόπος ἴδιος is hell.

f) Finally, τόπος occurs in adv. phrases. Ἐν παντὶ τόπῳ, *everywhere,* reflects the idea of the universal Church (1 Cor 1:2), the scope of Paul's missionary activity (2 Cor 2:14), and the spreading of the news of a church's faith (1 Thess 1:8). Κατὰ τόπους, *in various places,* refers to the earthquakes that will appear in the last days (Mark 13:8 par.). Εἰς ἕτερον τόπον, *to another place,* is used of Peter's departure (to an unknown place, Acts 12:17), and ἐπὶ τόπον (πλέων), *from place to place,* refers to the travels of coastal sailors (Rev 18:17; see Conzelmann).

3. Τόπος is used fig. in only a few cases.

a) Τόπος refers to a specific *position* in the Church, either the τόπος τῆς διακονίας ταύτης καὶ ἀποστολῆς that became vacant when Judas left the circle of the Twelve and thus had to be filled anew (Acts 1:25a), or the τόπος τοῦ ἰδιώτου occupied by the nonecstatic as a layperson, to the extent that this one does not understand the ecstatic prayer of the person speaking in tongues (1 Cor 14:16). The former usage perhaps presupposes a technical administrative term; the latter perhaps envisions a precise seating order such as that in Qumran.

b) As already in general Greek usage, τόπος in the NT occasionally refers to the *opportunity* or adequate *room* for something, e.g., Paul's lack of opportunity for further mission activity in the east (Rom 15:23); his legally entitled opportunity for self-defense (Acts 25:16); Esau's lost opportunity for repentance (Heb 12:17); and the place for divine wrath (Rom 12:19), for the devil (Eph 4:27), and for a second covenant (Heb 8:7).

c) In Luke 4:17 τόπος refers to the scriptural passage Jesus finds, here Isa 61:1f. This phrase, presumably influenced redactionally, has its nearest parallel in *1 Clem.* 8:4: καὶ ἐν ἑτέρῳ τόπῳ λέγει.

d) 2 Pet 1:19 uses αὐχμηρὸς τόπος metaphorically as a reference to the present world, in which the light of the prophetic word shines for Christians (cf. 2 Esdr 12:42).

                          G. Haufe

τοσοῦτος, αύτη, οὗτο(ν) *tosoutos* so great, so much, so strong*

This correlative adj. occurs both with and without nouns. In both instances it can refer to either (a) quantity or (b) quality.

1. With a noun: a) Matt 15:33 (bis); Luke 15:29; John 12:37; 14:9 (21:11); 1 Cor 14:10; Heb 4:7; Rev 18:7, 17. b) Matt 8:10 par. Luke 7:9 (*such* faith); Heb 12:1.

2. Without a noun: a) John 6:9; Acts 5:8 (bis). b) Gal 3:4. In Heb 1:4 and 10:25 τοσούτῳ (with comparative) corresponds to ὅσῳ: "*(by) as much . . . as.*" In 7:22 κατὰ τοσοῦτο follows καθ' ὅσον (v. 20).

τότε *tote* at that time; then, thereupon

This correlative adv. of time occurs 160 times in the NT and is esp. preferred by Matthew (90 occurrences; 21 in Acts, 15 in Luke, 10 in John, 6 in Mark). Two kinds of usage can be distinguished.

1. Τότε refers to far off, more distant time. a) The past *(at that time):* Matt 2:17; 4:17; 16:21; 26:16; 27:9, 16; Luke 16:16; Gal 4:8, 29; Heb 12:26; 2 Pet 3:6. b) The future *(then):* Matt 13:43; 1 Cor 13:12 (bis). c) Time defined by a condition *(then):* 2 Cor 12:10.

2. Τότε in the sense of *thereafter* introduces that which (immediately) follows temporally (BDF §459: nonclassical): Matt 2:7, 16; 3:13, 15; 4:1, 5, 10, 11; 8:26; 12:22, and elsewhere; Luke 11:26; 14:21; 21:10; 24:45; Acts 1:12; 4:8. Καὶ τότε occurs in Matt 7:23; 16:27; 24:10, 14, 30 (bis); Mark 13:21, 26, 27; Luke 21:27; 1 Cor 4:5; Gal 6:4; 2 Thess 2:8. Τότε οὖν ("so *then*") occurs in John 11:14; 19:1, 16; 20:8. Often ὅταν (with aor. subjunc.) is used in conjunction with τότε ("when . . . *then*"): Matt 24:16; 25:31; Mark 13:14; Luke 5:35; 21:20; John 8:28; 1 Cor 15:28, 54; 16:2; Col 3:4.

τούναντίον *tounantion* on the contrary*

Τούναντίον (= ἐναντίον with art.) occurs in the NT only in 2 Cor 2:7; Gal 2:7; 1 Pet 3:9. BDF §18.

τοὔνομα *tounoma* by name*

Τοὔνομα (from τὸ ὄνομα, acc.; cf. BDF §§18; 160) occurs in the NT only in Matt 27:57 (differently in Mark).

τράγος, ου, ὁ *tragos* male goat*

Heb 9:12, 13, 19 and 10:4 mention *male goats* with other sacrificial animals; cf. *Barn.* 2:5; 7:4, 6, 8, 10.

τράπεζα, ης, ἡ *trapeza* table; meal*

Τράπεζα usually refers to the *table* upon which meals are set (Mark 7:28 par. Matt 15:27; Luke 16:21; 22:21; Rom 11:9 [Ps 68:23 LXX]). Luke 22:30 refers to the table of the heavenly meal. Τράπεζα can also refer to the *meal* itself (Acts 6:2; 16:34). The contrast "*table* of the Lord" and "*table* of demons" (1 Cor 10:21) hardly presupposes the idea of pagan cultic meals (*contra* BAGD s.v. 2; with L. Goppelt, *TDNT* VIII, 213f., cf. also H. Conzelmann, *1 Cor* [Hermeneia] ad loc.). Heb 9:2 speaks of the *table* on which the bread of the Presence lay (Exod 25:23-30 LXX). Finally, τράπεζα is the *table* with the coins of the money changers (Mark 11:15 par. Matt 21:12/John 2:15) and (thence) the *bank* in which one deposits money for interest (Luke 19:23). L. Goppelt, *TDNT* VIII, 209-15; *TWNT* X, 1281 (bibliography); B. Klappert, *DNTT* II, 520f.

τραπεζίτης, ου, ὁ *trapezitēs* money changer*

Matt 25:27: βάλλω τοῖς τραπεζίταις, "invest money with the *bankers*"; cf. Luke 19:23 (→ τράπεζα). Spicq, *Notes* I, 430-35.

τραῦμα, ατος, τό *trauma* wound (noun)*

The Samaritan "bound up [the man's] *wounds*" (Luke 10:34).

τραυματίζω *traumatizō* wound (vb.)*

Luke 20:12 (different in Mark): "This one, too, they *wounded* (τραυματίσαντες) and cast out"; Acts 19:16: The sons of Sceva fled *wounded* (from the evil spirit).

τραχηλίζω *trachēlizō* lay bare*

Heb 4:13: "Everything is open (γυμνός) and *laid bare* (τετραχηλισμένος, pf. pass. partc.)" before God's eyes, to whom we are accountable.

τράχηλος, ου, ὁ *trachēlos* neck, throat*

Mark 9:42 par. Matt 18:6/Luke 17:2 mentions a millstone hung "around one's *neck*" (περὶ τὸν τράχηλον) in order to drown a person. The noun occurs in Luke 15:20 and Acts 20:37 in the phrase "fall upon someone's *neck*" (ἐπὶ τὸν τράχηλον) in greeting or farewell; in both instances it is combined with καταφιλέω. Acts 15:10 uses τράχηλος fig. in the expression "put a yoke upon one's *neck*," as does Rom 16:4 in "risk one's *neck* for someone."

τραχύς, 3 *trachys* rough, uneven*

Luke 3:5 (citing Isa 40:4 LXX): "The crooked shall be made straight, the *rough* (αἱ τραχεῖαι [*sc.* ὁδοί, ways]) shall be made smooth." In Acts 27:29 the τραχεῖς τόποι are probably "reefs."

Τραχωνῖτις, ιδος *Trachōnitis* Trachonitis*

Τραχωνῖτις is the fem. of Τραχωνίτης (an inhabitant of Trachonitis). Philo and Josephus use Τραχωνῖτις absolutely to refer to the district south of Damascus. Luke 3:1 uses the noun as an adj. in ἡ Τραχωνῖτις χώρα, "Trachonitis." This district, like Ituraea (→ Ἰτουραῖος), belonged to the region of the Herodian Philip. Schürer, *History* I, 336-39.

τρεῖς, τρία *treis, tria* three

1. Occurrences in the NT — 2. As an exact or approximate number — 3. Descriptive usage

Lit.: G. DELLING, *TDNT* VIII, 216-25. — P. HOFFMANN, "Mk 8,31. Zur Herkunft und Rezeption einer alten Überlieferung," FS Schmid (1973) 170-204. — J. JEREMIAS, "Die Drei-Tage-Worte der Evangelien," FS Kuhn 221-29. — K. LEHMANN, *Auferweckt am dritten Tag nach der Schrift* (1968). — R. MEHRLEIN, *RAC* IV, 269-310. — For further bibliography see Lehmann; *TWNT* X, 1281.

1. The ordinal number three occurs 67 times, which makes it the fifth most frequent number; occurring more often are the numbers one (346 occurrences), two (132), seven (88), and twelve (75). After seven and twelve, three is the number with the strongest symbolic significance in the NT. The frequency of τρεῖς in Acts (14 occurrences) is striking (it appears also 29 times in the Synoptic Gospels, 3 times in John, 10 in the Epistles, and 11 in Revelation).

2. Exact and emphatic usage probably occurs only in Gal 1:18 in the phrase "after *three* years," which corresponds to the customary way of counting in antiquity according to which partial years (already started) are counted in full; the meaning is then "after about two years" (F. Mussner, *Gal* [HTKNT] 93). In the remaining occurrences the number three is used more as a round number not intended primarily to provide exact or independent information (e.g., Luke 10:36). In isolated instances it has the secondary implication of "much" (Matt 13:33 par. Luke 13:21: "*three* seahs" = *ca.* forty liters) or "little" (1 Cor 14:27: "two or at most *three*" should speak in tongues). Luke esp. uses τρεῖς as an approximate period of time (Luke 1:56; 2:46; Acts 5:7; 7:20; 9:9; 17:2; 19:8; 20:3; 25:1; 28:7, 11, 12, 17).

3. The descriptive function of τρεῖς was common in antiquity (see the thorough discussion in Mehrlein). The NT demonstrates such usage, esp. in its OT references.

a) Τρεῖς is associated with OT legal ideas through Deut 19:15 (2 Cor 13:1; 1 Tim 5:19; Matt 18:16; cf. John 8:17; 1 John 5:7, 8). Heb 10:28 cites Deut 17:6. This understanding of testimony might resonate in Acts 10:19 (v.l. δύο) and 11:11, perhaps also in Luke 12:52. Does not also the smallest assembly in Jesus' name carry legal standing (Matt 18:20)?

b) Mark 8:2 par. and 9:5 par. acquire more profound meaning from the perspective of OT passages. Noah had three sons (Gen 6:10); three men visited Abraham (Gen 18:2); Israel journeyed three days in the wilderness (Exod 15:22; cf. 3:18); three times in the year Israel should appear before the Lord (23:14-17; 34:23), etc. (Mehrlein 298-300). Without being mentioned explicitly, the number three frequently plays an important role in parables and narratives (examples in Delling 223f.). Paul solemnly calls faith, hope, and love τὰ τρία ταῦτα (1 Cor 13:13). Three and one-half can also refer to the time of distress; Luke 4:25 and Jas 5:17 refer to 1 Kgs 17f. (*three* years and six months). Rev 11:9, 11 uses the traditional apocalyptic weekly scheme of three and one-half days.

c) Jesus' "three-day sayings" occupy a special place in the Gospels. The temple logion (Mark 14:58 par.; 15:29 par.; Matt 27:63) is almost universally attributed to the historical Jesus. John 2:19 attributes the saying to Jesus as well (Jeremias 221 considers this the original attestation). What is conceived as a brief time of tribulation will first occur, then the change in eras, the day of salvation (Jeremias 221f.; Lehmann 170f.). John 2:20 associates the temple logion with the three-day pattern of the resurrection sayings. In the suffering predictions only Mark has μετὰ τρεῖς ἡμέρας (8:31; 9:31; 10:34), meaning the same thing as "on the third day" (BAGD s.v.). Matt 12:40 (cf. 16:1-4) refers Jonah 2:1 to Jesus' own fate (→ Ἰωνᾶς); cf. also → τρίτος 3.   W. Feneberg

Τρεῖς ταβέρναι *Treis tabernai* Three Taverns*

Τρεῖς ταβέρναι is the Greek form of the Latin place name *Tres tabernae* ("three taverns"), a station on the Via Appia 33 Roman miles from Rome (Cicero *Epistulae ad Atticum* 2.10; *CIL* IX, 593; X, 684). Paul met here with emissaries from the Roman Christians (Acts 28:15). → ταβέρνα.

τρέμω *tremō* quake, tremble; be afraid*

Mark 5:33 par. Luke 8:47: the Syrophoenician woman fell down *trembling* before Jesus; 2 Pet 2:10: false teachers *are* not *afraid* to revile the angelic powers.

τρέφω *trephō* nourish, feed; rear, bring up*

Matt 6:26 par. Luke 12:24, of the birds or ravens (→ κόραξ), which God *feeds;* Acts 12:20, with inf. τρέφεσθαι, either "feed oneself" (mid.) or "be fed" (pass.); Luke 4:16: ἦν τεθραμμένος, "he was *brought up*/he *had grown up*"; Matt 25:37; Luke 23:29; Jas 5:5; Rev 12:6, 14. C. Moussy, *Recherches sur* τρέφω *et les verbes grecs signifiant "nourrir"* (1969); Spicq, *Notes* II, 890-93.

τρέχω *trechō* run; strive forward*

Literal in Mark 5:6; 15:36 par. Matt 27:48; Matt 28:8; Luke 15:20; 24:12; John 20:2, 4; 1 Cor 9:24a (bis); Rev 9:9. All other occurrences—most of them in Paul—use τρέχω fig., with the metaphor of the stadium race in the background: Rom 9:16 *(strive forward with great exertion);* 1 Cor 9:24c, 26; Gal 2:2 (bis); 5:7; Phil 2:16 (εἰς κενόν as in Gal 2:2). 2 Thess 3:1 speaks of the swift *spreading* of the "word of the Lord" (cf. Ps 147:4 LXX); Heb 12:1: τρέχω τὸν ἀγῶνα, "*run* in the race" (→ ἀγών 5). O. Bauernfeind, *TDNT* VIII, 226-33; *TWNT* X, 1281 (bibliography); G. Ebel, *DNTT* III, 945-47.

τρῆμα, ατος, τό *trēma* opening, hole; eye of a needle
→ ῥαφίς.

τριάκοντα *triakonta* thirty*

Mark 4:8 par. Matt 13:8 and Mark 4:20 par. Matt

13:23 refer to the thirtyfold yield of the grain harvest. Matt 26:15 and 27:3, 9 mention the τριάκοντα ἀργύρια *(thirty* pieces of silver) Judas received as payment (→ ἀργύριον). At the commencement of his public ministry Jesus was "about *thirty* years of age" (Luke 3:23; see G. Schneider, *Luke* [ÖTK] I, 95). John 6:19 uses the word in reference to distance: "When they had rowed twenty-five or *thirty* stadia" (*ca.* four miles). In John 5:5 τριάκοντα [καὶ] ὀκτὼ ἔτη ἔχων refers to the man who had been ill thirty-eight years, which hardly can be interpreted symbolically (cf. Deut 2:14); cf. R. Schnackenburg, *John* I (Eng. tr., 1968) ad loc. Τριάκοντα appears in the number "four hundred and thirty" in Gal 3:17.

τριακόσιοι, 3 *triakosioi* three hundred*

Mark 14:5 and John 12:5 estimate the value of the ointment (→ μύρον) at (more than) three hundred denarii.

τρίβολος, ου, ὁ *tribolos* thistle*

Matt 7:16 and Heb 6:8: pl. with ἄκανθαι ("thorns"; cf. Gen 3:18; Hos 10:8 LXX).

τρίβος, ου, ἡ *tribos* way, path*

Mark 1:3 par. Matt 3:3/Luke 3:4 (citing Isa 40:3 LXX): "Make his *paths* straight."

τριετία, ας, ἡ *trietia* period of three years*

Acts 20:31: Paul recalls his "three-year" stay in Ephesus (probably the source of τριετία in 20:18 D).

τρίζω *trizō* whir; gnash*

Mark 9:18 uses the vb. trans. in the phrase τρίζω τοὺς ὀδόντας, "*grate* one's teeth together/*gnash* one's teeth."

τρίμηνος, 2 *trimēnos* of three months*

Heb 11:23, used subst.: (fem. [or neut.]) τρίμηνον, "a period of three months." The acc. τρίμηνον here answers the question "how long?" (BDF §161).

τρίς *tris* three times*

Τρίς occurs in the context of Peter's threefold denial of Jesus (Mark 14:30, 72 par. Matt 26:34, 75/Luke 22:34, 61/John 13:38). In Acts 10:16 and 11:10 ἐπὶ τρίς refers to "three times over" or, perhaps better, "yet a third time." Paul wrote of his experiences, "*three times* I have been beaten with rods . . . *three times* I have been shipwrecked" (2 Cor 11:25); "*three times* I besought the Lord" (12:8). G. Delling, *TDNT* VIII, 216-25, esp. 222.

τϱίστεγον, ου, τό   *tristegon*   third story*

The sleeping young man Eutychus fell down from the *third story* (Acts 20:9).

τϱισχίλιοι, 3   *trischilioi*   three thousand*

Acts 2:41: three thousand people were converted at Pentecost.

τϱίτος, 3   *tritos*   third

1. Occurrences in the NT — 2. As a numeral — 3. Descriptive usage

Lit.: G. DELLING, *TDNT* VIII, 216-25. — H. GRASS, *Ostergeschehen und Osterberichte* (⁴1970). — K. LEHMANN, *Auferweckt am dritten Tag nach der Schrift* (1968). — H. K. MCARTHUR, "On the Third Day," *NTS* 18 (1971/72) 81-86. — For further bibliography see Lehmann.

1. Of the 56 occurrences of τϱίτος, 23 are in Revelation, and 13 of these are in Revelation 8. Luke also has a certain predilection for τϱίτος, using it 10 times. Elsewhere it appears in Matthew (7 times), Mark (3), John (4), Acts (4), 1 Corinthians (2), and 2 Corinthians (3).

2. Τϱίτος never indicates special emphasis or additional significance when it occurs within an enumeration: the third of seven men (Mark 12:21 par.), the third of four creatures (Rev 4:7; 6:5), the third of seven seals (6:5), the third of seven angels (8:10; 16:4) or of four angels (14:9), the third of twelve foundation stones (21:19).

Τϱίτος is used similarly whenever reference is made to the time of day. Even at "the *third* hour" (i.e., 9:00 A.M.), the householder sees unemployed persons in the marketplace (Matt 20:3). At this hour the disciples cannot be drunk (Acts 2:15); at this hour, too, Jesus is crucified (Mark 15:25). According to the Roman division of the night into watches, the master can come "at the *third* watch" (or 3:00 A.M.; Luke 12:38). Acts 23:23 mentions the "*third* hour of the night" (9:00 P.M.).

The use of τϱίτος is probably also unemphatic in Acts 27:19; 1 Cor 12:28; 2 Cor 12:2; Rev 11:14. In John 2:1 τϱίτος in popular parlance could refer to the wedding day, the day of happiness (cf. the twofold "good" in Gen 1:10, 12; S. Ben Chorin, *Bruder Jesus* [1972] 84f.).

3. Revelation 8 uses τὸ τϱίτον (with gen.) 12 times of *a third* (of the earth, of the trees, of the sea, etc.); so also 9:15, 18; 12:4. This division is traditional in both Jewish and Hellenistic thinking (R. Mehrlein, *RAC* IV, 270).

Repeating a statement three times renders it legally binding; indeed, in a mnemonic culture this practice can virtually replace written contracts (J. B. Bauer, *SacVb* III, 911). Jesus goes away and prays a third time (Matt 26:44) and finds the disciples sleeping (Mark 14:41). Only after

the third servant does the owner send his son (Luke 20:12). Pilate questions the Jews three times to render their judgment legally binding (Luke 23:22). Jesus appears a third time to his disciples (John 21:14), a third time he asks Simon about his love, and a third time Simon "repents" of his own denial (v. 17). Paul, too, implies legal considerations when he says he will come to Corinth a third time (2 Cor 12:14; 13:1).

In twelve instances the "*third* day" refers to the day of salvation, either Jesus' resurrection (1 Cor 15:4; Matt 16:21 par.; 17:23; 20:19 par.; Luke 9:22; 18:33; 24:7, 46 [cf. 24:21]; Matt 27:64; Acts 10:40) or the day of completion (Luke 13:32). The meaning of this statement is disputed. Virtually no one subscribes any longer to a historical derivation from the finding of the empty tomb (cf., however, → ἡμέϱα 3.a) or from the first epiphanies (cf. P. Hoffmann, *TRE* IV, 482f., who recently considers the new possibility of derivation from the mystery religions as an alternative to a derivation from OT Targums). Since an early Sunday liturgy cannot establish the initial meaning (Hoffmann 482f.; H. Conzelmann, *1 Cor* [Hermeneia] 256), derivation from OT scriptural exegesis seems most likely, which then corresponds to later targumic interpretation (Conzelmann 256; Lehmann 159-230; McArthur, and others).

The Feast of Weeks takes place in the third month (cf. Exod 19:1); the revelation at Sinai takes place on the third day (Exod 19:11, 16); on the third day Abraham sees his place of testing (Gen 22:4). The third day is the day salvation commences (Lehmann 264). This significance corresponds to use of the third day in Jonah 2:1 and Hos 6:2. Rabbinic writing also interpreted the latter passage eschatologically.

                                      W. Feneberg

τϱίχινος, 3   *trichinos*   made of hair*

Rev 6:12: The sun became like a garment *made of hair* (σάκκος τϱίχινος).

τϱόμος, ου, ὁ   *tromos*   trembling, quaking (noun)*

Τϱόμος is used with ἔκστασις (Mark 16:8) and with φόβος (1 Cor 2:3; 2 Cor 7:15; Phil 2:12; Eph 6:5).

τϱοπή, ῆς, ἡ   *tropē*   turn, return; change (noun)*

Jas 1:17 asserts that with God there is no παϱαλλαγή or τϱοπῆς ἀποσκίασμα ("variation or shadow *of a change*"). The context suggests an astral sense here for τϱοπή, which perhaps indicates an eclipse caused by a change of the constellations; cf. BAGD s.v.

τϱόπος, ου, ὁ   *tropos*   way, manner*

The relative phrase ὃν τϱόπον *(as)* occurs in Matt 23:37

par. Luke 13:34; further Acts 1:11; 7:28; 2 Tim 3:8; Acts 15:11 (καθ᾽ ὃν τρόπον, "in the same *way* as"); 27:25. Paul uses the phrases κατὰ πάντα τρόπον, "in every *respect*" (Rom 3:2), and παντὶ τρόπῳ, "in every *way*" (Phil 1:18); cf. 2 Thess 2:3; 3:16. In Heb 13:5 τρόπος refers to one's turn of mind or character. In Jude 7 τὸν ὅμοιον τρόπον τούτοις is used of "just like these" or "in a *way* similar to these."

τροποφορέω *tropophoreō* bear with someone's manner*

Acts 13:18 (Deut 1:31 B* LXX), of God's patience with his people during the sojourn in the wilderness. 𝔭74 A^c C* al read → τροφοφορέω.

τροφή, ῆς, ἡ *trophē* nourishment, food*

Literal in Matt 6:25 par. Luke 12:23 ("life is more than *food*"); Matt 3:4; 10:10; 24:45; John 4:8; Acts 2:46; 9:19; 14:17; 27:33, 34, 36, 38; Jas 2:15. Fig. in Heb 5:12, 14 ("solid *food*" in contrast to "milk").

Τρόφιμος, ου *Trophimos* Trophimus*

Acts 20:4 mentions Trophimus together with Tychicus (→ Τυχικός) as "coming from [the province of] Asia"; 21:29 specifies that Trophimus comes from Ephesus. He accompanied Paul on the final journey to Jerusalem and unwittingly provided the occasion for Paul's arrest in Jerusalem. According to 2 Tim 4:20 Paul left Trophimus in Miletus (on a later journey).

τροφός, οῦ, ἡ *trophos* nurse; mother*

1 Thess 2:7: The apostle treated the church in Thessalonica like a *mother* taking care of her children.

τροφοφορέω *trophophoreō* care for

Acts 13:18 𝔭74 A^c C* al (cf. Deut 1:31) in place of → τροποφορέω. During the sojourn in the wilderness God *carried* his people in his arms *like a nurse* (→ τροφός); i.e., he cherished and cared for them.

τροχιά, ᾶς, ἡ *trochia* course, wheel track*

Heb 12:13 (cf. Prov 4:26 LXX): "Make straight *paths* for your feet, so that lame members may not be put out of joint but rather be healed."

τροχός, οῦ, ὁ *trochos* wheel*

Jas 3:6: ὁ τροχὸς τῆς γενέσεως, "the *wheel* of existence /of life" (→ γένεσις 3). BAGD s.v.; M. Dibelius, *Jas* (Hermeneia) 195-98, esp. 196ff.; F. Mussner, *Jas* (HTKNT) ad loc.

τρύβλιον, ου, τό *tryblion* bowl, dish*

Mark 14:20 par. Matt 26:23 speaks of the *dish* (at Jesus' last supper) into which one dips one's hand together with another. This idiom expresses the intimacy of table fellowship (Mark). In Matthew Jesus thus identifies his betrayer.

τρυγάω *trygaō* gather (fruit), pick (grapes)*

Luke 6:44 (differently in Matt 7:16): "For figs are not gathered from thorn plants, and from a bramble bush one does not *harvest* grapes"; Rev 14:18, 19 (metaphorically): the angel "*gathered* the grapes from the vine of the earth."

τρυγών, όνος, ἡ *trygōn* turtledove*

Luke 2:24 speaks of a pair of *turtledoves* as the sacrifice of poor people (Lev 12:8 LXX). H. Greeven, *TDNT* VI, 69f.

τρυμαλιά, ᾶς, ἡ *trymalia* hole; eye of a needle → ῥαφίς.

τρύπημα, ατος, τό *trypēma* (drilled) hole; eye of a needle → ῥαφίς.

Τρύφαινα, ης *Tryphaina* Tryphaena*

A Christian woman greeted in Rom 16:12.

τρυφάω *tryphaō* lead a life of self-indulgence, carouse*

Jas 5:5, in an accusation directed toward the rich: "You have lived in luxury on the earth."

τρυφή, ῆς, ἡ *tryphē* indulgence; luxury, splendor*

Luke 7:25: "Those who are gorgeously clothed and live in *luxury* are in kings' palaces"; 2 Pet 2:13, of false teachers: "They consider as pleasure their *reveling* [even] in the daytime."

Τρυφῶσα, ης *Tryphōsa* Tryphosa*

Rom 16:12: a Roman Christian woman to whom Paul sends greetings.

Τρῳάς, άδος *Trōas* Troas*

A city in Asia Minor on the Aegean Sea (actually [ἡ] Ἀλεξάνδρεια Τρῳάς, "Alexandria Troas," as, e.g., in Polybius v.111.3). Troas is used with the art. in 2 Cor 2:12 and probably refers to the region of this name in northwest Asia Minor (cf. v. 13: Macedonia). Otherwise, except in Acts 20:6, the art. is absent, as is customary for place names (BDF §261). Paul visited the city of Troas twice: Acts 16:8, 11 and 20:5f. A Christian church existed in Troas (20:7-12). The reference to Troas in 2 Tim 4:13 might be a literary invention; see N. Brox, *Die Pastoralbriefe* (RNT) ad loc. A. Wikenhauser, *LTK* X, 370; C. J. Hemer, "Alexandria Troas," *Tyndale Bulletin* 26 (1975) 79-112.

Τρωγύλλιον, ου   *Trōgyllion*   Trogyllium

A promontory and city south of Ephesus where, according to Acts 20:15 Koine (D), Paul remained for one night.

τρώγω   *trōgō*   chew, eat*

Matt 24:38 speaks of the people before the great flood τρώγοντες καὶ πίνοντες, "*eating* and drinking." Τρώγω appears four times in John 6:54-58 (variously ὁ τρώγων, with the objs. μου τὴν σάρκα, με, and τοῦτον τὸν ἄρτον) in reference to the eucharistic food. In addition to *eating,* the drinking of Jesus' blood is also mentioned. Eternal life is promised to the person eating and drinking (vv. 54, 57, 58). In 13:18 (citing Ps 41:10) Jesus says, "He who *ate* my bread has lifted his heel against me." L. Goppelt, *TDNT* VIII, 236f.; R. Schnackenburg, *John* II (Eng. tr., 1979) 62; C. Spicq, "ΤΡΩΓΕΙΝ: Est-il synonyme de ΦΑΓΕΙΝ et d'ΕΣΘΙΕΙΝ dans le NT?" *NTS* 26 (1979/80) 414-19.

τυγχάνω   *tynchanō*   meet, attain; happen, turn out*

1. Occurrences, forms, meaning — 2. Τυγχάνω with an obj. — 3. Εἰ τύχοι — 4. Τυγχάνω in an adv. sense — 5. Τυγχάνω with negation

Lit.: BAGD s.v. — O. BAUERNFEIND, *TDNT* VIII, 238-43. — BDF, index s.v.

Τυγχάνω occurs 12 times in the NT: once in Luke, 5 times in Acts, 3 times in 1 Corinthians, once in 2 Timothy, and twice in Hebrews. Its uses are varied: in 7 instances τυγχάνω has a gen. obj. and is used of *attain /obtain;* twice it appears in the opt. clause εἰ τύχοι, *if it should happen, for example, perhaps;* once it is a partc. used adv. of *perhaps;* and twice it appears negated with a partc. used adj. referring to something *unusual.* In every instance, as in writings outside the NT, the element of chance or of the unusual resonates (which does not extend to the related noun τύχη).

2. When τυγχάνω takes an obj. it refers either to an eschatological element of salvation or to earthly salvation. In the former case one *attains* the future world (Luke 20:35), salvation mediated through Christ Jesus (2 Tim

2:10), a better resurrection (Heb 11:35), or Christ's special high-priestly ministry (8:6), all of which it is presupposed that God has made possible. In the latter case one *obtains* lasting peace through the governor Felix (Acts 24:2), God's aid (26:22), and the care of one's friends (27:3). Τυγχάνω thus always signifies a gift, never one's own work.

3. The idiomatic phrase εἰ τύχοι, which developed during the Hellenistic period, refers either to a possible example (1 Cor 15:37: "a bare kernel, *perhaps* of wheat") or to an indefinite quantity (14:10: "There are *who knows how many* languages in the world").

4. The aor. partc. τυχόν occurs in 1 Cor 16:6 in an adv. sense: "*Perhaps* I will stay with you." Τυγχάνω here refers to the open-ended nature of Paul's travel plans.

5. The intrans. partc. with negation is used adj. and refers to an *unusual* event: God performs "*extraordinary* miracles (δυνάμεις οὐ τὰς τυχούσας) through the hands of Paul (Acts 19:11, referring to the unusual healings in v. 12); the natives of Malta show "*unusual* hospitality" (οὐ τὴν τυχοῦσαν φιλανθρωπίαν) to Paul after the shipwreck (28:2).

                                 G. Haufe

τυμπανίζω   *tympanizō*   martyr, torture (vb.)*

Heb 11:35, of the ancient witnesses of faith: "Others were *tortured* (ἐτυμπανίσθησαν) and did not accept release." This vb. derives from τύμπανον, an instrument of torture. E. C. E. Owen, *JTS* 30 (1929) 259-66.

τυπικῶς   *typikōs*   as a model or representative
→ τύπος.

τύπος, ου, ὁ   *typos*   prefiguration, model; impression, copy; foreshadowing*
ἀντίτυπος, 2   *antitypos*   antitypical, representative; subst.: antitype, copy*
τυπικῶς   *typikōs*   as a model or representative*

1. Occurrences in the NT — 2. Semantic presuppositions of NT usage — 3. General usage — a) John 20:25 — b) Acts 7:43; 23:25 — 4. Τύπος as "example" in Paul — a) 1 Thess 1:7 — b) Phil 3:17 — 5. Τύπος as "model" in post-Pauline letters — a) 2 Thess 3:9 — b) 1 Tim 4:12; Titus 2:7; 1 Pet 5:3 — 6. Τύπος διδαχῆς in Rom 6:17 — 7. "Typological" meaning? — a) 1 Cor 10:6, 11 — b) Rom 5:14 — 8. Typologies — a) Hebrews — b) 1 Pet 3:21 — 9. Post-NT writings

Lit.: E. AUERBACH, "Figura," *idem, Neue Dantestudien* (Istanbuler Schriften 5, 1944) 11-71. — H. D. BETZ, *Nachfolge und Nachahmung Jesu Christi im NT* (BHT 37, 1967), esp. 137-89. — A. VON BLUMENTHAL, "ΤΥΠΟΣ und ΠΑΡΑΔΕΙΓΜΑ," *Hermes* 63 (1928) 391-414. — R. BULTMANN, "Ursprung und Sinn der Typologie als hermeneutischer Methode," *idem, Exegetica* (1967) 369-80. — K. GALLEY, *Altes und neues Heilsgeschehen bei Paulus* (AzT I/22, 1965), esp. 54-57. — L. GOPPELT, *Typos: The Typological Interpretation of the OT in the NT* (1982). — *idem, TDNT* VIII, 246-59. — U. LUZ, *Das Geschichtsverständnis des Paulus* (BEvT 49, 1968), index s.v. Typologie. — H. MÜLLER, *DNTT* III, 903-7. — SPICQ, *Notes* II, 894-97. — A. TAKAMORI, *Typologische Auslegung des AT? Eine wortgeschichtliche Untersuchung* (Diss. Zurich, 1966). — For further bibliography see *TWNT* X, 1281.

1. Τύπος occurs 15 times in the NT: 5 times in Paul (additionally τυπικῶς in 1 Cor 10:11), 3 in deutero-Pauline letters, and further in John 20:25 (bis); Acts 7:43, 44; 23:25; Heb 8:5; 1 Pet 5:3. Ἀντίτυπος occurs only in Heb 9:24 and 1 Pet 3:21.

2. In secular Greek τύπος is used to describe the process of casting and forming and refers both to that which has been cast and to that which itself forms, whether a mold and its impression (e.g., a signet ring or a die [for coins]) or a raised form such as a relief or a sculpture. This basic meaning develops from the concrete to the abstract, so that τύπος comes to be used of "pattern, model, copy, prototype, outline sketch, general impression, version of a document."

3. a) In John 20:25 (bis) τύπος exhibits a meaning atypical for the NT in its almost crass realism. Thomas's demand ("unless I see in his hands the *print* of the nails, and place my finger in the *print* of the nails [v.l. variously τόπος in place of τύπος] and place my hand in his side, I will not believe") seems stylized. (Nails are mentioned only here and in Luke 24:39; in contrast, the στίγματα τοῦ Ἰησοῦ Paul carries on his own body [Gal 6:17] are scars that, like the brands on slaves, identify the apostle as a slave of his Lord.) The conditional clause and double negation, as in John 8:51f.; 16:7, and elsewhere, express assertorial certainty. As in 4:48 the concern here is for critical specification of the basis of faith. The condition of having seen the Lord in order to believe is granted as an exception only here. Henceforth the testimony of witnesses is fully adequate. Although an antidocetic point does not appear to be intended, it does suggest itself (cf. Ign. *Smyrn.* 3:1f.).

b) Commensurate with the concrete meaning "copy, statue," τύπος (pl.) in Acts 7:43 in an OT citation (Amos 5:25-27) renders Heb. ṣelem. Even the Hebrew text does not clearly indicate whether the reference is to pictures or to statues; what is clear is that *images of idols* are meant. In Acts 23:25 Luke announces that a formal letter is being cited in the "following *version*" (τὸν τύπον τοῦτον; RSV *to this effect*); τύπος occurs with the same common Hellenistic meaning in 3 Macc 3:30 and *Ep. Arist.* 34 as well.

4. Paul uses τύπος in the context (explicit or otherwise) of → μιμέομαι (4) in a sense usually rendered by "example." The concept of example is admittedly unfortunate, since what comes

readily to mind is the idea of an ethical ideal or guide that one chooses or is offered as something to imitate or realize. A certain degree of critical reflection on historical or ideological considerations is thus unavoidable.

a) In 1 Thess 1:6f. Paul writes in the context of the preamble: "You became imitators (μιμηταί) of us and [thereby] of the Lord, for you received the word in much affliction, with joy [as given by] the Holy Spirit, so that you became a *strikingly formed model* (τύπος) for believers in Macedonia and Achaia." V. 8 then establishes and explains what this means: First, they are τύπος in that through them the word of the Lord has acquired a reputation that sounds forth in a way that cannot be ignored (on ἐξηχέω cf. Joel 3:14 LXX). Second, the Church as such is τύπος in its concretely lived faith and obedience to the Lord, who will deliver the members from judgment (v. 10). They are not τύπος because they live "exemplary" lives or serve as an "example"; rather, they have become τύπος because they have accepted the word.

Paul uses μιμέομαι, a term from the Hellenistic mystery cults (Betz), to describe the acceptance in personal faith and the obedient recognition of being formed by the call of the gospel and of the Kyrios. The living Christ and Kyrios, who is the crucified Jesus, is active both in the gospel and in the apostle's own life. If the Church allows itself to be formed by the gospel's call and power, it becomes an "imitator" of the apostle and thereby also of the Kyrios. Third, what becomes clear is that the Church is τύπος for all believers, i.e., before a public (i.e., eschatological) forum that stands under the claim of the gospel, is interpreted by the apostle, and is recognized in faith (cf. also 1 Thess 2:14).

b) Phil 3:17 makes it imperative that the Church itself live out what the apostle shows in his own life to be the power of the gospel: "Become my fellow travelers (fellow imitators), brethren, and orient yourselves toward those who live as you have a *prefiguration* in us." Here as elsewhere there is no thought of exemplary ethical behavior; the substance of Paul's identity as τύπος, i.e., the "typically Christian" features of his existence, he has already presented in vv. 4-11, 12-16, where from his own life he explicates the decisive elements of his sense of theological responsibility toward the gospel. Hence τύπος refers to the forming of one's life by Christ that endures during one's entire life; it offers, not an example of a perfectly rounded life, but the pattern of a life to be fulfilled in the future. (To that extent it is correct to say that, in his own life formed by Christ, Paul views the prefiguration of the "affirmation . . . of tribulation and of the cross" [J. Gnilka, *Phil* (HTKNT) ad loc.] and the renunciation of all ecstatic experience of perfect fulfillment.)

5.a) 2 Thess 3:9 shows clearly how the meaning of τύπος eases into the Hellenistic understanding of an ethicizing, moral-aesthetic evaluation of human existence. Referring now to a "standard, exemplary model," it thus becomes assimilated to the meaning of παράδειγμα and ὑπόδειγμα. (In the NT cf. ὑπόδειγμα, "example, model," in John 13:15; Jas 5:10; Heb 4:11; 2 Pet 2:6; similarly ὑπογραμμός, "model, pattern," in 1 Pet 2:21. On the alternation between παράδειγμα and τύπος in the LXX, cf. Exod 25:9, 40; 4 Macc 6:19; on the semantic correlation between παράδειγμα, "example, model," and τύπος, "mold," in secular Greek, cf. Blumenthal 410ff.) It is no longer Paul himself who speaks in his understanding of apostolic existence, but rather an image of Paul. The author of 2 Thessalonians uses 1 Thessalonians as a source and transfers it into his own writing in order to displace it and offer 2 Thessalonians as the (only) letter Paul wrote to the Thessalonians (cf. W. Marxsen, *2 Thess* [ZBK] 33f.).

2 Thess 3:6 alters 1 Thess 5:14 into a directive to withdraw from any brother living in an undisciplined way and not according to tradition. This tradition is explicated by the example Paul himself gives, which, as the readers already know, must be imitated (2 Thess 3:7). The substance of this passage, by recalling 1 Thess 2:9; 4:11, and perhaps even beyond that also 1 Cor 4:12; 9:6, 14, and the legend of Paul (Acts 18:3; 20:34; cf. H. Conzelmann, *Acts* [Hermeneia] ad loc.), relates that by working day and night himself, Paul earned his own keep. He did this even though he had the apostolic right to be supported by the Church (2 Thess 3:9a; cf. 1 Cor 9:4), "that we might be an *example* for you to imitate" (2 Thess 3:9b). Hence in contrast to the general formative meaning of being an apostle (→ 4), specific behavior is elevated to the status of a normative example. Disregard of this exemplary norm now becomes constituted as "undisciplined conduct" (v. 11); additionally—and this is genuinely disturbing—the assertion is made that disregard for this particular posited example requires separation from the Church. In this function the exemplary image of Paul is virtually equated with transmitted doctrine.

b) The category of exemplary ethical behavior also encompasses the meaning of τύπος in 1 Tim 4:12, Titus 2:7, and 1 Pet 5:3. The instructions to Church leaders in 1 Tim 4:11–5:2 begin with the command to "set the believers an *example* in word and conduct, in love, in faith, and in purity." Even if it is unclear how the Church leader can be an example in proclamation of the word (as regards proper faith? or in one's use of words?), the sense of being an example in conduct is unmistakable. Even if the false teachers surpass the (still young) Church leader in age, experience, education, and reputation, all the more should the latter see that in his own piety and behavior he offers an incisive example of the proclamation of the properly believing Church. The trio "love, faith, purity" explicates this exemplary feature and sketches perhaps "the first outlines of a priestly ethical code" (V. Hasler, *Die Briefe an Timotheus und Titus* [ZBK] 37).

A reflection on the Church itself in Titus 2:7 also

includes instructions to the Church leader: "Show yourself in all respects a *model* of good deeds." Even more clearly than in 1 Tim 4:12 the point of the exhortation to be a model both of saintly seriousness as regards doctrine and of moral and ecclesiastical integrity is characterized as the following: The opposing faction should stand ashamed and have no possible opportunity to "say evil of us" (v. 8). 1 Pet 5:1-4 first admonishes the presbyters not to "tend" the individual churches out of greed or desire for domination, and then gives the positive directive to "be examples to the flock" (v. 3); there is no indication, however, of what they are supposed to be examples.

6. Rom 6:17 is problematic. The awkward attraction of the parenthetical insertion almost certainly is to be resolved thus: ὑπηκούσατε . . . τῷ τύπῳ διδαχῆς, εἰς ὃν παρεδόθητε. In the phrase τύπος διδαχῆς, unique in early Christian writings, τύπος refers to the "formal *version* of a document (letter, decree, etc.)."

This and further exegetical observations force the conclusion that v. 17b is a marginal gloss from Church tradition that made its way into the text at an early stage (cf. R. Bultmann, *Exegetica* [1967] 283). If the phrase in question were genuinely Pauline (so, e.g., E. Käsemann, *Rom* [Eng. tr., 1980] 180-82; and U. Wilckens, *Rom* [EKKNT] II ad loc.), then one would have to postulate that this expression, already fixed in the tradition and taken up by Paul—somewhat as a contrasting term to the Jewish μόρφωσις τῆς γνώσεως καὶ τῆς ἀληθείας (Rom 2:20)—refers to a gospel credo passed along at baptism, to which the baptized person is committed (Käsemann 181), or to a summary of the content of Christian doctrine (Wilckens ad loc.). If those baptized have been "given over" to this content (and not vice versa, as elsewhere), then the Pauline τύπος would have to characterize Christ—as is indeed the case in *Barn.* 12:10: "Jesus Christ, the Son of God, appeared depicted [τύπῳ; E. J. Goodspeed: *symbolically revealed*] in the flesh."

Ign. *Magn.* 6:2 presents a similar view and even attests paratactically the phrase τύπος καὶ διδαχή. Here Christians should constitute a unity with the bishop—as the representative copy of God (*Trall.* 3:1; *Magn.* 6:1 v.l.)—and with the leaders as a representative copy and teaching of immortality. As little as this meaning of τύπος (διδαχῆς) can be forced onto Pauline theology (*contra* Wilckens, *Rom* ad loc.), all the more strongly does the assumption suggest itself that we are dealing with a gloss in Rom 6:17b. The editor is referring to a solemn version (prefigured in heaven) of the apostolic doctrine to which—elevated to celestial proportions and thus characterizing Christ — the baptized could be committed.

7. We consider here those texts in which τύπος in one way or another is conceived "typologically." This leads to discussion of "typological exegesis" as a hermeneutical method.

a) It is highly unlikely that Paul associated two completely disparate meanings with the one word τύπος. Hence in 1 Cor 10:6, 11 one should proceed from the exegetically proven use *formative model, prefiguration*.

This passage agrees with 1 Thess 1:7 and Phil 3:17 (and Rom 5:14) in identifying as τύποι neither "occurrences" (*contra* H.-D. Wendland, *1 Cor* [NTD] ad loc.), nor events, nor things, but rather only human beings to the extent that they are touched by the eschatologically qualified divine event. (The use of ταῦτα in 1 Cor 10:6 seems to contradict this, yet the pl. ἐγενήθησαν seems significant here, as it doubtless takes up the subj. of κατεστρώθησαν; thus ταῦτα could be the acc. of relation [cf., however, also Luz 120, 396].) The differences are twofold: First, 1 Cor 10:6 is referring to people from a past age, namely, "all our fathers," i.e., Israel during its exodus from Egypt. Second, it is not μιμεῖσθαι κτλ. that corresponds to these τύποι ἡμῶν but rather a negative warning (εἰς τὸ μὴ εἶναι ἡμᾶς ἐπιθυμητὰς κακῶν); this negation is mediated when the events themselves in which the fathers became τύποι ἡμῶν— which thus happened to them τυπικῶς (v. 11)—were written down for us as a warning deserving our attention, since it is to us that the end of time has come.

This means: First, τύπος here does not refer to the "real," spiritual meaning of a text or of a narrated event gained through allegorical interpretation, though neither should we disregard the fact that Paul does indeed interpret persons as τύποι who by no means present themselves as such in the OT text. Second, in the Pauline interpretation those forefathers from Israel are not τύποι ἡμῶν only subsequently and through the medium of interpretation; at the time of their existence they are already such, although they are removed from themselves as τύποι ἡμῶν. Third, although inaccessible to themselves, they are τύποι ἡμῶν because even at that time they were already touched and formed in their own existence by the eschatological event (vv. 2-4; the rock was [already] Christ—his preexistence is presupposed). Fourth, this idea is not inconsistent, given the presupposition that the eschatological event also qualifies past existence (the dead). Even then they were already a "model" because now, in the eschatological time, eschatologically qualified existence can be portrayed through that model—though now admittedly it comes to us only as a written warning deserving our attention. It is thus part of apostolic encouragement (παρακαλεῖν) and not itself a model of eschatological existence. For the ancients disregarded the gift of divine presence corresponding to the Spirit by engaging in worship of idols and in immorality. Thus eschatological future judgment can be narrated and portrayed in past events (v. 11).

The question of the extent to which in the midrash in 1 Cor 10:1ff. Paul is following Jewish "typological" exegesis can be passed over for present purposes. There is no support at least in Paul for L. Goppelt's definition: "Only historical facts, i.e., persons, deeds, events, and institutions can be the object of typological interpretation, and words and portrayals only to the extent they are concerned with such objects. A typological interpretation of these objects occurs when they are conceived as exemplary representations set by God, i.e., 'types' of future, and indeed of more perfect and greater facts" (18f.). Only eschatologically qualified and interpreted human existence can be τύπος; furthermore, present existence is perceived as τύπος in the fashion of μιμεῖσθαι, and past existence is so perceived critically and antithetically because it is already written down. Hence if 1 Corinthians 10 employs "typology" at all, then it is in the critical-antithetical use of Scripture.

b) Only Rom 5:14 focuses on something like past history as a whole. Here, too, it is viewed as history represented by one man, Adam, and is qualified negatively in the eschatological sense by the eschatological event of grace in Christ.

Adam is the "antithetical correspondent" to the coming second man, namely, Christ (cf. 1 Cor 15:45ff.). From the perspective of the present eschatological event, Adam is the one that points toward Christ. As a result of sin, however, what Adam is as τύπος is inaccessible to him and to all those in his sphere, i.e., all those who are in the story of Adam (cf. also Rom 3:23); hence Christ as an antithetical movement corresponds in his own death, which was a deed of obedient love, to the "empty space" represented by Adam.

8. Τύπος occurs in Heb 8:5 and Acts 7:44, just as also ἀντίτυπος in Heb 9:24 and 1 Pet 3:21, in an expressly hermeneutical and technical sense that calls for so-called typological exegesis.

The following differentiation seems in order:

First, "typology" as traditio-historical hermeneutics is at work whenever a historically new, usually eschatological institution of salvation and judgment is expressed in terms of a temporally preceding institution. Since the older is thus surpassed by what is eschatologically newer, or is critically or antithetically suspended by the latter, it thus appears as a superseded prefiguration of the newer. Typology that is synthetic and oriented to salvation history develops secondarily relative to typology that is defined more as antithesis to what precedes. The former is then continued in a certain way in "figural interpretation" (cf. Auerbach). The lack of strict differentiation between "typological" interpretation on the one hand, and correspondence between prediction and fulfillment conceived from the perspective of salvation history on the other, impairs a great many assertions made concerning the subject of typology. Despite Bultmann's misconception of typology as an unhistorical and mythological thought structure that simply repeats similar elements, his criticism of Goppelt's inflationary expansion of typological elements within the NT is appropriate.

Second, the apocalyptic understanding of history can alter typology such that an eschatological event can appear to have been prefigured from the very beginning. It thus enjoys both temporal and objective priority over against its corresponding counterpart (cf., e.g., *2 Bar.* 4:1-7).

Third, in Hellenistic Judaism, esp. in Philo, we encounter the speculative cosmological idea that the world of tangible, earthly things was created as a copy of its prototype. *Op.* 16, 19, 36 is exemplary: At creation God first formed the ἀρχέτυπος and the νοητὴ ἰδέα, and the tangible, earthly creation was then produced as a copy of this τύπος or παράδειγμα—an activity, however, comprehensible only to the Spirit. See also *Som.* i.206 on Exod 25:40: The divine prototype of the tabernacle became visible to Moses in the Spirit as τύπος or παράδειγμα; only then, and according to this model, did Bezalel produce an imitation or copy (μίμημα or σκιά), namely, the tangible, earthly tabernacle itself. In textual exegesis τύπος refers to what actually should be shown and what should be disclosed in its hidden meaning through allegory (*Op.* 157).

a) In Hebrews this Hellenistically conceived relationship between the "perfect heavenly prototype" and the "earthly copy and shadow" is clearly transferred into the historical dimension of the eschatological Christ-event; in the process, the conscious use of the (exegetically acquired) key term τύπος produces a "typological interpretation" of the OT in the technical hermeneutical sense. Its conception should thus probably be sought in this early Christian formation within the tradition, represented by the letter to the Hebrews, and not in Paul.

In a "typological" understanding of Exod 25:40, Heb 8:5 characterizes priestly service in the old covenant by asserting that those priests "serve a copy and shadow of the heavenly sanctuary; for when Moses was about to erect the tabernacle, he was instructed by God, saying, 'See that you make everything according to the *pattern* that was shown you on the mountain.'"

Within the LXX citation, as in Acts 7:44, τύπος is the translation of Heb. *taḇnît* (building plan, model, picture) and is not used elsewhere in the letter to the Hebrews. Yet in Heb 10:1 εἰκών occurs in the same way as in 8:5 opposite an OT σκιά ("the law has but a shadow of the good things to come instead of the true form of these things"). 9:23f., initially recalling the ratification of the OT covenant with blood (vv. 15-22), speaks of the "copies (ὑποδείγματα) of the heavenly things"; immediately thereafter, however, the expression ἀντίτυπος, "antitype," occurs, which also acquires a technical meaning and here parallels ὑπόδειγμα. This term emphasizes the contrast between the sanctuary (or cultic objects?) of the old covenant on the one hand, and the true sanctuary on the other: "For Christ did not enter into a sanctuary made with hands, an *antitype* of the true one, but into heaven itself, now to appear in the presence of God on our behalf."

In Hebrews this scheme of correspondence between heavenly prototype and earthly copy is clearly a consciously chosen hermeneutical device, though not in the service of any "vertically" conceived cosmological doctrine of salvation. The correspondence, rather, has a typological function: The eschatologically unsurpassable, one-time sacrifice of the true high priest and mediator is realized in the event of Jesus' death occurring even now, which therefore suspends once and for all the OT institutions of dispensing salvation. This suspension turns those very institutions into their own linguistic "copies" and historical "shadows."

b) 1 Pet 3:21 uses ἀντίτυπος in what appears to be an already familiar typological sense. Mediated through the idea that Christ preaches salvation to the dead (v. 19), Noah's deliverance through water (the flood) appears as an event against which saving baptism is thrown into relief for the reader as an antitype, perhaps intended as a warning. Although the idea of correspondence hinges here on that of water, neither the linguistic relationships nor the train of thought is wholly transparent. In v. 21a, ὅ hardly refers to the act of deliverance, but rather to the water, "in correspondence to which as an antitype baptism now delivers you as well." Cf. also *2 Clem.* 14:3: Christ's flesh (the Church) is the ἀντίτυπος ("representative") of the Spirit, which is αὐθεντικόν.

9. In two usages, τύπος in writings after the NT seems to be a virtually fixed concept.

a) Τύπος is the earthly copy of a heavenly model: superiors as a copy of God (*Did.* 4:11; *Barn.* 19:7), the bishop as copy of the Father (or of God; Ign. *Trall.* 3:1). A variation of this usage is "essential image" (*Barn.* 6:11). The term is then transferred to visionary images of apocalyptic realities (*Herm. Vis.* iii.11.4; iv.1.1; iv.2.5; iv.3.6; *Sim.* ii.2).

b) Τύπος is an OT prefiguration of events and circumstances realized in the salvation history of Jesus Christ; this is excessively the case in *Barn.* 7:3, 7, 10, 11; 12:2, 5, 6, 10; 13:5. The same sense appears in Justin *Dial.* 42.4 (cf. 90.2), where one after another of Moses' instructions are presented as τύπους καὶ σύμβολα καὶ καταγγελίας of the future Christ-events.

G. Schunack

τύπτω *typtō* beat (vb.)*

Most of the 13 NT occurrences are in Luke (4) and Acts (5). Τύπτω is used fig. in two instances: Acts 23:3a refers to blows dealt by God (frequently also in the LXX), and 1 Cor 8:12 to the wounding of a weak conscience. Τύπτω is used with a personal acc. obj. in Matt 24:49 par. Luke 12:45; Acts 18:17; 21:32. People are *struck* on the mouth (Acts 23:2, 3b), the head (Mark 15:19 par. Matt 27:30), and the cheek (Luke 6:29). To *beat* one's breast is a sign of grief and perplexity (Luke 18:13; 23:48). G. Stählin, *TDNT* VIII, 260-69.

τύραννος, ου, ὁ *tyrannos* despotic ruler, tyrant

Acts 5:39 D, in an expansion: "neither you nor kings nor *tyrants.*" *TCGNT* ad loc.

Τύραννος, ου *Tyrannos* Tyrannus*

A man in Ephesus mentioned in Acts 19:9, in whose auditorium (σχολή) Paul was able to hold lectures. Tyrannus was perhaps an orator himself, or he owned the hall.

τυρβάζομαι *tyrbazomai* trouble oneself excessively with

Luke 10:41 TR in Jesus' words to Martha: "You *are troubling yourself* with many things."

Τύριος, ου, ὁ *Tyrios* a Tyrian*

An inhabitant of → Τύρος. Acts 12:20 mentions Tyrians with Sidonites.

Τύρος, ου *Tyros* Tyre*

The NT frequently mentions the Phoenician city Tyre together with Sidon (in most Gospel occurrences: Mark 3:8; 7:31; Matt 11:21, 22 par. Luke 10:13, 14; Matt 15:21; Luke 6:17). In Mark 7:24 and Acts 21:3 Tyre is the destination of travel (εἰς), in Acts 21:7 the point of departure (ἀπό). Acts 21:4 presupposes that there was a church in Tyre, with which Paul stayed a week. M. Liverani, *ISBE* IV, 932-34; H. P. Rüger, *BHH* 2035f.; W. Röllig, *KP* V, 1027-29; A. H. McDonald and J. H. Simon, *OCD* 1102.

τυφλός, 3 *typhlos* blind (adj.); blind person

1. Occurrences in the NT and usage — 2. Jesus' healings of the blind — 3. The saying about the blind guide — 4. Ethical sayings

Lit.: BILLERBECK I, 524f. — A. VAN DEN BORN, *BL* 250f. — A. ESSER, *Das Antlitz der Blindheit in der Antike* (^{2}1961). — G. GERLEMAN, "Bemerkungen zur Terminologie der 'Blindheit' im AT," *SEÅ* 41/42 (1976/77) 77-80. — F. GRABER, *DNTT* I, 218-20. — J. HEMPEL, *Heilung als Symbol und Wirklichkeit im biblischen Schrifttum* (^{2}1965), esp. 247f. — E. LESKY, *RAC* II, 433-46. — J. M. LIEU, "Blindness in the Johannine Tradition," *NTS* 34 (1988) 83-95. — F. NÖTSCHER, *Gotteswege und Menschenwege in der Bibel und in Qumran* (1958), index s.v. Blind (125). — J. ROLOFF, *Das Kerygma und der irdische Jesus* (1970) 119-41. — W. SCHRAGE, *TDNT* VIII, 270-94. — K. SEYBOLD and U. B. MÜLLER, *Sickness and Healing* (1981) 143-45. — H. J. STOEBE, *BHH* 257f.

On Mark 10:46-52: E. S. JOHNSON, JR., "Mark 10:46-52: Blind Bartimaeus," *CBQ* 40 (1978) 191-204. — K. KERTELGE, *Die Wunder Jesu im Markusevangelium* (1970) 179-82. — V. K. ROBBINS, "The Healing of Blind Bartimaeus (10:46-52) in the Marcan Theology," *JBL* 92 (1973) 224-43. — ROLOFF, *Kerygma* (see above) 121-26.

On John 9: G. BORNKAMM, "Die Heilung des Blindgeborenen," *idem, Aufsätze* IV, 65-72. — G. REIM, "Tradition und zeitgenössische messianische Diskussion," *BZ* 22 (1978) 245-53. — ROLOFF, *Kerygma* (see above) 135-41. — S. SABUGAL, *La curación del ciego de nacimiento* (1977).

1. a) Τυφλός occurs 50 times in the NT, 46 of these in the Gospels (17 times in Matthew, 5 in Mark, 8 in Luke, 16 in John). It occurs otherwise only in Acts 13:11; Rom 2:19; 2 Pet 1:9; Rev 3:17. Τυφλός refers to *blind*, either in the literal sense (in most instances in the Gospels and Acts 13:11) or fig. (Matt 15:14a bis; 23:16, 17, 19, 24, 26; John 9:39, 40, 41; Rom 2:19; 2 Pet 1:9; Rev 3:17).

b) In most instances—esp. in the Gospels—τυφλός is used as a subst. *(the blind person);* adj. usage occurs less frequently (Matt 12:22; 15:14a; 23:16, 24, 26; Mark 10:46; John 9:1, 18, 24, 25, 40, 41; Acts 13:11; 2 Pet 1:9; Rev 3:17).

In Luke 4:18 τυφλός appears in a citation from Isa 61:1 LXX. In the LXX the adj. is a translation of the Heb. *'iwwēr*. The *blind* are often mentioned together with the lame (χωλοί); persons with these afflictions were considered to be esp. hopelessly infirm and wretched (Matt 11:5 par. Luke 7:22; Matt 15:30, 31; 21:14; Luke 14:13, 21; John 5:3; cf. further LXX Lev 21:18; Deut 15:21; 2 Kgdms 5:8; Job 29:15; Mal 1:8; further 1QM 7:4).

In general, antiquity considered the healing of blindness possible only by means of a miracle (Schrage 273-75; see esp. Seybold and Müller). This view is reflected in the promise that the blind will be healed at the eschatological time of salvation (Isa 29:18; 35:5; 42:7; 61:1 LXX). Fig. use of τυφλός is widespread outside the NT as well; "τυφλός is most commonly used in the sphere of the capacity for knowledge and function of understanding" (Schrage 276f.; cf. Isa 43:8; 59:10; CD 1:9; 16:2). In Gnosticism esp. the unredeemed, world-blinded non-Gnostics are described as "blind" (*Gos. Truth* 29:32–30:15; *Gos. Thom.* 28; *Gos. Phil.* 56; *Pistis Sophia* 141).

2. All four Gospels contain stories of Jesus' healings of the blind. In them the final redactors view not only the fulfillment of "messianic" prophecies (→ 1.b) but also a metaphorical reference to the "sight" Jesus opens up within faith (cf. Roloff 119-21).

a) The Evangelist Mark associates Mark 8:22-26 with the "blindness" of the disciples (vv. 14-21), as Jesus must open their spiritual eyes to revelation. Mark interprets the healing of blind Bartimaeus (10:46-52) in terms of the idea of discipleship (v. 52c). Both the Synoptic parallels dependent on this pericope (Matt 20:29-34 and Luke 18:35-43) and the doublet Matt 9:27-31 also emphasize the significance of faith (esp. Matt 9:29). Outside the miracle stories, Jesus' healings of the blind signal the inbreaking of the eschatological time of salvation (Matt 11:5 par. Luke 7:21f.; Luke 4:18). Matthew also emphasizes through redactional addenda that Jesus healed the blind (Matt 12:22 [differently in Luke]; 15:30, 31 [differently in Mark]; 21:14 [differently in Mark; cf. the "suspension" of the prohibition of 2 Kgdms 5:8]).

b) Perhaps the reader of John 9:1-41, the story of the healing of the man blind from birth (vv. 1, 2, 19, 20, 32), is expected to apply the story to human beings in general, to human beings as they are "by nature" (vv. 39-41). The man's blindness to the light of revelation (cf. vv. 2f.) is eliminated by Jesus, who makes both the blind see and also those with sight become blind (v. 39b; cf. 3:19; see also → τυφλόω in 12:40). John 10:21 recalls the healing of the blind (John 9) and rejects the idea that Jesus might be possessed by a demon. 11:37 asks why Jesus, who opened the eyes of the blind, could not keep Lazarus from dying; vv. 38-44 then show that Jesus also has the (greater) power to awaken the dead.

3. Luke probably preserves the original version of the saying about the blind guides (Matt 15:14b; Luke 6:39), which comes from the logion source (cf. the context 6:37f.): One should refrain from "judging." Matthew refers the logion to the interpretation of the law offered by the Pharisees, who are blind to God's will (15:16f.; 23:16, 17, 19, 24, 26). They themselves even consider the people to be blind and want to be their guides. According to Rom 2:19, the Jew raises a similar claim over against the "blind" (Gentiles), who do not know the Mosaic law.

4. a) In Luke Jesus exhorts his listeners to invite the poor, the maimed, the lame, and the blind as guests after the model of the host at the great banquet (Luke 14:13, 21). According to Acts 13:11 Paul inflicted the punishment of blindness upon the magician Bar-Jesus (cf. the parallels from antiquity in Schrage 271f.).

b) In the parenesis of later NT writings the faulty ethical condition of Christian communities is characterized as blindness. 2 Pet 1:9 castigates the unfruitfulness of the ἐπίγνωσις, Rev 3:17 probably the self-satisfaction of the church at Laodicea.   G. Schneider

τυφλόω *typhloō*   make blind, deprive of sight*

All 3 NT occurrences use the vb. metaphorically (as in Isa 42:19 LXX). John 12:40 cites Isaiah: "He *has blinded* their eyes and hardened their heart." The citation itself (Isa 6:10) corresponds neither to the Hebrew text nor to the LXX and has probably been recast by the Evangelist with an eye on his own agenda. 1 John 2:11 shows that hatred makes a person blind: "Whoever hates his brother is in the darkness (→ σκοτία) and walks in the darkness, and does not know where he is going, because the darkness *has blinded* his eyes." 2 Cor 4:4 speaks of unbelievers, before whom the gospel remains concealed: "The god of this world *has blinded* their thoughts (νοήματα)." W. Schrage, *TDNT* VIII, 270-94; *TWNT* X, 1281 (bibliography); F. Graber, *DNTT* I, 218-20.

τύφομαι *typhomai*   (pass.) smoke, smolder*

Matt 12:20: "He will not quench a *smoldering* wick (λίνον τυφόμενον)" (cf. Isa 42:3: λίνον καπνιζόμενον).

τυφόομαι *typhoomai*   be puffed up, conceited; become foolish (?)*

Τυφόομαι (pass. of τυφόω, "becloud") occurs in the NT only in the Pastoral Epistles. A new convert who was appointed bishop could *become puffed up with conceit* (1 Tim 3:6). A teacher who does not offer the sound words of tradition but instead teaches strange things "is *puffed up with conceit* and understands nothing" (6:4). In the "last days" people will (among other things) be "treacherous, reckless, *swollen with conceit*" (2 Tim 3:4). Spicq, *Notes* II, 898.

τυφωνικός, 3 *typhōnikos*   like a whirlwind*

Acts 27:14: ἄνεμος τυφωνικός, "a *whirlwind*." Radermacher, *Grammatik* 28f.

Τύχικος, ου *Tychikos*   Tychicus*

One of Paul's companions from the province of Asia (Acts 20:4). Col 4:7 par. Eph 6:21 calls him "the beloved brother and faithful servant in the Lord." Both passages say that Tychicus will tell the letter's recipients about Paul, and the Pastorals view his task similarly: 2 Tim 4:12 speaks of sending him to Ephesus, Titus 3:12 of sending him to "Titus."

Y υ

ὑακίνθινος, 3 *hyakinthinos* hyacinth colored*

Rev 9:17: The riders had "breastplates the color of fire (πυρίνους) and of *hyacinth* [i.e., dark red] and of sulphur (θειώδεις)."

ὑάκινθος, ου, ὁ *hyakinthos* hyacinth*

Rev 21:20: the eleventh of twelve jewels on the foundations of the heavenly Jerusalem is hyacinth.

ὑάλινος, 3 *hyalinos* transparent as glass*

In its description of God's heavenly throne (introduced with ὡς), Rev 4:6 mentions a θάλασσα ὑαλίνη: "a *glassy* sea" (with the addition: "like crystal"); similarly 15:2a, b ("mingled with fire"; beside this "sea" the "conquerors" stand with harps).

ὕαλος, ου, ἡ *hyalos* glass, crystal (noun)*

Rev 21:18: "The city is pure gold like pure *glass*"; v. 21: "The street of the city is pure gold, transparent as *glass*."

ὑβρίζω *hybrizō* mistreat, abuse, insult*
ὕβρις, εως, ἡ *hybris* arrogance; disaster; mistreatment*

1. Occurrences in the NT — 2. Paul — 3. Other NT occurrences

Lit.: G. BERTRAM, *TDNT* VIII, 295-307. — For further bibliography see *TWNT* X, 1282.

1. The vb. occurs only 5 times in the NT, the noun 3 times.

2. Paul uses ὑβρίζω in reference to the sufferings he underwent during his first proclamation of the gospel in Philippi (1 Thess 2:2; this does not enhance the historical credibility of the events reported in Acts 16:22-24). 2 Cor 12:10 envisions the same phenomenon, where ὕβρις appears in second position within a "catalog of sufferings"

(cf. W. Schrage, "Leid, Kreuz und Eschaton. Die Peristasenkataloge als Merkmale paulinischer theologia crucis und Eschatologie," *EvT* 34 [1974] 141-75): Paul is "content in weaknesses (ἀσθενείαις), *mistreatment,* hardships (→ ἀνάγκη 2), persecutions (διωγμοῖς), and calamities (→ στενοχωρία)." Hence in Paul both vb. and noun reflect physical mistreatment, which he understands dialectically as strength because of its purpose ("for the sake of Christ," 2 Cor 12:10), or which prompt him to proclaim the gospel all the more joyfully (1 Thess 2:2).

3. In the rest of the NT ὕβρις occurs only in the verbatim speech of the Lukan Paul (Acts 27:10, 21). In both places it refers together with ζημία to "*injury and damage/loss*" that will befall the ship's crew during the sea journey (27:9-11 and 27:21-26 are two episodes the author of Acts has inserted into the narrative of a sea journey; cf. H. Conzelmann, *Acts* [Hermeneia] ad loc.).

Ὑβρίζω appears additionally in four other passages in the NT. In Matt 22:6 it stands in a sequence after → κρατέω (3) and before → ἀποκτείνω and refers to the act of mistreating the messengers sent by God. Luke 11:45 uses it in an objection by νομικοί to an alleged insult by Jesus. In 18:32 Luke uses the vb. in the third prediction of suffering as an amplification with → ἐμπαίζω (2) and → ἐμπτύω. In Acts 14:5 ὑβρίζω appears with λιθοβολέω: The excited crowd (Gentiles and Jews) in Iconium prepare to mistreat and stone Paul and Barnabas.

G. Lüdemann

ὕβρις, εως, ἡ *hybris* arrogance; disaster; mistreatment
→ ὑβρίζω.

ὑβριστής, οῦ, ὁ *hybristēs* person who is violent or insolent*

Ὑβριστής occurs twice in the NT in enumerations of wicked persons: Rom 1:30, with ὑπερήφανος, and 1 Tim 1:13, with βλάσφημος and διώκτης. G. Bertram, *TDNT* VIII, 295-307; E. Güting, *DNTT* III, 27f., 29.

ὑγιαίνω *hygiainō* be healthy*

Lit.: M. DIBELIUS and H. CONZELMANN, *The Pastoral Epistles* (Hermeneia) 24f. — F. KUDLIEN, *RAC* X, 902-45. — U. LUCK, *TDNT* VIII, 308-13. — D. MÜLLER, *DNTT* II, 169-71.

This vb. refers to physical health (Luke 5:31; 7:10; 15:27; 3 John 2). The Pastorals use ὑγιαίνω in the metaphorical sense in reference to Christian doctrine, specifically διδασκαλία (1 Tim 1:10; 2 Tim 4:3; Titus 1:9; 2:1; see C. Burini, *Vetera Christianorum* 18 [1981] 275-85) and λόγοι (1 Tim 6:3; 2 Tim 1:13). Christian teaching is thus characterized as correct or reasonable in contrast to false teachings, which deviate from received doctrine. A similar usage appears in ὑγιαίνω (ἐν) τῇ πίστει (Titus 1:13; 2:2).

ὑγιής, 2 *hygiēs* healthy*

In 11 instances this adj. refers to physical health (Matt 12:13; 15:31; Mark 5:34; John 5:4, 6, 9, 11, 14, 15; 7:23; Acts 4:10). Only once, in Titus 2:8, is it used fig.: λόγος ὑγιής here is "*healthy/sound* speech" (cf. the use of → ὑγιαίνω in the Pastorals). For bibliography → ὑγιαίνω.

ὑγρός, 3 *hygros* moist*

Luke 23:31: in his words to the lamenting women, Jesus mentions *moist/green* wood.

ὑδρία, ας, ἡ *hydria* water jar*

John 2:6, 7: the six stone *jars* at the wedding at Cana that Jesus orders to be filled with water; 4:28: the Samaritan woman's *water jar.*

ὑδροποτέω *hydropoteō* drink water*

In 1 Tim 5:23 this vb. connotes a life of strict abstinence; its opposite is "drink wine" (so also Aelian *Varia Historia* ii.38; cf. Dan 1:12 LXX). Cf. → οἶνος.

ὑδρωπικός, 3 *hydrōpikos* suffering from dropsy*

Luke 14:2: ἄνθρωπος ὑδρωπικός, "a man *suffering from dropsy,*" whom Jesus healed on the sabbath (vv. 3f.).

ὕδωρ, ατος, τό *hydōr* water

1. Occurrences and meaning in the NT — 2. Literal meaning — 3. Ritual usage — 4. Symbolic meaning

Lit.: BAGD s.v. — O. BIEHN, *LTK* X, 962f. — J. BLANK, *John* (NTSR) on 4:10ff. — O. BÖCHER, *Christus Exorcista* (BWANT 90, 1972), index s.v. — idem, *DNTT* III, 988-91. — idem, "Wasser und Geist," FS Stählin 197-209. — F. M. BRAUN, *Jean le Théologien. Sa Théologie* (1972) II, 61-65 (on John 7:37-39). — R. BULTMANN, *John* (Eng. tr., 1971) 181-86. — L. GOPPELT, *TDNT* VIII, 314-33. — F. HAHN, "Die Worte vom lebendigen Wasser im Johannesevangelium," FS Dahl 51-70. —

H. LEROY, *Rätsel und Mißverständnis* (BBB 30, 1968) 88-99 (on John 4:10-15). — F. MUSSNER, *LTK* X, 963-65. — F. PORSCH, *Pneuma und Wort. Ein exegetischer Beitrag zur Pneumatologie des Johannesevangeliums* (1974) 61-65. — R. SCHNACKENBURG, *John* I (Eng. tr., 1968) 425-28 (on 4:10). — H.-J. VENETZ, "'Durch Wasser und Blut gekommen.' Exegetische Überlegungen zu 1 John 5:6," *Die Mitte des NT* (FS E. Schweizer; 1983) 345-61. — For further bibliography see Schnackenburg.

1. Of the 78 total occurrences of ὕδωρ in the NT, 45 are in the Johannine writings (23 in John, 4 in 1 John, 18 in Revelation). Ὕδωρ is a basic human item (cf. Biehn); in references to *water,* various levels of meaning appear throughout the NT, with the symbolic most apparent in John, 1 John, and Revelation. Literal usage refers to the vital need for ὕδωρ or to the pain and death where it is lacking, as well as to subjection to the unrestrained elements (i.e., the experience of the flood) and to the use of water for purification. The ritual use of water fits under all of these categories. Although the point of departure is purification, the idea of immersion into a new realm (→ βαπτίζω 4) and new life (→ 4) is probably always intended as well. NT usage is an independent development of OT thought (cf. Hahn); in its symbolic use it is influenced by Gnostic ideas only peripherally.

2. The literal usage predominates in 30 instances.
a) Water for drinking is referred to in the cup of fresh water (Mark 9:41), the man carrying a jar of water (Mark 14:13 par. Luke 22:10), and the dipping of the end of one's finger into water (Luke 16:24); fresh water is mentioned in Jas 3:12 (cf. Rev 8:10f.; 11:6; 14:7; 16:4f., 12; Goppelt 324f.).
b) In 17 places, ὕδωρ refers to water in (often hostile) nature. In Matt 8:32 (par. Mark 5:13 θάλασσα) the swine perish in the waters. Peter asks permission to walk upon the water, and then indeed dares to do so (Matt 14:28f.). The demon casts the boy into fire and water (Mark 9:22 par. Matt 17:15). In specifically Lukan language Jesus threatens "the wind and the waves *of the water*" and commands "the winds and the *water*" (8:24f.). Eight souls are rescued from the flood, i.e., δι' ὕδατος (1 Pet 3:20). 2 Pet 3:5f. predicts the certain end of the world by drawing from Jewish cosmogony, from ideas about the origin of the world out of and by means of ὕδωρ, and from the parallel—also familiar to Jewish thinking—between the past end of the world through water and the future end through fire (Goppelt 328; W. Grundmann, *2 Pet* [THKNT] ad loc.). Revelation uses ὕδωρ 6 times in flood imagery (1:15; 12:15; 14:2; 17:1, 15; 19:6).

3. Ritual usage includes Jewish and Christian practices as well as those from John the Baptist. These should be distinguished but not absolutely separated.
a) Specifically Jewish foot washing is mentioned both in Luke 7:44 (the Pharisee does not offer it to Jesus) and

in John 13:5 (Jesus performs it on the disciples). Following the Jewish purification ritual, Pilate washes his hands before the crowd (Matt 27:24). In John 2:7, 9 (cf. 4:46) Jewish purification water is turned into wine. John 5:4, 7 reflects popular Jewish belief in the supernatural power of holy water (Böcher, *Christus* 22-24).

b) References to baptism manifest varying relationships to Christian baptism itself; sometimes water baptism is emphasized, and sometimes Spirit baptism (Mark 1:8 par.; John 1:26, 31, 33; Acts 1:5; 11:16). Since Ign. *Eph.* 18:2 the notion was common that the ὕδωρ from which Jesus emerged after his own baptism (Mark 1:10 par. Matt 3:16) was sanctified (cf. Goppelt 332f.). John the Baptist baptized "near Salim, because there was much *water* there" (John 3:23; perhaps this passage intends to associate "peace" and "water").

c) In specifically Christian thinking the tension continues between baptism with ὕδωρ on the one hand, and spiritual gifts on the other (Acts 8:36-39; 10:47); ὕδωρ itself remains a symbol of purification (Eph 5:26; Heb 10:22; cf. 9:19).

4. John 3:5 views water and the gift of the Spirit as a unity. John 4:7-15 associates ὕδωρ (8 times) with true life; according to 7:38 this "living water" flows out of Jesus (Schnackenburg, Braun ad loc.) or out of the believers (Hahn, 60, and others). "Blood and *water*" flow from Jesus' side (19:34), i.e., eucharist and baptism (*contra* G. Richter, "Blut und Wasser aus der durchbohrten Seite Jesu, Joh 19,34b," *MTZ* 21 [1970] 1-21); cf. 1 John 5:6, 8. Revelation uses OT imagery in the expression "living *water*" (7:17; 21:6; 22:1, 17; on the intertestamental history of tradition cf. Hahn; on the relationship between John and Revelation cf. Goppelt 325f.).

W. Feneberg

ὑετός, οῦ, ὁ *hyetos* rain (noun)*

Ὑετός is sg. in Acts 28:2; Heb 6:7; Jas 5:18 (5:7 Koine); Rev 11:6. The pl. appears in Acts 14:17 (with "fruitful seasons"; cf. Jas 5:18).

υἱοθεσία, ας, ἡ *hyiothesia* appointment or acceptance as a son, adoption*

Lit.: J. BLANK, *Paulus und Jesus* (SANT 18, 1968) 258-78. — W. VON MARTITZ and E. SCHWEIZER, *TDNT* VIII, 397-99. — W. THÜSING, *Per Christum in Deum* (NTAbh N.F. 1, 1965) 116-21.

On Rom 8:23: H. R. BALZ, *Heilsvertrauen und Welterfahrung* (BEvT 59, 1971) 55-66. — F. DE LA CALLE, "La 'huiothesian' de Rom. 8,23," *EstBib* 30 (1971) 77-98. — J. SWETNAM, "On Romans 8:23 and the 'Expectation of Sonship,'" *Bib* 48 (1967) 102-8.

This originally legal t.t. (see L. Wenger and A. Oepke, *RAC* I, 99-112) is attested in the NT in Paul (4 times) and

Eph 1:5. Rom 9:4 applies it to God's acceptance of the people of Israel (cf. Exod 4:22; Isa 1:2, which do not use υἱοθεσία [it does not appear in the LXX]). NT usage centers on the "adoption" of someone through God in Christ: Gal 4:5 asserts that the "Son" of God redeems those under the law and thus effects their υἱοθεσία (cf. also v. 6, further Eph 1:5). The Spirit received by the believers is πνεῦμα υἱοθεσίας (and not δουλείας) and allows them to experience the new father-son relationship (Rom 8:15). The firstfruits (→ ἀπαρχή) of the πνεῦμα establishes in us the anticipation of the full consequences of this adoption, the "redemption of our bodies" (v. 23). → υἱός 4.c.1.

υἱός, οῦ, ὁ *hyios* son

1. Occurrences in the NT — 2. General usage — a) Physical progeny — b) Fig. sense — 3. "Son" and "Son of God" as christological titles — a) Background — b) Jesus — c) Synoptics — d) Paul — e) Johannine writings — f) Other NT writings — 4. The divine sonship of human beings — a) Background — b) Synoptics — c) Other NT writings — d) Comparison with the Johannine writings — 5. "Son of Man" — a) Background — b) Usage in the NT — c) Jesus — d) Synoptics — e) John — f) Outside the Gospels — 6. "Son of David" — a) Background — b) Usage

Lit.: General: O. CULLMANN, *The Christology of the NT* (²1963) 109-92, 270-305. — R. H. FULLER, *The Foundations of NT Christology* (1965). — HAHN, *Titles* 15-53, 240-346. — JEREMIAS, *Theology* 61-68, 257-76. — W. VON MARTITZ, G. FOHRER, E. LOHSE, and E. SCHWEIZER, *TDNT* VIII, 334-92.

"Son of God": B. BYRNE, *"Sons of God"—"Seed of Abraham"* (1979). — G. DELLING, "Die Bezeichnung 'Söhne Gottes' in der jüdischen Literatur der hellenistisch-römischen Zeit," FS Dahl 18-28. — idem, "Die 'Söhne (Kinder) Gottes' im NT," FS Schürmann 615-31. — A. DESCAMPS, "Pour une histoire du titre 'Fils de Dieu,'" *L'Évangile selon Marc* (ed. M. Sabbe; 1974) 529-71. — F. HAHN, "Exegese und Fundamentaltheologie," *TQ* 155 (1975) 262-80. — M. HENGEL, *The Son of God: The Origin of Christology and the History of Jewish-Hellenistic Religion* (1976). — P. HOFFMANN, "Die apokalyptischen Voraussetzungen und ihre Verarbeitung im Q-Logion Mt 11,27 par Lk 10,22," *Kairos* 12 (1970) 270-88. — C. R. KAZMIERSKI, *Jesus the Son of God* (1979). — J. D. KINGSBURY, "The Title 'Son of God' in Matthew's Gospel," *BTB* 5 (1975) 3-31. — W. KRAMER, *Christ, Lord, Son of God* (1966). — W. R. G. LOADER, "The Apocalyptic Model of Sonship," *JBL* 97 (1978) 525-54. — idem, *Sohn und Hohepriester* (1981). — F. MUSSNER, "Ursprünge und Entfaltung der neutestamentlichen Sohneschristologie," *Grundfragen der Christologie heute* (ed. L. Scheffczyk; 1975) 77-113. — B. M. NOLAN, *The Royal Son of God: The Christology of Matthew 1-2 in the Setting of the Gospel* (OBO 23, 1979). — E. RUCKSTUHL, "Jesus als Gottessohn im Spiegel des markinischen Taufberichts," *Die Mitte des NT* (FS E. Schweizer; 1983) 193-220. — W. SCHLISSKE, *Gottessöhne und Gottessohn im AT* (1973). — R. SCHNACKENBURG, *John* II (Eng. tr., 1979) 172-86. — H.-J. STEICHELE, *Der leidende*

Sohn Gottes. Eine Untersuchung einiger alttestamentlicher Motive in der Christologie des Markusevangeliums (BU 14, 1980). — M. VELLANICKAL, *The Divine Sonship of Christians in the Johannine Writings* (1977). — D. VERSEPUT, "The Role and Meaning of the 'Son of God' Title in Matthew's Gospel," *NTS* 33 (1987) 532-56. — A. VÖGTLE, *Messias und Gottessohn* (1971). — C. A. WANAMAKER, "Phil. 2:6-11: Son of God or Adamic Christology?" *NTS* 33 (1987) 179-93. — For further bibliography see *TWNT* X, 1282f.

"Son of Man": M. BLACK, "Jesus and the Son of Man," *JSNT* 1 (1978) 4-18. — F. H. BORSCH, *The Christian and Gnostic Son of Man* (1970). — *idem, The Son of Man in Myth and History* (1967). — J. BOWKER, "The Son of Man," *JTS* 28 (1977) 19-48. — C. C. CARAGOUNIS, *The Son of Man: Vision and Interpretation* (WUNT 38, 1986). — C. COLPE, *TDNT* VIII, 400-477. — J. COPPENS, *Le Fils de l'Homme néotestamentaire* (1981). — P. DOBLE, "The Son of Man Saying in Stephen's Witnessing: Acts 6:8-8:2," *NTS* 31 (1985) 68-84. — J. A. FITZMYER, "Another View of the 'Son of Man' Debate," *JSNT* 4 (1979) 58-68. — H. GEIST, *Menschensohn und Gemeinde. Eine redaktionskritische Untersuchung zur Menschensohnprädikation im Matthäusevangelium* (FzB 57, 1986). — G. GERLEMAN, *Der Menschensohn* (1983). — V. HAMPEL, *Menschensohn und historischer Jesus. Ein Rätselwort als Schlüssel zum messianischen Selbstverständnis Jesu* (1990). — A. J. B. HIGGINS, *Jesus and the Son of Man* (1964). — *idem, The Son of Man in the Teaching of Jesus* (SNTSMS 39, 1980). — M. D. HOOKER, *The Son of Man in Mark* (1967). — J. JEREMIAS, "Die älteste Schicht der Menschensohn-Logien," *ZNW* 58 (1967) 159-72. — R. KEARNS, *Die Entchristologisierung des Menschensohnes* (1988). — *idem, Das Traditionsgefüge um den Menschensohn* (1986). — *idem, Vorfragen zur Christologie* (3 vols.; 1978-82). — S. KIM, *"The 'Son of Man' " as the Son of God* (WUNT 30, 1983). — H. S. KVANVIG, *Roots of Apocalyptic: The Mesopotamian Background of the Enoch Figure and of the Son of Man* (WMANT 61, 1988). — R. LEIVESTAD, "Exit the Apocalyptic Son of Man," *NTS* 18 (1971/72) 243-67. — B. LINDARS, *Jesus Son of Man* (1983). — *idem,* "Re-Enter the Apocalyptic Son of Man," *NTS* 22 (1975/76) 52-72. — E. LOHSE, "Der Menschensohn in der Johannesapokalypse," *idem, Die Vielfalt des NT. Exegetische Studien zur Theologie des NT* (1982) 82-87. — R. MADDOX, "The Function of the Son of Man according to the Synoptic Gospels," *NTS* 15 (1968/69) 45-74. — *idem,* "The Quest for Valid Methods in 'Son of Man' Research," *ABR* 19 (1971) 36-51. — I. H. MARSHALL, "The Synoptic Son of Man Sayings in Recent Discussion," *NTS* 12 (1965) 327-51. — F. J. MOLONEY, *The Johannine Son of Man* ([2]1978). — K. MÜLLER, "Menschensohn und Messias," *BZ* 16 (1972) 161-87; 17 (1973) 52-66. — M. MÜLLER, *Der Ausdruck "Menschensohn" in den Evangelien. Voraussetzungen und Bedeutung* (1984). — N. PERRIN, "The Creative Use of Son of Man Traditions by Mark," *Union Seminary Quarterly Review* 23 (1968) 357-65. — *idem,* "The Son of Man in the Synoptic Tradition," *BR* 13 (1968) 3-25. — R. PESCH, "Über die Autorität Jesu (Lk 12,8f)," FS Schürmann 25-56. — *idem, Die Vision des Stephanus* (1966). — R. PESCH and R. SCHNACKENBURG, eds., FS Vögtle. — A. POLAG, *Die Christologie der Logienquelle* (1977). — E. RUCKSTUHL, "Die johanneische Menschensohnforschung," *TBer* 1 (1972) 171-284. — H. SAHLIN, "Wie wurde ursprünglich die Benennung 'Der Menschensohn' verstanden?" *ST* 37 (1983) 147-79. —

G. SCHWARZ, *Jesus "der Menschensohn." Aramaistische Untersuchungen zu den synoptischen Menschensohnworten Jesu* (1986). — E. SCHWEIZER, "Menschensohn und eschatologischer Mensch im Judentum," *idem, NT und Christologie im Werden. Aufsätze* (1982) 104-20. — J. THEISOHN, *Der auserwählte Richter* (1975). — H. E. TÖDT, *Der Menschensohn in der synoptischen Überlieferung* ([3]1969). — G. VERMES, "The 'Son of Man' Debate," *JSNT* 1 (1978) 19-32. — *idem,* "The Use of bar nāsh/bar nāshā' in Jewish Aramaic," *idem, Post-Biblical Jewish Studies* (1975) 147-65. — P. VIELHAUER, "Gottesreich und Menschensohn in der Verkündigung Jesu," *Festschrift für Günther Dehn* (ed. W. Schneemelcher; 1957) 51-79. — A. VÖGTLE, "Bezeugt die Logienquelle die authentische Redeweise Jesu vom 'Menschensohn'?" *idem, Offenbarungsgeschehen und Wirkungsgeschichte. Neutestamentliche Beiträge* (1985) 50-69. — *idem,* "Der 'Menschensohn' in der paulinischen Christologie," *SPCIC* 1961 (AnBib 17-18, 1963) I, 199-218. — *idem,* "Eine überholte 'Menschensohn'-Hypothese?" *Wissenschaft und Kirche* (FS E. Lohse; Texte und Arbeiten zur Bibel 4, 1989) 70-95. — W. O. WALKER, "The Son of Man Question and the Synoptic Problem," *NTS* 28 (1982) 374-88. — *idem,* "The Son of Man: Some Recent Developments," *CBQ* 45 (1983) 584-607. — For further bibliography see Kim; Lindars, *Jesus; TWNT* X, 1283-86.

"Son of David": C. BURGER, *Jesus als Davidssohn* (1970). — J. D. KINGSBURY, "The Title 'Son of David' in Matthew's Gospel," *JBL* 95 (1976) 591-602. — E. LOHSE, *TDNT* VIII, 478-88. — G. RUGGIERI, *Il Figlio di Dio Davidico* (1968). — For further bibliography see *TWNT* X, 1286f.

1. Υἱός occurs a total of 379 times in the NT (*VKGNT* II, 282f.), in all writings except Ephesians, the Pastorals, Philemon, 3 John, and Jude. It is closely related to → τέκνον (99 occurrences) and also touches on the meaning of → παῖς, παιδίον (24 and 52 occurrences), and → σπέρμα, which in most cases (36 of its 43 occurrences) is used to refer to descendants in the literal or fig. sense.

Noteworthy among the attestations for υἱός are the 41 instances of the absolute phrase ὁ υἱός (9 times in the Synoptics, 1 in Paul, 6 in Hebrews, 25 in the Johannine writings) and one instance of ὁ υἱὸς ὁ μονογενής (1 John 4:9). "Son of God" is used to refer to Jesus in 80 cases, to human beings in 15. In this context a variety of expressions appear: ὁ υἱὸς τοῦ θεοῦ, υἱὸς θεοῦ, υἱὸς ὑψίστου, ὁ υἱός μου, ὁ υἱὸς αὐτοῦ, etc. Ὁ υἱὸς τοῦ ἀνθρώπου occurs 82 times (14 times in Mark, 30 in Matthew, 25 in Luke, 12 in John, 1 in Acts), and υἱὸς ἀνθρώπου occurs 3 times (John 5:27; with ὅμοιος in Rev 1:13; 14:14). Υἱὸς Δαυίδ occurs 15 times (3 times in Mark, 9 in Matthew, 3 in Luke).

2. General usage.

a) Physical progeny.

1) Biological sons are mentioned in healing stories (Mark 9:17 par. Matt 17:15/Luke 9:38, 41; John 4:46, 47, 50, 53; 9:19f.; Luke 7:12: μονογενὴς υἱός), in parables (Matt 7:9 par. Luke 11:11; Mark 12:6; Matt 21:37f. par. Luke 20:13; Matt 17:25f.; 22:2; Luke 15:11, 13, 19, 21a,

b, 24, 25, 30), and in Jesus' own sayings (Matt 10:37; Luke 12:53; 14:5). In Matt 21:5 υἱός refers to a young animal.

2) Patronymics are common: υἱοὶ Ζεβεδαίου (Mark 10:35 par. Matt 20:20f.; Matt 26:37; 27:56; Luke 5:10; cf. Mark 1:19f. par.); Σίμων ὁ υἱὸς Ἰωάννου (John 1:42; cf. Matt 16:17); ὁ υἱὸς Τιμαίου Βαρτιμαῖος (Mark 10:46); Ζαχαρίας υἱὸς Βαραχίου (Matt 23:35); John the Baptist as ὁ Ζαχαρίου υἱός (Luke 3:2); Jesus as ὁ τοῦ τέκτονος υἱός (Matt 13:55), as υἱὸς Ἰωσήφ or υἱὸς τοῦ Ἰωσήφ (Luke 3:23; 4:22; John 1:45; 6:42; cf. Matt 1:16, 18, 25), or as υἱὸς τῆς Μαρίας (Mark 6:3); from the OT: Σαοὺλ υἱὸς Κίς (Acts 13:21).

3) The birth of a son is mentioned in Luke 1:13, 36, 57 (John the Baptist) and 1:31; 2:7; Matt 1:21, 23, 25 (Jesus); cf. further Rev 12:5.

4) Other occurrences include Isaac as the son of Abraham or Sarah (Jas 2:21; Rom 9:9), Abraham's two sons (Gal 4:22, 30a, b), Jacob's sons (John 4:5, 12), Joseph's sons (Heb 11:21), Moses' adoption (Acts 7:21; Heb 11:24), Moses' sons (Acts 7:29), Timothy as the son of a Jewish mother (Acts 16:1), Sceva's seven sons (19:14), and the son of Paul's sister (23:16).

b) Fig. sense.

1) A genealogical context is presupposed by the expressions υἱοὶ Ἰσραήλ (Matt 27:9; Luke 1:16; Acts 5:21; 7:23, 37; 9:15; 10:36; Rom 9:27; 2 Cor 3:7, 13; Heb 11:22; Rev 2:14; cf. 7:4; 21:12), by υἱὸς (υἱοὶ) Ἀβραάμ (Matt 1:1; Luke 19:9; Acts 13:26; cf. Gal 3:7), and in a specific sense by υἱοὶ Λευί (Heb 7:5) and υἱοὶ Ἐμμώρ (Acts 7:16); reference is also made in a general sense to descendants (Acts 2:17).

2) Nongenealogical membership is expressed positively in a variety of phrases: υἱοὶ τῆς βασιλείας (Matt 8:12; 13:38; cf. 17:25f.), υἱοὶ φωτός or τοῦ φωτός (Luke 16:8; John 12:36; 1 Thess 5:5), υἱοὶ ἡμέρας (1 Thess 5:5), τῆς ἀναστάσεως υἱοί (Luke 20:36), υἱὸς εἰρήνης (10:6), υἱὸς τῶν προφητῶν καὶ τῆς διαθήκης (Acts 3:25), υἱοὶ τοῦ νυμφῶνος (Mark 2:19 par. Matt 9:15/Luke 5:34).

3) The same construction is used to express a negative judgment: υἱοὶ τοῦ αἰῶνος τούτου (Luke 16:8; 20:34), υἱοὶ τοῦ πονηροῦ (Matt 13:38), υἱοὶ τῶν φονευσάντων τοὺς προφήτας (Matt 23:31), υἱοὶ τῆς ἀπειθείας (Eph 2:2; 5:6), υἱοὶ ὑμῶν (sc. τῶν Φαρισαίων) (Matt 12:27 par. Luke 11:19, cf. Matt 12:24); further in the sg.: υἱὸς γεέννης (Matt 23:15 referring to a person proselytized by the Pharisees), υἱὲ διαβόλου (Acts 13:10 referring to the magician Elymas), υἱὸς τῆς ἀπωλείας (John 17:12 referring to Judas Iscariot; 2 Thess 2:3 to the Antichrist).

4) Paul speaks of himself in a neutral sense as υἱὸς Φαρισαίων (Acts 23:6); 1 Pet 5:13 refers to Mark as ὁ υἱός μου in the sense of discipleship. In two instances Aramaic names are explained: Βοανηργές by υἱοὶ βροντῆς (Mark 3:17) and Βαρναβᾶς by υἱὸς παρακλήσεως (Acts

4:36). Finally, the idea of adoption provides the background for γύναι, ἴδε ὁ υἱός σου (John 19:26).

5) Occasionally the phrase υἱὸς ἀνθρώπου or υἱοὶ τῶν ἀνθρώπων, common in both the OT and the LXX, occurs as a designation for human beings (sg. in the citation from Ps 8:5 in Heb 2:6; pl. in Mark 3:28; Eph 3:5); → 5.

3. "Son" and "Son of God" as christological titles.

These titles involve three fundamental conceptions: 1) Jesus' sonship is established in his relationship to God as the Father; 2) the position of the Son of God is, in the messianic sense, the appointment to the office of Savior; 3) divine sonship is a statement concerning the supernatural divine essence. These three conceptions cannot always be distinguished, and particularly the third increasingly predominates over the other two.

a) Background.

1) OT Jewish presuppositions can be seen clearly in the messianic tradition, though they are also discernible in the idea of sonship dependent on the relationship with the Father (cf. the concept of "knowledge" in Matt 11:27 par. Luke 10:22 and the idea of commissioning in the sense of authorization and assignment in Gal 4:4f.; Rom 8:3f.; John 3:17; 1 John 4:9). The messianic assertions are concerned with the adoption and installation of the acceding or expected king (2 Sam 7:14; Pss 2:7; 89:27f.; Isa 9:5). One attestation for the continuation of this idea in the post-OT tradition appears in Qumran (4QFlor 1:11-13; cf. 1QSa 2:11f.; further rabbinic attestations: b. Sukk. 52a [Bar.]; Tg. Ps 80:16; but cf. Tg. Ps 2:7). The question remains open whether in addition to the idea of the Messiah as God's son the actual title "Son of God" was used; on the basis of NT usage this seems likely, though it has not yet been documented.

2) The OT and Judaism understand the idea of divine sonship from the perspective of authorization and commissioning. It is, to be sure, not appropriate to juxtapose antithetically this functional conception characterized primarily by legal categories with one oriented toward "essence," since every statement concerning function implies an assertion about essence. A different question is whether other religio-historical influences are discernible. For NT texts the answer is partly so. Attempts at derivation from a specific Hellenistic tradition, however, whether Gnosticism or the idea of the θεῖος ἀνήρ, are disputed and have become increasingly unlikely. It is more likely that an already extant designation for Jesus as the Son of God from OT Jewish tradition was amplified by Hellenistic components in which the divine origin of extraordinary persons played a role. This assumption provides the prerequisites for a different, metaphysically oriented ontological conception with only incipient development in the NT. Aside from the general conceptual climate in the Hellenistic sphere of early Christianity, this modification suggested itself because in contrast to early Jewish tradition it was not the future or otherworldly aspect of the divine salvation reality that was to be expressed but its inbreaking through the appearance of Jesus as the Son of God.

b) Jesus himself used the address "Father." The Aramaic form → ἀββά is a characteristic of ipsissima vox (Jeremias 36f.; cf. Mark 14:36; Luke 11:2), and the Church took over this prayer salutation (Gal 4:6; Rom 8:15). The Jesus tradition consistently distinguishes between "my Father" and "your Father" (Matt 6:9 is no exception, since it is a prayer intended for the disciples). It is disputed whether Jesus spoke of himself as "son"; the two texts in question (Matt 11:27 par. Luke 10:22 and Mark 13:32 par. Matt 24:36) do show strong overlayering by post-Easter reflection.

c) Although a unified overall conception has been carried through redactionally in the Synoptic Gospels, the individual elements of tradition can still be discerned.

1) Matt 11:27 par. Luke 10:22, using ὁ υἱός absolutely, speak first of a comprehensive authorization, and then of the mutual "knowledge" (ἐπιγινώσκειν or γινώσκειν) between "Father" and "Son," language that in OT usage refers to total personal correlation.

The exclusivity of this relationship establishes the Son's revelatory function, whereby human beings are granted participation in this knowledge and correlation. This mutual knowledge does not, however, imply equality between the Son and Father; cf. Mark 13:32 par. Matt 24:36, where not having knowledge of "that hour" also applies to the Son. Matt 28:19, with its triadic baptismal formula, exhibits a stronger inclination to equate the two, and v. 18 speaks again of full authorization (here of the resurrected Jesus).

2) The brief hymn in Luke 1:32f. picks up the messianic idea and speaks of the bestowal of the name υἱὸς ὑψίστου, the ascension to the "throne of David," and the unlimited reign over the "house of Jacob." The story of Jesus' baptism also contains messianic elements (independent of the citation from Ps 2:7 in Luke 3:22 D it). The simultaneous reference to Isa 42:1 does not abrogate the substance of this assertion; the text of Mark 1:11 par. Luke 3:22, with its element of praise, still shows that the original idea was that of appointment to divine sonship, something no longer of concern to the Evangelists and expressly corrected in the parallel passage Matt 3:17 by the element of proclamation.

The temptation story from Q ("Son of God" twice in Matt 4:3, 6 par.) was originally understood in the messianic sense (4:8-10 par.) and then later associated with the Son of God's miraculous powers (4:3f., 5-7 par.). The concept "my beloved Son" from the baptism tradition was then altered even more drastically in the transfiguration story, as shown by the declamatory assertion in Mark 9:7b par. and particularly by the motif of metamorphosis. Finally, the question directed to Jesus in Mark 14:61 par. Matt 26:63 (differently in Luke 22:69f.) with its combination ὁ υἱὸς τοῦ εὐλογητοῦ and σὺ εἶ ὁ χριστός stands in the messianic tradition; Jesus' self-confession in Mark 14:62 par. Matt 26:64 then associates this with the expectation of the future Son of man. Whereas the idea of divine sonship in Luke 1:32f. and Mark 14:61f. par. Matt 26:63f. remains future oriented, Mark 1:11 par. is thinking of a messianic func-

tion in the context of Jesus' earthly history (also Matt 4:3, 6 par.; Mark 9:7 par.).

3) The "Son of God" exhibits a different character in the miracle stories. Mark 5:1-20 par. Matt 8:28-34/Luke 8:26-39 is characterized by the idea of Jesus' supernatural power over the demons' equally supernatural power. The adjuratory phrase in Mark 5:7 (with υἱὲ τοῦ θεοῦ τοῦ ὑψίστου, cf. Matt 8:29; Luke 8:28) may originally have been understood (like Mark 1:24 par. Luke 4:34 with the address ὁ ἅγιος τοῦ θεοῦ) from the perspective of Jesus' particular powers (Mark 3:22-27 par.) and was then interpreted from the perspective of his supernatural being (cf. what is probably a pre-Markan arrangement regarding Mark 5:21-43 par., esp. vv. 28ff. par.). Mark thus took up the motif into the collective report in 3:11; the same thing happened in Matt 14:33.

The transfiguration story should be understood in the same way: Jesus' supernatural being is to be revealed to the disciples through the metamorphosis in Mark 9:2b par. The question can remain open to what extent this transformation, which presupposes Hellenized thinking, already occurred on Palestinian soil, and to what extent it occurred only later, in the climate of early Hellenistic Christendom.

Finally, this complex includes Luke 1:35 (cf. vv. 30f., 34), where Jesus' divine sonship is set alongside the virgin birth (differently in Matt 1:18-25, where it is only a matter of the fulfillment of Isa 7:14; the idea of divine sonship is then introduced redactionally in Matt 2:15).

4) The Gospels unify the individually transmitted traditions. Mark has created an interesting matrix: Whereas divine sonship characterizes Jesus' hidden essence revealed and made manifest already during his lifetime in isolated instances, sayings about the Son of man (→ 5) characterize Jesus' path and commission. After 1:11 and 9:7 the (redactionally inserted) confession of the Gentile centurion to Jesus as the Son of God in 15:39 is formulated in retrospect regarding Jesus' earthly life and death (cf. 12:6-8). The Christ confession in 8:29 combines statements about both his being and his function, as shown by vv. 30-33 and 9:2-13. The text-critically disputed 1:1, because of its correspondence with 8:29 and with 1:11; 9:7; 15:39, probably originally contained the predicate of divine sonship.

5) Although Jesus' divine sonship is self-evident for Luke, Acts shows (with explicit mention only in 9:20; 13:33, and 8:37 v.l.) that it is not central. The Evangelist expunged Mark 13:32, altered Mark 15:39, and replaced υἱὸς θεοῦ with δίκαιος in Luke 23:47. From the virgin birth onward he views Jesus' divine sonship as grounded in the activity of the Spirit. 3:22a, 4:1a, b, and 4:14, 18 show that he is interested in a christology of the Spirit. This general concern is evident in his treatment of the temptation story (4:3, 9), the demons' recognition (4:41;

8:28), the transfiguration (9:35), and the saying about the mutual knowledge between Father and Son (10:22). One peculiarity occurs in 22:67-70 during the interrogation before the Sanhedrin. The double question in Mark 14:61 is rendered by two separate questions in Luke 22:67-69, 70; the first, whether Jesus is the Christ, is answered by the assertion that the Son of man is (from now on) sitting at the right hand of God; the second, whether he is the Son of God, is answered by "I am."

6) Matthew exhibits the most fully developed christology of divine sonship (and also claims the most occurrences of the relevant phrases—15, vs. 8 in Mark and 10 in Luke). He calls Jesus the son of Abraham and the son of David (1:1) in order to characterize him as the fulfillment of OT promise and as the Messiah, adds first the Moses typology to the idea of virgin birth, and then introduces the predicate of divine sonship (2:15). The altered baptism story, the temptation, and the miracle traditions (3:17; 4:3, 6; 8:29; 14:33) all show that Jesus' essential being is that of the Son of God, which the saying about the mutual knowledge between Father and Son also asserts (11:27). The new rendering of 16:13-17, with its confession σὺ εἶ ὁ χριστὸς ὁ υἱὸς τοῦ θεοῦ τοῦ ζῶντος, shows that the idea of divine sonship in connection with that of messiahship has moved to the forefront. The story of the transfiguration (17:2) allows the supernatural features to emerge more strongly than does the Markan version, and esp. the Passion narrative (cf. also 21:37-41) emphasizes Jesus' divine sonship several times (26:63f.; 27:54 picking up Mark; 27:40, 43 redactionally). The Gospel concludes with the triadic baptismal formula following on the statement about full authorization (28:19). The fulfillment of OT promise thus culminates in Matthew in a pronounced Christian understanding of Jesus as the Son of God.

d) In the seven indisputably authentic Pauline Epistles "Son of God" occurs only 15 times (7 times in Romans, 2 in 1 Corinthians, 1 in 2 Corinthians, 4 in Galatians, 1 in 1 Thessalonians). This number contrasts with *ca.* 217 occurrences of "Christ" and 187 of "Kyrios." In the deutero-Pauline Epistles the predicate occurs only once each in Colossians and Ephesians.

1) Paul takes his cue from tradition. Rom 1:3b, 4a associates divine sonship with the installation into the heavenly office of Messiah on the basis of the resurrection; 1 Thess 1:9f., which speaks of the resurrected Jesus who will return, implicitly presupposes this view. In Gal 4:4f. the sending of the Son of God establishes the acceptance of human beings into sonship (amplified by Paul with vv. 4d, 5a, possibly also with v. 4c; used without amplification in Rom 8:3f.). Two additional passages, Gal 2:20 and Rom 8:32, combine the statement concerning divine sonship with the traditional formula of sacrifice.

2) The framework of the received tradition in Rom 1:3a, 4b shows that for Paul divine sonship characterizes Jesus' person and history in the larger sense. The focus here is on the content of the message of the gospel, as is also the case in Rom 1:9 and 2 Cor 1:19. In the commissioning formula Paul is esp. interested not only in the full authorization but also in the connection with the idea of preexistence and of heavenly origin, as shown by Rom 8:3f. (recalling Phil 2:6-8): πέμψας ἐν ὁμοιώματι σαρκὸς ἁμαρτίας (also presupposed in γενόμενος ἐκ γυναικός in Gal 4:4c). Jesus' death is central, as can be seen in Rom 5:10 and Gal 2:20, the ἐξαγοράζειν in Gal 4:5a, and the statement καὶ περὶ ἁμαρτίας κατέκρινεν τὴν ἁμαρτίαν ἐν τῇ σαρκί in Rom 8:3b. According to Gal 1:15f. Paul's own call to be the apostle to the Gentiles is grounded in the fact that God revealed to him his (exalted) Son.

For all believers it is a matter of the κοινωνία τοῦ υἱοῦ αὐτοῦ (1 Cor 1:9) and of a life of faith in the Son of God (Gal 2:20). Gal 4:6 speaks of the "Spirit of the Son of God" poured into the hearts of those participating in sonship. The statement concerning the conformation to the εἰκὼν τοῦ υἱοῦ αὐτοῦ (Rom 8:29, related to Phil 3:21) is characteristic of eschatological anticipation; according to 8:23 this stands in the same context as the υἱοθεσία in the sense of the ἀπολύτρωσις τοῦ σώματος ἡμῶν. The only absolute use of ὁ υἱός (1 Cor 15:28) also belongs in this context. What emerges is that the relatively few references to the Son of God in Paul nonetheless represent a comprehensive christological conception.

3) Col 1:13 speaks of redemption from the dominion of darkness and deliverance εἰς τὴν βασιλείαν τοῦ υἱοῦ τῆς ἀγάπης αὐτοῦ, which on the one hand adopts the motif of the "beloved son" from the baptism and transfiguration stories, and on the other, as in Rom 1:4a, focuses on the reign of the exalted Christ, in which the baptized participate (cf. v. 14). Eph 4:13 speaks of faith in and knowledge of the Son of God.

e) Several traditions converge in the Johannine writings. What is striking is the close association between "Son" or "Son of God" and "Son of man" (→ 5).

1) John and 1–3 John use ὁ υἱός and ὁ υἱὸς τοῦ θεοῦ alternately and without distinction (cf. John 3:16-18; 1 John 5:9-13). Various nuances in usage show the presence of different traditions. Ὁ υἱός is related not to ὁ θεός but rather to ὁ πατήρ; this explains the unusual combination ὁ υἱὸς τοῦ πατρός (2 John 3; cf. 1 John 1:3). Ὁ υἱὸς τοῦ θεοῦ betrays its origin within the confessional tradition: σὺ εἶ (John 1:49; 11:27); οὗτός ἐστιν (1:34); πιστεύω εἰς or ὅτι (3:18; 20:31 [cf. 3:36]; 1 John 3:23; 5:5, 10a, 13); ὁμολογέω ὅτι (1 John 4:15 [but cf. also 2:22f.]); οἴδαμεν ὅτι (1 John 5:20a); this includes the use of credo formulas (John 11:27; 1 John 1:7; 3:8; 4:9b, 10b; 5:20a).

Ὁ υἱός reveals the same tradition as in the Synoptics: the basic motifs are commissioning by the Father and full authorization. Traditional formulations appear in the context of the commissioning motif in John 3:16f. (redactionally reworked) and 1 John 4:14b; cf. the statements about the "Father who has sent me." Transferal of authority occurs in John 3:35 (cf. 3:3; 17:2) and is behind the redactionally structured section 5:19-27. The statement about the Father's love for the Son appears in 3:35 and 5:20, corresponding to the motif of knowledge in Matt 11:27 par. (though not mutual knowledge).

2) The Johannine conception understands the commissioning in the sense of a descent from heaven (John 3:13; 6:33, 38, 41f., 50f.) and of the incarnation of the preexistent Logos (1:14). The Son participates in the Father's divinity (1:1c). Because he says of himself υἱὸς τοῦ θεοῦ εἰμι (10:36), which ends up being the basis of his condemnation (19:7), he is accused of blasphemy, ὅτι σὺ ἄνθρωπος ὢν ποιεῖς σεαυτὸν θεόν (10:33; cf. 20:28). To him as the revealer God entrusts everything; whoever sees the Son and believes in him has eternal life (6:40; 3:36) and true freedom (8:36) but also simultaneously sees in him the Father (cf. 12:45; 14:9). For as little as the Son does anything of his own accord, all the more does he do everything that is the Father's will and work (5:19f.).

As the bringer of salvation for the world (3:16f.; 11:27; 1 John 3:8; 4:9f., 14), both judgment and ζωοποιεῖν are given over to him (John 5:21-23, 26f.); both are a present reality (5:24f.; cf. 3:18-21). Faith in the Son thus determines salvation or judgment (3:36; 5:24; 1 John *passim*), and whoever honors him also honors the Father (John 5:23). One must thus "abide" in the Son and in the Father (1 John 2:24; 5:20b; or in the "doctrine of Christ," 2 John 9). The glorification of the Son as well as of the Father thus takes place on earth (John 11:4; 14:13; 17:1a, b); the glorification of the Son includes his death on the cross, just as it does his resurrection and living presence (cf. John 7:39; 12:23-26; 13:31; 17:4f.).

3) The Johannine conception clearly has grown out of genuinely early Christian circumstances. Religio-historical influences from other quarters are unlikely and at most helped shape the consistent development of the christology of the Son. Christology and soteriology are intimately connected, emphasizing both the exclusive authoritative power of revelation and the unlimited power to mediate salvation. Jesus' position as the Son of God is an expression of his divine being, though at this point no metaphysical reflections play any role. As emphatically as the preexistence and present activity of the exalted Christ are emphasized, the incarnation and death on the cross still occupy the central position and are not weakened by the witness of faith acquired from the perspective of Easter (John 2:22; 12:16; 14:26). What is important is the witness of Jesus as the only bringer of salvation, the one who comes from and leads us to the Father.

f) Within the remaining NT writings the expression "Son" or "Son of God" occurs 12 times in Hebrews and once each in 2 Peter and Revelation.

1) For Hebrews Ἰησοῦς ὁ υἱὸς τοῦ θεοῦ is the common Christian confession, as shown by the exhortation κρατῶμεν τῆς ὁμολογίας (4:14). The same holds true in the context of a denial of the Son of God (6:6; 10:29). The Melchizedek typology shows that the "Son of God" is understood as an eternal, divine person (7:3). The fundamental understanding of the "Son" includes his mediation in creation, his function as maintainer, his salvation activity, and his seat at the right hand of God; he is described as the ἀπαύγασμα τῆς δόξης καὶ χαρακτὴρ τῆς ὑποστάσεως αὐτοῦ (i.e., θεοῦ) (1:2f.). At the same time, Hebrews picks up the messianic predictions of the OT (Ps 2:7 in Heb 1:5; 5:5; 2 Sam 7:14 in Heb 1:5; Ps 44:7f. in Heb 1:8). In contrast to Moses as θεράπων, Christ is the υἱὸς ἐπὶ τὸν οἶκον αὐτοῦ (i.e., θεοῦ) (3:5f.). Although he is indeed the Son, he had to learn obedience through suffering (5:8), though in so doing, he attained perfection forever (7:28). This motif then issues in the doctrine characteristic for Hebrews of Christ's high-priestly office (2:17; 4:14-16; 6:20; 7:1-10, 18).

2) 2 Pet 1:17 refers to the voice from heaven at Jesus' transfiguration. Rev 2:18, in the open letter to Thyatira, begins with τάδε λέγει ὁ υἱὸς τοῦ θεοῦ; at the same time, it picks up elements from the call vision in 1:14f., which described an epiphany of the Son of man (1:13). This shows that the two conceptions of majesty have merged.

4. The divine sonship of human beings.

a) In addition to the designation of heavenly beings as "sons of God" and the messianic use of "Son of God," the OT also uses the motif of divine sonship regarding Israel itself. Exod 4:22, which mentions Israel as the "first-born son" designated to serve Yahweh, is difficult to evaluate as regards tradition history. The oldest attestations include first Hos 2:1: "son of the living God," and 11:1: "out of Egypt I called my son"; it then occurs in Isaiah, Jeremiah, Deutero- and Trito-Isaiah, and Deuteronomy. It is always a matter of Israel's election and the Father's concern.

This idea continues in Palestinian Judaism, though faithfulness to the law becomes the criterion, which is why esp. the pious are viewed as sons of God (cf. Sir 4:10); additionally, this divine sonship as the substance of promise is also transposed to the eschaton (*Jub.* 1:24f.; *Pss. Sol.* 17:27, 30; *1 Enoch* 62:11; *T. Mos.* 10:3; *T. Jud.* 24:3). This tendency becomes even more pronounced in Hellenistic Judaism (cf. Wis 2:10, 13, 18; 5:5, and elsewhere). What began in the OT as fig. usage (Ps 103:13; Prov 3:11f.) is taken literally (cf. Wis 12:21; 16:10).

In Philo it is the wise and the perfect who become sons of God on the basis of true knowledge (cf. *Conf.* 145-48; *Spec. Leg.* i.317f.). Though he does emphasize God's role as Father of creation and refers to the cosmos itself as the "(younger) son of God" (*Imm.* 31f.; *Migr.* 193), Philo nonetheless avoids speaking of human beings as "sons" and instead prefers ἔκγονα (cf. *Op.* 10, 75).

b) This motif emerges only in isolated instances in the Synoptic Gospels. The amended statement in the context of the conversation with the Sadducees clearly refers to the future (Luke 20:36d; cf. Mark 12:25 par. Matt 22:30); the assertion is that those participating in the resurrection (υἱοὶ ἀναστάσεως) will be υἱοὶ θεοῦ. The juxtaposition with υἱοὶ τοῦ αἰῶνος τούτου is noteworthy, as is the statement οὐδὲ γὰρ ἀποθανεῖν ἔτι δύνανται, ἰσάγγελοι γάρ εἰσιν: participation in the heavenly world is here assumed.

In a corresponding fashion, Luke 6:35 promises eschatological reward and future divine sonship for loving one's enemies; the exhortation ἔσεσθε υἱοὶ ὑψίστου is grounded in the reference to God's goodness over against those who are ungrateful and evil. The parallel Matt 5:45 treats this a bit differently; on the basis of a realization of love for one's enemies it speaks of divine sonship possible already in the present (ὅπως γένησθε υἱοὶ κτλ.). This does not, however, refer to any general divine sonship for all human beings, but rather for those who emulate Jesus and who make righteousness a reality (5:20); God's present activity is the expression of his mercy toward all human beings, something he proves to them as their Creator.

Since the kingdom of God has already commenced, access to divine sonship has been disclosed. Matt 5:9 states that the εἰρηνοποιοί are blessed, and the addendum asserts: ὅτι υἱοὶ θεοῦ κληθήσονται. This future assertion serves, as does vv. 4-8, to motivate the promise of salvation in the present. Since, according to vv. 3, 10, participating in the βασιλεία τῶν οὐρανῶν is promised, the blessed may already participate in the substance of this future salvation (cf. 17:25f.). Whereas Luke follows Jewish tradition, Matthew exhibits a Christianized understanding of human beings as sons of God.

c) The view of the divine sonship of believers is more fully developed in the other NT writings.

1) Rom 8:19 shows that for Paul eschatological anticipation plays an essential role (creation awaits the revealing of the υἱοὶ τοῦ θεοῦ). V. 23 speaks of the → υἱοθεσία in the sense of the "redemption of the body." For Paul, however, sonship as a salvation possession is not one-sidedly future but rather already present: ὅσοι γὰρ πνεύματι θεοῦ ἄγονται, οὗτοι υἱοὶ θεοῦ εἰσιν (v. 14). Believers have received the "spirit of sonship" and can thus also cry "Abba! Father!" (v. 15). The Spirit itself bears witness that we are τέκνα θεοῦ and as such also κληρονόμοι who as Christ's fellow heirs move toward future glory (vv. 16f.).

Gal 3:26–4:7 is even more specific: human beings are υἱοὶ θεοῦ "through faith in Christ Jesus" (3:26) and because they are baptized into Christ (v. 27). This truth is grounded in the sending of the Son of God, since this sending happened ἵνα τὴν υἱοθεσίαν ἀπολάβωμεν (4:4f.). This is why God sent the "Spirit of his Son" into our hearts; it not only makes the cry "Abba!" possible (v. 6) but also liberates us from slavery, gives us freedom, and

makes us into heirs (vv. 1-3, 7). Sonship is the expression of participation in Jesus' own sonship, which is promised, strengthened by the Spirit as a "deposit" (Rom 8:23), and will find its completion in the future. Rom 9:26 transfers Hos 2:1 LXX to the salvation community composed of Jews and Gentiles (cf. 9:24).

The use of the legal t.t. for adoption → υἱοθεσία is noteworthy, since Gal 4:5 and Rom 8:15, 23 (similarly Eph 1:5) emphasize the bestowal of sonship. This word is, indeed, also used of the legal standing of sonship, since υἱότης is not yet common in classical and Hellenistic usage; so Rom 9:4 (also 8:23).

2) The letter to the Hebrews also ties participation in sonship and in eschatological perfection to the Son's own salvation work. Although 2:10 creates no direct relationship between the Son and the sons, Christ's sonship is the theme of 1:1-14, something underscored by the christological interpretation of Ps 8:5-7 in Heb 2:5-9. The phrase ἀρχηγὸς τῆς σωτηρίας in 2:10 refers to Christ's function in grounding salvation for the πολλοὶ υἱοί. Just as now the "Son" must suffer in solidarity with human suffering (2:10b, 14-18; 4:15; 5:7-9), so also must the "sons" endure suffering in the sense of chastisement imposed by God (12:5-8 citing Prov 3:11f.).

3) Rev 21:7 uses the motif of divine sonship in the context of participation in future salvation, doing so by referring the messianic promise in 2 Sam 7:14 to all those who are delivered. The same citation appears in a slightly altered and expanded form in the deutero-Pauline insertion 2 Cor 6:14–7:1, though here in v. 18 with reference to the earthly salvation community as ναὸς θεοῦ ζῶντος (v. 16).

d) John and 1–3 John can be briefly compared here. Υἱός is never used of believers, but only in an exclusively christological fashion. In substance, however, a certain correspondence does occur; for on the one hand these writings speak of τέκνα θεοῦ (John 1:12; 11:52; 1 John 3:1, 2, 10; 5:2), and on the other of "being begotten by God" or "from above" (John 1:13; 3:3-8; 1 John 2:29; 3:9a, b; 4:7; 5:1, 4, 18a, b; cf. 3:9: σπέρμα αὐτοῦ [i.e., τοῦ θεοῦ]). The Johannine tradition is clearly concerned with a present salvation condition (1 John 3:2a: νῦν τέκνα θεοῦ ἐσμεν) characterized by faith and love. Statements about being begotten betray their original context within the baptism tradition (cf. 1 John 2:26-29). In other respects, though, the eschatological horizon remains visible here also (3:2b).

5. "Son of man."

a) Background.

1) It is clear philologically that the unusual Greek phrase with two articles (ὁ υἱὸς τοῦ θεοῦ) derives from a Semitic construction. The OT uses ben-ʾādām of one person, thus applying ʾādām, which as a rule is used collectively, to an individual. The form with the definite article—ben- hāʾādām—is not attested until Qumran (1QS 11:20). The corresponding Aramaic expressions, since ʾādām does not occur in Aramaic, are bar-(ᵉ)nāš and bar- (ᵉ)nāšāʾ. Scholars agree that Aramaic makes no fundamental distinction between definite and indefinite forms and that both can be used collectively or of individuals (Vermes, Jeremias, Bowker).

There is some question concerning the comparison of *hāhû' gaḇrā'* and the use of *bar-nāš* or *bar-nāšā'* as a substitute for "I" (Fitzmyer *contra* Vermes). In contrast to *hāhû' gaḇrā'*, *bar-nāšā'* can certainly refer to the speaker, though it is not unequivocally a substitute for "I" (*contra* Jeremias). In the Gospels, if such a form can indeed be used for "I," then the sayings about the Son of man could be the point of departure for the tradition. If, however, the Aramaic term refers to "someone," "a person," or "the human being," then one would suspect its use in the sayings to refer primarily to a coming Son of man. Since the Greek form with two articles is probably not accidental, it is likely that the Aramaic word with the article *(bar-nāšā')* has been used in designating a specific figure distinct from the person speaking.

2) If "Son of man" derives from everyday language, then one cannot assume the presence of any religio-historical content and can only inquire where human existence as such is emphasized (Leivestad and others). Reference to a tradition of primal man has frequently been suspected (most recently Borsch, *Son of Man in Myth and History*), though it cannot be substantiated (Colpe), at least not in the sense of any direct dependence. Reference is sometimes made to Ezekiel's form of address *ben-'āḏām*, but this is improbable, not least because no vocatives occur.

Because of the allusions to Dan 7:13f. one must assume some connection with this text and its conceptual framework. It is disputed whether there is a primary or a secondary dependence on the text, and whether one should assume a direct dependence or one mediated through the post-Daniel tradition. A secondary dependence is extremely improbable. Any direct dependence, however, cries out for clarification concerning the transition from the comparative manner of speech "*like* a son of man" to the actual NT usage. Furthermore, the text of Daniel deals with an image for "the people of the saints of the Most High" (7:21f., 27); yet behind this vision stands an even older tradition (vv. 9f., 13f.). It is difficult to decide to what extent the reference is to an individual figure functioning as a mediator of salvation.

1 Enoch 37–71 could in any case be dependent on this (Theisohn). A dispute continues, however, concerning both the age and provenance of this imagery, which in contrast to other parts of the book of Enoch are not attested in Qumran, as well as concerning the overall character of the Ethiopic designation for the figure of the Son of man. 2 Esdr 13:2 again exhibits this comparative manner of speech, though the reference is to an individual person functioning both in judgment and salvation. Nowhere do any immediate prefigurations of the NT usage of "Son of man" become visible. One must probably reckon with a related tradition that can be disclosed from within the NT itself (Colpe).

In any case, extant early Jewish writing does attest the figure of a heavenly man whose primary function is one of judgment and salvation, and which in isolated instances is also integrated with inner-worldly or personal expectations (Müller). No evidence exists, however, attesting any titular usage (Leivestad, Vermes), and the question must remain open whether any existed in the pre-Christian period. Since the NT sayings about the Son of man reveal a strong influence of apocalyptic motifs (Lindars), including references to the ἐξουσία bestowed upon Jesus and the almost exclusive focus on the last judgment (Maddox, "Function"), it is extremely likely that the use of *bar-nāšā'* for a (different) human figure was already associated with this apocalyptic tradition.

b) Usage in the NT.

1) It is unmistakable that the Son of man in the NT is everywhere identical with Jesus. Son of man sayings occur only as self-assertions (differently in Acts 7:56 and in OT citations in Heb 2:6; Rev 1:13; 14:14). "Son of man" is thus exclusively a self-designation and exhibits quasi-titular meaning. The transition to direct titular usage can be recognized in John 9:35; 12:34c; Acts 7:56 (cf. also the combination with nouns in Matt 24:27, 30a, 37, 39; Luke 17:22, 26), though nowhere is it carried through fully. It is always reserved for Jesus' majesty. It is first used as a designation for Jesus' human side by Ign. *Eph.* 20:2, then *Barn.* 12:10; Justin *Dial.* 100:3 (on Heb 2:6 → f.2). Hence the translation for NT texts cannot be "a man" or "this man" but only, as in the Greek, the emphatic "Son of man."

2) The various Son of man sayings in the Synoptics can appropriately be divided into three groups, with respective focus on the Son of man as earthly, as suffering and resurrected, and as returning and exalted. Sayings about the earthly Son of man (2 in Mark, 7 in Matthew, 8 in Luke) and those about the suffering Son of man (4 in Mark, 6 in Matthew, 3 in Luke) or the suffering and resurrected Son of man (5 in Mark, 4 in Matthew, 3 in Luke) belong more closely together. Then there are those about the returning (3 in Mark, 13 in Matthew, 10 in Luke) and the exalted Son of man (1 in Luke, 1 in Acts, 2 in Revelation). In John all occurrences refer to Jesus' earthly ministry (13 times). This division also makes sense from the perspective of tradition history, though this has been disputed (Hooker; Maddox, "Quest").

3) Among the Synoptics, Matthew and Luke have to a large extent taken over the 14 Markan occurrences (Mark 8:31 is missing in Matthew, and Mark 9:9, 12; 10:45; and 14:21b, 41 are missing in Luke). To these 37 occurrences are added 14 from Q (7 each in Matthew and Luke) and 9 each from M and L. This does not include 3 occurrences in which υἱὸς ἀνθρώπου or οἱ υἱοὶ τῶν ἀνθρώπων is used of "human being(s)" (→ 2.b.5).

4) Comparisons of Son of man sayings with parallels that lack the phrase should not lead to an assumption that the Son of man designation is secondary. Rather, in each case the substance of the passage should be evaluated; usually one can assume that the original version of the sayings included "Son of man" (Borsch, *Christian and Gnostic Son of Man; contra* Jeremias).

5) In the matter of authenticity, one must assume that the logia have been reworked (Hooker), which does not mean, however, that all are of secondary origin (Vielhauer, Perrin). One point of contention now as earlier is whether the original sayings are those about the earthly Son of man, including possibly the sufferings sayings (Schweizer, Leivestad, Vermes, and others), or those about the heavenly Son of man (Tödt and others).

c) The question whether Jesus himself used the designation "Son of man" hinges on passages in which his own activity and that of the Son of man are juxtaposed. Although the formulation in Luke 12:8f. with "confess" and "deny" cannot be considered authentic (*contra* Pesch), nor that in the abbreviated version in Mark 8:38 with "be ashamed" (*contra* W. G. Kümmel, FS Vögtle 210-24), the basic structure of the statement might go back to Jesus: One's position regarding the person of Jesus is decisive for salvation, since this will be the standard for the Son of man at judgment. In all this Jesus expects that the judge will confirm his claim and identify with him. It is possible that other sayings about the future activity of the Son of man also go back to Jesus (Luke 17:24, 26f. par.), though no clear criteria can be set up, since everywhere the identification of the Son of man with Jesus is already presupposed.

d) On the surface the Synoptic tradition exhibits a multifarious use. At a deeper level, however, the different groups of Son of man sayings complement one another.

1) If one assumes that Jesus himself spoke of the heavenly Son of man, then what probably took place first in tradition history was an identification of the resurrected Jesus with the future Son of man. The expectation of the parousia was thus explicated with the help of a Son of man christology. This soon led to an understanding of Jesus' earthly life as also being a function of the Son of man. Through an additional process not presupposed in Q the suffering was then included, and then also Jesus' resurrection (and in isolated instances also his exaltation). In any case, the oldest layer of sayings about the Son of man clearly shows that we are dealing with an independent early Christian conception.

2) The sayings about the earthly activity of the Son of man emphasize Jesus' claim to full authority and majesty (cf. Mark 2:10 par. and 2:28 par.). This is presupposed in the blessing in Luke 6:22 and in the comparison with John the Baptist in Matt 11:18f. par. Luke 7:33f. This logion, however, makes it clear that the Son of man's majesty is hidden, to which Matt 8:20 par. Luke 9:58 alludes. Luke 17:(20f.)22 and 19:10 emphasize the soteriological function, and though Matt 12:32 par. Luke 12:10 also holds to such a view, this saying, which effectively divides salvation history into different periods, is focusing particularly on the activity of the Spirit after Easter.

3) Among the sayings about the Son of man's suffering and resurrection one must distinguish between the simple predictions of suffering on the one hand (Mark 14:21a, b, 41 par. Matt 26:24a, b, 45/Luke 22:22), and the double statements about suffering and resurrection on the other (Mark 8:31 par.; 9:31 par.; 10:33f. par.; Luke 9:44b par. Mark 9:31 has been redactionally shortened into a suffering logion). It is noteworthy that suffering at the hands of human beings is mentioned (cf. Mark 9:31 par.), without emphasizing the soteriological function of Jesus' death. Mark 10:45 par. Matt 20:28 occupies a special position and shows the influence of a different christological tradition. Whereas the suffering logia emphasize the hostile actions of human beings, the resurrection logia emphasize the Son of man's own powerful actions, as shown by the use of ἀνίστημι. Mark 10:33f. par., which in its present form is late (probably redactional), offers an outline of the story of suffering and resurrection. In similar fashion Matt 12:(38f.)40 undertakes a typological interpretation of the story of Jonah in reference to Jesus' death and burial (differently in the par. Luke 11:29f.).

4) The sayings about the future actions of the Son of man are referring to Jesus' sudden and unexpected parousia (so Luke 17:24 par. Matt 24:27; Luke 17:26f. par. Matt 24:37f.; Luke 17:(28f.)30 par. Matt 24:39; further Matt 10:23). Mark 14:62 par. Matt 26:64 speaks of the powerful epiphany of the Son of man, who will come sitting at the right hand of God. The whole world will see him and will see how he reveals himself and sends his angels to gather his elect (Mark 13:26f. par.; Matt 16:27 [cf. Mark 8:38b par. Luke 9:26b]). His function will then also be that of judge, as shown by the speech (laden with parable elements) about the last judgment in Matt 25:31-46 (with Luke 12:8f.; Mark 8:38 par. Luke 9:26 and Matt 13:41; 19:28).

5) The sayings about the suffering and resurrection of the Son of man do not yet play a role in Q, though both Jesus' earthly ministry and his future activity are placed under the purview of his authority as the Son of man. Even if the individual logia belong to an early stage of transmission (H. Schürmann, FS Vögtle 124-47) and not to the final redaction (so also Polag), their significance is unmistakable; Jesus' designation as the Son of man is clearly a dominating christological conception (Tödt).

6) The Son of man sayings in Mark occupy an esp. important position because the Evangelist is concerned with emphasizing Jesus' salvation-historical mission in addition to stressing the supernatural essence of the Son of man (→ 3.c). He distributes the groups of Son of man sayings throughout the three parts of his Gospel: 1:14–8:26 emphasizes the full authority of the earthly Jesus (2:10, 28), 8:27–10:45 focuses on the suffering and resurrection (8:31; 9:9, 12, 31; 10:33f.; 10:45), and 10:46–16:8 points beyond the Passion events to his eschatological function (13:26; 14:62). In the process, the second and third parts are bracketed together, since 8:38 already speaks of the coming Son of man, and 14:21a, b, 41b speaks anew of the suffering Son of man; furthermore, 14:24 picks up the statement concerning atonement in 10:45.

7) As a result of structural alteration Matthew no longer preserves Mark's divisions, and the perspective of the Son of God moves more prominently into the foreground. Though two statements each about the earthly Son of man (13:37; 16:13) and his suffering (12:40; 26:2) are indeed amplified, the sayings about the coming and judging Son of man acquire more weight by the acquisition from Q and M of additional material from tradition (10:23; 13:41; 16:28; 19:28; 24:27, 30a, 37, 39, 44; 25:31). Also, only Matthew speaks as well of the παρουσία of the Son of man (24:27, 37, 39; cf. 24:3).

8) Luke adds Son of man sayings from all three groups to the tradition he received from Mark. Luke 6:22 and 19:10 (L) supplement the statements about the earthly activity; 17:25 and 22:48 (redactional) supplement those

about suffering; and 24:7 (redactional) supplements those about suffering and resurrection. In Luke, too, statements concerning the future move into the foreground through the juxtaposition of the two eschatological speeches in 17:22-37 and 21:5-38, where Son of man sayings are central (cf. Luke 9:26 par. Mark 8:38; Luke 11:30; 12:8f., 40 [Q]; 18:8b [L]). The uniqueness of the Lukan conception becomes visible in 22:67-69, where Jesus responds to the high priest's question whether he is the Christ with the following words: ἀπὸ τοῦ νῦν δὲ ἔσται ὁ υἱὸς τοῦ ἀνθρώπου καθήμενος ἐκ δεξιῶν τῆς δυνάμεως τοῦ θεοῦ; thus for the first time the idea of exaltation is taken up unequivocally into the understanding of the Son of man (cf. Acts 7:56).

e) John applies the entire spectrum of exalted titles to Jesus (cf. 1:1-51), at the same time combining messianic traditions and conceptions of the Son of God together with the idea of the Son of man (cf. 5:25f., 27; 12:34a, b, c).

1) John 9:35 uses the phrase πιστεύω εἰς τὸν υἱὸν τοῦ ἀνθρώπου (v.l. υἱὸν τοῦ θεοῦ); cf. 3:(14)15. This is an innovation containing an implicit confession. The passage shows that "Son of man" is being used as a title and refers to the earthly Jesus. 1:51 is also referring to the earthly Jesus by using a motif from Gen 28:12: Jesus' unbroken connection to the heavenly world and thus also to the Father can be viewed through faith.

2) Exaltation sayings occupy a large space, and in them ὑψωθῆναι and δοξασθῆναι in the Johannine sense also encompass Jesus' death, which emerges from the typological statement in John 3:14, from 12:23 (24ff., 32f.), 34b, c, and 13:31. The same applies to the act. use of ὑψόω in 8:28. The phrase ἀναβαίνειν εἰς τὸν οὐρανόν (3:13) is related to this context and corresponds as well to the ἐκ τοῦ οὐρανοῦ καταβαίνειν (cf. 6:62: ἀναβαίνων ὅπου ἦν τὸ πρότερον). The coming of the preexistent Christ into the world, his death, and his ascension into heaven all provide the framework for his exaltation and glorification. Compared with the Synoptic tradition, John significantly modifies the conception of the Son of man. On the one hand he expands it to include a theology of preexistence and incarnation; on the other by his use of ὑψωθῆναι and δοξασθῆναι he establishes a close bracketing of sayings about Jesus' death and those about his ascension and enthronement.

3) Although John does not offer any sayings about the returning Son of man, it is quite significant that in view of Jesus' present activity 5:27 asserts that the υἱὸς ἀνθρώπου (a phrase occurring only here) receives the ἐξουσία to execute judgment (κρίσιν ποιεῖν). In 6:27 the Son of man bestows the gift of life; it is he who gives "the food that endures to eternal life." The deutero-Johannine section 6:51c-58 alters this motif in the sense of a eucharist saying: φαγεῖν τὴν σάρκα τοῦ υἱοῦ τοῦ ἀνθρώπου καὶ πιεῖν αὐτοῦ τὸ αἷμα (v. 53).

4) There is no direct dependence here on the Synoptic Son of man tradition, nor is it a case of more fully developing a received tradition. What is interesting is that precisely the apocalyptic sayings have been taken up and transformed. Aside from the function of judgment and the gift of life (John 5:27; 6:27), this is the case for ὑψωθῆναι (cf. Mark 14:62 par., sitting at the right hand of God), for δοξασθῆναι (cf. Mark 8:38 par.: ἐν τῇ δόξῃ), and for John 1:51 (on the opening of heaven and the descending angels cf. Rev 4:1; Heb 1:14; on ὄψεσθε cf. Mark 14:62). This complex also includes the reference to the eschatological hour in John 12:23 (13:1, 31) as well as the knowledge of who he is (8:28; cf. 19:37 and Matt 24:30; Rev 1:7).

Sayings about the suffering of the Son of man have also played a role (cf. John 3:14; 8:28; 12:23 [24-26]; 12:34; 13:31). On the one hand, though, originally future-oriented motifs have been transferred to the present, and on the other the statements concerning suffering and exaltation have been blended together. The idea of καταβαίνειν and ἀναβαίνειν in John 3:13 and 6:62 is then added as a new motif, though it is still disputed from which tradition this comes and whether it is a result of foreign influence. The most likely source is still the Jewish wisdom tradition, as it is also for the salient features of the idea of preexistence (cf. Prov 30:4; Wis 9:16; Bar 3:29).

5) Of decisive significance in John is the connection between preexistence and incarnation as well as with ascension to the heavenly world, topics always concentrated on the person of the earthly Jesus. According to 3:13 the man who has descended from heaven is the Son of man, and not vice versa; similarly, the crucified Jesus, and not the resurrected one, is exalted and glorified. According to 1:51 the heavenly reality is revealed in the Son of man. He is the giver of life (6:27), and God's own eschatological revelation takes place in his life and death. Whoever believes in him thus has eternal life. All these christological assertions focus on soteriology. Though in John, unlike in the Synoptics, the idea of the parousia is absent, that of realizing a complete salvation is very much present.

f) Outside the Gospels reference to the Son of man occurs only in citations from Dan 7:13 (Rev 1:13; 14:14) and from Ps 8:5 (Heb 2:6) and in Acts 7:56. An indirect reference to the Son of man tradition in Paul is unlikely.

1) Although Rev 1:13 and 14:14 both take up Dan 7:13 with the phrase ὅμοιον υἱὸν ἀνθρώπου (not from LXX or Theodotion), Revelation otherwise avoids references to the Son of man, as the parallel to Luke 12:8 in Rev 3:5b shows. The focus is on the exalted one set apart with divine majesty. He is the Lord of the Church (cf. the seven lampstands in 1:13) and the future judge (14:14).

2) The christological interpretation of Ps 8:5(6f.) in Heb 2:6 (5-9) has left some question whether this reference is to the early Christian Son of man tradition (Higgins), or whether with the help of the OT citation Jesus' existence as a human being is merely being emphasized as the ground of his eschatological dominion (E. Grässer, FS Vögtle 404-14). There is likely at least some association with the idea of the earthly and suffering Son of man. Hebrews, however, does not develop a Son of man christology, focusing rather on its Son christology, which is complemented by the idea of the high priest.

3) "Son of man" does not appear in Paul. Despite the citation from Ps 8:7b in 1 Cor 15:27 there is no reason to assume an indirect connection with the Son of man tradition (Vögtle, "Menschensohn"; U. Wilckens, FS Vögtle 387-403). The statements about Christ as "the man" (1 Cor 15:21, 47; Rom 5:15), which could well be a linguistically correct tr. of "Son of man," do not exhibit any relationship to the apocalyptically characterized conception of the Son of man; they presuppose, rather, a Hellenistic Jewish view of the primal man (cf. Philo) that has been eschatologically modified and typologically applied. One might more likely suspect a connection with the Son of man tradition in the deutero-Pauline text 1 Tim 2:5f. (cf. Mark 10:45 par.).

4) Outside the Gospels, the only appearance of "Son of man" independent of an OT citation is Acts 7:56, where Stephen sees the heavens opened and the Son of man standing at the right hand of God. The reference to "standing" (instead of "sitting") doubtless is significant, but it presents difficulties. It is unlikely that the martyr is to be received personally or that the exalted Son of man is preparing for the parousia. The reference is either to the function of the witness and supporter during a trial (in the sense of Luke 12:8) or to the judge, who rises to pronounce judgment (Isa 3:13 LXX; *T. Mos.* 10:3; so Pesch).

6. "Son of David."

a) Background.

1) The phrase υἱὸς Δαυίδ expresses a genealogical connection with the line of David (→ Δαυίδ 2, 3). Membership among the descendants of David, however, is also mentioned elsewhere (cf. the genealogies in Matt 1:6-16a, 17, 20; Luke 3:23b-31, and Luke 1:27; 2:4 [Joseph ἐξ οἴκου Δαυίδ).

2) The point of departure for Jesus' designation as the Son of David is the OT Jewish view of the Messiah, according to which the king of the time of salvation is to be a descendant of David, in whose activity the promises of 2 Sam 7:14; Isa 9:1-6; 11:1-10, and elsewhere will be fulfilled. This expectation was kept alive in post-OT Judaism (cf. *Pss. Sol.* 17:21; 4QFlor 1:11-13; the fourteenth of the Eighteen Benedictions, and elsewhere).

b) Usage.

1) The titular use of "Son of David" presupposes in all instances Jesus' inclusion among the descendants of David. Luke somewhat glosses over the issue of ancestry with ὡς ἐνομίζετο (3:23), though because of the marriage of the virgin Mary to Joseph he does presuppose such ancestry (1:27, 32f.). In contrast, Matthew emphasizes the fact of Joseph's adoption resulting from the divine visit (1:18-25), which is why the statement in v. 16b does not interrupt the genealogy but rather underscores the legal and fully valid inclusion.

2) The historical question whether Jesus did in fact belong to David's descendants is frequently answered in the negative (most recently Burger), and a reconstruction based on the messianic confession is alleged. At very least this question should be left open. Although genealogies were correctly kept only in priestly and levitical circles, the consciousness of belonging to a certain tribal and familial tradition was always quite pronounced in Israel (cf. the lists of those returning from the exile [Ezra 2:1ff.; 8:1ff.; Neh 7:6ff.; 11:3ff.] and Phil 3:5).

3) What is decisive is the fulfillment of the messianic promise. Here Jesus' birth in Bethlehem, "the city of David" (Luke 2:4, 11; cf. Matt 2:5f.), plays an important role, as Matt 2:1-12 and Luke 2:1-20 show. The tension between messianic promise and origin in Nazareth or Galilee was indeed felt (John 1:46; 7:42, 52; cf. Matt 2:23).

4) Jesus' messianic function, which finds multiple expressions in the NT (→ Χριστός), also shows up clearly wherever a passage refers to the promises made to King David (Luke 1:32f., 69; Acts 2:25-31, 34; 4:25-28; 13:22f.; 15:15-18; Heb 11:32f., 39f.; cf. also Mark 2:23-28 par.), or wherever specifically Davidic epithets are used (Rev 3:7; 5:5; 22:16).

5) One special problem is the actual substance of the reference to the Son of David. Υἱὸς Δαυίδ does not occur at all in the NT Epistles, though two confessions mention ἐκ σπέρματος Δαυίδ (Rom 1:3; 2 Tim 2:8; cf. Ign. *Eph.* 18:2; 20:2; *Trall.* 9:1). Here the juxtaposition of earthly existence as Son of David and resurrection as the enthronement of the exalted Son of God is characteristic, a situation showing "a Christology built up in two stages" (Hahn, *Titles* 246, building on previous work by E. Schweizer, "Der Glaube an Jesus den 'Herrn' in seiner Entwicklung von den ersten Nachfolgern bis zur hellenistischen Gemeinde," *EvT* 17 [1957] 11). In the Synoptic Gospels the conversation in Mark 12:35-37a par. shows that here, too, Davidic sonship is the prerequisite or preliminary stage of the κυριότης promised in Ps 110:1. As the Son of David, the earthly Jesus is the designated Messiah.

6) Other texts presuppose miraculous works, and Jesus is addressed with υἱὲ Δαυίδ, ἐλέησόν με (Mark 10:47f. par.). For Mark this occurs in the context of a Son of David discussion and implies a preliminary and secret recognition of Jesus' messianic function. Virtually the same is the case in Luke. Although the inbreaking of salvation is proclaimed at the birth in Bethlehem (Luke 2:11), according to Acts only the resurrection of Jesus itself fully establishes this messianic function (Acts 2:34; 13:33).

7) Matthew develops most clearly the idea of an independent function of the earthly Jesus as the Son of David; healing stories offer two additional instances where Jesus is addressed with ἐλέησον ἡμᾶς, υἱὸς Δαυίδ (9:27; 15:22; cf. 20:30f. par.). Furthermore, the people themselves pose the following question in the context of healings: μήτι οὗτός ἐστιν ὁ υἱὸς Δαυίδ; (12:23). Also, the acclamation ὡσαννὰ τῷ υἱῷ Δαυίδ, which occurs only here, is used not only at the entry into Jerusalem but also after the healings in the temple (21:9, 15). Jesus offers

the people healing as a visible sign of coming salvation, thus acting in this aspect of his earthly ministry as the Son of David.

8) Davidic sonship does not exhibit any theological significance for John (7:41f.). The NT contains no formal rejection of this sonship (as do *Barn.* 12:9f.; *Ps.-Clem. Hom.* 18:3, amid later premises oriented more thoroughly toward Jesus' divinity).

                                    F. Hahn

ὕλη, ης, ἡ   *hylē*   wood; forest*

Jas 3:5, regarding misuse of the tongue: "Behold, a small fire, and what a large *forest* it sets ablaze." Cf. Sir 28:10.

ὑμεῖς   *hymeis*   you (pl.)

1. Occurrences in the NT — 2. Usage — 3. Those addressed with ὑμεῖς

Lit.: BAGD s.v. σύ. — BDF §§277; 284; 288. — KÜHNER, *Grammatik* II/1, 555-60. — MAYSER, *Grammatik* II/1, 62-65.

1. The second person pl. personal pron. occurs quite frequently in the NT (altogether 1,847 times; cf. also → ἡμεῖς). It appears relatively less often in writings that contain less speech material (only 78 occurrences in Mark vs. 249 in Matthew; only 11 in Revelation) and more often in Epistles that use relatively more direct address (146 and 153 times in 1–2 Corinthians vs. 84 in Romans) or that are addressed to individuals (Pastorals, 3 John).

2. On the use of ὑμεῖς in nom. (esp. frequent in John and 1 Corinthians, never in the Pastorals, Philemon, Hebrews, 2–3 John, or Revelation) cf. → ἡμεῖς 2. Ὑμεῖς, too, is often combined with καί or δέ (*ca.* 55 and 32 times). Peter's sermons in Acts contain the combination ὃν ὑμεῖς (ἐσταυρώσατε or similar; 2:36; 3:13; 4:10; 5:30).

The gen. ὑμῶν occurs as a gen. absolute (Luke 22:10; 1 Cor 5:4; 11:18-20; 2 Cor 1:11; 1 Pet 4:4), is governed by the appropriate preps. (Matt 5:11, 12, e.g., κατά or πρό), and occurs esp. often as a substitute for the possessive pron. (e.g., 1 Thess 1:3, 4, 8; on word order see BAGD).

The dat. ὑμῖν is regularly a component of the salutations (χάρις ὑμῖν καὶ εἰρήνη . . .) in the Epistles (also Rev 1:4; exceptions: Pastorals, Hebrews, James, 1–3 John). In other environments, the dat.—like the acc. ὑμᾶς—is dependent on corresponding preps. and vbs., the latter esp. frequent in John 13–16 (with 50 occurrences), where vbs. of speaking and giving predominate (e.g., in the phrase ἀμὴν ἀμὴν λέγω ὑμῖν: 13:16, 20, 21; 14:12; 16:20, 23; elsewhere in John: 1:51; 5:19, 24, 25; 6:26, 32, 47, 53; 8:34, 51, 58; 10:1, 7; 12:24).

3. In letters those addressed with ὑμεῖς are the target Christian congregations. In the Gospels it is first Jesus'

listeners whom he thus addresses, in the Synoptics usually in a general sense the people or disciples, and in John often polemically "the Jews," in contrast with the disciples. The real addressees in the Gospels, however, are those for whom they are written, i.e., the Christians and their neighbors (cf., e.g., H. Schürmann, *Luke* [HTKNT] 320f.).

                                    W. Radl

Ὑμέναιος, ου   *Hymenaios*   Hymenaeus*

1 Tim 1:20: "*Hymenaeus* and Alexander" are men who have shipwrecked their own faith (v. 19) and whom "Paul" has "delivered to Satan"; 2 Tim 2:17: "*Hymenaeus* and Philetus" and other false teachers asserted that "the resurrection has already occurred" (v. 18).

ὑμέτερος, 3   *hymeteros*   your, yours*

The second person pl. possessive pron. occurs only 11 times in the NT; in most cases its meaning is conveyed instead by the personal pron. (ὑμῶν; BDF §285). In most occurrences ὑμέτερος exhibits possessive meaning (Luke 6:20; 16:12 [subst.: "that which is your own"]; John 7:6; 8:17; 15:20; Acts 27:34; 1 Cor 16:17; 2 Cor 8:8; Gal 6:13). Paul also uses ὑμέτερος for the obj. gen.: "by the mercy shown *to you*" (Rom 11:31); "my boasting *about you*" (1 Cor 15:31).

ὑμνέω   *hymneō*   praise, extol; sing (a hymn)*
ὕμνος, ου, ὁ   *hymnos*   song of praise, hymn*

1. Occurrences and meaning — 2. Intrans.: sing a hymn — 3. Trans.: sing a hymn to, praise (someone) — 4. Ὕμνος

Lit.: R. DEICHGRÄBER, *Gotteshymnus und Christushymnus in der frühen Christenheit* (SUNT 5, 1967) 188-214. — G. DELLING, *TDNT* VIII, 489-503. — H. GNILKA, *Col* (HTKNT, 1980) 200f. — J. KROLL, *Die christliche Hymnodik bis zu Klemens von Alexandreia* (Libelli 240, 1921-22, ²1968). — R. J. LEDOGAR, "Verbs of Praise in the LXX Translation of the Hebrew Canon," *Bib* 48 (1967) 29-56. — H. RINGGREN, *TDOT* III, 404-10. — R. WÜNSCH, PW IX/1, 140-83.

1. Ὑμνέω occurs 4 times in the NT (Mark 14:26 par. Matt 26:30; Acts 16:25; Heb 2:12), the noun ὕμνος twice (Eph 5:19; Col 3:16). The NT never uses these words in the secular sense of songs to human beings, but rather always in the religious sense referring to *praise* of God. The hymn is always performed publicly; like the psalm or ode, it represents a cultic song of the congregation.

Ὑμνέω follows LXX usage, where, along with → αἰνέω and → ἐξομολογέω (3), it is used primarily as a translation of *hll* (Piel), "to praise." As a synonym for → αἴνεσις, ὕμνος translates Heb. *tᵉhillāh*, "praise, hymn."

2. Only Mark 14:26 par. Matt 26:30 uses ὑμνέω in-

trans.: ὑμνήσαντες, *having sung the hymn* (see J. Elling-ton, "The Translation of 'Passover' in French-speaking Parts of Africa, and Elsewhere," *BT* 30 [1979] 445f.). The "hymn" here refers to the second part of the Hallel (prob-ably Pss 113–18), which is sung after the concluding prayer of the actual Passover meal over the fourth goblet of wine (see Billerbeck I, 845-49).

3. Only twice is ὑμνέω used trans. with the acc. of the person praised. According to Acts 16:25 Paul and Silas *sang hymns* to God while imprisoned in Philippi (ὕμνουν τὸν θεόν), "and the [fellow] prisoners were listening to them." Heb 2:12 cites Ps 21:23 LXX. Here ὑμνέω does not necessarily refer to a song; "in the midst of the con-gregation" Christ proclaims God's name and *praises* him.

4. The pl. of **ὕμνος**, *hymn, song of praise**, appears in Col 3:16 and Eph 5:19 between ψαλμοί and ᾠδαὶ πνευματικαί. No differentiation between the various terms appears to be intended, however; rather, this is probably a case of the influence of Jewish tradition, according to which it is customary to multiply terms for the praise of God (see Kroll 5f. n. 2). Possibly the intention is to distinguish psalms (a clearly biblical term) from *hymns* and odes (Hellenistic terms). It is at least questionable whether Col 3:16 refers to a parenetic use of psalms, hymns, and odes; in the case of Eph 5:19, however, such a use is probable (cf. also Deichgräber 188-96).

The addressee of the hymns in Col 3:16 is God. The v.l. τῷ κυρίῳ (C² D² Ψ*) represents an assimilation to Eph 5:19, where in a gradual distancing from the Jewish synagogue prayers, Christ moves more into the fore-ground of worship.   M. Rutenfranz

ὕμνος, ου, ὁ *hymnos*   song of praise, hymn
→ ὑμνέω (4).

ὑπάγω *hypagō*   go, go away

1. Occurrences in the NT — 2. Miracle stories — 3. Exorcisms — 4. Unspecific use — 5. Mark 14:21a — 6. John — 7. Later writings

Lit.: J.-A. BÜHNER, *Der Gesandte und sein Weg im vierten Evangelium* (WUNT II/2, 1977) 421-33. — G. DELLING, *TDNT* VIII, 504-6. — H. LEROY, *Rätsel und Mißverständnis* (BBB 30, 1968) 51-74. — L. SCHENKE, *Studien zur Passionsgeschichte des Markus* (FzB 4, 1971) 203-71. — G. THEISSEN, *The Miracle Stories of the Early Christian Tradition* (1983) 67f.

1. Ὑπάγω occurs 79 times in the NT, 39 of these in the Synoptics (19 in Matthew, 15 in Mark, 5 in Luke), 32 in John, 1 each in James and 1 John, and 6 in Rev-elation. This vb., which the NT uses only intrans., was not a part of standard Attic speech (BDF §§101; 308, s.v. ἄγειν).

2. The imv. *go* at the conclusion of miracle stories appears as a fixed expression. Jesus sends a healed man back home (Mark 2:11 par. Matt 9:6; Mark 5:19 [cf. Mark 8:26; Luke 8:39]) or to the priest for a confirmation of the healing (Mark 1:44 [cf. Luke 17:14]) or to the pool of Siloam (John 9:7). Elsewhere Jesus combines ὕπαγε with an affirmation of faith (Mark 5:34; 10:52; Matt 8:13) or uses it absolutely after a healing (Mark 7:29; John 11:44). The imv. *go (forth)* is also combined with a com-missioning for proclamation (Mark 5:19; 16:7; Matt 28:10); Mark 5 is referring to "what the κύριος has done," and Mark 16 par. Matt 28 to the epiphany of the resur-rected Jesus.

Only Mark 1:44a combines a specific commandment to be silent with the order ὕπαγε. The fact, however, that Pap. Egerton 2, 1, ll. 32ff. (see Hennecke/Schneemelcher I, 96f.) attests a literarily independent version of Mark 1:40-45 without "spiritual agitation" of the miracle worker (v. 43) and without the commandment to be silent (this is also missing in the parallels in Matthew and Luke) suggests that Mark 1:44b, c could be interpreted indepen-dently of vv. 43, 44a. Hence ὕπαγε as a fixed exhortation can be interpreted from the perspective of the substance of the version in Mark 5:34, 10:52, and Matt 8:13: To a person's trusting appeal for God's help in the person of Jesus, Jesus himself responds with a confirmation of faith (and peace, Mark 5:34) and discharges that one (ὕπαγε) into a redeemed future.

This express sending away from Jesus' immediate presence is the reason for the command to be silent in Mark 1:44a. (Jesus never exploits his actions for personal advantage, 10:45a.) The dismissal ὕπαγε, however, does not contain any topos from Hel-lenistic miracle tradition. The only documentation of such a procedure (although not in combination with ὕπαγε), namely, Lucian *Philops.* 16 and Diogenes Laertius viii.67, comes from the 2nd cent. and the 3rd or 4th cent. A.D. and thus cannot be compared with the Gospel material (*contra* Theissen 67f.).

3. Jesus uses ὕπαγε in an exorcism in Matt 8:32, then analogously in Matt 4:10 (against the tempter) and Mark 8:33 (against Peter).

4. The vb. is used unspecifically in Mark 10:21 par.; Matt 5:24; 18:15; Luke 12:58, and elsewhere.

5. On the one hand Mark 14:21a uses ὑπάγω as a euphemism for "die" (J. Gnilka, *Mark* [EKKNT] II ad loc.), and on the other it emphasizes Jesus' active progress toward death (E. Schweizer, *Mark* [Eng. tr., 1970] ad loc.). This latter usage, however, shows a departure from the other sayings concerning the suffering Son of man (8:31a; 9:12b; Luke 17:25; also Mark 9:31a; 14:41c; Luke 24:7).

Whereas other passages christologically or theologically qualify what happens to the Son of man (using the *passivum divinum*), in Mark 14:21a Jesus speaks actively of himself. If one eliminates as being later insertions both the Son of man predicate (C. Colpe, *TDNT* VIII, 446) and the scriptural proof (Dibelius, *Tradition* 184), and if one recognizes with Schenke (203-71) the redactional reworking of Mark 14:18-20 and the pre-Markan character of the cry of woe in v. 21b, c (cf. Luke 17:1f.), then what remains is a simple, unaffected statement (ὕπαγε is neither syntactically nor semantically attached to παραδίδοται in v. 21b, *contra* Schenke 261) of Jesus' conscious progress toward death (cf. Phil 2:6-11, esp. vv. 7f.).

6. John often uses ὑπάγω unspecifically (3:8; 4:16, and elsewhere; on 9:7; 11:44 → 2). In addition there are three rhetorical spheres in which Jesus uses the vb. in a consciously active fashion: a) "I *will go* to him who sent me" (7:33; 16:5a), or "I *go* to the Father" (16:10, 17); b) "I know whence I have come and whither I *am going*" (8:14a; 13:3), or "you do not know . . ." (8:14b); c) "Where I *am going,* you cannot come" (8:21, 22; 13:33), or as a question "Where *are you going?*" (13:36a; 14:5; 16:5b).

Each sphere has been overlaid by specific religio-historical influences: a) by prophetic-apocalyptic notions of rapture (Bühner 421); b) by the idea of the Gnostic path (R. Schnackenburg, *John* II [Eng. tr., 1979] 193); c) by wisdom speculation (the image of departing Wisdom; Leroy 51-74). Yet the aforementioned rhetorical spheres are not consistently structured according to these religio-historical conceptions. In sphere a) there is no emphasis on → κατάβασις, and no apocalyptic culmination takes place—e.g., by the addition of the title "Son of man"; in b) and c) the mode of attainment is missing (e.g., mediated through "knowledge"). Hence the statement about Jesus' conscious progress toward death remains as the basic structure. In formulating this statement, John emphasizes ὑπάγειν as the way of the cross (13:37), with which Jesus himself identifies (14:5f.). Only from this perspective does the goal of Jesus' path disclose itself (v. 4)—i.e., the Father (v. 6)—and the idea of following Jesus (13:36b) and of salvation (14:28; cf. 15:16) arise.

7. The later NT writings use ὑπάγω unspecifically to refer simply to *go* (→ 1).   H. Probst

ὑπακοή, ῆς, ἡ *hypakoē* obedience*
ὑπακούω *hypakouō* obey, be obedient*

1. Occurrences in the NT and meaning — 2. Synoptic Gospels and Acts — 3. Paul — 4. Deutero-Pauline Epistles — 5. Hebrews — 6. 1 Peter

Lit.: R. DEICHGRÄBER, "Gehorsam und Gehorchen in der Verkündigung Jesu," *ZNW* 52 (1961) 119-22. — K. S. FRANK, *RAC* IX, 390-430. — S. C. FREDERICK, *The Theme of Obedience in the First Epistle of Peter* (Diss. Duke University, 1975). — G. FRIEDRICH, "Muß ὑπακοὴ πίστεως Röm 1,5 mit 'Glaubensgehorsam' übersetzt werden?" *ZNW* 72 (1981) 118-23. — G. KITTEL, *TDNT* I, 216-25, esp. 224f. — O. KUSS, "Der Begriff des Gehorsams im NT," *TGl* 27 (1935) 695-702. — W. MUNDLE,

DNTT II, 179f. — L. NIEDER, *LTK* IV, 601f. — SCHNACKENBURG, *Botschaft,* index s.v. Gehorsam. — G. SEGALLA, "L'obbedienza die fede' (Rm 1,5; 16,26) tema della Lettera ai Romani?" *RivB* 36 (1988) 329-42. — C. SNOEK, *De idee der gehoorzaamheid in het NT* (1952). — SPICQ, *Notes* Suppl., 238-45. — A. STÖGER, *SacVb* II, 616-20.

1. Ὑπακοή and ὑπακούω, compounds derived from → ἀκούω, occur in the NT particularly in the Epistles. Only the vb. ὑπακούω is used (7 times) by the authors of the Synoptic Gospels (Mark 1:27; 4:41 par. Matt 8:27/Luke 8:25; Luke 17:6; Acts 6:7; 12:13). The other occurrences are for the most part in Paul: ὑπακοή 11 times, ὑπακούω 5 times (cf. also ὑπακούω in Col 3:20, 22; Eph 6:1, 5; 2 Thess 1:8; 3:14). Particular interest is also shown by Hebrews (ὑπακοή once, ὑπακούω twice) and 1 Peter (ὑπακοή 3 times, ὑπακούω once). Both words (as well as ὑπήκοος) are omitted entirely from John, 1–3 John, and Revelation.

These words are adequately rendered *obedience/obey;* as in English, they derive from "hear" (ἀκούω; Lat. *oboedio [= ob + audire]*). Only Acts 12:13 is probably using ὑπακούω in its literal sense: The woman at the door "listens" to the person seeking entrance, i.e., she is to open the door for him. In the NT, ὑπακοή and ὑπακούω do not refer to an "answering" on the part of God. In tracing the concept of obedience in the NT, one should consider other words (→ ἀκούω, ἐνωτίζομαι, ἐπακούω, πειθαρχέω, and the pass. of πείθω and ὑποτάσσω) as well as various idioms (see Deichgräber 120f.).

2. The Synoptic Gospels emphasize the idea that the "unclean spirits" (Mark 1:27) as well as wind and sea (4:41 par. Matthew/Luke) must obey Jesus. This amounts to subjection to Jesus' commands (ἐπιτάσσω, Mark 1:27; Luke 8:25). Luke 17:6 sees the same connection between command and obedience (differently in Matt 17:20) in the context of πίστις, even if such πίστις is only as large as a mustard seed. Acts 6:7, in a summary, speaks of obedient subjection to πίστις (here: "faith" in the objective sense; see G. Schneider, *Acts* [HTKNT] I, 430 n. 83): Ὑπακούω τῇ πίστει refers to "*subject oneself* to [the Christian] faith" or "come to faith" (cf. Rom 10:16; 2 Thess 1:8: τῷ εὐαγγελίῳ).

3. For Paul, faith (→ πίστις 6) is essentially a matter of obedience, just as lack of faith is understood as disobedience toward God and his message. This messenger of faith wants to move those he addresses with his gospel to "the obedience of faith," i.e., to subjection to the divine message. The act of faith is an act of obedience (Bultmann, *Theology* I, 314), as a comparison of Rom 1:8 with 16:19 makes clear. Paul thus can create the expression ὑπακοὴ πίστεως (1:5; cf. 10:16; 16:26; → πίστις 3.b), indicating thereby the goal of his apostleship (cf. 15:18). Justification

issues from the *obedience* of Christ, which Paul contrasts with the disobedience of the first man (5:19).

For humankind there is, according to Rom 6:16a, b, only the "either-or of slavery under sin or slavery under obedience (of faith), which lead to correspondingly different ends" (U. Wilckens, *Rom* [EKKNT] II, 34). The baptized receive this admonition: "Let not sin therefore reign in your mortal bodies, to make you *obey* their passions" (v. 12). Furthermore, "do you not know that if you yield yourselves to any one as *obedient* slaves, you are slaves of the one whom you *obey*, either of sin, which leads to death, or of *obedience*, which leads to righteousness? But thanks be to God, that you who were once slaves of sin *have become obedient* from the heart to the standard of teaching to which you were committed" (vv. 16f.). Paul can speak of a church's *obedience* when he praises their conduct (2 Cor 7:15; Phil 2:12; cf. Phlm 21). Referring to his adversaries, Paul asserts that he will "take every plot captive to *obey* Christ, being ready to punish every disobedience, when your *obedience* is complete" (2 Cor 10:5, 6).

4. With the phrase ὑπακούω τῷ εὐαγγελίῳ 2 Thess 1:8 is drawing from Pauline expressions (Rom 10:16), though it does add the gen. "of our Lord Jesus." 2 Thess 3:14 proscribes those who "refuse to *obey* what we say in this letter," a reference to the entire contents of this pseudepigraphic Pauline Epistle (cf. W. Trilling, *2 Thess* [EKKNT] 154).

Within the context of household codes Col 3:20 and Eph 6:1 admonish children to obey their parents (ὑπακούετε). Col 3:22 par. Eph 6:5 directs the same admonition to slaves regarding their masters. 1 Pet 3:6 can also be compared here; Sarah's obedience toward Abraham is presented as a model for wives (→ 6).

5. Heb 5:8f. makes a direct connection between Christ's obedience and that of Christians and their eternal σωτηρία: "Although he was a Son, he learned *obedience* through what he suffered, and being made perfect he became the source of eternal salvation to all who *obey* him." At the beginning of the section that speaks of Abraham, the father of faith (11:8-16), we read that in faith (πίστει) *he obeyed* God's command at his calling and set out on his journey (v. 8): "Faith responds, and precisely in so doing shows itself to be obedience" (O. Michel, *Heb* [KEK] 392).

6. 1 Peter concludes its admonitions to wives (3:1-6) with a reference to Sarah, who according to v. 6 obediently subordinated herself to her husband, for she called him her lord (Gen 18:12). The beginning of the letter (1:2) offers a triadic summary of Christian election: "destined by God the Father and sanctified by the Spirit for *obedience* and for sprinkling with Christ's blood" (cf.

L. Goppelt, *1 Pet* [KEK] 83-87). This election is grounded in the Father's resolution, mediated by the Spirit, and realized by obedience and by belonging to Christ. The expression "children of *obedience*" (1:14) is a Hebraism that refers here to the baptized (cf. "sons of disobedience," Eph 2:2). The addressees have purified their souls "by *obedience* to the truth" (ὑπακοὴ τῆς ἀληθείας; 1 Pet 1:22). What is meant here is the process of coming to faith (cf. 1:21; further Acts 15:9; Rom 1:5; 10:16). On the concept of obedience in 1 Peter see (besides Frederick) N. Brox, *1 Pet* [EKKNT] 260 (index s.v. Gehorsam).

G. Schneider

ὑπακούω *hypakouō* obey, be obedient
→ ὑπακοή.

ὕπανδρος, 2 *hypandros* subordinated to a man, married*

Rom 7:2, referring to a *married* woman (cf. Polybius x.26.3; Num 5:20, 29, and elsewhere in the LXX).

ὑπαντάω *hypantaō* go toward, encounter, meet*

In a neutral sense: Mark 5:2 par. Matt 8:28/Luke 8:27; Matt 28:9; John 4:51; 11:20, 30; 12:18; Acts 16:16; in a hostile sense: Luke 14:31. O. Michel, *TDNT* III, 625f.; W. Mundle, *DNTT* I, 324f.

ὑπάντησις, εως, ἡ *hypantēsis* meeting, encounter*

The NT uses this word only in the phrase εἰς ὑπάντησιν, "[in order] to meet/encounter": with dat. in Matt 8:34 and John 12:13; with gen. in Matt 25:1. For bibliography → ὑπαντάω.

ὕπαρξις, εως, ἡ *hyparxis* property, goods*

Acts 2:45, in a summary: The believers "sold their possessions (κτήματα) and *goods* (ὑπάρξεις)" and distributed the profits among the needy; Heb 10:34: "You joyfully accepted the plundering of your *property*." F. Selter, *DNTT* II, 845-47.

ὑπάρχω *hyparchō* be present; have, possess

1. Occurrences in the NT — 2. Synoptics and Acts — 3. Epistles and later writings

Lit.: H.-J. DEGENHARDT, *Lukas, Evangelist der Armen* (1965) 208-22. — W. PESCH, "Zur Exegese von Mt 6,19-21 und Lk 12,33-34," *Bib* 41 (1960) 356-78. — J. ROLOFF, *Acts* (NTD, 1981) 89-91. — G. SCHNEIDER, *Acts* (HTKNT, 1980) 290-95. — *idem, Luke* (ÖTK, 1977) 342-45. — A. WEISER, *Acts* (ÖTK, 1981) 134-38. — For further bibliography see Schneider, *Acts*.

1. This vb. occurs 60 times in the NT: 3 times in

Matthew, 15 in Luke, and 25 in Acts; Paul uses it once in Romans, 5 times in 1 Corinthians, twice each in 2 Corinthians, Galatians, and Philippians; it is also used in Heb 10:34, Jas 2:15, and 3 times in 2 Peter.

2. Among the Synoptics Luke's use is of particular interest. Ὑπάρχω occurs 6 times in the Gospel and 20 times in Acts in unspecific references for *have* or *be*. It is used of *possess* a total of 14 times in Luke, usually as a subst. partc. Only Luke 12:44 is taken from Q, while Luke 16:1 and Acts 7:55a come from L. Otherwise Luke uses ὑπάρχω independently (Luke 8:3; 11:21; 12:33; 14:33; 16:14; 19:8; Acts 4:32, 34). There the parables, told from the perspective of the kingdom of God, which has appeared in Jesus, address the impossibility of protecting great possessions in the long run (Luke 11:21) and both just (12:44) and smart (16:1) distribution of possessions (parable material in Matt 24:47 [Q]; 25:14 speaks similarly of attentiveness and clever initiative regarding one's *possessions* [τὰ ὑπάρχοντα]).

The admonitions warn against an accumulation of luxury, since otherwise one might easily define one's life from the perspective of such ὑπάρχοντα (Luke 12:15). This can be avoided by the sale and distribution of one's possessions as a gift of solidarity with the poor (v. 33a), for only this yields treasure that cannot be lost (v. 33b). Only total freedom over against "all your *possessions*" (πᾶσιν τοῖς ἑαυτοῦ ὑπάρχουσιν) makes discipleship possible (14:33). In addition, several exemplary stories demonstrate voluntary distribution of possessions both for the sake of fellowship with Jesus and for the sake of the early Church itself (Luke 8:3; 19:8; Acts 4:32, 34, 37).

These examples show how Luke wanted both such criticism of possessions and Jesus' command for renunciation on the other to be understood (cf. Luke 6:24; 16:19-31; Mark 10:23ff.; see also the analogous statements in Matt 19:21; 24:47 [Q]; 25:14). It was not to be the beginning of a complex theory of economics, but rather pointed to liberation from all fixation on objects (Luke 12:15). Luke's ethics of possession consists in sacrifice without falsity or resentment (Acts 5:4) whenever the life of the Church requires it. Such sacrifice (initial problems emerge in vv. 7, 11) essentially eliminates the function of ὑπάρχοντα. It is no longer these ὑπάρχοντα that contribute to the structuring or restructuring of the Church, but rather the Spirit alive in the Church (4:33). The last specific use of ὑπάρχω in Acts (7:55) refers significantly to Stephen's possession of the Holy Spirit.

3. Paul relativizes even complete renunciation of possessions, teaching that without love within the bodily, Spirit-induced fellowship of Christ (1 Cor 12), the most extreme radicality, even in self-renunciation, remains senseless (13:3). The author of Heb 10:34 presents as an example of Christian patience—doubtless gained from the Church's own experience—the joyful bearing of the plundering of τῶν ὑπαρχόντων, "since you knew that you yourselves had a better possession (ὕπαρξιν) and an abiding one." The remaining uses in Paul and in the later writings exhibit a less specific meaning.   H. Probst

ὑπείκω *hypeikō* submit*

Heb 13:17: "Obey your leaders and *submit* to them."

ὑπεναντίος, 3 *hypenantios* opposed, hostile*

Col 2:14 (with dat.) refers to the record that stood *against* us (ὃ ἦν ὑπεναντίον ἡμῖν); Heb 10:27 (subst.): "God's *adversaries/opponents.*"

ὑπέρ *hyper* with gen.: for, for the sake of, in place of; with acc.: above, more than; as adv.: yet more

1. Occurrences and meaning — 2. With gen. in soteriological formulaic language — 3. With acc.

Lit.: On preps. in general → ἀνά. — G. BRATCHER, " 'The Name' in Prepositional Phrases in the NT," *BT* 14 (1963) 72-80. — G. DELLING, "Die Entfaltung des 'Deus pro nobis' in Röm 8:31-39," *SNTU* 4 (1979) 76-96. — G. FRIEDRICH, *Die Verkündigung des Todes Jesu im NT* (idem, *Biblisch-theologische Studien* 6, 1982). — GOPPELT, *Theology* II, 92-98. — O. HOFIUS, "Τὸ σῶμα τὸ ὑπὲρ ὑμῶν 1 Kor 11,24," *ZNW* 80 (1989) 80-88. — J. JEREMIAS, *Abba* (1966) 191-216. — W. KRAMER, *Christ, Lord, Son of God* (1966) 115-19. — E. LOHSE, *Märtyrer und Gottesknecht* (FRLANT 64, [2]1963). — H. PATSCH, *Abendmahl und historischer Jesus* (1972), esp. 158-70. — W. POPKES, *Christus Traditus* (ATANT 49, 1967) 193-203. — H. RIESENFELD, *TDNT* VIII, 507-16. — J. ROLOFF, "Anfänge der soteriologischen Deutung des Todes Jesu," *NTS* 19 (1972/73) 38-64. — E. RUCKSTUHL, "Neue und alte Überlegungen zu den Abendmahlsworten Jesu," *SNTU* 5 (1980) 79-106. — K. WENGST, *Christologische Formeln und Lieder des Urchristentums* (SNT 7, [2]1973) 55-104. — U. WILCKENS, *Rom* (EKKNT) I (1978) 233-43. — For further bibliography see *TWNT* X, 1287.

1. Of the 150 occurrences, 130 involve ὑπέρ with gen. *for, in place of,* distributed in a striking manner throughout the NT. The Synoptics repress this usage (Matthew uses it only in 5:44, though cf. Luke 6:28, and all further parallels have been expunged; Mark 9:40 par. Luke 9:50 use it in a gnomic formulation, otherwise only in Mark 14:24 par. Luke 22:19f. in the tradition of the eucharist—as in 1 Cor 11:24, cf. John 6:51), whereas in John (in sacrifice or death formulas) and Acts (in name formulas) a fixed theological language emerges that dominates esp. in Paul (88 occurrences) and Hebrews (10 occurrences). Usage becomes increasingly formulaic and limited to soteriological contexts. Mss. (e.g., Luke 6:28; John 1:30) and parallels (e.g., Mark 14:24 par. Matt 26:28; Matt 5:44 par. Luke 6:28) sometimes exchange it

with περί, rarely with ἀντί (cf. 1 Tim 2:6 with Mark 10:45 par. Matt 20:28), probably without any shift in meaning. The opposite of ὑπέρ is κατά (Mark 9:40 par. Luke 9:50; Rom 8:31).

The prep. with acc. *above, more than* (19 occurrences) is avoided by Mark and the Johannine writings, and the few occurrences are distributed without any noticeable pattern. This prep. recedes outside the NT as well (Moulton/Milligan s.v.).

2 Cor 11:23 uses ὑπέρ as an adv.: ὑπὲρ ἐγώ, "I *even more* [than these]."

2. The rhetorical sphere of what is known as the ὑπέρ formula (Jeremias) is theologically significant in a soteriological context. The original *Sitz im Leben* of this tradition is the liturgy of the eucharist, in which the atoning significance of Jesus' death is stated and proclaimed to the Church. The phrase ὑπὲρ πολλῶν, "*for* many," spoken over the cup (Mark 14:24; cf. Matt 26:18) —this Semitism can probably be traced back to Heb. $b^e ad$ $rabbîm$ and Aram. $ḥ^a lāp$ (or $'al$) $sagî̂ în$—is interpreted by both Luke (22:19, 20) and Paul (1 Cor 11:24) in reference to the Church: "*for* us"; Matthew specifies "for the forgiveness of sins" (26:28). John 6:51 also preserves the universal sense: "*for* the life of the world [of human beings]." It is disputed just where the ὑπέρ phrase was originally used (over the cup and/or over the bread) and whether it represents a secondary explication of the words of interpretation. Much suggests that this (cf. also Mark 10:45) is the historical source of early Christian soteriology.

Extracted from the cultic liturgy, this universal assertion recurs with Hellenized language in christological formulas that speak of Jesus' atoning death ὑπὲρ πάντων (2 Cor 5:14f.; cf. 1 Tim 2:6; ὑπὲρ παντός, Heb 2:9), namely, "*for* sinners" (Rom 5:6; cf. 1 Pet 3:18), "*for* the people" (John 11:50-52; 18:14). In several instances the formula referring to Jesus' death is developed from the perspective of the Church: "*for* us" (Rom 5:8; 1 Thess 5:10) or "*for* our sins" (1 Cor 15:3), for the Christian brother (Rom 14:15), "*for* you" (1 Pet 2:21). The same variation recurs in the sacrificial formula "*for* all" (1 Tim 2:6), "*for* us" (Titus 2:14; Eph 5:2; 1 John 3:16), "*for* our sins" (Gal 1:14), for the Church (Eph 5:25). "*For* us all" (Rom 8:32) represents a mixed form.

Paul's own theological reflection refers the sacrificial formula to himself as well: "*for* me" (Gal 2:20). In his christological argumentation he made extensive use of the kerygmatic formulaic material passed down to him, giving it a profound interpretation. Most important it serves as the grounding of his doctrine of justification (Rom 5:6-8; 8:31f., 34; 2 Cor 5:21; Gal 3:13, and elsewhere) and as a means of deepening his own theology of the cross (1 Cor 1:13). Pauline soteriology, which heavily

colors his christology, is initially quite conservative and traditional and confronts the early Christian reader with familiar material before moving into his doctrine of justification or his theology of the cross. Paul's manner of theological explication also takes its existential motivation from his continual experience of the eucharist (Wilckens 242).

Paul's further use of this prep. cannot be systematically traced in terms of tradition history. For example, the idea of representative baptism on behalf of the dead does not exhibit any connection with the previous formulas (1 Cor 15:29). See also 2 Cor 5:20; Phil 2:13, and many other instances as well.

The letter to the Hebrews also uses the formulaic phrase when, within the high-priestly typology, it emphasizes that the high priest continually had to renew the temple sacrifice for human sins (5:1ff.; 7:27a; 9:7), whereas the one-time sacrifice of the high priest Christ expiates sins once and for all (10:12; 7:25, 27b), "*on our behalf*" (6:20; 9:24).

In John Jesus speaks in a formulation unique to him of giving up his life (→ ψυχή 5), both in a parable ("*for* the sheep," 10:11, 15) and in a speech to the disciples ("*for* his friends," 15:13). This sacrifice is limited to Jesus himself (13:37f.). In the parenesis Jesus' example is the basis for the corresponding obligation Christians have toward one another (1 John 3:16).

The typically biblical phrase "*for* the name" (Acts 5:41; 9:16; 15:26; 21:13) also occurs in Paul in an older formula-tradition (Rom 1:5) and in 3 John 7. Whereas OT rabbinic thinking refers to God in this phrase (cf. even *Did.* 10:2), the NT always refers, even if no other specification is made, to Jesus. The name is a metonym for the person (→ ὄνομα 4).

3. The prep. with acc. always expresses an intensification. It occurs (as a Septuagintism) after the comparative (Luke 16:8; Heb 4:12), as a substitute for the comparative (Matt 10:37 bis: "*more than* me"; Gal 1:14: "*more than* those my own age"; in context with a vb: 1 Cor 4:6a; 10:13; Phlm 21), or for the superlative (Eph 1:22: Christ is the "head *over* all things [ὑπὲρ πάντα] for the Church," i.e., "the head surpassing everything"; Phil 2:9: "the highest name"; cf. Eph 3:20). The sense is often *more exalted/superior* (Matt 10:24 bis par. Luke 6:40 referring to the relationship between teacher and disciple; cf. Phlm 16).   H. Patsch

ὑπεραίρομαι *hyperairomai* be overbearing*

Twice 2 Cor 12:7 uses ἵνα μὴ ὑπεραίρωμαι, "so that I do not *become overbearing*." 2 Thess 2:4 speaks of the "man of lawlessness" (v. 3) "who opposes (ἀντικείμενος) and *exalts himself* (ὑπεραιρόμενος) above everything called God or every object of worship."

ὑπέρακμος, 2 *hyperakmos* overripe*

1 Cor 7:36 refers either to a virgin, in the sense of *overripe/past her prime*, or to a man pledged to her, in the sense of *overly strong* ("if [his passions toward her are] *too strong*"). Cf. H. Conzelmann, *1 Cor* (Hermeneia) ad loc.

ὑπεράνω *hyperanō* above, high above*

Ὑπεράνω is used in a local sense in Eph 4:10 and Heb 9:5 as an improper prep. with gen. In Eph 1:21 the phrase ὑπεράνω πάσης ἀρχῆς καὶ ἐξουσίας refers to the superior status of the exalted Christ.

ὑπεραυξάνω *hyperauxanō* increase abundantly → αὐξάνω 3.

ὑπερβαίνω *hyperbainō* transgress; allow oneself to infringe*

1 Thess 4:6, in parenesis: "that no one *transgress* [against his rights] and deceive his brother in business." J. Schneider, *TDNT* V, 743f.; W. Günther, *DNTT* III, 583f.

ὑπερβαλλόντως *hyperballontōs* exceedingly, to a much greater degree*

2 Cor 11:23, in a catalog of sufferings: ἐν πληγαῖς ὑπερβαλλόντως, "with *far more* beatings." G. Delling, *TDNT* VIII, 520-22.

ὑπερβάλλω *hyperballō* exceed, surpass*

Only the partc. occurs in the NT, modifying various intangibles: ἡ ὑπερβάλλουσα δόξα, "the *surpassing* splendor" (2 Cor 3:10); God's χάρις (9:14); Christ's ἀγάπη (Eph 3:19); τὸ ὑπερβάλλον μέγεθος, "the *immeasurable* greatness" (1:19); and πλοῦτος, "wealth" (2:7). G. Delling, *TDNT* VIII, 520-22.

ὑπερβολή, ῆς, ἡ *hyperbolē* excess*

In the NT ὑπερβολή occurs 8 times in the Pauline Epistles. Besides καθ' ὑπερβολήν, "beyond measure, excessively" (Rom 7:13; 1 Cor 12:31; 2 Cor 1:8; 4:17; Gal 1:13), Paul also uses the combinations ὑπερβολὴ τῆς δυνάμεως, "*excess* of power/*extraordinary* power" (2 Cor 4:7); εἰς ὑπερβολήν, "immeasurable" (v. 17); ὑπερβολὴ τῶν ἀποκαλύψεων, "*abundance* of revelations/*extraordinary* revelations" (12:7). G. Delling, *TDNT* VIII, 520-22.

ὑπερεῖδον *hypereidon* overlook; disdain 2nd aor. of → ὑπεροράω.

ὑπερέκεινα *hyperekeina* beyond*

2 Cor 10:16: τὰ ὑπερέκεινα ὑμῶν (*sc.* μέρη), "the regions that lie *beyond* you." Cf. BDF §184.

ὑπερεκπερισσοῦ *hyperekperissou* quite beyond all measure (adv.)*

1 Thess 3:10: "praying *earnestly*"; 5:13: "esteem them *very highly* in love (ἡγεῖσθαι αὐτοὺς ὑπερεκπερισσοῦ ἐν ἀγάπῃ)"; Eph 3:20, with gen. of comparison: "*far more abundantly* than we ask (ὧν αἰτούμεθα)." F. Hauck, *TDNT* VI, 61f. → περισσεύω (1).

ὑπερεκπερισσῶς *hyperekperissōs* quite beyond all measure (adv.)
V.l. in Mark 7:37 D in place of ὑπερπερισσῶς and in 1 Thess 5:13 B D* al in place of ὑπερεκπερισσοῦ. F. Hauck, *TDNT* VI, 61f.

ὑπερεκτείνω *hyperekteinō* stretch out beyond*

2 Cor 10:14: "*We were* not *stretching out beyond* [i.e., we were not overextending ourselves]." E. Fuchs, *TDNT* II, 465.

ὑπερεκχύννομαι *hyperekchynnomai* (pass.) overflow*

Luke 6:38 (differently in Matthew): "a good measure, pressed down, shaken together, *running over.*"

ὑπερεντυγχάνω *hyperentynchanō* intercede*

Rom 8:26: The πνεῦμα "*intercedes* (Koine: ὑπὲρ ἡμῶν) with unspeakable sighs." O. Bauernfeind, *TDNT* VIII, 243f.

ὑπερέχω *hyperechō* project over; have power over; surpass*

In the NT ὑπερέχω appears only as a partc. and is used only fig. Of its 5 occurrences, 4 are in Paul. In Rom 13:1 and 1 Pet 2:13 this vb. refers to ἐξουσίαι or to βασιλεύς, and thus to "authorities." In Phil 2:3 (with gen. obj.) and 4:7 (with acc.) the partc. is used in the general sense *being superior to/surpassing* (something else). In Phil 3:8 the subst. τὸ ὑπερέχον τῆς γνώσεως refers to "the *unsurpassable* knowledge." G. Delling, *TDNT* VIII, 523f.

ὑπερηφανία, ας, ἡ *hyperēphania* arrogance, pride*

Mark 7:22, in a catalog of vices. G. Bertram, *TDNT* VIII, 525-29; E. Gütig and C. Brown, *DNTT* III, 28-32.

ὑπερήφανος, 2 *hyperēphanos* arrogant, proud*

Luke 1:51, used subst.: "He has scattered *those who show themselves proud* in the thinking of their hearts." The opposite is ταπεινός (Jas 4:6; 1 Pet 5:5). Like → ὑπερηφανία, this adj. appears in catalogs of vices (Rom 1:30; 2 Tim 3:2). P. L. Schoonheim, "Der alttestamentliche Boden der Vokabel ὑπερήφανος Lukas I 51," *NovT* 8 (1966) 235-46; G. Bertram, *TDNT* VIII, 525-29; E. Gütig and C. Brown, *DNTT* III, 28-32.

ὑπερλίαν *hyperlian* exceedingly*

Used as an adj. in the expression οἱ ὑπερλίαν ἀπόστολοι, "the *superlative* apostles" (2 Cor 11:5; 12:11), with which Paul describes his Corinthian adversaries; cf. R. Bultmann, *2 Cor* (Eng. tr., 1985) 203.

ὑπερνικάω *hypernikaō* vanquish, overcome*

Rom 8:37: "Yet in all this *we overcome* [we overcome all this] through him who loved us." O. Bauernfeind, *TDNT* IV, 945.

ὑπέρογκος, 2 *hyperonkos* swollen; arrogant, bombastic*

2 Pet 2:18: *bombastic* words; cf. also Jude 16 (ὑπέρογκα with vb. of speaking).

ὑπεροράω *hyperoraō* overlook; disdain*

Acts 17:30: "The times of ignorance God *overlooked*." Spicq, *Notes* II, 899f.

ὑπεροχή, ῆς, ἡ *hyperochē* superiority, advantage, superior position*

1 Cor 2:1: "I did not come with *superiority* (καθ' ὑπεροχήν with gen.) of word or wisdom"; 1 Tim 2:2: οἱ ἐν ὑπεροχῇ ὄντες, "those who are in *high positions*." G. Delling, *TDNT* VIII, 523f.

ὑπερπερισσεύω *hyperperisseuō* (cause to) overflow*

Rom 5:20, using the vb. intrans.: "Grace *was present in even greater abundance*"; 2 Cor 7:4, using it trans. in the pass.: "I *overflow* with joy." F. Hauck, *TDNT* VI, 58-61; → περισσεύω (1).

ὑπερπερισσῶς *hyperperissōs* beyond all measure (adv.)*

Mark 7:37: "And they were astonished *beyond all measure*" (at Jesus' miraculous healing). Cf. → περισσεύω (1).

ὑπερπλεονάζω *hyperpleonazō* be present in great number*

In 1 Tim 1:14 "Paul" says about himself: "The grace of our Lord *abounded* for me" (cf. 1 Cor 15:10). G. Delling *TDNT* VI, 263-66; W. Bauder and D. Müller, *DNTT* II, 130f.

ὑπερυψόω *hyperypsoō* raise to the loftiest height*

Phil 2:9: God *raised* [RSV *exalted*] Christ Jesus, humbled on the cross unto death (v. 8), *to the loftiest height* (cf. Ps 96:9 LXX). G. Bertram, *TDNT* VIII, 606-12.

ὑπερφρονέω *hyperphroneō* esteem oneself too highly*

Rom 12:3, in a wordplay with φρονέω: I say to everyone among you "not to *think of yourself more highly* (ὑπερφρονεῖν) than you ought to think (φρονεῖν), but rather to reflect (φρονεῖν) on being reasonable (σωφρονεῖν)."

ὑπερῷον, ου, τό *hyperōon* upper room, upstairs*

This noun is formed from ὑπερῷος, "above, situated up above" (originally *sc.* οἴκημα). Ὑπερῷον occurs in the NT only in Acts 1:13; 9:37, 39; 20:8.

ὑπέχω *hypechō* endure, suffer*

Ὑπέχω occurs in Jude 7 with the obj. πυρὸς αἰωνίου δίκην, "*suffer* the punishment of eternal fire."

ὑπήκοος, 2 *hypēkoos* obedient*

Ὑπήκοος γενέσθαι occurs in Acts 7:29 (as in Josephus *Ant.* ii.48) referring to how the Israelites refused to obey Moses. In 2 Cor 2:9 Paul writes "so that I might test you and know whether you are *obedient* in everything (εἰς πάντα)." Phil 2:8 refers to Christ Jesus: "He humbled himself and became *obedient* unto death." G. Kittel, *TDNT* I, 224; W. Mundle, *DNTT* II, 179f.

ὑπηρετέω *hypēreteō* serve, assist*

This vb. occurs in the NT only in Acts (cf. → ὑπηρέτης): 13:36 refers to David's service before God, 20:34 to Paul's manual labor to support himself and his companions, and 24:23 to Paul's ἴδιοι (his fellow Christians), who were permitted to *assist* him during his imprisonment in Caesarea. K. H. Rengstorf, *TDNT* VIII, 530-44.

ὑπηρέτης, ου, ὁ *hypēretēs* assistant, servant*

1. Occurrences in the NT and meaning — 2. Literal sense (pl.) — 3. "Servant (of the word)"

Lit.: A. FEUILLET, " 'Témoins oculaires et Serviteurs de la Parole' (Lc I 2b)," *NovT* 15 (1973) 241-59, esp. 242-46. — K. H. RENGSTORF, *TDNT* VIII, 530-44. — L. J. D. RICHARDSON, "ΥΠΗΡΕΤΗΣ," *Classical Quarterly* 37 (1943) 55-61. — SPICQ, *Notes* II, 901-6. — TRENCH, *Synonyms* 33f.

1. Ὑπηρέτης occurs 20 times in the NT, most often in John (9 times) and the Lukan work (twice in Luke, 4 times in Acts; the vb. → ὑπηρετέω also occurs 3 times in Acts). The remaining occurrences are distributed in Mark 14:54 par. Matt 26:58; Mark 14:65; Matt 5:25; 1 Cor 4:1.

Ὑπηρέτης derives from ὑπό and ἐρέτης ("rower") and thus according to its etymology means something like "subrower" (*EWG* 91). The NT always uses it in the more general sense of *assistant* or *servant* (of someone in a higher position), e.g., an assistant accompanying a superior (BAGD s.v.). Thus John Mark is Barnabas and Paul's ὑπηρέτης (Acts 13:5); Silas's role should probably be understood in the same way (15:40). Matt 5:25 speaks of the judge's ὑπηρέτης (*bailiff*) (cf. Diodorus Siculus xvii.30.4), and Luke 4:20 of the ὑπηρέτης at the synagogue worship service (the *attendant* receives the lectionary after the reading; see I. Elbogen, *Der jüdische Gottesdienst in seiner geschichtlichen Entwicklung* [³1931] 485-87). The sg. ὑπηρέτης occurs otherwise only in Acts 26:16 (with μάρτυς) in the fig. sense (referring to Paul, → 3); cf. also John 18:22: "one of the *attendants* of the high priest."

2. The overwhelming majority of occurrences use the pl. (οἱ) ὑπηρέται absolutely, with the context making clear the specific nature of the service rendered or of the relationship with the superior: Peter sits with the *attendants* in the courtyard of the high priest (Mark 14:54 par. Matt 26:58); the *servants* in the Sanhedrin strike Jesus (Mark 14:65); high priests and Pharisees send *servants* to seize Jesus (John 7:32, 45, 46). This last reference is probably to servants of the Sanhedrin as in 18:3. There we read that the high council put (armed) assistants at Judas's disposal; at Jesus' arrest they are called "the ὑπηρέται of the Jews" (v. 12). These *servants* (together with "slaves") make a charcoal fire in the courtyard of the high priest (v. 18; cf. Mark 14:54; variously *guards, officers*); one of the *officers* strikes Jesus at the interrogation before Annas (John 18:22; cf. Mark 14:65). John 19:6 reports the cry of the high priests and *officers* demanding Jesus' crucifixion. In this context it is significant that before Pilate (18:36) Jesus speaks of his own *servants* (οἱ ὑπηρέται οἱ ἐμοί), who would fight for him if his kingdom were "of this world." The Johannine Jesus thus contrasts his own (nonviolent) "servants" with the

"servants of the Jews" (v. 12). Acts speaks in the pl. of the *officers* of the Sanhedrin who were to bring forward the apostles (5:22, 26). Only Luke 1:2 and 1 Cor 4:1 use pl. ὑπηρέται metaphorically and variously accompanied by a gen. modifier (→ 3).

3. In 1 Cor 4:1 Paul calls Christian proclaimers "*servants* of Christ and stewards of the mysteries of God." In the context of the preceding verses (3:22f.), 4:1 does not apply to Paul alone. The introductory formulation "one should regard us as (ὡς) . . ." shows that Paul is making a comparison with ("secular") offices for which the *entrusted* task, the commission, stands in the foreground: What is important is the steward's (and servant's) trustworthiness (4:2). Acts 26:16 refers with fixed terminology to Paul's own calling to be "a *servant* and witness" of Christ.

This statement in Acts should be read in the light of Luke 1:2, where we read that the (twelve) apostles were "eyewitnesses from the beginning" and later (after Easter) became "*servants* of the word [i.e., of the word of proclamation]." Having accompanied Jesus during his ministry (cf. Acts 1:21f.), they were able to proclaim his word, and that proclamation was tied to that which they had experienced as witnesses. According to Acts 26:16 Paul, too, was called to be "a *servant* and witness"—though called in a different way: by the resurrected Lord. His witness, too, was authorized by an encounter with Christ and at the same time bound to that encounter. The apostles were "*servants* of the word." They stood *under* its authority; according to Luke this holds true in an analogous sense for Paul.

                                        G. Schneider

ὕπνος, ου, ὁ *hypnos* sleep (noun)*
ἀγρυπνέω *agrypneō* be awake; keep watch*
ἀγρυπνία, ας, ἡ *agrypnia* wakefulness*

1. The Gospels and Acts use ὕπνος in the literal sense. Matt 1:24 refers to Joseph, who woke ἀπὸ τοῦ ὕπνου. Luke 9:32 (different in Mark) speaks of Peter and his companions, who were overcome by *sleep*. In John 11:11-13 Jesus refers to the sleep of death (→ κοιμάομαι 3), though the disciples understand ὕπνος (v. 13) literally. Acts 20:9a, b speaks of Eutychus, who fell asleep and fell to his death from the upper story (having fallen into "a deep *sleep*," as in Sir 22:9 LXX; 3 Macc 5:12). Rom 13:11 uses ὕπνος fig.: It is time "for you to raise yourselves/wake *from sleep*," a reference to a turning away from "works of darkness" (v. 12, cf. v. 13). H. Balz, *TDNT* VIII, 545-56; L. Coenen, *DNTT* I, 441-43.

2. The opposite of ὕπνος is ἀγρυπνία, etymologically derived perhaps from ἀγρός and ὕπνος (referring to sleeping in an open field; cf. *EWG* 3; see also Luke 2:8: ἀγραυλέω). This noun occurs in the NT only in Paul

(2 Cor 6:5; 11:27 [pl., used in the literal sense]). Fig. usage (cf. → 1) of **ἀγρυπνέω** *(be alert, be watchful)* occurs in the repeated parenesis on watchfulness: Mark 13:33 (cf. Matt 25:13 → γρηγορέω); Luke 21:36 (*"watch at all times"*); Eph 6:18 (ἀγρυπνοῦντες ἐν πάσῃ προσκαρτερήσει, *"alert* in all perseverance"). Of ecclesiastical leaders Heb 13:17 says (metaphorically): "They *are keeping watch* over your souls/your lives." A. Oepke, *TDNT* II, 338f.

ὑπό *hypo* with gen.: by, under, by means of; with acc.: under, beneath, to

1. Occurrences and usage in the NT — 2. With gen. — 3. With acc. — a) Local meaning — b) Temporal meaning

Lit.: On preps. in general → ἀνά. — BAGD s.v. — BDF §§210; 232. — K. DIETRICH, "Die präpositionalen Präfixe in der griechischen Sprachentwicklung," *Indogermanische Forschungen* 24 (1909) 87-158. — KÜHNER, *Grammatik* II/1, 521-26. — LSJ s.v. — MAYSER, *Grammatik* II/2, 509-15. — RADERMACHER, *Grammatik* 114-19. — P. F. REGARD, *Contributions à l'étude des prépositions dans la langue du NT* (1919) 620-51. — SCHWYZER, *Grammatik* II, 522-33.

1. Occurring 220 times in the NT, ὑπό is eleventh in frequency among NT preps. (Morgenthaler [*Statistik* 160] counts only 217 occurrences, since he misses 1 in Luke and 2 in Romans; for correction cf. the concordances.) Ὑπό is distributed in all NT writings except Titus and Philemon and occurs particularly often in the Gospels and Acts. It appears with 29 different vbs. as part of a compound and is also used in connection with double preps. (Morgenthaler 162).

In contrast to classical Greek, in which—though less frequently— ὑπό is also used with dat. (cf. BDF §187), in biblical Greek (except in Job 12:5 v.l.) it is used only with gen. and acc. Although ὑπό does not replace other preps., in the case of the pass. agent or with vbs. with a pass. sense it is itself often replaced by ἀπό (Matt 11:19 par. Luke 5:35; Matt 16:21 par. Luke 9:22, but cf. Mark 8:31; 2 Cor 7:13; Jas 5:4; Rev 12:6, and elsewhere; in contrast cf. classical usage, e.g., Herodotus viii.94; Xenophon *HG* vi.5.43, and → ἀπό 4.b.6). Also, classical ὑπό is occasionally replaced by ἀπό in the case of causation, e.g., Luke 22:45 ("sleeping because of sorrow"). In pass. constructions in the NT the expected ὑπό with gen. is often replaced by διά with gen. or by παρά.

2. In biblical and early Christian literature ὑπό with gen. does not appear with a local meaning. This case is used here only in a metaphorical and fig. sense. First of all, in pass. constructions ὑπό with gen. of person or thing refers to the *agent* or *cause (by/as a result of)*.

a) With gen. of person: Matt 1:22: "to fulfill . . . *by* the Lord through the prophets" (cf. Gen 45:27; Josephus *Ant.* viii.223); John 14:21: "loved *by* my father"; 1 Cor 1:11: "it was reported to me . . . *by* Chloe's people"; Phil 3:12: "possessed *by* Christ," and elsewhere.

b) With gen. of thing *(as a result of/by means of):* Matt 8:24: "swamped *by* the waves" (cf. Xenophon *An.* i.5.5); Luke 7:24: "a reed shaken *by* the wind" (Appian *BC* iv.28.120; cf. Isa 7:2; Josephus *Ant.* iv.51); Acts 27:41: "*under [the influence of, by]* the force of the waves"; Rom 3:21: "attested *by [through]* the law"; 2 Cor 5:4: "so that what is mortal may be swallowed up *by* life." Ὑπό has the same sense in Rom 12:21; 1 Cor 10:29; Col 2:18; 2 Pet 2:17; Jude 12; Rev 6:13.

c) Ὑπό can also be used in act. sentences to designate the *agent:* Rev 6:8: ἀποκτεῖναι . . . ὑπὸ τῶν θηρίων, "power . . . to kill . . . *by* wild beasts" (cf. *Herm. Sim.* ix.1.2). Here the prep. with gen. indicates who carries out the intention of the vb.

d) The prep. is also used with vbs. or expressions that imply a pass. sense, and in this case the agent is introduced with ὑπό just as with genuine pass. Occasionally the prep. can approximate instrumental meaning. Matt 17:12: πάσχειν ὑπ' αὐτῶν, the Son of man will have to "suffer *through* them." It is used together with πάσχω elsewhere in the NT as well: Mark 5:26 and 1 Thess 2:14; 2 Cor 11:24: (πληγὰς) ὑπὸ Ἰουδαίων . . . λαμβάνω, "receive (lashes) *at the hands of* the Jews"; Heb 12:3: ὑπομένω ὑπὸ τῶν ἁμαρτωλῶν . . . ἀντιλογίαν, "suffer hostility *from* sinners." The construction γίνομαι ὑπό τινος indicates the source or origin of something, for which the translation *by* or *from* is usually appropriate (Luke 13:17; 23:8; Acts 20:3; 26:6; but Eph 5:12: "that which happens *through* them in secret").

e) In one instance in the NT ὑπό appears with a noun in attributive position: ἡ ἐπιτιμία αὕτη ἡ ὑπὸ τῶν πλειόνων, "this punishment *by/from* the majority [of the church]" (2 Cor 2:6; cf. Esth 1:20).

3. With acc.:

a) Local ὑπό answers the question "whither?": *under* or *beneath* (indicating the goal of the movement), in Matt 8:8 par. Luke 7:6: "*under* my roof"; Matt 23:37: "*under* her wings [for protection]"; Mark 4:21: "*under* a bed"; Jas 2:3: ὑπὸ τὸ ὑποπόδιόν μου, "*down at* my feet." It is used also in a fig. sense: Rom 16:20: "crush Satan *beneath/at* your feet"; 1 Cor 15:25 (cf. also v. 27): "put all enemies *under* his feet"; Eph 1:22: "put all things *at* his feet."

Ὑπό with acc. also answers the question "where?": *under/in the vicinity of,* in the literal meaning in Mark 4:32: "*under/in* its shade"; John 1:48: "*under* the fig tree." On the basis of Ps 104:39 (LXX) and *Mek. Exod.* 13:21[30a] we should also interpret 1 Cor 10:1 in the literal sense: οἱ πατέρες . . . ὑπὸ τὴν νεφέλην ἦσαν, "our fathers were . . . *under* the cloud" (cf. Exod 13:21); Acts 4:12: "*under* heaven [*sc.* on earth]," cf. also Luke 17:24 and Col 1:23; Jude 6: ὑπὸ ζόφον, "*under* the gloom/*in* darkness." In Rom 3:13 (citing Ps 139:4 LXX) it is uncertain whether ὑπὸ τὰ χείλη αὐτῶν, "*under* [or *upon*] their lips," is intended in the literal or fig. sense.

In a manner corresponding to classical usage, which attests ὑπό τινά εἰμι, "be *under* someone's *power*" (cf. Thucydides vi.86.4), the NT also uses ὑπό with acc. with fig. meaning, and also in the sense of *subordination*, of exercised *dominion, force,* and *power:* Matt 8:9a par. Luke 7:8a: ἄνθρωπός εἰμι ὑπὸ ἐξουσίαν, "I am a man *under* authority"; Matt 8:9b par. Luke 7:8b: "soldiers *under* me"; 1 Tim 6:1: "*under* the yoke of slavery"; 1 Pet 5:6: "humble yourselves *under* the mighty hand of God."

Esp. Paul uses this prep. with striking frequency to characterize the condition of the total subjugation of human beings, often using ὑπό with forceful connotations: Rom 3:9: "*under* the power of sin"; 6:14: "*under* the law" (vs. "*under* grace"); 7:14: "sold *under* sin"; 1 Cor 9:20: ὑπὸ νόμον (4 times; cf. Gal 4:21 and 5:18); Gal 3:10: "*under* the curse [of the law]"; 4:4: γενόμενος ὑπὸ νόμον, "*subject to* the law"; 4:5: "those *subject to* the law."

b) In the NT only Acts 5:21 uses ὑπό temporally: ὑπὸ τὸν ὄρθρον, "*toward/just at* daybreak" (cf. *Jos. As.* 11:1). Ὑπό does not occur in the NT writings in fixed phrases and idioms such as ὑφ' ἕν, *at one stroke* (cf. Wis 12:9; *Barn.* 4:4), or ὑπὸ χεῖρα, *continually* (Josephus *Ant.* xii.185; *Herm. Vis.* iii.10.7; *Man.* iv.3.6; cf. BAGD s.v. 2.d).

D. Sänger

ὑποβάλλω *hypoballō* instigate secretly*

Acts 6:11, with acc. obj.: "They *secretly instigated* men" who were to accuse Stephen.

ὑπογραμμός, οῦ, ὁ *hypogrammos* model, example*

1 Pet 2:21 refers to the *example* of Christ (who suffered "for you"). *1 Clem.* 16:17; 33:8, and Pol. *Phil.* 8:2 also use ὑπογραμμός to refer to the example of Christ. G. Schrenk, *TDNT* I, 772f.

ὑπόδειγμα, ατος, τό *hypodeigma* example, model; copy*

In 4 of its 6 NT occurrences, ὑπόδειγμα refers to an *example* or *model:* of Jesus (John 13:15), of the prophets (Jas 5:10), of falling into ruin (as a result of disobedience, Heb 4:11); of Sodom and Gomorrah as a warning (2 Pet 2:6): They are ὑπόδειγμα μελλόντων ἀσεβεῖν, "an *example* to those who will be ungodly," i.e., to the godless in the future. In Heb 8:5 and 9:23 ὑπόδειγμα refers to a kind of (shadowy) *copy* (of the heavenly things). H. Schlier, *TDNT* II, 32f.; Spicq, *Notes* II, 907-9.

ὑποδείκνυμι(-νύω) *hypodeiknymi(-nyō)* show; give instructions; prove*

Ὑποδείκνυμι is used in the NT only fig., in some instances referring roughly to "teach" (with dat. of person). It occurs in Matt 3:7 par. Luke 3:7 in the speech of John the Baptist: τίς ὑπέδειξεν ὑμῖν with a following inf. φυγεῖν ("so that you escape the coming judgment of wrath"). In Luke 6:47 (different in Matthew) and 12:5 (different in Matthew) it occurs in the words of Jesus: ὑποδείξω (δὲ) ὑμῖν, "I *will show* you." In Acts 9:16 the exalted Lord speaks: "I *will show* him [i.e., Paul] how much he must suffer for the sake of my name"; in 20:35 it occurs in Paul's farewell speech: "I *have shown* you. . . ."

ὑποδέομαι *hypodeomai* (mid.) tie underneath*

This vb. is used in reference to footwear (cf. → ὑπόδημα), specifically σανδάλια (Mark 6:9; Acts 12:8). Metaphorical in Eph 6:15: "*having shod* your feet with readiness for the gospel." A. Oepke, *TDNT* V, 310-12.

ὑποδέχομαι *hypodechomai* receive as a guest*

This vb. occurs with acc. of the person received in Luke 10:38 (Martha receives Jesus); 19:6 (Zacchaeus receives Jesus); Acts 17:7 (Jason receives Paul and Silas); Jas 2:25 (Rahab receives the messengers; cf. Josh 2:1-21).

ὑπόδημα, ατος, τό *hypodēma* sandal*

Ὑπόδημα refers to the leather sole fastened to the foot by means of a strap. The NT usually uses the pl.: Mark 1:7 par. Matt 3:11/Luke 3:16 (Mark and Luke have "whose *sandals* I am not worthy to untie"; Matthew reads "whose *sandals* I am not worthy to carry [= take off]"); Matt 10:10 par. Luke 10:4 (in Jesus' prohibition against taking sandals); Luke 15:22 (sandals for the prodigal son); 22:35 (reference to 10:4). The sg. refers collectively to *footwear* (John 1:27; Acts 7:33; 13:25). A. Oepke, *TDNT* V, 310-12.

ὑπόδικος, 2 *hypodikos* guilty; accountable*

Rom 3:19: ὑπόδικος τῷ θεῷ, "*guilty* before God." C. Maurer, *TDNT* VIII, 556-58.

ὑποζύγιον, ου, τό *hypozygion* beast of burden; donkey*

All NT occurrences refer to a donkey (Matt 21:5 [citing Zech 9:9 LXX, different in Mark]; 2 Pet 2:16 [cf. Num 22:28 with its reference to Balaam's donkey]).

ὑποζώννυμι *hypozōnnymi* undergird*

Acts 27:17 uses this word as a nautical t.t.: "to equip a ship with ὑποζώματα [cables, braces]." Such cables were fastened around the ship's external hull during rough seas; cf. Polybius xxvii.3.3. BAGD s.v. (bibliography); R. Hartmann, PW Suppl. IV, 776-82.

ὑποκάτω *hypokatō* (adv.) underneath, below*

This word occurs in the NT as an improper prep. with gen., 4 times in the phrase ὑποκάτω τῶν ποδῶν, "*at* your feet" (Mark 12:36 par. Matt 22:24 [citing Ps 110:1, different in Ps 109:1 LXX], further Heb 2:8 [Ps 8:7 LXX] and Rev 12:1). Other phrases occur in Mark 6:11 ("*on* your feet"); 7:28 ("*under* the table"); Luke 8:16 ("*under* a bed"); John 1:50 ("*under* the fig tree"); Rev 5:3, 13 ("*under* the earth"); 6:9 ("*under* the altar").

ὑπόκειμαι *hypokeimai* lie below

A defective deponent vb. (Luke 6:42 D it) meaning *lie below*: "Behold, the log *lies below* [i.e., is found] in your own eye."

ὑποκρίνομαι *hypokrinomai* pretend, play a role → ὑπόκρισις 1, 3.

ὑπόκρισις, εως, ἡ *hypokrisis* godlessness, hypocrisy*
ὑποκρίνομαι *hypokrinomai* pretend, play a role*

1. Occurrences and meaning — 2. Ὑπόκρισις — 3. Ὑποκρίνομαι

Lit.: R. A. BATEY, "Jesus and the Theatre," *NTS* 30 (1984) 563-74. — H. FRANKEMÖLLE, " 'Pharisäismus' in Judentum und Kirche. Zur Tradition und Redaktion in Mt 23," *Gottesverächter und Menschenfeinde?* (ed. H. Goldstein; 1979) 123-89. — H. GIESEN, *Christliches Handeln. Eine redaktionskritische Untersuchung zum δικαιοσύνη-Begriff im Matthäusevangelium* (EHS XXIII/181, 1982) 151-57, 216-19. — W. GÜNTHER, *DNTT* II, 468-70. — E. HAENCHEN, "Mt 23," Haenchen I, 29-54. — W. PESCH, "Theologische Aussagen der Redaktion von Mt 23," FS Schmid (1973) 286-99. — SPICQ, *Notes* Suppl. 655f. — U. WILCKENS, *TDNT* VIII, 559-71. — B. ZUCCHELLI, Ὑποκριτής. *Origine e storia del termine* (1963). — For further bibliography see *TWNT* X, 1287f.

1. The noun ὑπόκρισις occurs 6 times in the NT: once each in the Synoptic Gospels and 3 times in the Epistles. The vb. occurs only in Luke 20:20. The stem ὑποκρ- derives originally from theatrical language; first it referred to "playacting," and then later also to "hypocrisy." The NT, however, usually follows LXX usage, in which ὑποκριτής twice renders *hānēp* (Job 34:30; 36:13), referring to a person whose conduct is not determined by God and is thus "godless." By using ὑποκριτής κτλ. in this

manner, the Bible succeeds in stigmatizing godless behavior, which permeates human activity generally. God exposes such behavior as "playacting," which is why it has no validity before him.

2. In Mark 12:15 ὑπόκρισις does not refer to hypocrisy (*contra* J. Ernst, *Mark* [RNT] 345; J. Gnilka, *Mark* [EKKNT] II, 152), but rather to the interrogators' godless maliciousness (cf. R. Pesch, *Mark* [HTKNT] II, 226). Jesus sees that they are trying to deceive him (v. 13) with their leading question (v. 14) and are trying to find an excuse to have him arrested (v. 12). Jesus, however, does not fall into their trap. According to Matt 23:28, although the scribes and Pharisees do outwardly appear righteous, they are nonetheless full of godlessness and malice (here *lawlessness*, ἀνομία), since their behavior is not determined by God's will. Luke 12:1 also refers to the Pharisees' perverted behavior as ὑπόκρισις, which the image of the leaven illustrates. The context of the cries of woe (11:37) underscores the godlessness of such behavior.

According to Gal 2:13, the fact that Cephas withdrew with the other Jewish Christians from table fellowship with Gentile Christians (v. 12) is also ὑπόκρισις. Because Paul thus considers Cephas condemned (before God), he dares oppose him to his face (v. 11). Here ὑπόκρισις is neither hypocrisy (*contra* F. Mussner, *Gal* [HTKNT] 142f.) nor deception (*contra* H. Schlier, *Gal* [KEK] 85) but rather a betrayal of the gospel (v. 14) and thus an expression of unbelief (cf. also vv. 15-17). In 1 Tim 4:2 ὑπόκρισις refers to the behavior of heretics, who advocate demonic teachings and thus transgress against God's truth (v. 3c). As the eschatological adversaries of Christians, they sin against the order of creation (vv. 3-5). 1 Pet 2:1, in a catalog of vices, uses the pl. of ὑπόκρισις ethically in the sense of expressions of *hypocrisy*.

3. The vb. can also refer to *play a role, pretend*. Trying to trap Jesus, the scribes and high priests sent spies who *pretended* to be sincere (v. 20). Luke thus interprets ὑπόκρισις (Mark 12:15, → 2) in the sense of the original Greek usage.   H. Giesen

ὑποκριτής, οῦ, ὁ *hypokritēs* godless person*
ἀνυπόκριτος, 2 *anypokritos* without hypocrisy, genuine*

1. Occurrences in the NT — 2. Ὑποκριτής — 3. Ἀνυπόκριτος

Lit.: → ὑπόκρισις.

1. In the NT ὑποκριτής occurs only in the Synoptic Gospels (18 times): once in Mark, 3 times in Luke, and 14 in Matthew (including the v.l. Matt 23:14). It appears only in the words of Jesus. The adj. ἀνυπόκριτος occurs

6 times in the NT, only in the Epistles. On variations of meaning → ὑπόκρισις 1.

2. In the context of the question of purity (Mark 7:1-23 par. Matt 15:1-20) Jesus addresses his adversaries as ὑποκριταί (Mark 7:6/Matt 15:7), since they substitute human tradition for God's commandment (Mark 7:8f./ Matt 15:3b); Jesus introduces Isa 29:13 LXX to support his position (Mark 7:6c, 7/Matt 15:8f.). They show themselves to be practical atheists. Whoever does not correctly interpret the present time (a different matter from interpreting signs of the weather) is a *godless person* (12:56) to the extent that that person is closed to Jesus' message, which is present in his deeds as a sign. Jesus similarly addresses the ruler of the synagogue and those he represents as godless (Luke 13:15) because they take offense at the healing of the woman on the sabbath. They are adversaries of both Jesus and God (v. 17), in whose name he acts (cf. also v. 13).

Whoever judges a brother (Matt 7:1) instead of forgiving him (Luke 6:37) resists God's will as proclaimed by Jesus and is in this sense *godless* (Matt 7:5/Luke 6:42), as shown in the figure of the speck and the log. Matthew uses three examples from the religious sphere (6:2: giving alms; v. 5: praying; v. 16: fasting) to illustrate why the Pharisees are ὑποκριταί: in their actions they seek their own honor (v. 2) instead of the Father's (cf. 5:16), since they are concerned with excelling before human beings (6:5, 16). Thus do they miss the righteousness demanded by God (6:1). They want to be seen by people (6:1; 23:5). Hence in Matthew 23 Jesus repeatedly unmasks them as *godless* (23:13 [14], 15, 23, 25, 27, 29). They are so blinded (vv. 16, 17, 19) that they cannot act other than they do. When Jesus exposes his adversaries' malice concerning the question of taxes and recognizes the covert temptation, the term ὑποκριτής targets their unbelief (Matt 22:18). According to Matt 24:51 the unfaithful servant shares the lot of the *godless*.

3. The adj. **ἀνυπόκριτος** characterizes love (Rom 12:9; 2 Cor 6:6), brotherly love (1 Pet 1:22), faith (1 Tim 1:5; 2 Tim 1:5), and wisdom (Jas 3:17) as being *genuine, without falsity, deception,* or *hypocrisy.*   H. Giesen

ὑπολαμβάνω *hypolambanō*   take up; support; assume, believe*

Acts 1:9: "a cloud *took* him *up*"; 3 John 8, of the hospitable reception of brothers who are strangers; Luke 10:30: ὑπολαβὼν εἶπεν, "he *seized* the opportunity to speak." In Luke 7:43 and Acts 2:15 the vb. means *believe/think.* G. Delling, *TDNT* IV, 15; B. Siede, *DNTT* III, 747, 749.

ὑπολαμπάς, άδος, ἡ *hypolampas*   window

Acts 20:8 D in place of → λαμπάς. Cf. Passow II s.v.: "a kind of window that, without letting in fresh air, nonetheless faintly illuminated the room and allowed one to see out onto the street."

ὑπόλειμμα, ατος, τό *hypoleimma*   remnant*

Rom 9:27: τὸ ὑπόλειμμα σωθήσεται, "a *remnant* will be saved"; cf. Isa 10:22, where the LXX, however, reads κατάλειμμα. G. Schrenk, *TDNT* IV, 194-214; W. Günther and H. Krienke, *DNTT* III, 247-53.

ὑπολείπομαι *hypoleipomai*   (pass.) be left*

Rom 11:3 quotes Elijah from 3 Kgdms 19:10 (14): "I alone *am left.*" Cf. → ὑπόλειμμα.

ὑπολήνιον, ου, τό *hypolēnion*   vat placed beneath a winepress*

Mark 12:1: "A man planted a vineyard, set a hedge around it, dug out a *trough for the winepress,* built a tower . . ." (different in Matt 21:33 → ληνός, "winepress"). This refers to the trough in which the juice gathers during pressing. G. Bornkamm, *TDNT* IV, 254-57.

ὑπολιμπάνω *hypolimpanō*   leave behind*

1 Pet 2:21: Christ "*left* an example (→ ὑπογραμμός) for you."

ὑπομένω *hypomenō*   stay behind; take upon oneself; hold out, endure*

1. Occurrences — 2. Basic meaning and constructions — 3. Theological meaning

Lit.: → ὑπομονή; see also BAGD s.v.

1. Differently than in the LXX (→ ὑπομονή 1), ὑπομένω, with 17 occurrences, appears only about half as frequently as its related noun. It occurs 4 times in Hebrews and not at all in the Johannine writings (cf. in contrast → μένω).

2. Luke (and only he) uses ὑπομένω exclusively of *remain* in the spatial sense, referring to the twelve-year-old Jesus, who in contrast to his parents "*stayed behind* in Jerusalem" (Luke 2:43), and to Silas and Timothy, who initially *stay behind* in Beroea while Paul travels on to Athens (Acts 17:14).

Fig. ὑπομένω refers to staying as opposed to fleeing, to holding out and enduring misfortune (never people), as well as to perseverance in difficult circumstances— never, however, to waiting and trusting in someone, as exemplified by the already formulaic "waiting for the Lord" in the OT (e.g., Ps 36:9, 34 LXX). Although ὑπομένω can be used absolutely (Mark 13:13 par.; 2 Tim 2:12; Heb 12:7; Jas 5:11), it usually specifies its obj., which appears in either acc. (Heb 10:32; 12:3; Jas 1:12; πάντα: 1 Cor 13:7 and 2 Tim 2:10; the cross that Jesus [perhaps literally] *takes upon himself:* Heb 12:2) or dat. ([in] tribulation: Rom 12:12), or else takes a partc. as complement (1 Pet 2:20a, b). Heb. 12:7 mentions the purpose of ὑπομένω (εἰς παιδείαν), Mark 13:13 par. its temporal goal (εἰς τέλος).

3. The Gospels include this sentence 3 times, without variation: ὁ δὲ ὑπομείνας εἰς τέλος οὗτος σωθήσεται, "the one who *endures* to the end will be saved." Jesus demands such endurance in Mark 13:13 in the face of the hatred and persecution that Christians will experience before the end. Matthew, too, emphasizes this call for perseverance during the time of general chaos and distress before the end (24:13), though it is equally valid for the present persecution under which Jesus' disciples will be suffering (10:22). Other writings also assert that the proclamation of the gospel and one's confession of it will lead to distress. Such tribulation is a part of apostolic experience (2 Tim 2:10, 12) and of the Christian life in general (Rom 12:12; Heb 10:32; 12:7). Christians know that this allies them with the suffering Christ through his example (Heb 12:2, 3), and that through this common experience it allies them with him even beyond such suffering (2 Tim 2:11, 12).

In a general ethical sense ὑπομένω refers to perseverance in the face of any kind of temptation to evil (Jas 1:12; 5:11). It also is the attitude that accepts such wrongdoing instead of requiting it; Paul attributes it to love, which "*endures* all things" (1 Cor 13:7). Slaves must often suffer hardship, i.e., mistreatment. Having this kind of *patience* "for punished mistakes" (K. H. Schelkle, *1 Pet* [HTKNT] 79), i.e., for something incurred through one's own guilt, is admittedly no great thing (1 Pet 2:20a); for something not self-incurred, however, it is "grace with God" (v. 20b, c).   W. Radl

ὑπομιμνῄσκω *hypomimnēskō* remind; pass.: remember*

Act. forms, used of "*remind* (someone of something) or *recall* (something)," occur in John 14:26 (referring to the Paraclete); 2 Tim 2:14 and Titus 3:1 (imv.); 2 Pet 1:12; 3 John 10; Jude 5. Only Luke 22:61 (different in Mark 14:72) uses the pass. form, which is used of *remember:* "Peter *remembered* the word (τοῦ ῥήματος) of the Lord." K. H. Bartels, *DNTT* III, 230f., 242.

ὑπόμνησις, εως, ἡ *hypomnēsis* remembrance*

Twice the author of 2 Peter attempts to "arouse" his readers "by way of *reminder*" (1:13; 3:1). 2 Tim 1:5 uses ὑπόμνησις in a pass. sense referring to *remembrance:* ὑπόμνησιν λαβὼν τῆς ἐν σοὶ ἀνυποκρίτου πίστεως, "I am *reminded of* your [i.e., Timothy's] sincere faith."

ὑπομονή, ῆς, ἡ *hypomonē* perseverance, patience; expectation*

1. Occurrences — 2. Meaning and usage — 3. Chracteristic examples — a) Jesus — b) Paul — c) Later apostolic writings

Lit.: BAGD s.v. — S. Brown, *Apostasy and Perseverance in the Theology of Luke* (1969) 48-50. — J. S. Croatto, "Persecución y perseverancia en la teología lucana," RevistBib 42 (1980) 21-30. — U. Falkenroth and C. Brown, *DNTT* II, 772-76. — P. Goicoechea, *De conceptu "ὑπομονή" apud S. Paulum* (1965). — F. Hauck, *TDNT* IV, 581-88. — P. Ortiz, Valdivieso, *La* hypomone *en el Nuevo Testamento* (Diss. Rome, 1965). — F. J. Schierse, *HTG* I, 436-41. — M. Spanneut, *RAC* IX, 243-94. — Spicq, *Notes* Suppl. 658-65.

1. While ὑπομένω occurs 80–85 times in the LXX, and ὑπομονή only *ca.* 25 times (some 15 of those in Sirach and 4 Maccabees), the NT uses the vb. only 17 times and the noun 32 times. The latter occurs 7 times in Revelation, though not at all in John or 1–3 John. The other occurrences, apart from Luke 8:15 and 21:19, are distributed among the letters.

2. Derived from ὑπο-μένω, ὑπομονή refers to steadfastness and perseverance "under" certain circumstances, and also to remaining expectant in the face of passing time. The first meaning exhibits a certain shift of emphasis compared with standard Greek usage, and the second when compared with the OT concept of ὑπομονή (or of *miqweh*). In standard Greek ὑπομονή refers overwhelmingly—and positively—to independent, unyielding, defiant perseverance in the face of aggressive misfortune, and thus to a kind of courageousness; in the negative sense it refers also to the enduring of humiliation (attestations in Hauck 581f.). In contrast, the NT considers this latter case to be praiseworthy (2 Thess 1:4), and ὑπομονή, rather than being the expression of one's own personal strength, is made possible by Christian hope (Rom 8:25; on self-control mentioned in 2 Pet 1:6, see Hauck 586). In contrast to the OT "hope of Israel" (Jer 14:8; 17:13) in the sense of trusting in God, the NT speaks of waiting for Christ (Rev 1:9; cf. 1 Thess 1:3).

Commensurate with these definitions, the NT attributes the attitude of ὑπομονή only to human beings, i.e., to Christians. The gen. Χριστοῦ in 2 Thess 3:5 refers either to him who bestows ὑπομονή (cf. BAGD) or, more probable in this context, to the person who is anticipated (obj. gen.); the same is true of μου in Rev 3:10 (if it does not refer to λόγος; so A. Wikenhauser, *Rev* [RNT] 45).

3. a) Ὑπομονή does not occur in the authentic witnesses of Jesus' own proclamation. He calls for ὑπομονή neither in the sense of perseverance in trouble nor in that of anticipation. He aids many sufferers himself, and for him the kingdom of God, which will end all trouble (cf. Luke 6:20f.), is about to commence.

b) For Paul "the new creation" (2 Cor 5:17; Gal 6:15) is already a reality in Christ (through faith and baptism), though the comprehensive renewal with resurrection and judgment is still to come. In ὑπομονή a Christian spans this tension between justification, which has already occurred, and the still-anticipated consummation. In the experience and belief that they possess the Spirit as a "firstfruit" (Rom 8:23) and "guarantee" (2 Cor 1:22; 5:5), Christians can compose themselves in patience and can persevere in patient expectation (Rom 8:25). Present afflictions can only strengthen and keep them in this perseverance (5:3, 4). Thus patience is often mentioned along with encouragement (παράκλησις: Rom 15:4, 5; 2 Cor 1:6) and as a characteristic of Christian hope (1 Thess 1:3). As "servants of God" (2 Cor 6:4), who is "the God of *patience*" (Rom 15:5; cf. Col 1:11), Paul and his fellow workers persist "in great *endurance*" (2 Cor 6:4)—indeed, "in all *patience*" (12:12; H. Lietzmann, *1–2 Cor* [HNT] 158: "in difficult circumstances").

c) The postapostolic writings associate ὑπομονή esp. frequently (cf. already 1 Thess 1:3) with πίστις and/or ἀγάπη: with πίστις alone in 2 Thess 1:4; Jas 1:3; Rev 13:10; 14:12; with ἀγάπη in 2 Thess 3:5; with both in 1 Tim 6:11; 2 Tim 3:10; Titus 2:2; Rev 2:19 (cf. Rom 5:2-5). In addition, or along with these (cf. again 1 Thess 1:3), ὑπομονή also occurs with ἔργον (ἔργα) and/or κόπος (Jas 1:4; Rev 2:2; 2:19; 14:12f.).

In referring to one of the familiar Christian virtues, ὑπομονή thus becomes "a watchword and keyword of ecclesiastical preaching" (Schierse 440). Ὑπομονή now no longer applies as much to the tension between present and future statements. On the one hand the focus is on the great tribulation threatening to engulf the Christian, tribulation in which one must steadfastly anticipate the redemption of the parousia or accept martyrdom; on the other hand the preaching addresses the whole span of one's life, during which one may not give in but must live steadfastly and faithfully as a Christian until death. The first esp. characterizes Revelation in its appeal to oppressed churches (1:9; 2:2, 3, 19; 3:10; on martyrdom see 13:10; 14:12). The second is true of the admonitions issued by the Pastorals (1 Tim 6:11; 2 Tim 3:10; Titus 2:2) and in 2 Pet 1:6 (bis) and Luke 8:15 (different in Mark; cf. Rom 2:7).

Perseverance in faith is also mentioned in Hebrews

(10:36; 12:1), James (1:3, 4; 5:11), and Luke 21:19 (differently in Mark 13:13, where—with the vb.—the reference is probably to holding out during the final tribulations). In contrast, John and 1–3 John speak not of ὑπομονή but rather of "remaining" in Christ, in his love, etc. (cf. → μένω 3).

W. Radl

ὑπονοέω *hyponoeō* suspect (vb.)*

Acts 25:18, with a following acc. (ὧν πονηρῶν showing attraction of the relative); 13:25 and 27:27, with acc. and inf. J. Behm, *TDNT* IV, 1017f.

ὑπόνοια, ας, ἡ *hyponoia* suspicion; presumption*

1 Tim 6:4: ὑπόνοιαι πονηραί, "base *suspicions*," following βλασφημίαι in a catalog of vices. J. Behm, *TDNT* IV, 1017f.

ὑποπλέω *hypopleō* sail under (the lee)*

In the NT in references to sea travel "under the lee of an island" (name of the island in the acc.), i.e., along an island such that the island shields the wind: Acts 27:4: "*we sailed under the lee of* Cyprus"; v. 7: "*we sailed under the lee of* Crete."

ὑποπνέω *hypopneō* blow gently*

Acts 27:13: ὑποπνεύσαντος νότου, "when the south wind *blew gently*."

ὑποπόδιον, ου, τό *hypopodion* footstool*

Jas 2:3 uses ὑποπόδιον in the literal sense. It also refers fig. to God's *footstool* (Matt 5:35; Acts 7:49) and, with reference to Ps 109:1 LXX, to total subjection in the phrase "make someone a footstool for someone else" (Luke 20:43 [different in Mark 12:36 → ὑποκάτω]; Acts 2:35; Heb 1:13; 10:13; also *1 Clem.* 36:5; *Barn.* 12:10).

ὑπόστασις, εως, ἡ *hypostasis* basis, foundation; reality; undertaking*

1. Occurrences in the NT — 2. Meanings — 3. Usage

Lit.: C. ARPE, "Substantia," *Philologus* 94 (1941) 65-78. — H. DÖRRIE, "'Ὑπόστασις. Wort- und Bedeutungsgeschichte," NAWG.PH 3 (1955) 35-92. — idem, "Zu Hbr 11,1," *ZNW* 46 (1955) 196-202. — F. ERDIN, *Das Wort Hypostasis* (FTS 52, 1939). — E. GRÄSSER, *Der Glaube im Hebräerbrief* (MTSt 2, 1965) 46-51, 99-102. — G. HARDER, *DNTT* I, 710-14. — H. KÖSTER, *TDNT* VIII, 572-89. — M. A. MATHIS, "Does 'Substantia' Mean 'Realization' or 'Foundation' in Heb 11:1?" *Bib* 3 (1922) 79-87. — idem, *The Pauline πίστις-ὑπόστασις according to Heb 11:1* (Diss. Catholic University of America, Washington, D.C., 1920). — A. SCHLATTER, *Der Glaube im NT* (⁴1927, ⁵1963) 614-18. — SPICQ, *Notes* II, 910-12. — R. E.

WITT, "ʽΥΠΟΣΤΑΣΙΣ," *Amicitiae Corolla* (FS J. R. Harris; 1933) 319-43. — For further bibliography see *TWNT* X, 1288.

1. In the NT the noun occurs only 5 times: twice in 2 Corinthians and 3 times in Hebrews. The corresponding vb. (ὑφίστημι/-αμαι) does not occur at all.

2. ʽΥπόστασις originally referred to "that which stands under," the "basis," from which developed a range of meanings in secular Greek: "basis, foundation, support, guarantee, possession, existence, deposit." The last-mentioned meaning in turn led to the philosophical usages "realization, presence, reality." With reference to human behavior ὑπόστασις refers to "undertaking, plan, venture" as well as "venturing, holding out."

The complexity of this expression also manifests itself in the LXX (and in early Judaism). It occurs 20 times in the LXX, rendering 12 different Hebrew equivalents. If, as seems justified, one understands the term from the perspective of Greek, not Hebrew, one sees that its usage in the LXX exactly follows that of secular Greek. The usage "confidence, trust" cannot be documented, including in instances where ὑπόστασις is the rendering of Heb. *tiqwāh* or *tôḥelet* ("hope"; Ruth 1:12; Ps 38:8 LXX; Ezek 19:5).

3. The NT also uses ὑπόστασις in various ways. It refers to *undertaking, project* in 2 Cor 9:4, where ἐν τῇ ὑποστάσει ταύτῃ parallels the phrase ἐν τῷ μέρει ("matter of concern") τούτῳ. The ὑπόστασις refers here to the collection the Corinthians have undertaken but not yet finished (see 9:2, 5, and 8:11f., where it is no accident that the vb. is ἐπιτελέω; cf. Herodotus iii.127.2; Diodorus Siculus i.3.2; xvi.33.1, 3). ʽΥπόστασις also refers to *undertaking* in 2 Cor. 11:17, though this time in the sense of *resolve, daring.* Paul even says of himself that he is speaking "as a fool," and only if the reader keeps this in mind may Paul dare to "boast" here. So this boasting doubtless parallels the act of "courageousness" (τολμάω; see v. 21 and 10:2; cf. Polybius vi.55.2; Thucydides i.144.4). A similar meaning is intended in Heb 3:14. Here ὑπόστασις parallels "frankness" and "pride in hope" (see 3:6 and cf. 10:23, 35f.) and refers to *resolve* or *point of departure* (τὴν ἀρχὴν τῆς ὑποστάσεως = τὴν κατ᾽ ἀρχὴν ὑπόστασιν).

In Heb 1:3 ὑπόστασις is used more or less philosophically of *reality* or *being:* Jesus Christ as the Son is the "stamp of God's [immortal and transcendent] *being*" (cf., e.g., Wis 16:21; *Diog.* 2:1; Tatian *Or. Graec.* 15:3f.). Heb 11:1 probably also uses ὑπόστασις philosophically. True faith, i.e., faith that one keeps to the end (see 10:39), is the (obj., not subj.) *guarantee* of salvation (πίστις ἐλπιζομένων ὑπόστασις). The believer is assured of receiving that which is not yet present but which is promised by God (see esp. 6:12, 15; 11:33; → πίστις 8).

H. W. Hollander

ὑποστέλλω *hypostellō* draw back; mid.: withdraw, shy away from*

Gal 2:12, with ἑαυτόν: "draw back" (if ἑαυτόν is not

the obj. here of ὑποστέλλω, then it is used intrans. with the same meaning). The other NT passages use ὑποστέλλω in the mid.: Acts 20:27, *shrink from;* Heb 10:38 (Hab 2:4), *withdraw/shrink back;* Acts 20:20, *keep silent about* (something). K. H. Rengstorf, *TDNT* VII, 597f.

ὑποστολή, ῆς, ἡ *hypostolē* timidity*

Heb 10:39: οὐκ ἐσμὲν ὑποστολῆς, "we have nothing to do with *timidity*" (contrasting πίστις). K. H. Rengstorf, *TDNT* VII, 599.

ὑποστρέφω *hypostrephō* return*

This vb. occurs only intrans. in the NT (35 times, 32 of these in Luke and Acts). It occurs with εἰς and local acc. in Luke 1:56; 2:45; 4:14; 7:10; 8:39; 11:24; 24:33, 52; Acts 1:12; 8:25; 12:25; 13:13, 34 (εἰς διαφθοράν, "to the grave"); 14:21; 21:6; 22:17; 23:32; Gal 1:17. It occurs with διά and local gen. in Acts 20:3; with ἀπό and local gen. in Luke 4:1; 24:9; Acts 1:12 (cf. Heb 7:1); and with ἐκ in 2 Pet 2:21. ʽΥποστρέφω stands absolutely in Luke 2:20, 43; 8:37, 40; 9:10; 10:17; 17:15, 18; 19:12; 23:48, 56; Acts 8:28. Concerning the Gospel of Luke, W. Schenk (*SE* VII [1982] 443-50) has ascertained that ὑποστρέφω "functions as a doxology indicator," esp. in episodic conclusions.

ὑποστρωννύω *hypostrōnnyō* spread out underneath*

Luke 19:36: ὑπεστρώννυον τὰ ἱμάτια αὐτῶν (different in Mark 11:8: ἔστρωσαν), "they *spread out* their garments [on the road]" (cf. Josephus *Ant.* ix.111).

ὑποταγή, ῆς, ἡ *hypotagē* subjection, subordination; obedience*

Lit.: BAGD s.v. — R. BERGMEIER, "Loyalität als Gegenstand paulinischer Paraklese," *Theokratia* I (ed. K. H. Rengstorf; 1970) 51-63, esp. 61f. — G. DELLING, *TDNT* VIII, 27-48, esp. 46f. — E. S. GERSTENBERGER and W. SCHRAGE, *Woman and Man* (1981) 167-69. — H. VON LIPS, *Glaube—Gemeinde—Amt* (FRLANT 122, 1979) 106-43. — R. R. RUETHER, "Frau und kirchliches Amt in historischer und gesellschaftlicher Sicht," *Concilium* (German) 12 (1976) 17-23. — For further bibliography → ὑποτάσσω.

1. There are 4 occurrences in the NT (Paul and the Pastorals); in a pass. sense, each refers to existing or asserted authority. In the LXX ὑποταγή occurs only as a misspelling of ἐπιταγή (Wis 18:15 A).

2. In Gal 2:5 τῇ ὑποταγῇ (dat. of manner) refers to *in subjection* or *with docility* (cf. ὑπετάγη in 2 Macc 13:23). 2 Cor 9:13 uses ὑποταγή in reference to *obedience* that proves itself in the acknowledgment of the apostolic proc-

lamation of Christ. The organization of the local church and its officeholders is modeled after the organizational authority of the domestic household, at the head of which stands the patriarch and educator. A church leader thus "ought to bring up his children in *obedience* and proper respect" (1 Tim 3:4). "In this model there can be no question of any exercise of authority in the Church by women" (von Lips 143). "Let a woman learn in silence and *complete subordination*" (2:11; for critique, cf. Ruether, also Gerstenberger and Schrage).

R. Bergmeier

ὑποτάσσω *hypotassō* subject, subordinate (vb.)*

1. Occurrences in the NT — 2. Usage — a) Act. — b) Pass. and mid.

Lit.: H. R. BALZ, *Heilsvertrauen und Welterfahrung* (1971) 36-51. — J. BAUMGARTEN, *Paulus und die Apokalyptik* (1975) 76-82, 99-106, 170-78. — R. BERGMEIER, "Loyalität als Gegenstand paulinischer Paraklese," *Theokratia* I (ed. K. H. Rengstorf; 1970) 51-63. — N. BROX, *1 Pet* (EKKNT, 1979). — J. E. CROUCH, *The Origin and Intention of the Colossian Haustafel* (1972). — G. DELLING, *TDNT* VIII, 27-48, esp. 39-46. — F. FROITZHEIM, *Christologie und Eschatologie bei Paulus* (1979) 144-57, 245-56. — E. S. GERSTENBERGER and W. SCHRAGE, *Woman and Man* (1981) 167-69, 193-200. — J. GNILKA, *Col* (HTKNT, 1980) 203-18. — E. KAMLAH, "Ὑποτάσσεσθαι in den neutestamentlichen 'Haustafeln,'" FS Stählin 237-43. — H. VON LIPS, *Glaube—Gemeinde—Amt* (1979) 106-43. — E. SCHWEIZER, *Col* (Eng. tr., 1982) 213-20. — SPICQ, *Notes* II, 913-16. — K. THRAEDE, "Zum historischen Hintergrund der 'Haustafeln' des NT," *Pietas* (FS B. Kötting; JAC Ergänzungsband 8, 1980) 359-68. — U. WILCKENS, *Rom* (EKKNT) II (1980). — idem, "Röm 13,1-7," idem, *Rechtfertigung als Freiheit* (1974) 203-45. — For further bibliography on Rom 13:1-7 → τάσσω; on 1 Cor 15:27f. → τάγμα; see further *TWNT* X, 1278.

1. Ὑποτάσσω occurs 38 times in the NT (Luke, the Pauline corpus, Hebrews, James [4:7], 1 Peter). Its usage corresponds to that in the LXX (Delling 40); the mid. meaning reflects the social structures of Hellenistic-Roman antiquity.

2. a) The act. is used of *subject, subordinate, place under.* God is the subj. in Rom 8:20b (cf. Balz 39-51; Wilckens, *Rom* II, 154f.); Heb 2:5, 8a (citing Ps 8:7b LXX; the same citation occurs in 1 Cor 15:27a); Eph 1:22 (→ πούς 3). Ὑποτάσσω αὐτῷ τὰ πάντα (cf. also Philo *Op.* 84) appears in 1 Cor 15:27c, 28c; Phil 3:21; Heb 2:8b.

b) The pass. is used of *be subjected to, be placed under* (Rom 8:20a; 1 Cor 15:27b, 28a; Heb 2:8c; 1 Pet 3:22 [cf. Dan 7:27]).

The mid. usage occurs most frequently: *submit to, subordinate oneself to, yield to, be subject to, obey,* usually with the dat.: to God in 1 Cor 15:28b; Heb 12:9; Jas 4:7 (cf. Ps 61:2, 6 LXX; Epictetus *Diss.* iii.24.65); to God's law in Rom 8:7; to God's righteousness in 10:3;

to Christ in Eph 5:24a. "The spirits of prophets *are subject to* prophets" (1 Cor 14:32); evil spirits *are subject to* the disciples (Luke 10:17, 20; cf. *T. Sim.* 6:6). The child Jesus *was obedient to* his parents (Luke 2:51).

The vb. can be used parenetically—most often in the household codes—of *subordination, obedience:* to political authorities (Rom 13:1, 5; 1 Pet 2:13f.; Titus 3:1); wives toward their husbands (Col 3:18; Eph 5:24b; 1 Pet 3:1, 5; Titus 2:5); in a general sense (1 Cor 14:34; cf. 1 Tim 2:11 [→ ὑποταγή 2]); slaves toward their masters (1 Pet 2:18; Titus 2:9); the younger toward elders (1 Pet 5:5; cf. Josephus *B.J.* ii.146); and the Christians in Corinth toward fellow workers in the Church (1 Cor 16:16). "Subordination has become such a fundamental, required behavior in the early Christian tradition that in Eph 5:21 and 1 Pet 2:13 it is given in a general form as an introductory commandment itself, before the specific exhortation" (Kamlah 237; on Eph 5:21 cf. 1QS 5:23: obey one another, namely, the lesser is to obey the superior).

R. Bergmeier

ὑποτίθημι *hypotithēmi* lay down; mid.: recommend*

Rom 16:4 (act.), in the phrase "*offer/lay down* one's neck (τράχηλον)," i.e., "*risk* one's neck"; 1 Tim 4:6 (mid.): "Timothy" should *put* the proper teaching (see vv. 1-5) *before* the brethren, i.e., should *recommend* it to them.

ὑποτρέχω *hypotrechō* run under*

Acts 27:16, as an expression from the language of sailors: νησίον δέ τι ὑποδραμόντες, "*running under* [i.e., sailing under the lee of] a small island."

ὑποτύπωσις, εως, ἡ *hypotypōsis* model, prototype, example*

1 Tim 1:16 speaks of the *prototype* Christ gives by the patience he showed with "Paul." 2 Tim 1:13 asserts that Timothy should hold fast to "the *pattern* of sound words" he has heard from "Paul." L. Goppelt, *TDNT* VIII, 248, 250; H. Müller, *DNTT* III, 903-6.

ὑποφέρω *hypopherō* bear, endure*

2 Tim 3:11 speaks of "*enduring* persecutions"; 1 Pet 2:19 of "*enduring* grief." In 1 Cor 10:13, where the vb. is used absolutely, the context suggests that the reference is to withstanding temptation.

ὑποχωρέω *hypochōreō* withdraw, retire*

Luke 5:16 (different in Mark): Jesus "*withdrew* (ἦν ὑποχωρῶν) to the wilderness and prayed"; 9:10b (different in Mark): Jesus "took them [i.e., the apostles] and *withdrew* to a city called Bethsaida."

ὑπωπιάζω *hypōpiazō* strike under the eye, strike in the face; torment*

Literal in Luke 18:5: "so that she does not *strike me in the face*"; 1 Cor 9:27, fig., alluding to boxing (cf. v. 26): ὑπωπιάζω μου τὸ σῶμα, "I *torment* my body." K. Weiss, *TDNT* VIII, 590f.

ὗς, ὑός, ἡ *hys* sow (noun)*

2 Pet 2:22, in a proverb: "The *sow* is washed only to wallow in the mire."

ὕσσωπος, ου, ἡ (ὁ) *hyssōpos* hyssop*

In the LXX ὕσσωπος is masc. or fem. and refers to a small bush with highly aromatic leaves used in purification rituals (Exod 12:22; Lev 14:4; Num 19:6, 18; Ps 50:9 LXX). The NT uses the word twice: Heb 9:19 and John 19:29. The latter usage presupposes (incorrectly?) that hyssop is a plant with a rigid stem. This may be an allusion to the atoning effects of hyssop, which according to Exod 12:22 was used esp. during Passover. E. Nestle, "Zum Ysop bei Johannes, Josephus und Philo," *ZNW* 14 (1913) 263-65; BAGD s.v.; R. Schnackenburg, *John* III (Eng. tr., 1982) 283f.; B. Hartmann, *BHH* 2197f.

ὑστερέω *hystereō* come too late; be in need of, lack; pass.: do without*

Act. forms appear in Heb 4:1 *(fail);* 12:15 (with ἀπό τινος, "*fall away* from something"); Luke 22:35 *(lack);* 2 Cor 11:5 and 12:11 with gen. of comparison ("*be inferior* to"); Matt 19:20 *(be wanting);* Mark 10:21 and John 2:3 *(be missing).* The pass., used of *be lacking,* occurs esp. in Paul (Rom 3:23; 1 Cor 1:7; 8:8; 12:24; 2 Cor 11:9; Phil 4:12; further Luke 15:14 and Heb 11:37). U. Wilckens, *TDNT* VIII, 592-601.

ὑστέρημα, ατος, τό *hysterēma* deficiency*

Of the 9 occurrences in the NT 7 are in the Pauline letters: 1 Cor 16:17 (with ἀναπληρόω: "make up for *the absence* [of a person]," i.e., represent someone who is absent); 2 Cor 8:14 (bis; contrasted with περίσσευμα); 9:12; 11:9; Phil 2:30; 1 Thess 3:10. It also appears in Luke 21:4 (different in Mark 12:44, ὑστέρησις) and Col 1:24 (ἀνταναπληρόω τὰ ὑστερήματα, "fill out *what is yet lacking*"). U. Wilckens, *TDNT* VIII, 592-601.

ὑστέρησις, εως, ἡ *hysterēsis* deficiency; poverty*

Mark 12:44 refers to the poor widow who ἐκ τῆς

ὑστερήσεως αὐτῆς ("from what *little* she *possessed*") gave all she had; Phil 4:11: καθ᾿ ὑστέρησιν, "from *want*." U. Wilckens, *TDNT* VIII, 592-601.

ὕστερος, 3 *hysteros* latter, last*

Of the 12 occurrences in the NT 7 are in Matthew. Apart from the masc. in 1 Tim 4:1, only the neut. form ὕστερον occurs (as an adv.), used of *later* (Matt 4:2; 21:29, 32; 25:11; Mark 16:14; John 13:36; Heb 12:11) or *last of all* (Matt 21:37; 22:27; 26:60; Luke 20:32). Ὕστερος is used as (superlative) adj. in 1 Tim 4:1: "in the *last* times." U. Wilckens, *TDNT* VIII, 592-601.

ὑφαίνω *hyphainō* weave

Luke 12:27 D syr[s, c]: οὔτε νήθει οὔτε ὑφαίνει, referring to the κρίνα ("lilies"), which "neither spin nor *weave.*"

ὑφαντός, 3 *hyphantos* woven*

John 19:23: Jesus' tunic (→ χιτών) was "*woven* from top to bottom" and without seam (ἄραφος).

ὑψηλός, 3 *hypsēlos* high; exalted, haughty*

Ὑψηλός is used in the literal sense to refer to ὄρος, "mountain" (Mark 9:2 par. Matt 17:1; Matt 4:8 [different in Luke]; Rev 21:10); τεῖχος, "wall" (Rev 21:12); βραχίων, "*(uplifted)* arm" (Acts 13:17). The comparative ὑψηλότερος is used in Heb 7:26 with gen. of comparison ("*higher* than [heaven]"). In Heb 1:3 the subst. τὰ ὑψηλά, *heights,* refers to heaven.

The fig. sense of ὑψηλός *(haughty, proud)* occurs in Luke 16:15 ("*what is exalted* among men"); Rom 11:20 (ὑψηλὰ φρονέω, "harbor *proud* thoughts"); 12:16 (τὰ ὑψηλὰ φρονέω, "strive after *higher things*"). Cf. 1 Tim 6:17 ℵ (ὑψηλὰ φρονέω in place of → ὑψηλοφρονέω).

ὑψηλοφρονέω *hypsēlophroneō* be haughty*

1 Tim 6:17: "Admonish the rich in this world not *to become haughty.*" Cf. Rom 11:20 TR (in place of ὑψηλὰ φρονέω).

ὕψιστος, 3 *hypsistos* highest; subst.: the Most High (God), the highest (heaven)*

1. Hellenistic Greek and LXX — 2. Usage — a) The Most High — b) The highest heaven

Lit.: G. BERTRAM, *TDNT* VIII, 614-20. — BILLERBECK II, 99f. — HENGEL, *Judaism,* index s.v. hypsistarians.

1. In the Hellenistic environment of the NT ὕψιστος often occurs as a predicate of Zeus. Nonetheless, the LXX also uses it as a translation of ῾elyôn as an epithet for Yahweh, and it often serves as a designation for God in Hellenistic-Jewish texts and

inscriptions. Hence ὕψιστος used subst. is a general designation for the highest being.

2. LXX usage continues in the NT, where the 13 occurrences of ὕψιστος refer to God (9 times) and to the heavens (4 times).

a) Outside of Mark 5:7 and Heb 7:1, ὕψιστος as a designation for God is limited to the Lukan dual work. The birth story calls Mary's promised child "Son *of the Most High*" (Luke 1:32), whose mother the "power *of the Most High*" will overshadow (v. 35). Jesus' precursor, John the Baptist, accordingly receives the designation "prophet *of the Most High*" (v. 76). The Gerasene demoniac addresses Jesus as "Son of God, *of the Most High*" (Mark 5:7/Luke 8:28), which has a parallel in Acts 16:17: The soothsaying girl calls Paul and his companions "servants of God, *of the Most High.*" The two remaining occurrences in Luke's writings correspond to this usage: Luke 6:35 (those who carry out Jesus' words will be "sons *of the Most High*"); Acts 7:48 ("*the Most High* [i.e., God] does not dwell in houses made with human hands"). Heb 7:1, quoting Gen 14:18, refers to Melchizedek as a "priest *of the Most High.*"

b) In Mark 11:10 (par. Matt 21:9/Luke 19:38) ὕψιστος designates the celestial regions (cf. the par. Ps 148:1). In these passages (similarly Luke 2:14) the heavenly powers are exhorted to join in the praise ("Sing Hosanna, you in *the highest*"). It is improbable that Mark 11:10 par. is "an invocation of God" ("Help, thou in the highest"), "the name of God being replaced by a designation of place in Jewish fashion" (Bertram 619).   G. Lüdemann

ὕψος, ους, τό   *hypsos*   height*

In Eph 3:18 and Rev 21:16 ὕψος refers in the literal sense to the dimension of height, in other instances to the concrete place (heaven: Luke 1:78; 24:49; Eph 4:8). In Jas 1:9 ὕψος refers in the fig. sense to high position. G. Bertram, *TDNT* VIII, 602-5; J. Blunck, *DNTT* II, 198-200.

ὑψόω   *hypsoō*   raise up; make great*

1. Occurrences in the NT — 2. Ὑψόω as the opposite of "to humble" — 3. The christological context — 4. John

Lit.: G. R. BEASLEY-MURRAY, "John 12:31-32: The Eschatological Significance of the Lifting Up of the Son of Man," FS Greeven 70-81. — G. BERTRAM, *TDNT* VIII, 606-13. — H. HOLLIS, "The Root of the Johannine Pun ὑψωθῆναι," *NTS* 35 (1989) 475-78. — L. RUPPERT, "Erhöhungsvorstellungen im AT," *BZ* 22 (1978) 199-220. — W. THÜSING, *Erhöhungsvorstellung und Parusieerwartung in der ältesten nachösterlichen Christologie* (SBS 42, 1970). — For further bibliography see *TWNT* X, 1288.

1. Ὑψόω occurs 20 times in the NT. In Acts 13:17 it refers to *make great,* otherwise to *raise up.*

2. One group of occurrences focuses on the contrast with "to humble" (→ ταπεινόω); cf. the Jesus saying in the Synoptics concerning self-humiliation and self-exaltation (Matt 23:12 par. Luke 18:14 [cf. Luke 14:11 bis and Luke 1:52; also Matt 11:23 par. Luke 10:15]), which reflects OT Jewish influence (cf. Ezek 21:31 [= 21:26 LXX] and Billerbeck I, 921). "Along the lines of the OT revelation of God all exaltation on man's part is repudiated. Exaltation is the act of God alone" (Bertram 608). This same line of tradition includes sayings such as those in Jas 4:10 ("humble yourselves before the Lord and he *will exalt* you") or 1 Pet 5:6 ("humble yourselves therefore under the mighty hand of God, that in due time he *may exalt* you").

The contrasting pair "humble-*exalt*" occurs in a different context in the Pauline corpus. In 2 Cor 11:7 the Corinthians' exaltation consists in the fact that they have accepted the gospel (without cost), whereas (ironically) Paul humbled himself by his unpaid proclamation.

3. Ὑψόω acquires special meaning in christology, where it refers to the appointment of Jesus to his position of dominion. This is the case in the pre-Pauline Philippians hymn (Phil 2:6-11; v. 9: ὑπερυψόω) and in what are probably old traditions in Acts 2:33 and 5:31. Exaltation here is identical to resurrection, regardless of what relationship obtained between the two concepts during the earliest period (cf. Thüsing 41-55).

4. Ὑψόω occurs 5 times in John and exhibits there a pronounced theological sense. In all 5 instances it possesses double meaning, referring to Jesus' being raised up on the cross, which simultaneously means his exaltation into heaven (3:14 bis; 8:28; 12:32, 34). John no longer speaks of a suffering Son of man who goes to his death, or of the scandal of the cross in the Pauline sense; his view thus allowed for a docetic christology of glory.
     G. Lüdemann

ὕψωμα, ατος, τό   *hypsōma*   that which has been raised, that which towers above; height*

In Rom 8:39 ὕψωμα is used as an astronomical t.t. referring to the region over the horizon: "neither *height,* nor depth (βάθος)." In 2 Cor 10:5 πᾶν ὕψωμα ἐπαιρόμενον refers to "everything *that rises up,* or, more specifically, all *pride* that rises up in opposition." G. Bertram, *TDNT* VIII, 613-14.

Φ φ

φάγος, ου, ὁ *phagos* glutton*

Matt 11:19 par. Luke 7:34, in the charge against Jesus (used with οἰνοπότης): "A *glutton* (ἄνθρωπος φάγος) and drunkard, a friend of tax collectors and sinners."

φαιλόνης, ου, ὁ *phailonēs* cloak*

Φαιλόνης is a Latin loanword *(paenula)* and originally was spelled φαινόλας or φαινόλης. "From these by metathesis came φαιλόνης" (BAGD s.v.). On the pseudepigraphic character of the remark in 2 Tim 4:13 ("When you come, bring the *cloak* I left with Carpus at Troas") cf. P. Trummer, " 'Mantel und Schriften' (2 Tim 4,13). Zur Interpretation einer persönlichen Notiz in den Pastoralbriefen," *BZ* 18 (1974) 193-207. Spicq, *Notes* II, 917f.

φαίνω *phainō* shine; appear*

1. Occurrences and meaning of the act. — 2. Usage in the pass. — 3. The partc. φαινόμενα

Lit.: R. BULTMANN and D. LÜHRMANN, *TDNT* IX, 1-10. — H.-C. HAHN, *DNTT* II, 487f. — C. MUGLER, *Dictionnaire historique de la terminologie optique des Grecs* (1964) 406-13.

1. Φαίνω occurs 31 times in the NT (13 times in Matthew, 2 in Mark, 2 in Luke, 2 in John, 3 in Paul, 4 in Revelation, and once each in Hebrews, James, 1 Peter, 2 Peter, and 1 John). The act. form occurs 9 times, 7 of these in the Johannine writings; its basic meaning is *shine, appear.* Since Homer it is used intrans. to refer to the illumination and shining of various sources of light, such as the sun, the moon, lamps, and fire. In the NT it maintains this meaning when speaking, e.g., of the shining of a lamp (→ λύχνος).

2 Pet 1:19 compares the prophetic word of Scripture to the shining light of a lamp: "And we have the prophetic word made more sure. You will do well to pay attention to this as to a lamp *shining* in a dark place, until the day dawns and the morning star rises in your hearts." Using motifs from Psalms 105, 118, and 2 Esdr 12:42 ("For of all the prophets you alone are left to us, like a lamp in a dark place"), this verse understands the prophetic word of Scripture as a reference to Christ and his parousia, since Christ's transfiguration has revealed his divine being. The christological promise of Scripture shines like a light in the present darkness of the world (cf. Matt 4:16; John 1:5; Eph 6:12). The light of the prophetic word will shine until the eschatological day dawns (cf. Rom 13:12 [the day of the parousia will end the night] and 2 Cor 4:4-6 [the divine light has both cosmic and individual dimensions]).

The "morning star" in 2 Pet 1:19 might be an allusion to the messianically interpreted star in Num 24:17. The metaphor is applied to a person in John 5:35, where the Johannine Jesus compares John the Baptist to a lamp: "He was a burning and *shining* lamp." In the context of the cursing of Babylon (Rev 18:23) the avenging angel declares that "the light of a lamp *shall shine* in thee no more; and the voice of bridegroom and bride shall be heard in thee no more."

Rev 1:16 christologically applies the metaphor of the sun's light to the appearance of the Son of man: "And his face was like the sun *shining* in full strength" (cf. Matt 17:2; Dan 7; Ezek 1:24ff.). The apocalyptic vision of the destruction of the world should also be understood within this context of the eschatological parousia, as alluded to in Rev 8:12. The prologue in John 1:5 uses φαίνω in a thoroughly christological fashion ("the light *shines* in the darkness . . ."), whereas 1 John 2:8 christologically grounds the ethics of the "new commandment": "I am writing you a new commandment, which is true in him and in you, because the darkness is passing away and the true light *is* already *shining.*"

Phil 2:15 uses the metaphor in an ethical context that emphasizes the believer's role as example: "That you may be blameless and innocent, children of God without blemish in the midst of 'a crooked and perverse generation' [Deut 32:5], among whom you *shine* as lights in the world. Hold fast to the word of life." In Rev 21:23 the apocalyptic seer similarly views the heavenly Jerusalem as the city in which the Lamb Christ shines: "The city has no need of sun or moon to *shine* upon it, for the glory of God is its light, and its lamp is the Lamb." The christological meaning allies itself here with an ecclesiological one, since the natural sources of light—sun and moon— are superfluous if God's own glory will be illuminating the heavenly Jerusalem, the Church on earth. All these passages posit the mighty superiority of Christ's own light. It is an existential faith-motif of positive mastery over the world, and it triumphs over the darkness of one's experience of the world.

2. The pass. form φαίνομαι occurs 22 times, 17 of those in the Synoptic Gospels (including Mark 16:9); it is used of *shine, appear, come to light, be seen, be visible, be revealed, be illuminated.* It refers, e.g., to the appearance of the star (Matt 2:7), the dream appearance of the angel of God in the Matthean history before Jesus' birth (1:20; 2:13, 19), the appearance of Elijah (Luke 9:8), the appearances of the resurrected Jesus (Mark 16:9), and the parousia appearances of the returning Son of man (Matt 24:27, 30). In this semantic context it signifies an epiphany event (→ ἐπιφάνεια) emphasizing God's illuminating inbreaking into the experience of the world's darkness, all the while presupposing the apocalyptic and eschatological background of the antithesis between light and darkness (→ σκότος, φῶς).

A related motif is that in which God's power appears in the deeds of the earthly Jesus; cf. the witnesses' reaction to Jesus' exorcism of demons during the healing of the demoniac (Matt 9:33): "Never *was* anything like this *seen* in Israel." The pass.-mid. construction expresses God's revelation in Jesus' deeds. The vb. occurs in Jas 4:14 in a parenetic context: "What is your life? For you are a mist that *appears* for a little time and then vanishes." 1 Pet 4:18 cites Prov 11:31 with similar meaning within an admonishment: "And if the righteous man is scarcely saved, where will the impious and sinner *appear?*" The parable of the weeds among the wheat exhibits similar usage (Matt 13:26): "So when the plants came up and bore grain, then the weeds *appeared* also."

The following occurrences refer to the contrast between concealment and public disclosure: Matt 6:5 (so that they may be seen by others); v. 16 (so that others see that they are fasting); v. 18 (so that your own fasting is not seen by others); and the cry of woe over the scribes and Pharisees (Matt 23:27f.): "You are like white-washed tombs, which outwardly *appear* beautiful, but within they are full of dead men's bones and all uncleanness." 2 Cor 13:7 also focuses on this discrepancy between appearance and reality before God: "Not that we may *appear* to have met the test, but that you may do what is right."

The high priest uses the vb. at Jesus' trial before the Sanhedrin in an expression referring to one's forming an

opinion by a process of critical evaluation (Mark 14:64): "How *does it seem* to you?" Luke 24:11 uses φαίνομαι similarly in its reference to the apostles' reaction to the women's testimony concerning the resurrection ("But these words *seemed* to them an idle tale, and they did not believe them"), and Rom 7:13 in its reference to the Pauline reflection concerning the relationship between law and sin ("in order that sin *might become visible* as sin . . .").

3. Heb 11:3 uses φαίνω in a philosophical-epistemological context, which in the sense of creatio ex nihilo views God's creative word as the primal foundation of the visible world (the βλεπόμενα): "By faith we understand that the world was created by the word of God, so that what is seen has not come to be from *what is perceivable by the senses* (φαινόμενα)." The intention here is to reject a materialistic understanding of creation derived from an evolutionary cosmogony. What is suggested instead is faith in a theocentric creation and its accompanying teleology of ordered cosmic determination by God (cf. Schelkle, *Theology* I). The vb. occurs with the same meaning in Ign. *Rom.* 3:2f.; *Pol.* 2:2.

P.-G. Müller

Φάλεκ *Phalek* Peleg*

Indeclinable personal name in Jesus' genealogy in Luke 3:35 (Gen 11:16-19; 1 Chr 1:25 LXX).

φανερός, 3 *phaneros* visible, evident, clear; public*

1. Occurrences in the NT — 2. Of what can be known

Lit.: R. BULTMANN and D. LÜHRMANN, *TDNT* IX, 2f.

1. Φανερός occurs 18 times in the NT. It comes from classical Greek, where it refers to "visible, exposed to view, apparent, clear, public" and, in reference to persons, "splendid, excellent." Φανερός occurs 19 times in the LXX. Besides these usages, φανερός appears in the NT in theologically significant contexts where Paul uses it in arguments from evidence for what exists; furthermore, it is used in the context of specific revelatory terminology.

2. Paul uses φανερός within the framework of his theology of paganism (Rom 1:19), where he views the salvation of the Gentiles as possible precisely because they clearly recognize God and experience his deeds within themselves: "For what can be known about God is *plain* to them, because God has shown it to them" (on this view of God's self-revelation in the Gentiles, cf. D. Lührmann, *Das Offenbarungsverständnis bei Paulus und in paulinischen Gemeinden* [1965] and the bibliograpy for → ἀποκαλύπτω). When Paul then comes to speak of the salvation of the Jews and the soteriological relevance of circumcision (the physical mark of Jewish

identity), he emphasizes that the external, public, demonstrative aspects of being a Jew are not decisive; rather, what is decisive is the attitude of the heart before God and the inner integrity of faith of a genuinely pious person (Rom 2:28): "For he is not a real Jew who is one *outwardly,* nor is true circumcision something *external* and *physical.*" Such a formulation reflects OT motifs (Deut 10:16; 30:6; Jer 4:4; 6:10; 9:25; Ezek 44:7, 9; 1QpHab 11:13; *Odes Sol.* 11:1-3; *Jub.* 1:23f.; cf. H. Schlier, *Rom* [HTKNT] 89f.). Jesus' instructions concerning secret piety are similar (Matt 6:4, 6, 18).

Gal 5:19 speaks of this in an ethical-parenetic sense in introducing a catalog of vices: "The works of the flesh are *clear.*" 1 Tim 4:15 reads similarly: "So that your progress [toward perfection] may be *visible* to all," as does 1 John 3:10: "By this *do* the children of God and the children of the devil *reveal* themselves." In Acts 4:16 the Sanhedrin speaks of the apostles' *"manifest* miraculous signs." The word is used repeatedly to contrast what has been previously concealed and not perceived (Mark 4:22 par.): "For there is nothing hid, except to be made manifest; nor is anything secret, except to come to *light*"; so also Luke 8:17; Mark 3:12 (par. Matt 12:16): The response to the question "Are you the Son of God?" is the commandment to keep the messianic secret, "not to make him *known.*"

Φανερός also occurs in Mark 6:14 in this simple sense of "make known" (John the Baptist's name is known, including to King Herod); Acts 7:13 (Joseph makes himself known to his brothers); 1 Cor 11:19 (factions, so that those who are genuine among you may become *revealed*); 14:25 (the secrets of his heart are *disclosed* when an unbeliever is called to account by all); Phil 1:13 (it became known that Paul endures his imprisonment in Christ). The disclosure of works stands in the eschatological context of the last judgment in 1 Cor 3:13: on the day of the Lord "each man's work will become *visible.*" In summary one can say that the adj. is used both to criticize an overly forensic and external understanding of piety and to emphasize the open, public, and eschatological nature of the disclosure of good and evil.

                                               P.-G. Müller

φανερόω *phaneroō* reveal; pass.: appear, become visible; become known

1. Occurrences in the NT — 2. Pauline and deutero-Pauline usage — 3. Johannine usage (including Revelation)

Lit.: M. N. A. BOCKMUEHL, "Das Verb φανερόω im NT," *BZ* 32 (1988) 87-99. — R. BULTMANN and D. LÜHRMANN, *TDNT* IX, 3-6. — E. JENNI, *THAT* I, 753-55.

1. Φανερόω, which appears to be newly coined in

Hellenistic Greek, occurs 49 times in the NT. The LXX attests it only in Jer 40(33):6, where *gālāh* (Piel) is the Hebrew equivalent. Synoptic usage is confined to the proverb-like pronouncement in Mark 4:22: "For there is nothing hid, except *to be made manifest,*" which occurs in a slightly altered form in the version from the logia source Luke 12:2 par. and has probably also influenced Luke 8:17. The Markan context alludes to the secret of understanding Jesus' parables.

2. Paul uses φανερόω and ἀποκαλύπτω almost synonymously, as becomes clear in the repetition of Rom 1:17 in 3:21. The former asserts that "in every person who believes—for the Jew and also for the Greek— God's righteousness *is revealed* (ἀποκαλύπτεται)." The latter emphasizes the same justification through faith: "But now the righteousness of God *has been manifested* (πεφανέρωται) apart from law," referring to the one-time event of Christ and its soteriological efficacy. One sees that for Paul the vb. is a key term for the revelation of God's salvation (1:19) in the gospel of Jesus Christ (cf. 16:26: "my gospel . . . *is* now *disclosed* and . . . is made known to all nations").

In a striking usage, φανερόω occurs 9 times in a polemical context in 2 Corinthians, where Paul may be employing one of his adversaries' catchwords. "Through us he *reveals* the fragrance of the knowledge of him everywhere" (2:14); hence in Paul's proclamation God's revelation occurs through Jesus Christ. "*For all to see,* you are a letter from Christ, delivered by us" (3:3); "we always carry in the body the death of Jesus, so that the life of Jesus *may* also *be manifested* in our bodies" (4:10; in his suffering Paul attests an existential imitation of Christ); "so that the life of Jesus *may be manifested* in our mortal flesh" (v. 11).

1 Cor 4:5 uses φανερόω within the context of eschatological judgment: "The [coming] Lord will bring to light the things now hidden in darkness and *will disclose* the purposes of the heart"; cf. further 2 Cor 5:10: "for we all *must appear* before the judgment seat of Christ"; v. 11: "what we are *is known* to God, but I hope it *is known* also to your conscience"; 7:12: "so that your zeal for us *might be revealed* among you before God"; in 11:6 in a different context, Paul emphasizes his knowledge, which he *has made plain* in every way.

The Pauline school continues this synonymous usage of φανερόω and ἀποκαλύπτω within the framework of a revelatory scheme borrowed from the pre-Pauline tradition, and it does so in order to express God's revelation in Jesus Christ taking place in the proclamation of the gospel. The light-darkness parenesis, however, becomes stated much more strongly than in Paul himself. Eph 5:13f.: "But everything brought to light becomes *revealed;* for anything that is *revealed* is light"; Col 1:26:

"the mystery hidden for ages and generations but now *made manifest* to his saints"; 3:4: "when Christ who is our life *appears,* then you also *will appear* with him in glory." Although life with and in Christ from baptism to the parousia is yet hidden, what is hidden will appear in the eschatological coming of the Messiah; cf. 1 John 3:2: "we know that when he *appears* we shall be like him."

The relationship between Christ and life has already been established in Phil 1:21: "For to me to live is Christ" (cf. Gal 2:20: "Christ lives in me"). In Col 4:4, the apostle is commissioned to *reveal clearly* the mystery of Christ. 1 Tim 3:16 uses φανερόω in an extremely old, pre-Pauline hymn about the mystery of the incarnation: "He *was revealed* in the flesh." 2 Tim 1:10 speaks of our calling, "which now *became known* through the appearance of our savior Christ Jesus." Titus 1:3: "God *manifested* his word at the proper time through the preaching with which I have been entrusted." A variation of the same revelatory scheme appears in an eschatological version in 1 Pet 1:20: "He was destined before the foundation of the world but *was made manifest* at the end of the times for your sake." Heb 9:8 also emphasizes the Christ-event as a caesura: "The way into the sanctuary *was* not yet *revealed* as long as the outer tent was still standing"; v. 26: "but as it is, he *has appeared* once for all at the end of the age to put away sin by the sacrifice of himself."

3. The Johannine theology of revelation uses φανερόω and γνωρίζω as synonyms and largely avoids ἀποκαλύπτω (except John 12:38, citing Isa 53:1). Whereas Paul adopted revelatory terminology more from mysticism, John is concerned precisely with concrete appearance and its value for knowledge in emphasizing God's salvific activity in the signs and words of the earthly and resurrected Jesus. Jesus reveals God's reality (John 7:4), God's name (17:6), God's works (3:21; 9:3). Indeed, Jesus is God's revealer in the larger sense, as the prologue (1:5, 16-18) already emphasizes. According to 21:1, 14, however, the resurrected Christ also reveals God's deed (cf. Mark 16:12, 14).

1 John 3:5, 8 and 4:9 similarly understand Jesus as the one who reveals God's love, whereby this same revelation continues in the Church's own living tradition of Jesus (cf. 1:2: "the life *appeared,* and we saw it, and testify to it, and proclaim to you the eternal life which was with the Father and *appeared* to us"). The language of the christological creed as transmitted within the Church's tradition is grounded in the original witnesses' concrete experience of the appearance of the divine essence in the earthly and resurrected Jesus. To abide within the apostolic tradition of the Church ensures true faith (cf. 1 John 2:19: "They went out from us, but they were not of us; for if they had been of us, they would have remained with us, but it had to be *plain* that not

all are of us"). This "abiding in Christ" should be maintained until his appearance at the parousia (cf. 2:28). What the baptized are is still concealed under the eschatological reservation (cf. 3:2).

1 John 3:5 emphasizes the soteriological aspect of the incarnation: "He *appeared* in order to take away sins"; similarly 3:8b; 4:9: In this the love of God *became visible* among us, that God sent his only Son into the world, so that we might live through him" (cf. J. P. Miranda, *Der Vater, der mich gesandt hat* [1972] 82-100).

The pass. of φανερόω appears in Rev 3:18 and 15:4 in a hymn ("your just deeds *have been revealed*") without any particular theological significance.   P.-G. Müller

φανερῶς   *phanerōs*   openly, publicly; clearly, distinctly*

Mark 1:45: "so that he could no longer *openly* enter a town"; John 7:10 (in contrast to ἐν κρυπτῷ): "then he also went up [to Jerusalem], not *publicly,* but [as it were] in private"; Acts 10:3: "in a vision (ἐν ὁράματι)" Cornelius *clearly* saw an angel of God coming in. R. Bultmann and D. Lührmann, *TDNT* IX, 3.

φανέρωσις, εως, ἡ   *phanerōsis*   revelation, announcement*

Used twice in Paul: φανέρωσις τοῦ πνεύματος, "the *revelation* of the Spirit" (1 Cor 12:7), and φανέρωσις τῆς ἀληθείας, "*open proclamation* of the truth" (2 Cor 4:2). Trench, *Synonyms* 356-57; R. Bultmann and D. Lührmann, *TDNT* IX, 6.

φανός, οῦ, ὁ   *phanos*   lamp, lantern*

John 18:3 uses φανοί with λαμπάδες: the cohort sent to arrest Jesus was equipped "with torches, *lanterns,* and weapons." Cf. → λαμπάς 2, 3.

Φανουήλ   *Phanouēl*   Phanuel*

Indeclinable personal name in Luke 2:36, the father of the prophetess Anna, of the tribe of Asher.

φαντάζομαι   *phantazomai*   pass.: become visible*

Heb 12:21: τὸ φανταζόμενον, the *appearance,* referring to the Sinai theophany. R. Bultmann and D. Lührmann, *TDNT* IX, 6.

φαντασία, ας, ἡ   *phantasia*   pomp, pageantry*

Acts 25:23: Agrippa (II) came μετὰ πολλῆς φαντασίας, "with great *pomp/pageantry.*" Cf. Radermacher, *Grammatik* 12.

φάντασμα, ατος, τό *phantasma* appearance; ghost*

In Mark 6:49 par. Matt 14:26 the disciples think that Jesus, who is walking on the water, is a *ghost* (ὅτι φάντασμά ἐστιν). Φάντασμα also occurs in place of → πνεῦμα in Luke 24:37 D in the report of the appearance of the resurrected Jesus. R. Bultmann and D. Lührmann, *TDNT* IX, 6.

φάραγξ, αγγος, ἡ *pharanx* ravine*

Luke 3:5: "Every *ravine* shall be filled" (citing Isa 40:4 LXX).

Φαραώ *Pharaō* Pharaoh*

Indeclinable name (actually the title) of the Egyptian kings (Gen 12:15; Exod 1:11 LXX, and elsewhere). In the NT it refers to the Pharaohs at the time of Joseph and Moses (Acts 7:10, 13, 21; Rom 9:17 [cf. Exod 9:16]; Heb 11:24). E. Winter, *LTK* VIII, 437f.; B. Reicke, *BHH* 1445-47 (bibliography).

Φάρες *Phares* Perez*

Indeclinable personal name in Jesus' genealogy (Matt 1:3a, b; Luke 3:33 [cf. Gen 38:29; 1 Chr 2:4, 5 LXX).

Φαρισαῖος, ου, ὁ *Pharisaios* Pharisee

1. Occurrences in the NT — 2. Usage in the NT — a) Mark — b) Matthew — c) Luke and Acts — d) John — 3. Portrayal in Jewish sources — a) Josephus — b) Rabbinic writing — 4. Jesus and the Pharisees — 5. Paul as a Pharisee

Lit.: G. BAUMBACH, *Jesus von Nazareth im Lichte der jüdischen Gruppenbildung* (1971) 72-97. — A. I. BAUMGARTEN, "The Name of the Pharisees," *JBL* 102 (1983) 411-28. — W. BEILNER, "Der Ursprung des Pharisäismus," *BZ* 3 (1959) 235-51. — J. T. CARROLL, "Luke's Portrayal of the Pharisees," *CBQ* 50 (1988) 604-21. — M. J. COOK, "Jesus and the Pharisees," *JES* 15 (1978) 441-60. — D. GOODBLATT, "The Place of the Pharisees in First-Century Judaism," *JSJ* 20 (1989) 12-30. — J. KAMPEN, *The Hasideans and the Origin of Pharisaism: A Study in 1 and 2 Maccabees* (1988). — B. LINDARS, "Jesus and the Pharisees," FS Daube 51-63. — D. LÜHRMANN, "Die Pharisäer und die Schriftgelehrten im Markusevangelium," *ZNW* 78 (1987) 169-85. — U. LUZ, "Jesus und die Pharisäer," *Judaica* 38 (1982) 229-46. — J. MAIER, *Geschichte der jüdischen Religion* (1972) 71-79. — R. MEYER and H. F. WEISS, *TDNT* IX, 11-48. — R. L. MOWERY, "Pharisees and Scribes, Galilee and Jerusalem," *ZNW* 80 (1989) 266-68. — J. NEUSNER, *The Rabbinic Traditions about the Pharisees before 70* (3 vols.; 1971). — *idem,* "The Use of the Later Rabbinic Evidence for the Study of First-Century Pharisaism," *Approaches to Ancient Judaism: Theory and Practice* (Brown Judaic Studies 1, ed. W. S. Green; 1978) 215-28. — E. P. SANDERS, *Paul and Palestinian Judaism*

(1977). — K. SCHUBERT, *Die jüdischen Religionsparteien in neutestamentlicher Zeit* (1970) 22-47. — SCHÜRER, *History* II, 381-403. — D. R. SCHWARTZ, "Josephus and Nicolaus on the Pharisees," *JSJ* 14 (1983) 157-71. — M. SIMON, *Jewish Sects at the Time of Jesus* (1967) 27-43. — C. THOMA, Maier/Schreiner 254-72. — H. F. WEISS, "Pharisäismus und Hellenismus," *OLZ* 74 (1979) 421-33. — U. C. VON WAHLDE, "The Terms for Religious Authorities in the Fourth Gospel: A Key to Literary-Strata?" *JBL* 98 (1979) 231-53. — R. A. WILD, "The Encounter between Pharisaic and Christian Judaism: Some Early Gospel Evidence," *NovT* 27 (1985) 105-24. — J. A. ZIESLER, "Luke and the Pharisees," *NTS* 25 (1978/79) 146-57. — For further bibliography see *TWNT* X, 1288f.

1. The 99 occurrences of Φαρισαῖος in the NT (including John 8:3) are with one exception (Phil 3:5) found in the Gospels (89 times) and Acts (9 times).

2. a) Mark uses Φαρισαῖος 12 times, though only between 2:16 and 12:13 and only in connection with disputes in which the Markan church defends against Jewish charges its freedom to engage in religious praxis apart from the law. Thus these references to the Pharisees do not allow any conclusions to be drawn concerning their actual theological profile. The mention of Pharisees and Herodians together (3:6; 8:15; 12:13) is also historically questionable, since this follows the agenda of disqualifying the Pharisees by casting them in the mold of Herod, thus portraying them as murderous (cf. 3:6; 8:11; 10:2; 12:13, 15).

b) Φαρισαῖος occurs most frequently in Matthew (29 times). With the exception of 22:16 Matthew avoids mentioning Pharisees and Herodians together, though several times he does mention Pharisees together with Sadducees (3:7; 16:1, 6, 11, 12) as well as Pharisees and high priests (21:45; 27:62). This completes an assimilation to the old Passion tradition in which the high priests appear as Jesus' primary adversaries, thus allowing the Pharisees to participate actively in Jesus' elimination. In addition, Matthew changes "scribes" to "Pharisees" on several occasions (cf. Mark 12:28, 35 with Matt 22:34, 41) in order to characterize Jewish opposition emphatically as Pharisaic. He shows the same motives in dealing with the Q-tradition by having John the Baptist and Jesus direct their invectives against the Pharisees (cf. 3:7ff.; 23:2ff. with Luke 3:7; 11:39ff.).

Matthew stereotypically calls the Pharisees "hypocrites" (6:2, 5, 16; 7:5, and elsewhere) and characterizes them as self-contradictory (23:3), lawless (23:28), and godless (15:12-14), since they do not practice what they teach (23:3, 23). In this way Matthew sets up a kind of fence around both Judaism and false teachers (cf. 24:11ff.; 7:15ff.). The Pharisees simultaneously function as a model for false prophets and as an antitype for Jesus, who fulfills the Torah in an exemplary fashion. By following Jesus, the Church realizes in its own life a far better righteousness than that of the Pharisees and scribes (cf. 5:20).

c) Betraying dependence on Mark, Luke also presents disputes against Pharisees and scribes (cf. 5:30, 33; 6:2, 7; 12:1), though only rarely does he insert Pharisees as Jesus' adversaries (cf. 5:17, 21; 7:30). Luke uses the tradition from Q in various ways (cf. 3:7ff.; 11:39ff., 45ff.). He accuses the Pharisees particularly of greed and of a resulting self-righteousness and unwillingness to repent (cf. 16:14f.; 18:9), so that they represent both the model of unconverted cosmopolitans called to renounce possessions (cf. 11:41; 12:33, and elsewhere) and the antitype of Jesus, who is portrayed as being poor.

Luke does not, however, attribute any murderous intentions to the Pharisees or have them participate in Jesus' death. Rather, he reports invitations (7:36ff.; 11:37f.; 14:1ff.) and well-intentioned advice (13:31) Jesus receives from Pharisees, as well as amicable behavior on the part of Pharisees who are members of the Sanhedrin (Acts 5:34; 23:6ff.). In addition, Luke mentions converted Pharisees (Acts 15:5) and emphasizes Paul's own membership in the Pharisees (23:6; 26:5), whom he describes as "the strictest αἵρεσις" (26:5). Since Luke considers the resurrection of Jesus to be the decisive salvation event (cf. Acts 2:24; 3:15; 4:10, and elsewhere), he portrays the Pharisees, who did believe in resurrection, more positively than did Mark and Matthew.

d) In John the Pharisees act in concert with the high priests (cf. 7:32, 45; 11:46, 47; 18:3) as representatives of Jewish authority residing in Jerusalem. They already appear as John the Baptist's adversaries (1:19, 24). They take offense at Jesus' freedom from sabbath regulations (5:1ff.; 9:1ff.) as well as his interest in the ὄχλος, or ʿam hāʾāreṣ (7:49). The Pharisees represent "the Jews," who from the very start are intent on eliminating Jesus (cf. 7:32; 11:46ff.) and are therefore associated with the devil as murderers (cf. 8:44ff.). This charge effectively casts as diabolic all Judaism, as so defined in terms of the Pharisees. John draws this Judaism into the stark dualism between the divine sphere of salvation and the world's sphere of ruin, so that the Pharisee or Jew becomes a model for the unbeliever.

3. a) Josephus, who according to *Vita* 12 claimed to have been a Pharisee himself, offers us more dependable information about the Pharisees than do the Gospels. In his historical work he mentions the Pharisees first during his portrayal of the time of Jonathan (*Ant.* xiii.171ff.). After the schism among the Hasidim during the middle of the 2nd cent. B.C. they organized into what was initially a strongly politically oriented group opposed to the sacral kingship of the Hasmoneans. Their influence increased after the time of Salome Alexandras (76-67 B.C.). *Ant.* xiv.41 suggests that they viewed Pompey's intervention in the affairs of the Jewish state as a righteous divine judgment and thus did not oppose Roman rule. Neither did they oppose in principal the reign of the half-Jew Herod (40-4 B.C.; cf. *Ant.*

xiv.172ff.; xv.3), though some Pharisees did object to the eagle fixed on the temple as a sign of Herod's (divine?) power (*B.J.* i.648ff.; *Ant.* xvii.149ff.).

Apparently the Pharisees were concerned above all with the sanctification of God's name (cf. *Ap.* ii.171, 192) and with the separation from all that was unholy. Their name also alludes to this emphasis (Φαρισαῖοι and *pᵉrûšîm* refer to "separated ones"), which their adversaries used in the derogatory sense of "separatists."

According to *Ant.* xvii.41 the Pharisees were proud of their precise knowledge of the patriarchal laws and boasted of their adherence to the law. They were known as the most accurate interpreters of the law, among which they counted not only the written Torah but also the oral Torah, the patriarchal traditions (*B.J.* ii.162); according to *Ant.* xiii.297 they "preserved many commandments not written in the laws of Moses." Since they were concerned with using the oral Torah to help people fulfill the Torah in their concrete daily lives, and thus with helping them attain salvation, they were considered more philanthropic and thus had "the great mass of people on their side" (*Ant.* xiii.298, cf. 288, 401f.)—probably primarily the urban middle class, which was relatively open-minded concerning new ideas.

Not only did the Pharisees develop religious law through a multitude of updated regulations, they also introduced new ideas in eschatology. They believed in the resurrection of the good and in an eternal punishment of the bad (*B.J.* ii.163; *Ant.* xviii.14). With this they accentuated a person's own ethical decisions, which according to *B.J.* ii.162 and *Ant.* xviii.13f. they viewed as the result of cooperation between God's own providence and human will. The communal life of this → αἵρεσις, which Josephus praises in *B.J.* ii.166, was of great significance. According to *Ant.* xvii.42 there were over six thousand Pharisees at the time of Herod.

b) The rabbinic writings offer no dependable information concerning the Pharisees before the destruction of the temple. The Pharisees appear here as a movement concerned with the sanctification of every aspect of one's life. To this end they posited a multitude of regulations (i.e., the oral Torah) as a fence around the written Torah in order to preserve the faithful from transgressions and also to give the average person access to salvation (cf. *m. 'Abot* 1:1; 3:3; *b. Roš. Haš.* 16b, 17a). The scribes as bearers of the oral tradition thus acquired great significance. Because this interpretation of law focused on what was humanly possible, apocalyptic groups accused the Pharisees of being compromising hypocrites (cf. 4QpNah 1:2; CD 1:11-19, and elsewhere). As the statements about the seven Pharisees in *y. Ber.* 9:14b (cf. *y. Soṭa* 5:20c) show, the Pharisees were aware of their own weaknesses.

From *b. Bek.* 30b; *y. Dem.* 2:2; *t. Dem.* 2:2 one can conclude that the Pharisees lived together in societies that had common meals and fixed times for prayer. Those who wished to join had to commit themselves to regular giving of the tithe and to the practice of levitical purity, and also had to undergo a period of probation. In contrast to the Qumran community the Pharisaic brotherhoods did not make any claim to exclusivity but rather affirmed the unity of the elect (cf. *m. Sanh.* 10:1). They viewed their own task as that of winning many adherents and, through common Torah study, building up Israel itself such that it might live up to the task of its own election according to Isa 60:3, namely, to be a light to the nations (cf. *m. 'Abot* 1:1; *'Abot R. Nat.* 1:3; *b. Ber.* 63b). As for the future, they anticipated on the one hand the coming of the Messiah, which according to *y. Ta'an.* 1:64a (cf. *b. Šabb.* 118b) will be prepared by obedience to the law, and on the other hand the resurrection of the dead (cf. *m. Sanh.* 10:1-3; *b. Sanh.* 98a).

4. Since the aforementioned three main sources for the Pharisees were edited only after A.D. 70, it is very difficult to answer the question concerning Jesus' own relationship to the Pharisees. Critical evaluation of these sources allows us to ascertain both (a) common ground and (b) differences.

a) Jesus, too, was concerned with gathering in the entire people of Israel (cf. Luke 7:22 par.; 13:34 par.), and not with a holy remnant. To this end he won adherents, whom he then had participate in his ministry and to whom he gave rules for fellowship and prayers (cf. Mark 3:14 par.; 10:42ff. par.; Matt 6:9ff. par.). The sanctification of God's name by the observance of God's will was an essential concern of Jesus' own proclamation (cf. Matt 6:9f. par.; Mark 3:35 par.; 12:28ff. par.). He seems to have reckoned with a resurrection of the dead (cf. Mark 12:18ff. par.).

b) Jesus' own behavior and message were determined primarily by the nearness of the kingdom of God, which is why the prophetic-eschatological element predominated in his proclamation. Preparation for God's advent is the pressing commandment of the hour. This call was directed without exception to every person in Israel and called into question the current scale of values (cf. Luke 7:36ff.; 14:16ff.; 15:11ff.; 18:10ff.). Accordingly, the Pharisees must have found Jesus' behavior particularly offensive, since it was characterized by disregard for purity and tithing regulations and by association with tax collectors and sinners (cf. Mark 2:15ff. par.; 7:15 par.; Matt 11:19 par.). In view of the distribution of actual power during that period, however, they cannot be considered the instigators of Jesus' death.

5. Paul's letters represent an authentic testimony of a Pharisee. According to these documents, Pharisees distinguished themselves through their attitude toward the law, which took the form of zeal for complete fulfillment of the written and oral Torah (cf. Phil 3:5f.; Gal 1:14). Additionally, Paul showed himself to be a particularly active enthusiast in his persecution activity (Gal 1:13). Although, because of the antithesis between righteousness by faith and righteousness by works, he describes his conversion as a radical change from his identity as a Pharisee (Phil 3:7ff.), Paul as a Christian apostle nonetheless remained a product of his Pharisaic past: in his attitude toward his people (cf. Rom 9:1ff.; 11:25f.) and toward the Romans (cf. 13:1ff.), in his recognition of Scripture as the source of divine revelation, in his efforts concerning its correct interpretation, in his affirmation of the enduring nature of one's obliga-

tion to the Torah as God's will (cf. 7:12ff.; 9:6ff.; 13:8ff.), and in his reservations concerning ecstatic phenomena (cf. 1 Cor 14:1ff., 19).

G. Baumbach

φαρμακεία, ας, ἡ *pharmakeia* sorcery, magic*

Gal 5:20, in a catalog of vices; Rev 18:23, in reference to "Babylon's" *sorcery,* through which "all nations were deceived"; also in Rev 9:21 A al (φαρμακείων in place of φαρμάκων). *TCGNT* ad loc.

φαρμακεύς, έως, ὁ *pharmakeus* mixer of poisons; magician

Rev 21:8 TR in place of → φαρμακός.

φάρμακον, ου, τό *pharmakon* poison; magic charm*

Rev 9:21: People "did not repent of their murders or their *magic potions* or their immorality." BAGD s.v. 2.

φαρμακός, οῦ, ὁ *pharmakos* magician*

Pl. in Rev 21:8 and 22:15 in vice catalogs (sometimes accented φάρμακος).

φάσις, εως, ἡ *phasis* announcement, report*

Acts 21:31: ἀνέβη φάσις τῷ χιλιάρχῳ . . . ὅτι . . . , "a *report* came up to the tribune [i.e., up to the fortress Antonia] that. . . ."

φάσκω *phaskō* assert*

Acts 24:9 and 25:19 use φάσκω with acc. and inf. An assertion concerning oneself uses the nom. of the partc. with a following inf. with pred. nom.: φάσκοντες εἶναι σοφοὶ ἐμωράνθησαν, "*by claiming* to be wise, they became fools" (Rom 1:22).

φάτνη, ης, ἡ *phatnē* manger*

Luke 2:7, 12, 16: ἐν (τῇ) φάτνῃ, "in the *manger,*" referring to Jesus, who was placed in a feeding manger after his birth. 13:15 refers to the ox or donkey one looses "from the *manger*" in order to lead it to water. M. Hengel, *TDNT* IX, 49-55.

φαῦλος, 3 *phaulos* bad, evil*

Φαῦλος is used in the moral sense in Rom 9:11 (πράσσειν τι ἀγαθὸν ἢ φαῦλον); John 3:20 and 5:29 ([τὰ] φαῦλα πράσσειν); Jas 3:16 (πρᾶγμα); Titus 2:8 (μηδὲν ἔχων λέγειν περὶ ἡμῶν φαῦλον, "having nothing *evil* to say of us"). In 2 Cor 5:10 εἴτε ἀγαθὸν εἴτε φαῦλον hardly refers to "reward or punishment from the judge" (*contra* BAGD s.v.

2), but more likely to that which a person has done in this earthly life (cf. R. Bultmann, *2 Cor* [Eng. tr., 1985] ad loc.). Trench, *Synonyms* 317f.; E. Achilles, *DNTT* I, 564.

φέγγος, ους, τό *phengos* radiance, light*

Lit.: C. MUGLER, *Dictionnaire historique de la terminologie optique des Grecs* (1964) 425-28.

1. The use of φέγγος in referring to *radiance, light* is attested since Homer. It occurs 24 times in the LXX and frequently refers to the radiance, light, and blinding effects emanating from the appearance of the Lord, esp. from the face of the Lord (2 Kgdms 22:13: "Out of the *brightness* before him coals of fire flamed forth"). The righteous person, however, also shines in this way (2 Kgdms 23:4: "When one rules justly, ruling in the fear of God, he dawns on them like the *morning light,* like the sun shining forth upon a cloudless morning"). See further Job 3:4; 22:28; 38:12; 41:10; as well as Wis 7:10; Hos 7:6; Amos 5:20; 2 Macc 12:9. The word occurs 5 times in the vision in Ezekiel 1, and also in Ezek 10:4 ("and the court was full of the *brightness* of the glory of the Lord"); 43:2 ("And behold, the glory of the God of Israel came from the east; and the earth *shone* with his glory"). The use in Ezekiel (and Wis 7:10) appears to provide the background for its two occurrences in the NT.

2. The citation from Isa 13:10 is included within the framework of the speech on the return of the Son of man in Mark 13:24 par. Matt 24:29: "The sun will be darkened and the moon will not give its *light.*" This prophecy foretells the darkness that will arise when God's light, which is bestowed in the radiance of the sun and moon, is taken from the world. The background here includes the motifs of "the day of judgment" (after Isa 34:4; Joel 2:10f.; 3:4; 4:15f.) and "the day of darkness" (after Zeph 1:15). The eclipse of the sun, the extinguishing of the moon, and the falling of the stars from heaven are all metaphors of judgment indicating the cosmic dimensions of Christ's parousia. Cf. A. Vögtle, *Das NT und die Zukunft des Kosmos* (1970) 28-31, 67-71; F. Hahn, FS Vögtle 240-66.

P.-G. Müller

φείδομαι *pheidomai* spare; refrain from something*

This mid. deponent vb. appears with a gen. obj. in 1 Cor 7:28 ("I *would spare* you that") and 2 Cor 1:23 (φειδόμενος ὑμῶν). It occurs frequently with a negative ("not *spare*": Acts 20:29; Rom 8:32; 11:21a, b; 2 Cor 13:2; 2 Pet 2:4, 5). In 2 Cor 12:6 an inf. as obj. (τοῦ καυχᾶσθαι) is implied: "But I *refrain* from it [i.e., from boasting]."

φειδομένως *pheidomenōs* sparingly, sparsely*

Constructed from the partc. φειδόμενος ("one who is stingy"), this adv. occurs twice in 2 Cor 9:6 modifying first σπείρω, "sow," and then θερίζω, "reap."

φέρω *pherō* carry, bring, bear; lead; endure; uphold*

1. Occurrences in the NT — 2. Usage — a) Carry, bring (along) — b) Bring (someone) — c) Bear (fruit) — d) Bring (a legal matter) — e) Lead (locally) — f) Endure — g) Bring (a teaching) — h) Uphold

Lit.: R. BORIG, *Der wahre Weinstock. Untersuchungen zu Joh 15,1-10* (SANT 16, 1967). — J. A. FITZMYER, "The Use of *Agein* and *Pherein* in the Synoptic Gospels," FS Gingrich 147-60. — K. WEISS, *TDNT* IX, 56-59. — For further bibliography see *TWNT* X, 1289.

1. Of the 66 occurrences in the NT 50 are in the Gospels and Acts alone. Within the Synoptic Gospels (19 occurrences), φέρω is clearly preferred by Mark (15 occurrences); in 4 instances Matthew replaces φέρω (πρός) by → προσφέρω (8:16; 9:2; 17:16; 22:19; cf. Fitzmyer 150ff.).

2. a) In Luke 23:26 (differently in Mark 15:21/Matt 27:32 [αἴρω]/John 19:17 [βαστάζω]) Simon of Cyrene "carries" the burden of the cross "behind Jesus" (cf. Plutarch *Moralia* 554A; compared with the other readings, Luke's use of φέρω emphasizes more the idea of forward movement than that of picking up). From the perspective of Luke 14:27 Simon of Cyrene thereby becomes the first disciple (→ μαθητής 4.c) who picks up the cross and follows Jesus. Fig. in Heb 13:13 of personal acceptance of Jesus' suffering: "Let us . . . *bear* abuse for him" (cf. Ezek 34:29; 36:6).

In reference to other objects φέρω refers to *bring (along):* in Mark 6:27f. par. Matt 14:11 (bis) the head of John the Baptist (cf. *Esth. Rab.* 1:19, 21 [Billerbeck I, 683]; Diogenes Laertius ix.58; Appian *BC* iv.20.81); in Mark 11:2, 7 (differently in Matt 21:2, 7/Luke 19:30, 35 [→ ἄγω 2]) the colt; in Luke 15:23 the fatted calf; in 24:1 the spices the women had prepared for Jesus' body (see also John 19:39); in 2 Tim 4:13 a cloak. Cf. further John 2:8 (bis); 4:33: "*Has* anyone *brought* him food?"; Acts 4:34, 37; 5:2; 14:13: the priest of Zeus brings sacrificial offerings "to the city gates," a reference found esp. frequently in the LXX (see Weiss 56); 1 Pet 1:13: the grace "that *is brought* to you at the parousia (→ ἀποκάλυψις 4)."

According to Mark 12:15f. (differently in Matt 22:19 [ἐπιδείκνυμι]/Luke 20:24 [→ δείκνυμι 2]), Jesus has someone *bring* him a denarius. In Matt 14:18 he tells his disciples: "*Bring* them [i.e., five loaves and two fish] here to me" (cf. John 21:10). In John 20:27 Thomas receives the challenge: "*Put* your finger here . . . and *put out* your hand. . . ." In Rev 21:24 the kings of the earth *bring* their → δόξα (2), and in v. 26 the nations *bring* their δόξα and τιμή into the heavenly Jerusalem (allusion to Isa 60:3, 5, 11; cf. Pss 67:30 LXX; 71:10f. LXX) and hand them over.

b) Φέρω occurs frequently in Mark's exposition of miraculous healings: People *bring* or *carry* the sick and possessed (Mark 1:32; 2:3 par. Luke 5:18/Matt 9:2; 7:32 [different in Matt 15:30]; 9:17, 19f. par. Matt 17:16f.; cf. Acts 5:16) and *lead* the blind (Mark 8:22) to Jesus to be healed by him. In Mark 15:22 they *bring* Jesus himself to Golgotha. John 21:18 is possibly reworking a proverb (cf. R. Bultmann, *John* [Eng. tr., 1971] 713) that is reinterpreted to refer to the martyrdom of Peter: "When you were young . . . you walked where you would; but when you are old . . . another . . . *will lead* you where you do not wish to go" (on his martyrdom see v. 19).

The pass. occurs in Acts 27:15, 17: The sailors *are driven* by the wind, which in 2:2 is itself described as φερομένη πνοὴ βιαία, "a *rushing,* mighty wind" (cf. Ptolemy *Apotel.* i.11.3 [οἱ φερόμενοι ἄνεμοι]; Isa 64:5). 2 Pet 1:17f. mentions the voice that *was borne* from heaven at Jesus' transfiguration (Mark 9:7 par. Luke 9:35: ἐγένετο). Fig. in 2 Pet 1:21b in juxtaposition with v. 21a (→ g): The prophets did not speak of their own free will, but rather spoke from God as they were "*moved* by the Holy Spirit" (cf. Job 17:1 LXX).

Heb 6:1 employs a fixed expression that also occurs in Euripides *Andr.* 392f. (ἀλλὰ τὴν ἀρχὴν ἀφεὶς πρὸς τὴν τελευτὴν . . . φέρῃ): "Therefore let us leave (ἀφίημι) the beginnings (ἀρχή) of the doctrines of Christ and *go on* (φερώμεθα) to τελειότης."

c) Mark 4:8, John 12:24, and 15:2, 4f., 8, 16 all use the metaphor of "*bringing forth* fruit" (καρπὸν φέρω; see also → καρποφορέω), which also frequently occurs outside the NT (documentation in Borig 84ff., 112ff., 162ff.). According to Mark 4:8 the seeds that fell into good soil *brought forth* grain "thirtyfold and sixtyfold and a hundredfold" (i.e., thirty, sixty, and one hundred seeds are in one ear of grain), whereas those that fell along the path, onto rocky ground, and among thorns yielded nothing. The hyperbolically amplified contrast within the parable itself, which should first be distinguished from its "interpretation" (vv. 14-20), is supposed to show that in the final analysis the yield of Jesus' proclamation will far surpass what at first glance appears to be its apparently larger failure.

John 12:24 mentions the example of the grain of wheat that must fall away and die in order to "*bear* much fruit" later. This example explains first the paradox of Jesus' own death, through which the path to his glorification must lead (v. 23; see Bultmann, *John* ad loc.; → δοξάζω 3); it then also explicates (v. 25 [ecclesiastical redaction?]) the dialectic of the call to the disciples, according to which life "is won exactly when we give it up" (Bultmann 425; T. Baumeister, *Die Anfänge der Theologie des Martyriums* [Münsterische Beiträge zur Theologie 45, 1980] 150).

In the speech about the true vine (John 15:1-10; see

Borig 237ff.), the metaphor of the vine and its branches is transferred to Jesus and his disciples (v. 5), who can "*bear* fruit" only if they "abide" (→ μένω 3) in him, though the metaphor is never resolved (for interpretation suggestions see Borig 237f., who himself interprets it from the perspective of vv. 9f. as "keeping the commandments" [241]). Probably, however, no internal interpretation is being solicited; the linguistic image itself does not point beyond itself but seeks only to establish the requirement of μένειν ἐν ἐμοί. Not until v. 12 is the content of the phrase "*bear* fruit" filled out by the context as ἀγαπᾶν ἀλλήλους.

d) In a legal context one can *bring* a charge or accusation or even "a reviling judgment" (John 18:29; Acts 25:18; 2 Pet 2:11 [cf. Jude 9: ἐπιφέρω]). Heb 9:16 refers to legal argumentation (see F. Field, *Notes on the Translation of the NT* [1899] 230): "Where a will is involved, the death of the one who made it [i.e., public proof of the death] *must be brought forth*" (cf. Demosthenes *Or.* 58.22; Polybius xxxiii.11.2; Josephus *B.J.* vii.33; *Ant.* xx.47; Plutarch *Cat. Mi.* 19).

e) According to Acts 12:10 the iron gate *leads* into the city (this local or geographic meaning also occurs in Demosthenes *Or.* 47.53; Xenophon *HG* vii.2.7; Herodotus ii.122, and elsewhere).

f) Φέρω occurs in the sense of *endure* in Rom 9:22: God has not immediately destroyed the "vessels of wrath" (Israel) made for ἀπώλεια (→ ἀπόλλυμι 2) but rather *has endured* them ἐν πολλῇ μακροθυμίᾳ (cf. Jer 51:22 LXX). Heb 12:20 shows the same usage with the negative.

g) 2 John 10 refers to the contents of teaching: "If anyone comes to you and *does not bring* ταύτην τὴν διδαχήν [i.e., this particular christological teaching, see v. 7] . . ." (cf. Pindar *Pythia* viii.38: λόγον φέρω); 2 Pet 1:21a: "no prophecy ever *issued* from human impulse."

h) In Heb 1:3 (see O. Michel, *Heb* [KEK] ad loc.), the statement that Christ "*bears* the world through his mighty word" reflects Jewish usage (Heb. *sābal;* cf., e.g., *Exod. Rab.* 36:4: "God carries his world"; *Tg. Yer. I* Deut 33:27; see Billerbeck III, 673; *Herm. Sim.* ix.14.5f.: "The name of the Son . . . carries the entire world"; see also Num 11:14; Deut 1:9 referring to Moses [φέρω τὸν λαὸν τοῦτον/ὑμᾶς]; Plutarch *Luc.* 6:3: φέρω τὴν πόλιν). This usage also expresses the thought that Christ has attained world dominion (see vv. 3d, 4).

                                                        M. Wolter

φεύγω *pheugō* flee, escape; avoid*

The following occurrences refer to physical flight: Mark 5:14 par. Matt 8:33/Luke 8:34; Mark 13:14 par. Matt 24:16/Luke 21:21; Mark 14:50 par. Matt 26:56 (all the disciples); Mark 14:52 (the young man); 16:8 (the women); Matt 2:13 and 10:23 imv. (with εἰς); John 10:5, 12; Acts 7:29; 27:30; Jas 4:7; Rev 9:6; 12:6. Nonphysical escape or running away from is referred to in Matt 3:7 par. Luke 3:7 (from the coming judgment of wrath); Matt 23:33 (from the sentence of hell); Heb 11:34 (from the sword).

The following occurrences refer to the ethical sphere *(avoid):* with acc. obj. in 1 Cor 6:18 (πορνεία); 1 Tim 6:11 (ταῦτα); 2 Tim 2:22 (the passions of youth; the opposite of φεύγω is διώκω), and with ἀπό τινος in 1 Cor 10:14 *(hold oneself back* from the worship of idols).

In Rev 16:20 φεύγω is best translated *vanish* (referring to "every island"), probably also in 20:11 (referring to "earth and sky"; here, however, it may refer to *flee*).

Φῆλιξ, ιχος   *Phēlix*   Felix*

Lit.: E. HAENCHEN, *Acts* (Eng. tr., 1971) 657ff. — P. VON ROHDEN, PW I, 2616-18. — SCHÜRER, *History* I, 459-66. — E. M. SMALLWOOD, *The Jews under Roman Rule* (SJLA 20, 1976) 266ff. — R. D. SULLIVAN, "The Dynasty of Judaea in the First Century," *ANRW* II/8 (1977) 296-354, esp. 330f.

1. (Marcus) Antonius Felix, according to Acts 23–24 the Roman procurator of Judaea who interrogated Paul (23:24, 26; 24:3, 22, 24, 25, 27 bis; 25:14), was a freedman born to Antonia, who was the mother of the emperor Claudius and a daughter of Marc Antony (hence the name and surname; cf. Sullivan). Felix was appointed by Claudius in A.D. 52/53 and was previously the leader of a cohort and of a contingent of troops (Suetonius *Claudius* 28; on his preceding activity in Judaea, reported only in Tacitus *Ann.* xii.54, cf. Smallwood 266f. n. 32). His tenure in office was characterized by serious internal dissatisfaction (see Josephus *Ant.* xx.160-81; *B.J.* ii.252-70). Not surprisingly this period saw a strengthening of the Zealot movement, the emergence of the Sicarii (which Felix, according to *Ant.* xx.162-64, himself employed to have the high priest Jonathan murdered, who had intervened with Claudius to have Felix appointed in the first place but who then criticized him because of his rule), the appearance of an Egyptian prophet (cf. Acts 21:38), and other unrest that was half-political and half-criminal.

Ancient historians consider Felix coresponsible for these developments. Tacitus (*Hist.* v.9) passes the summary judgment that Felix "per omnem saevitiam ac libidinem ius regium servili ingenio exercuit" ("he reveled in cruelty and lust, and wielded the power of a king with the mind of a slave" [see BAGD s.v.]; cf. also *Ann.* xii.54: "cuncta malefacta sibi impune ratus tanta potentia subnixo" ["(Felix) thought that he could do any evil act with impunity, backed up as he was by such power"]; Tertullus's gratitude to Felix in Acts 24:2 for "peace and reform" is strictly pro forma).

According to Suetonius *Claudius* 28, Felix was married to three queens: Drusilla, a daughter of Herod Agrippa I; another Drusilla (possibly a mixup with this name), a granddaughter of Marc Antony and Cleopatra (Tacitus *Hist.* v.9); the third is unknown.

The time of Felix's removal is disputed (A.D. 55 at the earliest, 60 at the latest; cf. A. Suhl, *Paulus und seine Briefe* [1975] 333ff.; H. Koester, *History, Culture, and Religion of the Hellenistic Age* [*Introduction to the NT* I, 1982] 399f.; Schürer, *History* I, 465f. n. 42). According to Josephus *Ant.* xx.182, although Felix subsequently was charged in Rome because of his

administration, the intervention of his influential brother Pallas with Nero prevented him from ever being punished.

2. Luke does not portray Felix as negatively as do Tacitus and Josephus, since he is concerned with allowing the relationship between Christendom and the Roman authorities, represented here by Felix, to appear as untroubled as possible. Also, "this is the second of those four appearances in which Paul after his apology has his innocence attested by the judge concerned" (Haenchen 658; also after the tribune [Acts 23:29] and before Festus [25:18f.] and Agrippa II [26:31f.]). Even if Felix may have been genuinely interested in the substance of Paul's message (Haenchen 658), this interest was in any case weaker than his hope of making financial gains from Paul's imprisonment (24:26), as shown by his delay of the trial and failure to release Paul after two years' imprisonment at the end of his administration (24:27 bis; 25:14; on his visit to Paul with Drusilla [24:24f.] → Δρούσιλλα).

                        M. Wolter

φήμη, ης, ἡ   *phēmē*   report*

Used with ἐξῆλθεν in referring to the *report* that spread concerning Jesus (Luke) and his activity (Matthew): Matt 9:26, at the end of a miracle narrative (different in Mark), and Luke 4:14b, at the beginning of Jesus' ministry in Galilee (different in Mark).

φημί   *phēmi*   say, express, assert*

1. Occurrences in the NT — 2. Usage — 3. Meaning

Lit.: BAGD s.v. — BDF, index s.v. φάναι. — R. BULTMANN, *Der Stil der paulinischen Predigt und die kynisch-stoische Diatribe* (FRLANT 13, 1910). — H. FOURNIER, *Les verbes "dire" en grec ancien* (Collection Linguistique 51, 1946). — KÜHNER, *Grammatik* II, 353. — LSJ s.v. — J. J. O'ROURKE, "The Construction with a Verb of Saying as an Indication of Sources in Luke," *NTS* 21 (1974/75) 421-23.

1. The following forms of φημί appear in the NT:

a) ἔφη 14 times in Matthew, 6 in Mark, 7 in Luke, 2 in John, 14 in Acts, also as v.l. in Matt 13:29; 19:18b; John 9:36; Acts 2:38; 25:22a;

b) φησίν 2 times in Matthew, 1 in Luke, 1 in John, 11 in Acts, and 1 each in 1 Corinthians, 2 Corinthians, and Hebrews; also as v.l. in Matt 19:18a and possibly Acts 2:38;

c) φημί 4 times in 1 Corinthians;

d) φασίν in Rom 8:3 and as v.l. in 2 Cor 10:10; a total of 66 occurrences.

2. As an introduction to direct discourse ἔφη can appear either before (e.g., Mark 10:29) or after (e.g., Matt 14:8) its subject. The person addressed stands in the dat. (Matt 4:7; 17:26; 19:21; 21:27; 25:21, 23; 26:34; 27:65; Mark 9:38; 12:24) or with πρός in the acc. (Luke 22:70b;

Acts 2:38 v.l.; 10:28; 16:37; 26:1). The vb. alone occurs frequently with contrasting or connective δέ (Mark 9:12; 10:20; 14:29; Matt 13:28, 29 v.l.; 19:18b v.l.; 22:37; 27:11, 23; Luke 22:58b; Acts 7:2; 21:37; 22:27, 28; 26:32; John 9:38). Τέ appears in place of δέ in Acts 10:28; 23:5, or καί in 10:30. Luke is esp. inclined to expand by means of a more specific partc. (Luke 7:44; 15:17; 22:58a; 23:3, 40; Acts 16:30; 17:22; 23:17; also Matt 8:8). In Matt 26:61 false witnesses cite Jesus' temple saying with οὗτος ἔφη. Simple ἔφη in John 1:23 is not citing, since John the Baptist is the subj. Ἔφη occurs in medial position like Lat. *inquit* in Acts 23:35; John 9:36 v.l. Ellipses occur in Acts 2:38; 25:22a v.l., and 26:28. Ἔφη is never taken over from a source but is used rather as a free redactional stylistic device.

Φησίν introduces Matt 13:29 (with ὁ δέ), stands in medial position in Matt 14:8, and occurs as v.l. in Matt 19:18a; it appears postpositively in Luke 7:40b. Φησίν also occurs in medial position in Acts 25:5, 22b; 26:25; with indefinite subj. in 1 Cor 6:16 (citing Gen 2:24 LXX), Heb 8:5 (citing Exod 25:40 LXX), 2 Cor 10:10 (referring to the objection directed against Paul). An introductory καὶ φησίν appears in Acts 8:36; 10:31; 22:2; 23:18; 25:24; John 18:29. Other combinations occur with partc. (Acts 19:35) and with gen. absolute and dat. of manner (26:24). Its appearance in Acts 2:38 is disputed (see *TCGNT* 300f.). In Rom 3:8 and 2 Cor 10:10 (v.l.) φασίν reports slanderous charges. Paul uses φημί in 1 Cor 7:29; 10:15, 19; 15:50 to formulate authoritatively apostolic doctrine and instruction (cf. J. Weiss, *1 Cor* [KEK] on 7:29 and 15:50).

3. With a background of mantic and prophetic usage (cf. H. Krämer, *TDNT* VI, 783), φημί preserves traces of its original demonstrative character in its uses as subjective expression and authoritative proclamation. In its formal use in introducing direct speech it loses its emphatic meaning, is reduced to common parlance, and becomes formulaic. In this process, however, the NT authors are adhering to stylistic literary devices of the Hellenistic vernacular of their time. Corresponding parallels occur in Philo and Epictetus, among others. Even Jesus' own words exhibit this weakening in their alternation with λέγω, though even more in the fact that the saying thus introduced often supplies its own affirmative elements (such as ἀμὴν λέγω ὑμῖν, → ἀμήν 4).   V. Hasler

φημίζω   *phēmizō*   spread by word of mouth

Pass. as v.l. in Matt 28:15 (ℵ al) and Acts 13:43 (E al).

Φῆστος, ου   *Phēstos*   Festus
Πόρκιος, ου   *Porkios*   Porcius*

As the Roman procurator in Palestine, Festus was the successor of Felix (→ Φῆλιξ), although the beginning and ending dates of his administration cannot be precisely determined. Under his rule Paul's trial was passed on to the imperial court in Rome. Πόρκιος (Acts 24:27) is the clan name of Festus. In the NT Φῆστος appears in Acts 24:27; 9 times in 25:1-24; and in 26:24, 25, 32. Schürer, *History* I, 467f.; M. Stern, "The Province of Judaea," *The Jewish People in the First Century* (Compendia 1) I (1974) 308-76, esp. 320, 368-70; Wikenhauser, *Geschichtswert* 354-58; J. Schmidt, *LTK* IV, 101; B. Reicke, *BHH* 479.

φθάνω   *phthanō*   reach, arrive; come before*

1. Occurrences in the NT — 2. The Jesus tradition — 3. Paul

Lit.: E. Best, *1–2 Thess* (BNTC, 1972) 109-23. — C. Demke, "Theologie und Literarkritik im 1 Thessalonicherbrief," FS Fuchs 103-24. — G. Fitzer, *TDNT* IX, 88-92. — E. Grässer, "Zum Verständnis der Gottesherrschaft," *ZNW* 65 (1974) 3-26. — N. Hyldahl, "Auferstehung Christi— Auferstehung der Toten," *Die paulinische Literatur und Theologie* (ed. S. Pedersen; 1980) 119-35. — W. G. Kümmel, *Promise and Fulfillment* (1957) 105-9. — W. Marxsen, "Auslegung von 1 Thess 4,13-18," *ZTK* 66 (1969) 22-37. — O. Michel, "Fragen zu 1 Thess 2:14-16," *Antijudaismus im NT?* (ed. W. Eckert, et al.; 1967) 50-59. — G. E. Okeke, "1 Thess 2:13-16: The Fate of the Unbelieving Jews," *NTS* 27 (1980/81) 127-36. — B. A. Pearson, "1 Thess 2:13-16: A Deutero-Pauline Interpolation," *HTR* 64 (1971) 79-94. — W. Schmithals, *Paul and the Gnostics* (1972) 123-218.

1. Φθάνω occurs 7 times in the NT: Matt 12:28 par. Luke 11:20 (Q); Rom 9:31; 2 Cor 10:14; Phil 3:16; 1 Thess 2:16; 4:15.

2. Matt 12:28 par. Luke 11:20: The Q church understood Jesus' exorcism healings to be individual breakthroughs of God's dominion into the demon-plagued generation that preceded the end. The hand of God ("finger of God," Exod 8:15; 31:18) pursued the people in the miraculous deeds of Jesus, who was the designated Son of man filled by the Holy Spirit (not just any eschatological prophet). This did not constitute the commencement of the heavenly kingdom of God announced by Jesus as being near at hand (ἤγγικεν, Matt 10:7; Mark 1:15; Luke 10:9). Only his power over demons *has come before* his adversaries' eyes (aor. ἔφθασεν and ἐπί with acc.). From Q Matthew takes up (cf. 19:24; 21:31, 43) the formulation βασιλεία τοῦ θεοῦ, since he understands Jesus as Immanuel, "God with us" (1:23), who tried in vain to establish his dominion in Israel. For Luke the miraculous exorcisms constitute merciful providential epiphanies in the time of salvation of Jesus' earthly ministry (cf. Luke 10:18; 17:21).

3. Paul regrets in Rom 9:31 that, despite the revelation

of justification by faith, Israel continues to pursue an alleged justification based on law and thus misunderstands the salvation-historical purpose of the Torah (Rom 10:2-4; Gal 3:22-25); hence Israel has not *attained* the law's purpose. In 2 Cor 10:14 he defends the scope of his missionary activity, which *has taken him as far as* Corinth, and boasts that he has not exceeded the limits God has apportioned. His adversaries, however, boast with unfettered missionary zeal that recognizes no limits. The "more perfect ones" in Philippi strive enthusiastically for a higher level of faith not limited to a fellowship in suffering with the crucified Lord. In Phil 3:16 Paul admonishes them to hold to his own example and be content with what they have already *attained*.

In 1 Thess 2:14ff. Paul adopts traditional elements of OT and anti-Jewish polemic. He compares Gentile persecution with Jewish persecution in Palestine and says that the eschatological "wrath of God already *has come*" upon those Gentiles and Jews (cf. 1:10; *T. Levi* 6:11). In 1 Thess 4:15ff. Paul assures his readers with an apocalyptic saying of the Lord (cf. Matt 24:30f.) that the believers who will actually experience the parousia *will* not *precede* those who have already fallen asleep (i.e., died).

V. Hasler

φθαρτός, 3 *phthartos* perishable
→ φθείρω.

φθέγγομαι *phthengomai* speak, proclaim*

Acts 4:18, used absolutely (in contrast to "be silent"); 2 Pet 2:16, referring to Balaam's donkey: it "*spoke* with human voice"; v. 18, with acc. obj.: "*speak* haughty words (ὑπέρογκα)."

φθείρω *phtheirō* corrupt (vb.)*
ἀφθαρσία, ας, ἡ *aphtharsia* imperishability*
ἄφθαρτος, 2 *aphthartos* imperishable*
φθαρτός, 3 *phthartos* perishable*
φθορά, ᾶς, ἡ *phthora* corruption, destruction*

1. Occurrences and origin — 2. Φθείρω — a) Literal — b) Of "the old nature" — 3. The word group in references to the world and its future — a) General — b) 1 Corinthians 15 — c) Eschatological expectations in Paul — d) Aspects of the present in the post-Pauline sphere — 4. Φθορά in 2 Peter — 5. Liturgical usage in 1 Tim 1:17

Lit.: G. HARDER, *TDNT* IX, 93-106. — F. MERKEL, *DNTT* I, 467-70. — D. VETTER, *THAT* II, 891-94. — For further bibliography see *TWNT* X, 1289.

1. In the NT this word group occurs only in the Epistles (but not in Hebrews or 1–3 John) and Revelation. Φθείρω, manifesting the widest distribution (9 occurrences), occurs in Paul, Ephesians, 2 Peter, Jude, and

Revelation; φθορά occurs just as frequently, but only in Paul and 2 Peter. Ἀφθαρσία and ἄφθαρτος occur 7 times each: the former in Paul, Ephesians, and the Pastorals, and the latter in Paul, the Pastorals, and 1 Peter. Φθαρτός, finally, occurs 6 times, and only in Paul and 1 Peter.

The word group plays a role in Greek philosophy and Hellenistic religion in their attempt to comprehend the essential structure of the world; this also influenced its usage in Hellenistic Judaism (cf. Harder 94f., 98-102). Jewish apocalyptic thought determined the substance of the theologically honed usage in the NT, and esp. that of Paul, with its strict differentiation between the perishability of the present world and the imperishability of God's world to come.

2. a) Φθείρω is used in the literal sense of *corrupt, destroy*. It appears in a completely secular sense in Paul's defense in 2 Cor 7:2: "We have wronged no one, we *have corrupted* no one, we have taken advantage of no one," referring apparently to financial matters. The quotation from Menander in 1 Cor 15:33 (*Thais* [*FAC* III/B, frag. 218]) speaks of *ruinous* association, something Paul applies to any association with heretics. 2 Cor 11:3 uses the term similarly, only more sharply: Just as the serpent deceived Eve, so do the false apostles *corrupt* the thoughts of the believers; the construction with → ἀπό (2.b) appears to indicate deception, while the vb. itself, as suggested by the context, is apparently focusing on seduction (cf. BAGD s.v. φθείρω 2.b; see also Titus 2:7: ἐν τῇ διδασκαλίᾳ ἀφθορίαν).

The statements in Jude 10 and, influenced by them, in 2 Pet 2:12 are directed against the false teachers themselves. Instead of possessing healthy understanding, these people, who are like irrational animals, have insight that only *leads them into ruin*. 2 Pet 2:12 makes the comparison even more clear by drawing attention to the fate of animals as capture and *destruction* (φθορά), and by portraying their *destruction* as a reflection of the fate of the heretics. Although a reference to eschatological fate does lie behind this comparison, it does not predominate, something confirmed by the strengthening of the imagery in 2 Peter.

The statement in 1 Cor 3:17 can be understood first as a general warning in which φθείρω speaks in both parts about *destroying* within time; Paul understands the first part metaphorically (referring to the destruction of the Church), the second as a reference to God's eschatological judgment. (On Käsemann's characterization of this as "a sentence of holy law" in *NT Questions of Today* [1969] 66-68, see K. Berger, "Zu den sogenannten Sätzen heiligen Rechts," *NTS* 17 [1970/71] 10-40, esp. 31f.) No fixed terminology is apparent here. Rev 19:2 amplifies the usage *corrupt:* The harlot representing the idolatrous power of the world has *led* the world *into corruption*.

b) Only Eph 4:22 uses the vb. more abstractly to qualify the nature of the world, namely, as one that is passing away. The "old nature" that the baptized should put off *perishes* through its subjection to deceitful lusts.

3. a) The usage of **φθαρτός** and **φθορά** expresses even more forcefully the perishability of the world. Both words are used almost exclusively in explicit antithesis to their antonyms **ἄφθαρτος** or **ἀφθαρσία**. Ἄφθαρτος occurs only in juxtaposition with φθαρτός, and ἀφθαρσία only in 1 Pet 1:18 without an explicit contrasting term. There the world's means of purchasing—silver and gold—are called *perishable things,* compared with the blood of Christ. In 1 Cor 9:25 Paul calls the athlete's wreath *perishable* and contrasts it with the *imperishable* one of the eschatological goal. Rom 1:23 contrasts the *imperishable* God with *mortal* human beings, whom people have made into objects of worship alongside animals. Col 2:22 demonstrates the *perishability* (φθορά) of foodstuffs by referring to their purpose, namely, consumption, thus countering their estimation as religiously valuable.

b) These words acquire special significance in the Pauline discussion of the reality of resurrection (1 Cor 15:42-54): φθαρτός occurs twice (vv. 53f.), φθορά twice (vv. 42, 50), ἀφθαρσία 4 times (vv. 42, 50, 53f.), and ἄφθαρτος once (v. 52). Here the positive terms refer to the sphere of present human reality, qualified negatively as *perishability.* In v. 50 φθορά parallels "flesh and blood," referring to a person in this earthly confinement; the parallel terms in vv. 43f. (ἀτιμία, ἀσθένεια, σῶμα, ψυχικόν) show the negative evaluation, which may, however, be understood only as a religiously focused one. *Imperishability* is contrasted with this, paralleling in v. 50 the βασιλεία θεοῦ, and in vv. 43f. δόξα, δύναμις, and σῶμα πνευματικόν (cf. Rom 2:7: glory, honor, and *imperishability* find their goal in eternal life). Both in these sentences and in vv. 53f. Paul articulates through this antithesis the radical otherness of the resurrection reality compared to the reality of earthly life; it is disengaged life, no longer life destined for the death of this world (cf. vv. 53f., with contrast between θνητός and ἀθανασία).

c) According to Rom 8:21 all of creation will participate in the liberation from subjection to *perishability* and will move toward the eschatological perfection of the children of God. *Perishability* does, however, remain the ultimate fate of those who cast their lot with creaturely existence, just as those who cast it with the Spirit will attain eternal life (Gal 6:8).

d) Post-Pauline writings accentuate more strongly the significance of imperishability in Christians' present existence. Through the gospel Christ Jesus brought "life and *immortality"* to light (2 Tim 1:10). Rebirth through God's living and abiding word grows not from *perishable* seed but from *imperishable* (1 Pet 1:23 [cf. v. 18]) and has as

its end the *imperishable* inheritance of salvation kept in heaven (1 Pet 1:4). Thus the *"imperishable manner* of the gentle and quiet spirit" (1 Pet 3:4) characterizes the hidden person of the heart, "the human spirit characterized by God's spirit" (L. Goppelt, *1 Pet* [KEK] 217). The concluding greeting in Eph 6:24 also belongs here; ἐν ἀφθαρσίᾳ concludes the benediction and refers thus to χάρις.

4. In 2 Peter the **φθορά** as (active) *corruption* plays an important role. Christians will participate in the divine nature (eschatologically; see K. H. Schelkle, *1–2 Peter, Jude* [HTKNT] 188f.) because they have escaped (aor. partc., referring to baptism) the *corruption* "that is in the world because of passion" (1:4). In contrast, the seducers proclaiming freedom are slaves of *corruption* (2:19); δοῦλοι and the following clause show that the reference is to an existing power. The metaphorical usage in 2 Pet 2:12 (influenced by Jude 10) has been discussed above (→ 2.a).

5. Finally, the predication in 1 Tim 1:17 belongs to Hellenistically influenced (Jewish-Christian) liturgical language: "To the king of ages, *imperishable,* invisible, the only God."

                                                                    T. Holtz

φθινοπωρινός, 3 *phthinopōrinos* belonging to late autumn*

Jude 12, in a fig. evaluation of false teachers: "fruitless trees *in late autumn"* (with "waterless clouds").

φθόγγος, ου, ὁ *phthongos* sound, noise; tone*

Φθόγγος refers to the human voice (Rom 10:18, citing Ps 18:5 LXX) and to the tones of musical instruments (1 Cor 14:7).

φθονέω *phthoneō* envy (vb.)*

Gal 5:26, in parenesis: "Let us have no self-conceit, no provoking of one another, no *envy* of one another."

φθόνος, ου, ὁ *phthonos* envy, jealousy*

Φθόνος appears in catalogs of vices in Rom 1:29; Gal 5:21 (pl.); 1 Tim 6:4; 1 Pet 2:1 (cf. Titus 3:3), and in the phrase διὰ φθόνον, "out of *envy,"* in Mark 15:10 par. Matt 27:18; Phil 1:15.

In Jas 4:5 πρὸς φθόνον ἐπιποθεῖ τὸ πνεῦμα should perhaps be translated "he [God] yearns *jealously* for the Spirit." It is also possible that τὸ πνεῦμα is the subj.; cf. → ἐπιποθέω. A. Vögtle, *Die Tugend- und Lasterkataloge im NT* (1936) 218-21; P. Walcot, *Envy and the Greeks: A Study on Human Behavior* (1978); Spicq, *Notes* II, 919-21.

φθορά, ᾶς, ἡ *phthora* corruption, destruction → φθείρω.

φιάλη, ης, ἡ *phialē* bowl, offering bowl

12 occurrences in the NT, all in Revelation: "golden *bowls*," with incense (5:8); "[seven] *bowls* of wrath" (16:1: "*bowls* of the wrath of God"; further 15:7; 17:1; 21:9); and referring individually to the seven *bowls* of wrath (16:2-17).

φιλάγαθος, 2 *philagathos* loving what is good*

In the list of bishop's qualifications in Titus 1:8 φιλάγαθος stands between φιλόξενος, "hospitable," and σώφρων, "self-controlled." W. Grundmann, *TDNT* I, 18.

Φιλαδέλφεια, ας *Philadelpheia* Philadelphia*

A city in Lydia founded by Attalus II Philadelphus. After 133 B.C. it was under Roman control. The sixth letter in Revelation (3:7-13) is directed to the Christian church in Philadelphia (1:11; 3:7), as is Ign. *Phld.* C. Burchard, *KP* IV, 733f.

φιλαδελφία, ας, ἡ *philadelphia* brotherly love*
φιλάδελφος, 2 *philadelphos* loving one's brother, brotherly*

Lit.: C. BRADY, *Brotherly Love: A Study of the Word φιλαδελφία and Its Contribution to the Biblical Theology of Brotherly Love* (Diss. Fribourg, 1961). — C. SPICQ, "La charité fraternelle selon 1 Th. 4,9," *Mélanges bibliques* (FS A. Robert; 1957) 507-11.

The noun occurs 6 times in the NT, the adj. once (1 Pet 3:8). A significant shift in meaning has occurred over against secular Greek. In the latter the word group always refers to "love of one's brother [or sibling]" in the literal sense (cf. Hellenistic ruler titles [*OGIS* I, 185, 1; 329, 6]; tomb inscriptions [Preisigke, *Sammelbuch* III, 6234f.]; Epictetus *Diss.* iii.3.9; and Plutarch's treatise Περὶ φιλαδελφίας [*De fraterno amore*]). In contrast, the NT uses the terms only fig. to refer (as → ἀδελφός [5, 6] also frequently does) to *brotherly love* between Christians united through their common status as children of God (cf. Rom 8:29; Heb 12:5ff.). Only 2 Macc 15:14, where φιλάδελφος refers to "loving those belonging to one's own people," attests a non-Christian fig. use of this word group.

In the NT φιλαδελφία always appears within the framework of parenesis (1 Pet 3:8; 2 Pet 1:7 bis) in catalogs of virtues. Rom 12:9f. and 2 Pet 1:7 attest it as a particular realization of ἀγάπη. Rom 12:10, 1 Thess 4:9, and 1 Pet 1:22 all draw attention to its special reference regarding one's fellow Christians: they should love one another

(ἀλλήλους). 1 Thess 4:9 characterizes φιλαδελφία as something taught by God (which is probably a biblicism; see Spicq 510). It expresses itself in sincere goodwill of the sort family members show to one another (φιλό-στοργος) and recognizes no conflicts of rank; it lacks all hypocrisy, it endures (1 Pet 1:22), and it is hospitable (Heb 13:1). N. Brox (*1 Pet* [EKKNT] 86 [on 1:22]) emphasizes quite justifiably that during times of persecution this kind of brotherliness was highly valued and must have strengthened "the perseverance of Christians."

E. Plümacher

φιλάδελφος, 2 *philadelphos* loving one's brother, brotherly
→ φιλαδελφία.

φίλανδρος, 2 *philandros* loving one's husband*

Titus 2:4, in reference to young women, who should be φίλανδροι ("loving their husbands") and φιλότεκνοι ("loving their children").

φιλανθρωπία, ας, ἡ *philanthrōpia* love for humankind, kind behavior*
φιλανθρώπως *philanthrōpōs* benevolently, kindly*

Lit.: H. I. BELL, "Philanthropia in the Papyri of the Roman Period," *Hommages à J. Bidez et F. Cumont* (1948) 31-37. — U. LUCK, *TDNT* IX, 107-11. — A. PELLETIER, "La philanthropia de tous les jours chez les écrivains juifs hellénisés," *Paganisme, Judaïsme, Christianisme* (FS M. Simon; 1978) 35-44. — C. SPICQ, "La philanthropie hellénistique, vertu divine et royale," *ST* 12 (1958) 169-91. — *idem*, *Notes* II, 922-27. — M. D. VAN VELDHUIZEN, *"Philanthropia" in Philo of Alexandria* (Diss. University of Notre Dame, 1982). — For further bibliography see *TWNT* X, 1289; Luck; Spicq, *Notes* s.v.

1. Whereas φιλανθρωπ- originally referred to benevolent behavior on the part of divine beings toward human beings, from the 4th cent. B.C. onward it was used increasingly to characterize human relationships themselves (Demosthenes *Or.* xiii.17; xxv.81), frequently with a certain undertone of condescension (L. Heinemann, PW Suppl. V, 298). During the Hellenistic period φιλανθρωπία—"a keyword in this period" (Spicq, *Notes* II, 922) and highly valued (cf. esp. Plutarch: R. Hirzel, *Plutarch* [1925] 25ff.)—referred to "benevolence toward human beings (love of humankind)" both on the part of the deity (Philo *Virt.* 77, 188; Josephus *Ant.* i.24; Musonius [ed. O. Hense, 1905] p. 90, l. 12; Xenophon Ephesius v.4.10) and on the part of rulers, who claimed it as an exemplary virtue (2 Macc 14:9; *Ep. Arist.* 290; *FGH* II, 75, frag. 2 [135.9f.]), and also officials, who used it in administrative language (ÄgU II, 522 [a centurion]; Pap. Oxy. no. 1102 l. 7).

Beyond this, one also characterized as φιλανθρωπία every gracious, noble, or simply friendly act of civilized persons toward one another, as well as such behavior in general (*IG* V, 491; *Pap. Greci et Latini* [ed. G. Vitelli et al.] I, 94; Achilles Tatius v.22.2), even on the part of animals (Achilles Tatius iv.4.7). Φιλανθρωπία is frequently mentioned along with other virtues, such as gentleness and goodness (πραότης, e.g., Pap. London VI, 1912, 83; Plutarch *Mar.* 8.2; χρηστότης, e.g., Philo *Leg. Gai.* 67; Musonius p. 39, ll. 12f.). Both philosophical ethics and Hellenistic Judaism posited a relationship between φιλανθρωπία and piety (Philo *Abr.* 208; *Decal.* 108ff.) and viewed God as a model for human φιλανθρωπία, particularly on the part of rulers (*Ep. Arist.* 208; A. Dihle, *Der Kanon der zwei Tugenden* [1968] 26, 31f.).

2. The NT uses this word group only in Acts 27:3; 28:2; Titus 3:4. Using a common phrase (φιλανθρώπως/ φιλανθρωπία χρήσασθαι, cf. Pap. London II, 1178, 23f.; *OGIS* I, 51, 8; Diodorus Siculus xx.17.1), Acts 27:3 notes that the centurion guarding Paul *treated him kindly;* also the Maltese βάρβαροι (Acts 28:2) showed the shipwrecked sailors *unusual kindness (hospitality).* The hieratically stylized formulation in Titus 3:4 (epiphany of "the goodness and *loving kindness* of God our Savior") might derive from the context of the cult of the ruler, whose terminology the Pastorals occasionally reflect (M. Dibelius and H. Conzelmann, *Pastoral Epistles* [Hermeneia] 101f., 143f.); cf. the cultic veneration of Tiberius's φιλανθρωπία (Dio Cassius lix.16.10). To be sure, revealed deities were adorned in other instances as well with φιλάνθρωπος (e.g., Asclepius and Hygieia: *CIG* III, 6813, 3).   E. Plümacher

φιλανθρώπως *philanthrōpōs* benevolently, kindly*
→ φιλανθρωπία.

φιλαργυρία, ας, ἡ *philargyria* love of money, avarice*

1 Tim 6:10 sees in φιλαργυρία "the root of all evils." G. Finkenrath, *DNTT* I, 138.

φιλάργυρος, 2 *philargyros* fond of money, avaricious*

Luke 16:14: the Pharisees are *fond of money;* 2 Tim 3:2: a catalog of vices includes φιλάργυροι; cf. → φιλαργυρία. Spicq, *Notes* II, 928f.

φίλαυτος, 2 *philautos* selfish, self-centered*

The pl. occurs in 2 Tim 3:2 at the beginning of a catalog of vices (claiming to describe people at the end time) before φιλάργυροι: self-love and avarice are the root of all evil; cf. 1 Tim 6:10 (→ φιλαργυρία).

φιλέω *phileō* love; kiss (vb.)*

1. Φιλέω and ἀγαπάω — 2. Synoptics — 3. John — 4. Other NT writings

Lit.: BAGD s.v. — R. F. BUTLER, *The Meaning of Agapao and Phileo in the Greek NT* (1977). — W. GÜNTHER, *DNTT* II,

547-49. — R. JOLY, *Le vocabulaire chrétien de l'amour est-il original? Φιλεῖν et ἀγαπᾶν dans le grec antique* (1968). — M. LATTKE, *Einheit im Wort. Die spezifische Bedeutung von ἀγάπη, ἀγαπᾶν und φιλεῖν im Johannesevangelium* (SANT 16, 1975). — M. PAESLACK, "Zur Bedeutungsgeschichte der Wörter φιλεῖν 'lieben,' φιλία 'Liebe,' 'Freundschaft,' φίλος 'Freund' in der Septuaginta und im NT (unter Berücksichtigung ihrer Beziehungen zu ἀγαπᾶν, ἀγάπη, ἀγαπητός)," *TViat* 5 (1953/54) 51-142. — C. SPICQ, *Agape in the NT* (3 vols.; 1963-65) III, 86-102. — idem, *Notes* I, 15-30. — G. STÄHLIN, *TDNT* IX, 113-46. — For further bibliography see Spicq, *Notes* s.v.; → ἀγάπη.

1. Φιλέω and ἀγαπάω are synonymous in the NT (Stählin 128 and elsewhere; for John see R. Bultmann, *John* [Eng. tr., 1971] 253 and elsewhere; R. Schnackenburg, *John* III [Eng. tr., 1982] 362f.). Variations in connotation or nuance by one of the two are usually taken over also by the other. "Like" (ἀγαπάω) is juxtaposed with *(strong, emotional, fervent) love* (φιλέω) (Stählin 116; R. Schnackenburg, *John* II [Eng. tr., 1979] 104). Stählin postulates what amounts to a reversal in "the relationship of mood and content" for the NT: "far from being less warm than φιλέω, ἀγαπάω is now deeper and more inward" (Stählin 117).

Why, in sharp contrast to secular usage, does φιλέω recede so noticeably in the LXX (15 occurrences, vs. 266 of ἀγαπάω) and (doubtless dependent on this) also in the NT (25 occurrences vs. 143)? Φιλέω and ἀγαπάω each can denote secular, erotic love (Stählin 125). Is ἀγαπάω more specific (Joly)? Is the consonance of ἀγαπάω with *'āhab*, the central OT word for "to love," the reason for this development (Stählin 124 n. 115)? Is it "the frequent nuance of 'preference' " in the case of φιλέω (Spicq, *Notes* I, 19)?

2. In the Synoptics φιλέω is multifaceted and theologically unemphatic. Matt 10:37 demands that for discipleship one must "love" Jesus "more than . . ." (par. Luke 14:26, μισεῖν). Apart from this weighty logion from Q φιλέω is also used negatively in a warning against the prayers of hypocrites (Matt 6:5) and against the scribes' and Pharisees' misuse of religious authority (Matt 23:6, par. Luke 20:46 against the scribes). It refers also to Judas's *kiss* of Jesus (Mark 14:44 par. Matt 26:48/Luke 22:47 [attempted only]).

3. John 12:25 is a reworking of Matt 10:37. The "original meaning" of φιλέω, namely, "to love what belongs to or is one's own" (Stählin 129), emerges in the almost dualistic statement about the world, which *loves* its own (John 15:19). Given John 11:3, 36, however, where Jesus *loves* Lazarus as his friend, we may agree that "φιλέω is at the very least one of the ambivalent expressions in John" (Stählin 130).

Reference to God's love for Jesus (John 5:20) and for the disciples (16:27) is expressed in only two instances by φιλέω (otherwise always with ἀγαπάω). John 20:2 uses φιλέω once for the beloved disciple (otherwise 4 times ἀγαπάω); 21:15-17 uses it 5 times (4 of those spoken by Peter, once in Jesus' third question to Peter as a variation of ἀγαπάω in the first two questions). Attempts to determine in these two passages distinctions that transcend mere feeling for language are not persuasive (Schnackenburg, *John* III [Eng. tr., 1982] 362f.).

4. 1 Cor 16:22 ("if anyone *loves* the Lord . . .") is a liturgical formula, probably from the eucharist. Titus 3:15 is a formula of greeting, Rev 3:19 a free rendering of Prov 3:12 LXX, and Rev 22:15 (πᾶς φιλῶν καὶ ποιῶν ψεῦδος) is the conclusion of a short catalog of vices introduced by οἱ κύνες (Stählin 136-38).   W. Feneberg

φιλήδονος, 2 *philēdonos* pleasure loving*

In the NT only in 2 Tim 3:4 in a catalog of vices. G. Stählin, *TDNT* II, 918, 925f.; E. Beyreuther, *DNTT* I, 458-60.

φίλημα, ατος, τό *philēma* kiss (noun)*

The kiss of greeting is mentioned in Luke 7:45; 22:48 (of Judas). It also occurs in the closing of Paul's letters in the exhortation to greet one another ἐν φιλήματι ἁγίῳ, "with a holy *kiss*" (Rom 16:16; 1 Cor 16:20; 2 Cor 13:12 [ἐν ἁγίῳ φιλήματι]; 1 Thess 5:26). 1 Pet 5:14 uses the phrase ἐν φιλήματι ἀγάπης. K.-M. Hofmann, *Philema hagion* (1938); G. Stählin, *TDNT* IX, 113-46, esp. 138-41; W. Günther, *DNTT* II, 547-49; H.-J. Klauck, *Herrenmahl und hellenistischer Kult* (NTAbh N.F. 15, 1982) 352-56.

Φιλήμων, ονος *Philēmōn* Philemon*

Lit.: J. D. M. Derrett, "The Functions of the Epistle to Philemon," *ZNW* 79 (1988) 63-91. — J. Gnilka, *Phlm* (HTKNT, 1982) 5f., 15f. — P. N. Harrison, "Onesimus and Philemon," *ATR* 32 (1950) 268-94. — W.-H. Ollrog, *Paulus und seine Mitarbeiter* (WMANT 50, 1979) 42-44. — K. Staab, *LTK* VIII, 445f. — P. Stuhlmacher, *Phlm* (EKKNT, 1975) esp. 20-24, 29-31.

The name Philemon is frequently documented. In the NT Philemon is the name of a man (probably in Colossae; see also Gnilka 5f.) who became a Christian through Paul. His slave Onesimus (→ Ὀνήσιμος) escaped from him and went to Paul (who was imprisoned at the time: Phlm 9, 23), who also won Onesimus over to the Christian faith (v. 10). Paul sent him back to his master and gave him a letter of reference, namely, the NT letter to Philemon. The name Philemon occurs only in Phlm 1 in the salutation (Paul and Timothy "to beloved Philemon") and in the subscript to the letter. V. 1 identifies Philemon as Paul's → συνεργός. Perhaps Apphia (᾽Απφία, v. 2) was his wife (Stuhlmacher 30; Gnilka 16).   G. Schneider

Φίλητος, ου *Philētos* Philetus*

A heretic mentioned only in 2 Tim 2:17 (with → Ὑμέναιος).

φιλία, ας, ἡ *philia* friendship, love*

Jas 4:4: "*Love* of the world means enmity toward God." G. Stählin, *TDNT* IX, 146-71; W. Günther, *DNTT* II, 547-49.

Φιλιππήσιος, ου, ὁ *Philippēsios* a Philippian*

In Phil 4:15 Paul addresses his readers as Φιλιππήσιοι.

Φίλιπποι, ων *Philippoi* Philippi*

The Macedonian city *Philippi* dates back to Philip of Macedonia. After *ca.* 167 B.C. it was under Roman rule. Paul founded the first Christian church on European soil in Philippi (Acts 16:12[-40]; 20:6; Phil 1:1; 1 Thess 2:2). J. Schmidt, PW XIX/2, 2206-44; O. Volk, *LTK* VIII, 458f.; T. J. Cadoux, *OCD* 816; J. Gnilka, *Phil* (HTKNT) 1-5; W. Elliger, *Paulus in Griechenland* (1978) 23-77.

Φίλιππος, ου *Philippos* Philip*

1. Philip, son of Herod — 2. Philip, one of the Twelve — 3. Philip the evangelist

Lit.: On 1: J. Blinzler, "Herodes Philippos," *LTK* V, 266. — S. Perowne, *The Later Herods: The Political Background of the NT* (1958) 20f., 23-26. — Schürer, *History* I, 336-40.

On 2: Hennecke/Schneemelcher I, 271-78 (the Gospel of Philip). — A. Wikenhauser, "Philippus, Apostel," *LTK* VIII, 465f.

On 3: E. Bishop, "Which Philip?" *ATR* 28 (1946) 154-59. — A. M. Johnson, Jr., "Philip the Evangelist and the Gospel of John," *Abr-Nahrain* 16 (1975/76) 49-72. — G. Schneider, *Acts* (HTKNT, 1980) 428, 480-509. — H. Waitz, "Die Quelle der Philippusgeschichten in der Apg 8,5-40," *ZNW* 7 (1906) 340-55. — W. Wikenhauser, "Philippos," *LTK* VIII, 464. — For further bibliography see Schneider.

1. In the NT the common Greek name Philip refers first to a son of Herod the Great and the Jewess Cleopatra of Jerusalem. After his father's death (4 B.C.), Philip became the tetrarch of Gaulanitis, Trachonitis, Auranitis, Batanea, and Paneas (Josephus *Ant.* xvii–xx) and, according to Luke 3:1, also of Ituraea. He is responsible for rebuilding Paneas near the source of the Jordan into "Caesarea *Philippi*" (Mark 8:27 par. Matt 16:13), and Bethsaida into Julius. He was married to Salome, Herodias's daughter (though Mark 6:17 par. Matt 14:3 makes him Herodias's first husband; → Ἡρῳδιάς 3), and died in A.D. 34. Thereafter his territory was annexed for a short time to the Roman province of Syria, and in 37 was given to Agrippa I.

2. A man named Philip also belonged to the circle of Jesus' twelve disciples. He came from Bethsaida (John 1:44; 12:21) and probably became a disciple quite early. Listings of the twelve disciples mention him fifth (after the two prominent pairs of brothers: Mark 3:18 par. Matt 10:3/Luke 6:14; Acts 1:13). He plays a special role in the fourth Gospel, being mentioned in John 1:43, 45, 46, 48 (stories of his call by Jesus); 6:5, 7 (dialogue with Jesus concerning the purchase of bread); 12:21, 22a, b (involvement with Greeks who want to meet Jesus); 14:8, 9 (asking Jesus, "Show us the Father").

The *Acts of Philip,* from the 4th or 5th cent., identifies Philip with the evangelist of the same name (→ 3); Hennecke/Schneemelcher II, 577. On the Coptic-Gnostic *Gospel of Philip* (*NHC* II, 3) see H.-M. Schenke, "Das Evangelium nach Philippus," *TLZ* 84 (1959) 1-26; J. É. Ménard, *L'évangile selon Philippe* (1967); K. Koschorke, "Die 'Namen' in Philippusevangelium," *ZNW* 64 (1973) 307-22; R. M. Wilson, *IDBSup* (1976) 664f. On the "Letter of Peter to Philip" (*NHC* VIII, 2) see J. É. Ménard, *La lettre de Pierre à Philippe* (1977).

3. The third person the NT mentions with this name is Philip "the evangelist" (Acts 21:8), one of "the seven" associated with Stephen (6:5). 8:5-13 tells of his missionary activity in Samaria (vv. 5, 6, 12, 13), and vv. 26-39 relate that he baptized an Ethiopian court official who had made a pilgrimage to Jerusalem (vv. 26, 29, 30, 31, 34, 35, 38, 39). These Philip stories in Acts show that very early the "Hellenists" around Stephen expanded the more narrow Jewish horizon of missionary activity. 8:40 notes that Philip preached in the cities from Ashdod (Azotus) to Caesarea. He later settled in Caesarea and received Paul as a guest (21:8); he had four prophetically gifted daughters (v. 9).

G. Schneider

φιλόθεος, 2 *philotheos* loving God*

2 Tim 3:4: "loving pleasure (→ φιλήδονος) rather than *loving God."*

Φιλόλογος, ου *Philologos* Philologus*

A Christian to whom greetings are sent in Rom 16:15; perhaps the spouse of Julia, who is also mentioned here. Spicq, *Notes* II, 930f.

φιλονεικία, ας, ἡ *philoneikia* contentiousness, dispute*

Luke 22:24 (introducing the pericope 22:24-30) mentions the *dispute* that arose among Jesus' disciples concerning "which of them was to be regarded as the greatest."

φιλόνεικος, 2 *philoneikos* contentious*

1 Cor 11:16: "If anyone is disposed to be *contentious* (φιλόνεικος εἶναι). . . ."

φιλοξενία, ας, ἡ *philoxenia* hospitality*

Rom 12:13 and Heb 13:2, in parenetic contexts. G. Stählin, *TDNT* V, 1-36; H. Bietenhard, *DNTT* I, 690; Spicq, *Notes* II, 932-35.

φιλόξενος, 2 *philoxenos* hospitable*

1 Tim 3:2 and Titus 1:8, in the list of qualifications for bishop; 1 Pet 4:9: "Be *hospitable* to one another without grumbling." For bibliography → φιλοξενία.

φιλοπρωτεύω *philoprōteuō* want to be the first*

3 John 9, in a criticism of Diotrephes, "who *wants to be the first* among them [i.e., the Christians in the Church]"; → Διοτρέφης.

φίλος, 3 *philos* beloved, loving; subst.: friend, guest*

1. Occurrences — 2. Meaning — 3. Luke-Acts — 4. John and 3 John — 5. James

Lit.: W. GÜNTHER, *DNTT* II, 549. — H. HIERS, "Friends by Unrighteous Mammon," *JR* 38 (1970) 30-36. — R. SCHNACKENBURG, *John* III (Eng. tr., 1982) 124-28. — SPICQ, *Notes* II, 936-43. — G. STÄHLIN, *TDNT* IX, 146-71. — H. THYEN, " 'Niemand hat größere Liebe als die, daß er sein Leben für seine Freunde hingibt' (Joh 15,13)," FS Dinkler, 467-81. — H. TIMM, *Geist der Liebe. Die Ursprungsgeschichte der religiösen Anthropotheologie (Johannismus)* (1978). — K. TREU, *RAC* VIII, 418-24. — For further bibliography see Spicq; Thyen.

1. The unequal distribution of the 29 total occurrences is striking: Luke (15 occurrences), Acts (3), John (6), 3 John (2), James (2), and Matthew (1). Use in Luke's writings and in John and 3 John is comparable, and James occupies a special position (Stählin 159).

2. Only Acts 19:31 uses φίλος possibly as an adj. (BAGD s.v.; *contra* G. Stählin, *TDNT* IX, 114). The subst. usage is widely distributed (→ 1; cf. M. Paeslack, *TViat* 5 [1953/54] 126-39).

3. Except for Luke 7:34 (par. Matt 11:19), Luke never calls Jesus himself φίλος, probably an example of his discretion and reserve as a Hellenist. The rarely expressed but central OT metaphor of God as the friend of human beings might underlie the imagery of the friend in need (Luke 11:5a, b; 6:8; cf. Exod 33:11 and elsewhere). Usually the Lukan usage corresponds to what at that time was the common, secular usage of *friend* (Luke 7:6; 21:16; Acts 10:24; 27:3). The political dimension emerges in Luke 23:12 and John 19:12 (φίλος

as a "court title"; cf. Stählin 147). Luke 12:4 (perhaps also 16:9) reflects specifically NT usage. The principle of mutuality—a fundamental cultural rule in antiquity —is called into question in Luke 14:12. Luke 14:10 shows how the uses *friend* and *guest* are almost the same, though here without eliminating the tension between them. Φίλος is one who loves and is loved in return; this implies both shared joy and concern for the fate of the φίλος (Luke 15:6, 9, 29).

4. Only John 3:29 attests the metaphor of the selfless joy of "the bridegroom's special friend" in reference to the relationship between John the Baptist and Jesus, imagery grounded in a Jewish wedding custom. The φίλος waits before the bridal chamber and rejoices with his φίλος when the latter confirms that his bride is yet chaste (cf. Schnackenburg, *John* I [Eng. tr., 1968] 453f.). John 11:11 calls Lazarus a φίλος of Jesus and the disciples.

The statement about the love of one's friend that extends to death (John 15:13, 14, 15) has many parallels in antiquity. Jesus' love has parallels with these maxims, showing that "Hellenistic thought was influential in Johannine Christianity" (Schnackenburg, *John* III, 110). Election makes φίλοι from δοῦλοι (a contrasting pair), though fulfillment of Jesus' commission becomes the criterion of his friendship. The particular language Christians use with one another is grounded in that friendship (3 John 15).

5. The divine pronouncement concerning Abraham (F. Mussner, *Jas* [HTKNT] 144) in Jas 2:23 uses φίλος in the context of God's own love. Dualistic thinking is in the background here, since friendship with God and with the world mutually exclude one another (4:4).

W. Feneberg

φιλοσοφία, ας, ἡ *philosophia* philosophy*

Col 2:8 characterizes the (Gnostic) false teaching as φιλοσοφία and κένη ἀπάτη, "empty deceit." Bornkamm, *Aufsätze* I, 139-56; P. W. Gooch, *Partial Knowledge: Philosophical Studies in Paul* (1987) 1-7; O. Michel, *TDNT* IX, 172-88; H. Weigelt, *DNTT* III, 1034-36.

φιλόσοφος, ου, ὁ *philosophos* philosopher*

Acts 17:18: "Epicurean and Stoic *philosophers*" conversed with Paul in Athens. O. Michel, *TDNT* IX, 172-88; H. Weigelt, *DNTT* III, 1034-36.

φιλόστοργος, 2 *philostorgos* loving dearly*

Rom 12:10: "[Be] *devoted* to one another in brotherly love (φιλαδελφία)." Spicq, *Notes* II, 944-48.

φιλότεκνος, 2 *philoteknos* loving children*

Titus 2:4, in reference to young women, who should love their husbands and children; → φίλανδρος.

φιλοτιμέομαι *philotimeomai* consider it an honor; make it one's ambition*

In the NT only Paul uses this vb., always with a following inf.: in Rom 15:20 (to preach the gospel where it is not yet known) and 2 Cor 5:9 (to please the Lord). It also occurs in the parenesis to the Thessalonians in 1 Thess 4:11: They should *have it as their ambition* to lead a quiet life and to work.

φιλοφρόνως *philophronōs* in a friendly manner*

Acts 28:7: Publius "received us [on Malta] and entertained us (ἐξένισεν) *hospitably* for three days."

φιλόφρων, 2 *philophrōn* friendly, kind
1 Pet 3:8 TR, in place of → ταπεινόφρων, "humble."

φιμόω *phimoō* tie shut; silence (vb.)*

1 Tim 5:18, in the literal sense: one should not *muzzle* threshing oxen (Deut 25:4 LXX). The other NT uses are fig.: Matt 22:34 (to silence); 1 Pet 2:15 and Matt 22:12 (pass.: become silent); Mark 1:25 par. Luke 4:35 (imv., in an exorcism); Mark 4:39 (to the sea: "Keep silent, *be still*").

φλαγελλόω *phlagelloō* scourge (vb.)
Mark 15:15 D (Lat. *flagello*), in place of → φραγελλόω.

Φλέγων, οντος *Phlegōn* Phlegon*

Φλέγων is attested esp. as the name of freedmen or slaves. Rom 16:14: "Greet Asyncritus, *Phlegon* . . . and the brethren who are with them." H. Lietzmann, *Rom* (HNT) 126.

φλογίζω *phlogizō* set on fire*

Jas 3:6 (bis), of the tongue as a fire (πῦρ): "It *sets on fire* the cycle of life and *is set on fire* by hell."

φλόξ, φλογός, ἡ *phlox* flame*

Luke 16:24 speaks of being in anguish "in this *flame*," i.e., in the torments of the underworld (cf. v. 23). Acts 7:30 tells that the angel appeared to Moses (Exod 3:2) ἐν φλογὶ πυρὸς βάτου, "in a *flame* of fire in a bush"; similar are πυρὸς φλόξ, "*flame* of fire" (Heb 1:7; cf. Ps 104:4), and φλὸξ πυρός (Rev 1:14; 2:18; 19:12, in comparisons). 2 Thess 1:8 speaks of Jesus revealing himself "in *flaming* fire (ἐν πυρὶ φλογός)." P. Katz, "Ἐν πυρὶ φλογός," *ZNW* 46 (1955) 133-38.

φλυαρέω *phlyareō* talk nonsense*

3 John 10, of Diotrephes: "He *prates* against us (φλυαρῶν ἡμᾶς) with evil words." Spicq, *Notes* II, 949.

φλύαρος, 2 *phlyaros* gossipy, foolish*

1 Tim 5:13, in a prediction concerning the "younger widows": "Not only do they become idlers, but also *gossips* and busybodies (→ περίεργος)." Spicq, *Notes* II, 949.

φοβέομαι *phobeomai* become frightened, be afraid*
ἀφόβως *aphobōs* fearlessly, without shyness, shamelessly*

1. Occurrences in the NT and usage — 2. Meanings and usage among the Greeks — 3. General NT usage — 4. Gospels — 5. The "God-fearers" — 6. Epistles — 7. Revelation

Lit.: W. C. ALLEN, " 'Fear' in St. Marc," *JTS* 48 (1947) 201-3. — BAGD s.v. φοβέω. — H. BALZ, "Furcht vor Gott? Überlegungen zu einem vergessenen Motiv biblischer Theologie," *EvT* 29 (1969) 626-44. — H. BALZ and G. WANKE, *TDNT* IX, 189-219. — B. J. BAMBERGER, "Fear and Love of God in the OT," *HUCA* 6 (1929) 39-53. — J. BECKER, *Gottesfurcht im AT* (AnBib 25, 1965). — H. BELLEN, "Συναγωγὴ τῶν Ἰουδαίων καὶ Θεοσεβῶν," *JAC* 8/9 (1965/66) 171-76. — BULTMANN, *Theology* I, 320-22; II, 213f. — A. DIHLE, J. H. WASZINK, and W. MUNDLE, *RAC* VIII, 661-99. — P.-E. DION, "The 'Fear Not' Formula and Holy War," *CBQ* 32 (1970) 565-70. — T. M. FINN, "The God-Fearers Reconsidered," *CBQ* 47 (1985) 75-84. — O. GLOMBITZA, "Mit Furcht und Zittern. Zum Verständnis von Philip. II 12," *NovT* 3 (1959) 100-106. — P. W. VAN DER HORST, "Can a Book End with γάρ? A note on Mark XVI.8," *JTS* 23 (1972) 121-24. — A. T. KRAABEL, "The Disappearance of the 'God-Fearers,'" *Numen* 28 (1981) 113-26. — K. LAKE, "Proselytes and God-Fearers," *Beginnings* V, 74-96. — I. H. MARSHALL, " 'Fear Him Who Can Destroy Both Soul and Body in Hell' (Matt 10:28 RSV)," *ExpTim* 81 (1969/70) 276-80. — C. MAURER, *RGG* II, 1794f. — W. MUNDLE, *DNTT* I, 621-24. — S. PEDERSEN, " 'Mit Furcht und Zittern' (Phil. 2,12-13)," *ST* 32 (1978) 1-31. — S. PLATH, *Furcht Gottes. Der Begriff* jrʾ *im AT* (AzT II/2, 1963). — K. ROMANIUK, "Der Begriff der Furcht in der Theologie des Paulus," *BibLeb* 11 (1970) 168-75. — idem, "La crainte de Dieu à Qumran et dans le NT," *RevQ* 13 (1963) 29-38. — idem, "Die 'Gottesfürchtigen' im NT," *Aegyptus* 44 (1964) 66-91. — idem, *TRE* XI, 756-59. — R. SANDER, *Furcht und Liebe im palästinischen Judentum* (BWANT 68, 1935). — W. SCHMITHALS, *Der Römerbrief als historisches Problem* (SNT 9, 1975) 69-91. — F. SIEGERT, "Gottesfürchtige und Sympathisanten," *JSJ* 4 (1973) 109-64. — M. SIMON, *RAC* XI, 1060-70. — A. STROBEL, "Furcht, wem Furcht gebührt. Zum profangriechischen Hintergrund von Röm 13,7," *ZNW* 55 (1964) 58-62. — M. WILCOX, "The 'God-Fearers' in Acts," *JSNT* 13 (1981) 102-22. — For further bibliography see *TWNT* X, 1289; BAGD; Schmithals n. 199.

1. Φοβέομαι occurs 95 times in the NT. It is particularly frequent in the Gospels (58 times: 18 in Matthew, 12 in Mark, 23 in Luke, 5 in John) and in Acts (14 times); it also occurs 7 times in Paul (Romans, 2 Corinthians, Galatians), 4 times in Hebrews, 3 times in 1 Peter, 6 times in Revelation, and once each in Ephesians, Colossians, and 1 John. The act. form φοβέω does not occur at all. The adv. ἀφόβως occurs 4 times: Luke 1:74; 1 Cor 16:10; Phil 1:14; Jude 12. Because semantically related words such as → ἐξίστημι, εὐλαβέομαι, → θαμβέω, τρέμω occur much less frequently, φοβέομαι together with the noun → φόβος are at the heart of the NT expression of "fear." In addition to various secular and theologically unspecific uses, the concept occurs esp. in statements about fear in the face of the mighty deeds of God or of his representatives, and about fear of God as a fundamental aspect of faith.

2. Φοβέομαι is etymologically related to φέβομαι ("flee") and originally referred to the concrete reaction of "being frightened, terrified," indeed of "panic" (cf. Homer *Il.* viii.139 ["flight"]; xvi.689 ["fright"]; Plato *Phdr.* 254a ("anxiety"). Greek tragedy sought to elicit fear in its spectators in the face of the inescapability of human fate (cf. Aristotle *Po.* 6.1449b). In philosophical language, in contrast, the pre-Socratics down to the Stoics and Epicureans usually rejected φόβος as a reaction contrary to reason (cf. Aristotle *De An.* i.1.403a; Epicurus *Frag.* 102, 116). Esp. the Stoics counted fear among the four emotions (λύπη, φόβος, ἐπιθυμία, ἡδονή, Diogenes Laertius vii.110), from which the genuinely pious person was free: ἄφοβος . . . ἔσει καὶ ἀτάραχος (Epictetus *Diss.* iv.1.84).

In popular and proverbial parenesis, however, fear (as reverence) before the powerful as well as before the law did play an unequivocally positive role: τὸ κρατοῦμ ("the powerful") φοβοῦ (*SIG* III, 1268, 2, 17; cf. also Stobaeus Joannes *Eclogae* iii.1.76; Plutarch *Sept. Sap.* 11). Here fear is also prompted by the divine (τοὺς μὲν θεοὺς φοβοῦ, Pseudo-Isocrates *Orationes* i.16), just as the epiphanies of divine power in miraculous events elicit fear (cf. Homer *Il.* xx.130f.; *PGM* I, 4, 367). For details see Balz, *TDNT* IX, 189-97. Statements about fear thus characterize in a special way the desire for protection and self-preservation in the face of overwhelming powers, whether earthly or divine.

3. In about 30 instances the NT uses φοβέομαι generally of *be afraid:* with acc., of certain persons or of the people (Luke 19:21; 20:19; Acts 9:26; John 9:22; Gal 2:12, and elsewhere); with ἀπό (Matt 10:28a par. Luke 12:4; cf. BDF §149); with acc. and following μή ("*be afraid* [on someone's account] that . . .": Gal 4:11); with μή ("*fear* that . . .": Acts 5:26; 23:10; 27:17, 29; 2 Cor 11:3; 12:20); with inf. (Mark 9:32; Matt 1:20; 2:22); used absolutely (Matt 14:30; 25:25; John 19:8; Acts 16:38; 22:29; Rom 11:20; 13:4; Heb 4:1; 13:6; 1 John 4:18, and elsewhere).

Herod Antipas fears John the Baptist (Mark 6:20) as his sharp critic and fears also the people (Matt 14:5) such that he initially does not dare have John put to death. The religious and political leaders, in their plans against John and Jesus, also fear the people (Mark 11:32 par.; 12:12 par.; Luke 22:2); according to Mark 11:18 they fear Jesus himself because of the people. Here φοβέομαι not only refers to the fear of those in positions of power before the authority of the "public"; it also shows that the people, despite all blindness, stand closer to God's eschatological messenger than do its leaders, whose actions are determined by this world and its power.

In John it is noteworthy that a corresponding element of fear manifests itself concerning the representatives of Jewish authority itself, so that the parents of the man blind from birth offer no information concerning the healing of their son "out of fear of the Jews" (φοβούμενοι τοὺς Ἰουδαίους, 9:22) and the threat of exclusion from the synagogue (→ ἀποσυνάγωγος). Even Pilate becomes increasingly afraid (μᾶλλον ἐφοβήθη, 19:8) in the face of the hatred of the Ἰουδαῖοι, since they coerce him through their law (v. 7) to execute Jesus.

4. In the Gospels the motif of fear in the presence of an epiphany carries particular theological weight, as does the exhortation μὴ φοβοῦ (or similar) that often accompanies these epiphanies as well as the exhortation to disciples not to be swayed by false fear.

a) The revelation of God's power in extraordinary occurrences (Matt 27:54; Luke 2:9) and in Jesus' own deeds evokes astonishment, fear, and terror in witnesses. The corresponding exhortation "fear not" turns this terror in the face of the incomprehensible into trust, since it is the power of the benevolent and saving God that appears in Jesus' deeds. Fear is elicited by the miraculous calming of the storm (Mark 4:41: ἐφοβήθησαν φόβον μέγαν; Luke 8:25: φοβηθέντες δὲ ἐθαύμασαν; Matt 8:27 weakened to ἐθαύμασαν), by Jesus walking on the water (John 6:19: ἐφοβήθησαν; Matt 14:26: ἀπὸ τοῦ φόβου ἔκραξαν [Mark 6:49 has only ἀνέκραξαν]), and by healings, including the healing of the demoniac (Mark 5:15 par. Luke 8:35: ἐφοβήθησαν; cf. Luke 8:37: φόβῳ μεγάλῳ συνείχοντο), of the paralytic (Matt 9:8: ἐφοβήθησαν; in contrast Mark 2:12: ἐξίστασθαι; Luke 5:26: ἔκστασις, ἐπλήσθησαν φόβου), of the hemorrhaging woman (Mark 5:33: φοβηθεῖσα καὶ τρέμουσα; Luke 8:47 has only τρέμουσα), and a raising from the dead (Luke 7:16: φόβος). Luke 1:12, 65 (φόβος), and 2:9 (ἐφοβήθησαν φόβον μέγαν) also belong in this context. This fear then issues in praise and worship of God (Matt 9:8 par.; 27:54; Luke 7:16; 8:25; cf. Mark 4:41; 5:33 par.).

The preceding passages are concerned with Jesus' significance as the mediator of divine power that causes a godless world to shudder (here esp. the stylistic devices of Hellenistic aretalogy play a role; see Balz and Wanke 194). The transfiguration and Easter stories, however, associate this fear motif in a special way with the person

and destiny of Christ. The distance between the yet uncomprehending disciples and their Lord becomes apparent over against the immediacy between the Son and the Father (Mark 9:6: ἔκφοβοι γὰρ ἐγένοντο; cf. Luke 9:34; Matt 17:6).

The sight of the empty tomb and the news of the resurrection also fill the women with intense fear on Easter morning (ἔφυγον, τρόμος, καὶ ἔκστασις [only here in the NT and LXX], ἐφοβοῦντο γάρ, Mark 16:8; weakened in Matthew [ἀπελθοῦσαι . . . μετὰ φόβου καὶ χαρᾶς μεγάλης, 28:8], though Matthew does emphasize the fright of the [unbelieving] guards at the tomb, 28:4; Luke, in contrast, mentions only the women's perplexity because of the empty tomb [ἀπορεῖσθαι αὐτάς, 24:4] and their fright before the appearance of the angel [ἐμφόβων δὲ γενομένων αὐτῶν, 24:5], though Luke does emphasize the disciples' incomprehension and unbelief, 24:11, 22; cf. Mark 16:11, 14). In the Markan view both the disciples' and the women's fright in the face of God's revelatory deed in Jesus is a result of their lack of understanding and faith. They have not yet experienced the crucified Jesus as the resurrected and present Jesus.

Even today the discussion continues concerning whether Mark ended his Gospel with the women fleeing in panic, so that the later Markan conclusion (16:9-20) would not have displaced, e.g., an earlier and lost conclusion (for bibliography see Horst 121f.; on the dispute see Balz, TDNT IX, 210f.; J. Gnilka, Mark [EKKNT] II on 16:8 [n. 41]; on the text-critical problem see K. Aland, Neutestamentliche Entwürfe [TBü 63, 1979] 246-83). Even if the Gospel's conclusion without an epiphany presents problems, both Matthew and Luke as well as the first copyists doubtless used a text that ended with Mark 16:8. Short sentences such as ἐφοβοῦντο γάρ are both possible and documented as conclusions to units and independent books (BAGD 1.a; W. L. Knox, "The Ending of St. Mark's Gospel," HTR 35 [1942] 13-23; Horst).

If Mark did indeed conclude the tomb pericope and thus his entire Gospel with the statement about the women's fearful silence concerning their experience on Easter morning, one could suspect an apologetic agenda (outside the early Church, the discovery of the empty tomb remained unknown; so Aland 278f.), though more likely a theological concern (e.g., the incomprehensible nature of the Easter message even to those immediately and initially affected; cf. J. Roloff, "Das Markusevangelium als Geschichtsdarstellung," EvT 29 [1969] 73-93; E. Schweizer, Mark [Eng. tr., 1970] ad loc.; or the exhortation to faith on the basis of merely hearing the Easter message [16:6] without any visual "proof," cf. A. Lindemann, "Die Osterbotschaft des Markus," NTS 26 [1979/80] 298-317; also H.-P. Hasenfratz, Die Rede von der Auferstehung Jesu Christi [1975] 87-131). In any case, the conclusion of the Gospel of Mark with 16:8, i.e., with a commission, and with fearful silence concerning that commission, represents a theological treatment of the Easter message (cf. also 1 Cor 15:3ff.) that Matthew and Luke can no longer follow.

b) An exhortation to courage or a call to fearlessness transforms fear before God's or Jesus' power into trust. Thus Jesus, walking on the water, identifies himself to the terrified disciples (φάντασμα, ἀνέκραξαν, Mark 6:49): θαρσεῖτε, ἐγώ εἰμι, μὴ φοβεῖσθε (6:50 par. Matt 14:27/ John 6:20). In Matthew this complex includes 17:7 (only here does Jesus approach the awestruck disciples physically after the transfiguration and allay their fear: μὴ φοβεῖσθε); 28:5 (cf. Mark 16:6: μὴ ἐκθαμβεῖσθε); and Matt 28:10; cf. also 1:20. Luke's infancy story employs the allaying of fear within the stylistic device of the angels' message (μὴ φοβοῦ, 1:13, 30; μὴ φοβεῖσθε, 2:10; cf. also Acts 18:9; 27:24). At the conclusion to the miraculous catch of fish Jesus allays all fear and calls Peter to his new service (Luke 5:10). Elements of OT tradition stand behind the exhortation to be without fear (cf. Exod 20:20; Judg 6:23; Isa 41:10; Dan 10:12, 19). Similarly, John 12:15 introduces Zech 9:9 (*contra* LXX and MT) with the exhortation μὴ φοβοῦ (cf. Isa 40:9).

c) Uncomprehending fear before the power of God or of his representative is a sign of alienation from God, as is day-to-day fear concerning one's own life and security. Hence Jesus interprets the fear of the ruler of the synagogue concerning the death of his daughter (Mark 5:36 par. Luke 8:50) as groundless fear of death that can be overcome through faith: μὴ φοβοῦ, μόνον πίστευε. Because the disciples still cling to the concerns of this life, they cannot understand Jesus' prediction of his own suffering (Mark 9:32 par. Luke 9:45) and his decision to go on to Jerusalem (Mark 10:32: ἐθαμβοῦντο, οἱ δὲ ἀκολουθοῦντες ἐφοβοῦντο). Hence Jesus teaches his followers to overcome their fear of suffering and persecution by trusting in God, who loves them and is aware of all injustice (Matt 10:26, 31; Luke 12:7; cf. also ἀφόβως . . . λατρεύειν αὐτῷ, 1:74). How can the little flock of the elect be afraid (Luke 12:32) and live in anxiety concerning its earthly existence (Matt 10:28a par. Luke 12:4)? At most they should fear him who can destroy their imperishable life (Matt 10:28b par. Luke 12:5 ter).

5. In Acts the formulaic construction ὁ (οἱ) φοβούμενος(-οι) τὸν θεόν appears 5 times: 10:2, 22, referring to Cornelius; 13:16, 26, in Paul's address in Antioch of Pisidia specifically to "God-fearers" along with the Jews; 10:35, referring generally to the pious in every nation. In addition, in 6 instances Luke formulates in a more Hellenistic fashion σεβόμενος(-οι) (θεόν), → σέβομαι. The models here are the OT formulas "to fear God" (esp. in Deuteronomy: 6:13; 8:6; 14:23) or "fear of God" (esp. in the wisdom literature: Prov 2:5; 9:10; Ps 34:12), and "God-fearers" (esp. in the Psalms: 22:24; 60:6), constructions that refer comprehensively to Israel's piety and ethical life.

To these the rabbinic phrase *yir'ê šāmayim* (*Deut. Rab.* 2:24; *Mek. Exod.* 22:20; *y. Meg.* 3:74a; cf. also 2 Chr 5:6 LXX) was added to refer to those non-Jews who, although not circumcised, nonetheless believed in the one God, observed the most important Torah regulations (esp. what are known as the Noahic regulations), and lived in close association with the synagogue communities (see Bellen, Schmithals, Siegert, Simon). They were not the same as proselytes but rather were considered "sympathizers" (→ προσήλυτος 2). Josephus *Ant.* xiv.110 calls them οἱ σεβόμενοι τὸν θεόν (cf. *Ap.* ii.10.39) and mentions them (as in Acts 13:16, 26) next to the Jews. They constituted an important group in the Jewish communities of the Diaspora and were esp. open to early Christian missionary activity (cf. Schmithals 74ff.). Luke 1:50 (cf. Ps 102:17 LXX), 18:2, 4, and 23:40 are additional echoes of this OT usage.

6. In NT letters φοβέομαι has a theological function esp. in the context of exhortations. Believers should lead their lives with trust in God and simultaneously in fear before God's demanding will and judgment. Such fear keeps them from falling into false security and arrogance and prompts them to take seriously God's infinite power and freedom. That is why the (Gentile) Church cannot claim any superiority over (temporarily obstinate) Israel, since it too lives only from God's kindness: μὴ ὑψηλὰ φρόνει ἀλλὰ φοβοῦ (Rom 11:20). Although the selfish and unfruitful false teachers who find their way into the Church's love feasts show no reverence (συνευωχούμενοι ἀφόβως, Jude 12), those called to God's ultimate salvation should be in fear in the period until the fulfillment of that promise so that they do not (as did Israel in the wilderness) fall away, i.e., fail (φοβηθῶμεν οὖν, μήποτε . . . δοκῇ τις ἐξ ὑμῶν ὑστερηκέναι, Heb 4:1 [cf. 3:7ff.]).

In the context of the parenesis of household codes, the respect due earthly authorities is also based on the fear of God. Hence Christians should respect all persons, though esp. Caesar and his representatives (πάντας τιμήσατε, . . . τὸν θεὸν φοβεῖσθε, τὸν βασιλέα τιμᾶτε, 1 Pet 2:17, which both cites and qualifies Prov 24:21 [φοβοῦ τὸν θεόν, υἱέ, καὶ βασιλέα]), slaves should obey their masters (ὑπακούετε . . . φοβούμενοι τὸν κύριον, Col 3:22), and indeed wives should respect their husbands (ἡ δὲ γυνὴ ἵνα φοβῆται τὸν ἄνδρα, Eph 5:33; cf. v. 22: ὡς τῷ κυρίῳ), thus conforming to the order willed by God.

Such admonitions against enthusiastic disregard for existing order reflect parenetic elements from wisdom (→ 5) and Hellenistic thought (→ 2), and esp. a basic feature of early Christian anthropology (→ 4.c). Only fear of God and the respect based on that fear enable believers to live in the world free of any anxiety or fear of punishment (θέλεις δὲ μὴ φοβεῖσθαι τὴν ἐξουσίαν, Rom 13:3; cf. v. 4), something appropriate for believers not only on the basis of their own insight but above all because of their own conscience (v. 5). Thus φοβέομαι can be used both positively and negatively here.

According to 1 Pet 3:6 precisely those wives who, like

Sarah, are obedient (cf. vv. 1f.) live free from fear of any human intimidation (μὴ φοβούμεναι μηδεμίαν πτόησιν; cf. also Prov 3:25); indeed, the entire Church is no longer affected by fear of suffering and persecution (1 Pet 3:14 [citing Isa 8:12 LXX]). This kind of liberation from anxiety also frees one to proclaim the gospel without fear (περισσοτέρως τολμᾶν ἀφόβως τὸν λόγον λαλεῖν, Phil 1:14), just as in the larger sense faith makes action without fear possible (cf. Heb 11:23, 27; 13:6: κύριος ἐμοὶ βοηθός, οὐ φοβηθήσομαι [citing Ps 117:6 LXX]).

Finally, according to 1 John 4:18 the relationship between God and those loved by God has nothing more to do with fear (as fear of the wrathful judge—ὁ φόβος κόλασιν ἔχει): ὁ δὲ φοβούμενος οὐ τετελείωται ἐν τῇ ἀγάπῃ. The traditional OT Jewish rhetoric concerning fear of God is jettisoned here; the redeemed now also know the God of judgment only as the God of love, before whom they are already living, focused on Christ, in unlimited παρρησία (4:17; see also G. Klein, "'Das wahre Licht scheint schon.' Beobachtungen zur Zeit- und Geschichtserfahrung einer urchristlichen Schule," ZTK 68 [1971] 323f.).

7. Revelation uses φοβέομαι in the traditional way. The Lord who reveals himself in power identifies himself with the cry μὴ φοβοῦ (1:17; → 4.b); suffering is overcome in fearlessness (2:10); the members of the Church are called οἱ φοβούμενοι (τὸ ὄνομά σου/αὐτόν, → 5), οἱ μικροὶ καὶ οἱ μεγάλοι (11:18; 19:5; cf. Ps 115:13); one should fear, praise, and worship God the judge (14:7; 15:4).

H. Balz

φοβερός, 3 phoberos fearful, causing fear, terrible*

This adj. occurs 3 times in the NT, only in Hebrews. 10:27 mentions φοβερὰ ἐκδοχὴ κρίσεως, "a fearful prospect of judgment," i.e., apostates fall back into a life that in the view of believers becomes terrifying because of the prospect of inescapable judgment; 10:31 underscores the terrible effects of God's judgment by concluding, φοβερὸν τὸ ἐμπεσεῖν εἰς χεῖρας θεοῦ ζῶντος, whereby the author perhaps consciously reverses OT statements such as 2 Sam 24:14; 1 Chr 21:13; Sir 2:18 (it is better to fall into the hands of God than into human hands; cf. Heb 12:19; Matt 10:28; Luke 12:5; further Isa 19:16f.; 24:16ff.; Joel 2:11; 3:4; Pss 75:8, 13 LXX; 98:3 LXX; Sir 43:29; 1 Enoch 100:8ff.; 2 Esdr 7:80ff.); and 12:21 refers to God's terrifying epiphany to Moses at Sinai: Οὕτω φοβερὸν ἦν τὸ φανταζόμενον ("so terrible was the sight"; cf. also Deut 9:19; b. Šabb. 88b) as a sign of the earthly and preliminary character of the old covenant, against which is juxtaposed the ultimate invitation to the new covenant, i.e., to Mount Zion and the heavenly city of God (Heb 12:22ff.).

φόβητρον, ου, τό phobētron terrible occurrence, terrible thing*

Luke 21:11: φόβητρά τε καὶ ἀπ' οὐρανοῦ σημεῖα μεγάλα, "terrors and great signs from heaven," which will announce the coming of the Son of man (vv. 25-27) in the end time (after the persecution of Christians and the fall of Jerusalem, vv. 12-24). After previously mentioning wars, earthquakes, pestilences, and famine (vv. 10f.), Luke may be using φόβητρον to refer to the final signs such as rain of blood, miscarriages, and storms, accompanied by eclipses of the sun and moon and similar occurrences (cf. Sib. Or. iii.796-806; 2 Macc 5:2f.; Rev 16:1ff.).

φόβος, ου, ὁ phobos terror, fear, reverence, anxiety*

1. Occurrences in the NT and meaning — 2. Use in the NT — 3. The Gospels and Acts — 4. Letters — a) Paul — b) Post-Pauline writings

Lit.: → φοβέομαι.

1. Φόβος occurs 47 times in the NT, 14 of these in the Gospels (3 in Matthew, 1 in Mark, 7 in Luke, 3 in John), 5 in Acts, 12 in Paul (5 in Romans, 1 in 1 Corinthians, 5 in 2 Corinthians, 1 in Philippians), and 16 in the other post-Pauline writings (including 5 in 1 Peter, 3 in 1 John [4:17f.], 3 in Revelation). Thus φόβος occurs less frequently in the Gospels and Acts than does → φοβέομαι (1), but predominates in the letters. Like the vb., the noun also is used of panic-stricken terror, of numinous fear in the face of incomprehensible events, of fear as a fundamental attitude toward God and in divinely willed relationships of subordination in the sense of reverence, and finally of anxiety before threats and punishment.

2. On the one hand fear can be viewed (esp. in Luke) as an independent power that "befalls" human beings (ἐπιπίπτω, Luke 1:12, 65; Acts 19:17; Rev 11:11), "fills" them (πληρόω, Luke 5:26), "seizes" them (λαμβάνω, 7:16), "oppresses" them (συνέχω, 8:37), or "comes upon" or "arises in" one (γίνομαι with dat. in Acts 2:43; with ἐπί in 5:5, 11).

On the other hand it more frequently refers to an inner reaction or emotion that is then followed by a certain course of action or development: with ἀπό (Matt 14:26: cry out in fear; 28:4: tremble with fear; Luke 21:26: faint with fear); with μετά (Matt 28:8: μετὰ φόβου καὶ χαρᾶς μεγάλης; Phil 2:12; Eph 6:5: μετὰ φόβου καὶ τρόμου; 1 Pet 3:16: μετὰ πραΰτητος καὶ φόβου); with ἐν (1 Cor 2:3: ἐν ἀσθενείᾳ καὶ ἐν φόβῳ καὶ ἐν τρόμῳ πολλῷ; 2 Cor 7:1: ἐν φόβῳ θεοῦ; Eph 5:21: ἐν φόβῳ Χριστοῦ; 1 Pet 1:17; 2:18: ἐν παντὶ φόβῳ; 3:2; Jude 23); with διά (John 7:13; 19:38; 20:19 [always in the phrase διὰ τὸν φόβον τῶν Ἰουδαίων]; Rev 18:10, 15 [variously διὰ τὸν φόβον τοῦ βασανισμοῦ]).

The simple dat. φόβῳ is used either of *in fear* (Acts 9:31) or *out of fear* (Heb 2:15). In 2 Cor 7:5 the pl. φόβοι refers to *(inner) anxiety;* in Rom 13:3 the sg. refers to a *ground* or *occasion for fear* (of punishment). The cause of fear can be mentioned in gen. (Luke 21:26; John 7:13; 19:38; 20:19; Acts 9:31; 2 Cor 5:11; Heb 2:15; 1 Pet 3:14, and elsewhere). The combination φόβον φοβέομαι occurs in Mark 4:41; Luke 2:9; 1 Pet 3:14. Φόβος is accompanied by τρόμος (2 Cor 7:15; Phil 2:12; Eph 6:5), χαρά (Matt 28:8), προσδοκία (Luke 21:26), πραΰτης (1 Pet 3:16); its antonym is ἀγάπη (1 John 4:17f. ter; cf. also Rom 8:15).

3. The Gospels use φόβος almost exclusively in connection with the fear prompted by epiphanies (→ φοβέομαι 4.a). Mark only uses it to refer to the disciples' reaction to the calming of the storm (ἐφοβήθησαν φόβον μέγαν, 4:41 par. Matt 8:27 [ἐθαύμασαν]/Luke 8:25 [φοβηθέντες ἐθαύμασαν]); Matthew uses it in the story of Jesus walking on water (ἀπὸ τοῦ φόβου ἔκραξαν, 14:26 par. Mark 6:49 [ἀνέκραξαν]/John 6:19 [ἐφοβήθησαν]) and in the Easter story to refer to the guard's terror at the appearance of the angel (Matt 28:4) and that of the women at the angel's message (φόβος καὶ χαρὰ μεγάλη, 28:8 [different in Mark 16:8; → φοβέομαι 4.a]).

Esp. Luke emphasizes the reaction of astonishment and fear in view of Jesus' deeds. After the healing of the paralytic the witnesses are "beside themselves" (ἔκστασις, 5:26), so that they glorify God and "are filled *with awe*" (ἐπλήσθησαν φόβου, namely, fear in the face of the incomprehensible event: εἴδομεν παράδοξα σήμερον); the parallels have ἐξίστασθαι . . . καὶ δοξάζειν (Mark 2:12) or ἐφοβήθησαν καὶ ἐδόξασαν (Matt 9:8). Similarly, φόβος and δοξάζειν belong together in Luke 7:16 (L). In 8:37, *contra* the parallels, Luke inserts the fear motif that also accompanies miraculous events in Acts (5:5, 11), which can provide the occasion for glorifying God (19:17) as well as express reverence (2:43). 9:31 characterizes the pious behavior of the Palestinian community (→ 4.b) in OT Jewish language with the phrase φόβος τοῦ κυρίου (cf. Ps 34:12; Prov 23:17; → φοβέομαι 5). In the Lukan infancy narratives the appearances of the angel of the Lord (1:12; 2:9) and God's miraculous deeds (1:65) elicit fear, which is then immediately allayed (1:13; 2:10; → φοβέομαι 4.b). In 21:26 Luke adopts the apocalyptic motif of fear (of the godless) before the terrors of the end time (different in Mark/Matthew; cf. Ps 65:8f.; see further Rev 18:10, 15).

Only John uses φόβος exclusively in a theologically unspecific sense to refer to the fear of Jesus' followers or disciples before the Jews (7:13; 19:38; 20:19; → 2 and 4.b).

4. a) Paul views φόβος both positively and negatively. He reflects OT Jewish tradition (→ φοβέομαι 5) when he views those without the fear of God as being under the power of sin (φόβος θεοῦ, Rom 3:18 [citing Ps 35:2 LXX]). He himself, however, is governed by the φόβος τοῦ κυρίου in his own apostolic service (2 Cor 5:11); i.e., it both makes its claim on him and simultaneously gives him confidence. Christ's suffering and cross manifest themselves in the apostle's weakness, so that he ministered among the Corinthians "in fear and trembling" (1 Cor 2:3; cf. 2 Cor 7:5).

Through the same tribulations the Church also learns to persevere in fear (2 Cor 7:11, 15) that is not worldly anxiety but rather a challenge by God (cf. v. 10: ἡ κατὰ θεὸν λύπη . . . ἡ τοῦ κόσμου λύπη). Fear thus is a part of faith and characterizes Christian obedience. Since God effects both willing and acting in believers (Phil 2:13), they are called to submit to God's salvation plan "with *fear* and trembling" commensurate with Jesus' own example, thus working for their own σωτηρία (2:12; *contra* Glombitza). It is but a short distance to the post-Pauline parenetic use of φόβος (ἐπιτελοῦντες ἁγιωσύνην ἐν φόβῳ θεοῦ, 2 Cor 7:1, concluding the interpolation 6:4–7:1; cf. also 1 Pet 1:14-17; 3:2), though Paul himself does not yet employ φόβος as an independent parenetic motif.

Though he does consider the justified children of God, who are filled by the Spirit of God, to be dependent on God for everything, they have nothing further to do with the slavish anxiety of those who fear the imperious judging God (Rom 8:15), just as really any fear of legitimate punishment by earthly authorities (13:3) would contradict their conscience (v. 5). Thus in v. 7 (bis) φόβος refers perhaps to God himself (cf. 1 Pet 2:17), whereas only τιμή is to be rendered to the authorities (see U. Wilckens, *Rom* [EKKNT] ad loc.; *contra*, e.g., Strobel; it is questionable whether in Rom 13:7 one can attribute to Paul, on the basis on vv. 3f., the terminology of Hellenistic parenesis regarding the authorities [→ φοβέομαι 2]). Believers do not do in this world what is good and appropriate out of fear of punishment, but rather because they have overcome the world (cf. Rom 12:1f.). The fear of God, however, is not the response to power, but rather to God's love.

b) In the post-Pauline period φόβος becomes an independent parenetic motif. Fear of God now also corresponds to the reverential attitude within the context of earthly hierarchical relationships and order; believers' obedience to their heavenly Master basically manifests itself in reverence for their earthly masters. Thus the Church should preserve the reverence for Christ (ἐν φόβῳ Χριστοῦ, Eph 5:21) in mutual subordination; esp. the subjection of wives to their husbands as their "head" corresponds to their obedience to Christ (ὡς τῷ κυρίῳ, vv. 22f.), for the Church subordinates itself to Christ as its head in the same way (vv. 23f.; cf. v. 33: ἵνα φοβῆται τὸν ἄνδρα). The same holds true in a corresponding sense for slaves in their relationship to their earthly masters, to whom they as δοῦλοι Χριστοῦ are obedient in singleness of heart μετὰ φόβου καὶ τρόμου (6:5; cf. v. 6) or ἐν παντὶ φόβῳ (1 Pet 2:18), especially when they must suffer unjustly (v. 19).

Fear of God is an expression of the obedience (cf. 1 Tim 5:20) and knowledge of God's just judgment. It characterizes the entire life of the churches in their earthly exile (ἐν φόβῳ . . . ἀναστράφητε, 1 Pet 1:17; cf. Acts 9:31) and brings about their sanctification (cf. 1 Pet 1:13-16; 2 Cor 7:1; 1 Pet 3:2 speaks of the saintly behavior of wives ἐν φόβῳ). Although this fear of God does prompt in the pious the appropriate respect for the powers of this world (2:13-17; → φοβέομαι 6), it does not elicit in them any devotion to or esp. anxiety before human beings, since even in suffering and persecution for Christ's sake they do not fear their persecutors (τὸν δὲ φόβον αὐτῶν μὴ φοβηθῆτε μηδὲ ταραχθῆτε, 3:14 [citing Isa 8:12]). Rather, they are always able to give to their critics an account of the basis for this hope, and though they maintain appropriate respect (μετὰ πραΰτητος καὶ φόβου, 1 Pet 3:16), they nevertheless always act in good conscience.

Fear before human authorities or indeed before the powers of this world does not result from fear of God (cf. Heb 2:15: φόβος θανάτου is a sign of enslavement under the devil's power). It does, however, elicit a determination not to be defiled through association with fleshly persons (οὓς δὲ ἐλεᾶτε ἐν φόβῳ, Jude 23; cf. v. 19).

Only 1 John views φόβος and ἀγάπη as mutually exclusive antitheses (→ φοβέομαι 6). In 4:17f. (ter) φόβος refers to fear before God as the wrathful Judge and is thus not reconcilable with knowledge of the loving God that even now allows those loved by God to live in full παρρησία in the face of the day of judgment (4:17). Just as God's perfected love excludes any fear of judgment, so no believer is yet perfected in love as long as fear of failure and punishment still plays a role in his or her relationship with God: ἡ τελεία ἀγάπη ἔξω βάλλει τὸν φόβον, ὅτι ὁ φόβος κόλασιν ἔχει (". . . for fear has to do with punishment").

This negative evaluation of φόβος in the context of one's relationship with God already shows the considerable extent to which Johannine theology and anthropology—in contrast to Paul and the Pauline school—have sacrificed the OT Jewish opposites of love and wrath, fear and trust, for the sake of a new, already pre-Gnostic monism. This does not, however, diminish the parenetic decisiveness of 1 John (cf. 4:19-21), though believers' actions are now grounded primarily in the experience of God's love and in the commandment of love, and not in the demanding will of God as both the loving Father and future Judge.   H. Balz

Φοίβη, ης *Phoibē* Phoebe*

Lit.: BAGD s.v. — F. W. BEARE, *BHH* 1463. — H. W. BEYER, *TDNT* II, 93. — A. VAN DEN BORN, *BL* 1383. — E. J. GOODSPEED, "Phoebe's Letter of Introduction," *HTR* 44 (1951) 55-57. — E. KÄSEMANN, *Rom* (Eng. tr., 1980) 409-11. — W. MICHAEL, "Kenchreä (Zur Frage des Abfassungsortes des Römerbriefes)," *ZNW* 25 (1926) 144-54. — K. ROMANIUK, "Was Phoebe in Romans 16:1 a Deaconess?" *ZNW* 81 (1990) 132-34. — W. D. THOMAS, "Phoebe: A Helper of Many," *ExpTim* 95 (1983/84) 336f.

Φοίβη (Greek: "radiantly pure") is the (originally mythological) name of a Christian woman described in Rom 16:1 as ἡ ἀδελφὴ ἡμῶν, who probably came from Cenchreae and was active in the church there as a "deaconess" (οὖσαν διάκονον τῆς ἐκκλησίας τῆς ἐν Κεγχρεαῖς, probably referring to an emerging ecclesiastical office; cf. Phil 1:1; 1 Tim 3:8ff.; see W.-H. Ollrog, *Paulus und seine Mitarbeiter* [WMANT 50, 1979] 31 with n. 136; U. Wilckens, *Rom* [EKKNT] III ad loc.).

Phoebe may have been in a position in the (eastern) harbor of Corinth (→ Κεγχρεαί), also as a result of wealth and house ownership, to function as a → προστάτις ("protectress, assistant") for many Christians, including also arriving and departing missionaries and their fellow workers, in any case also for Paul (Rom 16:2b; cf. Ollrog 31 n. 136). Paul thus urges the Roman congregation (on the problem of the addressees see, e.g., H.-M. Schenke and K. M. Fischer, *Einleitung in die Schriften des NT* [1978] I, 136-41; W.-H. Ollrog, "Die Abfassungsverhältnisse von Röm 16," FS Bornkamm 221-44) for its own part to receive Phoebe in a worthy fashion (ἵνα αὐτὴν προσδέξησθε ἐν κυρίῳ ἀξίως τῶν ἁγίων, 16:2a) and to give her whatever support she requires.

Since Phoebe's arrival in Rome is mentioned first in the list of greetings in Romans 16, she is probably to be considered the courier of the letter to the Romans; this is in any case the indication given in the subscript to Romans in mss. of the Koine text and elsewhere.

Φοινίκη, ης *Phoinikē* Phoenicia*

Lit.: A. VAN DEN BORN and H. HAAG, *BL* 1383-87. — A. R. BURN, *OCD* 826f. — O. EISSFELDT, *PW* XX, 350-80. — D. HARDEN, *The Phoenicians* (1962). — M. LIVERANI, *ISBE* III, 853-62. — S. MOSCATI, *The World of the Phoenicians* (1968). — B. REICKE, *BHH* 1464-68. — W. RÖLLIG, *KP* IV, 796-98.

Φοινίκη is the name (attested since Homer) of the coastal strip along the Palestinian Mediterranean coast approximately from Mount Carmel in the south to the Eleutherus River (the Nahr el-Kebir) in the north. Cut off from the inland by mountains (Lebanon), the region is esp. oriented toward the Mediterranean. Important harbors are Acco (Judg 1:31), Tyre (1 Kgs 7:13; Matt 11:21; Mark 3:8; Acts 21:3), Zarephath (Sarepta: 1 Kgs 17:9; Luke 4:26), Sidon (1 Kgs 16:31; Isa 23:2; Matt 11:21), Berytus

(Beirût), Byblos (Heb. *gᵉbāl,* Ezek 27:9), Tripolis, and Arvad (Ezek 27:8).

Eustathius of Thessalonica (12th cent. A.D.) derives the name Φοινίκη from φοινός, "red-purple," which corresponds to Akk. *kinaḫḫu,* "purple." Thereby the Akkadian, Egyptian, and biblical designation "Canaan" is related to Phoenicia (cf. Isa 23:11; Ezek 16:29; 17:4; Matt 15:22: γυνὴ Χαναναία, *contra* Mark 7:26: Συροφοινίκισσα). More frequently, though, the inhabitants of Phoenicia are called Sidonians (1 Kgs 5:20; 11:5; Isa 23:12; Luke 4:26; Acts 12:20).

In the 8th-7th cents. B.C. the Assyrians ended the political and economic independence of the Phoenician city-states and their extensive mercantile relationships (cf. 2 Sam 5:11; 1 Kgs 5:18ff.). In 64 B.C. Pompey annexed Phoenicia into the newly-formed province of Syria.

In the NT the name Φοινίκη occurs 3 times in Acts. According to 11:19 the "Hellenists" expelled from Jerusalem dispersed as far as Phoenicia, Cyprus, and Antioch, pursuing their missionary activity only among Jews (Acts mentions Phoenician churches in Tyre [21:3ff.], Ptolemais [= Acco, 21:7], and Sidon [27:3]). According to 15:3 Paul travelled with Barnabas from Antioch through Phoenicia and Samaria to the apostolic assembly in Jerusalem. During his final journey to Jerusalem Paul again went through Phoenicia (21:2) and visited the churches there (21:3-7).

In addition to Acts 12:20, the area around the Phoenician cities of Tyre and Sidon also plays a role several times in the Gospels (Matt 11:21f. par.; Mark 3:8 par.; 7:24ff. par.; 7:31 par.): Jesus even spent time on Phoenician soil and encountered faith there among the "unclean" and the "Greeks" (Matt 15:28 [cf. 11:21f. par.]; Mark 7:26ff. par.).   H. Balz

φοῖνιξ (φοίνιξ), ικος, ὁ *phoinix* palm; date palm; palm branch*

The date palm was a common tall tree in Palestine (esp. in Jericho, Deut 34:3; Josephus *Ant.* xiv.54; often depicted on coins). Its green branches played a role in the Feast of Tabernacles (Neh 8:15). According to John 12:13 the crowd of Passover pilgrims went out with *palm branches* to meet Jesus as he entered Jerusalem (ἔλαβον τὰ βαΐα τῶν φοινίκων; → βαΐον). Mark 11:8 par. Matt 21:8 only speaks of freshly cut branches spread upon the road. John might be indicating the advent of the messianic ruler, using palm branches as a sign of joy and victory (cf. 1 Macc 13:51; 2 Macc 10:7; 14:4; also *b. Sukk.* 37b; see W. R. Farmer, "The Palm Branches in John 12:13," *JTS* 3 [1952] 62-66; R. Schnackenburg, *John* [Eng. tr., 1982] II, ad loc.). Φοίνικες also refers to *palm branches* as a sign of victory in Rev 7:9. J. Feliks, *BHH* 323f.

Φοῖνιξ, ικος *Phoinix* Phoenix*

Φοῖνιξ is a harbor city on the southern coast of Crete in the bay of Phineka, the harbor of which is suitable for wintering. According to Acts 27:12 it is open toward the southwest and northwest; it does, however, offer protection from northeast storms. Against Paul's advice not to leave → Καλοὶ λιμένες (vv. 8-10), the majority (οἱ πλείονες) on ship decided to make for Phoenix and did run into the predicted danger (vv. 14ff.). For details see E. Haenchen, *Acts* (Eng. tr., 1971) 700f., esp. n.7; R. M. Ogilvie, "Phoenix," *JTS* 9 (1958) 308ff.

φονεύς, έως, ὁ *phoneus* murderer, killer*

This noun occurs 7 times in the NT, including 3 occurrences in vice catalogs (1 Pet 4:15; Rev 21:8; 22:15). Acts 3:14 refers to Barabbas as an ἀνὴρ φονεύς (cf. → φόνος, Mark 15:7; Luke 23:19, 25). According to Acts 28:4 the natives of Malta (v. 2) suspected that Paul was πάντως φονεύς ("no doubt a *murderer*"; cf. v. 6: θεός). In 7:52, at the climax of Stephen's accusations, φονεύς is used of the Jews: "You have become betrayers and *murderers* [of the righteous]," as already "your fathers" persecuted the prophets (cf. also 1 Kgs 18:4, 13; 19:10, 14; 2 Chr 24:20f.; Neh 9:26; Jer 26:20ff.; *1 Enoch* 89:51ff.; Matt 5:12; 23:29ff.; Heb 11:36-38). The motifs of persecution and murder of the prophets characterize esp. the deuteronomistic tradition of criticism of Israel, a tradition that continued into the early Christian period (see O. H. Steck, *Israel und das gewaltsame Geschick der Propheten* [WMANT 23, 1967] 265-316; U. Wilckens, *Die Missionsreden der Apostelgeschichte* [WMANT 5, ³1974] 214-17). Matt 22:7 (ἀπώλεσεν τοὺς φονεῖς ἐκείνους) is influenced by the same tradition.

φονεύω *phoneuō* kill, murder*

Φονεύω occurs 12 times in the NT: 5 times in Matthew, 4 in James, and 1 each in Mark 10:19; Luke 18:20; and Rom 13:9.

8 of the 12 occurrences mention the sixth commandment of the Decalogue, οὐ/μὴ φονεύσεις (Exod 20:15 LXX; Deut 5:18 LXX): The prohibition of murder is picked up in the first antithesis of the Sermon on the Mount (Matt 5:21 bis), then also occurs in series of commandments (from the "second table") in sayings of Jesus (Mark 10:19 par. Matt 19:8/Luke 18:20), in Paul (Rom 13:9), and in Jas 2:11 (bis). Matthew and Paul follow the Hebrew text (negated impf.) and the LXX by formulating the commandment with οὐ and fut. ind. (see BDF §§362; 427) as a strict prohibition, while Mark, Luke, and James follow good Greek by using μή with the aor. subjunc.

In the LXX φονεύω almost always renders Heb. *rāṣaḥ* ("murder, kill") and *nākâ* ("kill"). The OT makes a clear legal distinction between murder and manslaughter: Premeditated murder can only be atoned by execution of the murderer (Gen 9:6; Exod 21:12, 14; Lev 24:17; Num 35:16ff.), but someone who kills a person without premeditation and intention has the right to asylum in a sanctuary or free city (LXX also uses φονεύω in this case, e.g., Exod 21:13; Num 35:6, 12, 22ff.). The Decalogue commandment, *lō' tirṣāḥ*, cannot, however, be fixed to a specific legal situation, but rather prohibits all willful and lawless transgression against human life as contrary to the good of the community and irreconcilable with human dignity and divine right (cf. Gen 9:6; Num 35:33-35; Deut 21:1ff.).

Matt 5:21(ff.) does not expand the Decalogue commandment in any way, but carries it rather, contrary to any casuistic reduction, to its logical extreme (cf. also Lev 19:18; Eccl 7:9; Sir 34:25-27; *b. B. Meṣ.* 58b; 1 John 3:15).

Jas 4:2 finds in human emotions the causes of "wars and fights": the actions described with φονεύετε καὶ ζηλοῦτε (with ἐπιθυμεῖτε, μάχεσθε καὶ πολεμεῖτε, αἰτεῖτε) belong to the realm of futile desires (ἡδοναί, vv. 1, 3), which destroy society. This powerful expression should probably be understood as extreme hyperbole (cf. the above-mentioned occurrences; further BAGD s.v.) in viewing zealous "desire to possess" (ζηλοῦτε) directly with that particular aggressive hatred (φονεύετε) that infringes on another's right to life. Since Erasmus this difficult conjunction of terms has been alleviated by emendation of φονεύετε to φθονεῖτε (cf. v.l. in Gal 5:21; 1 Pet 2:1; for details see M. Dibelius, *Jas* [Hermeneia] 217f.). This, however, substitutes a rationalization for the radicality of the image itself and fails to do justice to the author's intention to speak of πόλεμοι καὶ . . . μάχαι ἐν ὑμῖν (v. 1, cf. v. 2b).

Finally, after numerous charges, Jas 5:6 accuses the rich: ἐφονεύσατε τὸν δίκαιον. A similar exaggeration as in 4:2 now refers to the destructive injustice of the rich and powerful over against the oppressed and powerless poor (cf. Ps 37:14, 32; Wis 2:10f., 19f.).

Matt 23:31 sets the OT and Jewish tradition of the persecution and murder of the prophets into Jesus' criticism of the scribes and Pharisees (cf. vv. 29f., 34; → φονεύς). V. 35 applies it to the murder of Zechariah, son of Barachiah, in the temple (for details cf. → Βαραχίας). J. J. Stamm, *TZ* 1 (1945) 81-90; B. Reicke, *BHH* 1237f.; W. Kornfeld, *BL* 1170.

H. Balz

φόνος, ου, ὁ *phonos* killing, murder*

This noun occurs 9 times in the NT. Pl. φόνοι appears in vice catalogs in Mark 7:21 par. Matt 15:19, probably with the meaning *thoughts/intentions of murder* (cf. διαλογισμοί), what come from within a person and make him unclean (in Matthew, in accord with the second table of the Decalogue, at the beginning of the series, in Mark after πορνεῖαι, κλοπαί; cf. also Hos 4:2; Rev 9:21; similarly in Rom 1:29: sg. φόνος after φθόνος, probably as a play on words; cf. also Gal 5:21 v.l.). In Mark 15:7 par. Luke 23:19, 25 φόνος refers to a *murder* committed by Barabbas or his Zealot group (Luke: in Jerusalem) during an insurrection (→ Βαραββᾶς 1). Acts 9:1 (Σαῦλος ἔτι

ἐμπνέων ἀπειλῆς καὶ φόνου) also presupposes the literal sense of φόνος (cf. 26:10f., → ἐμπνέω). Heb 11:37: ἐν φόνῳ μαχαίρης ἀπέθανον (cf. Exod 17:13; Deut 20:13), "they died the death of the sword/they died, having been murdered by the sword."

φορέω *phoreō* bear (continually), wear*

6 occurrences in the NT: *(habitually) wearing* clothes (this sense common in Greek: Sophocles *El.* 269; Josephus *Ant.* iii.153); in Matt 11:8; Jas 2:3; in John 19:5, a crown of thorns and purple robe; Rom 13:4: τὴν μάχαιραν φορέω, probably referring to the Roman authority in punishment and police activity (cf. μαχαιροφόροι, of Roman policemen in Egypt, *CPJ* II, 152; see also Philo *Spec. Leg.* iii.92-95, 159-63; on this problem see J. Friedrich, W. Pöhlmann, and P. Stuhlmacher, *ZTK* 73 [1976] 131-66, esp. 140-45; → μάχαιρα 3); 1Cor 15:49 (bis): φορεῖν τὴν εἰκόνα, of the present or perishable (aor.) and future (fut.) fate of believers, who wear their present form of existence (as an image of Adam) like a garment (on similarities with Gnosticism → εἰκών 7.a) and only later will receive the ultimate form of their existence (as a copy of the heavenly Christ; φορέσομεν, v. 49b). K. Weiss, *TDNT* IX, 83f.

φόρον, ου, τό *phoron* forum, market
→ Ἀππίου φόρον.

φόρος, ου, ὁ *phoros* tribute, tax*

Lit.: A. VAN DEN BORN, *BL* 1647. — J. FRIEDRICH, W. PÖHLMANN, and P. STUHLMACHER, "Zur historischen Situation und Intention von Röm 13,1-7," *ZTK* 73 (1976) 131-66. — B. REICKE, *BHH* 1868f. — W. SCHWAHN, PW VIIA, 1-78, esp. 44-47. — F. X. STEINMETZER, *RAC* II, 969-72. — H.-F. WEISS, *BHH* 11. — K. WEISS, *TDNT* IX, 78-83.

Φόρος occurs 5 times in the NT, twice in Luke, and 3 times in Romans. In the idealized setting of a controversy dialogue between Jesus and the representatives of the Jewish authorities concerning taxes (on this genre cf. Bultmann, *History* 39-54) Luke 20:22 uses φόρος, while Mark 12:14 par. Matt 22:17 has the synonymous Latinism → κῆνσος. Both terms have "political occupation" implications that can best be rendered by *tribute* (cf. E. Stauffer, *Die Botschaft Jesu* [1959] 96): Φόρος is the direct tribute (property- or head-tax) of a subjected people to the foreign ruler, whereas τέλος refers to tolls and diverse taxes (sales taxes, transport taxes, etc.) as mediated (collected by tax farmers, → τελώνης 2) dues to the various administrative authorities (K. Weiss, *TDNT* IX, 80f.). The charge against Jesus of having called for a boycott of tribute payments to the emperor (Luke 23:2) is squelched by 20:20ff.: Jesus' "middle path" in the tax question between revolution and glorification of the emperor (cf. W. Schrage, *Die Christen und der Staat nach dem NT* [1971] 39) exposes the accusation as a lie.

According to Rom 13:6, 7 (bis) Paul considers it part of one's loyal conduct toward the authorities to pay taxes (v. 7 has τέλος with φόρος: ἀπόδοτε πᾶσιν τὰς ὀφειλάς, τῷ τὸν φόρον τὸν φόρον, τῷ τὸ τέλος τὸ τέλος). This ind. confirmation that the Roman church fulfilled its tax obligations to the authorities (v. 6a: φόρους τελεῖτε; cf. Josephus *B.J.* ii.403) is followed by a generally formulated admonition to further payment and appropriate respect for the Roman authorities. Some consider this a reference to the escalation of the state's collection of taxes and the protests that arose against it in Rome under Nero in the years before A.D. 58 (J. Friedrich, et al., esp. 153-59, with reference to Tacitus *Ann.* xiii.50f.).   W. Rebell

φορτίζω *phortizō* have someone carry, burden, load down*

Only fig. in NT: Matt 11:28: οἱ κοπιῶντες καὶ πεφορτισμένοι (pf. pass. partc.), "those who labor and *are heavy laden*," i.e., with the burden of scribal interpretation of the law (→ φορτίον); act. in Luke 11:46 in the same sense: φορτίζω φορτία δυσβάστακτα, "*load down* with burdens hard to bear." K. Weiss, *TDNT* IX, 86f.

φορτίον, ου, τό *phortion* burden*

There are 6 occurrences in the NT, both fig. and literal, as in the LXX. Literal in Acts 27:10 of a ship's *cargo.* Otherwise fig.: Matt 23:4: φορτία βαρέα, of unbearable burdens the pious endure through the scribes' and Pharisees' casuistic interpretation of the law; cf. Luke 11:46 (bis): φορτία δυσβάστακτα, which the νομικοί offer not even a finger to help carry. In contrast, Jesus' *burden* (φορτίον with ζύγος) is light (ἐλαφρόν, Matt 11:30) and gives rest to the weary (v. 28, → φορτίζω). This is not so much a matter of "unburdening" as of giving new strength to fulfill God's will in following Jesus (v. 29; cf. also Sir 51:23). In Gal 6:5 (ἕκαστος γὰρ τὸ ἴδιον φορτίον βαστάσει), within the context of a criticism of false arrogance, Paul is concerned that each person test his own ἔργον before God (v. 4), because he must himself carry (fut.) his own actions along with his trespasses as a *load* (in the sense of "burden") before God's judgment (→ βαστάζω 2; cf. also Rom 14:10-12; 2 Cor 5:10; Rev 14:13; 2 Esdr 7:35; *m. 'Abot* 6:9). K. Weiss, *TDNT* IX, 84-86.

φόρτος, ου, ὁ *phortos* load, cargo
Acts 27:10 TR in place of → φορτίον.

Φορτουνᾶτος, ου *Phortounatos* Fortunatus*
Φορτουνᾶτος (Latin: "blessed, fortunate") is the name

of a Corinthian Christian who according to 1 Cor 16:17 (cf. v. 15 v.l.) visited Paul in Ephesus with Stephanas and Achaicus. This probably refers to a delegation that brought inquiries to Paul from the Corinthian church (cf. 7:1 and elsewhere) and then took a letter of response or possibly 1 Corinthians itself back to Corinth (cf. 16:18). Paul emphasizes his joy at their arrival (παρουσία), which occurred toward the end of his stay in Ephesus and probably while he was composing 1 Corinthians. According to *1 Clem.* 65:1 Φορτουνᾶτος was also the name of a member of the delegation from the Roman church sent to Corinth.

φραγέλλιον, ου, τό *phragellion* whip, lash (noun)*

Φραγέλλιον is a loanword from Lat. *flagellum* (cf. BDF §5). According to John 2:15 (*contra* Mark 11:15 par.) Jesus made a "*whip* of cords" with which to drive out the merchants and money changers as well as the sheep and oxen from the temple. According to v. 16, however, those who sold pigeons were still present later. The Evangelist is thus probably referring primarily to Jesus driving out the animals with the whip, not to blows directed toward the merchants themselves, who more likely had to follow their animals out.

φραγελλόω *phragelloō* flog, scourge*

Φραγελλόω is a loanword from Lat. *flagello.* According to Mark 15:15 par. Matt 27:26 Pilate had Jesus *scourged* before the crucifixion (φραγελλώσας; Luke 23:25 weakens this). According to the Roman penal code, scourging (with the *horribile flagellum,* a leather whip with pieces of lead or bone attached) preceded execution and other humiliating punishments of slaves and inhabitants of the provinces *(verberatio),* thus esp. in the case of crucifixion (cf. Mark 10:34 par.; John 19:1 → μαστιγόω; Josephus *B.J.* ii.306; v.449; Livy x.9.4f.). C. Schneider, *TDNT* IV, 515-19; A. van den Born, *BL* 533f.; W. Waldstein, *RAC* IX, 469-90.

φραγμός, οῦ, ὁ *phragmos* hedge, fence, wall*

Mark 12:1 par. Matt 21:33 (cf. Isa 5:2): enclosing a vineyard by erecting a *hedge* or *fence;* Luke 14:23: *fences* around houses (where beggars can be found); fig. in Eph 2:14: τὸ μεσότοιχον τοῦ φραγμοῦ, of the law, which as a *barrier* around Israel had represented a dividing wall between Jews and Gentiles before Christ (cf. *Ep. Arist.* 139; *m. 'Abot* 3:13b; see further Billerbeck I, 693f.; III, 587f.; R. Schnackenburg, *Eph* [Eng. tr., 1991] 112-14).

φράζω *phrazō* announce, explain, interpret*

Imv. φράσον in Matt 15:15 and in 13:36 v.l.: *"Explain* this parable to us" (cf. Dan 2:4 LXX).

φράσσω *phrassō* shut, stop up*

Heb 11:33: φράσσειν στόματα λεόντων, *"stop/close* lions' mouths" (cf. Dan 6:23 Theodotion; Judg 14:5ff.; 1 Sam 17:34ff.; 2 Sam 23:20); fig. in Rom 3:19: "so that every mouth *may be stopped/may go silent* (ἵνα . . . φραγῇ)"; 2 Cor 11:10: ἡ καύχησις αὕτη οὐ φραγήσεται εἰς ἐμέ, "this boast [corresponding to καύχημα, → καυχάομαι 1] *shall* not *be silenced/hindered*" (cf. 1 Cor 9:15).

φρέαρ, ατος, τό *phrear* well, shaft*

7 occurrences in the NT: Luke 14:5: a *well* (cf. par. Matt 12:11: βόθυνος, "pit"; the rabbinic parallels have "pit, ditch": *b. Šabb.* 128; *m. Beṣa* 3:4), i.e., a wide and shallow pit giving access to groundwater or rainwater. In contrast, in John 4:11, 12 φρέαρ (βαθύ) refers to a shaft well (over 30 m. deep), that of Jacob at Shechem, which as a well for groundwater (in contrast to a cistern) yielded ὕδωρ ζῶν (vv. 10f.; cf. Gen 21:19; 26:19). Rev 9:1, 2 (ter): a deep *shaft* leading to the underworld (φρέαρ τῆς ἀβύσσου; → ἄβυσσος 2), from which emerges the smoke of subterranean hell (→ γέεννα) with its terrors ("locusts," vv. 3ff.). A. van den Born, *BL* 263f.; H. Haag, *BL* 802; L. Rost, *BHH* 275f.; H. Hegermann, *BHH* 798.

φρεναπατάω *phrenapataō* deceive*

Gal 6:3: φρεναπατᾷ ἑαυτόν, "he *deceives* himself." The vb. is attested only in Christian writings.

φρεναπάτης, ου, ὁ *phrenapatēs* seducer, deceiver*

Pl. in Titus 1:10, with ματαιολόγοι and ἀνυπότακτοι: *those who deceive* the Church.

φρήν, φρενός, ἡ *phrēn* sense, understanding, insight*

Pl. in 1 Cor 14:20 (bis) in the antithesis παιδία ταῖς φρεσὶν . . . ταῖς φρεσὶν τέλειοι. Because they serve edifying and persuasive prophecy, φρένες *(insight, reasonable thinking)* stand over against the ecstatic utterances of glossolalia (which do not use the understanding, vv. 6ff., 14, 18), just as maturity stands over against immaturity. In Greek φρήν/φρένες usually refers to a person's insight or inner reflection as opposed to indistinct emotions (cf. Homer *Il.* i.193; Aristotle *PA* iii.10.672b). G. Bertram, *TDNT* IX, 220-35.

φρίσσω *phrissō* shudder, quake, tremble*

Jas 2:19, in ironic criticism of belief (in the one God) apart from works, which even demons possess: καὶ τὰ δαιμόνια πιστεύουσιν καὶ φρίσσουσιν. The author is probably alluding to exorcism procedures during which either the monotheistic formula εἷς θεός (v. 19a) was used or in which the shuddering of the demons before God's power played a role (cf. *PGM* 3, 227; 4, 2541f.; Justin *Dial.* 49.8; *Acts Phil.* 132; Clement of Alexandria *Strom.* v.125.1; Pr Man 4; Deissmann, *Light* 256, l. 3017; 260, esp. n. 3; E. Peterson, *ΕΙΣ ΘΕΟΣ* [1926] 295-99; M. Dibelius, *Jas* [Hermeneia] ad loc.; BAGD s.v.). Such faith thus leads not to salvation, but to ruin.

φρονέω *phroneō* think, reflect; set one's mind on*

1. Occurrences in the NT — 2. Mark 8:33 (par.) — 3. Paul — 4. Acts 28:22

Lit.: G. BERTRAM, *TDNT* IX, 220-35. — J. GOETZMANN, *DNTT* II, 616-19.

1. Φρονέω occurs 26 times in the NT: 3 times in the Gospels and Acts, 22 in Paul, and 1 in Colossians.

2. In Mark 8:33 (par. Matt 16:23) Jesus' rebuke to Peter concludes the significant complex either of Peter's confession (8:27-30) or of the first prediction of suffering (v. 31).

The form-critical and tradition-historical problems of this unit are extraordinarily complex (from the literature cf. E. Haenchen, "Die Komposition von Mark 8:27-9 und Par.," *NovT* 6 [1963] 81-110; E. Stegemann, *Das Markusevangelium als Ruf in die Nachfolge* [Diss. Heidelberg, 1974] 232ff.). Even where to divide the text is unclear (vv. 27-33 or 31-33). Despite their differences the various hypotheses agree in postulating a pre-Markan history for the unit. It is without doubt no longer possible to determine whether v. 33a-b (or even just 33b) ever existed independently or has always required the present context to be understood. If v. 33b had a separate prehistory, it is a wisdom saying of a general nature (just as, positively formulated, we have in Col 3:2).

In the present context in Mark this statement concerns the understanding of discipleship and the refusal to follow: Both are manifested in Peter's behavior. The refusal to follow thus corresponds to the rejection of the eschatological necessity of suffering (v. 31; cf. the connection with vv. 34ff., esp. the relationship between v. 33 and the motif of discipleship in v. 34). The only possibilities are to set one's mind on the world or to set it on God, φρονεῖν τὰ τῶν ἀνθρώπων or φρονεῖν τὰ τοῦ θεοῦ. The rebuke to Satan, directed at Peter, sharpens this contrast even more.

3. Paul uses this word with striking frequency and usually expresses with it single-minded commitment to something and the conditions for such commitment.

(Neutral use occurs only in 1 Cor 13:11, where φρονέω stands in a series with λαλέω and λογίζομαι.)

Rom 8:5-8 is characteristic (cf. the connection with → φρόνημα in vv. 6f.). Dependence on σάρξ or on πνεῦμα determines the nature of the whole person, including all of a person's thoughts and aspirations. Therefore, Paul is consistent in employing an OT motif to exhort his readers to avoid arrogance (ὑψηλὰ φρονεῖν; cf. 11:20; 12:3, 16; also 1 Tim 6:17) while also speaking of setting one's mind on God (in Phil 3:19 implied by the antithesis to τὰ ἐπίγεια φρονοῦντες; cf. Phil 3:20 and esp. the deutero-Pauline letter to the Colossians [3:1f.]). In Rom 12:3 (and 12:16), too, Paul uses a motif from Hellenistic popular philosophy to underscore his exhortation to sober judgment: It is a matter both of "not thinking beyond what one must think," and of "making it one's concern to be reasonable" (with wordplay: φρονεῖν εἰς τὸ σωφρονεῖν).

Rom 14:6 shows that such φρονεῖν for Paul has its basis in the Kyrios: Concern with disputed "days" is reasonable only in reflection that is oriented toward the Kyrios (cf. also v. 7). Paul's use of the hymn in Phil 2:5ff. makes such interdependence quite clear: The Church's φρονεῖν has Christ as its standard; Christ is mentioned at the beginning of the parenesis as more than just an example. Rather, for Paul the Kyrios and the idea of the body of Christ determine one's φρονεῖν concretely: The Church is to have τὸ αὐτὸ φρονεῖν (on τὸ αὐτό cf. also 1 Cor 1:10; 11:20; 14:23), a oneness of mind in commitment to the Kyrios, which does not, however, mean uniformity. In Phil 2:2 Paul amplifies τὸ αὐτὸ φρονεῖν with τὴν αὐτὴν ἀγάπην and σύμψυχοι, and specifies it more closely with τὸ ἕν. While τὸ αὐτό does not occur in 3:15, it is implied in substance by ἑτέρως and τῷ αὐτῷ in v. 16 (cf. also the v.l. in v. 16). In 4:2 the formula is used in reference to a concrete situation. In 2 Cor 13:11 (similarly in Rom 15:5) the concluding parenesis adds the wish that God may bestow τὸ αὐτὸ φρονεῖν on the church. In Gal 5:10 Paul uses a negative formulation (alluding to 1:6ff.): He is convinced that the congregation's own thinking knows no other goal than that of the apostle himself. This can also lead to a goal-oriented φρονεῖν for others: Phil 1:7 speaks of Paul's own commitment to the church, while 4:10 speaks conversely of such feeling on the church's part toward the apostle.

4. In Acts 28:22 the Roman Jews ask Paul about his "view, opinion" (ἃ φρονεῖς) concerning the new αἵρεσις of the Christians, about which they know only that it evokes opposition.   H. Paulsen

φρόνημα, ατος, τό *phronēma* aim, aspiration; way of thinking*

This noun occurs 4 times in the NT, all in Romans 8 (vv. 6 bis, 7, 27). Paul juxtaposes the φρόνημα τῆς σαρκός

(vv. 6a, 7) with the φρόνημα τοῦ πνεύματος (cf. → φρονέω in v. 5) and thus describes two fundamentally different ways of orienting one's life and actions, corresponding to two mutually exclusive ways of standing—before faith (→ σάρξ 3.c) and in faith (→ πνεῦμα 3.b; cf. Gal 5:19-23). The law had to fail in its encounter with the φρόνημα τῆς σαρκός, since the *mind* of the fleshly person is set fundamentally against God (Rom 8:7) and is on the side of death (v. 6a). But in believers the Spirit brings about ζωὴ καὶ εἰρήνη (v. 6b). The φρόνημα τοῦ πνεύματος (v. 27) is the substance and intention of the "sighs" that the Spirit effects in the believer (στεναγμοὶ ἀλάλητοι, v. 26), which God answers even if they lack the form and language appropriate to God (→ στενάζω 4). G. Bertram, *TDNT* IX, 220-35.

φρόνησις, εως, ἡ *phronēsis* way of thinking, understanding, insight*

Luke 1:17, drawing loosely on Mal 3:23, mentions as one purpose of the "forerunner" John the Baptist that he will "bring the disobedient to the *way of thinking/insight* of the just (ἐν φρονήσει [= εἰς φρόνησιν] δικαίων)"; the turning of the hearts of the fathers to the children runs parallel to this (cf. Mal 3:23a). Luke may also be thinking, on the basis of Malachi, generally of the reconciliation of generations and the establishment of righteousness as signs of the eschaton. Concretely, however, the parallelism could also suggest that the fathers (who have fallen away) are to be converted to the (eschatological) righteousness of the sons (cf. *Jub.* 23:26; P. Winter, *ZNW* 49 [1958] 65-77; W. Grundmann, *Luke* [THKNT] ad loc.). In any case, in Hellenistic Jewish usage φρόνησις can refer to an independent virtue (cf. Prov 3:19f.; 10:23; Wis 8:7; 4 Macc 1:2).

In Eph 1:8 ἐν πάσῃ σοφίᾳ καὶ φρονήσει, given the context, probably refers to "wisdom and *insight*" that God bestows on believers (γνωρίσας in v. 9 belongs with what follows; cf. also vv. 17f.). The redemptive event of forgiveness of sins (πλοῦτος τῆς χάριτος αὐτοῦ, v. 7) and the endowment of believers with σοφία and (practical) φρόνησις belong together (cf. also Prov 8:14; 9:6; 10:23; Wis 8:21; in reference to God: Isa 40:24; Jer 10:12; see also R. Schnackenburg, *Eph* [Eng. tr., 1991] on 1:8). G. Bertram, *TDNT* IX, 220-35, esp. 225f., 233.

φρόνιμος, 2 *phronimos* sensible, insightful*

This adj. occurs 14 times in the NT (9 times in the Synoptic Gospels, 5 in Paul). In the LXX it occurs mainly in the wisdom literature (Prov 3:7; 11:12, 29; 14:6; Sir 22:4, and elsewhere).

In the Gospels it appears in didactic contexts (parables and imagery of Jesus): Matt 7:24, of one who does Jesus' words and has "comprehended the eschatological situation of mankind" (H. Preisker, *TLZ* 74 [1949] 89); proverbial in 10:16: γίνεσθε οὖν φρόνιμοι ὡς οἱ ὄφεις (cf. *Midr. Cant.* 2:14; Billerbeck I, 574f.); 24:45 par. Luke 12:42, of the *wise* and faithful steward who is ready when his master comes; in a parable in Matt 25:1-13 (M), of five maidens (among the ten, vv. 2, 4, 8, 9) who, in contrast to the foolish ones (→ μωρία 3), live in continual anticipation of the parousia; Luke 16:8, of the superior wisdom (φρονι-μώτεροι) of the "sons of this world," from whom Church members can learn to ensure their (eschatological) future and (according to Luke) to deal even now with "unrighteous mammon": distributing it to the poor (cf. vv. 9ff.; see G. Schneider, *Luke* [ÖTK] II, ad loc.).

Paul probably draws on a self-designation of the Corinthian pneumatics in 1 Cor 4:10 when he ironically refers to them as "*wise* in Christ" (in contrast to ἡμεῖς μωροί). His mockery is more clear in 2 Cor 11:19, where he exposes the Corinthians' foolish behavior toward the false apostles: ἀνέχεσθε τῶν ἀφρόνων φρόνιμοι ὄντες (cf. J. Zmijewski, *Der Stil der paulinischen "Narrenrede"* [1978] 204-12). Paul uses φρόνιμος without irony in 1 Cor 10:15 in appealing to the insight of the Corinthians, to whom he speaks "as to *sensible people* (ὡς φρονίμοις)."

According to Rom 11:25 Paul, as the superior teacher, wards off all arrogance on the part of Gentile Christians concerning Israel's failures, ἵνα μὴ ἦτε [παρ'] ἑαυτοῖς φρόνιμοι ("lest you rely on your own insight"). Φρόνιμοι παρ' ἑαυτοῖς occurs in a similar sense in parenesis in 12:16 ("do not think of yourselves as *smart*"). G. Bertram, *TDNT* IX, 234; J. Goetzmann, *DNTT* II, 619f.

φρονίμως *phronimōs* wisely, sensibly*

After the parable of the dishonest steward (Luke 16:1-7) "the Lord" (ὁ κύριος refers here, as frequently elsewhere in L, to Jesus: cf. 7:13; 10:39, 41, and elsewhere) "commended the dishonest steward for acting *prudently* (ὅτι φρονίμως ἐποίησεν)" (16:8): In view of the impending catastrophe the steward risked everything so that he could be rescued. The adj. → φρόνιμος is used similarly in parables and imagery (cf. esp. Matt 10:16). G. Schwarz (*BZ* 18 [1974] 94f.) assumes, however, that the Aramaic behind φρονίμως and ἐπήνεσεν in Luke 16:8a were originally intended *in sensu malo* and should therefore be taken as words of the "master" in the parable, not of Jesus. G. Bertram, *TDNT* IX, 220-35, esp. 234.

φροντίζω *phrontizō* be concerned/worried, take care*

Titus 3:8, with inf.: "that they *be careful* to apply themselves to good deeds." Spicq, *Notes* II, 950-52.

φρουρέω *phroureō* guard, hold in custody; preserve, protect*

2 Cor 11:32: "*guard* the city" (i.e., its city gates; cf. Josephus *Vita* 53); Gal 3:23: ὑπὸ νόμον ἐφρουρούμεθα, "we *were confined* [before faith came] under the law," i.e., the law as custodian or → παιδαγωγός (2) (vv. 24f.) took on the impossible (in view of sin's power) task of confining us by guarding and subjecting us to hard discipline; act. in Phil 4:7 and pass. in 1 Pet 1:5: *preserve*, i.e., both "hold fast" and "protect."

φρυάσσω *phryassō* puff up; be proud/arrogant*

Acts 4:25 (citing Ps 2:1 LXX): ἱνατί ἐφρύαξαν ἔθνη, "why *did* the nations *rage*" (rendering Heb. *rāgaš*).

φρύγανον, ου, τό *phryganon* dry wood, sticks*

Acts 28:3: φρυγάνων τι πλῆθος, "a bundle of *sticks*."

Φρυγία, ας *Phrygia* Phrygia*

Lit.: A. VAN DEN BORN, *BL* 1387. — W. M. CALDER, *OCD* 829. — G. DELLING, *BHH* 1468f. — R. FELLMANN, *LAW* 2319-21. — J. FRIEDRICH, PW XX, 781-891. — A. GOETZE, *Kleinasien* (²1957) 201-6. — G. NEUMANN and E. OLSHAUSEN, *KP* IV, 822-26. — W. M. RAMSAY, *Cities and Bishoprics of Phrygia* (1895-97).

A region in the mountainous part of western Asia Minor, south of Lydia and Bithynia and west of Galatia. After the death of Alexander the Great Phrygia belonged first to the Seleucid Empire. After *ca.* 120 B.C. it was part of the Roman province of Asia. According to Acts 2:10 Jews from Phrygia living in Jerusalem witnessed the events of Pentecost. According to 16:6 Paul passed through Phrygia and Galatia during his "second missionary journey"; 18:23 presupposes that churches were founded in these regions. But the church at Colossae in the upper Lycus valley was not founded by Paul, but probably by Epaphras (Col 1:7; 4:12).

φυγαδεύω *phygadeuō* cause to become a fugitive; intrans.: live in exile

Intrans. in Acts 7:29 D*: οὕτως καὶ ἐφυγάδευσεν Μωϋσῆς, in place of ἔφυγεν δὲ Μωϋσῆς; trans. in E gig p, etc.: ἐφυγάδευσεν δὲ Μωϋσῆν.

Φύγελος, ου *Phygelos* Phygelus*

An otherwise unknown Christian in the province of Asia mentioned in 2 Tim 1:15 with Hermogenes as one of the many (πάντες) who turned their backs on "Paul," thinking perhaps of Paul's sufferings and imprisonment as the reason for this abandonment (see N. Brox, *Die*

Pastoralbriefe [RNT] ad loc.). On the spelling of the name cf. BDF §42. A. van den Born, *BL* 1387.

φυγή, ῆς, ἡ *phygē* flight*

Matt 24:20 par. Mark 13:18: *flight* into the mountains in the face of eschatological tribulations (cf. Matt 24:16-18 par.; 1 Macc 2:28). → φεύγω.

φυλακή, ῆς, ἡ *phylakē* prison, dungeon, jail; guard, watch (noun)*

1. Meaning — 2. Literal "prison" — 3. "Prison" in the fig.-eschatological sense — 4. "The spirits in prison" — 5. Watches of the night as temporal designations

Lit.: BAGD s.v. — G. BERTRAM, *TDNT* IX, 236-44. — A. SCHLATTER, *Matt* (⁶1963) 174, 458, 469, 725.

1. Compared to secular Greek and OT usage the spectrum of meaning of the term φυλακή is considerably limited in the NT. Most NT occurrences use φυλακή in the meaning *prison* (→ 2-4). Use for *contingent of guards* in Acts 12:10 is unique. And it is used temporally to refer to a watch of the night (→ 5).

2. A *prison* might be where delinquents such as Barabbas are held in custody (Luke 23:19, 25: because of insurrection and murder), though also a place for detaining undesirable persons, as with John the Baptist, who was thrown into prison (Mark 6:17 par. Matt 14:3; Luke 3:20; viewed differently in John 3:24) and beheaded there (Mark 6:27 par. Matt 14:10), and with Christians who proclaimed the gospel (Acts 5; 12; 16). Saul excelled as one who persecuted Christians in this manner (Acts 8:3), something he unabashedly admits (according to 22:4; 26:10; cf. Gal 1:13; Phil 3:6; 1 Cor 15:9). Christian discipleship in suffering includes being thrown into prison (2 Cor 6:5; Rev 2:10), as already shown by the example of the pious in the OT (Heb 11:36). Thus according to Luke 22:33 Peter promises to follow Jesus to prison and to death, and in 2 Cor 11:23ff. Paul speaks of his own experiences in a catalog of sufferings (doubtlessly with autobiographical elements; cf. Acts 21:13). Such persecutions are viewed as part of the woes of the end time (Luke 21:12; Rev 2:10). Yet precisely in such situations Christians must persevere.

Φυλακή is part of the thematic vocabulary of portrayals of miraculous liberation (Acts 5, 12, 16). Topics within this genre include imprisonment and incarceration (12:4; 16:23, 37), safekeeping in a dungeon (12:5; 16:24: in the inner prison), detainment by strengthened contingents of sentries (12:5, 6), miraculous opening of the prison doors (5:19), and the disappearance of detainees from prison (v. 22)—either in the "narrated" world or in terms of confirmation of such (v. 25; 16:27) in the "related world" (cf. 12:17; 16:40 is a concluding and transition verse).

3. Literal usage moves into the metaphorical when in the framework of the Matthean Sermon on the Mount prison is foreseen as punishment for a person incapable of reconciliation with his adversary (Matt 5:25 par. Luke 12:58). The metaphorical part of the parable of the unmerciful believer, whose "debt" is forgiven but who has his own debtor thrown into prison (Matt 18:30), refers to equalizing justice in the eschaton (vv. 34f.). Visiting prisoners is counted among the Jewish (and, in the NT, expanded) works of love (cf. J. Jeremias, *ZNW* 35 [1936] 77f. = *idem, Abba* [1966] 109f.). In the parable of the great judgment (Matt 25:31-46) this becomes an ethical injunction for Christians (vv. 36, 39, 43, 44) and is elevated to eschatological significance (vv. 40, 45).

4. The basis of ancient cosmology is the idea of the underworld as the prison of evil spirits, demons, and the dead. (Fallen Babylon can also be the prison or dwelling place of unclean spirits, as a sign of its depravity [Rev 18:2].) The serpent, i.e., Satan, is bound in the abyss for a thousand years, then released for the eschatological battle (Rev 20:7), only to be vanquished for the last time (v. 10). The resurrected Christ preached to the spirits in prison, which indicates that he has defeated Satan and death (1 Pet 3:19).

5. Night was divided into four watches of three hours each so that φυλακή was used as a temporal designation. On this basis its theological usage in eschatological parables usually refers to watchfulness in view of the unanticipated end (Matt 24:43; Luke 12:38; cf. also Mark 13:33-37). That it was the fourth watch of the night when Jesus appeared, walking on the sea (Mark 6:48 par. Matt 14:25), indicates the motif of "God's help at morning" (cf. Exod 14:24; Ps 46:6; Isa 33:2, and elsewhere) within the framework of stories of epiphanies and miraculous rescues. The reference to night in Luke 2:8 is in accord with the event of epiphany, and the darkness-light symbolism might be playing a further role: "Keeping *watch* by night" is a typical activity of shepherds, and the shepherd setting is a messianic allusion (cf. 1 Sam 16:1-13; Mic 4:8; *Tg. Yer. I* Gen 35:21)   R. Kratz

φυλακίζω *phylakizō* throw into prison, arrest*

According to Acts 22:17-21 God himself directed Paul to leave Jerusalem and turn his attention to the Gentiles: The inhabitants of Jerusalem would not listen to him, since he had persecuted believers: ἐγὼ ἤμην φυλακίζων . . . τοὺς πιστεύοντας ἐπὶ σέ (22:19; cf. 8:3; 22:4; 26:10; 1 Cor 15:9).

φυλακτήριον, ου, τό *phylaktērion* phylactery*

Lit.: BAGD s.v. — BILLERBECK IV, 250-76. — A. VAN DEN BORN and H. HAAG, *BL* 522f. — K. G. KUHN, *BHH* 525f. — SCHÜRER, *History* II, 480f. — J. H. TIGAY, "On the Term Phylacteries (Matt 23:5)," *HTR* 72 (1979) 45-53. — G. VERMES, "Pre-Mishnaic Jewish Worship and the Phylacteries from the Dead Sea," *VT* 9 (1959) 65-72. — For further bibliography see BAGD; Schürer.

This noun means "safeguard, secure place" (cf. Plutarch *Moralia* 275a, 377b), though the NT (only in Matt 23:5: πλατύνουσιν γὰρ τὰ φυλακτήρια αὐτῶν) uses it only to refer to the Jewish *phylactery* (Heb. *ṭôṭāpōṭ* Exod 13:16; Deut 6:8; 11:18; in rabbinic writings usually *tᵉpil-lîn,* Aram. *tᵉpillāʾ*), worn as a reminder and also as protection from demons (cf. φυλάσσω). On the basis of a literal interpretation of Exod 13:9, 16; Deut 6:8; 11:18 Jewish men fastened on their foreheads and upper left arms small cube-shaped capsules of leather containing four Torah passages written on parchment: Exod 13:1-10, 11-16; Deut 6:4-9; 11:13-21 (cf. also *Ep. Arist.* 159; Josephus *Ant.* iv.213). Some *tefillin* found in Qumran also contain the Decalogue (cf. K. G. Kuhn, *Phylakterien aus Höhle 4 von Qumran* [1957]). Every adult male Israelite had to wear the *tefillin,* as a rule through the whole day, as a sign of remembrance of the Torah and subjection to it. According to Matt 23:5 Jesus accused the scribes and Pharisees of making their phylacteries broad and their fringes (→ κράσπεδον) long in order to display their piety.

φύλαξ, ακος, ὁ *phylax* guard (subst.)*

Φύλαξ occurs in the NT only in Acts 5:23; 12:6, 19, and always in the context of the traditions of miraculous deliverance. Strengthened guards are part of the framework of the motif of the secure detainment of prisoners within the exposition of this genre; this then throws the miraculous liberation even more sharply into relief in the middle of the miracle story (→ φυλακή 2; → τηρέω 1).

φυλάσσω *phylassō* guard, watch over, preserve, look out for; observe*

Lit.: BAGD s.v. — G. BERTRAM, *TDNT* IX, 236-44. — H. G. SCHÜTZ, *DNTT* II, 134f. — For further bibliography → τηρέω.

1. a) The semantic field of φυλάσσω corresponds essentially to that of Heb. *šāmar.* The literal meaning of φυλάσσω is first of all *keep watch* (intrans.), *guard* (trans.). The vb. is used in the NT absolutely in the literal meaning only in Luke 2:8 in an etymological figure (→ φυλακή 5). One guards one's property against intruders (Luke 11:21), objects against theft (Paul guards the garments of those who murdered Stephen, Acts 22:20), prisoners so that they do not escape (Peter in Acts 12:4, who is freed miraculously; 23:35: Paul in Caesarea; 28:16:

Paul in Rome). According to Luke 8:29 a demoniac is guarded with chains and fetters; the demonic powers ("Legion"), however, break the bonds.

b) Guarding can, however, also serve a person's security and protection, so that the vb. can mean *tend.* The background of the Johannine farewell discourse (John 17:12) is the image of the "good shepherd." Noah's *preservation* before the flood (2 Pet 2:5) can be understood similarly. The epistolary conclusion in Jude 24 praises God as the one with power to *keep* believers from every transgression.

c) This suggests the variation in meaning *preserve for* (*or until*) with an indication of goal or time. The paradox in John 12:25 (*preserve* "until eternal life") relativizes the value of this world over against that of eternal life. In 2 Timothy "Paul" refers to his own teaching and life in the service of the right faith as a model for Timothy: He is convinced that God has the power to *preserve* (1:12) what has been entrusted to his proclaimer, i.e., proper doctrine, faith, and love, "until that day" (of the parousia). So also should Timothy *hold fast* (v. 14) in the power of the Holy Spirit to this possession. This is also the sense of the concluding admonition in 1 Tim 6:20—there in connection with the warning against the false teaching of "Gnosis."

d) In the mid. or with a reflexive pron. φυλάσσω means *be on guard against.* Its objects are individual evils and vices (Luke 12:15; Acts 21:25; 2 Pet 3:17), idols (1 John 5:21), or persons (2 Tim 4:15). Such admonitions usually appear in epistolary conclusions. God himself, who is faithful (πιστός), will *preserve* those who live in faith (πίστις) from evil (2 Thess 3:3, act.).

2. Many NT occurrences of φυλάσσω speak of *observing* the law or commandments (used thus also in the LXX). The basic idea of "keeping a law etc. from being broken" (BAGD s.v. 1.f) yields the meaning *observe, follow, keep.* Initially this refers to observance of the Torah, the law as a whole (νόμον: Acts 7:53; 21:24; Gal 6:13), the commandments (ἐντολάς: Mark 10:20; Matt 19:20; Luke 18:21), or individual provisions among them (δικαιώματα: Rom 2:26). In the Synoptics as in Acts and Paul this usage is linked with criticism of Jewish observance of the law (a significant exception is Acts 21:24, where Paul is presented as being in agreement with the Jewish Christians).

John 12:47 views hearing and keeping Jesus' words as determinative of a person's response to salvation. According to Luke, on the other hand, hearing and doing God's word characterizes those who belong to the kingdom of God (11:28; cf. 8:21). According to Acts 16:4 Paul and Silas delivered to the churches decisions (δόγματα) of the Jerusalem authorities for their observance. 1 Tim 5:21 charges Paul's pupil to keep various rules. Cf. also → 1.c.   R. Kratz

φυλή, ῆς, ἡ *phylē* tribe, nation, people*

This noun occurs 31 times in the NT, 21 of those in Revelation (14 times in 7:4-9). Only 4 occurrences speak explicitly of the δώδεκα φυλαί, i.e., of Israel in its ideal and anticipated ultimate form (cf. Isa 49:6; → δώδεκα 2): Matt 19:28 par. Luke 22:30 in an apocalyptic context; Rev 21:12 in the description of the heavenly Jerusalem, i.e., the eschatological community; and Jas 1:1 in the epistolary salutation, in reference to the Christian churches dispersed through the world (see C. Maurer, *TDNT* IX, 249f.). A similar transferal takes place in Rev 7:4-8, where the number of the sealed is given as twelve thousand from each of the tribes "of Israel" (ἐκ πάσης φυλῆς υἱῶν Ἰσραήλ, v. 4). The enumeration begins with Judah (the tribe of David and the Messiah), and the tribe of Dan is replaced by Manasseh (perhaps in view of Judges 17–18; cf. *T. Dan* 5:6f.).

Rev 7:9 shows that this hope for the eschatological reestablishment of Israel refers to the eschatological Church of Jews and Gentiles (ἐκ παντὸς ἔθνους καὶ φυλῶν καὶ λαῶν καὶ γλωσσῶν). Here φυλή means generally *people* (as an ethnic collective) and is also used with this meaning in similar contexts in 5:9; 11:9; 13:7; 14:6 (cf. 1:7; Matt 24:30: πᾶσαι αἱ φυλαὶ τῆς γῆς; Gen 12:3; 28:14).

Tribal names as designations of lineage appear in Luke 2:36 (Asher); Acts 13:21; Rom 11:1; Phil 3:5 (Benjamin); Heb 7:13, 14; Rev 5:5 (Judah as the tribe of David and Christ). C. Maurer, *TDNT* IX, 245-50.

φύλλον, ου, τό *phyllon* leaf*

6 occurrences in the NT, all pl.: Mark 11:13 (bis) par. Matt 21:19; Mark 13:28 par. Matt 24:32: the *leaves* of the fig tree; Rev 22:2: the *leaves* of the eschatological tree of life, which heal the nations (cf. Ezek 47:7, 12).

φύραμα, ατος, τό *phyrama* dough, lump*

5 occurrences in the NT, all in Paul, 4 times of bread dough (made of flour, water, and salt). In Rom 11:16 (εἰ δὲ ἡ ἀπαρχὴ ἁγία, καὶ τὸ φύραμα) the term is a metaphor for Israel. Just as the firstfruits of the first dough of the grain harvest sanctify the dough for the entire year to God (Num 15:17-21), so also is all Israel sanctified by the ἀπαρχή, namely, the patriarchs. In 1 Cor 5:6 and Gal 5:9 Paul draws on the well-known metaphor (→ ζύμη 2) of the profound effect of a small amount of leaven on the entire lump of dough (μικρὰ ζύμη ὅλον τὸ φύραμα ζυμοῖ): The Church should consider how each transgression threatens its entire existence. 1 Cor 5:7 heightens this image: The leavened dough represents the old life (παλαιά → ζύμη [4]), but the Church should view itself as νέον φύραμα, i.e., as the unleavened bread of the ultimately redeemed paschal community (5:7b-8). The Pau-

line metaphor reveals that the leavening of dough was usually understood as a process of putrefaction, and that leavened bread was thus as a matter of principle never used for sacrifices and the cult (the bread of the presence). Also, the bread of the Exodus eaten at Passover, in accord with the hurried departure of the Exodus community, was likewise unleavened (Exod 12:15ff., 34, 39; 13:3ff.). Hence in the eschatological situation leaven can represent what is old in the larger sense, and fresh, unleavened dough can be a metaphor for the Church's purity and its identity as God's possession.

In Rom 9:21 the φύραμα is the *lump* or the kneaded *mass* of clay with which the potter works (cf. Isa 18:6; Wis 15:7). A. van den Born, *BL* 260-62; P. van Imschoot and H. Haag, *BL* 1115f.; J. Rogge, *BHH* 1939. → ἄρτος.

φυσικός, 3 *physikos* natural, in accordance with nature; subst.: natural being*

Paul uses the phrase φυσικὴ χρῆσις in Rom 1:26, 27 of *natural* sexual relations, which Gentiles, women and men, in their godlessness, have perverted into intercourse παρὰ φύσιν (v. 26; → φύσις 2.a), i.e., homosexual relations. He draws here on Greek philosophy and ethics (Plato *Lg.* 836c; Diodorus Siculus xxxii.10.9; cf. also Josephus *Ap.* ii.273), though in accordance with OT and Jewish tradition he also sees in these trespasses a transgression against God's creation order (Rom 1:25; cf. further Lev 18:22; 20:13; Wis 14:22-26; *Ep. Arist.* 152; Philo *Abr.* 135ff.; *T. Naph.* 3:4f.).

2 Pet 2:12 compares false teachers with irrational animals (ἄλογα ζῷα), which as *creatures of instinct* (RSV) are born only to be caught and killed (cf. Jude 12: → φυσικῶς). Φυσικός is thus understood negatively here and refers to lack of γνῶσις in those who are spoken of (ἐν οἷς ἀγνοοῦσιν βλασφημοῦντες). Their fate before God corresponds to that of the φυσικά, namely, ἐν τῇ φθορᾷ αὐτῶν καὶ φθαρήσονται (v. 12). H. Köster, *TDNT* IX, 251-77, esp. 272f., 275f.

φυσικῶς *physikōs* in accord with nature*

Jude 10 uses this adv. in its criticism of false teachers, whom the author exposes—against their own claims—as false Gnostics who live dissolutely, deny the Lord Jesus (v. 4), reject authority, and revile angels (v. 8). They thus show themselves to be profoundly ignorant (v. 10a) and understand God's actions (only) *in a natural way,* i.e., without gnosis given by the pneuma: φυσικῶς ὡς τὰ ἄλογα ζῷα ἐπίστανται. Hence they bring destruction on themselves from God (ἐν τούτοις φθείρονται). 2 Pet 2:12 takes over the context of Jude 10: → φυσικός.

φυσιόω *physioō* blow up, puff up; make conceited*

Φυσιόω is rare in non-Christian texts and occurs 7 times in the NT (6 times in 1 Corinthians, once in Col 2:18), always with the fig. meaning *make puffed up, conceited,* pass. *put on airs, be conceited* except act. in 1 Cor 8:1; 1 Cor 4:6: do not *become puffed up/self-important* for the one against the other (i.e., for Paul against Apollos and vice versa); v. 18 of Paul's critics; v. 19: the πεφυσιωμένοι should prove themselves not in λόγος but in δύναμις; 5:2: grief rather than arrogance (πεφυσιωμένοι ἐστέ) would be appropriate (οὐχὶ μᾶλλον ἐπενθήσατε . . . ;); 13:4, of love: οὐ φυσιοῦται. Thus for Paul the vb. characterizes false gnosis and lack of love (ἡ γνῶσις φυσιοῖ, ἡ δὲ ἀγάπη οἰκοδομεῖ, 1 Cor 8:1), which throws light on the behavior of the "pneumatic" who is still oriented toward the flesh. In this sense it is also true of the false teacher: εἰκῆ φυσιούμενος ὑπὸ τοῦ νοὸς τῆς σαρκὸς αὐτοῦ (Col 2:18; cf. further Ign. *Pol.* 4:3; *Trall.* 7:1).

φύσις, εως, ἡ *physis* nature; natural characteristics; creature, species

Lit.: G. BORNKAMM, "Gesetz und Natur. Röm 2:14-16," *idem, Aufsätze* II, 93-118. — H. KÖSTER, *TDNT* IX, 251-77. — For further bibliography see *TWNT* X, 1290.

1. Considering the significant use of φύσις in the language of Hellenistic philosophy, its rare use in NT texts is striking (14 occurrences, 10 of those in Paul [7 in Romans, 1 in 1 Corinthians, 2 in Galatians], 1 in Ephesians, 2 in James, 1 in 2 Peter).

Only the late text 2 Pet 1:4 uses "nature" of the sphere of the divine, speaking of the believers' participation in the "divine *nature* (θεία φύσις)." Such participation means salvation and liberation from the corrupting perishability of the cosmos: A dualistic amplification accentuates the religious meaning of φύσις.

In contrast, Jas 3:7 uses φύσις of the dominant position of human beings: Every *kind* of animal is subject to the human *species* and is thus dependent on human beings.

2. a) Among the Pauline texts with φύσις, only 1 Cor 11:14 views nature as an acting subject: Φύσις teaches that long hair is degrading for a man (ἀτιμία). This seems to echo the Stoic motif of the commensurability of human behavior with nature, but Paul was hesitant to use such motifs and uses this argument only in passing. Rom 1:26 refers to naturally given conditions and also recalls ideas of popular philosophy: Every sexual transgression is also a transgression against the natural order. Gal 4:8 (on textual problems cf. P. Vielhauer, "Gesetzesdienst und Stoicheiadienst im Galaterbrief," *idem, Oikodome* [1979] 183-95) might also be reproducing a motif from Hellenistic philosophy: Paul's warning regards a fall back into

paganism as worship of gods that "by nature" (φύσει) are not gods at all and thus equates ignorance of God with dependence on idols. The parallel statement in v. 9 concerning worship of the cosmic elements (στοιχεῖα) supports this, since the element of the natural also plays a significant role in such worship.

Paul uses φύσις in a general sense in the metaphor of the olive tree (Rom 11:21, 24: κατὰ φύσιν/παρὰ φύσιν). Here φύσις is what has grown naturally. Contrary to nature, the branches of the wild olive tree are grafted onto the cultivated tree. Rom 2:27 (on the content → b) speaks of the uncircumcised condition of Gentiles, which is determined by both nature and origin. Eph 2:3 (deutero-Pauline) speaks of τέκνα φύσει ὀργῆς, those who like the rest of mankind were once "*by nature* children of wrath." If "we" in this verse refers to Jewish Christians, then a statement from Jewish apologetic—contrary to its original intent—is applied to them as well: They, too, like the Gentile Christians, were once τέκνα φύσει ὀργῆς.

b) Rom 2:14 plays a special role in Pauline use of φύσις, because of the significance of this text both in Romans and in Pauline theology as a whole (from the literature see Bornkamm; F. Hahn, "Das Gesetzesverständnis im Römerbrief und Galaterbrief," *ZNW* 67 [1976] 29-63). The argument (1:18–3:21) focuses on the revelation of divine wrath and seeks to expose the inexcusability of those who have always been sinful *coram deo* (1:20; 2:1). 1:21-32 argues more strongly from the perspective of the situation of Gentiles, while 2:1-3 focuses more on Jewish behavior. In the final analysis, however, the transcendent, all-encompassing character of sin stands in the foreground (3:21). Only in 2:12ff., picking up the motif of divine judgment, is the theme of the law addressed. Vv. 12f. formulate the guiding thesis: What is decisive is that one actually does the law (v. 13). With this presupposition Paul then speaks of Gentiles in vv. 14ff.: Though they do not have the law, they perform its works φύσει, *by nature.* The implication is that in so doing they are a law to themselves. The close connection between φύσις and νόμος in v. 14 is common in Hellenistic philosophy, and Paul might have known this topos from Hellenistic Judaism and used it here. There may also be a connection with the idea of the "unwritten law" (cf. R. Hirzel, *ΝΟΜΟΣ ΑΓΡΑΦΟΣ* [ASGW 20/1, 1900]) in v. 15: What the law requires is written on the hearts of the Gentiles.

H. Paulsen

φυσίωσις, εως, ἡ *physiōsis* being puffed up, conceit*

Pl. in 2 Cor 12:20, with similar attitudes suggesting arrogance and contentiousness, which Paul fears may have grown among the Corinthians.

φυτεία, ας, ἡ *phyteia* plant, planting*

Matt 15:13 (M), in imagery directed by Jesus against the Pharisees (v. 12): a *plant* not planted by God (cf. Ign. *Trall.* 11:1; *Phld.* 3:1; on Israel as God's plant cf. Exod 15:17; Isa 5:7; 60:21; Jer 2:21; Amos 9:15; Ps 80:9; *Pss. Sol.* 14:3f.; of the godless in Jer 12:2). The Qumran community understood itself as God's "eternal plant" (1QS 8:5; 11:8; CD 1:7). → φυτεύω.

φυτεύω *phyteuō* plant, cultivate*

Φυτεύω occurs 11 times in the NT, 7 times in the Synoptic Gospels and 4 times in 1 Corinthians. Mark 12:1 par. Matt 21:33/Luke 20:9, in Jesus' parable of the evil vinegrowers: ἀμπελῶνα ἄνθρωπος ἐφύτευσεν (cf. Isa 5:1ff.; Jer 2:21; *Herm. Sim.* v.5.2; see also 1 Cor 9:7; → ἄμπελος). In Matt 15:13, with the figure of the plant that his Father has not planted and that will be uprooted, Jesus rejects the Pharisees' self-understanding (on the self-understanding of Israel and the Qumran community → φυτεία; on the motif of uprooting see Matt 3:10 par. and → ἐκριζόω). Luke 13:6, in the parable of the unfruitful fig tree: συκῆ πεφυτευμένη; 17:6, in the saying about the power of faith that can transplant a mulberry tree into the sea: ἐκριζώθητι καὶ φυτεύθητι ἐν τῇ θαλάσσῃ; 17:28, in a list of daily chores (ἐφύτευον), during which, as in the days of Lot, judgment will take people by surprise "in the days of the Son of man" (v. 26).

In 1 Cor 3:5ff. Paul clarifies the relationship between himself and Apollos, who had apparently attracted adherents in Corinth (cf. 1:12), in two metaphorical figures: planting (vv. 6-8) and building (vv. 10-15; on the connection between the two cf. Deut 20:5f.; Jer 1:10). Paul regards himself and Apollos as equal in rank: Despite the different tasks of the two (v. 6: "I *planted*, Apollos watered"), God is really the one acting, the one who causes the seed to grow (οὔτε ὁ φυτεύων ἔστίν τι οὔτε ὁ ποτίζων, v. 7; ὁ φυτεύων δὲ καὶ ὁ ποτίζων ἕν εἰσιν, v. 8). In the metaphor of building the statement shifts somewhat: Paul claims precedence by emphasizing that he laid the foundation in Corinth (cf. P. Vielhauer, *Oikodome* [1940] 85).

1 Cor 9:7 uses φυτεύω in Paul's defense of his fundamental right to support by his churches (τίς φυτεύει ἀμπελῶνα καὶ τὸν καρπὸν αὐτοῦ οὐκ ἐσθίει; [cf. Deut 20:6]). B. Reicke, *BHH* 1442f.

φύω *phyō* grow up, come up*

Only intrans. in NT (cf. BDF §309; on forms §76): Luke 8:6, 8, of the *emergence* of seed (2nd aor. pass. partc. φυέν; cf. par. Mark 4:6, 8/Matt 13:6, 8); fig. in Heb 12:15, of the danger of a "root of bitterness *springing up*" (ῥίζα πικρίας ἄνω φύουσα; cf. Deut 29:17 LXX) in

the Church when a member falls in regard to grace and defiles the entire congregation.

φωλεός, οῦ, ὁ *phōleos* hole, lair, nest*

Pl. in Matt 8:20 par. Luke 9:58: the *holes/dens* of foxes.

φωνέω *phōneō* (vb.) call, summon, cry, address*

Lit.: BAGD s.v. — O. BETZ, *TDNT* IX, 301-3.

1. Φωνέω occurs only *ca.* 27 times in the LXX, and not at all in the Church Fathers. In contrast, it occurs 43 times in the NT *(NTG)*, though not in the Epistles; it occurs in Rev 14:18 and in all four Gospels and Acts. 12 of the occurrences are in the four versions of Peter's denial.

2. In Greek usage and in the LXX φωνέω was used only rarely of musical instruments or thunder (see Betz 301f.), and in the NT it always refers to production of sounds by living beings. Still, not even half of the NT occurrences emphasize (→ a below) the (sometimes loud) sound as such: In most occurrences (→ b below) someone is *addressed* or—sometimes by messengers, or even "secretly" (John 11:28a)—*summoned*.

a) In referring to the sound φωνέω is used most frequently in the NT of the cock's *crowing* in connection with Peter's denial (Mark 14:30, 68, 72 bis Matt 26:34, 74, 75; Luke 22:34, 60, 61; John 13:38; 18:27). In Mark 1:26 it refers to the inarticulate *cry* with which an "unclean spirit" comes out, in Rev 14:18 to the command of the angel in heaven, in Luke 16:24 to the call for help of the rich man in hell, in Acts 16:28 to Paul's saving cry in the prison shaken by the earthquake, in Luke 8:8 to Jesus' admonishing cry, in 8:54 to his call awakening the dead girl (cf. par. Mark 5:41: λέγει), and in 23:46 to his cry of prayer before death. In such cases the finite form of φωνέω is sometimes complemented by λέγων (8:54; Acts 16:28; Rev 14:18) and the partc. by εἶπεν (Luke 16:24; 23:46). The vb. can also be followed pleonastically by φωνῇ μεγάλῃ (Mark 1:26; Luke 23:46; Acts 16:28; Rev 14:18).

b) Φωνέω can also mean *summon* or *direct* someone *to come*. Jesus' futile cry for help to Elijah (Mark 15:35 par. Matt 27:47; cf. Luke 16:24) and his summoning of Lazarus (John 12:17; cf. Luke 8:54) take place with a loud voice. But this need not be the case (esp. according to Mark) when Jesus has the blind man (or men) come to him (Mark 10:49 ter par. Matt 20:32), calls the Twelve to himself (Mark 9:35), has the steward (John 2:9) and Martha (11:28b) come, or—as in the parable—"*calls* his own sheep by name" (10:3). The same holds true in John 1:48; 4:16; 9:18, 24; 11:28a; 18:33; Luke 16:2; 19:15

(φωνηθῆναι with imv. sense); Acts 9:41; 10:7, 18 (in v. 18 omitting the person addressed).

Φωνέω can also refer to direct *address* (John 13:13: "you *call* me 'teacher' and 'lord'"; on nom. with art. instead of voc. cf. BDF §143) or to an *invitation* (Luke 14:12).   W. Radl

φωνή, ῆς, ἡ *phōnē*   sound; voice; call; language

1. Occurrences — 2. Meaning — 3. Constructions — 4. Theological significance

Lit.: BAGD s.v. — O. BETZ, *TDNT* IX, 278-301. — *idem, DNTT* II, 1436-39. — M. J. HARRIS, *DNTT* III, 113f. — C. J. LABUSCHAGNE, *THAT* II, 629-34.

1. Φωνή occurs more than 600 times in the LXX, usually as the tr. of *qôl,* and 139 times in the NT. It appears only in isolated instances in the letters (14 times), but 55 times in Revelation. In the narrative books it has 27 occurrences in Acts, 15 in John, and 28 in the Synoptic Gospels.

2. In the NT φωνή basically refers to what is audible, as suggested by its frequent use with ἀκούω (41 times). It is used both of sounds caused by things (→ a) and of human or heavenly voices (→ b, c), and also of what is spoken (→ d) and the whole system of speech, i.e., language (→ e).

a) Φωνή is used of *sound,* i.e., audible *tones* and *noises* in nature and in the human environment, e.g., the rushing of wind (John 3:8) and storm (Acts 2:6), the roaring of water (Rev 1:15; 14:2a; 19:6), the rumbling of thunder (6:1; 14:2; 19:6), the sound of a millstone grinding (18:22), and the clatter of many chariots and the whirring of wings (9:9). In this sense φωνή also refers to sounds produced by musical instruments: the *peal* of trumpets (1:10; 4:1; 8:13) and the *music* of harps (14:2; 18:22), also sounds of wailing (Matt 2:18) and spoken words (Luke 1:44; Heb 12:19) and the *noise* of the crowd (Rev 19:1, 6).

The φωναί in Rev 4:5; 8:5; 11:19; 16:18 are thunderclaps or some other noise accompanying lightning, thunder, and earthquake (perhaps trumpets and thunder, as in Exod 19:16 MT; LXX: φωναὶ καὶ ἀστραπαί; Rev 8:5: βρονταὶ καὶ φωναὶ καὶ ἀστραπαί).

b) Most often φωνή is used of the voice of someone speaking or calling. E.g., Peter "lifted up his *voice*" (Acts 2:14; cf. 4:24; 14:11; 22:22; Luke 11:27; 17:13). "The dead will hear the *voice* of the Son of God" (John 5:25; cf. the citation of Ps 94:7 LXX in Heb 3:7, 15; 4:7). A *voice* is often described as loud: "with a loud *voice*" (Mark 15:34). Sometimes φωνή refers to the distinctive voice of a particular person (Acts 12:14; John 10:4, 5). In Gal 4:20 Paul uses it of the *tone,* dependent on "mood," in which Paul speaks to the Galatians. In Acts 12:22, too,

φωνή probably refers to the element of fascination in Herod—concretely manifested by the sound of his voice —rather than to the content of his words. In a completely different fashion Jesus' wordless *cry* (Mark 15:37) is the expression of divine power (epiphany? victory? judgment [cf. esp. Matt 27:50 with Joel 4:15f. LXX]?).

c) Often φωνή is used to portray a voice itself as speaking, usually representing the unnamed heavenly speaker (φωνὴ λέγουσα in Matt 3:17; 17:5; Luke 9:35; Acts 9:4; 11:7; 22:7; 26:14; Rev 6:6, and elsewhere; ἀπεκρίθη φωνή in Acts 11:9; φωνή alone with direct speech in Mark 1:11 par. Luke 3:22). That φωνή can refer to the speaker as such is shown by the formulation in Rev 1:12 ("I turned to see the *voice* that was speaking to me"), the change from fem. to masc. in 4:1 and 9:13 (φωνὴ . . . λέγων, v.l. λέγουσα), and the identification of the φωνή with John the Baptist (Matt 3:3; John 1:23 *contra* par. Mark/Luke, → d).

d) At times φωνή also refers to the articulated sounds insofar as they say or announce something. Thus the individual tone of a musical instrument can be called φθόγγος (1 Cor 14:7), whereas the ordered sequence of tones, however, is called φωνή, be it the *melody* of flutes and harps (v. 7) or the *signal* of a trumpet (v. 8). In the sense of comprehensible utterances or calls, φωνή— sometimes quoted verbatim—refers to the "*cry* with one voice" in the theater at Ephesus (Acts 19:34), the many-voiced *cry* of the crowd before Pilate (Luke 23:23), God's call directed to Paul (Acts 22:14), the heavenly voice speaking to Jesus (2 Pet 1:17), Paul's provocative *statement* (Acts 24:21), and even words of the prophets from the written tradition, though always as they are read aloud (13:27; cf. Mark 1:3 par. Luke 3:4). In Rev 10:4 the *calls* of the thunders can be written down (v. 3; cf. Ps 29:3-9; though not their "crashing peals," as BAGD [2.c] translates).

e) In isolated instances φωνή means *language,* in 2 Pet 2:16 human language as opposed to utterances of animals and in 1 Cor 14:10, 11 a foreign language as opposed to one's own.

3. Φωνή is the subj. esp. of ἐγένετο (Mark 1:11; 9:7; Luke 1:44; 9:35; Acts 7:31; 10:13; 19:34; cf. Luke 3:22; 9:36; John 12:30; Acts 2:6; pl. in Rev 8:5; 11:15, 19; 16:18), of (ἐξ)ῆλθεν (John 12:28; Rev 16:17; 19:5), of the pass. of ἀκούω (Matt 2:18; Rev 18:22a, c, 23), and where there is no vb. (Mark 1:3 par.; Acts 10:15; Rev 14:2b; ἰδοὺ φωνή in Mark 3:17; 17:5). As an obj. φωνή is usually found with ἤκουσα (Acts 11:7; 22:7; 26:14; 17 times in Revelation; cf. 14:2b) and other forms of ἀκούω (8 times in John), sometimes acc. (ὡς φωνήν in Rev 6:6; 19:6 ter), sometimes gen. It can also be the obj. of (ἐπ)αίρω (→ 2.b). The most common attributive adj. is "loud, powerful," often in the adv. phrase φωνῇ μεγάλῃ (Mark 1:26;

5:7; 15:34 par.; Matt 27:50; Luke 4:33; 8:28; 19:37; John 11:43; Acts 7:57, 60, and elsewhere; with ἐν in Rev 5:2; 14:7, 9, 15; 19:17).

4. Φωνή has great theological significance first because its bearers are primarily God, Christ, spiritually gifted persons, and spiritual beings. Except in Acts 7:31 God is not named directly; rather, the φωνή sounds "from heaven" (ἐκ τοῦ οὐρανοῦ and similar phrases: Mark 1:11 par.; John 12:28; Acts 11:9; Rev 10:4, 8; 11:12; 14:2a, 13, 14; 18:4), "out of the cloud" (Mark 9:7 par.), or "from the temple" (Rev 16:1, 17). Though in Revelation such phrases can refer to angels' voices (so explicitly in 5:2, 11), φωνή does appear there with lightning, thunder, and earthquakes as a genuine element of theophany (→ 2.a). Φωνή also exhibits the character of epiphany where it evokes the sound of masses of water (1:15; 14:2; 19:6) and large crowds (19:1, 6) or—as Christ's voice— sounds like a trumpet (1:10; 4:1).

The φωνή is a prophetic-apocalyptic medium of revelation, and is such esp. often in the book of "Revelation," where the events of the end time are proclaimed, though also elsewhere in the NT, usually where Christ is proclaimed. In the heavenly voice at Jesus' baptism and transfiguration (cf. John 12:28, 30; on the *baṭ qôl* in the rabbinic tradition see Betz 288f.) God confirms him as his Son. In the speeches in John (esp. chs. 5 and 10) Jesus himself emphasizes the authority and redemptive power of his own φωνή. According to Mark his mystery discloses itself in the (epiphany?) cry of death (15:34), and according to Acts he reveals himself— calling to Paul and calling him to service—to Paul the persecutor (9:4, 7; 22:7, 9, 14; 26:14).

The φωνή of spiritually gifted persons also has revelatory power: the words of the prophets (Acts 13:27; Mark 1:3 par.) and the apostles' own proclamation (Acts 2:14; 22:22), the call of the "woman in the crowd" (Luke 11:27), and Mary's greeting (1:44). Even the φωνή of demons becomes manifest to Jesus (Mark 5:7 par.; Luke 4:33f.).

Conversely φωνή is also used of response to the revelation of God's power, be it as praise from grateful persons (Luke 17:15; 19:37; Acts 14:11) or as the wild protest of vanquished demons (Mark 1:26; Acts 8:7; cf. 7:57), though it can also be the call for such revelation (Mark 15:34 par.; Luke 17:13; Acts 4:24; 7:60).

W. Radl

φῶς, φωτός, τό *phōs* light, radiance; fire; lamp

1. Occurrences in the NT — 2. As a metaphor for the salvation proclamation — 3. In epiphany narratives — 4. In Johannine theology and ethics — a) The Prologue (John 1:1-18) — b) Nicodemus — c) Soteriology — d)

"Walking in the light" — e) Revelation — 5. The Pauline tradition — 6. "Fire"

Lit.: S. AALEN, *Die Begriffe "Licht" und "Finsternis" im AT, im Spätjudentum und im Rabbinismus* (1951). — *idem, TDOT* I, 147-67. — E. R. ACHTEMEIER, "Jesus Christ, the Light of the World: The Biblical Understanding of Light and Darkness," *Int* 17 (1963) 439-49. — S. AGRELO, "El tema bíblico de la luz," *Antonianum* 50 (1975) 353-417. — J. BEUTLER, *Martyria. Traditionsgeschichtliche Untersuchungen zum Zeugnisthema bei Johannes* (1972) 265-71. — O. BÖCHER, *Der johanneische Dualismus im Zusammenhang des nachbiblischen Judentums* (1965). — *idem, TRE* XXI, 83-107. — C. BROWN, *DNTT* II, 495f. — R. BULTMANN, "Zur Geschichte der Lichtsymbolik im Altertum," *idem, Exegetica* (1967) 323-55. — J. CHMIEL, *Lumière et charité d'après la Première Épître de saint Jean* (1971). — H. CONZELMANN, *TDNT* VII, 423-45; IX, 310-58. — M. DIBELIUS, "Die Vorstellung vom göttlichen Licht. Ein Kapitel aus der hellenistischen Religionsgeschichte," *Deutsche Literaturzeitung* 36 (1915) 1469-83. — C. EDLUND, *Das Auge der Einfalt. Eine Untersuchung zu Mt 6,22-23 und Lk 11,34-35* (1952). — E. R. GOODENOUGH, *By Light, Light* (1969). — F. HAHN, "Die Worte vom Licht Lk 11,33-36," *FS* Schmid (1973) 107-38. — H.-C. HAHN, *DNTT* II, 490-95. — J. JEREMIAS, "Die Lampe unter dem Scheffel," *idem, Abba* (1966) 99-102. — G. KLEIN, "Das wahre Licht scheint schon," *ZTK* 68 (1971) 261-326. — M. PULVER, "The Experience of Light in the Gospel of St. John, in the 'Corpus Hermeticum,' in Gnosticism, and in the Eastern Church," *Spiritual Disciplines* (Papers from the Eranos Yearbooks [Bollingen Series XXX] 4, ed. J. Campbell; 1960) 239-66. — R. SCHNACKENBURG, " 'Ihr seid das Salz der Erde, das Licht der Welt.' Zu Mt 5,13-16," *idem, Schriften zum NT* (1971) 177-200. — *idem, SacVb* II, 503-9. — G. SCHNEIDER, "Das Bildwort von der Lampe," *ZNW* 61 (1970) 183-209. — L. R. STACHOWIAK, "Die Antithese Licht-Finsternis, ein Thema der paulinischen Paränese," *TQ* 143 (1963) 385-421. — G. P. WETTER, *"Ich bin das Licht der Welt"* (1914). — For further bibliography see *DNTT* II, 496; *TDNT* IX, 310f.; *TWNT* X, 1290.

1. "Light" is one of the most widely attested of the "primal words" in the phenomenology of religion that address the archetypal human yearning for God. Johannine use of φῶς (23 occurrences in the Gospel, 6 in 1 John) is esp. noteworthy among the 73 NT occurrences. In every instance (even in OT citations and in the language of mission) one must ascertain the particular nuance of meaning. There are 15 occurrences in the Synoptics, 10 in Acts, 6 in Paul, 5 in Ephesians, 4 in Revelation, and 1 each in Col 1:12; 1 Tim 6:16; Jas 1:17; and 1 Pet 2:9.

2. The metaphor "see the *light*" is used of the Christian proclamation of salvation grounded in Jesus' person, words, and works (Luke 8:16; 11:33), though the word φῶς does not occur in the various tradition-historically older versions of this expression (Mark 4:21; Matt 5:15). The disciples' self-understanding and the attestation of their faith includes their being "the *light* of the world" (Matt 5:14), "shining before people" (v. 16), and (parenetically formulated) being oriented toward God

(6:23 par. Luke 11:35). Jesus' incarnation itself reveals God's ultimate fulfillment of all prophetic hopes for the Gentile nations (picking up statements from deutero-Isaiah: Isa 42:6; 49:6): Luke 2:32 (in the Nunc Dimittis, referring to Jesus); Acts 13:47 (an exhortation to mission work); 26:18, 23 reflect the language of mission, which in 1 Pet 2:9 characterizes conversion—and thus God's saving work—as a transition from darkness to light. This metaphor of contrast, probably taken from Jewish proselytism, portrays the transition to salvation in incisive language of "effective solicitation" with a predilection for extremes of expression: darkness— wonderful light. This theological viewpoint probably plays a role in the loose combination of quotations in Matt 4:16 (Isa 8:23; 9:1), the purpose of which is to allude, in Jesus' journey to "Galilee of the Gentiles," to the later opening of mission from "Israel" to the Gentiles (and literarily to end the first part of Matthew's Gospel: 1:1–4:16). The Q tradition, which presents itself as instruction for the disciples, also uses the contrast of darkness and light for fearless confession of faith (Luke 12:3 par. Matt 10:27).

3. The optical motif of "light" is characteristic of epiphany narratives (theophanies and angelophanies: Matt 17:2; Acts 9:3; 22:6, 9, 11; 26:13). In the same way the numinous divine power of the saving God is shown in the liberation of prisoners (Acts 12:7; 16:29). The portrayal of heavenly figures of light with other-worldly radiance identifies such events as originating within God's transcendent realm: From that realm, where the "Father of *lights*" lives (Jas 1:17), come the messengers of God's saving intervention for mankind in the accompanying light of epiphany. 1 Tim 6:16 employs one of the Jewish attributes for God when it portrays him as the one "who dwells in unapproachable light" and who thus cannot be seen directly by human beings.

4. For John faith is the direct response to the self-revelation of the one and only representative of God, who brings us revelation, life, light, and salvation. The profound symbolic value of language, formed in the realm of Hellenistic mysticism and the Gnostic systems (*Corpus Hermeticum, Odes of Solomon,* Mandaean writings), is clearly exploited here in the conceptual pair "light and life":

a) The prologue (John 1:1-18), based on a logos-hymn, uses "life" and *light* to express the reality of salvation granted to believers through Christ (v. 4). But the godless world decides against the *light* (v. 5 is redactional, but v. 11 belongs to the original hymn). John the Baptist witnesses to this (vv. 6-8 are redactional, even though they are qualified in 5:35), and the christological-soteriological significance of φῶς in v. 9 already anticipates the statement about the incarnation in v. 14.

b) The dialogue with Nicodemus (John 3:1-21),

against the moral background of the dualism of "decision" between light and darkness, reflects in vv. 19-21 both belief and unbelief (φῶς occurs 5 times).

c) The soteriological redeemer saying in John 8:12 (cf. 9:5) transcends the Jewish horizon (the use of lights during the Feast of Tabernacles) and presents Jesus as the eschatological redeemer (cf. the parallel construction with "*light* of life" in 8:12b). The final exhortation to "believe in the *light*" (12:36 is the only instance a light metaphor is constructed with πιστεύω εἰς) is able—once again recalling John 1–12—to emphasize the redemptive claim (12:46) of the saving Christ, who does not judge.

d) 1 John, picking up the dualistic manner of expression of early Judaism (e.g., *T. Levi* 19:1; 1QM ["The Book of the War of the Sons of Light and the Sons of Darkness"]; 1QS), makes a theological statement concerning the divine essence by portraying God's reality as *light* (1:5; similarly 4:16: "love"). In accord with early Christian baptismal parenesis (cf. Eph 5:8-13), this suggests the *moral* injunction to "walk in the *light*" (1:7). That is to say, brotherly love is the inviolable condition for fellowship with God (2:8-10).

e) In the apocalyptic vision of judgment in Revelation (Babylon's destruction, 18:23) the extinguishing of light is viewed as the end of all signs of life. On the other hand, in 21:24; 22:5 walking in the light (cf. the quotation of Isa 60:3) constitutes fullness of life for the new Jerusalem.

5. Eph 5:8-14, in a pastorally motivated paraclesis, enjoins the realization of Christian existence (περιπατέω). The salvation plan's perspective of "before" and "now" is expressed by the contrast of darkness and light. The paraclesis section of Romans (12:1–13:14: exhortation to Christian living) might have provided the model (Rom 13:12).

There is no privilege for the Jew (Rom 2:19) whose actual behavior contradicts the (written) law. 1 Thess 5:5 and esp. 2 Cor 4:6 already use the metaphor *light* to illustrate christologically (and from the perspective of creation theology) faith as knowledge of Christ bestowed by grace (negatively in 2 Cor 6:14; 11:14), a perspective also seen in Col 1:12.

6. Φῶς has the meaning *fire, place of fire* in rare instances (Mark 14:54 par. Luke 22:56). A source of light (e.g. a "torch") can also be spoken of in this way (Acts 16:29), where such a secular meaning is suggested by the context.

H. Ritt

φωστήρ, ῆρος, ὁ *phōstēr* heavenly light, star; radiance*

In Phil 2:15 Paul compares believers who walk amid this evil generation with lights illuminating the world (ἐν οἷς φαίνεσθε ὡς φωστῆρες ἐν κόσμῳ). In this context the focus is on the irreproachable and exemplary life of the congregation, a manner of life in which they should not slacken. Nonetheless, this Pauline image should probably not be interpreted in the sense of an illumination of the world through a model existence (the reminiscence of Mark 5:14-16 [φῶς τοῦ κόσμου] could be understood in this way). Rather, Paul emphasizes God's gift to the believers that Paul himself, as apostle, has mediated to them (λόγον ζωῆς ἐπέχοντες, v. 16). Thus do they "shine" to the world. Φωστήρ is thus to be rendered with Gen 1:14, 16; Wis 13:2; Dan 12:3 LXX (φαίνω, cf. 1 Enoch 104:2); T. Jud. 25:2; 2 Esdr 7:97, 125 in the sense of celestial light, star (contra E. Lohmeyer, Phil [KEK] ad loc.; citing Gen 6:16, S. K. Finlayson ["Lights, Stars, or Beacons," ExpTim 77 (1965/66) 181] suggests the tr. "beacons"). The statement's particular accent lies in the Pauline understanding of eschatology: Even now is fulfilled in the Church's relationship to the world what apocalyptic predictions foresaw for the righteous only at the end (hence the citation of passages from Daniel, 1 Enoch, and 2 Esdras; see also H. Conzelmann, TDNT IX, 346).

In Rev 21:11 φωστήρ refers to the radiance of the heavenly Jerusalem (on this meaning cf. 1 Esdr 8:76).

φωσφόρος, 2 phōsphoros light-giving*

2 Pet 1:19 uses this adj. subst. of the bringer of light, i.e., the morning star that will rise in the hearts of Christians (despite Mal 4:2, not the sun). This understands the φωσφόρος as a sign of Christ's ultimate coming after the period of the world's night. This rising "in your hearts" underscores that Christians are still connected with their coming Lord and will not be caught unaware at his day. Recognizable here is an individualistic understanding of the parousia (W. Schrage, 2 Pet [NTD] ad loc.). Cf. further Rev 2:28; 22:16 (→ πρωϊνός); Num 24:17; Isa 60:1-3; Ps 110:3. BAGD s.v. (bibliography); Spicq, Notes II, 953f. (bibliography).

φωτεινός, 3 phōteinos shining, bright, radiant*

Matt 6:22 par. Luke 11:34, 36 (bis), with the antonym → σκοτεινός (see for bibliography) of the body, which becomes full and completely bright if the eye is sound, as if a lamp were illuminating it with its light (→ φωτίζω 2). In the account of the Transfiguration only Matthew (17:5) speaks of a "shining cloud (νεφέλη φωτεινή)" as a sign of God's presence (cf. Exod 24:16f.; 34:5, 29f.; Rev 14:14). H. D. Betz, "Matthew vi.22f. and Greek Theories of Vision," FS Black (1979) 43-56 (= idem, Essays on the Sermon on the Mount [1985] 71-87).

φωτίζω phōtizō illuminate, light up; bring to light; shine*

1. Occurrences in the NT — 2. The Gospels — 3. The letters — 4. Revelation

Lit.: H. CONZELMANN, TDNT IX, 310-58. — F. HAHN, "Die Worte vom Licht Lk 11,33-36," FS Schmid (1973) 107-38. — G. P. WETTER, Phōs. Eine Untersuchung über hellenistische Frömmigkeit. Zugleich ein Beitrag zum Verständnis des Manichäismus (1915). — For further bibliography see TWNT X, 1290.

1. Φωτίζω occurs 11 times in the NT: twice each in Ephesians and Hebrews, 3 times in Revelation, and once each in Luke 11:36; John 1:9; 1 Cor 4:5; and 2 Tim 1:10.

2. Any understanding of the problematic statement in Luke 11:36b (ὡς ὅταν ὁ λύχνος τῇ ἀστραπῇ φωτίζῃ σε) must take into account its connection with the christologically significant λύχνος motif in v. 33, since → λύχνος (3.b) is reintroduced with no modifier in v. 36. As in v. 33, λύχνος in v. 36b functions simply as a source of light. The future sense of φωτίζῃ σε after ἔσται (cf. BAGD s.v. ὅταν 1.a; Hahn 129, esp. n.68) and the ἀστραπή motif (17:24; Matt 24:27) make an eschatological-forensic understanding most appropriate: Whoever is open to Jesus' redeeming presence (vv. 33, 34-36a) and whose entire existence is illuminated by it will be confirmed as an illuminated one when he or she meets the Son of man in the last judgment (cf. Hahn 131; G. Schneider, Luke [ÖTK] II, ad loc.; E. Schweizer, Luke [Eng. tr., 1984] ad loc.). One can, then, translate ambiguously: "as when a lamp with its rays illuminates (= enlightens) you."

According to John 1:9 the Logos is the true light "that illuminates everyone that comes into this world." The Evangelist, who is already speaking here (after 1:6-8) of the incarnate Logos, thereby emphasizes the uniqueness and exclusive nature of the revelation in Jesus over against John the Baptist (v. 8) and all other supposed revelatory figures. The "illumination of every person" does not yet mean faith, but rather the God-given possibility that can lead to faith in everyone who opens himself to the divine solicitation (vv. 11f.).

3. Paul justifiably rejects the Corinthians' right to criticize his service as an apostle by referring to the parousia (1 Cor 4:5). Only then will Christ "bring to light what is now hidden in darkness" (cf. 14:25; Rom 2:16; 2 Cor 5:10).

In his prayers for the Church the author of Ephesians mentions among other things "enlightened eyes of the heart" (1:18), i.e., recognition of the hope grounded in God's call, of the inheritance as the attainment of the heavenly δόξα, and of God's incomparable power that can be experienced even now (1:18b, 19). According to 3:9 the apostle received the grace to "bring to light the realization of the mystery" during his missionary activity among the Gentiles. Thus in the apostle's proclamation the divine implementation of salvation (→ οἰκονομία 4) comes to movement, which was once hidden and is now made known (1:9; 3:3-5; 6:19).

As in Eph 3:9 and similarly in the context of the scheme of revelation, 2 Tim 1:10 asserts that Christ "*brought* immortal life *to light* through the gospel," i.e., through the apostolic proclamation. This, too, refers to an effective manifestation and not to a mere announcement (cf. Conzelmann 349).

In Hebrews φωτίζω occurs twice (6:4; 10:32) as an aor. pass. partc. referring to the Christians being addressed. They are told that "those who *have* once *been enlightened*" (6:4) and have received the various gifts of the Spirit, cannot possibly renew their conversion once they have fallen from faith (6:4-6; cf. 10:26-31; 12:15-17). This one-time event of enlightenment might be baptism (cf. O. Michel, *Heb* [KEK] ad loc.; Conzelmann, 355, 357f.). 10:32, as well ("Recall the former days when, *after you were enlightened,* you endured a hard struggle with sufferings"), appears to refer to baptism as the beginning of Christian existence.

4. Rev 18:1 says of an angel, which here represents God (alluding to Ezek 43:2): "The earth *was made bright* with his splendor." In a variation of a citation from Isa 60:1, 19f., Rev 21:23 asserts that the heavenly Jerusalem needs neither sun nor moon, since God's radiance *has illuminated* it (cf. vv. 3, 11). The same idea occurs in similar form in 22:5: God's δοῦλοι (v. 3) will need the light neither of a lamp nor of the sun "since the Lord God *will shine* over them" so that night will be no more.

M. Winter

φωτινός, 3 *phōtinos* shining, bright, radiant
A variant spelling of → φωτεινός (so Westcott/Hort [1881; ²1896]).

φωτισμός, οῦ, ὁ *phōtismos* illumination; light*

1. Φωτισμός occurs only twice in the NT, both in Paul (2 Cor 4:4, 6).

2. In an apologetic defense of his apostolic office (2 Cor 2:14–7:4) Paul bases his confidence first on his divine commission (2:14–4:6). Neither in his conduct nor in his proclamation can he find fault (4:2; 1:12), since he has neither tampered with nor concealed God's word, but rather has openly stated it with its claim to truth (4:2f.). If his gospel nonetheless seems "veiled," it is such only for the ἀπολλύμενοι (v. 3). "In their case" (on ἐν οἷς cf. BDF §220.1) "the god of this world has blinded the minds of the unbelievers" (the ἄπιστοι in v. 4 are identical with the ἀπολλύμενοι in v. 3; cf. R. Bultmann, *2 Cor* [Eng. tr., 1985] ad loc.) "so that they do not see the *light* of the gospel of the glory of Christ, who is God's likeness" (v. 4).

No dispute exists concerning the act. intrans. meaning of φωτισμός in 2 Cor 4:4 (cf. Pss 26:1; 43:4; 77:14; Job 3:9). What is disputed is the understanding of φωτισμός· in v. 6: "For it is the God who said 'Let light shine out of darkness' who has shone in our hearts to *bring to light* the knowledge of God's glory in Christ's face."

Paul is not referring here to his own enlightenment (*contra* H. Windisch, *2 Cor* [KEK] ad loc., among others), but rather to the purpose of his proclamation (BAGD s.v.; Bultmann, *2 Cor,* ad loc.). Creation and conversion are juxtaposed in parallelism (on this analogy in the Jewish tradition cf. H. Conzelmann, *TDNT* IX, 324f., 346). This interprets the beginning of Christian existence as a divine creative act.

In v. 6, unlike v. 4 and with a causal connection to v. 5 (ὅτι), Paul understands his apostolic office as grounded in God's revelatory action (ὃς ἔλαμψεν ἐν ταῖς καρδίαις ἡμῶν), which both commissions and authorizes him to proclaim in his gospel (κηρύσσομεν, v. 5) the δόξα τοῦ θεοῦ/᾽Ιησοῦ Χριστοῦ (3:18) and thus to awaken γνῶσις (2:14; Gal 1:16).

On the history-of-religions evaluation of φωτισμός (Gnostic terminology?) cf. Bultmann, *2 Cor,* ad loc.; O. Michel, *Heb* [KEK] 241 n.2; Conzelmann, *TDNT* IX, 346 n.296.   M. Winter

X χ

χαίρω *chairō* be glad, rejoice

1. Occurrences and use in the NT — 2. Spiritual *(enthusiastisch)* and eschatological joy — 3. Exhortations to joy — 4. Suffering and joy — 5. Joy as reaction — 6. The apostle's rejoicing over the Church — 7. Shared joy — 8. Related terms

Lit.: → χαρά.

1. Χαίρω occurs 74 times in the NT and has theological significance esp. in Q, Luke, John, and Paul. It also occurs frequently as a greeting (8 of the occurrences), including in epistolary prescripts (cf. Acts 15:23; 23:26; Jas 1:1). Here a relationship exists with the Christian epistolary greeting with → χάρις (6) (cf. K. Berger, *ZNW* 65 [1974] 200f.). The vb. occurs in narrative texts in Matt 2:10; 18:13; Mark 14:11; Luke 15:5; 19:6; 19:37; 22:5; 23:8; John 8:56; 20:20; Acts 5:41; 8:39; 11:23; 13:48; 15:31; Rev 11:10. 1 Cor 7:30 and 13:6 evaluate χαίρω with some moral ambivalence, and Rev 11:10 evaluates it negatively.

2. In keeping with the charismatic and experiential *(enthusiastisch)* character of early Christianity, joy is an expression of participation in the heavenly world (cf. Philo *Abr.* 202: Rejoicing is wholly appropriate only for God)—as the reaction of witnesses in visionary rapture (Luke 24:52; Acts 8:39) or in visions (John 8:56, of Abraham [cf. *Jub.* 15:17; *Tg. Onq.* on Gen 17:17; Philo *Mut.* 154]; 20:20). Comparable to this is joy in the larger sense as the reaction to seeing (→ 5) or as a reaction to the activity of the Pneuma (1 Pet 4:13f.). Thus even now one can already rejoice in view of future rewards (Matt 5:12; Luke 10:20b). Therefore, the exhortation to rejoice in Matt 5:12 corresponds functionally to a blessing (cf. 1 Pet 4:13f.). Heavenly or eschatological salvation, however, is similarly described simply as rejoicing (Luke 6:23; 1 Pet 4:13), as is joy at harvest time and weddings (John 3:29; 4:36), and the future joy (John 16:20, 22: antithesis between disciples and the world; joy at Jesus' parousia).

3. Exhortations to rejoice generally refer to the manner of rejoicing or that over which one rejoices. Such exhortations occur as admonition or parenesis, in the three parables of Luke 15 (vv. 6, 9, 32), and as exhortations to share in another's joy, which probably refers to the acceptance of penitent sinners by those addressed. Often such exhortations exhibit features of consolation in the face of present grief (John 14:28: Jesus' departure) or persecution (Matt 5:12). They can also refer to the substance of hope (Rom 12:12) or endurance of suffering (1 Pet 4:13). The phrase "in the Lord" (typical in Philippians: 3:1; 4:4, 10) and the adv. "always," which also accompanies the exhortation to constant prayer (1 Thess 5:16), reveals the origin in spiritual experience of Christian joy. "Rejoice" in 2 Cor 13:11 is virtually a summation of Christian existence. In contrast, in 1 Cor 7:30 Christian existence manifests itself as autonomous aloofness over against the world's joy. According to Luke 10:20 the charismatic's joy over his fullness of authority should be replaced by the anticipatory joy of heavenly salvation—perhaps a reference to the dispute concerning present and future eschatology in early churches.

4. Suffering and joy are so often connected that the suffering person is called on to rejoice even in and because of his suffering. Analogies exist in Judaism, e.g., *2 Bar.* 52:6f.: "Rejoice in the suffering that you (pl.) suffer now. For why do you look for your enemies' decline? Prepare your souls for what is reserved for you and . . . for the reward that is preserved for you." What comes after suffering is so much more glorious that suffering itself takes on the character of a necessary preliminary stage.

Expressions of this idea vary: According to John 14:28 the disciples should rejoice because Jesus is departing. In 11:15 Jesus rejoices because Lazarus has died, thus providing an opportunity for the manifestation of glory in a miracle. In Col 1:24 the apostle rejoices in his suffering because it is "for" the Church. According to 1 Pet 4:13 the Church should rejoice in its fellowship of suffering with Christ, so that it may also rejoice at the revelation of his glory. Peter and John rejoice according to Acts 5:41 because they are "considered worthy to suffer dishonor for the name." Here, as in other NT texts, rejoicing indicates one's orientation toward basic values, enjoyment of them, and the determining of one's motivations and emotions by these values. A negative experience in the present is valued as the prerequisite for the greater that is to come.

5. Joy as the reaction to charismatic phenomena is esp. prevalent in Luke, who in the larger sense places special value on miraculous endings (cf. E. Schweizer, *Luke* [Eng. tr., 1984] 268) and who in such instances mentions both "glorifying God" and "rejoicing" (Luke 13:17; 19:37; also 10:17). In Matt 2:10 the magi react with joy to the miraculous sign of the star, and the hymn in Rev 19:7 speaks of the self-exhortation to rejoicing and exultation in view of God's victory.

Rejoicing can be the reaction to "seeing" (Matt 2:10; Luke 19:37; 23:8; John 8:56; 20:20; Acts 8:39; 11:23; 15:31; Phil 2:28; Col 2:5) and to hearing (John 3:29; 14:28; Acts 13:48). Although there is no mention of rejoicing for the death and resurrection of Jesus until *Apostolic Constitutions* vii.36, Luke 19:6 already mentions joy as a reaction to the encounter with Jesus as the bearer of salvation. Reference should also be made to use of vbs. of rejoicing with vbs. exhibiting possible cultic-liturgical significance (such as "praise, glorify": Luke 19:37; Rev 19:7; Acts 13:48; 1 Thess 5:17).

6. The apostle regularly writes in the first person about rejoicing over the churches to whom he is writing, and the praise he expresses in such instances often has the character of *captatio benevolentiae* (so Rom 16:19; 1 Cor 16:17; 2 Cor 2:3; 7:7, 9, 13, 16; Phil 4:10; Col 2:5; 1 Thess 3:9; 2 John 4; cf. also 3 John 3). It is not surprising, therefore, that the vb. does not occur in Galatians.

7. Emphasis on shared joy often reflects grievous problems within a church and occurs with surprising frequency in parables, such as Luke 15:5, 6, 9, 32 (receiving the lost member, i.e., the penitent sinner); John 3:29 (the bridegroom and his friend, i.e., Jesus and John the Baptist); 4:36 (the sower and the reaper, again Jesus and the Baptist). Shared rejoicing also plays a role in the parenesis in Rom 12:15 ("with those who rejoice"). In Phil 2:17f. shared rejoicing is an expression of the fellowship between the apostle and the church.

· 8. The most important relationships with other words are those with ἀγαλλίασις and related words (Luke 1:14; Matt 5:12; John 8:56; 1 Pet 4:13; Rev 19:7), δόξα and related words (Luke 13:17; Acts 13:48; 1 Pet 4:13; Rev 19:7), εὐφραίνομαι (Luke 15:24, 32), οὐρανός (Matt 5:12; Luke 10:20), vbs. of seeing (→ 5), the antonyms κλαίω (Rom 12:15; John 16:20; 1 Cor 7:30), πάθημα (Col 1:24;

1 Pet 4:13), θλῖψις (Rom 12:12; Phil 1:17f.; Col 1:24), and λύπη and related words (John 16:21; 2 Cor 2:3; 6:10; 7:7-9; Phil 2:28), and terms of abuse, hatred, and dishonor (Luke 6:22f.; Matt 5:11f.; Acts 5:41). Such antithetical combinations reflect the historical situation of early Christianity.

K. Berger

χάλαζα, ης, ἡ   chalaza   hail*

In the NT only in Revelation in reference to an eschatological plague from God (cf. Exod 9:18ff.; Josh 10:11; Job 38:22ff.; Pss 78:47; 105:32f.; 148:8; Hag 2:17): Rev 8:7: χάλαζα καὶ πῦρ μεμιγμένα ἐν αἵματι, following the first trumpet (cf. Exod 9:24; Ezek 38:22); 11:19: χάλαζα μεγάλη, with ἀστραπαί, φωναί, βρονταί, and σεισμός after the seventh trumpet (cf. Isa 29:6; *Sib. Or.* iii.689-92); 16:21a: χάλαζα μεγάλη ὡς ταλαντιαία (→ ταλαντιαῖος); v. 21b: πληγὴ τῆς χαλάζης at the seventh bowl of wrath. A. van den Born, *BL* 655; G. Morawe, *BHH* 624.

χαλάω   chalaō   let down*

7 occurrences in the NT: Mark 2:4: *letting down* a pallet through the roof; Luke 5:4, 5: *letting down* nets for a catch; Acts 9:25: *letting* a person (Paul) *down* over a wall ἐν σπυρίδι; pass. of the same incident in 2 Cor 11:33: ἐν σαργάνῃ. In technical nautical language χαλάω τὸ σκεῦος refers probably to *lowering* the anchor (Acts 27:17; → σκεῦος 2; BAGD s.v. σκεῦος 1.a) and χαλάω τὴν σκάφην refers to *lowering* the lifeboat (27:30).

Χαλδαῖος, ου, ὁ   Chaldaios   Chaldean*

Acts 7:4 refers to γῆ Χαλδαίων as Abraham's home (cf. v. 2 → Μεσοποταμία), from which he journeyed at God's behest (*contra* Gen 11:31; 12:1-3, 5) to Haran. According to Gen 11:28, 31; 15:7; Neh 9:7 Abraham came from Ur of the Chaldeans ('*ûr kaśdîm*, LXX χώρα τῶν Χαλδαίων) on the lower Euphrates. But this uses the name of the people anachronistically, since (according to 2 Kgs 24:2; 25:4f., and elsewhere; Jer 21:4, and elsewhere; Dan 1:4; 5:11; 9:1) the Chaldeans were the people of the Neo-Babylonian kingdom, perhaps its founders. Furthermore, Assyrian texts mention the Chaldeans from the 9th cent. B.C. on. According to Jdt 5:6-8, however, the Israelites themselves were thought to be descended from the Chaldeans. Dan 2:2, 4f., 10; 4:4; 5:7 attests the later Hellenistic view that the Chaldeans were esp. known as interpreters of dreams and soothsayers. A. van den Born, *BL* 282f.; R. Borger, *BHH* 296f.

χαλεπός, 3   chalepos   hard, bad, evil, dangerous*

Matt 8:28, of two demoniacs, who were "very *malicious/dangerous* (χαλεποὶ λίαν)" (par. Mark 5:4f. emphasizes the [one] demoniac's wildness and strength); 2 Tim 3:1: καιροὶ χαλεποί, *"difficult* times," referring to the appearance of false teachers and false Christians (3:2ff.). Spicq, *Notes* II, 955f.

χαλιναγωγέω *chalinagōgeō* guide with a bridle, bridle (vb.), hold in check*

Fig. in Jas 1:26: χαλιναγωγέω γλῶσσαν, *"bridle* [one's] tongue," as a criterion for piety as a whole; 3:2, in a similar context: one who (as a teacher) makes no mistakes in what he says and is thus perfect, "able to *bridle* the whole body" (χαλιναγωγῆσαι καὶ ὅλον τὸ σῶμα); cf. also Pol. *Phil.* 5:3: χαλιναγωγοῦντες ἑαυτοὺς ἀπὸ παντὸς κακοῦ.

χαλινός, οῦ, ὁ *chalinos* bit, bridle*

Jas 3:3; Rev 14:20 (cf. Isa 63:1-3), of the *bits* of horses (τῶν ἵππων), in Rev 14:20, those that tread grapes in a wine press (cf. Isa 63:1-3).

χαλινόω *chalinoō* bridle (vb.)
Jas 1:26 B in place of → χαλιναγωγέω.

χαλκεύς, έως, ὁ *chalkeus* coppersmith*

2 Tim 4:14 identifies Alexander, who according to 1 Tim 1:20 has failed in faith, as a *coppersmith.* Spicq, *Notes* II, 957f.

χαλκηδών, όνος, ὁ *chalkēdōn* chalcedony*

According to Rev 21:29 the third jewel in the foundation of the wall of the heavenly Jerusalem is *chalcedony.* On the enumeration of precious stones cf. Exod 28:17ff.; 39:10ff.; Isa 54:11f.; Ezek 28:13, where, however, χαλκηδών does not occur. Today "chalcedony" is the designation for a group of variously colored minerals, including agate (cf. Exod 28:19; 29:12), onyx, sardonyx, carnelian, etc. BAGD s.v.; W. Frerichs, *BHH* 362-65; R. G. Bullard, *ISBE* IV, 623-30.

χαλκίον, ου, τό *chalkion* copper vessel*

According to Mark 7:4 the Pharisees purify cups, pots, and *copper vessels* by washing them; cf. Matt 23:25: cups and (small) plates. → βαπτίζω 9; ῥαντίζω.

χαλκολίβανον, ου, τό *chalkolibanon* gold ore(?)*

Rev 1:15 (cf. 2:18), of Christ, who appeared in a vision and resembled the Son of man: His eyes were like a flame of fire (φλὸξ πυρός) and his feet ὅμοιοι χαλκολιβάνῳ (ὡς ἐν καμίνῳ πεπυρωμένης). This probably refers to a particularly hard or burnished metal or a similar alloy (cf. also Dan 10:6 LXX: πόδες ὡσεὶ χαλκὸς ἐξαστράπτων; Ezek 1:27: ὡς ὄψιν ἠλέκτρου). Suidas s.v. relates χαλκολίβανον to ἤλεκτρον and describes it as a gold alloy with silver that is more valuable than gold (cf. also Josephus *Ant.* vii.106: χαλκός, ὃν τοῦ χρυσοῦ κρείττον' ἔλεγον; Virgil *Aen.* xii.87: *orichalcum,* "bronze/ brass"). In any case, λίβανος, "incense," also "censer," does not permit any conclusions concerning the compound itself. BAGD s.v.; H. Kraft, *Rev* (HNT) on 1:15; G. Menestrina, "χαλκολίβανος," *BeO* 20 (1978) 192.

χαλκός, οῦ, ὁ *chalkos* brass, copper, bronze; copper coins; copper basin*

Rev 18:12: Πᾶν σκεῦος ἐξ . . . χαλκοῦ, valuable *brass* utensils. Otherwise χαλκός refers to *copper coins,* i.e., small change (Mark 6:8; 12:41, with gold and silver coins in Matt 10:9). 1 Cor 13:1: χαλκός ἠχῶν, "noisy *brass basin,"* used as a musical instrument (with → κύμβαλον ἀλαλάζον).

χαλκοῦς, 3 *chalkous* made of copper, brass, or bronze*

Rev 9:20: idols *of bronze* (with gold, silver, stone, and wood) that cannot see, hear, or walk (cf. Dan 5:4, 23; Pss 115:4-7; 135:15-17; Isa 2:20; Jer 10:1ff.).

χαμαί *chamai* to/on the ground*

John 9:6: ἔπτυσεν χαμαί; 18:6: ἔπεσεν χαμαί, of Judas.

Χανάαν *Chanaan* Canaan*

The indeclinable name Canaan (Heb. *kᵉnaʿan,* Gen 11:31) occurs in the NT only in Acts 7:11 (of the famine in Egypt and Canaan during the patriarchal period; cf. Gen 41:54ff.; 42:5) and 13:19 (the destruction of seven nations in Canaan during the conquest; cf. Deut 7:1). In Acts the name refers, as it usually does in the OT, to the region west of the Jordan as the land inhabited by the patriarchs (cf. Gen 12:5ff.) and promised to all Israel (cf. Gen 13:14ff.; Exod 15:15; Num 13:2ff.; Jer 3:18; Ezek 16:3). Cf. also → Φοινίκη. J. Hempel, *BHH* 926; A. van den Born, *BL* 914f. (bibliography).

Χαναναῖος, 3 *Chananaios* Canaanite*

Unlike Mark 7:26 (Ἑλληνίς, → Συροφοινίκισσα τῷ γένει), Matt 15:22 identifies the woman from Phoenicia (in the Roman province of Syria), whose daughter Jesus healed in the region of Tyre and Sidon (v. 21), as γυνὴ Χαναναία. Matthew is using the old regional designation for the Syrian coast and its hinterland, a designation related to Akk. *kinaḫḫu,* "purple" (→ Φοινίκη) that also occurs in the OT (cf. Gen 10:19; Judg 1:31f.; Isa 23:11). J. Hempel, *BHH* 926-30 (bibliography).

χαρά, ᾶς, ἡ   *chara*   joy

1. Occurrences and usage in the NT — 2. Joy and the Spirit — 3. Joy within the event of revelation — 4. Joy as an injunction — 5. Joy in suffering and after suffering — 6. Eschatological joy — 7. Joy on the part of the bearer of salvation — 8. Negatively evaluated joy — 9. Related terms

Lit.: P. J. BERNADICOU, "Christian Joy in the NT," *Cross and Crown* 29 (1977) 328-36. — E. BEYREUTHER and S. FINKEN-RATH, *DNTT* II, 356-61. — H. CONZELMANN, *TDNT* IX, 359-415, esp. 359-71. — C. DIETZFELBINGER, "Die eschatologische Freude der Gemeinde in der Angst der Welt, Joh 16,16-33," *EvT* 40 (1980) 420-36. — E. G. GULIN, *Die Freude im NT* (2 vols.; Annales Academiae Scientiarum Fennicae 26/2, 1932; 37/3, 1936). — O. MICHEL, *RAC* VIII, 348-418. — W. G. MOR-RICE, *Joy in the NT* (1984). — W. NAUCK, "Freude im Leiden," *ZNW* 46 (1955) 68-80. — E. OTTO and T. SCHRAMM, *Festival and Joy* (1980). — J. SCHNIEWIND, "Die Freude im NT," *idem, Nachgelassene Reden und Aufsätze* (1952) 72-80. — G. STRECKER, *1-3 John* (KEK, 1989) 72f. — A. B. DU TOIT, *Der Aspekt der Freude im urchristlichen Abendmahl* (1965). — *idem, TRE* XI, 584-86. — For further bibliography see *TWNT* X, 1290; Conzelmann; Michel.

1. Χαρά occurs 59 times in the NT, and is esp. common in Matthew (6 occurrences), Luke (8), John (9), and in Paul (19, 5 each in 2 Corinthians and Philippians, none in 1 Corinthians). Although in most NT occurrences joy is a primary mode of the appropriation of the eschatological event of salvation by human beings, it can also be the reaction of God or of his representatives to this appropriation.

2. If "Spirit" constitutes God's most characteristic presence in the world, then joy is to a large extent the result of God's presence among human beings. The Spirit generates joy, along with righteousness and peace, as its fruit (Gal 5:22; Rom 14:17). It enables a person to endure joyfully the suffering and trials of Christian existence (1 Thess 1:6). Being filled with joy and the Spirit is itself a sign of the legitimacy of the mission to the Gentiles (Acts 13:52 after 13:47f., 50f.). Cf. also Luke 10:21 (exultation in the Holy Spirit over the criteria for election) and the inspiration of joy according to Philo (*Som.* ii.249; *Abr.* 201). Hence joy in this world is viewed as a witness to the activity of God himself. Cf. also *1 Clem.* 63:2; *Herm. Vis.* iii.13.2 (renewal of the pneuma through joy).

3. NT use of "joy" shows particularly that the addressee is a constituent part of the revelatory event itself and participates in it within the mode of (divinely induced) joy. Thus "the word" is "received" with joy (Mark 4:16 par.; 1 Thess 1:6). One accepts with joy the renunciations that accompany conversion (1 Thess 1:6; Heb 10:34). Heb 10:34 and Matt 13:44 speak of the joy that can accompany even the loss of one's possessions. The good news or words of authority can call forth joy (Luke 2:10: εὐαγγελίζομαι; 1 John 1:4; 2 John 12). According to 2 Cor 1:24 and Phil 1:25 joy and faith run parallel, or joy is the way in which faith is present apart from "progress."

Those who see visions react with joy (Matt 28:8; Luke 24:41, 52, after the ascension). Joy can also be the reaction to miraculous signs: a star (Matt 2:10), the apostles' own deeds (Luke 10:17), or miracles (Acts 8:7f.; 12:14). The mission to the Gentiles is a miraculous process and thus results in joy (Acts 15:3; Rom 15:32; cf. Acts 13:52). The formulation in 1 Pet 1:8 shows to what degree joy is understood as divinely effected participation in the heavenly world: "Without having seen him you believe and rejoice with unutterable and glorious joy."

Thus prayer and joy are intimately connected (Phil 1:4; Col 1:11f.). Luke 1:14 says about John the Baptist that "he will be your joy and your gladness, and many will rejoice at his birth," thus identifying him as a prophet of revelation (cf. *Bib. Ant.* 51:6f. [on Samuel]: "Sing praises . . . because of the miracles God has performed for you. . . . Sing praises for the Lord's miracles. . . . And they departed and went out with mirth, rejoicing and exulting in heart for all the glory that God had brought about for them. . . . Let the prophet live among the people. . . .").

4. Like the vb. → χαίρω (3), the noun χαρά can also be used in imperatives (fruit of the Spirit, Gal 5:22; with righteousness in Rom 14:17; further Phil 2:18f., cf. v. 2). Thus, in disagreement with the prevailing modern understanding, joy primarily refers not to an involuntary and internal "emotion" but, like "righteousness" and "peace," to comprehensive, value-centered, complex behavior (such as friendliness, generosity, self-sacrifice, overcoming of adversity), which like "righteousness" can stand for the sum of Christian behavior (e.g., 2 Cor 1:24; also 13:11). Cf. also Philo *Mut.* 167 (whoever has virtue also has constant joy).

5. Again like → χαίρω (4), the noun is used of Christian behavior in the face of unjust suffering and tribulation as the overcoming of such adversity: joy in the midst of grief and temptation and perseverance in faith as the result of faith itself (1 Pet 1:6-8); joy in time of temptation and testing of faith, often with patience (Jas 1:2 [like 1 Peter 1]); joy overcoming the affliction that accompanies acceptance of the word (1 Thess 1:6 [like 1 Peter and James referring to the consequences of conversion]); joyous renunciation of possessions—probably loss of property resulting from conversion (Heb 10:34).

According to Pauline dialectic (wretchedness as the prerequisite for God's merciful activity) the apostle, too, can thus experience joy for just this reason amid all affliction (2 Cor 7:4). For the Church also, perseverance amid affliction has resulted in joy, and poverty has resulted in a wealth of generosity (8:2). Similarly, in Col 1:11 joy stands next to the power of patience and endurance.

Heb 12:2 views Christ's suffering as a preliminary stage toward the joy that lay before him, and v. 11 applies this to the Church's present discipline (similar to 1QH 9:24f.). Yet these two instances are different from the Pauline passages precisely because they do not refer to the joy that is able to overcome even now, in the present.

In contrast, Matt 5:11f.; Jas 1:2, 12; 1 Pet 4:13f. emphasize again that there is an intimate relationship between a pronouncement of blessing for the present suffering of the righteous and the accompanying element of joy.

The fundamental theological concept behind all these statements about "joy in suffering" (or joy after suffering) is that in view of the antithesis between this unrighteous age and the coming age of righteousness the present suffering and persecution of the righteous constitutes for them a reason for joy. Righteousness virtually proves itself in such persecution. But this understanding does not always maintain a connection to the suffering and glory of Christ (though 1 Pet 1:11 does, after 1:6-8); we are dealing here with two mutually independent parallel ideas that found expression in various ways, including in the idea of the election of the poor and humble.

6. Joy is the subjective component of appropriation of the eschatological salvation promise. The term is thus parallel to "the kingdom of God," as seen in the correspondence between Matt 25:21, 23 ("Enter into the *joy* of your master") and Rom 14:17 ("The kingdom of God consists *in . . . joy . . .*") and as attested by Heb 12:2. The relationship between joy and crown in 1 Thess 2:19f. and Phil 4:1 clearly refers to the parousia (judgment; thus also to the advent of the kingdom). Concerning joy as a salvation promise cf. K. Berger, *ZNW* 65 (1974) 198 n.33 (sources), esp. also *1 Enoch* (Greek) 5:9 ("years of their joy filled in exultation and peace"); 103:3 (joy and honor for the souls of the deceased righteous).

7. Joy is also the reaction of the one who brings or effects salvation to the acceptance of that salvation, whether that be God (Luke 15:7, 10, cf. Ezek 18:23; antithetical example in *t. Sanh.* 14:10), the bridegroom and his friend in joy over the wedding = time of salvation (John 3:29), on the part of the apostle over his congregation (1 Thess 3:9; 2 Cor 2:3; 7:13; Phil 1:4; 2:2; 4:1; cf. also Heb 13:17; Phlm 7).

8. Joy is viewed negatively when as a sign of penitence and humility it should turn to weeping (Jas 5:9).

Thus the joy of the unrighteous who have not yet repented stands over against the present sorrow of the righteous (John 16:20-22) and the joy of the righteous in suffering (→ 5).

9. "Joy" often appears with πληρόω: Persons are often filled with joy, or joy is made "perfect" (i.e., endowed with eschatological quality). Θλῖψις is the antithesis of joy (2 Cor 7:4; 8:2; John 16:21), which also appears in phrases with the root περισσ- (2 Cor 7:4; 8:2).

K. Berger

χάραγμα, ατος, τό *charagma* sign, mark, stamp; that which is formed*

Χάραγμα occurs with the meaning *formed image/construction* only in Acts 17:29: χάραγμα τέχνης καὶ ἐνθυμήσεως ἀνθρώπου, "*a construction* of human art and invention" cannot represent the divine (on this idea cf. Deut 4:28; Isa 40:18ff.; Jer 10:1ff.; Wis 13:10; Rom 1:23).

Otherwise χάραγμα occurs 7 times in Revelation in the sense of a *brand* or *mark* which a person, as ordered by the "second beast" (13:11ff.), must wear on the (right) hand or forehead (v. 16) as a sign of the "first beast" (vv. 1ff.); the mark contains the ὄνομα τοῦ θηρίου or the ἀριθμὸς τοῦ ὀνόματος αὐτοῦ (v. 17). Everyone is subject to this (v. 16) and must have it in order to transact any business (v. 17). All those who have worshiped the first beast and his cultic image (cf. 13:14f.) and have received his sign will incur God's judgmental wrath (14:9, 11; 16:2). At the end, the first beast and his false prophet (the second beast), who have deceived the bearers of the sign, will be destroyed forever (19:20). But those who paid with their lives for having rejected the cult and mark will be raised again to life and will enter the thousand-year messianic kingdom (20:4).

Χάραγμα can also be used of inscriptions, stamps on documents (esp. the seal of Caesar: cf. Deissmann, *Light* 340f.), brands on animals, impressions on coins (see BAGD s.v.; U. Wilckens, *TDNT* IX, 416), stigmatization of slaves, and religious stigmatization as a sign of belonging to a certain deity (→ στίγμα 1; σφραγίς 2; this was unacceptable for Jews: Lev 19:28; 3 Macc 2:29f.).

Revelation juxtaposes the χάραγμα of the beast to the seal of the living God (according to 7:2ff.; esp. 14:1ff.) which the redeemed wear on their foreheads (7:3; 9:4; 14:1; 22:4). Accordingly, it is above all a sign of the imperial cult and of the Empire's economic power. Marking on both forehead and right hand is unknown (at best a polemical reference in *b. Meg.* 24b). Χάραγμα as an impression on a coin (or as a coin) has nothing to do with the forehead and as a sign of possession or religious stigmatization has nothing to do with the hand. Therefore, the statements in Revelation are to be understood in a very fundamental sense (χάραγμα might at most allude to the stamp on imperial decrees: see Deissmann, *loc. cit.*).

Just as the → σφραγίς (4.b) of the baptized (cf. 2 Cor 1:22; Eph 1:13) is based on their placement with God and Christ, so also do those belonging to the "beast" have their own χάραγμα in the homage they pay the emperor as the all-encompassing master and also in their economic dependence on Roman power (cf. further H. Kraft, *Rev* [HNT] ad loc.; U. Wilckens, *TDNT* IX, 416f.).

H. Balz

χαρακτήρ, ῆρος, ὁ *charaktēr* impression, image, copy; form*

Heb 1:3, of Christ: ὃς ὤν . . . χαρακτὴρ τῆς ὑποστάσεως αὐτοῦ. Χαρακτήρ refers generally to the impression on a coin (esp. the image on the coin), the impression of a seal, indeed, ultimately to coins, stamps, or seals themselves (BAGD s.v.; G. Kelber, *TDNT* IX, 418f.). Philo in particular applies χαρακτήρ to mankind, which according to Gen 1:26f. received God's → εἰκών (5/6) as the basic imprint at its creation; i.e., in the logos mankind is imprinted by God (*All.* 95ff.; *Her.* 38; also *1 Clem.* 33:4).

Heb 1:3 focuses on the eternal being of the Son of God. In v. 3a δόξα and → ὑπόστασις (3) refer to God, and → ἀπαύγασμα (2) and χαρακτήρ refer to Christ. Thus Christ (alone) is viewed as "the reflection of the divine glory" and as "the *one imprinted* by the divine reality/ by God's essence" (concerning similar statements regarding σοφία cf. Wis 7:26). In Christ, i.e., in his immediate origin in God and in his path of redemption, believers can thus gain a vision of God's essence and reality (cf. εἰκὼν τοῦ θεοῦ, 2 Cor 4:4; Col 1:15; also Phil 2:6; Heb 3:14). Bornkamm, *Aufsätze* II, 188-203, esp. 197-200; E. Grässer, *Text und Situation* (1973) 182-228; G. Kelber, *TDNT* IX, 418-23 (bibliography); *TWNT* X, 1291 (bibliography); → ἀπαύγασμα (bibliography).

χάραξ, ακος, ὁ *charax* stake; palisade; bulwark*

Luke 19:43: → παρεμβαλοῦσιν χάρακά σοι καὶ περικυκλώσουσίν σε, "erect a *palisade* against you," the Roman technique of siege called *circumvallatio*; cf., however, also Ezek 4:2; 26:8; *Ep. Arist.* 139.

χαρίζομαι *charizomai* show, give, grant, hand over (something pleasant or pleasing); remit, forgive*

1. Occurrences in the NT — 2. "Grant" — 3. Legal usage — 4. "Forgive"

Lit.: BAGD s.v. — H. CONZELMANN, *TDNT* IX, 359-415, esp. 375, 393, 396, 397. — J. MERKEL, "Die Begnadigung am Passahfest," *ZNW* 6 (1905) 293-316. — H. SCHLIER, *Gal* (KEK, ⁵1971) 149 n.3. — H. WINDISCH, *2 Cor* (KEK, 1924 = 1970) 88.

1. Χαρίζομαι occurs 23 times in the NT, among the Gospels only in Luke (3 occurrences), 11 times in Paul, not at all in the Catholic Epistles.

2. The LXX uses the vb. with the meaning to *give, grant* and does so consistently (e.g., Esth 8:7: "if I gave you all my possessions"; 2 Macc 3:33: "since through him the Lord has granted you your life"). Thus is Acts 27:24 to be understood (God has *granted* Paul the lives of all his shipmates), and in Phlm 22 Paul hopes to be granted to the church again through their prayers, despite his imprisonment. According to Luke 7:21 Jesus grants the power of sight, just as according to Hellenistic authors "deliverance" is granted (cf. Appian *BC* i.79 [360]: χαρίζεσθαί τινι τὴν σωτηρίαν). According to Phil 2:9 God bestows on the exalted Christ his name (the form-critical parallels read "inherit" or "receive") as his title of heavenly sovereignty. 1 Cor 2:12 focuses on similar heavenly gifts for Christians: Through the Pneuma Christians recognize what God has bestowed on them, namely, glory (v. 7) and all that has been prepared for them (v. 9). According to Rom 8:32, the gift that God will grant us with the one he has already given up for us will be even more comprehensive, namely, "all things": according to Rom 8:28 the whole creation, as in 2 Cor 5:17f. the "new creation," and according to 1 Cor 3:21-23 the "world," life and death." Rom 8:32 speaks, therefore, not of forgiveness, but rather of "inheritance of the world" and ultimately of the fulfillment of the promise to Abraham (4:13).

Phil 1:29 uses the vb. of Christian existence in the comprehensive sense otherwise spoken of with χάρις: To the Church is granted both faith in Christ and suffering for his sake (just as Jews suffer "for the law"; cf. Acts 5:41: "for the name").

3. The following occurrences deal with legal matters in the narrower sense: According to Acts 3:14 Barabbas was *released/handed over* to the Jews. 25:11 and 25:16 relate similarly that Paul *was given over* to his accusers; χάριν καταθέσθαι ("do someone a favor") in (24:27) 25:9 and αἰτούμενοι χάριν ("ask a favor") in 25:3 echo as well. Paul views the transfer of his trial to Jerusalem as being handed over to the Jews (E. Haenchen, *Acts* [Eng. tr., 1971] 672).

Gal 3:18 uses the vb. in the sense of a show of favor on the part of the person granting an inheritance: Because the inheritance could be redeemed by the promise (and not by the law), God *showed* Abraham *favor* through it (cf. the legal term for inheritance in L. Mitteis and U. Wilcken, *Grundzüge und Chrestomathie der Papyruskunde* [1912] II/2, 305, 25ff.: a person maintains the right "to show others favor" in a deposition; 2 Macc 7:22 uses it perhaps in a fig. sense).

Luke 7:41-43 is also concerned with the legal process of remission of guilt (cf. also Philo *Spec. Leg.* ii.39: τὰ δάνεια . . . τοῖς ὁμοφύλοις χαριζομένων); 7:47f. also focuses on forgiveness of sins, even if the vb. does not occur there. Legal aspects of guilt also form the background of Col 2:13f.: After speaking of forgiveness of sins the author mentions the certificate of indebtedness.

4. The vb. acquires the special meaning "*forgive* trespasses/sins" only after the LXX, first in Josephus *Ant.* vi.144: οὐκ εἶναι δίκαιον ἁμαρτήματα χαρίζεσθαι παραιτήσει. In the NT it has this meaning probably only in the Pauline and deutero-Pauline writings. According to 2 Cor 2:7, 10 it refers to forgiveness among human beings (the parallel in v. 8 is "love"); according to v. 10 Paul has forgiven the transgressor "in Christ's presence," i.e., by summoning Christ as a witness, who thus becomes both witness and guarantor of the forgiveness. 12:13 also focuses on forgiveness among human beings: The church —ironically— should forgive Paul his wrongdoing.

Not until Colossians (and Ephesians?) does the NT use the vb. of forgiveness by God. Col 2:13 still remains close to the legal concept of guilt (the certificate of indebtedness, v. 14) and employs a phrase that occurs only here in the NT: χαρίζεσθαι τὰ παραπτώματα (through being raised again to life with Christ).

Col 3:13 and Eph 4:32 are closely related: Just as the Lord (or God in Christ) has forgiven (?) you, so also do you forgive (?) one another. If the passage is so translated it is an analogy to Matt 18:33. But it seems questionable whether Eph 4:32 is speaking of forgiveness, since there is no acc. obj. and since the context is concerned not with guilt but with kindness and compassion. Things are different in Col 3:13, since here the concern is with the complaints of one against another. Thus in Eph 4:32 the vb. is to be translated *be kind* (which is also the more general meaning), and the passage in Colossians is the only text in the NT, and thus the second after Josephus *Ant.* vi.144, in which the vb. is used of forgiveness of sins by God.

K. Berger

χάριν *charin* for the sake of; because of*

The adv. acc. χάριν occurs 9 times in the NT as an improper prep. with gen., and except in 1 John 3:12 (Hellenistic) always after its obj. (cf. BDF §§162; 216). Luke 7:47: the reason for something (οὗ χάριν . . . ὅτι, "for this reason . . . considering that"); 1 John 3:12: χάριν τίνος, "why(?)"; Eph 3:1 (anacoluthon), 14, in a transitional formula recalling what was said previously: τούτου χάριν (cf. R. Schnackenburg, *Eph* [Eng. tr., 1991] on 3:1); Titus 1:5; Gal 3:19, to indicate a goal: τῶν παραβάσεων χάριν, the law was added to the promises in order to make sin apparent in its effects, namely, transgressions (cf. H. Schlier, *Gal* [KEK] ad loc.); 1 Tim 5:14: λοιδορίας χάριν, "*for* reproach"; Titus 1:11: αἰσχροῦ κέρδους χάριν, "*for the sake of* shameful gain"; Jude 16: ὠφελείας χάριν, "to gain advantage from it."

χάρις, ιτος, ἡ *charis* grace, gratitude; esteem

1. Occurrences in the NT and meanings — 2. Bestowal of grace on the proclaimer — 3. Grace manifested as charismata — 4. Grace and ethics — 5. Grace for all the elect and converted — 6. Grace as the ultimate salvation possession — 7. "Thanks" and other meanings — 8. The goal of God's gracious actions

Lit.: T. D. ANDERSEN, "The Meaning of ἔχοντες χάριν πρός in Acts 2:47," *NTS* 34 (1988) 604-10. — D. C. ARICHEA, JR., "Translating 'Grace' (charis) in the NT," *BT* 29 (1978) 201-6. — K. BERGER, "Apostelbrief und apostolische Rede," *ZNW* 65 (1974) 190-201. — H. CONZELMANN, *TDNT* IX, 359-415, esp. 373-76, 387-402. — G. D. FEE, "Χάρις in 2 Cor 1:15: Apostolic Parousia and Paul-Corinth Chronology," *NTS* 24 (1977/78) 533-38. — Z. C. HODGES, "Grace after Grace—John 1:16," *BSac* 135 (1978) 34-45. — C. F. D. MOULE, "A Christian Understanding of Law and Grace," *Christian Jewish Relations* 14 (1981) 52-61. — J. NOLLAND, "Grace as Power," *NovT* 28 (1986) 26-31. — idem, "Luke's Use of χάρις," *NTS* 32 (1986) 614-20. — S. A. PANIMOLLE, "La χάρις negli Atti e nel quarto vangelo," *RivB* 25 (1977) 143-58. — R. PREGEANT, "Grace and Recompense: Reflections on a Pauline Paradox," *JAAR* 47 (1979) 73-96. — E. RUCKSTUHL, *TRE* XIII, 467-76. — SPICQ, *Notes* II, 960-66. — M. THEOBALD, *Die überströmende Gnade. Studien zu einem paulinischen Motivfeld* (FzB 22, 1982). — D. ZELLER, *Charis bei Philon und Paulus* (SBS 142, 1990). — For further bibliography see *TWNT* X, 1290f.

1. Χάρις occurs 156 times in the NT. In the Gospels it appears only in Luke (8 times) and John (4 times in 1:14-17); it also occurs 17 times in Acts. Its highest frequency is in Paul (24 times in Romans, 10 in 1 Corinthians, 18 in 2 Corinthians, 7 in Galatians, 3 in Philippians, 2 each in 1 Thessalonians and Philemon); otherwise it occurs in the letters above all in Ephesians (12 times), Colossians (5), the Pastorals (13), Hebrews (8), and 1 Peter (10). It is used in non-Christian writings to refer to both "generosity" and "gratitude," and also to "gracefulness" and "beauty"—thus to free, uncoerced, cheerfully bestowed openness toward one another, and thus in relationship to God both "salvation" granted by him and human "thanks." Aristotle (*Rh.* ii.7.1385a) already emphasizes the gratuitous nature of χάρις in contrast to reward.

2. Paul received special *grace* with his apostolic commission, grace that is actually identical with his gospel, since his calling and his reception of the gospel were one and the same (cf. Ezekiel 1–2; Gal 1:15; 2:9; 1 Cor 3:10; 15:10; 2 Cor 12:9; Eph 3:2, 7, 8, though also Rom 1:5). He can refer authoritatively to this grace (Rom 12:3; 15:15). It is the antithesis of earthly wisdom (2 Cor 1:12). The Church at most partakes of this grace (Phil 1:7; cf. also *Corp. Herm.* i.32): Paul's presence in a church means the presence of grace (2 Cor 1:15).

Judaism anticipates this understanding of grace (referring to prophets in *2 Bar.* 81:2-4; 2 Esdr 14:22 [with the Holy Spirit]; *Vit. Proph.* 14 [Jeremiah]; *Asc. Isa.* 11:36 [on the basis of Isaiah's vision God is glorified as the bestower of such grace on humans]; Josephus *Ant.* iv.60 [Moses]; *2 Enoch* 69:15 [the priest Methusalam]). This Jewish understanding has analogies esp. in Luke, not only in statements about Stephen (Acts 6:8), Moses (7:10), and Apollos (18:27), but also in Luke's christology and in the programmatic development of Luke 4:18f. within the Lukan work as a whole: It is to this that "words of *grace*" in Luke 4:22 refers and which Acts 4:33 and esp. 11:23 (mission to the Greeks) fulfill, as do 14:3 (signs and wonders) and 20:24 (gospel of grace). Only 15:11 deviates from this pattern by fixing grace essentially to the proclaimer in an antiquated fashion.

3. The various charismata are understood as concrete manifestations of the one grace bestowed on all. Such is the case in 1 Pet 4:10 ("stewards" refers to the social obligations of service with the gifts of grace); Rom 12:6; 1 Cor 1:4, 7; Eph 4:7 (cf. vv. 11f.). It is striking that "grace" does not occur in 1 Corinthians 12; instead, the chapter speaks of the one Spirit (and body). Col 3:16 views Christian singing as grace (or "thankfulness"; cf. K. Grözinger, *JSJ* 11 [1980] 66-77); "pneumatic" occurs in this context.

4. 2 Corinthians particularly grounds morality in grace. A strong relationship exists between the grace shown by God and Christ (see esp. 8:9: "he . . . became poor even though he was rich") and the grace to be shown by the church in the form of the gracious gift of the collection. God's deed becomes the church's, so that it has "abundance in this *grace*" (8:7; cf. 8:1f., 9, 19; 9:8 [here grace becomes a good work as in Titus 2:11-14], 14). Grace is thus not received in vain (6:1), and Christ's own deed is both the soteriological and ethical model (8:9). According to Col 4:6 a Christian's speech should also be "in *grace*."

Grace acquires special significance for Christian existence, and not just at its beginning, according to a series of texts in which the noun is used with various vbs.: "stand in *grace*" (Rom 5:2; 1 Pet 5:12), "grow in *grace* [and knowledge]" (2 Pet 3:18), "become strong in *grace*" (2 Tim 2:1, referring to instruction), "continue in *grace*" (Acts 13:43, the summary of an admonition), "fall from *grace*" (Gal 5:4, referring to the Galatians' circumcision), "fail to obtain God's *grace*" (Heb 12:15), and "insult the Pneuma of *grace*" (10:29, i.e., by Judaizing). The relationship to knowledge, correct doctrine, or the correct gospel is clear in almost every instance; thus this category should probably also include Jude 4 (in emancipation from Jewish Christianity God's grace has been perverted into licentiousness) and Heb 13:9 (the grace that strengthens the heart is grace without any Judaized elements).

Similarly, "standing in grace" also represents correct behavior or suffering as a righteous person (so in 1 Pet 5:12). 2 Thess 1:12 refers grace to the perfecting of the work of faith.

Jewish writings anticipate the relationship between grace and knowledge ("to find grace" in the reception of revelation). *2 Bar* 44:13f. speaks of those who have not renounced grace. Existence in grace is thus thought of as a process of growth for which the initial proclamation (cf. → 2) has provided enduring standards in the form of doctrine.

5. a) Grace is the opening of access to God in the larger sense precisely by God himself. In Jewish writings God's grace and love are the basis of election (*2 Bar.* 21:21; 75:5f.; also 77:11; *Jub.* 31:24); Paul takes this up in precisely the same sense in Rom 11:5, 6 (cf. 11:29; interestingly, grace is not mentioned in 9:11f.). 2 Tim 1:9 also speaks of God's call and "purpose" in election according to grace; Eph 1:6 speaks of such predetermination (blessed in Christ). Gal 1:15 and 2 Tim 1:9 also speak of the call, and 2 Tim 1:9 of being saved (σῴζω), as do Acts 15:11 (we believe that we will be saved through grace) and Eph 2:5, 8. Eph 1:7 speaks of redemption and forgiveness.

All these texts are concerned with passing over the threshold of belonging to God by means of God's own anticipatory action. Rom 5:2 makes this clear once more by speaking of "access" to God (πϱοσαγωγή). And since this threshold is otherwise described as "faith," grace and faith are thus oriented toward one another (Rom 4:16; 5:2; Eph 2:8; 1 Tim 1:14). (Acts 15:11 does not use "believe" in this technical sense.)

The antithesis between grace and works may not, however, be projected onto these texts without further consideration. They are concerned only with associating conversion with God's activity in order to elevate such conversion out of the realm of merely human, circumstantial events. Nothing is said of a person's activity, and viewing divine and human activity here as mutually exclusive leads only into the typical insoluble questions of systematic theology.

But certain statements do attest the antithesis between grace and works in the context of the question of one's fundamental belonging to God (and only in this context): Besides Rom 4:4 and 11:6 see esp. 2 Tim 1:9 and Titus 3:5-7 (it is the Pastorals that display what are usually thought to be Pauline views)—with clear analogies in Philo's theology of grace (cf. *All.* iii.77, 83). But even here it is not a matter of tension between performance and election. Rather, human works are portrayed as thoroughly futile and flawed. The focus is thus on God's saving grace in the face of universal sinfulness—again according to Jewish model (*Bib. Ant.* 19:9; 2 Esdr 8:36;

Philo *Imm.* 104-8). Since Paul shows how sin and law are related, his view is that works performed under the auspices of the law intensify even more the negativity of mankind outside grace (Gal 2:21; 6:14f.; Rom 4:16).

Therefore, only in the dispute with non- or post-Christian Judaism (Galatians and Romans) does Paul set the grace received at conversion over against what was earlier the Jewish path. Only where Paul's discussion focuses on "law without grace" does he emphasize—against the negative backdrop of the connection between law and sin—the gratuitous character of *grace* (with δωρεά[ν] in Rom 3:24; 5:15, 17; in antithesis to μισθός in 4:4). The advantage of Christian over Jewish initiation consists according to Paul in its mediation not only of election, but also of righteousness as a gift even now (3:24 in contrast to 11:29: the "banishment" of unrighteousness will occur only in the future according to 11:26). Thus it was Paul who through this connection with the quantity "law" historically located and terminated the "timeless" and thus in a certain sense "anthropological" antithesis between grace and works of the kind known to Hellenistic Judaism and the Pastorals.

b) Χάρις views the event of initiation from God's perspective, but that event is described from the human perspective as "faith" (though πίστις is not limited to the initiation) and with the related expression "humility/lowliness" (ταπεινο-), which admittedly refers more in the durative sense to the human prerequisite for grace (as in the use of Prov 3:34 LXX in 1 Pet 5:5; Jas 4:6: the connection with initiation is made clear by v. 7). It is equally a matter of a human prerequisite when under certain conditions one "finds grace" before God (confidence, Heb 4:16; further Luke 1:30; 2:52 and *T. Sim.* 5:2; Acts 7:46). It is by no means a contradiction, but just the other side of the same process, when it is asserted that God's grace was "on him" (Luke 2:40), or when according to the additions to *T. Levi* 2:3 in the Koutloumousiou ms. one asks for the Holy Spirit and power in order to attain grace before God on the basis of works, or when according to *T. Jud.* 2:1 God gave grace in all works (cf. 2 Thess 1:12).

Thus in Jesus' proclamation χάρις, with "reward," can also refer to God's reaction to human action: so Luke 6:32-34 and parallel v. 35 (par. Matt 5:46 speaks only of "reward"). The closely related passage 1 Pet 2:19f. (here, too, the concern is with suffering/renunciation) even complements "grace" with "credit" in the sense of esteem before God. Luke 6:32-34 and 1 Pet 2:19 should be considered closely together with 1 Pet 5:5 and Jas 4:6, for lowliness, humility, bearing of suffering, and renunciation of revenge together are the substance of the prerequisite for grace with God. Here Christian morality is grounded in the uniqueness of the Christian event of election (which in the NT is primarily formulated as a paradox). Given this presupposition, the v.l. χάριτι in Heb 2:9 also makes good sense, since according to v. 10 suffering is the prerequisite for perfection, so that suffering becomes the criterion of election, as in 1 Pet 2:19; 5:5, and elsewhere. This is why according to 1 Pet 5:12 suffering is now the true grace.

6. Under the auspices of God's sovereignty, which apocalyptic thinking strongly emphasizes, grace is the substance of salvation in the larger sense. Compare the "coming grace" of *2 Bar.* 82:2 with the coming of grace (under the prerequisite of the passing away of the "world") in *Did.* 10:6, and also statements about the future salvation of Christians: 1 Pet 1:10, 13; 3:7 (fellow heirs); 2 Thess 2:16 (cf. *1 Enoch* [Greek] 1:8; 5:7f.; *Bib. Ant.* 51:5; *Sib. Or.* iv.45f., 189; 2 Esdr 16:31f.; *2 Bar.* 78:7).

The word χάρις was naturally suited to describing that element of salvation already received in the present; so in the benedictions at the beginning and end of many NT letters, which may correspond to the blessing in nonepistolary writings in the formula "commended to the *grace* of God" (Acts 14:26; 15:40; 20:32). 1 Pet 5:10 offers a prayer to "the God of all *grace*," and although Heb 4:16 speaks of access to the throne of grace on the basis of the sacrifice of the high priest, nowhere is grace thought of with such strict christological parameters as in John 1:14, 16, 17 (over against Moses and the gift of the law). Titus 2:11f., with its mention of the grace that "trains," is an original description of the unity of justification and ethics, for it understands ethics as the determination of form under the auspices of the formative event of Jesus Christ's own sacrifice.

Statements about the superabundance of grace are of special interest, such as those found in Rom 5:15, 20; 6:1; 2 Cor 4:15 (cf. also *Bib. Ant.* 39:6: "Though our sins abound, nevertheless his mercy fills all the earth"; cf. also 49:3f.). Romans 5 relates the messianic category of superabundance to the apocalyptic vision of the increase of evil: The overabundance of evil is reversed and simultaneously eclipsed by increased fullness. Paul can assert that such a transition has already occurred and manifests itself in freedom from law and in the "principle of abundance" in ethics.

7. Χάρις is used in the sense of *thanks* in 2 Cor 2:14; 8:16; 9:15; Rom 6:17; 7:25; 1 Cor 10:30 (partake with *thankfulness* toward God); 15:57; 1 Tim 1:12; 2 Tim 1:3; Luke 17:9; Heb 12:28.

Acts 24:27 and 25:9 use χάρις in the sense of "do a *favor,*" and 25:3 "ask a *favor.*" Col 4:6 uses it in the sense of *graciousness,* and Eph 4:29 as *gracious kindness.*

8. The goal of God's gracious actions so strongly emphasized in the NT is both his own glory and that of

human beings (1 Pet 1:10f.; 4:10f.; 2 Cor 4:15; Eph 1:6; Heb 2:9f. also belongs in this context). Hence grace is not granted "pointlessly."

K. Berger

χάρισμα, ατος, τό   *charisma*   gift, gift of grace*

1. Occurrences in the NT and usage outside the NT — 2. Charisma as an individual gift — 3. Charisma as a fundamental gift — 4. General and individual gift

Lit.: E. BANNON, "The Charism of Teaching," *Clergy Review* 64 (1979) 431-36. — N. BAUMERT, "Zur Semantik von χάρισμα bei den frühen Vätern," *TP* 63 (1988) 60-88. — idem, "Zur Begriffsgeschichte von χάρισμα im griechischen Sprachraum," *TP* 65 (1990) 79-100. — U. BROCKHAUS, *Charisma und Amt* (1987). — H. CONZELMANN, *TDNT* IX, 359-415, esp. 402-6. — M. DUMAIS, "Ministères, charismes et Esprit dans l'oeuvre de Luc," *Église et Théologie* 9 (1978) 413-53. — D. FRAIKIN, "Charismes et ministères à la lumière de 1 Co 12–14," *Église et Théologie* 9 (1978) 455-63. — F. HAHN, "Charisma und Amt. Die Diskussion über das kirchliche Amt im Lichte der neutestamentlichen Charismenlehre," *ZTK* 76 (1979) 419-49. — J. JERVELL, "Der schwache Charismatiker," FS Käsemann 185-98. — K. KERTELGE, *Gemeinde und Amt im NT* (1972) 103-12. — R. LAURENTIN, "Charisms: Terminological Precision," *Charisms in the Church* (Concilium 109, ed. C. Duquoc and C. Floristan; 1978) 3-12. — H. VON LIPS, *Glaube—Gemeinde—Amt. Zum Verständnis der Ordination in den Pastoralbriefen* (FRLANT 122, 1979). — H. A. LOMBARD, "Charisma and Church Office," *Neot* 10 (1976) 31-52. — V. C. PFITZNER, "Office and Charism in Paul and Luke," *Colloquium* 13 (1981) 28-38. — K. W. RITTER, *Paul's Concept of Charisma and the Ministry of Laity* (Diss. Claremont, 1976). — K. H. SCHELKLE, "Charisma und Amt," *TQ* 159 (1979) 243-54. — W. D. SCHNEEBERGER, "Charisma und Agape," *CV* 19 (1976) 151-56. — J. H. SCHÜTZ, *TRE* VII (1981) 688-93. — S. SCHULZ, "Die Charismenlehre des Paulus," FS Käsemann 443-60. — A. B. DU TOIT, "Die Charismata," *Nederduitse Gereformeerde Teologiese Tydskrif* 20 (1979) 189-200. — B. N. WAMBACQ, "Le mot charisme," *NRT* 97 (1975) 345-55. — For further bibliography see *TWNT* X, 1291; Schütz.

1. Χάρισμα occurs 17 times in the NT, all in the letters: those of Paul (6 times in Romans, 7 in 1 Corinthians, and 2 Cor 1:11), the Pastorals (1 Tim 4:14; 2 Tim 1:6), and 1 Pet 4:10.

Before the NT the word apparently occurred only rarely. Philo (*All.* iii.78: "For all things in the world and the world itself is a free gift [δωρεά] and act of kindness [εὐεργεσία] and grace [χάρισμα] on God's part"—parallel to χάρις) and Alciphro (iii.17.4: χάρισμα δοὺς ἔχειν) are the most important attestations, to which perhaps also *T. Sol.* recension C 13:14 may be added (magical gifts beneficial to health and wealth); although *Sib. Or.* ii.154 is probably contemporaneous with Christianity (the soul as divine χάρισμα may not be defiled), its substance is not comprehensible from the perspective of the NT.

2. The oldest Christian usage of χάρισμα in the sense of individual gifts occurs throughout 1 Corinthians and in Rom 12:6; 1 Pet 4:10. The basic premise is that there are different charismata (1 Pet 4:10: "varied grace"; Rom

12:6: "different charismata") and that each person (ἕκαστος, 1 Pet 4:10; 1 Cor 7:7; 12:7: "to each") has his own (ἴδιος, 1 Cor 7:7). These texts exhibit a tendency toward sequential enumeration of various charismata (1 Cor 1:5: speech and knowledge; 12:8-10, 28, 29f. [in all three lists in 1 Corinthians 12 χαρίσματα is used only of healing]; Rom 12:6-8; 1 Pet 4:11: speech and service).

The variety of charismata can also be summarized under a unity. In 1 Cor 12:4 this is the one Spirit (cf. v. 7: to each is given the revelation of the Spirit) and in v. 5 the one Lord; the one Spirit apportions to each as he wills (v. 11). In Rom 12:4f. this unity is (as in 1 Cor 12:12) likened to one body with many members. 1 Pet 4:11 focuses on the glorification of God by all. The agreement between Rom 12:6f. and 1 Pet 4:11 extends further, since each (with ὡς or ἐν) provides the standard according to which the charismata are to be realized. Furthermore, in Rom 12:6 the first-mentioned, "prophecy" and "service," correspond to "speech" and "service" in 1 Pet 4:11.

Χάρις is also a uniquely employed quantity in these texts (Rom 12:6; 1 Pet 4:10; 1 Cor 1:4); its concrete development is the individual charisma. The model for this division is the tradition following Isa 11:2 concerning the various spiritual gifts (cf. K. Berger, *Exegese des NT* [UTB 658, ²1983] 46-48), of which the most familiar development is Armenian Ps.-Philo *De Sampsone* (German tr. by F. Siegert [1980] 24f.). The connection between charismata and Spirit is also attested by 1 Cor 12:4, 9, 11 as well as by the designation πνευματικά in 12:1 and 14:1. Only in these two instances, however, does Paul cautiously call charismata πνευματικά, which he otherwise calls simply χαρίσματα, probably in order to distinguish adequately the Spirit as the effective cause and mediator of the individual effects from the charismata themselves.

These findings show that 2 Tim 1:6f. also belongs to this textual group; the relationship between spiritual gifts and charismata is the reverse of that in 1 Corinthians 12: The one charisma subdivides into the Spirit of power, love, and understanding. Outside this tradition, Rom 1:11 also associates the Spirit with χάρισμα.

The gifts of healing apparently played a special role in Corinth, since in 1 Corinthians 12 (vss. 9, 28, 30) only they are called charismata, and probably bestowed special standing (since they were most useful; cf. the Gospel tradition). 12:31 should be understood either as a critical indicative, such that such striving is countered by love as the sign of all true spiritual gifts, or as an imperative portraying love as the principle of the other charismata. In any case, 1 Corinthians 14 is a concretization of 12:31a.

3. Rom 5:15f.; 6:23; 11:29 are quite closely related, since although they all focus on concrete and historically

ascertainable gifts from God (as in → 2), the reference is to gifts of a fundamental and general nature. Rom 11:29 speaks of the irrevocable gifts associated with Israel's election (i.e., the covenantal provisions spoken of in 9:4), and Romans 5–6 speaks correspondingly of the comparable new concrete dispensations; to be sure, the antithesis between trespass and gift of grace in 5:15 is not that between deed and consequence, since this gift of grace has of course been realized in Jesus' own counter-deed of obedience (v. 19). A surprising juxtaposition emerges between 5:15 (antithesis: death), 6:23 (eternal life/death), and 2 Cor 1:11: Everywhere in the charisma the God is at work who raises the dead and gives life. It has been suggested that χάρισμα in 6:23 refers to the *donativum,* the special wage paid on the ascension of a new ruler. More likely, however, "wages" and the antithesis charisma suggest the opposition presented in 4:4.

4. Hence for Paul the same holds true for χάρισμα as for πνεῦμα and πνευματικά: In addition to that which applies to everyone and is given to them at baptism or at the proclamation of the gospel itself (thus is Rom 1:11 to be understood; cf. also 15:27), there are also individual spiritual gifts and individual charismata. Just how structurally similar these two conceptions are can be seen not only in the fact that in both cases charisma is associated with calling (1 Cor 7:7, 17, 20; Rom 11:29), but also in the fact that according to 1 Cor 1:7 the individual charismata are provisional gifts anticipating the revelation of Jesus Christ in the same way that the Spirit common to all Christians is according to Rom 8:19-27.

Whereas the Spirit of baptism (the ἀπαρχή in Rom 8:23; the ἀρραβών in 2 Cor 1:22) is only indirectly visible in fruits at present, to be fully visible esp. at the resurrection (2 Cor 5:5-10), the best definition of individual charisma is that it is a "manifestation of the Spirit" even now (1 Cor 12:7). Thus it certainly does not include just any activity, but rather activity that astonishes and directs attention vertically. It thus probably includes, e.g., being unmarried as opposed to being married (1 Cor 7:7) and perhaps extraordinary demonstrations of God's power (2 Cor 1:11; note that the proemium in both Romans 1 and 2 Corinthians speaks of χάρισμα).

One should not hastily disqualify as "charisma of office" the χάρισμα which Timothy is granted through prophecy and the laying on of hands (by the elders/ "Paul") and which he is called on to rekindle within himself (1 Tim [1:18] 4:14; 2 Tim 1:6), since it is probably no different from what was already common among the so-called congregation-apostles and also in the case of Paul (cf. Acts 13:1-3) and which through prophecy/ speech of the Pneuma exhibits no lack of spirituality. The fact that the Pastorals do not speak in a general fashion about the charismata of the baptized does not allow us,

given the nature of the genre (among other things, personal addressees), to draw any reliable conclusions.

K. Berger

χαριτόω *charitoō* favor (vb.), bestow favor on, bless*

In the NT this vb. refers to divine grace: Eph 1:6: εἰς ἔπαινον δόξης τῆς χάριτος αὐτοῦ ἧς ἐχαρίτωσεν ἡμᾶς, "to the praise of his glorious grace which he *freely bestowed* on us." In the angel's message to Mary in Luke 1:28 the Greek formula of greeting χαῖρε (Homer *Od.* i.123; cf. Mark 15:18; Matt 26:49; 27:29; John 19:3, and further → χαίρω 1; see H. Conzelmann, *TDNT* IX, 367) is combined directly with χαριτόω: χαῖρε, κεχαριτωμένη, "Greetings, *favored one*" (Vg.: *gratia plena;* Luther: "du Holdselige"). Luke 1:30 then explains the reason for Mary's confusion and thus also the meaning of the angel's greeting: εὗρες γὰρ χάριν παρὰ τῷ θεῷ. S. Lyonnet, *Bib* 20 (1939) 131-41; A. Strobel, *ZNW* 53 (1962) 86-110; M. Cambe, *RB* 70 (1963) 193-207; I. de la Potterie, *Bib* 68 (1987) 357-82, 480-508.

Χαρράν *Charran* Haran*

The indeclinable name (Heb. *ḥārān,* Gen 11:31f.; 12:4f.; 27:43) of the place in which Abraham lived after leaving Mesopotamia and before entering Canaan (11:31; 12:5). Acts 7:2, 4 mentions Haran, though Luke places God's appearance to Abraham in the period before his move to Haran (πρὶν ἢ κατοικῆσαι αὐτὸν ἐν Χαρράν, v. 2); → Μεσοποταμία. M. A. Beck, *BHH* 647; A. van den Born, *BL* 286f.

χάρτης, ου, ὁ *chartēs* papyrus (roll); paper*

According to 2 John 12 the πρεσβύτερος of the congregation still has much to write, but does not want to do it διὰ χάρτου καὶ μέλανος ("with *paper [papyrus]* and ink"). He wants rather to relate what he has to say later face to face during a visit; cf. 3 John 13. On similar concluding phrases in writings of antiquity see R. Bultmann, *John* (Eng. tr., 1971) 697 n.2.

χάσμα, ατος, τό *chasma* cleft, gap, chasm*

Luke 16:26: a great, impassable *chasm* (χάσμα μέγα) in the realm of the dead between the place of the rich man's torment (→ ᾅδης 1; γέεννα) and the realm of the blessed, where Lazarus is (in the bosom of Abraham); cf. also *1 Enoch* 18:11; 22:1ff.; 2 Esdr 7:85, 93; Billerbeck II, 225-33.

χεῖλος, ους, τό *cheilos* lip; shore*

This noun occurs 7 times in the NT, always in connection with OT texts. The pl. refers to the lips as the organ that forms human speech. Mark 7:6 par. Matt 15:8 uses it in a citation from Isa 29:13 LXX in speaking about the people, which "honors me [God] [only] with their lips," while remaining far from him in their hearts (cf. further *1 Clem.* 15:2; *2 Clem.* 3:5). Rom 3:13 (citing Ps 139:4 LXX) speaks of "the venom of asps under the *lips*" (with λάρυγξ, γλῶσσαι, and στόμα) as a metaphor for speech defiled by sin (cf. further the use of Pss 5:10 LXX; 10:7 in Rom 3:13f.); cf. 1 Pet 3:10 (χείλη with γλῶσσα, citing Ps 33:14 LXX). 1 Cor 14:21 (citing Isa 28:11 LXX) refers to the activity of God, who will speak to his people "in strange languages and with strange *lips* (ἐν ἑτερογλώσσοις καὶ ἐν χείλεσιν ἑτέρων)"; thus Paul refers Isaiah's announcement of a renewed effort by God on behalf of his people through those "of stammering lips and strange tongues" (on this text and its interpretation → γλῶσσα 6) to the early Christian phenomenon of glossolalia, which God reckons not—like prophecy—to belief, but to unbelief (cf. 1 Cor 14:20, 22-25). Heb 13:15 uses the phrase καρπὸς χειλέων ὁμολογούντων τῷ ὀνόματι αὐτοῦ; cf. Hos 14:3) of the Church's continual sacrifice of praise.

The meaning "*shore* of the sea" (χεῖλος τῆς θαλάσσης; cf. Gen 22:17) occurs in Heb 11:12.

χειμάζομαι *cheimazomai* be tossed about by a storm*

Acts 27:18, in an account of a sea journey: σφοδρῶς δὲ χειμαζομένων ἡμῶν, referring to winter storms (cf. 27:9, 20). Ign. *Pol.* 2:3 uses the term fig.

χείμαρρος (χείμαρρους), ου, ὁ *cheimarros (cheimarrous)* seasonal stream, stream*

John 18:1: ὁ χείμαρρος τοῦ → Κεδρών. A χείμαρρος is a stream that has an adequate flow of water only in winter, i.e., in the rainy season (cf. Josephus *Ant.* viii.17; Suidas s.v.: ὁ ἐν τῷ χειμῶνι ῥέων ποταμός).

χειμών, ῶνος, ὁ *cheimōn* winter; stormy weather, violent storm*

There are 6 occurrences in the NT. The noun can refer to *winter* as the season of bad weather, which makes traveling, or certainly flight, significantly more difficult: Mark 13:18 (χειμῶνος, *in winter*) par. Matt 24:20 (χειμῶνος μηδὲ σαββάτῳ); 2 Tim 4:21 (πρὸ χειμῶνος, "before *winter*"). John 10:22 calls the season of the Feast of Dedication (→ ἐγκαίνια) *winter*: χειμὼν ἦν (celebrated as a memorial of the purification and rededication of the Jerusalem temple by Judas the Maccabee on the twenty-fifth of Chislev [November/December], 164 B.C.).

Acts 27:20, in a reference to being buffeted by a violent *storm*: χειμῶνός τε οὐκ ὀλίγου ἐπικειμένου (cf.

27:9, 18). In Matt 16:3 ℵ B, and others, the term refers generally to *bad weather;* see *TCGNT* ad loc.; W. Rordorf, *BHH* 795; J. Nelis, *BL* 793f.; Spicq, *Notes* I, 305f.

χείρ, χειρός, ἡ *cheir* hand

1. Occurrences — 2. Literal usage — 3. Fig. usage — 4. As part of a t.t. — a) Seizure, arrest — b) Laying on of hands

Lit.: N. ADLER, "Die Handauflegung im NT bereits ein Bußritus? Zur Auslegung von 1 Tim 5,22," FS Schmid (1963) 1-6. — *idem, Taufe und Handauflegung* (1951) 62-81. — BAGD s.v. — J. BEHM, *Die Handauflegung im Urchristentum* (1911 = 1968). — J. COPPENS, *L'imposition des mains et les rites connexes dans le NT et dans l'église ancienne* (1925). — *idem,* "L'imposition des mains dans les Actes des Apôtres," *Les Actes des Apôtres* (ed. J. Kremer; 1979). — K. GRAYSTONE, "The Significance of the Word *Hand* in the NT," FS Rigaux 479-87. — A. T. HANSON, *TRE* XIV, 415-22. — F. LAUBACH, *DNTT* II, 148-50. — E. LOHSE, *TDNT* IX, 424-37. — R. PÉTER, "L'imposition des mains dans l'AT," *VT* 27 (1977) 48-55. — A. S. VAN DER WOUDE, *THAT* I, 667-74.

1. Χείρ occurs frequently throughout the LXX (almost 27 columns in Hatch/Redpath!) and 178 times in the NT *(NTG)*. Of these, about 25 are in the Epistles and about 25 in the Synoptic Gospels, about 15 in John and about 15 in Revelation, and 46 in Acts.

2. In literal use χείρ usually refers to the part of the body with which a person "handles things." A speaker commences with appropriate motions of the hand (Acts 12:17; 13:16; 19:33; 21:40; 26:1). Jesus "stretches out his *hand*" to point to his disciples (Matt 12:49), to touch a leper (Mark 1:41 par.), and to catch Peter sinking in the water (Matt 14:31; 26:51: ἐκτείνω τὴν χεῖρα, to defend Jesus; Luke 22:53: directed against him). Peter extends his hand to Tabitha to lift her up (Acts 9:41); one day he will stretch out his hands to be crucified (John 21:18; cf. BAGD s.v. ἐκτείνω).

One carries a person on or with one's hands (Matt 4:6 par.), holds something in and with one's hands (Rev 1:16; 6:5; 7:9; 10:2, 8; 14:14; 17:4; 20:1), and works with one's hands; thus Paul emphasizes not "work of the hands" themselves, but rather the fact that each—even the apostle—supports himself (Acts 20:34; 1 Cor 4:12; Eph 4:28; 1 Thess 4:11). In a similar fashion Paul refers at the conclusion of a letter to his personal signature made "with his own hand" (τῇ ἐμῇ χειρί; 1 Cor 16:21; Gal 6:11; Col 4:18; 2 Thess 3:17; Phlm 19). 1 John 1:1 uses χείρ as a typical *pars pro toto* as a subj. ("what our *hands* [i.e., we] have touched . . ."). Similar usage occurs when a Hebraizing reference is made to deeds that occur διὰ χειρῶν (χειρός) τινος (= διά τινος), by someone (someone's hand), in which χείρ loses much of its inherent import (Mark 6:2; Acts 2:23; 5:12; 7:25; 11:30; 14:3;

15:23; 19:11; cf. 17:25; Gal 3:19; different in Acts 7:41; 19:26; Rev 9:20). In contrast, hands can also appear as an independently acting subj. (Mark 9:43 par.; Matt 5:30; cf. 1 Cor 12:15, 21).

The hand can also be the object of action. Hence Jesus takes or merely touches the hand of the sick woman (Mark 1:31 par. Matt 8:15; cf. Mark 5:41 par.; Mark 8:23; 9:27; Acts 3:7; 23:19). Mark 3:1-5 par. also focuses on what Jesus does to an outstretched (v. 5 bis) withered hand (vv. 1, 3). Peter would like to have his "*hands* and head" washed as well (John 13:9). The prodigal son receives a ring "on his *hand*" (Luke 15:22). Those who worship the beast in Revelation have a mark (χάραγμα) imprinted on their (right) hand or on their forehead (13:16; 14:9; 20:4). A prisoner is bound by "feet and *hands*" (Acts 21:11; cf. Matt 22:13; John 11:14; Acts 12:7). The resurrected Christ shows the disciples his wounded "*hands* and feet" (Luke 24:40; cf. v. 39) or "*hands* and his side" (John 20:20; cf. vv. 25, 27).

Hands can also be subj. or obj. of a symbolic act. Raised toward heaven they express blessing (Luke 24:50), prayer (1 Tim 2:8), or oath (Rev 10:5). Washing the hands can effect ritual purity (Mark 7:2, 3, 5; Matt 15:2, 20) or prove innocence (Matt 27:24; concerning the blood of guilt on one's hand cf. Rev 19:2). On laying on of hands → 4.b.

Hand appears in three OT citations in the context of metaphorical language about God's loving and redemptive activity for Israel: Rom 10:21 (Isa 65:2); Heb 8:9 (Jer 31:32); 12:12 (Isa 35:3). The *hand* is also a constituent part of metaphorical idioms concerning the immanence of judgment (Matt 3:12 par.: "His winnowing fork is in his *hand*") and the consequences of discipleship (Luke 9:62: "Whoever puts his *hand* to the plow . . .").

Χείρ stands at the threshold of fig. usage where, in accord with OT usage, it becomes the subj. of divine action. God's *hand,* i.e., God in his power, "made everything" (Acts 7:50 = Isa 66:2 LXX); the heavens are the work of his *hands,* i.e., his work (Heb 1:10 = Ps 101:26 LXX). "The *hand* of the Lord was with him/them" (Luke 1:66; Acts 11:21).

3. In fig. usage χείρ represents not the person as a whole, but rather abstract concepts. When the dying Jesus commits his life "into the *hands*" of the Father, he is commending himself to his protection (Luke 23:46). No one can rob him of what belongs to him (John 10:29; cf. v. 28). The Father has given all things to the authority of the Son (3:35; 13:3). He in his power (ἡ χείρ σου) has predestined everything (Acts 4:28) and can use his power for healing (v. 30). One should humble oneself under his dominion (1 Pet 5:6). He called Moses with the help (σὺν χειρί) of an angel (Acts 7:35). God's power is evoked

when his *hand* comes upon Elymas (13:11), or when a person falls into his *hands* (Heb 10:31).

Human hands always signify hostile power. The Son of man "will be delivered into the *hands* of men," i.e., given over to their control (Mark 9:31 par.; cf. 14:41 par.; Luke 24:7), just as Paul is delivered to the control of the pagan Romans (Acts 21:11; 28:17). In contrast, Jesus escapes from the power of the Jews (John 10:39), Paul from Aretas's search (2 Cor 11:33), and God delivers Peter from Herod's control (Acts 12:11) and Israel from its enemies (Luke 1:71, 74).

4. a) Χείρ is often part of a t.t. for the particulars of seizure or arrest: (ἐπι)βάλλω τάς χεῖρας ἐπί τινα (τινί), "lay *hands* on someone." This expression is used in reference to the arrest of Jesus (Mark 14:46 par.; Luke 20:19; John 7:30, 44), of Peter and the other apostles (Acts 4:3; 5:18; 12:1), of Paul (21:27), and of Christians in general (Luke 21:12).

b) Laying on of hands is expressed by ἐπιτίθημι τὰς χεῖρας or—though only in Acts 8:18; 1 Tim 4:14; 2 Tim 1:6; Heb 6:2— by ἐπίθεσις (τῶν) χειρῶν. By this action Jesus bestows blessing on children (Mark 10:16 par. Matt 19:[13] 15). The sick are healed by laying on of hands, both by Jesus (Mark 5:23 par.; 6:5; 7:32; 8:23, 25; Luke 4:40; 13:13) and by Christians (Mark 16:18 v.l.; Acts 9:12, 17; 28:8). Laying on of hands during baptism bestows the Holy Spirit (Acts 8:17, 18, 19; 19:6; probably Heb 6:2); fixing the Spirit to such a gesture separate from actual baptism, however, even after Luke, is the—ecclesiologically grounded— exception. Finally, Paul and Barnabas are sent off on their mission by laying on of hands (Acts 13:3), and others are installed in office (6:6: the Seven, see G. Schneider, *Acts* [HTKNT] I, 428f. [bibliography]; 1 Tim 4:14; 2 Tim 1:6: Timothy; 1 Tim 5:22); to them, too, divine power is thus mediated.   W. Radl

χειραγωγέω *cheiragōgeō* lead by the hand*

Acts 9:8 (χειραγωγοῦντες) and 22:11 (χειραγωγούμενος), of Paul, who was blinded by the radiance of the christophany and was led by his hand to Damascus like a helpless blind person. Like the cognate noun, χειραγωγέω appears only during the Hellenistic period, and elsewhere, too, often refers to leading the blind (cf. also Judg 16:26; Josephus *Ant.* v.315; Artemidorus Daldianus i.48). E. Lohse, *TDNT* IX, 435; Spicq, *Notes* II, 967.

χειραγωγός, οῦ, ὁ *cheiragōgos* one who leads by the hand, leader*

According to Acts 13:11 the magician Bar-Jesus/Elymas, after being temporarily blinded and rendered completely helpless, sought *people to lead him by the hand* (ἐζήτει χειραγωγούς; cf. *Corp. Herm.* vii.2; →

χειραγωγέω; E. Lohse, *TDNT* IX, 435; Spicq, *Notes* II, 967).

χειρόγραφον, ου, τό *cheirographon* handwritten document; signed certificate of indebtedness*

Lit.: C. BURGER, *Schöpfung und Versöhnung* (WMANT 46, 1975) 106-10. — E. LOHSE, *TDNT* IX, 435f. — SPICQ, *Notes* II, 968-70. — N. WALTER, "Die 'Handschrift in Satzungen' Kol 2,14," *ZNW* 70 (1979) 115-18. — K. WENGST, "Versöhnung und Befreiung. Ein Aspekt des Themas 'Schuld und Versöhnung' im Lichte des Kolosserbriefs," *EvT* 36 (1976) 14-26.

1. Χειρόγραφον occurs in the NT only in Col 2:14. Since the simple meaning *handwritten document* makes no sense here, it should be understood as a legal t.t. for a *certificate of indebtedness* personally prepared and signed by the debtor (examples in Deissmann, *Light* 330-34; Moulton/Milligan 687).
Only in this form ("without deletions or additions," ÄgU III, 717, 24) would it be recognized by the debtor in case of any disagreement (cf. Luke 16:6f.). Similarly, in the LXX (Tob 5:3; 9:5) the term refers to a *personally prepared receipt* by which a person assumes responsibility for deposited money. In *T. Job* 11:11, out of sympathy for unfortunate debtors, Job cancels the *certificate of indebtedness* (χειρόγραφον). In *Apoc. Zeph.* 3:6ff. χειρόγραφον appears to refer to provisional *notes* whose contents are later entered into the heavenly "ledgers."
In Phlm 18 Paul gives an examples of a personally attested certificate of indebtedness (with circumlocution of the t.t.) when on behalf of Onesimus he assumes responsibility for eventual debts or damages.

2. Exegesis of Col 2:14 does generally refer to technical usage and translate χειρόγραφον with *bond*. But this usually evokes the idea of a heavenly ledger in which debts are entered and under certain circumstances canceled. The understanding is usually that because of the cross God cancels our debt, which has been entered in the heavenly register of debts, and thus drops the charges against us (on dat. appositional τοῖς δόγμασιν → δόγμα 4).
But the assumption that χειρόγραφον is being used in its literal, legal-technical sense for indebtedness also makes good sense here (Walter). In that case it does not focus on charges made by God, but on the readers' own fear of sin: They recognize, as it were "by their own hand," their own guilt as binding, since it exists according to norms (δόγματα) that they in this fear consider valid; they are uncertain whether these debts really are "settled" through Jesus' self-sacrifice (hence their efforts at further "guarantees": cf. vv. 16-23). They are now told that God really does free them from their guilt, to which they themselves confess, for the sake of Christ's cross, and that he, like an accountant, has "nailed" their *bond* to the cross and thus "dispensed" with it and filed it as completed business.   N. Walter

χειροποίητος, 2 *cheiropoiētos* made with hands*

ἀχειροποίητος, 2 *acheiropoiētos* not made with hands*

Χειροποίητος occurs 6 times in the NT, ἀχειροποίητος 3 times. In all its occurrences χειροποίητος speaks of "the antithesis of what is made with men's hands to the work of God" (E. Lohse, *TDNT* IX, 436).

Both words occur as an antithetical pair in Mark 14:58 in the testimony of false witnesses against Jesus before the Sanhedrin: Jesus claimed he would destroy "the temple *made with hands*" (ναὸς χειροποίητος) and in three days build one *not made with hands*. This temple saying, because of its framework, is to be understood as inauthentic (so R. Pesch, *Mark* [HTKNT] II, 433; W. Schmithals, *Mark* [ÖTK] II, 688; cf. E. Linnemann, *Studien zur Passionsgeschichte* [1970] 116-27). It belongs to the theme of the misunderstanding of Jesus' true messianic mission (cf. 15:29-32): Jesus shows himself to be the Messiah not in an externally visible mighty deed (Judaism anticipated the splendid rebuilding of the city and temple in the eschaton: Tob 13:17; Bar 5:1-9; *1 Enoch* 61:8; 91:13; by the Messiah in *Tg. Isa.* 53:3), but rather in his descent.

Acts uses χειροποίητος in Stephen's speech (7:48: "the Most High does not dwell in houses *made by hands* [ἐν χειροποιήτοις]"), and in the Areopagus discourse (17:24: God "does not live in temples *made by hands* [ἐν χειροποιήτοις ναοῖς]"). Neither occurrence expresses any fundamental criticism of the temple; rather, both pick up the idea of the limitation of the temple's significance, already suggested in the OT itself (cf. 1 Kgs 8:27), and both—particularly the theology of mediation characterizing the Areopagus discourse—show a connection to Stoic thinking (cf. É. des Places, *Bib* 42 [1961] 217-23). The diminishing of the temple's significance (namely, the progression from Luke 1–2 and Acts 1–5 to Acts 7:48; 17:24) corresponds to the increase in the sphere of influence of the gospel from Jerusalem "to the end of the earth" (cf. Acts 1:8).

In Eph 2:11 χειροποίητος characterizes "circumcision in the flesh" as accomplished *by human hands* (περιτομὴ ἐν σαρκὶ χειροποίητος; cf. Col 2:11: περιτομὴ ἀχειροποίητος, "circumcision *made without hands*," referring to baptism [cf. v. 12]). In Heb 9:11, 24 χειροποίητος characterizes the heavenly sanctuary—contrasting it with the earthly one—as *not made with hands*. In 2 Cor 5:1 the οἰκία ἀχειροποίητος is contrasted with the ἐπίγειος οἰκία as the earthly condition of believers and refers to their future imperishable existence in heaven (→ οἰκία 2). E. Lohse, *TDNT* IX, 436; G. Biguzzi, *RivB* 26 (1978) 225-40 (on Mark 14:58).   W. Rebell

χειροτονέω *cheirotoneō* decide, elect, choose; appoint by raising hands*

2 Cor 8:19, of the choice by the Macedonian churches of a traveling companion for Paul during his gathering of the collection ([ἀδελφὸς] . . . χειροτονηθεὶς ὑπὸ τῶν ἐκκλησιῶν → συνέκδομος ἡμῶν; cf. further Ign. *Phld.* 10:1; *Pol.* 7:2; *Did.* 15:1). In contrast, in Acts 14:23 χειροτονέω refers to the appointment or installation of elders by Paul and Barnabas during the "first missionary journey" (χειροτονήσαντες δὲ αὐτοῖς κατ᾽ ἐκκλησίαν πρεσβυτέρους; cf. → πρεσβύτερος 3.b). On χειροτονέω in the sense of *appoint* cf. Josephus *Ant.* vi.312 (the king is appointed by God); Titus 1:9 v.l. (460: μὴ χειροτονεῖν διγάμους), and the postscripts to 2 Timothy and Titus. BAGD s.v.; E. Lohse, *TDNT* IX, 437.

χείρων, 2 *cheirōn* worse, more severe*

This comparative of κακός occurs 11 times in the NT: Mark 2:21 par. Matt 9:16, with σχίσμα; Heb 10:29, with τιμωρία; John 15:14: subst. χεῖρόν τι, "something worse"; Mark 5:26, of the hemorrhaging woman: μᾶλλον εἰς τὸ χεῖρον ἐλθοῦσα, "instead she became *even worse*"; 2 Tim 3:13: the false teachers, whose influence will become even greater during the eschaton (*contra* 2:9), will "go from bad to *worse*" (προκόπτω ἐπὶ τὸ χεῖρον), though they are the "deceived deceivers" (cf. M. Dibelius and H. Conzelmann, *The Pastoral Epistles* [Hermeneia] on 3:13). The phrase γίνεται τὰ ἔσχατα . . . χείρονα τῶν πρώτων (and similar), "afterward it is *worse* than before," occurs in Matt 12:45 par. Luke 11:26; 2 Pet 2:20; cf. Matt 27:64; "worse than . . ." (with gen.) also occurs in 1 Tim 5:8.

Χερουβίν *Cheroubin* cherubim*

Lit.: K.-H. BERNHARDT, *BHH* 298f. — H. BIETENHARD, *Die himmlische Welt im Urchristentum und Spätjudentum* (WUNT 2, 1951), index s.v. *kᵉrubim*. — A. VAN DEN BORN, *BL* 938-40. — D. N. FREEDMAN and P. O'CONNOR, *TWAT* IV, 322-34. — E. LOHSE, *TDNT* IX, 438f. — O. MOE, "Das irdische und das himmlische Heiligtum. Zur Auslegung von Hebr. 9,4f.," *TZ* 9 (1953) 23-29. — H. RINGGREN, *RGG* II, 1301f. — For further bibliography see *TWNT* X, 1291; Lohse; van den Born.

The indeclinable term Χερουβίν (Heb. *kᵉrûbîm*) occurs in the NT only in Heb 9:5: ὑπεράνω δὲ αὐτῆς (= ἡ → κιβωτός, v. 4) Χερουβὶν δόξης κατασκιάζοντα τὸ → ἱλαστήριον (2), "the cherubim of glory overshadowing the mercy seat" (cf. Exod 25:17-22; 37:7-9). The LXX and other Jewish texts render the pl. with various spellings: Χερουβίν, -βίμ, -βείμ, -βείν, βεῖς (Josephus *Ant.* vii.378: masc., viii.72: fem.; cf. BAGD s.v.; E. Lohse, *TDNT* IX, 438 n.2); a similar situation obtains in NT mss. at Heb 9:5 (Χερουβίν in א D, -βείν in B, -βείμ in A P, -βίμ in K L). This also explains the variations among different editions of the text.

In the ancient orient cherubim were originally mythic deities or hybrid creatures, part human and part animal (Akk. *karābu*).

In the OT they are clearly subordinated to God: They guard the Garden of Eden (Gen 3:24) or uphold the divine throne-chariot (Ezek 10:1ff.); God sits enthroned above them (2 Sam 6:2; 2 Kgs 19:15; Ps 80:2; Isa 37:16, and elsewhere), usually in connection with the ark of the covenant (cf. esp. 1 Sam 4:4). According to Exod 25:18ff., 37:7ff., and 1 Kgs 6:23ff. (and elsewhere) the cultic objects in the holy of holies included two (gold or gilded) representations of the cherubim, which stood facing one another at either end of the ark of the covenant so that their wings covered the ark's lid. They were there to suggest God's presence, and God announced himself from between them (Exod 25:22; Num 7:89). Ezekiel's vision particularly associates the cherubim with God's glory (1:4ff.; 9:3; 10:1ff.; 11:22). Cherubim were originally thought of as part human, part animal (with faces of human beings and lions, Ezek 41:19), but they came to be understood as angels (*1 Enoch* 61:10), and it was said that no one could describe their actual appearance (Josephus *Ant.* viii.73; cf. iii.137).

In Heb 9:5 the cherubim play a role in the description of the provisional earthly sanctuary. They are the concluding high point of the portrayal, since the discussion centers here on God's δόξα and on the place of atonement. At the same time, however, the author views the earthly sanctuary (v. 1) and its ultimately insufficient power of atonement (vv. 6ff.) merely as prefigurations of the true and perfect sanctuary in heaven, which is not made with human hands (v. 11) and where the ultimate atonement is made (vv. 12ff.; → χειροποίητος; σκηνή 4).   H. Balz

χήρα, ας, ἡ *chēra* widow*

1. Occurrences in the NT — 2. Meanings — a) The need for protection — b) The widow's unmarried status — 3. The office of widows

Lit.: L. BOPP, *Das Witwentum als organische Gliedschaft im Gemeinschaftsleben der alten Kirche* (1950). — A. VAN DEN BORN, *BL* 1892f. — H. KRAFT, *Die Entstehung des Christentums* (1981) 207-89. — J. LEIPOLDT, *Die Frau in der antiken Welt und im Urchristentum* (1962). — J. MÜLLER-BARDORFF, *BHH* 2177f. — A. SAND, "Witwenstand und Ämterstrukturen in den urchristlichen Gemeinden," *BibLeb* 12 (1971) 186-97. — S. SOLLE, *DNTT* III, 1073-75. — G. STÄHLIN, *TDNT* IX, 440-65. — *idem*, "Das Bild der Witwe," *JAC* 17 (1974) 5-20. — D. C. VERNER, *The Household of God: The Social World of the Pastoral Epistles* (SBLDS 71, 1983) 134-39. — For further bibliography see *TWNT* X, 1291.

1. Χήρα occurs 26 times in the NT: 3 times in Mark, 9 in Luke, 3 in Acts, 8 in 1 Timothy (5:3 bis, 4, 5, 11, 16 bis), and in 1 Cor 7:8; Jas 1:27; Rev 18:7; Matt 23:14 v.l.

2. In the NT the term χήρα exibits a technical sense in addition to the general meaning familiar also to us; in this additional sense it refers to an office of widows in the churches. Widowhood as an office existed in the first centuries of Church history and was absorbed in the later period of Church Fathers by the class of virgins and nuns.

Two aspects are important to the use of this expression in the NT: the need for protection and the unmarried life of widows.

a) From Mark 12:40 both Matthew (23:14—an uncertain textual tradition) and Luke (20:47) take over Jesus' condemnation of scribes who as legal advisers appropriate the property, i.e., houses, of widows they represent under the pretext of intercession. They can expect esp. severe punishment, "additional judgment." Mark (12:31-44) and Luke (21:1-4) use this saying in connection with the story of the widow's mite: Out of love for God she offers her whole living and thus does more than all those who contribute out of their abundance. In so doing she illustrates why the poor are closer to the kingdom of God than the rich.

Although the unjust judge in the parable in Luke 18:1-8 fears neither God nor mankind, the perseverance of a widow—who in her helplessness can do nothing but implore him—forces him to come to her aid, probably against a powerful adversary in court. All the more will the righteous God answer the incessant prayers of his elect for the coming of his kingdom.

The grounding of such election in God's inscrutable will is shown by the widow of Zarephath (Luke 4:25f.), whose commission from God to care for Elijah (1 Kgs 17:9) saved her from starvation. It is also shown by the raising of the young man of Nain (Luke 7:11-17), the only son of a widow. This story is anticipated in the OT in the revival of the Shunammite's son (2 Kgs 4:18-37). It is uncertain whether one should understand it as a reference to the raising of the dead or only to Jesus' mighty power.

b) The earliest Church was uncertain whether in view of the near end marriage was appropriate at all. At first it viewed remarriage of widows—which normally seemed quite natural in view of the problems facing widows—as an expression of carnal desire. Anna is praised (Luke 2:36-38) because after seven years of marriage she lived many years as a widow. In 1 Corinthians 7 (esp. vv. 39f.), in consideration of sexual drive, Paul allows widows to remarry, though he prefers that they remain unmarried.

With expanded justification and focusing on the weakness of the flesh, Paul's pupil, the author of 1 Timothy (5:14), regulates the remarriage of young widows. If a widow does not remarry, her care is the responsibility, first, of her family members (children and grandchildren: v. 16), then of all Christians (Jas 1:27) as "pure and undefiled service before God," and finally but not least of the community as a whole within the context of its provision for the poor.

3. This care for widows is to be distinguished from the institution of widows who serve the community and are compensated (originally by food, etc.). Convinced that the organization of life—offices and morality—of the eschatological community was predicted in the OT, the first Christians viewed God's commissioning of the widow of Zarephath to care for the prophet Elijah as the institution of an "office." Peter's mother-in-law (Mark 1:31; Matt 8:15; Luke 4:39) was the first to embody this. The official widows in the early Jerusalem church were responsible for collecting and preparing food for the meals taken communally in the various houses (Acts 6:1; 2:46). On this Jerusalem model there also arose in the churches of the first (Hellenistic) missions cooperatives of "saints," maintained by the "widows" ("saints and widows," 9:41). Tabitha, whom Peter brought back to life, was a disciple—a virgin or widow—in such an organization, and was responsible for making clothing.

Although Paul does view virgins and widows as a special class (1 Cor 7:8), nowhere does he write specifically concerning the office of widows; perhaps he did not count it among the charismatic offices. This may also explain why 1 Tim 5:3-14 deals with the official, compensated (v. 3), "real" widows together with ordinary widows. Enrollment in the office of widow is restricted to women who are unprovided for (vv. 4, 16) and at least sixty years old (v. 9), who have exhibited irreproachable conduct and have already proven themselves in deeds of love.

Rev 18:7 juxtaposes "queen and *widow*" as opposing possibilities for the fate of a woman—extreme power or helplessness.

H. Kraft

χθές *chthes* yesterday

A variant of the adv. → ἐχθές (which in the Hellenistic period was used in the majority of instances); cf. BDF §29.6.

χιλίαρχος, ου, ὁ *chiliarchos* leader of a thousand soldiers, leader of a cohort, commander, tribune*

Lit.: BAGD s.v. ἑκατοντάρχης. — A. VAN DEN BORN, *BL* 966f. — H. OPITZ, *BHH* 974. — SCHÜRER, *History* I, 366. — H.-E. WILHELM, *BHH* 657f. — G. GRUBEN, *LAW* 650f. — For further bibliography see BAGD.

Χιλίαρχος occurs 21 times in the NT, 17 of those in Acts. As a rule it refers to the *leader of a cohort* (a group of five hundred to a thousand soldiers; see Opitz; → σπεῖρα 1), Lat. *tribunus militum* (cf. Josephus *Ant.* xvii.215), though also more generally to any higher military *commander,* as with God's adversaries in Revelation (6:15, with βασιλεῖς, μεγιστάνες, ἰσχυροί, and others; 19:18, with βασιλεῖς, ἰσχυροί, and others). In Mark 6:21 it refers to members of the court of Herod Antipas (with μεγιστάνες and πρῶτοι τῆς Γαλιλαίας).

According to the Johannine Passion account Judas led

a → σπεῖρα (2) of Roman soldiers and officers of the high priest and Pharisees to arrest Jesus (18:3), which was commanded by a χιλίαρχος (v. 12). The Evangelist thus envisions a relatively large Roman and Jewish contingent gathered against Jesus and probably understands the χιλίαρχος to have been the Roman military tribune or at least a commanding officer (John does not use other designations for military officers). Probably, however, this stretches the historical truth (see R. Schnackenburg, *John* [Eng. tr., 1982] III, on 18:3); seeing in the σπεῖρα and the χιλίαρχος references to the Jewish temple police (so J. Blinzler, *Der Prozeß Jesu* [⁴1961] 90-99), is probably a mistake, since they are expressly mentioned in addition to the ὑπηρέται τῶν Ἰουδαίων (v. 12). The Evangelist's source probably referred to a Jewish crowd (cf. Mark 14:43 par.), and the Evangelist himself first introduced the Romans.

Acts refers (up to 25:23) to the tribune of the Roman cohort in the fortress Antonia at the time of Paul's arrest, whom 21:31 correctly calls the χιλίαρχος τῆς σπείρης (cf. Josephus *Ant.* vii.368; xii.301), and who according to 23:26 identifies himself in his letter to the procurator Felix as Claudius Lysias (cf. 24:7 [v.l.], 22). He protects Paul from the rage of the mob (cf. 21:32, 33, 37), permits him to deliver a speech to the people (cf. 21:37ff.), and plays a positive role in the further development of Paul's proceedings (cf. 22:24, 26, 27, 28, 29; 23:10, 15, 17, 18, 19, 22; 24:7 [v.l.], 22). In 25:23 the pl. probably refers to the tribunes of Caesarea (as a rule, five cohorts were stationed there), who together with the prominent men of the city listen to Paul.

χιλιάς, άδος, ἡ   *chilias* thousand*

Χιλιάς occurs 23 times in the NT, 19 of those in Revelation (13 times in 7:4-8). The reference is always to multiples of one thousand, whereby esp. in Revelation χιλιάς expresses the comprehensive nature of eschatological events. Luke 14:31 (bis) mentions ten/twenty thousand (soldiers); according to Acts 4:4 the Church grew to (about) five thousand men. According to 1 Cor 10:8 twenty-three thousand Israelites perished in the wilderness (*contra* Num 25:9: twenty-four thousand).

Rev 7:4 and 14:1, 3 give the number of sealed servants as one hundred and forty-four thousand; this number is comprised of twelve thousand sealed from each tribe (7:5-8; cf. → σφραγίς 4.b; φυλή). The earthquake kills seven thousand people (in Jerusalem, 11:13). The heavenly Jerusalem will measure twelve thousand stadia in length, breadth, and height (21:6; cf. also Ezek 48:16f.). Rev 5:11 describes the immense host of angels around the divine throne with the gen. constructions μυριάδες μυριάδων (→ μυριάς) καὶ χιλιάδες χιλιάδων: "ten thousands of ten thousands and thousands of thousands"

(cf. also Dan 7:10; *1 Enoch* 40:1; this partitive gen. represents a translation Hebraism; see BDF §164.1; cf. Gen 24:60). E. Lohse, *TDNT* IX, 466-71.

χίλιοι, 3 *chilioi* thousand*

Lit.: W. BAUER, *RAC* II, 1073-78. — H. BIETENHARD, *Das tausendjährige Reich* (²1955). — BILLERBECK III, 823ff.; IV, 989ff. — O. BÖCHER, *Die Johannesapokalypse* (EdF 41, 1980) (on recent exegesis). — G. BOUWMAN, *BL* 290. — E. LOHSE, *TDNT* IX, 466-71. — M. RISSI, *BHH* 1937f. — VOLZ, *Eschatologie* 71-77. — For further bibliography see Lohse.

This noun occurs 11 times in the NT: 9 times in Revelation and twice in 2 Pet 3:8.

It occurs in compound numbers in Rev 11:3 and 12:6, where it refers to the apocalyptic period of 1260 days (ἡμέρας χιλίας διακοσίας ἑξήκοντα), corresponding to the three and one-half (half of seven) years of the reign of terror under Antiochus IV Epiphanes (167-164 B.C.; cf. Dan 7:25; 12:7, 11f.; three and one-half years are spoken of differently in Rev 12:14 ["time and times and half of time"] and in 11:2 and 13:5 ["forty-two months"]). The 1600 stadia in 14:20, as a multiple of 4, might be understood as a number implying totality (→ τέσσαρες 2).

All the other occurrences speak of (τὰ) χίλια ἔτη, "(the) thousand years." According to 2 Pet 3:8 God's time (and patience, v. 9) cannot be measured by human standards: μία ἡμέρα παρὰ κυρίῳ ὡς χίλια ἔτη καὶ χίλια ἔτη ὡς ἡμέρα μία (cf. Ps 90:4). In Revelation the reference is to Christ's thousand-year reign (20:2-7) before the final onslaught of the nations and their destruction, before the judging of the dead, and finally before the the advent of the new heaven and new earth (vv. 7ff.). The dragon is bound for a thousand years (v. 2) and thrown into the netherworld (v. 3; → ἄβυσσος 2). Christian martyrs are awakened to life so that they might reign with Christ, while all the other dead remain in death until the final judgment (vv. 4-6). Finally, after the thousand years is finished, Satan is loosed once more to incite the hostile nations against God one final time and then to perish with them (20:7[-10]).

Jewish apocalyptic texts speak of a time of righteousness and judgment before God's final judgment and the appearance of the new heaven (cf. *1 Enoch* 91:12-14: two cosmic weeks; 2 Esdr 7:28f.: four hundred years as the time of the Messiah and those belonging to him [on this number cf. Gen 15:13; Ps 90:15]; *2 Bar.* 29:3–30:1; 40:3f.: a blessed messianic period before the resurrection of the dead and final judgment; see also *Sib. Or.* iii.652ff.). The author of Revelation probably refers to such ideas, which are an amalgamation of the expectations of an earthly, royal Messiah, and a heavenly, universal judge and savior. The reference to one thousand years might have something to do with the idea of a cosmic week of seven thousand years (cf. Gen 1:11ff. with Ps 90:4; *T. Abr.* recension B 7:16; recension A 19:7; *Bib. Ant.* 28:8; *2 Enoch* 33:1)—the seventh thousand years, as the cosmic sabbath, will usher in the reign of the Messiah (cf. *Barn.* 15:4f.; *T. Isaac* 8:6)—even if no unified conception can be discerned here. The idea of eschatological fullness may also have influenced the idea of the thousand years (cf. the thousandfold fruit, etc., in *1 Enoch* 10:17, 19; *2 Bar.* 29:5).

H. Balz

Χίος, ου *Chios* Chios*

According to Acts 20:15, on his final journey from Greece through Asia Minor to Jerusalem Paul reached Chios between Mitylene and Samos (κατηντήσαμεν ἄντικρυς Χίου). The island of Chios lies in the Aegean Sea off the west coast of Asia Minor on the same latitude as Smyrna. K. H. Rengstorf, *BHH* 299; A. van den Born, *BL* 290.

χιτών, ῶνος, ὁ *chitōn* undergarment, tunic; garment*

Lit.: A. van den Born, *BL* 960-62. — Billerbeck II, 565f. — Dalman, *Arbeit* V, 208-20. — G. Fohrer, *BHH* 962-65. — S. Krauss, *Talmudische Archäologie* (1910) I, 161. — F. Rundgren, "Χιτών," *Orientalia Suecana* 22 (1973) 73-77.

Χιτών, the Greek transliteration of Heb. *kuttōneṯ* (Gen 37:23, 31-33; 2 Sam 15:32, and elsewhere), was part of Greek vocabulary from Homer on (e.g., *Il.* 24.580; *Od.* 15.60; Lat. *tunica*). Its meaning was essentially identical with that of *kuttōneṯ*: the undergarment or tunic that developed from the simple *śaq* (a sacklike garment), with variously altered forms and styles, worn either against the bare skin or over a linen shirt. The χιτών was made of linen or wool, reached to the ankles or knees, had long or half-sleeves, and was worn by both rich and poor. Χιτών and → ἱμάτιον (*undergarment* and outer garment) together constituted one's clothing (cf. Matt 5:40; Luke 6:29; Acts 9:39).

Χιτών occurs 11 times in the NT. Mark 6:9 par. Matt 10:10/Luke 9:3 speaks of the vow of the Twelve to frugality, including renunciation of one of the two *tunics* usually taken on journeys (cf. Josephus *Ant.* xvii.136; on distributive ἀνά in Luke cf. BDF §§204; 248.1). In the Q saying about love for enemies (Matt 5:40 par. Luke 6:29) according to Matthew Exod 22:25f. and Deut 24:12f. are surpassed by the new righteousness: τῷ θέλοντι . . . τὸν χιτῶνά σου λαβεῖν, ἄφες αὐτῷ καὶ τὸ ἱμάτιον ("if any one would sue you and take your *undergarment,* let him have your cloak as well"). In the Lukan version the thief who takes one's cloak (τὸ ἱμάτιον) should not be denied the *undergarment* as well. The Lukan theology of renunciation of possessions as the basis of discipleship (cf. Luke

14:33) includes John the Baptist's call to repentance: "He who has two *tunics,* let him share with him who has none" (3:11). In Acts 9:39 χιτῶνες and ἱμάτια are used to describe the pieces of clothing that the deceased Δορκάς had made.

According to Mark 14:63 the high priest tore his χιτῶνες (here: *garments)* before the Sanhedrin because of Jesus' alleged blasphemy (cf. βλασφημία, v. 64; Josephus *Ant.* iii.153-56, 159-61 describes the official inner and outer garments of the high priest as χιτῶνες; on whether the high priest did in fact wear his ceremonial regalia during Jesus' interrogation and on the significance of this for the historical value of the trial accounts cf. P. Winter, *On the Trial of Jesus* [SJ 1, 1961] 16-19; J. Blinzler, *Der Prozeß Jesu* [⁴1969] 160f. n.71). At the crucifixion the soldiers cast lots for Jesus' "seamless *tunic*" (χιτών ἄραφος, John 19:23 bis). According to Roman privilege of spoils the soldiers performing the execution were given the condemned's clothing (cf. Blinzler, 369 n. 47). The seamless tunic as such should not be interpreted symbolically; "rather, the entire scene is to be understood as the expression of a comprehensive christological conception" (J. Becker, *John* [ÖTK] II, 589; cf. R. Bultmann, *John* [Eng. tr., 1971] 670f.; R. Schnackenburg, *John* III [Eng. tr., 1982] 273f.).

In Jude 23 believers are called on to hate "the *garment* spotted by the flesh" (τὸν ἀπὸ τῆς σαρκὸς ἐσπιλωμένον χιτῶνα) of those who err (so as not to be defiled by the impurity; on the interpretation of this passage see W. Grundmann, *Jude* [THKNT] 49).

W. Rebell

χιών, όνος, ἡ *chiōn* snow*

The NT uses imagery of snow for the divine radiance and purity in an epiphany (Matt 28:3: τὸ ἔνδυμα αὐτοῦ λευκὸν ὡς χιών; cf. Mark 8:3 TR; *1 Enoch* 14:20) and in a vision of the Son of man (Rev 1:14: ἡ δὲ κεφαλὴ αὐτοῦ καὶ αἱ τρίχες λευκαὶ ὡς ἔριον λευκὸν ὡς χιών; cf. Dan 7:9). Elsewhere *snow* is a metaphor for complete whiteness or purity (Ps 51:9; Isa 1:18; *1 Clem.* 8:4; 18:7), or for the whiteness of leprosy (Exod 4:6; Num 12:10). H. Haag, *BL* 1546.

χλαμύς, ύδος, ἡ *chlamys* mantle, soldier's cloak, war mantle*

According to Matt 27:28 the soldiers disrobed Jesus before mocking him and put a "scarlet *soldier's cloak* (χλαμύδα κοκκίνην)" on him. Afterward they took this off and put his own clothes back on him (v. 31). Emperors, field commanders, and esp. soldiers wore a scarlet cloak (*paludamentum,* χλαμύς; Appian *BC* ii.90; Philo *Flacc.* 37), so that the color scarlet was considered a sign of war. This garment was usually fastened over the right shoulder and represented imperial power. According to Matt 27:28ff. Jesus was thus scorned as a powerless "Messiah" unable to support his claim. Mark 15:17, 20 (πορφύρα) speaks rather of a royal purple robe (cf., however, also Appian *BC* ii.150, where πορφύρα also refers to the soldier's cloak). Passow II, s.v.; O. Michel, *TDNT* III, 813; F. Eckstein, *LAW* 580.

χλευάζω *chleuazō* mock, scorn*

Only intrans. in NT: Acts 17:32: οἱ μὲν ἐχλεύαζον; cf. 2:13 v.l. (in place of → διαχλευάζω).

χλιαρός, 3 *chliaros* tepid, lukewarm*

Used literally this adj. most often refers to lukewarm water (*Vitae Aesopi* i.1 [230.7]). But in the NT (as also in rabbinic usage: *Gen. Rab.* on 39:3) it is used fig.: of the church at Laodicea, which is *lukewarm*, i.e., "neither cold nor hot" (Rev 3:16: ὅτι χλιαρὸς εἶ, καὶ οὔτε ζεστὸς οὔτε ψυχρός). The judge will reject it—just as one spits out stale water—because of its tepidness, i.e., as the context suggests, because of its complacency, blindness, and false accommodation (vv. 17-20). A. Oepke, *TDNT* II, 876f.

Χλόη, ης *Chloē* Chloe*

According to 1 Cor 1:11 Paul heard "from Chloe's people (ὑπὸ τῶν Χλόης)" concerning the dissensions in Corinth. It is impossible to determine whether Chloe lived in Corinth or Ephesus (where 1 Corinthians was written) and whether she was herself a Christian, though that she was is probable. Since the Corinthians had sent a delegation to Paul (16:17) and since Paul was informed about the Corinthian dissension neither by that delegation nor by Chloe directly, but rather through her people (probably members of her household, possibly also slaves or freedmen), Chloe more likely lived in Corinth. Probably she had been visited by relatives from Ephesus, who then reported to Paul concerning the quarrels in the church. Or members of her household—possibly traveling on business—had traveled from Corinth to Ephesus. That the delegation had a commission from the church probably explains why Paul does not refer, in his explanation of his own position concerning the dispute, to the delegation (although 1:16 mentions Stephanas). The Corinthians had not yet recognized their divisions as a problem (cf. 3:1ff., 18ff.; 4:1ff.). BAGD s.v.

χλωρός, 3 *chlōros* yellow-green, light green; pale*

Mark 6:39; Rev 8:7: "*green* grass"; subst. in Rev 9:4: πᾶν χλωρὸν ("anything *green*") οὐδὲ πᾶν δένδρον (with χόρτος), referring to green plants (cf. Gen 2:5); Rev 6:8:

pale/sallow, of the ἵππος χλωρός of death (cf. χλωρός as the color of disease and death in Hippocrates *Prog.* ii.79.18; Sappho frag. 2.14 [Diehl, *Anthologia* I, 330]).

χοϊκός, 3 *choïkos* made of earth, earthly*

This adj., related to the subst. → χοῦς ("dust"), occurs in the NT only in 1 Cor 15:47-49 (4 times), where Paul explains the succession of perishable and imperishable (v. 42), i.e., of σῶμα ψυχικόν and σῶμα πνευματικόν (vv. 44f.), on the ground of Adam's (ὁ πρῶτος ἄνθρωπος, vv. 45, 47) creation (according to the creation story in J) "from the earth," as a *person of dust* (ἐκ γῆς χοϊκός, v. 47; cf. Gen 2:7: καὶ ἔπλασεν ὁ θεὸς τὸν ἄνθρωπον χοῦν ἀπὸ τῆς γῆς). The χοϊκοί (v. 48 bis), i.e., believers in their earthly existence, are like this χοϊκός. In their spiritual existence, however, they already belong to the later, "final," or "second" Adam (vv. 45, 47), i.e., the (heavenly) Christ. In accord with this succession of earthly and heavenly man (Adam, Christ), they also, according to v. 49, (still) bear the image of the earthly person (ἐφορέσαμεν τὴν εἰκόνα τοῦ χοϊκοῦ), and will (only later) bear the image of the heavenly person (φορέσομεν καὶ τὴν εἰκόνα τοῦ ἐπουρανίου).

Χοϊκός does not occur in the LXX and occurs only rarely outside the NT. It might have been constructed directly (by Paul?) from χοῦς (Gen 2:7 LXX). Thus it emphasizes that a person is made from dust and will return to dust, and thus lives only through the Spirit of God within (cf. in addition to Gen 2:7 also 3:19; Job 4:19; 8:19; 10:9; Eccl 3:20; 12:7; Pss 22:30; 104:29; 146:4; Dan 12:2).

Like Paul, *Sib. Or.* viii.445 also takes up Gen 2:7 (χοϊκὸς πλασθείς). But in complete contrast to Paul Philo juxtaposes the earthly and the heavenly person by interpreting Gen 1:26f. in the first creation story (P) as referring to the ideal person formed (not *made*—of dust) in God's image, and 2:7 as referring to the actual, earthly person (γήϊνον πλάσμα, *All.* i.31f.; cf. *Op.* 134-36). The two creation stories are thus interpreted as referring to two types of humanity that then fuse in every concrete human being, so that ultimately a fundamental moral concept emerges (cf. also *All.* ii.4f.; *Her.* 57; *Quaest. Gen.* i.8; *Quaest. Ex.* 46). Hence the existing and physically perceivable person lives in order to attain participation in both the external and internal element of the divine.

The Corinthian "Gnostics" may have held a position similar to Philo's, but Paul distinguishes sharply between human corruption and Christ's salvation gift and thus puts off the forming of the believer into the image of the heavenly or final person Christ to the future. In Gnosticism the Philonic view prevailed; the earthly was associated with this world and bound to the lower creation, with which the pneumatics no longer associate (cf. Hippolytus, *Haer.* v.7.15; 7.36; 8.22, and elsewhere). E. Brandenburger, *Adam und Christus* (WMANT 7, 1962) 124-27; E. Schweizer, *TDNT* IX, 472-79; H. Conzelmann, *1 Cor* (Hermeneia) 283-87 (on 15:45-47).

H. Balz

χοῖνιξ, ικος, ἡ *choinix* (unit of measure)*

Rev 6:6 (bis): χοῖνιξ σίτου, τρεῖς χοίνικες κριθῶν. The χοῖνιξ is used here as a measure of grain constituting a daily ration (Diogenes Laertius viii.18), *ca.* 1.1 liter (Vg.: *bilibris*). A. Strobel, *BHH* 1165f.

χοῖρος, ου, ὁ *choiros* (young) pig, swine*

There are 12 occurrences in the NT. Mark 5:11, 12, 13, 16 par. Matt 8:30, 31, 32/Luke 8:32, 33: Demons exorcised from a demoniac enter into a large (Mark 5:13: about two thousand, omitted in Matthew and Luke) herd of *swine* (ἀγέλη χοίρων, χοῖροι). The uncleanness of swine probably plays a role here (cf. Lev 11:7; Deut 14:8; Isa 65:4; *Barn.* 10:1-3); in the Hellenistic Decapolis (→ Δεκάπολις), however, large herds of swine were certainly possible, since among Greeks and Romans swine played a cultic role. According to Luke 15:15f. the "prodigal son" had to tend (unclean) swine in a distant land (βόσκειν χοίρους, v. 15). The saying in Matt 7:6 (M) mentions swine proverbially with (equally unclean) dogs (cf. Pap. Oxy. no. 840, l. 33), probably referring fig. to pagans or persecutors (cf. also Matt 15:26; 2 Pet 2:22; *Did.* 9:5; *Gos. Thom.* 93; *b. Ber.* 83a). BAGD s.v.; G. Sauer, *BHH* 1748f.; H. Frehen, *BL* 1562; F. Annen, *Heil für die Heiden* (FTS 20, 1976) 162-73; H. von Lips, "Schweine füttert man, Hunde nicht—ein Versuch, das Rätsel von Mt 7,6 zu lösen," *ZNW* 79 (1988) 165-86. → κύων (bibliography).

χολάω *cholaō* be angry*

John 7:23: the Jews' anger at Jesus' sabbath healing (ἐμοὶ χολᾶτε, ὅτι . . . ;).

χολή, ῆς, ἡ *cholē* gall, bile*

In the LXX χολή renders Hebrew expressions for bitterness, gall, and poison (cf. Job 16:13; 20:14; Prov 5:4; Lam 3:15; Ps 68:22 LXX). According to Matt 27:34 the soldiers gave Jesus "wine mingled with *gall*" to drink before his crucifixion (οἶνον μετὰ χολῆς μεμιγμένον), probably as a sedative, possibly an allusion to Ps 69:22 MT (par. Mark 15:23: ἐσμυρνισμένον οἶνον, "wine mingled with myrrh," which also tasted bitter; Matthew, in view of Ps 68:22 LXX, may have substituted *gall* for "myrrh"). A sedative drink before execution was in accord with Jewish custom (see Billerbeck I, 1037f.). Fig.

in Acts 8:23, in the story of Simon Magus: χολὴ πικρίας, "*gall* of bitterness" (cf. Deut 29:17; Lam 3:15). W. Bunte, *BHH* 512; A. van den Born, *BL* 510f.

Χοραζίν *Chorazin* Chorazin*

Jesus mentions Chorazin in his cry of woe (Matt 11:21 par. Luke 10:13) together with Bethsaida (οὐαί σοι, Χοραζίν). Χοραζίν is the indeclinable name of a Galilean city situated within the area of Jesus' ministry in the vicinity of Bethsaida and Capernaum (Matt 11:23 par.) northwest of the Sea of Galilee (cf. *b. Menah.* 85a [Billerbeck I, 605]). Eusebius *Onom.* 303 identifies Chorazin as a ruin in the vicinity of Capernaum. Today it is identified with Khirbet Kerâzeh, 3 km. northwest of Capernaum, where the ruins of a synagogue made of basalt stones (A.D. 2nd/3rd cent.) suggest that at least during this period it was a thriving city. H. Kohl and C. Watzinger, *Antike Synagogen in Galiläa* (1916) 41-58; Kopp, *Holy Places* 187-89; B. Reicke, *BHH* 301; A. van den Born, *BL* 292 (bibliography).

χορηγέω *chorēgeō* provide (enough), place at one's disposal, supply*

This vb. originally meant "pay the expenses for training a chorus," etc. The NT uses it in a more general sense. 2 Cor 9:10: God supplies seed to the sower and bread for food (cf. Isa 55:10; → ἐπιχορηγέω) and accordingly will also *supply enough* seed for the Church and multiply it (χορηγήσει καὶ πληθυνεῖ τὸν σπόρον ὑμῶν); 1 Pet 4:11: the "strength that God *supplies*" (ἐξ ἰσχύος ἧς [= ἧν] χορηγεῖ ὁ θεός); cf. also Sir 39:33.

χορός, οῦ, ὁ *choros* (circle-)dance (noun)*

Luke 15:25: ἤκουσεν συμφωνίας καὶ χορῶν, "he [the older brother] heard music and *circle-dancing*," which indicated that a celebration was occurring (cf. Exod 15:20; 32:19; Ps 150:4). Ign. *Eph.* 4:2; *Rom.* 2:2 use χορός with the meaning "chorus."

χορτάζω *chortazō* satiate; pass.: become full*

This vb. occurs 16 times in the NT, most in the literal sense of eating or drinking one's fill. Act. in Matt 15:33: χορτάσει ὄχλον; Mark 8:4: act. τούτους . . . χορτάσαι ἄρτων (cf. Ps 131:15 LXX). Pass. in miraculous feeding narratives: καὶ ἔφαγον πάντες καὶ ἐχορτάσθησαν, Matt 14:20; 15:37; Mark 6:42; similarly 8:8; Luke 9:17; John 6:26; cf. χορτασθῆναι τὰ τέκνα in Mark 7:27; οἱ πεινῶντες νῦν . . . χορτασθήσεσθε in Luke 6:21; χορτασθῆναι ἐκ τῶν κερατίων, 15:16; ἀπὸ τῶν πιπτόντων ἀπὸ τῆς τραπέζης τοῦ πλουσίου, 16:21; χορτάζεσθαι καὶ πεινᾶν next to περισσεύειν καὶ ὑστερεῖσθαι, Phil 4:12. Ironic in Jas 2:16:

θερμαίνεσθε καὶ χορτάζεσθε (if, i.e., one only speaks and does not act thus). Rev 19:21 (cf. Ezek 39:17-20), of birds: πάντα τὰ ὄρνεα ἐχορτάσθησαν ἐκ τῶν σαρκῶν αὐτῶν, all *were gorged* (with the flesh of God's slain eschatological adversaries). Fig., of those who hunger and thirst for righteousness: ὅτι αὐτοὶ χορτασθήσονται (Matt 5:6; cf. also Ps 17:15).

χόρτασμα, ατος, τό *chortasma* food, nourishment*

Acts 7:11, of the famine that was in all Egypt and Canaan during the time of the patriarchs (cf. Gen 41:53ff.; 42:5): οὐχ ηὕρισκον χορτάσματα. In the LXX the noun refers esp. to food for livestock (Gen 24:32; Deut 11:15).

χόρτος, ου, ὁ *chortos* grass, green crops, hay*

There are 15 occurrences in the NT, which (as in the LXX) exhibits various meanings. It refers generally to (green) grass and similar green growth in fields and meadows, e.g., to a meadow as the place where a crowd sits: Matt 14:19: ἀνακλιθῆναι ἐπὶ τοῦ χόρτου; Mark 6:39: ἀνακλῖναι . . . ἐπὶ τῷ χλωρῷ χόρτῳ; John 6:10: χόρτος πολύς; in a general sense in Rev 8:7: πᾶς χόρτος χλωρὸς κατεκάη (cf. also Isa 15:6; 42:15; Jer 12:4); 9:4: ὁ χόρτος τῆς γῆς (cf. also Ps 105:35; Amos 7:2) with πᾶν χλωρόν and πᾶν δένδρον. Matt 13:26 and Mark 4:28 refer to germinating grain seed, so that χόρτος itself refers to the delicate green stalk.

Matt 6:30 (χόρτος τοῦ ἀγροῦ) par. Luke 12:28 (ἐν ἀγρῷ ὁ χόρτος) speaks of wild, colorful blooms in the fields. Χόρτος here refers to the previously mentioned κρίνα ("lilies" or generally "wildflowers," Matt 6:28f. par. Luke 12:27; see BAGD s.v. κρίνον), which God splendidly adorns during their short period of blooming, an example of God's care.

The metaphor is used differently in Jas 1:10 (ὁ δὲ πλούσιος . . . ὡς → ἄνθος χόρτου παρελεύσεται); 1:11 (ὁ ἥλιος . . . ἐξήρανεν τὸν χόρτον); 1 Pet 1:24 (ter: πᾶσα σὰρξ ὡς χόρτος . . . πᾶσα δόξα . . . ὡς ἄνθος χόρτου· ἐξηράνθη ὁ χόρτος καὶ τὸ ἄνθος ἐξέπεσεν): In accord with Isa 40:6-8 (cf. also 51:12; Pss 37:2; 92:8; 102:12) wildflowers represent here the fragility of human power and institutions (cf. οὐκ ἐκ σπορᾶς φθαρτῆς, 1 Pet 1:23).

Finally, in 1 Cor 3:12 Paul speaks of *hay* as an inferior construction material (with → καλάμη; cf. Diodorus Siculus xx.65.1).

Χουζᾶς, ᾶ *Chouzas* Chuza*

Luke 8:3: Joanna (→ Ἰωάννα), the γυνὴ Χουζᾶ ἐπιτρόπου Ἡρῴδου. Chuza (Aram. *kûzā';* cf. BAGD s.v.) administered the property of Herod Antipas and was thus probably a court official (→ ἐπίτροπος). Rabbinic texts

mention similar stewards of public or royal property (*b. Šabb.* 121a *[Bar.];* *b. Sukk.* 27a; ἐπίτροπος appears to be a loanword in Hebrew and therefore probably a fixed title). Chuza was probably respected and well-to-do, which might also throw some light on the mention of his wife in the circle of Jesus' followers and on the concluding comment in Luke 8:3, namely, that the women supported the others ἐκ τῶν ὑπαρχόντων αὐταῖς. There is no evidence, however, linking Chuza with the royal official mentioned in John 4:46, and esp. not with Manaen, the → σύντροφος of Herod Antipas according to Acts 13:1. BAGD s.v. (bibliography); Billerbeck I, 164; A. Hastings, *Prophet and Witness in Jerusalem* (1958) 38-49; B. Reicke, *BHH* 310; A. van den Born, *BL* 298.

χοῦς, χοός, ὁ *chous* dust*

This noun occurs twice in the NT. Like → κονιορτός it always appears in formulaic expressions (cf. BDF §52). According to Mark 6:11 if any place does not receive the disciples sent out by Jesus, the disciples should leave and "shake off the *dust* on their feet as a testimony against them" (ἐκτινάξατε τὸν χοῦν τὸν ὑποκάτω τῶν ποδῶν ὑμῶν; cf. χοῦς in Isa 49:23; 52:2). The Synoptic parallels Matt 10:14 and Luke 9:5 and Luke 10:11; Acts 13:51 use → κονιορτός in the same context. Luke 10:11 esp. elucidates the meaning of the gesture: The disciples, who could not remain in one house, shake off the city's dust that clings to their feet as they leave the city in the way that a Jew shakes off the dust of a Gentile country when he returns to his own country from a journey; thus any form of fellowship is abrogated (cf. *m. Ṭohar.* 4:5; *b. Giṭ.* 8a *[Bar.];* *b. Ber.* 19b; Acts 18:6: ἐκτιναξάμενος τὰ ἱμάτια . . . καθαρὸς ἐγὼ ἀπὸ τοῦ νῦν εἰς τὰ ἔθνη πορεύσομαι; see further Billerbeck I, 571). The figure in Rev 18:19 (ἔβαλον χοῦν ἐπὶ τὰς κεφαλὰς αὐτῶν) refers to a common gesture of grief (cf. Josh 7:6; Lam 2:10).

χράομαι *chraomai* use, employ, make use of; act, proceed*

1. Occurrences and meaning — 2.a) 1–2 Corinthians — b) 1 Timothy — c) Acts

The 11 occurrences of this vb. in the NT are in 1–2 Corinthians (7 occurrences), 1 Timothy (2), and Acts (2). The mid. of χράω means *wish, require, lack.* With the dat. the vb. has the sense *make use of, experience* (undergo), and *treat* (cf. LSJ s.v.).

The LXX has both act. and mid. (together *ca.* 60 times, largely in the later writings). Used with the dat. (as it usually is) it means *make use of* (Wis 2:6; 13:18, and elsewhere); the same meaning occurs with the acc. (2 Macc 4:19).

In the NT χράομαι (with dat.) means *use* something (1 Cor 9:12, 15; 1 Tim 5:23; Acts 27:17; dat. is understood in 1 Cor 7:21 [see BAGD s.v. 1.a]). Here also the same meaning occurs with the acc. (1 Cor 7:31). The meaning *act, proceed* occurs in 2 Cor 1:17; 3:12. An adv. replaces the dat. in 13:10 (see 1 Tim 1:8) without changing the meaning. With dat. of the person and an adv. (Acts 27:3) the vb. means *treat* someone in a certain way (see BAGD s.v. 3); with dat. of the thing and amplified by an adv., χράομαι means *employ* (1 Tim 1:8).

2. a) 1 Cor 7:21 uses the example of a slave (cf. v. 22) to illustrate the Pauline principle that "everyone should remain in the state in which he was called" (v. 20). One called to slavery should *remain* (in that condition), even if he can gain his freedom. From the context, i.e., εἰ καί ("even if"), ἀλλά (emphatic "indeed"; J. Weiss, *1 Cor* [KEK] 188), and esp. μᾶλλον (understood correctly), one can conclude that dat. δουλείᾳ (so most exegetes; see BAGD s.v. 1.a), not ἐλευθερίᾳ (so most earlier exegesis, following Luther and Calvin), is to be supplied (despite the aor.; cf. H. Conzelmann, *1 Cor* [Hermeneia] 127). → μᾶλλον 3.d; see S. S. Bartchy, *ΜΑΛΛΟΝ ΧΡΗΣΑΙ: First-Century Slavery and the Interpretation of 1 Corinthians 7:21* (SBLDS 11; 1973); P. Trummer, *Bib* 56 (1975) 344-68.

1 Cor 7:31 (vv. 25-38 deal with unmarried women and men) directs itself to those who *make use of* the world as though they had no use for it (ὡς μὴ καταχρώμενοι; acc. τὸν κόσμον may be occasioned by the compound with κατά [see BDF §152.4]). The intensive compound → καταχράομαι (otherwise only in 1 Cor 9:18) refers to a χρᾶσθαι binding one too strongly to the world (cf. J. A. Bengel, *Gnomon Novi Testamenti* [1773] 411: *utendum, non fruendum* ["using, not enjoying"]). The v.l. παραχράομαι, attested in only one ms. (L), misunderstands the apostle's statement in the sense of Lat. *abuti*.

In 1 Cor 9:12 the vb. means *make use of* something. The verse speaks of those who claim access to the Corinthian Christians' material goods (v. 11) and emphasizes Paul's voluntary decision not to make use of this right. So also v. 15a: Just as temple service (v. 13) gives one the right to share in the benefits of this service, so also (in accord with a "command of the Lord": cf. Matt 10:10b; Luke 10:7b; 1 Tim 5:18) does service to the gospel. But Paul makes no use of this right, and it is this renunciation that constitutes the ground of his boasting. According to 2 Cor 1:17 the apostle was accused of irresponsibility (ἐλαφρία [with art.] is a hapax legomenon in the NT) and of making plans "according to the flesh." Paul rejects the accusation; he *acted* neither irresponsibly nor arbitrarily (v. 18). The same sense is intended in 3:12. Paul draws the conclusion (οὖν) from what has just been said (vv. 7-11); in doing so, he is *proceeding* with all confidence, and does so in contrast to Moses, who veiled himself (pl. "we" refers primarily to Paul himself, as shown by the change in number between 1:14 and 1:15 and between 2:13 and 2:14). This bold behavior (ind., not subjunc.) is more than merely courageous openness

in one's demeanor; it contains the fullness of certainty generated by hope. In 13:10 (as a summary comment on vv. 1-9) Paul justifies his apology by asserting that he would like to avoid having to be severe in his *use* of his authority while in Corinth. The adv. ἀποτόμως (otherwise only in Titus 1:13) expresses the authority (v. 10b) given by the Lord not only for building up, but also for devastating judgment ("tearing down"; cf. Wis 5:20; 6:5; 11:10; 12:9; 18:15). The use of such severity (of judgment) "might in this case result in the destruction of the community" (H. Köster, *TDNT* VIII, 108 [on ἀποτόμως]).

b) "The law is good, if any one *uses* it lawfully" (1 Tim 1:8). This statement does not directly reflect Pauline tradition (cf. Rom 7:12, 16), but as a statement modeled on Paul (see V. Hasler, *1 Tim* [ZBK] 14) it has its place in a dispute over correct morality with adversaries who recognize the law only for the righteous (v. 9). In accord with 1 Tim 5:17-22 (which probably makes conceptual associations with the anti-sarkic position of the heretics) the author advises the reader (v. 23) to *use (drink)* not only water (imv.), but also a bit of wine as well (cf. C. Spicq, *Saint Paul. Les Épîtres Pastorales* [ÉBib] 549).

c) Acts 27:3 (χράομαι with dat. and adv.) praises the centurion of the Augustan Cohort (27:1) for having *treated* Paul kindly during the sea journey to Rome (cf. also v. 43).

The interpretation of χράομαι in 27:17a is more problematic: Which of the two participles belongs to ἐχρῶντο? *NTG*[26] and *UBSGNT* leave this question open; *NTG*[25] associates the vb. with the first partc.: The sailors haul the lifeboat (σκάφη; cf. LSJ s.v. I.2) on board by *employing* (special) measures (cf. the four theories of interpretation in E. Haenchen, *Acts* [Eng. tr., 1971] 633 n.2); this presumably refers to nautical measures taken to avoid imminent danger (cf. Aristotle *Rh.* ii.5.18; Philo *Jos.* 33).

A. Sand

χράω *chraō* lend

Luke 11:5: 1st aor. imv. χρῆσον, which can be associated with pres. χράω or, more likely, with the alternate form → κίχρημι, which occurs in the LXX with the meaning "equip with (something), lend" (1 Kgdms 1:28; Ps 111:5). Cf. LSJ s.v. χράω (B) B.

χρεία, ας, ἡ *chreia* need, necessity

1. Occurrences and meaning — 2. Χρείαν ἔχω — 3. Other constructions

1. Most of the 49 NT occurrences of this noun are in the Synoptics (22, including those in Acts); it occurs rarely or not at all in the other NT writings.

Greek use of this term encompassed a variety of

meanings: *need, duty, service* (as a military term), *use, maxim* (a rhetorical t.t.; cf. LSJ s.v.). The same holds true in the LXX, where χρεία occurs almost exclusively in the later writings (about 52 times), and most often in the wisdom literature (about 25 times) and 1–2 Maccabees (15 times). The spectrum of meaning includes *worry* (Sir 3:22), *need* (29:2), *affliction* (8:9), *service* (1 Macc 3:28; 10:41, 42), and *office* (10:37). The idiom χρείαν ἔχω, which is already attested in secular Greek (LSJ s.v. I.1; III), occurs *ca.* 12 times in the LXX (Isa 13:17; Wis 13:16; Tob 5:7, 12 [א], and elsewhere). The NT partially preserves this variety of meanings (see BAGD s.v.).

2. a) With 3 exceptions (→ 3) the Synoptics (including Acts) use χρεία in the expression χρείαν ἔχω, "require, have need of." Thus Jesus says to John the Baptist: "I *need* to be baptized by you . . ." (Matt 3:14 [M]). The Father knows what the disciples "need" (Matt 6:8 [M]). The strong "do not need" a physician, but rather those who are sick (Mark 2:17 par.). In Luke 10:42, by putting ἑνός in first position and appropriately rendering the text (see the numerous textual variations and cf. *NTG* with *UBSGNT* ad loc.), the contrast between "one" and "many" comes even more clearly to expression: Only one thing is necessary, which is to hear the word (v. 39; cf. → 3 on Acts 6:3).

The idiom χρείαν ἔχω also predominates in use of χρεία in the rest of the NT writings (always in the Johannine corpus and Revelation, usually in Paul and Hebrews). The basic sense of the clause is always "have *need* of" (with negation in 1 Cor 12:21 in the style of personifying diatribe; cf. J. Weiss, *1 Cor* [KEK] 305), "need" (John 2:25; 13:10; on the exegetical difficulties in 13:10 see G. Richter, *Die Fußwaschung im Johannesevangelium* [1967] 308f., 320), and "require" (Rev 3:17: the Laodicean Christians maintain that they are rich in spiritual gifts and need no outside encouragement).

3. Used absolutely, χρεία represents *what is necessary* (Eph 4:29), the *situation of need* (Phil 2:25), and *what is needed* (Heb 7:11). Rom 12:13 uses χρεία in the pl. (otherwise only in Acts 20:34; 28:10; Titus 3:14): The Christians in Rome should concern themselves with the *needs* of the saints (BAGD s.v. 1.b); the v.l. μνείαις (D* F G it vg^mss), which T. Zahn (*Rom* [KNT] 550f. and n.47; *contra* W. Sanday and C. Headlam, *Rom* [ICC] 362) does not entirely exclude, is probably a later interpretation in the sense of a *memoria* (though not of veneration of martyrs) for already deceased saints (cf. E. Käsemann, *Rom* [Eng. tr., 1980] 346f.). Acts 20:34 also speaks of *needs* (pl.): Through his own work Paul provided his own means of support, i.e., the *necessities* of life. At his departure, the sick whom Paul healed on Malta (Acts 28:10) take care of *what is necessary* (for the continued journey; Koine has sg. χρεία; for the better attested v.l. see *NTG*

ad loc.). Acts 6:3: *duty, service, office* (see BAGD s.v. 4): Seven men are to be appointed for the *task* of table service so that service to the word of God does not suffer. "A correspondence in substance between Luke 10:38-42 . . . and Acts 6:1-7" emerges from this statement (G. Schneider, *Acts* [HTKNT] I, 426 n.48).

A. Sand

χρεοφειλέτης, ου, ὁ *chreopheiletēs* debtor*

Luke 7:41: δύο χρεοφειλέται, in contrast to δανειστής (cf. Prov 29:13); Luke 16:5: εἷς ἕκαστος τῶν χρεοφειλετῶν, both times in parables of persons owing money or commodities. On the form of the word (from χρέος and ὀφειλέτης) and its spelling see BDF §§35.2; 151.

χρή *chrē* it is necessary*

Jas 3:10, with acc. and inf.: οὐ χρή . . . ταῦτα οὕτως γίνεσθαι, "*this ought* not to be so" (χρή is not Hellenistic and occurs in the LXX only in Prov 25:27; 4 Macc 8:26 A; see BDF §358).

χρῄζω *chrēzō* have need of, require, need*

5 occurrences in the NT, all with gen. (cf. BDF §180.4): Matt 6:32 (χρῄζω τούτων ἁπάντων) par. Luke 12:30 (χρῄζω τούτων), of daily needs; cf. Luke 11:8: ὅσων χρῄζω; Rom 16:2, of *needing* someone for something; 2 Cor 3:1, of *needing* letters of recommendation.

χρῆμα, ατος, τό *chrēma* property, wealth, possessions; money*

This noun occurs 6 times in the NT. The pl. always refers to *wealth/(rich) possessions:* Mark 10:23 (cf. v. 24 v.l.), of those who have *riches*, i.e., wealthy people (οἱ τὰ χρήματα ἔχοντες; on this idiom cf. Xenophon *Mem.* i.2.45), who will find it difficult to enter the kingdom of God. Luke 18:24 inserts this saying (on its authenticity see Bultmann, *History* 105) into the preceding dialogue between Jesus and the rich synagogue ruler, has pres. εἰσπορεύονται, and makes it clear that complete renunciation of possessions is an absolute condition for following Jesus (cf. also 14:33; see L. Schottroff and W. Stegemann, *Jesus and the Hope of the Poor* [1986] 105-9; concerning criticism of trust in possessions and money cf. Sir 5:1, 8, and elsewhere).

Acts uses both sg. and pl. with the meaning *money.* Acts 4:37 is structured as a counterpoint to Luke 18:22ff. and illustrates the behavior of a true disciple: Barnabas sold a piece of property in order to put the *money* (sg. referring here to a definite sum of money; cf. Herodotus iii.38) at the apostles' disposal. According to 8:18 Simon Magus offered *money* (pl.) to the apostles Peter and John in an attempt to acquire the gift of bestowing the Holy

Spirit (→ Σίμων 10); in v. 20 χρήματα is used synonymously with → ἀργύριον (2) in Peter's apostolic curse of Simon. 24:26 uses χρήματα in characterizing the governor Felix as a corrupt official (cf. G. Schneider, *Acts* [HTKNT] II ad loc.) who hoped to get *money* (through bribery) from the imprisoned Paul (ὅτι χρήματα δοθήσεται αὐτῷ ὑπὸ τοῦ Παύλου). F. Selter, *DNTT* II, 845-47; B. Reicke, *TDNT* IX, 480.

χρηματίζω *chrēmatizō* give an injunction or warning, foretell, direct; bear a name, be called*

This vb. occurs 9 times in the NT, 7 times referring to injunctions or prophecies from God. Act. only in Heb 12:25: ἐπὶ γῆς . . . ὁ χρηματίζων, of God, who on Sinai *did* not yet *give* the ultimate *warning.* Pass. *receive a revelation from God, be directed,* in Matt 2:12: χρηματισθέντες κατ' ὄναρ, with inf.; 2:22: χρηματισθεὶς κατ' ὄναρ; Acts 10:22: ἐχρηματίσθη ὑπὸ ἀγγέλου ἁγίου, with inf.; Heb 8:5: καθὼς κεχρημάτισται Μωϋσῆς (cf. Josephus *Ant.* iii.212); 11:7: χρηματισθεὶς Νῶε περὶ τῶν μηδέπω βλεπομένων, here possibly also with the meaning *receive a prophecy,* which in any case lies behind Luke 2:26 (ἦν αὐτῷ κεχρηματισμένον ὑπὸ τοῦ πνεύματος τοῦ ἁγίου). The pass. does not occur in the LXX, which uses the vb. more in the sense of "speak, announce" (cf. Jer 32:30 LXX, referring to God; 33:2 LXX, referring to the prophet). The meaning *be called, be named* occurs in Acts 11:26 (χρηματίσαι . . . τοὺς μαθητὰς Χριστιανούς) and Rom 7:3 (μοιχαλὶς χρηματίσει). B. Reicke, *TDNT* IX, 480-82.

χρηματισμός, οῦ, ὁ *chrēmatismos* divine statement or direction*

Rom 11:4 (τί λέγει αὐτῷ [Elijah] ὁ χρηματισμός;), in reference to *God's reply* (1 Kgs 19:18) to the prophet's lament (1 Kgs 19:10, 14, taken up in Rom 11:3). On this meaning cf. 2 Macc 2:4 (χρηματισμοῦ γενηθέντος, "when a divine oracle had come"); *1 Clem.* 17:5 speaks of God's utterance to Moses from the burning bush. B. Reicke, *TDNT* IX, 482.

χρήσιμος, 3 *chrēsimos* useful, advantageous* ᛫

2 Tim 2:14: ἐπ' οὐδὲν χρήσιμον, "it [the dispute about words] serves no *useful purpose*" (v.l. εἰς οὐδέν).

χρῆσις, εως, ἡ *chrēsis* usage; relationship, association; sexual intercourse*

Rom 1:26, 27: "natural *relations/intercourse* (ἡ φυσικὴ χρῆσις)" between men and women (φυσικὴ χρῆσις τῆς θηλείας, v. 27), i.e., *sexual intercourse,* which the Gentiles in their godlessness have perverted into relations παρὰ φύσιν (v. 26), i.e., homosexual activity on the part

of both women and men (→ φυσικός; φύσις 2.a). Χρῆσις occurs in the sense of sexual intercourse also in Plato *Lg.* 841a; Plutarch *Moralia* 905b, and elsewhere, but not in the LXX.

χρηστεύομαι *chrēsteuomai* show kindness*

1 Cor 13:4: χρηστεύεται ἡ ἀγάπη, "love *shows goodness/kindness*" (Vg.: *benigna est*); cf. *1 Clem.* 13:2; 14:3 (χρηστευσώμεθα ἑαυτοῖς κατὰ τὴν εὐσπλαγχνίαν καὶ γλυκύτητα τοῦ ποιήσαντος ἡμᾶς); *Pss. Sol.* 9:6, referring to God's graciousness. The vb. is not attested in extrabiblical and non-Christian Greek. K. Weiss, *TDNT* IX, 491f.; Spicq, *Notes* II, 975f.; → χρηστότης.

χρηστολογία, ας, ἡ *chrēstologia* smooth speech, fine words*

Rom 16:18: διὰ τῆς χρηστολογίας καὶ εὐλογίας ἐξαπατῶσιν τὰς καρδίας τῶν ἀκάκων, of false teachers who deceive believers "with *sweet words* and flattery," since they serve their own belly rather than Christ and are bent on dissension (v. 17). Χρηστολογία in and of itself refers to the speech of a good person, though it is always used (esp. by Christian writers) in the negative sense of words not corresponding to action (cf., e.g., Origen *Frag. in Prov.* 5.3 [*PG* XVII, 157c]; see further Eustathius *Commentarii ad Iliadem* 1437.53); *christologus* (= χρηστόλογος) characterizes a person *qui bene loqueretur et male faceret* (*Scriptores Historiae Augustae* [ed. E. Hohl; 1927] I, *Pertinax* 13:5 [p. 125]). K. Weiss, *TDNT* IX, 492.

χρηστός, 3 *chrēstos* useful, good, kind, mild*

This adj. occurs 7 times in the NT. It sometimes has the basic meaning *useful/serving a certain purpose,* used of things, though also in the sense of *kind and helpful,* used of God and human beings (in the LXX it often renders *ṭôḇ,* referring to God in Pss 24:8; 105:1 LXX, and elsewhere). In Luke 5:39 it characterizes old wine, which—in contrast to new wine—is χρηστός, i.e., *pleasant-tasting, pleasant* (v.l. χρηστότερος); this saying evokes a familar proverb (cf. Sir 9:10; *b Ber.* 51a, and elsewhere; see H. Seesemann, *TDNT* V, 163). The Savior's call in Matt 11:30 speaks of Jesus' *gentle/mild* yoke (ὁ γὰρ ζυγός μου χρηστός, with φορτίον . . . ἐλαφρόν; on the "yoke" of wisdom cf. Sir 6:24, 29f.; 51:23ff., 26): Just as wisdom does not force upon a person the heavy yoke of the conqueror, but rather invites him into an intimate bond which is actually a form of joy and adornment, so also does Jesus. A connection with the OT statements about God's goodness is improbable.

In 1 Cor 15:33 Paul uses χρηστός of "morals (ἤθη)" in the sense of *honorable, good;* in so doing he employs a Greek proverb preserved as a fragment from a comedy of Menander, *Thais* (frag. 218; cf., e.g., also Philo *Det.* 38: ἤθη χρηστὰ διαφθείρεται; see further Spicq, *Notes* II, 973f.). In contrast, Rom 2:4 is concerned with God's *kindness* (τὸ χρηστὸν τοῦ θεοῦ; cf. χρηστότης αὐτοῦ in the same verse), his forbearance and patience, which open to mankind the possibility of conversion. Similarly in Luke 6:35 as a way of grounding Jesus' commandment to love one's enemy: ὁ ὕψιστος . . . χρηστός ἐστιν ἐπὶ τοὺς ἀχαρίστους καὶ πονηρούς (cf. Billerbeck I, 374ff.; Seneca *Ben.* iv.26.1); cf. also 1 Pet 2:3 (χρηστὸς ὁ κύριος, quoting Ps 33:9 LXX and referring to Christ). According to Eph 4:32 believers should treat one another with the same kindness and love (γίνεσθε εἰς ἀλλήλους χρηστοί, εὔσπλαγχνοι): As in Luke 6:35, God's kindness and forgiveness make corresponding behavior possible among believers. K. Weiss, *TDNT* IX, 483-89; Spicq, *Notes* II, 971-74; → χρηστότης.

χρηστότης, ητος, ἡ *chrēstotēs* goodness, uprightness, mildness, kindness*

1. Occurrences and meanings — 2. NT usage — a) Of God — b) Of Christians or people in general — 3. Theology of goodness — a) Paul — b) The deutero-Pauline Epistles

Lit.: E. BEYREUTHER, *DNTT* II, 105f. — I. HÖVER-JOHAG, *TDOT* V, 296-317, esp. 317. — M. A. SIOTIS, "La χρηστότης de Dieu selon l'Apôtre Paul," *Paul de Tarse* (ed. L. De Lorenzi; 1979) 201-32. — C. SPICQ, *Agape in the NT* (1963-66) III, 215-23. — L. R. STACHOWIAK, *Chrestotes. Ihre biblisch-theologische Entwicklung und Eigenart* (1957). — idem, *SacVb* 321-28. — K. WEISS, *TDNT* IX, 483-92. — For further bibliography see *TWNT* X, 1292.

1. This noun occurs 10 times in the NT, all in the Pauline and deutero-Pauline letters. As an abstract noun from → χρηστός, the verbal adj. based on χράομαι (= "make use of"), it originally referred to usefulness or effectiveness, then in an ethical sense to excellence and honesty, whereby the term "managed to combine the idea of moral perfection and sublimity with that of friendliness and loving kindness" (Stachowiak, *SacVb* 323).

In the LXX χρηστότης is one of the words used to translate Heb. *ṭôḇ* and its derivatives and acquires the nuances of meaning accompanying this term for *goodness* in the various passages. Except in Pss 13:1, 3; 52:4, where the noun is used of human uprightness and piety, and Esth 8:12c, where the reference is to the generosity of a ruler, χρηστότης in the LXX is used only of God and designates his kind and merciful disposition or actions (including the resulting gifts of fortune and redemption); in this sense it is often elucidated (or replaced) by words such as → χάρις, → ἔλεος (Heb. *hen* or *ḥeseḏ*), → δικαιοσύνη (Heb. *ṣᵉdāqâ* /*ṣedeq*), and others (cf., e.g., Pss 24:7; 83:12; 84:11ff.; 118:64f.; 144:7 LXX).

In the NT, too, χρηστότης refers to *goodness* (the

character trait or virtue manifesting itself in a kind disposition and behavior toward others) in its various nuances (*uprightness, mildness, kindness, graciousness,* etc.). The more specific meaning emerges (as in the LXX) from the various contexts, esp. from accompanying synonyms, parallel expressions, and contrasting terms.

2. a) The noun is used of God in Rom 2:4; 11:32 (ter); Eph 2:7; Titus 3:4 (cf. also Rom 9:23 v.l.). Rom 2:4 speaks of God's "riches of kindness" (πλοῦτος τῆς χρηστότητος; cf. 9:23; Eph 3:16: πλοῦτος τῆς δόξης; Eph 1:7; 2:7: πλοῦτος τῆς χάριτος). What χρηστότης (or the synonym used in the following clause: τὸ χρηστόν) refers to is specified more closely by the → ἀνοχή ("forbearance, consideration") and → μακροθυμία ("patience") and by the contrasting term → ὀργή ("wrath") in vv. 5 and 8. Accordingly, χρηστότης refers here to that particular *generosity* "in which God holds back (ἀνοχή) his wrath provoked by sin, so as with patience to give the sinner time to repent" (U. Wilckens, *Rom* [EKKNT] I, 124f.).

Χρηστότης occurs 3 times in Rom 11:22, the first 2 in contrast with → ἀποτομία ("severity"). "Kindness and severity" are "the two standards of divine righteousness" (O. Michel, *Rom* [KEK] 277) that constitute an inseparable unity. This juxtaposition is not accidental, but is rather "the expression of a certain theological schema also familiar in rabbinic thought and Hellenistic theology" (Michel 278; for rabbinic examples see Billerbeck III, 292; cf. also H. Köster, *TDNT* VIII, 106-8). Significantly, in this particular passage χρηστότης refers not only to God's considerate *generosity in judgment* (over against the chastising severity of a judge), but is virtually a substitute for χάρις, and is referring to his *merciful actions* in the larger sense. This is clearly thought of as a dynamic process: In addition to the salvation already effected in Christ himself (and received by human beings in faith), it also includes the enduring attestation of this redemption in a person's life by that person's "continuing in kindness" (ἐπιμένειν τῇ χρηστότητι = "standing in faith," v. 20; cf. Acts 14:22).

Eph 2:7 directly associates χρηστότης with God's χάρις. Ἐν χρηστότητι can be understood causally, i.e., as one of the "motivating causes" affecting the divine χάρις (so J. Gnilka, *Eph* [HTKNT] 120), or (probably more appropriately) in a modal sense, indicating the concrete "way" in which χάρις as God's *redemptive action* consummates itself in Jesus Christ (cf. H. Schlier, *Eph* [1963] 112; idem, *Rom* [HTKNT] 335 n.17).

In Titus 3:4 χρηστότες forms a conceptual pair with → φιλανθρωπία ("kindness toward human beings"; in the NT only here of God), thus describing (under two different aspects?) the *salvation* (appearing in Christ) of God the Savior (→ σωτήρ 3), his χάρις manifesting itself as σωτηρία (cf. the parallel statement in 2:11: grace "having appeared").

b) In Rom 3:12 (Ps 13:3 LXX) χρηστότης refers to human beings in general and allows the original sense of (ethical-religious) "usefulness" to resonate. As the parallel expressions δίκαιος ("righteous"), συνίων ("understanding"), and ἐκζητῶν τὸν θεόν ("seeking God") in vv. 10f. show, χρηστότης here refers to *uprightness* and *piety* (as a human character trait manifesting itself in corresponding action [ποιῶν!], the lack of which makes a person "useless," "unfit" [before God]; cf. v. 12a: πάντες . . . ἠχρεώθησαν, "all . . . have become useless").

In the other occurrences χρηστότης refers to a virtue or demeanor specifically characterizing Christians. In 2 Cor 6:6 it is in a small catalog of virtues, which itself is part of an extensive catalog of sufferings (6:3-10), i.e., a list of apostolic "qualities" (cf. R. Bultmann, *2 Cor* [Eng. tr., 1985] 167-75; J. Zmijewski, *Der Stil der paulinischen "Narrenrede"* [1978] 231, 310-14). In the list of virtues χρηστότης appears with μακροθυμία ("forbearance") after ἁγνότης ("purity") and γνῶσις ("knowledge"). The last two terms refer to a Christian's (or apostle's) "more fundamental existential character traits," and the first two refer to "those behavioral traits that manifest themselves more externally" (Zmijewski 312). Therefore, in accord with the setting in a catalog of sufferings, μακροθυμία might refer concretely to "the mastering of one's easily provoked anger" (H. Windisch, *2 Cor* [KEK] 206) against one's adversary, and (almost synonymous) χρηστότης to *kindness* that seeks to win over that adversary (in the positive sense). All four virtues are grounded "in the Holy Spirit" or "in genuine love [effected by the Spirit]" (v. 6b).

In Gal 5:22 χρηστότης also appears in a catalog of virtues (5:22b-23a). Its significance is underscored here by its placement precisely in the middle of the nine virtues (which are designated as "fruit of the Spirit," v. 22a) between μακροθυμία and ἀγαθωσύνη. This characterizes *kindness* as the Christian virtue that emerges from ἀγαθωσύνη ("the idea of essential goodness," Stachowiak, *SacVb* 322) and manifests itself essentially as μακροθυμία ("forbearance").

In the five-member catalog of virtues in Col 3:12 χρηστότης appears after σπλάγχνα οἰκτιρμοῦ ("heartfelt compassion") and before ταπεινοφροσύνη ("humility"), πραΰτης ("meekness"), and μακροθυμία ("forbearance"). This sequence might be explained as follows: "Heartfelt compassion" refers to what for Christian behavior is the decisive, fundamental disposition: The view of antiquity was that the σπλάγχνα were the seat of emotions and feelings (cf. H. Köster, *TDNT* VII, 548-59; J. Gnilka, *Col* [HTKNT] 194). The four terms that follow refer, then, to the resulting external behavior. Χρηστότης stands at the center, perhaps because it is considered the most impor-

tant, a characteristic that also (at least in part) encompasses the others. One must concede "a certain lack of delineation" here (Gnilka 195), since the meanings of the individual terms can hardly be distinguished.

3. a) Although Paul's statements about the χρηστότης of God or of human beings/Christians still strongly reflect the OT conception of goodness, in the final analysis they can really only be understood against the background of his own particular salvation-historical and christological conceptions. In Rom 2:4 Paul asks, "Do you think scornfully of the riches of his *kindness*, forbearance, and patience and not know that God's goodness [τὸ χρηστὸν τοῦ θεοῦ] is meant to lead you to repentance?" He asks this of the Jew who counts on finding forbearance in God even if he sins (cf. Wis 15:1-3 and elsewhere) and means to cut off "such refuge in God's kindness for the salvation-historically privileged person" (Wilckens, *Rom* I, 124) by presenting such confidence as a "misunderstanding" of this kindness, the only goal of which, after all, is repentance (→ μετάνοια 9.a). Paul apparently wants both to warn this Jew and to accuse him of having fallen prey to "a basic sin against goodness" (Stachowiak, *SacVb* 326), a blinded "misunderstanding" of its divinely willed goal, of not taking advantage of the time for repentance that God has granted in the time of the ἀνοχή (i.e., according to Rom 3:26, the time before Christ's atoning death); such a person has, rather, remained in his sins. The statement in Ps 13:3 (LXX) applies to this person: "No one does good, not even one" (Rom 3:12): The Jews, too, are guilty, and thus in need of redemption; all the worse that they "have met God's eschatological offer of salvation in Christ with hard and impenitent hearts," instead of completing "the decisive eschatological turning in faith to Christ" (K. Kertelge, *Rom* [NTSR] 32)—this, above all else, is probably what is meant by μετάνοια as the goal of God's goodness. The result is, as Paul warns, that the Jew "is storing up wrath" that will come upon him in its full force "on the day of wrath" (2:5).

In the metaphor of the cultivated and wild olive trees (11:17-24) the apostle makes clear that this consequence is already manifesting itself in Israel's (temporary) rejection and the election of the Gentiles. Here he exhorts the Gentile Christian: "Note then God's *kindness* and severity: severity toward those who have fallen, but God's *kindness* to you, provided that you continue in his *kindness*. Otherwise you also will be cut off" (v. 22). The intention here is not only to remind Gentile Christians that God's severity to the people of Israel, manifesting itself in rejection of them, is for him, the former pagan, a manifestation of God's goodness; God has, after all, taken him "into his χάρις and let him partake of the 'root' of the cultivated olive tree—the patriarchs and their blessing of the promise" (Schlier, *Rom* 335); Paul also wants to warn Gentile Christians that they, too, will meet the same fate as the fallen Jew: Because of "pride" (v. 20b) they, too, will be "cut off" if they do not "continue in this kindness," i.e., stand fast in faith (cf. v. 20a). An essential part of "standing in faith" is integration of this received kindness into one's life and action and manifestation of it in one's own kindness, which (like the other virtues) is part of the "fruit of the πνεῦμα" (Gal 5:22), of "the new vital principle, brought about by the Holy Spirit" (Stachowiak, *SacVb* 327). The apostle of Christ is called in a special way to this kind of goodness brought about by the Spirit (2 Cor 6:6); it proves itself for him particularly in the situation of suffering (cf. the catalog of sufferings in 6:3-10).

b) The authors of the deutero-Pauline Epistles (Ephesians, Colossians, and Titus) continue with slightly different accentuation the apostle's basic salvation-historical and christological premise. For them, too, the Christ-event is the decisive proof of God's kindness and Christ himself virtually its personification. Thus Titus 3:4, referring to Christ's incarnation, speaks of the "epiphany" of "the *goodness* and loving kindness of God our Savior." Thus also Eph 2:7 points out that "in Christ Jesus" God has sent us "the immeasurable riches of his grace in [the form of] *kindness* toward us." This focuses on the concrete appropriation of the Christ-event through baptism. (Titus 3:5 describes baptism as the "washing of regeneration and renewal in the Holy Spirit" effected for our deliverance according to God's mercy. Eph 2:4ff. describes baptism as "rising again and ruling with Christ in the heavenly world" [Weiss 491] on the basis of the love of the God who is "rich in mercy.") In this appropriation is grounded the new and still hidden manner of Christian existence that will reveal itself fully only in the future (cf. Eph 2:7; Col 3:1-4). This new manner of existence both enables the Christian to carry out a new morality and obligates the Christian to do so (cf. esp. Titus 3:1-8 in context): It manifests itself in "good works" (Eph 2:10; cf. Titus 3:8), in the fact that Christians, "as God's chosen ones, holy and beloved, put on compassion, *kindness*, humility, meekness, and patience" (Col 3:12), thus living in accord with the Kyrios himself (v. 13: καθὼς καὶ ὁ κύριος . . . οὕτως καὶ ὑμεῖς) and carrying forth "the way that God acts toward his people" that has become incarnate in the Kyrios (E. Schweizer, *Col* [Eng. tr., 1982] 206).

J. Zmijewski

χρῖσμα, ατος, τό *chrisma* oil for anointing; anointing*

In the NT this noun occurs only in 1 John 2:20, 27 (bis) and refers to (the *anointing oil* or) the *anointing* that the Church has received through Christ (χρῖσμα ἔχετε ἀπὸ τοῦ ἁγίου, v. 20), which abides in them (τὸ χρῖσμα . . . μένει ἐν ὑμῖν, v. 27a) and teaches them about everything (τὸ αὐτοῦ χρῖσμα διδάσκει ὑμᾶς περὶ πάντων, v. 27b; cf. οἴδατε πάντες, v. 20). Χρῖσμα means "oil for anointing, unguent" (so in the LXX: ἔλαιον χρῖσμα, "anointing oil," Exod 30:25 bis) and also the action of *anointing* (so in the LXX: ἔλαιον τοῦ χρίσματος, Exod 29:7; 35:15, and elsewhere).

In 1 John 2:20, 27 the χρῖσμα is probably the gift of Christ's Spirit to the Church (cf. John 14:17, 26; 15:26f.; 1 John 3:24; 4:6, 13). That the author speaks of χρῖσμα instead of πνεῦμα is probably explained by the polemical intention of 1 John 2:18ff. (cf. πνεῦμα in the corresponding section, 4:1ff.). The adversaries (2:18: ἀντίχριστοι πολλοί; cf. v. 22) might have referred to their own unique χρῖσμα (so that they are viewed together with the eschatological Antichrist?), which qualified them as authoritative teachers (this claim countered: v. 20: οἴδατε πάντες; v. 26: πλανῶντες ὑμᾶς; v. 27: οὐ χρείαν ἔχετε ἵνα τις διδάσκῃ ὑμᾶς . . . τὸ . . . χρῖσμα διδάσκει ὑμᾶς . . . καθὼς ἐδίδαξεν ὑμᾶς); they probably emphasized their own special reception of the Spirit, as did the Gnostics later. The author responds by emphasizing that only those have received true *anointing* who hold fast to what has been given them, namely, the correct confession of Jesus as the Christ (and who hold fast to life in the Church according to his commandment [vv. 3-8, 21, 24f.]).

Neither in 1 John's congregation itself nor among the adversaries does this necessarily presuppose a specific act of anointing, as was common later in baptism and the laying on of hands (cf. *Acts Thom.* 27). We are prevented from following 2 Cor 1:21f. and referring χρῖσμα only to the act of baptism both by the situation itself (the adversaries are also baptized: 1 John 2:19: ἐξ ἡμῶν ἐξῆλθαν) and by the fig. usage of → χρίω (3) in reference to the reception of the Spirit in 2 Cor 1:21.

So χρῖσμα is best rendered with *anointing* in 1 John, since it refers not to the Spirit in and for itself (the adversaries are, after all, claiming this for themselves), but only to the Spirit already received and active in and on behalf of the Church. I. de la Potterie, *Bib* 40 (1959) 12-69; W. Grundmann, *TDNT* IX, 572; commentaries on 1–3 John by R. Schnackenburg (HTKNT), K. Wengst (ÖTK), G. Strecker (KEK, 1989, pp. 125-28), and R. E. Brown (AB, pp. 341-48).

H. Balz

Χριστιανός, οῦ, ὁ *Christianos* Christian*

1. Occurrences and meaning — 2. Acts — 3. 1 Peter 4:16

Lit.: E. J. Bickermann, "The Name of Christians," *HTR* 42 (1949) 109-24. — BDF §24. — H. J. Cadbury, "Names for Christians and Christianity in Acts," *Beginnings* V, 375-92, esp. 383-86. — W. Grundmann, *TDNT* IX, 536f., 576. — R. A. Lipsius, *Über den Ursprung und den ältesten Gebrauch des*

Christennamens (1873). — H. B. MATTINGLY, "The Origin of the Name Christiani," JTS 9 (1958) 26-37. — O. MONTEVECCHI, "Nomen christianum," Paradoxos politeia (FS G. Lazzati; 1979) 485-500. — J. MOREAU, "Le nom des Chrétiens," Nouvelle Clio I/2 (1949/50) 190-92. — E. PETERSON, "Christianus," Miscellanea G. Mercati (Studi e Testi 121, 1946) I, 355-72. — J. D. SEARLE, "Christian—Noun, or Adjective?" ExpTim 87 (1975/76) 307f. — C. SPICQ, "Ce que signifie le titre de chrétien," ST 15 (1961) 68-78. — P. ZINGG, Das Wachsen der Kirche (1974) 217-22.

1. Χριστιανός occurs as a subst. 3 times in the NT: Acts 11:26; 26:28; 1 Pet 4:16. It occurs esp. frequently in the writings of Ignatius (Eph. 11:2; Magn. 4; Rom. 3:2; Pol. 7:3). In Trall. 6:1 Ignatius uses Χριστιανός as an adj. In the NT ℵ* attests the form Χρηστιανός, which models itself on the name Χρηστός (BDF); cf. also Tacitus Ann. 44.2 (Chrestiani). Pliny the Younger Epistulae x.96 (passim) attests the form Christiani. The name Χριστιανός is derived from Χριστός and formed like, e.g., Ἡρῳδιανός. It is translated Christian person or, better, simply Christian.

2. Acts 11:26 takes for granted that Χριστιανοί is a familiar designation for those who believe in Christ and indicates the situation in which the term originated: in Antioch when Barnabas and Paul were active there and the Hellenists had begun their mission to the Greeks (vv. 20f., 23-26a). The designation was probably applied to the Christians by outsiders (cf. Suetonius Nero 16.2; Lucian Alex. 25.38; Peregr. 11-13, 16) when, not least as a result of this missionary activity to the Greeks, they began to separate themselves from the synagogue congregations and acquire an identity as a separate group. Ignatius's letters (→ 1) confirm the origin of the name in Antioch. The name itself presupposes that confession of Christ constituted the characteristic feature of Jesus' adherents. Acts 26:28 attributes to King Agrippa II the following response to Paul: "You are almost persuading me to present myself as a Christian!" Here the name is spoken explicitly by an outsider.

3. 1 Pet 4:16 not only uses the name Christian from the perspective of Christians themselves, but also uses it parenetically in the context of persecution: Christians share Christ's own suffering (v. 13); they are reproached "for the name of Christ" (v. 14). Thus if someone suffers "as a Christian (ὡς Χριστιανός), let him not be ashamed; rather let him glorify God under that name" (v. 16). The formulation ὡς Χριστιανός presupposes "that Christians are familiar to the public as representatives of their own questionable religion; in the region between Rome and Asia Minor addressed by our letter that was the case only after Nero's police action in the year 64" (L. Goppelt, 1 Pet [KEK] 309).   G. Schneider

Χριστός, οῦ, (ὁ)   Christos   Christ
χριστός, οῦ, ὁ   christos   anointed one

1. General considerations — a) Derivation — b) Title or name? — c) Occurrences in the NT — 2. The prehistory of NT usage — a) Anointing and messianic hopes in the OT — b) Early Judaism — 3. Presuppositions in the story of Jesus — 4. Synoptic Gospels and Acts — a) Mark — b) Matthew — c) Luke-Acts — 5. Paul and the deutero-Pauline letters — a) Paul — b) 2 Thessalonians and Colossians, Ephesians and the Pastorals — 6. John and 1–2 John — 7. Other NT usage — a) Hebrews — b) 1 Peter — c) James, Jude, and 2 Peter — d) Revelation — 8) Tradition-historical considerations

Lit.: General: O. EISSFELDT and J. KOLLWITZ, RAC II, 1250-62. — W. GRUNDMANN, F. HESSE, M. DE JONGE, and A. S. VAN DER WOUDE, TDNT IX, 493-580. — K. H. RENGSTORF, DNTT II, 334-43. — A. S. VAN DER WOUDE, BHH 1197-1204.

OT: J. BECKER, Messianic Expectation in the OT (1980). — J. COPPENS, Le messianisme royal (1968). — idem, Le messianisme et sa relève prophétique (1974). — H. C. KEE, "Messiah and the People of God," Understanding the Word (FS B. W. Anderson, 1985) 341-58. — J. KLAUSNER, The Messianic Idea in Israel (1956). — E. KUTSCH, Salbung als Rechtsakt im AT und im alten Orient (1963) — T. N. D. METTINGER, King and Messiah (1976). — S. MOWINCKEL, He That Cometh (1956). — É. LIPINSKI, "Études sur les textes 'messianiques' de l'AT," Semitica 20 (1970) 41-57. — J. A. SOGGIN, THAT I, 908-20.

Early Judaism: J. A. FITZMYER, "Further Light on Melchizedek from Qumran Cave 11," JBL 86 (1967) 25-41 (= idem, Essays on the Semitic Background of the NT [SBLSBS 5, 1974] 245-67). — R. R. HANN, "Christos Kyrios in PsSol 17,32: 'The Lord's Anointed' Reconsidered," NTS 31 (1985) 620-27. — H. HEGERMANN, Jesaja 53 in Hexapla, Targum und Peschitta (1954). — M. HENGEL, The Zealots (1989) 290-312. — M. DE JONGE, "The Use of the Word 'Anointed' in the Time of Jesus," NovT 8 (1966) 132-48. — M. DE JONGE and A. S. VAN DER WOUDE, "11Q Melchizedek and the NT," NTS 12 (1965/66) 301-26. — K. G. KUHN, Achtzehngebet und Vaterunser und der Reim (1950). — idem, "Die beiden Messias Aarons und Israels," NTS 1 (1954/55) 168-79. — M. RESE, "Überprüfung einiger Thesen von Joachim Jeremias zum Thema des Gottesknechtes im Judentum," ZTK 60 (1963) 21-41. — P. SCHÄFER, Der Bar-Kokhba-Aufstand (1981) 51-77. — K.-D. SCHUNCK, "Die Attribute des eschatologischen Messias," TLZ 111 (1986) 641-52. — SCHÜRER, History II, 488-554. — S. TALMON, "Typen der Messiaserwartung um die Zeitenwende," idem, Gesammelte Aufsätze (1988) I, 209-24. — A. S. VAN DER WOUDE, Die Messianischen Vorstellungen der Gemeinde von Qumrân (1957).

NT: K BERGER, "Zum traditionsgeschichtlichen Hintergrund christologischer Hoheitstitel," NTS 17 (1970/71) 391-425. — idem, "Die königlichen Messiastraditionen des NT," NTS 20 (1973/74) 1-44. — idem, "Zum Problem der Messianität Jesu," ZTK 71 (1974) 1-30. — M. BOUTTIER, En Christ (1962). — L. CERFAUX, Christ in the Theology of St. Paul (1959) 480-508. — O. CULLMANN, Christology of the NT (1959) 111-37. — N. A. DAHL, "The Crucified Messiah," idem, Jesus the Christ (1991) 27-47 (= idem, The Crucified Messiah and Other Essays [1974] 10-36, 167-69). — idem, "The Messiahship of Jesus in Paul,"

Jesus the Christ 15-25 (= *The Crucified Messiah* 37-47, 170-72).
— M. Dömer, *Das Heil Gottes* (1978) 43-93. — G. Friedrich,
"Beobachtungen zur messianischen Hohepriestererwartung in
den Synoptikern," *ZTK* 53 (1956) 265-311. — R. H. Fuller,
The Foundations of NT Christology (1965), *passim*. —E. Gütt-
gemanns, "Χριστός in 1. Kor. 15,3b—Titel oder Eigenname?"
EvT 28 (1968) 533-54 (cf. *EvT* 29 [1969] 222f., 657f.). — Hahn,
Titles 136-239. — M. Hengel, *Between Jesus and Paul* (1983)
65-78, 179-88. — J. Jeremias, "Artikelloses Χριστός," *ZNW* 57
(1966) 211-15. — D. L. Jones, "The Title Christos in Luke-
Acts," *CBQ* 32 (1970) 69-76. — M. de Jonge, "The Use of O
ΧΡΙΣΤΟΣ in the Passion Narratives," *Jésus aux origines de la
christologie* (ed. J. Dupont; 1975) 169-92. — K. H. Kim, *Die
Bezeichnung Jesu als (O) ΧΡΙΣΤΟΣ. Ihre Herkunft und
ursprüngliche Bedeutung* (Diss. Marburg, 1981). — W. Kra-
mer, *Christ, Lord, Son of God* (1966) 19-64, 133-50, 203-14. —
E. Lohse, "Der Christus der Juden und der Messias der
Christen," *idem, Die Vielfalt des NT* (1982) 57-69. — R. N.
Longenecker, *The Christology of Early Jewish Christianity*
(1970) 63-82. — C. F. D. Moule, *The Origin of Christology*
(1977) 31-89. — S. Sabugal, *ΧΡΙΣΤΟΣ—Investigación ex-
egética sobre la cristologia joannea* (1972). — *idem*, "El titulo
Χριστός en el Apocalypsis," *Augustinianum* 12 (1972) 319-40.
— W. C. van Unnik, "Jesus the Christ," *NTS* 8 (1961/62) 101-
16. — G. Vermes, *Jesus the Jew* (1973) 129-59. — P. Vielhauer, "Erwägungen zur Christologie des Markus," *idem,
Aufsätze zum NT* (1965) 199-214.

For further bibliography see *DNTT* II, 346-48; *TWNT* X,
1292f. For frequency of occurrences with or without Ἰησοῦς,
see the chart in vol. II, p. 181.

1. a) Χριστός is a verbal adj. derived from → χρίω.
The vb. itself means "rub in," "spread liquid over (something)," and "anoint" (→ χρῖσμα, "anointing oil, anointing"), and accordingly the verbal adj. means either
"capable of being spread upon" or "besmeared" =
"anointed" (τὸ χριστόν = "unguent, salve"). Outside the
LXX and NT and writings dependent on them χριστός is
never applied to persons. In contrast, the NT uses it as a
tr. of μεσσίας exclusively in reference to persons, either
to the unknown but anticipated messianic figure or to
Jesus of Nazareth as the Messiah who has come. →
Χριστιανός, Χριστιανισμός (Ign. *Rom.* 3:3, and elsewhere), and → ψευδόχριστος are derived from this usage.

b) The question whether Χριστός in the NT is a title
or a name needs to be specified more closely. On the
basis of the word's OT and Jewish history it is first of all
a designation of function. The legitimate appropriation
of a commissioned task is associated with the motif or
act of anointing (even where the anointing ritual recedes
or is only fig.). The word refers to a predication applicable
to a figure from Israel's own history or from the eschaton.
The predication also makes an assertion concerning majesty. This is esp. the case where it is used of a concrete
person within the context of confessional statements with
σὺ εἶ or οὗτός ἐστιν. Here the predication acquires titular
character, esp. where (ὁ) Χριστός represents or replaces
the proper name, as occurred with ὁ υἱὸς τοῦ ἀνθρώπου.

Where Χριστός is used with Ἰησοῦς, it is not simply a
proper name, but rather an epithet (*cognomen);* the predicative character does recede, but the titular meaning is
preserved in its entirety, even when other statements of
a titular character are added. Hence nowhere is a simple
double name presupposed.

c) Χριστός occurs 531 times in the NT (in all the NT
writings except 3 John), including 7 times in Mark, 16
in Matthew, 12 in Luke, 19 in John, and 26 in Acts (with
8:37); the Pauline corpus (without Hebrews) has altogether 383 occurrences; Hebrew then adds 12 to this, the
Catholic Epistles 49, and Revelation 7 (cf. *VKGNT* II,
300f.).

2. a) OT: From the vb. *māšaḥ*, "anoint" (usually qal, rarely
niphal) are derived the partc. *māšûaḥ*, "anointed," and the noun
māšîaḥ, "anointed one" (usually construct state *mᵉšîaḥ yhwh* or
with a suffix; Ps 105:15 attests a pl. form with a suffix). Neither
noncultic use nor anointing of cultic objects is important for our
purposes; only the anointing of persons is.

1) The anointing of the king (32 occurrences, e.g., 1 Sam
9:16; 10:1; 16:3, 12f.; 1 Kgs 1:34f., 39) indicates legal installation, authority, and inviolability (cf. 1 Sam 24:7, 11; 26:9-11,
23; 2 Sam 1:14, 16), and in isolated instances also the bestowal
of the Spirit (1 Sam 10:6, 9-13; 16:13). The designation of a
king as *mᵉšîaḥ yhwh* (e.g., 1 Sam 12:3, 5; 2 Sam 19:22; 23:1;
Pss 18:51; 132:17) indicates his divinely grounded legitimacy
in accord with special election and promise for his descendants
(2 Sam 7:8-16). Apart from Saul, David, and the Davidic kings,
references to the anointing of kings occur only rarely (Jehu in
2 Kgs 9:3, 6, 12; Hazael in 1 Kgs 19:15; cf. the fable of Jotham
in Judg 9:7-15; in Isa 45:1 the Persian king Cyrus is "Yahweh's
anointed").

2) Reference to the anointing of the high priest occurs only
in the Priestly writing and in 1 Chr 29:22; Sir 45:15. The high
priest is called *hakkōhēn hammāšîaḥ* (probably attibutive; Lev
4:3, 5, 16; 6:15; in all probability the *māšîaḥ* in Dan 9:25f. is
also a high priest). It is disputed whether this anointing constitutes an independent ritual of purification and consecration
(Kutsch), or whether in the post-exilic period what were
formerly royal traditions were transferred to the high priest
(Hesse). The general anointing of priests presupposed in the
additions to the Priestly writing is secondary (e.g., Exod 40:15;
Num 3:3).

3) Only rarely is any reference made to anointing of prophets
(1 Kgs 19:16; Isa 61:1). Here, too, the focus is on legitimacy,
though esp. on bestowal of the Spirit (cf. 2 Kgs 2:9, 15f.; Isa
61:1a; cf. "my anointed one" in the reference to the patriarchs
as "prophets" in Ps 105:15).

4) *Māšaḥ* and *māšîaḥ* are not used in the OT to refer to
messianic expectation. Of decisive influence in that expectation
are Nathan's promise in 2 Sam 7:8-16 and hope of renewal of
the monarchy under a Davidic descendant. This is understood
as an event in history, as Isa 8:23–9:6 shows, even if an element
of heightening is evident. Motifs are taken from traditional kingship ideology (Pss 2:1-12; 89:2-5, 20-38; 110:1-4; 132:10-18),
and in Isaiah 11:1-5, 6-9 (10) also from the paradise traditions.
Judgment discourse combines with the promise of a completely
new beginning in the house of David (Isa 11:1; Mic 5:1-3; Jer
22:24-30; 30:8f.; Ezek 17:22-24; 34:23f.; Amos 9:11-15 [a later

addition]). Although messianic hope is not constitutive for the prophetic tradition, it is attested more or less continuously both before and during the Exile. After the return, however, it was vigorously revived: Cf. the expectations focused on the Davidic figure Zerubbabel (Hag 2:20-23), joined by the second messianic figure, the high priest Joshua (Zech 4:1-6a, 10b-14; cf. 3:1-10; 4:6b-10a). This hope takes on a special form where the Messiah, as the king who is himself poor and humble, ushers in the age of peace for the nations (9:9f.). Texts that focus on a renewal of the office or the dynasty apparently expected the death of the person currently occupying the office; Zech 12:10 (within 12:4–13:1) and Dan 9:24-26 both speak of violent death (in contrast, Isa 52:13–53:12 comes from a different tradition and originally had nothing to do with messianic thinking). So messianic thinking is always a matter of future expectation, though not of actual eschatological hope.

b) Apart from noneschatological conceptions and a consistently theocratic eschatology, early Judaism exhibits various forms of messianic thought. "Messiah" is now used to refer to the anticipated figure of the time of salvation; although attestations are few (usually in gen. constructions), a clear image does emerge. It is disputed to what extent absolute *hammāšîaḥ* and *māšîaḥ* without the art. can be documented (Jeremias, Güttgemanns). *Māšîaḥ* without the art. could function as a predication and possibly also refer to an anticipated person (like ὁ υἱὸς τοῦ ἀνθρώπου), and could also be used as a (sur-)name while preserving its titular character. Apparently, however, this only occurred in the Christian tradition.

1) The tradition of kingship also lived on in the post-OT period without association with eschatological expectation (1 Maccabees, Sirach); high-priestly office and royal dignity were combined in the Hasmoneans. Whereas Jonathan received the position of a vassal king in addition to the office of high priest (1 Macc 10:19-21, 62), his brother and successor Simon was recognized by the Jews themselves as "high priest, commander, and prince of the Jews" (13:42; 14:41, 47). The "praise of the fathers" (Sirach 50) shows the enormous significance attributed to this hereditary office of the high-priestly king. Already in the Maccabean period there was also an element of eschatological expectation (Daniel), and messianic hope remained alive. Different lines of tradition can be discerned: purely royal conception, expectation of two messianic figures, and a connection with the apocalyptic tradition.

2) The *Psalms of Solomon*, from the Pharisaic tradition of the 1st cent. B.C., constitute one witness to royal messianic expectation (chs. 17 and 18); they speak explicitly of the χριστὸς κυρίου or αὐτοῦ (17:32; 18:1, 5, 7). The same conception appears in the messianic petition of the Eighteen Benedictions, the oldest version of which might go back to the pre-Christian period (cf. Kuhn). Finally, this messianic understanding appears in the Targum on the Prophets, which, although a late literary piece, nonetheless preserves older traditions. This focuses variously on the Davidic figure who institutes a kingdom of peace, faithfulness to the law, and righteousness; under his rule the dispersed return, order is restored in the land, and the Gentiles come to worship. Independent of the tradition of Davidic sonship, this messianic thought also plays a role among the Zealots and in Bar Cochba (cf. Hengel, Schäfer).

3) The idea of dual messiahship, going back to Zechariah 4, appears in the hardly ascertainable original stratum of *T. 12 Patr.*

(*T. Levi* 17–18; *T. Jud.* 24) and above all in the Qumran writings. In addition to an eschatological prophet (in accordance with Deut. 18:18f.) presumably identified with the "teacher of righteousness," two messianic figures from Jacob and Levi are anticipated (in accordance with Num 24:15-17; Deut 33:8-11: 4QTestim 5–10; cf. 4QFlor 1:13a). The preeminence of the high-priestly Messiah (cf. esp. 1QSa 2:11-16) is connected here with the priestly-Zadokite tradition and is unique to the Qumran community. Even in the final struggle this messianic high priest has a decisive function (1QM 2:1; 15:4; 16:13; 18:5; 19:11). The two are called "anointed ones of (or from) Aaron and Israel" (cf. 1QS 9:11; CD 20:1); the royal Messiah is also called "the prince of the congregation" (1QSb 5:20; CD 7:20, and elsewhere) and the "branch of David" (4QBless 3-4 and elsewhere). The two messiahs are earthly figures, represent the true priesthood and kingship, and exhibit no superhuman characteristics.

4) Apocalyptic thought does not anticipate an earthly realization of salvation, but rather the end of the present aeon and the inbreaking of an other-worldly aeon. To the extent that a specific figure is anticipated in view of the eschaton, it is the "Son of man" (Dan 7:13f.; metaphorical language in *1 Enoch;* 2 Esdras 13; → υἱός 5). Occasionally messianic expectation is associated with this title. The identification of the "Messiah" with the "Son of man" (*1 Enoch* 48:10; 52:4) is less noteworthy than the idea that the messianic age precedes the coming aeon; *2 Baruch* presupposes a temporally limited function for the Messiah (30:1; 40:4; cf. also 74:2f.), and 2 Esdras emphasizes this with a reference to the Messiah's death (7:26-35; also 12:32, 34b, cf. 13:2ff.). This is related to the idea of the thousand-year reign (cf. Rev 20:1-6; → χίλιοι). Such an understanding of the messianic age as an interim period is also attested in the talmudic tradition and the midrashes (van der Woude, *TDNT* IX, 524-27).

5) The Messiah is a man and an earthly ruler, and immortality is not presupposed; accordingly, his death is expected. Although Tryphon admits in the dialogue with Justin that the Messiah's suffering is in accord with Scripture, he rejects Jesus' death on the cross on the basis of Deut 21:23 as contrary to the law (89:2; cf. 36:1; 39:7; 90:1). Because of the experiences of the Bar Cochba insurrection, the idea arose in the 2nd cent. of the initially concealed and later dying Messiah Ben Joseph. Nowhere, however, does the Messiah's death acquire redemptive significance. The idea of the suffering and dying Messiah is also independent of Isaiah 53 (the designation "servant of God" does not occur consistently in one context in deutero-Isaiah). Apparently it was in the Christian tradition that Isaiah 53 was first interpreted messianically; there is no evidence for pre-Christian Jewish texts attesting a messianic interpretation of this text; although the targumic tradition does interpret texts messianically, it reinterprets all statements of suffering into statements of exaltation (cf. Hegermann, Rese).

6) According to 2 Sam 7:14, Ps 2:7, and Isa 9:5f. the king is adopted as the "Son of God" at his enthronement. Documentation for the divine sonship of the Messiah in early Judaism is sparse, though it is clearly attested at least by 4QFlor 1:10-13. The question remains open whether there was also any independent titular application (→ υἱός 3.a). Within the framework of royal messianic thought this motif hardly carried any weight.

7) 11QMelch 18 unequivocally shows that the idea of prophetic anointing remained alive in connection with the tradition of Isa 61:2. There the messenger of joy of Isa 52:7 is spoken of

as *māšîaḥ* (cf. *mᵉšîḥîm*, CD 2:12; 6:1; 1QM 11:7). The v.l. *mᵉšîaḥ hārûaḥ* (de Jonge and van der Woude), though not secured, is probable on the basis of Isa 61:1.

3. a) Historical-critical examination does not enable us to determine from the Gospel texts the extent to which those who inquired about Jesus' function and dignity (Mark 8:28 par.) viewed him as the promised Messiah. Nor do we know whether Judas Iscariot harbored messianic hopes, did not see them fulfilled in Jesus, and for that reason handed him over.

b) Peter's confession of Jesus as Messiah in Caesarea Philippi plays an important role in later Church tradition (Mark 8:29 par.). Although Jesus accepts the confession as the narrative stands, the important connection to the saying about the suffering Son of man who will rise again (vv. 30f. par.) is secondary. The rebuke of Peter (vv. 32f. par.) might originally have referred to the messianic confession itself in view of its political implications. The result was that the early Church was initially reserved in its use of the messianic title.

c) No evidence of Zealotism can be documented in Jesus' demeanor or ministry, and this is shown positively in the statements of the Sermon on the Mount concerning nonviolence. This also holds true for Jesus' response to the question concerning the imperial tax (Mark 12:13-17 par.), the saying about taking by violence (Matt 11:12 par.), and the two sword sayings (Matt 10:34; Luke 22:36-38). Jesus' entry into Jerusalem (Mark 11:1-10 par.) cannot be taken as something like what the Zealots envisioned, nor can the temple cleansing (11:15-17 par.), which was not motivated by revolutionary-political considerations, but represents rather an eschatological act in the fashion of a parable pointing to the end of the earthly temple in view of the inbreaking kingdom of God. With its portrayal of Jesus' third temptation (Matt 4:8-10 par.) the later Church characterized clearly its own attitude toward any aspirations of the Zealots.

d) Particular significance was attributed to the fact that Jesus was crucified as an alleged Zealot and "King of the Jews" (Mark 15:26 par.). The early Church viewed this as a divinely willed event. Here the question arises again concerning a connection between messianic expectation and the death of the Messiah. The various versions of the interrogation before Pilate show that the originally political charge against Jesus was quickly understood in a salvation-historical sense.

e) The statements that "here is something greater than Jonah" and "here is something greater than Solomon" (Luke 11:31c, 32c par.), presumably going back to Jesus himself, reveal a self-understanding transcending that of prophet and teacher of wisdom. But it is doubtful that this necessarily evokes the idea of messiahship. If despite Jesus' clearly anti-Zealot attitude one nonetheless posits a messianic self-understanding on Jesus' part, then one would have to show how he transformed OT and Jewish messianic thinking. Such a process of transformation is clearly discernible in the post-Easter community, but whether this can be presupposed for Jesus is vehemently disputed. It is much more likely that Jesus himself did not apply to himself any of the traditional categories concerning such a figure of the time of salvation; otherwise the post-Easter tradition would attest a much more unified picture. The Church's struggle to determine appropriate predications shows that the Church had only indirect points of departure. And one should certainly reject the suggestion that pre-Christian Judaism already exhibited such corresponding modifications, which Jesus then merely had to apply to himself.

4. a) Among the 7 (8) occurrences in Mark, 8:29 and 14:61 occupy a central position. In these texts we begin to see that the Evangelist saw the two traditions of Jesus as "Son of God" and "Son of man" included in the designation ὁ χριστός (cf. 8:27–9:8; 14:61f.; → υἱός 3.c, 4). Also, 15:32 is of significance because here the secular term ὁ βασιλεὺς τῶν Ἰουδαίων, which occurs several times in 15:1-20, 26, is taken up with ὁ χριστός and the OT and Jewish expression βασιλεὺς Ἰσραήλ. Conscious use of Χριστός as a predication of majesty also occurs in 9:41 (and 1:34 v.l.), where it appears without the art. and its identity with the person of Jesus is presupposed, so that the titular character emerges even more clearly. Ἰησοῦς Χριστός occurs only in 1:1, where it is expanded by υἱὸς θεοῦ (this reading is to be preferred), without its titular function being sacrificed. The eschatological warning in 13:21 uses ὁ χριστός as a functional designation in the Jewish sense (v. 22 speaks of ψευδόχριστοι and ψευδοπροφῆται). 12:35 intends essentially the same thing when it inquires generally concerning the Messiah's Davidic sonship; this question does, of course, refer to Jesus' own person and directs itself to Ps 110:1 and Jesus' designation as κύριος.

b) Usage of χριστός in the 18 occurrences in Matthew is closely related to that of Mark, which is partially a result of the parallel tradition. In 16:16 (par. Mark 8:29) Matthew complements ὁ χριστός with the predication of divine sonship, but then in the commandment to silence in 16:20 explicitly inserts ὁ χριστός. 26:63 (par. Mark 14:61) is similarly picked up again in 26:68 with voc. χριστέ. The predicative character of ὁ χριστός is underscored by the Matthean expression Ἰησοῦς ὁ λεγόμενος Χριστός (not in the sense of "so-called," but rather "who is called": 1:16; 27:17, 22). Titular ὁ Χριστός replaces the name Jesus in 1:17; 2:4; 11:2; 23:8, 10. Although simple Χριστός does not occur, Ἰησοῦς Χριστός appears in 1:1, 18; 16:21 (v.l.). The query concerning Davidic sonship in 22:42 and the eschatological warning in

24:23(f.) exhibits essentially the same meaning as in Mark, except that in 24:5 Matthew has complemented the warning with ἐγώ εἰμι ὁ χριστός (Mark 13:6: ἐγώ εἰμι). It is clear that in Matthew the messianic traditions of the OT are to be taken up and applied to Jesus, which implies the rejection of all other messianic claimants. Jesus' messianic dignity is already emphatically portrayed in the infant stories, and further in connection with Peter's confession and in Jesus' condemnation. In this context 11:2 is noteworthy, since it refers to Jesus' miraculous deeds as τὰ ἔργα τοῦ Χριστοῦ, something not occurring in the traditional OT Jewish idea of the Messiah, but coming rather from a different stratum of tradition, which is combined here with the idea of Jesus' messiahship.

c) Luke and Acts offer a different picture. First, the author picks up the vb. χρίω in connection with the promise in Isa 61:1f. (Luke 4:18; Acts 4:27; 10:38). This is unmistakably related to the baptism story and to the well-developed Lukan Spirit christology. Then, however, we come on two typical OT formulations absent in the other Gospels: ὁ χριστός τοῦ θεοῦ in Peter's confession (Luke 9:20; cf. Mark 8:29; Luke 23:35) and ὁ χριστός κυρίου (Luke 2:26); to be sure, parallel use of χριστός and κύριος also occurs, on the basis of double use of κύριος (Luke 2:11; Acts 2:36; 4:26; cf. 11:17; 15:11, 26; 16:31; 20:21; 28:31). Another new element over against Mark and Matthew is use of ὁ χριστός in connection with Jesus' death and resurrection (Luke 24:26, 46; Acts 3:18; 17:3a; 26:23) and his resurrection and exaltation (Acts 2:30-36). Acts also attests the expression ἐν ὀνόματι Ἰησοῦ Χριστοῦ several times (cf. Mark 9:41 with 9:37-39 and Luke 9:49; Mark 13:6, 13 par. Luke 21:8, 17) in the contexts of baptism (Acts 2:38; 10:48) and miracles (3:6; 4:10; cf. 16:18). Finally, we encounter the unique expression ὁ προκεχειρισμένος ὑμῖν χριστός Ἰησοῦς in a statement concerning the parousia (3:19-21).

Otherwise use of χριστός follows what one already finds in Mark and Matthew. This is true of the query concerning Davidic sonship in Luke 20:41, the Passion narrative, and also the alterations and additions in 22:67-69; 23:2, 39 (cf. v. 35). As does 22:67-69, both Luke 4:41 and Acts 9:20 emphatically relate ὁ χριστός and ὁ υἱὸς τοῦ θεοῦ. In Acts the expression εὐαγγελίζομαι or κηρύσσω τὸν Χριστὸν (Ἰησοῦν) (5:42; 8:5; 9:20) is also noteworthy, as is the assertion that Paul convinced people that Jesus was the Christ (9:22; 17:3b; 18:5, 28). Except in text-critically disputed passages the expression Ἰησοῦς Χριστός is strikingly rare (Acts 9:34; 10:36; 15:26; 24:24).

An independent concept thus emerges. Without drawing on other christological traditions Luke has consciously taken up and broadly developed the concept of the Messiah within the framework of his own christology. The predicative and titular character emerges unmis-

takably, which also indicates that at the end of the 1st cent. Χριστός had by no means become merely a second proper name, but on the contrary had fully maintained its implications (the statement about John the Baptist in Luke 3:15 also shows this).

5. a) 1) The *ca.* 271 occurrences of Χριστός and Ἰησοῦς Χριστός (Χριστός Ἰησοῦς) in the seven undisputed Pauline letters show well-developed usage with an astonishing consistency and with no elements of fixed or formulaic inertness. Although this usage is in many respects characteristic of Paul himself, a general early Christian model lies behind it. Three groups can be discerned, which overlap to a certain extent: Ἰησοῦς Χριστός with κύριος or ὁ κύριος ἡμῶν, Ἰησοῦς Χριστός, and Χριστός or ὁ Χριστός (because of the frequent variant readings one can often give only approximate numbers; → vol. II, p. 181).

2) The first group discloses a relatively self-enclosed picture. Κύριος Ἰησοῦς Χριστός (*ca.* 14 occurrences) clearly shows its origin in the confessional tradition (1 Cor 8:6; Phil 2:11, also 3:20) and in the liturgical tradition (Rom 1:7; 1 Cor 1:3; 2 Cor 1:2; 13:13; Gal 1:3; Phil 1:2; 4:23; 1 Thess 1:1; Phlm 3:25; also Rom 13:14). Ὁ κύριος ἡμῶν Ἰησοῦς Χριστός (*ca.* 27 occurrences) also shows evidence of fixed language, as does its frequent use in expressions with διά (Rom 5:1; 7:25, and elsewhere), ἐν (Rom 6:23; 8:39; 1 Cor 15:31), or with ὄνομα (1 Cor 1:2, 10; 6:11). On the connection with liturgical tradition cf. also Rom 15:6; 2 Cor 1:3. Among gen. expressions (with ἡμέρα, ἀποκάλυψις, ἐλπίς, παρουσία) use of χάρις is striking (2 Cor 8:9; Gal 6:18; 1 Thess 5:28). When in Gal 6:14 Paul speaks of the σταυρὸς τοῦ κυρίου ἡμῶν Ἰησοῦ Χριστοῦ he is employing a new construction modeled on this usage (cf. v. 12).

3) Among the occurrences of the second group, those with Ἰησοῦς Χριστός or Χριστός Ἰησοῦς, certain combinations of words are noticeable. In the introductions to letters Paul speaks of himself as ἀπόστολος, δοῦλος, or δέσμιος Ἰησοῦ Χριστοῦ (Rom 1:1; 1 Cor 1:1; 2 Cor 1:1; Phil 1:1; Phlm 1, 9). He also speaks several times of πίστις Ἰησοῦ Χριστοῦ or εἰς Χριστὸν Ἰησοῦν (Rom 3:22; Gal 2:16a, b; 3:22). In isolated instances he also uses combinations with ἡμέρα (Phil 1:6), ἀποκάλυψις (Gal 1:12), λειτουργός (Rom 15:16), πνεῦμα (Phil 1:19), further also βαπτίζειν εἰς Χριστὸν Ἰησοῦν (Rom 6:3, cf. v.l.). Prepositional phrases with διά (*ca.* 6 occurrences) and ἐν (*ca.* 28) are significant. 10 (or 11) central christological statements show that use of Ἰησοῦς Χριστός is not just formulaic (Rom 5:15, 17 [8:34 v.l.]; 1 Cor 2:2; 3:11; 2 Cor 1:19; 4:5; 13:5; Gal 3:1; 4:14; Phil 2:21).

4) The most varied picture emerges in the third group, occurrences of either ὁ Χριστός or Χριστός without the art. Here there are numerous fixed combinations such as

εὐαγγέλιον τοῦ Χριστοῦ (9 occurrences and several times as v.l. in place of absolute usage), ἐκκλησία τοῦ Χριστοῦ (Rom 16:16; cf. Gal 1:22), σῶμα (τοῦ) Χριστοῦ (Rom 7:4; 1 Cor 10:16; 12:12, 27; cf. μέλη Χριστοῦ in 6:15), ἀγάπη τοῦ Χριστοῦ (Rom 8:35; 2 Cor 5:14), πίστις Χριστοῦ (Gal 2:16; Phil 3:9), and σταυρὸς τοῦ Χριστοῦ (1 Cor 1:17; Gal 6:12; Phil 3:18). Other gen. combinations are with νόμος (Gal 6:2; cf. ἔννομος Χριστοῦ, 1 Cor 9:21), βῆμα (2 Cor 5:10), ἡμέρα (Phil 1:10; 2:16), ὑπηρέτης or δοῦλος (1 Cor 4:1; 7:22), ῥῆμα (Rom 10:17), μαρτύριον (1 Cor 1:6), δύναμις (2 Cor 12:9), αἷμα (1 Cor 10:16), χάρις (Gal 1:6), πνεῦμα (Rom 8:9), and others. Prepositional phrases playing an important role are διὰ (τοῦ) Χριστοῦ (2 Cor 1:5; 3:4; 5:18), ὑπὲρ Χριστοῦ (2 Cor 5:20a, b; 12:10; Phil 1:29), σὺν Χριστῷ (Rom 6:8; Phil 1:23; cf. Rom 6:3f.; 8:17; Gal 2:19; 1 Thess 5:9f.), διὰ Χριστόν (1 Cor 4:10; Phil 3:7), εἰς τὸν Χριστόν (Rom 16:5; 2 Cor 1:21; 11:3; Gal 3:24; Phlm 6; βαπτίζειν εἰς Χριστόν in Gal 3:27), and particularly ἐν Χριστῷ (ca. 25 occurrences). To these we may then add the numerous occurrences of simple Χριστός (ca. 47) or emphatic ὁ Χριστός (ca. 17) and the additional occurrences of Χριστὸς Ἰησοῦς (ca. 10).

5) An evaluation of the significance for Paul of these different expressions must begin with independent use of Χριστός, ὁ Χριστός, and Ἰησοῦς Χριστός. Here we immediately notice that Jesus' death and resurrection are central, both in references to death and resurrection (1 Cor 15:3-5; Rom 6:3f.; 8:34; 14:9) and in statements just about Jesus' death (Rom 5:6, 8; 14:15; 15:3; 1 Cor 8:11; Gal 2:19, 21; cf. Rom 5:15, 17; 1 Cor 5:7), his crucifixion (1 Cor 1:23; 2:2; Gal 3:1, 13), or his resurrection (Rom 6:9; 8:11; 10:7; 1 Cor 15:12-17, 20, 23). We may then add explicit statements about Jesus' exaltation (Rom 8:34; 10:6), preexistence (1 Cor 10:4; 11:3a, b), and earthly existence (Rom 9:5; 2 Cor 5:16). The context of these statements about death, resurrection, and exaltation also includes all texts concerning the σῶμα Χριστοῦ and Χριστός ἐν ὑμῖν, etc. (1 Cor 1:13; 12:12; Rom 8:10; 1 Cor 3:23a; 2 Cor 10:7a, b; 13:5; Gal 2:20; 3:29; 4:19; 5:24) and statements about the proclamation of Christ (Rom 15:18, 20; 1 Cor 1:17, 23; 15:12; 2 Cor 1:19; 4:5; Gal 4:14; Phil 1:15, 17, 18). Statements about "putting on" and "imitating" Christ come from baptismal and parenetic traditions (Gal 3:27; Rom 13:14; 1 Cor 11:1; cf. Rom 15:7; 1 Cor 10:9; 2 Cor 11:2; Phil 2:21). To this are added christological statements of a more fundamental nature (Rom 10:4; 1 Cor 1:24; 3:11, 23; Gal 2:17; 3:16; 5:1; Phil 1:20) and a few special expressions (Rom 9:3; Gal 5:2, 4; 1 Cor 1:12f.; Phil 1:21; 3:8, 12).

As a rule Paul uses simple Χριστός, which as a title also replaces the name; in some passages Paul uses it with the art. (Rom 9:3, 5; 15:3, 7; 1 Cor 1:13; 10:4, 9; 11:3; 12:12; 2 Cor 11:2; Gal 5:24; Phil 1:15, 17). Special attention should be given to statements about the apos-

tle's own representative activity (cf. esp. ὑπὲρ Χριστοῦ, 2 Cor 5:20) and about the reality of the σῶμα Χριστοῦ transcending both space and time (1 Cor 12:12-27; cf. Rom 12:5), which in many (though not all) instances includes the ecclesiological ἐν Χριστῷ or ἐν Χριστῷ Ἰησοῦ as an abbreviated expression for ἐν (τῷ) σώματι (τοῦ) Χριστοῦ (e.g., 2 Cor 5:17; Gal 3:28). The title is understood from the perspective of the salvation event itself, the center of which is Jesus' death, resurrection, and exaltation.

b) 1) Among the deutero-Pauline letters, 2 Thessalonians exhibits fixed usage. Apart from formulaic expressions with κύριος Ἰησοῦς Χριστός (4 occurrences) and ὁ κύριος ἡμῶν Ἰησοῦς Χριστός (5 occurrences), we encounter only the gen. construction ὑπομονὴ τοῦ Χριστοῦ (3:5; cf. the v.l. in 2:2).

2) Colossians and Ephesians offer a different picture. Here Pauline usage is consciously and to a certain extent independently continued. We see fixed expressions with κύριος Ἰησοῦς Χριστός (Col 2:6; Eph 1:2; 6:23) and ὁ κύριος ἡμῶν Ἰησοῦς Χριστός (Col 1:3; Eph 1:3, 17; 3:11; 5:20; 6:24), the designation ἀπόστολος Ἰησοῦ Χριστοῦ (Col 1:1; Eph 1:1), and numerous gen. constructions with Χριστός or ὁ Χριστός—with διάκονος, δοῦλος, and δέσμιος (Col 1:7; 4:12; Eph 3:1; 6:6), πλοῦτος, ἀγάπη, and φόβος (Eph 3:8, 19; 5:21), εἰρήνη (Col 3:15; cf. Eph 2:14), δωρεά (Eph 4:7), λόγος (Col 3:16), quite emphatically αἷμα (Eph 2:13), σῶμα (Col 2:17; Eph 4:12, cf. 1:20-23), πλήρωμα (Eph 4:13), and μυστήριον (Col 4:3; Eph 3:4). To these are added in Colossians ὑστερήματα τῶν θλίψεων τοῦ Χριστοῦ and περιτομὴ τοῦ Χριστοῦ (1:24; 2:11) and in Ephesians βασιλεία τοῦ Χριστοῦ καὶ θεοῦ (5:5).

The significance of usage of Χριστός becomes even more clear when one considers independent statements with (ὁ) Χριστός. Colossians refers to the central mystery of salvation as Χριστὸς ἐν ὑμῖν (1:27). Χριστός, who sits at God's right hand (3:1b), is "our life" (3:4). Of those who have died and been raised again with him in baptism (2:20; 3:1a) it is said: ἡ ζωὴ ὑμῶν κέκρυπται σὺν τῷ Χριστῷ ἐν τῷ θεῷ (3:3); about the Church itself it is said: πάντα καὶ ἐν πᾶσιν Χριστός (v. 11).

The occurrences in Ephesians are even more striking. In accord with the fundamental assertion that the μυστήριον τοῦ Χριστοῦ consists in the unity of Jews and Greeks, the focus is on the function of Χριστός in bringing about salvation and peace (2:12f., 14-18), the κατοικῆσαι τὸν Χριστόν in one's heart (3:17), and living with Christ (2:5; cf. 2:6). "Christ loved us and gave himself up for us" (5:2), and wants to give us light (v. 14). In relation to the σῶμα/Church (Eph 4:12; cf. Col 1:18) Christ is the κεφαλή (Eph 4:15, cf. 1:20-23), an idea developed in connection with the parenesis for husbands and wives (5:23f., 29; cf. also 2:8; 4:20; 6:5). Because of these ecclesiological themes, ἐν Χριστῷ (5 occur-

rences) and ἐν Χριστῷ Ἰησοῦ (7 occurrences) play an
important role. The one use of independent Χριστός
Ἰησοῦς (2:20) is also noteworthy.

We see everywhere in these letters that Χριστός is
used in the titular sense. This is underscored in Ephesians
by the frequent use of the art. before Χριστός.

3) Among the 32 occurrences in the Pastorals, only
1 Tim 5:11 uses simple Χριστός (cf. v.l. in 1 Tim 2:7;
2 Tim 2:19). All others use Χριστός Ἰησοῦς or Ἰησοῦς
Χριστός. Among these are fixed gen. constructions with
ἀπόστολος (1 Tim 1:1; 2 Tim 1:1; Titus 1:1), διάκονος
(1 Tim 4:6), and στρατιώτης (2 Tim 2:3). Πίστις, ἀγάπη,
χάρις, σωτηρία, and ζωή are modified by ἡ ἐν Χριστῷ
Ἰησοῦ (1 Tim 1:14; 3:13; 2 Tim 1:2, 13; 2:1, 10; 3:15);
in accordance with this is εὐσεβῶς ζῆν ἐν Χριστῷ Ἰησοῦ
(2 Tim 3:12) and διαμαρτύρομαι ἐνώπιον τοῦ θεοῦ καὶ
Χριστοῦ Ἰησοῦ (1 Tim 5:21; 2 Tim 4:1; cf. 1 Tim 6:13).
Reference is made to both God and Christ Jesus in the
expression κατ' ἐπιταγὴν θεοῦ . . . καὶ Χριστοῦ Ἰησοῦ
(1 Tim 1:1) and in all probability also in ἐπιφάνεια τῆς
δόξης τοῦ μεγάλου θεοῦ καὶ σωτῆρος ἡμῶν Ἰησοῦ Χριστοῦ
(Titus 2:13). As elsewhere in the NT, the expression
Χριστὸς Ἰησοῦς ὁ κύριος ἡμῶν occurs (1 Tim 1:2, 12;
6:3, 14; 2 Tim 1:2); this is altered to Χριστὸς Ἰησοῦς ὁ
σωτὴρ ἡμῶν in Titus 1:4.

The Pastorals are noteworthy only where they cite the
kerygmatic tradition (1 Tim 1:15; 2:5f.; 6:13[-16]; 2 Tim
1:9f.; 2:8; 4:1; Titus 2:[11f.]13f.; 3:[4f.]6f.). Here the
expression is consistently Χριστὸς Ἰησοῦς accompanied
by a characteristic soteriological statement. This preference for placing Χριστός in the first position in the Pastorals shows that the titular character of the term is clearly
perceived and maintained (cf. also 1 Tim 1:16).

6. a) Although the idea of messiahship does not occupy a central position in Johannine christology, John
does refer to Jesus 19 times as Χριστός, and in all these
instances the predicative-titular character of the term
comes clearly to expression. John the Baptist insists that
he is not the Messiah (1:20, 25; 3:28). Reference is made
to OT expectation and its fulfillment (1:41; 4:25f., 29
[4:42 v.l.]; 7:26, 41a). John 1:41 and 4:25 use the transliteration of the Hebrew word, Μεσσίας, and translate it
for Greek readers. Questions of Jewish messianic hope
are also expressly discussed: the Messiah's origin (7:27,
41b, 42 [cf. also 4:25]), whether he performs miracles
(7:31; cf. Matt 11:2), and whether he remains forever
(12:34). In addition to predicative statements with οὗτός
ἐστιν ὁ Χριστός (4:29; 7:26, 41a) there are also statements
with εἰ σὺ/σὺ εἶ ὁ Χριστός (10:24; 11:27; cf. 6:69 v.l.),
and esp. the expression ὁμολογεῖν Χριστόν (9:22), which
alludes unmistakably to titular use and use in confessional
statements. This is also seen in the Gospel's conclusion
in 20:31: . . . ἵνα πιστεύσητε ὅτι Ἰησοῦς ἐστιν ὁ Χριστὸς

ὁ υἱὸς τοῦ θεοῦ. Use of Ἰησοῦς Χριστός, in contrast, is
rare, and is limited to the two traditional statements in
1:17 and 17:3.

b) In 1 John and 2 John we have 8 and 4 occurrences
of χριστός respectively, with esp. frequent use of Ἰησοῦς
Χριστός. There is no need to ascertain the reason for this.
As in John 9:22, 1 John 2:22 and 5:1 attest the confessional statements ὁ ἀρνούμενος ὅτι Ἰησοῦς οὐκ ἔστιν
ὁ Χριστός and ὁ πιστεύων ὅτι Ἰησοῦς ἐστιν ὁ Χριστός
(parallel to ὁμολογέω or πιστεύω ὅτι Ἰησοῦς ἐστιν ὁ υἱὸς
τοῦ θεοῦ in 1 John 4:15; 5:5). In accord with this, 2 John
9a, b speaks of the διδαχὴ τοῦ Χριστοῦ.

Use of Ἰησοῦς Χριστός harks back to confessional
statements; Jesus' messiahship as such is not the issue,
but rather its understanding. This is the case in 1 John
4:2 and 2 John 7: the issue is ὁμολογεῖν Ἰησοῦν Χριστὸν
ἐν σαρκὶ ἐληλυθότα/ἐρχόμενον ἐν σαρκί; accordingly,
1 John 5:6 uses Ἰησοῦς Χριστός. The other occurrences
of "Jesus Christ" are combined with further predications,
such as Son of God (1 John 1:3; 3:23; 5:20; 2 John 3) or
δίκαιος and παράκλητος (1 John 2:1).

c) A close relationship between messiahship and
divine sonship is characteristic of Johannine theology.
Although this is stated programmatically in John 11:27
and 20:31, it is also made quite clear in other passages.
In the Gospel this is evoked among other ways by use of
βασιλεὺς τοῦ Ἰσραήλ/τῶν Ἰουδαίων with υἱὸς τοῦ θεοῦ
(John 1:49; 18:33-37a; 19:7). Any docetic christology is
to be rejected on the basis of the divine sonship. Here the
reference is to the work of the antichrist(s) (1 John 2:18,
22; 4:3; 2 John 7), who are heretics, not unbelievers (cf.
1 John 2:19). This messiahship is thus to be understood
neither as simple humanity nor as pure divinity. The
predication "Messiah" is consciously maintained, and its
use in confessional statements predominates. Therefore,
as in Luke-Acts, at the end of the 1st cent. the predicative
and titular character of Χριστός is still fully maintained
even though other christological ideas have come to the
forefront.

7. a) Ἰησοῦς Χριστός occurs 3 times in Hebrews, and
in each case the titular character is clearly discernible
(10:10; fixed expressions in 13:8, 21). This titular significance is in any case assured in use of ὁ Χριστός (6
occurrences: 3:14; 5:5; 6:1; 9:14, 28; 11:26) and Χριστός
(3 occurrences: 3:6; 9:11, 24). The author speaks of ὁ τῆς
ἀρχῆς τοῦ Χριστοῦ λόγος (6:1), describes believers as
μέτοχοι τοῦ Χριστοῦ (3:14), and in the typology of witnesses of faith refers to the ὀνειδισμοὶ τοῦ Χριστοῦ
(11:26). He associates Χριστός with Jesus' divine sonship
(3:6) and his high-priestly office (5:5; 9:11, 14, 24, 28).
Confession of Jesus as Son of God is of fundamental
significance for Hebrews (4:14; cf. 6:6). This is developed with the aid of the idea of Jesus as high priest, and

at the same time the idea of Jesus' messiahship is consciously taken up. 9:11-28 shows this clearly, speaking of αἷμα τοῦ Χριστοῦ (v. 14), Christ's once-for-all sacrifice (v. 28a), and his return (v. 28b). Here as in 11:26 it becomes clear that the messianic statements are associated above all with Jesus' death, from which they acquire their significance.

b) 1 Peter contains a whole series of fixed expressions. Ὁ κύριος ἡμῶν is used in the introductory blessing formula (1:3) and in expressions with Ἰησοῦς Χριστός — with ἀπόστολος (v. 1), ἀποκάλυψις (vv. 7, 13), ῥαντισμὸς αἵματος (v. 2), and ἀνάστασις (1:3; 3:21), and with διά (2:5; 4:11). Fixed expressions occur with Χριστός without the art. only in ἐν Χριστῷ (3:16; 5:10, cf. v.l.; 5:14b), πνεῦμα Χριστοῦ (1:11a), and ἐν ὀνόματι Χριστοῦ (4:14, cf. v. 16). The other 8 occurrences of χριστός exhibit specific usage; 7 refer to Jesus' suffering, always using expressions from the stem πασχ-/παθ-: ἔπαθεν (2:21; 3:18), παθών (4:1), παθήματα (1:11b; 4:13; 5:1); to this is added the image of Χριστός as the unblemished and spotless lamb (1:19; cf. 1:2). As in Hebrews, here a tradition is taken up that understands "Christ" as a title, esp. from the perspective of Jesus' death. 3:18 shows that we are dealing here with confessional tradition. Following the traditional confessional statement in 2:21, Isaiah 53 is taken up (2:22-25). Characteristic are the reference to the fictitious author as μάρτυς τῶν τοῦ Χριστοῦ παθημάτων (5:1) and the statement about believers: κοινωνεῖτε τοῖς τοῦ Χριστοῦ παθήμασιν (4:13). A reference to the blessing formula in the prescript is seen when the readers are exhorted: κύριον δὲ τὸν χριστὸν ἁγιάσατε ἐν ταῖς καρδίαις ὑμῶν (3:15).

c) The only two christological statements in James speak of κύριος (ἡμῶν) Ἰησοῦς Χριστός, without thereby acquiring special significance (1:1; 2:1). We encounter the same combination in Jude, where aside from the prescript, which has twice the dual designation Ἰησοῦς Χριστός, the expression ὁ κύριος ἡμῶν Ἰησοῦς Χριστός occurs (vv. 4, 17, 21, 25), once in connection with ἀρνέομαι (v. 4). Ὁ κύριος ἡμῶν Ἰησοῦς Χριστός recurs in 2 Peter (1:8, 14, 16), in some cases expanded to ὁ κύριος ἡμῶν καὶ σωτὴρ Ἰησοῦς Χριστός (1:11; 2:20; 3:18). The prescript speaks only of the σωτὴρ Ἰησοῦς Χριστός and of the author as δοῦλος καὶ ἀπόστολος Ἰησοῦ Χριστοῦ. Of decisive importance for 2 Peter is the ἐπίγνωσις τοῦ θεοῦ καὶ Ἰησοῦ Χριστοῦ τοῦ κυρίου ἡμῶν (1:2; cf. vv. 11, 14, 16). The relationship between messiahship and κυριότης is old, as the received version of the query concerning Davidic sonship shows (Mark 12:35-37a par.), and long maintained a specific conception, as we see from these three letters.

d) Revelation exhibits three different kinds of usage. Ἰησοῦς Χριστός occurs several times in the introductory chapter (1:1, 2, 5, also 1:9a, b; 22:21 v.l.). Within the

visions themselves the expression καὶ τοῦ Χριστοῦ αὐτοῦ (sc. θεοῦ) occurs twice in doxologies (11:15; 12:10). Finally, the section concerning the thousand-year reign twice uses absolute ὁ Χριστός (20:4 [at the end], 6b). Whereas ch. 1 attests the already fixed Christian word combination, the other four occurrences use a manner of expression dependent on Jewish tradition, though the identification with Jesus is taken for granted. What was originally a functional manner of expression thereby becomes titular. It is noteworthy that Ἰησοῦς Χριστός serves as a designation for the exalted one who has brought about redemption through death and resurrection (1:5f.), whereas absolute usage refers to the eschatological consummation. Here the function of dominion is esp. emphasized, something also expressed in the introduction with καὶ ἐποίησεν ἡμᾶς βασιλείαν (1:6), and certainly in the four occurrences of absolute usage.

8. a) As far as tradition-historical considerations are concerned, all NT texts with Χριστός are related to the OT and Jewish traditions. There is no secondary influence from secular Greek usage, which never applied χριστός to persons. But one must ask which OT-Jewish tradition (or traditions) were determinative for NT christology. Only Hebrews shows any dependence on high-priestly messianic thinking (contra Friedrich). Derivation from the idea of the anointed (messianic) prophet does not clarify the situation (contra Berger), even if this conception did exert some influence and numerous elements from the wisdom tradition were taken up. Neither can one proceed on the basis of any general "salvation function within a universal-existential horizon" (contra Kim). The point of departure in royal messianic thinking is determinative.

b) Jesus' life did not offer the immediate prerequisites for early Christian use of the messianic title. His execution as "king of the Jews," however, did prompt reflection that led to a profound modification. Early Christian usage itself exhibits no consistency. The messianic designation is totally absent from Q, and occurs only in isolated instances in the material from tradition used by the Gospels; only the Gospels themselves invested it with greater significance.

But it is clear that the designation secured itself very early in the confessional tradition. This is where one should seek the primary crystallization point for the title of majesty (Kramer, Kim). What is decisive is that the Χριστός died, which obviously is related to Jesus' condemnation. This confession was associated on the one hand with the soteriological interpretation of death as the suffering of atonement, and on the other with the reference to Jesus' resurrection. Further christological statements were associated with this: The living presence of the resurrected Jesus was understood with the help of Ps

110:1 as exaltation and installation in the heavenly office of king, and his parousia as the institution of royal dominion at the consummation of salvation, whereby Jewish traditions of royal messianic thought could be taken over relatively unaltered (cf. Revelation). To this was added the idea that in Jesus' entire history and person the OT promises of salvation were fulfilled. Although the extent to which this structure developed in clearly distinguishable phases is very difficult to ascertain, this development in any case probably came about in stages.

c) We do have access to traditions of early Hellenistic Jewish Christianity. It is disputed whether there was a similar tradition in the oldest form of Aramaic-speaking Christianity, and individual texts usually only admit conjectures. Word usage itself is more important: A combination of Χριστός as an epithet or as a substitute for the name Jesus is hard to imagine without an older preceding tradition showing predicative use. The beginnings thus probably lie in the earliest traditions of Palestinian Jewish Christianity (with Hengel, *contra* Kim). There the association of this predication with Jesus' person as the bringer of salvation was completed at an early stage. The definite form ὁ Χριστός, frequently used by Paul and up to the end of the 1st cent., was used alternately with Χριστός and alludes to the titular character of the epithet (cf. Dahl; differently Hengel).   F. Hahn

χρίω *chriō* anoint*

1. Occurrences and meaning — 2. LXX quotations and allusions in Luke-Acts — 3. 2 Cor 1:21 — 4. Heb 1:9

Lit.: BAGD s.v. — K. BERGER, "Zum traditionsgeschichtlichen Hintergrund christologischer Hoheitstitel," *NTS* 17 (1970/71) 391-425. — *idem,* "Die königlichen Messiastraditionen des NT," *NTS* 20 (1973/74) 1-44. — C. A. BOUWMAN, "De oorsprong van de rituele zalving der koningen," *Dancwerc* (FS D. T. Enklaar, 1959) 64-85. — E. DINKLER, "Die Taufterminologie in 2 Kor 1,21f," *idem, Signum Crucis* (1967) 99-117. — *idem,* "Die Taufaussagen des NT. Neu untersucht im Hinblick auf K. Barths Tauflehre," *Zu K. Barths Lehre von der Taufe* (ed. F. Viering; 1971) 60-153. — W. GRUNDMANN, F. HESSE, A. S. VAN DER WOUDE, and M. DE JONGE, *TDNT* IX, 493-580. — T. HOLTZ, *Untersuchungen über die alttestamentlichen Zitate bei Lukas* (TU 104, 1968). — A. HUG, PW I/2A, 1851-66. — E. KÄSEMANN, *The Wandering People of God* (1984). — E. KUTSCH, *Salbung als Rechtsakt im AT und im alten Orient* (BZAW 87, 1963). — E. KUTSCH, G. DELLING, and C. A. BOUMAN, *RGG* V, 1330-34. — E. LOHSE, "Taufe und Rechtfertigung bei Paulus," *idem, Die Einheit des NT* (1973) 228-44. — D. MÜLLER, *DNTT* I, 121-23. — A. ORBE, "La unción del Verbo," *AnGr* 113 (1961) 629-56. — I. DE LA POTTERIE, "L'onction du Christ," *NRT* 80 (1958) 225-52. — M. RESE, *Alttestamentliche Motive in der Christologie des Lukas* (SNT 1, 1969). — D. SÄNGER, *Antikes Judentum und die Mysterien* (WUNT II/5, 1980) 167-74. — E. SEGELBERG, *BHH* 1646f. — For further bibliography see *TWNT* X, 1292f.

1. The vb. occurs only 5 times in the NT, 3 of those in Luke-Acts (Luke 4:18; Acts 4:27; 10:38) and twice in the Epistles (2 Cor 1:21; Heb 1:9). In contrast to general usage in antiquity, which does not always distinguish between the often synonymous terms ἀλείφω and χρίω (cf. Dioscorides ii.76.13ff.; Pliny *HN* 10.55; 24.55; 37.204; see Grundmann 493f.; Hug 1851-57), χρίω is fig. in all NT occurrences.

This fig. usage is essentially anticipated by the OT. There, apart from Exod 30:32, Deut 28:40, and Ezek 16:9, the vb. is the LXX rendering of Heb. *māšaḥ*, "spread with fat, oil, or grease, fatten." In the ancient Near East (cf. Kutsch, *Salbung* 20-22, 27-52), anointing with oil was intended to serve healing (Isa 1:6), energizing and strengthening (2 Sam 12:20; Ruth 3:3; Mic 6:15; cf. *Life of Adam and Eve* 36, 40f.; Josephus *B.J.* ii.123; *Ant.* xvii.172), and increasing one's well-being (Ps 133:2; Prov 27:9; Eccl 9:8; cf. Isa 61:3; Amos 6:6). But anointing possessed above all a legal-sacral character.

This becomes esp. clear in the case of the anointing of the king in Israel, which after the anointing of the priests and high priest is the most frequently mentioned use of anointing. When the people or their representatives anointed one of their own as king (1 Sam 16:3, 12f.; 2 Sam 2:4, 7; 5:3, 17; 12:7; 1 Kgs 1:34, 39; 1 Chr 29:22; 2 Chr 23:11; Ps 89:21, and elsewhere), this constituted an act of empowerment. With this anointing the king received honor, power, and might. In addition to this we find other statements in which the subj. of the anointing is Yahweh or someone commissioned by him (1 Sam 9:16; 15:17; 2 Sam 12:7; 2 Kgs 9:3, 6; 2 Chr 22:7; Pss 2:2; 20:7; 84:10; Hab 3:13, and elsewhere). Through this act of anointing by or on behalf of Yahweh the king as the "anointed of Yahweh" (cf. only 1 Sam 24:7 LXX) was made directly subject to Yahweh and as a rule given a specific commission (1 Sam 9:16; 10:1 LXX). He became a quasi-vassal of Yahweh (Kutsch, *Salbung*), though also directly authorized in his office. It is questionable, however, whether this second form of anointing can claim any historicity and is not rather a theologoumenon expressing the king's close relationship with Yahweh. If this anointing of the king intends to emphasize his special legal-sacral status, then the anointing of objects (altar, tabernacle, ark, or even shields) is also to be understood as an act of desecularization (cf. Exod 29:36; 40:9f.; Num 7:1, 10; 2 Sam 1:21 [conjecture]; Isa 21:5).

Isa 61:1 posits a causal relationship between anointing and the bestowal and possession of the Spirit in the case of the prophet. It is doubtlessly intended in the fig. sense here (cf. → χρῖσμα).

2. In his inaugural sermon in Nazareth, Jesus refers Isa 61:1 LXX to himself: "The Spirit of the Lord is upon me, because he has *anointed* (ἔχρισεν) me to preach good news to the poor" (Luke 4:18a; cf. 4:21). Bestowal and possession of the Spirit are bound to anointing.

Whereas Isa 61:1 intends this in a nonliteral sense, Luke refers the reception of the Spirit concretely to Jesus' baptism (Luke 3:21f.; cf. 1:35). As the one on whom God's Spirit has been bestowed, Jesus is the → χριστός (4.c) (Luke 2:11, 26; 9:20; 20:41; 22:67; 23:2; 24:26, and elsewhere), and thereby also the eschatological prophet chosen and empowered by God in the OT sense, as esp. Luke 4:21 makes clear (πεπλήρωται). The quotation of Isa 61:1 LXX in Luke 4:18a thus has a dual function: It shows first how consciously the content of the OT idea of anointing is taken up in Luke and transferred to Jesus, and it also identifies and interprets the reception of the Spirit—and in Luke this means Jesus' messiahship—through baptism.

Even though Acts 4:27 and 10:38 do not refer in exact terms to Isa 61:1, this OT passage probably does provide their background. Not only does ἅγιος παῖς σου Ἰησοῦς in Acts 4:27 recall the image of the eschatological prophet (see Berger, "Messiastraditionen," esp. 13f.), what follows, "whom thou didst anoint (ὃν ἔχρισας)"—instead of the t.t. χριστός—also shows that in the sense of Isa 61:1 this reference is to an anointing through which Jesus is legitimized in his prophetic office. Acts 10:38a asserts that "God anointed (ἔχρισεν) Jesus of Nazareth with the Holy Spirit and with power." This statement is introduced as common knowledge (ὡς in v. 38 is dependent on οἴδατε in v. 37). Again Isa 61:1 with its association of Spirit and anointing probably provides the background here, with allusion also to Jesus' baptism (cf. v. 37b). There Jesus received the Spirit and thus was installed by God in his prophetic office in a way recognizable by all (οἴδατε).

3. In 2 Cor 1:21f. Paul cites fixed expressions from legal terminology to underscore the legally binding character of baptism: "God himself establishes us (βεβαιῶν) with you in Christ, has anointed us (χρίσας), has put his seal on us (σφραγισάμενος), and has given us (δούς) his Spirit in our hearts as a guarantee." In contrast to the other NT occurrences of the vb., in which Christ is always the anointed one, in 2 Cor 1:21 the obj. of anointing is Christians (ἡμεῖς), and the subj. is God.

The understanding of χρίω is determined by the grammatical resolution of vv. 21f. Either one brackets the first two participles in v. 21 together within ὁ δὲ . . . θεός and views them as being developed in v. 22 by the two following participles added with καὶ . . . καί (so Grundmann 555f.), or one takes the three aor. participles together, which then explicate βεβαιῶν (so, e.g., Dinkler, "Taufterminologie" 102f.). In spite of the problematic fact that reference is made to the gift of the Spirit only in association with the fourth vb., the first alternative is preferable, so that the partc. χρίσας—as in all previous instances of χρίω—refers to reception of the Spirit.

In baptism God has given us over to Christ (note εἰς Χριστὸν . . . χρίσας and cf. 1 Cor 12:13; Gal 3:26-28)

and thereby assured us of his Spirit, which is active within us. 2 Cor 1:21, like the passages in Luke-Acts, uses χρίω fig. Baptism "can be characterized as anointing, because it grants the Spirit" (R. Bultmann, 2 Cor [Eng. tr., 1985] 42).

4. Heb 1:9 cites Ps 45:8 LXX: "You [sc. Christ] have loved righteousness and hated lawlessness; therefore God, your God, has anointed (ἔχρισεν) you with the oil of gladness before your comrades" (cf. Heb 1:3c, d). Christ is addressed here at his heavenly enthronement, during which God elevates him to the status of ruler of all (cf. only 1:3f.). Not only the citation from Ps 45:8 LXX, but esp. the act of enthronement presupposed here makes it probable that Heb 1:9 must be understood against the background of the anointing of the king as encountered in the OT (→ 1).

D. Sänger

χρονίζω   chronizō   put off one's arrival, hesitate*

Lit.: E. GRÄSSER, Das Problem der Parusieverzögerung in den synoptischen Evangelien und in der Apostelgeschichte (BZNW 22, ²1960) 90-92, 119f. — W. MICHAELIS, Der Herr verzieht nicht die Verheißung (1942). — H. WEDER, Die Gleichnisse Jesu als Metaphern (FRLANT 120, ²1980) 239-49.

1. Χρονίζω appears in eschatological contexts in Matt 24:48 par. Luke 12:45; Matt 25:5; and Heb 10:37 and in a noneschatological context only in Luke 1:21. The vb. is derived from → χρόνος and means put off one's arrival (return), give oneself time, stay a long time, hesitate.

2. Whether the parables in Matt 24:45-51 par. Luke 12:42-46 and Matt 25:1-13 in their original forms were spoken by Jesus and whether the statements in them using χρονίζω are original are closely related questions. This discussion also touches on the central question concerning Jesus' understanding of time and continues unresolved even today. Nonetheless, we can probably assume with Grässer (91) and others that χρονίζει μου ὁ κύριος (Matt 24:48; similar in Luke 12:45) was from the very beginning an essential part of the parable; the same is true for χρονίζων in Matt 25:5 (Grässer 120). This, however, then allows both parables to be interpreted most naturally as Church formations, directives responding to the problem of the delay of the parousia (contra, e.g., Jeremias, Parables 51ff., according to whom in the original parable Jesus was issuing a "warning in view of the imminent eschatological crisis" [53]). Weder is typical of exegesis that rejects the "category of near expectation" in Jesus' proclamation; he attempts to maintain Matt 25:1ff. as an authentic parable of Jesus by asserting that the nearness of the kingdom of God is not expressed in the "category of a given period of time" (94, 245).

This constitutes a peculiar reversal of positions. In the discussion of a few decades ago W. G. Kümmel, as an energetic proponent of near expectation, defended the authenticity of this parable (*Promise and Fulfillment* [1957] 57ff.), whereas E. Fuchs, who condemned any talk of near expectation as "misleading" (*Studies in the Historical Jesus* [SBT 42, 1964] 182) considered an interpretation focusing on the early Church more appropriate (*idem, Aufsätze* II, 70). Today, however, Weder defends the parable's authenticity by drawing substantively on the work of Fuchs.

H. Hübner

χρόνος, ου, ὁ *chronos* time, duration

1. Occurrences in the NT — 2. Meaning — 3. Significant theological usage — a) Gal 4:4 — b) Acts 3:21 — c) 1 Peter — d) Rev 10:6

Lit.: J. BARR, *Biblical Words for Time* (²1969). — J. BAUM-GARTEN, *Paulus und die Apokalyptik* (WMANT 44, 1975) 180-97. — T. Boman, *Hebrew Thought Compared with Greek* (1960) 123-54. — G. DELLING, *Das Zeitverständnis des NT* (1940). — *idem, Zeit und Endzeit* (BibS[N] 58, 1970). — *idem, TDNT* IX, 581-93. — G. EBELING, *The Truth of the Gospel* (1985) 197-205. — H. C. HAHN, *DNTT* III, 839-45. — E. JENNI, *THAT* II, 370-85. — J. MARSH, *The Fulness of Time* (1952). — J. MUILENBURG, "The Biblical View of Time," *HTR* 54 (1961) 225-71. — For further bibliography see *TWNT* X, 1293.

1. Of the 54 NT occurrences of χρόνος, 24—almost half—are in the Lukan writings (7 in Luke, 17 in Acts). 4 each are in John, 1 Peter, and Revelation, 3 each are in Matthew and Hebrews, 2 each are in Mark, Romans, 1 Corinthians, and Galatians, and 1 each in 1 Thessalonians, 2 Timothy, Titus, and Jude.

2. In Greek thought → καιρός refers above all to the moment determined by fate, though this is also a moment that should be both recognized and grasped by a person, a moment demanding decision (Delling, *TDNT* III, 455f.). Χρόνος, on the other hand (first in the sense of "time in its course, section of time," Delling *TDNT* IX, 581f.), became the dominant term for time in Greek philosophy (Delling 582ff.). The decisive passage in Plato is *Ti.* 37-41: Like others before him and esp. Aristotle after him, Plato associates χρόνος with the movement of the all. He thus views the origin of time as a consequence of the origin of the moving celestial bodies, though he integrates this doctrine of time into his doctrine of ideas. Aristotle's normative definition of χρόνος in *Ph.* iv.11.219b reads: ἀριθμὸς κινήσεως κατὰ τὸ πρότερον καὶ ὕστερον ("number of motion in respect of 'before' and 'after' "). This fixes χρόνος as a physical-cosmological concept and as such as a quantifiable entity (on the term's further history in Greek thought see Delling *op. cit.*, 583f.)

Even though the NT stands very much in the OT and Jewish tradition and emphatically understands human existence as temporal, nowhere does it reflect on time as such, and temporality is spoken of almost nowhere with χρόνος. This is because in the NT χρόνος does not occupy the same position it does in Greek philosophy. The main NT expression for "time" is καιρός, which in significant passages refers to time qualified by the Christ-event.

Χρόνος is usually used of *duration of time,* in accord with part of the spectrum of the term's meaning in Greek

philosophy from an early time (see above): In addition to expressions such as "a short *time*," "a long *time*," and "a considerable *time*" (ἱκανὸς χρόνος, only in Luke-Acts: Luke 8:27; Acts 8:11; 14:3; 27:9; pl. in Luke 23:8), one can mention esp. Matt 2:7 ("the span of *time* in which the star appeared"); Acts 7:17 (ὁ χρόνος τῆς ἐπαγγελίας, "the *period of time* for the fulfillment of the promise," BAGD s.v.); 7:23 (ὡς δὲ ἐπληροῦτο αὐτῷ τεσσερακοντ-αετὴς χρόνος, "when he had spent forty years [when he was forty years old]"; → πληρόω 2); similarly 13:18. The *times* of ignorance (17:30) encompass the entire existence of humanity before Christ. In Rev 2:21 God grants the church in Thyatira yet a certain *amount of time* to repent. The duration of time referred to can be very short and can even be reduced virtually to a *point in time* (Luke 1:57: "the *time* for giving birth"; καιρὸς τοῦ τεκεῖν in Eccl 3:2 is formulated from a different perspective; cf. Luke 4:5: ἐν στιγμῇ χρόνου, "in a moment of time"). Πρὸ χρόνων αἰωνίων ("*ages* ago") occurs only in the Pastorals and is literal only in 2 Tim 1:9, and not in Titus 1:2. The juxtaposition of χρόνοι and καιροί in the eschatological passages in Acts 1:7 and 1 Thess 5:1 is in all probability a hendiadys.

3. a) Gal 4:4 is perhaps the most theologically significant occurrence of χρόνος in the NT. The → πλήρωμα τοῦ χρόνου is *the* καιρός of world history. But the χρόνος here is not in itself the καιρός, but only in that it has come to fullness. The background of the argument in Galatians 3-4 is clearly the idea of linear time in which "an epoch distinguishes between two times," "the time of the law and the time of faith, the time of servitude and the time of freedom" (Ebeling 204). Paul thus frames the idea of time, though not reflecting on it as such, within the dialectic of law and gospel and thus within the doctrine of justification.

Jewish parallels notwithstanding (e.g., 1QpHab 7:2: *gᵉmar haqqēṣ,* "completion of time" in the sense of "end time"), "fullness of time" does not mean that "time, in the sense of the passage of time, . . . came to an end" (H. Schlier, *Gal* [KEK] 194; differently Delling, *TDNT* VI, 305, without mentioning Schlier; F. Mussner, *Gal* [HTKNT] 269). "Fullness of time" means rather that in the salvation event in Christ time has attained its goal within history, esp. considering that near expectation is not constitutive for the theological argumentation in Galatians (see also Baumgarten 192f.). The definition of the word "eschatological" determines the extent to which one uses it of this time that has come to fullness.

b) Acts 3:20f. (vv. 19-21 in translations) parallels καιροὶ ἀναψύξεως, "times of respite," and χρόνοι ἀποκαταστάσεως πάντων, "*times* of realization (→ ἀποκατάστασις) of all [the prophetic promises]." Καιροί and χρόνοι here, as already in 1:7 (cf. 1 Thess 5:1), refer to the eschaton. That Acts 1:7 and 3:21 are indeed parallel statements is supported as well by the correspondence between ἀποκαθιστάνω in 1:6 and ἀποκατάστασις in 3:21 (see Mal 3:23 LXX). It is disputed to what extent Acts 3:19-21 is based on preexisting material and to what extent Luke has reworked the text redactionally. Since ἄχρι χρόνων ἀποκαταστάσεως probably was originally formulated within the scheme "primal age = eschaton," this phrase can hardly be considered redactional (on the discussion see esp. G. Schneider, *Acts* [HTKNT] I, 323-27 [bibliography]).

c) Χρόνος is a key theological term in 1 Peter. "That life in history is for Christians the 'time of their παροικία' (1:17) is a fundamental motif throughout 1 Peter" (L. Goppelt, *1 Pet* [KEK] 80). At the same time, however, the Christian is already living ἐπ' ἐσχάτου τῶν χρόνων, "at the end of the *times*" (1:20; cf. Jude 18: ἐπ' ἐσχάτου τοῦ χρόνου [on the text-critical question see *NTG* ad loc.]; see also ἐπ' ἐσχάτου τῶν ἡμερῶν τούτων, Heb 1:2). As in 1 Pet 4:2f., where the believers' earthly time is juxtaposed, as "*time* in the flesh" (→ σάρξ 7.b), with the previous sinful *time,* the reference to the eschatological situation here also occurs out of parenetic considerations.

d) Rev 10:6 (χρόνος οὐκέτι ἔσται) does not mean that time as such will no longer exist metaphysically. The reference is rather to the terrible proximity of the end when the seventh angel will sound his trumpet: Then there will be no more *time!*   H. Hübner

χρονοτριβέω *chronotribeō* spend time, lose time*

Acts 20:16, of Paul, who on his way to Jerusalem sailed past Ephesus in order not to "*lose time* in the province of Asia" (χρονοτριβῆσαι ἐν τῇ ᾿Ασίᾳ); he wants to be in Jerusalem at Pentecost (v. 16b; something Acts does not, however, later pick up again). The avoidance of Ephesus was probably prompted primarily by the earlier persecutions in the city (19:23ff.).

χρυσίον, ου, τό *chrysion* gold; money
→ χρυσός.

χρυσοδακτύλιος, 2 *chrysodaktylios* with (a) gold ring(s) on one's finger(s)*

Jas 2:2: the rich man who "comes into the assembly *with gold rings on his fingers* (ἀνὴρ χρυσοδακτύλιος) and in fine clothing," contrasted with πτωχὸς ἐν ῥυπαρᾷ ἐσθῆτι; cf. Epictetus *Diss.* i.22.18: χρυσοῦς δακτυλίους ἔχων.

χρυσόλιθος, ου, ὁ *chrysolithos* chrysolite, olivine*

Rev 21:20: the seventh jewel in the foundation of the wall of the heavenly Jerusalem: ὁ ἕβδομος χρυσόλιθος (cf. Exod 28:20; 36:20; Ezek 28:13). Chrysolite is a light

green transparent mineral (peridot). Pliny *HN* xxxvii.42, and Diodorus Siculus ii.52, however, use the word in reference to yellow topaz. W. Frerichs, *BHH* 362-65, esp. 363; R. G. Bullard, *ISBE* IV, 626.

χρυσόπρασος, ου, ὁ *chrysoprasos* chrysoprase*

Rev 21:20: the tenth jewel in the foundation of the wall of the heavenly Jerusalem: ὁ δέκατος χρυσόπρασος (cf. Pliny *HN* xxxvii.113; the word does not occur in the LXX). Chrysoprase is a green, transparent variety of chalcedony; cf. also → χαλκηδών. W. Frerichs, *BHH* 362-65, esp. 363; R. G. Bullard, *ISBE* IV, 626.

χρυσός, οῦ, ὁ *chrysos* gold (noun)*
χρυσίον, ου, τό *chrysion* gold; money*
χρυσοῦς, 3 *chrysous* gold (adj.)
χρυσόω *chrysoō* gild, cover or adorn with gold*

1. Occurrences in the NT and meaning — 2. Gold as a precious metal — 3. Finished gold — a) Adornment and utensils — b) Money — 4. Χρυσοῦς

Lit.: G. BECATTI, *Oreficerie antiche* (1955). — H. BLÜMNER, PW VII, 1555-78. — A. VAN DEN BORN, *BL* 611f. — R. J. FORBES, *Studies in Ancient Technology* VIII (²1971). — W. FRERICHS, *BHH* 582f. — J. F. HEALY, *Mining and Metallurgy in the Greek and Roman World* (1978), index s.v. "gold" (306f.). — H.-J. HORN, *RAC* XI, 895-930. — F. N. PRYCE, *OCD* 471. — M. ROSENBERG, *Geschichte der Goldschmiedekunst* (1910-1925 = 1972). — K. H. SINGER, *Die Metalle Gold, Silber, Bronze, Kupfer und Eisen im AT und ihre Symbolik* (FzB 43, 1980). — R. F. TYLECOTE, *A History of Metallurgy* (1976).

1. The noun χρυσός occurs 10 times in the NT, 5 times in Matthew alone. Like the diminutive χρυσίον (12 occurrences in the NT) it represents *gold,* both as a raw material and used in adornment, utensils, or money. Whereas χρυσός refers to *money* only in Matt 10:9 (perhaps also Jas 5:3), this tr. applies more frequently to χρυσίον (Acts 3:6; 20:33; 1 Pet 1:18). The adj. χρυσοῦς (18 occurrences in the NT: 2 Tim 2:20; Heb 9:4a, b; 15 occurrences in Revelation) characterizes objects as *made of gold* and also refers to adornment with gold. This latter sense is also the case in the two NT occurrences of the vb. (Rev 17:4; 18:16).

Of a total of 42 NT occurrences of this word group, 24 are in Revelation, 5 in the Gospels (all in Matthew), and only 1 in the genuine Pauline letters (1 Cor 3:12: χρυσός). The numerical preponderance of χρυσίον over against χρυσός corresponds to the frequency of the two terms in the LXX, where they are synonyms (rendering the same Hebrew equivalents), though χρυσίον by far predominates.

2. In antiquity gold was mined, e.g., in Nubia, from which Egypt and other countries acquired the precious metal. It was also found in Asia Minor (Lydia), though not in Mesopotamia

or Palestine. The OT speaks of gold being imported (1 Kgs 9:28; 22:49; 2 Chr 3:6; 8:18; 9:21, and elsewhere). Gold was desired not only because of its beauty and rarity, but also because it was easily worked by artisans and did not oxidize. Esp. cultic and royal objects were made of gold or gilded (also the images of idols, e.g., the "golden calf"). Weighed gold was early used as barter, though only at a relatively late date was it struck into coins (in Lydia?).

Χρυσός is used of gold as a raw material and as that which is precious, esp. in lists. In Matt 2:11 it is included among the gifts of the magi to the royal (cf. v. 9) messianic child (with frankincense and myrrh). In 1 Cor 3:12; Rev 18:12 (cf. 9:7) it appears with silver and precious stones. Gold as what is precious is also spoken of in the occurrences of χρυσίον in 1 Pet 1:7; Rev 3:18 and χρυσίον καθαρόν (cf. Exod 25:11; 2 Chr 4:4, 8 LXX), "pure *gold*," in Rev 21:18, 21, referring to the heavenly Jerusalem.

3. a) Χρυσός is also used of gold objects or adornment (Matt 23:16, 17 bis: the *gold* of the temple; Jas 5:3: the *gold* of the rich; Acts 17:29: the material from which idols are made; cf. also *1 Clem.* 1:6, → 4.a). Χρυσίον refers to adornment with gold in 1 Tim 2:9 and 1 Pet 3:3 (women's adornment); further also Rev 17:4 and 18:16 (adornment of the harlot "Babylon," in both instances κεχρυσωμένη χρυσίῳ καὶ λίθῳ τιμίῳ). Heb 9:4 mentions the "ark of the covenant covered on all sides with *gold*" (cf. also → 4.b).

b) In Matt 10:9 (*contra* Mark 6:8; Luke 9:3) χρυσός appears with ἄργυρος and refers to *gold coins*: Jesus forbids his missionaries from taking money with them. Jas 5:3 (→ a) may also refer to gold coins. Gold in the form of coins, however, is usually rendered by χρυσίον, as in Acts 3:6; 20:33; 1 Pet 1:18 (in all instances with ἀργύριον: the double designation "silver and *gold*" can be rendered "money").

4. One cannot always clearly determine whether the adj. (on its declension see BDF §45) is referring to solid *gold* or *gilded* objects.

a) The numerous occurrences of the adj. in Revelation refer to objects revealed to the seer and belonging to the heavenly realm and in part prefigured in the cult of the old covenant: the seven lampstands, representing the seven churches (1:12, 20; 2:1; cf. Exod 38:17 LXX), the gold girdle of the one like a man (Rev 1:13; cf. Dan 10:5 Theodotion; Rev 15:6: gold girdles of the seven angels), crowns (4:4: on the heads of the twenty-four elders; 14:14: on the one like a man; cf. Esth 8:15 LXX; 1 Macc 10:20; 13:37; 2 Macc 14:4), bowls (Rev 5:8: with incense; 15:7: bowls of wrath), a censer (8:3), the altar (8:3; 9:13; cf. Exod 40:5, 26 LXX), and the measuring rod for measuring the heavenly Jerusalem (Rev 21:15). The gold cup of "Babylon" (17:4; cf. Jer 28:7 LXX) and the gold

idols (Rev 9:20), on the other hand, characterize arrogance and perversion.

b) Outside Revelation χρυσοῦς occurs only 3 times. 2 Tim 2:20 contrasts "*gold* and silver vessels" with vessels of wood or earthenware. Heb 9:4a, b mentions the precious cultic objects in Israel's "holy of holies": the "*gold* altar of incense (θυμιατήριον)" and the "ark of the covenant covered on all sides with *gold*," which contained a "*gold* urn holding the manna and Aaron's rod" (cf. Exod 16:33; Num 17:25).   G. Schneider

χρυσοῦς, 3 *chrysous* gold (adj.)
→ χρυσός (4).

χρυσόω *chrysoō* gild, cover or adorn with gold
→ χρυσός.

χρώς, χρωτός, ὁ *chrōs* skin*

Acts 19:12: Paul's handkerchiefs and aprons (→ σιμικίνθιον) were carried away "from his *skin*/[surface of the] body (ἀπὸ τοῦ χρωτὸς αὐτοῦ)" to the sick, whereupon their diseases left them. In the instruction concerning leprosy in Lev 13:1ff. LXX χρώς stands almost exclusively for Heb. *bāśār*.

χωλός, 3 *chōlos* lame, crippled*

This adj. occurs 14 times in the NT, outside the Gospels and Acts only in Heb 12:13. It usually refers to lameness of feet.

The lame and the blind are mentioned together esp. frequently (cf. in the OT 2 Sam 5:6-8; Job 29:15; Jer 31:8, and elsewhere). Lameness was viewed as a physical deficiency, not as a disease, and rendered a person (as did other defects) unsuitable for the priesthood (Lev 21:18-24). Corresponding regulations applied to sacrificial animals (22:19-25; Deut 15:21; Mal 1:8, 13). It was expected that such imperfections and disabilities would be eliminated during the time of salvation (Isa 33:23: "The lame will take the prey"; 35:5f.: "Then will the lame man leap like a hart"; cf. also Jer 31:8; Isa 29:18f.). In such passages the lame are often mentioned together with persons with other disabilities (the blind, deaf, mute, and poor). Some NT occurrences can be understood from the perspective of this hope.

In the NT the sg. occurs in Acts 3:2 and 14:8, referring both times to a "man *lame* from birth" (ἀνὴρ χωλὸς ἐκ κοιλίας μητρὸς αὐτοῦ) who is then healed.

Heb 12:13 uses neut. sg. fig.: "Make straight paths . . . so that what is lame (τὸ χωλόν) may not be put out of joint [or: not depart from the way]" (→ ἐκτρέπομαι). Here χωλός is a metaphor for weak or vacillating Church members who should be supported and maintained by the entire congregation.

In the saying concerning discipleship in Mark 9:45 par. Matt 18:8 χωλός, with the meaning *one-footed/with only one foot,* refers fig. to those who for the sake of the kingdom of God have renounced what separates them from salvation. The radical nature of this metaphor of self-mutilation stands for the absolute obedience that sets new standards of wholeness and completeness for discipleship.

All other occurrences are pl., in connection with healings or the hope of healing, and together with other infirmities: Acts 8:7: παραλελυμένοι καὶ χωλοί; Matt 11:5 par. Luke 7:22: χωλοί with τυφλοί (and others; χωλοὶ περιπατοῦσιν: the end of lameness represents the renewal of one's entire existence); Matt 15:30, 31: χωλοὶ περιπατοῦντες; 21:14: τυφλοὶ καὶ χωλοὶ ἐν τῷ ἱερῷ; John 5:3. It is not friends and the rich who constitute the new table fellowship, but rather the πτωχοί, ἀνάπειροι, χωλοί, and τυφλοί (Luke 14:13, 21; cf. Isa 58:7; Job 29:15f.). The wholeness of the infirm and deformed thus also manifests itself in a new form of fellowship. Billerbeck, I, 593-96; B. Reicke, *BHH* 1043; A. van den Born, *BL* 1009.

χώρα, ας, ἡ *chōra* land, country; district, region; field*

Lit.: H. W. BARTSCH, "Geographische Bezeichnung für Israel im NT," *Jüdisches Land—gelobtes Land* (Abhandlungen zum christlich-jüdischen Dialog 3, ed. H. Gollwitzer; 1970) 290-304. — BAGD s.v. — W. BRUEGGEMANN, *The Land* (Overtures to Biblical Theology, 1977), esp. 167-83. — H. CONZELMANN, *The Theology of St. Luke* (1982) 18-94. — W. D. DAVIES, *The Gospel and the Land* (1974). — P. DIEPOLD, *Israels Land* (BWANT 95, 1972). — K. DIETERICH, "Bedeutungsgeschichte griechischer Worte," *RMP* N.F. 59 (1904) 226-37. — E. LOHMEYER, *Galiläa und Jerusalem* (FRLANT 52, 1936). — E. S. MALBON, *Narrative Space and Mythic Meaning in Mark* (1986). — W. MARXSEN, *Mark the Evangelist* (1959) 54-116. — R. RENDTORFF, *Israel und sein Land* (TEH 188, 1975). — W. C. ROBINSON, *Der Weg des Herrn* (TF 36, 1964).

1. The noun χώρα occurs in the NT 28 times. Apart from one epistolary occurrence (Jas 5:4), it occurs only in the Gospels and Acts, 17 times in Luke-Acts alone.

2. The basic meaning of χώρα is uninhabited or sparsely settled *land* in contrast to cultivated area or cities (Mark 6:55; Luke 2:8; extrabiblical documentation in Dieterich 227f.). Occasionally it refers to a defined region as a whole (Mark 5:10; Luke 15:13, 14, 15; John 11:54; Acts 13:49). Sometimes the *region* or *district* is specified by reference to its inhabitants (χώρα τῶν Γαδαρηνῶν, Matt 8:28; χώρα τῶν Γερασηνῶν, Mark 5:1; Luke 8:26) or its name as a province (Judea in Mark 1:5 [in Mark, unlike Luke, Judea always refers to the southern province; cf. Mark 3:7; 10:1; 13:14]; Acts 8:1; 10:39; 26:20; Samaria in Acts 8:1; Galatia in Acts 16:6; 18:23) or administrative territory (Ituraea and Trachonitis in Luke 3:1; cf. Josephus *Ant.* xvii.81; the *country* of the king [Herod] in Acts 12:20; cf. Luke 19:12).

In other instances the specification takes other forms.

In Matt 2:12 χώρα refers to the home country of those spoken of: "They [the magi] departed to their own *country* by another way." In Acts 27:27 χώρα is dry land as opposed to water. In Jas 5:4, as in Luke 12:16; John 4:35, χώρα is cultivated *land*, a *field;* in every instance the image of harvest is associated with χώρα (despite BAGD, χώρα in Luke 12:16 is not a farm, and in 21:21 not a field). Χώρα is also used repeatedly as an explicit designation for Judea in distinction from Jerusalem (Luke 21:21; John 11:55; Acts 26:20; cf. H. Baarlink, *ZNW* 73 [1982] 214f.).

Matt 4:16 partially cites Isa 9:1 LXX (on the text-critical problem and Matthew's source see G. Strecker, *Der Weg der Gerechtigkeit* [FRLANT 82, ³1971] 63-66): "A light (φῶς) has risen over those who sit in the land (χώρα) and shadow of death." In accord with Isa 8:23, χώρα in Matt 4:15f. refers to the area of the ancient tribes Zebulun and Naphtali, thus the western shore of the Sea of Galilee. Through Jesus (cf. 4:12f.; φῶς in v. 16 refers to him) this *land* becomes the land of eschatological promise and fulfillment.

It is disputed whether in Luke χώρα, used of Judea, and "Judea" referred to without χώρα are Judea proper, perhaps in contrast to Galilee (so Conzelmann 18ff., whose agenda includes proving that the geographical dimension is an element of Luke's theological composition: Jesus' ministry is objectively differentiated from that of John the Baptist) or refer to the entire area of Jesus' ministry, functioning virtually as synonyms for Palestine (so Robinson 31, and *passim;* Bartsch 296ff.; W. Grundmann, *Luke* [THKNT] 422). Regardless of one's conclusion, the connection to geographical places, to the χώρα, signifies the indispensable concretization of Christian promise and fulfillment (cf. just Matt 4:15f.).

D. Sänger

χωρέω *chōreō* make room, find place; grasp, comprehend; go forward/away*

Lit.: BAGD s.v. — R. SCHNACKENBURG, *John* II (Eng. tr., 1979) 210 with n.82. — D. TABACHOVITZ, "Till betydelsen an χωρεῖν Joh. 8,37," *Acta philologica Suecana* 31 (1933) 71f. — ZORELL, *Lexikon* 1362-64.

1. Of the 10 occurrences in the NT, 4 are in Matthew, 3 in John, and 1 each in Mark, 2 Corinthians, and 2 Peter.

2. a) Literal use occurs in John 2:6 in reference to jars, each of which *held* two or three μετρηταί, and in 21:25 in the hyperbolic assertion that the world could not *contain* the books (on this idea cf. Amos 7:10; Philo *Ebr.* 32; *Post.* 144; *orbis non caperet* and similar expressions in Curtius vii.8.12; Livy vii.25; Cicero *Philippicae* 2.44); according to Mark 2:2 not even the area around the door *was room enough for* the many people. John 8:37 uses

the vb. intrans.: "because my word *finds* no *place* in you" (so Tabachovitz, Schnackenburg, and others), unless the well-documented meaning "attain one's goal, have success" applies (Herodotus iii.42; v.89; vii.10; viii.68; Aristophanes *Pax* 509f.; cf. 2 Thess 3:1).

Using the vb. fig. Paul petitions the Corinthians (2 Cor 7:2): "*Make room* for me," i.e., give me understanding, without narrow-mindedness (cf. 6:12). In Matt 19:11 χωρέω refers to *comprehension, understanding* (Plutarch *Cato Minor* 64; Pseudo-Phocylides 89 [Diehl, *Anthologia* I]). The meaning of the term is stretched (cf. "make room") in Matt 15:17: "Whatever goes into the mouth *passes* into the stomach." Fig. also in "*progress toward* repentance" (2 Pet 3:9).   J. B. Bauer

χωρίζω *chōrizō* divide, separate*

1. Occurrences in the NT — 2. Meaning — 3. Heb 7:26

Lit.: BAGD s.v. — R. L. ROBERTS, "The Meaning of χωρίζω and δουλόω in 1 Cor 7:10-17," *Restoration Quarterly* 8 (1965) 179-84. — ZORELL, *Lexikon* s.v.

1. Of the 13 occurrences in the NT, 3 are in Acts, 2 in Romans, 4 in 1 Corinthians, and 1 each in Matthew, Mark, Philemon, and Hebrews.

2. According to Rom 8:35, 39 nothing can *separate* us from Christ's love, not even death, which otherwise breaks off even the most intimate of familial relationships (parents and children: *nec iam pater,* Ovid *Metamorphoses* viii.231; *nec iam modo mater,* Sedulius *Paschale carmen* 125; spouses: *iam non tua,* Virgil *Georgics* iv.498). It could be said of a widowed woman that "with respect to her hitherto subsisting subordination under the law binding her to her husband she is absolved, free and rid of it" (H. A. W. Meyer, *Rom* [Eng. tr., 1884] 260 = [Eng tr., 1881] I, 318).

Of death rather than divorce: "What God has joined together," i.e., spouses (cf. Gen 2:22; 24:14, 44; Tob 6:18) "let not mankind [i.e., no person can] *break apart*" (Mark 10:9; Matt 19:6).

Pass. *be separated (get divorced)* (in marriage contracts, ÄgU 1101, 5; 1102, 8; 1103, 6; cf. Preisigke, *Wörterbuch* 767) in 1 Cor 7:10: A wife should not *be separated/divorced* from her husband. If she *does separate,* however, she should remain ἄγαμος ("single," which she then becomes again! v. 11). The same holds true (cf. 7:39; Rom 7:1-3) if an unbelieving husband *separates* from his wife, who is a believer (v. 15 bis): The wife should not prevent him from doing this out of missionary zeal (cf. E. Fascher, *1 Cor* [THKNT] I, 184-89).

The vb. can also mean *run away* (Phlm 15) or *depart* from (ἀπό, Acts 1:4; 18:2; ἐκ, 18:1).

3. Jesus, the high priest, is "*separated* from sinners," to whom he was close during his earthly life (cf. Mark 2:15; Matt 11:19), now that he has been "exalted above the heavens" (Heb 7:26). Κεχωρισμένος ἀπὸ τῶν ἁμαρτωλῶν, however, also connotes moral difference from sinners (Herodotus i.140, 172; Epictetus *Diss.* ii.10.2).   J. B. Bauer

χωρίον, ου, τό *chōrion* piece of land, field; land, estate*

This noun occurs 10 times in the NT, almost always referring to areas of land that either have a name or are associated with certain persons: χωρίον οὗ τὸ ὄνομα / λεγόμενον Γεθσημανί (Mark 14:32 par. Matt 26:36); Jacob's *field* (John 4:5; → Συχάρ); Judas's field (Acts 1:18, 19 bis; → Ἀκελδαμάχ/χωρίον αἵματος); "owners of *lands* or houses" sold them (4:34); proceeds from the sale of a *piece of property* (5:3: τιμὴ τοῦ χωρίου, Ananias and Sapphira; cf. v. 8); *pieces of property* or *estates* belonging to Publius on Malta (28:7).

χωρίς *chōris* separated, far from, apart from, without*

1. Occurrences in the NT — 2. Usage — Heb 2:9

Lit.: BAGD s.v. — BDF §§216.2; 487. — RADERMACHER, *Grammatik* 140. — C. SPICQ, *Heb* (ÉBib, 1952) I, 419. — ZORELL, *Lexikon* s.v.

1. Only John 20:7 (cf. Xenophon *Cyr.* iv.1.18; Ign. *Trall.* 11:2) uses this word as an adv.: The handerkerchief lay *separately.* Otherwise χωρίς is used as an improper prep. with gen. Of the 41 NT occurrences, 13 are in Hebrews (with 1 each in Mark and Luke, 3 each in Matthew, John, and 1 Corinthians, 6 in Romans, 2 in 2 Corinthians, 1 each in Ephesians, Philippians, and Philemon, 2 in 1 Timothy, 4 in James).

2. a) With gen. of the person χωρίς means *without, separated from:* "Without connection to me you can do nothing" (John 15:5); χωρὶς Χριστοῦ a person is ἄθεος (Eph 2:2); without Paul (1 Cor 4:8); without us (Heb 11:40). In the Lord woman is not *without* man, and man not *without* woman (1 Cor 11:11); the one sex is not considered at the cost of the other or without considering the other (cf. Gal 3:28). Also *apart from, other than:* "*besides* women and children" (Matt 14:21; 15:38; cf. Jdt 7:2); with gen. of the thing (2 Cor 11:28). *Without the participation of* the Logos (John 1:3); *without the activity of* the preacher (Rom 10:14).

b) With gen. of the thing, that which one does not need or use: *without* a foundation (Luke 6:49); "not *without* parables" = "only with the aid of parables" (Mark 4:34; Matt 13:34); without having sinned (Heb 4:15);

without having taken an oath (7:20); without grumbling (Phil 2:14); without anger (1 Tim 2:8; 5:21); without your consent (Phlm 14); without question (something holds true, Heb 7:7); not without (spilling) blood (9:7, 18, 22); without sympathy (10:28); faith "from which no works grow" (Jas 2:18, 20; cf. also 4 Macc 5:9: χωρὶς ὀνείδους; *Gos. Thom.* 8: χωρὶς πόνου; Pap. Oxy. no. 506, l. 19: χωρὶς ὑπερθέσεως, "without delay").

Without the presence of: Without the Spirit the body is dead, as is faith without works (Jas 2:26 bis); *as long as there is no* law, sin is dead, there is no transgression, no stimulus for transgression (Rom 7:8f.); without (if one has no) faith, one cannot please God (Heb 11:6); without holiness one cannot see the Lord (12:14); whoever does not experience discipline is not really a son (v. 8).

Without reference to sin (Heb 9:28); *independent of* the (redemptive efficacy of the) law (Rom 3:21), of works (4:6; 3:28).

Separated from: "*outside* the body" (2 Cor 12:3; cf. Plato *Phd.* 67a; see F. Pfister, *RAC* IV, 952-55).

3. Χωρὶς θεοῦ was possibly the original reading in Heb 2:9 (rather than χάριτι θεοῦ): "Far from God [instead of: by the grace of God] he was to taste death for everyone." This harsh expression for Jesus' abandonment by God at the crucifixion (Mark 15:34; *Gos. Pet.* 19) may have been replaced at an early stage—in the usual way, taking only gentle liberties with the traditional text—by the familiar phrase referring to God's grace (cf. *Gos. Eb.* 2: ἐγκρίς instead of ἀκρίδες; cf. also A. von Harnack, SPAW [1929] 62-68; recently: U. Wilckens, *Das NT* [²1971] 779f.).

J. B. Bauer

χῶρος, ου, ὁ *chōros* northwest (noun)*

According to Acts 27:12 the harbor at → Φοῖνιξ on Crete is open "toward the southwest and the *northwest*" (βλέποντα κατὰ . . . χῶρον).

Ψ ψ

ψάλλω *psallō* sing; sing praise*

This vb., which occurs 5 times in the NT, actually means "pluck/play a stringed instrument" or "sing to the accompaniment of a harp." In the NT it always refers to a song of praise to God (dat.). In the LXX ψάλλω usually translates Heb. *zāmar*, esp. in the Psalms, and can refer to the playing of an instrument (LXX Pss 32:2; 104:2; 146:7, and elsewhere) or, less frequently, to the praise itself that is sung (LXX Pss 9:3; 65:4; a taunt-song: Ps 68:12 LXX).

In Rom 15:9 Paul interprets ἐξομολογέομαι and ψάλλω (citing Ps 17:50 LXX) with δοξάζω; the (promised) praise of God by the nations (i.e., the Gentile Christians) shows the measure of God's mercy and cannot be the occasion for arrogance over against his people. 1 Cor 14:15 (bis) speaks of glossolalic singing (cf. vv. 10f., 14, 16), which is acceptable only with singing with understanding, i.e., singing in comprehensible words with the congregation (cf. v. 26): ψαλῶ τῷ πνεύματι, ψαλῶ δὲ καὶ τῷ νοΐ. Eph 5:19 similarly considers it a (genuine) effect of the Spirit when Church members are united through songs of thanksgiving: ᾄδοντες καὶ ψάλλοντες (cf. LXX Pss 26:6; 104:2, and elsewhere) τῇ καρδίᾳ ὑμῶν τῷ κυρίῳ (→ ψαλμός). This refers to "singing aloud" (cf. 1 Cor 14:26) and collective singing in the assembly: Τῇ καρδίᾳ refers not to inwardness but to full participation (cf. R. Schnackenburg, *Eph* [Eng. tr., 1991] ad loc.). Jas 5:13 refers to the praise of the individual who in times of well-being should express his joy and gratitude before God: κακοπαθεῖ τις ἐν ὑμῖν, προσευχέσθω· εὐθυμεῖ τις, ψαλλέτω. C. H. Roberson, "The Meaning and Use of *Psallo*," *Restoration Quarterly* 6 (1962) 19-31, 57-66; G. Delling, *TDNT* VIII, 490f., 493f., 499; K.-H. Bartels, *DNTT* III, 670-72; → ὑμνέω.

ψαλμός, οῦ, ὁ *psalmos* song; song of praise, psalm*

Lit.: K.-H. BARTELS, *DNTT* III, 670-72. — R. DEICHGRÄBER, *Gotteshymnus und Christushymnus in der frühen Christenheit* (SUNT 5, 1967) 106ff. — G. DELLING, *TDNT* VIII, 489-503. — *idem, Worship in the NT* (1962) 86-91. — H. GROSS, *BL* 1056f. — P. VAN IMSCHOOT, *BL* 1421. — F. SCHNUTENHAUS, *BHH* 1519f. — O. SÖHNGEN, *Leiturgia* (1961) IV, 2-15. — K. WENGST, *Christologische Formeln und Lieder des Urchristentums* (SNT 7, ²1973) 144ff. — C. WESTERMANN, *BHH* 1086-93. — For further bibliography see *DNTT* III, 675f.; *TWNT* X, 1287.

This noun occurs 7 times in the NT. In the LXX ψαλμός largely renders Heb. *mizmôr*, esp. in the superscripts to psalms, and as a rule refers to a song accompanied by a stringed instrument (cf., e.g., ψαλμὸς ᾠδῆς, Ps 67:1 LXX with Ps 45:1, where ψαλμός renders Heb. *šîr*, "song").

All Lukan uses of ψαλμός refer to scriptural psalms: Luke 20:42 (cf. par. Matt 22:43): Δαυὶδ λέγει ἐν βίβλῳ ψαλμῶν (Ps 110:1 follows this citation formula); Acts 1:20: γέγραπται γὰρ ἐν βίβλῳ ψαλμῶν (Ps 69:26 follows); pl. in Luke 24:44 (with νόμος Μωϋσέως and προφῆται) of the Psalter (cf. Philo *Mut.* 115 and elsewhere: ἐν ὑμνοῖς) representing here the *k^etûbîm;* Acts 13:33 explicitly citing "the second psalm": ὡς καὶ ἐν τῷ ψαλμῷ γέγραπται τῷ δευτέρῳ (Ps 2:7 follows).

1 Cor 14:26 speaks of the church's assembly for worship (ὅταν συνέρχησθε), during which each member can contribute: ἕκαστος ψαλμὸν ἔχει . . . , "one has a *psalm/song* [to contribute], another. . . ." This probably refers to songs composed by members of the congregation, which they then present in the worship service (cf., e.g., Luke 1:46ff., 68ff.; also the songs of the author of Revelation: 5:9f., 12, 13; 11:15, 17f.; 15:3f., and elsewhere; texts such as Phil 2:6-11, Col 1:15-20, 1 Tim 3:16, 1 Pet 2:21-24, though Rom 8:31ff. and 1 Cor 13:1ff., etc., can also be viewed in this context). OT psalms and later Jewish psalms might have been (but need not have been, on the basis of these NT texts) the model.

Eph 5:19 and Col 3:16, speaking of the worship service, refer to ψαλμοὶ καὶ ὕμνοι καὶ ᾠδαὶ πνευματικαί together without making any clear distinction (→ ὑμνέω 4). The adj. πνευματικαί does not distinguish the ᾠδαί as "spiritual" from the songs referred to with the other terms, since → ᾠδή is, like ψαλμός, a biblical term. Rather, the adj. modifies all three terms and characterizes the songs as "inspired by the Spirit" or "filled with the Spirit" (cf. Eph 5:18; see BDF §135.3). Λαλοῦντες ἑαυτοῖς (Eph 5:19) is not a reference to antiphony (cf. also Col 3:16a). Rather, it refers to freely presented or collectively performed songs without liturgical stylization. The songs are, thus, expressions of the Spirit, of grace (Col 3:16) experienced in the worship service, and of thanksgiving to Christ and God (Eph 5:20) and are also directly associated with mutual edification (Col 3:16a).

H. Balz

ψευδάδελφος, ου, ὁ *pseudadelphos* false brother*

In 2 Cor 11:26 and Gal 2:4 Paul speaks of *false [Christian] brethren* threatening him, his proclamation, and thus also his churches. In 2 Cor 11:26 they appear at the end of an enumeration of eight dangers to which Paul is exposed. According to Gal 2:4 they are παρείσακτοι ψευδάδελφοι (→ παρείσακτος) seeking to spy on Pauline freedom. Paul is thinking of Jewish Christian or Judaizing adversaries from churches not founded by him, whose behavior shows them to be ἀδελφοί in name only. He speaks of a failed Christian in one of his own churches as an ἀδελφὸς ὀνομαζόμενος (1 Cor 5:11). Cf. further Pol. *Phil.* 6:3.

ψευδαπόστολος, ου, ὁ *pseudapostolos* false apostle*

In 2 Cor 11:13 Paul calls his adversaries who have penetrated into the Corinthian church ψευδαπόστολοι and characterizes them further as "deceitful workmen, disguising themselves as apostles of Christ." The context (vv. 7f.) suggests that they cast suspicions on the authenticity of his own apostleship, esp. on the basis of his not taking advantage of financial support by the church. Paul responds by denying that they were commissioned by Christ, since they pursue primarily their own goals (v. 4) and expound their own superiority (ὑπερλίαν ἀπόστολοι, v. 5; 12:11) instead of being characterized by the suffering and cross of Christ. The term ψευδαπόστολος is not documented in extra-Pauline writings. For a parallel in substance cf. Rev 2:2. K. H. Rengstorf, *TDNT* I, 445f.; C. K. Barrett, *Essays on Paul* (1982) 87-107.

ψευδής, 2 *pseudēs* lying, false*

Acts 6:13: *"false* witnesses" in judicial proceedings (cf. → ψευδομαρτυρέω); subst. *liar* in Rev 2:2: εὗρες αὐτοὺς ψευδεῖς (referring to alleged apostles); 21:8: πᾶσιν τοῖς ψευδέσιν, at the end of a vice catalog (v.l. ψευσταῖς).

ψευδοδιδάσκαλος, ου, ὁ *pseudodidaskalos* one who teaches falsehood, false teacher*

2 Pet 2:1: "Peter" tells the churches that *false teachers* will come among them (ἐν ὑμῖν ἔσονται ψευδο-

διδάσκαλοι) and will bring destructive heresies, deny Christ, and be destroyed (cf. vv. 2ff.). Although the author likens these teachers, in connection with his explication of prophecy (1:19ff.), to the false prophets of Scripture (→ ψευδοπροφήτης), he denies them any prophetic gift by employing the construction ψευδοδιδάσκαλος, which is unique to him in the NT. The ψευδοδιδάσκαλοι thus bring false teachings, but are characterized above all by their false lives (→ ψευδολόγος). The reference is probably to Gnostic "teachers," who in early Christian polemic were esp. subject to the charge of immorality (cf. Jude 4ff., 10ff., 17ff.; also Pol. *Phil.* 7:1). K. H. Rengstorf, *TDNT* II, 160.

ψευδολόγος, 2 *pseudologos* speaking falsely, lying*

Subst. in 1 Tim 4:2 *(liar),* of false teachers (cf. vv. 1, 3ff.), whose words and teaching are the most profound hypocrisy (ἐν ὑποκρίσει). Through false teaching and false behavior (v. 2b) they thus manage to lead some astray. Ψευδολόγος belongs to elevated language. Spicq, *Notes* II, 977.

ψεύδομαι *pseudomai* lie (vb.)*

Lit.: U. BECKER and H.-G. LINK, *DNTT* II, 470-74. — H. CONZELMANN, *TDNT* IX, 594-603. — H. GIESEN, *Christliches Handeln. Eine redaktionskritische Untersuchung zum δικαιοσύνη-Begriff im Matthäusevangelium* (EHS XXIII/181, 1982) 110-12 (on Matt 5:11). — I. DE LA POTTERIE, *La Vérité dans Saint Jean* (AnBib 73-74, 1977) 905-54. — For further bibliography see *TWNT* X, 1293.

1. The vb. ψεύδομαι occurs 12 times in the NT, of those once in the Gospels, twice in Acts, 8 times in the letters, and once in Revelation. It stands over against truthfulness or characterizes the realm hostile to God, since falsehood originates with Satan.

2. Negated, the vb. is used as a formula of asseveration underscoring the truthfulness of a statement (οὐ ψεύδομαι, Rom 9:1; Gal 1:20; 2 Cor 11:31; 1 Tim 2:7).

3. According to Heb 6:18 it is impossible for God to lie (cf. Titus 1:2). Since he has given us a guarantee through his promise and oath (v. 17), there is refuge for the person reaching for the promise set before him (v. 18b).

4. According to Matt 5:11 Christians are blessed not because they have unjustly suffered shame and persecution but because they, like their Lord (Matt 26:59f.), have persevered in faith in situations of tribulation.

By withholding from the Church part of the proceeds from the sale of a piece of property, Ananias lies to the

Holy Spirit (Acts 5:3) or to God (v. 4) and (with Sapphira) tempts God's Spirit (v. 9). Such actions show him to be Satan's tool (v. 3).

In Col 3:9a the imv. not to lie summarizes all the vices belonging to the old epoch (3:5-7). Falsehoods, which threaten the Church's life, should no longer determine the salvation-historical situation of Christians, which is determined rather by baptism.

Jas 3:14f. explicitly characterizes lies as demonic. Whoever brings discord into the Church and boasts of his jealous and selfish behavior—that person is lying (v. 14).

If a Christian pretends to live in fellowship with God while actually walking in darkness, i.e., in the realm hostile to God (1 John 1:6a), he is lying and not living the truth (v. 6b), as is shown by the absence of brotherly love (cf. v. 7).

According to Rev 3:9a, b, those who say they are Jews are really "from the synagogue of Satan." They are adversaries of the church, namely, of those whom Christ has loved (v. 9d).   H. Giesen

ψευδομαρτυρέω *pseudomartyreō* give false testimony*

ψευδομαρτυρία, ας, ἡ *pseudomartyria* false testimony*

ψευδόμαρτυς, υρος, ὁ *pseudomartys* false witness*

1. Occurrences and meaning — 2. The Synoptics — 3. 1 Cor 15:15

Lit.: → μάρτυς. See also: A. Sand, "'Falsche Zeugen' und 'falsches Zeugnis' im NT," *Christuszeugnis der Kirche* (ed. P. W. Scheele and G. Schneider; 1970) 67-89.

1. The vb. occurs 5 times in the NT, though only in the Synoptics: 3 times in Mark, and once each in Matthew and Luke. Ψευδομαρτυρία occurs only in Matthew (twice). Matthew and Paul use ψευδόμαρτυς once each. On the basis both of the constituent parts of the words and their context the basic meaning of the vb. and the abstract noun is "(give) false testimony," always in the context of a court situation. Ψευδόμαρτυς in Matthew refers to a "false witness" in court. On 1 Cor 15:15 → 3.

2. This word group occurs in the Synoptics in three contexts, in which the Markan text variously constitutes the basis or point of departure. The vb. occurs in all three Synoptic accounts of the "rich young man": "Do not *bear false witness*" is mentioned here among the commandments of the Decalogue. Mark 10:19 and Luke 18:20 have imv. with μή, Matt 19:18 ind. with οὐ, as in the LXX (Exod 20:16; Deut 5:20). Even the Markan model has already dispensed with the complementary phrase in the LXX (κατὰ τοῦ πλησίον σου μαρτυρίαν ψευδῆ), probably

in order to give the commandment more emphasis. Mark and Matthew follow Exodus and Deuteronomy MT in the sequence of the commandments, while Luke assimilates the order to Deuteronomy LXX.

The pl. of ψευδομαρτυρία occurs in Matt 15:19 in the framework of a catalog of sins abbreviated and reworked from Mark 7:21f. Here also Matthew strives for a closer assimilation to the Decalogue (Sand 72f.).

In the Jewish trial of Jesus Mark 14:56, 57 uses the vb. twice, and Matt 26:59, 60 uses ψευδομαρτυρία and ψευδόμαρτυς. Mark regards the statement about Jesus temple saying as "false testimony," while Matthew does not. Instead, Matthew presents the introduction of witnesses against Jesus as consciously engineered false testimony against Jesus on the part of the high priest and the Sanhedrin, whereas Mark does not. Luke is either unfamiliar with this scene or has skipped it. But in the interrogation of Stephen in Acts 6:13 he mentions false witnesses (μάρτυρες ψευδεῖς) against Stephen. Although Sand (83) sees here the portrayal of the fate of the prophet, one could think both in Acts 6:13 and in the trial of Jesus of the suffering righteous person in the Psalms (cf. Pss 26:12; 34:11 LXX: μάρτυρες ἄδικοι; also Sus 60 LXX: ψευδομάρτυρες).

3. It was long disputed whether θεοῦ in 1 Cor 15:15 was to be read as obj. or subj. gen. The latter position, represented esp. by K. Holl (1914), is not considered viable today, since the ὅτι clause that follows clearly indicates in what sense Paul speaks of ψευδομάρτυρες τοῦ θεοῦ. Ψευδομάρτυρες here is thus not the title "witness" negativized. It refers, instead, to the actions described in the subsequent verses. On this discussion cf. Sand 83-87 and the bibliography for → μάρτυς.   J. Beutler

ψευδομαρτυρία, ας, ἡ *pseudomartyria* false testimony
→ ψευδομαρτυρέω.

ψευδόμαρτυς, υρος, ὁ *pseudomartys* false witness
→ ψευδομαρτυρέω.

ψευδοπροφήτης, ου, ὁ *pseudoprophētēs* false prophet, prophet of lies*

Lit.: D. E. Aune, *Prophecy in Early Christianity and the Ancient Mediterranean World* (1983), index s.v. "false prophets." — G. Friedrich, *TDNT* VI, 830. — D. Hill, "False Prophets and Charismatics: Structure and Interpretation in Matthew 7,15-23," *Bib* 57 (1976) 327-48. — M. Krämer, "Hütet euch vor den falschen Propheten. Eine überlieferungsgeschichtliche Untersuchung zu Mt 7,15-23/Lk 6,43-46/Mt 12,33-37," *Bib* 57 (1976) 349-77. — P. S. Minear, "False Prophecy and Hypocrisy in the Gospel of Matthew," FS Schnackenburg 76-93. —

J. REILING, "The Use of *PSEUDOPROPHETES* in the Septuagint, Philo, and Josephus," *NovT* 13 (1971) 147-56.

This noun occurs 11 times in the NT, with 3 each in Matthew and Revelation.

The false prophets of Scripture are the focus in Luke 6:26 (L) and 2 Pet 2:1. According to Luke 6:26 the false prophets of salvation always had the people on their side (cf. 1 Kgs 22:26ff.; Isa 28:7ff.; Jer 5:31; Ezek 13:1ff.; Mic 2:11; 3:5ff.), while true prophets were persecuted (Luke 6:23; cf. Jer 6:13 LXX; 33:7f. LXX; 36:8 LXX, and elsewhere: ψευδοπροφήτης; MT simply "prophets"). The author of 2 Peter compares the ψευδοδιδάσκαλοι of his own day with the *false prophets* in Israel (2:1).

The (eschatological) false teachers and deceivers of the Church are, however, themselves explicitly characterized as false prophets in Matt 7:15 (M; on the image of ravenous wolves in sheep's clothing cf. Ezek 22:27f.; Rom 16:18; 2 Tim 3:5; Rev 13:11); Matt 24:11 (M; cf. Mark 13:6 par.). Ψευδόχριστοι and ψευδοπροφῆται are used together in Mark 13:22 par. Matt 24:24: Through signs and wonders (cf. Deut 13:1ff.) they will lead astray the elect (cf. also Josephus *Ant.* xx.97, 169: alleged eschatological prophets; *B.J.* ii.261; vi.285f. has ψευδοπροφήτης in the same context). Similarly, according to 1 John 4:1, the activity of the false prophets (πολλοὶ ψευδοπροφῆται ἐξεληλύθασιν εἰς τὸν κόσμον) is related to the appearance of the antichrists (2:18; → ἀντίχριστος). On the whole it is presupposed that the false prophets will both spread false teachings and appear with illegitimate prophetic claims, and thus deceive the churches (cf. also *Did.* 11:5f., 8-10).

Acts 13:6 is to be understood differently. The magician Bar-Jesus/Elymas is said to be a ψευδοπροφήτης Ἰουδαῖος. Luke thus emphasizes that he opposes the Pauline proclamation and simultaneously falsely uses Jewish tradition for the sake of magic (and probably astrology).

In all three occurrences in Revelation ψευδοπροφήτης refers to the second beast, which is portrayed in 13:11ff. Through his signs and power he seduces people to worship the first beast (cf. on 13:11 esp. Matt 7:25; → χάραγμα). This probably refers to representatives of the imperial cult, who embody the anti-divine false prophecy of the eschaton, which is extremely dangerous for the churches. The culmination is reached in the figure introduced in the enciphered announcement in 13:18 (probably *Nero redivivus;* → θηρίον 3.b; σφάζω). According to 16:13f. the dragon (see 12:3), the first beast, and his ψευδοπροφήτης lead the rulers of the whole world into the eschatological battle against God and Christ. But they are vanquished, and the beast and his lying prophet are cast into the lake of fire (19:20; 20:10).   H. Balz

ψεῦδος, ους, τό *pseudos* lie, falsehood*

   Lit.: → ψεύδομαι.

1. The noun ψεῦδος occurs 10 times in the NT: once in John, 6 times in the Epistles, and 3 times in Revelation. Falsehood is never understood from a purely ethical perspective, but rather always as a sign of belonging to the old aeon and its ruler, the devil.

2. When the devil "tells *lies*" (John 8:44), he functions as the eschatological opponent of Jesus, who "has told the truth" and is thus rejected by the Jews (v. 40). The devil counters the truth, i.e., God's revelation, with falsehood as a kind of anti-revelation. Whoever allows himself to be influenced by the devil, as do the Jews, does not have God as his father (vv. 42, 47), but rather the devil (v. 44a; not "the father of the devil," *contra* H. Conzelmann, *TDNT* IX, 602, with R. Schnackenburg, *John* II [Eng. tr., 1979] 213, and others), who as a murderer from the beginning (v. 44b) seeks to separate mankind from God.

According to 1 John 2:21 no lie comes from truth. The lie denies that Jesus is the Christ (v. 22a) and results in exclusion from fellowship with God, since this fellowship is mediated through the Son (vv. 22b-25). In contrast, whoever is taught by the oil of anointing (a metaphor for the Spirit) is assured of learning the truth and not lies (v. 27).

3. According to Rom 1:25 the lie with which the Gentiles perverted God's truth (i.e., God's reality, which can be deduced from his creation) consists in the fact that they put the creation in the Creator's place by failing to recognize the referential character of creation.

Eph 4:25 forbids not only falsehood (*contra* Conzelmann, *TDNT* IX, 601; J. Gnilka, *Eph* [HTKNT] 234, and others), but also states the fundamental prerequisite (aor. partc.; cf. v. 22) for the following imvs. (vv. 25-32).

In the eschaton the evil one will come in the power of Satan (2 Thess 2:9a). His power, which manifests itself in signs and wonders, is characterized by falsehood (v. 9b). He can deceive only those who perish because they have not kept the love of truth to be saved (v. 10). Belief in what is false excludes belief in what is true (vv. 11-12a) and thus results in judgment (v. 12a) and loss of salvation (v. 10).

4. Whoever "practices abominations and *falsehood*" (Rev 21:27) or "loves and practices *falsehood*" (22:15) is excluded from the eschatological salvation portrayed in the the image of the New Jerusalem. Thus it can be said conversely of the 144,000 who are saved that no lie was found in their mouth (14:5). For whoever lies stands, like the false prophet (16:13; 19:20; 20:10), on the side of the anti-divine and the Antichrist.   H. Giesen

ψευδόχριστος, ου, ὁ *pseudochristos* false Messiah, false Christ*

   Mark 13:22 par. Matt 24:24: ψευδόχριστοι καὶ ψευδοπροφῆται who in the eschaton will lead the elect astray by means of signs and wonders. While the "signs" characterize eschatological false prophets (→ ψευδοπροφήτης; cf. also Josephus *B.J.* ii.261; vi.285f.), ψευδόχριστοι probably identifies them concretely as the "messianic" leaders and liberators who appeared esp. in the period before and during the first Jewish War (cf. Mark 13:14ff. par.; 13:21 par. Matt 24:23, omitted by Luke; see further Acts 5:36; 21:38). The reference to the desert (Matt 24:26) might also be understood in this context, unless "desert" in juxtaposition with "chambers" is referring to the distant and hidden in contrast to "what is visible everywhere" (v. 27). Josephus uses → ψευδοπροφήτης or similar expressions of Zealot leaders such as Theudas, the Egyptian, etc. Ψευδόχριστος is first documented only as a Christian term. Bousset/Gressmann 223f.; W. Grundmann, *TDNT* IX, 530.

ψευδώνυμος, 2 *pseudōnymos* falsely called, carrying a false name*

According to 1 Tim 6:20 the γνῶσις claimed by the false teachers is only an *alleged* (doctrine of) knowledge illegitimately calling itself γνῶσις. Similarly, e.g., Plutarch (*Moralia* 479e) speaks of a ψευδεπίγραφος φιλόσοφος. The statement in 1 Timothy presupposes that the author's adversaries have already used γνῶσις as a t.t. for their salvation message. This does not, however, refer to any fixed title of a book or anything similar (on this problem cf. N. Brox, *Die Pastoralbriefe* [RNT] ad loc.).

ψεῦσμα, ατος, τό *pseusma* lying (noun), untruthfulness*

Rom 3:7 speaks of fundamental human *dishonesty* before God (τὸ ἐμὸν ψεῦσμα, with ἀδικία in v. 5; contrasted with ἡ ἀλήθεια τοῦ θεοῦ in v. 7; cf. θεὸς ἀληθής, πᾶς δὲ ἄνθρωπος ψεύστης, v. 4). Paul formulates quite specifically the theologically impossible consequence implied by his own use of Pss 50:6 LXX and 115:2 LXX in Rom 3:4, namely, that God needs this alleged human unrighteousness and *dishonesty/unfaithfulness* and thus should not really be permitted to judge sinners. Paul does this because he wants from the very beginning to disarm such objections on the part of his adversaries. God's concern with the unrighteous and dishonest person is a pure gift; there is no cooperation of the sinner with God.

ψεύστης, ου, ὁ *pseustēs* liar*

This noun occurs 10 times in the NT, 2 times in John and 5 in 1 John. In OT and Jewish tradition God is considered the truthful and inherently faithful one (cf. Num 23:19; 1 Sam 15:29; Ps 33:4). Therefore, ψεύστης is usually used of the attitude of opposition to God and

the inclination toward what is worthless. It is not a matter of untrue or incorrect words, but rather of a person's opposition to God.

In Rom 3:4 Paul uses ψεύστης in this comprehensive sense: before the only true God every person is necessarily a *liar* (citing Ps 115:2 LXX), i.e., God is neither dependent on any person nor affected by any person's criticism (→ ψεῦσμα). In 1 Tim 1:10 the pl. appears in a catalog of vices (next to ἐπίορκοι; cf. Lev 19:11f.).

Titus 1:12 cites a proverbial verse about the Cretans and attributes it to a Cretan poet (or προφήτης): Κρῆτες ἀεὶ ψεῦσται, κακὰ θηρία, γαστέρες ἀργαί. The Cretans' proverbial falseness is used against false teachers on Crete who claim to know God, while in their works they deny him and are thus *liars* in the basic sense. According to Clement of Alexandria *Strom.* i.59.2 the quotation comes from the Cretan philosopher Epimenides, probably from his collection of oracular sayings (περὶ χρησμῶν; cf. Diels, *Fragmente* I, 31ff.; see further M. Pohlenz, *ZNW* 42 [1949] 101ff.). The saying was widely known (see M. Dibelius and H. Conzelmann, *The Pastoral Epistles* [Hermeneia], ad loc.; for bibliography see N. Brox, *Die Pastoralbriefe* [RNT], ad loc.).

According to John 8:44, the devil (→ ψεῦδος 2), the master and father of Jesus' adversaries, stands in complete opposition to truth: Ψεύστης ἐστὶν καὶ ὁ πατὴρ αὐτοῦ (= τοῦ ψεύδους, cf. BDF §282; *contra* H. Conzelmann, *TDNT* IX, 602). Ψεύστης characterizes fundamental opposition to God, which itself then leads to an attitude of falsehood, i.e., of rejection of God's truth in Jesus. If Jesus were to deny his own knowledge of God, he would separate himself from the truth and become like his adversaries: ἔσομαι ὅμοιος ὑμῖν ψεύστης (8:55).

This provides a transition to the polemical use of ψεύστης in 1 John. A person claiming knowledge of God without keeping the commandments (2:4), claiming to love God without brotherly love (4:20), and finally claiming faithfulness to God without confessing Jesus as the Christ and as the Son of the Father (2:22[f.]) is a ψεύστης who, even in the midst of the Church, already belongs to the → ἀντίχριστος and is thus to be excluded. When the adversaries claim to be sinless they are destroying God's truth and Christ's redemptive work (1:7-10), and when they do not believe in the Son they deny God's witness about him, i.e., as liars before God they in their blindness make God himself into a liar: Ψεύστην ποιέω αὐτόν (1:10; 5:10; cf. also Jer 5:12; 13:25; Hos 7:13). H. Conzelmann, *TDNT* IX, 594-603; U. Becker and H.-G. Link, *DNTT* II, 470-74.

H. Balz

ψηλαφάω *psēlaphaō* feel, touch (vb.)*

Touching establishes the corporeality of the resurrected Jesus: ψηλαφήσατέ με (Luke 24:39 [L]) and the

historicity of the life-giving word, i.e., of Jesus Christ: ὃ
... αἱ χεῖρες ἡμῶν ἐψηλάφησαν (1 John 1:1).

Heb 12:18 (οὐ ... προσεληλύθατε ψηλαφωμένῳ καὶ
κεκαυμένῳ πυρί) is concerned with the provisional yet
terrifying character of God's past revelation on Sinai,
which is eclipsed by the ultimate revelation (ἀλλὰ προσεληλύθατε Σιὼν ὄρει, v. 22). Numerous mss., as a parallel
to v. 18, add ὄρει to ψηλαφάω: "a mountain that may be
touched" (D Ψ Koine and others). According to Exod
19:12, however, the people are not to touch the mountain
either before or during the divine revelation (cf. 19:21,
23f.; Heb 12:20), while God identifies himself veiled in
fire (Exod 19:18; Deut 4:11ff.; 5:23; 9:3). Since Heb
12:18f. is closely associated with these statements,
ψηλαφάω probably refers to the fire's concrete and
dangerous materiality which one "feels when one touches
it" (cf. ψηλαφάω with similar meaning in Job 20:10 A) or
which one can "approach by touch" only with the greatest
of caution (cf. ψηλαφάω with similar meaning in Job 5:14;
12:25; Isa 59:10; Nah 3:1). The verse thus refers to "fire
that *singes* and glows" (cf. also Exod 24:17: πῦρ φλέγον).

Acts 17:27 uses ψηλαφάω fig.: The nations should
"seek God in the hope that they might *feel after* him and
find him (εἰ ἄρα γε ψηλαφήσειαν αὐτὸν καὶ εὕροιεν)"; cf.
Philo *Mut.* 126 (ψηλαφάω τὰ θεῖα); *Corp. Herm.* v.2. E. C.
Selwyn, "On ΨΗΛΑΦΩΜΕΝΩ in Heb. XII 18," *JTS* 12
(1911) 133f.

ψηφίζω *psēphizō* calculate*

Luke 14:28: ψηφίζω τὴν δαπάνην, "*calculate* the cost
[of building a tower]"; Rev 13:18, of reckoning the number of the beast: ψηφισάτω τὸν ἀριθμὸν τοῦ θηρίου,
namely, the number 666 (v.l. 616). This number might
be the sum of the numerical values of the letters of a word
or name written in Greek or Hebrew (e.g., θηρίον or Heb.
nrwn qsr) or a triangular number on a base of thirty-six,
which itself is a triangular number on a base of eight. For
details see BAGD 892 (bibliography); E. Lohse, *Rev*
(NTD) ad loc.; G. Braumann, *TDNT* IX, 604-7; H. Kraft,
Rev (HNT) on 13:18; 17:10.

ψῆφος, ου, ἡ *psēphos* pebble; stone used in voting*

According to Acts 26:10 Paul participated in sentencing
adherents of Christ and voted for the death sentence:
ἀναιρουμένων τε αὐτῶν κατήνεγκα ψῆφον (cf. the weaker
συνευδοκέω in 8:1; 22:20). Luke is probably referring to the
familiar votes with white *(pro)* and black *(contra)* pebbles
(cf. Plutarch *Moralia* 186e; 4 Macc 15:26; Josephus *Ap.*
ii.265). Ψῆφος appears in the postscript to Philemon with
the meaning *condemnation* (to martyrdom).

Rev 2:17 (bis) mentions the "white *stone*" (ψῆφος
λευκή) on which "a new name is written that no one
knows except the one who receives it"; this probably

alludes to God's ultimate decision of deliverance concerning "those who conquer." Just as Zion is to receive
a new name as a sign of redemption (Isa 62:2ff.), so also
will those who have remained faithful to Christ. God
gives them their new names directly so that no one
knows it beforehand or can misuse it for deception. This
image exhibits elements both of the amulet and of the
voting pebble (for acquittal). BAGD s.v. (bibliography);
G. Braumann, *TDNT* IX, 604-7, esp. 605f.; H. Kraft, *Rev*
(HNT) on 2:17.

ψιθυρισμός, οῦ, ὁ *psithyrismos* whispering, mut-
tering, gossip*

Pl. in 2 Cor 12:20, in a list of covertly or openly
aggressive and selfish activities, all destructive to the
Church, with καταλαλιαί ("slander") and approximately
synonymous with it (with → καταλαλιά also in *1 Clem.*
30:3 [sg.]; 35:3 [pl.]). Luther's translation of the noun
was *Ohrenblasen*, i.e., "gossip, scandal-mongering."

ψιθυριστής, οῦ, ὁ *psithyristēs* one who gossips,
whisperer*

Pl. in Rom 1:29, in a catalog of vices with κατάλαλοι
(v. 30). Luther translates *Ohrenbläser*, i.e., "gossip, tale-
bearer." U. Wilckens, *Das NT* (1970), translates *Zuträger*,
i.e., "informer, tattler."

ψιχίον, ου, τό *psichion* tiny bit, crumb*

Mark 7:28 par. Matt 15:27: *crumbs* (cf. ἄρτος, Mark
7:27 par. Matt 15:26) that fall from the table; Luke 16:21
v.l.

ψυχή, ῆς, ἡ *psychē* (soul) life, person

1. Occurrences and meaning — 2. Usage — 3. Paul and
the deutero-Pauline writings — 4. The Synoptics and
Acts — 5. The Johannine corpus — 6. Other writings

Lit.: J. B. BAUER, " 'Wer sein Leben retten will . . .' Mk 8,35
Parr.," FS Schmid (1963) 7-10. — E. BRANDENBURGER, *Fleisch
und Geist. Paulus und die dualistische Weisheit* (WMANT 29,
1968). — H. A. BRONGERS, "Das Wort 'NFŠ' in den Qumran-
schriften," *RevQ* 4 (1963) 407-15. — BULTMANN, *Theology* I,
203-10 (on Paul). — E. DE W. BURTON, *Spirit, Soul, and Flesh*
(1918). — O. CULLMANN, *Immortality of the Soul or Resurrection of the Dead?* (1958). — G. DAUTZENBERG, *Sein Leben bewahren. Ψυχή in den Herrenworten der Evangelien* (SANT 14,
1966). — idem, "Seele (naefaeš-psyche) im biblischen Denken
sowie das Verhältnis von Unsterblichkeit und Auferstehung,"
*Seele. Ihre Wirklichkeit, ihr Verhältnis zum Leib und zur mensch-
lichen Person* (ed. K. Kremer; 1984) 186-203. — A. DIHLE,
E. JACOB, E. LOHSE, E. SCHWEIZER, and K.-W. TRÖGER, *TDNT* IX,
608-60. — E. VON DOBSCHÜTZ, *1/2 Thess* (KEK, 1909; 1974)
230-34. — J. FICHTNER, "Seele oder Leben in der Bibel," *TZ* 17
(1961) 305-18. — G. HARDER, *DNTT* III, 676-86. — R. JEWETT,

Paul's Anthropological Terms (1971) 334-57. — X. Léon-Dufour, "Perdre sa vie, selon l'Évangile," *Études* 351 (1979) 395-409. — D. Lys, *Nèphèsh. Histoire de l'âme . . .* (1959). — R. Morisette, "L'antithèse entre le 'psychique' et le 'pneumatique' en I Corinthiens XV, 44 à 46," *RevScRel* 46 (1972) 97-143. — W. Rebell, " 'Sein Leben verlieren' (Mark 8,35 parr.) als Strukturmoment vor- und nachösterlichen Glaubens," *NTS* 35 (1989) 202-18. — B. Reicke, "Body and Soul in the NT," *ST* 19 (1965) 200-212. — J. Schmid, "Der Begriff der Seele im NT," *Einsicht und Glaube* (FS G. Söhngen, ²1963) 128-47. — O. Schilling, *Geist und Materie in biblischer Sicht* (SBS 25, 1967). — L. Schottroff, *Der Glaubende und die feindliche Welt* (WMANT 27, 1970). — E. Schweizer, "Zur Trichotomie von 1. Thess. 5,23 und der Unterscheidung des πνευματικόν vom ψυχικόν in 1. Kor. 2,14; 15,44; Jak. 3,15; Jud. 19," *TZ* 9 (1953) 76f. — W. D. Stacey, *The Pauline View of Man* (1956). — P. A. Stempvoort, "Eine stilistische Lösung einer alten Schwierigkeit in I Thess V.23," *NTS* 7 (1960/61) 262-65. — J.-W. Taeger, *Der Mensch und sein Heil* (SNT 14, 1982) 19-22 (on Luke-Acts). — M. Winter, *Pneumatiker und Psychiker in Korinth* (MTSt 12, 1975). — For further bibliography see *DNTT* III, 687-89; *TWNT* X, 1293f.; Dautzenberg, *Sein Leben bewahren;* Dobschütz 321-33.

1. Among the anthropological terms of the NT ψυχή is used surprisingly uncommonly (103 times). It does not occur in Galatians, Philemon, 2 Thessalonians, the Pastorals, or 2 John; it occurs relatively frequently in the Synoptics and Acts (53 times). The statistical evidence reveals no particular preference by any one NT author.

In the LXX ψυχή is usually the tr. of *nepeš*, which is used over 750 times and originally meant "gullet, throat," and then acquired esp. the sense of "breeze, breath": The *nepeš* makes a person into a breathing and thus living being and "signifies that which is vital in man in the broadest sense" (Von Rad, *Theology* I, 153). In the LXX writings with a Hebrew source ψυχή maintains this meaning: It is simultaneously *vital power* and *life,* the *person* himself or herself, capable of feeling and emotion. Although Hellenistic influence makes itself felt in Greek Jewish writings (Wis 3:1; 9:15; 14:26; 16:9), the overall view of the OT is preserved. The Qumran texts take over the anthropological conceptions of the OT. In Josephus and esp. in Philo a more Hellenistic-dualistic understanding characterizes the conception of the human being, according to which the ψυχή represents an independent, higher value.

2. a) As the *principle of life* ψυχή stands over against physical death (Rev 8:9 [of animals]; Luke 9:24; 12:20; Acts 20:10 [of human beings]); in death this *vital power* dissociates itself and lives on in a place outside the earth (Acts 2:27 [citing Ps 16:8-11b LXX]; 2:31 TR; Rev 6:9; 20:4). Ψυχή designates a person's *life* and *vital existence* in general, which one seeks (Matt 2:20; Rom 11:3), risks (Phil 2:30), sacrifices (Mark 10:45 par. Matt 20:28; Acts 15:26; 1 Thess 2:8; instead of διδόναι John uses τιθέναι: 10:11, 15, 17, and elsewhere), and loves (Rev 12:11). This *life* is maintained by taking in nourishment (Matt 6:25a, b par. Luke 12:22f.) or neglected for the sake of a higher good (Luke 14:26; Acts 20:24). Finally, the ψυχή

is the seat of desire (Luke 12:19) and emotion (Mark 14:34 par. Matt 26:38; Luke 2:35; John 12:26); this is asserted of God anthropomorphically (Matt 12:18; cf. Heb 10:38).

b) Ψυχή is used metonymically for the *person* himself or herself, the *whole person,* i.e., as a living person (Mark 3:4 par. Luke 6:9; 1 Cor 15:45; Rev 16:3); this is also the case when ψυχή occurs in the pl. (Acts 2:41; cf. 7:14; 27:37; 1 Pet 3:20). Πᾶσα ψυχή means "every individual *person*" (Acts 2:43; 3:23; cf. 27:22; Rom 2:9 [with ἄνθρωπος]; 13:1).

c) Through the ψυχή a person is connected with God, to whom one must be dedicated "with (all) one's *soul*" (Matt 22:37 par. Luke 10:27 [in contrast Mark 12:30: ἐκ . . .; cf. 12:33 TR; Luke 10:27 TR]; Eph 6:6; Col 3:23). The ψυχή is thus the "seat and center of life that transcends the earthly" (BAGD s.v. 1.c). As such it is saved (Jas 1:21; cf. 1 Pet 1:9; Heb 10:39) and rescued from death (Jas 5:20) and also subject to destruction (Matt 10:28a, b; 16:26a; Mark 8:35, 36, 37). It is a precious possession (Matt 16:26b; cf. Mark 8:37) that succumbs to temptation (1 Pet 2:11; 2 Pet 2:14) and must be purified (sanctified; 1 Pet 1:22). Christ is the shepherd and guardian of the (converted) ψυχαί, i.e., of human *lives* (1 Pet 2:25; cf. N. Brox, *1 Pet* [EKKNT] ad loc.).

In the texts that have been listed above, the ψυχή is not something higher in a person over against an inferior part. Instead, it characterizes a person in the comprehensive vitality through which he really is himself, can find or lose himself, save or give himself up, hate or preserve himself (2 Cor 1:23; 12:15; Heb 6:19; 13:17; esp. Mark 8:35 par. Matt 16:25; Matt 10:39; Luke 17:33; 21:19 [pl.]; John 12:25). This comprehensive catalog of usage should not lead us into dissolving the sense of ψυχή into the indeterminate and abstract. "Ψυχή is always *my* life, never the phenomenon of life as such" (Schweizer, *TDNT* IX, 654, emphasis added). Nor, on the other hand, does it imply any fundamental identity of ψυχή with physical life: To gain physical life is actually loss, but that element of a person's life called ψυχή does not end in death (Acts 2:27; cf. 1 Cor 15:50f.).

3. The clause "give one's *life*" dominates Paul's usage of ψυχή. According to Phil 2:30 the apostle confirms that Epaphroditus risked his *life* and was near death (cf. Rom 16:4: Prisca and Aquila risked their "necks"). In 1 Thess 2:8 ψυχή stands on the same level as "gospel": Paul and his fellow workers want to share both with the Church; therefore, ψυχή designates the highest good a person can offer. 2 Cor 12:15 speaks of the willingness to sacrifice for the *members of the Church.*

In Phil 1:27 μία ψυχή is parallel with ἐν πνεῦμα (πνεῦμα is used anthropologically here): In one spirit, "as one person." This is a neither dichotomous nor trichotomous statement (*contra* E. Lohmeyer, *Phil* [KEK] 75); rather "we simply have rhetorical variation" (Schweizer, *TDNT* IX, 649); ψυχή is thus not specially qualified as, e.g., a soul over against flesh (body). According to 2 Cor 1:23

Paul offers his *life* as a pledge that his calling on God as a witness for his actions is genuine (E. B. Allo, *2 Cor* [ÉBib] 30: an "oath formula").

The text of 1 Thess 5:23 does present the problem of anthropological trichotomy when Paul uses the trio πνεῦμα—ψυχή—σῶμα. Von Dobschütz (ad loc.) has shown that there was no trichotomous anthropology in the pre-Christian period and that Paul was not familiar with such. But von Dobschütz's interpretation (ψυχή = "human individuality") is only partially correct. Bultmann also rejects a trichotomous interpretation and understands the text as wishing "that the readers may be kept sound, each in his entirety" (*Theology* 205). Nonetheless, one cannot overlook the fact that at least terminologically a "differentiated anthropology" is asserting itself (cf. Brandenburger 43). But this usage is not characteristic of Paul; it may be that he is thus rejecting a tripartite division of the human being by the libertinists in Thessalonica (cf. Jewett 180; *idem, The Thessalonian Correspondence* [1986] 107f., 175f.).

If one considers the apostle's other anthropological statements, one sees that the three words are used in 1 Thess 5:23 against adversaries who incorrectly see and evaluate human beings dualistically.

In Col 3:23 and Eph 6:6 ψυχή has no theological significance and describes a person's commitment in acting or fulfilling God's will with his entire *vital energy*. This idea is found in Jewish tradition (Prov 11:17; Sir 6:26, and elsewhere; *T. Gad* 2:1; *T. Benj.* 4:5) and is prefigured in substance in Sir 51:30: "Do your work before the appointed time, and in God's time he will give you your reward."

4. In the Synoptic Gospels and Acts ψυχή has the meanings outlined under → 2 above. It is natural, earthly *life,* the seat and point of departure of emotional response and feelings, and human *vitality* in the widest sense.

The two-part mashal in Mark 8:35 (par. Matt 16:25; Luke 9:24) grounds the call to discipleship in v. 34. The saying also occurs in Q (Matt 10:39 par. Luke 17:33) and John 12:25 (cf. *Gos. Thom.* 67). Although the positive statement varies in what vb. is used, it always means "preserve one's *life* from death, stay alive" (cf. Dautzenberg 52-56); the negative part (all three traditions use ἀπόλλυμι) means: "lose one's *life* through death (destruction)." The references to holding fast and losing both look at ψυχή as essential *life,* which in judgment will either come to its end or be rescued beyond judgment.

Mark 8:36f. (par. Matt 16:26; cf. Luke 9:25) then explicates the mashal in v. 35 with a twofold rhetorical question: The first asserts that gaining the whole world means nothing if in doing so one is threatened with (eschatological) loss of *life.* The allusion to Ps 49:8f. in the second question (v. 37) varies this idea: Nothing is as valuable (→ ἀντάλλαγμα) as the human existence that is realized in discipleship.

Matt 10:28 (cf. Luke 12:4f.) juxtaposes God, who can destroy both σῶμα and ψυχή, and humans, who can destroy the body, but not the ψυχή: God can destroy the entire person ("the real Self," A. H. McNeile, *Matt* [1915 = 1961] 145), not only the limited earthly existence, but also the entire, actual *life* God originally gives to a person.

The Lukan statements about life beyond death (Luke 9:25; 12:4f.; Acts 2:31) presuppose the conviction that after death a person will abide in Hades or paradise (Luke 16:22f.; 23:43; cf. 24:21-27). In 9:25 the term used in the source (Mark 8:35), ψυχή, is replaced by the pron.; Luke 12:5 speaks of hell (Gehenna) as the place of sojourn; and Acts 2:31 replaces ψυχή in Ps 15:10 LXX with σάρξ in order to avoid asserting that the ψυχή is given over to Hades (cf. Schweizer, *TDNT* IX, 646). Luke is interested in a physical resurrection (the continued life of the whole person), not in "immortality" of the soul. According to Luke 12:20 God takes away the life of a person who irresponsibly disregards what will happen after death. As in Mark 13:13b (without ψυχή), Luke 21:19 also suggests an endurance guaranteeing life in the real sense beyond physical death; the idea of future (eternal) life resonates here.

5. Several times the Gospel of John uses the expression τιθέναι τὴν ψυχήν, "lay down one's *life*," either as a sacrifice or as a risk (10:11, 15, 17; 15:13 [of Jesus]; 13:37f. [of Peter]; cf. also 1 John 3:16). According to John 10:17f. Jesus has the power both to give his ψυχή and to take it again. Jewish thinking characterizes this statement (cf. Dautzenberg, *Sein Leben bewahren* 109f.), according to which Jesus can retrieve his *life* again. The "goal of regaining" the ψυχή "is the whole person" (Dautzenberg 111; cf. also John 12:25; → 4). The exhortation to sacrifice one's own life for the brethren (1 John 3:16), which emerges as an imv. in v. 18 from the ind. in v. 17, is the substantive consequence of Jesus' own sacrificial love (v. 16a; cf. John 15:13).

6. Jas 1:21 speaks of the implanted (deeply rooted) word (of God), which is able to save ψυχαί, i.e., *persons* (cf. Gen 19:17, 19; 32:31 LXX, and elsewhere; Matt 16:25). In Jas 5:20 ψυχή is synonymous with "sinner" and refers to the *person* to be saved in judgment from (eternal) death and for whom a multitude of sins are covered (cf. 2:13; *Did.* 4:6).

In 1 Pet 3:20 ψυχαί is used of the *persons* rescued from the Flood, who according to 1:9 attained salvation through faith (cf. also 4:19). Christ as the "guardian of your *souls*" (1 Pet 2:25) is the shepherd who watches out for the life of the *Church members*. Hellenistic influence can be discerned in 1 Pet 2:11 (→ σαρκικός): The ψυχή is the inward *person* in contrast to the external person oriented toward the flesh, though "a typically Hellenistic dichotomy" is not at work here (*contra* W. Schrage, *1 Pet* [NTD 10] 86). In 2 Pet 2:14 ψυχαί is used of unsteady *persons;* in contrast, v. 8 distinguishes between the ψυχή as the inner part of the righteous person on the one hand,

and the righteous person himself on the other, though it characterizes the ψυχή positively as δικαία.

Statements using ψυχή in Hebrews are largely traditional and refer thus to the *inner element* of a person, which stands before God (6:19), or to the *person* himself (10:38; 13:17). According to 4:12 God's word pierces like a two-edged sword into a person to divide *soul* and spirit, joints and marrow; the twofold use of this dual statement functions with καρδία to express the absolute and total nature of the judgment of a *person.* "No definite theological trichotomy is in view" (Schweizer, *TDNT* IX, 651).

In Revelation ψυχή refers similarly to a person's earthly *life* (12:11; 18:14) and then to the *person* himself (18:13). The meaning is theological where ψυχή refers to *life* enduring beyond death (6:9; 20:4 [both times pl.]). The reference is to the *lives* of the witnesses slaughtered for the sake of their testimony, who thus attained participation in eschatological salvation.   A. Sand

ψυχικός, 3 *psychikos* (pertaining to the soul in the sense of) earthly, worldly*

Lit.: → ψυχή.

1. In Greek usage ψυχικός is the complement of σωματικός, ὑλικός, and χοϊκός. It means *pertaining to the soul* and follows the generally accepted understanding of the *soul* in the Hellenistic world. The related adv. ψυχικῶς appears in 2 Macc 4:37; 14:24: "with one's (whole) heart"; this usage, however, is unique. 4 Macc 1:32 speaks of "spiritual" as opposed to physical desires. The 6 NT occurrences can probably be considered from a Gnostic understanding, since in Gnosticism ψυχικός stands over against the adj. πνευματικός or the subst. πνεῦμα; Paul's language esp. may have been provoked by Gnostic adversaries.

2. Paul uses the adj. in two contexts in 1 Corinthians; it is not part of his otherwise familiar vocabulary. In 1 Cor 15:44a, b, 46 ψυχικός is used (3 times) over against πνευματικός. There is an *earthly-worldly* body which is sown like all else that is perishable, dishonorable, and weak (vv. 42, 43). The one important thing is the pneumatic body, which can attain access to the kingdom of God (v. 50) through Christ's life-giving pneuma (v. 45). Ψυχικός thus designates the *earthly person* "of the dust," to which is juxtaposed a second person "of heaven" (v. 47). In 1 Cor 2:14, too, the ψυχικὸς ἄνθρωπος is the "[merely] *earthly-worldly* person" who does not understand what can only be understood through the power of the gift of the Spirit. With Winter (205f.) one can say "that Gnostic texts represent the direct linguistic and conceptual background of the Pauline antithesis." Paul does not, however, carry through this Gnostic dualism himself, but rather radically calls it into question (cf. Winter 231f.).

3. Jas 3:15 speaks of *worldly* wisdom, which is earthly (ἐπίγειος) and demonic (δαιμονιώδης). Since the earthly sphere is ruled by evil powers, it is impossible for "the wisdom from above" to determine a person's conduct (cf. v. 13). Jude 19 speaks even more distinctly of "those who cause divisions": They are merely *worldly* people oriented toward the here and now, those who do not possess the pneuma, who scoff against the eschaton and live in accord with ungodly passions. Both Jas 3:15 and Jude 19 come close to a dualistic understanding of the world and mankind (cf. M. Dibelius, *Jas* [Hermeneia] 210-12, esp. 212), though they do not take the final step in this direction.   A. Sand

ψύχομαι *psychomai* become cold*

Fig. in Matt 24:12 (M) in Jesus' eschatological discourse: ψυγήσεται ἡ ἀγάπη τῶν πολλῶν, "the love of most *will grow cold*" (cf. the reference to hope in Josephus *B.J.* v.472; cf. also 1 Thess 2:10; Rev 2:4).

ψῦχος, ους, τό *psychos* coldness*

The *cold* of night (John 18:18) or winter (Acts 28:2), in the face of which one warms oneself by a fire. According to 2 Cor 11:23-29 Paul's tribulations include ψῦχος (v. 27). Together with γυμνότης ("nakedness") ψῦχος here probably explicates the general theme of "lack of clothing" (cf. J. Zmijewski, *Der Stil der paulinischen "Narrenrede"* [BBB 52, 1978] 263).

ψυχρός, 3 *psychros* cold, cool*

Subst. in Matt 10:42: "a cup of *cold/cool water* (ποτήριον ψυχροῦ)," a gift to the disciples that will be rewarded (adj. in v.l.: ποτήριον ὕδατος ψυχροῦ); fig. in Rev 3:15 in chastisement of the church at Laodicea, which is neither *cold* nor hot (ζεστός) and will therefore be "spit out" (→ χλιαρός; cf. *Did.* 7:2). A. Oepke, *TDNT* II, 876f.

ψωμίζω *psōmizō* give to eat, feed; distribute (as alms)*

Rom 12:20, with acc. of person in parenesis: "If your enemy is hungry, *feed* him" (citing Prov 25:21 LXX v.l.; cf. *1 Clem.* 55:2); 1 Cor 13:3: the basic meaning "feed/use as fodder": ψωμίζω πάντα τὰ ὑπάρχοντά μου, "*use* all my possessions to feed the needy," i.e., "*distribute as alms*" (cf. Deut 32:13; Ps 79:6 LXX; Dan 4:32 LXX/Theodotion; metaphorical in Jer 23:15; Sir 15:3; symbolic in Ezek 3:2).

ψωμίον, ου, τό *psōmion* small piece of bread*

Ψωμίον, the diminutive of ψωμός ("crumb"), is used 4 times in the Johannine announcement of Judas's betrayal. Βάπτω τὸ ψωμίον, "dip the *morsel/small bit*" (John 13:26 bis), might refer to dipping of bitter herbs into fruit sauce, which was part of the Passover meal (*m. Pesaḥ.* 10:3), though it probably refers to dipping of a piece of bread into a common dish, a usual part of the Jewish meal (cf. the scriptural citation in John 13:18: ὁ τρώγων μου τὸν ἄρτον . . .). Whereas Mark 14:20 par. only attests the common meal taken from a single dish, John thus portrays Jesus' specific designation of the betrayer (see further John 13:27: μετὰ τὸ ψωμίον; 13:30: λαβὼν τὸ ψωμίον). This sign is also Satan's cue (13:27; cf. also Luke 22:3; see R. Schnackenburg, *John* III [Eng. tr., 1982] 30f. with n.95).

ψώχω *psōchō* rub*

The Lukan version of the story of plucking ears of grain on the sabbath goes beyond Mark 2:23 par. Matt 12:1 (plucking [→ τίλλω] and eating) in saying (Luke 6:1) that the disciples "*rubbed* the ears of grain in their hands" (ψώχοντες ταῖς χερσίν). For Luke this rubbing of the ears of grain is important as a prerequisite for eating. If picking ears of grain is already forbidden on the sabbath as part of the work of harvest (→ τίλλω), rubbing the ears of grain could represent an additional element of work equally forbidden on the sabbath, namely, threshing or grinding (cf. *m. Šabb.* 7:2) or preparing a meal (cf. *m. 'Ed.* 2:6; *m. Pe'a* 8:7; *Jub.* 2:29; 50:9), which would present further difficulties in regard to tithing (see Billerbeck I, 616f.). It is difficult to determine whether Luke was trying to compound the disciples' sabbath transgressions or was merely specifying more concretely the activity of plucking and eating.

Ω ω

Ὦ[μεγα], τό *Ō(mega)* Omega
→ Ἄλφα.

ὦ *ō* O*

17 occurrences in the NT, 16 of those as an exclamation before an address (usually voc.), only in Rom 11:33 in a simple outcry (before nom.). The majority of occurrences stand (emphatically) at the beginnings of sentences or clauses: with voc.: ὦ γύναι (Matt 15:28); ὦ ἀνόητοι . . . (Luke 24:25); ὦ ἄνθρωπε (Rom 2:1, 3; 9:20); ὦ ἀνόητοι Γαλάται (Gal 3:1); ὦ ἄνθρωπε θεοῦ (1 Tim 6:11); ὦ Τιμόθεε (v. 20); ὦ ἄνθρωπε κενέ (Jas 2:20); with nom.: ὦ γενεὰ ἄπιστος . . . (Mark 9:19 par. Matt 17:17/ Luke 9:41); ὦ πλήρης παντὸς δόλου . . . (vocatives follow, Acts 13:10). As a pure form of address with no particular accentuation: ὦ Θεόφιλε (Acts 1:1); ὦ Ἰουδαῖοι (18:14); ὦ ἄνδρες (27:21). An actual person can be addressed (Matt 15:28; Acts 13:10, and elsewhere), or, in the style of diatribe, a fictitious dialogue partner (Rom 2:1, 3; 9:20). The voc. is also frequently used—and in addressing God always so—without ὦ. BAGD s.v.; BDF §146.

Ὠβήδ *Ōbēd* Obed
TR spelling of → Ἰωβήδ (cf. Josephus *Ant.* v.336).

ὧδε *hōde* here, to this place*

Of the 61 NT occurrences 43 are in the Synoptic Gospels (18 in Matthew, 10 in Mark, 15 in Luke) and 5 in John; it is also found frequently in Acts (6 occurrences).

With local meaning, *here:* Matt 12:6, 41, 42 (= in Jesus' vicinity); 14:17; 16:28; 17:4 (bis); 20:6; 24:2; 26:38; 28:6; Mark 6:3 (= at this place); 8:4; 9:1, 5; 13:2; 14:32, 34; 16:6; Luke 4:23; 9:12, 33; 11:31, 32 (= in Jesus' vicinity); 15:17; 16:25; 22:38; 24:6; John 6:9; 11:21, 32; Acts 9:14 (cf. v. 2); Col 4:9 (τὰ ὧδε, "what has taken place *here*/how things are going for us *here*"); Heb 13:14 (= *here* on earth); ὧδε—ὧδε in Matt 24:23 means

"*here—there*"; similarly ὧδε—ἐκεί in Mark 13:21; Luke 17:21; cf. 17:23.

The local meaning *to this place* occurs in Matt 8:29; 14:18; 17:17; 22:12; Mark 11:3; Luke 9:41; 14:21; 19:27; 23:5; John 6:25; 20:27; Acts 9:21; Jas 2:3 (ὧδε—ἐκεί, "*over here*—over there"); Rev 4:1; 11:12 (*up to this place*).

In the other occurrences the local sense almost entirely gives way to reference to the situation at hand or statement under discussion: *on this place* (Matt 14:8); ὧδε λοιπόν, "*in this connection* moreover" in the sense of a conclusion leading the discussion further (1 Cor 4:2; → λοιπός 3; see also H. Conzelmann, *1 Cor* [Hermeneia] 82 n.2); ὧδε—ἐκεί, "*on the one hand*—on the other" (Heb 7:8); ὧδε (. . . ἐστίν), "*here* is/*this* constitutes/*here* it is a matter of" (Rev 13:10, 18; 14:12; 17:9).

ᾠδή, ῆς, ἡ *ōdē* song*

There are 7 occurrences in the NT, 5 of those in Revelation.

In the LXX ᾠδή usually refers to a song of praise or thanksgiving directed toward God (e.g., Exod 15:1[ff.]; Deut 31:19, 30 [the song follows in 32:1ff.]; Judg 5:1[ff.]; Pss 17:1 LXX; 90:1 LXX, and elsewhere; cf. Josephus *Ant.* vii.305). No real distinction in meaning can be discerned with → ψαλμός or ὕμνος; cf. ἐν ψαλμοῖς· ᾠδή (Ps 4:1 LXX); ψαλμὸς ᾠδῆς (29:1 LXX; 67:1 LXX); ᾠδὴ ψαλμοῦ (82:1 LXX, and elsewhere). Josephus (*Ap.* i.40) calls the OT songs ὕμνοι (cf. *Ant.* iii.64; viii.124; ix.269; David composed ᾠδὰς εἰς τὸν θεὸν καὶ ὕμνους, vii.305). Similarly, Philo consistently calls the scriptural psalms ὕμνοι (*Mut.* 115; *Conf.* 52, and elsewhere). *Psalms of Solomon* 10, 14, and 16 are identified with the term ὕμνος, whereas 2, 3, 5, 13, 15, 17, and 18 are called ψαλμός with no distinction in meaning.

For these reasons ψαλμοὶ (καὶ) ὕμνοι (καὶ) ᾠδαὶ πνευματικαί in Eph 5:19; Col 3:16 does not allow us to differentiate between the individual forms. Πνευματικαί does not characterize "worldly" songs as now being "spiritual," but rather modifies all three nouns; the reference is to singing during the worship service in expression of thanksgiving for the new life brought about by the Spirit (→ ψαλμός; ὑμνέω 4). Only later was the liturgical distinction made between the (OT) Psalms and the (other biblical) *cantica.*

In Rev 5:9 (ᾄδουσιν ᾠδὴν καινήν); 14:3 (bis); 15:3 (ᾄδουσιν τὴν ᾠδὴν Μωϋσέως . . . καὶ τὴν ᾠδὴν τοῦ ἀρνίου) ᾠδή is used of a (new) song of the four creatures and twenty-four elders (5:9), the 144,000 sealed ones (14:3), and "those who have conquered" (15:3). The texts of the ᾠδαί cited in 5:9f. and 15:3f. (cf. further 4:8, 11; 5:12f.; 7:10; 11:15, 17f.; 12:10-12; 19:1f., 5, 6-8) are strongly oriented to the context at hand and are thus literary constructs of the author, rather than songs taken directly from congregational worship (see G. Delling, *NovT* 3 [1959] 107-37; K.-P. Jörns, *Das hymnische Evangelium* [SNT 5, 1971]). The "new song" (5:9; 14:3; cf. Ps 95:1 LXX: ᾆσμα καινόν; Isa 42:10 LXX: ὕμνος καινός; Ps 143:9 LXX: ᾠδὴ καινή) is the song of the eschatologically redeemed, which no one else can learn (Rev 14:3). H. Schlier, *TDNT* I, 163-65; K.-H. Bartels, *DNTT* III, 672-75; for further bibliography see *TWNT* X, 960.

ὠδίν, ῖνος, ἡ *ōdin* birth pangs; woe*
ὠδίνω *ōdinō* suffer birth pangs*

Lit.: BAGD 895. — G. BERTRAM, *TDNT* IX, 667-74. — W. HARNISCH, *Eschatologische Existenz* (1973) 62-72.

1. Ὠδίν (instead of ὠδίς, cf. BDF §46.4) occurs *ca.* 34 times in the LXX, though in the NT only in Mark 13:8 par. Matt 24:8; Acts 2:24; 1 Thess 5:3 (the only sg. occurrence). The vb. occurs *ca.* 20 times in the LXX and in the NT only in Gal 4:19, 27; Rev 12:2.

2. Pl. ὠδῖνες refers to the *pangs* of a woman giving birth. In accord with this ὠδίνω means *be in birth pangs /suffer birth pangs,* though also *give birth amid throes.* These words are used both literally and fig.

In Rev 12:2 the seer sees a woman "in the *pangs* and anguish of delivery" (ὠδίνουσα next to βασανιζομένη τεκεῖν). The idea of pangs serves as a referent for comparison in 1 Thess 5:3 in two respects: As "suddenly" as travail comes upon a woman, just as suddenly will destruction come, and just as the woman cannot "escape" from these pangs, neither can one "escape" the destruction.

In Gal 4:27 Paul quotes from Isa 54:1 LXX the reference to "one who is not in travail" (οὐκ ὠδίνουσα parallel with οὐ τίκτουσα) and applies it to the heavenly Jerusalem in contrast to the present Jerusalem, in this context against the background of the contrast between —initially childless—Sarah and the slave Hagar (vv. 21-31). Paul uses the vb. fig. in v. 19 of Galatians as his "children," whom he "again must *bear amid pangs,*" namely, now, after their conversion, in his renewed and painful efforts on their behalf.

According to Acts 2:24 God "loosed the *pangs* of

death" when he raised Jesus, i.e., brought them to an end (BAGD s.v. λύω 4). Luke apparently thinks of the fact that death could keep Jesus as little (cf. v. 24b) as a pregnant woman can keep her child within her body. Therefore, he does not speak of "cords" (Ps 18:5: *ḥeḇel*), but rather (as in Ps 17:5 LXX) of *pangs* (Heb. *ḥeḇel*).

In Jesus' eschatological discourse (Mark 13:8 par. Matt 24:8) ἀρχὴ ὠδίνων refers first to afflictions as such, though perhaps also to the process of the world's rebirth.

W. Radl

ὠδίνω *ōdinō* suffer birth pangs, give birth amid throes
→ ὠδίν.

ὦμος, ου, ὁ *ōmos* shoulder*

This noun occurs only twice in the NT (though frequently in the LXX and in the postapostolic fathers): fig. in Matt 23:4, of the heavy burdens the scribes and Pharisees "put on people's *shoulders*" (cf. the frequently occurring image of the "yoke of the Torah": *m. 'Abot* 3:5; *b. Sanh.* 94b; Matt 11:29). Luke 15:5 refers to the lost sheep that the shepherd goes after and "lays on his *shoulder*" (ἐπιτίθημι ἐπὶ τοὺς ὤμους).

ὠνέομαι *ōneomai* buy*

Acts 7:16: the tomb that "Abraham *bought* . . . from the sons of Hamor in Shechem (ἐν τῷ μνήματι ᾧ ὠνήσατο Ἀβραάμ)." The background is Gen 23:1ff., 16ff. (Abraham's purchase of the cave of Machpelah, taken up in 25:9; 47:30; 49:29ff.; 50:5, 13f.) and 33:18f. (Jacob's purchase of a piece of land from the sons of Hamor, taken up—in the context of Joseph's burial—in Josh 24:32). The two traditions are blended together (→ Συχέμ).

ᾠόν, οῦ, τό *ōon* egg*

Luke 11:12 tells of the son who asks his father "for an *egg*": αἰτήσει ᾠόν; he will not receive a scorpion instead. A fish and serpent are mentioned earlier in the same context (v. 11).

ὥρα, ας, ἡ *hōra* hour (point in time, time of day); hour (interval in time)

1. Occurrences — 2. Neutral chronological usage — 3. The hour of a miracle — 4. Significant events (Jesus' Passion) — 5. As an interval of time — 6. Jesus' hour (John) — 7. Ecclesiastical-eschatological usage — 8. Πρὸς ὥραν

Lit.: G. DELLING, *TDNT* IX, 675-81. — G. FERRARO, *L'"ora" die Cristo nel quarto Vangelo* (Aloisiana 10, 1974). — H. C. HAHN, *DNTT* III, 845-49. — J. JEREMIAS, "Ἐν ἐκείνῃ τῇ ὥρᾳ, (ἐν)

αὐτῇ τῇ ὥρᾳ," *ZNW* 42 (1949) 214-17. — R. SCHNACKENBURG, *SacVb* I, 379-82. — For further bibliography see *TWNT* X, 1294.

1. The subst. ὥρα occurs 106 times in the NT, 76 of those in the Gospels, 11 in Acts, 9 in the Epistles, and 10 in Revelation. As in the LXX, it refers to a point or interval in time, with its specific meaning often determined by the context.

2. It is used in a neutral chronological sense in Mark 6:35 par. Matt 14:15; Mark 11:11; Acts 2:15; 23:23. The owner of the vineyard seeks workers in the parable at the third (Matt 20:3), sixth, and ninth hours (20:5). That all the workers receive the same pay—including those who have worked only an hour (20:12; cf. v. 9)—emphasizes that one's wages depend on the person paying, i.e., on God. "At that *hour*" (Luke 2:38; 7:21; Matt 18:1) or "in this *hour*" (Luke 13:31) indicates that one action occurs simultaneously with another. The same holds true when a gen. follows ὥρα: "*at the hour* of the banquet" (Luke 14:17), "*at the hour* of incense" (1:10), the latter referring probably to the evening Tamid offering at 3:00 P.M. (cf. Acts 3:1). In Acts 10:3 the indication of the ninth hour (again 3:00 P.M.) is probably meant to underscore Cornelius's piety (cf. 10:30). Peter's vision takes place at the sixth hour (v. 9).

3. *Hour* also indicates the immediate occurrence of an event. At the end of healing stories Matthew emphasizes in this way the correspondence between faith and its fulfillment (8:13; 9:22; 15:28; 17:18). Inquiry concerning the hour (John 4:52) serves to confirm a miracle taking place at a distance and leads a royal official and his household to faith (4:53). At Paul's command an evil spirit immediately leaves a woman (Acts 16:18), which proves the efficacy of Jesus' name. Paul's sight is restored as soon as Ananias speaks to him (22:13). As soon as the seventy have returned from their successful mission journey (Luke 10:17), Jesus reacts with rejoicing (10:21ff.). The jailer is baptized with his household just after caring for Paul's and Silas's wounds (Acts 16:33).

4. Reference to the hour occasionally emphasizes the significance of certain events. Two disciples of John the Baptist meet Jesus at the tenth hour (John 1:39). The sixth hour might similarly underscore the importance of Jesus' encounter with the Samaritan woman (4:6), though it initially indicates Jesus' fatigue and thirst (4:7).

Indications of the hour increase in frequency in the Passion accounts. "And when the *hour* came" in Luke 22:14 introduces the portrayal of the Passover meal. During the hour of the Passion the disciples will scatter (John 16:32). "At that *hour*," when Jesus is arrested, he turns to Judas's companions (Matt 26:55). The indication that the crucifixion occurred in the third hour (Mark 15:25) might be an allusion to liturgical practice (J. Ernst, *Mark* [RNT] 468). Before Jesus dies a profound darkness falls between the sixth and ninth hour (Mark 15:33 par.

Matt 27:45/Luke 23:44), which in the context of the prophetic-apocalyptic tradition (cf. Amos 8:9f.) might be interpreting Jesus' death as the commencement of the eschaton. In the ninth hour Jesus recites Psalm 22, which simultaneously expresses abandonment by and trust in God (Mark 15:34 par. Matt 27:46). Pilate's presentation of Jesus at the sixth hour as king (John 19:14) might be an allusion to the slaughter of the Paschal lambs: Jesus is the true Paschal lamb.

5. *Hour* is an interval of time when Jesus asks Simon (Mark 14:37) or the disciples (Matt 26:40) if they could not have watched with him "for one *hour*" (cf. also Luke 22:59; Acts 5:7; 19:34). "To the present *hour*" (1 Cor 4:11), i.e., "until now" (4:13), Paul has accepted all manner of dangers. On the basis of his belief in the resurrection of the dead Paul subjects himself to peril "every *hour*," i.e., all the time (1 Cor 15:30).

6. John refers to Jesus' *hour*, which is dependent only on the Father's will. "My *hour*" (2:4) is first a reference to Jesus' activity from the miracle at Cana (cf. 11:9). His glory, however, already manifests itself in the "sign" (2:11b; cf. 1:14), so that the disciples come to faith (2:11c). As long as Jesus' hour of death has not yet come, his adversaries cannot seize him (John 7:30; 8:20; cf. 7:6). The hour of death is the hour of Jesus' glorification (12:23; 17:1), in which he goes to the Father (13:1). This hour signifies both the world's judgment (12:31) and also the possibility of salvation for mankind (12:32). When the beloved disciple takes Jesus' mother to his home "from that *hour*" on (19:27b), this is an indication of the time; nonetheless one can hardly disregard the concrete point in time: Jesus' exaltation on the cross.

7. The *hour* also appears in ecclesiastical and eschatological contexts. In John's Gospel the joy (of the resurrection, 16:22) will relieve the disciples' grief over Jesus' death, as made clear by the image of the hour in which the woman gives birth (v. 21). "The *hour* is coming," and is already present, when genuine worship of God is no longer bound to one cultic place (4:21), but takes place rather in spirit and truth (v. 23). At this hour the dead are awakened to life (5:25). According to 5:28 (ecclesiastical redaction) this hour still lies in the future. The hour is coming when some believe that they are serving God by killing Jesus' disciples (16:2). That is "their *hour*," the hour of the enemies of Christians (v. 4).

The disciples should not be anxious about what they should say when on trial, since "in that *hour*" of interrogation the Spirit will tell them what to say (Mark 13:11 par. Matt 10:19/Luke 12:12). Because believers do not know at which hour the Son of man (Matt 24:44 par. Luke 12:40; Matt 24:50 par. Luke 12:46) or the bridegroom (Matt 25:13) will appear in judgment (cf. Rev 3:3), they are admonished to be continually prepared (like the householder who does not know at what hour the thief is coming: Luke 12:39; cf. Matt 24:43). In Rom 13:11 ὥρα refers to the eschatological hour of decision in which Christians must prove themselves (cf. 13:12f.). The appearance of the Antichrist, whom the antichrists (i.e., the false teachers) represent, is a sign of the "last *hour*" (1 John 2:18). The Son's own ignorance of the hour (Mark 13:32 par. Matt 24:36) is usually thought to refer to the time of the parousia.

The Christians of Philadelphia are assured of being spared from the hour of trial (Rev 3:10) because they have proven themselves in steadfastness. God has fixed the apocalyptic-eschatological events to the specific time and hour (9:15). The events accompanying the taking up of the two witnesses "at that *hour*" (11:13) recall the miracles accompanying Jesus' resurrection (Matt 27:52). The "*hour* of judgment" (Rev 14:7), which is called the "*hour* to reap" (v. 15), should be the occasion for the nations to praise and worship God (v. 6). The ten kings who will receive power for "one *hour*," i.e., for a short while, together with the beast (17:12), will succumb in the battle against Christ, the Lamb (v. 14). Within only "one *hour*" (18:10, 17, 19) judgment over Babylon will be carried out.

8. The prepositional phrase πρὸς ὥραν (John 5:35; Phlm 15; 2 Cor 7:8) means something like "for a while." Negated it means "not one moment," "never." Πρὸς καιρὸν ὥρας (1 Thess 2:17) also means "for a while."

H. Giesen

ὡραῖος, 3 *hōraios* lovely, beautiful, graceful*

Jesus' cry of woe over the Pharisees and scribes (Matt 23:27) illustrates their hypocrisy with the image of the "whitewashed tombs" (→ κονιάω, τάφος 2), "which outwardly appear *beautiful* (φαίνονται ὡραῖοι)," while inside they are full of skeletons and refuse.

Acts 3 mentions the temple's "*Beautiful* Gate" twice: ἡ θύρα τοῦ ἱεροῦ ἡ λεγομένη Ὡραία (v. 2) and ἡ ὡραία πύλη τοῦ ἱεροῦ (v. 10). Neither Josephus (*Ant.* xv.410ff.; *B.J.* v.190ff.) nor the Mishnah (*Mid.* 1:3ff.) mentions a temple gate by this name. Tradition has therefore often identified it with the eastern Shushan Gate leading into the temple area. More likely, however, it was a gate inside the temple area. Today it is usually identified with the gate of Corinthian bronze mentioned by Josephus (*B.J.* ii.411; v.201ff., and elsewhere) which connected the Court of the Gentiles from the east with the Court of Women. Rabbinic literature also mentions that it was made of radiant Corinthian bronze (*m. Mid.* 2:3; *b. Yoma* 38a), calls it the Nicanor Gate (*m. Mid.* 1:4; *m. Yoma* 3:10), and locates it (probably incorrectly *contra*

Josephus) in one instance between the Court of Women and the Court of Israel (cf. Billerbeck II, 623f.). Thus Acts 3:2, 10 probably refers to the Nicanor Gate, which because of its radiant material stood out among all the gates of the inner temple area (cf. also K. Lake, *Beginnings* V, 479-86; Billerbeck II, 620-25; G. Schrenk, *TDNT* III, 236; E. Stauffer, *ZNW* 44 [1952/53] 44-66; E. Haenchen, *Acts* [Eng. tr., 1971] on 3:2; G. Schneider, *Acts* [HTKNT] I on 3:2 [bibliography]).

In Rom 10:15 Paul freely cites an abbreviated version of Isa 52:7 with the words: ὡς ὡραῖοι οἱ πόδες τῶν εὐαγγελιζομένως [τὰ] ἀγαθά. He is closer to the Hebrew text ("How beautiful on the mountains are the feet of the one who brings good news") than to the LXX (πάρειμι ὡς ὥρα ἐπὶ τῶν ὀρέων, ὡς πόδες εὐαγγελιζομένου ἀκοὴν εἰρήνης, ὡς εὐαγγελιζόμενος ἀγαθά, 52:6f.). Paul's choice of ὡραῖος might have been prompted by ὥρα in the LXX, though it agrees both with the Hebrew text and the Targum and renders the sense of the Hebrew *contra* the LXX. Ὡραῖος is thus not (in connection with ὥρα) to be rendered "timely," though that meaning is attested elsewhere (*contra* BAGD s.v.; E. Käsemann, *Rom* [Eng. tr., 1980] ad loc.), but rather *lovely, pleasant*, in accord with Heb. *nā'â* or *nā'weh* (as elsewhere in the LXX: Cant 1:16; 2:14; Joel 1:19f.; Lam 2:2). Cf. also Billerbeck III, 282f.; P. Stuhlmacher, *Das paulinische Evangelium* (FRLANT 95, 1968) 148-50.

ὡρύομαι *ōryomai* roar*

1 Pet 5:8 likens the devil to a "*roaring* lion" (ὡς → λέων ὡρυόμενος περιπατεῖ, citing Ps 21:14 LXX; cf. also Judg 14:5; Jer 2:15); cf. B. Schwank, *Erbe und Auftrag* 38 (1962) 15-20; L. Goppelt, *1 Pet* (KEK) ad loc. "Roaring" emphasizes the predatory aspects of the lion and the danger associated with it; thus does the unrighteous world persecute the Church.

ὡς *hōs* how, in what way; as, like; after, while; approximately; when, while

1. NT occurrences — 2. Conjunction introducing the distinguishing characteristic — 3. Comparative particle and conjunction — 4. Temporal conjunction — 5. Other uses

Lit.: BAGD s.v. — BDF index s.v. — MAYSER, *Grammatik* index s.v. (II/3, 252f.). — MOULTON, *Grammar* III, index s.v. — RADERMACHER, *Grammatik* index s.v. (239).

1. Ὡς occurs 504 times in the NT (*VKGNT* II s.v.).

2. Introducing the characteristic of something that is of particular importance in the context, whether it be an actual characteristic (John 1:14; Rom 3:7; 1 Cor 3:10; 7:25; 2 Cor 6:4; 1 Thess 2:4, 7a; Col 3:12; Eph 5:1; 1 Pet

1:19; 2:2; 4:15a; with partc. indicating the reason for an action: Acts 28:19; 2 Pet 1:3), an imagined or asserted characteristic (Luke 23:14; Acts 3:12; 23:15, 20; 27:30; 1 Cor 4:7, 18), or a wrongly claimed or false characteristic (Rom 9:32; 2 Cor 10:2; 11:17; 13:7; 2 Thess 2:2a).

3. As a comparative particle indicating the manner in which an action occurs: 1 Cor 3:15a: "[be saved] *as* through fire"; 1 Thess 5:2: "[come] *like* a thief in the night"; Eph 5:33: "[love someone] *as* [one loves] oneself"; Col 3:18: "*as* is fitting"; with some words ellided in Rom 13:13; 1 Cor 13:11a; Gal 3:16; Heb 11:29. In this use the phrase with ὡς can be subj. or obj. of a clause (Matt 1:24; 15:28; 26:39a). Ἕκαστος ὡς, "each one *as/according to*" in Rom 12:3; 1 Cor 3:5; 7:17a, b; Rev 22:12. In indirect questions in Luke 8:47; 23:55; 24:35; Acts 10:38; 20:20; Rom 11:2; 2 Cor 7:15.

As comparative conjunction: *as*. Correlative with οὕτως in Acts 8:32; 23:11; Rom 5:15, 18; 2 Cor 1:7; similarly ὡς . . . καί in Matt 6:10; Acts 7:51; 2 Cor 13:2; Gal 1:9; Phil 1:20. Ὡς with a noun in place of noun or adj. (a Hebraism): ὡς τὰ παιδία (Matt 18:3); ὡς ἡ ἄμμος (Heb 11:12); ὡς χόρτος (1 Pet 1:24); ὡς θάλασσα (Rev 4:6). Introducing a supporting Scripture reference (ὡς γέγραπται, Mark 7:6; Luke 3:4; Acts 13:33) or an authoritative statement (Acts 17:28; 22:5; 25:10).

4. As a temporal conjunction (cf. BDF §455.2), esp. in Luke-Acts and John, with aor.: *when, after* (Luke 1:23, 41, 44; 2:15, 39, and elsewhere; John 2:9; Acts 5:24; 10:7, 25, and elsewhere), with pres. or impf.: *while* (Luke 12:58; 24:32; John 2:23; 8:7; 12:35, 36; Acts 1:10; 7:23; 9:23, and elsewhere), ὡς ἄν with subjunc., referring to a future event: *when* (Rom 15:24; 1 Cor 11:34; Phil 2:23).

5. Other uses: a) consecutive conjunction: *so that* (Heb 3:11; 4:3); b) final particle (Acts 20:24; cf. 17:14 TR); c) with vbs. of knowing, saying, and hearing: *that* (Luke 24:6; Acts 10:28; Rom 1:9; Phil 1:8; 1 Thess 2:10, 11a); d) with numerals: *about, approximately* (Mark 5:13; Luke 1:56; 8:42; John 1:39; 4:6, and elsewhere; Acts 4:4; 5:7, 36, and elsewhere; Rev 8:1); e) in exclamations: *how* (Rom 10:15; 11:33); f) with superlative: ὡς τάχιστα (Acts 17:15). G. Schneider

ὡσάν *hōsan* as it were, so to speak, as if

2 Cor 10:9 in *NTG²⁵: ὡσὰν ἐκφοβεῖν ὑμᾶς, "as it were* to frighten you/*as if* I wanted to frighten you"; in *NTG²⁶* ὡς ἄν. Cf. BDF §453.3.

ὡσαννά *hōsanna* hosanna*

Lit.: BAGD s.v. — A. van den Born, *BL* 761. — J. A. Fitzmyer, "Aramaic Evidence Affecting the Interpretation of

Hosanna in the NT," FS Ellis, 110-18. — T. Lohmanns, *BHH* 752. — E. Lohse, "Hosanna," *NovT* 6 (1963) 113-19. — *idem, TDNT* IX, 682-84. — E. Werner, " 'Hosanna' in the Gospels," *JBL* 65 (1946) 97-122. — For further bibliography see BAGD; *TDNT* IX, 682.

Ὡσαννά is the Greek transliteration of Heb. *hôšî'â nā'* (the imv. was often abbreviated to *hôša'*), *help now,* a cry for help to God (Pss 118:25 [LXX: σῶσον δή]; 12:2), to the king (2 Sam 14:4; 2 Kgs 6:26), or to God on behalf of the king (Ps 20:10). This cry came to be fixed in Jewish liturgical usage (documentation in Billerbeck I, 845-49) since Psalm 118 was among the Hallel Psalms recited at the pilgrimage festivals of Passover and Tabernacles by the pilgrims as they entered the temple area. As Tabernacles changed from a feast of petition to one of rejoicing (cf. Billerbeck II, 805-7), the meaning of *hôšî'â nā'* changed as well: The prayer for help became praise. Judaism gave Psalm 118 various eschatological-messianic interpretations (*Midr. Ps.* 118:22 on Ps 118:24; cf. J. Jeremias, *The Eucharistic Words of Jesus* [1955] 173-75), as did the early Church (cf. in Mark 12:10f. the use of Ps 118:22f., and in Matt 23:39 par. Luke 13:35 the use of Ps 118:26). After the commencement of the Christian era the synagogue, in order to distance itself from the early Church's understanding of the psalm, repressed this messianic interpretation (cf. E. Werner, *JBL* 65 [1946] 121).

In the NT all 6 occurrences of ὡσαννά are in the story of Jesus' entry into Jerusalem; in each case Ps 117:25f. LXX (. . . σῶσον δή . . . εὐλογημένος ὁ ἐρχόμενος ἐν ὀνόματι κυρίου) is taken up and characteristically employed (Mark 11:9, 10; Matt 21:9 bis, 15; John 12:13). In both Mark 11:9 and John 12:13 ὡσαννά is used absolutely. Mark 11:10 underscores the messianic significance of the citation by praising the coming kingdom of David: εὐλογημένη ἡ ἐρχομένη βασιλεία τοῦ πατρὸς ἡμῶν Δαυίδ. For Mark the messianic expectation of the future kingdom of David is fulfilled in Jesus' coming (on the expectation of the reign of David cf. R. Pesch, *Mark* [HTKNT] II, 185; on the close relationship between ὡσαννά and eschatological expectation cf. also *Did.* 10:6). The second hosanna in Mark (11:10) is followed by ἐν τοῖς ὑψίστοις, as also in Matt 21:9b; this is "either a cry of help to God (help now, you in the highest) or an exhortation for the angels to join in the praise (cry hosanna, you in the highest)" (J. Gnilka, *Mark* [EKKNT] II, 118). In Matt 21:9a, 15 the cry of exultation is directed to Jesus as the Son of David (ὡσαννά τῷ υἱῷ Δαυίδ). The widespread use of hosanna in the early Church is attested by the Gospel of John, which is not literarily dependent on the Synoptic Gospels: John 12:13 uses the citation from Ps 117:25f. LXX to describe the crowd "bringing in" Jesus (on this terminology cf. J. Becker, *John* [ÖTK] II, 377f.) as the messianic king. Luke (19:38) omits the hosanna since it would have been unintelligible to Hellenistic readers (cf. Lohse, *TDNT* IX, 683; *contra* W. Schmithals, *Luke* [ZBK] 189: for reasons of political apologetic). W. Rebell

ὡσαύτως *hōsautōs* similarly, in the same way*

17 occurrences in the NT, all in a modal sense. With ποιέω in Matt 20:5, "do *likewise*" (cf. 21:36: "do *the same* to someone"); with λέγω in Matt 21:30; Mark 14:31; with other vbs. in Matt 25:17; Luke 13:5; 20:31; 1 Tim 5:25 (supply εἰσίν); Titus 2:6. Ὡσαύτως δὲ καί, "*likewise* also" (Mark 14:31; Luke 20:31; Rom 8:26; 1 Tim 5:25 v.l.). Esp. in enumerations the vb. can be omitted and supplied from the context (Mark 12:21: ἀπέθανεν; Luke 22:20: καὶ λαβὼν . . .; 1 Cor 11:25: ἔλαβεν . . .; 1 Tim 2:9: βούλομαι; 3:8, 11: δεῖ εἶναι; Titus 2:3: εἶναι).

ὡσεί *hōsei* just like, as, like; about, approximately*

This word occurs 21 times in the NT, including 9 times in Luke and 6 in Acts. As a comparative particle it is approximately synonymous with ὡς, which is often replaced by ὡσεί immediately before nouns and before indications of number or measure. Hence the mss. readings occasionally vary (see below).

Ὡσεί occurs before nouns with the meaning *like, just like* (Matt 3:16; 9:36; Luke 22:44 v.l.; 24:11; Acts 2:3; 6:15; Heb 1:12 [citing Ps 101:27 LXX]); before an adj.: καὶ ἐγένετο ὡσεὶ νεκρός, "he lay there *as if* dead" (Mark 9:26); before a partc.: ὡσεὶ ἐκ νεκρῶν ζῶντες, "*as* those who have been brought from death to life" (Rom 6:13).

Before numerals ὡσεί means *approximately, about* (Matt 14:21; Luke 9:14 bis; Acts 1:15; 2:41; 19:7), as before designations of time (Luke 3:23: ὡσεὶ ἐτῶν, cf. 8:42: ὡς ἐτῶν; 9:28; 22:59; 23:44; Acts 10:3: ὡσεὶ περὶ ὥραν ἐνάτην, "at *about* the ninth hour"), or distance: ὡσεὶ λίθου βολήν, "*about* a stone's throw away" (Luke 22:41). In TR in place of ὡς in Matt 28:3, 4; Mark 1:10; Luke 1:56; 3:22; John 1:32; 4:6; 6:10; 19:14, 39; Acts 4:4; 5:36; 9:18; Rev 1:14; cf. also Mark 6:44; Acts 19:34.

Ὡσηέ *Hōsēe* Hosea*

In Rom 9:25f. Paul cites the prophet Hosea (2:25 and 2:1) with the formula ὡς καὶ ἐν τῷ Ὡσηὲ λέγει, "as indeed he [= God] says in Hosea" (v. 25). In view of the quotation (God's promise) from Hos 2:25 God is to be understood as the speaker; otherwise Paul uses the formula γέγραπται (cf. Rom 1:17; 3:4, 10; 8:36; 9:13, 33; 10:15) or has the scriptural authors themselves speak (cf. Rom 4:6; 9:27, 29; 10:19).

ὥσπερ *hōsper* just as, just as indeed, like*

This adv. occurs 36 times in the NT, including among others 10 times in Matthew and 6 in Romans. In 17 instances it is correlative in comparisons introducing a protasis followed by an apodosis beginning with οὕτως (καί), "*(just) as* . . . so (also)" (Matt 12:40; 13:40; 24:27,

37; Luke 17:24; John 5:21, 26; Rom 5:12 [ὥσπερ . . . καὶ οὕτως in anacoluthon], 19, 21; 6:4, 19; 11:30; 1 Cor 11:12 [without vb.]; 15:22; 16:1; Gal 4:29; Jas 2:26). 2 Cor 8:7 reads: ὥσπερ . . . ἵνα καί (with subjunc.), "*just as* . . . may you also."

In the remaining occurrences ὥσπερ introduces a comparison explicating a previous statement: *just as, (indeed) precisely as*. The vb. is sometimes present (Matt 6:2; 20:28; 25:32; 1 Cor 8:5 [ὥσπερ εἰσὶν θεοὶ πολλοί, "*as* indeed there are many gods"]; 10:7 ["*as* it is written"]; Heb 9:25; Rev 10:3) and is sometimes to be supplied from the context (Matt 6:7; 18:17; Luke 18:11; Rev 2:2 [ὥσπερ with gen. absolute]; 3:17; 11:15; 1 Thess 5:3; Heb 4:10; 7:27). At the beginning of a parable: ὥσπερ γὰρ ἄνθρωπος, "for it will be [with you] *as* with one who . . ." (Matt 25:14). V.l. in the TR in place of ὡς in Matt 5:48; 6:16; 24:38; 2 Cor 1:7; 9:5; Eph 5:24.

ὡσπερεί *hōsperei* as it were, like*

The term occurs in the NT only as a comparative particle in 1 Cor 15:8: ὡσπερεὶ τῷ ἐκτρώματι ὤφθη κἀμοί, "he appeared also to me, *as it were* to one untimely born [among the apostles]"; → ἔκτρωμα. Also in 1 Cor 4:13 v.l. in place of ὡς.

ὥστε *hōste* for this reason, therefore; so that; in order that

This word occurs 83 times in the NT, esp. in Matthew (15 occurrences), Mark (13), Acts (8), 1 Corinthians (14), and 2 Corinthians (7).

As a conjunction indicating result ὥστε introduces both independent and dependent clauses. In independent result clauses it means *therefore, for that reason,* and is followed by ind., imv., or hortatory subjunc. (only 1 Cor 5:8: "Let us *therefore* celebrate the festival"). In dependent result clauses it means *so that* and is followed by ind. (only Gal 2:13; John 3:16: οὕτως . . . ὥστε, "so . . . *that*"; cf. BDF §391) or, more often, acc. with inf. or (less frequently) simply the inf. It is also followed by the inf. with the meaning *for the purpose of, with the intention of,* referring to intended result (virtually synonymous with ἵνα; cf. BDF §391, esp. 1-3).

Examples of independent result clauses with ind.: ὥστε ἔξεστιν, "*therefore* it is permitted" (Matt 12:12); ὥστε οὐκέτι εἰσὶν δύο, "*so* they are no longer two" (19:6); *thus/therefore* (23:31; 2 Cor 5:17 [without vb.], and elsewhere). With imv. following from a preceding statement (1 Cor 3:21; 4:5; 11:33; 14:39; 15:58; Phil 2:12; 4:1; 1 Thess 4:18; 1 Pet 4:19). Dependent result clauses with acc. and inf. (Matt 8:24; 8:28 [ὥστε μή]; 12:22; 13:2, 32, 54); οὕτως ὥστε (Acts 14:1); τοιαύτη . . . ὥστε, "of such a kind/such *that*" (1 Cor 5:1; 2 Cor 1:8; 1 Pet 1:21, and elsewhere); without acc. (Matt 15:33; 24:24; Mark 3:10; Acts 5:15; 1 Cor 13:2, and elsewhere); with inf. in a final sense (Matt 10:1; 27:1; Luke 4:29; 9:52; 20:20; Acts 20:24 v.l.). T. Muraoka, *NovT* 15 (1973) 205-19.

ὠτάριον, ου, τό *ōtarion*   ear, earlobe*

The diminutive of οὖς refers to the outer part of the *ear* (→ ὠτίον) and is used in Mark 14:47 and John 18:10 of the severed (John: right) *ear* of the high priest's slave (v.l. variously ὠτίον, as in par. Matt 26:51 /Luke 22:51; John 18:26; in Luke 22:50: οὖς). J. Horst, *TDNT* V, 559.

ὠτίον, ου, τό *ōtion*   ear, earlobe*

The diminutive of οὖς refers (as does → ὠτάριον) both to the outer part of the *ear,* the *earlobe,* and, in Hellenistic usage, including the LXX, also to the *ear* in general. In the NT it is used only of the severed ear of the high priest's slave (Matt 26:51 [*contra* Mark 14:47: ὠτάριον), in Luke 22:51 (L) to Jesus' healing of the ("right," v. 50: οὖς . . . δεξιόν) *ear.* John 18:26 mentions a relative of the the man whose (right, 18:10: ὠτάριον . . . δεξιόν) *ear* Peter had cut off. Cf. further Mark 14:47; John 18:10 v.l. J. Horst, *TDNT* V, 558.

ὠφέλεια, ας, ἡ *ōpheleia*   use, advantage*

Rom 3:1: τίς ἡ ὠφέλεια τῆς περιτομῆς, "Of what *use* is circumcision?" (cf. 2:17ff., 25ff.); Jude 16: ὠφελείας χάριν, "in order to gain *advantage"* (v.l. ὠφελία; cf. BDF §23).

ὠφελέω *ōpheleō*   help, benefit, support (vb.); pass.: be of value*

1. Occurrences in the NT — 2. Meanings — a) *Be of use, accomplish* — b) *Benefit* — 3. Secular and theological usage

Lit.: BAGD s.v. — BDF §§151.1; 159.2. — M. SÆBØ, *THAT* I, 746-48.

1. The vb. ὠφελέω and its derivatives → ὠφέλεια and → ὠφέλιμος occur altogether 21 times in the NT, including 9 times in the Gospels and 12 times in the Epistles. Ὠφελέω and ὠφέλεια (further → ὄφελος [1 Cor 15:32; Jas 2:14, 16]) serve in the LXX largely as translations of Heb. y῾l (Hiphil), "help, be of use."

2. As in classical Greek, ὠφελέω is used with acc. or absolutely of a person (Matt 27:24: οὐδὲν ὠφελεῖ, "he *is accomplishing* nothing"; John 12:19: "you *are accomplishing* nothing") or of a thing (Rom 2:25: ὠφελεῖ: *it is of value;* negated in John 6:63).

a) With the meaning *be of use, accomplish* ὠφελέω,

like Heb. y῾l, is used only with negation (except in Rom 2:25): directly with the indefinite pron. οὐδέν or μηδέν (Matt 27:24; Mark 5:26; 1 Cor 13:3; Gal 5:2) or with the negative particle οὐκ (John 6:63; 12:19; Heb 4:2; 13:9), indirectly in rhetorical questions anticipating a negative response (Mark 8:36 par. Matt 16:26/Luke 9:25 [the textual variants for these passages are the result of harmonization attempts]; 1 Cor 14:6: τί ὑμᾶς ὠφελήσω ἐὰν μὴ . . . ;).

b) Only Mark 7:11 par. Matt 15:5 uses ὠφελέω in the sense of *benefit, support.* The words δῶρον, ὃ ἐὰν ἐξ ἐμοῦ ὠφεληθῇς, "[let] temple offerings [be] the *benefit you might have* from me," correspond precisely to a Jewish vow formula (e.g., *m. Ned.* 8:7). The person taking the vow could also get out of the claims made by the person addressed without having to render anything to the temple (cf. Billerbeck I, 711).

3. The NT uses ὠφελέω predominantly in theological, though also in purely secular contexts.

a) Ὠφελέω is used in secular senses of unsuccessful human undertakings on the part of Pilate (Matt 27:24), the Pharisees (John 12:19), or the woman with the chronic hemorrhage (Mark 5:26) and of benefit from material goods that parents would have from a son (Mark 7:11 par. Matt 15:5).

b) More frequently ὠφελέω is used of a (negated) benefit or aid regarding salvation. The benefit of "gaining the whole world," as a symbol of ultimate human success and human security, is questioned in view of the loss of life itself in death (Mark 8:36 par.). "It is the Spirit that gives life, the flesh *is of no avail"* (John 6:63). The vb. is also used of the value or uselessness of circumcision over against the real advantage of salvation in Jesus Christ (Rom 2:25; Gal 5:2), of the uselessness of human works for attaining salvation, if such works are not characterized by love (1 Cor 13:3), and the uselessness of speaking in tongues without interpretation or teaching (14:6). Finally, it is used of the inefficacy of the gospel itself if it does not meet with faith in the hearers (Heb 4:2) and of the uselessness of a life based only on food regulations for attaining grace (13:9).   M. Rutenfranz

ὠφελία, ας, ἡ *ōphelia*   use, advantage
A common Hellenistic spelling of → ὠφέλεια.

ὠφέλιμος, 2 *ōphelimos*   useful, advantageous*

This noun occurs 4 times in the NT, all in parenetic contexts in the Pastorals. According to 1 Tim 4:8 (bis) "bodily training is *useful* only for some things, while godliness is *of value* in every way" (πρὸς ὀλίγον ὠφέλιμος . . . , πρὸς πάντα ὠφέλιμος; cf. A. Oepke, *TDNT* I, 775f.). The context suggests that the idea of "training, physical fitness" is to be appropriated for the realm of piety, alluding to the ascetic goals of the adversaries in vv. 1ff. (cf. N. Brox, *Die Pastoralbriefe* [RNT] on 4:8). 2 Tim 3:16: πᾶσα γραφή . . . καὶ ὠφέλιμος πρὸς διδασκα-λίαν . . . , "*useful/profitable* for teaching. . . ." Titus 3:8: "good deeds" (καλὰ ἔργα) are expected of Church members, since they are καλὰ καὶ ὠφέλιμα τοῖς ἀνθρώποις, "good and *profitable* for people."

INDEX TO VOLUMES 1–3

barley κριθή, 2:317

barley flour, made from κρίθινος, 2:317

barn ἀποθήκη, 1:129

Barnabas Βαρναβᾶς, 1:199

barracks παρεμβολή, 3:38

barren στεῖρα, 3:272

Barsabbas Βαρσαββᾶς, 1:199

Bartholomew Βαρθολομαῖος, 1:198

Bartimaeus Βαρτιμαῖος, 1:200

baseness ῥυπαρία, 3:215

basin for washing the feet ποδινιπτήρ, 3:123

basis θεμέλιον, 2:139; θεμέλιος, 2:139; ὑπόστασις, 3:406

basket κόφινος, 2:313; σαργάνη, 3:229; σπυρίς, 3:267

bath βάτος (II), 1:209; λουτρόν, 2:361

bathe λούω, 2:361

battle line παρεμβολή, 3:38

battle (noun) μάχη, 2:398; πάλη, 3:8; πόλεμος, 3:128

battle (vb.) μάχομαι, 2:398

be εἰμί, 1:392

be, cause to ἀποδείκνυμι, 1:126

beach αἰγιαλός, 1:36

beam δοκός, 1:343

bear (noun) ἄρκος, 1:152

bear (vb.) ἀνέχομαι, 1:98; τίκτω, 3:356; ὑποφέρω, 3:408; φέρω, 3:418

bear a name χρηματίζω, 3:474

bear children τεκνογονέω, 3:340

bear (continually) φορέω, 3:436

bear fruit καρποφορέω, 2:252

bear good fruit εὐφορέω, 2:86

bear ripe fruit τελεσφορέω, 3:346

bear with someone's manner τροποφορέω, 3:371

bear witness μαρτυρέω, 2:389

bear witness against καταμαρτυρέω, 2:264

bear witness in support of συμμαρτυρέω, 3:287

bear witness to beforehand προμαρτύρομαι, 3:158

bearable ἀνεκτός, 1:96

bearing καταστολή, 2:269

bearing evil calmly ἀνεξίκακος, 1:97

beast θηρίον, 2:148

beast of burden ὑποζύγιον, 3:402

beat δέρω, 1:287; κατακόπτω, 2:259; τύπτω, 3:376

beat (one's breast) κόπτω, 2:308

beat with a rod ῥαβδίζω, 3:206

beat (with a staff or rod) ῥαπίζω, 3:208

beatitude μακαρισμός, 2:379

beautiful ἀστεῖος, 1:173; καλός, 2:244; ὡραῖος, 3:508

beautifully καλῶς, 2:246

beauty εὐπρέπεια, 2:82

because διότι, 1:336; ἐπεί, 2:19; ἐπειδή, 2:19; καθότι, 2:226; ὅτι, 2:538

because of διά, 1:296; ἐκ (ἐξ), 1:402; ἕνεκα (ἕνεκεν), 1:452; περί, 3:71; χάριν, 3:457

become γίνομαι, 1:247

bed κλινάριον, 2:300; κλίνη, 2:300; κοίτη, 2:305; κράβαττος, 2:313

bedroom κοιτών, 2:305

bee, belonging to a μελίσσιος, 2:403

Beelzebul Βεελζεβούλ, 1:211

before ἔμπροσθεν, 1:446; ἔναντι, 1:449; ἐναντίον, 1:449; ἐνώπιον, 1:462; κατενώπιον, 2:271; πρίν, 3:150; πρό, 3:150

before all πρῶτον, 3:187

beg ἐπαιτέω, 2:17; προσαιτέω, 3:161

beget γεννάω, 1:243; τεκνογονέω, 3:340

beggar προσαίτης, 3:162

begin ἄρχω, 1:165; ἐνάρχομαι, 1:449

begin earlier προενάρχομαι, 3:154

begin speaking ἀποκρίνομαι, 1:133

beginning ἀρχή, 1:161

begotten γεννητός, 1:244

behave πράσσω, 3:145

behave foolishly παραφρονέω, 3:35

behave improperly ἀσχημονέω, 1:176

behave violently βιάζομαι, 1:216

behavior κατάστημα, 2:269

behead ἀποκεφαλίζω, 1:133; πελεκίζω, 3:67

behind μετά, 2:413; ὄπισθεν, 2:523; ὀπίσω, 2:523

behind, be διώκω, 1:338

behold (imv., interjection) ἴδε, 2:171; ἰδού, 2:173

behold (vb.) θεάομαι, 2:136

Beliar Βελιάρ, 1:212

believe δοκέω, 1:340; ἡγέομαι, 2:113; νομίζω, 2:470; πείθω, 3:63; πιστεύω, 3:91; ὑπολαμβάνω, 3:404

believe, fail to ἀπιστέω, 1:121

believing πιστός, 3:97

believing, not ἄπιστος, 1:121

bellow κραυγάζω, 2:316

belly κοιλία, 2:301

belonging to another ἀλλότριος, 1:64

belonging to the same body σύσσωμος, 3:312

belonging together σύμφυτος, 3:290

beloved ἀγαπητός, 1:8; φίλος, 3:427

below κάτω, 2:275; κατωτέρω, 2:275; ὑποκάτω, 3:403

belt ζώνη, 2:109

bend κάμπτω, 2:248; κλίνω, 2:300; συγκάμπτω, 3:283

bend down κύπτω, 2:328

bend over συγκύπτω, 3:283

bend over (in order to look into) παρακύπτω, 3:29

beneath ὑπό, 3:401

benefactor εὐεργέτης, 2:76, 77

beneficial σύμφορος, 3:290

beneficial to the community κοινωνικός, 2:305

benefit (noun) εὐεργεσία, 2:76; σύμφορος, 3:290

benefit (vb.) ὠφελέω, 3:511

benevolent ἵλεως, 2:186

benevolently φιλανθρώπως, 3:424

Benjamin Βενιαμίν, 1:212

bent, be completely συγκύπτω, 3:283

Beor Βεώρ, 1:213

bequeath διατίθεμαι, 1:314

bequeathed (by God), be προσκληρόομαι, 3:172

Berea, from Βεροιαῖος, , 1:213

Bernice Βερνίκη, 1:212

Beroea Βέροια, 1:213

beryl βήρυλλος, 1:216

beside oneself, be ἐκπλήσσομαι, 1:420

besprinkle ῥαντίζω, 3:207

best βελτίων, 1:212

best seat (in a synagogue) πρωτοκαθεδρία, 3:187

bestow περιτίθημι, 3:78

Bethabara Βηθαβαρά, 1:213

Bethany Βηθανία, 1:213

Bethesda Βηθζαθά (Βηζαθά), Βηθεσδά, 1:213

Bethlehem Βηθλέεμ, 1:214

Bethphage Βηθφαγή, 1:215

Bethsaida Βηθσαϊδά(ν), 1:215

betrayer προδότης, 3:154

betroth ἁρμόζω, 1:153

betrothed, be μνηστεύομαι, 2:436

better βελτίων, 1:212; κάλλιον, 2:244; κομψότερον, 2:307

between ἀναμέσον, 1:85; μέσος, 2:411; μεταξύ, 2:419

bewail κλαίω, 2:293

bewitch βασκαίνω, 1:208

beyond ἐπέκεινα, 2:20; ὑπερέκεινα, 3:398

deity εἴδωλον, 1:386; θεότης, 2:143

dejection κατήφεια, 2:273

delay (noun) ἀναβολή, 1:76; βραδύτης, 1:226

delay (vb.) ὀκνέω, 2:505

delegate ἀπόστολος, 1:142

deliberately ἑκουσίως, 1:419

deliver ἀναδίδωμι, 1:80

deliver blows with a stick ῥαβδίζω, 3:206

deliverance σωτηρία, 3:327; σωτήριον, 3:329

deliverer σωτήρ, 3:325

delusion ἄγνοια, 1:20

demand αἰτέω, 1:43; ἀπαιτέω, 1:114; ἐπιποθέω, 2:33; κελεύω, 2:280

demand back ἀπαιτέω, 1:114

demand one's right ἀνταποκρίνομαι, 1:108

Demas Δημᾶς, 1:295

demeanor καταστολή, 2:269

Demetrius Δημήτριος, 1:295

demolish διαφθείρω, 1:315; κατασκάπτω, 2:268

demon δαιμόνιον, 1:271; δαίμων, 1:271

demonic δαιμονιώδης, 1:274

demonstration ἔνδειξις, 1:450

den σπήλαιον, 3:264

denarius δηνάριον, 1:296

depart ἀναλύω, 1:84; διΐστημι, 1:324; μεταίρω, 2:414

depart from ἀστοχέω, 1:174

departure ἀνάλυσις, 1:84; ἄφιξις, 1:183; ἔξοδος, 2:8

departure, point of ἀφορμή, 1:184

deportation μετοικεσία, 2:420

depressed, be ταλαιπωρέω, 3:331

deprive of sight τυφλόω, 3:378

deprive of (the prize of) victory καταβραβεύω, 2:256

depth βάθος, 1:190

Derbe Δέρβη, 1:287

Derbe, from Δερβαῖος, 1:287

deride ἐκμυκτηρίζω, 1:419; καταγελάω, 2:256; μωμάομαι, 2:449

derision ἐμπαιγμός, 1:444

descendant ἔκγονος, 1:406

descendants σπέρμα, 3:263

descent γένεσις, 1:242; κατάβασις, 2:255

describe accurately διασαφέω, 1:310

desecrate βεβηλόω, 1:211

desert ἐρημία, 2:51

deserted ἔρημος, 2:51

desire (noun) ἐπιθυμία, 2:27; ἐπιπόθεια, 2:32; ἐπιπόθησις,

2:33; ἐπιποθία, 2:33; ἡδονή, 2:114; ὄρεξις, 2:531; ὁρμή, 2:533

desire (vb.) ἐπιθυμέω, 2:27; ἐπιποθέω, 2:33; θέλω, 2:138

desire to please (noun) ἀρεσκεία, 1:151

desire to please (vb.) ἀρέσκω, 1:151

desires, one who ἐπιθυμητής, 2:27

despair ἀπελπίζω, 1:437; ἐξαπορέομαι, 2:2

despairing, be ἐκκακέω, 1:410

despise καταφρονέω, 2:270; μισέω, 2:431; περιφρονέω, 3:80

despises, one who καταφρονητής, 2:270

despondent δειλός, , 1:281

despondent, be δειλιάω, 1:281

despotic ruler τύραννος, 3:376

destined to, be μέλλω, 2:403

destroy ἀπόλλυμι, 1:135; διαφθείρω, 1:315; ἐρημόω, 2:52; καθαιρέω, 2:217; καταλύω, 2:264; καταργέω, 2:267; κατασκάπτω, 2:268; καταφθείρω, 2:270; κενόω, 2:282; λυμαίνομαι, 2:362; ὀλεθρεύω, 2:506; ὀλοθρεύω, 2:508; περιαιρέω, 3:73; πορθέω, 3:137

destroyed, be ἀφανίζω, 1:180; καταφθείρω, 2:270

destroyer Ἀπολλύων, 1:136; ὀλεθρευτής, 2:506; ὀλοθρευτής, 2:508

destruction ἀναίρεσις, 1:81; ἀπώλεια, 1:135; ἀφανισμός, 1:180; διαφθορά, 1:315; ἐρήμωσις, 2:52; καθαίρεσις, 2:217; καταστροφή, 2:269; ὄλεθρος, 2:506; σύντριμμα, 3:311; φθορά, 3:422

determine διαγινώσκω, 1:298; ἐπικρίνω, 2:30; ὁρίζω, 2:531; τάσσω, 3:336

determine beforehand προετοιμάζω, 3:155; προτάσσω, 3:181; προτίθεμαι, 3:182

determine by lot κληρόω, 2:300

determined τακτός, 3:331

detest ἀποτρέπομαι, 1:147; βδελύσσομαι, 1:210

detestable στυγητός, 3:281

devastate πορθέω, 3:137

devastation ἐρήμωσις, 2:52

deviate ἀστοχέω, 1:174; παραβαίνω, 3:14

devil διάβολος, 1:297

devise slyly or craftily σοφίζω, 3:261

devote oneself to σχολάζω, 3:319

devour ἀναλίσκω, 1:84; καταπίνω, 2:266; κατεσθίω, 2:271

diadem διάδημα, 1:298

dialect διάλεκτος, 1:307

diarrhea δυσεντέριον, 1:361

Didymus Δίδυμος, 1:320

die ἀπογίνομαι, 1:125; ἀποθνῄσκω, 2:129; ἀπόλλυμι, 1:135; ἀποψύχω, 1:147; ἐκψύχω, 1:424; θνῄσκω, 2:153; νεκρόω, 2:461; τελευτάω, 3:346

die out γηράσκω, 1:247

die together συναπόλλυμαι, 3:298

die with συναποθνῄσκω, 3:298

different διάφορος, 1:315

different, be διαφέρω, 1:315

different teaching, spread a ἑτεροδιδασκαλέω, 1:317

differently ἑτέρως, 2:67

difficult βαρύς, 1:200; δύσκολος, 1:361

difficult, make things (more) παρενοχλέω, 3:38

difficult to explain δυσερμήνευτος, 2:54

difficult to interpret δυσερμήνευτος, 2:54

difficult to make intelligible δυσερμήνευτος, 2:54

difficulty μόχθος, 2:444

difficulty, with βαρέως, 1:198; δυσκόλως, 1:361; μόγις, 2:436; μόλις, 2:439

dig ὀρύσσω, 2:534; σκάπτω, 3:250

dig around σκάπτω, 3:250

dig up ἐξορύσσω, 2:9; ὀρύσσω, 2:534

dignity σεμνότης, 3:238

diligently ἐπιμελῶς, 2:31

dill ἄνηθον, 1:98

diminish ἐλαττόω, 1:426

Dionysius Διονύσιος, 1:336

Dioscuri Διόσκουροι, 1:336

Diotrephes Διοτρέφης, 1:336

dip βάπτω, 1:192; ἐμβάπτω, 1:442

dip into ἐμβάπτω, 1:442

direct βραβεύω, 1:226; προΐστημι, 3:156; συντάσσω, 3:309; χρηματίζω, 3:474

direction ἐπιταγή, 2:41

direction, divine χρηματισμός, 3:474

dirge θρῆνος, 2:154

dirt βόρβορος, 1:223; ῥυπαρία, 3:215; ῥύπος, 3:215

dirty ῥυπαρός, 3:215

dirty, become ῥυπαίνομαι, 3:215; ῥυπαρεύομαι, 3:215

disable καταναρκάω, 2:265

disadvantage ζημία, 2:101

draw to oneself παραλαμβάνω, 3:29
draw together συστέλλω, 3:313
draw up ἀνασπάω, 1:87
draw (water) ἀντλέω, 1:112
drawing up of borders ὁροθεσία, 2:533
drawn along, be συναπάγομαι, 3:298
dreadfully δεινῶς, 1:281
dream (noun) ἐνύπνιον, 1:462; ὄναρ, 2:517
dream (vb.) ἐνυπνιάζομαι, 1:462
dress ἐνδιδύσκω, 1:450; ἐνδύω, 1:451
dressing ἔνδυσις, 1:451
drift ἐκπίπτω, 1:420
drift away παραρρέω, 3:34
drilled hole τρύπημα, 3:208
drink (noun) πόμα, 3:134; πόσις, 3:140
drink (vb.) πίνω, 3:88
drink, cause to ποτίζω, 3:142
drink down καταπίνω, 2:266
drink together συμπίνω, 3:288
drink water ὑδροποτέω, 3:380
drink, strong σίκερα, 3:243
drinker μέθυσος, 2:401
drinker of wine οἰνοπότης, 2:505
drinking πόσις, 3:140; πότος, 3:143
drinking party πότος, 3:143
drinking vessel ποτήριον, 3:141
drive ἐλαύνω, 1:426; συνελαύνω, 3:303
drive away ἀπελαύνω, 1:120
drive out ἐκβάλλω, 1:405; ἐξωθέω, 2:13
drops θρόμβος, 2:156
drowned, be καταποντίζομαι, 2:267
drunk πάροινος, 3:42
drunk, be μεθύω, 2:401
drunk, get μεθύσκω, 2:401
drunk, make μεθύσκω, 2:401
drunkard μέθυσος, 2:401; οἰνοπότης, 2:505; πάροινος, 3:42
drunkenly dissolute πάροινος, 3:42
drunkenness μέθη, 2:401; οἰνοφλυγία, 2:505
Drusilla Δρούσιλλα, 1:354
dry (adj.) ἄνυδρος, 1:112; ξηρός, 2:486
dry (vb.) ἐκμάσσω, 1:419
dry, become ξηραίνω, 2:486
dry up ξηραίνω, 2:486
dry wood φρύγανον, 3:440
dull, make παχύνω, 3:62
dung heap κοπρία, 2:308
dungeon φυλακή, 3:441
dupe κατασοφίζομαι, 2:269
duration χρόνος, 3:488
during κατά, 2:253

dust κονιορτός, 2:307; χοῦς, 3:471
dwell καταμένω, 2:264; κατοικέω, 2:273; οἰκέω, 2:495
dwell, cause to κατοικίζω, 2:274; κατασκηνόω, 2:268
dwell in/among ἐγκατοικέω, 1:377
dwell in a tent σκηνόω, 3:252
dwell in the neighborhood περιοικέω, 3:74
dwell together συνοικέω, 3:309
dwell within ἐνοικέω, 1:456
dwelling κατοίκησις, 2:274; κατοικητήριον, 2:274; κατοικία, 2:274; μονή, 2:439; οἰκητήριον, 2:495; σκήνωμα, 3:253
dwelling among people as a stranger παρεπίδημος, 3:38
dwelling place, give a κατοικίζω, 2:274
dying νέκρωσις, 2:461
dysentery δυσεντέριον, 1:361

each ἕκαστος, 1:403
each one ἕκαστος, 1:403; καθεῖς, 2:221
each other ἀλλήλων, 1:63
eager σπουδαῖος, 3:267
eager, be ζηλεύω, 2:100
eagerly προθύμως, 3:156; σπουδαίως, 3:267
eagerness ὁρμή, 2:533; σπουδή, 3:267
eagle ἀετός, 1:34
ear οὖς, 2:547; ὠτάριον, 3:511; ὠτίον, 3:511
ear of grain στάχυς, 3:271
earlier πρίν, 3:150; πρότερος, 3:181
earliest πρῶτος, 3:188
earlobe ὠτάριον, 3:511; ὠτίον, 3:511
early πρόϊμος, 3:156; πρωΐ, 3:186; πρώϊμος, 3:187; πρωϊνός, 3:187
early fruits πρόϊμος, 3:156
early in the morning πρωΐ, 3:186
early morning ὀρθρινός, 2:531; ὄρθριος, 2:531
early rain πρόϊμος, 3:156
early things πρόϊμος, 3:156
earn προσεργάζομαι, 3:163
earth γῆ, 1:246
earth, made of χοϊκός, 3:469
earthen κεραμικός, 2:283; ὀστράκινος, 2:538
earthly ἐπίγειος, 2:24; κοσμικός, 2:309; χοϊκός, 3:469; ψυχικός, 3:503

earthquake σεισμός, 3:236
easily entangled εὐπερίστατος, 2:81
easily recognizable εὔσημος, 2:85
easy εὔκοπος, 2:78
easy to bear ἐλαφρός, 1:426
eat βιβρώσκω, 1:218; γεύομαι, 1:245; ἐσθίω, 2:58; ἔφαγον, 2:58; τρώγω, 3:372
eat a meal δειπνέω, 1:281
eat breakfast ἀριστάω, 1:152
eat salt together συναλίζομαι, 3:297
eat together συναλίζομαι, 3:297; συνανάκειμαι, 3:297; συνεσθίω, 3:305
eat up καταναλίσκω, 2:265; κατεσθίω, κατέω, 2:271
eaten by worms σκωληκόβρωτος, 3:256
eating βρῶσις, 1:228
eating, without ἄσιτος, 1:172
Eber Ἔβερ, 1:369
economic οἰκουρός, 2:505
edible βρώσιμος, 1:228
edification οἰκοδομή, 2:495
edifice οἰκοδομή, 2:495
education μόρφωσις, 2:444
effective ἐνεργής, 1:453
effective action ἐνέργεια, 1:453
effective power ἐνέργημα, 1:453
effort μόχθος, 2:444
egg ᾠόν, 3:506
Egypt Αἴγυπτος, 1:36
Egyptian (person) Αἰγύπτιος, 1:36
eight ὀκτώ, 2:506
eighteen δεκαοκτώ, 1:284
eighth ὄγδοος, 2:490
eighth-day ὀκταήμερος, 2:506
eighty ὀγδοήκοντα, 2:490
either ἤτοι, 2:125
Elamite (person) Ἐλαμίτης, 1:426
elapse διαγίνομαι, 1:298
elder γέρων, 1:245; πρεσβύτερος, 3:148
Eleazar Ἐλεάζαρ, 1:427
elect (adj.) ἐκλεκτός, 1:417; περιούσιος, 3:75
elect (vb.) ἐκλέγομαι, 1:416; χειροτονέω, 3:464
election ἐκλογή, 1:418
element στοιχεῖον, 3:277
eleven ἕνδεκα, 1:450
eleventh ἑνδέκατος, 1:450
Eli Ἠλί, 2:115
Eliakim Ἐλιακίμ, 1:434
Eliezer Ἐλιέζερ, 1:434
Elijah Ἠλίας, 2:115
Elisha Ἐλισαῖος, 1:435
Eliud Ἐλιούδ, 1:434
Elizabeth Ἐλισάβετ, 1:434
Elmadam Ἐλμαδάμ, 1:437

good ἀγαθός, **1**:5; καλός, **2**:244; χρηστός, **3**:474

good conduct ἀρετή, **1**:151

good deed εὐεργεσία, **2**:76; εὐποιία, **2**:81

good path, be on a εὐοδόω, **2**:81

good yield, have a εὐφορέω, **2**:86

goodness ἀγαθωσύνη, **1**:7; χρηστότης, **3**:475

goods ὕπαρξις, **3**:395

goodwill εὔνοια, **2**:80; προθυμία, **3**:156

gospel εὐαγγέλιον, **2**:70

gossip σπερμολόγος, **3**:264

gossip, foolish μωρολογία, **2**:450

gossips, one who ψιθυριστής, **3**:500

gossipy φλύαρος, **3**:429

govern the state πολιτεύομαι, **3**:130

government ἡγεμονία, **2**:112

governor ἡγεμών, **2**:112

grace χάρις, **3**:457

gracious ἵλεως, **2**:186

graft in/on ἐγκεντρίζω, **1**:377

grain καρπός, **2**:251; κόκκος, **2**:305; σῖτος, **3**:246; σπόριμος, **3**:266

grand μεγαλεῖος, **2**:398

grandchild ἔκγονος, **1**:406

grandeur μεγαλειότης, **2**:399

grandmother μάμμη, **2**:382

grant ἐπιχορηγέω, **2**:45; κατατίθημι, **2**:269; παρέχω, **3**:39; χαρίζομαι, **3**:456

grape σταφυλή, **3**:271

grapes βότρυς, **1**:224

grasp ἐπιλαμβάνομαι, **2**:30; καθάπτω, **2**:218; καταλαμβάνω, **2**:260; κρατέω, **2**:314; λαμβάνω, **2**:336; συναρπάζω, **1**:157; χωρέω, **3**:491

grasp the true sense συμβάλλω, **3**:285

grass χόρτος, **3**:471

grasshopper ἀκρίς, **1**:55

gratification πλησμονή, **3**:113

gratitude χάρις, **3**:457

grave μνῆμα, **2**:434; μνημεῖον, **2**:434; τάφος, **3**:337

graze βόσκω, **1**:224

great μέγας, **2**:399

great, become μεγαλύνω, **2**:399

great, make ὑψόω, **3**:410

great number πλῆθος, **3**:103

greater μειζότερος, , **2**:402; μείζων, **2**:402; περισσότερος, **3**:77

greater degree, to a much ὑπερβαλλόντως, **3**:398

greatly μεγάλως, **2**:399

greatness μέγεθος, **2**:401

Greece Ἀχαΐα, **1**:185; Ἑλλάς, **1**:435

greed, in repulsive αἰσχροκερδῶς, **1**:41

greediness πλεονεξία, **3**:102

greedy person πλεονέκτης, **3**:102

greedy, repulsively αἰσχροκερδής, **1**:41

Greek (adj.) Ἑλληνικός, **1**:436

Greek (man) Ἕλλην, **1**:435

Greek (woman) Ἑλληνίς, **1**:435

Greek, in Ἑλληνιστί, **1**:437

green crops χόρτος, **3**:471

greet ἀσπάζομαι, **1**:173

greeting ἀσπασμός, **1**:173

grief πένθος, **3**:69

grieve πενθέω, **3**:69

grind ἀλήθω, **1**:61; λικμάω, **2**:353

grind down συντρίβω, **3**:310

grind one's teeth βρύχω, **1**:227

grinding of teeth βρυγμός, **1**:227

groan (noun) στεναγμός, **3**:272

groan (vb.) στενάζω, **3**:272

groan together συστενάζω, **3**:313

ground γῆ, **1**:246; ἔδαφος, **1**:381

ground, on the χαμαί, **3**:453

ground, to the χαμαί, **3**:453

group of people eating συμπόσιον, **3**:289

group of travelers συνοδία, **3**:308

grow αὐξάνω, **1**:178; μεγαλύνω, **2**:399; πληθύνω, **3**:105

grow, cause to αὐξάνω, **1**:178

grow in length μηκύνομαι, **2**:424

grow old γηράσκω, **1**:247; παλαιόω, **3**:8

grow strong ἐπισχύω, **2**:41

grow together συμφύω, **3**:290; συναυξάνομαι, **3**:299

grow up φύω, **3**:445

grow up together συμφύω, **3**:290

grown together σύμφυτος, **3**:290

growth αὔξησις, **1**:179

grudge, have a ἐνέχω, **1**:454

grumble γογγύζω, **1**:256; διαγογγύζω, **1**:256; ὀνειδίζω, **2**:517

grumbler γογγυστής, **1**:256

grumbling γογγυσμός, **1**:256

guarantee μεσιτεύω, **2**:410

guaranteeing ἔγγυος, **1**:371

guarantor μεσίτης, **2**:410

guard (noun) κουστωδία, **2**:313; φυλακή, **3**:441; φύλαξ, **3**:442

guard (vb.) διαφυλάσσω, **1**:316; παρατηρέω, **3**:35; τηρέω, **3**:354; φρουρέω, **3**:440; φυλάσσω, **3**:442

guest ξένος, **2**:486; φίλος, **3**:427

guidance κυβέρνησις, **2**:327

guide εὐθύνω, **2**:77; κατευθύνω, **2**:271; ὁδηγέω, **2**:491

guide in another direction μετάγω, **2**:414

guide with a bridle χαλιναγωγέω, **3**:453

guileless ἄκακος, **1**:48

guilt ὀφειλή, **2**:550

guiltless ἀναίτιος, **1**:82

guilty αἴτιος, **1**:43; ἔνοχος, **1**:457; ὑπόδικος, **3**:402

gullet λάρυγξ, **2**:344

ha! ἔα, **1**:367

habit ἔθος, **1**:384; συνήθεια, **3**:306

habitation οἰκητήριον, **2**:495

Hades ᾅδης, **1**:30

Hagar Ἀγάρ, **1**:12

hail χάλαζα, **3**:452

hair θρίξ, **2**:156; κόμη, **2**:307

hair, made of τρίχινος, **3**:370

half ἥμισυς, **2**:122

half dead ἡμιθανής, **2**:122

half hour ἡμιώριον, **2**:122

Hallelujah ἁλληλουϊά, **1**:63

Hamor Ἐμμώρ, **1**:444

hand χείρ, **3**:462

hand, be at ἐνίστημι, **1**:455; ἐφίστημι, **2**:92

hand over ἀναδίδωμι, **1**:80; ἐπιδίδωμι, **2**:26; ἐπιτίθημι, **2**:42; παραδίδωμι, **3**:18; παρατίθημι, **3**:22

hand over (something pleasant or pleasing) χαρίζομαι, **3**:456

handed down from one's father or forefathers πατρικός, **3**:58

handed over ἔκδοτος, **1**:408

handkerchief σουδάριον, **3**:258

hands, not made with ἀχειροποίητος, **3**:464

handwritten document χειρόγραφον, **3**:464

hang κρεμάννυμι, **2**:316

hang on ἐκκρεμάννυμι, **1**:416

hang out ἐκκρεμάννυμι, **1**:416

happen συμβαίνω, **3**:285; τυγχάνω, **3**:372

happen earlier προγίνομαι, **3**:153

happen to be present παρατυγχάνω, **3**:35

happening on the fourth day τεταρταῖος, **3**:352

happiness ἱλαρότης, **2**:185

happy ἱλαρός, **2**:185; μακάριος, **2**:376

happy, be ὀνίναμαι, **2**:519

Haran Χαρράν, **3**:461

harbor λιμήν, **2**:353

immovable ἀμετακίνητος, 1:69; ἀσάλευτος, 1:168

impart κατηχέω, 2:273; μεταδίδωμι, 2:414

impartial ἀδιάκριτος, 1:31

impartially ἀπροσωπολήμπτως, 1:148

impede κωλύω, 2:332

imperishability ἀφθαρσία, 3:422

imperishable ἀνέκλειπτος, 1:96; ἀπαράβατος, 1:116; αρτος, 3:422

impervious, be ἀπαλγέω, 1:114

impervious, make παχύνω, 3:62

impious ἀνόσιος, 1:107

implanted ἔμφυτος, 1:447

implore ὁρκίζω, 2:532

important βαρύς, 1:200

impose regulations δογματίζω, 1:340

impossible ἀδύνατος, 1:33; ἀνένδεκτος, 1:97; πῶς, 3:202

impossible, be ἀδυνατέω, 1:33

impression χαρακτήρ, 3:456; τύπος, 3:372

imprison in hell ταρταρόω, 3:336

imprisoned αἰχμάλωτος, 1:44

imprisonment δεσμός, 1:288; τήρησις, 3:355

improvement διόρθωμα, 1:336; κατάρτισις, 2:268

imprudent talk εὐτραπελία, 2:86

impulsiveness ὁρμημα, 2:533

impure ἀκάθαρτος, 2:218; κοινός, 2:302

impurity ἀκαθαρσία, 2:218

impurity of thoughts ῥυπαρία, 3:215

in εἰς, 1:398; ἐν, 1:447

in fact δέ, 1:278

in front ἔμπροσθεν, 1:446

in front of ἔμπροσθεν, 1:446; πρό, 3:150

in need of no support αὐτάρκης, 1:179

in no way μηδαμῶς, 2:423; οὐδαμῶς, 2:540

in order that ὅπως, 2:525; ὥστε, 3:510

in place of ἀντί, 1:108; ὑπέρ, 3:396

in the eyes of ἐναντίον, 1:449

in the same way παραπλησίως, 3:33; ὡσαύτως, 3:510

in this way οὕτω, 2:549

in vain δωρεάν, 1:363; εἰκῆ, 1:388; μάτην, 2:397

in what sense? πῶς, 3:202

in what way ποταπῶς, 3:141; ὡς, 3:508

in what way? πῶς, 3:202

in which way ὅπως, 2:525

inanimate ἄψυχος, 1:187

inappropriate ἀνάξιος, 1:86

inappropriately ἀναξίως, 1:86

inasmuch as ἐπειδήπερ, 2:19

inaugurate ἐγκαινίζω, 1:377

incapable of being tempted ἀπείραστος, 1:119

incense θυμίαμα, 2:159; λίβανος, 2:352; λιβανωτός, 2:352

incense censer λιβανωτός, 2:352

incense offering θυμίαμα, 2:159

incense offering, make an θυμιάω, 2:159

incite ἀνασείω, 1:87; ἀναστατόω, 1:92; κινέω, 2:293; παροτρύνω, 3:43

inclination γνώμη, 1:255; πρόσκλισις, 3:172; ῥοπή, 3:213

incline κλίνω, 2:300

incline toward προσκλίνομαι, 3:172

inconspicuous, make ἀφανίζω, 1:180

incontestable ἀκατάγνωστος, 1:48

incontestably ὁμολογουμένως, 2:516

incorporated along with σύσσωμος, 3:312

incorruptibility ἀφθορία, 1:181

increase (noun) παράδοσις, 3:21

increase (vb.) αὐξάνω, 1:178; πληθύνω, 3:105; προστίθημι, 3:177

increase abundantly ὑπεραυξάνω, 1:179

increase, cause to αὐξάνω, 1:178

increase together συναυξάνομαι, 3:299

incredible παράδοξος, 3:21

indecent ἀσχήμων, 1:176

indecently, behave ἀσχημονέω, 1:176

indeed μέν, 2:406; μήν, 2:424; νή, 2:464

indescribable ἀνεκδιήγητος, 1:96

indestructible ἀκατάλυτος, 1:48

indication ἔνδειγμα, 1:449

indignant, be ἀγανακτέω, 1:8; προσοχθίζω, 3:176

indignation ἀγανάκτησις, 1:8

indivisible ἄτομος, 1:177

indulge σπαταλάω, 3:262

indulgence πλησμονή, 3:113; τρυφή, 3:371

industrious σπουδαῖος, 3:267

inexcusable ἀναπολόγητος, 1:87

inexhaustible ἀνέκλειπτος, 1:96

inexperienced ἄπειρος, 1:119

inexpressible ἀνεκλάλητος, 1:96; ἀνεκδιήγητος, 1:96; ἄρρητος, 1:158

infamous ἐπίσημος, 2:33

infant βρέφος, 1:227

inferior, be ἑσσόομαι, 2:60

inferior, make ἐλαττόω, 1:426

infertile στεῖρα, 3:272

inflamed, be πυρόομαι, 3:201

inflict injury ζημιόω, 2:102

inform ἀγγέλλω, 1:12

infringe, allow oneself to ὑπερβαίνω, 3:398

inhabit κατοικέω, 2:273; οἰκέω, 2:495

inhabited earth οἰκουμένη, 2:503

inherit κληρονομέω, 2:298

inheritance κληρονομία, 2:298

inheritance, give as an κατακληρονομέω, 2:259

inheritance, one who apportions an μεριστής, 2:409

inherited from one's father or forefathers πατρῷος, 3:58

inheriting together συγκληρονόμος, 3:283

iniquitous ἁμαρτωλός, 1:65

initiate μυέω, 2:444

initiated, be μυέω, 2:444

injunction, give an χρηματίζω, 3:474

injure ζημιόω, 2:102

injury, suffer ζημιόω, 2:102

ink μέλαν, 2:402

inn πανδοχεῖον, 3:9; ταβέρνα, 3:331

inner ἐσώτερος, 2:64

inner organs σπλάγχνον, 3:265

inner yearning σπλάγχνον, 3:265

innkeeper πανδοχεύς, 3:9

innocent ἀθῷος, 1:36; ἀναίτιος, 1:82; καθαρός, 2:218

innumerable ἀναρίθμητος, 1:87; μυρίος, 2:446

inquire διερωτάω, 1:323; ἐξεραυνάω, 2:3; ἐραυνάω, ἐρευνάω, 2:48; πυνθάνομαι, 3:197

inscribe ἐγγράφω, 1:371

inscription ἐπιγραφή, 2:25; τίτλος, 3:363

inscription, provide an ἐπιγράφω, 2:25

inscrutable ἀνεξεραύνητος, 1:97

inside ἐντός, 1:460; ἔσω, 2:64

inside, be ἔνειμι, 1:452

insidious δόλιος, 1:343

insight ἔννοια, 1:455; σύνεσις, 3:305

insightful συνετός, 3:305; φρόνιμος, 3:439

insignificant ἄσημος, 1:170; ταπεινός, 3:333

insist on βούλομαι, 1:225

insofar as καθό, 2:226; καθότι, 2:226

insolent person ὑβριστής, 3:379

Judea Ἰουδαία, 2:191
judge (noun) δικαστής, 1:336;
    κριτής, 2:322
judge (vb.) ἀνακρίνω, 2:321;
    βραβεύω, 1:226; κρίνω, 2:318
judge a person by appearances
    προσωπολημπτέω, 3:179
judges according to appearances, one
    who προσωπολήμπτης, 3:179
judgment γνώμη, 1:255; κρίμα,
    2:317; κρίσις, 2:318
judicial investigation, make a
    ἀνακρίνω, 2:321
judicial sentence ἀπόκριμα, 1:133
jug ξέστης, 2:486
Julia Ἰουλία, 2:198
Julius Ἰούλιος, 2:198
jump up ἀναπηδάω, 1:87
Junia Ἰουνία, 2:198
Junias Ἰουνιᾶς, 2:198
just δίκαιος, 1:324; ἔνδικος, 1:451
just as καθά, 2:217; καθάπερ,
    2:217; καθώσπερ, 2:226;
    ὥσπερ, 3:510
just as indeed ὥσπερ, 3:510
just like ὡσεί, 3:510
just the one who ὅσπερ, 2:537
justice δικαιοσύνη, 1:325;
    εὐθύτης, 2:78
justification δικαίωσις, 1:335
justify δικαιόω, 1:330
justly δικαίως, 1:324
Justus Ἰοῦστος, 2:198

keep διαφυλάσσω, 1:316; κρατέω,
    2:314; συντηρέω, 3:310;
    τηρέω, 3:354
keep concealed σιγάω, 3:242
keep in one's memory συντηρέω,
    3:310
keep secret σιγάω, 3:242
keep watch ἀγρυπνέω, 3:400
keeper of the prison δεσμοφύλαξ,
    1:290
keeping τήρησις, 3:355
Kenan Καϊνάμ, 2:229
key κλείς, 2:296
kick λακτίζω, 2:335
kid ἐρίφιον, 2:53
kidnapper ἀνδραποδιστής, 1:95
kidney νεφρός, 2:464
Kidron Κεδρών, 2:280
kill ἀποκτείνω, 1:134;
    διαχειρίζομαι, 1:316; θανατόω,
    2:133; καταστρώννυμι, 2:269;
    νεκρόω, 2:461; φονεύω, 3:435
killer φονεύς, 3:435
killing φόνος, 3:436
kin συγγένεια, 3:282

kind (adj.) ἐπιεικής, 2:26; πραΰς,
    3:146; φιλόφρων, 3:428;
    χρηστός, 3:474
kind (noun) γένος, 1:244; (noun)
    τάξις, 3:333
kind behavior φιλανθρωπία, 3:424
kindle ἀνάπτω, 1:87; ἅπτω,
    1:148; καίω, 2:236; περιάπτω,
    3:73
kindly φιλανθρώπως, 3:424
kindness ἀγαθωσύνη, 1:7;
    ἐλεημοσύνη, 1:428; πραΰτης,
    3:146; χρηστότης, 3:475
kindness, show χρηστεύομαι, 3:474
kindness toward strangers ξενία,
    2:485
king βασιλεύς, 1:205
king, be βασιλεύω, 1:207
kingdom βασιλεία, 1:201
Kish Κείς, Κίς, 2:293
kiss (noun) φίλημα, 3:426
kiss (vb.) καταφιλέω, 2:270;
    φιλέω, 3:425
knee γόνυ, 1:257
knock κρούω, 2:322
knoll βουνός, 1:226
know γινώσκω, 1:248; γνωρίζω,
    1:255; ἐπιγινώσκω, 2:24;
    ἐπίσταμαι, 2:36; νοέω, 2:469;
    οἶδα, 2:493; σύνοιδα, 3:309
know beforehand προγινώσκω,
    3:153
know, not ἀγνοέω, 1:20
knowable γνωστός, 1:248, 256
knowledge γνῶσις, 1:248;
    ἐπίγνωσις, 2:25
known γνωστός, 1:248, 256
known, become φανερόω, 3:413
known, make σημαίνω, 3:238
knows the heart, one who
    καρδιογνώστης, 2:251
Korah Κόρε, 2:308

labor κοπιάω, 2:307
lack ὑστερέω, 3:409
lack of appetite ἀσιτία, 1:172
lady κυρία, 2:328
lair φωλεός, 3:445
lake θάλασσα, 2:127; λίμνη, 2:354
lake, by the παραθαλάσσιος, 3:22
lamb ἀμνός, 1:70; ἀρήν, 1:70;
    ἀρνίον, 1:70; προβάτιον, 3:152
lamb, paschal πάσχα, 3:50
lame παραλυτικός, 3:31;
    παράλυτος, 3:32; χωλός, 3:490
Lamech Λάμεχ, 2:338
lament θρηνέω, 2:154; πενθέω,
    3:69; ταλαιπωρέω, 3:331
lamentation κοπετός, 2:307

lamp λαμπάς, 2:338; λύχνος,
    2:367; φανός, 3:414; φῶς,
    3:447
lampstand λυχνία, 2:366
lance λόγχη, 2:359
land γῆ, 1:246; χώρα, 3:491;
    χωρίον, 3:492
land, by πεζῇ, 3:62
land, piece of χωρίον, 3:492
lane ῥύμη, 3:213
language γλῶσσα, 1:251; φωνή,
    3:446
lantern φανός, 3:414
Laodicea Λαοδίκεια, 2:339
Laodicean Λαοδικεύς, 2:339
large, very πάμπολυς, 3:9
Lasea Λασαία, 2:344
lash φραγέλλιον, 3:437; μάστιξ,
    2:396
lash out λακτίζω, 2:335
lashes μάστιξ, 2:396
last ἔσχατος, 2:60; ὕστερος, 3:409
last year πέρυσι(ν), 3:80
lasting only a time πρόσκαιρος,
    3:171
late ὄψιμος, 2:554; ὄψιος, 2:555
late fig ὄλυνθος, 2:509
late fruit ὄψιμος, 2:554
late (in the day) ὀψέ, 2:554
late, that which is ὄψιμος, 2:554
Latin Ῥωμαϊκός, 3:216
Latin, in Ῥωμαϊστί, 3:216
latrine ἀφεδρών, 1:180
latter ἔσχατος, 2:60; ὕστερος,
    3:409
laud αἰνέω, 1:39
laugh γελάω, 1:240
laugh at καταγελάω, 2:256
laughter γέλως, 1:240
law νομοθεσία, 2:471; νόμος,
    2:471
law, act contrary to the παρανομέω,
    3:32
law, in accordance with the
    νομίμως, 2:471
law, not possessing the ἀνόμως,
    1:106
law, pertaining to the νομικός, 2:470
law, violation of the παράβασις,
    3:14
lawbreaker παραβάτης, 3:14
lawful ἔννομος, 1:455
lawgiver νομοθέτης, 2:471
lawgiver, be a νομοθετέω, 2:471
lawgiving νομοθεσία, 2:471
lawless ἄνομος, 1:106
lawless deed παρανομία, 3:33
lawlessness ἀνομία, 1:106
lawsuit κριτήριον, 2:321
lawyer νομικός, 2:470

linen cloth λέντιον, 2:349; ὀθόνιον, 2:493

linen, fine βύσσος, 1:229

linen garment λίνον, 2:354

linen, made of fine βύσσινος, 1:229

linen strip ὀθόνιον, 2:493

linger βραδύνω, 1:226; διατρίβω, 1:314

Linus Λίνος, 2:354

lion λέων, 2:351

lip χεῖλος, 3:461

list (noun) ἀπογραφή, 1:125

list (vb.) ἀπογράφω, 1:125

listen to εἰσακούω, 1:400; ἐπακροάομαι, 2:17

little βραχύς, 1:226; μικρός, 2:427; ὀλίγος, 2:506

little book βιβλαρίδιον, 1:217

little child τεκνίον, 3:340

little faith, of ὀλιγόπιστος, 2:506

little girl ταλιθα, 3:332

little while, a μικρόν, 2:427

live ἀναστρέφω, 1:93; βιόω, 1:219; ζῶ, 2:105; οἰκέω, 2:495

live among ἐνοικέω, 1:456

live as a foreigner παροικέω, 3:42

live coal ἀνθρακιά, 1:99

live in ἐνοικέω, 1:456

live (in a certain way) περιπατέω, 3:75

live in a certain way ἀναστρέφω, 1:93

live in peace εἰρηνεύω, 1:394

live luxuriously σπαταλάω, 3:262

live next to παροικέω, 3:42

live out of doors ἀγραυλέω, 1:23

live together συνοικέω, 3:309

live with συζάω, 3:284

livelihood διατροφή, 1:314

living being ζῷον, 2:109

living in the neighborhood περίοικος, 3:75

living quarters οἴκημα, 2:495

load γόμος, 1:257; ὄγκος, 2:491; φόρτος, 3:437

loam πηλός, 3:86

loan δάνειον, δάνιον, 1:276

local ἐντόπιος, 1:460

lock κλείω, 2:296

locust ἀκρίς, 1:55

Lod Λύδδα, 2:362

lodging κατάλυμα, 2:263; μονή, 2:439; ξενία, 2:485; πανδοχεῖον, 3:9

lodging, provide ξενίζω, 2:485

log δοκός, 1:343

logos λόγος, 2:356

loin ὀσφῦς, 2:538

loincloth σιμικίνθιον, 3:244

Lois Λωΐς, 2:369

lonely ἔρημος, 2:51

long ago ἔκπαλαι, 1:419; πάλαι, 3:7

long, become μηκύνομαι, 2:424

long hair, wear κομάω, 2:307

longed for ἐπιπόθητος, 2:33

longing ἐπιθυμία, 2:27; ἐπιπόθησις, 2:33; ἐπιπόθεια, ἐπιποθία, 2:33; ὄρεξις, 2:531

long-lived μακροχρόνιος, 2:381

look (noun) βλέμμα, 1:221

look (vb.) ἐμβλέπω, 1:442

look around (in a circle) περιβλέπομαι, 3:73

look at ἀποβλέπω, 1:125; ἐμβλέπω, 1:442; ἐπιβλέπω, 2:23; ἐπισκέπτομαι, 2:33; ἐπισκοπέω, 2:33; ἐποπτεύω, 2:46; ἐφοράω, 2:92

look at again and again ἀναθεωρέω, 1:81

look at (in a mirror) κατοπτρίζομαι, 2:274

look directly in the face ἀντοφθαλμέω, 1:112

look for ἀναζητέω, 1:80; προσδέχομαι, 3:162

look good εὐπροσωπέω, 2:82

look intently διαβλέπω, 1:297

look intently at ἀτενίζω, 1:177

look into παρακύπτω, 3:29

look out σκοπέω, 3:255

look out for φυλάσσω, 3:442

look up ἀναβλέπω, 1:76

loose λύω, 2:368

loose chatter ματαιολογία, 2:396

loosen ἀνίημι, 1:104; ἐπιλύω, 2:31

lord, Lord δεσπότης, 1:290; δυνάστης, 1:358; κύριος, 2:328

lord, be κυριεύω, 2:328

lord, become κατακυριεύω, 2:260

Lord, belonging to the κυριακός, 2:328

Lord (our), come! μαρανα θα, 2:385

lord, position as κυριότης, 2:331

lose ἀπόλλυμι, 1:135

lose heart ἐγκακέω, 1:377

lose one's senses ἐξίστημι, 2:7

lose time χρονοτριβέω, 3:489

lose validity ἐκπίπτω, 1:420

loss ἀποβολή, 1:125; ζημία, 2:101

loss of appetite ἀσιτία, 1:172

lost, be ἀπόλλυμι, 1:135

lot κλῆρος, 2:299

Lot Λώτ, 2:369

lot, divide by κατακληροδοτέω, 2:259

loud μέγας, 2:399

loud cry κραυγή, 2:316

love (noun) ἀγάπη, 1:8; φιλία, 3:426

love (vb.) ἀγαπάω, 1:8; φιλέω, 3:425

love, brotherly φιλαδελφία, 3:424

love for humankind φιλανθρωπία, 3:424

love of money φιλαργυρία, 3:425

lovely προσφιλής, 3:178; ὡραῖος, 3:508

loving φίλος, 3:427

loving children φιλότεκνος, 3:428

loving dearly φιλόστοργος, 3:428

loving God φιλόθεος, 3:427

loving one's brother φιλάδελφος, 3:424

loving one's husband φίλανδρος, 3:424

loving what is good φιλάγαθος, 3:424

low position, of ταπεινός, 3:333

low, make ταπεινόω, 3:334

lower (adj.) κατώτερος, 2:275

lower (vb.) καθίημι, 2:225

lowliness ταπείνωσις, 3:334

lowly ταπεινός, 3:333

Lucius Λούκιος, 2:361

Luke Λουκᾶς, 2:360

lukewarm χλιαρός, 3:469

lump φύραμα, 3:443

lure δελεάζω, 1:285

luxurious life, lead a στρηνιάω, 3:281

luxury στρῆνος, 3:281; τρυφή, 3:371

Lycaonia Λυκαονία, 2:362

Lycaonian language, in the Λυκαονιστί, 2:362

Lycia Λυκία, 2:362

Lydda Λύδδα, 2:362

Lydia Λυδία, 2:362

lying (adj.) ψευδής, 3:496; ψευδολόγος, 3:496

lying (noun) ψεῦσμα, 3:499

lying in ambush ἐγκάθετος, 1:376

lying, without ἀψευδής, 1:187

lyre κιθάρα, 2:293

lyre, play the κιθαρίζω, 2:293

Lysanias Λυσανίας, 2:364

Lysias Λυσίας, 2:364

Lystra Λύστρα, 2:364

Maath Μάαθ, 2:371

Macedonia Μακεδονία, 2:379

Macedonian Μακεδών, 2:379

made up πλαστός, 3:101

made with hands χειροποίητος, 3:464

madness μανία, 2:384

path τρίβος, 3:369
path, make a ὁδοποιέω, 2:491
patience μακροθυμία, 2:380;
  ὑπομονή, 3:405
patient ἀνεξίκακος, 1:97
patient, be μακροθυμέω, 2:380
patiently μακροθύμως, 2:380
Patmos Πάτμος, 3:57
Patrobas Πατροβᾶς, 3:58
Paul Παῦλος, 3:59
paved with stone or marble slabs
  λιθόστρωτος, 2:353
pay (noun) μισθός, 2:432
pay (vb.) τίνω, 3:360
pay attention to ἐπέχω, 2:21;
  ἐπισκοπέω, 2:33; καταμανθάνω,
  2:264; προσέχω, 3:169
pay back ἀνταποδίδωμι, 1:107
pay no attention to παρακούω, 3:29
pay out τελέω, 3:346
pay tithes δεκατόω, 1:284
payment μισθαποδοσία, 2:432
payment, without δωρεάν, 1:363
peace εἰρήνη, 1:394
peace, keep εἰρηνεύω, 1:394
peace, live in εἰρηνεύω, 1:394
peace, make εἰρηνοποιέω, 1:397
peaceable ἄμαχος, 1:69;
  εἰρηνικός, 1:397
peaceful εἰρηνικός, 1:397
pearl μαργαρίτης, 2:385
pebble ψῆφος, 3:500
peculiar to ἴδιος, 2:171
Peleg Φάλεκ, 3:412
penalty δίκη, 1:336
penny κοδράντης, 2:301
Pentecost πεντηκοστή, 3:70
people ἔθνος, 1:381; λαός,
  2:339; ὄχλος, 2:553; πατριά,
  3:57
people (crowd of) δῆμος, 1:296;
  λαός, 2:339
people of twelve tribes
  δωδεκάφυλον, 1:363
peoples ἔθνος, 1:381
perceive αἰσθάνομαι, 1:41; εἶδον,
  1:385; καθοράω, 2:226;
  συνοράω, 3:309
Perez Φάρες, 3:415
perfect παντελής, 3:10; τέλειος,
  3:342
perfecter τελειωτής, 3:346
perfection τελειότης, 3:344;
  τελείωσις, 3:346
perfectly τελείως, 3:345
perfidy δόλος, 1:343
perform magic μαγεύω, 2:371
Perga Πέργη, 3:71
Pergamum Πέργαμος, 3:71
perhaps ἴσως, 2:209; μήποτε,

2:424; μήτι, 2:426; πώς,
  3:202; τάχα, 3:338
period of life ἡλικία, 2:117
period of time καιρός, 2:232
perish with συναπόλλυμαι, 3:298
perishable φθαρτός, 3:422
perjured ἐπίορκος, 2:31
permit ἐάω, 1:368; ἐπιτρέπω, 2:43
permit to go farther προσεάω, 3:163
permitted ἐξόν, 2:9
permitted, it is ἔξεστιν, 2:5; ἐξόν,
  2:5
permitted, not ἀθέμιτος, 1:35
pernicious λοιμός, 2:360
perplexed, be greatly διαπορέω,
  1:310
perplexity ἀπορία, 1:141
persecute διώκω, 1:338
persecute vigorously ἐκδιώκω, 1:408
persecution διωγμός, 1:338
persecutor διώκτης, 1:338
perseverance ἐπιτέλεια, 1:422;
  προσκαρτέρησις, 3:172;
  ὑπομονή, 3:405
persevere in ἐμμένω, 1:444;
  προσκαρτερέω, 3:172
persevere with προσμένω, 3:175
Persis Περσίς, 3:80
persist in βούλομαι, 1:225;
  ἐπιμένω, 2:31
persistent ἐκτενής, 1:422
person ἄνθρωπος, 1:100; ψυχή,
  3:500
person of one's own age
  συνηλικιώτης, 3:306
persuade ἀναπείθω, 1:87; πείθω,
  3:63
persuaded, be πιστόω, 3:98
persuasion πειθώ, 3:63; πεισμονή,
  3:67
persuasion, art of πειθώ, 3:63
persuasive πειθός, 3:63
pervert ἐκστρέφω, 1:422
pestilence λοιμός, 2:360
pet κτῆνος, 2:324
Peter Πέτρος, 3:81
petition αἴτημα, 1:43
Phanuel Φανουήλ, 3:414
Pharaoh Φαραώ, 3:415
Pharisee Φαρισαῖος, 3:415
Philadelphia Φιλαδέλφεια, 3:424
Philemon Φιλήμων, 3:426
Philetus Φίλητος, 3:426
Philip Φίλιππος, 3:426
Philippi Φίλιπποι, 3:426
Philippian person Φιλιππήσιος,
  3:426
Philologus Φιλόλογος, 3:427
philosopher φιλόσοφος, 3:428
philosophy φιλοσοφία, 3:428

Phlegon Φλέγων, 3:428
Phoebe Φοίβη, 3:434
Phoenicia Φοινίκη, 3:434
Phoenix Φοῖνιξ, 3:435
Phrygia Φρυγία, 3:440
Phygelus Φύγελος, 3:440
phylactery φυλακτήριον, 3:442
physician ἰατρός, 2:171
pick τίλλω, 3:357
pick (grapes) τρυγάω, 3:371
pick up βαστάζω, 1:208
piece of money κέρμα, 2:284
pierce διϊκνέομαι, 1:324; νύσσω,
  2:483
pierce through ἐκκεντέω, 1:410;
  περιπείρω, 3:76
pierced, be κατανύσσομαι, 2:265
piercing κατάνυξις, 2:265
piety δεισιδαιμονία, 1:282;
  εὐσέβεια, 2:84
pig χοῖρος, 3:470
pigeon περιστερά, 3:78
Pilate Π(ε)ιλᾶτος, 3:87
pile up ἐπισωρεύω, 2:41
pillar στῦλος, 3:281
pillow προσκεφάλαιον, 3:172
pinnacle πτερύγιον, 3:191
pious δεισιδαίμων, 1:282;
  εὐλαβής, 2:79; εὐσεβής, 2:85;
  θεοσεβής, 2:142
piously εὐσεβῶς, 2:85
Pisidia Πισιδία, 3:91
Pisidian Πισίδιος, 3:91
pit βόθυνος, 1:223; σειρός,
  3:236; σιρός, 3:246
pitcher κεράμιον, 2:283
pitiable ἐλεεινός, 1:428
pity ἐλεημοσύνη, 1:428; ἔλεος,
  1:429
pity, have ἐλεάω, 1:429; ἐλεέω,
  1:429; σπλαγχνίζομαι, 3:265
pity, without ἀνέλεος, 1:96
place (noun) τόπος, 3:366
place (vb.) ἵστημι, 2:205; τίθημι,
  3:356
place around περιΐστημι, 3:74
place at one's disposal χορηγέω,
  3:470
place in the same category (as)
  ἐγκρίνω, 1:378
place (into a condition) περιτρέπω,
  3:80
place next to παρατίθημι, 3:22
place of assembly συναγωγή, 3:293
place of honor πρωτοκαθεδρία,
  3:187; πρωτοκλισία, 3:187
place of learning σχολή, 3:319
place of prayer προσευχή, 3:164
place on display θεατρίζω, 2:136

recall μιμνήσκομαι, 2:430

receive ἀναδέχομαι, 1:80; ἀπολαμβάνω, 1:134; δέχομαι, 1:292; εἰσδέχομαι, 1:400; λαμβάνω, 2:336; παραδέχομαι, 3:18; παραλαμβάνω, 3:29; προσδέχομαι, 3:162; προσλαμβάνομαι, 3:175

receive as a guest ἀναδέχομαι, 1:80; ἐπιδέχομαι, 2:26; ξενίζω, 2:485; συνάγω, 3:292; ὑποδέχομαι, 3:402

receive as a possession κληρονομέω, 2:298

receive (favorably) ἀποδέχομαι, 1:127

receive in full ἀπέχω, 1:120

receive in return ἀπολαμβάνω, 1:134

receive tithes δεκατόω, 1:284

received from one's father or forefathers πατροπαράδοτος, 3:58

recently προσφάτως, 3:177

reckless προπετής, 3:160

reckon λογίζομαι, 2:354

recline κατάκειμαι, 2:258

recline at table ἀνάκειμαι, 1:82

recline together σύγκειμαι, 3:283; συνανάκειμαι, 3:297; συναυλίζομαι, 3:299

recognition γνῶσις, 1:248; ἔπαινος, 2:16

recognition, without ἄτιμος, 1:177

recognizable, easily εὔσημος, 2:85

recognize ἀναγνωρίζω, 1:79

recommend ὑποτίθημι, 3:408

recompense ἀμοιβή, 1:72; ἀνταπόδοσις, 1:107

reconcile ἀποκαταλλάσσω, 2:261; καταλλάσσω, 2:261; συναλλάσσω, 3:297

reconcile oneself διαλλάσσομαι, 1:307

reconciled, be ἱλάσκομαι, 2:185

reconciliation καταλλαγή, 2:261

record ἀπογράφω, 1:125; ἐγγράφω, ἐνγράφω, 1:371; καταγράφω, 2:257

recover ἀπολαμβάνω, 1:134

recovery of sight ἀνάβλεψις, 1:76

recruit μισθόομαι, 2:432

recruit soldiers στρατολογέω, 3:280

red ἐρυθρός, 2:55; κόκκινος, 2:305

red, be πυρράζω, 3:201

redeem ἐξαγοράζω, 2:1

redeemer λυτρωτής, 2:366

redemption ἀπολύτρωσις, 1:138; λύτρον, 2:364; λύτρωσις, 2:366

reduce to ashes τεφρόω, 3:354

reed καλάμη, 2:240; κάλαμος, 2:240

reed pen κάλαμος, 2:240

reef σπιλάς, 3:265

reflect φρονέω, 3:438

reflect on διαλογίζομαι, 1:308

reflection ἀπαύγασμα, 1:117

reform διόρθωμα, 1:336

refrain from φείδομαι, 3:418

refresh ἀναπαύω, 1:86; ἀναψύχω, 1:95; καταψύχω, 2:270

refreshment ἀνάψυξις, 1:95

refuse (noun) περικάθαρμα, 3:74; σκύβαλον, 3:256

refuse (vb.) ἀπαρνέομαι, 1:153; ἀρνέομαι, 1:153; παραιτέομαι, 3:23

refutation ἀπελεγμός, 1:120

refute, totally διακατελέγχομαι, 1:302

region κλίμα, 2:300; μερίς, 2:409; ὅρια, 2:531; χώρα, 3:491

registration ἀπογραφή, 1:125

regret, without ἀμεταμέλητος, 1:69

regulation δικαίωμα, 1:334; παράδοσις, 3:21

regulations, impose δογματίζω, 1:340

Rehoboam Ῥοβοάμ, 3:213

reign βασιλεία, 1:201

reject ἀποδοκιμάζω, 1:129; ἀπωθέομαι, 1:148; παραιτέομαι, 3:23

reject faith σκανδαλίζω, 3:248

rejected ἀπόβλητος, 1:125

rejection ἀποβολή, 1:125

rejoice ἀγαλλιάω, 1:7; ὀνίναμαι, 2:519; εὐφραίνω, 2:86; χαίρω, 3:451

rejoice completely συνήδομαι, 3:306

rejoice with συγχαίρω, 3:283; συνήδομαι, 3:306

rejoicing ἀγαλλίασις, 1:7

rekindle ἀναζωπυρέω, 1:80

relate ἐξηγέομαι, 2:6

related συγγενής, 3:282

related by marriage, become ἐπιγαμβρεύω, 2:23

relationship χρῆσις, 3:474

relative συγγενεύς, 3:282

relative (female) συγγενίς, 3:282

relatives συγγένεια, 3:282

relax ἀναπαύω, 1:86

release (noun) ἀνάλυσις, 1:84; ἄφεσις, 1:181; λύσις, 2:364

release (vb.) ἀπαλλάσσω, 1:114; ἀπολύω, 1:140; ἀφίημι, 1:181

reliability ἀσφάλεια, 1:175; δοκιμή, 1:341

reliable βέβαιος, 1:210

relief ἄνεσις, 1:97

religion δεισιδαιμονία, 1:282; θεοσέβεια, 2:142; θρησκεία, 2:154

religious δεισιδαίμων, 1:282; θρησκός, 2:155

religious reverence, show σεβάζομαι, 3:235

relish προσφάγιον, 3:177

remain διαμένω, 1:308; διατρίβω, 1:314; ἐμμένω, 1:444; ἐπιμένω, 2:31; μένω, 2:407; παραμένω, 3:32

remain at προσμένω, 3:175

remain awake διαγρηγορέω, 1:298

remain behind περιλείπομαι, 3:74

remain in ἐμμένω, 1:444

remain with προσμένω, 3:175

remainder κατάλειμμα, 2:261; λεῖμμα, λίμμα, 2:347

remaining ἐπίλοιπος, 2:31; κατάλοιπος, 2:263; λοιπός, 2:360

remember μιμνήσκομαι, 2:430; μνημονεύω, 2:435; ὑπομιμνήσκω, 3:405

remembrance ἀνάμνησις, 1:85; μνεία, 2:434; μνήμη, 2:435; ὑπόμνησις, 3:405

remind ὑπομιμνήσκω, 3:405

remit χαρίζομαι, 3:456

remnant κατάλειμμα, 2:261; λεῖμμα, λίμμα, 2:347; ὑπόλειμμα, 3:404

remorse, feel μεταμέλομαι, 2:414

removal ἀπόθεσις, 1:129

remove ἀπεκδύομαι, 1:409; ἐκδύω, 1:409; ἐξαίρω, 2:1; κινέω, 2:293; μεθίστημι, 2:401; μετακινέω, 2:414; μετοικίζω, 2:420

remove a roof ἀποστεγάζω, 1:141

render powerless καταργέω, 2:267

renew ἀανακαινίζω, 2:229; ἀνακαινόω, 2:229; ἀνανεόω, 2:462; ἐγκαινίζω, 1:377

renewal ἀνακαίνωσις, 2:229

renounce ἀπολέγομαι, 1:135

rent μίσθωμα, 2:433

rented dwelling μίσθωμα, 2:433

rented, that which is μίσθωμα, 2:433

repayment ἀνταπόδομα, 1:107; ἀνταπόδοσις, 1:107

repays, one who μισθαποδότης, 2:432

repel ἀνακόπτω, 1:83

repent μεταμέλομαι, 2:414

Rephan Ῥαιφάν, 3:207

reply ἀποκρίνομαι, 1:133; προσλέγω, 3:175

rise up together, cause to
συνεγείρω, **3**:299
rising ἀνατολή, **1**:93
risk παραβολεύομαι, **3**:15;
παραβουλεύομαι, **3**:16
rite of cleansing καθαρισμός, **2**:218
river ποταμός, **3**:141
road ὁδός, **2**:491
road, wide πλατεῖα, **3**:101
roamer πλανήτης, **3**:101
roar ἠχέω, **2**:126; μυκάομαι,
2:445; ὠρύομαι, **3**:508
rob ἀποστερέω, **1**:142; συλάω,
3:285; συλαγωγέω, **3**:285
rob temples ἱεροσυλέω, **2**:179
robber ἅρπαξ, **1**:157; λῃστής, **2**:351
robbery ἁρπαγή, **1**:157; ἁρπαγμός,
1:156
robe στολή, **3**:278
rock πέτρα, **3**:80
rock crystal κρύσταλλος, **2**:324
rock in the sea σπιλάς, **3**:265
rocky πετρώδης, **3**:85
roll (noun) ἕλιγμα, **1**:434; κόλπος,
2:306
roll (vb.) ἑλίσσω, **1**:435; κυλίομαι,
2:327
roll away ἀνακυλίω, **1**:83;
ἀποκυλίω, **1**:134
roll up ἑλίσσω, **1**:435; πτύσσω,
3:192
roll up to προσκυλίω, **3**:173
rolling κυλισμός, **2**:327
Roman (adj.) Ῥωμαϊκός, **3**:216
Roman (adj. and noun) Ῥωμαῖος,
3:216
Roman citizen Ῥωμαῖος, **3**:216
Rome Ῥώμη, **3**:216
Rompha Ῥομφά(ν), **3**:213
roof δῶμα, **1**:363; στέγη, **3**:272
roof tile κέραμος, **2**:283
room οἴκημα, **2**:495
rooster ἀλέκτωρ, **1**:57; ὄρνις, **2**:533
root ῥίζα, **3**:211
root out ἐξολεθρεύω, **2**:8
rooted, be ῥιζόω, **3**:212
rope ζευκτηρία, **2**:99; σχοινίον,
3:319
rot σήπω, **3**:242
rot, cause to σήπω, **3**:242
rotten σαπρός, **3**:228
rough σκληρός, **3**:254; τραχύς,
3:368
rouse παραζηλόω, **3**:21
row ἐλαύνω, **1**:426
royal βασίλειος, **1**:205; βασιλικός,
1:208
rub ψώχω, **3**:504
rub on ἐγχρίω, **1**:378

rubbish περίψημα, **3**:80;
σκύβαλον, **3**:256
rue πήγανον, **3**:85
Rufus Ῥοῦφος, **3**:213
ruin (noun) ὄλεθρος, **2**:506;
ῥῆγμα, **3**:210; σύντριμμα, **3**:311
ruin (vb.) λυμαίνομαι, **2**:362
ruined, be καταφθείρω, **2**:270;
πταίω, **3**:191
rule ἄρχω, **1**:165; αὐθεντέω,
1:178; βασιλεύω, **1**:207;
ἡγέομαι, **2**:113
rule as tetrarch τετρααρχέω,
3:353; τετραρχέω, **3**:354
rule of conduct κανών, **2**:249
rule the house οἰκοδεσποτέω, **1**:291
rule with συμβασιλεύω, **3**:286
ruler ἄρχων, **1**:167; δυνάστης,
1:358; ἐθνάρχης, **1**:381;
κεφαλή, **2**:284
ruler, be ἡγεμονεύω, **2**:112
ruler over all παντοκράτωρ, **3**:11
run διώκω, **1**:338; τρέχω, **3**:369
run a risk κινδυνεύω, **2**:293
run about περιτρέχω, **3**:80
run after καταδιώκω, **2**:257
run aground ἐπικέλλω, **2**:30;
ἐκπίπτω, **1**:420; ἐποκέλλω, **2**:46
run ahead προτρέχω, **3**:182
run in εἰσπηδάω, **1**:402; εἰστρέχω,
1:402
run to προστρέχω, **3**:177
run together ἐπισυντρέχω, **2**:41
run under ὑποτρέχω, **3**:408
run with συντρέχω, **3**:310
running together συνδρομή, **3**:299
rush down κατατρέχω, **2**:270
rush headlong ὁρμάω, **2**:533
rush in εἰσπηδάω, **1**:402
rush out ἐκπηδάω, **1**:420
rust (noun) ἰός, **2**:191
rust (vb.) κατιόομαι, **2**:273
Ruth Ῥούθ, **3**:213

Sabaoth σαβαώθ, **3**:219
sabbath σάββατον, **3**:219
sabbath, day before the (Friday)
προσάββατον, **3**:161
sabbath observance σαββατισμός,
3:219
sabbath rest σαββατισμός, **3**:219
sack σάκκος, **3**:223
sackcloth garment σάκκος, **3**:223
sacrifice (noun) θυσία, **2**:161
sacrifice (vb.) θύω, **2**:161
sacrificial gift προσφορά, **3**:178
sacrificial meal θυσία, **2**:161
sacrificial offering προσφορά, **3**:178

sacrificial offering (slain) σφάγιον,
3:315
sad, be λυπέω, **2**:362
sad, become στυγνάζω, **3**:281
sad gaze, with a σκυθρωπός, **3**:256
sad, very περίλυπος, **3**:74
Sadducee Σαδδουκαῖος, **3**:222
sadness κατήφεια, **2**:273
safeguard ἀσφαλίζομαι, **1**:175
sail πλέω, **3**:103
sail across διαπλέω, **1**:310
sail along(side) παραλέγομαι, **3**:31
sail away ἀποπλέω, **1**:140
sail past παραπλέω, **3**:33
sail slowly βραδυπλοέω, **1**:226
sail toward καταπλέω, **2**:266
sail under (the lee) ὑποπλέω, **3**:406
sailor ναύτης, **2**:458
Salamis Σαλαμίς, **3**:224
Salem Σαλήμ, **3**:224
Salim Σαλείμ, **3**:224; Σαλίμ, **3**:225
Salmon Σαλμών, **3**:225
Salmone Σαλμώνη, **3**:225
Salome Σαλώμη, **3**:226
salt (noun) ἅλας, **1**:57
salt (vb.) ἁλίζω, **1**:57
salt, without ἄναλος, **1**:84
salty ἁλυκός, **1**:64
salutary σωτήριος, **3**:329
salutation ἀσπασμός, **1**:173
salvation σωτηρία, **3**:327;
σωτήριον, **3**:329
salve ἄρωμα, **1**:168; σμίγμα, **3**:257
Samaria Σαμάρεια (Σαμαρία), **3**:226
Samaritan (adj.) Σαμαρῖτις, **3**:226
Samaritan man Σαμαρίτης, **3**:226
Samaritan woman Σαμαρῖτις, **3**:226
same αὐτός, **1**:179
same trade, one who practices the
συντεχνίτης, **3**:310
same, almost the παραπλήσιος, **3**:33
same, the ταῦτα, **3**:337
Samos Σάμος, **3**:227
Samothrace Σαμοθρᾴκη, **3**:227
Samson Σαμψών, **3**:228
Samuel Σαμουήλ, **3**:228
sanctification ἁγνισμός, **1**:22
sanctify ἁγνίζω, **1**:22
sanctuary ἱερόν, **2**:175; σέβασμα,
3:235
sand ἄμμος, **1**:70
sandal σανδάλιον, **3**:228;
ὑπόδημα, **3**:402
sandy bank διθάλασσος, **1**:324
Sanhedrin συνέδριον, **3**:299
Sapphira Σάπφιρα, **1**:86
sapphire σάπφιρος, **3**:229
Sarah Σάρρα, **3**:233
Sardis Σάρδεις, **3**:229
sardonyx σαρδόνυξ, **3**:229

throw out ἐκβάλλω, **1**:405

throw out (in a circle) ἀμφιβάλλω, **1**:73

throw out the sounding lead βολίζω, **1**:223

throw to the ground ῥίπτω, **3**:212

throw up a defense προέχω, **3**:155

throwing ῥιπή, **3**:212

thrust out ἐξωθέω, **2**:13

thunder βροντή, **1**:227

thundercloud γνόφος, **1**:255

thus οὕτω, **2**:549; τοίνυν, **3**:364

Thyatira Θυάτ(ε)ιρα, **2**:158

Tiberias Τιβεριάς, **3**:355

Tiberius Τιβέριος, **3**:355

tie δέω, **1**:292

tie shut φιμόω, **3**:428

tie underneath ὑποδέομαι, **3**:402

till γεωργέω, **1**:246

Timaeus Τιμαῖος, **3**:357

time καιρός, **2**:232; χρόνος, **3**:488

time, appointed προθεσμία, **3**:156

time, at any πώποτε, **3**:201

time, at that τότε, **3**:367

time for, have σχολάζω, **3**:319

time, have εὐκαιρέω, **2**:78

time, have no ἀκαιρέομαι, **1**:48

time, small span of πῆχυς, **3**:86

time (span of) αἰών, **1**:44

time/opportunity, have no ἀκαιρέομαι, **1**:48

times, at all πάντη, **3**:11; πάντοτε, **3**:12

timid ὀλιγόψυχος, **2**:507

timidity ὑποστολή, **3**:407

Timon Τίμων, **3**:360

Timothy Τιμόθεος, **3**:359

tiny bit ψιχίον, **3**:500

tip ἄκρον, **1**:55

tire κάμνω, **2**:248; ἐκλύομαι, **1**:419; σκύλλω, **3**:256

tired πάρίημι, **3**:40

tired, be ἐκκακέω, **1**:410

tired, become ἐγκακέω, **1**:377; κοπιάω, **2**:307

tithe (noun) δεκάτη, **1**:284

tithe (vb.) ἀποδεκατεύω, **1**:127; ἀποδεκατόω, **1**:127

tithe, take a ἀποδεκατόω, **1**:127

Titius Τίτιος, **3**:363

Titus Τίτος, **3**:363

to εἰς, **1**:398; πρός, **3**:160; ὑπό, **3**:401

to be poured in βλητέος, **1**:222

to be sure καίτοιγε, **2**:236

to me μοι, **2**:436

to me also κἀμοί, **2**:248

to no purpose μάτην, **2**:397

to the contrary μενοῦν, **2**:406

to the degree that καθό, **2**:226

to this place δεῦρο, **1**:291; ἐκεῖ, **1**:409; ἐκεῖσε, **1**:410;; ἐνθάδε, **1**:454; ὧδε, **3**:505

to what place? ποῦ, **3**:143

to where ὅπου, **2**:524

today σήμερον, **3**:241

together ὁμόσε, **2**:517; ὁμοῦ, **2**:517

together (with) ἅμα, **1**:65

together with σύν, **3**:291

toil πόνος, **3**:135

tomb μνῆμα, **2**:434; τάφος, **3**:337

tomorrow αὔριον, **1**:179

tone φθόγγος, **3**:423

tongue γλῶσσα, **1**:251

too quickly ταχέως, **3**:338

tool ὅπλον, **2**:524

tooth ὀδούς, **2**:493

topaz τοπάζιον, **3**:365

torch λαμπάς, **2**:338

torment (noun) βάσανος, **1**:200

torment (vb.) βασανίζω, **1**:200; ὑπωπιάζω, **3**:409

tormented, be ὀχλέομαι, **2**:553

torture (noun) βασανισμός, **1**:200; βάσανος, **1**:200; μάστιξ, **2**:396

torture (vb.) βασανίζω, **1**:200; κακουχέω, **2**:239; τυμπανίζω, **3**:372

tortured, the act of being βασανισμός, **1**:200

torturer βασανιστής, **1**:200

tossed about by a storm, be χειμάζομαι, **3**:462

tossed to and fro by waves, be κλυδωνίζομαι, **2**:301

total παντελής, **3**:10

totally πάντως, **3**:12

touch ἅπτω, **1**:148; θιγγάνω, **2**:151; προσψαύω, **3**:179; ψηλαφάω, **3**:499

toward εἰς, **1**:398; πρός, **3**:160

tower πύργος, **3**:200

towers above, that which ὕψωμα, **3**:410

town πόλις, **3**:129

town, small κώμη, **2**:333

trace one's descent γενεαλογέω, **1**:242

Trachonitis Τραχωνῖτις, **3**:368

trade ἐμπορεύομαι, **1**:446; τέχνη, **3**:354

trade with καπηλεύω, **2**:249

tradition ἔθος, **1**:384; παράδοσις, **3**:21

train παιδεύω, **3**:3

training γυμνασία, **1**:265; παιδεία, **3**:3

traitor προδότης, **3**:154

trample πατέω, **3**:53

trample with the feet καταπατέω, **2**:265

tranquil ἡσύχιος, **2**:125

transform μετασχηματίζω, **2**:419

transgress παραβαίνω, **3**:14; ὑπερβαίνω, **3**:398

transgression ἀγνόημα, **1**:20; ἁμάρτημα, **1**:65; παράβασις, **3**:14

transgressor παραβάτης, **3**:14

translate διερμηνεύω, **2**:53; ἑρμηνεύω, **2**:53; μεθερμηνεύω, **2**:53, 401

translation ἑρμηνεία, ἑρμηνία, **2**:55

translator διερμηνευτής, **2**:53

transparent διαυγής, **1**:314; διαφανής, **1**:314

transparent as glass ὑάλινος, **3**:379

transplant μεθίστημι, **2**:401

transport (noun) ἔκστασις, **1**:421

transport (vb.) μετατίθημι, **2**:419

trap βρόχος, **1**:227; θήρα, **2**:148; παγίς, **3**:1

travel ὁδοιπορέω, **2**:491

travel by land πεζεύω, **3**:62

travel by sea πλέω, **3**:103

travel on foot πεζεύω, **3**:62

travel through διοδεύω, **1**:336

travel together συνοδεύω, **3**:308

traveler's bag πήρα, **3**:86

traveling company συνοδία, **3**:308

traveling companion συνέκδημος, **3**:303

tread on πατέω, **3**:53

treasure γάζα, **1**:231; θησαυρός, **2**:149

treasure chest θησαυρός, **2**:149

treasury γαζοφυλάκιον, **1**:232

treat deceitfully κατασοφίζομαι, **2**:269

treat scornfully καταφρονέω, **2**:270

treat shamefully ἀτιμάζω, **1**:177

treat with contempt ἐξουδενέω, **2**:9

treat with myrrh σμυρνίζω, **3**:257

tree δένδρον, **1**:285

tremble σείω, **3**:236; τρέμω, **3**:369

trembling ἔκτρομος, **1**:423; ἔντρομος, **1**:461; τρόμος, **3**:370

trial κριτήριον, **2**:321

tribe φυλή, **3**:443

tribune χιλίαρχος, **3**:466

tribute κῆνσος, **2**:287; φόρος, **3**:436

trip ὁδοιπορία, **2**:491; πορεία, **3**:136

Troas Τρῳάς, **3**:371

Trogyllium Τρωγύλλιον, **3**:372

troop σπεῖρα, **3**:262

troops στράτευμα, **3**:279

Trophimus Τρόφιμος, **3**:371

trouble (noun) κόπος, **2**:307